WESTERN NEVADA COMMUNITY COLLEGE
3 1439 00064 4743

S0-AVP-136

Handbook of North American Indians

Handbook of North American Indians

WILLIAM C. STURTEVANT
General Editor

VOLUME 13 PART 1 OF 2

Plains

RAYMOND J. DEMALLIE
Volume Editor

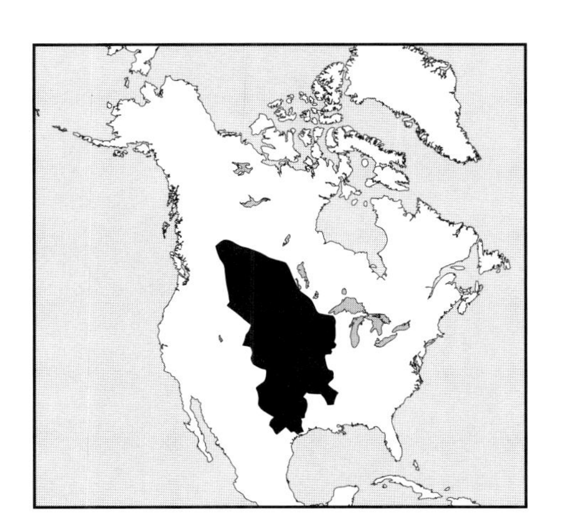

SMITHSONIAN INSTITUTION

WASHINGTON

2001

Library of Congress Cataloging in Publication Data

Handbook of North American Indians.

Bibliography.
Includes index.
CONTENTS:

v. 13. Plains.

1. Indians of North America.
I. Sturtevant, William C.

E77.H25 970′.004′97 77-17162

For sale by the U.S. Government Printing Office
Superintendent of Documents, Mail Stop: SSOP, Washington, DC 20402-9328

ISBN 0-16-050400-7

Plains Volume Planning Committee

Raymond J. DeMallie, Volume Editor

Douglas R. Parks, Associate Volume Editor

William C. Sturtevant, General Editor

W. Raymond Wood, Coordinator for Prehistory Chapters

Loretta Fowler

George Frison

Ives Goddard

Mildred Mott Wedel

Waldo R. Wedel

Contents

Special Topics

This map is a diagrammatic guide to the coverage of this volume; it is not an authoritative depiction of territories for several reasons. Sharp boundaries have been drawn and no area is unassigned. The groups mapped are in some cases arbitrarily defined, subdivisions are not indicated, no joint or disputed occupations are shown, and different kinds of land use are not distinguished. The simplified ranges shown are a generalization of the situation in the early 19th century, with those to the east showing earlier locations. Movements and changes in range were common and continual in this area, and territories at earlier and later dates were substantially different. Not shown are groups that came into separate existence later than the map period for their areas. For more specific information see the maps and text in the appropriate chapters.

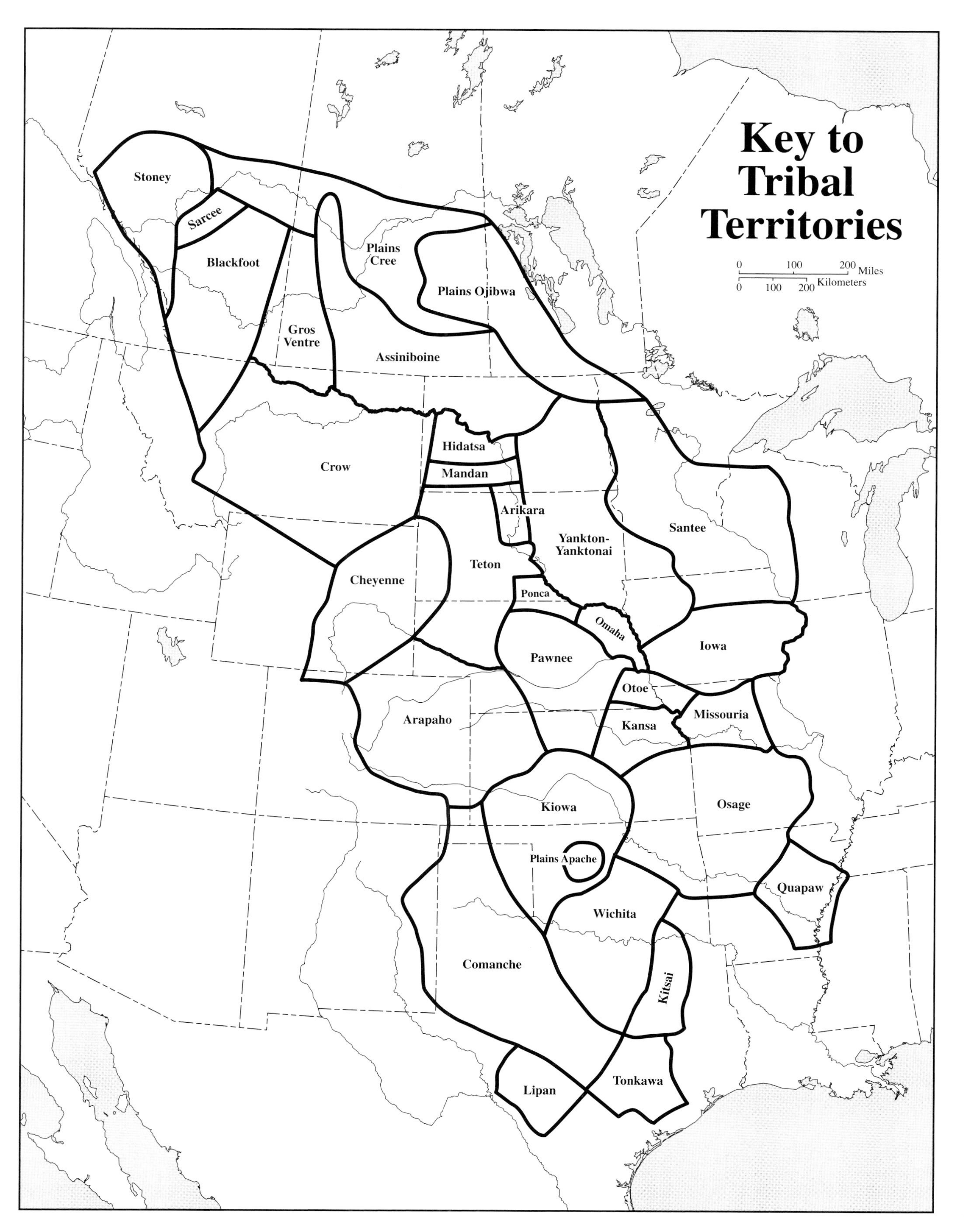
Key to Tribal Territories
0 100 200 Miles
0 100 200 Kilometers
Stoney
Sarcee
Blackfoot
Gros Ventre
Plains Cree
Plains Ojibwa
Assiniboine
Crow
Hidatsa
Mandan
Arikara
Yankton-Yanktonai
Santee
Cheyenne
Teton
Ponca
Omaha
Iowa
Pawnee
Otoe
Missouria
Kansa
Arapaho
Kiowa
Osage
Plains Apache
Quapaw
Wichita
Comanche
Kitsai
Lipan
Tonkawa

Technical Alphabet

Consonants

		bilabial	*labiodental*	*dental*	*alveolar*	*alveopalatal*	*velar*	*back velar*	*glottal*
stop	vl	*p*		*t*	*t*		*k*	*q*	*ʔ*
	vd	*b*		*d*	*d*		*g*	*ġ*	
affricate	vl			*θ̂*	*c*	*č*			
	vd			*δ̂*	*ʒ*	*ǯ, ǰ*			
fricative	vl	*ɸ*	*f*	*θ*	*s*	*š*	*x*	*x̣*	*h*
	vd	*β*	*v*	*δ, ð*	*z*	*ž*	*γ*	*γ̇*	
nasal	vl	*M*		*N*			*Ŋ*		
	vd	*m*		*n*			*ŋ*	*ŋ̇*	
lateral	vl				*ł*				
	vd				*l*				
semivowel	vl	*W*				*Y*			
	vd	*w*				*y*			

vl = voiceless; vd = voiced

Other symbols include: *λ* (voiced lateral affricate), *ƛ* (voiceless lateral affricate), *ʕ* (voiced pharyngeal fricative), *ḥ* (voiceless pharyngeal fricative), *r* (medial flap, trill, or retroflex approximant).

Vowels

	front	*central*	*back*
high	*i (ü)*	*ɨ*	*u (ɨ)*
	ɪ		*ʊ*
mid	*e (ö)*	*ə*	*o*
	ɛ		*ɔ*
		ʌ	
low	*æ*	*a*	*a*

Unparenthesized vowels are unrounded if front or central, and rounded if back; *ü* and *ö* are rounded; *ɨ* is unrounded. The special symbols for lax vowels (*ɪ, ʊ, ɛ, ɔ*) are generally used only where it is necessary to differentiate between tense and lax high or mid vowels. *ɨ* and *a* are used for both central and back vowels, as the two values seldom contrast in a given language.

Modifications indicated for consonants are: glottalization (*t̓, k̓,* etc.), retroflexion (*ṭ*), palatalization (*tʸ, kʸ, nʸ, lʸ*), labialization (*kʷ*), aspiration (*tʰ*), length (*t·*). For vowels: length (*a·*), three-mora length (*a:*), nasalization (*ą*), voicelessness (*A*). The commonest prosodic markings are for stress: *á* (primary) and *à* (secondary), and for pitch: *á* (high), *à* (low), *â* (falling), and *ǎ* (rising); however, the details of prosodic systems and the uses of accents differ widely from language to language.

Words in Indian languages cited in italics in this volume are written in phonemic transcription. That is, the letters and symbols are used in specific values defined for them by the structure of the sound system of the particular language. However, as far as possible, these phonemic transcriptions use letters and symbols in generally consistent values, as specified by the standard technical alphabet of the *Handbook*. Deviations from these standard values as well as specific details of the phonology of each language (or references to where they may be found) are given in an orthographic footnote in each tribal chapter.

No italicized Indian word is broken at a line end except when a hyphen would be present anyway as part of the word. Words in italicized phonemic transcription are never capitalized. Pronunciations or phonetic values given in the standard technical alphabet without regard to phonemic analysis are put in square brackets ([]) rather than in italics. Pointed brackets (⟨ ⟩) indicate an exact, unnormalized spelling or transcription. The glosses, or conventional translations, of Indian words are enclosed in single quotation marks.

Indian words recorded by nonspecialists or before the phonemic systems of their languages had been analyzed are often not written accurately enough to allow respelling in phonemic transcription. Where phonemic retranscription has been possible the citation of source has been modified by the label "phonemicized" or "from." Words that could not be phonemicized have in some cases been "normalized"—rewritten by mechanical substitution of the symbols of the standard technical alphabet. Words that have not been normalized sometimes contain letters used according to the values of other technical alphabets or traditional orthographies. The most common of these are ä for the *Handbook*'s *a*; c for *š*; ć for *č*; ch for *š* (in French sources) or for *x* or *h* (in German sources); eñ for *ę*; ğ or ġ for *γ*; ḣ or ȟ for *x*; j for *ž*, *ǯ*, or *y*; ⁿ or ŋ for nasalization; ň for *ŋ*; oñ for *ǫ*; 8 for French ou; q for *x*; ś for *š*; tc and tj for *č*; ź for *ž*; ' for *ʔ*; ' or ̣ for glottalization; and ʻ for *h* (or nondistinctive aspiration). All nonphonemic transcriptions give only incomplete, and sometimes imprecise, approximations of the correct pronunciation.

Nontechnical Equivalents

Correct pronunciation, as with any foreign language, requires extensive training and practice, but simplified (incorrect) pronunciations may be obtained by ignoring the diacritics and reading the vowels as in Italian or Spanish and the consonants as in English. For a closer approximation to the pronunciation or to rewrite into a nontechnical transcription the substitutions indicated in the following table may be made.

Technical	*Nontechnical*	*Technical*	*Nontechnical*	*Technical*	*Nontechnical*
æ	ae	*M*	mh	*Y*	yh
β	bh	*N*	nh	*ž*	zh
c	ts	*ŋ*	ng	*ʒ*	dz
č	ch	*Ŋ*	ngh	*ǯ*	j
δ	dh	*ɔ*	o	*ʔ*	’
δ̂	ddh	*θ*	th	*k̓*, *p̓*, *t̓*, etc.	k’, p’, t’, etc.
ε	e	*θ̂*	tth	*a·*, *e·*, *k·*, *s·*, etc.	aa, ee, kk, ss, etc.
γ	gh	*ϕ*	ph	*ą*, *ę*, etc.	an, en, etc.
ł	lh	*š*	sh	*kʸ*, *tʸ*, etc.	ky, ty, etc.
λ	dl	*W*	wh	*kʷ*	kw
ƛ	tlh	*x*	kh		

English Pronunciations

The English pronunciations of the names of tribes and a few other words are indicated parenthetically in a dictionary-style orthography in which most letters have their usual English pronunciation. Special symbols are listed below, with sample words to be pronounced as in nonregional United States English. Approximate phonetic values are given in parentheses in the standard technical alphabet.

ŋ: thing (*ŋ*)
θ: thin (*θ*)
ð: this (*δ*)
zh: vision (*ž*)
ă: bat (*æ*)

ä: father (*a*)
ā: bait (*ey*)
e: bet (*ε*)
ē: beat (*iy*)

ə: about, gallop (*ə*)
ĭ: bit (*ɪ*)
ī: bite (*ay*)
ô: bought (*ɔ*)

ō: boat (*ow*)
o͝o: book (*ʊ*)
o͞o: boot (*uw*)
u: but (*ʌ*)

ˈ (primary stress), ˌ (secondary stress): elevator (ˈeleˌvātər) (*élə̀vèytər*)

Conventions for Illustrations

- ● Native settlement
- ○ Abandoned settlement
- ■ Non-native or mixed settlement
- □ Abandoned settlement
- ▲ Modern reservations or archeological sites
- × Battlefield
- ⫽ Rapids
- / Dam
- + Mountain peak
- Mountain pass

Arapaho Tribe

Livingston Settlement

Black Hills Geographic feature

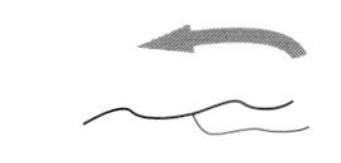
Movement/migration

Drainage

Reservation border

National border

State border

Railroad

Indian reservations and reserves

Precontact territory

Water

Credits and Captions

Credit lines give the source of the illustrations or the collections where the artifacts shown are located. The numbers that follow are the catalog or negative numbers of that repository. When the photographer mentioned in the caption is the source of the print reproduced, no credit line appears. "After" means that the Handbook illustrators have redrawn, rearranged, or abstracted the illustration from the one in the cited source. Measurements in captions are to the nearest millimeter if available; "about" indicates an estimate or a measurement converted from inches to centimeters. The following abbreviations are used in the credit lines:

Amer.	American	Lib.	Library
Anthr.	Anthropology, Anthropological	ms.	manuscript
		Mus.	Museum
Arch.	Archives	NAA	National Anthropological Archives
Arch(a)eol.	Arch(a)eology		
Coll.	Collection(s)		
Dept.	Department	Nat.	Natural
Dev.	Development	Natl.	National
Div.	Division	neg.	negative
Ethnol.	Ethnology, Ethnological	no.	number
		opp.	opposite
fol.	folio	p.	page
Ft.	Fort	pl(s).	plate(s)
Hist.	History	Prov.	Provincial
Histl.	Historical	Res.	Reservation (U.S.) Reserve (Canada)
Inc.	Incorporated		
Ind.	Indian	Soc.	Society
Inst.	Institute	St.	Saint
Lab.	Laboratory	U.	University

Metric Equivalents

100 cm = 1m	10 cm = 3.937 in.	1 km = .62 mi.	1 in. = 2.54 mi.	25 ft. = 7.62 m
10 mm = 1cm	1 m = 39.37 in.	5 km = 3.1 mi	1 ft. = 30.48 cm	1 mi. = 1.60 km
1,000 m = 1km	10 m = 32.81 ft.	10 km = 6.2 mi	1 yd. = 91.44 cm	5 mi. = 8.02 km

meters 0 1 2 3 4 5 6 7 8 9 10 11 12 13 14 15 16 17 18 19 20
feet 0 5 10 15 20 25 30 35 40 45 50 55 60 65

meters 0 10 20 30 40 50 60 70 80 90 100 110 120 130 140 150 160 170 180 190 200
feet 0 50 100 150 200 250 300 350 400 450 500 550 600 650

centimeters 0 1 2 3 4 5 6 7 8 9 10 11 12 13 14 15 16
inches 0 1 2 3 4 5 6

(actual size)

Preface

This is the twelfth volume to be published of a 20-volume set planned to give an encyclopedic summary of what is known about the prehistory, history, and cultures of the aboriginal peoples of North America north of the urban civilizations of central Mexico. Volumes 5–12 and 14–15 treat the other major culture areas of the continent.

Some topics relevant to the Plains area are excluded from this volume because they are more appropriately discussed on a continent-wide basis. Readers should refer to volume 1, Introduction, for general descriptions of anthropological and historical methods and sources and for summaries for the whole continent of certain topics regarding social and political organization, religion, and the performing arts. Volume 2 contains detailed accounts of the different kinds of Indian and Inuit (Eskimo) communities in the twentieth century, especially since 1950, and describes their relations with one another and with the surrounding non-Indian societies and nations. Volume 3 gives the environmental and biological backgrounds within which Native American societies developed, summarizes the early and late human biology or physical anthropology of Indians and Eskimos, and surveys the very earliest cultures. (Therefore the Paleo-Indian or Early Man period in the Plains receives major treatment in volume 3 rather than in this volume.) Volume 4 contains details on the history of the relations between Whites and Native American societies. Volume 16 is a continent-wide survey of technology and the visual arts—of material culture broadly defined. Volume 17 surveys the Native languages of North America, their characteristics, and historical relationships. Volumes 18 and 19 are a biographical dictionary; included in the listing are many Plains Indians. Volume 20 contains an index to the whole, which will serve to locate materials on Plains Indians in other volumes as well as in this one; it also includes a list of errata in all preceding volumes.

Preliminary discussions on the feasibility of the *Handbook* and alternatives for producing it began in 1965 in what was then the Smithsonian's Office of Anthropology. (A history of the early development of the whole *Handbook* and a listing of the entire editorial staff will be found in volume 1.) By 1971 funds were available and plans had advanced to the point where the details of the *Plains* volume could be worked out. In 1971 William W. Bittle agreed to serve as editor for the volume, and met with a planning committee (Robert E. Bell, Donald Lehmer, Beatrice Medicine, Abraham P. Nasatir, William W. Newcomb, Jr., and Symmes C. Oliver) to organize the contents and choose the authors to be invited. Many draft manuscripts were received, but work on this volume proceeded very slowly. Editorial attention was devoted to other volumes in the series, which advanced more rapidly.

After Bittle's resignation in 1983, Raymond J. DeMallie was appointed volume editor. In 1985 a new planning committee (listed on p. [*v*]) met in Washington with Sturtevant and Goddard to revise the outline of chapters and select a new list of authors. Many of the chapter topics and their authors in the 1971 plan were still appropriate and were carried over into the newly planned volume.

In September 1986 the Volume Editor contacted all authors to inform them that work on the *Plains* volume was imminent. Between February and August 1987 the Volume Editor sent each new author a brief description of the desired contents of the chapter. Authors remaining from the 1971 plan were sent new suggestions for revising and updating their chapters. Also sent each author was a "Guide for Contributors" prepared by the General Editor, which described the general aims and methods of the *Handbook* and the editorial conventions. One convention has been to avoid the present tense, where possible, in historical and cultural descriptions. Thus a statement in the past tense, with a recent date or approximate date, may also hold true for the time of writing.

Work on the *Plains* volume proceeded so slowly after 1987 that in 1992 other volumes in the series had to be given priority. Finally, in 1998 intensive work to complete the *Plains* volume was initiated. The contents of this volume reflect the state of knowledge in the 1990s, rather than in the early 1970s when planning first began.

As they were received, the chapter manuscripts were reviewed by the Volume Editor, the General Editor and his staff, and usually one or more referees, who frequently included a member of the Planning Committee and often authors of other chapters. Suggestions for changes and additions often resulted. The published versions frequently reflect more editorial intervention than is customary for academic writings, since the encyclopedic aims and format of the *Handbook* made it necessary to attempt to eliminate duplication, avoid gaps in coverage, prevent contradictions, impose some standardization of organization and terminology, and keep within strict constraints on length. Where the evidence seemed so scanty or obscure as to allow different authorities to come to differing conclusions, authors have been encouraged to elaborate their own views, although the editors have endeavored to draw attention to alternative interpretations published elsewhere.

The first editorial acceptance of an author's manuscript was on January 16, 1992, and the last on November 14, 2000. Edited manuscripts were sent from the Washington office to authors for their final approval between May 8, 1998, and December 15, 2000. These dates for all chapters are given in the list of Contributors.

Linguistic Editing

As far as possible, all cited words in Indian languages were referred to consultants with expert knowledge of the respective languages and rewritten by them in the appropriate technical orthography. In some cases a chapter author served as the linguist consultant. The consultants and the spelling systems are identified in the orthographic footnotes, most of which were written by Douglas R. Parks, others by the Linguistic Editor, Ives Goddard; all were edited by Goddard.

Statements about the genetic relationships of Plains languages have also been checked with linguist consultants, to ensure conformity with recent findings and terminology in comparative linguistics and to avoid conflicting statements within the *Handbook*. In general, only the less remote genetic relationships are mentioned in the individual chapters. The chapter "The Languages of the Plains: Introduction" discusses the wider relationships of those languages, and further information will be found in volume 17.

The Linguistic Editor served as coordinator and editor of these efforts by linguist consultants. A special debt is owed to these consultants, who provided advice and assistance without compensation and, in many cases, took time from their own research in order to check words with native speakers. The Linguistic Editor is especially grateful to Jean Charney, Eung-Do Cook, Raymond J. DeMallie, Donald G. Frantz, Randolph Graczyk, A. Wesley Jones, John E. Koontz, Wayne Leman, Mauricio Mixco, John D. Nichols, Douglas R. Parks, David H. Pentland, Robert L. Rankin, Willem J. de Reuse, David Rood, Scott Rushforth, Allan R. Taylor, Laurel Watkins, and H.C. Wolfart.

In the case of words that could not be respelled in a technical orthography, an attempt has been made to rationalize the transcriptions used in earlier anthropological writings in order to eliminate phonetic symbols that are obsolete and diacritics that might convey a false impression of phonetic accuracy.

Synonymies

Toward the end of ethnological chapters is a section called Synonymy. This describes the various names that have been applied to the groups and subgroups treated in that chapter, giving the principal variant, self-designations, the names applied to the groups in neighboring Indian languages, and the spellings used in European languages—English, French, and Spanish. For the major group names, an attempt has been made to cite the earliest attestations in English.

Throughout the ethnographic chapters more space has been devoted than in other volumes to presenting tribal synonymies that are as full and detailed as possible. The published literature is so replete with errors that accurate synonymies for Plains ethnonyms are a critical need. All synonymies were written by Douglas R. Parks to insure comparability of scope and detail. He provided linguistic forms, based on field elicitation, for Arikara, Assiniboine, Iowa-Otoe, Hidatsa, Mandan, Pawnee, Ponca, Sioux, Stoney, and Wichita. Parks wishes to acknowledge the following individuals who also provided data for the synonymies: Alice J. Anderton (Comanche); James Armagost (Comanche); Timothy A. Bernardis (Crow); Wallace L. Chafe (Caddo, Seneca); Jean Charney (Comanche); Eung-Do Cook (Sarcee, Stoney); David Costa (Illinois, Miami); Loretta Fowler (Arapaho); Donald G. Frantz (Blackfoot); Louanna Furbee (Iowa-Otoe); Talmy Givón (Ute); Ives Goddard (Arapaho); James Good Tracks (Iowa-Otoe); Randolph Graczyk (Crow); Robert Hollow (Mandan); A. Wesley Jones (Hidatsa); Thomas W. Kavanagh (Comanche); Geoffrey Kimball (Koasati); John E. Koontz (Omaha-Ponca); Wayne Leman (Cheyenne); G. Hubert Matthews (Crow); Wick R. Miller (Eastern Shoshone); Ken Miner (Winnebago); Mauricio Mixco (Mandan); John D. Nichols (Ojibwa); David H. Pentland (Plains Cree); Carolyn Quintero (Osage); Robert L. Rankin (Omaha-Ponca, Quapaw, Osage, and Kansa); Richard Rhodes (Ojibwa); David Rood (Wichita); Zdeněk Saltzmann (Arapaho) ; David Shaul (Eastern Shoshone); Demetri Shimkin (Eastern Shoshone); Allan R. Taylor (Blackfoot); Sarah G. Thomason (Salish); Randolph Valentine (Ojibwa); Paul Voorhis (Kickapoo); Laurel Watkins (Kiowa); H.C. Wolfart (Plains Cree).

These sections should assist in the identification of groups mentioned in the earlier historical and anthropological literature. They should also be examined for evidence on changes in the identifications and affiliations of groups, as seen by their own members as well as by neighbors and by outside observers. Questionable ethnonyms, and those not identifiable with a known tribe, are presented in the chapter "Enigmatic Groups."

Radiocarbon Dates

Authors were instructed to convert radiocarbon dates into dates in the Christian calendar. Such conversions have often been made from the dates as originally published, without taking account of changes that may be required by developing research on revisions of the half-life of carbon 14, long-term changes in the amount of carbon 14 in the atmosphere, and other factors that may require modifications of absolute dates based on radiocarbon determinations.

Binomials

The scientific names of animal and plant genera and species, printed in italics, have been checked to ensure that they reflect modern usage by biological taxonomists. Especially the plant names (but also most of the animal names) submitted in the chapter "Environment and Subsistence" were taken as standard. Binomials in other chapters have been brought into agreement with those in that chapter, or if they do not appear there, have been revised in consultation with curators in appropriate departments of the National Museum of Natural History.

Bibliography

All references cited by contributors have been unified in a single list at the end of the volume. Citations within the text, by author, date, and often page, identify the works in this unified list. Cesare Marino, the *Handbook* Researcher, served as bibliographer. Wherever possible, he resolved conflicts between citations of different editions, corrected inaccuracies and omissions, and checked direct quotations against the originals. The bibliographic information has been verified by examination of the original work or from standard reliable library catalogs (especially the National Union Catalog, the published catalog of the Harvard Peabody Museum Library, and the OCLC/PRISM on-line catalog). The unified bibliography lists all the sources cited in the text of the volume, except personal communications, and works consulted but not cited in the chapters. In the text, "personal communications" to an author are distinguished from personal "communications to editors." The sections headed Sources at the ends of most chapters provide general guidance to the most important sources of information on the topics covered.

Illustrations

Authors were requested to submit suggestions for illustrations: photographs, drawings, maps, and lists and locations of objects that might be illustrated. To varying degrees they complied with this request. Yet considerations of space, balance, reproducibility, and availability often required modifications in what was submitted. Much original material was provided by editorial staff members from research they conducted in museums and other repositories and in the published literature. Locating, collecting, and selecting suitable photographs, drawings, and paintings was the responsibility of the Illustrations Researcher, Joanna Cohan Scherer. Selection of and research on suitable artifacts to be photographed or drawn was the responsibility of the Artifact Researchers, Ernest S. Lohse, Thomas W. Kavanagh, and Christine A. Jirikowic during the initial period of volume preparation and Brenda G. McLain and Scherer during the later stages. During the final two years of volume preparation Candace S. Greene contributed valuable artifact research to many chapters in addition to the one she authored. All drawings are credited.

Maps for the "Key to Tribal Territories" and "Introduction" were produced by David Swanson of Equator Graphics, Inc. and for "Environment and Subsistence" by Roger Thor Roop. Maps for 23 tribal chapters were produced by Catherine Spencer while all others were by Daniel G. Cole of the Smithsonian Automatic Data Processing office. Digital sketch maps were created using information from the chapter manuscripts, from their authors, and from other sources. Final production (of all maps) was the responsibility of David Swanson, Alex Tait, and Dana Gantz of Equator Graphics, Inc.

Layout and design of the illustrations were the responsibility of the Scientific Illustrators, Catherine Spencer (1998–1999) and Roger Thor Roop (1999–) in coordination with Scherer. Captions for most illustrations were composed by Scherer; others were written by Lohse, Kavanagh, Jirikowic, McLain, Greene, Spencer, and Roop and for maps by Cole, with several by Swanson and Spencer. Native place-names in map captions were supplied by authors and edited by the Linguistic Editor and his consultants. All illustrations, including maps and drawings, and all captions have been approved by the Volume Editor, Technical Editor, and the authors of the chapters in which they appear.

The list of illustrations was compiled by Joanna Cohan Scherer.

Acknowledgements

During the first few years of this project, the *Handbook* editorial staff in Washington worked on materials for all volumes of the series. Since intensive preparation of this volume began in 1998, especially important contributions were provided by: the Editorial Liaison and Staff Coordinator, Paula Cardwell; the Production Manager and Manuscript Editor, Diane Della-Loggia; the Researcher and Bibliographer, Cesare Marino; the Scientific Illustrators, Catherine Spencer (1998–1999) and Roger Thor Roop (1999–); the Illustrations Researcher, Joanna Cohan Scherer; the Assistant Illustrations Researcher, Vicki E. Simon (1999–); the Artifact Researchers, Ernest S. Lohse (1985–1989), Thomas W. Kavanagh (1990–1992), and Christine A. Jirikowic (1994–1995); Brenda McLain (1998), Assistant Illustrations Researcher and Artifact Researcher; the Administrative Specialist, Melvina Jackson (until February 2000). Alex Young, Peta Joy Sosnowski, and Terrilee Edwards-Hewitt served as bibliographic assistants at various stages of volume preparation. Barbara Watanabe provided valuable back-up research assistance and technical support during critical periods of reduced staffing while Gabrielle Lawson provided additional typing. Between 1985 and 2000, the Illustrations Researcher was assisted at various times by Catherine J. Adams, Peggy Albright, Rosa Anchondo, Rebecca Blom, Amber Breiner, Monika Carothers, Christian Carstensen, Erica Davis, Francis Galindo, Billie Gutgsell, Jason Jones, Meredith Kilduff, Colleen Lodge, Timothy McCleary, Wendy Niece, Courtney O'Callaghan, Elizabeth Noznesky, Lynn Spriggs, Sarah Trabucchi, Laura Woodson, and Layla Wuthrick as interns, volunteers, or assistant illustrations researchers.

Candace S. Greene was assisted by Lea Foster and Marit Munson. Donald Tenoso (Hunkpapa Lakota) of the American Indian Program, National Museum of Natural History, helped document certain illustrations. Scientific Illustrators Karen B. Ackoff (until 1997) and Norman J. Frisch (Brockport, New York) prepared some drawings. Thanks are due to the many others (including student interns and volunteers) who provided assistance with the illustrations research effort at different stages of volume preparation. The index was compiled by Lee Gable of Coughlin Indexing Services, Inc.

Carolyn Rose served as Managing Editor in addition to her other duties as Deputy Chair and (since January 2000) Chair of the Department of Anthropology, National Museum of Natural History. She was particularly helpful in guiding the *Handbook* staff to work within an accelerated production schedule.

Throughout, Ives Goddard was of particular assistance on matters of historical and geographical accuracy. He served as Technical Editor as well as the *Handbook* Linguistic Editor and advisor to the General Editor.

Special thanks are owed to Stanwyn Shetler, Jerry Harasewych, and Phillip Angle, National Museum of Natural History, who were of particular assistance regarding scientific names of plants and animal genera and species.

Beyond the members of the Planning Committee and those individuals acknowledged in appropriate sections of the text, the Volume Editor would especially like to thank two individuals for their contributions to the volume—Douglas R. Parks who was asked by DeMallie to serve as Associate Volume Editor and to prepare the synonymies for the tribal chapters and Joanna Cohan Scherer who coordinated the majority of the illustrations for the volume. The Volume Editor also thanks W. Raymond Wood who graciously agreed to review final versions of the prehistory chapters after failing health prevented Waldo Wedel from continuing in his role as advisor in archeology. Special thanks are owed to the Volume Editor's research assistants, Lee Irwin (1989–1990) and Dennis M. Christafferson (1999–2000), who helped to finalize many of the chapters. Thanks also to Wallace E. Hooper, who oversaw the preparation of electronic files in Bloomington. Finally, DeMallie expresses his gratitude to graduate students at Indiana University who assisted him in editorial work on the volume: Christina E. Burke, Brenda Farnell, Erik D. Gooding, Jason Baird Jackson, Michael B. Moore, Mindy J. Morgan, and Joseph Sweeney. Other colleagues who provided support and advice include Carolyn R. Anderson, Morris W. Foster, Louis Garcia, Richard B. Henne, David Reed Miller, Jacqueline Peterson, David Smyth, Daniel C. Swan, and Arok Wolvengrey.

The following contributors to the volume would like particularly to acknowledge the support of various individuals and scholarly institutions that helped to make their research possible. Dennis Christafferson thanks Christina E. Burke and Mindy J. Morgan. Ian Dyck and Richard E. Morlan thank David A. Meyer, Rod Vickers, Ernest G. Walker, and the Canadian Museum of Civilization (especially the library staff). Ian A.L. Getty thanks Gerald Kaquits.

Acknowledgement is due to the Department of Anthropology, National Museum of Natural History, Smithsonian Institution (and to its other curatorial staff), for releasing Sturtevant and Goddard from part of their curatorial and research responsibilities so that they could devote time to editing the *Handbook*. The Department is also owed thanks for supporting the participation of Chair Carolyn Rose and Researcher Candace S. Greene. DeMallie acknowledges the support of Indiana University, Bloomington, especially George E. Walker, Vice-President for Research and Dean of the University Graduate School; the American Indian Studies Research Institute; and the Department of Anthropology.

Preparation and publication of this volume have been supported by federal appropriations made to the Smithsonian Institution.

February 11, 2001

William C. Sturtevant
Raymond J. DeMallie

Introduction

RAYMOND J. DEMALLIE

The Plains culture area is defined in this volume as the region of tall-grass prairies and short-grass high plains extending west from the Upper Mississippi River valley to the Rocky Mountains and from the Saskatchewan River valley south to the Rio Grande. The boundaries of the area, and in some respects the definition of the ethnic groups themselves, are arbitrary and based as much on subjective as objective criteria. Yet cultural commonalities and historical patterns of interaction attest to the practical value of this classification.

The geographical definition of the plains evolved over a long period of European and American exploration. The first written portrayal of the southern plains came from the 1540–1542 expedition of Francisco Vásquez de Coronado. Pedro de Castañeda, the expedition's chronicler, called the plains (*llanos*) "a vast level area," covered with very short grass (Hammond and Rey 1940:261). The earliest description of the northern plains is in the journal of Henry Kelsey, who in 1690 used the terms *champion land* (i.e., open land), *plain,* and *barren ground* to describe the area of the upper Saskatchewan, southeast of present Saskatoon (Kelsey 1929:8–9; G.M. Lewis 1975:27). During the eighteenth century the terms *plains, prairies,* and *meadows* were used interchangeably (A. Henry 1901:267).

While the definition of the Plains culture area was based on the expanse of grasslands, implicit in that definition were the vast herds of buffalo that inhabited the area. The lives of Plains peoples were dependent upon and dominated by buffalo hunting. During the time of European exploration, buffalo (*Bison bison bison*) were found throughout the entire plains and prairie area; prehistorically, the buffalo range extended far beyond, from the Hudson River almost to central California. In the far northwest, the Plains area overlapped slightly with the range of the wood buffalo (*Bison bison athabascae*) (W.R. Wedel 1961:41, 77; Roe 1970:map).

Physiographic delineation of the boundaries of the Plains is imprecise. The northern boundary may be considered as the Saskatchewan River drainage and the southern boundary as either the Rio Grande or the Texas coastal plain. From east to west the area has been defined as extending from 96, 98, or 100° west longitude to the Rocky Mountains, and frequently the line of 20-inch annual rainfall, which wavers back and forth across the 100th meridian, has been used as the limit of the high plains, with the area to the east as far as the Mississippi Valley being classified as prairie plains (W.R. Wedel 1961:20–45; B.M. Gilbert 1980:8–15). The ecological differences are reflected in the distinctive cultural adaptations of the nomadic tribes to the high plains and the semisedentary horticultural tribes to the prairie plains.

History of Classification

Cultural and linguistic study of Indians of the Plains began in the mid-nineteenth century, but use of the designation "Plains Indians" was slow to develop in anthropology. Most nineteenth-century classifications were based primarily on genetically defined linguistic families or stocks, without consideration of cultural or ecological factors. Albert Gallatin's *Synopsis of the Indian Tribes* (1836:120) recognized as a group those tribes west of the Mississippi River and east of the Rocky Mountains but did not give them a name; his study presented the first map of Indian tribes based on language. Ferdinand V. Hayden (1862) published the first ethnological and linguistic study of the Plains, but used the designation "Indian Tribes of the Missouri Valley." Lewis Henry Morgan (1871, 1877) studied the kinship and social systems of the Plains tribes, but he did not give them a name as a geographical or cultural unit. Although he posited a significant difference between "Village" (horticultural) and "Non-horticultural" tribes, with gradations in between, Morgan did not apply this distinction to the classification of Plains peoples. Daniel G. Brinton (1891) included the plains region within a broader "North Atlantic Group," under which tribes were classified by linguistic stock. John W. Powell's "Indian Linguistic Families North of Mexico" (1891) (vol. 17: map in pocket) followed Gallatin's model, but with the benefit of much additional data, particularly documenting the languages of western tribes, which allowed for a more accurate map of the entire continent. The general pattern of continuous distribution of each language family, Powell argued, proved that tribes had long occupied the areas in which they were met at first contact; therefore, American Indians should be considered as more fundamentally sedentary than truly nomadic (J.W. Powell 1891:30). However, he did not take the further step of considering such patterning in terms of culture.

Defining the Plains Culture Area

The classification of American Indian cultures into geographical areas developed in the context of museum displays. The U.S. National Museum building opened in 1881 and Otis T. Mason, a Smithsonian collaborator since 1872, became its curator of ethnology in 1884 (Hough 1908:662). To Mason fell the work of classifying and arranging the Smithsonian's ethnological collections, the largest part of which represented native North America. Mason devised an exhibit strategy based on technology, treating each object as if it were a biological specimen; by exhibiting, for example, bows and arrows in a single case, the variation from tribe to tribe would be apparent and would reflect the development of the underlying technology throughout the continent. The cumulative effect of many comparable exhibits would be to show the evolution of cultural forms, from simple to complex. Franz Boas, who in the 1880s was developing his critique of the "comparative method" that dominated nineteenth-century anthropology, argued that a more valuable perspective could be achieved by exhibiting specimens according to cultural group, thereby showing objects in context (Stocking 1974:57–67). Boas had the opportunity to demonstrate the effectiveness of such an organization at the World's Columbian Exposition held in Chicago in 1893, when he served as Frederick W. Putnam's assistant in preparing exhibits in the Anthropology building (Dexter 1966:330).

At the Chicago world's fair, Mason was in charge of developing the ethnological exhibit representing the U.S. National Museum. Abandoning the comparative technology approach, he designed the exhibit to show "the relation of the material activities of North America to the linguistic classification" (Mason 1894a:606). A 12 by 16 foot enlargement of Powell's map was displayed on a wall; artifacts were arranged in wall cases organized as much as possible in alcoves by linguistic stock. The focus of each alcove was a life group, appropriately costumed, of "lay figures" shown engaged in characteristic activities. Representing the Plains, the Siouan exhibits included a case showing two Sioux women dressing hides and another in which a Crow man was painting on hide; the Kiowa exhibit included a case showing a group of children around a child-size tepee, the boys playing the hoop and pole game (U.S. National Museum 1895:127–129).

As the world's fair exhibits were transferred to the U.S. National Museum, Mason abandoned the organization by linguistic stock and adopted Boas's method of organizing exhibits by culture. Mason classified the Americas into "culture areas," environmental regions whose resources had attracted various groups of people who, over time, developed commonalities of culture despite separateness of language, social structure, and religion. The availability of buffalo defined the culture area he called "The Rocky mountain region and Plains of the Great West," but Mason (1894:212–216) predicted that sorting out the history of cultural differences such as styles of houses, bows and arrows, and dress would prove difficult.

Mason soon systematized 10 "environments or culture areas" for North America, one of which he called "Plains of the Great West." Comprising "A piedmont sloping down to the immense prairies of the Missouri, the Platte, and the Arkansas," Mason (1896:649) defined the area both in terms of natural resources and prominent cultural characteristics. In a refinement of the culture area classification, Mason (in Hodge 1907–1910, 1:427–430), increased the number of culture areas to 12. In this scheme the "Plains" area was located "between the Rocky mts. and the fertile lands w. of the Mississippi. To the N. it stretches into Athabasca, and it terminates at the S. about the Rio Grande." The boundary with the Mississippi valley culture area directly to the east was left "loosely defined." In a discussion of the classification and arrangement of anthropological exhibits being implemented by the U.S. National Museum, William H. Holmes (1903b:268) referred to the system of "geo-ethnic or geographical culture districts," and provided a map of North America that illustrated Mason's culture areas (fig. 1).

Presentation by culture area became the norm for museum display of American Indian materials. Boas, hired in 1895 as curator of ethnology at the American Museum of Natural History in New York, arranged the exhibits by culture area. During the early twentieth century the Plains exhibits, displayed in a separate hall, were largely restricted to the High Plains tribes (Dorsey 1907c:587). A plan of the Plains Indian hall, published a few years after Boas was succeeded as curator by his student Clark Wissler, shows that the Hidatsa, Pawnee, and Wichita were the only Prairie Plains tribes represented; in addition to the High Plains tribes, cases representing the Shoshone, Ute, and Nez Perce—tribes later classified in the Basin and Plateau areas—were also included (Wissler 1912b:3). At the newly founded Field Columbian Museum, George A. Dorsey, a student of Putnam's, planned the transformation of Ayer Hall into a systematic presentation of the Plains area, organized by five language stocks: Algonquian, Siouan, Caddoan, Kiowan, and Shoshonean. Dorsey took a broad view, not strictly geographically based, including in the hall tribes of the Northeast (Delaware, Winnebago), Subarctic (Naskapi), and Great Basin (Shoshone, Bannock, Ute, Paiute) (Dorsey 1901; DeMallie and Parks 1999).

Based on his study of material culture collections in the American Museum of Natural History, and building on Mason's work, Wissler (1912b, 1914) presented a classification of nine North American "culture centers" north of Mexico. Placing tribal names on a map, but not delineating tribal territories, Wissler drew angular lines to define areas around each center. These lines were tentative and were not intended as boundaries between centers but rather as marking the points where the cultural traits of

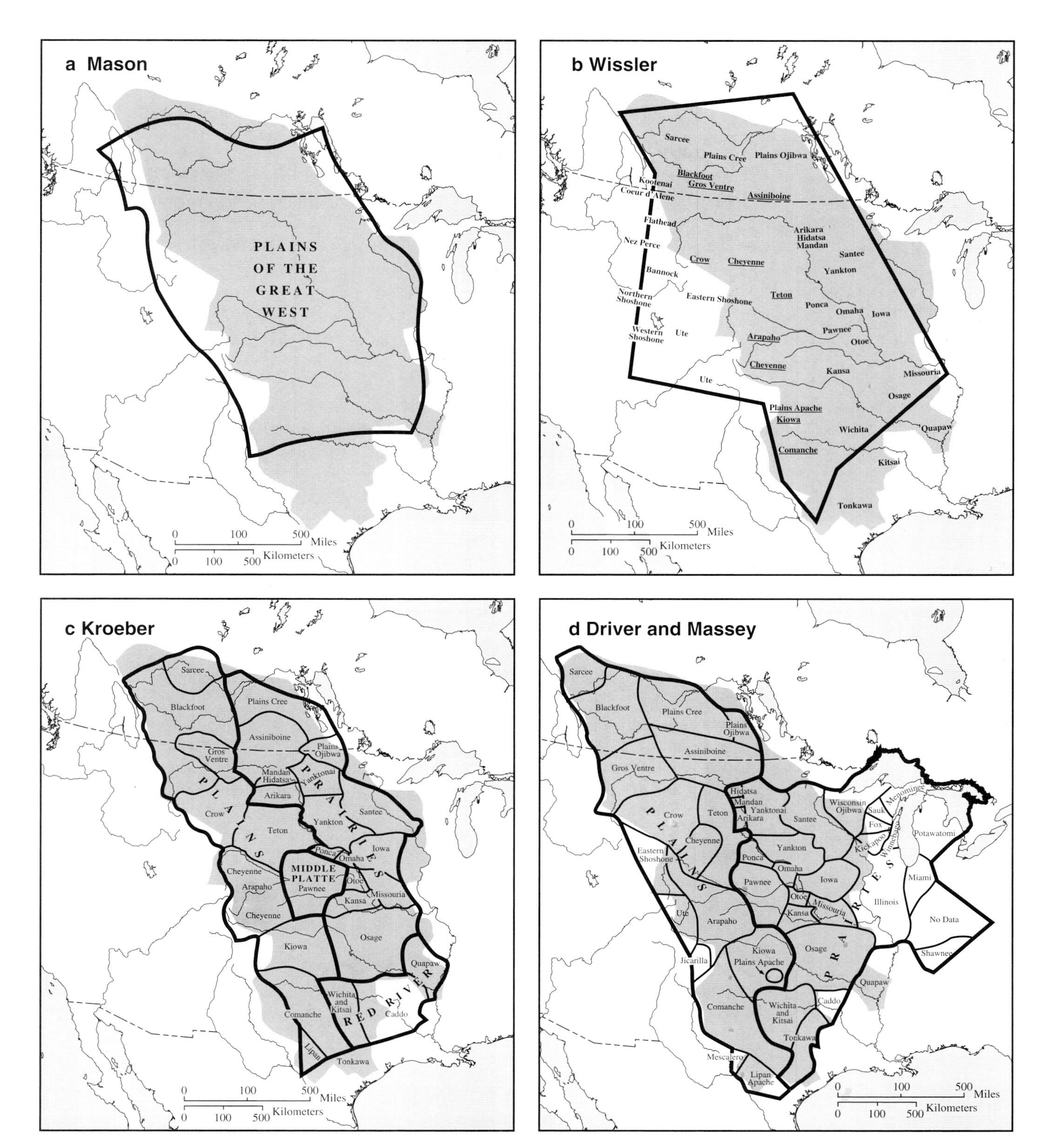

Fig. 1. The Plains culture area of the Handbook (tone) compared with other definitions: a, O.T. Mason, as mapped by Holmes 1903b; b, Wissler 1917 (with typical tribes underlined); c, Kroeber 1939; d, Driver and Massey 1957.

two centers were in balance (Wissler 1914:467n.1). Wissler's Plains area encompassed most of the Prairie Plains, all of the High Plains, and extended westward to include the Nez Perce and Eastern Shoshone as intermediate between the Plateau and Plains, and the Bannock and Ute as intermediate between the Southwest and Plains.

These areas were based on ethnological collections and were intended to represent the historic period—for the Plains, the seventeenth through the mid-nineteenth centuries, from the spread of the horse to the demise of the buffalo. The culture centers represented a static, rather than historical, perspective on native cultures.

Wissler (1917) extended his tribal classification by plotting food areas, archeological remains, and a variety of social and cultural traits ranging from clans to decorative designs. Combining those distributions again resulted in nine historical culture areas north of Mexico, providing additional empirical validation for the culture centers he had proposed earlier on the basis of material culture.

Wissler's conception of Plains culture was based on that of the nomadic, High Plains tribes. In an article summarizing the diffusion of Plains culture, he assumed that the nomadic, buffalo-hunting lifeway would not have been possible without horses (Wissler 1907a:44–45). Later, he noted that historical evidence, beginning with the accounts of the Coronado expedition, showed that nomadic hunting long predated the introduction of horses, and he concluded that Plains culture had been intensified and diffused as the horse was integrated into the older pattern (Wissler 1914a:25). Wissler defined the Plains area in terms of some 20 cultural traits, including dependence on buffalo; absence of fishing; absence of agriculture; use of tepees; land transportation only, using dog (later horse) travois; skin clothing; special rawhide work; rawhide shields; geometrical, nonsymbolic art; band-type social organization; men's societies; and the Sun Dance (Wissler 1917:206–208). Applying this definition, he identified 11 tribes whose culture was typical of the area; in addition, on the eastern border, 14 other tribes shared most of the Plains traits, as did two tribes on the west and two tribes on the northeast (fig. 1).

A more developmental picture of the Plains was suggested by classifying archeological materials, which revealed prehistoric areal patterning different from the ethnologically defined culture areas. Holmes (1914:414) reconstructed "cultural characterization areas" that divided the Plains among three archeologically defined areas. The High Plains region was classified, along with eastern Idaho and portions of Utah and Nevada west to the Sierras, as the "Plains and Rocky Mountains" area. The northern Prairie Plains was classified with the "Upper Mississippi and Lakes Region," and the southern Prairie Plains was classified with the "Middle and Lower Mississippi Valley Region"; both areas stretched eastward to the Appalachian Mountains. Wissler (1917:245–246) also plotted archeological areas, whose boundaries were largely similar to those proposed by Holmes. Those studies showed that, in terms of prehistory, the Plains was not a single area but was at the intersection of three distinct archeological areas, representing three distinct historical traditions. Wissler saw the horse as the element that united tribes from these three archeological areas into an intensified form of Plains culture during the historic period. Along the same lines, Edward Sapir (1916:45) suggested that the Plains culture area might be seen as a "reassortment" of older culture areas, a blending of peoples from the Northeast, Southeast, Plateau, and possibly the Southwest as well.

Alfred L. Kroeber (1939) provided the most thorough elaboration of the culture area concept (Driver 1962). He prepared a map defining tribal boundaries as the basis for drawing culture area boundaries, which he based on physiographic and vegetation regions as well as on cultural traits. Kroeber's intention was to move beyond Wissler's static classification and attempt to use culture areas to show historical as well as geographical relationships. Kroeber divided Wissler's Plains area into three areas: (1) Red River (Caddo, Wichita, Kitsai), transitional between the Southeast and the Plains, in which the Pawnee were classed as a Middle Platte subarea; (2) Plains, divided into Northern and Southern; and (3) Prairies, divided into Southern (Central Siouans), Central (Santee and Yankton-Yanktonai), Village (Hidatsa, Mandan, Arikara), and Northern or Canadian (fig. 1).

Kroeber recognized the difficulty of drawing meaningful culture area boundaries in eastern North America. For the Plains, his most valuable contribution was to make explicit the cultural distinctiveness between High Plains and Prairie tribes.

Robert Lowie's anthropological summary of the Plains followed Wissler's definition of the Plains area, excluding the Bannock, but adding the Kootenai and Jicarilla Apache (Lowie 1954:10–11). Like Wissler, Lowie discussed the Plains as a whole without differentiating between High Plains and Prairies.

The study of culture areas was carried forward by Harold E. Driver, one of Kroeber's students. Driver et al. (1953), following Kroeber, provided a tribal base map and classified all of North America east of the Rocky Mountains, south of the Subarctic, and north of Mexico into a single culture area with three subareas: Plains, Prairies, and East. Driver and Massey (1957), using detailed mapping of culture traits, presented 163 distributional maps that provided ethnographic support for Kroeber's more impressionistic study. Like Kroeber, they differentiated between Plains and Prairies culture areas, but their Prairies area was expanded to include the entire Midwest, encompassing Kroeber's Wisconsin (Wild Rice) and Ohio Valley areas (fig. 1). Driver (1961) refined the culture area classification and slightly reduced the Prairies by moving the Shawnee to the East culture area.

Statistical study of culture traits by George Peter Murdock and by Driver and his students revealed a variety of patterns for subdivisions within the Plains-Prairies area, none of which precisely matched any of the other classifications of the area (Scaglion 1980:26–32). Driver concluded that intuitively defined culture areas were preferable to the results of statistically determined groups, primarily because of the limitations of available data (Driver, Kenny, Hudson, and Engle 1972:321).

Although the *Handbook* culture areas in general follow Driver (1961), the definition of the Plains follows Mason, Wissler, and Lowie in combining Plains and Prairies into a single culture area. The *Handbook* differs in the inclusion or exclusion of some tribes assigned differently by others. The Wind River Shoshone and Ute have been placed in the Basin (vol. 11); the Bannock, Kootenai, and Nez Perce in the Plateau (vol. 12); the Jicarilla Apache in the Southwest (vol. 10); and the Caddo in the Southeast (vol. 14). The Lipan Apache and Tonkawa have been put in the Plains area rather than the Southwest and the Quapaw have been included in the Plains rather than the Southeast. Finally, for sake of inclusion in the ethnographic chapters of this volume, the Métis, originating at Red River, have been treated as a "tribe."

Social Units

The tribal units into which the Plains peoples have been organized for purposes of this volume reflect political consolidation subsequent to the establishment of formal relations with the governments of the United States and Canada, and the settlement of those peoples on reservations and reserves. During the early contact period, beginning in 1540, the written reports of European observers provide the first characterizations of the nature of Plains societies. Combined with native traditions and bolstered in some cases by the archeological record, the pattern of society of protohistoric Plains peoples is clear. The basic social units were extended families organized in nomadic bands or semisedentary villages, each independent but related to others speaking the same language and sharing the same culture. The political integration of bands or villages into tribal units was tenuous and incomplete. Scale was an important variable. Smaller groups were more easily united than larger ones, a distinction overlooked by the classification of all Plains peoples into tribes.

The size of residential units was to some extent dictated by ecological factors (Levy 1961; J.H. Moore 1982, 1987:127–175). Effective hunting of the large herds of buffalo that congregated each summer required the coordinated efforts of many hunters, whereas to survive when the herds were scattered, small social groups were optimal. Pasturage for horse herds was another important factor limiting the size or duration of residential groups. Seasonal variation in residence was a prominent part of Plains life.

Smaller tribes, those whose mid-nineteenth-century populations were 1,000 or less, were more likely to stay together throughout the year; they include the Sarcee, Plains Apache, Iowa, Otoe, Missouria, and Ponca. Larger tribes, in the range of 2,000–3,000, usually comprised a number of bands or villages that might come together only during the summer; they include the Cheyenne, Arapaho, Gros Ventre, Hidatsa, Arikara, Omaha, and Kansa. The most populous tribes, numbering in the 4,000–10,000 range, were comprised of divisions. Tribes this large rarely if ever congregated in one place at a single time, and the divisions themselves are better thought of as tribes in their own right. These include the Blackfoot (three divisions), Pawnee (four), Crow and Osage (two each), Teton Sioux (seven), and Comanche (four major and several minor). Such divisions ordinarily had their own territories and frequently were linguistically distinct. Some populous tribes comprised a large number of bands and lacked organization into divisions; these include the Assiniboine and Plains Cree.

Relations between tribal subgroups varied widely. The Cheyenne, for example, had a tradition of 10 bands, each with its own place in the camp circle, and each represented by four chiefs on the tribal council. The split of that tribe during the early nineteenth century into northern and southern divisions resulted in an imperfect replication of the band structure in both Montana and Oklahoma. The Omaha were similarly divided into 10 clans, each with its own place in the camp circle and with its own specialized responsibilities, and the tribe further divided into moieties, each of which provided one of the two head chiefs. Each of the Teton Sioux divisions had a tradition of elected chiefs and executive officials ("shirt wearers") that functioned during formal camp moves and the summer buffalo hunts. Among the village tribes, such as the Pawnee and Arikara, chieftainship was hereditary and balanced by a corresponding set of religious leaders. Many tribes, however, had no formal organization above the band level.

Social integration was largely accomplished through the kinship system. In general, lineage-type Omaha and Crow kinship systems among the Prairie tribes and generational systems among the High Plains tribes embodied the expected patterns of interaction between each pair of relatives and provided structure to social life. Since buffalo hunting required the cooperation of groups of men (classed together as "brothers"), Eggan (1937a:92–94, 1966:72) argued that tribes who came into the Plains with different social systems tended to develop similar kinship systems and social structures, based on the wide recognition of men of the same generation as brothers.

Tribal cohesiveness was based on a variety of social mechanisms as well as on commonalities of language, custom, and belief. Although detailed studies are lacking, it appears that in many tribes, marriages generally took place across bands, thereby forging immediate bonds of kinship among them. The Pawnee, among whom, at least in concept, each village was endogamous, are an exception. In a structural sense, it was important that Plains bands and villages were interrelated through an organization of men's societies that provided a strong force for social integration. Within each tribe, the societies were either formally age-graded—so that individual age cohorts passed through the system together from youth to maturity—or informally organized on the basis of age and social status. Each society had its distinctive regalia, songs, and dances. Societies were competitive with one another both in terms of war deeds and generosity toward the poor. In some tribes, like the Arapaho, the societies were intimately tied to the tribal religious hierarchy, but in most others they were more secular in nature.

During the nineteenth century, and occasionally in the twentieth century as well (e.g., Schlesier 1994:xxi), some writers suggested that the depopulation caused by epidemics and the disruptive influences of Euro-American civilization had resulted in the dissolution of formerly effective political confederacies of tribes. Based on traditions of a pre-European golden age, confederacies of tribes were said to have existed, such as that of the many Wichita and Kitsai villages, the 13 Skiri Pawnee villages, the 30 or so Arikara villages, and the "Seven Council Fires" said to have united all the Sioux. In fact, there is no historical documentation for such confederacies nor any reason to believe that they ever existed. As cultural ideals they perhaps functioned during the reservation period to provide Plains peoples with a counterpoint to the social disorganization caused by the disruption of their historical lifeway. But for the Plains from the late eighteenth century forward, all evidence points to the band or village as the basic social and political unit. The social and political systems reconstructed from historical documents and from the memories of Plains people during the late nineteenth and early twentieth centuries were not degenerate forms of earlier, more complex systems, but were fully functional ones that provided effective organization for life on the grasslands.

Cultural Characteristics of Plains Tribes

General cultural similarities of High Plains and Prairie tribes justify combining them into a single Plains culture area, while specific differences between them support the division of the culture area into two subareas (Holder (1970).

All definitions of Plains culture begin with dependence on the buffalo for subsistence (fig. 2) and the integration of the buffalo into all aspects of life: the hides for making clothing, shelter, and containers; the bones and horns for tools; hair for ropes; dried dung for fuel; and the spirit of the animal as an important part of religious life. For the Blackfeet, (Ewers 1955:150–151). 87 specific uses of the buffalo in addition to food have been identified. Linked to the buffalo in the historical period of Plains culture was the horse, which permitted mounted hunting. After their introduction on the Southern Plains in the early 1600s, horses spread northward from tribe to tribe and became as integral as buffalo to Plains culture (Ewers 1955:2–3).

The methods of Plains buffalo hunting are well-described in the literature (Wissler 1912b:19–28; Lowie 1954:16; Ewers 1955:152–170). Tribal groups gathered into large summer encampments to hunt the buffalo herds, since effective hunting required cooperative techniques. Before horses, the use of fire to surround a herd and drive the animals toward waiting hunters was recorded in the Prairie Region. On the High Plains, aboriginal methods included driving a herd over a cliff or into a corral, sometimes at the bottom of a slope or cutbank. A herd was lured by a buffalo caller, and as the animals moved between lines of rock piles or brush arranged as a funnel, increasingly constricting the herd, people shouted and waved robes to stampede the herd toward the precipice or into the corral (fig. 2).

After horses were in general use, two types of communal hunt were practiced. The first was the surround, in which hunters encircled the herd and attacked from all sides at once, causing the animals to mill about and giving the hunters maximum time to kill as many as possible. The second was the chase, in which hunters approached a herd, then charged alongside it, singling out animals to kill. The weapons used were lances and bows and arrows; during most of the historic period the only firearms were single-shot muzzle loaders, which were poorly adapted to mounted buffalo hunting. The chase method was easier to organize, required fewer hunters, and was less dangerous. By the mid-nineteenth century the Blackfeet had virtually abandoned the surround method in favor of the chase (Ewers 1955:154).

Throughout the year, small groups of men or lone hunters stalked buffalo using a variety of methods. For example, hunters disguised under wolf skins could crawl close enough to a small herd to make a kill. During winter, hunters on snowshoes drove buffalo into deep snow, where they could be killed as they floundered.

Differentiation of work according to male and female roles was a universal feature of Plains cultures. Men butchered the meat and brought it and the hides back to camp, where the kill became the responsibility of women. Surplus meat was sliced into thin sheets and dried in the sun for later consumption. Buffalo hides taken during the summer, when the hair was short, were used for making rawhide and soft-tanned buckskin for clothing and lodge covers. Winter hides, with long, dense hair, were tanned only on the inside and were used for cold-weather robes and bedding, as well as for the fur trade. To make rawhide, a hide was stretched out on the ground and pegged down with wooden stakes. Scraps of meat and fat were cleaned off using a toothed flesher of bone (fig. 3d,f), and the hide was allowed to cure in the sun. Then the skin was smoothed to an even thickness using an elkhorn scraper. The hair was removed from the other side using the scraper or a dehairing tool made from a knife blade (fig. 3e). To make buckskin (fig. 4), the rawhide was smeared with a mixture of brains, fat, and liver that was rubbed into the skin first with the hands, then with a smooth stone. After drying in the sun the hide was soaked in warm water, stretched back to its original size, and rubbed with a rough stone or a metal tool. Then the hide was softened by

Smithsonian, Dibner Lib.: top left, J. Franklin 1823; bottom, Hind 1860, vol. 1, neg. 90-6867; top right, U.S. Military Academy, West Point Mus. Coll., N.Y.:568.

Fig. 2. Buffalo hunting. top left, Assiniboine man on horseback driving buffalo into a corral. The man in the tree is the buffalo caller. Engraving after an unknown original by George Back, on the John Franklin Expedition 1819–1822. top right, Assiniboine method of chasing buffalo in the winter using snowshoes and dogs. Watercolor by Peter Rindisbacher, 1820 (computer enhanced). bottom, Plains Cree driving buffalo between lines of men and wooden logs or bundles of grass built up "like men" and into a pound, where they will be killed and butchered. Colored wood engraving after an unknown original made on Henry Hind Expedition of 1857–1858.

pulling it bank and forth through a loop of thong or twisted sinew. Finally, the hide might be smoked over a smouldering fire, which allowed it to dry soft and pliant after being wet (Ewers 1945:10–13; Weltfish 1965:369–372).

To make buffalo the focus of subsistence it was necessary to follow the seasonal movements, aggregations, and dispersals of the herds. Of necessity, all material possessions were portable. When Plains peoples were first described by Europeans, dogs were the only form of pack animals. Travois—poles fastened together where they crossed over a dog's withers, and sometimes with a small platform on the drag behind—were used to transport tepee covers and personal belongings ("Blackfoot," fig. 2, this vol.). Later, horses made larger loads possible. However, dog travois continued to be used after the introduction of horses, especially to haul firewood to camp.

Tepees were equally important as portable houses. Before horses, most of the Sioux, for example, lived in large, low tents housing multiple families. Each family was responsible for transporting a portion of the tepee cover. After horses, the historic form of the tepee developed: larger, taller, with wind flaps to control the flow of smoke out of the lodge. Constructed on three- or four-pole foundations, distinct tribal styles emerged. Social arrangements changed as well, since each tepee now housed a single married couple with their children and perhaps a widowed parent or other unmarried relative.

The High Plains tribes lived in tepees year-round, while the Prairie tribes used them only during their hunting expeditions. A unique expression of social solidarity of tribes or constituent bands was the camp circle, used on all formal occasions, including tribal hunts, religious ceremonies, and

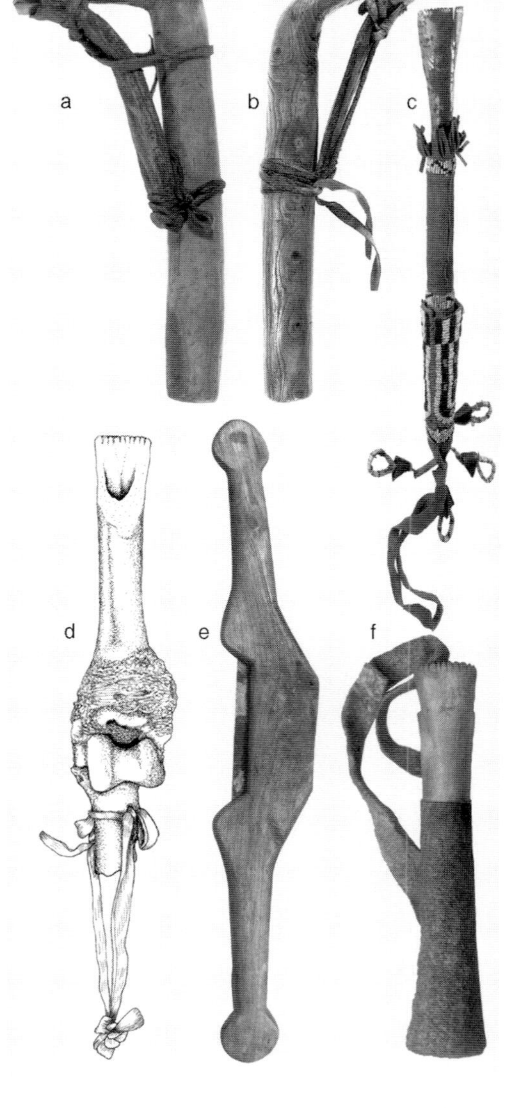

a
b
c
d
e
f

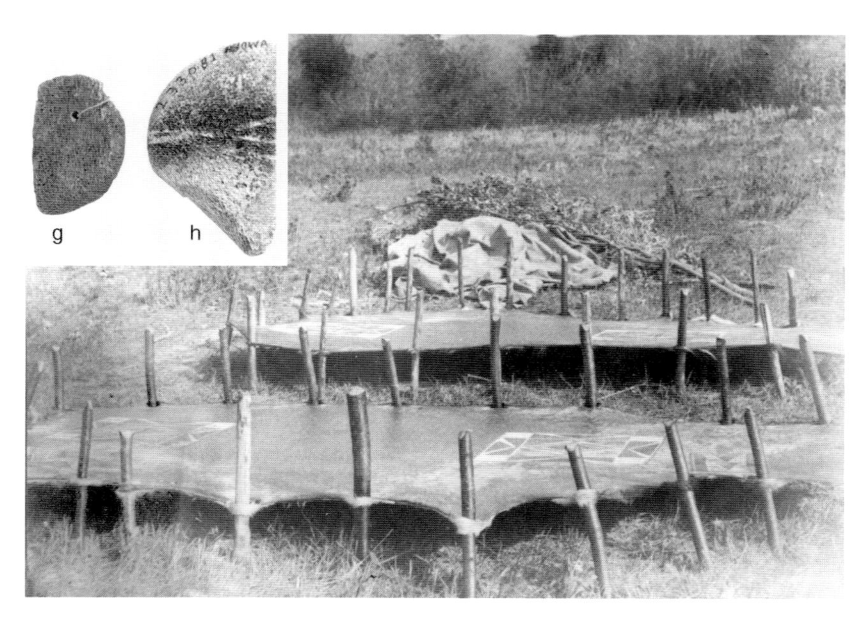

g
h

i

social festivities. Women pitched their tepees in a great circle, each band or clan arranged contiguously along a part of the arc. The whole represented the unity of the social group and frequently had cosmic symbolic significance as well. The Omaha camp circle, for example, was divided into moieties, one representing sky, the other earth, with a panoply of associated symbols and ritual duties.

The material culture of the Plains tribes shared a basic commonality of style, with regional and tribal variations. Horse travois, for example, among most of the northern tribes were constructed with woven platforms of saplings to support a load; the southern tribes improvised travois using tepee poles (Wissler 1912b:32). Rawhide containers, usually cylindrical or envelope-shaped parfleches, sometimes box-shaped, were used throughout the Plains. Clothing was made of buckskin, with regional stylistic variation, until the introduction of cloth and blankets supplemented and, by the late-nineteenth century, replaced hides. Similarly, common Plains patterns of stone, bone, and wood tools were gradually replaced after the late seventeenth century with Euro-American manufactured items provided in trade.

Like material culture, distinctive styles of women's art were common to the Plains. One was a geometrical style of painting on rawhide containers, by which women identified their belongings. Painting on tanned hide, predominantly robes, was likewise stylized. Quillwork, using porcupine or bird quills, was ubiquitous in the north. During the nineteenth century, after the introduction of manufactured glass beads, beadwork first enhanced, then ultimately replaced, most quillwork. Designs of both quillwork and beadwork were geometrical; early beadwork was restricted to large blocks of color, but later developed into distinctive tribal styles. On the northern and eastern edges of the Plains area, floral quillwork and beadwork traditions evolved, based on influences from Eastern tribes and perhaps from French Canadians. On the Southern Plains, the Comanche, Kiowa, and Plains Apache restricted beadwork to narrow borders, a style that Kroeber (1939:80) believed was borrowed from the Southwest.

Men's art styles were representational and were used to commemorate sacred visions and deeds in war on tepees, tepee liners, robes, and clothing. Some painting was symbolic, such as stylized hoof prints for horses stolen and parallel bands to indicate war parties.

Common to the Plains was a fundamental belief in "power," variously conceptualized from tribe to tribe, which was shared by all living things but which was beyond knowing. Humans could share in that power and use it to their advantage by accessing it through dreams or visions and by participation in rituals. Specialists—medicine men and priests—were those individuals with the greatest experience with power, who had garnered more power than the average person and who could use that power in war, hunting, and curing. Medicine bundles were collections of symbolic objects as diverse as bird and mammal skins, sacred stones, and ritual equipment that could be used in a wide variety of ritual contexts for the implementation of power. The realm of power was primarily that of men; women played essential roles in sacred ceremonies but did not play the role of intermediary between humans and the powers in the public way that men did. Medicine bundles were owned by individuals, who sometimes held them in trust for a clan, village, or tribe.

For most tribes, sacred power was acquired through the ritual of seeking a vision, in which men—usually young men—went away from the village to pray for communication from the powers. Fasting, prayer, and in some traditions, such as the Crow, Hidatsa, and Mandan, the sacrifice of a finger joint or other types of physical mortification were integral to the quest. Spirit beings, representing the powers, would appear to a successful visionary as a bird, animal, or other natural phenomenon that might then transform into a human. Spirits gave visionaries prayers and songs to recreate the vision experience and tokens of their power to be preserved in medicine bundles. Among many tribes, a man could sell or loan power objects so that

top left, Colo. Histl. Soc., Denver:F-41697; bottom left, Eastern Wash. State Histl. Soc., Cheney Cowles Mus., Allard Coll., Spokane:203. Smithsonian, Dept. of Anthr.: a, 418506, neg. 78-12581; b, 165785, neg. 75-8971; c, 200304, neg. 78-12409; g, 152912, neg. 92-10861-16; h, 233081, neg. 92-10861-16; i, 165918, neg. 37263-A; Harvard U., Peabody Mus., Cambridge, Mass.: d, 27576; neg. N3774; Smithsonian, Natl. Mus. of the Amer. Ind.: e, 6/7994, neg. N23614; f, 6/7923, neg. N23614.

Fig. 3. Rawhide processing. top left, Crow women stretching out a hide with wooden stakes; strips of meat are drying on racks. Photographed about 1900. center left, Mrs. Peter Lefthand, Crow, using an elkhorn scraper to reduce the skin to uniform thickness. Photograph by Fred Voget, Lodge Grass, Mont., 1940. top right, Hide processing tools. a, Northern Arapahoe elkhorn hide scraper with a thin iron blade. Collected by Ethel Cutler Freeman, Wyo., 1936; length 31cm. b, Southern Arapaho hide scraper with a thin iron blade and wooden handle. Collected by H.R. Voth, Southern Cheyenne and Arapaho Agency, Okla. Terr., 1882–1891; length 33 cm. c, Northern Arapahoe gun barrel hide flesher. The end of the barrel is split and notched to form the scraping edge. The handle is covered with beaded buckskin. Collected by Emile Granier, Wyo., before 1890; length 32.4 cm. d, Omaha flesher made of the femur of an animal, possibly buffalo. Collected by Alice Fletcher, Omaha Res., Nebr., 1882; length 25 cm. Drawn by Roger Thor Roop. e, Teton Sioux wooden dehairing tool with metal blade. Collected by Frances Densmore, Standing Rock Res., S. Dak., before 1917; length 48.3 cm. f, Teton Sioux flesher made of bone; handle covered with red painted buckskin and strap. Collected by Frances Densmore, Standing Rock Res., S. Dak., before 1917; length 24.8 cm. g–h, Kiowa paint applicators of porous bone used for lining out designs on rawhide and for applying paint to the pattern. Collected by James Mooney, Okla., 1904; h, height 10.1 cm, g to scale. bottom left, Crow stretched rawhides painted for constructing parfleches. Photographed about 1900. bottom right, Southern Cheyenne parfleche for carrying clothing. Collected by H.R. Voth, Southern Cheyenne and Arapaho Agency, Okla. Terr., 1882–1891; length 62 cm.

protection in war or the ability to heal might be shared more widely, and in some tribes sacred bundles and other power objects were passed down through the generations by gift or purchase.

Religious rituals were focused on individuals' demonstration of power through vision reenactments and on healing through the use of sacred songs and actions. Tribal rituals are exemplified in the Sun Dance, when all the constituent groups of a tribe gathered for a summer religious festival that involved prayer, sacrifice, and celebration. The coming together of a people in a single camp circle symbolized tribal unity. The multiday ceremony involved the erection of a tree, around which men and sometimes women danced and prayed, seeking power and frequently fulfilling a vow to perform the ritual in thanksgiving for surviving a difficult ordeal or for the good health of a loved one. Not all Plains tribes practiced the Sun Dance in this form, but all tribes had comparable summer rituals that involved entire social groups.

Relations among social groups on the Plains vacillated between hostility and alliance (Albers 1993). Even within tribes, bands or villages occasionally engaged in horse raiding or other hostilities against one another. Bonds of kinship and marriage, common language and culture, and the functioning of men's societies as camp police provided mechanisms for social integration that countered the tendency for groups to fractionalize (Provinse 1937).

Warfare was ubiquitous (M.W. Smith 1938; Newcomb 1950). Rather than an occasional state of affairs, warfare was a permanent relationship that united tribes together against one another. Group motives included competition over horses, hunting grounds, or access to European traders, while individual motives for warfare were vengeance for past deaths and the desire to gain horses, war honors, and social prestige. Forms of warfare varied from small, informal parties of men on foot intent on stealing horses from enemy camps, to large tribal parties of hundreds of mounted men traveling openly to seek vengeance. A system of graded "coups," symbolized by feathers variously worn and decorated, commemorated a man's war deeds.

Alliances, even between warring tribes, were common. Such temporary truces permitted periods of trade that were initiated by ritual pipe smoking and frequently a formal pipe-adoption ceremony, in which a man from one tribe adopted a man, or his child, from the other tribe in a ritual that was accompanied by lavish gift-giving. The bestowal of gifts was reciprocated, and periods of truce were at the same time periods of active trade. With the Cheyenne as trade middlemen from the late eighteenth to the early nineteenth century, European manufactured goods, particularly guns, flowed from the east and north of the Plains through the Missouri River village tribes in exchange for horses coming from the south and west (Jablow 1951). These trade patterns, undoubtedly prehistoric (vol. 4:351–353), included the exchange of horticultural surplus produced by the Prairie tribes for surplus meat, hides, and other products provided by the High Plains tribes.

Characteristics of the Prairie Tribes

Unlike the tribes of the High Plains, the Prairie peoples built permanent villages of large, multifamily dwellings. The Upper and Middle Missouri tribes, from the Hidatsa south to the Pawnee, constructed large, dome-shaped earthlodges; the more eastern tribes, from the Santee Sioux on the Mississippi and Minnesota rivers south to the Kansa, built rectangular bark-covered lodges. The Kansa also built oval or rectangular lodges covered with bark, hides, or mats, in the style of the Osage and Quapaw. Farther south, the Wichita and Kitsai made beehive-shaped houses covered with bundles of grass. Whatever the house style, these peoples built their villages on water courses, where women planted gardens of corn, beans, and squash in the bottomlands. The Sioux were, in general, exceptions; among the Santee Sioux, only the Mdewakanton had permanent villages of bark-covered lodges and small gardens of corn, while only some Yankton and Yanktonai experimented in the nineteenth century with building earthlodges and raising crops.

All the Prairie tribes inhabited their villages during the planting and harvest seasons and spent much of the rest of the year hunting buffalo. While traveling, all the tribes lived in tepees. In this way, living arrangements shifted throughout the year from multifamily lodges in the village to single-family tepees.

Most of the Prairie tribes were organized in matrilineal or patrilineal clans. Village unity was represented by sacred bundles preserved from generation to generation, accompanied by origin stories unique to each clan. Central to the Prairie tribes was the distinction between priests, who used the sacred bundles in their rituals for the benefit

Amer. Mus. of Nat. Hist., New York: top left, 23418; top right, 24396; center right, 284064; bottom right, 118957; bottom left, State Histl. Soc. of N. Dak., Bismarck; insert, Smithsonian, Dept. of Anthr.: 165971.

Fig. 4. Processing rawhide into buckskin. top left, Blackfeet woman rubbing fat into a hide. top right, Blackfeet women pulling a hide across a twisted loop of sinew tied to a tepee pole. A metal strap was also used for this purpose ("Plains Cree," fig. 2, this vol.). top left and right, Photographs by Clark Wissler, near Browning, Mont., 1904. center left, Winona Frank, Plains Cree, soaking a hide in water. A metal strap is attached to the post above the bucket. Photograph by Thomas Kehoe, Little Pine Reserve, Sask., 1973. center right, Plains Cree woman (married to an Assiniboine) wringing out a deerskin after soaking. Photograph by Robert H. Lowie, Ft. Belknap, Mont., 1908. bottom left, Weasel Woman, Crow-Sioux, graining hide using a metal-bladed scraper. Photograph by Monroe Killy, Elbowoods, Ft. Berthold Res., N. Dak., 1942. insert, Cheyenne graining tool, wooden handle with metal blade. Collected by H.R. Voth, Southern Cheyenne and Arapaho Agency, Okla. Terr., 1882–1891; length 15.2 cm. bottom right, Crow woman smoking skin. Photograph by Robert H. Lowie, Crow Indian Res., Mont. (computer enhanced), 1910–1916.

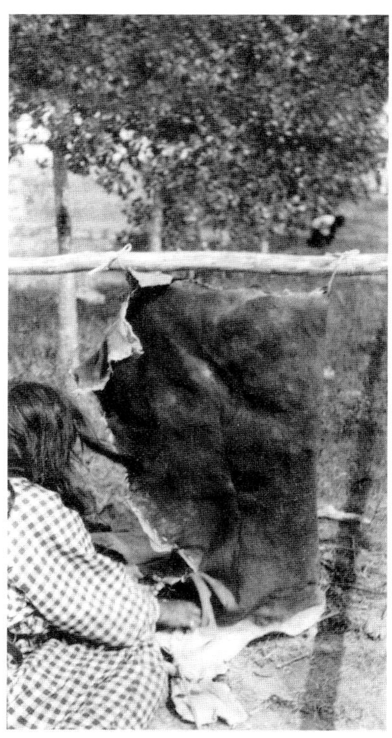

of the tribe as a whole, and medicine men or doctors, who used their vision powers to cure the sick and wounded and to perform magic. While sharing in all the other Prairie characteristics, the Caddoan tribes were distinctive in their lack of clans and unilineal descent. Kin relations were tightly correlated with status among the Prairie tribes; clan or family connections determined access to the status of chief or priest and in general dictated social standing. The Santee and Yankton-Yanktonai Sioux were again exceptions, lacking unilineal descent, hereditary status, and the distinction between priests and medicine men.

Characteristics of the High Plains Tribes

High Plains tribes had recognized hunting territories and annual patterns of camp movements that allowed them access to the variety of resources of their environment, including animals and plants. With the exception of the matrilineal Crow, they lacked unilineal descent and were organized instead in loosely structured bilateral bands, which tended to be kinship units comprising extended families or groups of extended families. Each nuclear family lived separately in its own tepee.

Sacred bundles among the Blackfoot, Gros Ventre, Cheyenne, Arapaho, Teton Sioux, and Kiowa symbolized tribal unity, but, unlike those of the Prairie tribes, they were not the basis for social hierarchies. The formal camp circle was the most important expression of tribal unity. Chieftainship tended to follow family lines but was not in concept hereditary. Band councils, composed of adult men, elected or appointed chiefs based on personal ability and charisma. Band membership tended to be fluid, with frequent movement between bands.

History

Anthropological studies generally equated Plains culture with the "typical" nomadic tribes of the High Plains; tribes of the Prairie Plains were "marginal" or "atypical." Wissler (1914a:25) argued that "the whole basic structure of the later horse Indian culture was in existence when the horse came." The horse shifted the balance of power from the older, semisedentary horticultural tribes of the Missouri River valley to the horse-mounted nomadic tribes, many of whom—like the Sioux and Cheyenne—were recent arrivals on the High Plains, but who had long resided in the Prairie Plains. Kroeber (1928:394–396) argued that the tribes along the eastern margin of the Plains were Woodland peoples, ultimately originating in the Southeast; the western High Plains were largely uninhabited. He proposed that, before the horse, "there was no important Plains culture, the chief phases in the area being marginal to richer cultures outside" (Kroeber 1939:76).

However, archeological investigations during the 1930s began to reveal both the antiquity and richness of prehistoric cultures in Nebraska and elsewhere in the Central Plains. Strong (1933:271) pointed out the paradox implicit in Wissler's analysis. If the basic structure of Plains culture was in place before the horse and was represented by the semisedentary horticulturalists, and if the effect of the horse was to "intensify" and diffuse that culture, then it does not follow that the horticulturalists should have been eclipsed by the horse-mounted nomads. Instead, Strong conceptualized the horticulturalist way of life as characteristic of the prehistoric Plains, and the mounted buffalo-hunting way of life as a new development during the historic period that involved many tribes who were newcomers to the area (Strong 1933:285). At issue was the extent to which buffalo hunting, as opposed to horticulture, was basic to prehistoric Plains culture.

Lowie (1955a:67), defending Wissler's conception of the Plains, characterized the pre-horse plains as "one of the well developed and characterized cultures of the continent," and argued that the importance of the horse to the hunting lifeway of the Plains was exaggerated. In an insightful culture history of the Plains written from the perspective of the village tribes, Holder (1970) examined the dual challenges to the older, semisedentary lifeway by the developing horse-mounted nomads and the slowly encroaching Euro-American civilization. The resultant picture situates the village tribes not as anachronisms, left behind in the florescence of mounted nomadism, but as culturally dynamic, responding and adapting to the rapid changes that engulfed the entire Plains area.

No change was more significant than the devastation wrought by epidemics. European diseases caused significant population decreases. In the absence of written records those losses are not possible to quantify.

The actual size of prehistoric populations remains a matter of conjecture. Mooney (1928:33; Ubelaker 1976:287) estimated the Plains population at 141,800, calculating the population of the Southern Plains in 1690 at 41,000 and the Northern Plains in 1780 as 100,800. Kroeber (1939:142) revised Mooney's estimate downward, calculating the entire Plains population at 129,400. Whatever figures are used, there is little controversy that European diseases during the eighteenth and nineteenth centuries decimated tribes, reducing the total Plains population by 50 to 75 percent. Working with both Mooney's and Kroeber's material, and basing his estimates on population densities of 5 or 10 per square kilometer, Ubelaker (1992:172–174) estimated the Plains population at the time of contact at 140,700 to 284,900; for his purposes he proposed a population of 189,000 in the year 1700. Ubelaker calculated the population in 1800 at 120,330 (a 36% decrease), in 1850 at 103,136 (a 46% decrease), and in 1900 at 62,656 (a 67% decrease). From the nadir in 1900, population levels increased in the twentieth century, rising steadily: 1925, 76,591; 1950, 123,513; 1960, 169,613; 1970, 211,701.

In developing a historical picture of the Plains, no problem presents greater challenges than the identification of archeological remains with historic tribes. The "direct historical approach" (W.R. Wedel 1938), the method by which archeological sites identifiable in the historical record are linked with specific tribes, has been successful with Pawnee, Iowa, and Cheyenne village sites. However, pressed to paint a fuller picture of the past, some archeologists have resorted to speculation based on the identification of prehistoric archeological complexes with tribes resident in the area in historical times (see various authors in Schlesier 1994; Wood 1999). Methodologically, this presupposes Powell's hypothesis, based on language distributions, of stable residence of North American peoples over long time periods. Since in the absence of historical documentation archeologically recovered artifacts cannot in any other manner be assigned to specific tribal traditions, speculative identification with historic tribes has assumed methodological currency, particularly in response to the necessity of assigning prehistoric physical remains to contemporary tribes for reburial under the Native American Graves Protection and Repatriation Act of 1990. This volume takes a more conservative approach since, as a reference work, hypothetical identifications are liable to be misconstrued as fact. Therefore, in the prehistory chapters, care has been taken to limit speculation about tribal origins even at the expense of providing an overall portrayal of the continuity of Plains history and prehistory.

Organization of the Volume

The volume begins with historical summaries of research in archeology, ethnology, and ethnohistory as well as a chapter on environment and subsistence. A survey of Plains languages is followed by more detailed discussions of the three largest families in the area: Algonquian, Caddoan, and Siouan. Particular attention is paid to Caddoan and Siouan since most of the languages in these two families are in the Plains area.

Eleven chapters are devoted to prehistory, outlining archeological manifestations: the Hunting and Gathering tradition, beginning about 8000 B.C. and lasting into the nineteenth century, represented by the nomadic High Plains tribes; Plains Woodland, on the eastern edge of the area, dating from about 500 B.C. to A.D. 1000; and the various Village traditions, extending from about A.D. 700 and lasting into the nineteenth century, represented by the semisedentary village tribes of the Missouri River valley.

The history of the Plains area is reviewed in the next four chapters, which summarize relations between Indians and Whites from contact through the twentieth century. The chapters are intended as background for the tribal chapters and emphasize general themes and outline important events during the period of exploration and in the course of official dealings of Plains peoples with the United States and Canadian governments.

At the heart of the volume are ethnographic chapters that focus on prereservation history and ethnography but also deal more succinctly with the late nineteenth and twentieth centuries. For the purposes of the *Handbook*, 32 ethnic units have been identified and treated in separate chapters. In some cases those units have been defined for convenience of reference, and they therefore do not necessarily reflect comparable social groups. For example, the three Blackfoot tribes are treated together, based on commonalities of culture and history. Similarly, the Otoe and Missouria, as well as the Yankton and Yanktonai Sioux, are treated in single chapters. To have done otherwise would have resulted in repetition of basic cultural description. The Métis are included among the tribal chapters in order to signal their significant role in Plains history. While not a tribe in the usual sense, the Métis (recognized in Canada as a First Nation) are descended from French and British fur traders and their Indian wives; the group originated in the Red River area of Manitoba in the early nineteenth century and developed a distinctive language and ethnic identity. Three topical chapters treat the Hidatsa, Mandan, and Arikara after their consolidation on the Fort Berthold Reservation in North Dakota and the Sioux tribes in the early and late periods. The final chapters of the volume are devoted to significant topics that cross-cut tribal chapters.

History of Archeological Research

WALDO R. WEDEL AND RICHARD A. KRAUSE

Nineteenth-century archeological work in the Plains was guided by a gentlemanly antiquarianism that on occasion lapsed into vandalism. Curious traders, explorers, militiamen, and homesteaders observed and circulated accounts of the burial mounds, earthworks, and village ruins they encountered and occasionally looted. Many of them did make desultory inquiries of the "stone age" implements they found, and some published accounts of their work. But most of the specimens acquired by avocational digging were at best described, displayed, or stored by material of manufacture. Many have been lost (Wedel 1981:16–20).

For the history of Plains archeology in Canada, see "Hunting and Gathering Tradition: Canadian Plains," this volume.

Early Surveys

The first observations and excavations by anthropologically trained scholars began around 1900. Most of this work was guided as much by chance or opportunity as by a sense of problem. George A. Dorsey (1900), for example, described a quartzite quarry in eastern Wyoming after a visit sponsored by the Field Columbian Museum, Chicago. William H. Holmes (1903) investigated the Afton Sulphur Spring in Oklahoma for the Smithsonian Institution, followed by Stephen C. Simms's (1903a) examination of the Bighorn Medicine Wheel in northern Wyoming, also sponsored by the Field Museum. The controversial 1902 "Lansing Man" finds near Atcheson, Kansas, involved both geologists and anthropologists as did Robert F. Gilder's 1906 Nebraska "Loessman" near Omaha (Gilder 1907a). Both finds were thought by their protagonists to bear on the debate about the antiquity of man in America. As evidence for Early Man neither of these finds, nor Newton H. Winchell's alleged Paleolithic flint workers of the Kansas Flint Hills, gained acceptance (Wedel 1981:16–20).

While early twentieth-century ethnologists were refining the social dimensions of the Great Plains as a culture area, their archeological colleagues were creating a different version of Plains culture. The archeologists' goal was to identify spatially restricted and, if possible, stratigraphically sequent prehistoric components or trait complexes as "archeological cultures." For instance, the Nebraska State Historical Society, Lincoln, commissioned E.E. Blackman to make a preliminary reconnaissance of the state—a labor he began in 1901 and continued for 30 years. In 1903, Robert F. Gilder began a program of reconnaissance and excavation of Nebraska culture remains near Omaha. Fredrich H. Sterns did the same in southeast Nebraska, northeast Kansas, and western Iowa (Blackman 1903, 1907, 1930; Gilder 1907, 1907a, 1908, 1908a, 1913, 1916; Sterns 1914, 1915, 1915a). Stone-chambered mounds near Kansas City were excavated in 1907 (Fowke 1910), and house and mound sites in southeast Nebraska were described (M.E. Zimmerman 1918).

In the Middle Missouri subarea, Orin G. Libby and A.B. Stout located and mapped sites along the Missouri River in North Dakota (W. Wedel 1981:23). In 1905, George F. Will and Herbert J. Spinden (1906) tested the Double Ditch Mandan site and surveyed other sites along the Missouri (Will 1924). Henry Montgomery (1906, 1908) reported the results of his work on earthen mounds in the Northeastern Plains. Reports on the slabhouse ruins in the Canadian and North Canadian valleys in Texas and Oklahoma were published as early as 1908 (Wedel 1981:16–20). From 1912 to 1915 William Nickerson tested mounds in Manitoba (Capes 1963).

The pace of organized fieldwork quickened in the next decade. In 1919 J. Walter Fewkes explored burnt rock middens and other sites in central Texas (Pearce 1932:44–54). William E. Myer dug into mound and village sites near Sioux Falls, South Dakota, and tested Osage sites in western Missouri (Myer 1922). In the mid-1920s Matthew Stirling excavated prehistoric cemetery sites near Mobridge, South Dakota (Wedel 1955), Charles R. Keyes (1927, 1930, 1949, 1951) organized a productive survey program in Iowa, and A.T. Hill revitalized the survey work of the Nebraska State Historical Society. Hill also introduced new excavation procedures and from 1926 to 1929 applied them to Pawnee earthlodge ruins. In Texas Cyrus N. Ray was reporting on deeply buried antiquities in the Abilene district, and in 1928 he took the lead in organizing the Texas Archaeological and Paleontological Society (Wedel 1981:25–27).

In 1928 the Smithsonian Institution began a matching fund program (Public Law 248) that supported work by the University of Nebraska, Lincoln, whose representatives applied Hill's new techniques to sites along the Missouri, Platte, and Republican rivers. The same program supported the work of Beloit College's Logan Museum on Middle Missouri sites and the Denver Museum of Natural

History survey of the Colorado High Plains (Wedel 1981:25–27). The Nebraska fieldwork resulted in several landmark Plains publications, among them William Duncan Strong's (1935) survey of Nebraska archeology, and Waldo R. Wedel's (1935b) classification of Nebraska and Kansas cultures.

Early Taxonomic Issues

W.C. McKern (1939) and his associates introduced the Midwestern Taxonomic System (MTS) to the archeological community, and Wedel introduced it to the Plains. The advent of the MTS led many Plains archeologists—Strong, Wedel, Paul L. Cooper, G.H. Gilmore, and John L. Champe among them—to reclassify previously introduced archeological cultures as components, foci, aspects, or phases of the new content-based taxonomic hierarchy. In the manuscript of *Introduction to Nebraska Archeology*, for example, Strong had refined Gilder's Nebraska culture, identified an Upper Republican culture, summarized Wedel's work on Pawnee archeology, and discussed other regional cultures. In the published version, however, he identified all the original cultures (except Dismal River) as aspects of the MTS (Strong 1935:1–2). A year after Strong's monograph was published, major revisions were proposed. Gilmore (E.H. Bell and Gilmore 1936) introduced a Nehawka focus of the Nebraska aspect; John L. Champe (1936) defined a single component Loup River focus of the Upper Republican phase, and Paul L. Cooper (1936) removed the Saint Helena focus from the Nebraska aspect and placed it in the Upper Republican aspect. In 1940 Wedel accepted the previous modifications, revised Strong's original foci, and grouped Nebraska and Upper Republican aspects into a Central Plains phase (Wedel 1940).

Early taxonomic discussions were fueled by the data gathered through the federal government's Works Progress Administration projects in the Central Plains in the 1930s. Whether construed as cultures, components, foci, aspects, or phases these units themselves became the subjects of analytical attention and for archeologists throughout North America, correlating them in time and space became the sine qua non of archeological interpretation (W.W. Taylor 1948:53). Plains archeologists participated fully in this paradigm of inquiry and to promote its aims used the evidence provided by house remains, ceramic, stone, bone, and shell tools for chronology building. In sum, culture history, as the approach was called, stressed systematic attempts to order archeological remains into local and regional sequences (Willey and Sabloff 1974:64).

The Direct Historic Approach

In the Plains, however, culture history shared the research limelight with attempts to trace the prehistoric roots of historically documented ethnic groups. The basic idea here was both intellectually demanding and cogent. If historically documented sites could be located and a suitable archeological sample drawn and analyzed, then (within certain limits) an ethnic identity could be assigned to co-occurring ceramic styles, house types, burial practices, and tool technologies. The work of George F. Will and Herbert J. Spinden (1906), W.E. Myer (1922), Matthew Stirling (Wedel 1955) and others was motivated by this aim. Will and Spinden used a mixture of oral history, ethnography, history, and archeology in their study of the Mandan. Strong (1935) used a similar mix of information; Waldo Wedel (1936) honed the approach in his introduction to Pawnee archeology; and Mildred Mott (1938) used it to detail the relationship of historic tribes to archeological manifestations in Iowa. Strong (1940) synthesized the ethnographic, historic, and archeological data available for the Arikara, Mandan, and Hidatsa remains in North and South Dakota (figs. 1–2), and William T. Mulloy (1942) used a similar integration of sources to suggest a Crow origin for the Hagen site in eastern Montana.

Cultural Ecology

The 1926–1928 finds near Folsom, New Mexico, added yet an additional warp to the fabric of early archeological inquiry in the Great Plains. The Folsom discoveries unequivocally documented the association of humans with an extinct form of bison and renewed an interest in mankind's New World antiquity (Figgins 1933; Wilmsen and Roberts 1978). The Folsom discoveries were soon followed by others demonstrating an association of man with mammoth (Sellards 1940:17–46). Two distinct forms of fluted points, one found primarily with mammoth, and the

State Histl. Soc. of N. Dak., Bismarck: #200-670.

Fig. 1. Camp, under the direction of William Duncan Strong, during excavation of the Leavenworth Arikara historic village on the west side of the Missouri River. left to right, Unidentified; Eric Jacobson; William H. Over, curator, University Mus., Vermillion, S. Dak.; unidentified, Jean Strong, wife of William Duncan Strong; George F. Will, chairman, Mus. Committee, State Historical Society of N. Dak., Bismarck; Michael O'Heeron, Baylor U., Dallas; Maurice E. Kirby, geologist-surveyor; Mathew Stirling, chief of the Bureau of American Ethnology, Smithsonian; Lee Daniels, Dept. of Sociology, U. of Nebr., Lincoln; and William Duncan Strong, Bureau of American Ethnology. Photograph by Russell Reid, Cottonwood Creek, Corson County, S. Dak., Aug. 1932.

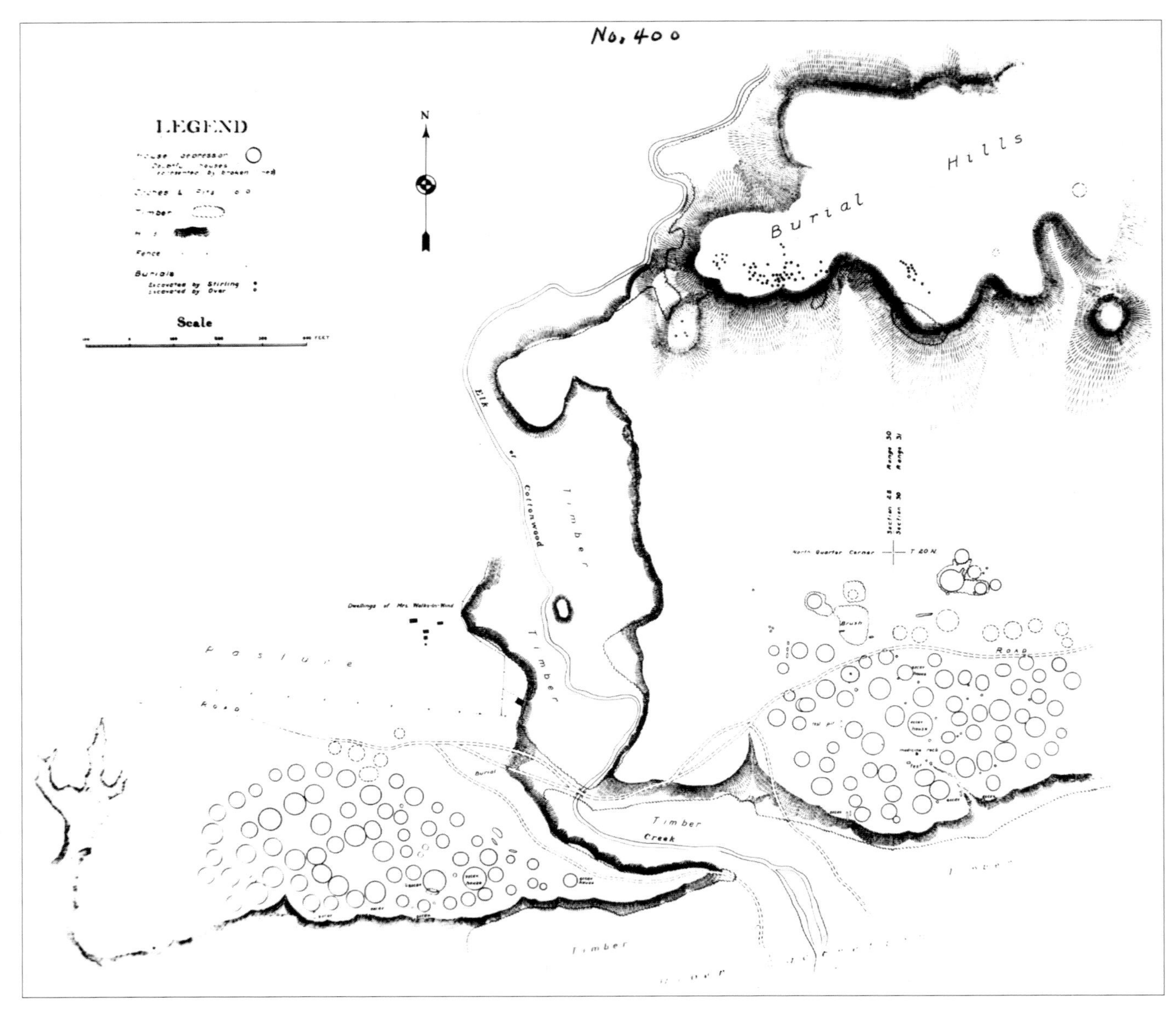

Smithsonian, NAA: 99-10125.

Fig. 2. Map of the Leavenworth site, S. Dak., at the time of Strong's excavations in 1932. An Arikara village along the Missouri River, the site yielded numerous artifacts including potsherds; bone implements such as awls, knives, hoes, and shaft straighteners; stone hammerstones; mortars; pestles; whetstones; and scrapers.

other with extinct bison, and the stratigraphic superposition of the two at the Clovis site (Sellards 1940:29–31), established a sequence of early mammoth and later bison hunters. The food requirements of mammoths exceeded those that could be supplied by modern steppe grasses; hence, a more luxuriant plant cover was posited for the past and the evidence for it sought.

The picture that emerged was one of a cooler, moister climate, which supported a lush prairie grassland where steppe or desert later prevailed. Many of the mammoth kills were in or near ancient ponds, streams, or river channels, and a significant proportion of the slaughtered beasts were female, young, or immature, leading some to infer selectivity on the part of the hunters. With the disappearance of the proboscideans—for reasons not yet clear—hunting and harvesting peoples turned to smaller but more abundant grazing animals, chief among them a bison of larger than modern size. Mass kills resembling drives, or pounds, and opportunistic surrounds or ambushes at water holes or in the breaks along water courses replaced the earlier pattern of repetitious single animal kills. In short, the work on Early Man in the western Plains focused attention on the relationship between prehistoric Plains cultures and their natural settings. This emphasis was most cogently expressed in Wedel's (1941) essay on environment and subsistence in the Central Plains. In this and related essays Wedel (1947, 1963) carefully outlined the role a prehistoric Plains environment might have played in shaping aboriginal social life.

Later Taxonomic Issues

From the 1940s to the 1960s a Smithsonian-sponsored, multi-institutional, salvage effort accompanied dam construction in the Middle Missouri. As a consequence time, money, and manpower were diverted to the Dakotas. The accumulating body of data thus produced was ordered within the Midwestern Taxonomic System with difficulty. Emergent classificatory problems were discussed by Gordon Baldwin, J.L. Champe, C.S. Smith, W.R. Hurt, and R.L. Stephenson during a 1955 trip to the Fort Randall and Oahe reservoirs and led to a spontaneous informal gathering upon the party's return to Lincoln. The published version (R.L. Stephenson 1954) of this gathering's deliberations identified 10 foci and six aspects for the Middle Missouri, eight foci and four aspects for the Central Plains. The Middle Missouri taxa went unchallenged, but a revision of those in the Central Plains engendered a decade of debate. At issue was Champe's reclassification of Upper Republican and Nebraska phases as foci of a single and inclusive Aksarben aspect. Wedel (1959) saw little merit to Champe's proposals. He introduced instead a three-aspect scheme for the classification of Central Plains materials.

In the 1940s the usefulness of the MTS was not seriously questioned, but in the early 1950s dissatisfaction began to grow, related to the body of data on social development in the Middle Missouri. Lehmer (1954) was the first to forthrightly address it. He delineated three developmental traditions, Central Plains, Middle Missouri, and Coalescent. These did not embody violent contrasts in social, economic, or manufacturing practices. Instead they reflected subtle distinctions best described as stylistic variations on a set of common themes (Lehmer 1954:140–147). Recognizing these subtly different lifeways as traditions was a stroke of genius. They have endured. The remainder of this first attempt to supersede the MTS was, however, a taxonomic nightmare. It combined the MTS focus with the Southwest time-space integrator the "branch." These units did not work very well and Lehmer worried about why, as he tried to replace them.

Early in the 1960s Lehmer collaborated with Warren W. Caldwell in the first comprehensive attempt to apply the Willey and Phillips system to Great Plains materials. The Willey and Phillips (1958) classification is based on taxa created through the interaction of time, space, and content. The basic units are the phase, horizon, and tradition; the phase is a classificatory taxon and the horizon and tradition are integrative ones. Phases are the basic content units. Their relationship to traditions and horizons may be summarized as follows:

1. Phases must have the greatest content
2. Traditions must have the greatest time depth
3. Horizons must have the greatest spatial spread
4. Traditions must have less content than phases
5. Traditions must have less spatial spread than horizons
6. Horizons must be less durable than traditions.

Lehmer and Caldwell (1966) proposed two major traditions: Middle Missouri and Coalescent each divided into horizons identified as initial, extended, and terminal. But the Lehmer-Caldwell use of horizon was a clear violation of principles 3 and 5 above. While Lehmer pondered the consequences of modifying the Willey and Phillips horizon, Lionel A. Brown (1966) tried to reorder Central Plains complexes using Lehmer and Caldwell's scheme. He integrated three phases: Smokey Hill, Upper Republican, and Nebraska with the Central Plains tradition but in doing so violated principle 2.

The problems with these initial attempts to use the Willey and Phillips system were discussed by Krause (1969:82–96) as a background for revising Central Plains taxonomy. The suggested revisions can be summarized as follows: (1) replace the Upper Republican phases with three phases—Solomon River, Classic Republican, and Loup River phases; (2) replace the Nebraska phase with two phases—Doniphan and Douglas phases; (3) retain the designation Central Plains for a subareal tradition and add two regional variants, Nebraska and Upper Republican; and (4) recognize a Saint Helena phase as a product of fusion between the two regional variants. Krause argued that these alterations, based on the use of Lehmer's idea of variant (devised in 1968 but not published until 1971) would bring Central Plains classificatory practices into accord with those being developed for the Middle Missouri region and with the provisions of the Willey and Phillips system. Criticism centered on how the Nebraska culture materials were to be handled (Blakeslee and Caldwell 1979).

In 1971 Lehmer published an *Introduction to Middle Missouri Archeology*, in which he resolved his taxonomic misgivings. He replaced the Lehmer and Caldwell (1966) horizon with the variant that he described as: "a unique and reasonably uniform expression of a cultural tradition which has a greater order of magnitude than a phase and is distinguished from other variants of the same tradition by its geographic distribution, age and/or cultural content" (Lehmer 1971:32). If Lehmer had described the variant as he used it he would have called it a mid-range integrative taxon with less content, greater time span, and greater spatial spread than a phase but less time span than a tradition and less spatial spread than a horizon. Thus defined, the variant fits securely within the logic of the Willey and Phillips system. Lehmer used it to provide a lucid and productive comparison of Middle Missouri artifact complexes, settlement patterns, and village types. With the variant, Lehmer achieved harmony between taxonomy and culture history.

Middle Missouri specialists have embraced and refined Lehmer's scheme. By separating the Initial variant of the Middle Missouri tradition into eastern and western components and systematically adding phases to most of the variants, they have facilitated a smooth and orderly transition from systematic-morphological to processual-interpretative classifications for the region's post-Woodland remains.

An equivalent shift in taxonomic practices has been uneven in the Central and Southern Plains. Although Kenneth L. Brown (1985) redefined the Pomona aspect as a variant integrating Clinton, Wolf Creek, May Brook, and Apple Valley phases, and Mary J. Adair (1988:33–44) viewed Smokey Hill, Keith, and Kansas City Hopewell as variants, Blakeslee and Caldwell (1979) rejected the use of the taxon in their appraisal of the Nebraska phase. Very few Central Plains specialists have used it since. Phases, however, have been proposed with increasing frequency. Vis and Henning (1969:253–271) framed cogent arguments for recognizing an early Little Sioux and a later Little Sioux phase for the Mill Creek manifestations. Hofman (1978:6–35) reformulated Oklahoma's Custer and Washita River foci as phases. Ludwickson (1978:94–108) expanded and refined the Loup River phase (ultimately renaming it the Itskari phase). Grange (1979) demonstrated the coherence and interpretative force of a proto-Pawnee Lower Loup phase, and Adair (1988) identified Bemis Creek and Steed Kisker as phases in her study of the emergence of food production in the Great Plains.

Efforts to form phases from Archaic and Woodland stage materials have been sporadic. In Nebraska, C.M. Wright (1982) identified Kivett's (1962) Logan Creek materials as an Archaic stage phase. In Kansas Witty (1982) defined an Archaic stage Munkers Creek phase, Grosser (1970) introduced a Chelsea phase, Rohn, Stein, and Glover (1977) a Colvin phase, Grosser (1970) and Artz (1981) a Walnut phase. Grosser (1973) defined an El Dorado phase, and Schmits (1980a) a Black Vermillion phase for Archaic deposits in eastern Kansas, Reid (1983) a Nebo Hill phase and M. Kay (1983) a Sedalia phase for similar materials in Missouri. Woodland stage phases defined for Kansas include: Lake City (K.L. Brown 1981); Trowbridge, Kansas City, Edwardsville (A.E. Johnson 1979, 1983); Bowlin (Schmits and Bailey 1986); Walnut (Grosser 1977); Hertha (Blakeslee and Rhon 1982–1986, 2); and Butler (Grosser 1973). Reynolds (1977) has also identified a Grasshopper Falls phase; Witty (1982), a Greenwood phase; and J.O. Marshall (1972), a Cuesta phase for Kansas Woodland complexes.

The shift in classificatory practices was uneven and for the most part was not accompanied by a shift in research emphasis. Changes in the popularity of artifact types or attributes of use and manufacture were still primarily used to infer the temporal relatedness of Willey and Phillips' phases, or MTS aspects and foci. Bone, stone, and shell tool types were formed by combining the evidence for their use with a description of their shape and size. Plains specialists have been remarkably consistent in their approach to shell, stone, and bone artifacts due in part to the limited options offered by the materials from which they were made and in part to historical descriptions of the manufacture and use of similar implements.

The analysis and description of pottery was a different matter. Paul Cooper produced the first systematic study of Plains ceramics in 1949. On the basis of differences in surface finish, vessel form, and rim and lip design, he divided the known Middle Missouri ceramic sample into three types he identified as simply A, B, and C (P.L. Cooper 1949:303). In 1951 Lehmer refined and revised Cooper's types in a study that became the model for most subsequent research. Lehmer (1951:3) used three of Cooper's criteria to define wares that "may be thought of as groups of types which share such fundamental characteristics as...the surface finish, the general form, and the basic rim form." Types in Lehmer's scheme were to be determined by differences in decoration and lip shape. "The types themselves have all the characteristic features of the ware but are distinguished by the decorative treatment and sometimes variation in form" (Lehmer 1951:3).

In defining types most followed Lehmer's lead. L.A. Brown (1966), Calabrese (1972, 1977), Caldwell (1966), Caldwell and Jensen (1969), Frantz (1962), J.J. Hoffman (1967), Husted (1965), Jensen (1965), A.E. Johnson (1979), R.B. Johnston (1967), Sperry (1968a), Stephenson (1962, 1969), Weakley (1971), Wood (1967), and Woolworth and Wood (1964) used Lehmer's criteria for ware and type formation in their Middle Missouri work. A.D. Anderson (1961), Blakeslee and Caldwell (1979), L.A. Brown (1966), Gunnerson (1952), Henning (1961), Ives (1955), Tiffany (1978), Sigstad (1969), and Wedel (1959) applied similar criteria to the study of Central Plains ceramics.

Lehmer's approach to pottery classification was successful because he combined the right elements of manufacture with the right elements of decoration. Morphological practices (with the exception of lip shaping and minor modifications of rim form) carry a relatively high risk of product loss. Decorative practices are not so risky. Innovation and experimentation in decorative embellishment and ornament may proceed with little or no risk of product loss. Therefore, stability in major morphological practices and change in minor manufacturing practices and decorative embellishments may be expected. Thus Lehmer's types, since they were defined by the least conservative morphological characteristics (i.e., lip form and rim construction) and by decoration were expectably sensitive time indicators within the continuum of the conservative morphological practices that defined his wares.

Processual Archeology

In the 1960s American archeology experienced a paradigm modification; a shift from culture history to a form of inquiry its adherents called processual archeology. To the most intractable processualists the culture history done by previous generations of archeologists had the interpretative appeal of a series of traits, artifact types, or taxonomic units hung on the clothesline of time. They preferred instead a perspective in which culture itself was considered a system, that is, an interconnected set of parts or subsystems with human behavior as the point of subsystem articulation. Variation in human behavior, and by extension variation in its products, artifact manufacture and use, were seen as both the results of subsystem reorganization and the means for re-establishing systemic harmony once it had been disrupted. Since most processualists considered culture an extrasomatic means of adaptation (Binford 1962:217), they emphasized the role of environmental variables in their work—an emphasis that revived a previous Plains interest in the interplay of technology, environment, and social organization.

Adaptation became a key issue in Plains work of the late 1960s. Detecting ecological boundaries beyond which elements of technology or social practice gained or lost adaptive significance became and remained an important regional research goal. Wood and his collaborators (1969a), for instance, argued that population density and distribution, together with domestic group size, composition, and degree of permanency had adaptive significance for Upper Republican and Nebraska peoples in the Central Plains. Caldwell (1966) and Lehmer (1970) claimed a significant relationship between climatic change and episodes of post-Woodland stage population expansion and contraction in the middle reaches of the Missouri River Trough. In a similar vein Dee Ann Story and S. Valestro (1977) argued for environmentally induced dislocations of cultural systems in Texas between the thirteenth and fifteenth centuries. In Oklahoma James A. Brown and his colleagues (1978) concluded that during this same interval there was a dispersal of households into many small communities as a consequence of attempts to spread the risk of crop failure.

For some time, environmentally focused research in the Western and Northwestern Plains had focused on the much earlier and more dramatic effects of the Hypsithermal (Altithermal), a period characterized by generally higher temperatures and lower rainfall than today (Antevs 1955; Deevey and Flint 1957). Early investigations suggested a cultural hiatus during this period. Mulloy (1943:433) even posited an abandonment as climatic conditions forced human groups into new settings. Human habitation has since been demonstrated (Reeves 1973:1223–1227), but there are relatively few Hypsithermal period sites in the Northwestern Plains, and the majority of them seem to be located in its mountainous parts. Surveys in the Pryor Mountain-Bighorn Canyon region indicated that Hypsithermal period peoples occupied higher elevations than their more recent counterparts (Lowendorf 1971:130), and numerous bison kill sites in the Big Horn Mountains suggest that this area was an oasis for both bison and bison hunters (Benedict and Olson 1978; Frison 1974; Reher 1970).

Wedel (1986) discussed the effects that higher temperatures and lower rainfall may have had upon the region's hunting and harvesting populations. He saw a gradual, if uneven, warming and drying that led to at least some redistribution of plants and animals. The human inhabitants, he argued, responded by adjusting their hunting tools and techniques, extending and perhaps intensifying their collecting practices, and equipping themselves with more efficient tools and implements for the preparation of plant foods. One gets the impression from his discussion that the better-watered regions served as focal areas, pockets of periodic but more restricted and intense interaction between humans, plants, and animals.

In the plains at large, post-Hypsithermal differences in fauna and flora seem to have shaped a mosaic of adjustment on the part of Woodland tradition hunters and harvesters. Among the elements of this mosaic were: (1) a highly mobile pattern of herd animal hunting and High Plains foraging in the western shortgrass plains, (2) a less mobile, mixed woodland and tall grass plains form of hunting and harvesting along the network of creek and river courses in the Central Plains, and (3) a yet more sedentary woodland-adapted pattern of hunting and gathering focused upon the broad-forested bottom lands of the major river valleys and feeder streams that edged the Plains on the east (Wedel 1961; Krause 1987:339; Adair 1988:24–36).

Although ecologically focused programs dominated the 1960s, an interest in the direct historical approach continued. Waldo Wedel (1959) used it to identify the remains expected of Kansas and Wichita Indians (fig. 3) (see also Bell and Bastian 1974), and Gunnerson (1960) used it to claim Plains Apache authorship for the Dismal River materials. Wood also used the approach to assign, following Strong's 1940 lead, a Cheyenne identity to the Biesterfeldt site (Wood 1971a) and to assess Mulloy's identification of Hagen as a Crow site (Wood and Downer 1977: 83–100). By far the most daring use of the direct historical approach came from the Southern Plains where Jack T. Hughes (1974) attempted to push Caddoan origins back to the Archaic stage.

The nature of archeological sites in the Western Plains (temporary camps, hunting stations, and kill sites) made a rigorous application of the direct historical approach difficult if not impossible (Reher and Frison 1980:29–34). Nevertheless,the general idea of working from the historic known to the prehistoric unknown was used to identify loosely defined pottery complexes such as Crow (Frison 1976; Mulloy 1958; Wedel 1954) or Shoshone (A.B. Kehoe 1959; Mulloy 1958; Wedel 1954). Although it may be a questionable practice, linguistic or ethnic identities were also sometimes assigned to prehistoric projectile point types (T.F. Kehoe 1966:827–841).

Federal Government Sponsorship

In retrospect the 1930s was a major turning point in Plains archeology. The Depression's adverse effects of institutional salary and budget cuts, reduced field allowances, and other economies were offset, in part at least, by work relief programs, particularly the Works Progress Administration. Functioning through sponsoring state universities, historical societies, and other agencies, the Works Progress Administration supported field and laboratory projects in many states, including Montana, Wyoming, the Dakotas, Nebraska, Oklahoma, and Texas. This work produced the masses of data and specimens that made some of the early syntheses that are now classics possible. In part it also stimulated the intellectual ferment that engendered the first Conference for Plains Archeology held in Vermillion, South Dakota, in 1931. Eighteen persons, representing Colorado, Iowa, Nebraska, North and South Dakota, Michigan, Minnesota, Wisconsin, and the Smithsonian's Bureau of American Ethnology took part. With an annual meeting since its fifth session in 1947, the Plains Conference remains a significant part of the regional scene, with site reports, symposia, and workshops. Six annual newsletters were issued from 1947 to 1953. Beginning in 1954, the *Plains Anthropologist*, the journal of the conference, has been an important publishing outlet for those specializing in Plains prehistory.

Smithsonian, NAA: 72-8413.

Fig. 3. Waldo R. Wedel, on right, and George S. Metcalf at excavation in Rice County, Kans. The area was occupied at contact by semihorticultural people believed to be ancestral to one or more of the Wichita-speaking tribes. Wedel began excavation here in the 1940s and resumed in 1965–1967. George Metcalf, a self-taught archeologist and collections manager of the Dept. of Anthr. at the Smithsonian's National Museum of Natural History, served as Wedel's assistant on 8 expeditions to the Plains states. In Rice County they investigated the council circles of the Little River focus (Wedel 1967, 1968a). Photographed in 1970.

Archeology by work relief, or otherwise, ended in 1941 and was not resumed until after World War II. As the war drew to a close, archeologists learned that the federal government planned a nationwide water-control program, including construction of numerous dams and related works, on major streams. Recognizing a grave threat to the nation's prehistorical resources, archeologists, government administrators, and planners created the Interagency Archaeological Salvage Program. This effort initially involved the National Park Service; the Bureau of Reclamation, Department of the Interior; the Corps of Engineers, Department of the Army; and the Smithsonian Institution. Other agencies were added from time to time.

The largest project in the Great Plains was in the Missouri River basin. Both federal and state agencies participated. State agencies that at first were self-supported later were funded by contracts with the National Park Service. Work in North Dakota, for example, was conducted by the State Historical Society of North Dakota (fig. 4); the University of North Dakota, Grand Forks; Montana State University, Bozeman; and the Smithsonian Institution's River Basin Surveys office in Lincoln, Nebraska. River Basin Surveys personnel (fig. 5) also worked in South Dakota as did representatives of the University of South Dakota, Vermillion; the University of Kansas, Lawrence; the Nebraska State Historical Society, Lincoln; the University of Idaho, Moscow; the University of Wisconsin, Madison; the State Historical Society of North Dakota, Bismarck; the University of Nebraska; Dana College, Blair, Nebraska; and the University of Missouri, Columbia.

The River Basin Surveys, funded by the National Park Service, continued under Smithsonian direction from 1946 to 1969, when the unit was transferred to the National Park Service and became the Midwest Archaeological Center based first in Omaha then later in Lincoln, Nebraska. As the Dakota impoundments were closed in the 1960s, work in that region diminished and attention turned to a series of U.S. Department of the Interior, Bureau of Reclamation, flood control projects ancillary to the Missouri River drainage in Kansas and Nebraska. Here again a National Park Service-sponsored multi-institutional effort was launched, this time including contributions from the Kansas State Historical Society, Topeka; the Nebraska State Historical Society; the University of Kansas; the University of Missouri; and the University of Nebraska. Much of this work, shaped by lessons learned in the Dakotas, stimulated the efforts to

State Histl. Soc. of N. Dak., Bismarck: 32ML2.

Fig. 4. Like-a-Fishhook Village, Ft. Berthold, N. Dak., aerial view from northeast. Excavation of Ft. Berthold I is on right surrounded by the circular remains of the earthlodge settlement of the Hidatsa, Mandan, and Arikara tribes. The village, built in association with Ft. Berthold, was excavated before it was inundated by Garrison Reservoir on the Missouri River; the encroaching waters are evident. The excavations were conducted by the State Historical Society of North Dakota and the River Basin Surveys of the Smithsonian Institution under contracts with the National Park Service, 1950–1954. Photograph by Alan R. Woolworth, 1954.

rework cultural classifications and to refine knowledge of the interplay among elements of technology, sociology, and environment. Then too, a cooperative chronology program initiated by the Smithsonian Institution, River Basin Surveys, Missouri Basin office in 1958, aimed at integrating the findings from dendrochronology, radiocarbon, and other dating techniques, materially aided Plains specialists in their quest for an understanding of ethnogenesis, their search for a workable systematics, and their desire for a human ecology with explanatory value.

With the growing dominance of "processual" interests in the mid- to late 1960s, American archeologists began to realize that future fieldwork would require a broadened research effort—an effort that could only be achieved through an expansion of archeology's financial, technological, and intellectual base. To find the resources to fund them Carl Chapman, Charles McGimsey, and others began an intense lobbying effort that achieved success with passage of federal enabling legislation. This legislation, Public Law 93–291, the Archaeological and Historical Preservation Act of 1974, both provided an expanded financial base for American archeology and brought agencies of the United States government, the Army Corps of Engineers, the National Park Service, the Bureau of Reclamation, the National Forest Service, and others into the research arena as brokers of and for archeological inquiry. These government agencies maintained archeologists on their staffs to conduct, in compliance with President Richard Nixon's executive order 11593, archeological surveys and cultural resource mitigation efforts as well as to let and monitor contracts with state agencies, academic institutions, and private corporations. Plains archeology has benefited from contemporary salvage efforts, now called cultural resource management. Because expanded highway construction, land-leveling, and other alterations of the landscape require attention to mitigating the effects of the damage they may do, the region's cultural resources Plains specialists will continue to benefit.

Smithsonian, NAA: River Basin Survey 39 HU00-63.

Fig. 5. The 17½ Plains Conference at Pierre, S. Dak. Such conferences, usually held in summer, were opportunities for the Plains archeologists to gather during their fieldwork to discuss informally taxonomy and their field problems. left to right around the table, Frank H.H. Roberts, Jr., head of the Missouri Basin Project; unidentified; Ward Weakly; Dick Jensen; W. Raymond Wood; John Corbett; Cal Burroughs, Warren Caldwell; Paul Beaubein; G. Hubert Smith; and unidentified crewman. Photograph by William M. Bass, III, Pierre airport, July 1960.

State and federal governments have responded to Native American concerns about the use of human skeletal remains, funerary artifacts, and sacred objects. These concerns led to the National Museum of the American Indian Act (Public Law 101–185) and Nebraska's Unmarked Human Burial Sites and Skeletal Remains Protection Act, both enacted in 1989. The Nebraska law, with its standard of evidence provisions, seems to have been the prototype for the 1990 federal Native American Graves Protection and Repatriation Act (Public Law 101–601). This mandate has forced state and federally supported institutions to comply with reasonably stringent standards for excavating, analyzing, curating, displaying and, in a number of cases, repatriating research and display collections (Wood 1998).

History of Ethnological and Ethnohistorical Research

RAYMOND J. DEMALLIE AND JOHN C. EWERS*

Even though the Great Plains is an inland area, the earliest descriptions of some of its Indian inhabitants antedate the first references to many Indian tribes who lived nearer the seacoast in other parts of North America. The literature on the historic tribes of the Plains comprises a vast and rich collection of writings by a host of contributors that date from 1541 and include soldiers, missionaries, traders, artists, naturalists, colonial officials, Indian agents, Euro-American settlers, and literate members of Plains Indian tribes, as well as anthropologists and historians.

Exploration of the Great Plains by the colonial powers of Spain, France, and England proceeded gradually from the south and east so that some tribes in the north and west of this area did not become known until much later than those of the southern and eastern portions of the Plains. Thus, the Wichita on the Arkansas River were seen and described as early as 1541 (Coronado in Hammond and Rey 1940), but the first eyewitness account of the Crow in their Yellowstone Valley homeland dates from only 1805 (Larocque in Wood and Thiessen 1985). The terminal date for direct observation of prereservation cultures also varied.

During the end of the nineteenth and the first half of the twentieth centuries, anthropologists were able to learn about Plains Indian cultures in prereservation times from the memories of living people. Since then, study of the large body of firsthand observations of tribal life preserved in printed and archival sources has become crucial for understanding the past while twentieth-century Plains Indian life has became a new focus of study.

The Sixteenth Century: Accounts of the Coronado Expedition, 1541

In the history of Plains Indian studies the earliest eyewitness accounts are especially important. Uniquely so are the observations on the Southern Plains tribes recorded during the summer of 1541 by members of the Francisco Vásquez de Coronado Expedition, who described aboriginal Indian cultures well before extensive European contact (Hammond and Rey 1940). They reported two major Plains Indian subcultures—nomadic buffalo hunters and more sedentary horticulturalists—at the time of first White contact. Brief as were their acquaintances with these Indians, the transient Spanish explorers reported a number of basic traits among the nomadic hunters—their skill in killing buffalo with bows and arrows, and in dressing hides; their use of buffalo for food, of buffalo hides for clothing and for covering their portable dwellings, of buffalo sinew for thread, bladders for water vessels, bones for awls, and dried dung for fuel. They also wrote of Indian use of dogs for packing and to drag lodge poles when moving camp, of their use of a sign language, their worship of the sun, and their trade with both the eastern Pueblos and the horticultural tribes of the Plains. In contrast to these nomads, the Indians of Quivira (ancestral to the Wichita) lived in villages of round, grass-covered houses and raised crops of maize, beans, and squash. These first European observers also reported intertribal warfare among the Plains Indians. The nomadic Querechos and Teyas were enemies, and the Quivirans were enemies of the Gaus (Osage).

Seventeenth- and Eighteenth-Century Accounts

French traders and missionaries who paddled their canoes westward through the Great Lakes during the mid-seventeenth century in quest of furs and unknown tribes to Christianize first met and briefly described the Santee Sioux. Father Claude Allouez encountered some Santee Sioux near the head of Lake Superior during the mid-1660s. He described them as a people living to the west toward the Mississippi, in a prairie country rich in game, who cultivated only tobacco and gathered wild rice from the lakes in late summer. They were able bowmen who were at war with all their neighbors (Allouez in Kellogg 1917:122).

During his descent of the Mississippi in 1673 Father Pierre Marquette first met and briefly described the Quapaw near the mouth of the Arkansas. He observed that they traveled in wooden canoes, lived in bark-covered cabins, and raised three crops of maize a year, yet "their wealth consists in the skins of wild cattle." Even at that early date their aboriginal culture was being modified by the acquisition of hatchets, knives, and beads obtained from the Illinois and other Indian intermediaries in the westward-expanding fur trade. Gun-using Indians

* Ewers drafted this chapter in 1973; after his death in 1997 DeMallie expanded and revised it. Ewers is the primary author for the chapter up to the section Nineteenth- and Early Twentieth-Century Anthropology; DeMallie is the primary author for the remainder of the chapter.

downriver barred their access to the sea (Marquette in Kellogg 1917:254–256).

As early as 1687 Frenchmen of René-Robert Cavelier, sieur de La Salle's ill-fated Texas settlement saw Wichita or Caddo Indians on horseback lancing buffalo—early proof that Indians of the Southern Plains had acquired Spanish horses and were using them effectively in hunting their traditional big game (Cavelier 1938:81).

In 1690, Hudson's Bay Company trader Henry Kelsey, traveling with an Assiniboine band, became the first White man to reach the Northeastern Plains. The Indians of the area had no horses and surrounded the buffalo on foot, but they "hunt their Enemies, and with our English guns do make [the]m flie" (Kelsey 1929:4). During his intimate association with these Indians Kelsey learned of some of their religious beliefs and customs—their dependence upon birds and animals as supernatural helpers; their shamanistic rites associated with hunting, curing, and witchcraft; and their use of sacred pipes and feather bonnets in war—and briefly described their lifeways long before they were reported in greater detail by later observers.

During the first half of the eighteenth century French traders extended their contacts with previously unknown tribes west of the Mississippi and the Red River of the North, although many pioneer French trader-explorers left no descriptions of the tribes they encountered. Landmark French accounts during those years include Pierre-Charles Le Sueur's descriptions of the Sioux with whom he traded on Blue Earth River (Minnesota) in 1700 (M.M. Wedel 1974a). Claude-Charles Dutisné and Jean-Baptiste Bénard de La Harpe's reports of their meetings with the Wichita and their neighbors in 1719 (Boimare 1831; M.M. Wedel 1971, 1972, 1973a), and Étienne Venyard, sieur de Bourgmont's observations on the Kansa and the Padouca (Plains Apache) in 1724 (Giraud 1958; Norall 1988). Pierre Gaultier de Varennes, sieur de La Vérendrye traded with and wrote of the Plains Cree and Assiniboine west of the Red River for several years before he marched overland to the Mandan villages on the Missouri in 1738 and observed that tribe and its flourishing intertribal trade with more distant Indians (Burpee 1927). In 1751 Jean-Bernard Bossu, a French naval officer, wrote the only extant account of the Quapaw before their culture was transformed by contact with Europeans (Bossu 1771, 1962). Before French dominion in North America ended in 1763, their officials gained some knowledge of the Pawnee and of tribes on the Missouri as far upriver as the Omaha and Ponca above the mouth of the Platte.

Meanwhile, the Spaniards in New Mexico and Texas were less successful in establishing peaceful relations with the Southern Plains tribes. They began to learn of the Comanche as warlike raiders as early as 1706, but their knowledge of them was acquired slowly and sporadically before Gov. Juan Bautista de Anza of New Mexico negotiated a peace with them 80 years later (Kavanagh 1996). Much of the Spanish knowledge of Plains Indians prior to the nineteenth century appears in official documents of soldiers and administrators (Bolton 1914, 1916; Kinnaird 1946–1949, 1958; Nasatir 1952; A.B. Thomas 1932, 1935, 1940, 1941).

During the last decade of the eighteenth century Saint Louis traders, licensed by Spain, pushed up the Missouri, established themselves among the Arikara, and briefly visited the Mandan. One of them, Jean-Baptiste Truteau, wrote an extensive description of the Arikara just as they were becoming acquainted with Europeans, as well as observations on the Cheyenne and Teton Sioux, including the first substantive account of the Sioux Sun Dance (Truteau 1912, 1921; Parks 1993).

Even before the French withdrawal in 1763, the Hudson's Bay Company, their English rival in the north, sent Anthony Henday up the Saskatchewan River in a vain attempt to induce the tribes near the Rockies to bring furs to their posts on Hudson Bay. Henday's journal contains the first brief account of the Gros Ventre, and the first evidence that the tribes of the Northwestern Plains had acquired horses and were riding them on buffalo hunts (A. Hendry 1907). After the French withdrew, English traders from Montreal competed with the Hudson's Bay Company men for the lucrative trade with the Indians of the Saskatchewan Valley. Traders' writings offer much information on the tribes of the Canadian Plains in subsequent years, and the archives of the Hudson's Bay Company provide a rich documentary resource ("History of the Canadian Plains Until 1870," figs. 5, 7, 8; vol. 17:196). Significant published accounts include those of Mathew Cocking on the upper Saskatchewan in 1772–1773 (Cocking 1908), Alexander Henry among the Assiniboine in 1776 (Henry 1809), Alexander Mackenzie's description of various tribes about 1790 (Mackenzie 1927), and Duncan McGillivray's journal of his trade with the Blackfoot and their neighbors in the 1790s (A.S. Morton 1929).

Nineteenth-Century Accounts

Traders

The writings of David Thompson and Alexander Henry the Younger during the late eighteenth and early nineteenth centuries are indispensable sources on the Indian tribes of the Northern Plains. These traders' accounts are rich in detailed information based upon their long and close observation of the Plains Cree, Plains Ojibwa, Assiniboine, Gros Ventre, Sarcee, and the three Blackfoot tribes, as well as their briefer contacts with the Mandan, Hidatsa, and Cheyenne on the Missouri River (Coues 1897; Glover 1962; Gough 1988–1992). Thompson not only recorded observations of contemporary life but also questioned Blackfoot Indians to reconstruct from their memories the nature of warfare before they obtained horses (Tyrrell 1916:328–332).

In the early nineteenth century several traders wrote accounts of tribes on the Missouri River. Pierre-Antoine Tabeau, a trader from Saint Louis, lived with the Arikara in the first years of the nineteenth century and wrote an account that provides a wealth of detail on the Arikara and Teton Sioux, as well as information on other tribes of the Middle Missouri region (A.H. Abel 1939). The journals of 1804–1805 by François-Antoine Larocque, a North West Company trader, include information on the tribes of the Upper Missouri; in 1805 he traveled with the Crow and wrote the first account of their culture (Wood and Thiessen 1985:129–220). Francis A. Chardon, a trader at Fort Clark, kept a journal from 1834–1839 that provides cultural detail on the Hidatsa and Mandan and presents an eyewitness account of the devastation caused by the smallpox epidemic of 1837 (A.H. Abel 1932). Among the most informative accounts of other traders and mountain men who described the Indian tribes of the upper Missouri and Rocky Mountain region are those of James P. Beckwourth (1856), Henry A. Boller (1868), Capt. Benjamin L.E. de Bonneville (in W. Irving 1868), Warren A. Ferris (1940), Charles Larpenteur (Coues 1898), Zenas Leonard (1959), Osborn Russell (1955), and Nathaniel J. Wyeth (1899).

Among fur traders, the most prolific writer was Edwin T. Denig, who knew the Arikara, Assiniboine, Crow, Plains Cree, and Teton Sioux for two decades after 1833 (Denig 1930, 1961). Father Pierre-Jean de Smet encouraged Denig's writing and included some of his accounts of the Assiniboine in one of his own books (de Smet 1905). Ferdinand V. Hayden (1862) incorporated much material from Denig in his ethnological study of the tribes of the Missouri Valley. Especially noteworthy are Denig's accounts of intertribal warfare (fig. 1) and prominent chiefs, as well as his lengthy monograph on the Assiniboine, which is the most detailed and insightful description of any Plains tribe before the reservation period.

No extensive traders' accounts exist for the Southern Plains. M.C. Fisher (1869), wrote a brief account of the Arapaho, Kiowa, and Comanche, and Anthony Glass kept a journal of his activities on the Texas frontier in 1808–1809 (Flores 1985). John Sibley (1922), sometime Indian agent at Natchitoches, wrote a valuable account of the tribes of the Southern Plains in 1807.

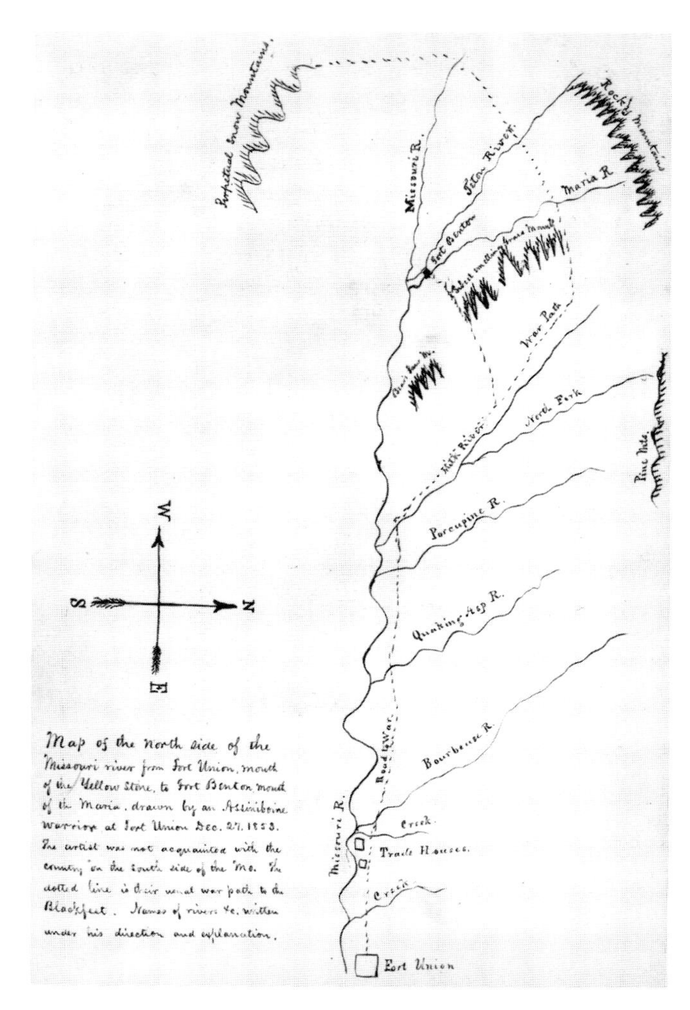

Smithsonian, NAA: 42,514-C.

Fig. 1. "Map of the North side of the Missouri river from Fort Union, mouth of the Yellow Stone to Fort Benton, mouth of the Maria, drawn by an Assiniboine warrior at Fort Union Dec. 27, 1853. The artist was not acquainted with the country on the south side of the Mo. The dotted line is their usual warpath to the Blackfeet. Names of rivers &c. written under his direction and explanation." Copied by Edwin T. Denig, about 1854.

Exploring Expeditions

The purchase of the vast territory of Louisiana by the United States in 1803 initiated an era of intensive exploration of the Plains south of 49° latitude. President Thomas Jefferson's instructions to Meriwether Lewis charged the explorers of the Lewis and Clark Expedition with responsibility for obtaining information on the Indian tribes. While they wintered near the Mandan on the Missouri in 1804–1805, the leaders collected data on the populations, locations, occupations, intertribal relations, and trading prospects of the large number of tribes known to the Indians and traders in that vicinity. A significant amount of that information came from the trader Tabeau. Tabulated, and published under the title *A statistical view of the Indian nations inhabiting the territory of Louisiana, and the countries adjacent to its Northern and Western boundaries*, it was a major contribution to knowledge of Plains Indians. The journals of the expedition's officers contain more detailed observations on the Plains tribes they met, particularly the Mandan and Teton Sioux, during their trek to the Pacific and return (Lewis and Clark 1832; Thwaites 1904–1905; Moulton 1983–; D. Jackson 1992).

Lt. Zebulon Pike headed government-sponsored explorations of the Upper Mississippi in 1805 and of the Central and Southern Plains in 1806–1807 (Z.M. Pike 1810; Coues 1895; D. Jackson 1966). Following the model of Lewis and Clark, he also provided tabulated data on Indian tribes and details of tribal culture in his narratives.

In 1817 Maj. Stephen H. Long of the U.S. Topographical Engineers led a small party to map the Mississippi up to Prairie du Chien. His journals provide important details on the Santee Sioux (S.H. Long 1889; Kane, Holmquist, and Gilman 1978:49–77).

In 1819–1820 Long led a scientific expedition to explore the Lower Missouri, Platte, and Arkansas rivers. Thomas Say, the expedition's naturalist, with the assistance of the trader John Dougherty, later an Indian agent, wrote a detailed account of the Omaha during the winter of 1819–1820. Say's observations the following summer on the Pawnee, Arapaho, Kiowa, Plains Apache, and Comanche would have been more extensive if his field notebooks had not been stolen by army deserters shortly before the expedition reached Fort Smith on their return from the Rocky Mountains (E. James 1823). Capt. John R. Bell (1957), official journalist of the expedition, included observations of the Indians in his record.

In 1823 Long returned to chart the upper Mississippi and Red rivers to Lake Winnipeg, and the reports of the expedition again provide valuable ethnographic material on the Santee Sioux and other tribes of the region (Keating 1824; Kane, Holmquist, and Gilman 1978:113–327). He was accompanied for part of this trip by G.C. Beltrami, an Italian traveler, who published an account that includes additional information on the Indians he met on the Upper Mississippi (Beltrami 1824, 1828); Beltrami also acquired a Santee Sioux vocabulary (1995) and one of the earliest collections of Santee Sioux and Métis material culture (Vigorelli 1987).

During 1829–1830 the Mexican Boundary Commission explored a portion of Texas under instructions to obtain information on the Indian tribes as well as the natural resources of the region. José Francisco Ruiz, a native Texan who had lived eight years among the Comanche, furnished many details on the cultures of the Comanche, Wichita, and their neighbors to members of the commission (Ruíz 1972; Mexican Boundary Commission 1857–1859). Jean Louis Berlandier, the expedition naturalist, described the customs of the Comanche, Tonkawa, and Wichita. The drawings by the Mexican artist Lino Sánchez y Tapia, which accompany Berlandier's text (1969), are important pictorial records for the Southern Plains.

Santee Sioux culture and language were further documented during the late 1830s through the field observations of the French scientist Joseph N. Nicollet (1843), employed by the War Department to map the upper Mississippi basin (E.C. Bray and M.C. Bray 1976).

Naturalists

The naturalists Henry M. Brackenridge and John Bradbury accompanied Saint Louis traders as far up the Missouri as the Mandan villages in 1811, and each recorded observations of the Indians and natural resources (Brackenridge 1814, in Thwaites 1904–1907, 6; Bradbury 1819, in Thwaites 1904–1907, 5). Thomas Nuttall described the Quapaw in 1819 (Nuttall 1980). In 1835 Charles Augustus Murray went on a summer buffalo hunt with the Pawnee and described their life before they were decimated by smallpox (Murray 1839). In 1833 John Treat Irving (1835) and his uncle Washington Irving (1868) accompanied a treaty commission to the Pawnee villages where they witnessed one of the last occurrences of the Pawnee Morning Star ceremony and recorded observations of Pawnee life. Victor Tixier (1940), a French physician, wrote a detailed description of the Osage with whom he traveled on an extended buffalo hunt in 1840.

Among those by naturalists, the most important study of Plains Indians during the second quarter of the nineteenth century resulted from the close collaboration of Maximilian, Prince of Wied-Neuwied, and the Swiss artist, Karl Bodmer. In 1833 they ascended the Missouri as far as Fort McKenzie, at the mouth of the Marias, where they observed and pictured the Blackfoot tribes for a month. Then they wintered at Fort Clark near the Mandan and Hidatsa villages. Maximilian's scholarly observations and Bodmer's exquisitely detailed portraits (fig. 2 right), and scenes of Indian life are indispensable ethnographic sources for the Upper Missouri tribes (Maximilian 1839–1841, 1843, in Thwaites 1904–1907, 22–24; Bodmer 1984).

Artists and Photographers

The earliest artist who documented Plains tribes was Peter Rindisbacher, whose drawings provide a graphic record of the Indians and Métis on Red River prior to 1826 (Josephy 1970).

The best-known artist who depicted Plains Indians is George Catlin, who in 1832 was aboard the first steamboat to reach Fort Union on the Upper Missouri. Although he pictured and described all the tribes he met, he was most impressed by the Mandan (fig. 2 left), and Catlin's major contribution was his illustrated, eyewitness account of their major tribal ceremony, the Okipa ("Mandan," fig. 5, this vol.) (Catlin 1967; C.F. Taylor 1996). In 1834 Catlin extended his picture-making travels to the Southern Plains. In 1835 and 1836 he met the Santee Sioux on the Upper Mississippi and visited the famed pipestone quarry in southwestern Minnesota, the stone from which was named "catlinite" in his honor. Through exhibitions of his paintings in eastern cities and abroad and profusely illustrated books (Catlin 1841) Catlin popularized Plains Indians and stimulated field studies of them (see Truettner 1979).

Noteworthy artist-observers of Plains Indians include Alfred Jacob Miller, who attended the Shoshone Rendezvous in present Wyoming in 1837 (M.C. Ross 1968); John Mix Stanley, who traveled on the Southern Plains during the 1840s and across the Northern Plains

left, Natl. Gallery of Art, Washington:1965.16.184; right, Joslyn Art Mus., Omaha, Nebr.

Fig. 2. Artists. left, George Catlin painting the portrait of Mah-to-toh-pa, Mandan (*mąɫó tópa* 'four bears') (d. 1837). Oil painting by George Catlin, 1861–1869. right, Pehriska-Ruhpa (*pé·ricka nupa* 'two ravens'), Hidatsa, principal leader of the Dog Society, dressed in his society regalia and decorated with facial and body paint. The headdress was made of magpie tail feathers with a wild turkey tail in the middle. He wears a whistle (probably eagle-leg bone) around his neck and carries a dewclaw rattle with beaded handle. Watercolor and pencil by Karl Bodmer, Ft. Clark, in present-day N. Dak., 1834.

with Governor Isaac I. Stevens's railroad exploration party in 1853 (Kinietz 1942; I.I. Stevens 1859, 1860); Father Nicolas Point, pioneer missionary to the Blackfoot and Gros Ventre in 1846–1847 (Point 1967); Paul Kane, who twice crossed the Canadian Plains during the late 1840s (P. Kane 1859; Harper 1971); Rudolph F. Kurz, who traveled on the Missouri as high as Fort Union in 1848–1852 (Hewitt 1937); Capt. Seth Eastman, who depicted the Santee Sioux during the 1840s and who illustrated the books by his wife Mary H. Eastman (1849, 1975, 1995); Frank Blackwell Mayer, who sketched the Santee Sioux in 1851 (Heilbron 1932); Balduin Möllhausen, on the Platte in 1851, and the Southern Plains in 1853 (Taft 1953; Hartmann 1963); Gustavus Sohon, at the first Blackfoot and Flathead treaty councils in 1855 (Ewers 1948a; H. Stevens 1900); Richard Petri, near Fredericksburg, Texas, prior to 1857 (Pinckney 1967); and Charles Wimar, on the Missouri as high as Fort Benton in 1858 and 1859 (R. Stewart 1991).

During the mid-nineteenth century the developing art of photography provided another medium for the preservation of American Indian images.† One of the first photographers to document Northern Plains Indians was Alexander Gardner, from Washington, D.C., who preserved an invaluable record of the Sioux, Cheyenne, Crow, and Shoshone participants in the 1868 treaty council at Fort Laramie, Wyoming (DeMallie 1981). William H. Jackson, whose studio was in Omaha, Nebraska, documented the Pawnee in the late 1860s and served as photographer on the Hayden Survey from 1870 to 1879, recording images of both the Northern and Southern Plains tribes (W.H. Jackson 1877, 1940; Fleming and Luskey 1986:106–108; Hales 1988). After learning photography from Mathew Brady, Stanley J. Morrow moved to Yankton, Dakota Territory, in 1868; he joined the 1873 Yellowstone Expedition and photographed Indians throughout the Northern Plains, establishing a studio at Fort Keogh, Montana Territory, in 1878 (Hurt and Lass 1956; Hedren 1985; Mitchell 1987). In 1879 Morrow sold out to Laton Alton Huffman, who made one of the most extensive and best-known nineteenth-century photographic records of the Cheyenne, Sioux, Crow, and other Northern Plains tribes (M.H. Brown and Felton 1955; Karson 1990). Huffman had learned his trade from Frank Jay Haynes, who had a studio in Fargo, Dakota Territory, and traveled for the Northern Pacific Railroad photographing scenery as well as Plains Indians (Fleming and Luskey 1986:195–203). William H. Illingworth, of Saint Paul, Minnesota, accompanied the 1866 Fisk Expedition to the gold fields of Montana as well as the 1874 Black Hills Expedition led by Lt. Col. George A. Custer; his photographs include the Sioux as well as the Arikara, Hidatsa, and Mandan of Fort Berthold Reservation (Grosscup 1975).

†Information on photographers was provided by Joanna Cohan Scherer.

Other late nineteenth-century photographers on the Northern Plains included: George and Ernest Trager and Clarence Grant Moreledge, who photographed on the Pine Ridge Reservation and documented the aftermath of the Wounded Knee massacre of 1890–1891 in a series of well-publicized images (Jensen, Paul, and Carter 1991); Orlando Scott Goff and David F. Barry, of Bismarck, North Dakota, and Frank Bennett Fiske, of Fort Yates, all of whom photographed the Sioux at Standing Rock (J.S. Gray 1978; Heski 1978; North Dakota Heritage Foundation 1983); John A. Anderson and Jesse Hastings Bratley, on the Rosebud Sioux reservation (H.W. Hamilton and J.T. Hamilton 1971; P. Dyck 1971; D. Doll and J. Alinder 1976; Jacobsen 1990); Sumner Matteson who photographed the Assiniboine and Gros Ventre of Fort Belknap Reservation (Horse Capture 1977; Casagrande and Bourns 1983); and Roland Reed who photographed Blackfoot, Cheyenne, and Crow in Montana (Ruby 1981).

A number of late nineteenth-century Canadian photographers worked among Plains tribes in Alberta and Saskatchewan (Silversides 1994), including: Frederick Steele: Assiniboine, Blackfoot, Cree; William Hanson Boorne: Blackfoot (including well-known images of the Blood Sun Dance; Scherer 1999), Cree, Sarcee; Charles W. Mathers: Cree, Stoney, Métis, Sioux (Provincial Archives of Alberta 1989); George Anderton: Assiniboine, Blackfoot, Cree, Sioux; and Geraldine Moodie: Cree, Assiniboine (D. White 1998).

On the Southern Plains, William S. Soule, based at Fort Sill, Indian Territory, made images of the Kiowa, Comanche, Plains Apache, Arapaho, Cheyenne, and Wichita from about 1869 to 1875 (Belous and Weinstein 1969; Current 1978; Kavanagh 1991); William S. Prettyman, of Arkansas City, Kansas, photographed Indians in the Oklahoma area 1880–1909 (Cunningham 1957); George A. Addison photographed around Fort Sill (Fleming and Luskey 1986:232); and James Mooney photographed Arapaho, Cheyenne, Kiowa, and Plains Apache in the course of his field studies for the Bureau of American Ethnology (Moses 1984; Jacknis 1990).

Some of the earliest images of Plains Indians were preserved in portraits taken of delegations that traveled to Washington on official business (Scherer 1998). James McClees and Julian Vannerson's studio, A. Zeno Shindler, Alexander Gardner, Charles M. Bell, Mathew Brady's studio, John K. Hillers, DeLancey Gill, and many other photographers took delegation photographs from the 1850s well into the twentieth century (Glenn 1983; Fleming and Luskey 1986:20–44). Many of these portraits are preserved in the Bureau of American Ethnology Collection, National Anthropological Archives, Smithsonian Institution.

Missionaries

Missionary writings on the Plains Indians are too numerous to mention in detail. Jesuit contributions to documenting Indians of the Northwestern Plains in the 1840s include the writings of de Smet (1905) and the drawings and paintings by Point (1967). The culture and language of the Santee Sioux in Minnesota were documented by Congregationalist missionaries, including Stephen Return Riggs (1852, 1869, 1887, 1893) and Samuel William Pond (1908). The writings of Protestant missionaries John Dunbar ("Caddoan Languages," fig. 1, this vol.) and Samuel Allis (J. Dunbar 1910; J. Dunbar and Allis 1918; W.R. Wedel 1985), and Dunbar's son, John B. Dunbar (1880, 1880a) document the Pawnee in the 1830s, before their removal from Nebraska to Oklahoma.

Army Officers

During the late nineteenth century Army officers were detailed to carry out cultural and linguistic studies of various Plains tribes. Surgeon Washington Matthews (1877) described Hidatsa culture, wrote a grammatical sketch of the language, and compiled a lexicon. James H. Bradley (1896–1923) described Blackfoot culture and collected Crow traditions. W.P. Clark (1885), Garrick Mallery (1877, 1881), and Hugh L. Scott (1912–1934) studied Plains sign language (fig. 3) (vol. 17:276–277). Mallery also undertook an intensive investigation of Teton Sioux pictorial winter counts (1877, 1886, 1893) (vol. 17:286) and H.L. Scott (1911), while stationed at Fort Sill, recorded descriptions of the Sun Dance and obtained pictorial representations from Silverhorn ("History of the United States Plains Until 1850," fig. 3, this vol.), a Kiowa soldier under his command. John G. Bourke (1894) recorded observations of the 1881 Sun Dance at Pine Ridge Agency as well as valuable ethnographic material on other Plains tribes (Sutherland 1964; Porter 1986).

Government Reports

The greatest wealth of contemporary source material on Plains Indians from the mid-nineteenth century on is preserved in the official reports, correspondence, and records of the Bureau of Indian Affairs and of the War Department in the National Archives in Washington and of the Department of Indian Affairs in Ottawa (see E.E. Hill 1981). Particularly valuable for the study of native cultures are the verbatim transcripts of treaty councils, meetings, and delegations to Washington, which provide insight into Indian understandings of the critical events of the second half of the nineteenth century. Some of these are published in the U.S. Congressional Serial Set (see S.L. Johnson 1977), including the *Annual Reports of the Commissioner of Indian Affairs* (ARCIA 1824–1848, 1849–), which include individual reports from local agencies and reservations. Comparable for Canadian reserves are the *Annual Reports of the Department of Indian Affairs*, published in the Sessional Papers of the Canadian Parliament.

left, Milwaukee Public Mus., Wis.:43856; Smithsonian, NAA:neg. 13A and 13B.

Fig. 3. Sign communication. left, Horn Weasel, a deaf Assiniboine, using signs at a Fourth of July celebration. His perforated buckskin shirt decorated with beadwork and ermine trim had protective powers. Photograph by Sumner W. Matteson, Ft. Belknap, Mont., July 1905–1906 (cropped). right, Red Shirt, Oglala Sioux, while visiting Washington, D.C., with a delegation from Red Cloud (Pine Ridge) Agency, Dak. Terr., photographed demonstrating signs for a publication. By holding "the flat hand edgewise, pointing upward before the right side of the chest, then throwing it outward and downward to the right" (Mallery 1881:441) he signs "no" or "not." Photographed by Charles M. Bell, Washington, 1880. In the corresponding engraving in Mallery (center) Red Shirt's suit has been redrawn as a traditional Plains fringed buckskin shirt.

Nineteenth- and Early Twentieth-Century Anthropology

Ethnographic studies of American Indians during the late nineteenth and into the beginning of the twentieth century were dominated by an evolutionary perspective that measured human progress from simple to complex social and cultural forms classified in a series of developmental stages (savagery, barbarism, civilization). In the United States, the work of Lewis Henry Morgan (1871, 1877) defined the terminology and approach used by anthropologists during this period. Anthropological field study of Plains Indians began with Morgan's investigations of kinship among the tribes on the Missouri and the Red River of the North in 1859–1862. Morgan's travel journals also contain information on social groups (bands, clans, men's societies) as well as ceremonies and daily life based on information supplied by missionaries, traders, and Indians themselves (L.H. Morgan 1959). Morgan's (1877) *Ancient Society*, which summarized the results of his American Indian studies, placing them in an evolutionary, world-wide context (from ancient Greece and Rome forward), became the first textbook in anthropology, a resource used by virtually all American anthropologists for the remainder of the century.

Anthropology was stimulated by national expositions: the Centennial Exposition in Philadelphia in 1876, the Columbian Historical Exposition in Madrid in 1892, and the World's Columbian Exposition in Chicago in 1893. At this time anthropology was being established in natural history museums, including the U.S. National Museum at the Smithsonian Institution in Washington, the American Museum of Natural History in New York, and the Field Columbian Museum in Chicago. The need to acquire objects for display and to form coherent collections drove much early research (figs. 4–5).

Bureau of American Ethnology

Founded in 1879 by John Wesley Powell as a means of organizing anthropological research relating to American Indians, the Bureau of Ethnology (after 1894, the Bureau of American Ethnology), situated within the Smithsonian Institution, played a central role in defining the parameters of anthropological research (Hinsley 1981). Most Bureau members and collaborators focused on recording firsthand ethnographic information and preparing ethnological comparisons cross-tribally. Powell and his close associate WJ McGee reserved for themselves theorizing about how the data fit into the larger anthropological picture. In practice, this meant comparing customs and institutions in terms of relative complexity and assigning them to positions on Morgan's evolutionary continuum. The result, beneficial for later generations who abandoned the evolutionary approach, was largely to divorce theory from description and firmly lay the groundwork for the distinctive Americanist tradition in anthropology. Linguistic precision was important for this tradition, which required the

Smithsonian, NAA: top, S.I. 76-4464; bottom left, 82-11677; bottom right, 91-17921.

Fig. 4. 19th-century exhibits of Plains material culture. top, Centennial Exposition in Philadelphia, displaying an Arapaho council tepee collected by the artist Vincent Colyer in 1869 from Little Raven. Made of 14 buffalo-cow skins and the best-preserved, full-size tepee cover from that time (Ewers 1982b:47), it was on display in the National Museum of Natural History's North American Indian and Eskimo Hall from 1957 to 1998. Photograph by the Centennial Photographic Company, 1876 (cropped). bottom left, Wax figure, probably the earliest manikin of a Plains Indian man displayed in a museum. It was dressed in a buckskin shirt decorated with porcupine quills, beads, and both human and horsehair trophies. The shirt appears to be the one given to William O. Collins by Sota (*šóta* 'smoke') an Oglala Teton Sioux chief, before his death in 1864. The figure holds a Yankton Sioux drum (Army Medical Mus. #90/8390) collected in Dak. Terr. by Dr. A.B. Campbell before June 1868. The split horn headdress (Warren coll.: #1941), Central Plains and probably Sioux, was collected by G.K. Warren, 1855–1857 (Hanson 1996:66). Photograph by C. Seaver, Jr., at the Smithsonian Institution, Washington, D.C., about 1870. bottom right, Manikins at the Columbian Historical Exposition, Madrid, 1892. The figure on the far left was identified as Big Bow, Jr., or Ongotoya, Kiowa. The second manikin, with eagle-feather headdress, wears the same buckskin shirt as the wax figure. The third manikin from the left was identified as Rosa White Thunder, Sioux, wearing a stroud dress decorated with elk teeth, and long dentalium hair ornaments ("History of the United States Plains Since 1850," fig. 8). The fourth manikin is a Zuni male; the fifth is a Kiowa woman with a baby in a cradleboard. Photographer not recorded.

systematization of an orthography for presenting Indian languages (J.W. Powell 1877, 1880). The hallmark of the Americanist enterprise was the recording of texts in native languages as a basis for linguistic study (including the compilation of dictionaries and the writing of grammars) as well as for the documentation of cultures (Darnell 1998, 1999).

One of the original members of the Bureau of Ethnology was a Plains specialist, James Owen Dorsey (vol. 17:249), who in 1871 had undertaken mission work for the Episcopal Church among the Ponca and learned the Omaha-Ponca language. On the basis of a manuscript dictionary and grammar, Powell in 1878, anticipating Congressional approval for the Bureau, hired Dorsey to collect Omaha-Ponca texts and to study traditional society, religion, and culture in general. Dorsey's (1884) *Omaha Sociology* is the first systematic study of a Plains Indian social system. He also published an extensive body of Omaha-Ponca texts, prepared with the aid of Francis La Flesche, an educated Omaha (Dorsey 1890, 1891a), and a study of Omaha material culture (1896). Throughout his short career Dorsey expanded his studies to the Siouan linguistic family in general, publishing a comprehensive monograph on Siouan religions based on both fieldwork and historical study (1894), a comparative study of Siouan social organization (1897), and a brief but invaluable collection of Osage ritual texts (1888b). Working with Dorsey in 1887–1888, George Bushotter, a young Sioux literate in Lakota (vol. 17:252), wrote an extensive collection of texts that included autobiographical accounts; myths; historical tales; and ethnographic accounts of ceremonies, men's societies, and games (DeMallie 1978). During this period Dorsey edited Stephen Return Riggs's publications on Dakota: a dictionary (1890) and a study of grammar, texts, and ethnography (1893), adding comparative Lakota material from Bushotter and others.

Contemporary with Dorsey was Alice C. Fletcher, who began fieldwork with the Teton Sioux and Omaha in 1881 (for a biography see Mark 1988). Affiliated with the Peabody Museum at Harvard University, after the turn of the century she became a collaborator of the Bureau of American Ethnology. She wrote the first anthropological accounts of Sioux and Omaha rituals based on direct observation (Fletcher 1883, 1884a) as well as a monograph on Omaha music that is the first anthropological study of American Indian music (Fletcher 1893). She was the pioneer on the Plains in using the graphaphone to record music and ritual speech. With James R. Murie (vol. 17:251), a mixed-blood Pawnee, she coauthored a study of the Plains intertribal pipe adoption ceremony, which they called the Hako (1904). This study was carried out among the Pawnee because the ceremony was no longer practiced

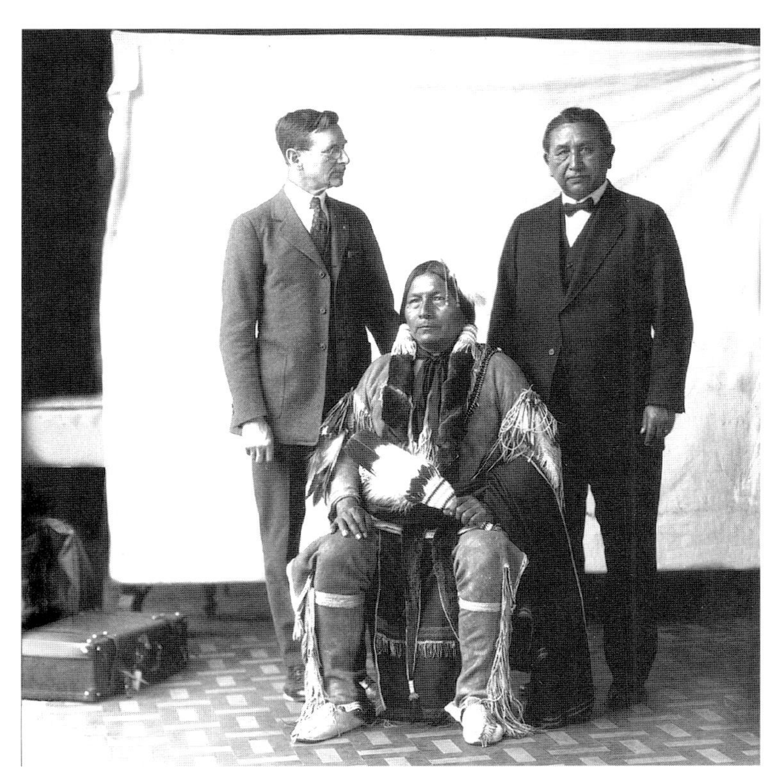

left, Smithsonian, NAA: S.I. 4877-D; right, Smithsonian, Dept. of Anthr., Physical Anthr. Div.: cat. no. 380,831, neg. 91-16317.

Fig. 5. Anthropological research at the Smithsonian Institution. left, William H. Egberts, Smithsonian employee of the Dept. of Anthr. who made casts and busts for the National Museum; Albert Attocknie ('Another House'), Comanche; Francis La Flesche, Omaha. Photograph by De Lancey Gill, 1926. right, Bust of Attocknie, age 45. The mold was made by Egberts and the bust by A. Joseph Andrews, Dept. of Anthr. conservator, 1939. Three casts, one face and 2 busts, exist of Attocknie.

or remembered by the Omaha. Their account is especially valuable for the care with which the ritual is situated in the context of Pawnee social life and for the detail, including all the song lyrics transcribed in Pawnee by Murie, with English translations. Fletcher collaborated for many years with Francis La Flesche, whom she adopted as a son; together they wrote an encyclopedic study of the Omaha (1911) that stands as a monument to nineteenth-century Americanist ethnography. Employed by the Office of Indian Affairs, La Flesche was transferred to the Bureau of American Ethnology in 1910 and carried out his own studies on Osage rituals, publishing over 2,000 pages of texts and an Osage dictionary (1921, 1925a, 1928, 1930, 1939; Mark 1988:324–353).

In 1885 James Mooney joined the Bureau (see Moses 1984; Colby 1977). His comparative study of the Ghost Dance ritual and its spread from tribe to tribe, based on fieldwork throughout the Plains and in the records of the Bureau of Indian Affairs and Department of War, is a classic in the study of American Indian nativistic movements (Mooney 1896). Beginning in 1891 he carried out extensive fieldwork with the Kiowa and published a landmark study (1898) of their calendar histories (winter counts) that presents the first native perspective on the Plains Indian past; he also published an account of Cheyenne history and culture (1907). His larger project, under the joint sponsorship of the Bureau of American Ethnology and the Field Columbian Museum, Chicago, was a study of heraldry (tepee and shield decoration) among the Kiowa and Cheyenne; this was never completed, but his notes and sketches have been preserved in the National Anthropological Archives, Smithsonian Institution. Similarly, his planned study of the spread of the Peyote religion (later incorporated, with Mooney's direct involvement, as the Native American Church) was left uncompleted.

Stewart Culin, who was associated from 1890–1903 with the University of Pennsylvania, Philadelphia, and from 1903–1929 with the Brooklyn Institute of Arts and Sciences (later the Brooklyn Museum), published his monumental study of American Indian games, including much Plains material from his own and George A. Dorsey's work, through the Bureau (1907; see Lawrence and Wythe 1996).

Frances Densmore (fig. 6) specialized in the study of Indian music (vol. 17:256). However, her monograph on Teton Sioux music (1918) is also a major ethnographic source on ritual and religion. Likewise, her study of Teton Sioux material culture (1948), based on her collection deposited in the Museum of the American Indian, is a valuable contribution. Subsequent works on the Mandan and Hidatsa (1923), Pawnee (1929), and Cheyenne and Arapaho (1936) are largely limited to the structure of music.

Similarly, Inez Hilger published her work on American Indian childhood through the Bureau, including a study of the Arapaho (1952).

Independent Researchers

A number of individuals who had no ongoing affilation with museums or academic institutions made important contributions to Plains ethnography. One was the naturalist and conservationist George Bird Grinnell. While on a paleontological expedition in 1872 he hunted buffalo with the Pawnee on that tribe's last great hunt, and in 1874 he accompanied Lt. Col. George A. Custer's exploring expedition in the Black Hills. He continued his association with Plains Indians throughout his career, beginning long-term study of the Cheyenne in 1890 (fig. 7) (Reiger 1972). He published a valuable ethnographic study and collection of tales from the Pawnee (1889), a similar volume on the Blackfoot (1892), a collection of Blackfoot tales (1913a), and a volume including both Pawnee and Blackfoot stories (1901a). His major work is on the Cheyenne, including a history (1915), collection of tales (1926), and comprehensive ethnography (1923).

Walter McClintock, who began his association with Blackfoot in the United States and Canada while working for the United States Forest Service in 1896, published a valuable ethnographic study elaborately illustrated with his own photographs (1910). Later, he was affiliated with

Minn. Histl. Soc., St. Paul: 8145-A.

Fig. 6. Frances Densmore and *makʰá waštéwį*, 'good earth woman', Susan Windgrow (b. 1849, d. 1938), Santee Sioux. Windgrow was Densmore's principal consultant of the Santee community of Prairie I., Minn. Photographed early 1930s.

the Southwest Museum, Los Angeles, which published some of his work (1930, 1948).

Edward Curtis's (1907–1930) ethnographic studies of Plains Indians, carried out with his assistant, W.E. Myers, are remarkable for linguistic accuracy and comparable encyclopedic coverage of many Plains tribes, from the Sarcee and Blackfoot in the north to the Cheyenne and Arapaho in the south. Curtis's publications on the Teton Sioux, Assiniboine, and Arikara, to chose some examples, provide invaluable details not found elsewhere on ritual, society, and customs. As a photographer, Curtis focused on his own distinctive portraits and evocative images of tribal customs, and it is for this that he is best known (B.A. Davis 1985; Lyman 1982; Day 1997; Gidley 1998). However, Curtis's two-decade long study, funded by J. Pierpont Morgan, was remarkable as an independent scholarly enterprise. The text of his work has received less scholarly attention than it deserves.

Boasian Studies: The American Museum of Natural History, the Field Columbian Museum, and Others

Franz Boas's strategy for North American ethnology was outlined in his landmark essay on "The Limitations of the Comparative Method of Anthropology" (1896), in which he argued for distributional studies among neighboring tribes of particular customs in relation to the total culture of a tribe as a means of understanding the origins and development of those customs. His position at the American Museum of Natural History in New York, beginning in 1895, gave him the institutional base for undertaking such large-scale studies, and his appointment at Columbia University in 1899 as professor of anthropology provided him access to graduate students who could carry them out (Kroeber 1942). Having already begun studies on the Northwest Coast and organized the Jesup North Pacific Expedition to examine cultural relations on both sides of the Bering Strait, Boas turned next to the Plains.

To maintain support for research in the museum it was necessary to send collectors to Indian reservations to procure specimens of material culture to fill the exhibit halls. Boas sent two of his first students to the Plains: Alfred L. Kroeber to the Arapaho and Gros Ventre in 1899 and 1900 (vol. 17:46) and Clark Wissler to the Sioux, Blackfoot (fig. 8), and other Northern Plains tribes from 1901 to 1905. In addition to collecting they were to investigate the symbolism of beadwork designs in an attempt to determine whether abstract designs in primitive art represent degenerate forms of realistic designs; at the same time they were to record as much as possible about the culture and mythology of the peoples they visited. The results of the design studies (Kroeber 1900, 1901, 1902–1907; Wissler 1904, 1905a, 1907) confirmed that the symbols in Plains beadwork were not derived from naturalistic designs although abstract shapes were given conventional names.

Encouraged by preliminary results—Kroeber used the Arapaho design study for his Ph.D. dissertation at

Natl. Park Service, Glacier Natl. Park, W. Glacier, Mont.

Fig. 7. George Bird Grinnell (third from right) with a group of Northern Cheyenne men. His interpreter Willis Rowland may be the man writing notes on the far right. Photographed at Lame Deer, Mont., 1890–1937.

Columbia University (1901)—Boas proposed a plan to study the organization of men's societies and the tribal ritual of the Sun Dance throughout the Plains. When he left the museum in 1905 for a full-time position at Columbia, implementation of those comparative studies fell to Wissler, who supervised the research from 1907 to 1916. The published results are among the most impressive products of Plains anthropology: *Societies of the Plains Indians* (Wissler 1912–1916) and *Sun Dance of the Plains Indians* (Wissler 1915–1921). Both volumes comprise separate monographs by many authors and cover most of the Plains tribes, although the museum's collaborators avoided tribes already adequately documented and those among which active work was being carried out by other institutions. The summary essays to each volume—written by Wissler (1916) and Lowie (1916) for the volume on societies and by Leslie Spier (1921) for the Sun Dance volume—are comprehensive, covering the entire Plains area. Spier's essay, regarded as the classic model of distributional studies of culture traits, served as his Ph.D. dissertation at Columbia.

Although the distributional culture trait method failed to provide as clear a picture of historical development as Boas had hoped (for critique of Spier's Sun Dance study see Bennett 1944), the hypotheses raised were still being debated at the end of the twentieth century. The ethnographic material published in the two systematic comparative volumes supplements other publications of the American Museum of Natural History. By presenting material in topically organized monographs, Wissler published on all aspects of Blackfoot culture (1910, 1911, 1912, 1913, 1918; Wissler and Duvall 1908) as did Lowie on the Crow (1912, 1913a, 1913b, 1915b, 1917, 1918, 1919a, 1922, 1922a, 1922b, 1924); both followed and expanded upon the model set by Kroeber in his publications on the Arapaho (1902–1907; G.A. Dorsey and Kroeber 1903) and Gros Ventre (1907, 1908). Lowie, in addition, carried out briefer field studies (and collecting trips) with many Plains tribes, including the Assiniboine and Stoney (1909), Santee Sioux (1913), Hidatsa and Mandan (1917, 1919, 1939), Arikara (1915), Comanche (1912a, 1915a), and Kiowa (1916a). Pliny E. Goddard published on his field studies of the Plains Cree (1919a), Plains Ojibwa (1919b), and Sarcee (1919). In the long run, the record compiled by the American Museum for the Plains offers the single richest source of Plains ethnographic data.

Amer. Mus. of Nat. Hist., New York: top, 2A18377; center, 286528; bottom, Minn. Histl. Soc., St. Paul: 42346.

Fig. 8. Boasian anthropologists. top, Researcher, probably Clark Wissler, photographing skin dressing among the Blood. Photographed in 1901–1905. center, Frederick Wilson taking notes as Mahidiwiats, Hidatsa (*maxíriwiac* 'buffalo bird woman'), weaves a basket. Photograph by Gilbert Wilson, 1912. bottom, Gilbert Wilson holding his research notebook and a baby, probably Raymond Goodbird. Photographed in 1914.

After leaving the American Museum for a teaching position at the University of California, Berkeley, Lowie reworked material from his monographs to produce a comprehensive ethnography of the Crow (1935); after his death his collection of Crow texts (1960) and Crow dictionary (1960a) were published.

Many publications of the American Museum describe collections of material culture made for the museum. Kroeber on the Arapaho (1902–1907) and Gros Ventre (1907), Lowie on the Assiniboine (1909) and Crow (1922, 1922a), and Wissler on the Blackfoot (1910) are notable. Wissler (1910) includes extensive comparative notes, making it an invaluable study of Plains Indian material culture in general. Wissler also published comparative studies of Plains Indian riding gear (1915a), costume (1915, 1916a), and moccasin decoration (1927) based primarily upon the museum's collections.

Part of the success of the American Museum was Wissler's ability—again, following Boas's lead—to find dedicated individuals on Indian reservations who would work independently, then send their research materials to the American Museum for editing and publishing. One was Gilbert L. Wilson, who began fieldwork among the Hidatsa in 1906 as a Presbyterian minister but used the material he recorded as his Ph.D. dissertation in anthropology at the University of Minnesota. Collaborating with his brother Frederick, an artist, the Wilsons (fig. 8) continued summer fieldwork through 1918, producing a series of publications on agriculture, material culture, architecture, and religion (G.L. Wilson 1917, 1924, 1928, 1934; Weitzner 1979; Gilman and Schneider 1987). Wilson also published significant Hidatsa autobiographies (1914, 1921).

Most of the American Museum collaborators were not professional anthropologists. David C. Duvall, a Montana Blackfoot, recorded tales and ethnographic material that became central to Wissler's own studies (Wissler and Duvall 1908; A.B. Kehoe 1995a), as did James R. Walker (agency physician) and Richard and Charles Nines (interpreters) among the Sioux of Pine Ridge Reservation (Wissler 1912a; J.R. Walker 1917, 1980, 1982, 1983). Other anthropologists, not full-time associates of the American Museum, were also involved in Plains fieldwork to fill gaps in the comparative studies of men's societies and the Sun Dance, including Alanson Skinner among the Plains Cree (1914a, 1919), Plains Ojibwa (1914c, 1919a), Iowa (1915), Kansa (1915b), Ponca (1915a), and Santee Sioux (1919b), as well as Wilson D. Wallis among the Santee Sioux (1919).

The ethnographic studies of George A. Dorsey at the Field Columbian Museum, carried out from 1900 to 1907, complemented those of the American Museum. Although not a student of Boas (Dorsey was trained in physical anthropology at Harvard) he emulated the work of the Boasians. In addition to aggressive collecting of material culture for the Field Columbian Museum, Dorsey conceptualized his own plan to study the Sun Dance and men's societies. While the American Museum collaborators collected their material through interviews, without ever seeing actual performances of surviving rituals, Dorsey made a point not only of carrying out firsthand observations of Sun Dances but also of having them photographed. His studies of the Arapaho and Cheyenne Sun Dances (1903, 1905b) are unmatched in the anthropological record for the detail of ritual description supplemented by photographic images. In the Arapaho case, he was able to bring one of the Sun Dance leaders to Chicago to go over his notes on the performance of the ceremony and amplify the symbolism and significance of ritual acts. Dorsey also published shorter studies of the Ponca Sun Dance (1905) and the Osage Mourning-War Ceremony (1902). He published collections of oral traditions for the Arapaho (1903, authored jointly with Kroeber), the Cheyenne (1905a), and the Osage (1904c).

Collaborating with Murie, Dorsey carried out an ambitious comparative project with the Caddoan tribes, investigating myths, ritual, and social organization for the Arikara (1904), Pawnee (1904b, 1906), Wichita (1904a), and Caddo (1905c). Another product of the collaboration between Dorsey and Murie was an extensive manuscript on Skiri Pawnee society and religion, only a portion of which has been published (G.A. Dorsey and Murie 1940).

Unable to unlock satisfactorily the meanings of ritual symbolism, Dorsey became convinced that understanding them could take place only through the native language itself. He hired James R. Murie to work with him on his Caddoan studies, and together they recorded a huge quantity of ritual songs as well as texts on wax cylinders. In order to better translate and analyze his material, in 1907 Dorsey took Murie and a selection of the recordings to New York to enlist Boas's help in devising a proper orthography and working out the fundamentals of the grammar. With the large collection of dictated texts by Roaming Scout, a Skiri priest, nearly complete, and a large manuscript on Skiri society and religion virtually ready for publication, Dorsey turned his attention away from American Indians and never returned to the work, leaving an enormous ethnographic and linguistic legacy for the future (DeMallie and Parks 1999).

Murie continued to work on ethnographic projects throughout the remainder of his life. With the assistance of Wissler, he wrote the monograph on Pawnee societies for the American Museum's comparative study (1914) and again under Wissler's supervision, but with the support of the Bureau of American Ethnology, compiled a very large manuscript entitled "Ceremonies of the Pawnee," complete with transcriptions of the lyrics of hundreds of songs recorded on wax cylinders (1921).

Other institutions that made extensive Plains Indian collections also sponsored and published field research. Alanson Skinner's work on the Iowa (1926) was published by the Milwaukee Public Museum; the National Museum of Canada, Ottawa, published Diamond Jenness's studies

Nebr. State Histl. Soc., Lincoln.

Fig. 9. Melvin R. Gilmore recording Omaha singers with an Edison recorder, Nebr. State Histl. Soc. expedition. Photograph probably by Addison E. Sheldon, Omaha Res., Nebr., 1905.

of the Sarcee (1938) and Marius Barbeau's stories from the Stoney and other tribes of Alberta (1960); the Museum of the American Indian, Heye Foundation, New York, published brief papers by Melvin R. Gilmore (fig. 9) on the Sioux (e.g., 1929, 1929a) and Arikara (1925, 1925a, 1926a, 1927), Skinner on the Santee Sioux Midewiwin ceremony (1920), and William Wildschut's studies of Crow Indian medicine bundles and beadwork (Wildschut 1960; Wildschut and Ewers 1959). The Nebraska State Historical Society, Lincoln, published Gilmore's study of Teton Sioux ethnobotany (1913) and the Bureau of American Ethnology published his comparative study of Northern Plains ethnobotany (1919). Gilmore, who taught at the University of Michigan, Ann Arbor, also published in the Michigan Academy of Science, Arts, and Letters (e.g., 1930, 1931, 1933) and wrote a popular book on Plains Indian traditions (1929b); see Woolworth (1987) for a bibliography of Gilmore's brief, but numerous, ethnographic papers on the Arikara, based on his field studies. Between 1929 and 1932 Martha Warren Beckwith, a student of Boas, recorded significant collections of folklore and traditions among the Teton Sioux (1930) and the Mandan and Hidatsa (1937).

Columbia University

A number of Boas's later students, and the students of his students, also turned to Plains Indian research. Wilson D. Wallis worked among the Santee Sioux in Canada in 1914 (1919, 1923, 1947). Ruth Benedict wrote her dissertation on a comparative study of the vision quest, bringing together material from throughout the Plains (1922). Working with Boas and Benedict from 1927 to 1948, Ella C. Deloria, herself a native speaker of Sioux, recorded texts in the Lakota and Dakota dialects as well as ethnographic material (DeMallie 1988; Medicine 1999). Deloria published one volume of texts (1932), but most of her material, together with her extensive retranscriptions and retranslations of historical texts, is unpublished and is archived with the Boas Collection in the American Philosophical Society Library, Philadelphia. (Bowdlerized versions of some of the texts are printed in Rice 1992, 1993, 1994.) Deloria coauthored the standard grammar of Lakota (Boas and Deloria 1942) and published a popular book, Speaking of Indians (1944), that provides insightful cultural understanding of the Sioux and places American Indians within the broader context of the United States.

After Alexander Lesser expressed interest in undertaking a comparative kinship study for his dissertation, Boas suggested he study the Siouan family (Parks 1985). Based on Teton Sioux kinship data from Ella Deloria in New York, fieldwork with many Siouan tribes, and published sources, Lesser's study (1928, 1929, 1958) is a model of Boasian comparativism, designed to test the relationship between kinship systems and social structure and to reconstruct the historical development of kinship systems within the family. He also prepared a similar, briefer study of Caddoan kinship systems (1979). Coordinating his research with that of his wife, Gene Weltfish, Lesser carried out fieldwork from 1928 to 1931. Pawnee ethnology was a topic of mutual interest, in which they had the benefit of Murie's unpublished manuscripts from the Field Museum and the Smithsonian Institution. In 1929–1930 Lesser documented Kitsai, a Caddoan language whose last fluent speaker lived with the Wichita, compiling texts (working from Kitsai to Wichita to English, since the Kitsai speaker did not speak English), grammatical notes, and lexical material. At the same time he recorded comparative ethnographic and linguistic material on the Wichita. Lesser and Weltfish (1932) wrote the definitive classification of Caddoan languages. Lesser devoted 1930–1931 to field study of Pawnee ethnology. Out of this work came his study of the Pawnee Ghost Dance Hand Game (1933), a remarkable combination of documentary history with field investigation that examines what began as a nativistic religious movement and ultimately became institutionalized in Pawnee culture. It is a classic in the literature on culture change.

In 1928 Boas suggested to Gene Weltfish that she work on the Pawnee, starting with language (Parks and Pathe 1985). From 1928 through 1931 she carried out field research on Pawnee, completing a collection of South Band Pawnee texts (1937) and retranscribing the song texts in Murie (1921). In 1935, using in part Murie and Dorsey's manuscripts from the Field Museum, Weltfish again carried out fieldwork to reconstruct the social and economic life of the Skiri Pawnee in the mid-nineteenth century. From her voluminous field notes she published a comprehensive historical ethnography of that tribe (1965).

Under Boas's direction, Ruth Landes undertook a comparative study of traditional social institutions among Prairie tribes; she worked with the Santee Sioux at Prairie Island in 1935 (Landes 1968).

Field Schools

During the 1930s three summer field schools among Plains Indians provided training for anthropology graduate students and resulted in significant contributions to the ethnographic record. In 1933, Ralph Linton (fig. 10), of the University of Wisconsin, Madison, who would become Boas's replacement as chair of the anthropology department at Columbia University from 1938–1946, organized a Comanche field party for the Laboratory of Anthropology in Santa Fe, New Mexico, consisting of Gustav G. Carlson, J. Nixon Hadley, E. Adamson Hoebel (and his wife), Claiborne Lockett, and Waldo R. Wedel. For the first few weeks the students took notes while Linton interviewed consultants; later the students worked independently. Although a planned ethnographic monograph failed to appear, a number of publications based on the summer's work were produced (G.G. Carlson and V.H. Jones 1940; Hoebel 1939, 1940, 1941; Linton in Kardiner et al. 1945:47–100). Hoebel's field notes are in the American Philosophical Society Library, and Wedel's are in the National Anthropological Archives, Smithsonian Institution. The field notes by Carlson, Hoebel, and Wedel are collated in Kavanagh (1991). During summer 1934 Jeanette Mirsky, also a Columbia student, carried out independent fieldwork with the Comanche, and some of her material was used in the publications of the field school members.

Hoebel continued to develop the case-study method for analyzing traditional systems of law and did comparative fieldwork with the Fort Hall Northern Shoshone in 1934 and with the Northern Cheyenne in 1935. In collaboration with Karl N. Llewellyn, of the Columbia University Law School, Hoebel coauthored an analysis of Cheyenne law that is a landmark in legal anthropology (Llewellyn and Hoebel 1941) and wrote a general book entitled *The Law of Primitive Man* incorporating material from his field studies (Hoebel 1954).

Smithsonian, NAA: Wedel Coll.

Fig. 10. Ralph Linton (center), with Quasyah, Comanche, and unidentified man. Photograph by Waldo Wedel, Walters, Okla., 1933.

In 1935 Alexander Lesser organized a field party at Columbia University to study the Kiowa, also under the auspices of the Laboratory of Anthropology. The members were William Bascom, Donald Collier, R. Weston LaBarre, Bernard Mishkin, and Jane Richardson. Each student chose a topic for study but as they interviewed consultants they attemped to be as comprehensive as possible, recording material relating to the other students' interests as well. Field notes were typed with multiple carbons and shared among all members of the party. Mishkin, writing on rank and warfare (1940), and J. Richardson, writing on law (1940), both published volumes resulting from this fieldwork. Copies of these field notes are deposited in the National Anthropological Archives (J. Richardson et al. 1935).

In 1939 Ruth Benedict organized a field party for the Columbia University Laboratory of Ethnography jointly with the University of Montana, Missoula, to carry out an ambitious comparative study of the Blackfoot tribes in the United States and Canada (Goldfrank 1978:127–150). Harry D. Biele, Esther S. Goldfrank, and Marjorie Lismer worked with the Blood; Lucien M. Hanks, Jr., and Jane Richardson worked with the Blackfoot; Oscar Lewis and his wife Ruth worked with the Canadian Peigan; and Rae Walowitz, Sylvia Susan Sommers (later Dietrich), and Gitel Steed and her husband Bob worked with the Piegan in Montana. A number of publications developed from this field season (Goldfrank 1945; Hanks and Richardson 1945, 1950; O. Lewis 1942; Lismer 1974; A.B. Kehoe 1996). Goldfrank's field notes are in the National Anthropological Archives, Smithsonian Institution, and J. Richardson's are in the Glenbow-Alberta Institute, in Calgary.

The University of Chicago

A distinctive approach developed in the 1930s at the University of Chicago that combined Boasian culture history represented by Fay-Cooper Cole with the British social anthropology of A.R. Radcliffe-Brown. Focusing on kinship and social structure, Fred Eggan (fig. 11), a student of both men, combined their perspectives in his own unique approach that had a major influence on generations of students trained at Chicago (DeMallie 1994). Eggan began by summarizing the literature on Plains kinship and social systems for Radcliffe-Brown, then carried out fieldwork among the Cheyenne and Arapaho of Oklahoma in 1933. From 1933–1934 J. Gilbert McAllister carried out a comparable study with the Plains Apache. These, the first descriptions of Plains social systems to follow a structural-functional approach, were published in Eggan (1937). In 1939 Donald Collier did fieldwork with the Teton Sioux and Crow, and wrote a summary study of Plains camping groups (1940a). Karl and Iva Schmidt worked with the Wichita and other Caddoan tribes studying kinship and social organization (1952). Eggan (1955) wrote a masterful summary of the state of American Indian kinship studies, providing much new information about the Plains tribes.

During the same period Alfred Bowers began his in-depth ethnographic studies at Fort Berthold Reservation, complementing archeological studies he made under the auspices of the Logan Museum at Beloit College, Wisconsin (Parks 1992). From 1929 to 1931 he worked with the Mandan (fig. 11) and from 1932 to 1934 principally with the Hidatsa, attempting to make as detailed a record as possible of social and religious organization and the ceremonies and myths that were their foundation. Using census records, he reconstructed geneaologies and the paths through which sacred bundles and ritual knowledge passed. In the process he recorded texts in English and in the native languages and fashioned his cultural reconstructions around them. In 1947 Bowers returned to record an extensive autobiography by Crow's Heart, a Mandan, who was the last survivor of the elders with whom he had originally worked. His publications on the Mandan (1950) and Hidatsa (1965) are rich sources of ethnographic data and analytically they combine the insights of British social anthropology with the Boasian culture-historical approach, extended to explore the intersection of myth and society.

Other Plains Studies

Other significant ethnographic work was carried out independently of major universities or museums. Unique among them is the volume by James Larpenteur Long, an Assiniboine who worked for the Federal Writers' Project. He compiled stories and reminiscences from the older members of his tribe (J.L. Long 1942; M.S. Kennedy 1961). Long's grandfather, Charles Larpenteur (1898, 1933), a French fur trader, knew and described the Assiniboine and their neighbors on the Upper Missouri.

Alice L. Marriott, who received an M.A. at the University of Oklahoma, carried out extensive field study with the Kiowa beginning in 1935 and published a historical ethnography (1945), collections of tales (1947, 1963), and a study of culture change (1968). One of the organizations with which Marriott was associated was the Indian Arts and Crafts Board of the Department of the Interior, created in 1935, which founded the Museum of the Plains Indian in Browning, Montana, and the Southern Plains Indian Museum in Anadarko, Oklahoma. The board fostered popularization of American Indian arts and crafts. Among signifiant studies sponsored by the board are Carrie Lyford on Teton Sioux quill and beadwork (1940), Ewers on Blackfoot crafts (1945), and Mable Morrow on painted rawhide (1975).

Psychological and Acculturation Studies

In the 1930s acculturation studies developed along with the psychological approaches that came to be known as culture and personality studies. Fieldwork for two of these studies was carried out in the summer of 1930. Wissler's student, H. Scudder Mekeel, began his work with the Oglala Sioux on Pine Ridge Reservation, returning the next summer as well. He studied contemporary Sioux life, including political and economic structures, and collected representative individual life histories for purposes of studying the psychological dimensions of modern reservation life for both full bloods and mixed bloods (Mekeel 1932a, 1936, 1943; see Biolsi 1997). The summer of 1930 Margaret Mead worked on the Omaha Reservation with her husband, Reo Fortune. Out of that work she wrote *The Changing Culture of an Indian Tribe* (1932), disguising

top, Wichita & Affiliated Tribes, Anadarko, Okla.; bottom, U. of Idaho, Bowers Lab. of Anthr.

Fig. 11. Anthropologists from U. of Chicago. top, left to right, Fred Eggan; McCarty "Bocardi" Stephenson, Wichita; Gilbert McAllister; Cora McAllister; Fanny Stephenson, Wichita; R.L. Boak, trader; and Rolland Stephenson, Wichita. Photographed near Anadarko, Okla., 1933. bottom, left to right, Bear on Flat, Mandan; Crows Heart, Mandan; and Alfred Bowers at an eagle-trapping site, Ft. Berthold Res., N. Dak. Photographed 1930–1931.

the identity of the tribe by using the pseudonym "Antlers." Mead's was the first published study of acculturation among North American Indians in the reservation period. Her approach was distinctive in Plains ethnography in that she worked extensively with women, who, she argued, found adaptation to reservation life less traumatic than did men.

The psychologist Erik Erikson, accompanied by Mekeel, studied child training briefly at Pine Ridge in 1937 and wrote about childhood and education among the Sioux (1939, 1950:98–140). His psychological interpretations provide a useful foil to those of anthropologists. From 1935 to 1938 Ralph Linton used ethnographic material from his Comanche field school as a contribution to Abram Kardiner's seminars on psychology at Columbia University (Kardiner et al. 1945:47–80; see A. Linton and Wagley 1971:49–60). In the late 1940s George Devereux undertook an extensive psychological study of a Plains Indian World War II veteran (1951, 1969).

The Committee on Indian Education Research, organized jointly by the University of Chicago and the Bureau of Indian Affairs, undertook a comparative project to study American Indian personality. Gordon Macgregor headed a team that carried out psychological testing of 200 school children at Pine Ridge in 1942. The resulting book, *Warriors without Weapons* (1946), discusses social change and contemporary reservation conditions to assess their effects on personality development of Oglala Sioux children. Royal B. Hassrick, a member of the Pine Ridge team, carried out fieldwork at Rosebud Reservation (1944) and completed an ethnography of the Teton Sioux (1964) written from a psychological perspective.

Formal studies of acculturation were stimulated by the subcommittee on acculturation of the general committee on personality and culture of the Social Science Research Council. From 1935 to 1938 Linton served as a member of the committee and in that capacity he organized and edited a volume on acculturation among seven Indian tribes, written by his students, and prepared summaries of each ethnographic case as well as a general evalution (1940). The Plains was represented by the Northern Arapahoe, who were studied by Stanley Elkin. Edward Spicer's comparative study of American Indian acculturation (1961), which takes a more historical and cultural perspective, has become a standard work on the subject. In that volume the Plains area is represented by Edward Bruner's sketch of the Mandan.

Fred Voget (fig. 12), a graduate student at Yale University, began field study of the modern Crow in 1939 to provide data for George Peter Murdock's cross-cultural survey. He arrived just at the time that the Shoshone Sun Dance was being introduced to the Crow; this became the subject of his Ph.D. dissertation (1948). Voget continued to chronicle the Sun Dance over several decades as it developed into a major feature of twentieth-century Crow culture (1984).

Historical Approaches

While nineteenth-century scholars had used historical materials as background for their cultural reconstructions based on field studies, the first systematic mining of printed and manuscript documents for the purpose of developing an overall picture of Native America was carried out in conjunction with the writing of the Bureau of American Ethnology's *Handbook of American Indians North of Mexico* (Hodge 1907-1910). That work was hurried, and writers relied on secondary sources and translations rather than seeking out primary sources. Similarly, the historical syntheses produced by the Boasians tended to be thorough summaries of easily available printed material. The result was to foster a tradition of uncritical use of documentary sources, accepting or rejecting the observations of missionaries, explorers, travelers, and military men according to the degree to which the information presented fit with larger cultural patterns worked out through fieldwork. At the Smithsonian Institution the ongoing work of John R. Swanton, while centered primarily on the Southeast, was important in stimulating anthropologists to

top, Sask. Arch. Board, Regina: R85-169; bottom, Smithsonian, Handbook of North Amer. Indians Photo. Coll.

Fig. 12. Anthropologists in the field in the 1930s. top, David Mandelbaum with the Plains Cree. Second from left is Solomon Blue-horn and the elder sitting in front holding a pipe is Maskwa. Photographed at Sweet Grass Res., Alta., 1934. bottom, Fred Voget and his sixth-grade class at Lodge Grass school, Lodge Grass, Mont., made up of both Crow and non-Indian children. Voget was doing research for his dissertation at the time and supported himself in the field by teaching in the school. Photographed in 1940.

incorporate primary historical sources in their ethnological studies. The festschrift for Swanton (Smithsonian Institution 1940) includes important essays by W. Duncan Strong (1940) and Waldo R. Wedel (1940) that demonstrate the feasibility and importance of linking documentary evidence with archeological sites.

Beginning about 1930 anthropologists turned to the examination of historical materials for the light they could throw on American Indian cultures and culture change. Wissler taught at Yale University from 1924 to 1940, where his interests turned toward history and he began to write a historical ethnography of the Northern Plains. (The planned book, never completed, is documented by his papers in the Department of Anthropology at Ball State University, Muncie, Indiana.) Mekeel synthesized the historical literature on the Sioux (1932). David Mandelbaum's (fig. 12) dissertation, a study of Plains Cree culture change (1936, 1940, 1979), is rich in ethnographic detail and presents a careful historical reconstruction using primary sources. John C. Ewers (fig. 13), a student of Wissler, wrote a comparative study of Plains Indian hide painting based on museum specimens (1939). He served as founding curator of the Museum of the Plains Indian, where he carried out extensive fieldwork with the Blackfeet. After joining the staff of the Department of Anthropology, U.S. National Museum (later the National Museum of Natural History) in the Smithsonian, and following Wissler's lead closely, Ewers published a monograph assessing the effects of horses and their role in Blackfoot culture, including comparative material from throughout the Plains (1955). He published prolifically on Plains Indian art (1986), history, and culture (1968, 1997).

Historical studies were also emphasized at Columbia University, reflecting the Boasian culture-historical approach exemplified by Lesser and Weltfish, as well as the influence of W. Duncan Strong, who went to Columbia in 1937. As an archeologist, Strong was interested in the processes of cultural and social change associated with networks of intertribal and Indian-White trade on the Plains (Hoebel 1980:18-19; Solecki and Wagley 1963; J. Vincent 1990:232-241). Strong encouraged a group of students to write Ph.D. dissertations on a variety of historical topics, several of which have become classics: Bernard Mishkin's study of Kiowa rank and warfare, focusing on the effects of the introduction of horses and guns (1940), Oscar Lewis's analysis of the effects of the fur trade on the Blackfoot (1942), and Joseph Jablow's study of the role of the Cheyenne in Plains trade networks (1951). Under Weltfish's supervision Preston Holder did fieldwork with the Arikara and wrote a dissertation on Plains Caddoans concerned with the distinctive features of social stratification characteristic of the Plains village tribes (1949); the published version (1970) includes an insightful historical survey of relations between the village tribes of the Upper Missouri River and the nomadic tribes but omits the comparative material on the Pawnee found in the dissertation.

Another center of historical study in anthropology was the University of Chicago where, under the rubric of ethnohistory, Fay-Cooper Cole facilitated the development of a consortium of Midwestern universities and libraries to study systematically the historical material relating to the greater Midwest, including the Prairie Plains. The initial purpose for the project was to provide historical context to explicate archeological findings, a method that came to be called "the direct historical approach" (W.R. Wedel 1938). One important result of the project was the publication of a collection of historical maps from European and American sources that document the development of Euro-American knowledge of tribal locations (Tucker 1942), with a supplement (Temple 1975) and a companion volume that takes the scope farther west onto the High Plains (Wood 1983).

Stemming directly from the Chicago project was the annual Ohio Valley Historic Indian Conference, begun in 1953, and its journal, *Ethnohistory*, the first issue of which was published in April 1954 (E.W. Voegelin 1954). The conference developed into a professional society of anthropologists and historians, in 1966 renamed the American Society for Ethnohistory, which through its annual meetings and journal has played a major role in increasing anthropologists' awareness of the need to meet the standards of textual criticism developed in history in order to use documentary source materials responsibly.

The need to write tribal histories to evaluate Indian land claims was a further stimulus to the use of historical documents. After the Indian Claims Commission was founded in 1946 many anthropologists (and historians as well) were enlisted to compile documentary evidence for the court. Although they were primarily chronological digests designed to document Indian land use, these histories

Fig. 13. John C. Ewers. The buffalo hide painting, showing war exploits, was made about 1835 by a Plains Indian of the Upper Missouri and collected by the War Department in 1866 (Maurer 1992:151). The Teton Sioux human effigy, used in a victory dance, was collected by George Keiser Sanderson in 1876–1887 (Ewers 1986:144). Both objects are in the Smithsonian collections. This photograph was made for and was part of a research case exhibit on Ewers's work installed May 1978. It shows Ewers's research interests in Plains Indian painting and sculpture. Photograph by Chip Clark, Washington, D.C., January 1978.

proved to be valuable resources and stimulated further work. At Indiana University, for example, Erminie W. Voegelin organized a massive project that involved many graduate students and faculty to carry out research and compile documents for the Justice Department in claims relating to the greater Midwest. (N.A. Ross 1973 lists the Indian Claims Commission reports.) Harold Hickerson's work on the Chippewa developed into two valuable published monographs (1962, 1970). He demonstrated the necessity of looking at tribes not in isolation, but in the context of their neighbors as well. Through analysis of warfare between the Chippewa and the Santee Sioux Hickerson discovered that an unoccupied buffer zone developed between the two tribes during the eighteenth century. The archeological correlate of this ecologically distinctive buffer zone was confirmed by Watrall (1968a). Likewise, Ewers expanded his report on the Blackfeet of Montana for the Indian Claims Commission into a tribal history (1958) that integrates cultural description and historical events.

Late Twentieth-Century Cultural Anthropology

Cultural anthropology of Plains Indians from the 1960s to the 1990s continued the two previous traditions: ethnographic description and the testing of anthropological theories using Plains data. Publications resulting from this work are too numerous to survey encyclopedically; the following selection attempts to describe a variety of trends.

Ethnographies

Although tribal ethnographies were less emphasized during this period, some important studies were written. Hoebel (1960) is a succinct but masterful summary that abstracts the premises of Cheyenne life to a series of epistemological postulates. James H. Howard compiled a comprehensive summary of the ethnographic and historical material on the Ponca, incorporating his own field interviews (J.H. Howard 1965). Howard also published an ethnography of the Canadian Sioux, based closely on his field notes (J.H. Howard 1984). For the Teton Sioux, two ethnographies of contemporary life make a nice contrast: Daniele Vazeilles (1977) presents a reflexive account of her fieldwork at Cheyenne River while Elizabeth Grobsmith (1981) offers a concise but thorough overview of Rosebud Reservation. Jeffrey Anderson's (1999) ethnography of contemporary Northern Arapahoe life uses native language concepts to explore the underpinnings of cultural behavior.

Historical Studies

A wide variety of approaches to history characterized Plains ethnography during this period. Noteworthy are the works of Loretta K. Fowler. Her history of the Northern Arapahoe from 1851 to 1978 (Fowler 1982) combines ethnohistorical method with symbolic (interpretive) anthropology to focus on political processes and reveals remarkable cultural continuities over time despite major transformations in lifeways and social organization. Fowler's (1987) parallel study of the Gros Ventre investigates cultural continuity and innovation as that tribe embraced an ideal of "progress" as a means of succeeding in reservation life. Drawing on the concept of "cohort groups," Fowler also explicates the "generation gap" that became so apparent during the cultural revivals of the 1970s. She concludes with a thoughtful analysis of the meaning of history, investigating the competing histories of the Gros Ventres and Assiniboines who share the Fort Belknap Reservation.

Writing about the Cheyenne, John Moore (1987) investigates the formation of the Cheyenne as a tribe out of disparate bands, reconstructs subsequent changes in the social order, and traces the ecological correlates of Cheyenne life down through the reservation period. Moore (1996) also published an ethnography of the Cheyenne set in historical perspective through the early 1990s. Father Peter John Powell (1979), restricting his focus to the chiefs' and warriors' societies of the Northern Cheyenne, wrote a massive narrative history tracing individual bands and leaders throughout the nineteenth century until settlement on the Tongue River Reservation in 1879. An interpretive ethnohistory, the work is written in a narrative style based on Powell's understandings of historical Cheyenne culture and, in particular, takes the perspective of a Cheyenne religious leader.

While most tribal histories were written by historians, works by anthropologists include Thomas Kavanagh's meticulous reconstruction of Comanche political and social bands and divisions through time (1996) and Benjamin Kracht's study of the Kiowa, which focuses on the native concept of 'power' and its manifestations through time (1992). David Reed Miller (1987) chronicled the history of the Assiniboine in Montana and DeMallie (1986) wrote a history of the Sioux in Montana, 1869–1884.

Reservation histories are represented by Ernest L. Schusky's study of the Lower Brule Sioux (1975), which brings their story up through the devastation caused by the flooding of the reservation's best lands by the building of the Missouri River dams. Carolyn R. Anderson (1997) wrote the history of the Prairie Island Sioux of Minnesota tracing them from the 1600s through their renaissance as a small, but casino-rich tribe. Irene Castle McLaughlin wrote an in-depth study of ranching during the reservation period at Fort Berthold (1993) and Thomas Biolsi took an anthropological perspective on the New Deal as it played out among the Sioux on Rosebud Reservation (1992).

Tribal and Ethnic Identity

Taking a perspective from interpretive anthropology, Robert E. Daniels wrote an important analysis of identities on the

Pine Ridge Reservation (1970). A study by Neils Braroe (1975), part of a larger project designed by John W. Bennett (1969) to look comparatively at the Northern Plains region, investigates shifting identities among Plains Cree of Saskatchewan as they interact with neighbors, Indian and White. Malcolm McFee studied acculturation and identity among the Blackfeet in Montana (1968, 1972). Anne S. Straus, writing from twin perspectives of psychological and symbolic anthropology, investigated identity in relation to the life cycle among the Northern Cheyenne (1976, 1977, 1978). A study of the Comanche by Morris W. Foster (1991) argues for the perpetuation of the Comanche over time through social interactions rather than cultural symbols. Working in Bennett County, South Dakota, until 1911 a part of Pine Ridge Reservation, Paula Wagoner (1997, 1998) explored the tangle of identities that characterized Indians, mixed bloods, and Whites in an area perpetually politically charged.

Historical Documents

John Parker (1976) edited the 1766-1767 journals of Jonathan Carver that provide important material on the Santee Sioux. The 1794-1796 journal and "Description of the Upper Missouri" by the French-Canadian fur trader Jean-Baptiste Truteau (1912, 1921), which are rich in ethnographic detail, were edited for publication by Douglas R. Parks (1993). Edmund C. Bray and Martha Coleman Bray (1976) edited the 1838-1839 journals of mapmaker Joseph N. Nicollet, who worked among the Sioux and Ojibwa; DeMallie (1976) edited Nicollet's ethnographic notes on the Sioux.

William Wildschut's manuscript on the life of Two Leggings, a Crow warrior, was edited for publication by Peter Nabokov (1967). The account of the life of the Gros Ventre religious leader Bull Lodge, recorded in the 1930s by tribal member Fred P. Gone, was published with an introduction by George Horse Capture (1980a), also a tribal member. The ethnographic writings, 1897-1917, on the Oglala Sioux by Pine Ridge Reservation physician James R. Walker were edited by DeMallie and Elaine A. Jahner (J.R. Walker 1980, 1982, 1983). DeMallie (1984) also edited the 1931 and 1944 interviews by John G. Neihardt of Oglala Sioux religious leader Nicholas Black Elk, from which Neihardt wrote his popular books *Black Elk Speaks* (1932) and *When the Tree Flowered* (1951).

Religious Belief and Ceremony

The most important material on Plains religion published during this period was Murie's account of Pawnee ceremonialism edited by Douglas R. Parks (1981), a rich resource that serves as a basis for reanalyzing the religious systems of the Caddoan tribes.

Much attention has been paid to the Teton Sioux. Major publications include J.R. Walker (1980), which provides first-person narratives that give individual perspectives on belief and ritual from the turn of the twentieth century. Stephen E. Feraca (1963, 1998) documented ceremonialism at Pine Ridge in the 1950s, revealing both continuities and innovations. William K. Powers presented an overall picture of Oglala religion (1977) that combines materials from the late nineteenth to the twentieth century and gives a timeless reconstruction that obliterates change. His monograph on *yuwipi*, a ceremony performed for healing and conjuring (1982), is a valuable ethnographic contribution, contextualizing the ritual in reservation life. Luis Kemnitzer (1968, 1970, 1976) also studied yuwipi at Pine Ridge. Thomas Mails compiled a valuable record of the Sun Dance at Rosebud and Pine Ridge reservations in the 1970s (1978). Thomas Lewis's study of Pine Ridge medicine men (1990) offers a sympathetic portrayal from the late 1960s, with many direct quotes from practitioners. A collection of papers originating in a 1982 symposium that brought together both practitioners and scholars of all varieties of Sioux religion presents a wide variety of viewpoints characteristic of the contemporary scene (DeMallie and Parks 1987). Raymond Bucko published a thorough summary of the historical literature on the most basic of Sioux rituals, the sweatlodge, together with his own observations and experiences at Pine Ridge (1998).

P.J. Powell (1969, 2) published a detailed ethnography, with copious photographic documentation, of contemporary Cheyenne ceremonialism, and Margot Liberty published accounts of the Sun Dance and Sacred Hat ritual (1965, 1967, 1968). Karl Schleisier (1987) published an account of the development of Cheyenne ceremonialism that is guided by contemporary understandings and offers an idealized reconstruction that relates more to the present than the past.

Peter Nabokov wrote an important dissertation (1988) on the Crow Tobacco society, with an account of ritualism in the 1980s. Rodney Frey (1979) studied the practice of the Shoshone-Crow Sun Dance and associated belief system among the Crow. Robin Ridington and Dennis Hastings, a tribal member, published a comprehensive account of the Sacred Pole of the Omaha and documented the process and effects of its repatriation to the tribe from the Peabody Museum of Harvard University (Ridington and Hastings 1997).

Completing a lifetime of study of the Native American Church, primarily in the Great Basin and Southwest, Omer C. Stewart (1987) published a historical account of the Peyote religion that includes material on many Plains tribes, from Oklahoma to Montana. Daniel C. Swan (1999) examined art associated with the Peyote religion in a beautifully illustrated study.

Kinship and Social Organization

Most studies of kinship and social organization on the Plains were stimulated by the combination of British social anthropology and American historical anthropology exemplified in the work of Fred Eggan (1955, 1966). Starting with an interest in the effects of ecology, Symmes C. Oliver (1962) systematically examined the kinship and social systems of the nomadic tribes of the Plains, concluding that ecological factors accounted for the similarities among them, despite disparate tribal origins. This study was a valuable comparative survey but was limited by the inadequacies of the ethnographic record and by the dearth of historical research required to substantiate origins and patterns of relationship among Plains tribes.

In his Lewis Henry Morgan lectures, delivered at the University of Rochester, New York, Eggan (1966) again synthesized the available material on Plains kinship, and a number of his students took up the study of American Indian kinship systems. DeMallie worked on the Western Sioux (1971, 1979, 1994), Joseph E. Maxwell undertook a comparative study of the nomadic tribes (1971, 1978), and Anne S. Straus worked on the Northern Cheyenne (1976, 1977, 1994).

Other significant studies of Plains kinship include R.H. Barnes (1984) who skillfully synthesized the literature on the much-discussed kinship system of the Omaha tribe, and John H. Moore's evaluation of Cheyenne kinship (1988). L. Johnson (1994a) reconstructed the Crow-type kinship system of the Tonkawa using data collected by Albert S. Gatschet in 1884 and Alexander Lesser in 1929, and R.H. Barnes (1996) assessed L.H. Morgan's presentation of Pawnee kinship data.

A study by Jane Collier (1988) is unique in using published data on the Kiowa, Comanche, and Cheyenne to test theories of social inequality in classless societies.

Texts

A great many texts were recorded during the twentieth century, although most of them were not published. The important collection of native-language texts by the Skiri Pawnee religious leader Roaming Scout was translated and edited by Douglas Parks (1995, 1999b; Parks and DeMallie 1992a). Similarly, the collection of Lakota texts by George Sword (vol. 17:252), written in the early 1900s at Pine Ridge, was translated and edited (DeMallie 1993, 1999; Parks and DeMallie 1992). Parks (1991) also published a large collection of Arikara texts, recorded from 1970-1987 from the last speakers of the language. Collections of contemporary texts in Plains Cree were published by H. Christoph Wolfart and Freda Ahenakew, a native scholar (1992, 1993, 1997, 1998). Wayne Leman (1987) published a collection of contemporary Northern Cheyenne texts, and H.H. St. Clair (1909) and Eliot D. Canonge (1958) contributed Comanche texts.

Music and Dance

The study of Blackfoot music by Bruno Nettl (1989) continued the tradition of the analysis of music structure begun by Densmore. Gloria A. Young (1981) wrote a study of the powwow on the Southern Plains that is rich in historical context and contemporary description. Orin Hatton (1974, 1986) has written on Northern Plains powwows. Luke E. Lassiter (1998) published a book on Kiowa song, and Virginia Giglio published two volumes of Southern Cheyenne women's songs (Giglio 1994; Little Coyote and Giglio 1997).

Other Topics

Significant work on other topics includes the study by Murray Wax, Rosalie Wax, and Robert V. Dumont of education on the Pine Ridge Reservation (1964), an insightful analysis that situates the educational experience within the broader context of Lakota culture and society. Rosalie Wax's account of the experiences at Pine Ridge that formed the basis for that study is an informative inside look at the dynamics of fieldwork (1971). *The Modern Sioux* (Nurge 1970) is a valuable collection of papers on Sioux culture including such diverse topics as food, politics, identity, and music and dance; it is the only such multisided presentation for any Plains tribe. Other valuable collections of papers include Patricia Albers and Beatrice Medicine's (1983) volume on Plains Indian women and John Moore's (1993) on Plains Indian political systems.

Few collaborations between anthropologists and Plains people have resulted in the publication of Indian autobiographies. John Stands in Timber and Margot Liberty's *Cheyenne Memories* (1967) is an important exemplar. Other significant works in this genre include C.S. Brant's (1969) life story of a Plains Apache man, and David E. Jones's (1972) book on a Comanche medicine woman.

Brenda Farnell (1995) described Assiniboine sign language from the last fluent signers at Fort Belknap Reservation ("The Languages of the Plains: Introduction," fig. 2, this vol.), documented the interaction between sign and speech, and provided textual analysis of selected performances.

Environment and Subsistence

WALDO R. WEDEL AND GEORGE C. FRISON

The Plains is here defined as that portion of the northern temperate grassland lying largely west of 96° west longitude between 32° and 52° north latitudes. Occupying an area of some two million square kilometers, the plains extend 2,300 kilometers north from the Rio Grande to the Saskatchewan River and have a breadth of about 900 kilometers east and west exclusive of the Prairie Peninsula (fig. 1). At the time of discovery by Whites in the mid-sixteenth century, the area was a vast grassland with generally low to moderate relief; a continental climate featuring cold dry winters, hot dry summers, and a scanty and unpredictable precipitation pattern; and vegetation of perennial grasses with trees largely confined to stream valleys, scarp lands, and hilly to mountainous tracts.

Despite the uniformity implied in their usual designation, the Plains exhibits considerable diversity of terrain. Topographically, they consist of flatlands, table lands, dune sands, deep V-shaped gullies, terraced stream valleys, and isolated mountain masses. There are, in addition, intermontane basins, particularly in Wyoming—notably the Bighorn, Wind River, and Wyoming basins—that demonstrate ecological conditions similar to the Plains but with distinctive characteristics as well. High-elevation areas such as the North Park in northern Colorado and the Jackson Hole Basin in nothwest Wyoming demonstrate plains characteristics, although they are completely surrounded by mountains. Floral and faunal resources were plains-like as were the human populations found there prehistorically.

During the late Paleo-Indian period, the cultural evidence indicates a strong dichotomy in foothill-mountain and plains subsistence strategies while at other times the two subsistence strategies appear to merge. The causes are proposed as environmentally determined (Frison 1988a) and demonstrate the problem of attempting to separate culturally the foothills-mountain biome from that of the plains.

Topography

The land surface on which the Plains developed is essentially a product of repeated uplifts of the Rocky Mountain region in Tertiary time, some 10 million years or more ago, and continuing into Pleistocene time. This upwarping eventually produced a zone of highlands 10,000–11,000 feet high. The streams that developed to carry the runoff from these heights actively deepened, widened, and lengthened their valleys and deposited enormous quantities of eroded materials where their gradient eased and their erosive power lessened. As the sediment-laden streams slowed, they shifted from side to side and their growing alluvial fans merged into a vast apron of waste, hundreds of feet thick and sloping gently eastward from the mountain base. This apron of gravels, sands, silts, clays, and other materials eventually covered the southern part of what is now the Prairie Provinces of Canada, much of Montana and eastern Wyoming, and most of North and South Dakota to a distance of 80 to 120 kilometers beyond the Missouri River, where the Missouri Coteau marks its approximate limit. In the Central Plains, most of Nebraska and more than half of Kansas was mantled in the sections now classed as the High Plains and the Plains Border. Farther south, the outwash belt may have included western and central Oklahoma. Here the Plains province narrows greatly, and southward it is best shown in the Llano Estacado and Edwards Plateau of Texas. Millennia of erosion have greatly modified much of this outwash plain (Fenneman 1931:1–91).

A few streams only—the North and South Saskatchewan, the Missouri (fig. 2), the Platte, and the Arkansas—cross the Plains from the Rockies. Most, along with many of the lesser waterways, run on sandy beds in bluff-bordered, flat-floored valleys, characteristically lined by flood-free terraces. The western or High Plains are in general the region of least relief. Over large areas, their flatness is

Fig. 1. Physiographic provinces of the Plains (C.B. Hunt 1974; Osterkamp et al. 1987), including quarries and salt resources. Canada: 1, Paskapoo (chert); 2, Blue (pipestone); 3, Hand Hills (chert); 4, Swan River (chert); 5, Top of the World (chert); 6, Livingston (chert). United States: 7, Knife River (flint); 8, Three Waters (chert); 9, Catlinite (pipestone); 10, Flint Hill/Battle Mountain (quartzite); 11, Spanish Diggings (quartzite); 12, Bijou Hills (quartzite); 13, Hartville Uplift (hematite); 14, Wamsutter (chert); 15, Flattop (limestone); 16, Salt Creek Saline (salt); 17, Newhawka (flint); 18, Kremmling (chert); 19, Graham Jasper (chalk); 20, Jamestown Saline (salt); 21, Tuthill Saline (salt); 22, no name (chert); 23, Great and Little Rock Saline (salt); 24, Great Salt Plain (salt); 25, Kay County (Clovis artifacts); 26, Peoria (flint); 27, Alibates (dolomite); 28, Tecovas (dolomite); 29, Frisco (chert); 30, Pisagah Ridge (chert); 31, Edwards Plateau (chert).

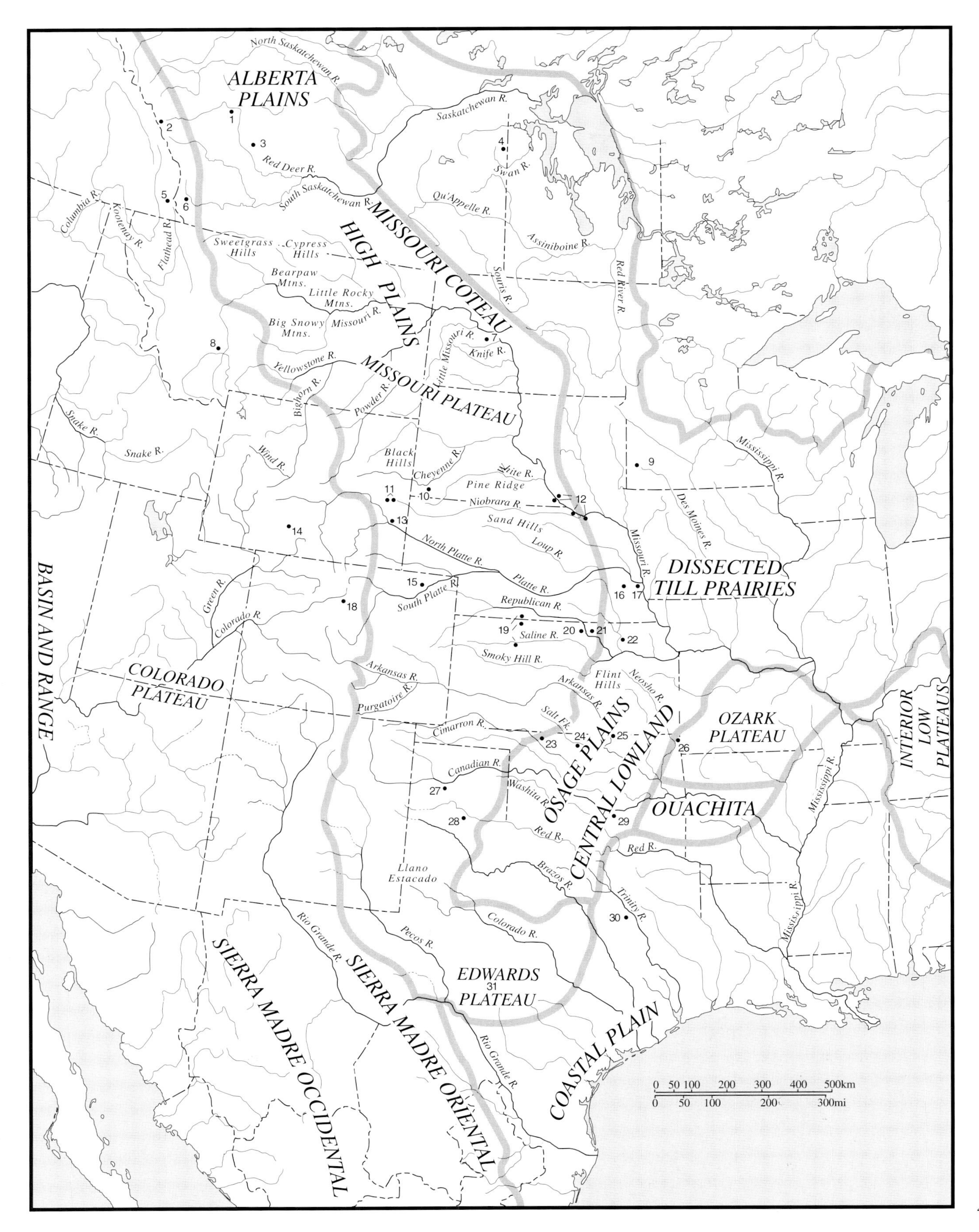
ALBERTA PLAINS
MISSOURI COTEAU
HIGH PLAINS
MISSOURI PLATEAU
DISSECTED TILL PRAIRIES
BASIN AND RANGE
COLORADO PLATEAU
OSAGE PLAINS
CENTRAL LOWLAND
OZARK PLATEAU
INTERIOR LOW PLATEAUS
OUACHITA
EDWARDS PLATEAU
COASTAL PLAIN
SIERRA MADRE OCCIDENTAL
SIERRA MADRE ORIENTAL
North Saskatchewan R.
Saskatchewan R.
Red Deer R.
South Saskatchewan R.
Swan R.
Qu'Appelle R.
Assiniboine R.
Souris R.
Red River R.
Columbia R.
Kootenay R.
Flathead R.
Sweetgrass Hills
Cypress Hills
Bearpaw Mtns.
Little Rocky Mtns.
Big Snowy Mtns.
Missouri R.
Little Missouri R.
Knife R.
Yellowstone R.
Bighorn R.
Powder R.
Snake R.
Wind R.
Black Hills
Cheyenne R.
White R.
Pine Ridge
Niobrara R.
Sand Hills
Loup R.
North Platte R.
Platte R.
South Platte R.
Republican R.
Saline R.
Smoky Hill R.
Green R.
Colorado R.
Arkansas R.
Purgatoire R.
Flint Hills
Neosho R.
Salt Fk.
Cimarron R.
Canadian R.
Washita R.
Red R.
Brazos R.
Trinity R.
Llano Estacado
Pecos R.
Rio Grande R.
Mississippi R.
Des Moines R.
0 50 100 200 300 400 500km
0 50 100 200 300mi

relieved by numerous basins including buffalo wallows and playa lakes. These vary greatly in size and depth, ranging from a few meters in diameter to hundreds of hectares in extent. Some of the larger lakes may hold rainwater for weeks or even months during the rainy season; and like the springs in which many plains streams head, they were important foci of interest to Indian populations on their hunting forays into the bison country. The lush stands of vegetation around these waterholes were an added attraction to the game herds.

Sandy areas occur in several places—along the Cimarron and Arkansas in western Kansas, between the Republican River headwaters and the Platte in southwestern Nebraska and northeastern Colorado, along the North Platte in Wyoming, the Green River and Wyoming basins in Wyoming, and locally elsewhere. The largest area, by far, some 51,800 square kilometers, is north of the Platte River in central Nebraska. With their high summer temperatures, reduced precipitation, and often unstable soils, these were in the twentieth century primarily a grazing area, as they were mostly a hunting ground in pre-agricultural days. The Nebraska Sand Hills (fig. 2 bottom right) may have been a major source of wind-transported materials during the Altithermal climatic episode whereby much of the preceding Paleo-Indian activity was masked (Ahlbrandt, Swinehart, and Maroney 1983).

The predominantly flat surface of the High Plains, "as flat as any land surface in nature" (Fenneman 1931:14), gives way north of the Pine Ridge escarpment to a rough hilly terrain designated the Missouri Plateau. Isolated mountain masses of varied origins are found there, including the Black Hills, the Big Snowy, Little Rocky, and Bear Paw mountains, and the Sweetgrass and Cypress hills. Badlands (fig. 2 bottom left) are found along the Missouri, Yellowstone, Little Missouri, and White rivers and in the intermontane basins of Wyoming. Uninviting as these may appear, there is evidence in the White River section, in widely scattered fireplaces of varying ages, that food-gathering was undertaken for many centuries before Whites undertook ranching in the nineteenth century. These prehistoric features continue throughout the area to the west and even well into the Rocky Mountain foothills. Along with grinding tools, they may indicate a shift to a greater dependence on plant food resources.

Climate

The climatic characteristics of the Plains have been no less important to its human occupants than the land surface. Precipitation varies from about 100 centimeters in the east to about 35 centimeters in eastern Colorado and 25 centimeters in southern Alberta and Manitoba. Toward the west the annual amount declines fairly regularly as far as the 50 centimeter isohyet, roughly at 100° west longitude. On the High Plains of the Texas Panhandle, there is a rainfall increase of 12–15 centimeters. In the Black Hills of South Dakota, the annual moisture received may exceed that on the surrounding plains by 15–20 centimeters. Increases of lesser magnitude have been noted on the divide between the Platte and Republican in southwestern Nebraska, in the Bear Paw Mountains, in the Cypress Hills, and in other elevated localities. In the intermontane basins of Wyoming, which are in the direct rain shadows of the mountains, yearly precipitation may be as low as 18–20 centimeters, which results in true desert conditions.

The Plains lie in the rain shadow of the Rocky Mountains, and their climate results from the interaction of three major air masses whose movements are largely from west to east (Borchert 1950). Mild rain-laden air moving eastward from the Pacific Ocean has lost most of its moisture content by the time it crosses the Great Basin and the Rockies, where it meets moist warm subtropical air pushing north from the Gulf of Mexico and cold dry Arctic air moving south and east out of Canada. A strong flow of westerlies results in an expanding aridity in the Plains, which is most pronounced in the west. As changing circulation patterns weaken the westerlies and permit intrusion of moisture-laden tropical air, the regional precipitation may increase significantly. Such changes in climatic behavior— varying greatly in frequency, intensity, and duration—and the resulting fluctuations in abundance and distribution of plants and animals are familiar features of the environmental setting in the twentieth century. There is accumulating evidence that such changes have been going on for a long time. For large portions of the Plains region, the moisture available is very often marginal, whether for crop growing in the eastern portions or for pasturage and grazing in the western range lands. These vagaries of nature are clearly reflected in the archeological record.

Throughout the multimillennial human occupation of the Plains there have been frequent variations in the characteristics of the land, notably in the climate and in the flora and fauna. Available evidence from the molluscan record (Frye and Leonard 1952:180) suggests a progressive drying up of the region since mid-Pleistocene times, culminating in a biologically severe climate of hot dry summers and cold dry winters perhaps as far back as 12,000 years ago. Botanical and pollen evidence indicates that until possibly 14,000 years ago, when the Des Moines lobe of the continental ice sheet stood at its maximum southward extensions in present Iowa, a spruce forest extended from Iowa across northeastern Kansas, Nebraska, and the Dakotas, to merge with the western coniferous forest running eastward from the Rocky Mountains. The character of the contemporary vegetation in the present steppe country of western Kansas and Colorado is still unclear. However, pollen evidence from the Powder River Basin in Wyoming and the drainage of the Little Missouri River in southeastern Montana indicates the grasslands there were well established before Clovis times (Scott-Cummings 1996; Markgraf and Lennon 1986).

Lib. of Congress, Prints and Photographs Div: top left, LC-USF 342-30758-A, top right, LC-USF 34-4514-D, center left, LC-USF 34-27232-D; center right, Smithsonian, NAA: River Basin Survey, neg. 39 FA 65-187; bottom left, S. Dak. Dept. of Tourism, Pierre; bottom right, Nebr. Dept. of Economic Dev., Lincoln.

Fig. 2. Plains terrain. top left, Stream valley grassland of McKenzie Co., N. Dak. Older eroded landforms are in the background. Photograph by Russell Lee, Oct. 1937. top right, Pennington Co., S. Dak. In the foreground and distance are eroded landforms. A stream valley and grasslands along the valley floodplain are visible. Photograph by Arthur Rothstein, May 1936. center left, Missouri R., Broadwater Co., Mont. The cottonwood trees and willow thickets are typical of vegetation along stream valleys. Photograph by Arthur Rothstein, June 1939. center right, Plains terrain with the interfingering of stream-bottom vegetation and upland grasslands, southeast of the Black Hills, S. Dak. Photograph by Richard P. Wheeler, 1950. bottom left, Deeply dissected badlands in Badlands National Park, S. Dak. Photograph by Paul Horsted, 1989. bottom right, Nebr. Sandhills. The area includes rolling grass-covered hills and hundreds of natural lakes. The sand dunes are stabilized by vegetation. Photographed 1978–1982.

The boreal coniferous forest was replaced by deciduous forest, and this in turn gave way to grassland about 8,000–10,000 years ago. By 10,000 years ago, considerable portions of the Plains were suited to occupation by large gregarious herbivores (Bryson and Wendland 1967), and the archeological evidence indicates that such occupation was taking place. Open forests and parklands, varying from time to time in composition and extent, apparently persisted along the southwestern margin (Wendorf and Hester 1975).

In historic times, the grasses and other native vegetation of the Plains varied from east to west in accord with the observed precipitation and other climatic factors. In the west, beyond 100° west longitude, there was a north to south belt of short grasses, preponderantly *Bouteloua* and *Buchloë*, peculiarly adapted to dry soils and to a short growing season, with 37.5 centimeters or less of annual precipitation. Eastward, where precipitation rises to 60 and finally to 100 centimeters annually, the steppe gave way to mixed grasses and then to tall-grass bluestem prairie. All of this region lies within the needlegrass-pronghorn-grama grass biome (Shelford 1963:328). It is also the heart of the former range of the bison (*Bison bison*), ecologically a dominant in the short- and mixed-grass zone and a resource of prime importance to the human inhabitants throughout most of their residence in the region.

Lithic and Mineral Resources

Among the natural resources available to the ancient plainsmen, materials of prime importance were the varied lithic, mineral, and other items obtainable for the manufacture of artifacts and for other uses. For more detail on chert and quartzite occurrences, see Banks (1984, 1990) and figure 1. (In late precontact times, Plains Indians traveled to quarries outside the Plains for chert and pipestone.)

• ALIBATES DOLOMITE Quarries of this material were situated in the Texas panhandle about 50 kilometers north of Amarillo. Hundreds of pits of widely varying sizes and depths are scattered over the hills there, reflecting sources of stone utilized from Folsom times to late prehistoric and early historic village Indians of Texas, Oklahoma, Kansas, and neighboring states. The stone is identified as an agatized dolomite, varying greatly in color but chiefly in reds, blues, and grays, much of it streaked. It outcrops in two separate stratigraphic zones within the Permian-aged exposures of the panhandle Quartermaster formation (K. Bryan 1950; Shaeffer 1958:189; Lintz 1984:335). Tecovas chert, an inferior stone that is not always readily distinguishable from Alibates, is obtainable in quantity near Quitaque, southeast of Amarillo, and was widely used in the region.

• KAY COUNTY QUARRIES In the Flint Hills of Oklahoma and Kansas, extensive chert deposits occur in the Permian-aged Florence formation. There is considerable variability in the character and tractability of the stone from various localities. In situ samples tend to be mainly grayish-yellow and blue-gray; archeological specimens tend to be in the reds or pinks, reflecting heat treatment by the craftsmen. Some pieces are strikingly color-banded; others include numerous wheat-grain shaped Fusulinid fossils, often whitish in color and imparting an attractive color and textural note to artifacts chipped from them. Stone from these quarries, where pits and refuse piles are abundant and sizable, was much used from about A.D. 1000 to 1400 by flintsmiths in Oklahoma, Kansas, New Mexico, and adjacent areas (Kidder 1932:31; W.R. Wedel 1959:476).

• PEORIA QUARRIES The Peoria quarries are located in the Tahlequah chert member of the Mississippian-aged Moorefield formation in Oklahoma (Holmes 1894; Banks 1984). From these pits, not more than three to five meters deep originally and up to 12 meters in diameter, was taken a cream-colored chert that was tough and at the same time very tractable and easily worked. Excavations in northeast Oklahoma suggest use of the rock and possibly of the quarries themselves beginning by about 5000 B.C. until about A.D. 1000.

• GRAHAM JASPER Also known as Smoky Hill or Republican River or Alma jasper, this stone is dense brown to yellowish-brown, but with frequent variation in color and tractability. It is thought to have originated as a silicified chalk peculiar to the upper beds of the Smoky Hill chalk in the Cretaceous Niobrara formation. As lenses and layers of variable thickness or as nodules along the Republican, Smoky Hill, their tributaries, and other streams of the central Plains, this material is widely distributed through Nebraska and Kansas. Aboriginal workings have been noted on Dutch Creek, Nebraska; in the Big Creek drainage in the vicinity of Collyer, Kansas; and at Norton, Kansas. Because of its wide availability and suitability, it was very popular with the prehistoric flintsmiths over a wide area in the Plains and for a long time (G.F. Carlson and Peacock 1975; W.R. Wedel 1986:28; Frye and Swineford 1946:56–60). Its use certainly dates back to the Hell Gap people, about 7000 B.C., if not earlier, and continues to about A.D. 1300.

• FLAT TOP QUARRIES This aggregation of ancient diggings is situated on an isolated flat-topped butte in Logan County, Colorado, about 28 kilometers north and west of Sterling, where considerable quantities of grayish-purple streaked chert were obtained in prehistoric times. The stone has been recognized in late prehistoric village sites, A.D. 1000 to 1300, on the Republican and Smoky Hill rivers nearly 300 kilometers to the southeast, and in Paleo-Indian contexts much farther afield (W.R. Wedel 1986:66, 111).

• SPANISH DIGGINGS Innumerable scars of ancient diggings are scattered over hundreds of hectares on the hills and ridges of the Muddy Creek drainage in eastern Wyoming. Immense quantities of broken stone and miscellaneous debris are associated with these diggings, which range up to 12–15 meters in diameter and two to five meters deep. Stone tepee rings, workshop areas where the workmen reduced the quarried materials to manageable proportions for transportation and further processing, and hammerstones have been found in the debris. How early this quarrying began it is impossible to tell, but the Hell Gap people certainly were using it perhaps as early as 9000 B.C., and its use continued through the late prehistoric. Quartzite artifacts thought to have originated in the Spanish Diggings have been identified at least as far east as the Missouri River near Omaha (G.A. Dorsey 1900; Holmes 1919).

• FLINT HILL QUARRIES These quartzite quarries are situated on Flint Hill, about 10 kilometers due south of Minnekahta, at the south edge of the Black Hills near Edgemont and Hot Springs, South Dakota. Here, and on Battle Mountain six kilometers to the north, there are extensive ledges of quartzite, and the characteristic stone is represented at many archeological sites in the nearby Angostura reservoir and elsewhere in the region. The ancient diggings occupy about 150 hectares on a high tableland. They include scores of large and small pits and adjacent piles of rough workshop debris. Large quarry blanks are or once were plentiful, all of quartzite in colors that varied from gray and purplish through reds and browns to yellows. Tepee rings are abundant in the neighborhood and are reported to extend northward for some kilometers to the Black Hills proper (Darton and Smith 1904; W.R. Wedel 1961:272)

• BIJOU HILLS QUARRIES Quartzite from the Bijou Hills in Gregory County, South Dakota, provided an important source of flint for prehistoric peoples of the region (Zimmerman 1985:41).

• KNIFE RIVER QUARRIES In the Knife River basin of North Dakota, south of the Missouri River, a prevalently dark molasses-colored flint was extensively quarried and distributed throughout the northern Plains. Archeological evidence indicates more or less continuous use from Paleo-Indian times through the protohistoric. Pebbles and cobbles transported from the present primary area by alluvial and glacial processes have made the stone available over a wide area of the Northern Plains (M.L. Gregg 1987a:367).

• CATLINITE A fine-grained grayish-red to dark red claystone, often attractively mottled or speckled, catlinite was a favorite pipe-making material on the plains, especially from the seventeenth century onward. Decorated slabs and palettes, as well as miscellaneous articles for ceremonial and religious purposes or for personal adornment, were also made from it. Catlinite occurs as a thin stratum embedded in quartzite. When freshly quarried it is soft enough to be easily carved with stone or metal knives and drills. (The name derives from the artist George Catlin, who first brought it to the attention of mineralogists about 1839.) The quarries near Pipestone, Minnesota (fig. 3), are noted as early as 1702 (Delisle 1702). Warring tribes are said to have forborne hostilities when meeting at the quarries during periodic visits to obtain the stone. Catlinite, widely traded throughout the Plains from prehistoric times, became an important commodity in the trade between Euro-Americans and Indians during the nineteenth century. In two years during the mid-1860s, for example, the North West Company manufactured and distributed to the tribes of the upper Missouri nearly 2,000 pipes, and by 1892 it was estimated that only one percent of catlinite pipes were manufactured by Indians (Holmes 1907; Woolworth 1983).

• FREDERICK-SUNRISE HEMATITE MINES South of the Spanish Diggings and east of the Platte River in eastern Wyoming is the Hartville uplift, long noted for its iron ore deposits. There, in the Frederick-Sunrise district in Platte and Goshen counties (fig. 1, no. 13), hematite in both hard and soft forms was readily obtainable in abundance. Long before European contact Indians were mining there, running drifts some 15 meters into the hillsides and sinking shafts to depths of six to eight meters. Sledges and hammers were found in these Indian diggings and around their entrances. How widely, how early, and by and to whom these pigment materials were carried and traded is unknown (W.R. Wedel 1959:274; E.P. Snow 1895; Gilder 1908a).

• SALT The extent to which the Plains Indians utilized salt in the seasoning and preservation of foodstuffs, in skin dressing, and for other purposes is unclear. Saline marshes and creeks extensively drawn upon by early Euro-American settlers and possibly also by Indians were available at Tuthill Marsh on Salt Marsh Creek in Republic and Cloud counties, Kansas (fig. 1, nos. 20, 21; W.R. Wedel 1986:31). Important sources also were two large salines in northern Oklahoma, the Great Saline on the Salt Fork of the Arkansas River about six kilometers east of Cherokee, and the Rock Saline, or Big and Little Salt Plains on the Cimarron River just south of the Kansas boundary (fig. 1, no. 23). Other salines were available in the vicinity of Lincoln, Nebraska, around the head of Salt Creek (fig. 1, no. 16). At all these localities, salt could be easily obtained by evaporation of the highly saline ground waters, or it could be dug from the accumulated deposits left by natural evaporation of the saline outflows. In historic times, and perhaps before, Indians were sometimes attracted to such salt licks by large gatherings of bison and other game animals assembled there (see McDermott 1940:224; W.R. Wedel 1986:31).

• SOAPSTONE Among the lithic materials that figured in native trade from the Rocky Mountains into and across the Plains was steatite, easily worked into pots and jars, and fire-resistant. Limited observations by geologists refer to a deposit in Fremont County, Wyoming, "on the north side of Rattlesnake Mountain, on the headwaters of South Powder River"; a small occurrence of "massive soapstone and fibrous talc" on Badger Creek, on the west side of the Teton Range (Osterwald and Osterwald 1952:159–160); and a locality northeast of Driggs, in Teton County, Idaho, where a prospector reported "an exposed face on which lie

State Histl. Soc. of Wis., Madison: WHi(X3)44156.

Fig. 3. Quarrying catlinite. A wedge or bar would be placed in the fracture plane of the rock and hit to dislodge the consolidated quartz overburden, which allowed access to the catlinite. Big Thunder (John Wakerman), Santee Sioux, is standing in the pit wearing white gloves and holding a sledge hammer. The building in the background on left is part of the federal Indian Industrial Training School. Photographed at Pipestone, Santee Sioux Res., Minn., 1894.

partially cut away blocks of soapstone, with fragments of broken pots at the foot of the exposure" (W.R. Wedel 1961:264).

Mammals

The earliest known human evidence, that pertaining to Clovis hunters, indicates use of the mammoth, extinct species of bison, pronghorn (*Antilocapra americana*), and an occasional American camel, musk-ox, and horse. By 9000 B.C. the mammoth was extinct and probably also the musk-ox and the horse. By about 8000 B.C. there may have been a few camels left, but the fauna was essentially a modern one. The ecology of small mammal populations found in the stratified Agate Basin site in eastern Wyoming demonstrates significant climatic changes between 9000 and 8000 B.C. (D.N. Walker 1982). Similar changes were postulated on the basis of pollen data from Minnesota (Bryson and Hare 1974).

Animal food resources were available in abundance and variety. Less numerous than the bison and not so widely distributed was the pronghorn, wanted for its pelt and its flesh. Deer were found in areas of brush and rough topography. Mountain sheep (*Ovis canadensis*) were common in rough areas, in the foothills, and in the higher slopes of the Rocky Mountains. Other plains upland species taken were the coyote (*Canis latrans*), gray wolf (*C. lupus*), badger (*Taxidea taxus*), black-tailed prairie dog (*Cynomys ludovicianus*), and black-footed ferret (*Mustela nigripes*). These were supplemented by woodland and forest-edge animals whose range extended far into a primarily grassland environment by way of the narrow winding ribbons of woodland edging the watercourses. Thus became available elk or wapiti (*Cervus elaphus*), mule deer (*Odocoileus hemionus*), white-tailed deer (*O. virginianus*), grizzly bear (*Ursus horribilis*), black bear (*U. americanus*), mountain lion (*Felis concolor*), bobcat (*Lynx rufus*), beaver (*Castor canadensis*), river otter (*Lutra canadensis*), raccoon (*Procyon lotor*), mink (*Mustela vison*), muskrat (*Ondatra zibethicus*), desert cottontail (*Sylvilagus audubonii*), jackrabbits (*Lepus* spp.), and other small furbearers.

Birds

Bird species from the eastern and western United States met and shared habitats in the Plains. Gallinaceous birds included the wild turkey (*Meleagris gallopavo*), ranging west as far as trees for roosting and shelter could be found and grasshoppers could be substituted for oak mast; also sharp-tailed grouse (*Tympanuchus phasianellus*), greater prairie chicken (*T. cupido*), and sage grouse (*Centrocercus urophasianus*). Upland ponds and water holes from southern Canada to the High Plains of Texas provided nesting and feeding places for resident waterfowl and stopping places for migrating myriads of ducks, geese, swans, and other nonresident water birds. A numerous and varied population of passerine and song birds was present, and there were eagles, hawks, owls, and other raptors whose feathers, talons, feet, heads, and bones supplied materials for ceremonial, decorative, and ritual items (Ubelaker and Wedel 1975; Parmalee 1977). By comparison with mammals, birds furnished a relatively small and insignificant part of the human diet in the plains.

Fish and Shellfish

Fish and shellfish appear to have been usually of secondary importance in the food quest, although they were to be found in most Plains streams with permanent water. There were fish in abundance in the Missouri River, some of considerable size, and the lower reaches of its major tributaries also offered good possibilities.

At the beginning of contact times, the middle Missouri tribes—Arikara, Mandan, and Hidatsa—used fish traps (fig. 4) and weirs ("Plains Cree," fig. 2, this vol.). These were anchored in shallow waters near the stream bank, baited with maggoty or rotten meat, and used to take mainly catfish, which were prepared for human consumption by boiling. Archeology has shown that there was widespread use of the curved single-piece bone fishhook, unbarbed but notched or knobbed for line attachment. These have been found at prehistoric village sites even on small secondary creeks that carry water now only during rainy times, suggesting that a millennium ago, with a higher water table, these streams may have been much more dependable for fishing. Bone fishhooks have been recorded on the middle Missouri soon after A.D. 950, from 1000 to 1350 in Nebraska and Kansas, and at around 1250 at Washita River sites in Oklahoma.

Fish were also taken by spearing, although not much is known about details of this operation. At prehistoric sites along the Missouri in eastern Nebraska, bone or conical antler tip points, socketed to receive a shaft or foreshaft and provided with a perforated tang at one side for line attachment, have come to light. It is difficult to resist the notion that these were designed as togglehead harpoon heads. Larger points made from heavier bone or antler and with two lateral barbs on one side may have been designed for larger fish such as sturgeon or they may have been beaver or muskrat spears.

There is no record of leisters in the Plains or of the use of fish poisons.

The relative scarcity of fish bones at many archeological sites as compared to bones of other animals has resulted in the comparatively limited identification of the fish species used by the Indians. There was undoubtedly as much variation in size of the fish taken as in the species harvested. Perhaps the most common was the catfish. This was available in several species, including the blue (*Ictalurus furcatus*) weighing up to 100 pounds; the flathead (*Pylodictus olivaris*), up to five feet long and weighing nearly 100 pounds; the channel (*Ictalurus punctatus*), seldom over 25 pounds; and the black bullhead (*I. melas*), two pounds or less but highly nutritious and present almost everywhere water could be found (Lewis and Clark in Moulton 1983–, 2:432, 486).

In the Washita River sites of central Oklahoma, R.E. Bell (1984a:314) reported remains of blue and flathead

State Histl. Soc. of N. Dak., Bismarck: left, #16; right, #17.

Fig. 4. Fish trap made by Black Bear, Hidatsa, near the mouth of Shell Creek, south of Van Hook, N. Dak., in the Missouri R. right, Close-up of same trap. Photographs by Russell Reid, Aug. 1929.

catfish, freshwater drum (*Aplodinotis grunniens*), white sucker (*Catostomus commersoni*), and shortnose gar (*Lepisosteus platostomus*). Curved one-piece bone fishhooks and straight bone gorge hooks in the village sites suggest that the fish were taken with hand lines.

Occasionally, significant pockets of fish bones of widely varying size are encountered in trash pits. These suggest the random end-of-the-summer harvest, when temporary ponds created by spring overflows were drying up and the aquatic life they contained was being concentrated in progressively smaller areas where it could be easily scooped out by children and adults. By this strategy, using a net or drag, a highly varied assortment of fish, mussels, amphibians, reptiles, and insects could be gathered. From this assemblage, the fish, turtles, crayfish, and frogs considered large enough to be dressed and eaten were taken to be boiled up together while the small fry, snakes, and other trash were abandoned to such predators and scavengers as raccoons and water birds, or to their inevitable death as oxygen in the water gave out and the water itself finally disappeared beneath the August sun.

A clue to the former presence of Indians on a given piece of ground is the finding of quantities of mussel shells and shell fragments. Freshwater mussels are found at most village and camp sites, though usually in limited quantities. Unworked unionid valves were used as spoons, corn shellers (Gradwohl 1982:145–148), paint receptacles, and pottery scrapers. Occasional trash pits at Upper Republican sites at Medicine Creek have yielded hundreds of unmodified valves of the mapleleaf mussel (*Quadrula quadrula*) for whose presence other than as refuse of the food quest it is difficult to account (Wedel 1986:126). Shellfish rank fairly high as a source of protein, but large quantities would have to be consumed to replace bison meat. It seems questionable that a stream like Medicine Creek could by itself long sustain an Indian population of the size implied by its archeological remains through shellfish production alone. On the other hand, many prairie streams probably were well populated with mussels (Lewis and Clark in Moulton 1983–, 2:483).

Most of the molluscan materials found in the Plains are presumed to have come from localities within the region. An exception is a worked specimen of onyx rocksnail (*Leptoxis praerosa*) recovered at the Graham ossuary (25HN5) in southern Nebraska. This species was reported to be common in the Wabash and Ohio rivers and southward, but as not occurring naturally west of Illinois (Strong 1935:111, 113).

Wild Plants

There was an abundance of wild plants that figured in various ways in Indian subsistence economies. Some have been found in burned-out houses, cache pits, and trash deposits. Others are known to have been used by neighboring or distant natives as food or medicine—grasses and forbs whose seeds, spring shoots, leaves, tubers, and other parts were used.

Of primary interest was the Indian breadroot or prairie turnip (*Psoralea esculenta*) (fig. 5), which grew on well-drained hillsides and produced nutritious starchy tubers, one per plant. These were collected in considerable quantity by the women with digging sticks in May or June, peeled out of their heavy rind, to be eaten fresh, dried, or boiled with vegetables, or alternatively were peeled, braided in meter-long strings, and hung in the lodges for later sale, barter, or consumption (W.R. Wedel 1978; K.C. Reid 1977; Kindscher 1987). On the tribal hunts the villages sometimes planned their route of march to make stops at the turnips practical for the women. In the streamside bottoms grew the groundnut (*Apios americana*), a twining vine with long stringy roots on which tubers grew like beads on a string. With these there often grew another vine, the hog-peanut (*Amphicarpaea bracteata*), producing both small aerial "beans" and large underground seeds coveted by small rodents and humans alike. The underground beans were preferred; they were gathered by the Indian women where they grew or, with luck, from a previously collected underground cache made by a prairie vole (*Microtus ochrogaster*).

Other food plants included the sunflower (*Helianthus annuus*), grown for its oily nutritious seed; the Jerusalem artichoke (*H. tuberosus*) and purple poppy mallow (*Callirhoe involucrata*), for their thickened rootstocks; the bush morning glory (*Ipomoea leptophylla*) for its huge but not very palatable root, used mainly when other starchy foods were unavailable; the American lotus (*Nelumbo lutea*), which grew in the bottoms of lakes, ponds, and sluggish streams, where its fast-growing tubers and aerial nutlike seeds were collected by women, the tubers to be roasted, the seeds to be boiled. The spring shoots of cattails (*Typha* spp.) and the roots of the arrowheads (*Sagittaria* spp.) were other edible foods from wet locations, streamside marshes, and around springs. Certain grasses that were heavy seed producers in late summer and early fall, including sand dropseed (*Sporobolus cryptandrus*), vine mesquite (*Panicum obtusum*), barnyard grass

Smithsonian, Natl. Mus. of the Amer. Ind.: 12/6311.

Fig. 5. Prairie turnips. Collected from the Omaha by Melvin R. Gilmore in 1924.

(*Echinochloa muricata*), and pignut (*Hoffmannseggia glauca*) were utilized in season. Prickly-pear cacti (*Opuntia* spp.) grew widely and its fruit, tuna, was a popular food. In pre-horse days, pigweed (*Amaranthus* spp.) and giant ragweed (*Ambrosia trifida*) may have been of much greater importance, providing seeds, spring shoots, and tubers. Ground plum (*Astragalus crassicarpus*), wild onion (*Allium* spp.), lamb's quarters (*Chenopodium album*), ground cherry (*Physalis heterophylla*), purslane (*Portulaca* spp.), curly dock (*Rumex crispus*), and prairie spiderwort (*Tradescantia occidentalis*) were also useful plants. Sego lilies (*Calochortus nuttallii*) grow profusely in the foothills and on the open plains, and a few minutes with a digging stick can yield enough bulbs to provide a tasty meal either raw or roasted. Yucca pods (*Yucca glauca*) are plentiful during good years and, before they become too mature, can be roasted and are excellent food. Wild plums (*Prunus* spp.) and chokecherries (*P. virginia*), silver buffalo berries (*Shepherdia argentea*), and other fruits were gathered in season to be eaten fresh or dried. In the south, mesquite beans (*Prosopis* spp.) were available, as were piñon nuts (*Pinus edulis*) on the southwestern periphery in Colorado and New Mexico. Farther north, the smaller nuts of the limber pine (*Pinus flexilis*) were harvested for human consumption as is indicated by the presence of grinding stones in the vicinity of limber pine stands.

The hackberry (*Celtis occidentalis*) in the Plains is widespread, and its seeds are usually abundant enough at archeological sites to suggest use of its sugary fruits as foods, eaten fresh or ground up and mixed with dried meat. The fruits of black walnut (*Juglans nigra*) and sometimes those of shagbark hickory (*Carya ovata*), gathered in streamside forests, provided edible fats. Cottonwoods (*Populus* spp.) and willows (*Salix* spp.) grew creekside and on valley bottoms nearly everywhere, providing fuel and low-grade building material. Oaks, elms, and hackberries supplied good building material, as did the juniper (*Juniperus* spp.) which grew widely, and was much more durable than the hardwoods in contact with the soil. Hardwoods were generally preferred for house building. Straight growing poles for tepee frames were obtained at stands of pine on Lodgepole Creek in the Laramie and Bighorn mountains of eastern Wyoming, in the Black Hills of South Dakota, and elsewhere (fig. 6).

Subsistence Strategies

The vegetational and climatic differences between the eastern and western subareas of the Plains were reflected in the distribution of Indian peoples in historic times. The semiarid western steppe has always been primarily an area of hunting and gathering subsistence economies in which human settlement and activities were concentrated along the stream valleys and around the springs and water holes where the game herds also tended to congregate (Wendorf and Hester 1962; W.R. Wedel 1963). In the sixteenth century, this was the range of the Apachean dog nomads (D.A. Gunnerson 1956). After introduction of the horse in the mid-seventeenth century, these lands were taken over by other tribes drawn from surrounding areas by the abundance and ready availability of the bison. The customs of these linguistically and culturally diverse newcomers were reshaped by environmental factors (Oliver 1962) into the more or less uniform lifeway of mobile horse-using bison hunters whom Wissler (1922:22) designated the "typical" Plains tribes—the Sioux, Cheyenne, Arapaho, Comanche, Kiowa, and others. Most of these tribes spent the greater part of their hunting time west of 100° longitude, where rainfall deficiencies precluded the maize-bean-squash-sunflower hoe subsistence economy of the village Indians along the waterways. The upland grasslands were generally too tough to till with bone-bladed hoes and wooden tools, but stream-valley bottoms, easily worked with primitive technologies, made possible an increasingly rewarding food producing subsistence economy. In good seasons, there were often sufficient crop surpluses to encourage trade with the nonhorticultural tribes roaming the western grasslands and usually able to take by force that which the villagers were not strong enough to defend.

The villagers, mainly Caddoan and Siouan speakers, appear to have been deeply rooted in the same localities where they first met the European invaders. Their lifeway—divided between seasonal bison hunting and horticulture—had at least 500 years of development before the earliest Whites arrived. In its horticultural practices and crops, its houses and settlement patterns, its ceramic and other industries, there are clear relationships to the Eastern Woodland peoples of the Mississippi-Ohio basin, whence the material culture and perhaps most of the people as well, were apparently derived. By contrast, the nonhorticultural equestrian bison hunters of the short-grass steppe were only the last variants in a long succession of peoples following a Plains lifeway based on mobility, portability of possessions, and primary reliance on the bison.

The Hunting and Gathering Tradition

Very little is known about the lifeways of the Late Pleistocene and Early Holocene elephant hunters of the Plains, either Clovis or pre-Clovis. Most finds consist of skeletal remains of one to a dozen animals, generally associated with springs, streams, lake margins, upland ponds, waterholes, and the like. Sociopolitically, a sparse and scattered population, probably consisting of roving family units (Hammond and Rey 1940:262, 301) with seasonal or otherwise recurrent coalescence into larger groups for social functions, including communal hunts, may be hypothesized.

Bison species could undoubtedly have been taken singly or in small groups by stalking, ambush, or other methods available to solitary hunters or to small parties working

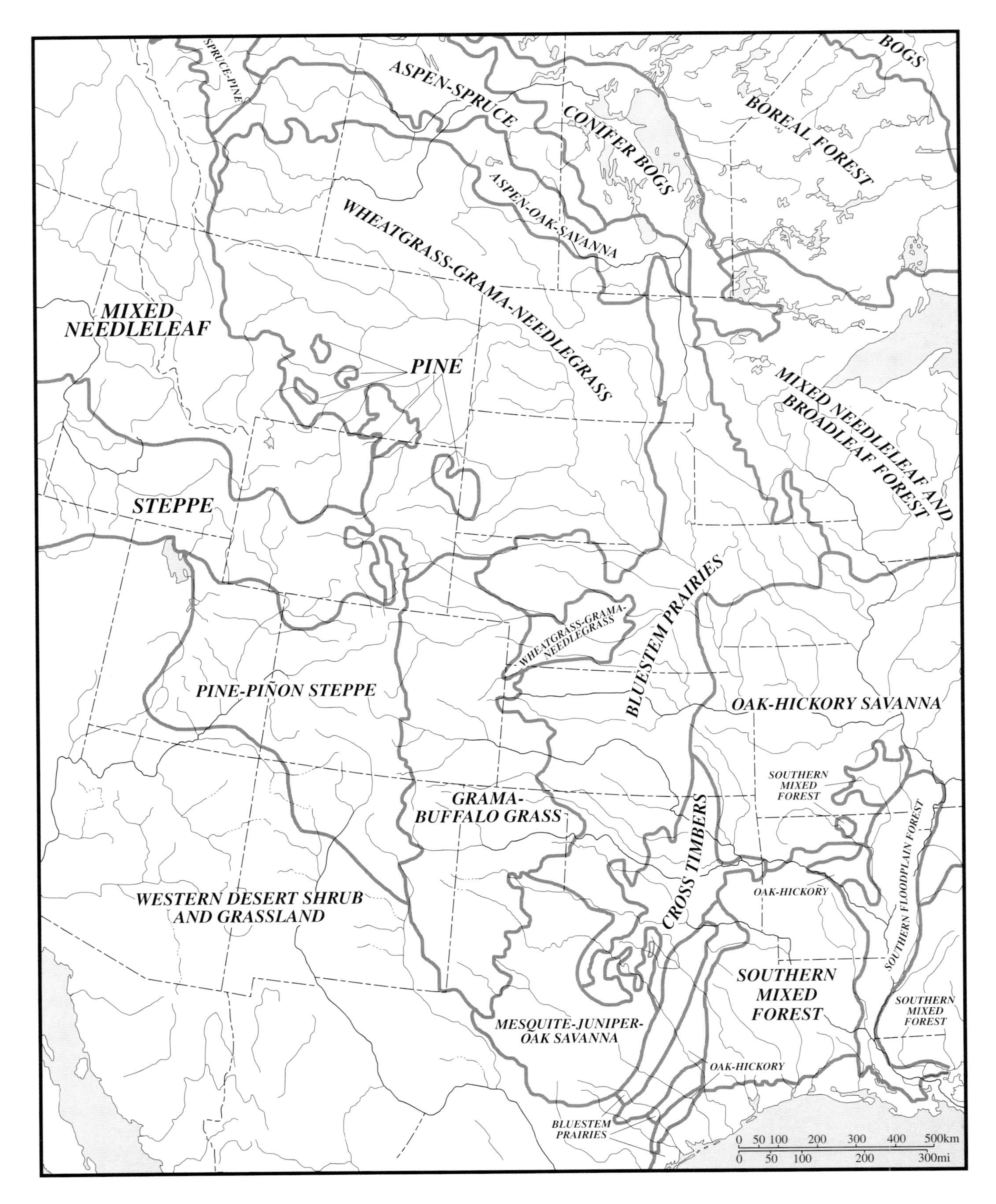

 Fig. 6. Potential natural vegetation (U.S. Geological Survey 1970; Energy, Mines and Resources. Canada 1974; Bonine et al. 1970).

along game trails, near waterholes, from blinds, with grass fires in season, or in deep snow where suitable conditions existed. Upland ponds and lakes and the nearby grassy flats attracted bison, who were hunted from brush blinds with spears and large bows. Bison meat, fat, and hides were traded by these Indians to the pueblos on the west and to the semisedentary village Indians to the east and southeast. In winter, the plainsmen moved to the vicinity of these same settlements, abandoning the treeless and inhospitable plains along with the bison, who sought shelter in the stream valleys and in broken terrain.

The Plains Indians devised effective methods for procuring adequate to abundant meat supplies through communal hunting. The success of these techniques rested on the gregarious behavior of the animals and their tendency to stampede when threatened. By the proper exploitation of these characteristics, the hunters achieved the mass killing of dozens to hundreds of bison by cooperative methods. Along with the development of effective meat-preservation techniques, such as drying and perhaps freezing in suitable environments, these kills provided large stores of food for use in winter and at other times when the bison were not available.

Successful mass kills were the product of careful planning, good organization, coordinated execution, and good luck insured by appropriate ritual sanction. The techniques varied widely, depending on circumstances such as the number of animals and hunters available, the nature of the terrain, and the weather.

For the Northern Plains, the bison procurement methods have been reviewed in detail (Arthur 1975). By the time of contact, the horse was supplementing or replacing the dog for traction and other uses. The winter's meat supply was regularly obtained by cooperative drives that involved construction of a corral or pound of logs, brush, or stones (fig. 7) (Wissler 1910:34– 36). Into these, bison to the number of 200 or more were driven through converging lines of piles of stones, sods, brush, or buffalo chips. The ends of these lines began far apart on the uplands where the herd was gathered for the final drive. In prehorse days, when the range of gathering operations was more limited, the animals were frequently driven over a cliff, cut bank, or "jump," perhaps with a holding pen below where animals not killed or disabled by the fall could be dispatched by spear, dart, or arrow. There is no eyewitness account of a jump operation, though their general nature is not difficult to reconstruct from the evidence, but there are dramatic descriptions of the death scenes at the pound (Hind 1859:55).

The lifeway of the historic bison-hunting nomads was characterized by high mobility and ready portability of gear, both of which were vastly facilitated by adoption of the horse. During summer, the Indians followed the buffalo over the plains, and in the winter they camped along sheltered waterways (Warren 1875:18). The hunts were usually communal, featuring the surround on horseback,

Mont. Histl. Soc., Helena: top and middle.

Fig. 7. Hunting big mammals. top, Madison buffalo jump near Logan, Mont. middle, Drive line from an animal trap, near Daily Lake, Paradise Valley, Mont. top and middle, Photographs by John Smart, 1988. bottom, Corral used to trap mountain sheep near Dubois, Wyo. Not shown in this photograph but associated with this site is a shaman's hut to the left and a second corral, in case the animals missed this one. Photograph by George Frison, 1978.

with impounding customary in the Northern Plains. Impoundment appears to have been usual among the Canadian Indians even in winter (Arthur 1975). Wintering grounds regularly or frequently used by the Plains Indians included the canyon of the Purgatoire in eastern Colorado, where deer were available in great numbers; the canyons and foothill breaks around the Arkansas River where it emerges from the mountains; the South Fork of Cheyenne River in present Weston County, Wyoming; the Lodgepole Creek valley; the Big Timbers of the Arkansas, where the Cheyenne, Arapaho, and Kiowa could find bison in winter; the Big Timbers of the Republican, frequented by the Cheyenne and Arapaho; the North Fork of Red River for the Kiowa and Comanche; and the forest margins and foothills in Canada (W.R. Wedel 1963). These localities, in addition to shelter from the winter winds and snows of the uplands, also harbored deer, antelope, and smaller game. No less important were the stands of cottonwood, the bark and twigs of which were a primary, and often the only, food for the horses during the winter months.

Noteworthy is the practice of a sort of herding of bison, reported for the Northwestern Plains. Near the Black Hills, for example, the Teton Sioux blocked the southward movement of large herds, killing only stragglers, pending development of the hides to their maximum stage for winter robe manufacture (G.K. Warren 1875:19). It is also possible that during prehorse times bison herds were penned in valleys and killed as needed, a tactic reported for the Eastern Shoshone (W.F. Raynolds 1868:86). This type of impoundment might have been employed at topographically suitable settings such as Palo Duro Canyon and other Southern Plains locations with flat-floored grassy valleys and steep walls that could be scaled by large mammals only with great difficulty.

The surrounds on horseback often yielded as heavily as the jumps and pounds of the western and northwestern Plains. Observers traveling with the Pawnee summer hunt of 1835 (J. Dunbar and Allis 1918; C.A. Murray 1839) reported the killing of 200–300 animals at a time. Much of the 50,000 to 100,000 pounds of meat thus made suddenly available was eaten fresh; the rest could be reduced by drying ("Assiniboine," fig. 3, this vol.) to perhaps 20 percent of its original weight and bulk. Depending upon the proportions of fat mixed with the dried lean, the resulting product could yield as much as 3,200 to 3,500 calories per pound (Wentworth 1957) and would keep for months if protected from moisture. In 1868, the United States Army found nearly five tons of dried bison meat, the equivalent of perhaps 45 to 50 packhorse loads, at one Cheyenne camp (W.R. Wedel 1986:204–205).

That the Plains Indians ever relied exclusively on one or two large species, like the bison, is highly unlikely. Antelopes were taken in a trap, consisting of a stockaded circle, lane, and pit (W.F. Raynolds 1868). Frison (1978:251) has provided details and an important archeological perspective. Mountain sheep were likewise taken by drives. Deer, bear, elk, mountain sheep, rabbits, and other animals were also hunted (fig. 8). The occasional presence of shellfish, reptilian and amphibian remains, as well as ducks and turkeys, has been recorded. All this suggests a catholicity of food tastes among these people and the incorporation of whatever edible items came their way if and when larger quarry was not available (E.M. Johnson 1977).

Probably the early hunters, like the mounted ones of historic times, made extensive use of wild roots, tubers, seeds, nuts, fruits, young shoots, and other vegetal products that became available from season to season and in various localities. Grinding tools have been recovered, and their use in reducing vegetal items for food is commonly inferred. The documentary record for the historic Plains tribes clearly attests the importance of plant foods to the bison-hunting equestrian Indians, among whom dried and stored meat from summer and fall hunts was seldom sufficient to carry the group through the winter and who not infrequently had difficulty locating the herds. At such times, plant foods were often the only way to survive.

Food Production and the Village Tradition

The beginnings of maize-bean-squash-sunflower hoe gardening in the eastern Plains are uncertain, but it seems likely that by the tenth century, and perhaps as early as the eighth or ninth, the Woodland complexes in the eastern plains were giving way to, or developing into, others of more sedentary character. These later complexes involved more or less fixed settlements of substantial earth- or grass-covered habitations with circular, elliptical, or subrectangular floor plans and a subsistence economy divided between hunting-gathering and crop production. They were scattered along many of the permanent river and creek valleys throughout the tall grass prairies and westward into the mixed grass zone from the Dakotas to Texas and possibly into the short grass steppe west of 102° west longitude in eastern Colorado. The principal crops included maize (*Zea mays*), beans (*Phaseolus* spp.), squashes (*Cucurbita* spp.), and sunflowers. The tools were the bone-bladed wooden-handled hoe, a rake of deer or elk antler, and presumably a wooden digging stick (fig. 9). Usually associated with these settlements were subterranean storage pits of variable size, eventually used for disposal of trash and garbage; grinding slabs with handstones or wooden upright mortars; and charred remains of cultigens in the middens along with the bones of game animals, birds, fish, shellfish, turtles, and other lost and discarded items. Possibly excepting the sunflower, a native of the plains, the cultigens can all be regarded as of Eastern Woodland derivation and ultimately from the tropics.

At the beginning of White contact with the Plains Indians, the northern limits of native Plains maize cultivation were at the Knife River villages of the Hidatsa at 47°30′ north latitude. In the 1850s maize was ripening at Fort Qu'Appelle and at Portage la Prairie, at and beyond 50° north latitude (Hind 1859:34, 49, 12 7; Palliser 1863:13, 51). In the central plains of Kansas and Nebraska, the western limits were at approximately 99° west longitude. Earlier, the western limits may have been

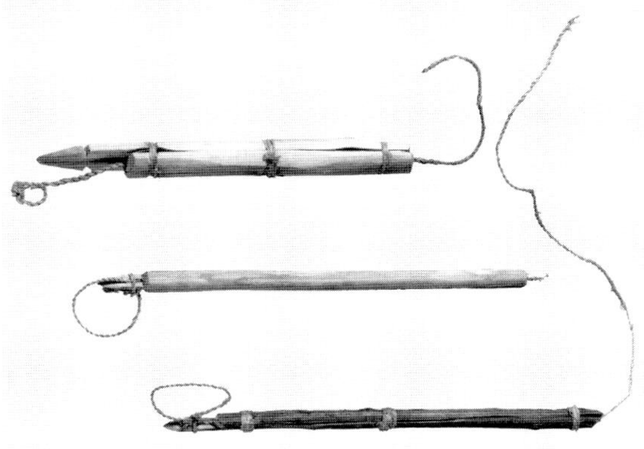

left, U. of Wyo., Amer. Heritage Center, Laramie: 705. top right, Amer. Mus. of Nat. Hist., New York: 286516; bottom right, Minn. Histl. Soc., St. Paul: 7059.69a–c, neg. 09026-1.

Fig. 8. Hunting technology. left, Crow or Cheyenne arrowmaker using sinew to fasten feathers to the shaft. The points are of trade steel. A bow and quiver with additional arrows are in the foreground. Photograph by Richard Throssel, 1902–1910. top right, Wolf Chief, Hidatsa, making a bow. He is in the process of smoothing the sinew backing with a rib bone. The bow is bound to a piece of wood while drying. To his right is a model of a tobacco fence; a tobacco plant is hanging from the window screen for drying. Historically the tobacco plants were tied to sticks and suspended from the earthlodge timbers. Photograph by Gilbert Wilson, Independence, N. Dak., 1912. bottom right, Hidatsa rabbit snares made from box elder sticks with the pith cores hollowed out, tied with sinew or plant fiber strings. Collected by Gilbert Wilson in 1916. Length of top, 25 cm; rest to scale.

somewhere between 101° and 102° west longitude in the Republican River basin. Whether introduction of irrigation to the Plains Apache by fugitive Pueblo Indians from the Rio Grande during the turbulent days leading up to, and including, the Pueblo Revolt of 1680 made possible the westerly expansion of Plains Indian horticulture is not clear. Horticulture was practiced by the prehistoric Panhandle dwellers in Oklahoma and Texas, and as far south as the Brazos River at approximately 32° north latitude by the seventeenth-century Wichita.

All the Village Indians of the eastern Plains practiced some measure of horticulture, but the depth of commitment to this activity varied considerably from locality to locality and from time to time. On the Middle Missouri, among the Arikara, Mandan, and Hidatsa, the ground under cultivation varied from one-third to one acre per person. At the other extreme, among the Osage and Kansa who relied to a greater extent on hunting, about one-third acre per head seems to have been more characteristic. Between these extremes were the Wichita and Pawnee. Archeological and documentary evidence suggests that among the Pawnee in the sixteenth and seventeenth centuries, and perhaps also among the Wichita of that period, the scale of gardening activity and the success of the effort may have approached that reported for the Middle Missouri tribes.

Flint, flour, and sweet corn, in varieties with 8–14 rows of kernels, were in use. The Mandan and Pawnee had 13 or more varieties each, the Arikara had 11, the Omaha had 12, the Poncas had five, and the Otoe had two (Will and Hyde 1917:284). The northern flint, widespread throughout the northern United States, is thought to have been derived from the eight-rowed *maíz de ocho* of Mexico (Galinat and Gunnerson 1963), introduced into the Plains in Late Woodland–Central Plains tradition times and probably an important factor in the rapid spread of maize horticulture through the Plains. The various strains were maintained by exercising great care in the selection, drying, and storing of the seed. Long ears, with straight rows of kernels filled to the tip, were braided and dried by themselves (fig. 10), and were stored separately from the corn for eating. Among the Mandan, Arikara, Pawnee, and

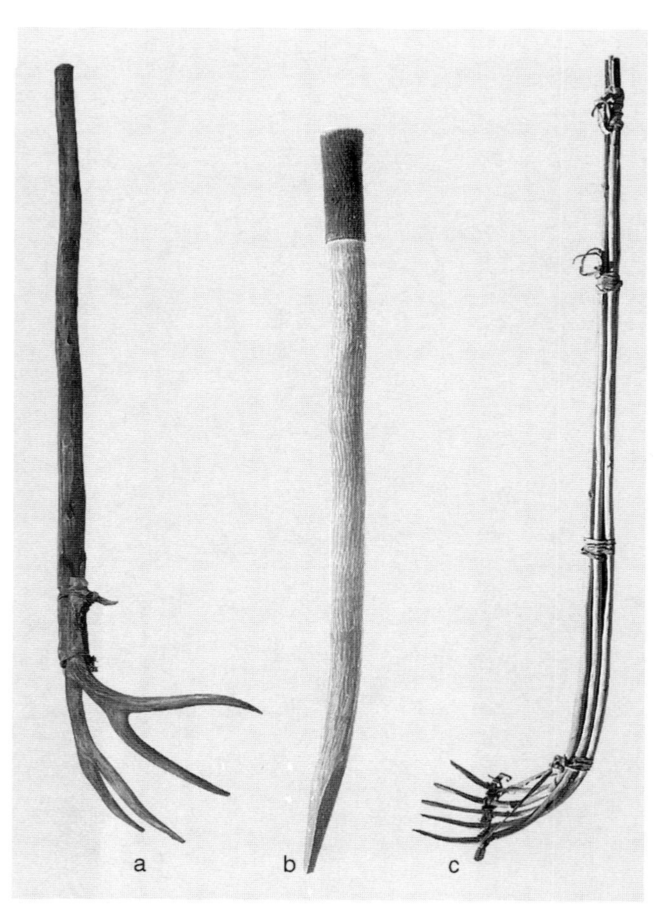

Minn. Histl. Soc., St. Paul: top left, 9448-A; bottom left, 09107#12; a, 7059.43a, neg. 09049-7; Smithsonian, Dept. of Anthr.: b, 419111-A, neg. 91-19236; Smithsonian, Natl. Mus. of the Amer. Ind.: c, 12/2991.

Fig. 9. Horticultural tools. top left, Sioux Woman, Hidatsa, hoeing squash using a traditional bone hoe, which had been obsolete for about 50 years (Gilman and Schneider 1987:206). Photograph by Gilbert Wilson, Independence, N. Dak., 1912. bottom left, Vegetables frequently grown in Hidatsa gardens: Mandan Banquet (winter) squash, corn, Hidatsa pole beans, and sunflower seeds. Seeds for these were preserved by anthropologists in the early 20th century and grown by Fred Schneider in 1986 (Gilman and Schneider 1987:207). a, Deer antler rake, Hidatsa. Collected by Gilbert Wilson, about 1914; length 128 cm. b, Digging stick for prairie turnips. Made by an Assiniboine on the Ft. Belknap Res., Mont., in 1953; length 99 cm. c, Wooden rake, Arikara. Collected by Melvin R. Gilmore, Ft. Berthold Res.; length 125 cm.

Omaha, careful women gardeners kept two years' supply of seed corn on hand at all times.

Everywhere in the Plains, cultivation was the responsibility of the women, except that tobacco was grown by the men in separate garden plots closed to other persons. Maize was planted in hills, between which were beans and squash, with sunflowers used to fence off the plots and sometimes planted among the corn hills. Plots were individually owned and tilled; most were small by modern standard, but around the larger villages they were sometimes so closely spaced as to give the impression of continuous fields. Among the nineteenth-century Pawnee the plantings were usually in patches of one-quarter to one acre, scattered over the bottoms and along the creeks wherever loose, easily worked soil was available and where there was some protection from the hot drying southerly winds that sometimes seemed to blow endlessly. Around the larger communities there was at times such shortage of suitable garden ground that the women reportedly traveled afoot 8–10 miles from their home village to the gardens, at great risk to their lives from Teton Sioux raiders (J.T. Irving 1955:138; Oehler and Smith 1974:29). There is no record that fertilizers were used by the Plains Village Indians or that irrigation was practiced except by the casual use of seep springs at the base of the valley bluffs by Pawnee (Carleton 1983:75).

Among the sixteenth-century Wichita in what is now southern Kansas, each hut was surrounded by "a small cultivated plot where maize, beans, and calabashes were raised" (Hammond and Rey 1953:746–877). The Indians merely pulled up the grass to make holes in which the corn was planted (Hammond and Rey 1953:755). Among the abundant stocks of corn was some that was kept in the ear on the ground in the houses. For milling corn, these Indians had stone metates. Outside the houses there were silos or storage pits for other surpluses (W.R.Wedel 1959).

The harvested crops, when not used fresh or green, were dried and stored chiefly in underground caches. When properly dried, these reserves could remain edible for months. Inadequate drying or protracted rains that penetrated the caches sometimes resulted in heavy losses and severe food shortages. There was also danger of loss from rodent activity by which the seal was broken and the food stores were left unprotected. Even greater was the danger of theft of the stored food by other tribes or villages during absence of the owners on tribal hunts when everyone except the aged and infirm left the home village for weeks or months at a time.

In historic times, the crop yields of the Plains Villagers seem to have averaged around 20–25 bushels of corn an acre, but with wide fluctuations from year to year. Erratic rainfall and frequent droughts, excessive moisture and floods, high winds, hail storms, grasshopper infestations, predatory animals and birds—these were among the hazards that confronted Indian gardeners. The Indians also risked loss of their crops by enemy action. In an earlier day, and on the western and northern peripheries, prehistoric corn yields may have been significantly lower. At prehistoric Upper Republican village sites on Medicine Creek, Nebraska, reduced corn yields are suggested by the smaller and often less abundant cache pits. Usually, these

top left, U. of Wyo., Amer. Heritage Center, Laramie: I87; Minn. Histl. Soc., St. Paul: top right, 42269, inset bottom, 7059.38, neg. 09066-2; bottom left, 42278, bottom right, 9627-A. inset top, Mus. für Völkerkunde, Berlin: IV-B-6148.

Fig. 10. Preparation of foods for storing. top left, Crow or Cheyenne women making pemmican. They are using modern metal axes as well as a more traditional pestle to pound the dried meat. The pulverized meat is mixed with melted fat and dried fruit such as chokecherries. The pemmican is then stuffed into skin bags where, if kept dry, it will last 4–5 years. Photograph by Richard Throssel, 1902–1910. top right, Owl Woman, Hidatsa, making chokecherry balls for drying. A stone mortar and pestle was used for crushing the chokecherries into a pulp. inset top, Teton Sioux mortar, pestle, and raw hide bowl. Collected by Clark Wissler, 1904. Diameter of bowl, 38 cm. bottom left, Owl Woman, putting sliced squash on spit to dry. inset bottom, Hidatsa buffalo scapula knife used to slice squash. Collected by Gilbert Wilson about 1914. Length 15.5 cm. bottom right, Husked corn being braided before drying. top right, bottom left, and bottom right, Photographs by Gilbert Wilson, Independence, N. Dak.; top right and bottom left, 1916, bottom right, 1909.

do not much exceed one meter in depth and diameter, with a capacity of perhaps 50 bushels. From the prehistoric gardens on this westerly frontier, the yield may have been as much as five bushels an acre below that of the Pawnee and Wichita in reservation days, whose storage pits were up to two meters deep and broad and probably had a capacity of 150 bushels or more, besides being more numerous than those at Upper Republican villages.

The extent to which cultivated crops—maize, beans, squash, and perhaps others—dominated the diet of the Village Indians is difficult to judge, but it appears that they outweighed that derived from communal hunts plus the wild vegetal foods gathered by the women and children from the prairies and streamside woodlands. This is the impression one gets from the reports of the commissioners of Indian affairs from the 1830s to the 1870s. When the garden crops failed or fell short, even a good hunt scarcely sufficed to carry the villagers through the winter. Conversely, even a successful crop did not insure adequate sustenance if the hunt fell short. For instance, in 1837 the Pawnee agent credited them with an estimated harvest of 10,000 bushels of corn from "about four hundred acres of ground, in small patches, scattered about in the ravines" to provide for a population of about 6,000, or less than two bushels a head (Dougherty 1837:548). Whether this included the green harvest or only the final ripe harvest is not clear. For the Osage, Iowa, and Kansa, Jedidiah Morse (1822) reported 15 to 30 bushels of maize and beans per family. G. K. Warren (1875:205) reported an 1854 average of four bushels per capita for the Arikara, Mandan, and Hidatsa. These Middle Missouri tribes often produced surpluses for sale or trade to Whites and neighboring Indian tribes. Total crop failures were rare among Middle Missouri tribes, and in historic times they were more often due to grasshoppers than drought (Will and Hyde 1917:70).

The horticultural activities of the Village Indians were adjusted to their needs for large supplies of meat to supplement the vegetal diet. Each year there were two hunts in which all able-bodied members of the tribe or village participated. The summer hunts were staged from approximately mid-May to mid-July, beginning after the second hoeing of the corn and ending in time for the green maize harvest. In September or October, following the mature maize harvest, another communal hunt began and lasted into or through the winter, or until the food carried along from the village ran out and planting time was at hand. On these hunts there were usually hundreds of Indians, moving generally westward from the permanent villages to the country where the bison might be found in sufficient numbers to merit a large-scale group effort. In addition to the meat, much tallow, and an abundance of hides, hair, sinew, and bones for various purposes were procured. The Pawnee winter hunt of 1865 yielded a reported 1,600 bison, elk, pronghorn, and deer (ARCIA 1865:385). On these hunts, which sometimes involved hundreds of miles of travel under extremely difficult conditions, the villagers lived in skin tepees, used the horse and dog travois, and behaved much like the equestrian nomads of the western plains. Hunt police to maintain order and forestall premature attacks on the target herds by individual hunters were a regular and important feature of the social structure.

The Languages of the Plains: Introduction

IVES GODDARD

The peoples of the Plains spoke a large number of languages from at least seven distinct linguistic families (fig. 1). Their linguistic diversity was much greater than the diversity of other aspects of their cultures and must be a retention from a time when they had less contact with each other and were culturally more distinct. This conclusion correlates with traditional, historical, and archeological evidence that many of the peoples of the High Plains are relatively recent immigrants and that even those of the Prairie Plains have expanded into the Plains area in late prehistoric and early historic times (vol. 17:94, 99, 102–105; Bradbury 1819:139; W.P. Clark 1885:39, 99–100; Mooney 1907:361–373; Grinnell 1923, 1:30, 35, 47; Jelinek 1967; Wood 1971a; Vehik 1993). The general picture that is suggested is of diverse peoples retaining their distinct ancestral languages while adopting new and to a large extent shared lifeways after entering the Plains and coming into contact with each other.

The language groups represented in the Plains area are: Algonquian (a branch of the Algic family), Athapaskan (in Nadene), Caddoan, Kiowa-Tanoan, Siouan (in Siouan-Catawba), Tonkawa (a language isolate), and Uto-Aztecan. There is ethnohistorical and traditional evidence that speakers of Kootenai (an isolate) and of Salishan languages (Plains Salish and Flathead) were also formerly on the Northern Plains (vol. 12:225, 226, 297). Because there is no direct linguistic evidence from a number of groups named in tribal traditions and the early historical literature, it is possible that there were additional linguistic units in the Plains area in the recent past. The three families with the largest number of Plains languages are treated separately ("Algonquian Languages of the Plains," "Caddoan Languages," and "Siouan Languages," this vol.). This chapter treats the remaining families. The Athapaskan, Uto-Aztecan, and Kiowa-Tanoan languages are also covered within the context of their relatives outside the Plains in "Historical Linguistics and Archeology" (vol. 9), "Northern Athapaskan Languages" (vol. 6), and "Uto-Aztecan Languages" and "Apachean Languages" (vol. 10). Additional information on all the languages is in volume 17.

Linguistic Diversity

The diversity of the languages spoken on the High Plains was evident to the earliest European observers at the beginning of the nineteenth century. Pierre-Antoine Tabeau (1939:154) reported that the eight "nations" that before 1804 traded with the Cheyenne and Arikara near the Black Hills spoke seven languages. In his list of these, names for the Arapaho, Nawathinehena, Comanche, Plains Apache (Kiowa Apache), and Kiowa can be recognized with some confidence. The other two groups listed as having distinct languages were the Datami (or Datamixes) and the Tchiwâk, whose identities are unknown. The Datami, called the Dotame by Meriwether Lewis and William Clark (1832; Moulton 1983–, 3:422, 425), were located near Arapahoan peoples and others (W. Clark, in Moulton 1983–, 1:map 32a). What Clark refers to as "subsequent information" that the Dotame and others of these groups were subdivisions of the Padoucas (which would make them Apacheans) is clearly wrong (Moulton 1983–, 3:439). The Tchiwâk are referred to in Clark's notes as To-che-wah-coo and War too che work koo, renderings of an Arikara name *tUhčiwáku?* that literally means 'fox village' (Moulton 1983–, 3:136, 217). Jean-Baptiste Truteau called them the Tokiouako and located them on a tributary of the Cheyenne River in 1796 (Nasatir 1952, 2:379, 384). Tabeau's impressionistic description of their language seems to imply the presence of vowelless sequences, a prominent feature of Salishan languages, and it is conceivable that they were the Plains Salish or the Flathead, who were in contact with the Plains tribes (Teit 1930:320). In this connection it may be significant that Clark gives the name of the Flathead in an unspecified Indian language as Tut-seé-wâs (Lewis and Clark 1832), although a Shoshone explanation for this name has also been proposed (vol. 12:312).

In addition to there being a multiplicity of language families on the Plains, there was also greater diversity within some subfamilies and languages at the beginning of the nineteenth century than in the twentieth century. Arapahoan began with five languages and became reduced to two, and there were major dialects of Cheyenne, Arikara, Kiowa, Tonkawa, and Wichita that later disappeared, in some cases without a trace.

The diversity of the different families represented in the Plains area as well as the similarities of languages related in language families can be seen in a comparative vocabulary of basic words (table 1). Languages related to each other in the Algonquian, Caddoan, Athapaskan, and Siouan language families show many similarities, and within these

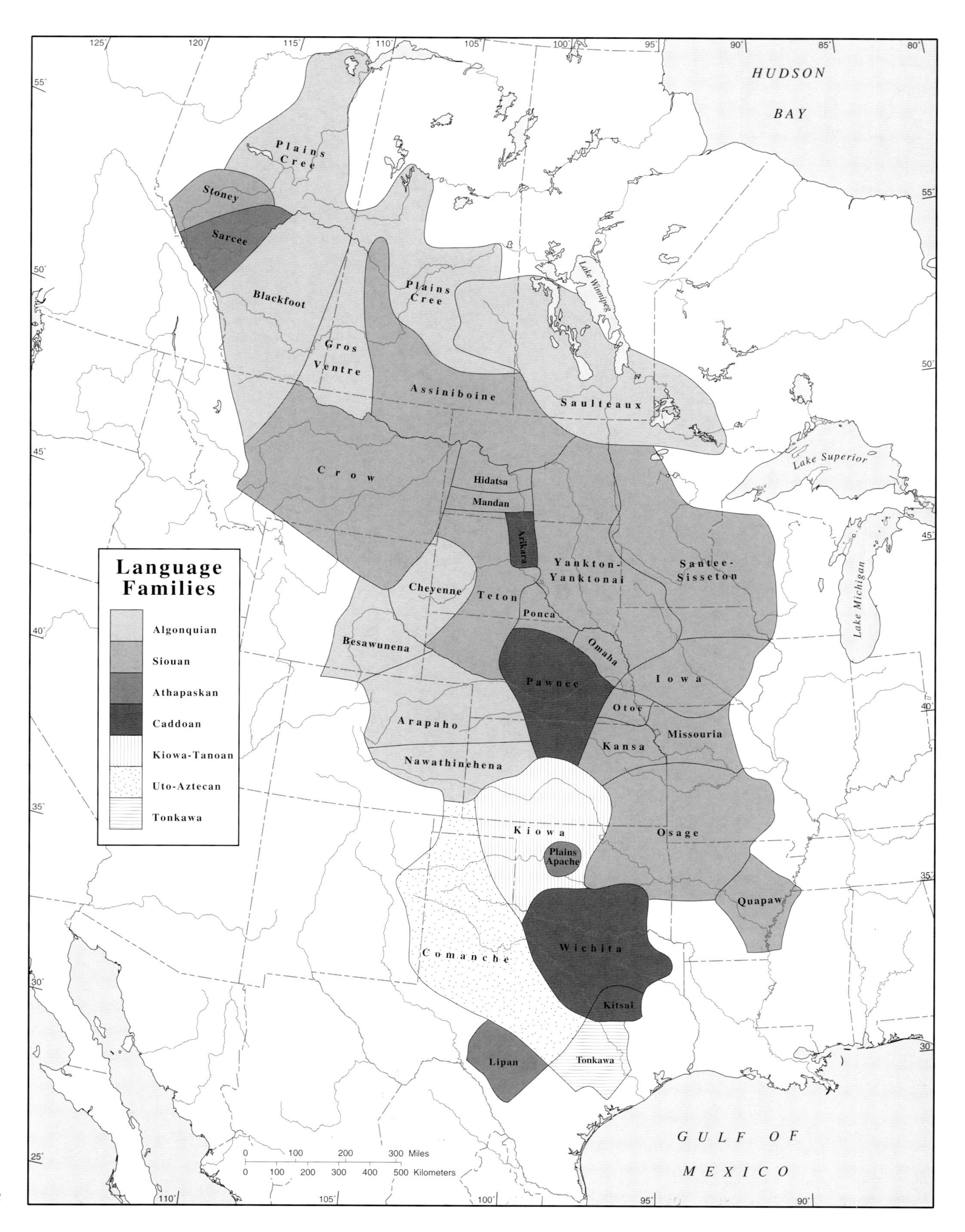
HUDSON
BAY
Lake Winnipeg
Lake Superior
Lake Michigan
GULF OF
MEXICO
Language Families
Algonquian
Siouan
Athapaskan
Caddoan
Kiowa-Tanoan
Uto-Aztecan
Tonkawa
Plains Cree
Stoney
Sarcee
Blackfoot
Plains Cree
Gros Ventre
Assiniboine
Saulteaux
Crow
Hidatsa
Mandan
Arikara
Yankton-Yanktonai
Santee-Sisseton
Cheyenne
Teton
Ponca
Omaha
Besawunena
Pawnee
Iowa
Otoe
Arapaho
Kansa
Missouria
Nawathinehena
Kiowa
Osage
Plains Apache
Quapaw
Wichita
Comanche
Kitsai
Lipan
Tonkawa
0 100 200 300 Miles
0 100 200 300 400 500 Kilometers

families subgroups are also apparent. In Algonquian, Arapaho and Gros Ventre are obviously quite close, being members of the Arapahoan subgroup. Arikara and Pawnee are more similar to each other than either is to the other two Caddoan languages. In Siouan, Crow and Hidatsa form a subgroup; Santee, Teton, Assiniboine, and Stoney are all in another subgroup (sometimes call Dakotan); and Omaha, Ponca, Kansa, Osage, and Quapaw make up the Dhegiha branch, with Omaha and Ponca the most similar pair. This pattern of similarities and differences would be confirmed by additional word comparisons and by the comparison of grammatical forms and structures.

Further matches between words in related languages can be recognized when the history of the divergent sound changes that the languages have undergone is worked out. For example, all occurrences of **k* in the Proto-Algonquian parent language are lost without a trace in Arapaho and Gros Ventre, and this historical change accounts for the divergence in the shape of several words when compared to Cree and Saulteaux: see 'bear', 'beaver', 'day', 'fire', 'ice', 'skunk', 'snow', 'star', 'woman'. Cheyenne loses many occurrences of original **k* and **p*. In contrast, the dissimilarities in Blackfoot appear to be the result of the widespread replacement of words with new coinages. The only Blackfoot words on this list that are related to words listed for the other Algonquian languages are those for 'day', 'dog', 'fish', 'man', and 'snow', and even some of these are problematical.

Some words reflect relatively recent usages. For example, the words given for 'house' are in several cases used specifically for houses of European type; the Cree and Saulteaux words referred originally to a fort, the Arapaho word is etymologically 'earthlodge', and the Sarcee word is 'buffalo pound where the fire is'. The Saulteaux expression for 'buffalo' is literally 'prairie cattle'; *pišikki* was the original word for 'buffalo' but now means 'cow, domestic cattle'. In many cases additional matches could be found if words with similar meanings were also compared. Thus, the Arapaho, Gros Ventre, and Cheyenne words for 'tree' go back to the Proto-Algonquian word for 'poplar', and the Blackfoot word reflects the word for 'aspen'. Stoney *wiyá, wiyé, wi·* 'buffalo' is cognate with Santee-Sisseton *wíye* 'female animal', a shift that reflects the preference for female buffalo as game. The general Dhegiha Siouan word for 'bear' is etymologically 'the black one', referring specifically to the black bear; the Mandan and Sioux-Assiniboine word was originally the word for 'grizzly bear' (Robert L. Rankin, personal communication 1999). The Crow and Hidatsa words for 'skunk' are from a word that in other languages means 'badger' (Robert L. Rankin, personal communication 1999). The Mandan and Santee words for 'snake' are members of a set of words applied to various vermin; the Iowa-Otoe word reflects one that means 'spirit, sacred' in Sioux-Assiniboine-Stoney and Dhegiha but is 'snake' also in Saponi, an extinct Siouan language of Virginia (Robert L. Rankin, personal communication 1999). The existence of multiple words with slightly different meanings and slight shifts in usage also accounts for some of the differences within families in the words given for 'dirt'.

Words given for 'eagle' may be generic terms or names for specific species, or both. In Arapaho an eagle may be referred to as *ni·ˀéhi·*, which is also the general word for 'bird', or as *he·béθi·ˀéhi·* 'big bird'; similarly, the Comanche word is also literally 'big bird', the Tonkawa is 'much bird' or perhaps 'real bird', and the Kiowa is 'real bird'. The words for 'eagle' in Cheyenne, Cree, and Saulteaux all reflect the Proto-Algonquian word for 'golden eagle'; this has become a generic term for "eagles and vultures" in Cheyenne (Petter 1913–1915:420) and has perhaps also come to be used generically in the other two languages. This may also be the case with Gros Ventre *nɔ́·kɔtiyéíhi* 'eagle', since it literally means 'whitetail', just like Arapaho *hi·no·kóθonít* 'golden eagle' (Hayden 1862:331; Salzmann 1983). The reference is not to the all-white tail of the bald eagle, but to the mostly white, dark-tipped tail feathers of the immature golden eagle (called the war eagle), which were prized. The words listed for 'eagle' in Santee, Teton, Mandan, Crow, and perhaps other Siouan languages, and in Arikara and Pawnee refer specifically to the immature golden eagle (Hayden 1862:360, 406, 440; Riggs 1852:222; Buechel 1970:540; Medicine Horse 1987:3, 111). The Hidatsa form was specifically the name of this variety in the nineteenth century and was later used generically (W. Matthews 1877:185; A. Wesley Jones, personal communication 1999). The Stoney word is probably cognate with Sioux-Assiniboine *wíyaka* 'wing or tail feather'.

In some cases the phonemic transcription used makes words more similar than they are in actual pronunciation. For example, Crow, Hidatsa, and Mandan are all written with the phonemes *w* and *r*, but the actual pronunciations of these phonemes are conditioned by the phonetic context in which they occur, according to patterns that differ in the three languages and that changed over time. In word-initial position Crow *w* is usually pronounced [b], while Hidatsa *w* is pronounced [m], and between vowels *r* is [r] in Hidatsa but generally [l] in Crow, at one time a characteristic of women's speech, which replaced earlier [r] (Kaschube 1967:8–9). In Mandan, *w* and *r* are pronounced [m] and [n] before nasal vowels, including the vowel inserted automatically between a consonant and an *r*. Thus of the words for 'water', Crow *wiré* is pronounced [bilé] and was earlier [biré] and in the early nineteenth century [mini]; Hidatsa *wirí* is [mirí], in the nineteenth century [midi], [bidi],

Fig. 1. Languages and language families of the Plains in the first half of the 19th century. The indicated areas are approximations, as the distributions of the languages overlapped in many areas and shifted through time. The areas in which the Plains Cree and Saulteaux languages are spoken extend beyond the Plains into the Subarctic and the Northeast. Groups whose languages are undocumented are omitted; if they were included, the map would show pockets of unclassified languages in the central Plains and in Texas.

Table 1. Comparative Vocabulary of the Languages of the Plains

	Algonquian						Uto-Aztecan
	Blackfoot	Arapaho	Gros Ventre	Cheyenne	Plains Cree	Saulteaux	Comanche
1. bear	*kiá·yowa*	*wóx*	*wɔ́s*	*náhkohE*	*maskwa*	*makkwa*	*wasapeʔ*
2. beaver	*ksísskstakiwa*	*hébes*	*hɛ́bis*	*hómaʔE*	*amisk*	*amikk*	*haʔni·*
3. bird	*sisttsíwa*	*ni·ʔéhi·*	*ni·ʔíhi·*	*véʔkésE*	*piye·si·s*	*pine·ššį·*	*huhcu·ʔ*
4. buffalo	*i·ní·wa*	*hí·θeino·n*	*ʔí·tɛ·nɔ́·n*	*ésevonE*	*mostos*	*maškote·-pišikki*	*taʔsiwo·ʔ*
5. corn	*áóhpi·ki·na·ttsi·stsi*, pl.	*bésko·té·*	*béskɔ·tɛ́·*	*hoóʔkóhtsEstsE*, pl.	*mahta·min*	*manta·min*	*haniβi*
6. day	*ksi·stsikóyi*	*hí·siʔ*	*ʔí·si*	*èšE*	*ki·sika·w*	*ka·-ki·šikakk*	*taβe* 'day, sun'
7. dirt	*ksá·hkoyi*	*hóʔ*	*ʔɔ́ʔ*	*héšeʔkE; hoʔE* 'earth'	*asiskiy; askiy* 'earth'	*ašiški; akki* 'earth'	*ohtapi*
8. dog	*imitá·wa*	*héθ*	*ʔɔ́t*	*hótamE* (arch.); *oeškēsE*		*atim*	*animošš*
sari·ʔ							
9. eagle	*pí·ta·wa*	*he·béθi·ʔéhi·*	*nɔ́·kɔtiyéíhi*	*netsE*	*kihiw*	*kiniw*	*piahuhcu·ʔ*
10. fire	*pakóyittsiyi*	*hisíte·*	*ʔisítɛ·*	*hoʔēstA*	*iskote·w*	*iškote·*	*kohto·hpɨ*
11. fish	*mamí·wa*	*néb, nówoʔ*	*nɔ́wo*	*nómaʔnE, nómaʔhE*	*kinose·w*	*ki·kǫ·*	*pe·kwi*
12. five	*ni·sitoyi*	*yo·θón*	*yɔ·tɔ́n*	*nòhO, nóhone-*	*niya·nan*	*na·nan*	*moʔoβetɨ*
13. four	*ni·só-*	*yéín*	*yɛ́·n*	*nèvE, néve-*	*ne·wo*	*ni·win*	*hayarokwetɨ*
14. house	*moyísi*	*hoʔóowuʔ*	*bɛ·yéθɔo*	*mAhēōʔO*	*wa·skahikan*	*wa·kka·ʔikan*	*kahni*
15. ice	*kokótoyi* (also #22)	*woʔów*	*wɔ́ʔɔwo*	*máʔomE*	*miskwamiy*	*mikkwam*	*tahkaβi* 'ice, snow'
16. man	*nína·wa*	*hinén*	*ʔinén*	*hetanE*	*na·pe·w*	*inini*	*tenahpɨ*
17. mountain	*mi·stáki*	*hóheʔ, hóheʔn*		*ʔɔhʔɛ́n*	*hoʔhonáevosE*	*waciy*	*wačiw toyaβi*
18. night	*koʔkóyi*	*tééeʔ*	*tíčeʔ*	*taaʔE*	*tipiska·w*	*ka·-tipikkakk*	*tukani*
19. rock	*ó·hkotoka*	*hohʔonó·ke·*	*ʔɔ́hʔɔnɛ́·čɛ·*	*hoʔhonááʔE*	*asiniy*	*assin*	*tɨpi*
20. skunk	*á·pi·kayiwa*	*xo·ó*	*θɔ́ɔ·, θóou*	*xāōʔO*	*sika·k*	*šika·k*	*pisuni·ʔ*
21. snake	*pitsí·ksi·na·wa*	*sî·sí·yei*	*sî·sí·yɛ·*	*šéʔšenovOtsE*	*kine·pik*	*kine·pik*	*kwasinaβo·ʔ*
22. snow	*ko·na* 'ice, snow'	*hi·í*	*ʔíi·*	*héstaʔsE*	*ko·na*	*ko·n*	*tahkaβi* 'ice, snow'
23. star	*kakatóʔsiwa*	*hóθoʔ*	*ʔɔ́toʔ*	*hotòhkE*	*acahkos*	*anank*	*tahcinupi*
24. sun	*na·tóʔsiwa*	*hi·sî·s*	*ʔí·sî·s*	*éšeʔhE*	*pi·sim*	*ki·siss*	*taβe* 'day, sun'
25. three	*nió·kska-*	*nê·só*	*nɛ̂·θ*	*naʔhE, naʔhe-*	*nisto*	*nisswi*	*pahihtɨ*
26. tobacco	*pisstá·hka·ni*	*sî·so·wo·*	*cî·θɔ́·wɔ·*	*tseʔnémooʔO*	*ciste·ma·w*	*asse·ma·*	*pahmu*
27. tree	*mi·stsísa*	*hohó·t*	*ʔɔhɔ́·tʸ*	*hoòhtsEstsE*	*mistik*	*mittik*	*hu·hpi*
28. two	*na·toʔk-, ná·tsi-*	*ní·s*	*ní·θ*	*nèšE, néše-*	*ni·so*	*ni·š*	*wahahtɨ*
29. water	*aohkí·yi*	*néč*	*níc*	*mahpE*	*nipiy*	*nipi*	*pa·*

	Caddoan				Athapaskan		
	Arikara	Pawnee	Kitsai	Wichita	Sarcee	Plains Apache	Lipan
1. bear	*kú·nUx*	*ku·ruks*	*oríni*	*wiraʔa*	*nīnīγá*	*šaš*	*šaš*
2. beaver	*čítUx*	*kituks*	*kitakwát*	*kitiskata·hicʔa*	*mīčàdīkòdí*	*ča·*	*ča·ʔ*
3. bird	*níkUs*	*rikucki*	*kocáki*	*ichiri*	*ìċáγá*	*ʔíža·š*	*cidí*
4. buffalo	*tanáhaʔ*	*tarahaʔ*	*tánaha*	*ta·rha* (female)	*xānítíí*	*ʔížą·de*	*ʔiyání*
5. corn	*né·šuʔ*	*re·ksuʔ*	*kotai*	*té·s*	*gūwà*	*ʔida·dą́·ʔ*	*ʔina·dą́ʔ*
6. day	*šakú·nuʔ*	*saku·ruʔ*	*tiasakónu*	*sa·khirʔa* 'sun, day'	*ʒínīs*	*ǯį·*	*ǯį*
7. dirt	*hItká·nuʔ*	*itka·ruʔ*	*hunána*	*hira·rʔa*	*gūƛ̓ìs*	*nǫ·*	*łe·š*
8. dog	*xá·tš*	*asa·ki*	*anósa*	*wáseʔekʔa*	*ƛ̓íčà*	*łį·če·h*	*ni·ʔłį*
9. eagle	*né·tAhkas*	*re·tahkac*		*ko·s*	*dīłóní*	*ʔíča·h*	*ʔicáh*
10. fire	*če·káʔuʔ*	*ke·kauʔ*	*karon*	*he·cʔa*	*kù*	*kǫʔ*	*kǫ·ʔ*
11. fish	*čiwáhtš*	*kaci·ki*	*nitát*	*ka·cʔa*	*ƛúk̓á*	*kak̓íčį*	*łǫ́ʔ*
12. five	*šíhUx*	*sihuks*	*ikstáweʔu*	*iskʷi·cha*	*gúùłāā*	*ʔašλaʔ*	*ʔa·šλiʔ*
13. four	*či·tíʔIš*	*kskit·tiʔiks*	*kinákt*	*tá·kʷicha*	*dīīčí*	*dį·čiʔ*	*dį·ʔí*
14. house	*aká·nuʔ*	*aka·ruʔ*	*kosánu*	*akha·rʔa*	*násʔóγákùwá*	*łe·š*	*go·γąh*
15. ice	*na·xí·tuʔ*	*ra·si·tuʔ*	*ahonánis*	*na·hicʔa*	*nīstīní*	*kóšíčįhí·*	*kįh*
16. man	*wí·tA*	*pi·ta*	*wí·ta*	*wi·c*	(*dīná*) *k̓àłíní*	*de·ná·*	*diⁿdí*

Table 1. Comparative Vocabulary of the Languages of the Plains *(continued)*

	Caddoan				Athapaskan		
	Arikara	Pawnee	Kitsai	Wichita	Sarcee	Plains Apache	Lipan
17. mountain	wá·u?	pa·u?	naha	nawa·re?erhárih	cáčū	ʒił	ʒił
18. night	hínAx	ratkaha·ru?	natkat	ckha·r?a	īƛ̓íyì	ƛ̓é·g	ƛ̓í·?
19. rock	kanítš	karitki	katánu	ika·?a	cá	ce·h	cí
20. skunk	níwIt	riwit	hiwi·it	niwi·c	náázíγà	do·kač̓įłčesá	k̓e·łíšé
21. snake	nút	rutki	kini·ca	hi·c	nàduzáγá	gǒ·?	gó·
22. snow	huná·u?	ura·u?	naóa	hira·?a	zòs	zas	zas, yas
23. star	sáka·?A	u·pirit	nikwírik	hí·k^{w}irik?a	sùh	sǫ·	sǫ·s
24. sun	šakú·nu?	saku·ru?	sakónu	sa·khir?a	č̓āłáγà	ša·	ǯį·?na·?áí
25. three	táwIt	tawit	ta·wiku	tawha	táák̓í	kák̓i	káí?í
26. tobacco	na·wIšká·nu?	ra·wiska·ru?	wióko	wí?i·k?a	īkáčīnà	dá·łod	?ináłodi
27. tree	nAhá·pI	raha·pi	yakwi	tiya·hkwi	īčī	kǫ?é·h	cį
28. two	pítkUx	pitku	cúsu	wicha	àkíyí	da·či?	na·ki
29. water	tstó·xu?	ki·cu?	akicónu	kic?a	tú	kó·	kó
30. woman	sápat	capat	cakwákt	ka·hi·k?a	čìká	če·čą·	?isʒání

	Siouan						
	Mandan	Crow	Hidatsa	Santee	Teton	Assiniboine	Stoney
1. bear	wąt6?	raxpiččê·	raxpic^{h}í	mat^{h}ó	mat^{h}ó	mąt^{h}ó	ožįča
2. beaver	wráp	wirápe	wirápa	č^{h}ápa	č^{h}ápa	č^{h}ápa	č^{h}ápa
3. bird	wą́·rek	rakâ·ke	caká·ka	zitkádą	zįtkála	zitkána	ziktán
4. buffalo	ptį́·re, ptį́·-	wišê·	wité·	pté	pté	pté	wiyá, wiyé, wi·
5. corn	kó·xą?te	xó·xa·še	kó·xxa·ti	wamnáheza	wagmíza	wakmúhaza	įskésken
6. day	hąpé	wa·pé	wa·pí	ąpétu	ąpétu	ą́pa	ą́pa
7. dirt	wárat	pu·xké; awé 'earth'	áwa 'earth'	mak^{h}á	mak^{h}á	mąk^{h}á	ųpšíya
8. dog	wrįs-wé·rut	wiškė́	wašúka	šų́ka	šų́ka	šų́ka	šų́ka
9. eagle	wą́·hsi	rêaxka·še	wa·-išú	wąmdí	wąblí	wamní	wiyá·
10. fire	wára?re, wára?-	wirê·	wirá?a	p^{h}éta	p^{h}éta	p^{h}éta	įtkų́
11. fish	pó?	wúá	wúa	hoγą́	hoγą́	hoγą́	hoγą́
12. five	kíxų	čiaxxó	kixxú	záptą	záptą	záptą	záptą
13. four	tó·p, tó·pa-	šo·pé	tó·pa	tópa	tópa	tópa	ktųsá
14. house	tí?, otí?	awa·sû·a	atí	t^{h}ípi	t^{h}ípi	t^{h}ípi	t^{h}ípi
15. ice	xó·re	wurúxe	warúxi	č^{h}áγa	č^{h}áγa	č^{h}áγa	č^{h}áγa
16. man	rųwą́?k	wačé·	wacé·	wič^{h}ášta	wič^{h}áša	wįč^{h}á	wįč^{h}á
17. mountain	xáre, xá-	awaxa·wé	awaxa·wí	xé	xé	įyąxe	įyáxe
18. night	ištú	ô·ččia	ó·kcia	hąyétu	hąhépi	hąhépi	hąhépi
19. rock	wį?re, wį?-	wi·á	wí?i	įyą	įyą	įyą	įp^{h}ápin
20. skunk	šų́xte	xúáhče·	xúhke	maká	maká	mąká	šičamnán
21. snake	wá·krux	îaxasse·	wa·púkša 'vermin'	wamdúška	zuzéča	snohéna	t^{h}ahmų́sisin
22. snow	wá?he	wî·a	wá·	wá	wá	wá	wá
23. star	xkéke, xkék-	ihké	ihká	wič^{h}ą́xpi	wič^{h}áxpi	wįč^{h}áxpi	yahyą́hįken
24. sun	wį·rą?k	áxxa·še	wirí	wí	wí	wí	wahįyąpa
25. three	rą́·wrį	râ·wi·a	rá·wi	yámni	yámni	yámni	yámni
26. tobacco	wrą́še, wrą́š-	ô·pe	ó·pi	č^{h}ądí	č^{h}ąlí	č^{h}ąní	įtuk^{h}ápi
27. tree	wą́rąh	warapâ·re	wirá	č^{h}ą́	č^{h}ą́	č^{h}ą́	č^{h}ą́
28. two	rų́p, rų́pa-	rû·pe	rú·pa	nų́pa	nų́pa	nų́pa	núm
29. water	wrį?	wiré	wirí	mní	mní	mní	mnį
30. woman	wį·he	wîa	wía	winóxįča	wįyą	wįyą	wįyą

Table 1. Comparative Vocabulary of the Languages of the Plains *(continued)*

	Siouan						Kiowa-Tanoan	Tonkawa
	Omaha	Ponca	Kansa	Osage	Quapaw	Iowa-Otoe	Kiowa	
1. bear	*wasábe*	*wasábe*	*wasábe*	*wašápe*	*wasá*	*mų́·ǯe*	*sét*	*nencopan*
2. beaver	*žábe*	*žá·be*	*žá·be*	*žápe*	*žáwe*	*rá·we*	*pó·*	*heylapanekaman*
3. bird	*wažį́ga*	*wažį́ga*	*wažį́ga*	*wažį́ka*	*wažį́ka*	*wa·yį́ŋe*	*kú·tò, i̓ę̀·né*	*ko·lʔa*
4. buffalo	*tte*	*tte*	*ččedǫ́ga*	*cce*	*tte*	*č^{h}e·*	*kɔ́l* 'herd, cow', *p^{h}ɔ́·* 'bull'	*ʔawasatak*
5. corn	*wat^{h}ą́zi*	*wat^{h}ą́zi*	*wak^{h}ózü*	*hápa*	*wat^{h}ą́se*	*wadú·ǯe*	*ʔé·t^{h}âl*	*tolʔaxan*
6. day	*ą́ba*	*ą́ba*	*hǫ́ba*	*hǫ́pa*	*hą́pa*	*hą́·we*	*k^{h}í·*	*taxas*
7. dirt	*manį́kka*	*mąðį́kka*	*moį́kka*	*máįkka*	*maníkka*	*máha*	*dɔ́m* 'ground, earth', *p^{h}ą́y* 'dust, dirt'	*ha·c*
8. dog	*šínuda*	*šínuda*	*šǫ́ge óyüda*	*šǫ́ke*	*šǫ́ke*	*sųk^{h}én^{y}į*	*cę̂·hį̀·*	*ʔek^{w}an*
9. eagle	*xiðá*	*xiðá*	*xüyá*	*xüðá*	*xidá*	*xra·*	*kú·tòhį̀·*	*ko·lʔa·tak*
10. fire	*ppé·de*	*ppé·de*	*ppé·ǯe*	*ppé·ce*	*ppétte*	*p^{h}é·ǯe*	*p^{h}í· ~ p^{h}yá-*	*mʔelʔan*
11. fish	*húhu*	*huhú*	*ho*	*ho*	*ho*	*ho·*	*ʔɔ́·pį́·*	*neswalʔan*
12. five	*sáttą*	*sáttą*	*sáttą*	*sáttą*	*sáttą*	*θá·t^{h}ą*	*ʔɔ́ni̓ɔ̀·*	*kask^{w}a*
13. four	*dú·ba*	*dú·ba*	*dó·ba*	*tópa*	*tówa*	*dó·we*	*yí·kyá*	*sikit*
14. house	*tti*	*tti*	*čči*	*cci*	*tti*	*č^{h}i·*	*tó·*	*na·ho·n*
15. ice	*núγe*	*núγe*	*nóγe*	*ną́γe*	*tóγe*	*nú·xeθrį*	*tę́·gyà*	*nestikan*
16. man	*niašį́ga*	*niášiga*	*níkka*	*níkka*	*níkka*	*wą́ŋe*	*k̓í·, k̓yą́·hį̂ ·*	*ha·ʔako·n*
17. mountain	*ppahé maše*	*ppahé mąši*	*bahéxta*	*paxó sce*	*maší ttąka*	*ahé maše*	*k̓óp*	*na·to·n*
18. night	*hą*	*hą*	*hąye*	*hą*	*hą*	*hą́·he*	*gį́·-; gį́·gyá* 'at night'	*ʔo·ʔa*
19. rock	*íʔe*	*į́ʔe*	*į*	*į*	*į*	*ʔį·no*	*č̓ép, č̓ó·*	*yatexan*
20. skunk	*mą́ga*	*mą́ga*	*mǫ́ga*	*mą́ka*	*mą́ka*	*mų́k^{h}a*	*tâl*	*heka·new*
21. snake	*weṡá*	*wéṡa*	*weċá*	*wéċa*	*wiṡá*	*wa·k^{h}ą́*	*są̀·né*	*se·nan*
22. snow	*ma*	*ma*	*bahúya*	*pa*	*poíde*	*ba·hú*	*i̓ól*	*maslakelan*
23. star	*mikkáʔe*	*mikkáʔe*	*mikkák̓e*	*mikkák̓e*	*mikkáẋe*	*bi·k^{h}áẋe*	*tą́·*	*tawsew*
24. sun	*mi*	*mį*	*míǫba*	*mi*	*mi*	*bi·*	*páy*	*taxas*
25. three	*ðá·bðį*	*ðá·bðį*	*yá·blį*	*ðá·brį*	*dá·bnį*	*dá·n^{y}į*	*p^{h}ą́·ò·*	*metis, metʔis*
26. tobacco	*niníži*	*niní*	*nǫnű́*	*nanű́hü*	*tanní*	*rá·n^{y}į*	*t^{h}á·bɔ́t*	*nepaxkan*
27. tree	*xðábe*	*xðábe*	*žą*	*žą*	*žą*	*ną·*	*ʔá·dɔ̀*	*heylapan*
28. two	*ną́ba*	*nąbá*	*nǫbá*	*ðǫ·pa*	*nąpá*	*nų́·we*	*yí·*	*ketay*
29. water	*ni*	*nį*	*ni*	*ni*	*ni*	*n^{y}į·*	*t^{h}ǫ́·*	*ʔa·x*
30. woman	*waʔú*	*waʔú*	*wak̓ó*	*wak̓ó*	*waẋó*	*hį·náge*	*mà·yį́*	*k^{w}a·n*

SOURCES: This table is based on one compiled by Allan R. Taylor and David S. Rood (communication to editors 1975); data credited with no date are from this compilation. Revisions incorporating new data and analyses were made by Ives Goddard (Algonquian), Douglas R. Parks (Caddoan and Siouan), Robert Rankin (Siouan), and Laurel J. Watkins (Kiowa).

Arapaho data from: Salzmann (1983; communication to editors 1975), with some reanalysis; Arikara: Douglas R. Parks (personal communication 1999); Assiniboine (Ft. Belknap, Mont.): Douglas R. Parks and Raymond J. DeMallie (personal communication 2000); Blackfoot: Frantz and Russell (1995), Donald G. Frantz (personal communication 1999); Cheyenne: Wayne Leman (personal communication 1996); Comanche: John E. McLaughlin (personal communication 1999); Cree: H. Christoph Wolfart; Crow: Medicine Horse (1987), Randolph Graczyk (personal communication 1999); Gros Ventre (conservative pronunciation): A. R. Taylor (1967, 1994; communication to editors 1975), respelled; Hidatsa: A. Wesley Jones (personal communication 1999); Iowa-Otoe: Franklin Murray, Truman Dailey, Lizzie Harper, and Liess Valentine, transcribed by Robert L. Rankin and John E. Koontz (Robert L. Rankin, personal communication 1999); Kansa: Maude Rowe and Robert L. Rankin (personal communication 1999); Kiowa: Laurel J. Watkins (personal communication 1999); Kitsai: Alexander Lesser; Lipan: Morris Opler and Harry Hoijer, Hoijer (1955:225–226), Scott Rushforth (personal communication 1999); Mandan: Otter Sage and Richard T. Carter (Robert L. Rankin, personal communication 1999), Mauricio Mixco (personal communication 1999); Omaha: Elmer Blackbird and Jim Thompson (Robert L. Rankin, personal communication 1999); Osage: Frances Holding and Carolyn Quintero (Robert L. Rankin, personal communications 1999); Pawnee (South Band): Douglas R. Parks (personal communication 2000); Plains Apache: William Bittle, Bittle (1963); Ponca: Parrish Williams and Kathleen Shea (Robert L. Rankin, personal communication 1999); Quapaw: Odestine McWatters, Alice Gilmore, Maude Supernaw, Mary Red Eagle, and Robert L. Rankin (Robert L. Rankin, personal communication 1999); Santee: Riggs (1852, 1893), phonemicized; Sarcee: Eung-Do Cook, Gary Donovan, Brian Potter, and Bruce Starlight (personal communication 1999); Saulteaux: Paul H. Voorhis (personal communication 1999); Stoney: Allan R. Taylor and Eung-Do Cook (personal communication 1999); Teton: Allan R. Taylor; Tonkawa: Hoijer (1933, 1949); Wichita: David S. Rood.

NOTES:

2. Comanche: also *piakwasiʔ* 'big-tail', *pawihtima* 'water-dammer'; Tonkawa: 'tree-gnawer'.
4. Comanche: 'paws earth with foot'; Kansa: 'buffalo bull' (*ččemí* 'buffalo cow'); Mandan and Teton: 'buffalo, buffalo cow'.
8. Mandan: 'excrement-eating "horse" '; *wrį́se* (*wrį́s-*) 'horse' is archaically also 'dog'.
9. Comanche: also *kwihnai.*
11. Arapaho: *nówoʔ* was the old plural, later used as a singular and stem (Hayden 1862:331; Goddard 1998:191).
21. Comanche: 'striped-tail'.
22. Tonkawa: 'falling white'.
27. Crow: 'growing wood' (*waré* 'wood'); Kiowa: contains *-dɔ̀* (singular).

[mini]; Hidatsa *wirí* is [mirí], in the nineteenth century [midi], [bidi], and [mini]; and Mandan *wrį̨ʔ* is [mįnį̨ʔ] (Lowie 1960:370; Thomas Say in James 1823:lxxix; W. Matthews 1877:192). Similarly, words in Assiniboine and Stoney would look different if transcribed in the more innovative dialects of these languages. For example, the general Sioux-Assiniboine-Stoney word *tʰípi* 'house' is pronounced [tʰíbi] by speakers of Assiniboine born in the twentieth century and by the Mountain Stoney.

Among some Plains groups, a word similar to the name of a deceased person was replaced in the speech community. This practice is reported for the Kiowa, Plains Apache, and Tonkawa (vol. 17:212; Goddard 1979a:359–363). The social mechanisms for replacing a word and for possibly later reviving it are not known, but this custom can be expected to have had some permanent impact on vocabulary turnover.

The Plains peoples learned each other's languages to only a minimal extent, although there were some regional lingua francas, including Blackfoot within the Blackfoot Confederacy, Plains Cree on the Northern Plains, and Comanche on the Southern Plains (vol. 17:118–120). The borrowing of words from other languages was rare, the largest category being perhaps tribal names. For example, Mandan *šóta* 'Cheyenne' (Mauricio Mixco, personal communication 1999) is from Cheyenne *sóʔtaaʔe* 'Sutaio', a former Cheyenne band; Cree *sa·si·w* 'Sarcee' (vol. 17:438) is from Blackfoot *sa·hsiwa* (Frantz and Russell 1995:194). Unusual cases are the borrowing of the Dhegiha Siouan word for '(black) bear' into Comanche, perhaps from Osage (see table 1), and the borrowing of Kiowa *séndé*, the name of the culture hero, as Crow *čé·te* 'wolf; bogeyman' (Robert L. Rankin, personal communication 1999). Related languages whose speakers were in proximity to each other may show some convergence in vocabulary as a result of mutual influence; the clearest cases of this kind are Plains Cree and Saulteaux, in the Algonquian family, and Mandan and Hidatsa, in Siouan.

The most widespread means of coping with the linguistic diversity of the region was through the use of Plains Indian sign language (vol. 17:275–282), a moderately elaborate conventional language of gestures used throughout the Plains, with some local variation (fig. 2). The sign language seems to have originated in the heavily polyglot region of southern Texas and the Gulf Coast and to have spread north within the early historical period (Goddard 1979a:355–356; Wurtzburg and Campbell 1995). In this area Álvar Nuñez Cabeza de Vaca found a fully developed sign language in use already in the years following 1527 (Wurtzburg and Campbell 1995:154–158). There is a credible reference to a comprehensive sign language being used by the Querechos and Teyas in eastern New Mexico and west Texas in 1541–1542 in the records of the Francisco Vásquez de Coronado expedition (A.R. Taylor 1978a; cf. Samarin 1987:66). The Querechos were probably Plains Apacheans (vol. 10:382, 387, 393; Habicht-Mauche 1992:154–255), and at least some Apacheans had trade relations with Gulf Coast groups (Goddard 1979a:369, 383). The Teyas may have been Caddoans (Habicht-Mauche 1992:255–256). In contrast, in the accounts of the journey of Louis-Joseph Gaultier de La Vérendrye and his brother François Gaultier Du Tremblay in 1742–1743 (vol. 4:28, 358) there is one unspecific reference to the use of "signs," but otherwise the Frenchmen communicated with various Northern Plains groups through Spanish or by learning a little of the local languages. The impression is left that there was then as yet no sign language in general use in that region (Burpee 1927:406–432).

Languages Other Than Algonquian, Caddoan, and Siouan

Athapaskan

Three Athapaskan languages were spoken on the Plains in the nineteenth and twentieth centuries: Sarcee, Lipan, and Plains Apache (referred to in vols. 6, 9, 10, and 17 as Kiowa Apache or Kiowa-Apache). Sarcee is a northern Athapaskan language (vol. 6:67–85), and Lipan and Plains Apache are members of the Apachean branch of the family (vol. 10:393–400). Apachean was also presumably spoken by other groups of Plains Apacheans that were encountered in the early historical period. (The Plains Apacheans were referred to collectively as the Plains Apache in vol. 10.)

• SARCEE Sarcee does not have close dialectal ties with other northern Athapaskan languages and has a number of features that set it off sharply from its nearest Athapaskan-speaking neighbors, with whom its speakers had little contact (vol. 6:84–85). It has been described in a grammar by E.-D. Cook (1984). The first publication on Sarcee was a brief vocabulary obtained by Umfreville (1790); additional publications are given in volume 17:751. Edward Sapir's manuscripts on Sarcee, recorded in 1922, are in the American Philosophical Society, Philadelphia (Kendall 1982:90). In 1999 there were 52 speakers remaining (E.-D. Cook, personal communication 1999).

• LIPAN Within the Apachean branch of Athapaskan Lipan and Jicarilla form the Eastern Apachean subbranch. The earliest vocabulary was collected by Berlandier and Chowell (1828–1829). Most of what is known of the language is from the work done in 1940 by Harry Hoijer, whose main publication is an analyzed text dictated by Augustina Zuazua (Hoijer 1975; vol. 17:739). Some other texts collected by Hoijer are in the American Philosophical Society, Philadelphia (Kendall 1982:64), but he apparently discarded his field notes before his death and no copies are known. In 1999 some individuals remained on the Mescalero Apache Reservation who identified themselves as of Lipan descent, but the distinctive Lipan variety of Apachean was no longer used. A few people retained knowledge of some Lipan words and expressions, but the language was effectively extinct (Scott Rushforth, communication to editors 1999).

• PLAINS APACHE Plains Apache forms one of the three subbranches of Apachean, together with Western Apache and Eastern Apache, but it is the most divergent language in the Apachean branch, the other two subbranches being linguistically closer to each other than they are to it (vol. 10:393–400; Huld 1983:189). The most extensive studies of Plains Apache were conducted by Harry Hoijer in the 1930s and William E. Bittle (1956, 1963) in the 1950s and 1960s; their papers are in the Alaska Native Language Center, Fairbanks; the American Indian Studies Research Institute, Indiana University, Bloomington; and the Western History Collection, University of Oklahoma, Norman. The earliest extant documentation was made by Gatschet (1884b); Pliny E. Goddard's field notes from 1903–1911 are in the American Philosophical Society, Philadelphia (J.F. Freeman 1966:80).

There were about 10 fluent speakers in 1980, and in 1999 three speakers remained, all in their 80s or 90s (Liebe-Harkort 1980:88; Willem de Reuse, personal communication 1999). Pursuant to the Indian Education Act of 1972 (Public Law 92–318), an after-school language program for children was begun in 1973 and continued for two years, using an alphabet based on English that omitted the marking of tones and vowel nasalization (Liebe-Harkort 1980:88, 90–91). A grant was received in 1999 to support a language mentoring program and school instruction (Pamela Innes, personal communication 1999).

Other Families

• COMANCHE Comanche is the sole representative of the Uto-Aztecan language family on the Plains. It is a member of the Central subbranch of the Numic branch of the family, but although clearly an offshoot of the Shoshone language it has diverged enough to become a separate language since separating from its congeners in the Great Basin and Wyoming (vol. 10:113–124, 11:99, 101).

The earliest record of Comanche is the band and chiefs' names and scattered words that appear in Spanish documents after the middle of the eighteenth century (A.B. Thomas 1929; Pino 1812:36–39; synonymy in "Comanche," this vol.). In that period Comanche had not yet undergone the loss of nasal segments in clusters, an innovation that would later distinguish Comanche from Shoshone. For example, the band name Yamparica appears for later Comanche *yaparihka* 'yampah root (*Perideridia gairdneri*) eaters', and Cuchantica and Cuchuntica for *kuhcutihka* 'buffalo eaters'. The earliest vocabulary was recorded by Berlandier and Chowell (1828–1829).

Comanche grammar has been described by Charney (1993), and Casagrande (1954–1955) treats aspects of the language that reflect recent innovation, particularly in the lexicon, with some information from nineteenth-century vocabularies; see also the section on sources in "Comanche," this volume, and volume 17:729–730.

In 1999 there were fewer than 100 fluent speakers of

left, Mont. Histl. Soc., Helena.

Fig. 2. Use of sign communication in the 20th century. Oral narratives were often accompanied by signs using the pan-Plains sign language, a method of intra- and intertribal communication. left, Brave Wolf, Cheyenne, using signs in interview with Olin D. Wheeler, wearing beaded moccasins, (second from left, taking notes). Brave Wolf relates a narrative about the Battle of the Little Bighorn while his wife, Corn Woman, listens to the account. Squint Eye, the interpreter, on the right, is also taking notes. Photograph by Laton A. Huffman, Cheyenne Res., Mont., 1901. right, James Earthboy, Assiniboine, using signs in a modern narrative. He is describing Assiniboine territory (Farnell 1995:59–116). Photograph by Philip Deloria, at Snake Butte, Ft. Belknap Res., Mont., 1988.

Comanche; they were mostly over the age of 70, with the youngest being 55. About 500 more, all 50 and older, were semispeakers. The Comanche tribe sponsored a master-apprentice language immersion program and a dictionary development program (Bill Southard, personal communication 1999).

• KIOWA Kiowa forms a branch of the Kiowa-Tanoan language family; the other branches of this family—Jemez, Tiwa, Tewa, and Piro—are or were spoken by Pueblo peoples of the Southwest. The name Kiowa-Tanoan reflects the fact that this family unites two of the stocks recognized by Powell (1891), Kiowan and Tañoan, but the "Tanoan" languages of the Pueblos do not form a distinct branch of the family more closely related to each other than to Kiowa (I. Davis 1979:401–403; vol. 9:171, 17:95–96). The membership of Kiowa in this family was shown by Harrington (1910) and further documented in other studies (W.R. Miller 1959; Trager and Trager 1959; K.L. Hale 1962, 1967; vol. 17:317). Linguistic evidence sheds no light on the question of whether the family originated in the Puebloan Southwest or on the Plains.

It is possible that there were dialects of Kiowa at one time. Kiowa tradition reports that a band called the K'úato (**kʰúttɔ́* 'the ones who pulled themselves out'), who were wiped out in the late eighteenth century, spoke "a peculiar dialect" (Mooney 1898:157–158; Laurel Watkins, personal communication 1999). The nineteenth-century Kiowa may have incorporated a group called the Wetapahato or Pitapahoto that Truteau implies spoke a different language (Moulton 1983–, 3:421–422; Truteau in Nasatir 1952, 1:301, 304, 309, 2:379); nothing is known of their speech, but, despite Truteau and their Northern Caddoan name, it is conceivable that they spoke a Kiowa dialect. However, although there is some variation in Kiowa, no clearly defined dialects are known.

Kiowa has been described in a grammar by Watkins and McKenzie (1984) and a dictionary with paradigms by Harrington (1928); see also volume 17:737. Parker P. McKenzie (b. 1897, d. 1999), a Kiowa speaker who worked with John P. Harrington beginning in 1918 (McKenzie and Harrington 1948), spent his life compiling Kiowa materials, which he wrote in a fully phonemic transcription of his own devising. Writings by him are in the National Anthropological Archives, Smithsonian Institution, and in the Oklahoma State Historical Society, Oklahoma City, which has a set of the privately duplicated primers and wordlists that he prepared. The first Kiowa vocabulary to be published was collected by Lt. Amiel W. Whipple in 1849 (Whipple, Ewbank, and Turner 1855:78–80).

In 1999 there were perhaps 200 fluent speakers of Kiowa, probably none of whom was younger than 60, and some younger semispeakers. There were no tribally sponsored language programs, but some language classes were conducted intermittently in various locations, including the University of Oklahoma, Norman (Laurel Watkins, personal communication 1999).

• TONKAWA Tonkawa is a language isolate. Suggested distant relationships with various other language families have not received general support (vol. 17:314, 316,319).

There is some evidence that dialects of Tonkawa or a similar language were spoken by some of the political allies of the Tonkawa that were absorbed by them in the late eighteenth and early nineteenth centuries, but some claims about other Tonkawa speakers have been shown to be unlikely. Tonkawa tradition recalls one such Tonkawa-speaking tribe as the Yakwal (Gatschet in Hodge 1907–1910, 2:985–986). Sibley (1832:722) listed the Mayeye (as "Mayes") in 1805 as speaking "a language of their own," distinct from those of all their neighbors, including the Tonkawa, but a Tonkawa recalled in 1884 that they (the "Méye" or "Míyi") had spoken a Tonkawa dialect (Gatschet 1891:36–37). Herbert E. Bolton made the influential claim that the Ervipiame, Mayeye, and Yojuane, who were prominent allies of the Tonkawa in the eighteenth century, spoke languages related to Tonkawa in a group he called Tonkawan (Hodge 1907–1910, 2:783). Bolton's claim was most strongly supported by documentary indications that the mission of San Francisco Xavier de Horcasitas was founded in 1748 for these three tribes, that this mission was one of three on the San Gabriel River to which the Spaniards had the express policy of assigning Indians on the basis of linguistic affinity, and that the Tonkawa were later assigned to this mission (Bolton 1908a; Bolton in Hodge 1907–1910, 1:432, 2:354, 438, 778–779, 998–999; Fletcher and Bolton in Hodge 1907–1910, 1:824–825; Goddard 1979a:358–359). However, Bolton's conclusion was called into question by evidence that the Ervipiame were one of several small groups that had migrated from northeastern Coahuila to east-central Texas after 1708, and that Tonkawas had never, in fact, moved to San Francisco Xavier mission (T.N. Campbell 1979:13–14, 1988:75, 138–139; vol. 10:346; "Tonkawa," this vol.). Bolton (in Hodge 1907–1910, 2:422–423, 779) also conjectured that Tonkawa dialects might have been spoken by the Sana, Emet, Cagua (Cava), Toho, and Tohaha, small bands known not to have spoken Coahuilteco that were along the middle and upper Guadalupe and Colorado rivers between the Tonkawa speakers and the Coahuilteco speakers in the eighteenth century. The distinctness of the Sana language can be confirmed from the phonological shape of Sana names (L. Johnson and T.N. Campbell 1992), but there is no evidence that it was related to Tonkawa. It remains possible that some of the bands known historically to have been allied with the Tonkawa became partly bilingual or even adopted Tonkawa speech, but none of them can be definitely shown to have been original speakers of Tonkawa or a related language.

The earliest information on Tonkawa is a vocabulary recorded by Rafael Chowell and a few words noted by Jean Louis Berlandier (Berlandier and Chowell 1828–1829; Berlandier 1980, 2:313, 383). Most existing knowledge of Tonkawa comes from the publications of Harry Hoijer, which were based on fieldwork conducted in 1927–1931;

these include a grammar (1933, 1946a), a dictionary (1949), and texts (1972). Gatschet's (1884c) field notes contain additional information. Tonkawa kinship terminology was examined by Troike (1969, 1970), who found evidence for contact with Caddo. Hoijer's field notes and other manuscripts on Tonkawa are not extant; apparently he discarded them before his death (Rudolph C. Troike, personal communication 1999).

The impact of the custom of replacing a word similar to a deceased person's name probably accounts for the differences in basic vocabulary seen in Tonkawa vocabularies recorded at different dates. (All examples that have been identified are nouns.) For example, words given for 'hand' are: ⟨cheque⟩ (Berlandier and Chowell 1828–1829), ⟨nāt-a-pan′⟩ (A. Pike 1861c), ⟨nonton⟩ (i.e. *no·nto·n*) (Oscar Loew in Gatschet 1876:101), and *nonoto·n* 'hand, fingers' (Hoijer 1949:27, 28). The last two forms are derived from a verb meaning 'touch with the hand or fingers', and the second form also has the shape of a noun based on a verb. In some cases a word appears to have been replaced and then later revived, as with the words for 'woman': ⟨cuan⟩ (Berlandier and Chowell 1828–1829), ⟨pa´-ho-e-tan´⟩ (A. Pike 1861c), ⟨bekhueta⟩ (Oscar Loew in Gatschet 1876:99), *k^wa·n* (Hoijer 1949:34). This suggests that it was possible for replaced words to come back into use, perhaps as replacements themselves, and there is other evidence that knowledge of proscribed words was retained in the speech community (Goddard 1979a:362). If Tonkawa dialects were formerly spoken in more than one speech community, these could also have served as reservoirs of replacement words. Nevertheless, over time this custom would have accelerated the turnover of nouns in the basic vocabulary, and the resulting need to coin new words probably accounts for why so many basic nouns in Tonkawa are derived from verbs (Hoijer 1933:101–102), for example: *ha·ʔako·n* 'man' (< *ha·ʔakewa-* 'to copulate'), *yamʔacxan* 'nose' (< 'sneeze'), *yak^{w}an* 'leg' (< 'kick'), *nencopan* 'bear' (< 'dip meat in grease'), *heylapan* 'tree' (< 'stand'), *sʔe·tan* 'rope' (< 'cut with a knife').

Tonkawa is extinct, although one fairly proficient semi-speaker was living in the late 1980s (Rudolph C. Troike, personal communication 1999).

The Algonquian Languages of the Plains

IVES GODDARD

There are seven languages spoken in the Plains area that are members of the widespread Algonquian family: Plains Cree, Saulteaux, Mitchif, Blackfoot, Gros Ventre, Arapaho, and Cheyenne. Outside the Plains, Algonquian languages are found in the Subarctic (vol. 6:52–66) and in the Northeast (vol. 15:70–77, 583–587).

Three of the Algonquian languages of the Plains are varieties of languages whose speakers are located predominantly in other culture areas. Plains Cree and Mitchif are dialects of Cree, and Saulteaux is a dialect of Ojibwa. Blackfoot, Gros Ventre, Arapaho, and Cheyenne, in contrast, are spoken only by Plains tribes and are conventionally referred to as the Plains Algonquian languages. These do not form a linguistically distinct branch of the family but are grouped together simply because of their geographical location. Blackfoot and Cheyenne are each single languages with a minimal amount of internal dialectal variation, but Gros Ventre and Arapaho are closely related members of an Arapahoan subgroup that includes several additional, extinct languages as well.

Plains Cree

Plains Cree is the westernmost dialect of the Cree language. It is most readily distinguished from other dialects by the use of *y* for the original **r* (or **l*) of Proto-Algonquian, the reconstructed ancestral protolanguage of the Algonquian family:

Proto-Algonquian	Moose Cree	Plains Cree
**ro·tenwi* 'the wind blows'	*lo·tin*	*yo·tin*

Plains Cree also lacks the contrast between *s* and *š* retained by some other dialects and differs in vocabulary and in the details of inflections:

Proto-Algonquian	Moose Cree	Plains Cree
**name·ʔsa* 'fish'	*name·s* 'fish'	[not in use]
**kenwešye·wa* 'pike'	*kinoše·w* 'pike'	*kinose·w* 'fish'
**wa·pameθankwe* 'that he sees us (incl.)'	*e·-wa·pamitahk*	*e·-wa·pamikoyahk*

The Plains Cree ending *-ikoyahk* 'he (acting) on us (inclusive)' in the last example is one of a set of recent innovations in the forms for action between a third-person and a first- or second-person plural in the conjunct order. Religious translations made in the nineteenth century show older forms identical to those in Moose Cree still in use in Plains Cree (Dahlstrom 1989). In the twentieth century Plains Cree was distinct enough from other varieties to be considered a separate language.

Within Plains Cree there are two subdialects; in the northern dialect *e·* merges with *i·*:

Proto-Algonquian	Southern Plains Cree	Northern Plains Cree
**na·pe·wa* 'man'	*na·pe·w*	*na·pi·w*

Northern Plains Cree is spoken by people classified ethnographically as the Western Woods Cree of the Subarctic area (see vol. 6:256). It is distinct from the Woods Cree language, which has ð as the reflex of Proto-Algonquian **r*.

Plains Cree has been widely used as a contact language by Euro-Canadians and by Indians other than Crees (Scollon and Scollon 1979; A.R. Taylor 1981:178; Rhodes 1982). In fact, some ethnic Ojibwa, Saulteaux, and Assiniboine individuals and communities speak Plains Cree as their dominant or only Indian language. This is the case, for example, in the Assiniboine communities on the Mosquito and Grizzly Bear's Head reserves, Saskatchewan, and among the Turtle Mountain Chippewa of North Dakota, who also speak Mitchif.

There is a large literature on Plains Cree, including grammars (vol. 17:390–439), dictionaries (Bloomfield 1984; Wolfart and Ahenakew 1998), and text collections (see vol. 17:748). Vernacular writing in Plains Cree is mostly in the Cree syllabary, or syllabics (vol. 17:175). The first extensive descriptions of Plains Cree as distinct from other varieties were by Albert Lacombe (1874, 1874a) and James Hunter (1875); earlier vocabularies were collected by Daniel Harmon (1820:385–403), Thomas Say (in Keating 1824, 2:450–459), and Prince Maximilian (1839–1841, 2:505–515).

Mitchif

Mitchif, also called French Cree, Métif, Michif, and Métchif, was historically the in-group language of the Métis communities of the northern Plains, whose members used French or Plains Cree, and later English, in dealing with outsiders. It can be described as a variety of Plains Cree in which almost all the nouns, in fact most of the components of the noun phrase, and some other words are borrowed from a variety of western Canadian French (vol. 6:56, 17:113–114, 132–133; Rhodes 1977, 1986; Papen 1987; Bakker 1990, 1992, 1997).

Saulteaux

Saulteaux (ˈsōtō) is the westernmost dialect of Ojibwa, spoken from the area of the Lake of the Woods across southern Manitoba and reaching as far west as several locations in Saskatchewan and the O'Chiese Reserve (Rocky Mountain House) in Alberta (vol. 6:54, 56–58; Valentine 1986). The western dialects are spoken in the Plains area by people known as Saulteaux in Canada and Plains Ojibwa in the United States, and the eastern dialects are spoken by the Saulteaux of the Subarctic area. There is a fair amount of internal diversity within Saulteaux, often reflecting dialectal ties with different non-Saulteaux dialects. There is noticeable influence from Plains Cree on some local forms of Saulteaux. In Saskatchewan Saulteaux the general Ojibwa contrast between *s* and *š* is lost, as in Plains Cree, with phonetic [š] used before front vowels and phonetic [s] before back vowels in the reflexes of both segments (Paul Voorhis, personal communication 1990).

Belcourt's (1839) grammar of Saulteaux was the first grammar of an Algonquian language to mark vowel length. The pedagogical grammar by Voorhis (1977) includes dialectal variants.

Blackfoot

Of all the Algonquian languages, Blackfoot (figs. 1–2) differs most from the others. It is not clear to what extent this divergence may be an archaic feature, reflecting a stage of Algonquian earlier than that continued by all the other languages, or the result of extensive innovations, or a combination of these factors (Goddard 1994:187–189). Typically, for example, the correspondences outside Blackfoot of many of its phonological patterns are obscure, but all the correspondences that have been worked out involve innovations, often extensive, on the part of Blackfoot rather than on the part of the rest of the languages as a group (A.R. Taylor 1978, Thomson 1978, Proulx 1989). There is a very slight degree of variation among the local forms of Blackfoot spoken on different reserves in Canada and in the United States, mostly in certain idiomatic expressions. Frantz and Russell (1989:ix) have pointed out that "there is as much variation between speakers from the same reserve as there is between speakers from different reserves."

For Blackfoot both a grammar (Frantz 1991) and a dictionary (Frantz and Russell 1989, 1995) are available. Blackfoot was first known from brief vocabularies

Glenbow-Alberta Inst., Calgary, Alta.: NA 250-4.

Fig. 1. Interior of St. John the Divine Anglican Mission church, Blackfoot Res., Alta. The first Anglican mission on the reserve, it was built by Rev. John W. Tims in 1883. The Bible verses in Blackfoot on the wall hangings are, left to right: 'Christ Jesus came to this earth to rescue sinners' (1 Timothy 1:15), 'The blood of Jesus Christ erases our sins' (1 John 1:7), and 'God so loved all people that he gave his only son to die so that these people might not die but live forever' (John 3:16). Photograph by William H. Boorne of the Boorne and Ernest G. May studio, 1886.

Glenbow-Alberta Inst., Calgary.: NA-1713-16/ translation M4359.

Fig. 2. Blackfoot letter in syllabics sent to King George V, on the occasion of the 25th year of his reign, 1935. Devised in the 1890s by Anglican missionaries Harry Stocken, John W. Tims, and Joshua Hinchliffe, the Blackfoot syllabary was used in tracts printed at the Calgary Indian Industrial School between 1905 and 1907, when the school closed. The script then gradually went out of use. Written on rawhide.

The accompanying translation reads:

"Your Majesty King George V, may the Supreme Being grant you all that is good, so you may lead us to happiness, prosperity, usefullness and long life.

You have reigned over us Twenty Five years and may the Supreme One spare you to reign over us a long time.

Duck Chief. Paul Little Walker. Turned Up Nose. One Gun. Linden Many Bears. Heavy Shield. Pilor Fox. Philip Backfat. Teddy Yellowfly.

Blackfoot Indian Tribe, Gleichen, Alberta Canada.

Blackfoot Tribal Motto—'Be Wise and Persevere.'"

collected by traders in the eighteenth century, and by the end of the following century the first grammars and extensive vocabularies had appeared (vol. 17:23, 30). Prince Maximilian (1839–1841, 1:584–585, 2:474–480) published an extensive vocabulary, as did Hayden (1862:266–273); both took exceptional care in their work and despite imperfections in transcription their publications contain much useful information on a number of Plains languages. John W. Tims, a Protestant missionary among the Canadian Blackfoot, published a grammar and dictionary (1889). The Dutch scholar C.C. Uhlenbeck did fieldwork among the Blackfeet of Montana in 1910 and 1911, producing two volumes of texts (1911, 1912), a grammar (1938), and a two-volume dictionary (Uhlenbeck and van Gulik 1930, 1934; see also vol. 17:724–725). Josselin de Jong (1914) is a collection of Blackfoot texts with an English translation. A.R. Taylor wrote a grammar (1969) and a paper on ethnobotany (1989).

Cheyenne

Cheyenne (fig. 3) exhibits considerable superficial divergence from other Algonquian languages, as a result of extensive innovations, particularly in the phonology, most of which have been worked out in considerable detail (Goddard 1988). The most unusual of these innovations is the restructuring of the Proto-Algonquian opposition of long and short vowels into a tone system with four contrastive level tones derived from an underlying opposition of high and low tones (Leman 1981). The Northern Cheyenne and Southern Cheyenne speak the language in identical form, the only divergences being very occasional differences in idiomatic detail and meaning, especially in relatively recent expressions. For example, 'apples' is Northern Cheyenne *maˀxemèno* (animate gender) but Southern Cheyenne *maˀxemènOtse* (inanimate gender), and the inanimate-gender form that means 'apples' in Southern Cheyenne means 'plums' in Northern Cheyenne (Glenmore and Leman 1984:8).

Few definite traces have been found of the dialect of the Sutaio (Cheyenne *sóˀtaeoˀo*, sing. *sóˀtaaˀe*), who were absorbed into the Cheyenne in the nineteenth century (Goddard 1978). One Cheyenne speaker in the 1970s labeled variant forms of many words as Sutaio (Alford and Leman 1976), but most of these are in fact simply the nondiminutive forms of words that are usually used in a diminutive form. (The nondiminutive often lacks a *k* or *hk* found in the corresponding diminutive.) It is possible that Cheyenne speakers of Sutaio descent tended to favor nondiminutive forms. J.H. Moore (1984:293–294) reports the dropping of *k* as one of the features characteristic of the speech of Southern Cheyennes "representing" the Sutaio, but he gives no examples. The relative uniformity of the language of the Cheyenne is consistent with their unity as a tribe in the nineteenth century and the fact that their division into northern and southern groups was not an old feature of their political organization.

The Sutaio ("Chouta") were mentioned in 1796 as one of three bands of Cheyennes along branches of the Cheyenne River of South Dakota near the Black Hills, the others being the Ouisy (or Ouisay) and the Cheyenne proper, who were the largest (Jean-Baptiste Truteau in Nasatir 1952, 1:304, 2:379). By 1804 the Cheyenne are described as being in two villages, on opposite sides of the Cheyenne River, one that the Arikaras called by their name for the Cheyenne (*ša·héˀ*) and the other called We hee Shaw (Lewis and Clark in Moulton 1983–, 3:136, 138, 420). It is likely that whatever dialectal differentiation may have existed in these bands rapidly disappeared after they consolidated in the nineteenth century.

There were also traces in Cheyenne of a distinctive men's pronunciation, in which the *k* in *ke* was pronounced as [t^y] or [č] and the *sk* of other speakers was pronounced *šk*. This distinction gradually disappeared in the course of the twentieth century, with the generalization of the men's

Mennonite Indian Leaders Council, Busby, Mont.

Fig. 3. Title page and 3 hymns from a Cheyenne hymn book (Mennonite Indian Leaders Council 1982). Some of the hymns were translated or adapted by missionaries from English or German hymns, and others were composed by Cheyenne church members. Drawing by Hazel Shorey.

pronunciation in the case of *šk* and the other pronunciation in the case of *ke* (Goddard 1978:77–78; Michelson 1935:156). The exact social conditions for the use of the men's speech are not known.

Descriptive materials for Cheyenne include a grammar with extensive paradigms (Leman 1980), a preliminary topical dictionary (Glenmore and Leman 1984, 1985), and texts (Leman 1987; Croft 1988). The first records of Cheyenne were those of Prince Maximilian (1839–1841, 2:487–489) and of Lieut. James W. Abert, who worked with John S. Smith, a White trader who spoke the language, at Bent's Fort in present eastern Colorado in 1846 (Abert 1848:11–14; Mooney 1907:428, 435, 441). Smith's own vocabulary of Cheyenne was published by Schoolcraft (1851–1857, 3:446–459). Hayden (1862:283–320) obtained an extensive vocabulary and grammatical information. The Swiss Mennonite missionary Rodolphe Petter, who worked among the Southern Cheyenne from 1891 to 1947, produced a massive dictionary, which includes much cultural information, as well as grammatical descriptions (Petter 1907, 1913–1915, 1952; Mooney 1907:438–439; vol. 17:727).

Arapaho

The Arapahoan languages were, in traditional north-to-south order, Gros Ventre (sometimes called Atsina), Besawunena, Arapaho, and Nawathinehena. They formed a group that shared certain innovations not found elsewhere in Algonquian, most noticeably the loss in all positions of Proto-Algonquian **k* and the later or concomitant shift of Proto-Algonquian **p* to Arapahoan **k* (with subsequent palatalization in certain environments; table 1). There was a fifth traditional Arapahoan language, Ha'anahawunena (*hó·ˀonohowû·nénnóˀ*), but not a single word of it was ever recorded. The first three of these languages were similar enough so that in aboriginal times their speakers probably could understand each other with a little practice, but Nawathinehena was phonologically very different.

Arapaho was spoken in the historical period in nearly identical form by both the Northern Arapahoe and the Southern Arapaho. The two dialects differ only in a few expressions, especially for items of recent introduction. For example 'harness' is Northern Arapahoe *číítooˀoyóó* Southern Arapaho *čečehnóókuθóó* (Salzmann 1960:40).

There is a grammar of Arapaho (Salzmann 1963), partly published (Salzmann 1956, 1961, 1965, 1965a, 1967), a dictionary (Salzmann 1983), and a collection of texts (Salzmann 1956a, 1956b). The first published vocabulary of Arapaho was one compiled by John S. Smith (Schoolcraft 1851–1857, 3:446–459), and Hayden's (1862:328–339) vocabulary has significant data. A.L. Kroeber studied Arapaho and the other extant Arapahoan languages during his 1899–1901 fieldwork (Kroeber 1916; vol. 17:723). His field notes and those from Truman Michelson's 1929 fieldwork are in the National Anthropological Archives, Smithsonian Institution.

Table 1. Representative Comparative Vocabulary of the Plains Languages

Gloss	*Proto-Algonquian*	*Arapaho*	*Gros Ventre*	*Nawathinehena*	*Cheyenne*	*Blackfoot*
'dog'	*aθemwa	*héθ*[a]	*ʔɔ́t*	⟨hăʹtam⟩	*hótame*[b]	*imitá·wa*[c]
'man'	*erenyiwa	*hinén*	*ʔinín*	⟨hitĕʹn⟩	*hetane*	*nína·wa*[d]
'woman'	*eθkwe·wa	*hísei*	*ʔíθɛ·*	⟨hĭhĩĭʹ⟩	*hēʔe*	(*a·kí·wa*)[e]
'hare'	*wa·poswa	*nó·ku*	*nɔ́·kɔ́·c*[f]	⟨māa^{n}kŭʹt⟩	*vóóhe*[g]	(*a·pátsínnapisiwa*)[h]
'water'	*nepyi	*néč*	*níc*	⟨nêʹtc⟩	*mahpe*[i]	(*aohkí·yi*)[j]
'bowstring'	*meʔtekwa·pyi	*be·téyo·k*	*bɛ̂·tíyɔ·c*	—	*maʔtāno*	—

NOTE: Forms in italics are phonemic according to the sources; Nawathinehena forms in shallow-pointed brackets reproduce the original impressionistic field transcription. Parenthesized forms are not cognate.

SOURCES: Salzmann (1956, 1983), A.R. Taylor (1967), Kroeber (1899), Glenmore and Leman (1984), Frantz and Russell (1989).

[a] With vowel assimilation before regular final syllable loss.

[b] Final syllable restored; tone not original.

[c] Cognate assuming consonant metathesis and reshaping of the end (cf. 'man').

[d] Cognate assuming consonant assimilation and reshaping of the end (cf. 'dog')

[e] Similar but probably not cognate because of first vowel and lack of cluster; Blackfoot *ohki·mi-* 'have a wife' appears to reflect Proto-Algonquian **we(te)θkwe·mi-* 'have a woman', a verb of possession derived from **eθkwe·wa* 'woman'.

[f] Has added *nɔ́·k-* 'white'.

[g] More commonly *vóhkóóhe*, with the addition of *vóhk-* 'crooked'.

[h] A new coinage, literally 'long hind legs'.

[i] First consonant assimilated in position to the second.

[j] Etymology unknown.

Gros Ventre

Arapaho, Gros Ventre, and Besawunena share certain innovations that set them apart as a subgroup within Arapahoan. For example, Proto-Algonquian **w*, when not following a consonant, became *n* in these three languages but remained as a labial (variously written) in Nawathinehena (table 1, 'hare'). Such shared innovations show that these three languages descend from a single intermediate common language spoken sometime in the past, but they had already developed into distinct languages by the time of the earliest historical records. By the accident of having come into contact with Canadian traders in the eighteenth century, the Gros Ventre were the first Arapahoan group to have specimens of their language recorded, and these records already show distinct features of the Gros Ventre language, albeit with some archaic details (Umfreville 1954:104; G. Williams 1969:211; Pentland 1979:110).

A distinct men's pronunciation has been described for Gros Ventre (Flannery 1946; Salzmann 1969; A.R. Taylor 1982), but the details are uncertain. Apparently for the *č* of men's speech, and for t^y if this was a distinct phoneme, women's speech had the pronunciation [k], or perhaps [k^y]. Pentland (1979:113–114) argues that this distinction was not present before the second half of the nineteenth century, since early vocabularies (those of Umfreville, Maximilian 1839–1841, 2:499–500, and Hayden 1862:344–345) consistently show spellings of k^y for later men's *č* (apparently distinct from t^y). Taylor's experience suggests that the matter may be more complex.

A preliminary dictionary of Gros Ventre includes extensive material on inflectional paradigms (A.R. Taylor 1994). An earlier vocabulary from the same author, with a comparative vocabulary of Arapaho, records a conservative pronunciation of Gros Ventre men's speech that preserved some contrasts not found in the later material (A.R. Taylor 1967).

Besawunena

Besawunena is known from a word list collected by Kroeber (1916:74–76; vol. 17:46), and there were speakers as late as the late 1920s among the Northern Arapahoe (Michelson 1935:131). Apparently the phonology differed only slightly from that of Arapaho, but a few additional sound changes resemble those in Gros Ventre. The Besawunena dialect must have earlier been used by a distinct Besawunena people, but such a group is not known for certain outside Arapaho tradition. Their Arapaho name is usually given as *bê·sô·wû·nénnoʔ*, literally 'big-lodge people' (Goddard 1967a; cf. Salzmann 1983:10), but the translation 'wood-lodge people' (Mooney 1896:955; Kroeber 1916:73–76) would imply a form *bésô·wû·nénnoʔ*. The name is also explained as meaning 'brush-hut people' (Kroeber 1902–1907:6–7; Curtis 1907–1930, 6:138). It is possible that the speakers of Besawunena were a tribe referred to as the Skihitanes (Squihitanes) or Staetan, who are described as speaking the same language as the Northern Arapahoe in the early nineteenth century but later disappear as a distinct group (Tabeau 1939:154; Jefferson 1806:32; Lewis and Clark 1832:707–721, in Moulton 1983–, 3:423).

Nawathinehena

Nawathinehena was the former language of the Southern Arapaho, who switched to speaking Arapaho (originally the language of only the Northern Arapahoe) in the course of the nineteenth century (Hayden 1862:321; Mooney 1896:955; Curtis 1907–1930, 6:138; Jesse Rowlodge in Michelson 1929:29). The language, known only from a vocabulary obtained among the Southern Arapaho in 1899 (Kroeber 1916:74–76), differs considerably from Arapaho. For example, it has the unusual sound shift of Proto-Algonquian **s* to [t] (table 1, 'hare'), in contrast to Arapaho and Gros Ventre, in which Proto-Algonquian **s* became *h* (subject to dropping word-finally) and *n* (word-initially). (One possibility is that **s* shifted to **z* in Nawathinehena, and word-initially in Arapaho–Gros Ventre; then **z* shifted to **r*; and then **r* underwent its regular shifts to Nawathinehena [t] and Arapaho–Gros Ventre *n*.) The distinctness of the Nawathinehena language must reflect a long period of separation between the ancestors of the Northern and Southern Arapaho, a separation also reflected by the fact that different signs are used for the two Arapaho groups in the Plains Indian sign language (W.P. Clark 1885:38–39; Mooney 1896:954; Kroeber 1902–1907:6). It is possible that the original Nawathinehena (Arapaho *no·wóθi·néhe·noˀ*, sing. *no·wóθi·néhe·*) are to be identified with the Nemousin (Nimoussine) referred to in accounts of Plains tribes in the early nineteenth century (Tabeau 1939:154; Jefferson 1806:33; Lewis and Clark 1832:707–721, in Moulton 1983–, 3:424–425). The name Nemousin has the same sequence of consonants as the former Cheyenne name for the Southern Arapaho, recorded as Nomsĭn'néo (Mooney 1907:424; cf. Keim 1885:188), and these are the regular Cheyenne correspondents of the first four consonants in the Arapaho name *no·wóθi·néhe·nóˀ*, but the disagreement in the first vowel is unexplained.

Diffusion among Plains Algonquian Languages

Although the Plains Algonquian languages do not form a subgroup of the family, they do share some features that reflect contact among them. They have all undergone two sound changes found in all Algonquian languages outside of Eastern Algonquian: the shift of Proto-Algonquian **we* to **o* (when not after a vowel) and of word-initial Proto-Algonquian **e* to **i*. (The outcomes of these changes are subject to further changes in some cases.) Cheyenne and the Arapahoan languages all merge Proto-Algonquian *i*-quality and *o*-quality vowels (with the contrast of vowel length preserved). They also underwent some similar or identical phonological innovations in different sequences, producing different outcomes (Goddard 1974:106–107, 1994:193; Pentland 1979). For example, Arapaho–Gros Ventre, Nawathinehena, and Cheyenne share the merger Proto-Algonquian **w* and **y* to **y* (unconditional in Arapaho–Gros Ventre; postconsonantal in Nawathinehena and Cheyenne); a loss of Proto-Algonquian **k* (unconditional in Arapahoan; with exceptions in Cheyenne); and a shift of **y* to *n* (initially and after vowels in Arapahoan; initially and after vowels and *h* in Cheyenne). Because Arapahoan shifted **y* to *n* before the loss of **k*, while Cheyenne underwent the parallel changes in reverse order, Proto-Algonquian **kw* is reflected by *y* in Arapaho–Gros Ventre (**kw* > **ky*; nonpostconsonantal **y* > *n* before **ky* > *y*) and by *n* in Cheyenne (**kw* > **ky* > **y* > *n*); see table 1 ('bowstring'). Such patterns of partially shared innovations suggest that linguistic influences spread back and forth between the Arapahoan languages and Cheyenne, and thus that there must have been a fairly extended period after these languages were distinct when they were in repeated close contact.

The Plains Algonquian languages also share a number of expressions, some of which are found in non-Algonquian Plains languages as well. For example, the name of the trickster–culture hero is used for 'White man': Arapaho *nihˀó·θo·*, Gros Ventre *níhˀɔ·to*, and Cheyenne *véˀhoˀe* (all cognate with Cree *wi·sahke·ča·hk*, the name of the trickster–culture hero, with some reshaping in Cheyenne), and Blackfoot *ná·piwa* (literally 'old man', from Proto-Algonquian **na·pe·wa* 'man'), which has the meaning 'White man' in derivatives (e.g., *ná·pi·koana* 'White person', with *-koan-* 'person'). In addition, the name of the trickster–culture hero in Arapaho, Gros Ventre, and Cheyenne is used as the word for 'spider', an equation also found in Sioux (Santee-Sisseton *ųktómi*, Teton *iktómi*).

In all the Plains Algonquian languages the word for 'horse' was a coinage literally meaning 'elk-dog': Arapaho *wóxu·hô·x*, earlier *hiwóxu·hô·x* (*hiwóxu·h-* 'elk' + *-ô·x* 'dog'), Gros Ventre *ˀiwɔ́si·hɔ̂·θ* (*ˀiwɔ́si·h-* 'elk' + *-ɔ̂·θ* 'dog'), Cheyenne *moˀéhnoˀha* (*moˀéh(n)-* 'elk' + *-oˀha* 'dog'), Blackfoot *ponokáómita·wa* (*ponoká-* 'elk' + *-ómita·-* 'dog'). Typically for these languages, the constituent elements in the first three have clear Algonquian roots, but those in Blackfoot do not. The words for 'elk' in Arapaho, Gros Ventre, and Cheyenne (as well as in Besawunena and Nawathinehena) reflect Proto-Algonquian **wemaško·swa* 'elk', and the elements for 'dog' go back to the noninitial element **-aˀθemw-* 'dog'. The phonetic changes are extensive but completely regular, and the Algonquian pedigree is clear. In contrast Blackfoot *ponoká-* 'elk' is apparently a descriptive coinage, with second element *-ká-* 'foot, leg', from Proto-Algonquian **-ka·-* 'leg'. Blackfoot *-ómita·wa* is a noninitial variant of *imitá·wa* 'dog', which may continue Proto-Algonquian **aθemwa* 'dog' (see table 1). The idea of referring to the horse as 'elk-dog' has thus clearly spread independently of the specific elements used with these meanings. As this is not the concept used in the Plains Indian sign language, some level of former bilingualism is indicated.

In some cases the Plains Algonquian languages refer to a feature of the Plains environment with a word whose cognates in Algonquian languages to the east refer to a feature of the woodland environment. For example, in Arapaho, Gros Ventre, and Cheyenne the reflexes of Proto-Algonquian **mo·swa* 'moose' (whence Plains Cree *mo·swa* 'moose') have shifted their meaning to 'buffalo cow': Arapaho *bí·* (Kroeber1916:76, phonemicized), Gros Ventre *bʸí·h*, Cheyenne *méhe*. There is evidence from Arapaho of an earlier meaning 'buffalo (in general)', and the narrowing of reference to 'buffalo cow' parallels that in Sioux *pté* 'buffalo cow', which reflects the old Siouan word for 'buffalo' (Goddard 1974:114-115). Buffalo cows were preferred over bulls as game. The shift of the term for 'moose' to 'buffalo, buffalo cow' must reflect the shift from reliance on moose as the largest game animal to buffalo when the ancestors of the Arapaho–Gros Ventre and of the Cheyenne moved from the woodlands to the Plains. A similar shift is found in Arapaho *hóteʔ* 'bighorn sheep' (later applied to domestic sheep), from Proto-Algonquian **atehkwa* 'caribou'.

Borrowings

The Plains Algonquian languages have borrowed very few words directly from other languages, but a few loanwords reflect early contacts. Blackfoot *napayíni* 'bread' (cf. *óʔkapayini* 'flour', with *oʔk-* 'raw') is from French *la farine* 'flour' and must have been borrowed from early traders who spoke French. In Blackfoot a person of French descent is called *ni·tsá·pi·koana*, literally 'original White person'. Arapaho *wó·keč* 'cow' (pl. *wó·keči·*), and Gros Ventre *wɔ́·kɔ̌č* must come ultimately from Spanish *vacas* 'cows', and indeed the Arapaho were in contact with Spaniards from New Mexico who came to the Green River to trade (Bolton 1913a:63–64; E. Williams 1913:197; Luttig 1920:76–77). The Spaniards did not bring cows with them over the mountains, though, and the only opportunity for borrowing the word for 'cow' would have been one of the trading expeditions to Santa Fe and other Spanish settlements that the Upper Missouri Indians undertook in the early nineteenth century (Wheat 1957–1963, 2:56, maps 289, 290). In fact, the word may have been borrowed in the Southwest through the intermediary of another Indian language (e.g., Zuni *wa·kaši* 'cow, cows').

Some words that appear to be innovations shared by Arapaho–Gros Ventre and Cheyenne have no clear Algonquian etymology. In some cases the sound correspondences exactly match what would be expected in old cognates. For example, the words for 'coyote', Arapaho *ko·ʔóh* (pl. *ko·ʔóhwu·*; Gros Ventre *kɔ·ʔɔhwóh*), and Cheyenne *óʔkOhómE*, would both regularly reflect Proto-Algonquian **pa·xkahamwa*. This has the form of a type of noun regularly derived from a certain class of transitive verbs and would mean '(the one that) opens (it) by tool', but as a word for the coyote, an animal not found in the woodlands in earlier times, it must be an innovation of Arapaho–Gros Ventre and Cheyenne. The words for 'buffalo herd', Arapaho *hí·θeino·n*, Gros Ventre *ʔí·tɛ·nɔ́·n*, Cheyenne *ésevone*, also correspond, but no etymology is suggested by any of the several possible reconstructions (**ki·čye·wa·niwa*, **ko·θwe·wa·niwa*, etc.). In other cases there is a close similarity, allowing for regular sound changes, but not an exact match, as, for example, in the words for 'magpie', a western species: Arapaho *wo·ʔúhʔei*, Nawathinehena ⟨mōŭ'xtiäⁿ⟩, Cheyenne *moʔēʔha*.

Implications for Prehistory

The grammatical and phonological divergences separating Arapahoan, Cheyenne, and Blackfoot point to a lengthy separate existence for these three western branches of the Algonquian family. At the same time, enough of the linguistic history of Arapahoan and Cheyenne has been worked out to establish firmly that these are ordinary Algonquian languages that have undergone a comparatively large amount of innovation, especially in phonology, and what is known of reconstructed Blackfoot history is consistent with a similar interpretation of Blackfoot divergence. There is no linguistic support for the conjecture that any of the Plains languages might represent the relics of an earlier more general Algonquian occupation of the Plains. Rather, the linguistic evidence supports the hypothesis that the Plains Algonquian languages moved westward onto the Plains with their speakers, separating from other Algonquian speakers who remained in the woodlands about the Upper Great Lakes. Even if archaisms not found elsewhere in Algonquian are eventually identified in Blackfoot (Goddard 1994:188–189), the overwhelmingly Algonquian character of Blackfoot grammar would rule out the conjecture (e.g., by Robins 1962:16–17) that Blackfoot in some way represents an intermediate stage between the rest of Algonquian and the distantly related Ritwan languages (Wiyot and Yurok) of northern California.

As divergent as they are superficially, the Plains Algonquian languages have remained similar enough to the non-Plains languages for their affinity to be noticed by native speakers. The Ojibwa-speaking historian William Warren (1957:33–34, 68) in the mid-nineteenth century concluded from similarities he had observed between Blackfoot and Ojibwa that Blackfoot was an Algonquian language. An Arapaho speaker interviewed in Oklahoma in 1967 pointed out cognates that linked his language to that of the Oklahoma Sac and Fox (Goddard 1967a). These retained similarities explain why the Plains Cree call the Cheyenne *ka·-ne·hiyawe·sicik* 'those whose language is a little like Cree', and why the Sioux call the Cheyenne 'the little Cree' (Teton *šahíyela*; Santee-Sisseton, Yankton-Yanktonai, Assiniboine *šahíyena* [the source of the English name]; cf. Assiniboine *šahíya* 'Cree'). Such expressions need not date back to a period when the languages were more similar, as Pentland (1979:115) suggests.

The similar words innovated in both Arapahoan and Cheyenne for some elements of the Plains environment indicate that when the ancestral speakers of these languages moved from the woodlands to the Plains they were in contact with each other. Also, the diffusion of these words must have taken place at a time when the phonologies of the languages were much less divergent than what is attested by their historically recorded shapes. This suggests that the extensive phonological innovations in Arapahoan and Cheyenne postdate the movement of these groups onto the Plains. The fact that some phonological innovations diffused between these languages would be consistent with such a conclusion. Because Cheyenne shares some of these diffused innovations with Nawathinehena but not the rest of Arapahoan, they must date to a period when Nawathinehena was in contact with Cheyenne but the rest of Arapahoan, presumably being located farther to the north, was not.

Goddard (1967) suggested that a date for these innovations within the last two or three centuries might be indicated by parallelisms in the development of the verbal inflections in Arapaho and Cree and by the fact that Arapaho *kokúy* '(long-barreled) gun' was cognate with Miami *papikwani* 'gun', since these parallel developments would have to have taken place before the extensive phonological changes in Arapaho if they are to be explained as resulting from diffusion (cf. Pentland 1979:114). However, diffusion is unlikely or impossible in both these cases. Dahlstrom (1989) has shown that the Cree innovations in question arose in the course of the nineteenth century. Kroeber (1916:117) glosses Arapaho *kokúy* as 'tube, gun, whistle', and of these meanings, 'tube' and 'gun' must be later extensions of 'whistle', which continues Proto-Algonquian **papikwani* 'flageolet, end-blown flute' (derived from **papikwe·wa* 'he plays music, as on the flageolet'). The meaning 'gun' in Arapaho and Miami is most reasonably explained as arising by independent parallel developments in the two languages.

Another piece of evidence pointing to a westward movement of the Plains Algonquian languages is the typological character of the resulting phonologies of these languages, whose reduced consonant and vowel inventories seem more similar to Caddoan languages than to other Algonquian languages. For example, the 13 consonants of Proto-Algonquian (**p*, **t*, **č*, **k*; **s*, **š*, **h*; **m*, **n*, **θ*, **r*; **w*, **y*) were reduced by regular sound changes to nine consonants in the intermediate common language of Arapaho and Gros Ventre (**t*, **k*, **ʔ*; **θ*, **š*, **h*; **m*, **n*, **y*). This reduction was produced by the loss of Proto-Algonquian **k*, by sound shifts, notably the change of Proto-Algonquian **p* to a new **k*, and by mergers, like the falling together of Proto-Algonquian **č* and **θ* to **θ* and of Proto-Algonquian **s* (noninitially) and **h* to **h*. (Later conditioned splits increase the number of consonants in both languages.) This inventory can be matched nearly one-to-one with that of Wichita, a Caddoan language: *t*, *k*, *k*ʷ, *ʔ*; *c*, *s*, *h*; *w*, *r* (realized as [r] and [n]), *y* (Rood 1971; vol. 17:583). Also, Arapahoan reduces the four vowel qualities of Algonquian (**i*, **e*, **a*, **o*) to three (**i*, **e*, **a*, subject to subsequent splits), which are the same as the three basic vowels of Wichita. The precise implications of this phonological parallelism are not clear, not the least since Wichita is spoken on the Southern Plains, and even the generally accepted earier location of the Wichita in Kansas is not very near the assumed more northerly prehistoric location of the Arapahoans. It is possible, though, that in the early years of its movement onto the Plains, Arapahoan was in contact with and influenced by a Caddoan or other language with an inventory something like that of Wichita.

Language Survival

By the 1990s the Plains Algonquian languages exhibited a great variety in the the degree of robustness with which they were spoken and used.

Blackfoot had the most speakers, estimated at 5,000 to 8,000. In Canada most adults were speakers, primarily living on the Blackfoot (Siksika), Blood, and Peigan reserves in southern Alberta. A few children were learning Blackfoot as a first language in one community of the Blood Reserve and in a few other families. In the United States, there were fewer than 100 elderly speakers on the Blackfeet Reservation in northwestern Montana (Frantz and Russell 1989:ix; Donald Frantz, personal communication 1999). Blackfoot was taught at the University of Lethbridge and at several community colleges in Canada, and there were Blackfoot language programs on the Blackfeet Reservation, Montana, in the Blackfeet Community College, and in the Browning public schools (fig. 4).

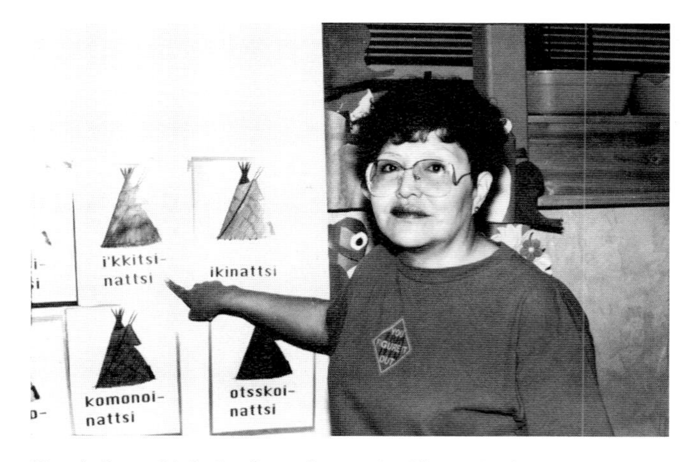

Fig. 4. Lena Little Leaf, teacher at the Piegan Institute, Moccasin Flat School, Blackfoot Language Immersion Program, Browning, Mont. The lesson is on colors and the captions read: (top left) 'gray', (top right) 'pink', (bottom left) 'violet', and (bottom right) 'blue, green'. Photograph by Joe Fisher, 1996.

There were an estimated several hundred fluent speakers of Arapaho in Oklahoma and Wyoming, including "a number of proficient speakers among the older members of the tribe" but few if any of these were teenagers or younger (Salzmann 1983:8; Zdeněk Salzmann, personal communication 1990). Literacy materials were developed for use in the schools in the Wind River Reservation area and in the Arapaho Studies curriculum of the Wyoming Indian High School.

There were about 2,000 speakers of Cheyenne in Montana and 500 in Oklahoma. Most Cheyennes over 40 in Montana were fluent, and the children in a few families were speakers, but in Oklahoma most fluent speakers were over 60. A Title VII Bilingual Education Program was initiated among the Northern Cheyenne in the 1970s (Alford and Leman 1976), and a phonemic orthography was developed that was officially adopted by the Cheyenne Tribal Council on April 21, 1997 (Wayne Leman, personal communication 1999).

Only a very few semispeakers of Gros Ventre remained in Montana.

Plains Cree and Saulteaux were spoken in the 1990s by the majority of members of these groups, including substantial numbers of children. Literacy programs and language instruction at all levels were widespread in areas where these languages were spoken.

Caddoan Languages

DOUGLAS R. PARKS

In the twentieth century the Caddoan family comprised five languages: Arikara, Pawnee, Kitsai, Wichita, and Caddo. Until the late eighteenth century speakers of these languages formed an almost unbroken population continuum extending over the tall grass prairies of the eastern Plains from South Dakota to southeastern Texas and western Louisiana ("The Languages of the Plains: Introduction," fig. 1, this vol.). That continuum was the historical result of a gradual northward movement from the southeastern Plains of the people who were the ancestors of the modern Northern Caddoan tribes. The Arikara were in the vanguard of that movement, while the Caddo remained in what is presumed to be the Caddoan homeland and are, as a consequence, the southernmost member of the family, straddling the Plains and Southeast culture areas.

Historically the Caddoan peoples were diverse socially and linguistically, forming numerous tribes and bands. However, as a result of large population losses during the eighteenth and nineteenth centuries, surviving tribes, bands, and villages coalesced into the five historically known tribes, and their former dialectal diversity gradually disappeared, until in the twentieth century only vestiges of it survived.

Arikara

The northernmost Caddoan language is Arikara, which was spoken by a large, diverse population in present South Dakota until the early nineteenth century, when the remnants of the tribe moved north into present North Dakota. Since 1862 the tribe has resided on what is now the Fort Berthold Reservation in the west-central part of the state.

In the earliest historical sources from the late eighteenth and early nineteenth centuries, fur traders and explorers who visited the Arikara observed significant dialectal diversity among them and at the same time recognized the close linguistic relationship between the Arikara bands and the Pawnee (Parks 1979a). In 1804 the Saint Louis fur trader Pierre-Antoine Tabeau, who for two years lived in one of the three Arikara villages—all that remained of more than a dozen before a series of smallpox epidemics in the late eighteenth century—wrote that there were at least 10 distinct dialects still spoken, representing former Arikara "tribes" or divisions. He stated that those dialects, jealously maintained, were characterized by marked differences in pronunciation and lexical usage that hindered mutual intelligibility, creating "linguistic confusion" even within families. He noted further that there were two major dialect groups—one whose speech was "drawling," perhaps more closely resembling contemporary Pawnee, and another whose speech was markedly different, apparently more closely resembling that of contemporary Arikara (Abel 1939:125–126; see also Clark in Thwaites 1904–1905, 1:188).

Although by the late twentieth century almost all the former diversity within Arikara speech had been leveled, there were vestiges of it in both vocabulary and phonology. A systematic phonological difference is exemplified by alternate forms of the stem for 'wood' in word-initial position: speakers in one community use the form *ha·k-*, while those in other communites have *nak-* (cf. Pawnee *ra·k-*, Kitsai *yak-*, and Wichita *ha·k-*) (Parks 1986a). Compare, for example, the following pairs illustrating the alternation in Arikara:

ha·karíkA	*na·karíkA*	'Branch Sticking Out', a village sacred bundle
ha·katá·rIt	*nakatá·rIt*	'cupboard'
ha·hna·wIškáhtš	*nAhna·wIškáhtš*	'pipe'

Writers have generally considered Arikara to be a divergent dialect of Pawnee (Gallatin 1836:129; Lesser and Weltfish 1932:2–4; A.R. Taylor 1963:54), and Arikara and Pawnee speakers in the twentieth century recognized a close lingustic relationship between their speech, some, in fact, claiming mutual intelligibility. Although in a strict linguistic sense Arikara and Pawnee are divergent dialects, Arikara has undergone numerous phonetic and phonological changes and preserved several older morphological features that Pawnee has lost. Those changes, together with extensive semantic shifts and lexical replacements, mask the underlying similarities and create on the surface what seem like greater differences than there really are. However, Arikara and Pawnee in the twentieth century, and probably for at least a century earlier, were not mutually intelligible. For that reason, as well as the political and geographical distinctness of the two groups, their speech should be considered to represent separate languages (Parks 1979:198–203).

Until the late twentieth century, documentation of the Arikara language was sparse, represented almost exclusively by relatively short wordlists. Although Tabeau recorded the names of Arikara bands and chiefs in 1804

(Abel 1939:125), Alexander Philipp Maximilian, Prince of Wied-Neuwied, recorded in 1833–1834 the earliest extensive wordlist, which is notable for its phonetic accuracy (Maximilian in Thwaites 1904–1907, 24:210–214). His list was followed by a less accurate one that George Catlin (1926, 2:299–302) published in 1841; and it in turn was followed by a list that Ferdinand V. Hayden (1862:351–363) published. Lewis Henry Morgan (1871:293–382) published a list of Arikara kinship terms, and in 1909 Edward S. Curtis (1907–1930, 5:59–100, 148–152) included in his sketch of Arikara culture a significant amount of cultural vocabulary that is also distinguished by its phonetic accuracy. Charles L. Hall, the Congregational missionary on Fort Berthold Reservation, compiled a manuscript list of verb forms and short sentences (C.L. Hall 1876–1890) organized by English gloss.

In the early twentieth century, during the course of field studies, four anthropologists collected Arikara vocabulary, including kinship terms: Melvin Gilmore from 1916 to 1923; Alexander Lesser and Gene Weltfish in 1930; and Preston Holder in 1938. Most of that material is still unpublished. In 1960 the linguist Allan R. Taylor recorded a short collection of texts (A.R. Taylor 1977:20–26) as well as vocabulary. Francesca Merlan undertook summer fieldwork from 1971 to 1973 that resulted in a doctoral dissertation on syntax (Merlan 1975). In 1970 Parks began a long-term documentary study of the language that resulted in a four-volume collection of texts (Parks 1991), a reference dictionary database (Parks 1999c), as well as an array of pedagogical materials.

Pawnee

Throughout most of the historical period Pawnee speakers lived immediately south of the Arikara, primarily in present east-central Nebraska, until the tribe moved to Indian Territory in 1874–1876 and settled on a reservation in present Pawnee County, Oklahoma. The language, at least in recent historical times, was spoken in two distinct but mutually intelligible dialects, Skiri and South Band, the latter spoken by the formerly autonomous Chawi, Kitkahahki, and Pitahawirata bands. The distinctness of those two dialects was maintained through the end of the twentieth century, despite a tendency among some Pawnees beginning earlier in the century to develop a mixed dialect (Lesser and Weltfish 1932:3–4; Parks 1965–1999).

The salient differences between the two dialects are phonological and lexical. Skiri has three vowels (*i*, *a*, *u*) in contrast to the four vowels of South Band (*i*, *e*, *a*, *u*). Skiri also shortened many vowels that are long in South Band and developed a distinct accentual pattern. As a consequence, there are various phonological rules for vowel contraction and length reduction that are specific to Skiri. There are, in addition, two consonant cluster reductions peculiar to Skiri—South Band *hr* was reduced in Skiri to *h*, and South Band *kt* became Skiri *tt* for most speakers—while word-initial and intervocalic *h* is retained in Skiri but dropped in South Band. Lexical differences, which include replacement and modification of forms, the latter a feature characteristic primarily of Skiri, amount to less than 10 percent of vocabulary. South Band was, in short, the more conservative dialect, preserving older or more archaic linguistic traits, while Skiri was the more innovative.

There are no historical references to, or traditions of, dialectal differences among the Skiri. Early in the twentieth century older South Band speakers claimed that formerly, when the three bands lived separately, there were differences among the speech of the Chawi, Kitkahahki, and Pitahawirata. However, no evidence of such dialectal diversity has been documented (Lesser and Weltfish 1932:4).

The earliest substantive Pawnee vocabulary was recorded by Thomas Say, zoologist on Stephen H. Long's expedition to the Rocky Mountains (James 1823, 2:lxx–lxxviii; James in Thwaites 1904–1907, 17:290–298). Hayden (1862:347–351) published a longer, more accurately transcribed vocabulary compiled by William Hamilton, a missionary to the Skiri, and an expanded vocabulary with verb forms and a translation of the Lord's prayer based on his own fieldwork (Hayden 1868:390–406). Morgan (1871:292–382) published kinship schedules for the Chawi and Kitkahahki bands.

In 1836 the Presbyterian missionary John Dunbar published a Pawnee primer (fig. 1) using an orthography he devised that is essentially phonetic, generally, but not always, distinguishing long from short vowels. His son, John B. Dunbar, who apparently learned to speak Pawnee as a child, wrote the first grammatical sketch of the language (in Grinnell 1890:409–437) and compiled a manuscript dictionary (J.B. Dunbar 1911). Although his Pawnee orthography in both works is quasiphonetic, words can generally be reconstituted phonemically, making the dictionary an invaluable resource.

During the first decade of the twentieth century Alice C. Fletcher began to collaborate with James R. Murie, an educated Skiri Pawnee, who until his death in 1921 worked with a succession of anthropologists studying the Pawnee and was primarily responsible for the rich linguistic record of the language compiled during the first two decades of the century. Fletcher and Murie recorded on wax cylinders the Calumet ritual song texts, which Murie transcribed and translated into English. The value of Murie's work is diminished by his use of an idiosyncratic alphabet that failed to distinguish vowel length and to record certain consonant distinctions as well as by translations that divide polysynthetic words into putative morphemes assigned meanings that are often misleading or erroneous (Fletcher and Murie 1904).

In 1906, after Murie began working with George A. Dorsey, ethnologist at the Field Columbian Museum,

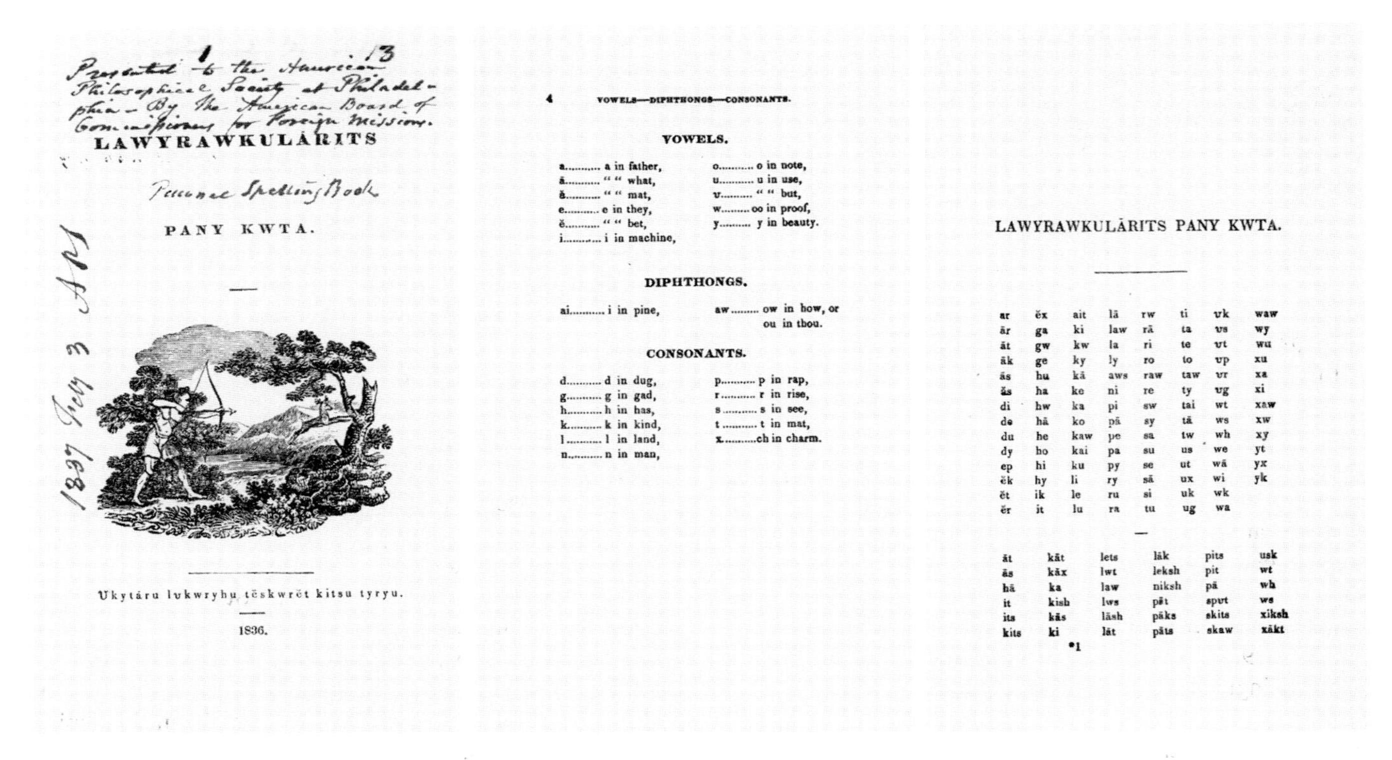

LAWYRAWKULĀRITS

PANY KWTA.

ʊkytāru lʊkwryhu tĕskwrĕt kitsu tyryu.

1836.

4 VOWELS—DIPHTHONGS—CONSONANTS.

VOWELS.

a..........	a in father,	o..........	o in note,
ā..........	" " what,	u..........	u in use,
ă..........	" " mat,	ʊ..........	" " but,
e..........	e in they,	w..........	oo in proof,
ĕ..........	" " bet,	y..........	y in beauty.
i..........	i in machine,		

DIPHTHONGS.

ai..........	i in pine,	aw..........	ow in how, or ou in thou.

CONSONANTS.

d..........	d in dug,	p..........	p in rap,
g..........	g in gad,	r..........	r in rise,
h..........	h in has,	s..........	s in see,
k..........	k in kind,	t..........	t in mat,
l..........	l in land,	x..........	ch in charm.
n..........	n in man,		

LAWYRAWKULĀRITS PANY KWTA.

ar	ĕx	ait	lā	rw	ti	ʊk	waw
ār	ga	ki	law	rā	ta	ʊs	wy
āt	gw	kw	la	ri	te	ʊt	wu
āk	ge	ky	ly	ro	to	ʊp	xu
ās	hu	kā	aws	raw	taw	ʊr	xa
ăs	ha	ke	ni	re	ty	ʊg	xi
di	hw	ka	pi	sw	tai	wt	xaw
de	hā	ko	pā	sy	tā	ws	xw
du	he	kaw	pe	sa	tw	wh	xy
dy	ho	kai	pa	su	us	we	yt
ep	hi	ku	py	se	ut	wā	yx
ĕk	hy	li	ry	sā	ux	wi	yk
ĕt	ik	le	ru	si	uk	wk	
ĕr	it	lu	ra	tu	ug	wa	

āt	kāt	lets	lāk	pits	usk
ās	kāx	lwt	leksh	pit	wt
hā	ka	law	niksh	pā	wh
it	kish	lws	pĕt	spʊt	ws
its	kās	lāsh	pāks	skits	xiksh
kits	ki	lāt	pāts	skaw	xākt

*1

Amer. Philosophical Soc., Philadelphia.

Fig. 1. Pawnee primer, title p. and p. 4–5 (J. Dunbar 1836). The title is Lawyrawkvlārits Pany Kwta 'The Pawnee Book' and the text at the bottom of the title p. reads Vkytāru Ivkwryhu tĕskwrĕt kitsu tyryhu 'big village near the big water'. Compiled by the Presbyterian missionary John Dunbar and published in Boston in 1836 by the American Board of Commissioners for Foreign Missions, it represents the earliest attempt to develop Pawnee literacy to aid in Christian proselytization. The book is made up of a key to pronunciation, examples of syllables, lists of words, and short paragraphs in Pawnee.

Chicago, the two men recorded on wax cylinders a large corpus of ethnographic, autobiographical, and mythological texts from Roaming Scout, a Skiri priest, an endeavor that was one part of Dorsey's larger Caddoan documentary project (DeMallie and Parks 1999). Murie transcribed those texts and again provided a literal, putatively etymological interpretation of words; later, Dorsey emended the Skiri texts, but he, too, failed to record vowel length and preconsonantal *h*. As part of their study of Skiri ceremonialism, Dorsey and Murie also recorded a large number of ritual songs that Murie transcribed and translated, but neither collection of texts was ever published. In the course of that language documentation, Dorsey became interested in Pawnee linguistic structure and planned to write a grammar of the language, but all that remains of his plans is a single notebook filled with paradigmatic forms of Pawnee verbs (G.A. Dorsey 1907b).

A decade later, when Murie was engaged by the Bureau of American Ethnology to document surviving Pawnee ceremonialism, he recorded a vast corpus of songs for three South Band doctors' dances and wrote out their texts; and later, while working on Skiri ceremonialism with Clark Wissler, curator at the American Museum of Natural History, New York City, he transcribed another large corpus of Skiri song texts (Murie 1981). In 1919 and 1920, when the ethnomusicologist Frances Densmore recorded Pawnee songs, Murie transcribed and translated the texts (Densmore 1929).

Other shorter collections of Pawnee linguistic data from the early twentieth century include two wordlists (Swanton 1921; Harrington 1900), a list of stream names (Grinnell 1913), and a collection of plant names (Gilmore 1919).

In 1929 Gene Weltfish, a student of Franz Boas, initiated the modern linguistic study of Pawnee. Working with contemporary speakers, she retranscribed in phonetic form and retranslated many of the Roaming Scout texts and most of the song texts that Murie recorded while working with Dorsey and Wissler and for the Bureau of American Ethnology. She wrote a grammatical sketch of South Band Pawnee (Weltfish 1940) and published an analyzed text and a collection of texts in that dialect (Weltfish 1936, 1937) presented in phonetic transcription. Other data from her linguistic research appear in her ethnographic writings (Weltfish 1965) as well as in unpublished field notes. She and Alexander Lesser collected extensive kinship data that are largely unpublished.

In 1965 Douglas R. Parks began linguistic documentation of Pawnee. Results of that work include a description of South Band phonology and morphology (1976) and a small collection of Skiri and South Band texts (1977) as well as a retranscription and retranslation of the song and other linguistic texts compiled by Murie and Wissler and retranscribed by Weltfish (Murie 1981). Parks also retranslated and edited the Roaming Scout texts (fig. 2) (1995) and compiled dictionary databases for both the Skiri (1999) and South Band (1999a) dialects.

Kitsai

Extinct since the mid-twentieth century, Kitsai was spoken by a small tribe that throughout most of the historic period lived below the Red River in north-central Texas, between Caddo groups on the east and ancestral Wichita groups on the west and north. One group of Kitsai allied itself politically and socially with the Caddo, while another allied itself with Wichita bands. In the late nineteenth century the remnant Kitsai population settled among the Wichita in what is now Caddo County, Oklahoma, and lost its identity as a tribe. Their language is intermediate between Pawnee and Wichita, and in vocabulary and phonology it is more closely related to Pawnee (Mooney 1896:1095; Lesser and Weltfish 1932:9; Parks 1979:203).

The only nineteenth-century documentation of Kitsai is a poorly recorded vocabulary list collected in 1853–1854 by Amiel Weeks Whipple in the course of a survey for a southern railway route to the Pacific Ocean (Whipple, Ewbank, and Turner 1856:65–69). In 1929 and 1930 Alexander Lesser, a student of Franz Boas, recorded a large corpus of texts, vocabulary, and morphological data from the last fluent speaker of the language (Bucca and Lesser 1969; Lesser 1977:44–64).

Wichita

Formerly, the Wichita, like other Caddoan tribes, were organized in autonomous bands that apparently shared a single language. Until 1872, when they settled on a reservation in present Caddo County in central Oklahoma, their territory extended first from central Kansas through central Oklahoma and later shifted southward to north-central Texas, placing them immediately south of the Pawnee. In the twentieth century the Wichita spoke a single dialect, but native tradition and twentieth-century native testimony held that the speech of the Tawakoni and Waco, the westernmost Wichita groups, differed from that of the other bands, suggesting dialectal diversity. However, it is now impossible to characterize precisely the nature of the differences that existed.

The only published nineteenth-century sources on Wichita are three poorly transcribed wordlists. In 1852 Capt. Randolph Marcy collected Wichita vocabulary in the Red River country of Texas and Louisiana (Marcy 1854:273–276; Marcy in Schoolcraft 1851–1857, 5:709–711). Whipple published a Waco vocabulary (Whipple, Ewbank, and Turner 1856:65–69).

Early twentieth-century linguistic material includes cultural and other vocabulary (Curtis 1907–1930, 19:35–104, 223–224, 230–238) and kinship terminology (Spier 1924), as well as a small corpus of unpublished texts and vocabulary collected by Lesser (1929–1930). Between 1947 and 1950 Karl Schmitt and Iva Schmitt (1952) collected extensive kinship data, including terminology. Paul L. Garvin undertook the first significant linguistic fieldwork with Wichita in 1949 (Garvin 1950); most of his work, including extensive lists of verbal paradigms, remains upublished. In 1965 David S. Rood began a long-term documentary study of Wichita, the results of which include a grammar (Rood 1976), a grammatical sketch (vol. 17:580–608), a small collection of texts (Rood 1977), and articles on aspects of Wichita phonology and grammar (Rood 1971, 1971a, 1973, 1975, 1975a).

Smithsonian, NAA.

Fig. 2. Nora Pratt (Skiri Pawnee) and Douglas R. Parks reviewing their retranscriptions and retranslations of the Roaming Scout texts, one of the most important ethnographic and linguistic records of the Skiri Pawnee. Photograph by William Howell, near Pawnee, Okla., 1994.

Internal Relationships

In his 1836 classification of American Indian languages, Albert Gallatin (1836:116–117, 128–129) ennumerated many of the bands comprising the Caddo, Wichita, and Pawnee tribes, noted dialectal diversity among the Caddo groups, and stated that the Pawnee and Arikara spoke a single language. He also suggested that Pawnee and Wichita might be related languages, but he did not propose any other relationships. The first individual to posit the affinity of all the northern Caddoan tribes was Josiah Gregg (1844, 2:251), who remarked that "The Pawnees and Rickaras of the north, and the Wacoes, Wichitas, Towockanoes, Towyash and Keechyes, of the Red River, are of the same origin," but he did not provide any linguistic evidence. William Wadden Turner (Whipple, Ewbank, and Turner 1856:68) compared Arikara, Pawnee, Kitsai, Wichita, and Waco vocabulary lists, and concluded on the basis of 15 cognate sets that the languages probably comprised a Pawnee stock. He also compared those cognate sets with related Caddo forms and found six possible cognates that led him to suggest that

Caddo might be related to the other languages (Whipple, Ewbank, and Turner 1856:70). At the same time Johann Carl Eduard Buschmann (1859:448) compared Caddo with Wichita, Waco, and Kitsai and, on the basis of the few similarities that he found, concluded that Caddo was an independent language, not related to those in the Pawnee family.

Later nineteenth-century classifications included Caddo, at first provisionally, with the other members of the family. Latham (1860:400, 1862:470–475) stated that Pawnee and Arikara were "Caddo languages," and he suggested that Wichita, Waco, and Kitsai were also related to Caddo. A.H. Keane (1878:478) grouped Caddo tentatively as the fourth member of the Pawnee family, the other three members being Pawnee proper, Arikara, and Wichita. Albert S. Gatschet (1884–1888,1:42–44) and Daniel Brinton (1891:95–97) placed Caddo unambiguously in a "Pani" family or stock, but they also did not include Kitsai. John Wesley Powell named the family Caddoan and included Kitsai in it. Although Pani or Pawnee had become established as the designation for the family, Powell chose Caddoan to replace it because the entry for Caddo appears a few pages before, and separate from, that for Pawnee in Gallatin's 1836 survey (Smithsonian Institution, Bureau of [American] Ethnology 1885; Powell 1891:58–62, 1891a; vol. 17:299–304).

Adai (Adaize, Adaes), a language that became extinct in the early nineteenth century, is possibly Caddoan. It was spoken by a small tribe that attached itself to the Caddo and lived near present Robeline in Natchitoches Parish, Louisiana. In 1802 Sibley (1832:722) visited the remnants of the tribe in a settlement on Lake Macdon near an affluent of the Red River, when their population comprised 20 men and a larger number of women, and wrote down a 250-word vocabulary, the only record of the language. Sibley wrote that Adai "differs from all others, and is so difficult to speak or understand that no nation can speak ten words of it." On that basis Gallatin (1836:116, 306) and subsequent writers, including Powell (1891:45–46), classified Adai as a language isolate.

Gatschet compared Sibley's vocabulary with words in several Caddoan dialects and, despite the fact that the Adai had borrowed many Caddo words, he concluded that since "a considerable percentage of the Adái words have a more or less remote affinity with Caddoan," it was a Caddoan dialect (Powell 1891:46). Powell, like most later students, did not accept the relationship because the amount of data necessary to establish it was insufficient and the data were too poorly recorded (A.R. Taylor 1963:57–58; Chafe 1976:16), but he adopted it soon after his classification was published (vol. 17:305). Lesser and Weltfish (1932:14) tentatively classified Adai as a divergent Caddo dialect, and Swanton (1952:196) accepted Gatschet's conclusion as an established fact. A.R. Taylor (1963a:131) also accepted it as Caddoan but was uncertain where to place it within the family—as an independent branch, or as a part of the Northern or Southern branches.

The first subgrouping of the Caddoan languages based on linguistic fieldwork is presented in Lesser and Weltfish (1932:1–2). They divided the family into two groups: Pawnee, Kitsai, and Wichita; and Caddo. Pawnee comprises three dialects: South Band, or Pawnee proper; Skiri; and Arikara. Wichita comprises two dialects, Wichita proper and a tentative divergent dialect spoken by the Tawakoni and Waco bands. Caddo is similarly presented as spoken in two major dialects, Caddo proper and Hainai, and in a possible third one, Adai. They state that the three northern languages are equally divergent from each other, except that Kitsai is closer to Pawnee in phonetic structure and lexical forms.

A.R. Taylor (1963a) published the first comparative study of the Caddoan languages. He compiled an extensive set of vocabulary for each of the languages, except Kitsai, based on a combination of data from historical sources and limited fieldwork by contemporary linguists. On the basis of those data he presented 113 cognate sets, from which he was able to reconstruct the outlines of Proto-Caddoan phonology. In addition to establishing the sound correspondences that obtain among Arikara, Pawnee, Wichita, and Caddo, Taylor's study also supported the Lesser and Weltfish classification and corroborated those writers' conclusion that Arikara is not a branch of Skiri Pawnee, as both tradition and writers had claimed. Arikara and an earlier form of Pawnee actually split before the Skiri-South Band dialect division occurred (fig. 3). Discussions of the internal relationships among Caddoan languages include Chafe (1976, 1979a), who sketched some of the features of comparative Caddoan phonology and morphology.

In a review of historical and contemporary evidence for dialectal diversity among the northern languages, including Kitsai, Parks (1979) showed that all the languages, except Kitsai, were formerly characterized by significant internal diversity that resulted from their social organization in small, widely dispersed settlements. Preceding the late eighteenth century, before the smaller groups had coalesced, Northern Caddoan territory was apparently characterized by areas of dialect clusters or continua. Southeastern South Dakota, where the ancestors of the modern Arikara lived, was perhaps the most complex area, representing more diversity than historical Pawnee territory in east-central Nebraska (Parks 1979a:218, 236–237) and probably Wichita territory as well. Beginning in the late eighteenth century that diversity was leveled when the remnants of Northern Caddoan populations regrouped into larger villages, former bands amalgated, and the modern languages emerged.

Dating

There are two means of estimating time-depth within a language family. One, glottochronology, is a controversial statistical technique for dating language separation by

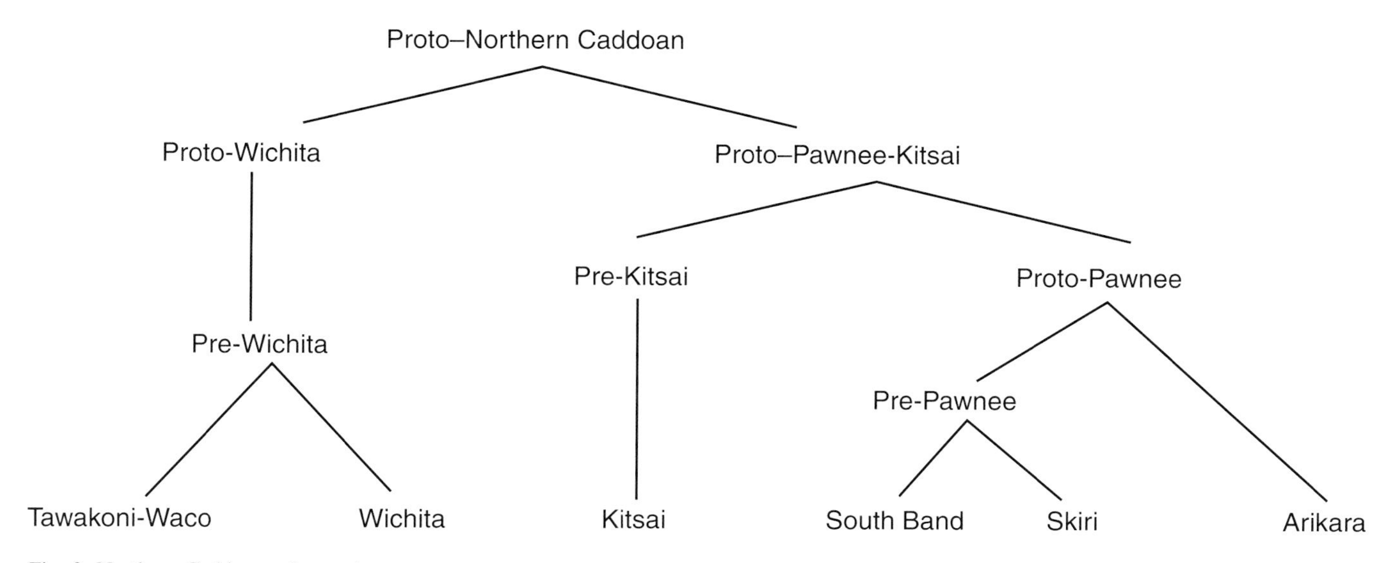

Fig. 3. Northern Caddoan subgroupings.

measuring lexical replacement. The other means is an impressionistic one, in which an estimate of time-depth is offered based on a knowledge of the languages being dated and on a comparison of their differences with those among comparable languages for which there are historically recorded dates of separation.

In 1955 Morris Swadesh and Gene Weltfish made the first glottochronological comparison of Caddoan languages in a study that included Arikara, Pawnee, Wichita, and Caddo. Because there were unsolved phonological and etymological problems in the data, as well as an incomplete Arikara lexical list, the authors considered their results provisional and publishd only part of them (Swadesh 1958:673). However, Jack T. Hughes (1968:81–84) reported their results fully. Parks (1979:205–212; Hollow and Parks 1980) gave the results of a glottochronological study of the Northern Caddoan languages (table 1) that utilized the full 100 wordlist and is derived from recently recorded data for all the languages except Kitsai, the forms for which came from Lesser's fieldwork. Parks (1979:204–205) also offered approximate impressionistic dates of separation among the languages that differed somewhat from the lexicostatistical ones. Although the authors of both studies emphasized the limitations of their techniques, their results do provide approximate, if imprecise and varying, dates for gauging time-depths. Parks's study also demonstrates that in basic vocabulary Kitsai is closer to Pawnee than it is to Wichita.

External Relationships

In his reductionist classifications of North American languages, Edward Sapir (1921, 1929) grouped Caddoan and Iroquoian in his Hokan-Siouan superstock. That stock was listed next to an "Eastern Group" that included Siouan and Yuchi as well as Natchez and Muskogean, implying that Caddoan and Iroquoian were related in some manner to Siouan. The classification also suggested that Caddoan was related to the other stocks in Hokan-Siouan: Tunican, Keres, Yuki, and Hokan-Coahuiltecan. Sapir did not present any

Table 1. Time-Depths of Separation among Caddoan Languages: Glottochronological Studies

	Swadesh and Weltfish 1955 (in J.T. Hughes 1968:81–84)		*Parks 1979*	
Language Pair	*Percent Cognate*	*Years of Separation*	*Percent Cognate*	*Years of Separation*
Pawnee-Arikara	85	500	88	300
Pawnee-Kitsai			60	1,200
Arikara-Kitsai			61	1,200
Pawnee-Wichita	67	1,400	45	1,900
Arikara-Wichita	55	2,000	43	2,000
Kitsai-Wichita			44	1,950
Pawnee-Caddo	36	3,300		
Arikara-Caddo	34	3,500		
Wichita-Caddo	40	3,000		

evidence for the proposed relationships, relying instead on his hypothesis, based in large part on typological similarities, that they would ultimately be shown to be related.

Although Swadesh (1967:287–289) stated that his exploratory examinations confirmed the grouping of Caddoan with Iroquoian and Siouan, Chafe (1973, 1976) has presented the only data in print to support a Macro-Siouan stock composed of the three families. To support a Siouan-Caddoan connection he gave three sets of data: five sets of lexical resemblances; a comparison of Siouan (specifically Winnebago) instrumental prefixes with what seem to be comparable elements in Caddo verb bases; and the occurrence in verbs in the languages of both families of elements that specify position (sitting, lying, standing). The data presented to bolster a Caddoan-Iroquoian relationship, the first put forth, include four lexical similarities between Caddo and Seneca, and a comparison of the verb structure of the languages in the two families with some notable similarities of Caddo and Seneca prefixes, particularly person and number categories and forms. Although the material that Chafe presented is attractive, it is only suggestive; and no other investigator since then has found additional, compelling evidence (Hollow and Parks 1981:81; L. Campbell 1997:262–269).

Swadesh (1967:287, 292–294) concluded that a relationship between Caddoan and Keres seemed promising based on a set of 100 lexical comparisons between Caddo, Keres, and Oneida. From impressionistic evidence, he found that 32 Keres-Caddo and 15 Keres-Caddo-Oneida similarities showed some possibility of being cognate. Rood (1973) subsequently pointed out that Swadesh's Caddo forms were actually Wichita and then, based on six pairs of similar words, he proceeded to formulate tentative sound correspondences and 11 rules to account for them. However, Eric Hamp (in Rood 1973) and Irvine Davis (1974) undermined Rood's claims, leaving the possibility of a relationship between the two groups unresolved.

Northern Caddoan Phonologies

Northern Caddoan languages are characterized by unusually small sound inventories.

Consonants

Arikara has 12 consonants, while Kitsai has 10 and the two Pawnee dialects and Wichita have nine. The consonantal systems of each language, which are nearly identical, comprise three voiceless unaspirated stops, one affricate, and the glottal stop; two to four voiceless fricatives; and two or three resonants. The consonant correspondences among the Northern Caddoan languages, together with their reconstructed forms in Proto–Northern Caddoan (PNC), are presented in table 2. (These correspondences are in part based on A.R. Taylor 1963a and Chafe 1979a.)

Table 2. Northern Caddoan Consonant Correspondences

Arikara	*Pawnee*	*Kitsai*	*Wichita*	*Proto–Northern Caddoan*
p	*p*	*kw*	*kw, w-*	**p*
t	*t*	*t*	*t, c*	**t*
k, č	*k*	*k*	*k*	**k*
ʔ	*ʔ*	*ʔ*	*ʔ*	**ʔ*
s	*c*	*c*	*c, s*	**c*
x, š	*s*	*s*	*s*	**s*
h	*h/Ø*	*h*	*h*	**h*
w	*w, p-*	*w*	*w*	**w*
r, n-	*r*	*r, n-*	*r*	**r*
n	*r*	*n*	*r, n-*	**n*
h, h-/n-	*h, r-*	*y*	*y, h-*	**y*

NOTE: a consonant followed by a hyphen is the outcome in word-initial position.

Arikara has several innovations that differentiate its consonant system from PNC and other Northern Caddoan languages. It innovated a phoneme *č* that developed from the palatalization of **k* before the vowel *i* (compare 'bone' and 'horn' in table 3). The PNC affricate **c*, which has remained in the other languages, changed to *s* in Arikara (see 'intestine' and 'up'), while PNC **s* developed as two fricative sounds in Arikara: *š* when occurring before the two front vowels *i* and *e* (see 'bone'), and *x* before the other, nonfront vowels *a*, *o*, and *u* (see 'one'). The PNC resonant **r* changed to *n* in word initial position in Arikara but remained *r* in medial position before vowels (compare 'intestine' and 'horn'). Finally, the PNC resonant **y* became Arikara *h* medially ('tree'); in word-initial position it became *h* in one dialect and *n* in another ('wood' and examples above).

The Pawnee consonant system has remained close to the PNC system. The major change in Pawnee was the merger of PNC **n* and **y* with *r* (see 'tail', 'buffalo', and 'wood'), leaving Pawnee with only two resonants, *w* and *r*. Two other developments were the change of **w* to *p* in word-initial position in both dialects (see 'man') and the dropping of *h* in word-initial position in the South Band dialect (see 'tongue').

Kitsai retained the PNC consonant system almost fully intact. The only notable change was replacement of PNC **p* with *kw* in Kitsai, a change that also occurred in Wichita and probably was borrowed from one language to the other in the course of their close historical contact (see 'egg' and 'blood').

In Wichita, there were several changes among stops and the affricate. PNC **p* was replaced by *w* in word-initial position and *kw* medially (see 'egg' and 'blood'). PNC **t* was replaced by Wichita *c* in syllable-final position and remained *t* elsewhere (see 'tongue', 'three', and 'spit out'). And PNC **c* was replaced by Wichita *s* after *a* in word-medial position ('up'). The resonants **r* and **n* appear to have merged in Wichita to *r*, although the reflex of PNC **n* is *n* in word initial position, an allophone of *r* (see 'stand', 'buffalo', 'gerundial'). Finally, PNC **y* became Wichita *h* initially and was kept as *y* medially ('tree' and 'wood').

Vowels

Arikara has five vowels, while South Band Pawnee and Kitsai have four, and Skiri Pawnee and Wichita have only three. All those vowels occur short and long, and in Skiri and Wichita they also occur extra long as a result of contractions of long and short vowels. Characteristic of all the languages except Kitsai is devoicing of unstressed vowels in word-final position. In Arikara, vocalic devoicing is even more pervasive: all unstressed vowels in words devoice when occurring before a fricative (*s*, *š*, *x*, *h*), before *t* when it is the first element in a consonant cluster or is in final position, and when they are in word-final position. When preceding a voiceless vowel, resonants (*w*, *n*, *r*) also devoice.

The vowel correspondences among the Northern Caddoan languages, together with their reconstructed forms in Proto-Caddoan, are given in table 4. Examples of the correspondences are given in table 3.

Although most of the vowel correspondences are identical, there are several notable features. Wichita merged Proto-Caddoan **u* with **i* (see 'sun'), so that both of the earlier vowels are *i* in Wichita, with the result that Wichita has no high back vowel. The third Wichita vowel is *e*, which also occurs as *e* in all the other languages except Skiri Pawnee, where it is *i* (see 'intestine'). In all the modern languages the vowel *e* usually occurs long and is only rarely short. It is the result of a contraction of various sequences of **a* and **i* that sometimes had an intervening resonant or laryngeal (see 'intestine', where in Kitsai the noncontracted form alternated with the contracted form). Arikara has an additional vowel *o* not shared by the other languages. It, too, usually occurs long and frequently is the

Table 3. Northern Caddoan Cognates

English	*Arikara*	*South Band Pawnee*	*Skiri Pawnee*	*Kitsai*	*Wichita*
egg	*nipí·kuˀ*	*ripi·kuˀ*	*ripi·kuˀ*	*nikwí·kuˀ*	*nikwi·kˀa*
blood	*pá·tuˀ*	*pa·tuˀ*	*pa·tuˀ*	*kwá·tuˀ*	*waackicˀa*
tongue	*há·tuˀ*	*a·tuˀ*	*ha·tuˀ*	*há·tuˀ*	*hacˀa*
three	*tawihk-*	*tawihk-*	*tawihk-*	*táwihku*	*tawha·*
spit out	*-hawat-i*	*-hawat-i*	*-hawat-i*	*-hawati*	*hawati*
horn	*arí·kuˀ*	*ari·kuˀ*	*ari·kuˀ*	*arí·kuˀ*	*ˀarikˀa*
bone	*čí·šuˀ*	*ki·suˀ*	*kí·suˀ*	*kí·suˀ*	*ki·sˀa*
intestine	*né·suˀ*	*re·cuˀ*	*ri·cuˀ*	*kiré·cuˀ*, *kiriacuˀ*	*niya·cˀa*
up, above	*áskAt*	*ackat*	*ackat*		*askat*
sun	*šakú·nuˀ*	*saku·ruˀ*	*saku·ruˀ*	*sakú·nuˀ*	*sa·khirˀa*
one	*áxkU*	*asku*	*asku*	*arísku*	*ass*
man	*wí·tA*	*pi·ta*	*pi·ta*	*wi·ta*	*wi·c*
arrow	*ní·šuˀ*	*ri·ksuˀ*	*ri·ksuˀ*	*níksuˀ*	
tail	*nItkú·ˀuˀ*	*ritku·ˀuˀ*	*ritku·ˀuˀ*	*nitkuhu*	
stand	*arik-*	*arik-*	*arik-*	*ariki*	*ariki*
buffalo	*tanáhaˀ*	*tarahaˀ*	*tarahaˀ*	*tanáhaˀ*	*ta·rha*
tree	*nAhá·pI*	*raha·pe*	*raha·pi*	*ayákwi*	*tiya·hkw*
wood	*há·kuˀ* 'box'	*ra·kuˀ* 'box'	*ra·kuˀ* 'box'	*yá·kuˀ*	*ha·kˀa*
gerundial	*na-*	*ra-*	*ra-*	*na-*	*na-*

Table 4. Northern Caddoan Vowel Correspondences

Arikara	*South Band Pawnee*	*Skiri Pawnee*	*Kitsai*	*Wichita*	*Proto-Caddoan*
i	*i*	*i*	*i*	*i*	**i*
a	*a*	*a*	*a*	*a*	**a*
u	*u*	*u*	*u*	*i*	**u*
e	*e*	*i*	*e*	*e*	**i* + **a*[a]
o	*u*	*u*	*u*	*i* (?)	**a* + **u*[b]

[a] This set of correspondences results from combinations of *a and *i.

[b] This set of correspondences results from combintions of *a and *u.

result of contractions of *a* and *u*, which in the other languages result in *u·* (but *i·* in Wichita; cf. vol. 17:584).

Despite their small sound inventories and relative phonetic simplicity, Northern Caddoan languages are typologically fusional when combining morphemes into words and consequently are distinguished by complex sets of rules to account for the sound changes that occur in word formation. As a result it is often difficult to identify all the morphemes comprising fully formed words.

Structural Characteristics of Northern Caddoan Languages

On the basis of morphology there are only three word classes in Northern Caddoan languages: nouns, verbs, and adverbs. Derivation is employed extensively in the formation of words in all three classes, but inflection is limited to just two classes, nouns and verbs. Of those two, inflection is restricted to a small number of categories in nouns, while it is represented by an unusually large number in verbs. The elaborate array of inflectional, as well as derivational, categories that enter into the verbal system in large part characterizes the structure of these languages, making them prototypical examples of polysynthesis.

Although on the surface each of the Northern Caddoan languages looks quite different from the others, they are in fact similar, and sometimes nearly identical, in their underlying morphology and syntax. Consequently, Pawnee will serve here as a representative illustration of Northern Caddoan, even though all of its grammatical features are not found in the others. For a more detailed overview of a contrasting Northern Caddoan structure, see the sketch of Wichita (vol. 17:580–608).

Noun and Verb Derivation

In Pawnee a relatively small number of noun and verb roots occur independently or are stems ready for inflection. For example, there are approximately 100 active verb roots. Most verb stems are derived by the use of prefixes and suffixes and, more commonly, by compounding various elements. Active verb stems, for example, are constructed from active roots by compounding them with various combinations of other, nonactive verb stems (descriptive and locative), as well as with noun roots. Similarly, most independent nouns are derived by compounding various elements or by use of gerundial forms of verbs.

Noun Inflection and Classification

Most Pawnee nouns in their independent form have an absolutive suffix *-uˀ*, which has no meaning but serves only to mark a noun as such. Many other nouns have an archaic diminutive suffix *-ki* that no longer has any meaning. Both suffixes are dropped whenever a noun is incorporated into a verb or is followed by an inflectional or derivational element. For example, *ásuˀ* 'foot' becomes *as-* in such compounds as *asikitawiˀuˀ* 'bicycle' (literally 'foot astride') and *astahku·kuˀuˀ* 'footwear' (literally 'covering the feet').

Most nouns are inflected for locative and instrumental cases. There are three locative suffixes, each of which occurs with specific classes of nouns, and there is one instrumental suffix, which is identical in form to one of the locatives. A plural morpheme optionally occurs before some locatives.

Kinship terms, which always occur in possessed form, constitute the only class of nouns inflected for possession. First- and second-person possessors are marked by prefixes, while third-person possessor is marked by a combination of prefix and suffix. For other nouns, possession is indicated by prefixes in the verb and, occasionally, by a separate gerundial construction that translates as 'the one that is mine', 'the one that is yours', etc.

Pawnee classifies all nouns according to shape as well as other characteristics, and when referring to a noun, a positional verb is required. The position (sitting, standing, lying), or alternatively movement (going, coming, passing), of an animate noun is always indicated by an appropriate positional or movement verb when referring to it. When modifying a noun with a demonstrative construction (a demonstrative prefixed to a gerundial verbal form) or when referring to the location of an object (where it is or was), the appropriate positional or movement verb is used rather than a verb of being, as in English. Thus, English 'this man' has Pawnee equivalents like *tira·ku pi·ta* 'this-one-sitting man', *tira·riki pi·ta* 'this-one-standing man', *tira·sa pi·ta* 'this-one-lying man', in which the modifying demonstrative construction is a gerundial verb form.

Inanimate nouns are similarly classified by shape and require a positional verb. Horizontally elongated objects (like a log, board, or automobile) are classified as 'lying,' while round or square objects (like a book, bowl, or body of water) are 'sitting'. Anchored, upright objects (such as dwellings and trees) are 'anchored, vertically upright,' and unanchored, vertically upright and celestial objects (like a table, star, or the sun) are 'standing'.

In addition to position, many nouns belong to one of eight categories based on specific characteristics. Those categories are: mass or granular object, liquid in a container, cooked food, a wooden object, a string object, a building or structure, a social activity, or a vocal activity. Nouns that fall into these categories will take a verb with either a subject plural prefix (mass nouns) or an incorporated noun that designates the class (all other nouns) and that co-occurs with the specific, independent noun or referentially in lieu of it. Those incorporated nouns are class agreement morphemes. For example, when asking for a pipe, a speaker will incorporate the noun root *ha·k-* 'wood' in an accompanying verb, saying *kuksa·ku rakta·wiska·ruˀ* 'give-me-a-piece-of-wood a-pipe,' that is, 'give me the pipe!' If the noun pipe is modified, it too will incorporate the noun root, as in *kuksa·ku tiraha·kca rakta·wiska·ru?* 'give-me-a-piece-of-wood this-wood-lying pipe,' that is, 'give me this pipe!' When it is obvious that the speaker is referring to a pipe, the independent form for pipe can be omitted in these sentences.

Verbs

Verbs fall into four classes characterized by distinctive inflectional properties: (1) active verbs, both transitive and intransitive; (2) stative verbs, in which generally an action befalls an individual and what is interpretively the subject pronoun is grammatically an object pronoun; (3) descriptive verbs, which in general are the equivalent of adjectives in English; and (4) locative verbs, which usually designate the location of an object and are the equivalent of English prepositions or prepositional phrases.

Only two categories in verbs are marked by suffixes: aspect and subordination. Active and stative verbs occur in one of two basic aspects, perfective and imperfective. Other aspects that are built on one or both of these include an intentive (indicating when something is going to happen), a habitual (indicating when something regularly happens), and an inchoative (indicating when something is beginning to happen). All verbs also occur in both independent and subordinate forms. While independent forms in all classes do not take a suffix, subordinate forms take a subordinate suffix that in part defines the class. Descriptive stems, for example, take a suffix *-u*, while locative verbs take a suffix *-wi*. Active and stative verbs, in contrast, belong to one of four subclasses, of which two are marked by different vowel suffixes, one by a final-syllable stress change, and one by the lack of a suffix.

Verbal prefixes fall into two groups: a large inner group whose members are more closely bound phonologically to one another and to the verb, and an outer group whose members are more loosely bound to the verb complex and can be classed more properly as proclitics, although most cannot occur independently. The inner prefixes include the following grammatical and semantic categories.

• MODE Every verb must be inflected for one of 12 independent or four subordinate modes. Independent modes include the indicative, negative indicative, assertive, imperative, contingent, potential, and absolutive, while subordinate modes are the conditional, gerundial, subjunctive, and infinitive.

• PERSON AND NUMBER Pronominal subjects and objects, both direct and indirect, occur following the modal prefixes. Pawnee, like other Northern Caddoan languages, distinguishes three persons—first, second, and third—as well as three numbers—singular, dual, and plural. In both the dual and plural numbers there is a further distinction between inclusive (including the person spoken to) and exclusive (excluding the person spoken to). There is, in addition, an obviative prefix that designates an indefinite third-person subject or a change in third-person subject. In active intransitive, descriptive, and locative verbs there is a marked distinction between collective and non-collective plural subjects, and in many transitive verbs there are separate prefixes for animate and inanimate third-person plural objects.

• POSSESSION AND BENEFACTION Both subject and object possession, as well as indirect objects, are marked by either single prefixes and combinations of prefixes. There is a distinction between regular and partitive possession, and between simple subject ownership and actual subject physical possession. Independent possessive constructions, which are gerundial forms of the verb 'to be one's' and serve as modifiers of nouns, are rarely used.

• EVIDENTIALS Members of this category indicate a speaker's source of information or judgment of the validity of a statement, making explicit the kind of evidence supporting it. There are four evidentials in Pawnee. One is a quotative that is used extensively in narratives to indicate that the speaker is repeating what he was told. Related to it is an evidential proper that is also used in narratives and in conversation as well to signify that the speaker either was or was not an eyewitness to an activity or state. The other two are an inferential (indicating the speaker knows that an act occurred on the basis of inference) and a dubitative (indicating that the speaker, who did not witness an activity or state, is in doubt about its occurrence).

• TENSE As a grammatical category, tense is little developed in Pawnee. There is only one tense prefix, an aorist, that is optionally used to indicate past time. Most verb forms are tenseless and translate temporally as either past or present or sometimes future. The potential mode and intentive aspect frequently translate into English as a future tense, but their meanings are wider than that.

• EXHORTATION There are many constructions that are used to form commands and requests of varying degrees of urgency. The most common one comprises the contingent mode and a morpheme that is identical in shape to the aorist prefix.

• ADVERBIALS Occurring after all prefixes except those for subject and object number are two adverbial morphemes, one translating as 'now, finally' and the other as 'even, at least'.

The outer prefixes in Pawnee fall into five categories. Some are more loosely attached to the verbal complex than others.

• REFLEXIVE AND RECIPROCAL A single prefix marks reflexive and reciprocal subjects.

• NEGATIVES Although there is a negative indicative mode that parallels the indicative mode, other modes require one of several negative prefixes that precede the modal prefixes.

• INTERROGATIVES There are six interrogative prefixes that translate as, for example, 'who', 'when', 'where', 'how many', as well as form 'yes-no' questions.

• ADVERBIAL PROCLITICS There are several adverbial proclitics that serve as introductory or transitional elements (translating as 'then', 'and so') and as temporal anchors ('now', 'then').

• DEICTICS Five deitics indicate both temporal and spatial location.

In addition to the preceding prefixes, Pawnee, like the other Northern Caddoan languages, generally incorporates nouns that are the subjects of intransitive verbs and the objects of transitive verbs. Among the nouns that typically incorporate rather than appear in independent form in sentences are those for body parts and body products, natural phenomena, foods, and cultural products. In the word *rira·wisurahcat* 'he blew smoke to the ground,' the noun object *ra·wi·su?* 'smoke' is incorporated with the verb stem *hurahcak* 'to blow smoke to the ground'. Often more than one noun is incorporated, as in the form *tiha·ktariwiha·hka?u·kut* 'he took the poles to the game ground,' in which the incorporated noun object *ha·k-* 'pole' is followed by the plural marker *rar-*, and that in turn is followed by the verb stem *riwiha·hka?u·kuk* 'take to a game ground,' which has the noun *wiha·ru?* 'game ground' in its composition.

Borrowings

Northern Caddoan languages are notable for relatively few borrowings from neighboring Indian or European languages. In both Arikara and Pawnee, lexical borrowings from other tribes are restricted to a small number of personal names, ethnonyms, and miscellaneous nouns, most of which speakers recognized as nonnative. The Arikara personal names *wa·to·ná·šA* and *ho·wá?Aš*, for example, are borrowings of, respectively, Sioux *matʰó naγi* 'Bear's Ghost' and *howášte* 'Good Voice'. The Pawnee name *kahi·ki* 'Captain' comes from a Dhegiha Siouan language, while the personal names *iskata·pi?* and *pa?i·kasape?* (no translations) come from an unidentified Siouan or Algonquian language. These Pawnee names, which belonged to prominent individuals, were undoubtedly bestowed during a Calumet or other intertribal ceremony. Other Arikara borrowings are *hi?éskA* 'interpreter' from Sioux *iyeska* 'interpreter; mixed blood' and *či·?é?* 'friend' from Sioux *cʰiyé* 'male's older brother'.

In all the Northern Caddoan languages there are tribal ethnonyms that have a wide geographical distribution and are often of uncertain provenience. Arikara examples include *ka?íwA* 'Kiowa', *ši?A* 'Chippewa; Cree', and *ša·hé?* 'Cheyenne'. Pawnee forms include *sahe?* (Skiri *sahi?*) 'Cheyenne', *u·kahpa* 'Quapaw' (from the Quapaw designation of one of their villages), and *sari?itihka* 'Arapaho' (from Comanche *sari·tihka* 'dog eater'), as well as the Pawnee self-designation *pa·ri*, which is the Dhegiha Siouan term for the Pawnee. Similar Wichita borrowings are *ká·hi·wah* 'Kiowa' and *sá·ri?itika?a* 'Arapaho'. The languages also have loan translations of names that are widely distributed; for example, Arikara *panIšúkAt* and Skiri Pawnee *pahiksukat* 'Sioux' (literally, 'cuts the throat'); Arikara *tUhká·ka?* and Pawnee *tuhka·ka?* 'Crow' (literally, 'raven village'); Arikara *xUhkátit* and Pawnee *asuhka·tit* 'Blackfoot' (literally, 'black moccasin').

Borrowings from European languages are restricted to a few names for food items and domestic animals. Arikara *patát* 'potato' is apparently borrowed from French *patate* 'potato, spud', while *ápos* 'apples', *káwitš* 'cabbage', *ótwi?Iš* 'oatmeal', and *paná·ni* 'banana' were borrowed from English. Pawnee borrowings from English are *aksi* 'ox, oxen; cow', *aracis* 'orange', and *apu* 'apple'. In addition to those nouns, which occur only as independent forms, Arikara borrowed four English nouns that occur only as dependent forms incorporated into verbs. The nouns are *čo·tš-* 'church', *iskun-* 'school', *pe·tš-* 'page', and *tšu·-* 'tobacco' (from 'chew'). Thus, *čo·tš-* occurs in the stem *čo·tšaka·* 'to be a church,' as in the form *ni·načo·tšaká·wI* 'where the church is' (comprised of *ni·-* 'where' + *na-* 'gerundial mode' + *čo·tš-* 'church' + *aka·* 'be a dwelling' + *-wi* 'locative subordinate'). Similarly, *pe·tš-* occurs in such stems as *pe·tšwi·na·hn* 'to turn a page' and *pe·tšta·nu·* (*ut*...) 'to be (so many) pages'.

Certain areal features found in Arikara, and not in the other Northern Caddoan languages, are undoubtedly the result of linguistic diffusion. The Arikara consonant inventory, which includes the voiceless palatal and velar fricatives *š* and *x*, illustrates the influence of surrounding Siouan languages, all of which have these sounds.

Vowel devoicing, which occurs only in word final vowels in Pawnee and Wichita, is pervasive in Arikara, occurring in the same environment as well as in any unstressed syllable preceding a fricative or the stop *t* in final position or preceding another consonant. Resonants (*w*, *r*, *n*) also devoice preceding a voiceless vowel. Examples include *wAhúx* [WAhúx] 'squash', *kú·nUx* [kú·NUx] 'bear', and *nAhki·sAhka?á·hnA* [NAhki·sAhka?á·hNA] 'when he walked around the village'. Similar devoicing occurs pervasively in Cheyenne, a tribe with whom the Arikara were in close contact in the eighteenth and early nineteenth centuries, and to a lesser extent in Comanche and Assiniboine, tribes with whom they had less contact, supporting the suggestion that this phonetic feature spread through areal diffusion.

Another areal feature found in Arikara is consonantal symbolism. The fricatives *š* and *x* are freely replaced by *s* to indicate a diminutive or small object:

kunAhúx 'old man'	*kunAhús* 'little old man'
wi·náxtš 'boy'	*wi·násts* 'little boy'
xá·tš 'dog'	*xá·ts* 'little dog'
	sá·ts 'newborn puppy'

There is, in addition, one example of the affricate *č* changing to *ts*:

sUxčítA 'shrew'	*sUstsítA* 'spring peeper'

Since consonantal symbolism of this type is not found in any other Caddoan language but is found in Plains Siouan languages and is reconstructible in Proto-Siouan, the most plausible explanation of it is diffusion to Arikara through the extensive cultural contact that the tribe had with Sioux groups in the eighteenth and nineteenth centuries (Parks 1986a).

Language Use and Survival in the Twentieth Century

In the late nineteenth and early twentieth centuries most Northern Caddoan people became bilingual in English after attending boarding or day schools. In 1909, for example, the Indian agent at Fort Berthold Agency reported that two-thirds of the reservation population (including Arikaras, Hidatsas, and Mandans) spoke English (C.W. Hoffman 1909).

A few of the first generation of students to go to boarding schools in the late nineteenth century also became literate in their languages. Among the Pawnee was James R. Murie, who worked at the Pawnee Agency recording Pawnee names on censuses and legal documents and accompanied tribal delegations to Washington, D.C., as interpreter. Among the Arikara, Peter Beauchamp, Sr., and John P. Young performed similar duties. Young, together with other educated members of the Congregational Church, including Ernest Hopkins, the first Arikara minister, learned to write Arikara in the alphabet developed for writing Sioux that was taught at Santee Normal Training School, Nebraska (Case and Case 1977:173–174). The legacy of that effort is a hymnal (fig. 4) comprising scriptural passages and the texts of hymns presented in Arikara for use in church services (C.L. Hall 1900) as well as a religious tract translated into Arikara (Hopkins and Hall 1900). Beyond those limited efforts, there were no systematic attempts to develop and sustain literacy among the Arikara, Pawnee, or Wichita.

Children born between the second decade of the twentieth century and World War II grew up with parents and grandparents speaking their native language in the home and in many social contexts outside the home but most did not become fluent speakers themselves, although they generally understood the language when it was spoken. Nevertheless, as late as 1970 there were a few elderly Pawnees and Arikaras who had never attended school and were monolingual in their native language. In the homes of those monolinguals, as well as in a relatively small number of others, Pawnee and Arikara were spoken by elderly people whose native language was their first one and by those who cared for their older relatives.

In the 1960s and 1970s, Arikara, Pawnee, and Wichita had approximately 200 speakers each, all over the age of 50 and of varying fluency. By then native language use was generally limited to social and ritual situations, although elderly people would generally converse in it when visiting each other. Among the Pawnee and Arikara,

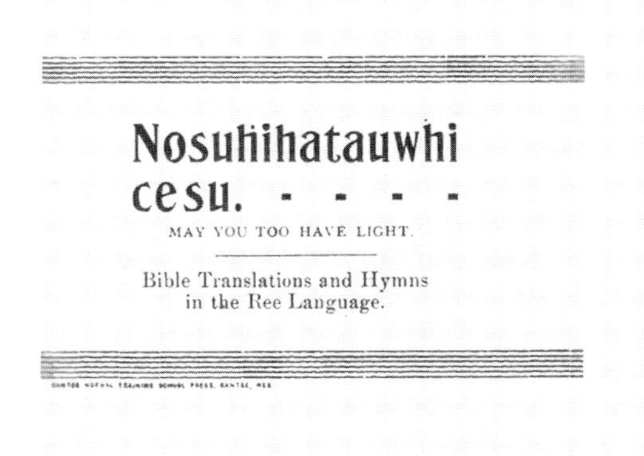
Nosuȟihatauwȟi cesu. - - - -
MAY YOU TOO HAVE LIGHT.
Bible Translations and Hymns in the Ree Language.

4

The Sounds of the Ree Language are represented by

a e i o u as in German or Dakota; au, dipthong, as ou in out, English; c h ȟ k n p s ś t w as in the Dakota;

g like ġ in Dakota;

r as in English;

' the apostrophy represents a terminal breathing or aspirate.

There are some obscure terminal half sounds, reduplications, or contractions, that can only be correctly given by those who have been in the habit of hearing them.

23

Kanic Naracśicit.
Rock of Ages.

1. Kanciś naracśicit
Nonagiu' śkuȟitipana.
Tstoȟu patu natskawa,
Niśinonikȟiwawiha.
Nikananatu'nera,
Tsu kuneśkunakiwara.

2. Ciku kakatutawan,
Nohunu nakutawe,
Na atsuȟausawanu
Iksuhausciritskawa,
Natsu kanenetu'ne
Weneśkunanowaa.

3. Ciku kakanaiśta,
Neśanu notginihit
Nonagiu' wetatota,
Nonagiu' wetatoteri't,
Aȟkunanowaana,
Jesus kogikuriciśt.

4. Ninikukot i cesu
Anuaskat kogtiat;
Christ kogtuteri't ceśu
Ninarokawakarok.
Kaniciś naracśicit,
Nonagiu' śkuȟitipana.

E. C. Hopkins, April, 1899.

State Histl. Soc. of N. Dak., Bismarck: Charles Lemon Hall Papers, #10005, box 3, file 6.

Fig. 4. Arikara hymnal (C.L. Hall 1900), title p. and pp. 4 and 23. Arikaras who attended Santee Normal Training School during the 1890s learned the contemporary missionary alphabet used for writing and printing Sioux and, under the direction of Rev. Charles L. Hall, Congregational missionary for the Ft. Berthold Res., they translated Bible passages and Christian hymns into Arikara. It was reprinted in successively expanded editions in 1905 and 1924. Tribal members sang these hymns in Congregational church services throughout the 20th century.

for example, prayers, both in homes and at public events, were offered in the native language by elders, and rituals such as the mourning feast, bestowal of a native name, and giving a young woman the right to wear an eagle plume in dances required that the officiant conduct the ritual in the native language. Among both tribes there was the belief that the efficacy of rituals depended on their being conducted in the native language, since that was the sole medium by which the living could communicate with spirits and deities. At dances announcers would occasionally speak in the native language, and among the Arikara an elderly person would often harangue the crowd in Arikara, admonishing people to live by the teachings of their elders, just as elderly people did on such occasions in the past (Weltfish 1937:38; Parks 1991, 4:675).

Two linguistic symbols of Arikara and Pawnee tribal identity during the twentieth century were personal names and songs. Throughout the first half of the twentieth century nearly every individual had an Arikara or Pawnee name in addition to a legal English name. Native language names had usually belonged to deceased relatives and hence could be drawn upon by family members in younger generations. After World War II many families began to disregard the tradition of giving their children native names, but beginning in the 1970s and continuing through the closing decades of the twentieth century that trend was reversed, when a reawakening of tribal pride developed among younger people and once again most Arikaras and Pawnees took a native name. Although individuals usually did not understand the significance of their names, they bore them as a mark of tribal and personal identity.

A second symbol of identity throughout the twentieth century was music, both traditional and Christian. All three Northern Caddoan tribes maintained their earlier musical traditions, which were integral to social and ritual events, and through song lyrics they preserved an important linguistic genre. Singers continued to sing older dance and ritual songs with native lyrics, and as late as the 1970s some individuals among the Arikara and Pawnee were still creating new songs to honor individuals serving in the armed forces. The lyrics of those songs alluded to the person's exploits or those of an ancestor. The songs were sung at dances and on other public occasions. In the final two decades of the century, after the last generation of Arikara- and Pawnee-speaking singers had died, younger singers knew songs only as memorized texts.

Christian hymns that had been translated into Arikara and Pawnee early in the twentieth century represented a related linguistic symbol of identity. In Christian churches, Arikaras and Pawnees continued to sing those hymns throughout most of the century; and in Native American Church services among the Pawnee, songs and prayers were always in the native language.

By the end of the twentieth century there were among the Arikara, Pawnee, and Wichita fewer than 10 fluent speakers of each language, and there was a relatively small but indefinite number of semi-speakers. By the early 1990s the languages were rarely heard in public.

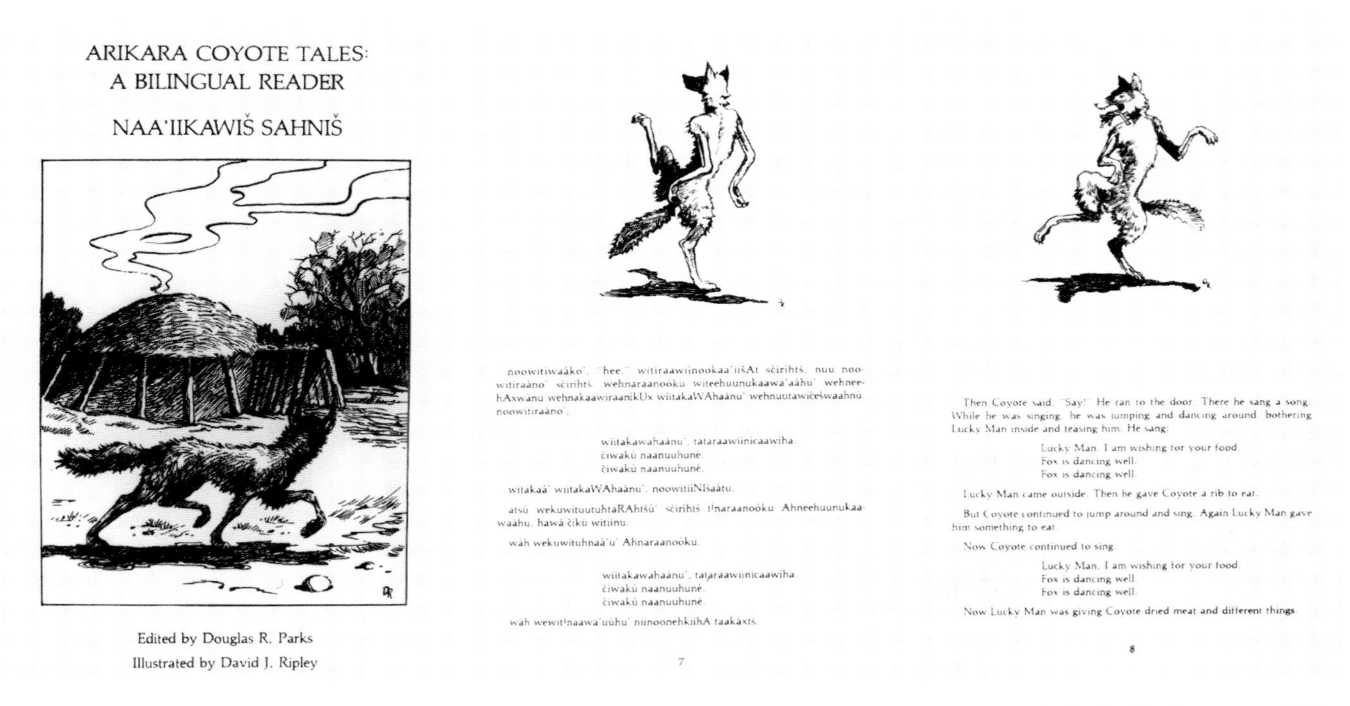

ARIKARA COYOTE TALES:
A BILINGUAL READER

NAA'IIKAWIŠ SAHNIŠ

Edited by Douglas R. Parks
Illustrated by David J. Ripley

noowitiwaáko', "hee," witiraawiinookaa'iišAt sčirihtš. nuu noowitiraáno' sčirihtš. wehnaraanoóku witeehuunukaawa'aáhu' wehneehAxwánu wehnakaawiraanikUx wiitakaWAhaánu' wehnuutawičešwaahnú. noowitiraáno'.

wiitakawahaánu', tataraawiinicaawiha.
čiwakú naanuuhuné.
čiwakú naanuuhuné.

witakaá' wiitakaWAhaánu'. noowitiiNIšaátu.

atsú wekuwituutuhtaRAhtšú' sčirihtš t^{I}naraanoóku Ahneehuunukaawaáhu. hawá čikú witiinu.

wáh wekuwituhnaá'u' Ahnaraanoóku.

wiitakawahaánu', tataraawiinicaawiha.
čiwakú naanuuhuné.
čiwakú naanuuhuné.

wáh wewit^{I}naawa'uúhu' niinoonehkiihA taakáxtš.

7

Then Coyote said, "Say!" He ran to the door. There he sang a song. While he was singing, he was jumping and dancing around, bothering Lucky Man inside and teasing him. He sang:

Lucky Man, I am wishing for your food.
Fox is dancing well.
Fox is dancing well.

Lucky Man came outside. Then he gave Coyote a rib to eat.

But Coyote continued to jump around and sing. Again Lucky Man gave him something to eat.

Now Coyote continued to sing:

Lucky Man, I am wishing for your food.
Fox is dancing well.
Fox is dancing well.

Now Lucky Man was giving Coyote dried meat and different things.

8

Fig. 5. Title p. and p. 7–8 from *Arikara Coyote Tales: A Bilingual Reader* (Parks 1984). The story "Coyote Fools Lucky Man" was recorded in 1977 by Parks from Alfred Morsette, Sr. (Not Afraid of the Enemy), a noted Arikara reconteur. A typical trickster story, it tells how Coyote through deceit obtained all of Lucky Man's food supply. The booklet, made up of 9 stories in Arikara with English translation on facing pages, was prepared for use in Arikara language classes in the White Shield School, Roseglen, N. Dak. Drawings by David J. Ripley, Arikara, 1984.

Revival and Retention Programs

Beginning in the early 1970s and continuing through the next two decades, when many American Indian communities became concerned about the loss of their languages and cultural heritage, the Arikara were the first among Northern Caddoan tribes to actively attempt to revive and maintain their language. In 1976 the White Shield School, a predominantly Arikara institution in the seat of the Arikara community on the Fort Berthold Reservation, instituted daily language instruction in elementary classes. For over a decade the instructional program comprised a team of an elder speaker and a teacher's assistant who was a nonspeaker; later it was reduced to an elder speaker alone. Teaching materials for the classes (fig. 5) included a teacher's guide, readers, and a dictionary (Deane 1977; Howling Wolf 1977; Parks 1984, 1986; Parks and Beltran, 1976, 1999; Parks, Beltran and Waters 1979, 1998, 1998a). In the late 1970s the Fort Berthold Community College (New Town, North Dakota) and Mary College (now Mary University, Bismarck, North Dakota) began offering Arikara language classes that utilized a college-level textbook written for them (Parks, Beltran, and Waters 1979).

In the 1990s, when there were no longer elderly speakers to provide language instruction, Parks, with support from the White Shield School, began development of a comprehensive set of language curriculum materials for both elementary and secondary levels (Parks, Beltran, and Waters 1998, 1998a). An integral part of the language program was the creation of multimedia language lessons that incorporated sound recordings of native speakers. In fall 1998 the school instituted a one-year Arikara language requirement for secondary level students.

In the 1980s and 1990s the Pawnee tribe periodically offered evening language classes for adults and youth in an effort to revive the language; and the Pawnee High School, a predominantly non-Indian institution, provided language instruction utilizing a textbook and tape recordings (McNeil and Tennant 1979). In 1997 Parks, in collaboration with the Pawnee tribe, began development of a set of secondary-level curriculum materials that included language lessons in printed and multimedia formats as well as elementary dictionaries for both dialects of the language.

In the 1990s efforts to revive the Wichita language were also undertaken. David S. Rood, working with an elderly speaker, developed a set of lessons in printed and sound-recorded form for use in adult education and several sound-recorded lessons for young children. Various Wichita speakers conducted weekly language classes held at the Wichita tribal office, and an extracurricular Wichita language class was offered at Riverside Indian School in Anadarko, Oklahoma (David S. Rood, personal communication 1999).

Siouan Languages

DOUGLAS R. PARKS AND ROBERT L. RANKIN

In the twentieth century the Siouan family was represented by 12 languages on the Plains: Crow, Hidatsa, Mandan, Sioux, Assiniboine, Stoney, Chiwere (Iowa, Otoe, and Missouria), Omaha-Ponca, Osage-Kansa, and Quapaw. In the late eighteenth and early nineteenth centuries those languages were spread from western Alberta and southern Manitoba through the Plains to Arkansas. Siouan languages spoken outside the Plains area included Winnebago (Wisconsin), Ofo and Biloxi (Mississippi), as well as Tutelo, Saponi, and probably Occaneechi and Moniton (Virginia). The distribution of Plains Siouan languages represented a gradual westward movement of the northern tribes, of whom the Stoney were in the vanguard, followed by the Assiniboine and Crow, as well as the Teton, Yanktonai, and Yankton Sioux.

Published surveys of linguistic scholarship in the Siouan family include Chafe (1973, 1976), Rood (1979), and de Reuse (1987).

Survey of Languages and Sources

Crow

The Crow formerly inhabited eastern Montana and northern Wyoming. In the late nineteenth century the major divisions of the tribe settled on the Crow Reservation, Montana. Before the divisions settled on the Crow Reservation in 1883, there was minor dialectal variation (W. Matthews 1877:78), but in the twentieth century the language was characterized as uniform (Lowie 1935:3–4; Randolph Graczyk, personal communication 1999).

The earliest documentation of the Crow language was a recording of the numbers from 'one' to 'ten' about 1743 (Isham 1949:36). Short vocabularies were collected in the nineteenth century by Thomas Say, zoologist on Stephen H. Long's expedition to the Rocky Mountains in 1819–1820 (E. James 1823:lxxix; in Thwaites 1904–1907, 17:299), Alexander Philipp Maximilian, Prince of Wied-Neuwied, recorded in 1833–1834 (Maximilian 1839–1841, 2:490; in Thwaites 1904–1907, 24:222); and Ferdinand Vandeveer Hayden (1862:395–420), who included comments on Crow grammar. Lewis Henry Morgan (1871:291–382) presented a set of Crow kinship terms, while Edward S. Curtis (1907–1930, 4:3–126, 175–180, 189–196) included native terms throughout his ethnographic sketch of the Crow and provided a comparative Crow-Hidatsa vocabulary.

During the closing decade of the nineteenth century and the early decades of the twentieth century, Jesuit missionaries on the Crow Reservation, including Edward M. Griva and Aloysius Vrebosch, compiled several manuscript Crow–English and English-Crow dictionaries, and John Boschi wrote a grammar of the language structured on a Latin model (Carriker, Carriker, Carroll, and Larsen 1976:25–26).

In the early twentieth century Lowie initiated the modern study of the Crow language, producing a text with grammatical notes (Lowie 1930); an analyzed text and grammatical sketch (Lowie 1941); and a susbstantial collection of texts and an accompanying Crow-English, English-Crow glossary that were edited posthumously (Lowie 1960, 1960a). He also published papers on Crow oral literary genres and style, including prayers and proverbs (Lowie 1914b, 1932, 1933, 1950, 1959a). Although Lowie's materials suffer from technical deficiencies (he was not trained as a linguist), they provide a wealth of linguistic documentation.

Professional linguists who studied Crow included Dorothea V. Kaschube, G. Hubert Matthews, Randolph Gracyzk, Ray Gordon, and Karen Kay Wallace. Kaschube (1960), Graczyk (1990), and K. Wallace (1993) wrote grammatical descriptions as dissertations. Kaschube later published her structuralist sketch (1967) as well as a collection of texts (1978). Graczyk's work is a comprehensive description that is the standard reference on Crow grammar. Gordon and Graczyk (1985) prepared a Crow dictionary. Smaller modern Crow dictionaries are Tushka (1979) and Medicine Horse (1987), both of which were prepared for students in Crow bilingual education programs. Gracyzk (1984, 1991), Gordon, and G.H. Matthews (1981) were all engaged in missionary and bilingual education activities on the Crow Reservation at the end of the twentieth century, and Matthews was translating the Bible.

Hidatsa

The Hidatsa (locally called Gros Ventre and formerly also Minitari) lived in central North Dakota. In the early nineteenth century their language, which is closely related to Crow, was spoken by three autonomous divisions—Awaxawi, Awatixa, and Hidatsa proper—that reportedly spoke separate dialects. The Awaxawi, who lived south of the other divisions, were more closely associated with the

Mandan than the other divisions, were often portrayed as a separate tribe and dialectally the most divergent. After the 1837 smallpox epidemic the remnants of the three divisions and the Mandan moved to Fort Berthold and established Like-a-Fishhook Village, in which the two tribes maintained separate sections. After this relocation and coalescence, the linguistic diversity that had existed among the Hidatsa divisions gradually leveled, so that by the late nineteenth century it was not possible to determine the distinctive features of the former dialects and by the twentieth century the vestiges of those dialects had essentially disappeared (W. Matthews 1877:80; Z. Harris and C.F. Voegelin 1939:178–179; Parks 1992:xii–xiii). In the late twentieth century the Hidatsa were the dominant population of the western and northern portions of the Fort Berthold Reservation, in and around Mandaree, New Town, and Parshall.

The first documentation of Hidatsa was the vocabularies recorded by Say (E. James 1823:lxx–lxxviii, lxxxiv–lxxxv; in Thwaites 1904–1907, 17:290–298, 304), Maximilian (1839–1841, 2:562–590; in Thwaites 1904–1907, 24:261–276), and Hayden (1862:424–426). L.H. Morgan (1871:291–382) presented Hidatsa kinship terminology.

The earliest extensive studies of Hidatsa were conducted from 1865 to 1872 by Washington Matthews, a U.S. Army surgeon, who published a Hidatsa grammar and dictionary (W. Matthews 1873–1874, 1877). The Congregational missionary Charles L. Hall compiled a Hidatsa vocabulary (1878–1908) and prepared a hymnal (1895) that included translations of Bible passages. Curtis (1907–1930, 4:129–172, 180–186, 189–196) recorded cultural and general vocabulary.

In the 1930s, the anthropologist Alfred Bowers recorded a small number of mythological texts in Hidatsa; in the 1960s he sound-recorded retranslations of an autobiography of Crows Heart from English into both Hidatsa and Mandan. None of these materials has been published. In 1911 Robert H. Lowie wrote down a small collection of Hidatsa texts that in the 1930s Zellig Harris and Carl F. Voegelin sound-recorded and transcribed; they published five of them in a modern orthography together with an outline of Hidatsa phonology and notes on the morphemic composition of words in the texts (Z. Harris and C.F. Voegelin 1939). Their study of Hidatsa was continued by Florence M. Robinett, who, in a dissertation based on Harris and Voegelin's material as well as her own, described its phonology and morphology within an item-and-arrangement model (Robinett 1955; G.H. Mattews 1965:18–28). Robinett also sound-recorded a large corpus of linguistic material, including vocabulary, examples of morphological constructions, and texts, among which is a woman's autobiography (Urciuoli 1988). G. Hubert Matthews (1965) published a description of Hidatsa syntax within the framework of an early version of generative grammar. His monograph includes a critical discussion of previous work on the language. A. Wesley Jones compiled a Hidatsa-English, English-Hidatsa glossary and a small collection of texts for classroom use (1978, 1979) and published on Hidatsa phonology and morphology (1979a, 1983, 1983a, 1991, 1992).

Mandan

In the late eighteenth century the Mandan lived in villages along the Missouri River near present Bismarck, North Dakota, and in the early nineteenth century near the mouth of the Knife River, where they were closely associated with the Hidatsa.

As late as the mid-nineteenth century, Mandan was spoken in at least two dialects, Nuptare and Nuetare. After the 1837 smallpox epidemic Mandan survivors moved with the Hidatsa to Like-a-Fishhook Village and later, after land allotment, occupied the southern segment of the Fort Berthold Reservation, where they eventually formed the village of Twin Buttes, with many living in Hidatsa communities as well. In the twentieth century only the Nuetare dialect survived, and Mandans who spoke it also spoke Hidatsa.

Nineteenth-century documentation of Mandan is represented primarily by vocabularies, the most important of which are those of George Shannon (Rafinesque 1832–1833:132–133); Maximilian, who includes notes on Mandan grammar as well as a separate comparative vocabulary of the Nuptare and Nuetare dialects that provides the only extant documentation of Nuptare (Maximilian 1839–1841, 2:514–561; Thwaites 1904–1907, 24:250–261; R.T. Carter 1991); George Catlin (1841:261–265); James Kipp (Schoolcraft 1851–1857, 3:255–256, 446–459); and Hayden (1862:435–444), who also provides grammatical notes. L.H. Morgan (1871:291–382) published kinship terms. Charles L. Hall compiled a Mandan-English vocabulary (1878–1908a) and prepared a Mandan hymnal for Congregational mission churches that included translations of Bible passages (1905).

In the early twentieth century more extensive documentation of Mandan is represented by the work of George F. Will and Herbert J. Spinden (1906:188–219), who included a grammatical sketch and vocabulary in their descriptive monograph on Mandan culture. Will (1906–1951) compiled additional linguistic materials that were never published. Curtis (1907–1930, 5:3–55, 143–148, 169–177) published cultural terms and general vocabularies. In the early 1930s Edward Kennard, a student of Franz Boas, undertook fieldwork with the language, published a grammar (1936), and recorded interlinear texts (1936a).

Robert C. Hollow recorded Mandan linguistic data, including texts, and compiled a dictionary and grammatical sketch of the language as his dissertation (1970). Hollow's (1965–1975) unpublished material, which includes a reelicitation and retranslation of Kennard's texts, provides the basis for a Mandan grammar and dictionary, but since Hollow failed to record vowel length and, often, vowels with glottal constriction, his transcriptions are deficient (R.T. Carter 1991:483). In 1993 Mauricio J. Mixco began fieldwork with the few remaining speakers of the language with the goal of completing a grammar and dictionary. He published a sketch of Mandan grammar (1997) and an article on switch reference (1997a).

Stoney

Stoney has been spoken in Alberta east of the Rockies since the eighteenth century. There were two major tribal divisions, the Mountain Stoney in southern Alberta and the Wood Stoney farther north. In the late nineteenth century the Stoney were settled on what were later five reserves. The Mountain Stoney, comprising the Bearspaw, Chiniki, and Wesley bands, shared a reserve at Morley, near present Calgary, as well as two satellite reserves, Big Horn and Eden Valley, about 100 miles farther north. The Wood Stoney lived on two reserves about 50 miles west of Edmonton: the Alexis Reserve at Lac Sainte Anne, near the town of Glenevis, and Paul's Reserve on Lake Wabanum, near Duffield. In the late twentieth century distinct dialects were spoken on the northern and southern reserves, presumably continuing dialectal differences between the two divisions, but little information on their characteristics was available (E.-D. Cook 1995:227).

Stoney is part of a dialect continuum that includes Assiniboine and Sioux. In the nineteenth century the close historical relationship of the Stoney and Assiniboine resulted in frequent confusion of their identities (Laurie 1957–1959, 1:22). Throughout most of the twentieth century Stoney was generally assumed to be a Canadian, or Alberta, variety of Assiniboine (Chafe 1976:29, 32), sometimes also called Northern Assiniboine (Curtis 1907–1930, 18:163), but in the mid-twentieth century Stoney and Assiniboine were mutually unintelligible and constituted separate languages that were in turn distinct from Sioux. Stoney was the most divergent member of this group (Harbeck 1969:19; A.R. Taylor 1983b; Parks and DeMallie 1992).

The earliest recorded Stoney linguistic material is a vocabulary collected by Alexander Henry the Younger about 1808 (Coues 1897, 2:640–642; A.R. Taylor 1983b). An extensive dictionary, with grammatical notes, was compiled by the Oblates of Mary Immaculate missionary Valentin Végreville (1875–1881). Anna E. Barker (1886) recorded a Mountain dialect vocabulary; and Edward S. Curtis (1907–1930, 18:163–176, 214–218) included accurately transcribed vocabulary, including a set of kinship terms, in his ethnographic sketch and in a separate list. In 1907 Lowie (1909:263–264, 1960b:20–30) recorded several Stoney texts that were presented in interlinear form. The first extensive and accessible documentation of Stoney is a manuscript grammar and dictionary of Morley speech compiled by John L. Laurie (1959, 1959a), a Calgary teacher.

In the late twentieth century several linguists worked with Stoney. Ernest Jay Bellam (1975) wrote a thesis describing aspects of Stoney phonology and morphology, and Warren Harbeck, a Summer Institute of Linguistics missionary, collected material but did not publish most of it (Bellam 1975:85–86). In her study of phonological and morphological processes in Sioux dialects, Patricia Shaw (1976, 1985) included Stoney data that she collected; and, after limited fieldwork, Allan R. Taylor (1981a) described the salient phonological characteristics of the language and noted the influences of Cree speech on Stoney. Eung-Do Cook (1995; E.-D. Cook and Owens 1991), also conducted fieldwork on the language.

Assiniboine

The Assiniboine in the nineteenth century ranged throughout southern Saskatchewan and northern Montana. In the late nineteenth century they settled on reserves in Saskatchewan:-Mosquito, Lean Man, and Grizzly Bear's Head, later a single reserve designated Mosquito-Grizzly Bear's Head Reserve; Carry The Kettle Reserve; and White Bear Reserve, some residents of which in the 1990s moved to Pheasant's Rump and Ocean Man reserves. On both the Mosquito-Grizzly Bear's Head and White Bear reserves, Assiniboines were a minority among Cree populations, and all Assiniboines there spoke Cree as well as Assiniboine. The population of Carry The Kettle Reserve included both Cree and Santee-Sisseton speakers, and most Assiniboines there spoke either Cree or Santee-Sisseton as well.

The U.S. Assiniboine settled on: Fort Belknap Reservation in Blaine and Phillips counties, Montana, which is shared with the Algonquian-speaking Gros Ventre tribe; and Fort Peck Reservation in Valley and Roosevelt counties in Montana, shared with various Sioux groups, primarily Yanktonai. Most Montana Assiniboines did not speak Cree, unless they came from Saskatchewan; and only a few, primarily at Fort Peck, spoke any dialect of Sioux (Parks and DeMallie 1992:248).

Despite its wide geographical distribution, Assiniboine is a discrete language with only minor internal differentiation. One of its two major dialects is spoken at Fort Peck Reservation, and White Bear Reserve, including Pheasant's Rump and Ocean Man reserves. The second dialect is spoken at Fort Belknap, Montana, and at Mosquito-Grizzly Bear's Head and Carry The Kettle. The dialectal differences are primarily lexical, although there is one notable phonological change differentiating the Assiniboine of Mosquito-Grizzly Bear's Head and Carry The Kettle, which has the metathesis of *tk* to *kt* found in Stoney. Thus Fort Belknap speakers have *yatką́* 'to drink', while those on the two Saskatchewan reserves have *yaktą́*.

The earliest documentation of Assiniboine is represented by wordlists recorded in Saskatchewan in 1785 by Edward Umfreville (1790:folding sheet facing p. 202;

Gallatin 1836:374) and in 1808 by David Thompson (Coues 1897, 2:534–538). Later lists include ones recorded by Maximilian (1839–1841, 2:474–480; Thwaites 1904–1907, 24:215–217), Edwin Thompson Denig (Schoolcraft 1851–1857, 4:416–431), and Hayden (1862:389–391). Assiniboine vocabulary occurs throughout the ethnographies of Denig (1930), Curtis (1907–1930, 3:127–133), and Lowie (1909).

Lowie (1909:365–370; 1960b:1–20) recorded at Fort Belknap a small corpus of Assiniboine texts that were published in interlinear form. Ella C. Deloria wrote on Fort Belknap (1936) and published an Assiniboine text with a parallel Teton version in interlinear form (Boas and Deloria 1941:182–183). Valery Drummond (1976) and Emily Schudel (1997) present small collections of Assiniboine texts recorded at Carry The Kettle Reserve. Schudel also gives an overview of Assiniboine grammar.

There is no grammar of Assiniboine. Norman Balfour Levin's (1964) description, based on data recorded at Fort Peck Reservation, is not accurate. Papers describing aspects of the language include a note on phonology by Robert C. Hollow (1970a), who collected material at Fort Peck and Fort Belknap, and a discussion of relative clauses by Drummond (1976a), whose data were recorded at Carry The Kettle. Based on work in all Assiniboine communities, but primarily Fort Belknap and Carry The Kettle, Parks and DeMallie (1999) compiled a multimedia dictionary database and recorded an extensive collection of texts.

Sioux

Until the mid-nineteenth century the Sioux occupied most of present Minnesota, northwestern Iowa, North and South Dakota, and parts of eastern Wyoming and Montana and northern Nebraska. Later in the nineteenth century Sioux groups settled on 17 reservations in the United States and 8 reserves in Canada.

The Sioux language has three major dialects, corresponding to the three major Sioux divisions; those divisions in turn comprise numerous subdivisions or bands, which often speak separate subdialects:

(1) Santee-Sisseton, the dialect of the Eastern, Santee, or Dakota division. The Santee dialect is that of the Mdewakanton, Wahpekute, and Wahpeton bands, and the Sisseton subdialect that of the Sisseton.

(2) Yankton-Yanktonai, the dialect of the Central, or Wichiyena, division. Yankton is the subdialect of the Yankton, and Yanktonai that of the Lower Yanktonai.

(3) Teton (Lakhota in vol. 17), the dialect of the Western, Teton, or Lakota division. The northern subdialect of Teton is spoken by the Minneconjou, Two Kettles, Sans Arcs, Blackfoot, and Hunkpapa, and the southern subdialect by the Oglala and Brule. The differences among the dialects and subdialects are primarily phonological and lexical, and they generally do not prevent mutual intelligibility.

The three major dialects of Sioux, and their close relationship to Assiniboine and Stoney, were recognized early in the nineteenth century (Gallatin 1836:124; S.R. Riggs 1852:viii–ix). The most salient phonological feature distinguishing them is the use of *d*, *n*, or *l*. Santee-Sisseton and Yankton-Yanktonai have *d*—although Yankton-Yanktonai and Sisseton, as well as some varieties of Santee, also have *n*—where Teton has *l* and Assiniboine and Stoney have *n*. For example, the term of self-designation is Santee-Sisseton and Yankton-Yanktonai *dak^{h}óta*, Teton *lak^{h}óta*, and Assiniboine and Stoney *nak^{h}óta*. In the twentieth century these three sounds were generally but incorrectly assumed to define three dialects, and Yankton-Yanktonai was mistakenly identified as an *n* dialect, from which Assiniboine and ultimately Stoney were said to have derived historically (Hodge 1907–1910, 1:376; Lowie 1954:8; J.H. Howard 1960:249, 1966a:4). The inaccuracy of this scheme is discussed in Parks and DeMallie (1992) and Shaw (1976:4–5).

• SANTEE-SISSETON The earliest published Sioux vocabularies are recordings of Santee by the explorer Jonathan Carver (1778:433–441), and by John Marsh, the first schoolteacher in Minnesota, who also wrote a short description of Sioux grammar and compiled a vocabulary in 1827 (in Atwater 1831:149–172). Joseph N. Nicollet (1836–1840) recorded Santee vocabulary and wrote an outline of Sioux grammar. Later nineteenth-century vocabularies include one for Sisseton collected by William H. Gardner (1868), a military surgeon, and a short comparative vocabulary that includes Santee (L.H. Morgan 1871:181–182). L.H. Morgan (1871:167–169, 293–382) gives a comparative chart of kinship terms for Santee, Sisseton, Yankton, Yanktonai, Oglala, Brule, Hunkpapa, and Blackfoot Sioux.

Protestant missionization began among the Santee in Minnesota in 1834, and over the ensuing century a small, dedicated group of missionaries compiled and published major reference works on the language, translations of the scriptures that ultimately resulted in the entire Bible, and instructional materials for promoting literacy (T.S. Williamson and S.R. Riggs 1880; Pilling 1887). Samuel W. Pond and Gideon H. Pond recorded the first collection of Santee texts (1840), and in 1842 Samuel Pond compiled a Hebrew-Dakota dictionary intended to facilitate translation of the scriptures from Hebrew into Santee (Plaut 1953). The first Dakota grammar and dictionary were compiled by members of the Dakota Mission (fig. 1), including Thomas S. Williamson, and edited by Stephen Return Riggs (1852; Folwell 1922–1930, 1:447–452); a shorter version of the dictionary was published by Riggs's wife, Mary Ann Clark Riggs (1852). After Riggs's death, James Owen Dorsey edited the missionaries' materials and published an expanded Dakota-English dictionary (S.R. Riggs 1890) as well as a volume comprising the grammar, with texts and ethnographic notes (S.R. Riggs 1893). Culminating this missionary tradition was an

English-Dakota dictionary that included Yankton and Teton forms published by John P. Williamson (1886, 1902), son of Thomas S. Williamson. Although all these publications suffer from the missionaries' failure to distinguish between aspirated and unaspirated consonants, they remain the primary resources on Santee.

The first linguist to study Sioux in the twentieth century was Franz Boas, who wrote a combined description of the Teton and Santee dialects based on Teton textual material extracted by John R. Swanton and on Santee material from Riggs's publications (Boas and Swanton 1911). Between 1928 and 1938, Ella C. Deloria, a Sioux who was Boas's collaborator throughout most of his study of the language, collected Santee texts and compiled lexical material (Freeman 1966:119–122; Kendall 1982:37).

Descriptive material on late-twentieth-century Santee collected among the Wahpeton of Sioux Valley Reserve appears in a study of phonological and morphological processes in Sioux dialects (Shaw 1976, 1985a). Paul War Cloud (1967) privately published an English-Sioux glossary that is said to represent the "Santee-Yankton and Teton dialects" and in which Sioux words are written in a quasi-phonetic alphabet.

• YANKTON-YANKTONAI Early vocabularies include a Yanktonai list recorded by Maximilian (1839–1831, 2:491–498; in Thwaites 1904–1907, 24:223–226) and a Yankton one from Thomas Say (E. James 1823:lxxiv–lxxviii, lxxxiv; in Thwaites 1904–1907, 17:290–298, 304). For Yankton, the missionary Joseph Witherspoon Cook (1880–1882) filled out in their entirety the schedules in J.W. Powell's *Introduction to the Study of Indian Languages* (1880) (fig. 2). Curtis (1907–1930, 3:152–159) provided a comparative Teton-Yanktonai-Assiniboine vocabulary, Deloria (1932:165–166; Freeman 1966:120) recorded several Yankton texts, and Parks (1999e) compiled a Yanktonai dictionary.

• TETON After Maximilian's short wordlist (1839–1841, 2:498; in Thwaites 1904–1907, 24:226), the earliest significant Teton vocabularies were those of the painter Albert Bierstadt (1863); the military officers Joseph K. Hyer and William S. Starring (1866), collected at Fort Laramie; Capt. A.H. Corliss (1874); and the government scouts Willis Eugene Everette (1881), whose material was recorded in Sitting Bull's camp in Montana Territory in 1878; and E.H. Allison (1897, 1899), who filled out a copy of Powell's schedules at Standing Rock Reservation and recorded two texts in interlinear format. In addition to Morgan's lists, James R. Walker (1914) published a set of Oglala kinship terms. Curtis (1907–1930, 3:1–118,

WICOIE WOWAPI
Wowapi Pehanpi kin.
The Word Book Wall Roll
BY A. L. RIGGS, A.M.
Published for the DAKOTA MISSION, by the
AMERICAN TRACT SOCIETY,
NEW YORK CITY.

Moody County Mus. and Histl. Soc., Flandreau, S. Dak.: no. 65-1888.

Fig. 1. Cover and lesson one of a Sioux (Santee dialect) language wall chart, 1881, by Alfred L. Riggs (vol. 4:679). The 25-page chart, nailed to a wooden rod, was used in teaching the language in Dakota Mission schools. Lesson 1 ("Woonspe I") of "Wicoie Wowapi Kin" ('the word book') teaches ⟨śunka⟩ 'dog' and ⟨inmu-śunka⟩ 'cat'.

152–159) provided Teton cultural terms and a Teton-Yanktonai-Assiniboine vocabulary.

The first collections of Teton texts were recorded by native speakers: George Bushotter (1887–1888), who was educated at Hampton Normal and Agricultural Institute in Virginia, wrote out 257 texts for James Owen Dorsey at the Bureau of Ethnology (see DeMallie 1978:98–102); and George Sword (1909; E.C. Deloria 1929), a prominent Lakota political and religious leader on the Pine Ridge Reservation, wrote texts for the reservation physician James R. Walker (see Parks and DeMallie 1992). Deloria retranscribed and translated many of those texts in the 1930s, and Raymond J. DeMallie (1998), collaborating with Vine V. Deloria, Sr., retranscribed and translated the remainder of the collection.

From 1904 to 1954, the Jesuit missionary Eugene Buechel documented the Teton dialect, producing a grammar (1939) and—posthumously edited—the most comprehensive dictionary of any Sioux dialect (1970) and two editions of a collection of texts, one in Teton (1978) and the other in Teton and English (1998). The grammar, which is presented within a traditional English model and relies on biblical translations for illustrations of usage, is an important resource. Although Buechel distinguished aspirated from unaspirated consonants in his dictionary slip file, that phonemic distinction is not indicated in his texts or consistently in the published dictionary.

E.C. Deloria (1932, 1929, 1954) recorded a large number of Teton texts representing a wide range of genres, but most remain unpublished. She and Boas published a paper on characteristics of Teton (Boas and Deloria 1933) that was integrated into a detailed Teton grammar with comparative material on the Santee and Yankton dialects (Boas and Deloria 1941). Other studies include two of Teton music (Densmore 1918; N.B. Curtis 1907:37–90) and one of kinship based on material recorded in 1928 (Lesser 1958).

Several linguists have written dissertations on Teton phonology and grammar. Richard T. Carter (1974) described phonology using data recorded at the Lower Brule Reservation; Robert Detrick Van Valin, Jr. (1977) discussed aspects of syntax within the framework of role and reference grammar; Janis S. Williamson (1984) described the major systems of syntax using government and binding theory; and Trudi Alice Patterson (1990) portrayed various aspects of phonology and morphology in a lexical phonology framework. Allan R. Taylor and David S. Rood provide a comprehensive overview of phonology and morphology (vol. 17:440–482). DeMallie (1971, 1979, 1994) wrote a dissertation and articles on kinship terminology, and Elizabeth S. Grobsmith (1976) wrote a dissertation on contrasting language use in two communities on the Rosebud Reservation. For additional studies, see de Reuse (1987).

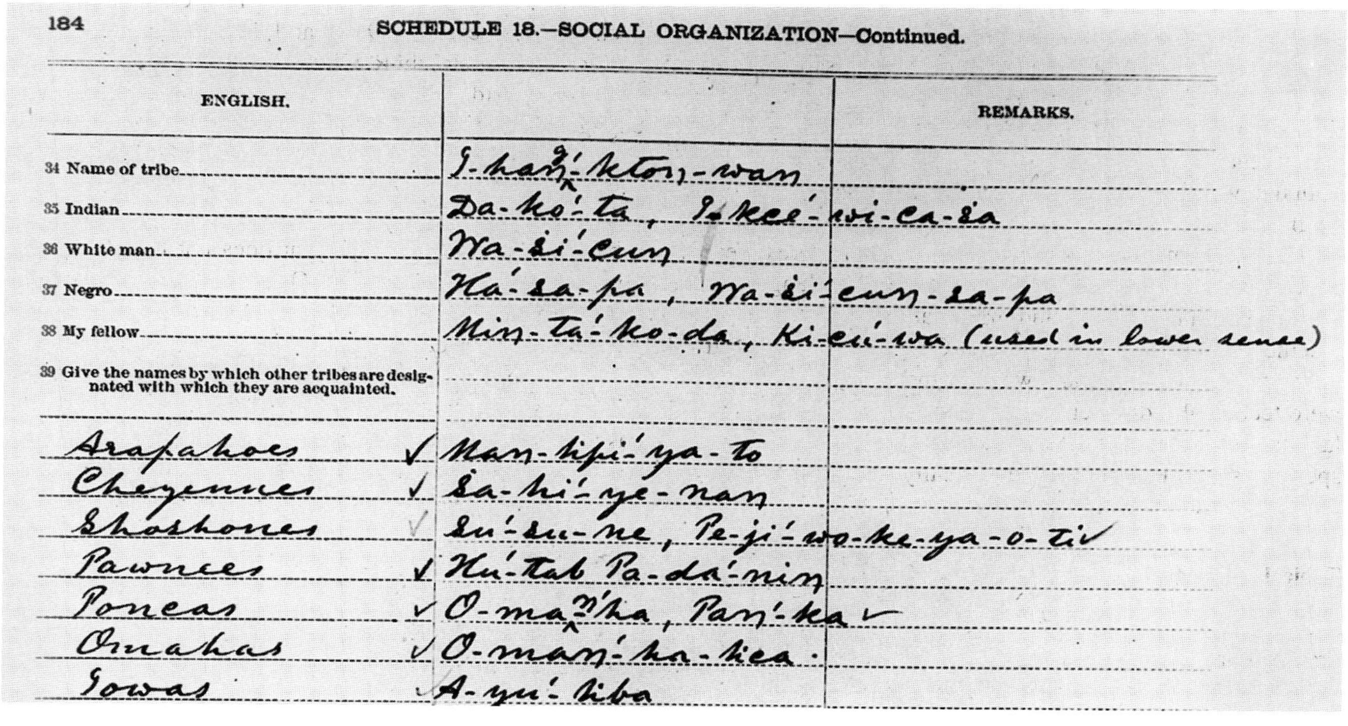

184 SCHEDULE 18.—SOCIAL ORGANIZATION—Continued.

ENGLISH.		REMARKS.
34 Name of tribe	I-hañ-kton-wan	
35 Indian	Da-ko'-ta, I-kce'-wi-ca-śa	
36 White man	Wa-śi'-cun	
37 Negro	Ha'-sa-pa, Wa-śi'-cun-sa-pa	
38 My fellow	Min-ta'-ko-da, Ki-cu'-wa (used in lower sense)	
39 Give the names by which other tribes are designated with which they are acquainted.		
Arapahoes ✓	Man-hpi'-ya-to	
Cheyennes ✓	Śa-hi'-ye-nan	
Shoshones ✓	Su'-su-ne, Pe-ji'-wo-ke-ya-o-ti ✓	
Pawnees ✓	Hu'-tab Pa-da'-nin	
Poncas ✓	O-mañ'-ha, Pan'-ka ✓	
Omahas ✓	O-mañ'-ha-kica.	
Iowas ✓	A-yu'-hba	

Smithsonian, NAA: ms. 1486.

Fig. 2. Yankton Sioux vocabulary in Powell's (1980) schedules, recorded 1880–1882 along the Missouri River, west of Yankton City, Dak. Terr., by Joseph W. Cook with the aid of Charles S. Cook, Alfred C. Smith, Battiste Defond, and Frank Vassar. Cropped.

Dhegiha

The Omaha, Ponca, Osage, Kansa, and Quapaw are separate tribes that formerly spoke varieties of a single language or language complex called Dhegiha (ðegēhä). In the late eighteenth and early nineteenth century, the Omaha and Ponca lived along the Missouri River in northeastern Nebraska and nearby South Dakota. In the twentieth century the Omaha continued to reside in their former territory on the Omaha Reservation, Nebraska. Some Poncas lived on a reservation in Knox and Boyd counties, Nebraska, but most of the tribe relocated to Indian Territory in 1877 and since that time lived in the area of their former reservation in present Noble County, Oklahoma.

The name Dhegiha was introduced by J.O. Dorsey (1884, 1885), whose published and unpublished materials are the most extensive documentation of Dhegiha. It is from an Omaha-Ponca term for 'those dwelling here', which Dorsey wrote ¢egiha. He first presented Dhegiha as comprising two groups: Omaha-Dhegiha, with the three dialects Omaha-Ponca, Osage, and Kansa; and Kwapa-Dhegiha (Dorsey 1884:211). Later, he divided Dhegiha into four languages: Omaha-Ponca (which he called Dhegiha), Osage, Kansa, and Quapaw (Dorsey 1890:xv). Fletcher and La Flesche (1911:35) wrote that the speech of the five tribes "as yet have hardly differentiated into distinct dialects."

One feature differentiating the Dhegiha languages is the development of Proto-Siouan oral vowels (table 1). In all Dhegiha **u* fronted to *ü*, which is retained in Osage-Kansa. This *ü* unrounded to *i* in Quapaw and Omaha-Ponca (see 'shoot') and Proto-Siouan **o* raised to *u* in Omaha-Ponca (see 'woman'). Other phonological distinctions affect the glottalized fricatives (see 'snake', 'elder', and 'woman').

In the twentieth century Omaha and Ponca still formed a single language, while Osage and Kansa, also mutually intelligible, formed another. Quapaw, which is more divergent, was a third language. Although the three languages are very similar lexically and grammatically, it is unclear whether Omaha-Ponca and Kansa-Osage speakers could understand one another and whether the two speech forms were technically distinct languages or dialects of a single language. La Flesche (1932:1), who was a native Omaha speaker, stated that they were mutually intelligible, even though "terms in their rituals and songs varied." In the mid-twentieth century some Osages testified that they could understand Omaha-Ponca with difficulty, but claimed that Quapaw was completely unintelligible (Wolff 1952:63).

• OMAHA-PONCA The earliest vocabularies of Omaha and Ponca include those recorded by Maximilian (1839–1841,2:599–612, 632; in Thwaites 1904–1907, 24:280–285, 294), Say (E. James 1823:lxx–lxxviii, lxxxi–lxxxiii), and Hayden (1862:448–452). L.H. Morgan (1871:291–382) gave Omaha and Ponca kinship terms.

Dorsey's Ponca primer (Dorsey 1873) and unpublished grammar (Dorsey 1877) were based on linguistic work done as an Episcopal missionary. Subsequently, supported by Powell and the Bureau of Ethnology, he published sample Omaha texts in interlinear format (Dorsey 1879c, 1881d) and a voluminous collection of texts in Omaha and Ponca (Dorsey 1890, 1891a). He also compiled a large Omaha-Ponca slip file dictionary for the texts (Dorsey 1883–1891). His monograph on Omaha sociology (Dorsey 1884) contains linguistic data, a comparative paper on Dhegiha phonology has Ponca forms (Dorsey 1885), and another paper lists Omaha and Ponca personal names (Dorsey 1886a). He wrote and compiled numerous unpublished manuscripts on Omaha-Ponca linguistics and ethnology (Dorsey 1872–1894) and comparative Siouan linguistics and ethnology (Dorsey 1878–1894). Boas (1907) published a sketch of Ponca grammar based on Dorsey's texts and notes.

Twentieth-century sources include vocabulary in the Omaha ethnography written by Alice C. Fletcher and Francis La Flesche (1911) and in the ethnobotanical publications of Melvin R. Gilmore (1913a, 1919:139–145, 147–148). Frida Hahn (1935), a student of Boas who engaged in fieldwork in the 1930s, wrote a grammar of Ponca. Mark Swetland (1977) compiled an English-Omaha glossary.

• OSAGE-KANSA Osage and Kansa are mutually intelligible dialects of a language that does not have an inclusive, single-term designation. Osage formerly had five or more subdialects (Dorsy 1890:xv), but their differences were not described.

In the late eighteenth and early nineteenth centuries, the Kansa resided along the Kansas River in present northeastern Kansas, and the Osage occupied the territory along the Osage River in present Missouri, eastern Oklahoma,

Table 1. Development of Proto-Siouan Oral Vowels in Dhegiha Languages

	'throw, shoot'	*'snake'*	*'elder'*	*'woman'*	*'vomit'*
Proto-Siouan	**hku·te*	**wes̓á*	**š̓áke*	**wax̓ó*	**kré·pe*
Omaha-Ponca	*kkí·de*	*wes̓á*	*įš̓áge*	*waˀú*	*gðé·be*
Kansa	*kkü·ǯe*	*wec̓á*	*c̓áge*	*wak̓ó*	*lé·be*
Osage	*hkü·ce*	*wéc̓a*	*ic̓áke*	*wak̓ó*	*lé·pe*
Quapaw	*kkítte*	*wis̓á*	*š̓áke*	*wax̓ó*	*kdé·we*

WAͣSHASHE WAͣGERESSA PAHY̱GREH
TSE.

THE OSAGE FIRST BOOK.

BOSTON:
PRINTED FOR THE AMERICAN BOARD OF COMMISSIONERS
FOR FOREIGN MISSIONS, BY CROCKER & BREWSTER
1834.

14

Tabera breo.
I am going a hunting.
Maͣhi dihta hoah.
Give me your knife.
Mih pe dikiueh ?
Who gave you a blanket ?
Mi mih brimio.
I bought a blanket.
Cheh mi̱h ilaleo.
I saw a buffalo.
Chehhĭ hoa̱ke stiusa ?
Where did you get the kettle ?
Kauah laͣgeni a̱ͣkiupe.
He gave me a fine horse.
Hoa̱kithʋh latshia ?
Where did you come from ?
Mi hoa̱kithʋh shuah ?
At what time did you start ?
Hathaͣnche'laͣgari ?
When did you come ?
Hathanda laͣgareh'tatsheo ?
When will you go ?

15

Kauah dihta ka̱hsakio.
Your horse is swift.
Tah-ha hana wahni nikshe ?
How many deer-skins have you ?
Tata hnʋh sthimi tahnikshe ?
What will you buy ?
Maͣshaͣ hoaͣke talabera tahnikshi ?
Where will you hunt ?

Pe minche dikshiheh ?
Who made the bow for you ?
Maͣh dihta laͣgenimpio.
Your arrows are good.
Tah wiuke minche itselale eskah ?
Did you ever kill a deer with an arrow ?
Nikashika noampaͣh hoampaͣtʋh tah tseleh ?
How did the old men kill deer ?
Maͣhity̱ga maͣh to̱hpenahi̱h ?
Have the Americans arrows ?

Shunke hiuch y̱keini y̱kathau.
We have a great many dogs.
Maͣhitʋnga shunke ihtape wy̱ke velale eskah ?
Did you ever see American dogs ?
Eh shumekaͣse ori̱keh nʋmpio ?
They catch wolves.
Tah-skah ʋppa wachuhta laͣgenimpio.
Sheep are good animals.
Hinkeh hahhi ikahheh nʋmpio.
Blankets are made of their wool.

Fig. 3. Cover and pages 14–15 of *The Osage First Book* (W.B. Montgomery and W.C. Requa 1834), representative of mid-19th-century primers that missionaries prepared for Plains Indians. The first section of this book comprises simple Osage sentences with interlinear English translations. Subsequent sections include Osage translations of the Ten Commandments and selections from Genesis, Proverbs, Isaiah, and several books of the New Testament. In the sentences illustrated here many verbs have the endings ⟨-o⟩ or ⟨-au⟩ of male speech, showing that the lesson was designed for boys.

and southeastern Kansas. In the late nineteenth century the two tribes settled on reservations in Indian territory, later Oklahoma—the Osage in present Osage County and the Kansa in Kay County, where their members lived in the twentieth century.

Nineteenth-century vocabularies include ones by Albert Pike (Adelung and Vater 1806–1817, 3:273–274), John Bradbury (1817:213–219), Dr. Murray (Vater 1821:53–62), Say (E. James 1823:lxx–lxxviii; in Thwaites 1904–1907, 17:290–298), and Maximilian (1839–1841, 2:504, 637–645; in Thwaites 1904–1907, 24:229, 296–300; Rankin 1994b). The missionaries William B. Montgomery and William C. Requa (1834) published *The Osage First Book*, which is a combined primer and collection of biblical passages presented in Osage (fig. 3). Kansa and Osage kinship terms are given in L.H. Morgan (1871:291–382).

Dorsey (1888b) published a collection of Osage texts, and his study of comparative phonology (1885) includes Osage and Kansa data. He also compiled an Osage-English slip file vocabulary, a file of Osage personal names, and other shorter manuscripts that were never published (Dorsey 1880–1883). For Kansa Dorsey compiled parallel sets of unpublished materials: collections of texts, a slip file Kansa-English vocabulary, files of personal names and geographical names, as well as other manuscripts (Dorsey 1882–1890).

La Flesche (1932) published an Osage dictionary that incorporated Dorsey's materials and is the standard source on the language. He also published collections of Osage ritual texts presented in a standard format of free translation separate from the Osage text and followed by a set of notes giving word composition (1921, 1925a, 1928, 1930, 1939).

The linguist Hans Wolff (1952, 1952a) published papers on Osage phonology and morphology, but the value of his material is diminished by his failure to record Osage sounds correctly. Carolyn Quintero (1997) wrote a description of Osage phonology and verb morphology based on fieldwork with contemporary speakers and, based in part on lexical material collected in the 1970s by Robert Bristow, she compiled a manuscript Osage dictionary (Quintero 1995). Robert L. Rankin (1987) compiled a manuscript Kansa dictionary based on Dorsey's lexical material and his own fieldwork.

• QUAPAW The Quapaw formerly occupied an area near the junction of the Arkansas and Mississippi rivers; in the late nineteenth century they settled on a reservation in Indian Territory, in what is now Ottawa County, where they continued to reside after allotment.

The earliest Quapaw vocabulary was collected by George Izard (1827; Gallatin 1836:307–367). The most extensive Quapaw linguistic materials were recorded by Dorsey; they include a Quapaw-English vocabulary, the only collections of texts, files of personal names and names for other tribes, and other manuscripts (Dorsey 1882–1894). In 1940 Frank T. Siebert, Jr. (1989) collected a short Quapaw vocabulary and first noted vowel length as a phonemic distinction in the language. Rankin compiled a Quapaw glossary based on Dorsey's and his own materials (1991a) and wrote a grammatical sketch (1999).

Chiwere

The Chiwere (chĭ'werē) language, which Dorsey (1885:919) also named, was spoken by the Iowa, Otoe, and Missouria, each in separate dialects. Chiwere is most closely related to Winnebago, with which it forms a subgroup.

In the late eighteenth century the Iowa lived in present Iowa, and after 1827, in northwest Missouri; in 1837 they moved to a reservation on the west side of the Missouri River that straddled Nebraska and Kansas, in Richardson and Brown counties, respectively. From the early eighteenth to the mid-nineteenth centuries, the Otoe lived near the confluence of the Platte River with the Missouri; from 1855 to 1881 they occupied a reservation in southeastern Nebraska that crossed into northeastern Kansas. From the late seventeenth century the Missouria were located along the Missouri River at its junction with the Grand River but at the close of the eighteenth century most of the survivors joined the Otoe. In the late nineteenth century part of the Iowa moved to Indian Territory, where they settled on a reservation in the present Oklahoma counties of Payne, Lincoln, Oklahoma, and Logan. The Otoe and Missouria also removed to a reservation in Indian Territory and after allotment continued living in the area of Red Rock, Oklahoma.

Nineteenth-century vocabularies of Chiwere include Otoe lists recorded by Say (E. James 1823:lxx–lxxviii, lxxx; in Thwaites 1904–1907, 17:290–298, 300) and Maximilian (1839–1841, 2:612–630; in Thwaites 1904–1907, 24:285–293; Rankin 1994), and an "Iowa, or Oto" list by Hayden (1862:452–456). L.H. Morgan (1871:291–382) printed two sets of kinship terms, one for Iowa and another for Otoe-Missouria. The Protestant missionaries William Hamilton and Samuel M. Irvin published an Iowa grammar (1848), spelling book (1843), and primer (1849).

James Owen Dorsey's unpublished manuscripts are the most extensive documentation of Chiwere, and include texts, a short grammar and descriptions of the verb, collections of personal names, and a slip file vocabulary. Dorsey also retranscribed material from the manuscripts of William Hamilton and Iowa agent M.B. Kent (Dorsey 1878–1881).

In the twentieth century William Whitman, an ethnologist who studied under Boas, published a short grammatical description (Whitman 1947:233–248); and Gordon H. Marsh (1936), also a student of Boas, collected extensive materials for an Iowa grammar and dictionary. Lila Wistrand-Robinson (1972) prepared an Iowa-Otoe glossary for a language program, and Jimm G. Good Tracks (1992) compiled an Iowa-Otoe-Missouria dictionary based on material from historical and contemporary sources (fig. 4). In the 1980s Louanna Furbee and Jill Davidson recorded linguistic material from the last speakers of the language.

Internal Relationships

The relationship of the Plains Siouan languages was recognized in the mid-nineteenth century, when vocabularies for each of the languages became available. Gallatin (1836:120–128, 306) presented the first classification of Siouan, grouped under the name Sioux, comprising four subdivisions: Winnebago; Sioux proper and Assiniboine, including "doubtful[ly]" (and erroneously) Cheyenne; Minetare, comprising Mandan, Hidatsa, and Crow; and "southern Sioux," consisting of Osage-Kansa, Quapaw, Iowa, Otoe-Missouria, and Omaha-Ponca. His scheme was later reflected in other publications of the period (Prichard 1847:408; Berghaus 1845–1848:map 17). Subsequently, Gallatin applied geographical names to all the subdivisions, listing the first two as North and labeling his Minetare group West (Schoolcraft 1851–1857, 3:402).

Bancroft (1834–1875, 3:243) introduced the family designation Dahcota that in various spellings was followed by others such as Hayden (1862:232), L.H. Morgan (1871:150, 170), A.H. Keane (1878:460, 470), and Berghaus (1887:map 72). Although Hayden merely listed the members of the family, Morgan (1871:170–189) divided them into five groups based on degree of affinity: Dakota nations proper, including most Sioux divisions and bands; Missouri tribes, including all the Dhegiha and Chiwere groups; Winnebago; Mandan; and Hidatsa and Crow. Morgan's classification was followed by that of Keane (1878:470–471), who reduced the subgroups to three: a Dakota branch, comprising the Sioux and Assiniboine bands; a Winnebago branch that includes all the Dhegiha and Chiwere tribes; and an Upper Missouri branch comprising the Crow, Hidatsa, and Mandan. Dorsey (1885:919) restricted the name Dakota to Sioux-Assiniboine, and J.W. Powell (1891:114–115) used it only for the Sioux.

In 1870 Horatio Hale (1883, 1883a; J. Anderson 1872) recorded a vocabulary from one of the last speakers of Tutelo, a language spoken in colonial times in Virginia,

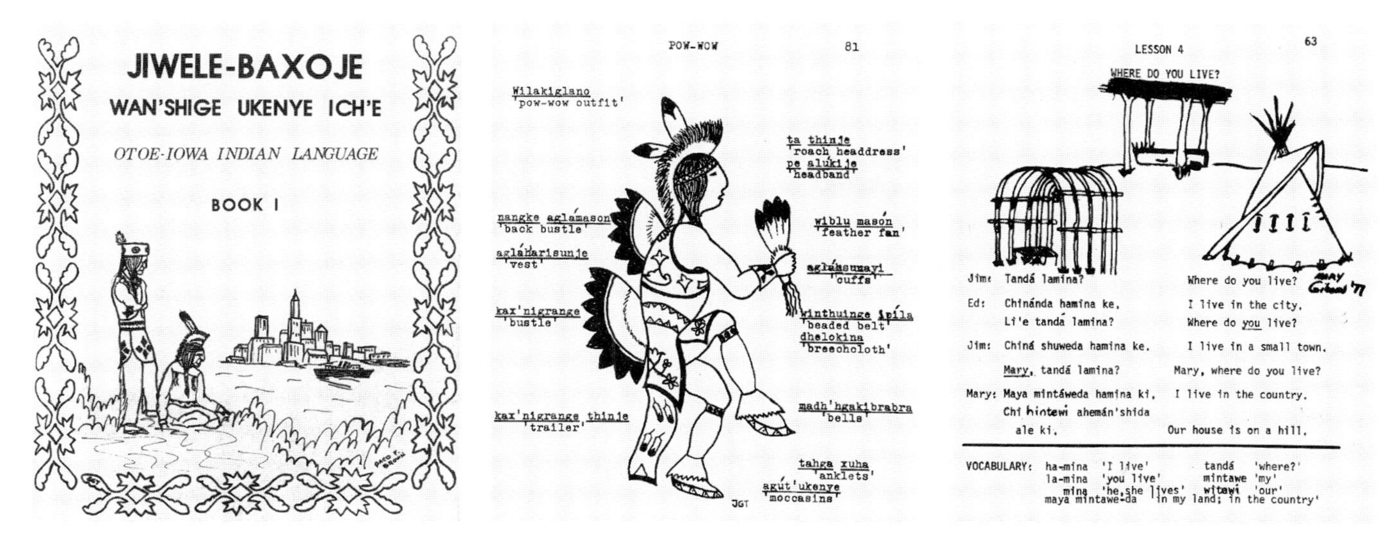

Fig. 4. Cover and excerpts from "Jiwele-Baxoje Wan'shige Ukenye Ich'e," Otoe-Iowa Indian Language Book No. 1 (Wistrand-Robinson et al. 1977), a primer used in native literacy programs. (The title page has "uk'enye.") The book consists of 111 pages of alphabet, conversational phrases, drills, and photographs and drawings. center, Lesson 14 on powwow clothing. right, Lesson 4, conversations on getting acquainted. Drawings by Jimm Good Tracks (center) and Mary Gibson (right).

and demonstrated that it was related to the "Dakotan" languages. In 1881 Albert S. Gatschet recorded linguistic material from Catawba speakers in South Carolina and suggested a Siouan relationship for that language, which Dorsey (J.W. Powell 1891:112) corroborated and Siebert (1945) later confirmed; and in 1886 Gatschet identified Biloxi, a language spoken on the Gulf coast of Mississippi, as Siouan (Dorsey 1894c; Dorsey and Swanton 1912:9–10). These languages were first included in the family by Powell (1891:111–118), who established the name Siouan for the language family, although it had actually first appeared in publications by Dorsey (1884, 1885). Powell listed 18 Siouan-speaking tribes, including the Woccon of North Carolina. Swanton (1909, 1923) later added Ofo, another language formerly spoken in Mississippi.

Swanton (1923:43) proposed an internal classification of Siouan that recognized four largely geographical groups: a northeastern comprising Hidatsa, Dakota, Biloxi, Ofo, as well as Tutelo and other languages of Virginia; a southeastern comprising Catawba and Woccon; a southwestern comprising the Dhegiha dialects; and a northwestern comprising the Chiwere dialects and Winnebago. He omitted Mandan from the classification since he was not certain where it belonged. Later, Swanton (1936) reiterated that Tutelo and Catawba belong to different subgroups, and C.F. Voegelin (1939, 1941) strengthened the evidence first that Biloxi and Ofo belong to a single subgroup and then that Crow and Hidatsa also belong to a single subgroup.

C.F. Voegelin (1941) presented the first classification based on sound correspondences. It recognizes four subgroups: an Eastern group comprising only Catawba; an Ohio Valley group (so named because Voegelin thought these tribes dispersed from the Ohio River Valley prehistorically) comprising Ofo, Biloxi, and Tutelo; a Missouri River group comprising Hidatsa and Crow; and a Mississippi Valley group comprising Chiwere and Winnebago, Dhegiha, Dakota (i.e., Sioux and Assiniboine), and Mandan. That classification, which became the standard for Siouan, has required only two modifications. First, Mandan is sufficiently different from the other Mississippi Valley languages to suggest its placement in a separate group; and, second, Catawban (Catawba and Woccon) is more distantly related to the other Siouan languages than they are among themselves and thus stands apart from them. The internal classification of Siouan is presented in table 2.

The Missouri River Siouan languages appear surprisingly different, both phonologically and grammatically, from languages in the other subgroups, and it is often difficult to recognize related vocabulary. Both Crow and Hidatsa retain initial unaccented syllables where portions have been lost in Mandan and the better-known Mississippi Valley languages (table 3) They have also lost nasality as a distinctive phonological feature, although each has phonetic [m] and [n], which are positional variants of *w* and *r* or *l*, respectively. Moreover, Proto-Siouan nasal vowels have all denasalized in both Crow and Hidatsa (see 'water') (C.F. Voegelin 1941a).

Mandan shares the loss of certain short, unaccented, initial syllable vowels with the languages of the Mississippi Valley subgroup (table 3), and it appears to have borrowed much vocabulary from Hidatsa. Those two factors cause Mandan to resemble superficially both the Missouri River and Mississippi Valley subgroups and make it the most

Table 2. Classification of Siouan Languages

Subgroup	*Languages*	*Major Dialects*
Missouri River	Crow Hidatsa	
Mandan	Mandan	Nuptare, Nuetare
Mississippi Valley		
Sioux-Assiniboine-Stoney	Sioux	Santee-Sisseton, Yankton-Yanktonai, Teton
	Assiniboine Stoney	
Chiwere-Winnebago	Chiwere	Iowa, Otoe, Missouria
	Winnebago	
Dhegiha	Omaha-Ponca	Omaha, Ponca
	Kansa-Osage	Kansa, Osage
	Quapaw	
Ohio Valley		
Virginia Siouan	Tutelo, Saponi, Moniton, Occaneechi	
Mississippi Siouan	Biloxi Ofo	

Table 3. Words Illustrating Development of Proto-Siouan Initial Syllables

English gloss	*'bison'*	*'dog (horse)'*	*'water'*
Proto-Siouan	*wité·	*wišų́ke	*wirį́
Crow	wišé· ([bišé·])	wiš ké ([biške])	wirí ([bilí], [birí])
Hidatsa	wité· ([mité·])	wašúka ([mašúka])	wirí ([mirí])
Mandan	p tį·		w rį́ ([mįnį́])
Sioux	p te	šų́ka	m ni
Winnebago	če·	šų́·k	nį·
Iowa-Otoe	č^{h}e·	sų́k-hén^{y}i	n^{y}i
Omaha-Ponca	t te	šą́ge	nį
Kansa	č če	šǫ́ge	ni
Osage	h ce	šǫ́ke	ni
Quapaw	t te	sǫ́ke	ni
Biloxi		cǫ́ki	ani
Ofo		ač^{h}ų́ki	áni
Tutelo		č^{h}ų́ki	mani

difficult of the Siouan languages to place. Because Mandan morphology is significantly different from the languages of both the Missouri River and Mississippi Valley subgroups and seems to share few clear innovations with either group, it stands alone as a distinct subgroup.

Dating

To gauge the time-depth of separations among languages within the Siouan family, several linguists made comparisons of basic vocabulary and calculated dates of separation using the technique of glottochronology (Headley 1971; Hollow in Hollow and Parks 1980; Grimm 1985; vol. 17:101). Hollow's results, which are based on more accurate or fuller data, are given in table 4. Springer and Witkowsky (1983) utilized Headley's study to develop an interpretation of Siouan prehistory and its implications for Oneota archeology.

In three separate glottochronological comparisons of Crow and Hidatsa, Pierce (1954) obtained a time-depth of 1,182 years for their separation from each other, while W.R. Wood and Downer (1977), in a methodologically flawed study, gave a time-depth of 654–970 years, and G.H. Matthews (1979) , in a critique of Wood and Downer, presented more reliable data and obtained dates ranging between 317 and 800 years.

Impressionistically, there is a somewhat greater divergence among Siouan languages than there is within the Romance, Germanic, or Slavic language families. Such an analogy with European language families suggests for Proto-Siouan a time-depth of 2,000 to 3,000 years before present, which is significantly less than that arrived at by glottochronology.

Proto-Siouan Homeland

The distribution of the four major Siouan subgroups in the seventeenth century suggests a relatively late prehistoric location for the Plains Siouan groups in the northern Mississippi Valley. Because three of the four major Siouan subgroups were represented in the area of the Dakotas at that time, some Siouanists assumed diffusion from that area. However, the remaining subgroup, Voegelin's Ohio Valley Siouan, had representatives in Virginia and Mississippi; and the Dhegiha tribes (within the Mississippi Valley subgroup) had oral traditions linking them to the lower Ohio Valley.

Table 4. Time-Depth of Separation among Selected Siouan Languages

Language Pair	*Years of Separation*
Crow-Hidatsa	600
Crow-Mandan	1,900
Crow-Sioux	2,200
Crow-Kansa/Osage	3,200
Hidatsa-Mandan	1,500
Hidatsa-Sioux	2,100
Hidatsa-Kansa/Osage	2,800
Sioux-Mandan	1,600
Sioux-Kansa/Osage	1,200
Mandan-Kansa/Osage	2,100

SOURCE: Hollow and Parks (1980:80).

Swanton (1923, 1943), an early champion of an Ohio Valley homeland for Plains Siouan peoples, proposed a northwestwardly movement of the Plains groups and a southerly and easterly movement of Tutelo, Biloxi, and Ofo from a prehistoric location somewhere in the Ohio Valley. He also recognized the distinctness of Catawban from Siouan. His conclusions were challenged by archeologists, notably James B. Griffin (1942, 1960), but neither side was ultimately able to marshal convincing proof for their claims. When Catawban in the Carolinas, with its greater time-depth, is added to the wider Siouan grouping, and the possible relationship with Yuchi, also in the Southeast, is considered, the possibility of an earlier point of origin in the East may be strengthened, but the question of the Siouan homeland remains unresolved.

External Relationships

Nineteenth-century speculation on the external relationships of Siouan to other North American language families that presaged twentieth-century ideas began with Robert Gordon Latham (1856:58, 1860:327), who thought that the Siouan and Iroquoian families belonged to a larger class that also included Catawba and Woccon, Cherokee, Choctaw, and perhaps the Caddoan languages. L.H. Morgan (1871:151) offered the opinion that the Iroquoian family was an offshoot of the Dakotan family.

In his reductionist classifications of North American languages, Edward Sapir (1921, 1929) placed Siouan-Yuchi in an Eastern group within the now-abandoned Hokan-Siouan superstock (L. Campbell 1997:262–269). Hokan-Siouan included Iroquois-Caddoan and numerous other language families, including Keresan in the Southwest and Yukian in northern California. The classification posited a close relationship between Siouan and Yuchi and of these in turn with Natchez and Muskogean, but it did not imply a close relationship between Siouan and the other groups comprising the superstock. Except for Iroquoian and Caddoan, no evidence for most of those interfamilial relationships was ever presented.

Evidence to support a relationship between Siouan and Iroquoian was offered by Louis Allen (1931) and Wallace L. Chafe (1964). Chafe (1976:7–9) proposed the term Macro-Siouan for a stock that includes Siouan, Iroquoian, and Caddoan, arguing that the evidence for such a relationship is based on similar structural characteristics—polysynthesis and morphological fusion—as well as seemingly cognate words. However, despite those similarities, the evidence to date is insufficient to prove a relationship among the three language families (Hollow and Parks 1980:81; L. Campbell 1997:262–269).

Other remote, and even more tenuous, relationships have been suggested for Siouan that would, were there evidence to support them, interconnect virtually all the language families of North America east of the Rockies. Based on lexical similarities, Mary R. Haas (1951, 1952, 1958, 1963, 1964) sought to strengthen Sapir's hypothesis of a relationship between Siouan and Yuchi as well as to establish numerous, more distant connections. At the same time William W. Elmendorf (1963, 1964) presented resemblances between Siouan, Yuchi, and the Yukian languages of California (Yuki, Huchnom, and Wappo) that he thought pointed to a possible relationship among those groups. Siebert (1945) previously demonstrated the relationship of Siouan and Catawban, and Rankin (1998) bolstered the Siouan-Yuchi hypothesis by citing morphological correspondences between Siouan-Catawban and Yuchi classificatory prefixes and pronominals. A survey of attempts to find external relationships for Siouan appears in L. Campbell (1997).

Comparative Studies

James Owen Dorsey (1885) undertook the first comparative study in Siouan, when he described certain phonological features and sound shifts in Sioux, Dhegiha, Chiwere, and Winnebago. Nils Holmer (1945, 1947) published two articles on Proto-Siouan consonant clusters that utilized data published by Dorsey. Hans Wolff (1950–1951) reconstructed Proto-Siouan phonology, as well as roots, stems, and pronominal prefix morphology. G. Hubert Matthews's (1958) dissertation provided an expanded and more accurate reconstruction, set of sound correspondences, and cognate sets, as well as a grammatical outline that includes the forms of affixes, roots, and the stem class system. G.H. Matthews also reconstructed Proto-Siouan kinship terminology (1959a) and described Proto-Siouan continuants and their development in contemporary Siouan languages (1970). Allan R. Taylor (1976) reconstructed Siouan verbs of motion and traced their development in the daughter languages, and Rankin (1977) showed how certain Proto-Siouan verbs for position (lying, sitting, and standing) have taken on an aspectual function in some languages and developed into a noun classifier system in others. David S. Rood (1979) critically assessed the sources for comparative studies and twentieth century work on subgroupings, historical phonology, historical grammar, and semantic subsystems.

In the 1980s and 1990s a group of linguists, including Richard T. Carter, A.W. Jones (1983, 1992), Koontz (1980, 1983, 1985a, 1986), Rankin (1977, 1987, 1994), and Rood were engaged in comparative studies. Carter, Jones, and Rankin, collaborating with Rood, began in 1985 a long-term project to reconstruct Proto-Siouan and to compile a comparative dictionary, and briefly surveyed Proto-Siouan phonology and grammar (Rankin, Carter, and Jones 1998).

Phonologies

The sound systems of most Siouan languages are similar in their inventories and basic contrasts.

Consonants

Characteristic of Siouan consonantal inventories are the following features:

(1) A contrast between aspirated and unaspirated stops. Most phonologies possess this contrast for labial, dental, and velar stops, and often a palato-alveolar affricate. Aspiration in Proto-Siouan was probably predictable in accented syllables, but other changes in the history of the family have rendered it distinctive now in every language except Crow, Hidatsa, and Mandan, which have lost Proto-Siouan aspiration entirely (Rankin 1994) (table 5).

(2) A contrast between glottalized (ejective) and nonglottalized stops. The Mississippi Valley languages have a series of glottalized stops that are lacking in the Ohio and Missouri valley languages as well as in Mandan.

(3) Contrasting voiced, voiceless, and glottalized fricatives in the Mississippi Valley languages.

(4) Fricatives that typically are dental, palato-alveolar, and velar in point of articulation.

(5) A coronal sonorant variously produced and perceived as *r*, *l*, *n*, *y*, *t*, or *d*, depending on the language, dialect, or phonological environment.

(6) Lack of a nasal distinction among consonants. In Crow, Hidatsa, Mandan, and perhaps Tutelo and Proto-Siouan, nasality is not distinctive among consonants; thus the phonemes *w* and *r* have phonetically nasalized variants [m] and [n], respectively.

Vowels and Accent

There are two primary characteristics of Siouan vowel systems: a contrast between oral and nasal, and a contrast between long and short. Most languages have five oral and three nasal vowels that occur both short and long.

Accent in Proto-Siouan generally fell on the second syllable of the phonological word. Stress accent systems that count from the beginning of the word are rare in the world's languages, but pitch accent systems often do so. Crow and Mandan have pitch accent systems (Gordon 1972; Graczyk 1991; R.T. Carter 1991:488), and Hidatsa probably does (A. Wesley Jones, personal communication 1999), suggesting that Proto-Sioux had pitch accent as well.

Structural Characteristics

Typologically, Siouan languages are primarily agglutinating, freely combining elements to create larger words with only a mild degree of phonological fusion, with the result that morphemic constituents of words are generally transparent or easily recognizable. Derivation by compounding, prefixation, and suffixation is used to form new verbs and nouns from a relatively small set of roots. Inflection is primarily associated with the verb, although there is limited noun inflection.

Derivation

Nouns are derived by the compounding of various elements, such as two or more nouns, or a noun and a stative or active verb. Prefixes, expressing meanings such as 'place where' and 'instrument for' are extremely common in noun derivation; common suffixes are diminutives, plural markers, and aspectual enclitics like the habitual. Verbs are also freely nominalized.

New verb stems are derived by a relatively small number of prefixes and suffixes, as well as by compounding various elements. Some of the more common derivational processes employ morphemes from the following categories:

(1) Locative prefixes. Most languages have three locative prefixes that express location (place where something occurs, 'in', 'on', or 'against'), as in Yanktonai Sioux *o'íde* 'to burn in', from *idé* 'to burn' (Parks 1999d), and in

Table 5. Words Illustrating the Development of Proto-Siouan Aspirated and Unaspirated Voiceless Stops

	'fire'	'four'	'blue/green'	'throw, shoot'	'mark'
Proto-Siouan	*ahpé·te	*tó·pa	*htóho	*hkú·te	*ká·xe
Crow		šo·pá	šu·a		-ka·xi
Hidatsa		to·pá	tóˀo-		-ka·xe
Mandan	pte	top	toho-	-kų·te	-kax-
Sioux	p^{h}éta	tópa	t^{h}o	k^{h}uté	káγa
Winnebago	pe·č	ǰo·p	čo·		ga·x
Iowa-Otoe	p^{h}é·ǯe	do·we	t^{h}o	k^{h}ú·ǯe	gá·xe
Omaha-Ponca	ppé·de	dú·ba	ttúhu	kkí·de	gá·γe
Kansa	ppé·ǯe	dó·ba	ttóho	kküǰe	gá·γe
Osage	hpé·ce	tó·pa	htóho	hkü·ce	ká·γe
Quapaw	ppétte	tó·pa	ttóho	kkítte	ká·γe
Biloxi	peˀti	topa	tóhi	kité	
Ofo	ap^{h}éti	tópa	it^{h}óhi		
Tutelo	pé·ti	to·pa	oto·	kité·	

Assiniboine *akápsų* 'to accidently spill on', from *kapsų́* 'to accidently spill' (Parks and DeMallie 1999).

(2) Instrumental prefixes. All the languages have a set of seven to nine instrumental prefixes that are freely added to verb roots to denote different types of agency, such as by pressure with the hands or body, with the foot, with an instrument or by means of a blow, and by means of the mouth or teeth (table 6). Frequently these prefixes change the class of a verb, making stative verbs active or even transitive.

(3) Indefinite prefix. In most of the languages there is a prefix *wa-* that changes transitive verbs to intransitive ones and denotes indefinite, plural objects or people: for example, Assiniboine intransitive (with indefinite prefix) *wanáxʔų* 'to listen; to hear (things)', derived from transitive *naxʔų́* 'to hear (someone or something)' (Parks and DeMallie 1999); Osage intransitive (with indefinite prefix) *waðáhtą* 'to drink (things)', from transitive *ðáhtą* 'to drink (a specific liquid)' (Quintero 1997:191).

(4) Causative suffixes. Each language has one or more causative suffixes or auxiliary forms that follow stative and intransitive verbs to make them transitive. Thus, the Osage intransitive stem *híhce* 'to hurry' becomes, with the addition of the causative suffix *-ðe*, the transitive stem *híhceðe* 'to hurry (someone)' (Quintero 1997:209).

(5) Compounding. Siouan languages allow speakers to form compound verb forms by combining another verb, an adverb, or a noun to the basic root or stem. Compounding of nouns with verb stems, sometimes termed noun incorporation, occurs extensively in Sioux and Assiniboine, illustrated by Yanktonai *čʰabʔígmųka* 'to trap beaver' from *čʰápa* 'beaver' + *igmų́ka* 'to trap' (Parks 1999d). It is described in Teton by de Reuse (1994).

(6) Sound symbolism, a prominent trait of Siouan, is a productive derivational process in all Mississippi Valley languages. There are many examples in which two fricatives occur as contrasting pairs, and some in which three occur. Examples in Quapaw are: *wasá* 'something black (a bear)', and *wašá* 'something dark (melanoma)'; *bdáze* 'burst', and *bdáže* 'spread apart' (Rankin 1991a). A three-member set in Sioux is *zí* 'yellow', *ží* 'tawny', and *γí* 'brown' (Boas 1937:139).

Inflection

Nouns are generally inflected only for possession and definiteness.

Siouan languages, which typologically are active-stative (or split intransitive), distinguish between two major verb classes: stative verbs, comprising what in English are largely adjectives, and active verbs that are transitive and intransitive. The subjects of stative verbs and the objects of active transitives take the same pronominal affixes, while the subjects of active verbs, both transitive and intransitive, take a different set of pronominal affixes.

Verbs are typically inflected for person. There are both subject (agent) and object (patient) pronominal affixes (prefixes or infixes) for first, second, and inclusive (you and I) forms, but there is no affix for third person. Separate affixes or enclitics indicate subject and object pluralization in a weakly developed number-marking system. Reflexive, reciprocal, subject possessor, dative, and benefactive forms of verbs are also formed by prefixes or infixes.

Other verbal categories—aspect, mode, negation, and evidentiality—are marked by particles that are enclitic to the verb. Verbs are normally inflected for aspect rather than tense and have a number of distinct modalities that are signaled by post-verbal enclitics that mark assertion, emphasis, imperatives of different kinds, interrogative, and other modes.

In the Mississippi Valley Siouan languages, gender is also generally marked by different enclitics for male and female speakers. In Sioux, Assiniboine, and Stoney, for example, gender of the speaker is indicated by different declarative, interrogative, and imperative particles, while in Mandan the gender of the person addressed is marked by separate enclitics (Boas and Deloria 1941:109–112; Hollow and Jones 1976; Trechter 1995). In Biloxi the gender of both the speaker and addressee can be marked (Dorsey and Swanton 1912:3).

Syntax

All Siouan languages have the basic word order subject-object-verb (SOV), together with many of the syntactic

Table 6. Quapaw Instrumental Prefixes and Illustrative Stems Based on the Root *baγe* 'to sever'

Instrumental prefix	*Example*
pá- 'by cutting, by bladed tool'	*pábaγe* 'to cut in two with a blade'
ba- 'by pushing'	*babáγe* 'to break by thrusting'
bi- 'by pressing'	*bibáγe* 'to break by pressure; to sit on and break'
pó- 'by shooting'	*póbaγe* 'to shoot (a rope or cord) in two'
da- 'by use of the mouth'	*dabáγe* 'to bite in two'
na- 'by use of the feet'	*nabáγe* 'to break with the feet'
di- 'by pulling, by use of the hands'	*dibáγe* 'to break by pulling'
ka- 'by striking'	*kabáγe* 'to cut in two by striking, to chop in two'
tá·- 'by extreme temperature'	*tá·baγe* 'to burn in two'

orderings that verb final languages tend to have: postpositions (in contrast to prepositions); main verb preceding auxiliary verb; inalienable possessor prefixed to noun; and subordinate clause preceding main clause. Siouan languages also have several secondary syntactic patterns that are congruent with their overall (S)OV structure: adverbials precede the main verb; and number, tense, aspect, and modal particles are enclitic to the verb. Adjectives follow their nouns in Siouan languages, but those adjectives are actually stative verbs and thus may be considered the syntactic heads of their constructions.

Most Siouan languages classify nouns according to shape or position. In languages such as Assiniboine and Sioux, that classification is reflected in partially overlapping sets of verbs of position (standing, sitting, lying) that are used when referring to the location of animate and inanimate objects (Boas and Deloria 1941:126–127; University of Colorado Lakhota Project 1976, 2:12/7–13). The position of animate objects is determined by their actual or characteristic position, while for inanimate objects the use of positional verbs is determined by a classification based on physical shape (tall, standing; short, sitting; long, lying; and randomly scattered). In the Dhegiha languages there is a similar classification of nouns that is reflected in definite articles that modify nouns. Those articles are marked for animacy (animate versus inanimate), position (sitting, standing, lying), and movement (Rankin 1977; Quintero 1997:239–349).

Parallel sentences in four Siouan languages that illustrate transitive clauses and case marking, noun-adjective order, and article usage are given in table 7, set 1. These sentences show grammatical differences as well as closely parallel patterns. The verb 'kill' is a compound of 'die' plus a causative auxiliary in Omaha-Ponca and Biloxi but is a lexical verb in Teton Sioux. Crow, Teton, and Omaha-Ponca require definite articles with the subject, but Biloxi does not, and the articles are not cognate across the other languages; hence the origins of that morphology remain unclear. Case marking for nouns is not general in Siouan but exists in the Dhegiha subgroup, where *ak^{h}a* marks animate, stationary subjects.

Clauses illustrating intransitive-active order, some case marking, and the use of postpositions are given in table 7, set 2. Although intransitive word order is always SV, there are important differences among the languages: the postpositions, suffixes, and enclitics are not cognate among the subgroups, although cognate postpositions and enclitics among these languages do exist.

Clauses illustrating intransitive-stative order and a relative clause are in table 7, set 3. In Biloxi the relative clause 'who killed the deer' is preposed to its head, while in the other languages the relative clause appears postposed to its head. Articles and demonstratives (Crow *-š*, Teton *kį hé*, Omaha-Ponca *ak^{h}a*, and Biloxi *ya*) serve as relativizers in all the languages, but none is cognate from one subgroup to the next.

Table 7. Clause Structure and Syntactic Features in 4 Siouan Languages

Set 1	*Transitive clauses and case marking, noun-adjective order, and article usage*
Crow	*i·sâ·kši-w háčke·-š û·xa-w dappé·-k* young.man-HEAD tall-DEF deer-a kill-DECLAR 'The tall young man killed a deer.'
Teton	*k^{h}oškálaka hą́ske kį (he) t^{h}áxča wą kté* young.man tall the DEM deer a kill 'The tall young man killed a deer.'
Omaha-Ponca	*núžįga snéde ak^{h}a ttáxti wį ṫé-ða biamá* boy tall SUBJ deer a die-CAUS they.say 'The tall boy killed a deer.'
Biloxi	*sįtó tudé máyą té-ye* boy tall turkey die-CAUS 'The tall boy killed a turkey.'
Set 2	*Intransitive active clause order, some case marking, and the use of postpositions*
Crow	*i·sâ·kše·-š â·še kuss-basâ·-k* young.man-DEF river toward-run-DECLAR 'The young man is running to the river.'
Teton	*k^{h}oškálaka kį wakpála ektá íyąke* young.man the river toward run 'The young man is running to the river.'
Omaha-Ponca	*núžįga ak^{h}a wat^{h}íška k^{h}e ttáðišą ttąðį́ biamá* boy SUBJ river the.lying toward run they.say 'The boy ran toward the river.'
Biloxi	*sįtó ayixyą́ mą́kiwayą tąhį́* boy bayou toward run 'The boy ran toward the bayou.'
Set 3	*Intransitive-stative clause order and a relative clause*
Crow	*i·sâ·kši-w û·xe·-š ak-dappê·-š háčka-k* young.man-HEAD deer-DEF REL-kill-DEF tall-DECLAR 'The young man who killed the deer is tall.'
Teton	*k^{h}oškálaka wą t^{h}áxča kį kté kį hé hą́ske* young.man a deer the kill the DEM tall 'The young man who killed the deer is tall.'
Omaha-Ponca	*núžįga ak^{h}a ttáxti ṫé-ðe ak^{h}a snéde abiamá* boy SUBJ deer die-CAUS REL tall they.say 'The boy who killed the deer is tall.'
Biloxi	*itá té-ye yą sįtó tudé* deer die-CAUS REL boy tall 'The boy who killed the deer is tall.'

Borrowings

Siouan languages are characterized by a strong resistance to lexical and grammatical borrowing from neighboring Indian as well as European languages. The number of lexical borrowings, for example, ranges from a dozen or fewer identifiable forms in Mandan and Sioux to perhaps 20 or somewhat more words in Dhegiha languages. Such borrowings are also generally restricted to a small number of semantic domains—ethnonyms, garden plants, animals, and personal names—in which vocabulary was typically being added in the course of cultural contacts and innovation. In Siouan languages, however, almost all new vocabulary for cultural and other innovations was derived using native linguistic elements to form descriptive designations.

Of the major divisions within Siouan, the Dhegiha group shows evidence of contact with Algonquian speakers. Those older influences, which undoubtedly preceded the late eighteenth century, seem to include two phonological changes and a replacement in the numeral system:

(1) The complex consonant clusters that occur in Sioux and Mandan are reduced in Dhegiha to only the types permitted generically in central Algonquian for fricatives and clusters of *h* followed by a stop (e.g., **pt* and **kt* become *ht* or *tt*, **ks* becomes *ss* or *s*).

(2) In two Dhegiha languages, Omaha-Ponca and Quapaw, the common Siouan five-vowel system has been replaced by a four-vowel system as in Algonquian languages.

(3) In Chiwere, as well as Dhegiha, the Siouan decimal counting system has been replaced with a partial quinary system in which 'seven' and 'eight' are based on 'two' and 'three', respectively, combined with a derivational affix, as in Algonquian.

Identifiable loanwords from Algonquian languages are few and include words for 'bow', 'squash', and 'beans' (Koontz 1986; Rankin 1994a).

Tribal ethnonyms that have a wide geographical distribution and are often of uncertain provenience occur in all the Siouan languages. One commonly borrowed ethnonym is the name for the Cheyenne that occurs as Teton Sioux *šahíyela* (Buechel 1970:460), and Santee-Sisseton Sioux and Assiniboine *šahíyena* (S.R. Riggs 1890:440; Parks and DeMallie 1999); compare Pawnee *sahe?* and Arikara *ša·hé?* (Parks 1999, 1999c). The term for Cree and Ojibwa is another such borrowing: Assiniboine *šahíya* (Parks and DeMallie 1999), Mandan *šahí* (Hollow 1970:223), Hidatsa *šahí* (A.W. Jones 1979:63); cf. Arikara *šAhí?A* (Parks 1999c). So also is the term for Spaniard or Mexican, which derives from French *espagnol* 'Spaniard': Santee-Sisseton *spaníyo wič^hháša* (J.P. Williamson 1902:217), Teton *spayóla* (Raymond J. DeMallie, personal communication 1999), Mandan *íšpari?ori* (Hollow 1970:385), and Osage *į́špaðǫ* 'European' (Carolyn Quintero, personal communication 1999), Kansa *éspanone* (Rankin 1987:42), and Quapaw *spái?ą* (Rankin 1991a:52). A similar borrowing is ultimately from older French *(le)s anglois* 'the English': Assiniboine *šakná* 'mixed-blood; Métis' (Parks and DeMallie 1999), Santee-Sisseton *sagdáši̜* and *sagdáša*, Teton *šagláša* 'Englishman' (S.R. Riggs 1890:430, 440), Omaha Ságanasch, Otoe Sanganasch, Osage Sanganásch 'Englishman' (Maximilian in Thwaites 1904–1907, 24:281, 287, 297); the intermediary was older Ojibwa Ságanasch 'Englishman' (Maximilian in Thwaites 1904–1907, 24:277), later *ša·kana·šš* (J.D. Nichols and E. Nyholm 1995:174, retranscribed).

At least two European domestic animal terms that are distributed widely over North America occur in various Siouan languages. One is the term for 'hog' or 'pork', derived from dialectal French *coucouche* (A.R. Taylor 1990), which occurs as Sioux *k^hukhúše* (S.R. Riggs 1890:299; Buechel 1970:319); Assiniboine *kukúša* (Parks and DeMallie 1999); Omaha-Ponca *kkukkusi* (Dorsey 1891a, retranscribed); Kansa-Osage *kkokkósa* (Rankin 1987:82; La Flesche 1932:88, retranscribed); cf. Arikara *kúhkUx* and Pawnee *kuhkus* (Parks 1999, 1999a). Another is the English term *puss* or *pussy* 'domestic cat', which occurs as Assiniboine *púza* (Parks and DeMallie 1999), Teton *pusíla* (Raymond J. DeMallie, personal communication 1999), Mandan *pús* and *pusé* (Hollow 1970:159), Hidatsa *pu·šíhke* (A.W. Jones 1979:17); Cheyenne *póéso* (Glenmore and Leman 1985:4); and Pawnee *pús* (Parks 1999a). Other borrowed animal terms include Osage *hkáwa* and Kansa *kkawáye* 'horse' from Spanish *caballo* (Carolyn Quintero, personal communication 1999; Rankin 1987:78).

Some ethnonyms are loan translations of designations that are common among many tribes and are often reflected in the sign language designation for a group; others are direct or indirect borrowings of a tribe's own name for itself (see the synonymies, this vol.).

Examples of miscellaneous borrowings include Crow *akíssatre·* 'soldier' from Sioux *akíc^hita* 'soldier' and *wáre·* ([bále·]) 'money' from English (Randolph Graczyk, personal communication 1999). Osage *lą́ðe* and Kansa *lą́ye* 'big' come from Spanish grande (Carolyn Quintero, personal communication 1999; Rankin 1987:83).

Among the Sioux and Assiniboine in the twentieth century there were occasional local borrowings that were used on a specific reservation or in a specific community. Illustrating those are the English kinship terms *p^hapá* 'papa, daddy' and *mamá* 'mama, mommy' used on the Pine Ridge Reservation (A.R. Taylor and D.S. Rood in University of Colorado Lakhota Project 1976, 1:7–33, 7–34). Assiniboine *múniya* 'White man', from Plains Cree *mo·niya·w* 'White person' (Ahenakew 1987a:237), was formerly used only on Carry The Kettle and White Bear reserves (Parks and DeMallie 1999). Other borrowings were restricted to a single dialect, as English *baby*, borrowed as Teton Sioux *bébela*, with diminutive suffix *-la*.

Literacy

The development of materials to promote literacy was one of the first efforts of Christian missionaries among Siouan tribes in the early nineteenth century. For Protestant missionaries on the eastern Plains, who undertook that work as early as the 1830s, their first products were primers that typically presented a writing system as well as translations of English words, sentences, and biblical stories or passages. Primers were printed for Osage (W.B. Montgomery and W.C. Requa 1834), Santee-Sisseton Sioux (Stephens 1836; S. R. Riggs 1877, 1881), Otoe (M. Merrill 1837), Iowa (Hamilton and Irvin 1843, 1849), Omaha (E. McKenney 1850), and Ponca (Dorsey 1873). Subsequent native language materials usually included hymnals, representative of which are ones for Otoe (M. Merrill 1834), Iowa (Hamilton and Irvin 1843a), Omaha (Hamilton 1887), Santee-Sisseton Sioux (Renville and Williamson 1842; Hinman 1869, 1871, 1874), Hidatsa (C.L. Hall 1895), and Mandan (C.L. Hall 1905). They also included translations of books of the Bible, such as those for Santee-Sisseton (see Pilling 1887:6), Iowa (Hamilton and Irvin 1850; Pilling 1887:32), and Omaha (Hamilton 1868); as well as catechisms, like those for Santee-Sisseton (Renville and Williamson 1837; S.W. Pond 1844; S.R. Riggs 1864), Iowa (Hamilton and Irvin 1850a), and Yankton Sioux (J.W. Cook and C.S. Cook 1882).

Roman Catholic missionization, which began among the Santee in Minnesota in the 1840s, is represented primarily by a native language summary of doctrine, prayers, Bible history, and songs (Ravoux 1843, 1876; see Pilling 1887:58). At Saint Paul's Mission on the Fort Belknap Reservation, Edward M. Griva (1894–1895) compiled an Assiniboine dictionary and translated a short catechism with prayers into the language; at Saint Francis Xavier and Saint Charles missions on the Crow Reservation, Griva and Aloysius Vrebosch also prepared Crow catechisms with prayers, Peter Paul Prando compiled translations of Old and New Testament history, and an unknown author translated hymns (for a list of manuscripts and mimeographs see Carriker, Carriker, Carroll, and Larsen 1976:25–28; Missionaries of the Society of Jesus 1891). Of the Jesuit missionaries among the Sioux, only Eugene Buechel promoted the use of Sioux as a medium of instruction and, using the orthography of the Protestant missionaries, he published a Bible history (1924) and a combined prayer book and hymnal (1927) in the Teton dialect. Beginning in 1879, Benedictines from St. Meinrad Abbey, among them the priest Jerome Hunt, missionized on the Standing Rock and Devils Lake reservations and published a prayer book (J. Hunt 1907) and a hymnal (B. White and J.C. Baine 1919).

One of the most successful efforts to establish literacy among a North American Indian people was that of the Protestant missionaries among the Sioux. Members of the Dakota Mission had the indispensable assistance of Joseph Renville, a mixed-blood French-Dakota trader fluent in both French and Santee, who until his death in 1846 either made or supervised all translations of the gospels and other religious materials prepared by the missionaries. Development of Sioux-language biblical translations, hymnals, and other tracts, as well as native language primers and readers to aid in building literacy, continued over the ensuing decades of the nineteenth century. These materials were used in the Dakota Mission schools, including Santee Indian Training School, which established a press for printing Indian language materials. An important part of the general effort to promote literacy was publication of Sioux-language newspapers—the Congregational *Iapi Oaye/The Word Carrier* (1871–1939), the Episcopal *Anpao Kin/The Day Break* (1878–1937), and the Catholic *Šina Sapa Wocekiye Taeyanpaha/The Catholic Sioux Herald* (1892–1939). By the end of the nineteenth century and throughout the first half of the twentieth century, most adult Sioux people were literate in their language. After publication of the Sioux language newspapers ceased during the 1930s and native language use waned in reservation communities after World War II, literacy in Sioux was no longer taught and most individuals failed to learn to read and write their language.

During the World War II era, in a reversal of previous policy to stamp out native languages, the U.S. Indian Service attempted to promote literacy and preserve native language use by introducing bilingual readers to Sioux, Navajo, and Hopi students in government boarding

THE HEN OF WAHPETON

The War-Bonnet family
lived at Wahpeton
in a small log house
and a big canvas tent
with a goat and a hill
and a tree and a dog,
a fine root cellar
and a place with a fence
that could be used
for a chicken yard.

UNJINCILA WAȞPETʿUN
ETANHAN KIN HE

Wapʿaha tʿiwahe kiŋ
Waȟpetʿuŋ oyaŋke el tʿipi.
Cʿaŋtʿipi waŋ cikʾala otʿipi
na wakʿeya tʿipi waŋ tʿaŋka
kʿo otʿipi,
tʿatʿokala waŋ, na paha waŋ
na cʿaŋ waŋ, na šuŋka waŋ
hecʿel wicʿayuhapi makʿatʿipi
waŋ lila wašte na owaŋka kiŋ
okšaŋ acʿuŋkaška he
he kʿokʿoyaȟʾaŋla otʿi tʿiʾokšaŋ
kiŋ el uŋpʿica kiŋ hecʿa.

7

Fig. 5. Title p. and p. 7 from *About the Hen of Wahpeton* (1943). This is the first of 9 Indian Service readers in English and Teton Sioux. Printed by students at Haskell Indian School. Drawings in the book are by Andrew Standing Soldier, a well-known Sioux artist.

schools. Between 1941 and 1947 a Sioux series of nine readers at different grade levels was printed bilingually, with Teton and English text on facing pages. The stories, with titles like *The Hen of Wahpeton* (fig. 5) and *Singing Sioux Cowboy* (A.H. Clark 1943, 1947), were composed in English by children's writer Ann Clark, then translated into Lakota by Emil Afraid-of-Hawk (Pine Ridge Reservation), and presented in a phonemic orthography created by linguist Edward Kennard. The readers did not have a significant impact on Sioux education, and their orthography never gained currency.

Language Revival Programs

In the late 1960s the bilingual education movement, in which non-English speaking students were first taught in their native language and then gradually transitioned to instruction in English, took form in the United States. At the same time an interest in native-language instruction began to develop among younger people in many Plains Siouan reservation communities. Over the ensuing three decades, with funding primarily from the U.S. Department of Education, language programs were established in reservation school districts and tribal colleges across the Northern Plains. Programs were also initiated in some Oklahoma schools that served members of Siouan tribes.

Sioux

In the late 1960s schools in many Sioux communities began to take an active role in initiating bilingual education programs, the earliest of which were Loneman (Loud Hawk et al. 1969) and Holy Rosary elementary schools on the Pine Ridge Reservation and Saint Francis School on the Rosebud Reservation. By 2000 nearly all reservation schools had some form of language instruction that usually began in Headstart programs and continued through high school; but in the 1990s, when most elementary and secondary students no longer learned Teton at home, the programs had become language revival or enrichment efforts.

Among the Sioux the late twentieth-century native language revival movement generally ignored the missionary orthographies and instructional materials that had been used for over a century; instead, each program, operating independently, developed its own writing system and teaching materials. Despite attempts at numerous conferences over several decades to establish a uniform orthography, none gained general acceptance. Although many programs developed their own teaching materials or eschewed written materials in favor of oral instruction, the interest in language instruction generated several useful textbooks. Foremost among them is the set produced by linguists David S. Rood and Allan R. Taylor (University of Colorado Lakhota Project 1976) that includes a two-year two-volume college-level language textbook, an elementary bilingual dictionary, and a reader for Teton as spoken on the Pine Ridge and Rosebud reservations. In part derivative from it is a textbook by Albert White Hat, Sr. (1999), who is a member of the Rosebud Sioux tribe. Another useful textbook for Teton was developed for use in secondary schools on the Rosebud Reservation (Hairy Shirt, et al. 1973), but it suffers from use of a nonphonemic orthography. For Santee-Sisseton there is also a college-level textbook (Decora, Flute, and Dunnigan 1972–1973).

In addition to language programs in local communities, several universities offered language courses in the Teton and Santee-Sisseton dialects. The first courses began in the early 1970s at the University of Colorado, Boulder (Teton), and the University of Minnesota (Santee-Sisseton). Subsequently, courses were regularly offered at other universities in North and South Dakota and Nebraska.

Assiniboine

Beginning in the 1980s Assiniboine was taught in elementary and secondary schools on the Fort Belknap and Fort Peck reservations and at Fort Belknap and Fort Peck colleges, as well as at Saskatchewan Federated Indian College in Regina. Here, too, each school relied largely on materials prepared by current language teachers. At Fort Belknap College in the late 1990s a comprehensive set of instructional materials was developed, including a one-year language textbook, multimedia language lessons that incorporate sound recordings, student and verb paradigm dictionaries, and a reader (Parks, Ditmar, and Morgan 1999).

Stoney

In the 1990s Stoney was taught in the elementary school at Morley.

Crow

In 1974 both a bilingual education project and a Bilingual Materials Development Center were established on the Crow Reservation. The goal of the program, which served primary grades in elementary schools in Crow Agency, Lodge Grass, and Hardin, was to transition Crow-speaking children to speaking English. The program, which continued through the early 1980s, established a practical orthography for writing Crow and printed curriculum materials, including readers, two dictionaries (Tushka 1979; Medicine Horse 1987), and instructional guides. After a hiatus of a decade, new bilingual programs were started in Lodge Grass and Hardin schools. The most extensive and effective program was one serving all grades at Pretty Eagle School, the Roman Catholic mission school established by Jesuits. Little Big Horn College also offered courses in Crow language since its founding in 1983

(Carlene Old Elk and Timothy McLeary, personal communication 1999).

Hidatsa and Mandan

In the late 1970s the North Dakota Indian Languages Program (Mary College, Bismarck, North Dakota) produced curricular materials that were used for teaching Hidatsa in the Mandaree School, Mandaree, North Dakota, and Mandan in the Twin Buttes Elementary School (Hollow and Jones 1976). Language instructional programs continued through the end of the century in both those schools, as well as in New Town and Parshall schools. When founded in the mid-1970s, Fort Berthold Community College mandated native language instruction as a fundamental goal of the college. However, no suitable textbook or dictionary was available for teaching either Mandan or Hidatsa.

Dhegiha and Chiwere

In the 1990s elementary Omaha was taught in the public schools and Nebraska Indian Community College in Macy, Nebraska. During the same period informal Ponca language classes were organized several times in White Eagle, Oklahoma, and beginning in fall 1999 a Ponca class was offered in Frontier School in Red Rock, Oklahoma. Beginning in the 1980s Osage was taught sporadically by a speaker-facilitator team at the White Hair Memorial Center, Fairfax, Oklahoma; and after 1994 Carolyn Quintero regularly taught Osage to adults in Tulsa, Oklahoma. Quintero (1999) wrote a textbook that was used in her classes, in informal language classes in Hominy, Oklahoma, and, beginning in 1999, in the Skiatook, Oklahoma, public schools. There were no instructional programs for Kansa, Otoe, or Quapaw.

Language Use in the Late Twentieth Century

By the end of the twentieth century there were no fluent speakers of two Dhegiha dialects—Quapaw and Kansa—or Chiwere. Table 8 gives the number of fluent or near-fluent speakers of each Plains Siouan language in 1999. For each language there are, in addition, indeterminate numbers of semifluent individuals.

Only Crow, Sioux, and Stoney—and perhaps Hidatsa—were first languages for, or actively used by, relatively large numbers of speakers. Among other Plains Siouan tribes, in which there were relatively few speakers, usually all elderly, native language use was generally limited to social contexts in which its use served to define an event symbolically as a tribal occasion (fig. 6). At public gatherings—particularly at funerals, religious meetings, and dances—an opening prayer was offered by an elderly speaker in the native language, and if an announcer knew his language, he would occasionally announce in it. At dances singers sang songs with native lyrics when they knew them. In the same contexts elderly speakers bestowed native names on individuals, particularly on children or young people who wanted that symbol of tribal identity or whose parents wanted the next generation to carry on family names.

Crow speakers were notable among Plains Indians for an unusually strong commitment to using only their native language with other Crow speakers, regardless of conversational topic or the presence of non-Crow speakers (Graczyk 1992). As a consequence, Crow remained viable through the end of the twentieth century. However, during the last three decades of the century there was a progressive decline in its use among children. In 1969, for example, Read (1978:91) found that 82 percent of a sample of Crow children were primary speakers of Crow who had

Table 8. Estimated Fluent Speakers of Plains Siouan Languages, 1999

Language or Dialect	*Estimated Speakers*	*Source*
Crow	4,500	Randolph Gracyzk, personal communication 1999
Hidatsa	400	A. Wesley Jones, personal communication 1999
Mandan	6	Mauricio J. Mixco, personal communication 1999
Santee-Sisseton	600	Raymond J. DeMallie, personal communication 2000
Yankton-Yanktonai	300	Raymond J. DeMallie, personal communication 2000
Teton	5,000	Raymond J. DeMallie, personal communication 2000
Assiniboine	100	Raymond J. DeMallie, personal communication 1999
Stoney	3,000	Eung-Do Cook, personal communication 1999
Iowa	0	Louanna Furbee and Jimm Good Tracks, personal communications 1999
Otoe-Missouria	0	Kathleen Shea and Jimm Good Tracks, personal communications 1999
Omaha	40	Margery Coffey, personal communication 1999
Ponca	25	Margery Coffey, and Kathleen Shea and Parrish Williams, personal communications 1999
Kansa	0	Robert L. Rankin, personal communication 1999
Osage	6	Carolyn Quintero, personal communication 1999
Quapaw	0	Robert L. Rankin and Gloria Young, personal communications 1999

Lib. of Congress, Amer. Folklife Center.

Fig. 6. Welcoming sign at the Omaha annual powwow. Photograph by Carl Fleischhauser, Omaha, Nebr., 1983.

learned it as their first language and spoke it with family and friends, while only 18 percent had English as their primary language. In 1976, the children whose first language was Crow or who were equally proficient in Crow and English had dropped to 73 percent, while the number of those whose primary language was English had grown to 26.5 percent (Read 1978:94–95). In 1992 only 33 percent of children spoke Crow as a first language, 27 percent understood but did not speak it, and 28 percent did not understand it (LaForge in Graczyk 1992:7).

The number of Hidatsa speakers declined steadily during the late twentieth century, but by 2000 there were still families in which the language was used, primarily in the Mandaree, New Town, and Parshall communities. At dances and other social events in those communities it was not uncommon to hear Hidatsa spoken by an announcer, and in religious ceremonies it was always used. In the 1980s the language was occasionally used by Hidatsa members of the Fort Berthold Tribal Council in meetings.

As in most other northern Plains communities, Hidatsa also survived in traditional music, where old songs as well as new ones with recently composed Hidatsa lyrics were sung by both younger and older men. Most Hidatsas also symbolically maintained their linguistic heritage by taking Hidatsa personal names that were passed down in families.

Around 2000, Stoney was the primary language of about 80 percent of the population at Morley and half the population on Alexis and Paul's Band reserves (fig. 7). At Morley political meetings were conducted in Stoney, but minutes were taken in English (Eung-Do Cook and David R. Miller, personal communications 2000).

The largest number of Teton speakers was on the Pine Ridge and Rosebud reservations, although there were significant numbers of speakers on Lower Brule, Cheyenne River, and Standing Rock reservations. On Pine Ridge Reservation, Sioux was the dominant language in outlying communities such as Wanblee, Slim Buttes, Red Shirt, and Potato Creek, while English was the dominant language in Pine Ridge Village and other towns with large mixed-blood populations. On Rosebud Reservation there were contrasts among communities like Spring Creek and Ring Thunder, in which Sioux was the first language of most adult members, and larger, more acculturated communities like Mission, Rosebud, and Antelope, in which English was the first language of the majority. On the Cheyenne River Reservation members of remote communities like Red Scaffold and Iron Lightning generally spoke Sioux as their first language, but in Dupree and Eagle Butte English was the first language of most people. On Standing Rock Reservation the majority of Teton speakers were found in the Little Eagle and Bullhead communities in South Dakota, while relatively few fluent speakers lived in Wakpala and McLaughlin, South Dakota, and Fort Yates, North Dakota.

Through the mid-twentieth century the majority of Pine Ridge Sioux spoke their language, but in the second half of the century the knowledge and use of Lakota declined rapidly. Maynard (1968:12–13) found that although 75 percent of the population spoke Lakota, they used English more than Lakota. Even though 99 percent of full bloods were Lakota speakers, only 14 percent of full-blood households were entirely or primarily Lakota-speaking. Only 28 percent of mixed bloods under 30 spoke Lakota, as opposed to 55 percent over 30.

Over the ensuing two decades language use continued to decline among both full and mixed bloods, and in the 1990s most children, including even those living in Lakota active communities, spoke primarily English. On other reservations most children grew up speaking little or no Lakota.

Despite the relatively large number of active Teton speakers, there were two striking features of Lakota language usage in the late twentieth century. One was frequent interspersion of English words, phrases, and idiomatic expressions in Lakota conversation and even occasionally in speech in ceremonial contexts. Such code switching indicated that Lakotas often preferred to use English for expressing Western objects and concepts rather than to use native terms for them (E.S. Grobsmith 1981:91–95). The other striking feature among speakers on all Teton reservations was a contrast between the speech of

Stoney Cultural Education Program, Morley, Alta.

Fig. 7. Mountain Stoney alphabet, developed in 1970 in cooperation with the Summer Institute of Linguistics, based on Roman orthography. top, Alphabet; bottom, poster used in the language program, © 1972. The text translates: "People! These days it's good to have relatives so hold on to them!"

older, fluent speakers and younger individuals, generally middle-aged adults. Younger speakers in most communities developed a generational dialect characterized by contractions, shortened forms of words, slang expressions, and indifference to many of the phonological distinctions in Lakota, particularly the contrasts between aspirated, unaspirated, and glottalized stops, as well as by a limited vocabulary and simplified morphology and syntax.

There were relatively few Yankton speakers in the area of the former Yankton Reservation and only small numbers of elderly Yanktonai speakers on the Crow Creek, Devils Lake, and Fort Peck reservations. Most Yanktonai speakers lived in the Cannon Ball community on Standing Rock Reservation, where in the late twentieth century the language was still actively used in some homes and even spoken by a small number of children.

In communities in Minnesota, North and South Dakota, and Nebraska, Santee-Sisseton was no longer actively used by a significant population in the late twentieth century. In Manitoba language use varied dramatically. At Sioux Valley and Oak Lake reserves in the late 1970s at least 75 percent of the population, including children, spoke their language. In 1999, however, only five children at Sioux Valley spoke it. In the same year at Birdtail Reserve the percentage of speakers was relatively small, and at Dakota Tipi Reserve there was only a small number of speakers (Paul Voorhis, personal communication 1999). On the Saskatchewan reserves the situation was comparable: the language was spoken by individuals over 40 years of age on the Standing Buffalo, Moose Woods, and Sioux Wahpeton reserves. On the Sioux Wahpeton Reserve, those adults generally spoke Cree as well (David R. Miller, personal communication 1999).

In Sioux communities throughout the twentieth century, the language remained a strong symbol of identity, even when a significant number of people did not speak it. Rituals were always conducted in Sioux, so that ritual leaders who spoke Sioux regularly served communities in which there was no local speaker to fill that role. At public events—dances, powwows, dedications of buildings—elders offered introductory prayers in Sioux, singers sang songs with Sioux lyrics, and announcers would generally switch between Sioux and English, even when the audience was primarily English-speaking. Young people who were not speakers often learned a small stock of words that served to identify themselves as Lakotas. Similarly, nonspeakers who attended native rituals were instructed beforehand to use certain key Lakota terms or phrases—*mitákuye oyásʔį* 'all my relatives'—at appropriate times if they were to participate. Finally, in Christian church services worshipers continued to sing the songs in Sioux-language hymnals compiled in the nineteenth and early twentieth centuries.

In the late twentieth century there were efforts to bring Sioux into public discourse and to adapt the language to the linguistic needs of contemporary life. The *Lakota Times*, for example, originally a Pine Ridge–based newspaper serving Sioux reservations in the Northern Plains, carried a column written in the language. And there were attempts to create and standardize Teton terms for contemporary objects and activities, such as stockcar race, welfare recipient, U.S. Forest Service, and items in office technologies (Starr 1994).

Hunting and Gathering Tradition: Canadian Plains

IAN DYCK AND RICHARD E. MORLAN

The Canadian Plains stretch from the Rocky Mountains to the Manitoba Lowlands and from 49° west longitude to the North Saskatchewan River. This northernmost part of the Plains contains 540,000 square kilometers of open grasslands bordered by aspen parklands (fig. 1).

The Canadian Plains were buffalo country from the time of deglaciation until the advent of historic agriculture. For 12,000 years, buffalo hunting was the mainstay of subsistence. Other game and wild plants were used as supplements or as last resorts in times of scarcity, but never as long-term alternatives. Aboriginal people in southern Manitoba even attempted agriculture, about A.D. 1400, but that northernmost example of prehistoric agriculture was short-lived (McLeod 1987:42–44).

Canadian Plains prehistory is organized into the Early or Paleo-Indian period (12,000–6500 B.C.), and the Middle (6500–2000 B.C.) and Late (2000 B.C.–A.D. 1750) periods, corresponding to the Hunting and Gathering or Plains Archaic tradition in the United States. The Middle and Late periods are treated here; the Early Period is discussed in volume 3 of the *Handbook*. The Middle period is characterized by atlatl dart-size projectile points. The Late period is represented by mixed use of atlatl dart and arrow-size projectile points, a substantial increase in mass bison hunting, and, in its later part, the use of pottery.

Which sort of human groupings may be correlated with an archeological complex is not precisely known. For the Plains, it may be something on the order of a long-lived regional association of bands. Thus, a complex shows the greatest integrity. An aggregate may contain more than one complex with the perceived ambiguity involving roughly contemporaneous entities. A series may also contain more than one complex, but the ambiguity includes sequent entities. Closely related contemporaneous complexes may be combined to form a composite, and related serial complexes may comprise a tradition. This scheme constitutes an amalgamation and reworking of several existing classifications (Reeves 1970, 1983; Syms 1977; I. Dyck 1983; Foor 1985; M.L. Gregg 1986).

The chronology used here is based upon evaluation and calibration of hundreds of radiocarbon dates (Buchner 1979, 1980; L.B. Davis 1982; I. Dyck 1983; Brumley and Rushworth 1983; M.L. Gregg 1986; Morlan 1988, 1993, 1999; Beaudoin 1991; Frison 1991). Calibrations were performed with the CALIB computer program using the 20-year (bi-decadal) data set for dates in the range 0–8,140 radiocarbon years before present (Stuiver and Reimer 1986). Calibrated dates are given in Gregorian calendar years (A.D. or B.C.).

Middle Period, 6500–2000 B.C.

Mummy Cave Series

By 7000 B.C., the people of the Northern Plains began to participate in a continent-wide stylistic changeover from lanceolate and stemmed projectile points to smaller side-notched points. It is generally believed that this change reflects the adoption of a new weapons system with throwing and thrusting spears being replaced by smaller darts propelled with an atlatl or throwing stick; however, there is little direct evidence for the propulsion mechanism.

The earliest examples of side-notched points have been subsumed under the label Mummy Cave complex in the west (Reeves 1969), the Logan Creek complex in the east (Kivett 1959, 1962; Buchner 1980), or the Logan Creek/Mummy Cave complex (M.L. Gregg 1986). E.G. Walker (1992) uses discriminant analysis to define five point types that form a sequence, with overlap, spanning more than 2,500 years: (1) Blackwater Side-Notched, known from Mummy Cave in northwestern Wyoming and the Stampede site in Alberta, 6400–6000 B.C.; (2) Northern or Bitterroot Side-Notched, widespread in Alberta, Montana, and Wyoming, 6000–4900 B.C.; (3) Hawken Side-Notched, known from Wyoming 5400–4100 B.C., perhaps persisting somewhat later on the Colorado Plateau; (4) Gowen Side-Notched, from Montana and Alberta eastward to south-central Saskatchewan, 4900–4350 B.C.; and (5) Mount Albion Corner-Notched (fig. 2), widespread in the Colorado Front Range from about 4600 to perhaps 3200 B.C.

The earliest notched points in Alberta are associated with lanceolate points that mark a transition from late Paleo-Indian styles. These date to 7200 B.C. at Hawkwood (Van Dyke and Stewart 1985) and 6610 B.C. at Boss Hill Locality 2 (M. Doll 1982). Both components, as well as many others in Alberta, are found stratigraphically below Mazama tephra that dates to about 5650 B.C. (Bobrowsky et al. 1990). Mummy Cave series components also occur above Mazama tephra, and a date of 3980 ± 170 B.C. (GX-6394A) at the Mona Lisa site (M.C. Wilson 1983) may approximate the end of Mummy Cave time in Alberta. At

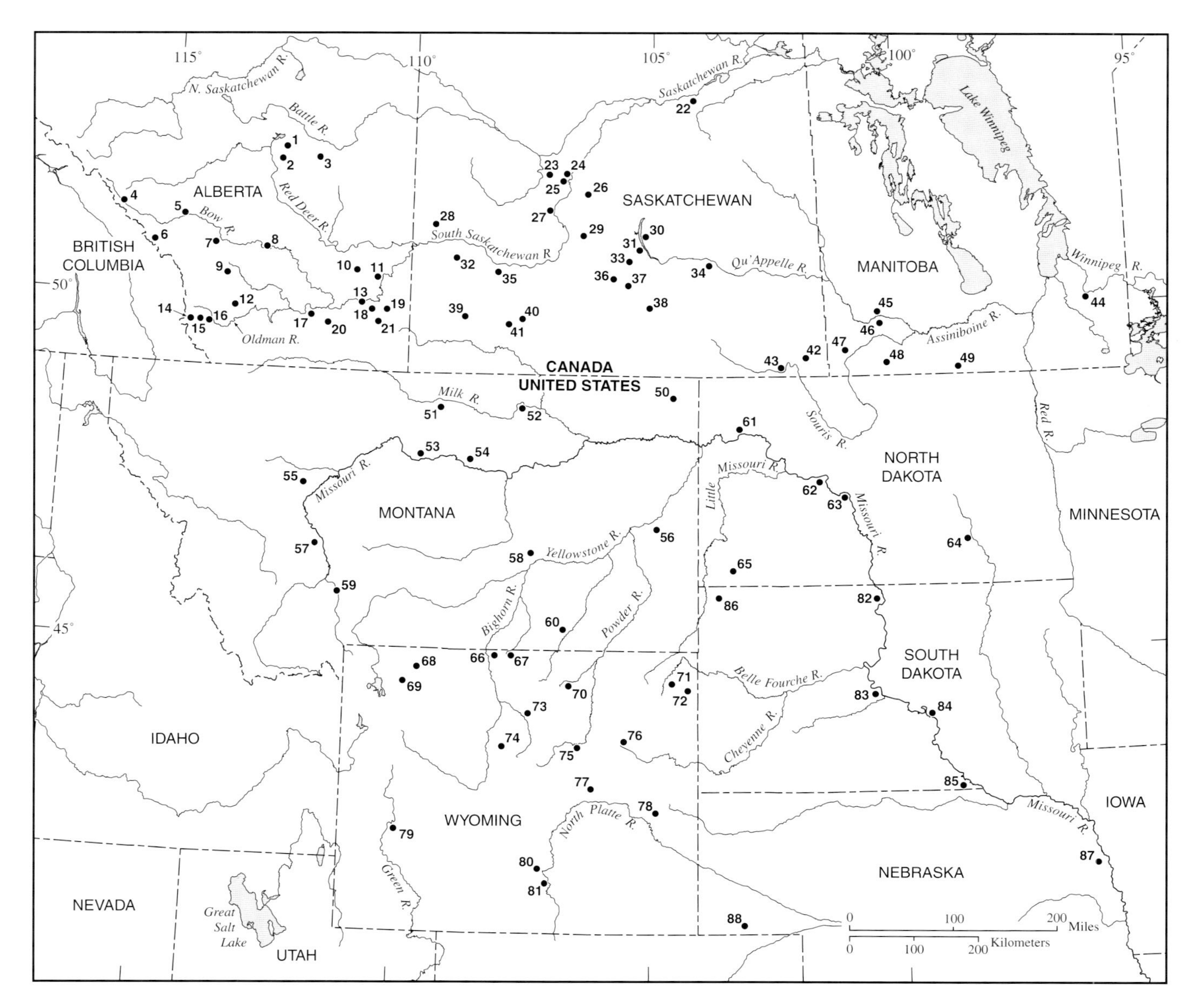

Fig. 1. Hunting and Gathering tradition archeological sites of the northern and central plains. Alberta: 1, Boss Hill Loc 2 (FdPe-4); 2 Muhlbach (FbPf-1); 3, Castor Creek (FbOw-1); 4, Vermillion Lakes (EhMv-8); 5, Coal Creek (EhPp-1); 6, Sibbald Creek (EgPr-2); 7, Hawkwood (EgPm-179) and Mona Lisa (EgPm-3); 8, Cluny (EePf-1); 9, Old Women's (EcPl-1); 10, Ramillies (EcOr-35); 11, Cactus Flower (EbOp-16); 12, Calderwood (DkPj-27) and Head-Smashed-In (DkPj-1); 13, Southridge (EaOq-17); 14, Mapleleaf (DjPo-46); 15, DjPm-44 and DjPm-98; 16, DjPl-11; 17, Cranford (DlPb-2); 18, Ross Glen (DlOp-10); 19, Larson (DlOn-3); 20, Fletcher (DjOw-1); 21, Stampede (DjOn-26). Saskatchewan: 22, Crown (FhNa-86) and Bushfield West (FhNa-10); 23, Harder (FbNs-1) and Tschetter (FbNr-1); 24, Amisk (FbNp-17), Redtail (FbNp-10), and Thundercloud (FbNp-25); 25, Gowen 1 (FaNq-25), Gowen 2 (FaNq-32), Hartley (FaNp-19), Fitzgerald (ElNp-8), and Norby (FaNq-56); 26, Bradwell (EkNm-1); 27, Sjovold (EiNs-4); 28, Elma Thompson (EiOj-1); 29, Melhagen (EgNn-1); 30, Lake Midden (EfNg-1); 31, Bethune (EeNg-6); 32, Heron Eden (EeOi-11); 33, Stoney Beach Midden (EdNh-1); 34, Lebret (EeMw-26); 35, Gray (EcNx-1a); 36, Walter Felt (EcNm-8); 37, Mortlach (EcNl-1); 38, Avonlea (EaNg-1); 39, Gull Lake (EaOd-1); 40, Niska (DkNu-3); 41, Napao (DkNv-2); 42, Oxbow Dam (DhMn-1); 43, Long Creek (DgMr-1) and Woodlawn (DgMr-6). Manitoba: 44, Whitemouth Falls (EaLa-1); 45, Stott (DlMa-1); 46, Lovstrom (DjLx-1); 47, Brockinton (DhMg-7); 48, Richards Kill (DhLw-2) and Richards Mounds; 49, Star Mound (DgLq-1). Montana: 50, Tufton; 51, Wahkpa Chu'gn (24HL101); 52, Henry Smith (24PH794); 53, Lost Terrace (24 CH68); 54, Keaster (24PH401); 55, Sun River (24CA74); 56, Ayers-Frazier (24PE30); 57, Pilgrim (24NW675); 58, Stark-Lewis (24GV401); 59, Schmitt (24BW559); 60, Kobold (24BH406). North Dakota: 61, 32WI12; 62, High Butte (32ME13); 63, 32OL270; 64, Naze (32SN246); 65, Red Fox (32BO213). Wyoming: 66, Bottleneck Cave (48BH206); 67, Wortham Shelter (48BH730); 68, Dead Indian Creek (48PA551); 69, Mummy Cave (48PA201); 70, Billy Creek; 71, McKean (48CK7); 72, Hawken (48CK303); 73, Leigh Cave (48WA304); 74, Wind River Canyon (48HO10); 75, Leath; 76, Ruby (48CA302); 77, Dunlap-McMurry (48NA675); 78, 48PL21; 79, Wardell (48SU301); 80, Sand Creek; 81, Scoggin (48CR304). South Dakota: 82, Stelzer (39DW242) and Swift Bird (39DW233); 83, LaRoche (39ST9); 84, Truman Mounds (39BF224); 85, Scalp Creek (39GR1); 86, Lightning Spring (39HN204). Nebraska: 87, Logan Creek (25BT3); 88, Sidney (25CN55).

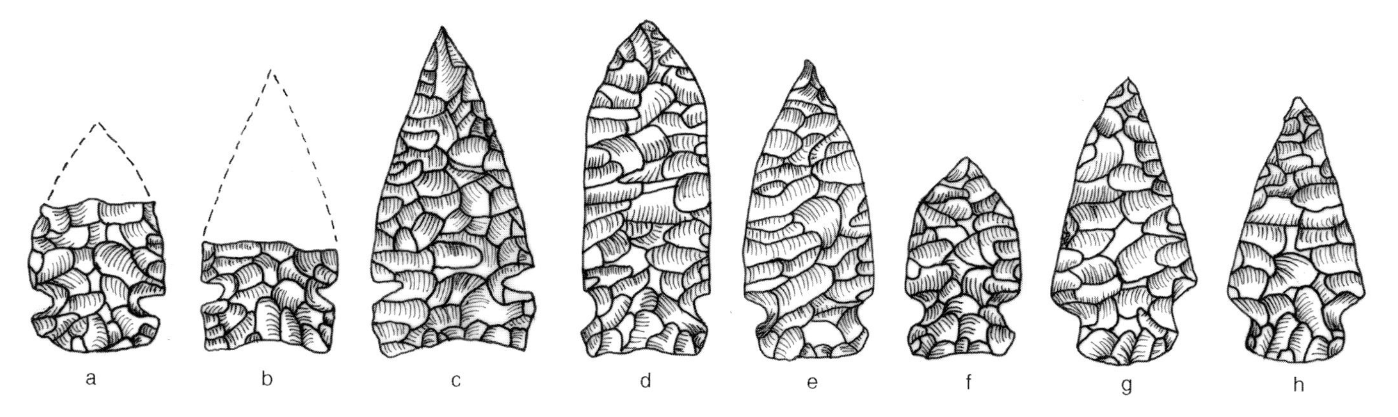

after E.G. Walker 1992:fig. 23.

Fig. 2. Idealized projectile point types of the Early Middle Prehistoric period, Mummy Cave complex. a, Blackwater Side-Notched; b–c, Northern (Bitterroot) Side-Notched; d–e, Hawken Side-Notched; f, Gowen Side-Notched; g–h, Mount Albion Corner-Notched. Length of c 4 cm. Drawn by Roger Thor Roop.

a number of Alberta sites, Mummy Cave components occur stratigraphically below younger complexes such as Oxbow (Stampede) (Gryba 1976) or within sequences containing both younger and older complexes (Vermilion Lakes) (Fedje 1986). However, in Saskatchewan, Mummy Cave components have not been found beneath younger stratified sequences, and the best sites—Gowen 1, Gowen 2, and Norby—are situated on a distinctive landform known as the Saskatoon Terrace (E.G. Walker 1992; Zurburg 1991). These sites date to 4850–4500 B.C., and the difference in site setting, as compared with Alberta, may signify a delay in the evolution of modern landforms in the middle course of the Saskatchewan River system.

The time span of the Mummy Cave series roughly corresponds to the warm dry Altithermal climatic interval proposed by Antevs (1955), and failures to find sites dated to this period (6300–2550 B.C.) were attributed to climatically induced abandonment of the Plains by people and bison, hence the hiatus shown in many sequences (Mulloy 1958; Wormington and Forbis 1965). It is clear that the Plains area was not abandoned (Hurt 1966; Reeves 1973; Mackinnon and Stuart 1987; E.G. Walker 1992), although people and bison may have experienced episodic and regional fluctuations (Vance, Matthews, and Clague 1992). Climatic changes may have transgressed from west to east (Barnosky, Grimm, and Wright 1987) and from south to north (E.G. Walker 1992). However, even the most rapid changes probably took place over several human generations, and these can hardly be invoked as causes of rapid cultural change (Schweger 1987:374). In fact there is little evidence of cultural change in the Northern Plains throughout the two or more millennia of the Mummy Cave series. Climatic influences may be seen in the short duration, limited areal extent, sparse assemblage content, and close adjacency to reliable water sources that characterize most Mummy Cave series sites. The people seem to have comprised "mobile bands using large territories within a thinly populated region" (Shay 1971:72).

Both technology and typology suggest sparse population with little opportunity for frequent communication and trade. The projectile points are highly variable (fig. 3a–f), and when found out of context they may be confused with late prehistoric artifacts (Reeves 1973:1246; I. Dyck 1983:92; M.L. Gregg 1986:104; Frison 1991:87–88). Exotic stone types are relatively rare in Mummy Cave components, although most assemblages contain at least a trace of them. Perhaps the most interesting lithic suite from this time period has been found in the Norby site on the Saskatoon Terrace. Swan River chert is predominant, followed by Knife River flint among the formed tools and fine-grained quartzite in the debitage. Less common are Gronlid siltstone from near the forks of the Saskatchewan River, fused shale from the Estevan area of southeastern Saskatchewan, and a distinctive agate from western Montana. The Gowen sites, also on the Saskatoon Terrace, exhibit heavy reliance on quartzite cobbles and split chert pebbles (fig. 3g–k), the pebbles involving a bipolar technology used to make scrapers and wedges throughout the Northern Plains (E.G. Walker 1992; M. Doll 1982; M.C. Wilson 1983; Quigg 1984; Van Dyke and Stewart 1985).

Bone artifacts, relatively rare, include a needle (Stampede), a chopper (Mona Lisa), and an antler flaking tool (Boss Hill). The Gowen sites contain the most interesting bone industry with awls or perforators, flaking tools, flaked bone knives, and a bone tube made on a pronghorn metacarpal. The Gowen 2 site yielded possible examples of a netting hook and a paint dauber as well as a tentatively identified bison effigy made of bitumen.

All Mummy Cave series faunal assemblages are dominated by bison. Post-Mazama bison at Mona Lisa Locality C are "near or above the [size] limit for modern bison" (M.C. Wilson 1983:367), and all three sites on the Saskatoon Terrace contain bison slightly larger than

Canadian Mus. of Civilization, Hull, Que.: a–f, FANq-32, g–k, FaNq-25.

Fig. 3. Mummy Cave series chipped stone tools. a–f, Projectile points from the Gowen 2 site, Saskatoon Terrace, Sask. g–k, Split chert pebbles from the Gowen 1 site, Saskatoon Terrace, Sask. Width of i, 3.9cm; rest same scale.

modern (Zurburg 1991; Morlan 1992). These findings, tentatively suggesting that *Bison bison occidentalis* is represented, are consistent with the Hawken site analysis in Wyoming (Frison, Wilson, and Wilson 1976) and with M.C. Wilson's (1978) model of Holocene bison evolution.

The biometric studies also provide information on the age and sex structure of the intercepted herds and the season of procurement. The lower post-Mazama bone bed at Mona Lisa represents a nursery herd killed in the winter, whereas the Norby site contains the remains of a bull herd killed during the winter. Both Gowen sites contain nursery herd samples, probably procured during the late summer or early fall. Nowhere is the method of procurement clear, and various authors have speculated about snowdrift traps, ambush at watering sites or crossing places, or miring in a marsh as at Mapleleaf (Landals 1990). Although the Mummy Cave components at Head-Smashed-In have been interpreted as the remains of a bison jump (Reeves 1978), no other sites of this age have been shown to be bison jumps. It may be noteworthy that Early Plains Archaic people used the Kobold site in Montana as a campsite whereas later occupations used the site as a bison jump (Frison 1970, 1991).

While bison was the economic mainstay, other animals were exploited occasionally. Wapiti (elk) and deer are found at several sites, and ground squirrels, often assumed to be self-intruded, may have been consumed at Stampede (see Gryba 1975:143). Abundant canid bones at Gowen 1 (n=111) and Gowen 2 (n=164) raise the question of the role of canids in human society (Krozser 1991). Only a few could be positively identified as wolf, coyote, or fox, and dogs or wolf/dog hybrids may account for most of the bones (E.G. Walker 1992). In any case, they represent large canids that could have supplied hides suitable for use as camouflage while hunting bison (Catlin 1841:illus. no. 110). The Gowen sites also yielded bones of muskrat, pocket gopher, chipmunk, and deer mouse, although the reasons for their presence are unclear. A clearer picture of the role of small mammals is seen at Boss Hill Locality 2 where swift fox and snowshoe hare bones are broken and charred, and teeth representing several species of rodents were screen-washed from hearth matrix (M. Doll 1982). Unlike Early Plains Archaic sites to the south, there is little evidence for plant use in Canadian Mummy Cave components. Goosefoot (*Chenopodium* spp.) seeds at Gowen 1 could well have been introduced to the site as smudge materials or in bison dung used as fuel (E.G. Walker 1992). The significance of the chokecherry seed at Boss Hill is not clear, and the associated "milling stones" are nondescript pieces of sandstone that might have served any of several functions.

The manufacture of bone grease is a very important innovation that can be traced to sites of the Mummy Cave series. Reeves (1990:170) presents a good summary concerning the importance of bone grease in "pemmican technology . . . represented in archaeological sites by rocks fractured during stone boiling, bone boiling pits, extensively smashed selected bones, and bone spill piles." In his review of Northern Plains sites, Reeves finds no evidence for bone grease manufacture before about 2800 B.C. However, E.G. Walker's (1992) report on the Gowen sites clearly reveals 2,000 years earlier all the diagnostic traits of bone grease manufacture at both localities. Limb bone ends were especially targeted for this purpose, with the result that bison gender analysis depends entirely on carpal and tarsal bones. Hundreds of small fragments of limb bone articular surfaces are associated with large quantities of fire-broken rock, hearths, boiling pits, and bone spill piles. Bone grease manufacture was a seasonal activity best performed in the fall when bison were in prime condition and water could be boiled with heated rocks outdoors. Gryba (1975:146) suggests that bone grease was made in the Mummy Cave component at the Stampede site.

Pit houses like those at Early Archaic sites in Wyoming (Frison 1991:83–86) have not been found on the Canadian Plains. Component 1 at Hawkwood yielded evidence of one or more tepeelike shelters outlined by cobbles used as hold-downs (Van Dyke and Stewart 1985). Similarly, little is known of burial practices for the Mummy Cave series. Two burials dated to this period—Dunlap-McMurry and Whitemouth Falls Feature 10-76—lack diagnostic artifacts (Buchner and Pujo 1977; Zeimens et al. 1976). Although now within the forest, the Whitemouth Falls site is thought to have been within the grassland zone when an adult female was interred in a flexed position and covered with a patina of red ocher (Buchner 1980:125–126). An ocher-filled clamshell dish was found near the skull, and a bison skullcap smeared with ocher had been placed over the lower leg region. At the Gray site, a large burial ground primarily associated with the Oxbow complex, two burial units contain large side-notched points (Millar 1978), and the earliest dates extend into the temporal period of the Mummy Cave series (Morlan 1993).

Oxbow Complex

By 4000 B.C. side-notched points exhibit a widespread stylistic change with basal thinning producing a concave basal outline and a distinctive eared appearance (fig. 4a–f). The points were named for the Oxbow Dam site (D'A.C. Greene 1998), and the Oxbow culture in Long Creek Levels 7 and 8 defined the complex (Wettlaufer and Mayer-Oakes 1960).

Oxbow points have been found throughout the grassland and parkland areas northward from western Nebraska (G.F. Carlson et al. 1999), northern Wyoming (Husted 1969), and western Montana (S.T. Greiser et al. 1983; S.T. Greiser, T.W. Greiser, and S.M. Vetter 1985). In Alberta the Oxbow complex is found stratigraphically above Mummy Cave series components (Stampede, Hawkwood), but in Saskatchewan this is the earliest complex found in stratified sequences (Long Creek, Amisk-Amundson 1986). Formal characteristics of projectile points from some of the earliest components (Oxbow Dam, Long Creek Level 8) can be seen as transitional between the Mummy Cave series and Oxbow, and many aspects of lithic technology exhibit continuity. In addition to the projectile points, the tool kit includes point preforms, ridged and flat-topped end scrapers, flake perforators and gravers, unifacial and bifacial knives, spokeshaves, wedges, a variety of choppers, hammerstones, and anvils. Bipolar split-pebble technology continues, particularly for the manufacture of scrapers and wedges. Most stone tools are made with locally available raw materials. Knife River flint is known from several sites, but the Southridge Oxbow component contains a remarkably small amount of exotic stone (Brumley 1981).

Although such scarcity of imported lithics might seem to imply limited trade connections, the Oxbow complex reveals the first evidence of long-distance trade in nonlithic materials, including copper, presumably from the Great Lakes region, and beads made of marine shells from the Atlantic coast. Both shell and bone were used to make ornaments such as beads and gorgets, and bird tracheal segments were worn as beads (fig. 4g–j). A copper crescent, certainly traded westward to Alberta from the Great Lakes Old Copper culture, has long been attributed to the Oxbow complex, although it was actually found in the bed of Castor Creek some 15 meters downstream from the deposit that contained the Oxbow points (Forbis 1970). Excavations covering about 60 percent of the Gray burial ground have revealed 99 burial units containing the remains of 304 individuals (Millar 1978, 1981). Both primary extended interments and secondary bundle burials incorporating as many as 14 people were placed in this site over several millennia. Red ocher was found in many graves, either rubbed on the bones or mixed with the pit fill, and eagle talons were found with a few of the burials. One grave also contained the primary interment of a dog. Radiocarbon dates on the Gray site range from 4400 to 1700 B.C. (Millar 1978; Morlan 1993), and it is not certain that the younger dates (<2400 B.C.) are associated with the Oxbow complex. Oxbow points were found in only seven burial units, three of which have been dated (4150–3300 B.C.).

The largest known Oxbow habitation site is the Harder site, which covers about 1,000 square meters (I. Dyck 1977). Although architectural features were lacking, the outlines of circular dwelling floors, perhaps once covered by tepeelike houses, were inferred from the distribution of artifacts and faunal remains. Stone hold-downs were not found, but the location of the site in a sand hill area distant from water suggests a winter season occupation during which snow could be used to secure pegged lodge covers and to provide drinking water. Bison tooth eruption and

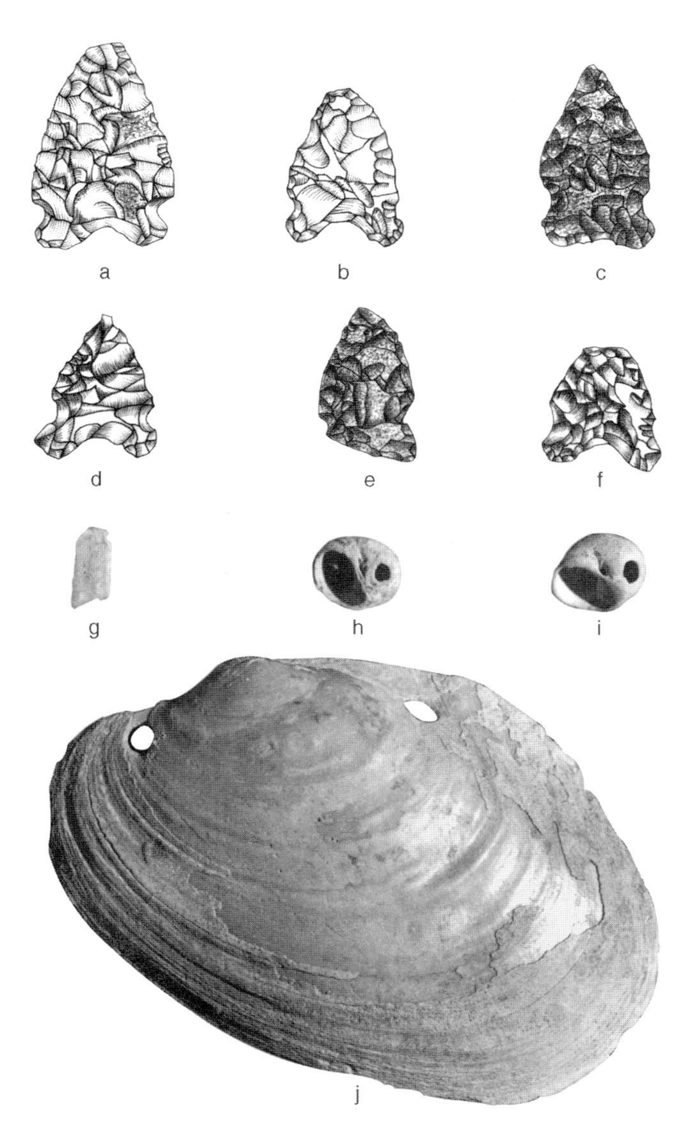

a–f, Canadian Mus. of Civilization, Hull, Que.: FbNs-1. g–j, U. of Sask., Dept. of Anthr., Saskatoon: EcNx-1.

Fig. 4. Oxbow complex artifacts. a–f, Projectile points from the Harder site, Sask. Drawn by Roger Thor Roop. g–j, Shell ornaments from the Gray site, Sask. Width of h, 1.6 cm; rest same scale.

wear patterns confirm the winter occupation, and both male and female bison were taken (Morlan 1994). I. Dyck (1977) estimated that perhaps 50 people and 30–40 dogs were supported for three to six weeks by procuring approximately 100 bison.

There is no known kill site where a specific method of bison procurement can be inferred for the Oxbow complex. At Harder individualistic and small-group kills of one or a few bison each contributed to the maintenance of the habitation site. Once again, canid bones comprise a noteworthy component of the fauna, second only to bison, and all five species are present—wolf, dog, coyote, red fox, and swift fox (Morlan 1994). Wolves are most abundant, especially with cranial elements, and it may be that camouflage robes with the unbutchered head still in place were used to hunt bison until the robes were damaged and discarded in the campsite. A stress-induced pathology at the distal end of a dog radius may reflect the use of this animal in heavy traction such as pulling a travois (see also Millar 1978:365–367). Although Oxbow hunters usually focused on bison, they also took other game. At Sun River they procured every ungulate native to the northern Plains with pronghorn predominant in one component (S.T. Greiser, T.W. Greiser, and S.M. Vetter 1985).

The temporal duration of the Oxbow complex is not clear. Most radiocarbon dates indicate a termination around 2450 B.C. (Morlan 1993), but several dates suggest a continuation to 1200 B.C. There is evidence, mostly from poorly stratified sites, for a persistence of the Oxbow complex in parkland and forested areas, and the issue is by no means settled (T.H. Gibson 1981).

McKean Series

Around 3700 B.C. new projectile point styles appeared in the headwaters of the Yellowstone drainage and quickly became widespread in the Wyoming basins. Named for the McKean site, this series includes the lanceolate McKean, stemmed Duncan, and side-notched Hanna types. The McKean series "has been proposed as originating from all four cardinal directions as well as the mountains" (Kornfeld and Frison 1985:43; see also J.B. Benedict and B.L. Olson 1973). Forbis (1985:29) observes that indigenous development on the Central and Northern Plains should also be considered. The McKean series appears some 500 years earlier in northern Wyoming than in the Canadian Prairie provinces, and in Canada it appears suddenly in territory already occupied by the Oxbow complex. For example, the Cactus Flower (Brumley 1975), Redtail (C.L. Ramsay 1993), and Thundercloud sites (Mack 1999; S.M. Webster 1999) contain multiple McKean components.

It is not clear whether the northward spread of McKean represents a movement of people or the diffusion of ideas. Favoring the movement of people are the ongoing persistence of Oxbow and a notable difference in mortuary style between Oxbow and McKean. McKean interments have been recovered from the living floors of habitation sites without accompanying red ocher, whereas all known Oxbow burials are ocher-covered in large burial grounds or isolated graves (E.G. Walker 1986). Favoring the diffusion of ideas, such as projectile point styles, is a change in subsistence economy as McKean spreads northward. The recovery of charred seeds from McKean sites in Wyoming, Montana, and the Dakotas and the even more common occurrence of handstones and milling slabs are characteristics that prompt comparisons with Desert culture in the Great Basin (Keyser 1986), but these traits have not been found in Canadian sites where the subsistence base is clearly focused on bison (Brumley 1975). However, throughout the entire region McKean peoples evince highly adaptable responses to local resources, relying on mountain sheep and deer in the foothills (Husted and Edgar 1968; Lahren 1976; Frison and D.N. Walker 1984), wapiti and moose in the southern boreal forest of Saskatchewan (Quigg 1986a), and pronghorn along with bison in the grasslands (Brumley 1975; Keyser and Davis 1984). There are even hints that fishing may have played a minor subsistence role, from channel catfish (*Ictalurus punctatus*) spines at Bottleneck Cave and Cactus Flower (M.A. Graham, M.C. Wilson, and R.W. Graham 1987:417) and suckers at the Crown site.

The McKean method of bison procurement remains obscure. The Scoggin site clearly functioned as a fenced surround (Lobdell 1973), but it is unique for this time period. At Cactus Flower, bison were ambushed at a river crossing (Brumley 1975). The widespread occurrence of more solitary ungulates, such as sheep, deer, and moose, shows that McKean peoples were skilled opportunistic hunters.

Hints of a variety of dwellings are associated with the McKean series. There are many rockshelter occupations in Wyoming and Montana, and features at the McKean and Dead Indian Creek sites are thought to represent pit houses (Frison 1991:97–100). A partially exposed large, shallow depression at the Red Fox site in southwestern North Dakota may have been a dwelling floor (Keyser 1982), and a circular pattern in an artifact distribution at Cactus Flower probably reflects the former location of a tepee with a central hearth and an east-facing entrance (fig. 5).

McKean tool kits from Canadian sites include a variety of bifaces, gravers, end and side scrapers, spokeshaves, pebble cores, cobble tools, hammerstones, and anvils. Bone was used to make awls, scrapers, and beads, while antler was used for percussion and pressure flakers. Shell beads and disks, a stone pipe and a fossil ammonite septum are known from Cactus Flower (Brumley 1975). Ammonite septa, called buffalo stones by the Blackfoot, were carried as personally owned effigies of bison (Forbis 1960:158; T.F. Kehoe 1965). The Crown site yielded a dentalium shell that reflects participation in long-distance trade extending to the Pacific coast (Quigg 1986a). Some

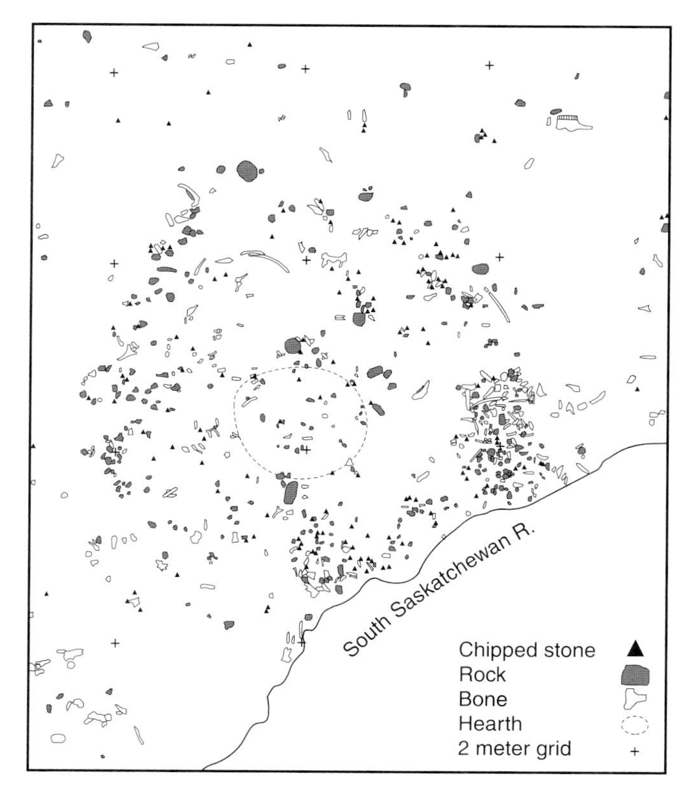

after Brumley 1975: fig. 7.

Fig. 5. McKean dwelling floor plan. Circular concentration of debris in Layer VIII of the Cactus Flower site, Alta. Drawn by Roger Thor Roop.

of the normally perishable items known from dry sites such as Mummy Cave and Leigh Cave must also have accompanied the northward spread of McKean, including wooden foreshafts, cordage, basketry, sinew, hide clothing, and moccasin padding made of grass and hair (Frison and Huseas 1968; Husted and Edgar 1968; Wedel, Husted, and Moss 1968).

The co-occurrence of the McKean, Duncan, and Hanna point styles may have several explanations. Syms (1969, 1970) suggested that each represents a different ethnic group and that co-occurrence reflects interactions among groups. Reeves (1969) and Brumley (1975) see the styles as forming a temporal sequence beginning with McKean and leading to Duncan and Hanna (R.P. Wheeler 1954; Morlan 1993). C.M. Davis and J.D. Keyser (1999) propose a functional interpretation with some points used for atlatl darts and others for spears.

Late Period, 2000 B.C.–A.D. 1750

Pelican Lake Series

Pelican Lake refers to archeological remains characterized by corner-notched projectile points and dating from 1850 B.C. to A.D. 350 (Wettlaufer 1955; Wettlaufer and Mayer-Oakes 1960; Reeves 1970, 1983; Syms 1980:365; I. Dyck 1983:105–107; Brumley and Dau 1988:33–35; Keyser and Davis 1984:50–54).

By about 1850 B.C. forests and peatlands on the northern fringes of the Plains had begun to encroach 50–100 kilometers farther south into lands previously covered by parklands and grasslands. This shift, apparently completed by about 650 B.C., was caused by a change toward cooler and/or wetter summers like those of modern times. Grasslands, parklands, and forests have remained in roughly constant positions from that time until the present (R.S. Hoffman and J.K. Jones 1970:360–61; Ritchie 1983; Vance, Emerson, and Habgood 1983; Zoltai and Vitt 1990). While vegetation zones were making their adjustments, changes also appeared in the archeological record. One example was the introduction of barbed corner-notched projectile points. Another was a substantial increase in mass bison hunting, particularly in the techniques of the pound and the jump (Foor 1982:111; Reeves 1990).

Pelican Lake materials are found in mass kills at Head-Smashed-In (fig. 6), Old Women's, Walter Felt, Keaster, Ayers-Frazier, and Stark-Lewis sites. Proliferation of mass hunting during Pelican Lake times may have been due to an increasing density in bison populations (Foor 1982:162–166).

Pelican Lake remains are found throughout the Northern Plains from the South Platte River in Colorado to the North Saskatchewan River in Saskatchewan, and from the Rocky Mountains in Alberta, Montana, Wyoming, and possibly Colorado, to the parklands of southeastern Manitoba. The southeastern boundaries, presumably in the Dakotas, are not well defined (Reeves 1983:2–4, 317; Foor 1982). The Pelican Lake series is well represented within the Rocky Mountains from Alberta to Wyoming (Reeves 1983:2–4), and there are also occasional occurrences in the boreal forest of northern Saskatchewan (D. Meyer 1983:155, 159–160). In north-central and western parts of the Northern Plains Pelican Lake components are more numerous than those of any predecessors (Conaty, Hanna, and Melit 1988:17; Van Dyke et al. 1991:43–46; Ruebelmann 1983:63–64; Greiser 1981:44–45).

The oldest Pelican Lake sites, dating to about 1850 B.C., span much of the study area: Layer XX at Sjovold, the Pilgrim site, the Wind River Canyon Burial and Cache, CMU-12 at DjPm-44, and Layer II at Cactus Flower. In all known multicomponent sequences containing both McKean series and Pelican Lake components, Pelican Lake is always younger. Thus, even though there is some temporal variance from one district to another, it appears that Pelican Lake generally replaced McKean. Later, occurrences of Pelican Lake shared the Northern Plains with the Besant series for perhaps 1,000 years. Finally, about A.D. 350, Pelican Lake disappeared just as the Besant series was entering a period of florescence and as the Avonlea complex was making its first appearance.

The most common and distinctive elements of the Pelican Lake tool kit are chipped-stone projectile points

Fig. 6. View of the Head-Smashed-In buffalo jump site, Alta., from the southeast. Photograph by Ted J. Brasser, 1980s.

(fig. 7a–e), the major type being straight-based, with straight to gently convex sides and U-shaped corner notches. This type exhibits a trend toward increasing basal width and decreasing notch width in younger components. Thus, both basal and neck widths tend to be broader in later forms. Unnotched versions of the late straight-based variant, presumably projectile point preforms, are found in small numbers in some sites (cf. G.R. Clark and M.C. Wilson 1981:34–35; Reeves 1983:81). A second Pelican Lake point type has straight sides, corner notches, and a convex base. This variety appears about midway through the Pelican Lake sequence and co-exists with straight-based types until the end. Projectile points that fall within the Besant range of variation are also found in some Pelican Lake components, particularly later ones. There is noticeable variation in Pelican Lake point size. Most points are 30–50 millimeters long and have a combination of measurements (D.H. Thomas 1978) that suggests use on atlatl darts. However, a few smaller specimens with measurements indicative of arrowhead use are found in early Pelican Lake assemblages (I. Dyck 1983:107; Brumley and Dau 1988:33). Thus, bow and arrow weaponry may have been known while remaining subordinate to atlatls and darts during Pelican Lake times. For additional information about the Pelican Lake tool kit, see Reeves (1983:94–96) and Foor (1982:73–80).

Circular shelters, probably hide-covered tepees, are the only kind of habitation structure known for Pelican Lake. The clearest examples are those outlined by stone tepee rings, as at 48PL21, Pilgrim, Schmitt, DjPl-11, DjPm-98, and Cranford. Pelican Lake campsites all seem to be of a small, transitory, or task-specific type, and large base camps have not been found. This may reflect a dispersed kind of settlement system (Keyser and Davis 1984:45).

Pelican Lake burials were usually secondary bundle interments, placed in shallow pits, infused with red ocher, accompanied by a diverse assemblage of grave goods, sometimes covered by rock cairns, and usually situated in prominent spots overlooking water or on high hill slopes (Brink and Baldwin 1988:131). The Wind River Canyon burial is a mountain variant placed at the base of a steep sandstone wall on a low terrace 10 meters above the river. The Bradwell and Sand Creek burials are variants involving primary flexed interments.

Pelican Lake subsistence rested firmly on bison. Foor's (1982:92–97) study shows that 94 percent of components with identifiable faunal remains contain bison and that 70 percent of identified mammal bones are bison. Other mammals represent only a small proportion of faunal debris: rabbit/hare 10 percent; other small animals 10 percent; deer, dog, bighorn sheep, antelope, 2 percent each; wapiti and beaver 1 percent each; and bear, a trace. Clamshell is present in substantial quantities in some sites, while fish, bird, and reptile bones occur in only minute amounts (fig. 7f–t) (Foor 1982:93; Reeves 1983:311).

Chipped-stone tools and debitage reflect the use of local chert, siltstone, quartzite, petrified wood, and basalt sources and of materials sometimes obtained at a distance such as cherts from Montana (L.B. Davis 1987), red and gray siltstones from Montana and Wyoming (Reeves 1983:86), Knife River flint from North Dakota (Reeves 1983:86; Buchner 1979:42–44), and Top-of-the-World

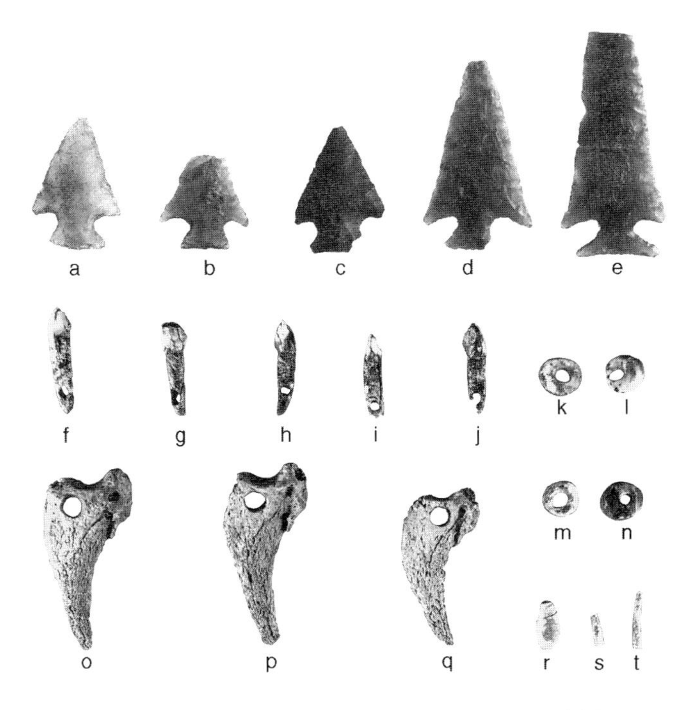

a–e, Royal Sask. Mus., Regina:DgMr-1; f–t, Prov. Mus. of Alta., Edmonton: EePk-272.

Fig. 7. Pelican Lake complex artifacts. a–e, Projectile points from Level 4 of the Long Creek site, Sask. f–t, Perforated shell, bone, and tooth ornaments from the Highwood River site, Alta. Length of r, 1.6 cm; rest same scale.

chert from British Columbia (Choquette 1981; Reeves 1983:4). Pelican Lake peoples had access through trade to decorative materials from more remote sources: olivella and dentalium shells from the Pacific coast (Brink and Baldwin 1988; L.B. Davis 1987) and native copper from the Great Lakes (D.R. King 1961; E.G. Walker 1982; Brink and Baldwin 1988).

The question of Pelican Lake origins is perplexing. The evidence that Pelican Lake was adapted to bison hunting from the beginning opens an argument for in situ development on the Plains. Continuities between certain Hanna and Pelican Lake tool forms—drills, ovate bifaces, pointed unifaces, and dome side-scrapers—and the common use of basin-shaped rock-filled hearths provide support for this idea (Reeves 1970, 1983). The Pelican Lake entity seems to have appeared quite suddenly over a broad area. Additional signs of discontinuity have been found in subsistence economies and burials. McKean subsistence varied from bison hunting to small game hunting and plant food collecting, while Pelican Lake subsistence was clearly focused on bison hunting (Keyser and Davis 1984:51–52). Pelican Lake burials turn out to have been more like Oxbow burials than those of the McKean series (Brink and Baldwin 1988:131–132). Such differences cast doubt on the idea that there was a simple evolutionary transition from McKean to Pelican Lake. Reeves (1983:7) offered an alternative hypothesis to the effect that Pelican Lake was intrusive from the west and arose out of interaction between Plains and Mountain cultures. This idea receives some support from the grouping of early and late Pelican Lake dates on the western half of the Northern Plains.

The fate of Pelican Lake is another question. Mountain subphases of Pelican Lake could have been ancestral to the Avonlea complex (Reeves 1970, 1983:164–166). However, Pelican Lake's fate remains enigmatic (Reeves 1983:18).

Besant Series

About 650 B.C. a new type of chipped-stone point came into use among bison hunters of the far Northern Plains (Reeves 1978:fig.17.22; I. Dyck 1983:107–108). Outlook points are distinguished by straight to slightly concave bases, side-notching, narrow necks and relatively small size (I. Dyck and Morlan 1995:433–437). These points have the dimensions of arrowheads (D.H. Thomas 1978) but could have been used on composite fletched darts of small diameter (Christenson 1986). Identifying a specific origin for these Outlook points is a problem. One has to reach a fair distance outside the region to find appropriate comparative material of contemporary age. However, a similar form is found in one of two varieties of the Black Sand type in the Early Woodland period of Illinois (Montet-White 1968:fig.26.11). Given an expansion of the Woodland tradition at this time, a relationship between the northern and the Black Sand types does not seem out of the question. As to the fate of the small northern points, closest comparisons are with younger forms known in the Northern Plains as Besant. Thus, Outlook points, apparently derived from an Early Woodland source, mark the initiation of the Besant series on the Northern Plains.

Additional evidence for Early Woodland influence in the Besant series appears about 500 B.C. as remains of an unusual post-in-ground daub-covered habitation structure at the Naze site (fig. 8). Associated with it were cordmarked pottery and small side-notched and corner-notched projectile points. Although the dwelling and ceramics were clearly inspired by the Woodland tradition, the mode of subsistence was dominated by bison hunting in conformity with the traditional Northern Plains pattern.

In central Saskatchewan, a distinctive side-notched, basally concave dart point known as Sandy Creek (Wettlaufer 1955; I. Dyck 1983) appeared about 500 B.C. The type is similar to the much older Oxbow form as well as the contemporary and slightly older Northwestern Plains type called Yonkee (Frison 1978:201–211) and to the second of two Black Sand varieties known in Illinois (Montet-White 1968:fig.46-F) and Iowa (Straffin 1971:fig.3.1B). Thus, Sandy Creek may be evidence for continuity with older Plains types and for Plains influence on Woodland cultures. Whatever its source, Sandy Creek appears to be another contributor to the range of projectile points found later in the Besant series (cf. A.M. Ramsay 1991:fig.5.2, no. 10865).

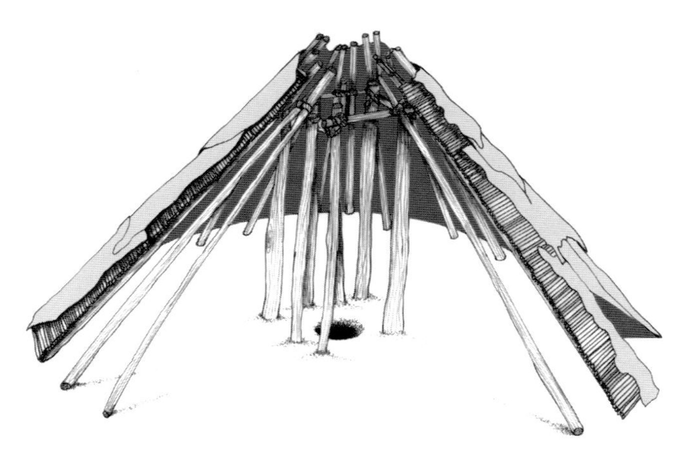

after M.L. Gregg 1990:35.

Fig. 8. Reconstruction of Besant series post-in-ground dwelling, Naze site, N. Dak. Drawn by Roger Thor Roop.

By about A.D. 50, the Northern Plains manifestations described above seem to have coalesced into a highly successful bison-hunting complex known as Besant. First identified at the Mortlach site, Besant spanned the whole Northern Plains (Reeves 1970, 1983; Syms 1977). The remains include side-notched to corner-notched projectile points in both dart and arrowhead sizes with straight, slightly concave, or slightly convex bases (Reeves 1970; T.F. Kehoe and A.B. Kehoe 1968; T.F. Kehoe 1974). Endscrapers are generally well-worked, trianguloid, and occasionally side-notched or side-removed (Neuman 1975:pl.9k; I. Dyck 1972:fig.10). In many components Besant chipped-stone tools reveal a strong preference for Knife River flint (Reeves 1983). Such an emphasis on particular chipping materials was a hallmark of the Illinois Hopewell culture, whose far-flung trading relationships and cultural influences penetrated the Missouri River area A.D. 1–300 (Willey 1966:273, 280). Besant ceramics, the first on the Northern Plains, are present in a few sites, predominantly though not exclusively in the eastern part of the range. Vessel shapes are conoidal; exterior surfaces are usually cordmarked, occasionally smoothed or plain; the most common decoration is an encircling row of punctates one to two centimeteres below the lip (M.L. Gregg 1986:119–121).

The great bulk of Besant subsistence, as in previous Northern Plains complexes, focused on bison hunting. One favored technique was the pound, as shown by massive bone middens peppered with Besant projectile points at the Ruby, Muhlbach, Melhagen, and Richards kill sites. They also used bison jumps at Old Women's, Calderwood, and Wahkpa Chu′gn. Their campsites are numerous (Reeves 1983; I. Dyck 1983). Besant housing seems to have included post-in-ground structures (Mortlach, LaRoche) reminiscent of Early Woodland dwellings. At the High Butte site, an arcing line of six shallow depressions may represent a small community of somewhat similar dwellings. However, portable shelters, presumably hide-covered tepees, were probably the more common Besant shelter. Although the remains of tepees are often hard to identify, fairly convincing Besant tepee floors, ringed with stones, have been found at the Elma Thompson, Coal Creek, Ross Glen, and 32OL270 sites.

Bone uprights are a common feature in Besant sites (fig. 9), one which is apparently rare in sites of other Northern Plains complexes. The feature consists of a small hole, 15–40 centimeters in diameter and 10 or more centimeters in depth, into which have been inserted one or more vertically aligned bison bones (Gruhn 1971:139; Frison 1971:80–81). The bones were generally shoved into the hole sharp end down, leaving an unaltered articular end protruding above the occupation surface. Bone uprights have been found in linear arrangements in association with a bison kill midden, where they have been interpreted as wedge-filled posts outlining the base of a pound enclosure (Frison 1971). They have also been found in more random arrangements near the exterior edges of tepee rings, where they have been interpreted as bone stakes or as bone-wedged wooden stakes used to anchor tepee guy-lines (L.B. Fredlund, Herbort, and Munson 1985:128). Another innovative but less compelling interpretation is that they served as hide-covered anvils for stone chipping (Neuman 1975:32).

Burials are known almost exclusively from mound sites in the southeast portion of the range. Built singly or in small groups along the edges of high river terraces, these low earthen tumuli have basal diameters of 16.8 to 30.5 meters and heights of from 0.4 to 2.1 meters (Neuman 1975). In most cases the human interments were secondary burials, disarticulated or partially articulated clusters of bones placed within a subfloor pit beneath the center of the mound. Accompanying grave goods include a sampling of potsherds; a ceramic pipe bowl; chipped-stone projectile points, endscrapers, knives, gravers and drills; serrated bone fleshers; pendants of shell, tooth, or bone; beads of

Fig. 9. Besant features. Bone upright feature, Muhlbach site, Alta. Photograph by R. Gruhn, 1965.

bone, shell, and rolled copper; atlatl weights of stone or shell; bone awls and pins; red and green pigments; basketry; grass or bark matting; pieces of timber used in covering the pits; and bones of bison, beaver, bear, elk, deer, canids, along with smaller animals and birds. An intriguing aspect of Besant mounds is the universal inclusion of articulated bison skeletons. For example, at the Swift Bird site two articulated bison skeletons were found on the floor of Mound 1 lying parallel to the long axis of the burial pit and a short distance to the west (Neuman 1975:40–41). In addition bison skulls had been placed at the north and south edges of the burial pit. Neuman (1975:89,95) interprets the bison skeletons and skulls, quite convincingly, as being offerings indicative of considerable forethought, effort, and ritual. Besant bison ritualism was not limited to burial mounds. A row of bison skulls within a post-in-ground ceremonial structure associated with a bison pound has been found at the Ruby site.

Outside the southeastern portion of its range the nature of Besant burials is poorly known. Burial mounds are numerous in southern Manitoba (Capes 1963). Some of them, the Richards mounds, for example, may turn out to be Besant. The only Besant burial known for the western half of the range is the Tufton site, a vandalized rock cairn in northeastern Montana that appears to have covered secondary burials. Neuman (1975) has tried to make a case for grouping the North and South Dakota burial mound materials, together with some nearby campsite materials, into a separate complex called Sonota. Given Besant's extensive geographic and temporal distribution, it is certainly conceivable that it might have been contained regional variants. Yet, in trying to understand what makes Sonota distinct from the main body of Besant materials one immediately encounters definitional problems. Distinguishing traits—subsistence, artifact types and styles, house types, feature types, raw material preferences, indications of ritualism, overlapping distributions and age—all yield powerful impressions of sameness (for a dissenting opinion see Syms 1977:91–92; for a rebuttal see Reeves 1983:10–13). The only trait that really distinguishes the two is the presence of burial mounds in parts of North and South Dakota (Sonota) and the absence of burial information for the rest of the range (Besant).

The fate of the Besant people is not known. A strong and continuing suspicion is that they evolved into the Old Women's culture (Reeves 1970, 1983; I. Dyck 1983; Vickers 1994).

Avonlea Complex

About A.D. 200 a group of bison hunters who specialized in bow hunting appeared in the grasslands of southern Saskatchewan and Alberta (fig. 10a–c). Bow-and-arrow technology may have been in use along with atlatl and spear weaponry as far back as Pelican Lake time. However, Avonlea peoples were the first to rely almost exclusively on bows and arrows. The points are small and thin with tiny side notches placed close to a slightly concave, or occasionally straight, base (T.F. Kehoe 1973). This point type, and later the whole material complex, were named after the site in Saskatchewan where Avonlea materials were first recognized (Wettlaufer and Mayer-Oakes 1960; T.F. Kehoe and McCorquodale 1961, 1961a). Their bows are unknown, but arrowshafts have been discovered at Wortham Shelter. Pottery types associated with the Avonlea complex are net-impressed, parallel-grooved (fig. 10d), and plain (Byrne 1973; R.G. Morgan 1979; Quigg 1988; A.M. Johnson 1988). Avonlea is concentrated in a North-central and Northwestern Plains core area, with late extensions into the Kootenay River Trench of the Rocky Mountains and the parklands of Saskatchewan and Manitoba (L.B. Davis 1966; Reeves 1983; D. Meyer, Klimko, and Finnigan 1988; Joyes 1988). The evidence in South Dakota is spotty (A.M. Johnson 1988; Neuman 1960; Hannus and Nowak 1988). Overall distribution is similar to that of the Besant series, which preceded Avonlea and, in some places, was its contemporary.

Avonlea appeared first in the Upper and Middle parts of the Saskatchewan River basin just as the damp Sub-Atlantic period was drawing to a close. Two hundred years later, during the warm dry Scandic period, it had spread south into the basins of the Upper Missouri and Yellowstone rivers (Morlan 1988). A climax occurred around A.D. 800, about the same time that Plains Village horticulture was being established along the Missouri River in South Dakota (L.J. Zimmerman 1985:73). By about A.D. 1000, near the beginning of the warm moist Neo-Atlantic period, Avonlea had extended west into the Kootenay River basin and east into the Lower Saskatchewan River basin, but by this time it was beginning to disappear from the Middle Saskatchewan basin. In another 200 years it was gone from the Upper Missouri and Yellowstone basins. Avonlea seems to have persisted until about A.D. 1300 in the Lower Saskatchewan and perhaps another hundred years longer in the Upper Saskatchewan and Kootenay portions of its range.

Plains bison were the key element of Avonlea subsistence. Avonlea hunters were adept at communal hunting methods that allowed them to bring together and dispatch dozens of animals at one time. Pounds and jumps, such as those at Gull Lake, Head-Smashed-In, Ramillies, Henry Smith, and Wardell, have left substantial bone middens and, in some cases, the remains of pound structures where bison were killed and butchered. Often there are extensive campsite remains nearby where bison parts were processed for storage or cooked and consumed. Avonlea people did not rely exclusively on bison. Larson, a winter campsite, yielded the broken bones of five bison, one pronghorn antelope, one dog, one swift fox, and one mustelid. Lebret was apparently a fishery, but other game including bison, deer, beaver, river otter, hares, and various waterfowl were also consumed there. At Lost Terrace,

Canadian Mus. of Civilization, Hull, Que.: EiNs-4.

Fig. 10. Avonlea complex artifacts. a, Projectile point; b, endscraper; c, minimally retouched tool; d, parallel grooved pottery from Layer VI, the Sjovold site, Sask. Width of b, 2 cm; rest same scale.

apparently during a time of food shortage, Avonlea people focused on secondary resources such as antelope. They were also capable of occupying and exploiting the boreal forest (D. Meyer, Klimko, and Finnigan 1988; Tamplin 1977).

The people probably lived in portable tepees. Avonlea materials have been found within stone tepee rings at several sites (Brumley 1983; Reeves 1977 cited in Reeves 1983:17 and in Brumley and Dau 1988:43; Head 1985). Burials are poorly known. The Truman mounds contain Avonlea parallel-grooved pottery, which indicates that burial mounds may have been used at least in southeastern portions of Avonlea distribution. A disturbed Avonlea burial on a knoll near Bethune contained a mixture of seven primary and secondary interments dating to about A.D. 620. The remains, buried in a 59-centimeter-deep pit, were associated with a rectangular arrangement of stones reminiscent of stone rectangles seen in the Truman mounds. Cultural items that escaped a raid by pothunters included an arrowpoint, a chipped-stone biface, a painted turtle carapace, and an ocher-stained bone tube. Much richer assemblages of projectile points, bone beads, shell pendants, chipped-stone bifaces, and flakes have been recovered from the Billy Creek and Leath burials.

The question of Avonlea origins has prompted several hypotheses. The speculation that Avonlea people were northern Athapaskans (T.F. Kehoe 1966:839, 1973:77) has not found archeological support; there are no clear precedents for Avonlea material culture in the northern boreal forests. Nevertheless, the proposition retains some currency, partly because an alternative origin has not been convincingly demonstrated and partly because there remains a need for a prehistoric link between northern and southern Athapaskan tribes (Frison 1988; D.R. Wilcox 1988). The proposed in situ development for Avonlea (Reeves 1983) with supposed ancestors being foothills or mountain cultures of the Pelican Lake aggregate draws some support from vague similarities between late Pelican Lake and Avonlea projectile point forms and from appropriate geographic and temporal distributions (Reeves 1983:18). The place of Avonlea origins could be the Saskatchewan-Montana area if a different Pelican Lake complex was the precursor (Brumley and Dau 1988:44–45). Yet another possibility is that Avonlea developed out of Besant (Ruebelmann 1983:65–66).

It is suspected that Avonlea eventually developed regional variants, the Beehive complex of Wyoming being one example (Frison 1988; L.B. Fredlund 1988; Reeves 1988), late variants in the northeastern parklands (D. Meyer, Klimko, and Finnigan 1988) and the Kootenay Valley (Roll 1988) being others. Avonlea seems also to have had contacts with contemporaries such as Besant and Laurel (D. Meyer, Klimdo, and Finnigan 1988). In the core area Avonlea and Besant occupations often occur in the same district, but not frequently in the same site. Examples of mixed Avonlea and Besant components, where compressed stratigraphy is not the chief cause of mixing, are rare. Avonlea and Besant components do occasionally appear within the same multicomponent site, and in those cases Avonlea is always younger (Morlan 1993). Nevertheless, there must have been contact between peoples of the two complexes since their occupation of the Northern Plains overlapped, at minimum, during the period A.D. 300–600. One sign of such contact may be the appearance of an Avonlea-like projectile point style called Samantha (T.F. Kehoe 1974) in the Besant complex after about 400. Meanwhile, in the northern parklands Avonlea and Laurel ceramics and ceramics sharing attributes of both complexes are mixed together in single components (D. Meyer, Klimko, and Finnigan 1988; D. Meyer and H.T. Epp 1990), which suggests more direct contact than with Besant. Avonlea points have also been found in Initial Middle Missouri Villages in South Dakota (Husted 1968:68), which indicates contacts there as well. In fact, Avonlea people may also have been in contact with Woodland cultures of South Dakota. Woodland pottery referred to as Randall Incised at the Scalp Creek site looks similar to the Avonlea parallel grooved type. The Scalp Creek Woodland components also produced net-impressed pottery, which is another commonality with Avonlea.

It has been noted that Avonlea components are relatively rare in comparison to the numbers of Besant and Old Women's components (I. Dyck 1983; Vickers 1986). Two factors that might govern this situation are population size and length of regional occupancy. Since Avonlea, Besant, and Old Women's cultures are similarly long-lived, one turns to population size and the idea that Avonlea populations may have been smaller. Contrary to this, Brumley and Dau (1988:46) have proposed that Avonlea might have had a different settlement system, one in which they had fewer sites that were occupied by larger groups for longer periods of time.

The fate of Avonlea people has also been a matter for speculation. According to the Athapaskan hypothesis (T.F. Kehoe 1973; D.R. Wilcox 1988) the Avonlea people moved south where they emerged during historic times as the Apache and Navajo. Although this idea has been strongly questioned (Reeves 1983:167–169; Byrne 1973:456; G.F. Adams 1977:142; Wedel 1986:151), a comparison of Avonlea archeological remains with those of a later Central Plains (Athapaskan) complex such as the Dismal River complex (J.H. Gunnerson 1960) has not been attempted. There are sufficient similarities in at least two kinds of artifacts (chipped-stone arrowpoints and parallel-grooved body treatment of pots) and in one type of feature (rock-floored roasting pits) (Wedel 1986:141; Brink and Dawe 1989:42–62) to justify additional work on this hypothesis. On the other hand, there is evidence for continuity between Avonlea and later Northern Plains complexes. The alternative holds that Avonlea people stayed in or near the Northern Plains contributing to the development of the Old Women's phase in Alberta and Saskatchewan (Byrne 1973:468–70; Reeves 1983:18; Brumley and Dau 1988:49; G.M. Clarke 1995), to the Tobacco Plains phase of the Kootenay Valley of the Rocky Mountains (Reeves 1983:19–20), and to late variants of Avonlea in the forest fringe of Manitoba and Saskatchewan (D. Meyer, Klimko, and Finnigan 1988). It has also been suggested that peoples of the Avonlea complex were involved in the formation of village cultures of the Middle Missouri tradition (Husted 1968:68). It is, of course, possible that the fate of the Avonlea culture took more than one twist.

The Last Millennium

Ceramics with finishes and decorations similar to Woodland, Mississippian, and Plains Village ceramics spread from east to west, southeast to northwest, and possibly also south to north during this period. The use of burial mounds for disposal of the dead was prominent in eastern parts of the area. Horticulture was attempted as a supplement to traditional hunting and gathering, particularly in the eastern area. However, nomadic bison hunting remained the dominant mode of subsistence.

• OLD WOMEN'S AGGREGATE Westernmost of Late Period assemblages are those of the Old Women's aggregate. The Old Women's phase (Reeves 1969) refers to most southern Alberta bison hunters' camp and kill site remains dating A.D. 800–1850. Diagnostic artifacts for the Old Women's phase are the series of small side-notched projectile points (Forbis 1962) at the Old Women's buffalo jump. These are better known by the type names Prairie Side-Notched (fig. 11a–j) and Plains Side-Notched (fig. 11k–v) (T.F. Kehoe 1966). In western parts of the Northern Plains, Prairie Side-Notched points appeared as early as A.D. 250 and dominated assemblages from 800 to 1300. The Plains Side-Notched type predominated from about 1300 until early historic times (T.F. Kehoe 1966).

Eight components in southwest Alberta are a regional expression of the Old Women's phase, the Pass Creek Valley subphase. Excavations yielded Plains Triangular and Side-Notched, Catan, Prairie Side-Notched and Flake arrowpoints; cordmarked and check-stamped pottery; a variety of specific stone and bone tool types; a split pebble technology referred to as the Rundle Technology; an unusually frequent use of petrified wood; and use of several hearth types and of several seasonal types of hunting and camp sites (Reeves 1972:109–111). An ethnic affiliation was proposed for the Old Women's phase in which regional and temporal variants represented tribal constituents such as North Peigan, Blood, and Gros Ventre (Reeves 1983:20).

Two major ceramic complexes were present in southern Alberta, namely, a long-lived Saskatchewan Basin complex, which originated in southern Saskatchewan and Manitoba; and a late, shorter-lived Cluny complex. Byrne (1973) subdivided the Saskatchewan Basin complex ceramics into Early and Late varieties and attributed the Late variety to the Old Women's phase. Vickers (1994:21, based on Byrne 1973) summarizes the numerous shapes, finishes, and modes of decoration of Saskatchewan Basin Late Variety ceramics:

> Vessels have an elongated globular form, shoulders are common and often pronounced, necks are shallow and short, rims either flare or are vertical, and lips are usually flat. Most vessel exteriors were textured by the application of a cord-wrapped paddle or through fabric/net impressing. About one-third of the vessels were then smoothed, almost obliterating the textured surface. Another one-third of the vessels show truncation of the surface finish; that is, the surface was not completely obliterated. The vessels bear little decoration; punctation is the most common technique although incision and impression also occur. Motifs are simple and include oblique impressions on the lip or at the lip edge. Decoration below the lip consists of a few rows of elements, usually oriented horizontally.

In attempting to sort out the late prehistory of southeastern Alberta, Brumley and Dau (1988:26, 50–63) have proposed a division of materials into four complexes: Old Women's complex, A.D. 1250 to Early Historic, occupying southern Alberta and represented by Prairie and Plains Side-Notched projectile point types, Saskatchewan Basin ceramics, a Blackfoot-type memorial medicine wheel attributed to prehistoric Blackfoot groups; the Cluny complex, thought to represent Siouan groups; the aceramic Saddle Butte complex, A.D. 1100–1300, of Montana, which utilized Prairie and Plains Side-Notched projectile points and is related to one of the preceding complexes; and the

Highwood complex, A.D. 1300–1450, of central Montana, southern Alberta, and southern Saskatchewan, characterized by Buffalo Gap single spurred and Emigrant basal-notched varieties of projectile points, and possibly reflecting Uto-Aztecan groups. In Saskatchewan, D. Meyer (1988) proposes that remains from a number of sites dating 800–1300 belong within the Old Women's construct. He projects the distribution throughout the grasslands of southern Saskatchewan with at least one occurrence in the parklands and hypothesizes that after 1300 Old Women's materials may be limited to the western border of the province.

• BLACKDUCK COMPLEX The Blackduck complex is found on the eastern edge of the Northern Plains. Its core area lies at the southwest margin of the boreal forest, stretching along the north shore of Lake Superior through the northern third of Minnesota into the lowlands of Manitoba, around Lakes Winnipeg and Winnipegosis, with an extension into the parklands of southwest Manitoba (Buchner 1979; vol. 6:86–96). Lenius and Olinyk (1990) limit the complex to what was formerly known as "Early or Classic" Blackduck, which ranges 650–1100. Throughout most of its geographic range Blackduck subsistence was based on a variety of forest resources: sturgeon, moose, beaver, black bear, birds, martin, turtle, muskrat, snowshoe hare, wolf, clams, and, at least in southern parts of the range, wild rice. In parts of southwestern Manitoba, such as at the Stott site (Tisdale 1978), Blackduck peoples ran very successful bison pounds.

The most distinctive Blackduck artifact is a type of round-based pottery with constricted necks and flattened and thickened lips. Decoration occurs on the neck and rim, on the lip, and occasionally on the inner rim. The most common decorative elements are horizontal and oblique cord-wrapped stick impressions and exterior punctates. Manufacture was either by paddle-and-anvil technique, or involved formation inside of a fabric container. As a consequence the undecorated portions of the vessels are either cord-impressed or fabric-impressed (S. Anfinson 1979). Associated artifacts and features may include small triangular and side-notched projectile points, a variety of stone and bone hide-scraping tools, ovate knives, stone drills, smoking pipes, bone awls, needles, harpoons and spatulas, bear and beaver tooth ornaments, small copper tools and ornaments, and burial mounds (MCHR 1989). The origins of the complex appear to lie in the preceding and partially contemporary Laurel composite (Evans 1961; Buchner 1979; vol. 6:86–96). At the end of its span Blackduck merged with the Laurel composite and became two new composites, Rainy River (Lenius and Olinyk 1990) and Selkirk (D. Meyer and D. Russell 1987).

• RAINY RIVER COMPOSITE Extending eastward only as far as the western end of Lake Superior, the Rainy River composite consists of at least three regional complexes that lasted from 1100 to the late 1600s. One of these, the Bird Lake complex, 1200–1350, has been found in the parklands of southwestern Manitoba at the Stott and Brockinton sites (Lenius and Olinyk 1990:84, fig. 8.12), giving a Plains bison hunting aspect to a complex that was otherwise forest or forest-edge adapted. Bird Lake ceramic vessels are generally simple necked jars with pronounced outflaring rims. The constriction of the neck forms an exterior angle that is right-angled to acute and an interior ridge that is rounded rather than sharply ridged. Surface finishes are generally textile-impressed or smoothed. The one design element common to all vessels belonging within this complex are various patterns of small ovoid or triangular stamped impressions (Lenius and Olinyk 1990:93–96). The linguistic identity of those who created the Rainy River composite, as for Blackduck and Laurel, is assumed to have been Algonquian (Lenius and Olinyk 1990:101).

after Dyck 1983:130–131.

Fig. 11. Projectile points. a–j, Prairie Side-Notched projectile points from the Tschetter site, Sask., FbNr-1. k–v, Plains Side-Notched projectile points from Layer 3 of the Gull Lake site, Sask. Drawn by Roger Thor Roop. Length of e, 3.2 cm; rest same scale.

• SELKIRK COMPOSITE Four related Late Prehistoric complexes are distributed through the boreal forest of central Saskatchewan, central Manitoba, and northwestern

Ontario (D. Meyer and D. Russell 1987; Lenius and Olinyk 1990; David Meyer, personal communication 1992). One of these, the Pehonan complex, extended into the parklands of east-central Saskatchewan (T.H. Gibson 1998; McKeand 1995; D. Meyer 1984). The covering name for the whole group is Selkirk Composite, and it is thought to date 1200–1700. Collectively, the Selkirk complexes are characterized by late side-notched projectile points and fabric-impressed Selkirk ware pottery, variants of which are important in distinguishing the regional complexes. The Pehonan complex shows evidence for contact with Plains complexes in its occasional uses of obsidian and Knife River flint for stone tools and of check-stamped pottery. Finds of Selkirk-like ceramics have been made in the grasslands of southern Saskatchewan (A.B. Kehoe 1959), but whether these are due to occupation by an unidentified plains-oriented Selkirk complex or to exchange due to warfare or trade is not known (D. Meyer and D. Russell 1987:20–21). The Selkirk composite originated in north-central Manitoba, and the Laurel and Blackduck complexes contributed to its formation (D. Meyer and D. Russell 1987). Selkirk remains were probably left by Cree peoples, the separate complexes possibly representing regional Cree populations (J.V. Wright 1968, 1971; Hlady 1971; D. Meyer and D. Russell 1987).

• DEVILS LAKE–SOURISFORD BURIAL COMPLEX The Devils Lake-Sourisford Burial complex was defined by Syms (1979) to draw together mortuary goods from burial mounds in southwestern Manitoba, southeastern Saskatchewan, and northeastern North Dakota with similar materials from isolated nonmound burials in a broader distribution along the Northeastern Plains grassland-parkland interface. The definitive traits are smoothed-surface mortuary vessels with incised designs and distinctive lip decoration, incised and plain gorgets made from marine whelk shell, pendants and beads made from the columella or spiral axis of the marine whelk shell, tubular pipes, and incised stone "tablets." Other traits include birchbark baskets, curved bone "anklets, bracelets, collars or wrist guards," washer-shaped shell beads, notched trapezoidal shell pendants, copper beads, and head bands, antler tine handles for beaver tooth gouges, bird-bone beads, bone harpoons, fresh water clamshell "spoons" or containers, and perforated small marine shells (Syms 1979:284). The densest concentration of remains is centered between Devils Lake, North Dakota, and Sourisford, Manitoba, but scattered finds have been recorded as far south as the James River of North Dakota and as far west as south-central Saskatchewan. The complex appeared approximately 1000–1150 and persisted into at least the late 1300s with a few elements persisting into the historic period (Syms 1979:301). Comparisons show that Devils Lake–Sourisford ceramic designs, whelk gorget designs, and certain traits of other items have many similarities to Mississippian tradition artifacts. Therefore, those responsible for the Devils Lake–Sourisford burial complex could have been Hidatsa-Crow, Mandan, Santee Sioux group, Assiniboine, or a Teton Sioux group (Syms 1979:303–304). Artifactual evidence narrows the focus to the Hidatsa (Swenson and Gregg 1988). Discovery of a possible case of blastomycosis among Devils Lake–Sourisford burials at the Woodlawn site (E.G. Walker 1983) could be supportive of a Hidatsa identification, since the disease is caused by a soil-borne pathogen, is common among agricultural people, and the Hidatsa were the closest contemporary agriculturalists (Ahler, Thiessen, and Trimble 1991).

• WANIKAN COMPLEX Materials of the Wanikan culture were first recognized in north-central Minnesota, where they share an overlapping distribution in time and space with the Blackduck complex (Cooper and Johnson 1964). The most distinctive feature of the Wanikan complex is its Sandy Lake Ware pottery, which includes smooth-surfaced, vertically cordmarked and check-stamped varieties and whose simple decorations, when present, consist of lip notching, interior lip notching, or interior punctates (cf. S. Anfinson 1979). Other Wanikan traits, particularly in the woodland and parkland parts of the complex's range, are mound burials, small triangular projectile points, ricing jigs or threshing pits, and small seasonally occupied sites. The Wanikan distribution is focused in a core area near the headwaters of the Mississippi River between the northwest side of Lake Superior and the southeast corner of Lake Winnipeg, but traces of its ceramics are also found in eastern North Dakota (PLSBW 1988), northern North Dakota (Michlovic 1983:28), and the parklands of southwestern Manitoba (B.A. Nicholson 1990).

Bison hunting appears to be the main means of subsistence in the plains and parkland sites, but at the Lovstrom site where Sandy Lake ware was only a small part of the ceramic remains, corn horticulture seems also to have been practiced (B.A. Nicholson 1990). Wanikan complex dates range 1100–1750. In Late Prehistoric and Early Historic sites in the eastern part of the Wanikan distribution, Sandy Lake Ware is sometimes found overlying components containing Blackduck ware and sometimes found in association with ceramics belonging to Blackduck, Clam River, and Selkirk wares (L.R. Cooper and E. Johnson 1964; Arthurs 1978). Debates about probable ethnic affiliation, based on age, distribution and similarities to Mississippian tradition materials have focused on two possible identities, proto-Assiniboine and protohistoric Santee (S. Anfinson 1979:176).

• MORTLACH AGGREGATE A suite of abundant late prehistoric and protohistoric Northern Plains assemblages have been grouped into what is variously known as the Mortlach phase (Joyes 1973; Walde 1994), the Mortlach complex (Syms 1977), or the Mortlach aggregate (F.E. Schneider and Kinney 1978; D. Meyer and Epp 1990). The remains seem to be characterized by well-made pottery including check-stamped, plain, cord-wrapped paddle, grooved paddle, scored and fabric-impressed surface finishes, and displaying a variety of decorative techniques—oblique dentate stamping or cord-wrapped rod impressions on the lips and combinations of cord-wrapped and dentate impressions and punctates on the rims, pinching (on the shoulders), and incising being common modes of decoration (Syms 1977:125). Other material culture includes Plains Side-Notched and triangular projectile points, a diverse bone industry with polished pendants, awls, spatulas, arrow shaft wrenches, knapping tools, notched and incised pottery decorating tools, and snow slider heads incised with animal and geometric designs, plus large schist chitho scrapers, a range of chipped-stone end-scrapers, perforators and cutting edges, and tubular stone pipes (Syms 1977; D. Meyer and Epp 1990; Orchard 1946). Bison bones dominate the faunal assemblages from these sites, but carnivores, birds, and other herbivores are also present (Syms 1977:125).

Substantial midden deposits believed to be associated with large winter camps and attributable to this aggregate have been found at the Lake Midden, Stoney Beach Midden, and 32WI12 sites (Walde 1994; Malainey 1991). Cluny, an unusual fortified earthlodge village dating to about 1740, is also thought to belong in the group. Mortlach aggregate sites have been found throughout south-central and southeastern Saskatchewan south of the parklands, as well as in northwestern North Dakota, northeastern Montana, and southeastern Alberta. Dated components yield an age range about 1500–1800 (F.E. Schneider and Kinney 1978:33). From the time of their earliest discovery, materials of the Mortlach aggregate have been likened to materials from the Mandan-Hidatsa agricultural villages of North Dakota (Orchard 1946). While there are some generic resemblances in the pottery and specific similarities in the bone industry, the likeness is only general and the Mortlach aggregate forms an entity distinct from Plains Village remains.

Hunting and Gathering Tradition: Northwestern and Central Plains

GEORGE C. FRISON

From about 9000 to 6000 B.C., the Paleo-Indian lifeway on the Plains specialized in the hunting of big game. This gave way to a cultural adaptation based on broad-spectrum hunting and gathering. In the Northwestern and Central Plains, the Hunting and Gathering tradition may be characterized as the Plains Archaic, defining Archaic as "the stage of migratory hunting and gathering cultures continuing into environmental conditions approximating those of the present" (Willey and Phillips 1958:107).

The Plains Archaic began to develop by at least 8000 B.C. in the foothills and mountains at the western edge of the plains. Seed grinding tools and small cache pits found archeologically date to as early as 6500 B.C., although the former were not yet the fully developed manos and metates that became common a thousand years later. Shortly after about 6000 B.C., the peoples living on the short grass plains also adopted the Archaic lifeway. The trend toward drier climate that began in the late Pleistocene reached sufficient proportions at the beginning of the Altithermal period (Antevs 1948, 1955) to force most of the bison out of their natural habitat on the short grass plains. The effects of the Altithermal were felt for nearly 3,000 years because the economic base to sustain big game hunting no longer existed, forcing human populations to adjust to the changed conditions.

Cultural Boundaries

Cultural boundaries for the Plains Archaic must be somewhat arbitrary (fig. 1). The Northwestern area includes extreme western Minnesota, North and South Dakota, Wyoming, the eastern part of the Snake River plain in Idaho, and southern Montana east of the Continental Divide. A short distance north of the Wyoming-Montana border, evidence of the Archaic adaptation begins to disappear from the archeological record in favor of an economy based on bison hunting.

The Central Plains area includes extreme western Iowa and Missouri, Nebraska, Kansas, and Colorado, including the Front Range and farther west to include part of the western slope of the Rockies in northern Colorado.

The western portions of these areas are the most difficult to describe because they include regions that usually have not been considered part of the Plains area. However, during Archaic times, the same populations utilized both areas. There are intermontane basins that are often more reminiscent of the Great Basin than the Plains. There are many small enclaves of Plainslike environments, some at relatively high elevations. In the upper Green River basin, there is a broad flat area of sagebrush steppe that merges with the mountain slope. Even the interiors of the relatively small Jackson Hole and Sunlight basins in northwest Wyoming, which are completely surrounded by high mountains, can be regarded ecologically as Plainslike environments. The area around the headwaters of the Missouri and Colorado rivers can also be included.

Chronological Frameworks

Based on fieldwork in Montana and Wyoming, Mulloy (1958) used the expression Middle Period rather than Archaic. Mulloy recognized an Early Period corresponding to the Paleo-Indians as well as a time period between these two for which there was no evidence of human occupation. Now this time gap is called the Early Plains Archaic, Mulloy's Early Middle Period is the Middle Plains Archaic, and his Late Middle Period is the Late Plains Archaic.

Investigators in southwest Wyoming postulated an Early Archaic dating from about 5200 to 2600 B.C., divided into Great Divide and Green River phases. They eliminated the Middle Plains Archaic and defined a Late Plains Archaic dated from about 2600 B.C. to A.D. 1, divided into Pine Spring and Deadman Wash phases. Complicating this picture is evidence for Middle Plains Archaic (McKean) in the area, probably arising from the intrusion of Great Basin elements into the Wyoming Basin (Zier et al. 1983; Metcalf 1987).

The Archaic chronology for the eastern plains is different also. For example, in the Kansas City area, the Early Archaic is 8000–5000 B.C., Middle Archaic is 5000–2500 B.C., and Late Archaic is 2500 B.C. to A.D. 1.

Northwestern Plains

Late Paleo-Indian Foothill-Mountain Paleo-Archaic Groups

The peoples living in the foothills and mountains at the western edge of the Plains during Paleo-Indian times were oriented toward broad-spectrum hunting and gathering. At the Medicine Lodge Creek site (fig. 2) (Frison 1976a)

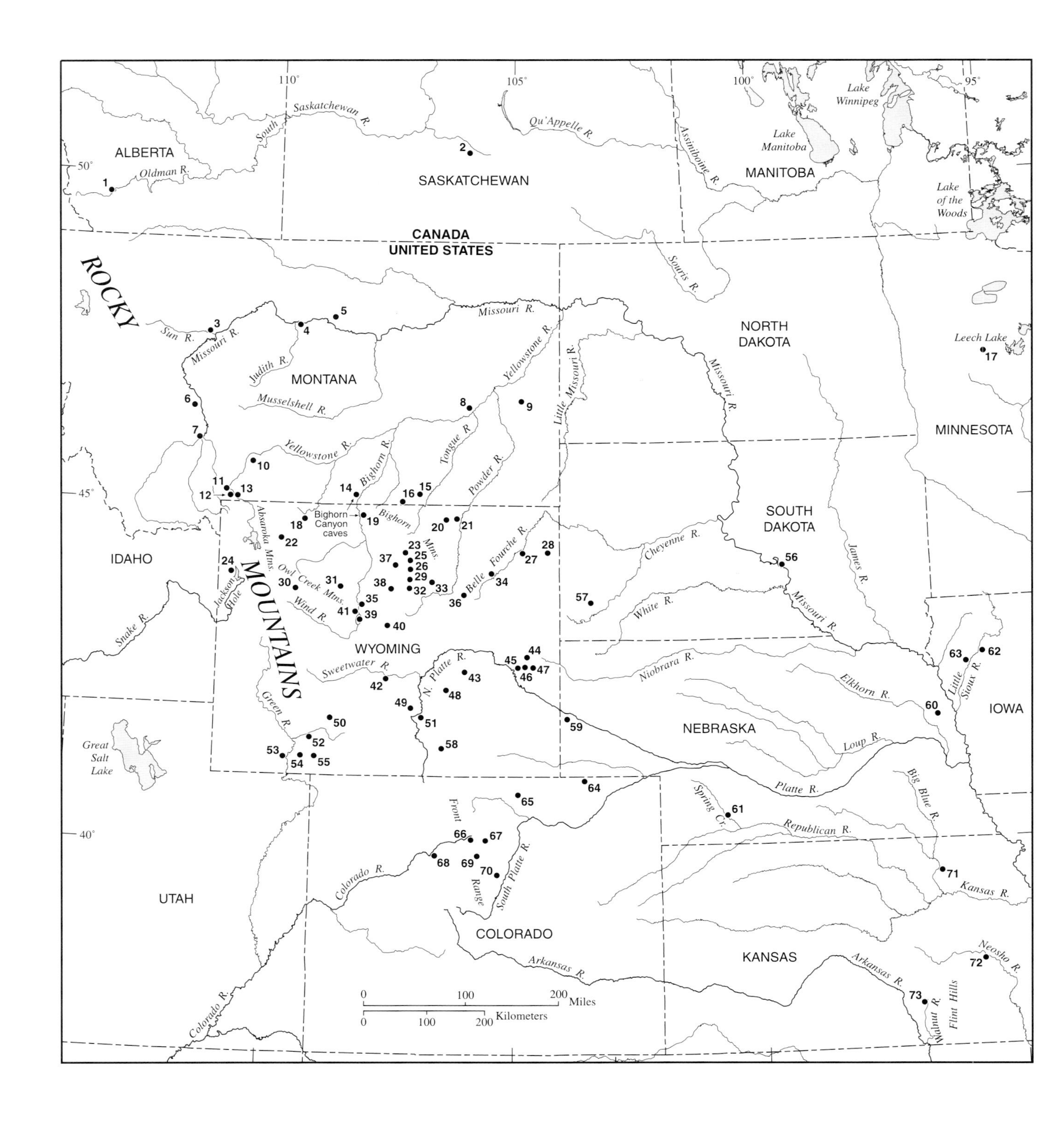

there were six meters of stratified deposits with at least 31 occupation levels dating from 8000 to 6000 B.C. A bone midden dated to 7500 B.C. yielded partial remains of several hundred small mammals mostly bushy-tailed wood rats or "packrats" (*Neotoma cineria*) but only one deer, two mountain sheep, and a single bison (D.N. Walker 1975). Simple food-grinding tools that presage better-developed types in following Archaic periods appear in late Paleo-Indian times in the Bighorn Canyon caves (Husted 1969) and at Medicine Lodge Creek (Frison 1991:69–71). Small pits, in protected areas (Frison 1991:342–343), presumably for short-term storage of dried foodstuffs—plant or animal—also appeared at Medicine Lodge Creek. At Schiffer Cave on the eastern slope of the Bighorn Mountains, several species of seeds were recovered from what were also believed to have been cache pits of about the same age

Fig. 1. Archeological sites of the Hunting and Gathering tradition of the Northwestern and Central Plains. Alberta: 1, Head-Smashed-In-Buffalo-Jump. Saskatchewan: 2, Mortlach. Montana: 3, Sun River (24CA74); 4, Holmes Terrace (24FR52); 5, Keaster (24PH401); 6, Pilgrim (24BW675); 7, Schmitt (24VW559); 8, Powers-Yonkee (24PR5); 9, Ayers-Frazier (24PE30); 10, Myers-Hindman (24PA504); 11, Carbella (24PA302); 12, Rigler Bluffs (24PA401); 13, Sphinx (24PA508); 14, Pretty Creek (24CB4), Sorenson (24CB202) and Mangus (24CB221); 15, Kobold (24BH406); 16, Benson's Butte (24BH1726). Minnesota: 17, Itasca Bison Kill site (21CE1). Wyoming: 18, Dead Indian Creek (48PA551); 19, Bottleneck Cave (48BH206); 20, Mavrakais-Bentzen-Roberts (48SH311); 21, Powder River (48SH312); 22, Mummy Cave (48PA201); 23, Shelter 3 (48BH332), Beehive (48BH346) and Medicine Lodge Creek (48BH499); 24, Lawrence (48TE509); 25, Laddie Creek (48BH345) and Southsider Cave (48BH364); 26, Leigh Cave (48WA304); 27, McKean (48CK7); 28, Hawken Bison Kill site (48CK303); 29, Daugherty Cave (48WA302); 30, Lookingbill (48FR308); 31, Legend Rock (48HO4); 32, Spring Creek Cave (48WA1); 33, Schiffer Cave (48JO319) and Schiffer Ranch Trail (48JO1513); 34, 48CA1391; 35, Wedding of the Waters Cave (48HO301); 36, Ruby Bison Pound (48CA302); 37, Ten Sleep Ridge site (48WA53); 38, Joe Emge (48WA303); 39, Boysen Reservoir (48FR16); 40, Long Butte (48FR261); 41, Birdshead Cave (48FR54); 42, Split Rock Ranch (48FR1484); 43, Shirley Basin (48AB301); 44, 48NO50; 45, 48PL24; 46, 48PL48; 47, 48GO40; 48, Muddy Creek Stone Circles (48CR324, 325, and 1737); 49, Scoggin (48CR304); 50, Deadman Wash (48SW1455); 51, Shoreline (48CR122); 52, Sweetwater Creek (48SW5175); 53, Pine Spring (48SW101); 54, Maxon Ranch (48SW2590); 55, Bozner (48SW5809); 56, Garret Allen (48CR301). South Dakota: 57, Beaver Creek Shelter (39CU779); 58, Medicine Crow (39BF2). Nebraska: 59, Signal Butte (25SF1); 60, Logan Creek (25BT3); 61, Spring Creek (25FT31). Iowa: 62, Cherokee Sewer (13CK405); 63, Simonson (13CK61). Colorado: 64, Dipper Gap (5LO101); 65, Wilber Thomas Shelter (5WL45); 66, Granby (5GA151); 67, Hungry Whistler (5BL67); 68, Yarmony (5EA799); 69, Fourth of July Valley (5BL120: 70, LoDaiska (5JF142) and Magic Mountain (5JF223). Kansas: 71, Coffey (14PO1); 72, Williamson (14CF330); 73, Snyder (14BU9).

(Frison 1973). The foothill-mountain groups also tended to use local sources of stone for flaking materials in contrast to the Plains Paleo-Indian groups, who obtained exotic materials such as Knife River flint from distances up to several hundred kilometers. Differences between the foothill-mountain and the plains groups are in fact as much a matter of degree as of kind.

Sufficient data are available to define the Pryor Stemmed complex for the foothill-mountain groups (Frison and Grey 1980), named after a distinctive projectile point type (fig. 3 b, i, j) from the Bighorn Canyon Caves along the Bighorn River in Wyoming and Montana (Husted 1969). Another projectile point type, Lovell Constricted (fig. 3 e–g), is slightly older than Pryor Stemmed.

While the plains Paleo-Indians produced large quantities of projectile points for big game hunting, the foothill-mountain Paleo-Archaic groups did not. This may in part reflect different procurement strategies, for example, the use of large, reinforced nets for taking animals such as mountain sheep (Frison et al. 1986). Nonetheless, tool assemblages of the Paleo-Archaic groups demonstrate definite relationships with plains Paleo-Indians. The most complete record of Paleo-Archaic foothill-mountain projectile points was recovered from the Medicine Lodge Creek site (fig. 3).

Investigations in southwest Montana may prove significant in understanding Paleo-Indian age groups in foothill-mountain environments. The Barton Gulch site (24MA171) on a drainage of the Ruby River has produced materials of late Paleo-Indian age that typologically do not fit into the Plains chronology and may be a local variant of the foothill-mountain groups that adapted to a somewhat different and unique ecological area (Davis, Aaberg, and Greiser 1988).

U. of Wyo., Dept. of Anthr., Slide Coll., Laramie.

Fig. 2. Location of the deeply stratified Medicine Lodge Creek site (arrow) at the base of the Bighorn Mts., Wyo. Photograph by George Frison, 1973.

Early Archaic

The depositional context of early Plains Archaic sites was adversely affected by the climatic conditions of the Altithermal. Cave and rockshelter sites provide a higher proportion of the available data; open sites producing good stratified sequences of Early Archaic materials reflect unusual conditions. For example, the Laddie Creek site

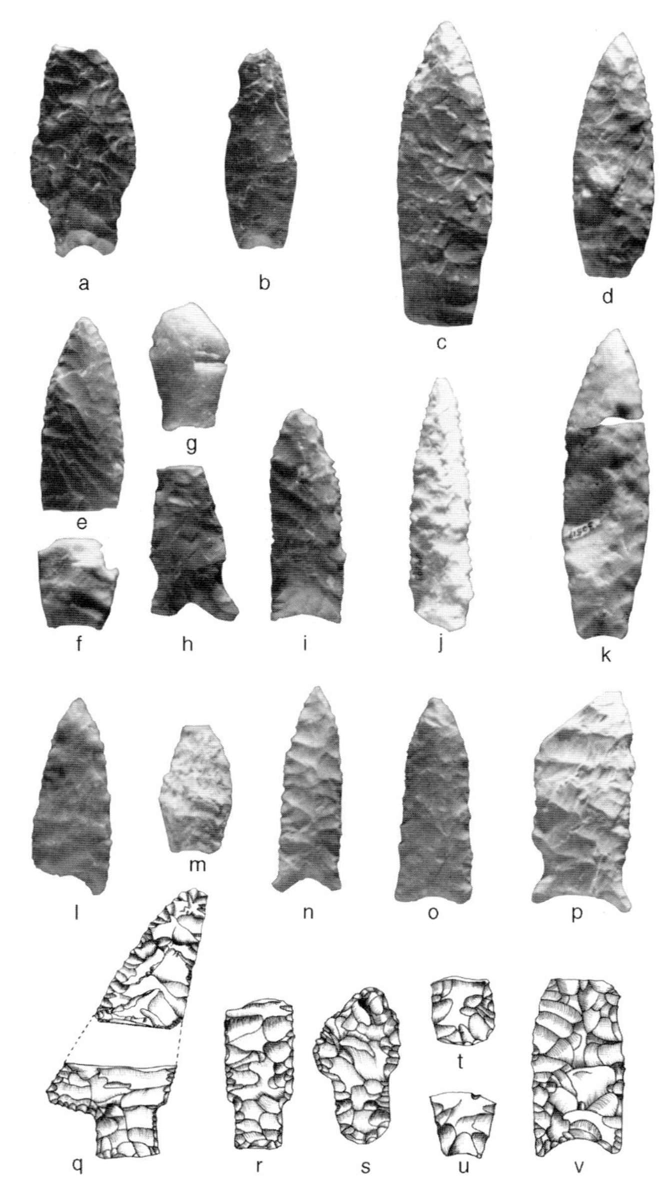

U. of Wyo., Dept. of Anthr., Laramie: a, 30577; b, 30007; c, 31922; d, 32036; e, 30048; f, 32026; g, 30519; h, 31902; i, 30050; j, 34793; k, 30517-32037; l, 30029; m, 31908; n, 30020; o, 30379; p, 34807; q, 30686-32003; r, 30031; s, 34996; t, 31996; u, 30642; v, 30062.

Fig. 3. Paleo-Archaic projectile points from the Medicine Lodge Creek site dating from about 7850 to 6100 B.C. (a–v). Named projectile point types include the Pryor Stemmed (b, i, j) and Lovell Constricted (e, g); also named is an Eden point (m) and a Cody knife (n), both dating to about 6880 B.C. Length of c, 6.8 cm, rest to same scale. q–v, Drawn by Roger Thor Roop.

(Frison 1991:82–84; Larson 1990), produced at least four stratified levels of Early Plains Archaic occupation because springs that flowed throughout the period created artificial conditions of aggradation (Karlstrom 1977). In contrast, at Medicine Lodge Creek, only remnants of in situ Early Plains Archaic cultural levels were found lying on the youngest Paleo-Indian level. Loss of the Early Plains Archaic levels indicates site degradation that lasted until the beginning of the Middle Plains Archaic at approximately 3000 B.C.

The Early Archaic witnessed the development of more sophisticated vegetal grinding tools in the form of simple manos and grinding slabs. Along with these are pits, usually filled with fire-fractured rock and charcoal, believed to have been designed for the preparation of vegetable food products and noticeably different from hearths of the earlier Paleo-Indian period. All these elements are present in an in situ level at the Lookingbill site (48FR308) dated at 5,190 ± 160 B.C. (RL-554) (Frison 1983a).

Archaic fire pits are basin-shaped, usually about 50–80 centimeters in diameter. It is generally accepted that fires were built in these pits and after there was a bed of hot coals, stones were added to hold heat for cooking (fig. 4). Since there was no means of controlling the amount of heat, the stones eventually fractured; when they disintegrated into fragments too small to hold heat effectively, the pit was either abandoned or cleaned out and reused. Some pits were deep enough that sequences of fire and stones were added before being abandoned or cleaned for reuse. Some of these fire pits may have served a second and equally important purpose of heating the inside of small living structures.

There are earlier radiocarbon dates for the period: these include 5735 ± 580 B.C. (UGa-957) at the Pretty Creek site (24CB4) in Montana (Loendorf Dahlberg, and Western 1981), 5700 ± 200 B.C. (RL-669) at Southsider Cave in Wyoming (48BH363) (Frison 1991:74–76), and 5680 ± 170 B.C. (I-1588) at Mummy Cave in Wyoming (McCracken 1978). The large side-notched projectile point is the most obvious diagnostic marker for the period.

The change in projectile point morphology from the lanceolate, stemmed, and laterally restricted styles of the Late Paleo-Indian period to the side-notched styles of the Early Plains Archaic (fig. 5 a–d) occurred suddenly. Whether this reflects a local development, the acceptance of new ideas from the outside (Frison 1983), or whether

Fig. 4. Typical Plains Archaic stone-filled fire pit, located at the Joe Emge site, Wyo. Photograph by George Frison, 1971.

these new ideas were brought to the area by actual population movement (Husted 1969:88; Reeves 1983a) is unknown.

At the Lookingbill site, tool assemblages in the Early Archaic levels demonstrate a carryover of some types from the Paleo-Indian period; these had gradually disappeared by the end of the period at around 3000 B.C. (Frison 1983a:13). On the other hand, the beveled biface Archaic knife appeared by at least 7,000 years ago (Frison 1983a:12) and the addition of side notches produced the Altithermal Side-Notched Knife (fig. 6a–b) (Heffington 1985), which persisted into Middle Archaic times. This gradually changed to the Late Archaic beveled edge knife (Frison 1991:129), which reached its maximum expression in the Late Plains Archaic period with the addition of notches (fig. 6c–d) more likely for the purpose of attaching a thong for carrying purposes rather than for the application of a handle.

In the Southsider Cave site the latest Early Archaic level contained two cache pits, averaging 58 centimeters diameter and 45 centimeters deep, which resemble those in the Late Paleo-Archaic levels at Medicine Lodge Creek. They strongly suggest the continuation of a caching strategy present in the area a millennium earlier. The pits contained rocks and trash. However, in order to preserve a cache pit of this nature for reuse once it is emptied, it must be refilled with something or the sides will collapse within a short period. The easiest way to preserve them was to fill them with trash, which was removed when the pit was reused.

Faunal remains are relatively scarce in Early Archaic components. Medium-size animals recorded include mountain sheep and deer; smaller ones include jackrabbit, cottontail rabbit, marmot, and woodrat. Notably, bison are scarce or absent. However, the Early Archaic Hawken site (48CK303) in the Black Hills in Wyoming (Frison, Wilson, and Wilson 1976) is an arroyo bison kill radiocarbon-dated at 4520 ± 170 B.C. (RL-185) and 4320 ± 170 B.C. (RL-437). Perhaps the Black Hills was an oasis during the Altithermal, or perhaps there were periods when drought conditions ameliorated enough to allow the bison populations to increase to a point where communal procurement was possible. Evidence indicates also what appears to have been communal pronghorn procurement in northwest Wyoming at about 3850 B.C. (Francis and Miller 1992).

The Beaver Creek Shelter (39CU779) in Wind Cave National Park, South Dakota, produced a series of radiocarbon dates from 3550 to 4570 B.C. as well as at least one side-notched projectile point that is a diagnostic of the Early Plains Archaic (Martin, Alex, and Benton 1988).

In the Wyoming Basin in southwest Wyoming, the Deadman Wash Site (48SW1455) yielded stratifed deposits from Late Paleo-Indian through Early, Middle, and Late Archaic and into the Late Prehistoric period (Armitage, Creasman, and Mackey 1982). The earliest Early Archaic radiocarbon date for the site is 4890 ± 90 B.C. (Beta 3924). The Bozner site (48SW5809) (Anonymous 1985) in the same area has a similar stratigraphic and cultural record but lacks the radiocarbon dates.

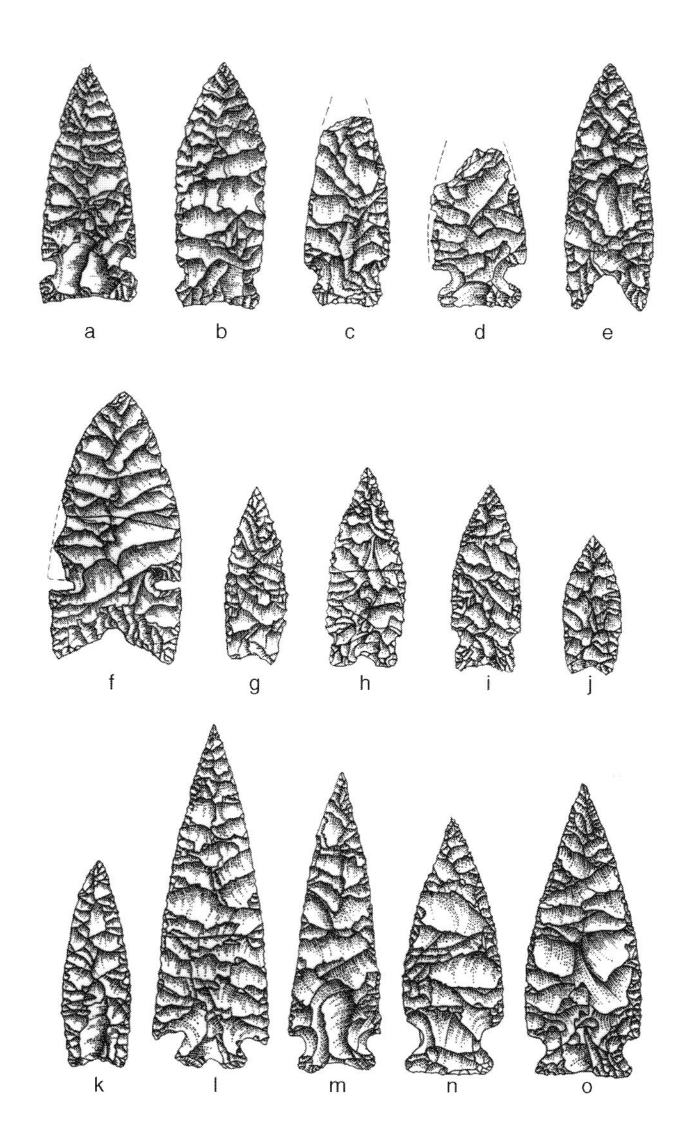

U. of Wyo., Dept. of Anthr., Laramie: a, 7067; b, 60191; c, 2272; d, 32096; e, 79088; f, 79141; g, 65084; h, 65098; i, 65732; j, 65082; k, Q0792; l, 63500; m, 76136; n, 12287; o, 12050.

Fig. 5. Plains Archaic projectile points from: Early Archaic, a–d; Middle Archaic, e–k; and Late Archaic, l–o. Side-notched points from the a, Lookingbill site; b, Hawken Bison Kill site; c, Wedding of the Waters Cave site; and d, Laddie Creek site. McKean and McKean variant points from the e, Scoggin site; g–j, Dead Indian Creek site; and k, Southsider Cave site. f, Mallory point from the Scoggin site. Yonkee points from the l, Kobold and m, Roberts sites. n–o, Besant points from the Ruby Bison Pound site. Length of o, 6.75 cm, rest to same scale. Drawing by Norm Frisch.

A significant development in the archeology of the Plains is the discovery of housepits in all the Archaic periods. A number of sites in southwest, central, and northern Wyoming have yielded housepits leaving no doubt that these features figured prominently in survival strategies. In fact, it is difficult to envision winter survival on the

Northwestern Plains without adequate protection from the elments. Many interior and exterior features such as fire pits and post holes are present (Frison 1991:83–86; Harrel and McKern 1986; Newberry and Harrison 1986; Eakin, Francis, and Larkin 1997: Miller and McGuire 1997).

Although the Powder River basin in Wyoming and southern Montana is an area in which a great deal of contract archeology has been done, except for caves and rockshelters on the eastern slopes of the Big Horn Mountains, no significant Early Archaic sites have been recognized even though the diagnostic artifacts are regular surface finds. Until the factors that determine site formation and destruction are better understood, the relative lack of Early Archaic sites in this part of the plains should not be attributed to a lack of human occupation, particularly in light of the evidence of Early Archaic communal bison hunting at the Hawken site and in open camp and rockshelter sites in the Big Horn Mountains.

The Bitterroot cultural complex was in place in the Birch Creek valley in Idaho between the Lemhi and Beaverhead mountain ranges by 6550 and 6050 B.C. (see Swanson, Butler, and Bonnichsen 1964; Swanson and Sneed 1966) according to data from stratified rockshelters. The Bitteroot diagnostic is the side-notched projectile point similar to those from Early Archaic sites to the east in Wyoming at about the same time period.

The Oxbow complex is well represented in northern Montana and the Canadian provinces, but there is only one radiocarbon-dated Oxbow site in Montana, the Sun River site (24CA74) near Great Falls, Montana, with dates from about 1550 to 3250 B.C. (Greiser et al. 1983). Oxbow as a cultural complex is known by a projectile point type, and there are examples of this type found in sites in northern Wyoming, including Mummy Cave (McCracken 1978) and Dead Indian Creek (Frison and Walker 1984).

Middle Archaic

The end of the Early Plains Archaic and the beginning of the Middle Plains Archaic (or Early Middle Period as most archeologists in Montana and the Plains of Canada prefer) can be documented stratigraphically in a number of sites. Numerous caves and rockshelters along the slopes of the Bighorn and Absaroka mountains adjacent to the Bighorn basin demonstrate continuous deposition from Early to Middle Archaic and an abrupt end to the diagnostic side-notched projectile points at about 3050 B.C. Middle Plains Archaic diagnostics appear at about the same time with relatively little overlap of the two. The McKean complex is the first recognizable entity of the Middle Plains Archaic, identified by several projectile point types and variants (fig. 5 e, g–k). Reliable radiocarbon dates range from about 1150 to 2950 B.C.

In contrast to the Early Plains Archaic, bison remains appear in relatively large numbers in most sites. Fire pits filled with fire-cracked rock, which are probably food preparation features, along with plant-grinding tools, carry over from the preceding period and continue in the tool assemblages. The McKean site in northeast Wyoming (Mulloy 1954a) is located at an ecotone: on one side are the open plains and on the other side are the timbered breaks of the Black Hills, each producing a wide variety of plant and animal food resources. Nearby are the riparian resources of the Belle Fourche River. Freshwater mussels (*Lampsilis* sp.) were gathered in quantity and presumably used for food at the McKean site as well as other Archaic sites along the river. The McKean site area, ideal for a broad spectrum hunting and gathering subsistence strategy, was apparently reoccupied many times. Several other significant Middle Archaic sites were investigated by R.P. Wheeler (1996).

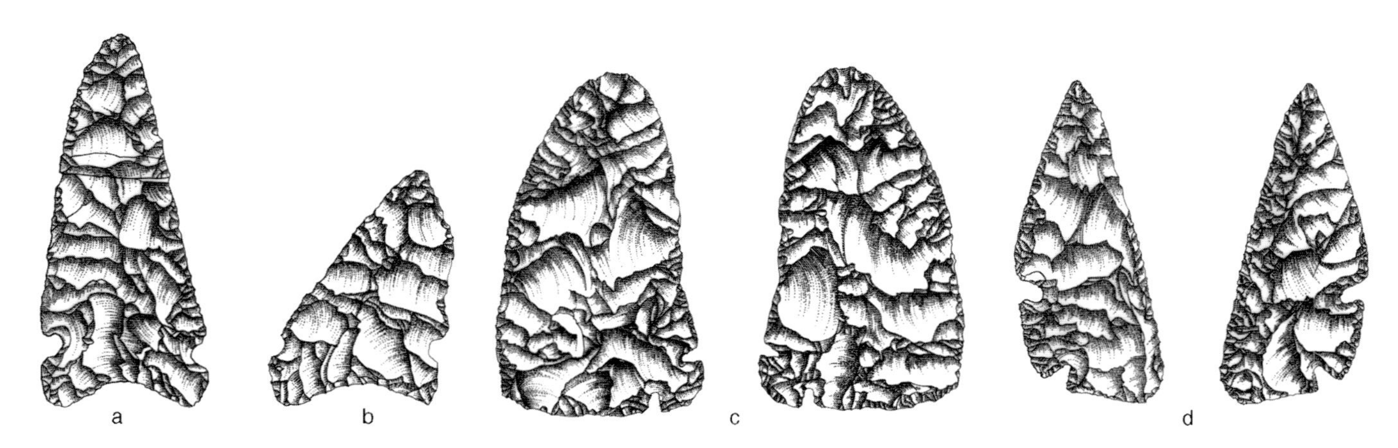

U. of Wyo., Dept. of Anthr., Laramie: a, 2512; b, 2527; c, GA-2; d, Saratoga Mus., Wyo.

Fig. 6. Archaic stone knives. a–b, Early and Middle Archaic side-notched stone knives from the Ten Sleep Ridge site, Wyo. c, d, Late Archaic single-beveled and notched stone knives from the Garrett Allen site, Wyo. a, c, Knives are each in an early stage of use, c being in almost pristine condition; b, d, knives are each in an advanced stage of use, showing extensive resharpening. Length of a, 6.25 cm, b to same scale; length of c, 10 cm, d to same scale. Drawing by Norm Frisch.

The major segment of the Black Hills lies in South Dakota, and McKean sites are present there and in the surrounding area (Tratebas 1985). Another area of known McKean site occurrence is in the butte country of northwestern South Dakota and the adjoining area of southwestern North Dakota. Another McKean site has been investigated in North Dakota just south of the Missouri River. Six sites within this widespread expanse have yielded 16 radiocarbon dates between 1450 and 2240 B.C. (Keyser and Davis 1984, 1985; Tratebas and Vagstad 1979). In addition, Gregg et al. (1996) have compiled a useful overview of the Archaic in central and western North Dakota.

Lacking at the McKean site but very much in evidence in what is considered a Middle Archaic context at Signal Butte in western Nebraska (Strong 1935) is a projectile point type commonly referred to as Mallory (Forbis, Strong, and Kirby 1950). This is a large, side-notched type but quite different in technology and appearance from the Early Archaic side-notched varieties. McKean lanceolates along with the Mallory type projectile points (fig. 5 f) were found in good context at the Scoggin site (48CR304), a bison kill near the Platte River in Wyoming and dated at 2590 ± 110 B.C. (RL-174) (Lobdell 1973). Mallory type points were recovered in three sites in northeastern Colorado (E.A. Morris, Blakeslee, and Thompson 1985) but were absent in other sites, particularly at another butte location in northeastern Colorado (M.D. Metcalf 1974), which is not far from Signal Butte. Mallory type points are known to appear occasionally in Middle Plains Archaic levels in caves and rockshelters in the Bighorn Mountains, and large surface sites producing Mallory type points have been exposed on terraces along the North Platte River in central Wyoming.

Benson's Butte is another butte campsite located in the Wolf Mountains in Montana. This isolated topographic feature rises abruptly about 50 meters from the surrounding countryside and has an area about 50 by 100 meters near the top that was suitable for occupation. Features and artifacts recovered there indicate both a Middle (McKean) and a Late Archaic occupation. Grinding stones suggest use of plant resources, and faunal remains indicate hunting of a wide variety of small and large mammals (L.B. Fredlund 1979). Farther north of Benson's Butte in Montana, the plant-grinding tools gradually disappear.

In the Wyoming basin, dated McKean sites are relatively rare, although surface finds of all McKean variants occur in numbers that are not commensurate with the small number of recorded sites. Radiocarbon dates there compare well with other McKean sites.

At the Dead Indian Creek site (48PA551), a winter campsite in the Sunlight basin in northwest Wyoming (Frison and Walker 1984), all variants of projectile points in the McKean complex occur together (fig. 5 g–j). Included also were several projectile points that fit typologically into the Oxbow type as it is known farther north (see Nero and McCorquodale 1958; Reeves 1978). At least part of the Dead Indian Creek site occupation occurred during the winter months (based on tooth eruption and wear on a large sample of deer mandibles; T. Simpson 1984). Mountain sheep were also well represented in the faunal assemblage along with small numbers of bison, pronghorn, and elk. In addition there were significant numbers of manos and metates, which suggests that there was an equally strong orientation toward plant-food gathering, probably representing a different seasonal occupation. The site lies at 2,028 meters elevation, although its location in a small basin extending back into the Absaroka Mountains gives the feeling of a more mountainlike environment than is actually the case. This site is also located at an ecotone with mountain slope, open basin, and stream bank resources readily available. Three radiocarbon dates are from 1850 to 2450 B.C.

A site feature at Dead Indian Creek was interpreted in 1972 as an occupation in an old channel cut (Frison and Walker 1984:46), but upon reexamination it is almost certainly a housepit (fig. 7 top) with a large central fire pit and other features, one of which could be a deep storage pit. A profile through a large fire pit during the 1983 excavations at the McKean site (Kornfeld and Todd 1985) revealed a dark, stained area about 50 centimeters thick extending just over a meter on each side of the pit. Other small, shallow features suggest post holes, and this also appears to have been a housepit. Housepits of Middle Archaic age (or late Early Archaic age and early Late Archaic age in the proposed Wyoming basin chronology) were found in southwestern Wyoming (Harrell and McKern 1986; Newberry and Harrison 1986). These discoveries extend the range of known Archaic housepits over much of the Northwestern Plains.

Another unusual feature at the Dead Indian Creek site in Sunlight basin was an arrangement of mule deer skull caps with antlers attached (fig. 7 bottom), which strongly suggests ceremonial treatment of the species that represented a major food source. Mountain sheep were also an important food source at the site, but there is no evidence of special treatment of their skulls.

Middle Plains Archaic sites have been documented along the upper Yellowstone River in Montana outside of Yellowstone National Park. These include the Carbella (24PA302), Rigler Bluffs (24PA401) (Arthur 1966), Myers-Hindman (24PA504) (Lahren 1976), and Sphinx (24PA508) sites (Lahren 1971).

Small amounts of perishable material have been found in the McKean level at Mummy Cave, including several pieces of two-strand, twisted vegetable fiber cordage, some of which were incorporated into three net fragments; a fragment of coiled basketry; and a dart foreshaft. These were dated at 2470 ± 150 B.C. (I-1428) (Husted 1978:116).

At Leigh Cave (48WA304) (Frison and Huseas 1968) in the foothills of the Bighorn Mountains, a much larger assemblage of perishable materials was recovered. The floor of the McKean level was a consolidated mat of vegetable material that, along with grass and other plant fibers, contained several hundred outer coverings of wild onion (*Allium* spp.) bulbs, which presumably had been used as food.

Remains of other plants that were probably used as food included silver buffalo berry seeds (*Shepherdia argentea*), plains prickly-pear cactus leaves and seeds (*Opuntia polyacantha*), chokecherry pits (*Prunus virginiana*), limber pine nuts (*Pinus flexilis*), immature yucca pods (*Yucca glauca*), and wild rose hips (*Rosa woodsii*). A large sample of two-strand twisted cordage fragments ranges in diameter from 0.7 to 3.7 millimeters with a wide variation in maceration, tightness, and overall quality. Bast, leaf, and bark fibers used for cordage include milkweed (*Asclepias* spp.), yucca, juniper bark (*Juniperus* spp.), and at least two unidentified grasses. Two pieces of unidentified hide appear to have been parts of clothing that were sewed together with two-strand, twisted vegetable fiber cordage. Part of the material in the packed floor consisted also of wood shavings and a few discarded ends from woodworking identified as chokecherry, cottonwood (*Populus* spp.), willow (*Salix* spp.), and western birch (*Betula occidentalis*). Two manos and a broken metate or grinding slab were also recovered.

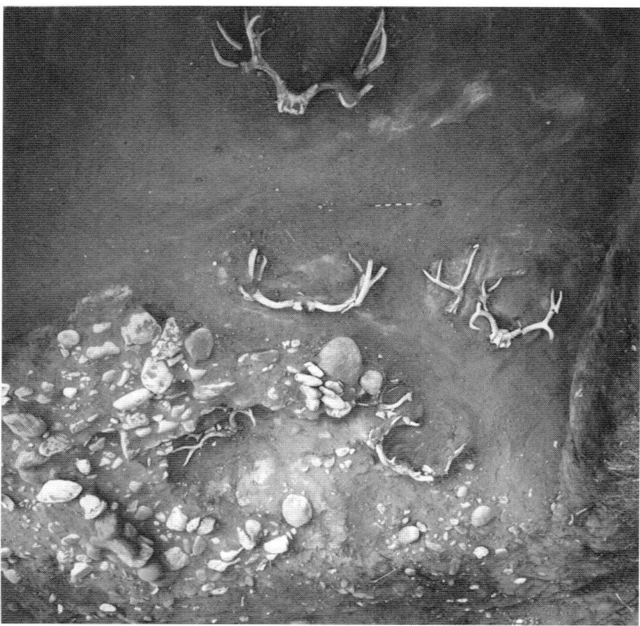

U. of Wyo., Dept. of Anthr., Slide Coll., Laramie.

Fig. 7. Dead Indian Creek site, northwest Wyo. top, Profile of a Middle Archaic pit house. Photograph by George Frison, 1970. bottom, Arrangement of mule deer antlers suggesting ritual activity. Photograph by George Frison, 1969.

The surface of the area immediately adjacent to a fire pit filled with fire-fractured rock in Leigh Cave was littered with the partially charred remains of several hundred mormon crickets (*Anabrus simplex*), large insects similar to locusts that were apparently being roasted for food.

In general, the faunal and floral evidence from known archeological sites of the McKean period indicate a widespread but closely related subsistence strategy that favored ecotonal situations that provided the widest possible range of plant and animal resources. Differences in subsistence strategies observed from one site to another were largely determined by the resources available in any given area at any given time. Not surprising is a strong Great Basin influence in the Wyoming basin and a Northern Plains influence in southern Montana and northern Wyoming.

A cultural manifestation in the Powder River basin in Wyoming and Montana has been called Yonkee, a name derived from the Powers-Yonkee site (24PR5) in southeastern Montana. During the first investigations of the site in 1961 (Bentzen 1962), a charcoal sample was submitted that yielded a date of 2500 ± 125 B.C. (I-410). This date along with what was first thought to be a similarity in morphology of projectile points (fig. 5 l–m) resulted in Yonkee being proposed as part of the Middle Archaic McKean complex (see Frison 1978:49–50). Many other sites in the Powder River area of northern Wyoming and southern Montana have been identified as Yonkee. These and a reinvestigation of the original Yonkee site have produced a series of radiocarbon dates that range from about 500 to 1150 B.C. (Bentzen 1963; Frison 1991:34, 103–106; 1968a; Tom E. Roll, personal communication 1988) indicating that the first Yonkee site date is probably in error. Another site in the Powder River basin in Wyoming with definite Yonkee affiliations suggests one incidence of a possible preference of pronghorn over bison (McKibbin et al. 1988). These data indicate that Yonkee follows McKean in time and, although possibly derived from McKean, it would have to be placed within the early part of the Late Archaic period. Bison jumping was apparently part of the subsistence strategy at the Kobold site (24BH406) in southern Montana (Frison 1970).

Late Archaic

Little in the way of subsistence strategies can be documented to separate the Late Archaic (or Late Middle

Period as some investigators prefer) from the Middle Archaic. The most visible diagnostic is the appearance of the Pelican Lake corner-notched projectile point. At the Medicine Lodge Creek site there is an uninterrupted sequence of occupation levels through the Middle and Late Plains Archaic: two radiocarbon dates on a level with a large sample of Pelican Lake projectile points are 1160 ± 170 B.C. (RL-559) and 1070 ± 140 B.C. (RL-96). At Mummy Cave good stratigraphic integrity exists and there is a Late Archaic date of 870 ± 135 B.C. (I-1427). From these data, it appears that around 3,000 years ago dates the appearance of this cultural manifestation.

The name Pelican Lake comes from the designation given to certain of the lower levels at the stratified Mortlach site in Saskatchewan (Wettlaufer 1955). The Pelican Lake projectile point type is recognized widely over the northern part of the Plains. A radiocarbon-dated Pelican Lake level at the stratified Head-Smashed-In Buffalo Jump in southern Alberta is 1090 ± 120 B.C. (GaK-1416). Late Archaic dates of 1250 to 1550 B.C. were obtained from the upper component at the McKean site (Mulloy 1954a) and from the Boysen Reservoir excavations (Mulloy 1954) in central Wyoming; however, these were among the earlier solid carbon dates and their accuracy is open to question. Pelican Lake bison kill sites (L.B. Davis and E. Stallcop 1965; G.R. Clark and M. Wilson 1981) and open-air campsites (L.B. Davis et al. 1982; Greiser et al. 1983) have been investigated in northern Montana.

The corner-notched dart point continued until around A.D. 500. Representative late radiocarbon dates include 390 ± 130 (RL-95) at Medicine Lodge Creek (Frison 1991:28); 430 ± 200 (SI-238) at Bottleneck Cave in the Bighorn River Canyon (Husted 1969); 480 ± 70 (GaK-2633) at the Myers-Hindman site in southwest Montana (Lahren 1976); and 625 ± 150 (M-971) at site 48PL24 (fig. 1, no. 45) along the Platte River, Wyoming (Mulloy and Steege 1967).

Immediately following the Late Archaic is the proposed appearance of the bow and arrow in contrast to the atlatl and dart (fig. 8) and the beginning of the Late Prehistoric period on the Plains. Avonlea is considered to be the earliest manifestation of the Late Prehistoric period although in the Wyoming area, Avonlea continued a definite Archaic lifeway. Avonlea appears around A.D. 100 at Head-Smashed-In Buffalo Jump (Reeves 1978), but its age is later in the southern Montana-Wyoming area. For example, in the uninterrupted stratigraphic sequence at Medicine Lodge Creek is a radiocarbon date of 590 ± 100 (RL-376); at Benson's Butte is a radiocarbon date of 440 ± 60 (Tx2795) (L.B. Fredlund 1979:92); and at the the Beehive site near the Medicine Lodge Creek site (Frison 1991:114, 115) is a date of 500 ± 100 (RL-538).

The Besant cultural manifestation, another name derived from the Mortlach site in the Besant valley of central Saskatchewan (Wettlaufer 1955), appeared in the Wyoming and Montana area between about A.D. 100 and 400. Besant hunters were apparently still using the atlatl and dart, and their projectile points (fig. 5 n–o) are distinctive in morphology and manufacture technology, utilizing the best of available raw materials. They may have been the most sophisticated bison-hunting group on the Northwestern Plains in prehorse times judging from evidence recovered in eastern Wyoming (Frison 1971; Reher 1983). Seasonality of the bison trapping in which man-made corrals were used is not known, since the faunal remains were not saved and the sites had been badly damaged by artifact hunters. However, the size and complexity of corrals, drive line fences, and ramps indicate a high level of familiarity with bison behavior. The short duration of their stay in the area could indicate a rapid depletion of the bison, either through overkill, unfavorable climatic factors, or both. Some, but not all, Avonlea and Besant sites yield small amounts of ceramics that can be used to suggest Woodland contact before they reached the Northwestern Plains.

Besant manifests the most convincing evidence for ritual activity associated with large animal procurement in the archeological record for Archaic times. At the Ruby

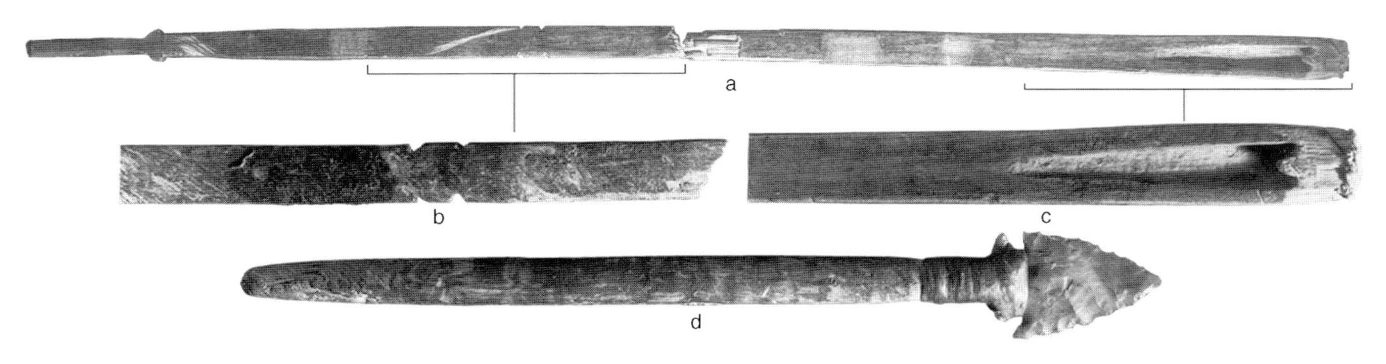

U. of Wyo., Dept. of Anthr., Laramie: a-c, 591; d, 597.

Fig. 8. Weapons from Spring Creek Cave site, Wyo. a, Atlatl; b, reversed and englarged portion of atlatl as indicated, showing the notches and adhesive suggesting the former presence of an atlatl weight; c, enlarged view of a portion of the atlatl's grooved end; d, Late Archaic projectile point mounted in a foreshaft, showing notches and adhesive. Length of a, 46 cm; d, 19.1 cm.

Bison Pound site buffalo corral (Frison 1971), alongside the drive lines as they terminated at the corral, was a structure approximately 12 meters long and 4 meters wide formed by two intersecting arcs of circles from points 16 meters apart and with radii of 10 meters. The structure had been partially roofed over, and bison skulls had been placed around one end. Other associated features and the lack of any evidence that would suggest use of the structure for living or hunting strongly suggests shamanistic activity associated with the corraling of the bison.

Dry caves and rockshelters along the western slopes of the Big Horn Mountains in northern Wyoming have yielded perishable materials from Late Archaic occupations (Frison 1962, 1965, 1968; Husted 1969). Birdshead Cave (Bliss 1950) on the southern slopes of the Owl Creek Mountains in central Wyoming yielded a large number of Late Archaic perishable items.

Unequivocal evidence of use of the atlatl and dart was demonstrated from Spring Creek Cave (Frison 1965) and Daugherty Cave (Frison 1968). The atlatl resembles the Southwest type: the one nearly complete specimen (fig. 8 a–c) is carved from a single piece of a local, extremely resilient wood known as skunk brush sumac (*Rhus trilobata*). Other fragments are of similar size and shape. Both proximal and distal ends of main shafts along with wooden foreshafts with hafted, corner-notched Late Archaic type projectile points (fig. 8) were also recovered.

Several fragments of coiled basketry (fig. 9) were recovered from Spring Creek and Daugherty caves. One was identified as a classic Fremont-style parching tray (Frison, Adovasio, and Carlisle 1986:166). All coiled basketry fragments from these and other sites in the area represent a technology found in Great Basin coiled baskets of similar age and indicate also a strong economic emphasis on seed gathering.

Sharpened sticks up to 28 millimeters in diameter and 40 centimeters long were first interpreted as stakes because of evidence of heavy use on the sharpened ends. These along with long, straight elk antler tines of similar size and with worn distal ends are regarded as probable digging sticks for bulbs and roots such as sego lily (*Calochortus nuttalli*), wild onion, biscuit root (*Lomatium cous*), and bitterroot (*Lewisia rediviva*). Both manos and grinding slab metates were present in the artifact assemblages. Several bulbs, seeds, berries, and leaves of edible plants were in the dry cave, Late Archaic assemblages. These perishable parts of the assemblages present a much stronger case for plant food use than do the lithic parts alone.

The Late Archaic witnessed a continual expansion of occupations into the interior parts of the intermontane basins as well as the foothills and mountains. This is evident mainly in the proliferation of fire pits, which take a myriad of shapes, sizes, and clusters. They occur singly and in pairs and are combined with other features such as stone boiling pits. All are believed to reflect different kinds of functional applications, mainly in food preparation.

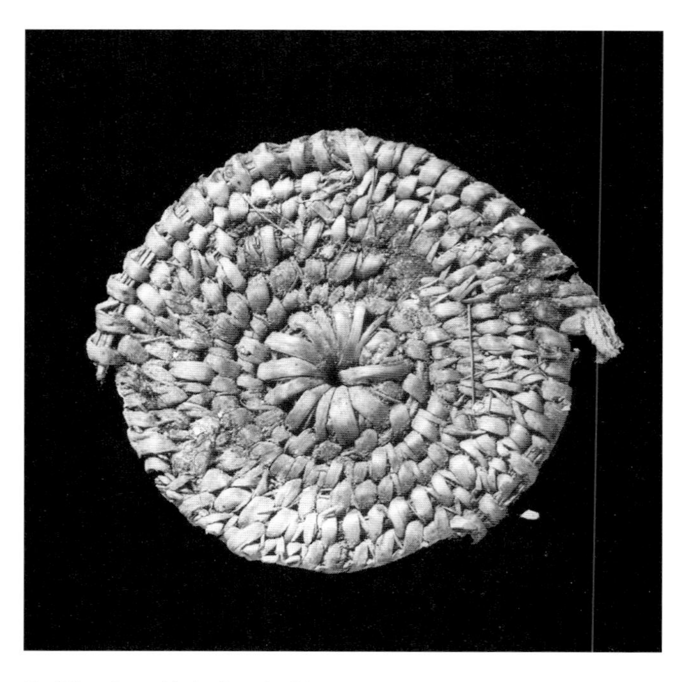

U. of Wyo., Dept. of Anthr., Laramie: 680.

Fig. 9. Coiled basketry fragment from Spring Creek Cave. Diameter 6.3 cm.

It is often difficult to establish boundaries for fire-pit sites since they are scattered over areas up to hectares in size. Associated artifacts consist mainly of manos, metates, and a few simple flake tools. Perimeters of individual fire pits often demonstrate red oxidation rings up to five centimeters thick where enough iron particles are present in the clay attesting to the amount of heat that was generated during use. Others are lined with sandstone slabs (fig. 10) or occasionally cobbles. Most contain fire-cracked rock, and the area surrounding some of these pits is covered with fire-cracked rock that was fragmented beyond usefulness and was cleaned out of the pits so that it could be replaced with fresh rock, thereby attesting to repeated use.

At least some of these features may also have served to provide heat for small structures. Although only in rare cases are these Late Archaic fire pits associated with anything that can be interpreted as a tepee ring, stones are not an absolute requirement for holding down the edges of a simple structure nor are stones of the proper size always available within reasonable distances. The subsistence strategy may have required frequent moves so that simple, portable structures were in common use (see Frison 1983b).

Shorelines of certain lakes formed by glaciers moving out of the Yellowstone plateau, and connecting mountain systems were occupied by Archaic groups. Most of these lakes have been raised to store water for irrigation projects so that the archeological sites have been affected by annual rising and lowering of lake levels. Jackson Lake in Teton National Park is one of these (see Connor 1986); the

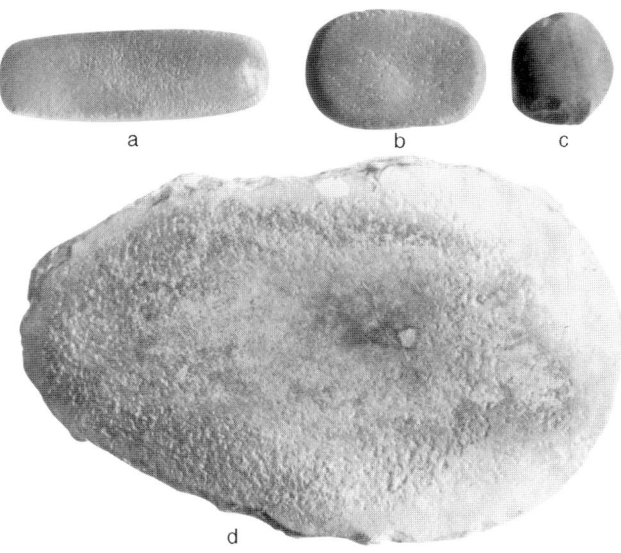

bottom, U. of Wyo., Dept. of Anthr., Laramie: a, JE-9; b, JE-5; c, JE-8; d, JE-1.

Fig. 10. Joe Emge site, northern Wyo. top, Late Archaic slab-lined stone-filled fire pit. Photograph by George Frison, 1971. bottom, Lake Archaic manos (a–c) and a grinding slab or metate (d). Length of a 20 cm, rest to same scale.

largest site on its shore, Lawrence, is characterized by large numbers of stone-filled fire pit features (Reeve, Wright, and Mecham 1979). Manos and grinding slabs (fig. 10) dominate the tool assemblage, and radiocarbon dates are of both Middle and Late Archaic age. The paucity of faunal remains suggests a strong orientation toward plant foods. The true functions of these fire pits remain unclear.

The Archaic as a lifeway continued well into the Late Prehistoric period in areas such as the Bighorn, Wind River, and Wyoming basins. For example, there is an occupation dated at A.D. 990 ± 90 years (RL-375); both that and Medicine Lodge Creek site are characterized by typical Late Archaic stonefilled fire pits and grinding stones. In contrast, in the areas that were more plainslike ecologically, the economy was more oriented toward bison hunting.

• STONE CIRCLES Tepee rings or stone circles (fig. 11) are probably the most visible feature on the Northwestern Plains in Late Prehistoric times but they began to appear in considerable numbers during the Late Archaic. There is a possibility that some of these were present during Middle Archaic times. They appear singly and in large groups; butte tops, barren ridges, minor topographic rises, and stream terraces were common locations for their placement. Cobble-filled teraces where stones were readily available were particularly attractive. They are found in the interior basins and plains, in the foothills, and with less freguency in the high mountains.

There is no total agreement on the function of stone circles, particularly the ones that appear during the Late Archaic (see L.B. Davis 1983). Mulloy (1954) believed that most of those he found in the Boysen Reservoir area were not the remains of living structures, citing as evidence the paucity of artifacts and features such as fires, cache pits, and the wide range of diameters (1.2 to 7.3m). Investigations along the North Platte River in southeastern Wyoming (Mulloy 1965; Mulloy and Steege 1967) produced numerous stone circles that were interpreted as the remains of habitation structures, while others were questionable enough that they might have served other purposes. T.F. Kehoe (1958, 1960) used mainly ethnological evidence from the Blackfeet Reservation to present a strong case that the great majority of stone circles were actually tepee rings used to hold down the outside skin coverings of conical pole structures.

Both Mulloy and Kehoe were probably right since they were interpreting different bodies of data. The great majority of stone circles are noted for their lack of cultural material, which suggests that if they do represent the remains of living structures, either the human groups involved were culturally impoverished or else the periods of occupation were very short. The visibility and numbers of stone circle sites is high and, consequenty, there is no need for the investigator to search for buried sites. However, in exposed situations with the highly visible circle of stones, the removal of certain classes of artifacts, particularly the diagnostics, is high, which tends to bias the archeological record.

Some complexities that arise in attempting to deal with stone circles can be demonstrated by a number of isolated site situations. For example, at the Beehive site a single, in situ Late Archaic stone circle was directly below but stratigraphically separated from a Late Prehistoric Avonlea component. A centrally located fire hearth on sandstone bedrock was 1.1 meters in diameter, and a stone flaking area with a large quantity of debitage was inside the circle.

top, U. of Wyo., Dept. of Anthr., Slide Coll., Laramie.

Fig. 11. Stone circles. top, Long Butte site, northern Wyo., part of 27 closely spaced stone circles occupying the entire surface of a flat-topped butte. Photograph by George Frison, 1969. bottom, Boysen Reservoir site, central Wyo., isolated Late Archaic stone circle or tepee ring. Photograph by William Mulloy, 1950.

Outside were large quantities of debitage, animal bone, and fire-fractured sandstone rock. Artifacts included manos and one grinding slab and several Late Archaic, corner-notched projectile points along with numerous less diagnostic tool types. The high integrity of this site component indicates that the stone circle was the base of some sort of living structure with an opening to the east. No details of the actual structure are known.

In contrast, a location in the Shirley basin in central Wyoming contains at least 100 stone circles with outside diameters 4.5–5.5 meters exposed at the surface. Many of the circles are contiguous; careful searching may reveal a flake or two that may or may not be related to the stone circles. No features were present inside or outside the circles tested.

Within a few kilometers of this site are the Muddy Creek stone circle sites, to which Reher (1983) has applied the term villages. These are associated with a large Besant bison corral and drive line system. The circles represent unquestionable clusters of living structures directly associated with the bison procurement events; and the amount of debitage, stone tools, and weaponry both inside and out of the circles presents a sharp contrast to numerous other nearby stone circle sites.

Extensive investigation of the Pilgrim stone circle site in Montana revealed long-term use that began in Pelican Lake times. Of 71 stone circles, 49 were systematically exacavated and the conclusions were that the main attraction was the presence of wild food plants, especially bitterroot and leafy wild parsley (*Musineon divaricatum*) (L.B. Davis et al. 1982a). Hunting was apparently a secondary consideration in this location.

• HUMAN BURIALS Archaic Period human skeletal material from the Northwestern Plains is relatively scarce. One flexed, mature male skeleton was recovered. The radiocarbon dates of 3300 ± 150 B.C. (RL-543) and 3400 ± 160 B.C. (RL-651), if correct, date the burial to the Early Plains Archaic. No grave goods were recovered (see Zeimens et al. 1978).

A probable female skull was recovered in the first McKean site investigations (Stewart 1954), and the partial remains of a child were recovered a short distance away (Haspel and D. Wedel 1985). Partial remains of another child were recovered in a small pit below the occupation floor at the Dead Indian Creek site (G.W. Gill 1984). A secondary burial with only a few bones along with grave goods consisting of projectile points, shell beads, bifaces, two pieces of cut and polished human bone, and a biface and flake cache was recovered in the southern Bighorn basin of Wyoming. All these items had been covered with a thick level of red ocher, and a fire had been built on top. The associated projectile points are strongly suggestive of Pelican Lake; however, a radiocarbon date on charcoal from the fire is 1570 ± 140 B.C., which would be the oldest known date for Pelican Lake. It is possible that the wood was several hundred years old at the time of burning. The occurrence is unique and provides insight into Archaic mortuary practices (Frison and Van Norman 1985).

The number of documented burials increases for the Late Archaic although the sample is still quite small (G.W. Gill 1981) and increases very slowly. There is considerable variation in Late Archaic burials from flexed (Scoggin 1978) to extended (Steege 1960), usually with small amounts of grave goods. G.W. Gill (1974, 1981, 1991) suggests the possibility of a distinctive cranial form for the Late Plains Archaic that changes during the Late Prehistoric period.

Perhaps of greatest significance in terms of Archaic subsistence strategies is the extreme wear on human teeth demonstrated in burials of the period. This wear is usually interpreted as the result of particulate matter derived from the grinding tools used in the preparation of plant foods (Scheiber and Gill 1996; J. Williams 1996).

• PICTOGRAPHS AND PETROGLYPHS Pictographs and petroglyphs are found in relatively large numbers over most of the Northwestern Plains but there is always the difficulty of correlating them with dated materials. Whether or not any of the "rock art" is actually of Archaic age is open to question. Buckles (1964) used evidence from a cave in which deposits were continually aggrading to suggest different petroglyph traditions, some of which might have been as much as 2,000 years old. Although this was an innovative approach, the deposits were not systematically excavated and the conclusions must remain tentative. Much has been published on pictographs and petroglyphs (Conner and Conner 1971; Hendry 1983), most of which are believed to have been executed in the last 1,000 years.

Evidence has been found for petroglyphs of Late Archaic age of petroglyphs in the Bighorn basin of Wyoming. A radiocarbon date of A.D. 30 ± 140 was obtained from an in situ cultural level that overlay a buried pecked figure at a large site known as Legend Rock (D.N. Walker and J.E. Francis 1989). Quantitative studies of rock art (Loendorf 1989) promise further insight into the problems of age and affiliation of petroglyphs and pictographs (see also Francis 1991, 1996).

• CAIRN LINES Widespread features that may be of both Late Archaic and Late Prehistoric age are lines of stone piles or cairns (see Frison 1981; Loendorf and Brownell 1980). The cairns, composed of stones of cobble size and larger (fig. 12), may be several meters in diameter or contain only a few stones. They may be contiguous for short distances and then be separated for several meters. They may be traced for a few meters or several kilometers and may be apparently discontinuous with single cairns marking a gap or a prominent location.

The function of these is as uncertain as their age. Sometimes they appear to mark trails, but in other cases they defy any rational explanation. The absence of datable material and the questionable context of diagnostic items leaves them even more frustrating to the investigator.

U. of Wyo., Dept. of Anthr., Slide Coll., Laramie.

Fig. 12. Three cairns (foreground) that are part of the Schiffer Ranch Trail, continuous meandering line of over 100 cairns in central Wyo., believed to be of Late Archaic age. Photograph by George Frison, 1975.

Central Plains Archaic

Archaic occupations are well-represented in northern Colorado from the western slope to the eastern Plains. The drainages of the Colorado River occupy most of the mountains of northwestern Colorado and form a series of river valleys, mountain slopes, and high alpine areas. In addition, the North Park area just south of the Wyoming border is an intermontane basin at 2,440 meters and above in elevation and forms the headwaters of the North Platte River, which flows northward into Wyoming and provided easy access for prehistoric groups into the northern Colorado mountains from the Plains.

The Colorado River headwaters constitutes an area of several thousand square miles that lies at considerable distance from the Central Plains, which begin at the base of the Colorado Front Range, and from the Northwestern Plains in Wyoming. The multiple component Yarmony site revealed evidence of Early Archaic occupations adapted to the ecological situations encountered there on a year-round basis, apparently requiring no migrations to the open plains. Much of this interpretation is strongly dependent on the discovery of Early Archaic, semisubterranean pit houses (M.D. Metcalf and K.D. Black 1988, 1997). This site and data from other western slope sites present a strong case for year-round, mountain Archaic occupations with pit houses as permanent winter residences. During the remainder of the year, base camps in strategic locations maximized the use of a wide variety of seasonally available floral and faunal resources from low to high elevations.

Evidence for wattle and daub structures of Early and Middle Archaic age has been found in the same general vicinity in the Middle Park area near Granby, Colorado (5GA151) at an elevation between 2,200 and 2,230 meters (C.W. Wheeler and G. Martin 1982). These structures may predate any other wattle and daub structures in the United States. At Vail Pass at timberline in the Colorado Rockies, Gooding (1981) recovered evidence of occupations throughout the Archaic periods with radiocarbon dates ranging from about 5050 to 250 B.C.

Cultural affiliations of the Early Archaic, Colorado River pit houses are thought to be in the direction of the northern Colorado Plateau and Great Basin. Certainly, the weaponry assemblage lacks the familiar side-notched styles found to the north and east on the Plains. However, the nearby North Park area has produced evidence of Middle Plains Archaic McKean diagnostics (Lischka et al. 1983). M.D. Metcalf and K.D. Black (1988, 1997) suggest an Archaic lifeway in place in the Colorado mountains by 9,000 years ago, which is believable since the same situation is well documented 1,000 years earlier in the Bighorn Mountains in northern Wyoming.

In the Colorado Front Range there are Archaic occupations from the foothills to above timberline. Best known for the Early Archaic is the Mount Albion complex (J.B. Benedict and B.L. Olson 1978). The diagnostic artifact is the Mount Albion corner-notched projectile point. One site is claimed to be a game drive and butchering site with radiocarbon dates from 3550 to 3830 B.C. Mount Albion diagnostics are recognized in several other surface and foothill rockshelters. The easternmost known occurrence of the Mount Albion point type is from a shelter near Carr, Colorado, well to the east of the Colorado Front Range (Breternitz 1971).

The Fourth of July Valley site at timberline in the Colorado Front Range west of Denver has produced radiocarbon dates from 3850 to 4050 B.C. Projectile points from the site are strongly reminiscent of the late Paleo-Indian lanceolate style—particularly the James Allen type (Mulloy 1959)—with parallel, diagonal pressure flaking and ground blade edges near the base. The investigators (J.B. Benedict and B.L. Olson 1973) suggest the site evidence can be used to propose a direct line of relationship for the development of the lanceolate McKean projectile point out of the late Paleo-Indian lanceolate type, which they believe occurred in the mountains of Colorado.

However, in other stratigraphic contexts, the lanceolate late Paleo-Indian projectile point style with ground edges and parallel oblique pressure flaking terminated with the late Paleo-Indian and was replaced with side-notched varieties.

The Albion Boardinghouse complex (not to be confused with the Mount Albion complex), with radiocarbon dates of around 3550 to 4050 B.C. from the Colorado Front Range (J.B. Benedict 1975), requires research. In this case the diagnostic artifact appears very similar to the Mallory projectile point as it is known from the Signal Butte site in western Nebraska and the Scoggin and Pine Spring sites (Sharrock 1966) in southern Wyoming with radiocarbon dates of around 2550 B.C.

Early Archaic age materials were found in the foothills of the Colorado Front Range at Magic Mountain, a deep, stratified site (Irwin-Williams and Irwin 1966). The earliest cultural manifestation there is the Magic Mountain complex, with earliest dates at about 4550 B.C. and lasting about 1000 years. The relationships between Magic Mountain and Mount Albion complexes, which were close chronologically, remain to be determined.

The LoDaisKa site is a rockshelter in the foothills of the Colorado Front Range. The earliest archeological evidence there, Complex D, is dated from about 3050 to 1550 B.C. and was thought to have affiliations with the Great Basin and the Desert culture (Irwin and Irwin 1959, 1961). Above this stratigaphically is Complex C, a McKean or Middle Plains Archaic manifestation dated from about 1600 B.C. to A.D. 500.

Another Archaic manifestation, the Apex complex (Irwin-Williams and Irwin 1966:216), is dated from about 3050 to 550 B.C. at the Magic Mountain site. The investigators see this as having roots in the Southwest. There is also a Magic Mountain Complex B, which is Late Archaic, beginning about 550 B.C. and lasting until about A.D. 750. It is recognizable by corner-notched projectile points reminiscent of the Pelican Lake type.

Farther east, away from the Front Range in Colorado and into Nebraska and Kansas, the Archaic is less well known. Wedel (1986) attaches importance to the Spring Creek site (25FT31) in Nebraska (Grange 1980), now inundated by reservoir water behind Red Willow Dam. The Archaic component was buried under as much as four meters of deposits, attesting to the difficulty of locating Archaic sites this far to the east along major rivers. The site was large, with cultural material scattered over as much as seven hectares. The faunal assemblage indicates heavy reliance on bison, claimed to have been of the modern subspecies with a radiocarbon date of about 3750 B.C. (Bison from the Hawken site in the Wyoming Black Hills [Frison, Wilson, and Wilson 1976], dated 4450 B.C., were determined to be intermediate in size between those of the Late Pleistocene at about 8050 B.C. and the modern *Bison bison*.) Along with other faunal materials was a wide range of typically Archaic tools and large side-notched projectile points diagnostic of the Early Plains Archaic and similar to those from the Logan Creek site in Burt County in eastern Nebraska.

Coffey, a deeply stratified site along the Big Blue River in Kansas (Schmits 1978, 1980), yielded a stratigraphic record of Archaic occupations between about 3550 and 3050 B.C. Other Archaic sites of importance in the Kansas Flint Hills include Williamson (Schmits 1980a) and Snyder (Grosser 1973). Archaic manifestations in eastern Kansas are subsumed under a number of phases including Munker Creek, El Dorado, Black Vermilion, Chelsea, and Walnut (see P.J. Obrien 1984).

The Nebo Hill complex of Late Archaic age is located in the Kansas City area on both sides of the Missouri River but is better known and represented farther east in Missouri (Reid 1983, 1984).

Middle Missouri and Northeast Periphery Archaic

The Logan Creek site contained four cultural zones representing a single Early Archaic complex; exacavations were conducted in only a small portion of a larger site. As at the Spring Creek site, bison dominated the faunal assemblage but no taxonomic studies were attempted. The entire artifact assemblage is strongly Archaic and there is a radiocarbon date of about 4650 B.C. The diagnostic artifact is the widespread side-notched projectile point (Kivett 1962) similar to those farther west.

Although just beyond the conventional eastern border of the plains, the Cherokee Sewer site in northeast Iowa is relevant to the study of the Plains Archaic. The site has a late Paleo-Indian level dated at about 6450 B.C. and two Early Archaic levels at about 5250 and 4400 B.C. Diagnostics in the 5250 B.C. level are similar to those of the Logan Creek complex, and the younger Archaic projectile points are of a more generalized corner-notched style. Paleoecological study concluded that there was relatively little change in the environment or human lifeways at the site from late Paleo-Indian through the two Archaic periods represented. There was the usual change in projectile point styles, and grinding stones appeared in the Archaic. Bison constitute the majority of the faunal collections. The taxonomy of the animals from the three components is not certain due mainly to the inadequate size of the sample and poor bone preservation (Anderson and Semken 1980).

Along the Missouri River in South Dakota at the Medicine Crow site complex, stratified Early Archaic (6050–5050 B.C.), Middle Archaic (5050–3050 B.C.), and Late Archaic (3050–1050 B.C.) components have been defined (Ahler and Toom 1989). Earliest is the Logan Creek complex with several reoccupations. Middle Archaic evidence is present but scanty; they were probably direct descendants of the earlier Logan Creek groups. In the Late Archaic, the evidence is strongly suggestive of Middle Archaic McKean from the Northwestern Plains. Uninvestigated Archaic sites have appeared in many locations exposed by wave action along shorelines of the Missouri River dam reservoirs (Toom 1996).

Along the James River in eastern North Dakota the Archaic is not well known from site data. Gregg and Picha (1988) use the Northwestern Plains Archaic chronology and mention only scattered Early Archaic surface finds with Logan Creek and Oxbow affiliations. Although out of the Plains, mention should be made of the Itasca bison kill site in northwest Minnesota (Shay 1971). It indicates an Early Archaic lifeway not unlike that represented at the Logan Creek, Cherokee Sewer, Medicine Crow, and Simonson sites (Agogino and Frankforter 1960). Fossil bison were confirmed at Itasca and Simonson and may have been present also at the Logan Creek and Medicine Crow sites.

Middle Plains Archaic evidence is rarely found in the James River area but Late Plains Archaic sites have been found and investigated with radiocarbon dates between about 1050 and 50 B.C. and cultural affiliations with the Pelican Lake complex. Besant is considered as Late Archaic on the Northwestern Plains but it and the Sonota complex are interpreted as having developed out of Early Plains Woodland between 500 B.C. and A.D. 600. Aside from the earliest known ceramic vessel production on the northern part of the Plains, the Early Plains Woodland groups were pursuing an Archaic lifeway (Gregg et al. 1996).

Conclusion

The Archaic lifeway was well established and in place in the foothills and mountains at the western edge of the Central and Northwestern Plains by 8000 B.C. In the Wind River and Bighorn basins in Wyoming, it continued well into the Late Prehistoric period. These areas during Archaic times were not able to support the bison populations found in the Powder River basin and areas to the north in Montana.

The entire Archaic Period on the Northwestern Plains and adjoining mountains was characterized by groups of band-level size that continually fragmented and aggregated in response to food resources. They continued to be viable because of the wide range of alternative food resources. However, the unpredictable nature of plant and animal resources over both the short and long term did not allow any permanency in settlements and required some form of short-term food caching to allow for bad winters.

In an area such as this where there is a delicate balance between good and bad years, human subsistence strategies had to shift along with the resource base. During a series of good years, the human groups could turn to communal hunting of large mammals. In less favorable periods, a return to hunting and gathering could not be avoided. The social organization of these groups had to be fluid enough to adapt to these changes (Yellen and Harpending 1972; Larson and Francis 1997).

Hunting and Gathering Tradition: Southern Plains

SUSAN C. VEHIK

Physiography

The physiographic boundaries of the Southern Plains are the Arkansas River on the north, the Rocky Mountains on the west, and the Balcones Escarpment on the south (fig. 1). The eastern boundary is uncertain physiographically (Gustavson et al. 1991; Madole et al. 1991; Thornbury 1965:213); culturally it is set by the transition from grasslands to forest.

The Southern Plains are divided into the western High Plains and the eastern rolling Plains. The High Plains are marked by very flat topography with elevations between 1,500 and 2,000 meters. The eastern edge of the High Plains has a series of escarpments marking the transition to the more eroded topography of the rolling Plains. At the eastern margin of the rolling Plains elevations average around 450 meters (Gustavson et al. 1991; Madole et al. 1991; Thornbury 1965:287–288).

Environment

Stone

The Southern Plains provide a variety of materials from which stone tools are manufactured (Banks 1990). The Ogallala Formation, a prominent source of stone tool materials, extends across the Southern Plains (T. Church 1994). Through its erosion, Ogallala quartzite as well as other cherts and quartzites became widely available across the area. Bedrock deposits of Alibates agatized dolomite in the Texas panhandle and Edwards chert in central Texas are sources of high-quality materials (V.T. Holliday 1997:244–252). Farther east, Permian limestone provided a variety of cherts. The streams that flow through the Southern Plains carry gravel of most of these cherts (Banks 1990; Kraft 1997; Wyckoff 1993). There was widespread use of high-quality lithics early in time and greater reliance on more local lithics later.

Vegetation

While most of the Plains are covered with grasses, forests can be found along streams. Nuts were a major fall food source for humans, deer, and turkey. There is variability in what grasses occur where (Parton, Ojima, and Schimel 1994:fig. 2). Not all grasses are of the same value to the grazing animals that are such a prominent feature of the Plains. After tall grasses mature and die they have little nutrient value for grazers. Short grasses such as buffalo and blue grama retain much of their nutrient value and provide excellent winter pasture (Weaver and Albertson 1956:32–37, 66, 319; Vallentine 1989:244; Stubbendieck, Hatch, and Butterfield 1992:33, 75, 89, 193). As short grasses dominate the High Plains, bison and other grazers were likely more common in short grass environments (Lynott 1979). Changes in rainfall and temperature regimes through time also altered the distributions of the grasses.

Only a few plant foods with nutritional value for humans in grassland settings were common enough to be major food sources (Drass 1997:27). Perhaps most important was prairie turnip (K.C. Reid 1977; Bruseth, McGregor, and Martin 1987:table 18–9). However, at certain times in the past, xerophytic plants such as sotol and yucca were major resources.

Animals

Large and small animal resources were utilized prehistorically. Bison are commonly assumed to be the primary animal resource, but the Southern Plains experienced pronounced fluctuations in the size and distribution of bison herds (S.T. Baugh 1986; Creel, Scott, and Collins 1990; Dillehay 1974; Flynn 1982; Huebner 1991; Lynott 1979). As defined by Dillehay (1974), there were three periods marked by the presence of bison (10,000–6000/5000 B.C., 2500 B.C.–A.D. 500, and A.D. 1200/1300–1550) and two marked by an absence of bison (6000–2500 B.C. and A.D. 500–1200/1300). Presence or absence is more accurately a matter of more or fewer (S.T. Baugh 1986; Flynn 1982; Creel, Scott, and Collins 1990).

Bison herds are a clumped and unpredictable resource compared to deer and other small animals that tend to be dispersed. This distinction has implications for the size and distribution of human social groups.

Paleoclimate

One of the more widely applied paleoclimatic schemes is that outlined by Wendland (1978). The episodes include the Atlantic of 6500 to 3000 B.C., which is a period of maximum warmth and dryness also known as the

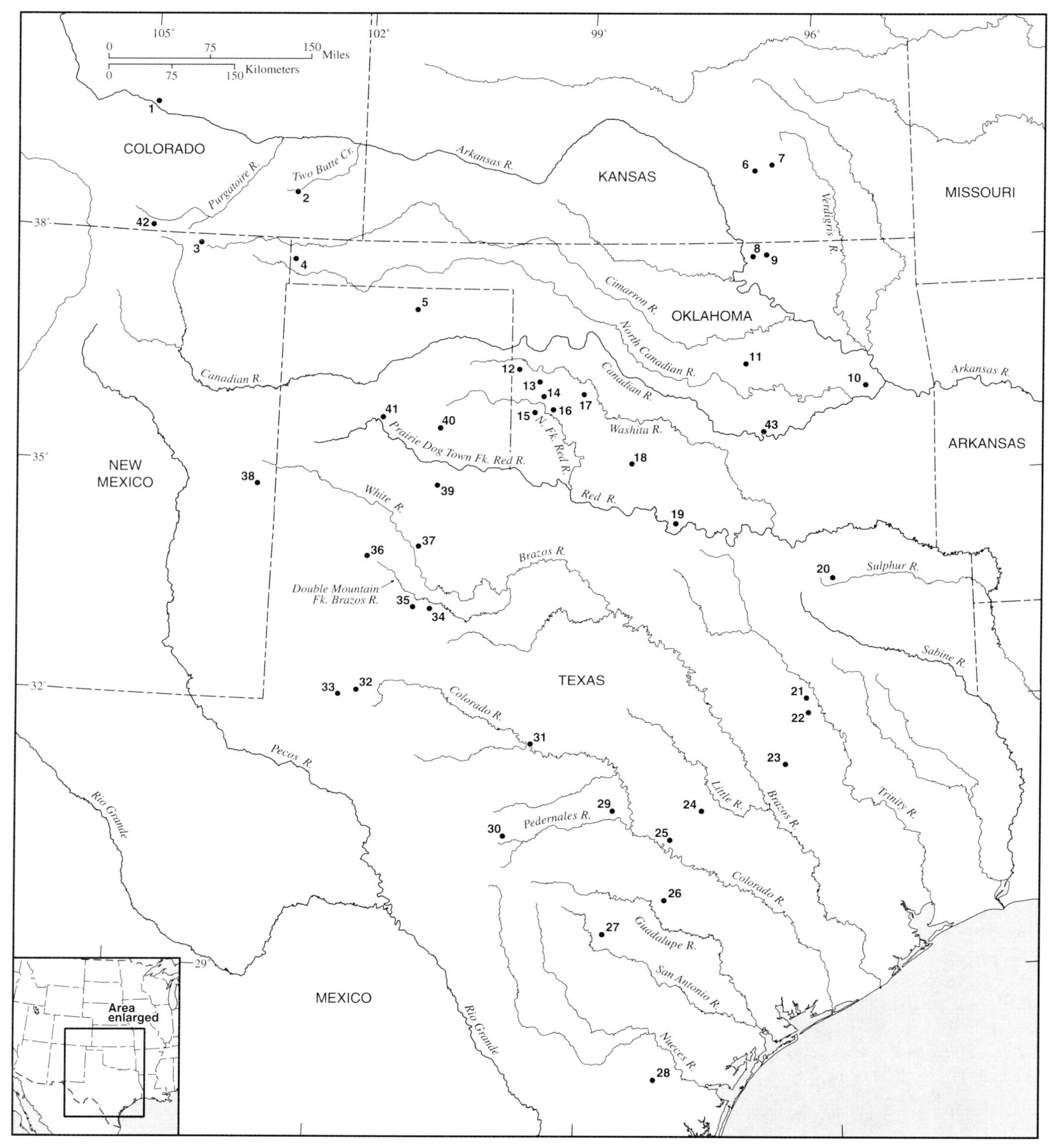

Fig. 1. Archeological sites of the Southern Plains: 1, Recon John Shelter; 2, McEndree Ranch; 3, Trinchera Cave; 4, Kenton Caves; 5, Sanders; 6, Snyder; 7, Two Deer; 8, Hammons; 9, Kubik; 10, Arrowhead Ditch; 11, Bellcow Shelter; 12, Swift Horse; 13, Beaver Dam; 14, Goodwin-Baker; 15, Edwards I; 16, Certain; 17, Duncan; 18, Gore Pit; 19, Frazier; 20, Finley Fan; 21, Irvine; 22, Bird Point I.; 23, Cottonwood Springs; 24, Loeve-Fox; 25, Wilson-Leonard; 26, Zapotec; 27, Jonas Terrace; 28, Clemente and Herminia Hinojosa; 29, Slab; 30, Buckhollow Encampment; 31, Turkey Bend Ranch; 32, Mustang Springs; 33, Salt Cedar; 34, Longhorn; 35, Sam Wahl; 36, Lubbock Lake; 37, Bridwell; 38, Blackwater Draw; 39, Kent Creek; 40, Greenbelt; 41, Chalk Hollow; 42, Running Pit House; 43, Roulston Rogers.

Altithermal and Hypsithermal. After 3000 B.C. there was a trend toward cooler and wetter conditions. The Neo-Atlantic of A.D. 700 to 1100 is considered to be warmer and wetter than today. These conditions gave way to a period of dryer weather known as the Pacific. The period of A.D. 1550 to 1850 is that of the Neo-Boreal with cooler climatic conditions than that of today. This period is also known as the Little Ice Age.

A simpler model presented by S.A. Hall (1988) describes the period of 5000–3000 B.C. as one of aridity, although central Texas and areas to the south may have had greater moisture. There then was a trend toward drier conditions, although the period 1000 to 1 B.C. was likely drier than today. Between A.D. 1 and 1000 the climate was comparatively moist. Since A.D. 1000 the trend has been toward drier conditions.

One or the other of these schemes is commonly used in interpreting Southern Plains archeological data. Agreement on the exact climatic conditions in any one period or place does not exist (D.O. Brown 1998; Frederick 1998; Fredlund, Bousman, and Boyd 1998; E.M. Johnson and Holliday 1995:528–529; L. Johnson and Goode 1994:fig. 2).

Chronology

The traditional temporal divisions for the Plains during the time under consideration here are Archaic, Woodland, and Plains Village or Late Prehistoric. These periods do not work well for the Western Plains. After various attempts to retain these period names it became apparent that a different organization was necessary. What is sometimes called the Early Archaic is here referred to as Early Mobile Foraging. What is often termed the Middle Archaic is referred to here as Late Mobile Foraging.

The main problem with traditional chronologies is in the use of Late Archaic and Woodland to describe people living between 3000 B.C. and A.D. 1000. These two terms are loaded with meanings derived from their use in eastern North America, and the Western Plains is a complex mix of indigenous, eastern, and southwestern peoples and influences. To try and place the Western Plains in its own setting, the period 3000 B.C. to A.D. 1000 is referred to as the Middle Prehistoric. Sedentism became an increasingly important feature of settlement behavior while subsistence was based on wild resources only occasionally supplemented with domesticated plants. The use of the term Middle Prehistoric negates the conflict between the traditional meanings of Archaic and Woodland and the realities of Plains life.

The period between A.D. 1000 and 1450 is referred to here as the Late Prehistoric. Around 1450 there were major transformations in Southern Plains subsistence and social behavior. This continued to some time after 1600 without significant Euro-American impacts. By 1680 Euro-American influences, even if they were mostly indirect, were sufficient to end the prehistoric era. The period 1450 to 1680 is referred to as Transitional Late Prehistoric.

Early Mobile Foraging Period, 8000–5000 B.C.

The main feature of the period 8000 to 5000 B.C. is that it is transitional both biologically and culturally. Extinct forms of fauna are associated with the early part of the period but by around 6500 B.C. fauna were fully modern (Kay 1998:173). For bison this may mean not only a transition to the modern form but also a retreat or decline in the Southern Plains or parts thereof.

Culturally, the period includes projectile point styles of Paleo-Indian affiliation, along with a bison-hunting adaptation, especially on the High Plains (Hofman and Graham 1998:103–116). In other settings, mainly off the High Plains, point styles such as Dalton, Golondrina, and San Patrice occur in association with evidence for a more diverse economy involving the hunting of deer, bison, and small mammals along with the collecting of mussels and plants. The Wilson component at the Wilson-Leonard site has evidence for bulb roasting around 6500 B.C. (M.A. Masson and Collins 1995:9). Between 6500 and 5000 B.C. mussel shell concentrations are associated with large burned rock hearths (Quigg et al. 1996:266–267). At the Turkey Bend Ranch site a possible structure (fig. 2) consisting of a ring of post supports around a large hearth feature is dated between 6500 and 6000 B.C. (Lintz, Treece, and Oglesby 1995:171). These occupations not uncommonly include Paleo-Indian point styles and even points with a mix of attributes (Bamforth 1991; Black 1989:25; Collins 1995:382; Fields 1995:304; Hill, Holliday, and Stanford 1995:385; Hofman and Graham 1998:103–116; E.M. Johnson and Holliday 1995:525–526; Thies 1990; Wyckoff 1992:177–178; Wyckoff and Taylor 1971). There may also be increased dependence on local stone resources and a restructuring of exploitation areas to follow east-west oriented interfluvial divides (Bruseth, McGregor, and Martin 1987:233; Wyckoff 1992:178). Still, the wide distribution of projectile point styles is interpreted as indicating a lack of regionalization. People were probably highly mobile (Prikryl 1990:71).

Late Mobile Foraging Period, 5000–3000 B.C.

Climatically this period is associated with the Altithermal or Hypsithermal episode. The Hypsithermal is assigned varying periods of time. For some it dates 4500–2500 B.C. (E.M. Johnson and Holliday 1995:526); for others it is 6700–3300 B.C. (L. Johnson and Goode 1994:20). For this discussion it is taken that the period of time between 5000 and 3000 B.C. was one of greater warmth and possibly regionally variable rainfall, especially toward the south; elsewhere it seems to have been quite dry.

In general there are comparatively few archeological remains that can be assigned to this period. This is taken by some to indicate that the Plains at this time was not a place favorable for human occupation (Mulloy 1958; Wedel 1961:254). Others argue that pronounced erosion and deposition associated with hot and dry climatic conditions removed or buried archeological sites dating to the period (Reeves 1973). Likely the truth is somewhere in between, and a movement of some people to nearby locations with more hospitable conditions may have taken place, especially along the margins of the Plains. Thus, people from the Western Plains may have moved to higher altitudes in the Rocky Mountains (Benedict 1979; cf. Stone 1999:56–57). There is very limited evidence for human occupation of southeastern Colorado (except at higher elevations), northwest Oklahoma, and southwest Kansas during this period (Gunnerson 1987:31; Hofman 1989:51).

The Gore Pit site in southwestern Oklahoma dates to between 5000 and 4000 B.C. This site, buried under six to seven meters of alluvium, consists of several large circular basins with burned rock, mussel shell concentrations, and some animal bones. These basins are presumed to represent earthen ovens. There is a large variety of projectile points present ranging from Paleo-Indian types to styles dating to A.D. 1. Other artifacts include Clear Fork gouges, scraper planes, flake tools, and grinding tools. Fauna include turtle, prairie dog, gopher, deer, and rabbit but no bison. A burial dating to around 5100 B.C. possibly represents death by violence. Gore Pit likely was a repeatedly visited base camp (Bastian 1964; Cheatum 1976; Hammatt 1976; Hofman 1989:54–55; Keith and Snow 1976).

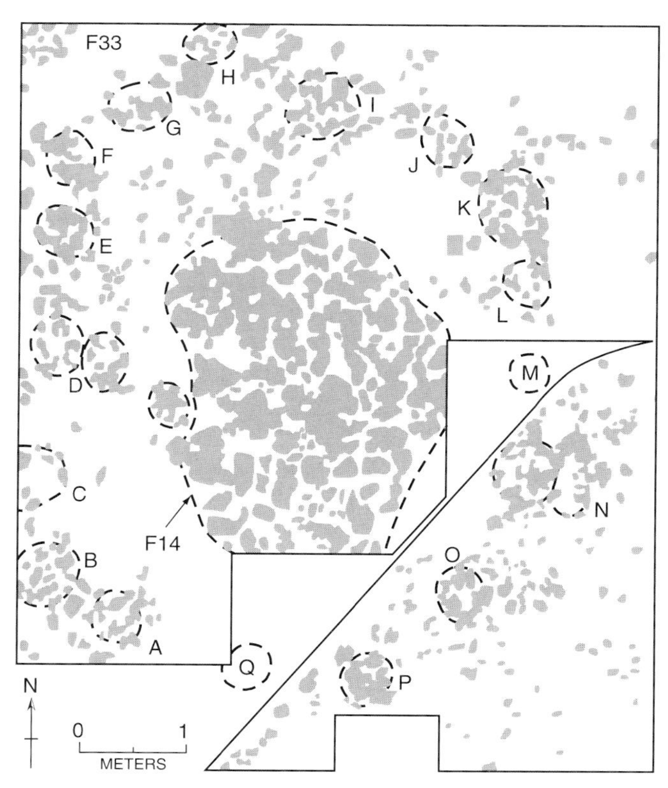

after Lintz, Treece, and Oglesby, 1995:fig. 3.

Fig. 2. Structure plan from the Turkey Bend Ranch site (41CC112), Tex., A - Q = post supports, with M and Q hypothetical. Drawn by Roger Thor Roop.

Bison dental abnormalities are present at kills from the Lubbock Lake area, suggesting the animals were under stress. These kills involved small numbers of animals. Plant use intensified throughout this period. The wells excavated at Blackwater Draw and Mustang Springs suggest shortages of surface water; wells were not excavated at Lubbock Lake (E.M. Johnson and Holliday 1986:44–45, 1995:526; Meltzer 1991; Meltzer and Collins 1987).

North-central Texas has few sites that date between 5000 and 3000 B.C. The Finley Fan site component from this period includes burned rock concentrations and a few expanding and stemmed dart points along with some ground and battered stone (Gadus et al. 1992). Population densities are thought to be low with occupations of any one place being infrequent (Bruseth, McGregor, and Martin 1987:233; Fields 1995:303–305).

In central Texas, there seems to be a concentration of occupation along the eastern and southern margins of the Edwards Plateau. Artifacts include grinding and hammering stones, Guadalupe bifaces, and Clear Fork gouges. Projectile points include forms with deep basal notching variously known as Calf Creek, Bell, or Andice along with unnotched triangular, corner-notched, and parallel stemmed forms. There is little evidence for either bison or pronghorn. The main game is deer supplemented by a variety of small animals. Burned rock features are argued to be earth ovens for bulb cooking (Black 1989:25–28; Collins 1995:383). Population density is low. Society consisted of small, highly mobile bands (Black 1989:25–28).

For the Edwards Plateau area, L. Johnson and Goode (1994:20–25, fig. 2) recognize three projectile point traditions. Earliest are those belonging to the Early Barbed or Early Corner-notched and the Early Split Stem traditions, beginning some time after 6000 B.C. and ending some time before 4000 B.C. These are thought not to have developed from local Paleo-Indian groups and thus to be intrusive from elsewhere. The few burials that can be assigned to these traditions suggest a low carbohydrate diet and low stress (L. Johnson and Goode 1994:22, 24).

The third tradition is Calf Creek, dating to around 3600 B.C., which may be intrusive from the eastern Woodlands. These people migrated into the area following a brief reappearance of buffalo (L. Johnson and Goode 1994:24–25). Most Calf Creek sites occur high on interfluvial divides and are severely deflated. Sites include Arrowhead Ditch (Wyckoff, Morgan, and Woodward 1994:307–328) and Kubik. Most dates overlap in the area around 3000 B.C. (Marjorie Duncan, personal communication 1998).

Extensive studies of lithic resource use and settlement locations provide some information on Calf Creek lifeways (Bartlett 1994; Duncan 1995). Lithic caches suggest the presence of residential base camps to which periodic returns were made. Calf Creek tools, especially the Calf Creek point, had long use-lives, were multifunctional, and extensively maintained and reworked.

The caches are predominantly composed of the nearest high-quality lithic material available. Nonetheless, many caches and most open sites have other high-quality lithics derived from farther away. These nonlocal materials may account for high percentages of assemblages at some open sites. This may indicate that exploitation areas were quite large, extending over a couple of hundred kilometers. Wyckoff (1992:181) proposed that four widely ranging bands exploited the rolling Plains in Oklahoma. On the other hand, the natural distributions of the various lithic resources during this time of extensive erosion and deposition are not known. Many presumed nonlocal resources may have been available at much closer distances compared to present.

The Arrowhead Ditch site contains the burned rock remains of a roasting oven. Plant resources represented include walnut, possibly hickory or black locust, Chenopodium and amaranth, and purslane (Marjorie Duncan, personal communication 1998). There is a possible bison kill at the Frazier site (Duncan 1995:133). Bellcow Shelter includes the remains of deer, bison, and turtle (Girard and Carr 1995:110–135).

For the Late Mobile Foraging period over much of the Southern Plains population densities were probably low. Small groups were tethered to periodically revisited base camps but also traveled widely for a diversity of resources.

Middle Prehistoric Period, 3000 B.C.–A.D. 1000

3000 to 1500 B.C.

About 3000 B.C. the Colorado foothills were inhabited by populations whose material culture had Southwest resemblances. To the east, the Chaquaqua Plateau includes sites with projectile point styles most closely tied to the Southern Plains. Other artifacts include side scrapers, grinding tools, and bone awls (Gunnerson 1987:35–36).

The presence of McKean complex projectile points in collections from eastern Colorado, western Kansas, and northwestern Oklahoma probably reflects occupations dating some time between 2900 and 1200 B.C. McKean complex is primarily a Northern and to some extent Central Plains phenomenon. For the Southern Plains little is known about the culture of those using McKean style projectile points. Recon John Shelter has a McKean component that indicates the use of prairie dog, rabbits, goosefoot, and hackberry (Frison 1998:163; Hofman 1996:87; Zier and Kalasz 1991:119–121, 133).

Along the Arkansas River and to its east in south-central Kansas the Chelsea phase dates between 2900 and 2100 B.C. This phase is best known from the Snyder site. Side- and corner-notched dart points are characteristic. Large and small animals were hunted, including bison. The presence of grinding stones indicates plant-processing activities, although it is uncertain what specific plants were being used. The El Dorado phase, also first defined at the Snyder site, dates 2100–1300 B.C. Stemmed and side-notched points are characteristic. Other artifacts include grinding stones, chipped-stone knives, axes, and choppers as well as bone beads and tools. Shell beads are of both freshwater and marine origin. Structures are possible but poorly defined. The same pertains to storage pits. Burials occur in occupation sites as well as in mounds. Occupation sites include burned rock concentrations of uncertain function, such as at the Kubik site (fig. 3). Fall bison hunting is indicated along with the exploitation of mammals and shellfish. Plant resources include hackberry, pigweed, and lamb's-quarter (L.E. Bradley 1973; Finnegan 1981; Grosser 1970, 1973, 1977; Hofman 1989:48–50, 1996:95–97; Root 1981; Schmits 1987).

This subperiod is poorly represented in western Oklahoma, eastern New Mexico, and the Texas panhandle. In west Texas about 3000 B.C. the Lubbock Lake area is associated with both camps and bison kill and butchering sites. Large basins filled with ash and capped with burned caliche cobbles may represent ovens. After 2500 B.C. intensive plant use declined (E.M. Johnson and Holliday 1986:45, 1995:528). The Little Sunday complex may have begun around 2000 B.C. (Boyd 1997; Gunnerson 1987).

For north-central Texas between 3000 and 1000 B.C. sites with small rock-lined hearths and substantial deposits of discarded mussel shell are characteristic. Roasting pits and concentrations of burned rock are present as well. The major projectile points are straight stemmed styles. Other artifacts include Waco sinkers and Clear Fork gouges. Major subsistence resources include turtle, rabbit, bird, fish, deer, hickory, and rhizomes (Bruseth, McGregor, and Martin 1987:234–236).

The schemes proposed for ordering archeological remains in central Texas (Black 1989; L. Johnson and Goode 1994; Prewitt 1981,1985; Weir 1976) all have substantial limitations (Collins 1995:371). The scheme presented by L. Johnson and Goode (1994) is used here. In central Texas the Taylor and Nolan-Travis cultural intervals or complexes likely date between 3000 and 2300 B.C. The Nolan and Travis projectile point styles are straight to expanding stem types that may have developed from similar styles in the lower Pecos valley. At least some burned rock features are involved with the processing of xerophytes such as sotol. Bison were apparently not part of the available fauna resources. The Bulverde interval begins around 2300 B.C. and is followed by the Pedernales interval, which may have ended around 1500 B.C. The Bulverde point style appears to have connections to northern or northeastern Texas while Pedernales may develop locally from Bulverde. Both the Bulverde and Pedernales intervals occur during a period of what is believed to be a rather dry climate. Burned rock middens are major site features. Grinding stones are commonly associated with

Fig. 3. Burned rock feature at the Kubik site (34KA354), Okla. Photograph by Richard Drass, 1998.

these features. During fall, nuts and deer were major resources available in the stream valleys. Skeletal remains from sinkhole burials give some indication that the diet may have been less healthy than earlier (Bement 1994; L. Johnson and Goode 1994:39). Important sites for the subperiod are Wilson-Leonard and Jonas Terrace.

1500 B.C. to A.D. 500

In southeastern Colorado, around 500 B.C. the Rocky Mountain foothills were associated with populations having greater similarities to Southwest Basketmaker cultures. People living farther east on the Chaquaqua Plateau used projectile points of small to medium form with corner notches, which resemble Southern Plains styles. Other artifacts include tools made on flakes, grinding stones, and bone and shell beads, including some marine shell. A diversity of small and large animals was exploited, with the former perhaps being of greater importance. The lower levels of Trinchera Cave show a mix of Plains and Basketmaker artifact styles (Gunnerson 1987:36–37). McEndree Ranch has a pit house with a ramp entrance, a slab-lined hearth, and a possible boiling pit (Cassells 1983; Shields 1980). Elements of bison were returned to the site for procurement of marrow and bone grease. Plants included yucca, flax, ephedra, knotweed, composites, and goosefoot or pigweed (Hofman 1989:51–52; L.J. Scott 1982).

For southeastern Colorado, southwestern Kansas, and adjacent parts of Oklahoma and New Mexico some phases are proposed for the period A.D. 1–900/1000, but their validity is questionable (Butler 1986, 1988; Gunnerson 1987:51–61). Floral remains include mostly wild seeds, fruits, nuts, and bulbs, with corn being very rare (Adair 1996:table 25; Eighmy 1994:225, 231). After A.D. 500 bison may have been less important. Many types of large and small mammals were utilized (Eighmy 1994:229–231).

Settlements included open sites (lacking evidence of structures), rockshelters, pit houses, and stone enclosures (houses). The Running Pit House site is a multiroomed construction of conjoined circular pits. Barrier or defensive walls occur at some later sites (Gunnerson 1987:36–37, 60). Most burials are isolated, apparently occurring where an individual died. However, the presence of several secondary bundle burials together also suggests curation of bodies for some periodic ceremony. Grave goods are primarily utilitarian tools and bone beads (Eighmy 1994:226, 231).

Ceramics, if present, are of types belonging to Plains Woodland complexes to the east. They are cord roughened, conoidal in shape, and generally tempered with sand or crushed stone. Sites with pit houses and no ceramics are often tied to the Southwest Basketmaker tradition (Gunnerson 1987:36–37). Projectile point styles appear to change from corner-notched dart and arrow forms to triangular side-notched forms over time. Other items include end scrapers, expanding base drills, stone pendants, bone awls, worked shell, and grinding stones (Adair 1996:120; Eighmy 1994:226–227, 232–233; Gunnerson 1987:36–37, 60; A.M. Johnson and A.E. Johnson 1998:209).

Sites in the Texas panhandle, northwest Texas, and western Oklahoma have been assigned to the Little Sunday complex dating from around 2000 B.C. to A.D. 500 (Boyd 1997:233–267). Bison kills such as the Certain site (fig. 4) (Bement and Buehler 1994; Buehler 1997; Kraft 1995) and bison processing facilities such as the Sanders site (Quigg 1997) are prominent site types, as are campsites including the Chalk Hollow site (fig. 5) (Wedel 1975), Swift Horse (Briscoe and Burkhalter 1986), and Beaver Dam (Thurmond 1988, 1988a, 1989). Burned rock middens are present, possibly involved in yucca processing. There are no known houses. Deer, small animals, and mussels were also utilized (Boyd 1997:250, 264; Briscoe and Burkhalter 1986; Quigg 1997:94). Grinding implements hint at plant processing but no particular resources were identified. There is no evidence of horticulture (Boyd 1997:264; Gunnerson 1987:37–38).

Primary, secondary, bundle, and cremation burials were usually covered by a rock cairn (Boyd 1995:35, 1997:253). Burial goods included both utilitarian and decorative, symbolic, or ritualistic items (Boyd 1997:253–256; Gunnerson 1987:38–39; B.R. Harrison and Griffin 1973). There is evidence for fairly frequent violent death (Boyd 1997:266; Button and Agogino 1986; F. Gettys 1991).

Projectile point styles are predominantly large dart points with broad blades having side to corner notches (Boyd 1997:233). Other artifacts include oval knives, unifacial scrapers, Clear Fork gouges, abraders, and manos and metates (Boyd 1997:243). Expedient bone tools, hafted bone skinning tools, bone awls, and deer antler billets or flaking tools also occur (Gunnerson 1987:37–38; Quigg 1997:143–160). Cordmarked and Jornada Mogollon ceramics and corner-notched arrow points occur infrequently (Boyd 1997:251–252; Quigg 1997:173–177).

Some of the deposits in the Kenton Caves likely date to this subperiod and may belong to the Little Sunday complex. Dry conditions have preserved highly perishable materials such as skin bags, cakes made of acorn and either cherries or plums, wooden spear throwers, foreshafts, fire drills, snare parts, and basket making tools. Woven fur, yucca leaf sandals, basketry fragments, and cordage are also present (Gunnerson 1987:40; Lintz and Zabawa 1984). Kenton Caves gives some idea of the range of other items in the material culture inventory of people living in the western High Plains.

In south-central Kansas the Walnut phase dates from 1000 to 1 B.C. and is defined from excavations at the Snyder site. Small corner-notched points are most common. Bison, deer, and small mammals were hunted. There are no data relating to floral resource use (Hofman 1989:50, 1996:97–98).

In central Oklahoma the settlement pattern seems to involve villages or residential bases at which extended occupations occur, such as the Hammons site (W.C. Young 1978). There are also many smaller sites, such as Roulston-Rogers, occupied for hunting and nut gathering during the fall (Drass 1979). Features at these and other similar sites include rock-lined hearths, large rock ovens, large pits of uncertain function, and a possible house (Drass 1997:8). Floral resources utilized were mostly acorns, walnuts, and hickory. There is no evidence for horticulture. Faunal remains indicate an emphasis on deer and small mammals with occasional occurrences of bison and pronghorn (Drass 1997:11). Projectile points include large, broad-bladed, corner-notched darts as well as other forms, especially those with contracting stems. There are circular and stemmed scrapers and Clear Fork gouges, as well as straight and expanding base drills. Grinding implements

Fig. 4. Bison kill bone bed at the Certain site (34BK46), Okla. Photograph by Leland Bement, 1993.

Smithsonian, NAA: Wedel Coll.: Aerial photos, contact sheet #13.

Fig. 5. Campsite at the Chalk Hollow site (41RD75), Tex. top, View of excavation. bottom, Detail showing stratigraphy. Photographs by Waldo Wedel, 1972.

include manos, metates, and nutting stones. Ceramics are infrequent but have both smoothed as well as cordmarked surfaces, with crushed stone, sand, clay, or bone temper. Bone tools are relatively uncommon (Drass 1997:10–11; Vehik 1984:186–192). Burials, which appear to have taken place at the location of death, seldom involved grave goods (Drass 1997:10–11).

In north-central Texas, this subperiod is associated with the exploitation of hickory, acorn, pecan, prairie turnips, and marsh elder. Corn may have been added later (Prikryl 1993:200). The major animal resources are deer and turtle (Bruseth, McGregor, and Martin 1987:239–240, table 18–6). Wylie pits are prominent features at some sites, such as Bird Point Island. These large pits are interpreted to be roasting ovens for processing seasonally abundant but spatially limited resources, such as prairie turnips and nuts. Because potential competition over these resources is seen as high, the pits are believed to reflect interband gatherings where feasting as well as mortuary activities took place. Ceramics are shell tempered (Bruseth, McGregor, and Martin 1987:236–237). Projectile point styles show affiliations with those to the north and east (Prikryl 1990:74).

In central Texas, the Montell interval or complex follows the Pedernales interval. Montell is likely a development from Pedernales. The Montell dart point combines Plains-derived corner notching with locally developed basal bifurcation. Burned rock middens reflect the continuation of xerophyte processing. Buffalo reappeared as a resource (L. Johnson and Goode 1994:29, 35).

Around 600 B.C. on the Edwards Plateau wetter conditions resulted in the retreat of xerophytic vegetation to the west and southwest. As a result, burned rock midden growth slowed and retreated in those directions. Still, a high intake of sotol, yucca, agave, or perhaps acorns is posited. Corner-notched styles, some with bifurcated bases, dominated projectile points. Similarities are seen to projectile point styles to the north and east. Houses, just east of the Balcones Escarpment, include small brush structures at the Slab site and larger, more formal structures at the Zapotec site (Garber 1987; Patterson 1987). There is an increase in objects that can be associated with ritual or symbolic functions, which may reflect eastern North American influences (Hopewell, Marksville) or contacts with the Texas Gulf Coastal Plain. In regards to the Gulf, strong fluctuations in resource availability may have been offset by resource sharing between the two areas (Black 1989:19, 21, 30; S.A. Hall 1998:6; L. Johnson and Goode 1994:36–39).

In the northern part of the eastern Texas prairie the period between 1650 and 150 B.C. is associated with a variety of straight and contracting stem projectile point styles. Other tools include various gouges and unifaces along with grinding stones. Sites like Finley Fan have hearths with burned rock (Gadus et al. 1992). Overall, sites are characterized by short-lived, infrequent occupations (Fields 1995:305).

Along the southern part of the east Texas prairie burned rock concentrations may also represent hearths. Shallow baking pits are present. A cemetery associated with the Cottonwood Springs site suggests that people may be tied to particular areas or territories. Artifacts include stemmed dart points, stone perforators and gouges, grinding stones, pitted stones, pigment, galena, and slate gorgets. Major resources were deer, turtle, hickory, and walnut (Fields 1995:307–309).

Contracting and straight stemmed dart points, perforators, and gouges dominated sites dating between A.D. 1 and 800 in this area. Grinding implements were present. Turtle, deer, rabbit, and mussels were the major animal resources. Bison occurred occasionally. Floral remains were dominated by hickory nuts with prairie turnip, acorn, and legume seeds also being present. There is no indication of maize. Ceramics are rare, but sandy paste wares with southeast Texas affiliations occasionally occur. Cemeteries, especially the Cottonwood Springs site, reflect relatively permanent populations (Fields 1995:305–309). Both cemetery burial and the wide variety of resources utilized indicate that people may have exploited defined areas or territories.

A.D. *500–1000*

In eastern New Mexico the Vermejo and Pedregoso phases, which occupied the area between the Canadian and Pecos rivers in northeastern New Mexico, are of Southwest Basketmaker affiliation. Circular houses of dry laid masonry occur at some sites (Baugh 1994:269–270; Gunnerson 1987:61–62). In east-central New Mexico the 18 Mile phase is of Jornada Mogollon affiliation (Hofman and Brooks 1989:66–67). Both phases are dependent to some extent on horticulture, especially later in time (Baugh 1994:269; Boyd 1997:279).

In south-central Kansas the Butler phase, defined at the Snyder site, involves hamlets or homesteads composed of one or two houses. Basin-shaped pits are probably for storage. Subsistence was primarily derived from wild resources. Wild plants included Chenopodium and amaranth, sunflower, smartweed, spurge, grape, pokeweed, black walnut, and hickory. Corn was present but very infrequent. Small corner-notched arrowpoints, scrapers, flake tools, celts, pitted stones, and grinding stones were present. Ceramics were cordmarked and tempered with crushed stone, sand, or clay (Hofman and Brooks 1989:62–64). By the time the Two Deer site was occupied, sometime around A.D. 1000, domesticated resources were a much more prominent part of subsistence (Adair 1996:118).

Little is known about this subperiod in Oklahoma. Likely the same trends defined for south-central Kansas are applicable.

Probably dating to after A.D. 500 is the Lake Creek complex (J.T. Hughes 1962), which includes sites in the Texas panhandle and adjacent western Oklahoma (Boyd 1997:282). Bison occurred only sporadically. Instead, deer, rabbit, turtle, and mussels were relied upon (Boyd 1997:283, 288). While grinding stones are frequent, there is no evidence for horticulture (Boyd 1997:293). Most sites are classed as campsites but a few may be villages. The Greenbelt site includes several pit houses (Boyd 1997:282–283; T.J. Campbell 1983).

Artifacts include small corner-notched arrowpoints and pottery that is cordmarked, thick, conoidal based, and tempered with crushed rock and/or bone. Other items include bone beads, occasional corner-notched dart points, knives, scrapers, and infrequent Southwest brownwares (Boyd 1997:282–290).

The Palo Duro complex partially overlaps the area occupied by the contemporary Lake Creek complex but the main area of occupation is between the Red and Brazos rivers (Boyd 1997:329). The primary animal resources were deer and pronghorn; bison were rare. No domesticated plants appear to have been used. Goosefoot, purslane, cucurbits, mesquite beans, prickly pear cactus, and acorns were collected. Substantial deposits of burned rock suggest extensive plant processing at some sites (Boyd 1997:299–308, 323).

Site types include villages, open sites, and rockshelters (Boyd 1997:295). Pit houses occurred at the Kent Creek village and Sam Wahl sites (Boyd 1995; Cruse 1989, 1992). Other features include storage and baking pits along with bedrock mortars (Boyd 1997:298–301). Burial occurred at the place occupied at the time of death. Conflict with other groups was responsible for some of those deaths (Boyd 1997:329).

Both darts and arrowpoints are present although the latter are more common. Arrow forms are corner notched or basal notched. Other stone tools include drills, end scrapers, bifacial knives, Clear Fork gouges, shaft abraders or awl sharpeners, and a wide variety of grinding implements. Bone was used to make awls and other items. Mussel shell pendants or scrapers occasionally are found. Ceramics, even though relatively rare, include a variety of Southwest and local brownwares (Boyd 1997:299–308, 318).

In central Texas, a burned rock midden has a large central cooking pit built into its top; its use is uncertain. The burned rock midden appears to be associated with bone grease production from deer and pronghorn (Ricklis and Collins 1994:8, 320).

The period 3000 B.C. to A.D. 1000 reveals limited evidence for trade over much of the Southern Plains. There are occasional marine shell items in most of the complexes discussed here, especially those in the east and south. There was some trade of obsidian as well. Long distance trade items were more common A.D. 1–300. It has been suggested that at least the period A.D. 300–1000 was a time of adequate resources with little need to establish external connections (Vehik 1984:190). Instead it seems that a shorter distance trade in stone and ceramics may be of greater importance (Boyd 1997:253–256, 264, 292, 301, 319; Eighmy 1994:226, 231; George 1981; Harrison and Griffin 1973; L. Johnson and Goode 1994:37–38; Vehik 1984:186–192; Vehik and Baugh 1994:253–256). This may reflect intensification of local political organization or tribalization (Braun and Plog 1982), perhaps under conditions of resource stress or conflict.

Throughout the Middle Prehistoric period there is evidence for an increasing reliance on locally available resources, especially lithics (Bruseth, McGregor, and Martin 1987:234–237; Prikryl 1993:195). A reduction in the size of areas exploited and increases in population density are posited as being reflected in the reliance on local resources. Likely this involves an increase in population size, but this is the subject of some debate (Black 1989:28–30; Bruseth, McGregor, and Martin 1987:234–237; L. Johnson and Goode 1994:36). Changing resource distributions, especially of bison, xerophytes, and perhaps nuts and prairie turnips may also have played a role in determining population density and exploitation area sizes.

The appearance of houses may reflect the presence of predictable, high density resources. Storage technology may have developed for much the same reason (Hofman 1996:110), but storing suggests resource availability was irregular. While resource predictability and density are part of the explanation, if they were the only variables, sedentism and storage would be more common earlier. Increasing population or increasing population densities and pressure on available resources also no doubt played a role.

The western High Plains during the Middle Prehistoric was occupied by people with both Plains and Southwest cultural affiliations, sometimes by people with a mix of those characteristics. The conflict in the area seems to have been between the two traditions. The role of xerophyte productivity in both population increase and conflict is an important issue.

For societies in the rolling Plains, conflict does not appear to be of importance. Possibly the lack of evidence for conflict reflects more adequate resources, the ability to make more effective use of horticulture, and the use of resource-sharing strategies (including intensification of political organizations) to mitigate shortages.

Late Prehistoric Period, A.D. 900–1450

Around A.D. 900–1000 horticulture became primary in Eastern Plains subsistence strategies. To the west the role of horticulture was less important and declined toward the end of the period (Adair 1988; Drass 1997). In southeastern Colorado, northwestern New Mexico, southwestern Kansas, the Oklahoma panhandle, northwest Oklahoma, and the northern part of the Texas panhandle are cultures that are assigned to the Upper Canark variant (Lintz 1986). Best known is Antelope Creek phase (Lintz 1986). Other phases include Buried City (D.T. Hughes and A.

Hughes-Jones 1987), Zimms (Flynn 1986), and Apishapa (Gunnerson 1989). These societies are horticultural to varying degrees and are discussed elsewhere in this volume.

Of importance to this discussion is that for Antelope Creek, and probably the other Upper Canark variant members, the role of bison hunting relative to horticulture increased over time, especially after A.D. 1350–1400 (Baugh 1994:278; DeMarcay 1986; Lintz 1991:102). Mobility increased through time as well (Lintz 1991:93). Also, defensive considerations played a role in the location of at least some Upper Canark sites (Baugh 1994:277; Lintz 1986). Violence is evident in the skeletal remains (R.L. Brooks 1994:318–319; Lintz 1991:93).

To the southeast the Redbed Plains variant Custer and Turkey Creek phases occupied west-central Oklahoma. These phases rely less on horticulture than do more eastern members of the variant. The role of bison increased over time (Drass 1997:112, 120–121, 141, 1998:428–429). Defensive considerations, rather than access to bison herds (M.C. Moore 1988:65–83), may explain the placement of settlements at high elevations.

Along the eastern edge of the Plains in Texas were several hunting and gathering societies (Bruseth, McGregor, and Martin 1987; Fields 1995). Best documented are the Richland Creek and Round Prairie phases, which date between A.D. 700 and 1300. The Irvine and Bird Point Island sites are the best representatives of these phases. Subsistence was based on deer and turtle along with a variety of small animals and fish. Bison and jackrabbit become more common over time. The main plant resources were hickory, prairie turnip, acorn, pecan, marsh elder, and vetch or peavine. Domesticated resources were rare in some settings but in others they were important (Fields 1995:319). Large roasting pits are a frequent site feature. Houses appear to be brush structures and may not have been occupied for long periods of time. Arrowpoints of various corner-notched and stemmed styles are present and have stronger relations with styles to the east (Fields 1995:323). Ceramics are of two traditions, a sandy paste plainware (of southeast Texas affiliation) and an occasionally decorated ware tempered with grog, grit, or bone. The decorations are possibly of Caddoan inspiration (Bruseth, McGregor, and Martin 1987:240–245).

To the south population densities were lower, and people may have been less sedentary (Fields 1995:322). Burned rock middens were important site features (Fields 1995:323).

During the period A.D. 1300–1650 the St. Elmo phase reflects readjustments of populations and changes in sedentism. Bison and pronghorn increased in importance. Floral remains emphasize nuts, prairie turnips, small seeds, and berries. Maize and squash are occasionally found. Ceramics and arrowpoints increased in importance. Plains influences are especially evident in the ceramics (Bruseth, McGregor, and Martin 1987:245–247; Fields 1995:311–313, 317, 319).

In the southern part of the Texas panhandle the Palo Duro complex disappeared between A.D. 1000 and 1200. After 1200 small villages composed of surface houses occurred around pluvial lakes and playas. The primary subsistence activity was bison hunting (Boyd 1997:364–368).

The Blow Out Mountain complex of extreme northwest Texas dates 800–1300, and possibly earlier. Bison were not present; instead the main resources were deer and a variety of small animals. Nothing is known about utilization of floral resources. There is no evidence for the use of ceramics. Projectile points were primarily small, contracting stem arrowpoints. Burials, which are found on hills, were covered by rock cairns. Violence was responsible for some of the deaths (Boyd 1997:280–281).

In east-central New Mexico the period 1200–1350 is associated with the McKenzie phase. Surface houses are replaced by contiguous room structures late in the phase. An economic switch to bison hunting along with abandonment of a sedentary lifeway occurred by 1350. Around 1450 the area was apparently abandoned (Boyd 1997:353–354; Couzzourt 1985, 1988:48–49; Jelinek 1967).

The Jornada Mogollon occupations east of the Pecos River are associated with pit house villages, but there is a transition to surface houses around 1200. Little is known about subsistence, but horticulture may have been relatively unimportant (Boyd 1997:278–279; R.H. Leslie 1979:179). Ceramics include locally produced brownwares (Boyd 1997:278). By around 1300 the material culture had a decidedly Plains appearance, including beveled knives and end scrapers. The people of the Ochoa phase and the Salt Cedar site (Collins 1966, 1968) were extensively involved in bison hunting and show no evidence of horticulture. Sites are near playas and include villages. There is evidence for violent death in some of the burials.

The Austin and Toyah phases or intervals occupied southern Texas. The Austin interval (800–1300) had small corner-notched arrowpoints but lacked ceramics. Gathering, along with deer hunting, were the main subsistence activities. The Loeve-Fox site had a cemetery utilized over a long period of time, and there is evidence for an increase in violent death during the Austin interval (Black 1989:32; Collins 1995:385; Prewitt 1982).

The Toyah interval covered a large area of southern Texas. Toyah, which began around 1300, was characterized by a contracting stemmed arrowpoint style called Perdiz. Other artifacts include end scrapers, beveled knives, and bone-tempered ceramics. Grinding stones also occur. It is uncertain if farming took place (Prikryl 1993:202). Primarily the economy is considered to be one of hunting and gathering, especially bison hunting. The Clemente and Herminia Hinojosa site is a good example of a campsite (Black 1986). Toyah pottery may derive from the Jornada Mogollon tradition. The same could also be true of the Perdiz point. It is possible that the ancestor of Toyah is the Palo Duro complex (Black 1989:32; Boyd 1997:361–364; Collins 1995:385–386; L. Johnson 1994:241–287). L.

Johnson (1994) provides a detailed discussion of the Toyah phase based on the Buckhollow Encampment site.

Exchange increased in importance through the Late Prehistoric period. This exchange tied groups with greater reliance on hunting and gathering (especially bison hunters) with those that were horticultural. At the same time, those that were predominantly horticultural increased their trading activity among one another. Evidence for trade among hunter-gatherers, especially those dependent on bison hunting, is limited (Vehik 1988; Vehik and Baugh 1994).

In summary, hunting and gathering continued to be an important adaptive strategy for Southern Plains societies into the Late Prehistoric period. Horticulture was present, but its importance seems quite variable. In western areas, when horticulture was adopted it declined in importance through time. Simultaneously, bison increased on the Southern Plains after about 1200. Either climatic conditions favoring an increase in bison were limiting to horticulture or bison were a more productive resource than horticulture. The increasing emphasis on bison hunting is associated with both mobile and sedentary settlement strategies. For those living in villages the period of residence likely declined in comparison to earlier in the Late Prehistoric period.

The conflict that characterized Middle Prehistoric period societies on the High Plains may have expanded and intensified during the Late Prehistoric period. The exact cause of the conflict is uncertain, although specialization on animal resources, primarily bison, along with potentially inadequate plant food resources, are probably factors. Trade increased after 1200 as well and no doubt was a strategy for mitigating conflict and subsistence difficulties. However, this trade also was important in the intensifying political complexity of eastern Plains horticulturists. These developments may be interrelated.

Transitional Late Prehistoric Period, A.D. 1450–1680

By 1450 bison hunting was a prominent adaptive strategy. For those in western parts of the Southern Plains bison hunting was the primary subsistence activity. The presence of burned rock middens, tepee encampments, and small corner-notched arrowpoints in southeastern Colorado may represent Apachean occupations. There are no ceramics. Later, ceramics classified as Ocate Micaceous are thought to reflect Apachean sites (Gunnerson 1987:107–108).

Sometime around 1450–1500 Antelope Creek people abandoned the panhandle areas of Texas and Oklahoma. Tierra Blanca complex is proposed to replace Antelope Creek phase and to be of Apachean affiliation (Habicht-Mauche 1992). The primary area of occupation was the Prairie Dog Town Fork of the Red River. The complex may date from as early as the fourteenth century, but mostly it belongs to the fifteenth through early seventeenth centuries. The economic focus was on bison hunting. Triangular projectile points, beveled knives, and end scrapers dominate lithic assemblages. Ceramics were either locally produced or imported from Puebloans. Although corn was present, farming implements are rare, and it is thought that little farming took place. Features include hearths, circular baking pits, tepee encampments, and wattle and daub surface structures. Apart from corn, floral remains include cattail, grasses, Chenopodium and amaranth, composites, goosefoot, and knotweed. Bison hunting by small groups took place in the spring, followed by communal bison hunting from spring into fall, with winter spent at residential base camps in stream valley bottoms (Baugh 1994:283–285; Boyd 1997:419,421, 426, 464, 469–481, table 120; Habicht-Mauche 1987, 1992).

In western Oklahoma, Wheeler phase (or Edwards and Wheeler complexes) replaced Turkey Creek and other late Redbed Plains and Upper Canark variant phases (Baugh 1982, 1986, 1991; Hofman 1984, 1989:95–98). There is evidence for heavy dependence on bison hunting and limited involvement in horticulture. Bison processing was extensive with both bone marrow and bone grease being important resources (Savage 1995:189–193). While some researchers see Wheeler phase as an indigenous development from Redbed Plains variant phases (Baugh 1982:217; Drass and Baugh 1997; Vehik 1986), others argue for an association with Plains Apacheans (Gunnerson 1987:110–111; Hofman 1984:358–359).

Wheeler phase houses (Goodwin-Baker) are smaller (fig. 6) than late Redbed Plains variant houses. Storage pits are rare. Occupation intensity declined (Swenson 1986:84, 88). Small triangular projectile points and end scrapers dominated lithic assemblages. Corn was present but less common than earlier. Wild seeds and nuts were major resources (Baugh 1991:table 7.1). Fortified settlements (Edwards I and Duncan) may be late fall bison hunting establishments (Baugh 1982:216; Savage 1995:139, 146, 193). Ceramics were dominated by Edwards Plain, a thin sand-tempered ceramic that some see as being analogous to Apachean ceramics (Gunnerson 1987:110). It needs to be kept in mind, however, that ceramics used to boil bones for grease may have different technological requirements than ceramics used to cook corn.

In 1601 the bison-hunting Escanjaque resided in the area associated with the Wheeler phase (Vehik 1986). The Escanjaque are argued to be Apacheans (Newcomb 1961; Wedel 1959:51), Kansa (Hodge 1907–1910, 1:653, 655), or Wichita (J.T. Hughes 1968:319; Newcomb and Campbell 1982:37; Schroeder 1962:18; Vehik 1992). The Escanjaque lived in sedentary villages for part of the year and went on long-distance bison-hunting excursions in late summer and fall (Hammond and Rey 1953; Savage 1995:146, 193).

On the upper Brazos River is the Garza complex, defined by Garza and Lott arrowpoints, which are of a style different from the small triangular points so common to much of the Plains. The complex may date as early as the twelfth and thirteenth centuries, but principally from the fifteenth and sixteenth centuries (Boyd 1997:419, 421,427). Garza complex material culture, in addition to the projectile points, is marked by drills, beveled knives, end scrapers, manos, metates, and thin plainware ceramics that may be locally made or imported from the Southwest (Boyd 1997:419, 447–452, table 104; Habicht-Mauche 1987). Garza complex site features include hearths, storage pits, and circular baking pits. Tepee encampments include the Longhorn site (Boyd 1997:173–183). The Bridwell site has a circular embankment that is of uncertain function (Parker 1982). Possibly the embankment represents fortifications similar to that of the Wheeler phase (Boyd 1997:table 121).

Garza people subsisted primarily on bison but also utilized deer, pronghorn, cattle, horses, and many other animals. The large number of furbearing animals included fox, bobcat, badger, skunk, raccoon, mink, and muskrats. Bone grease production was very important (Boyd 1997:464–465). If Garza complex people engaged in growing domesticated resources there is very little evidence for it. Major plant resources included grape, prickly pear, wild plum, cocklebur, hackberry, needlegrass, panicgrass, and ground cherry. The settlement system is posited to be much like that of Tierra Blanca complex (Boyd 1997:469–481).

Garza complex may be the archeological representative of the Teya encountered by Francisco Vásquez de Coronado's expedition in 1541 (Baugh 1994:285; Habicht-Mauche 1992; Word 1994). Some researchers think the Teya were Apacheans (Gunnerson 1956:363; Wedel 1959:20); others believe they were Plains Caddoans (Baugh 1982:217; Habicht-Mauche 1992:255–256; Schroeder 1974:99; Swanton 1942:34–35; Vehik 1992:328).

Toyah people also frequented the area utilized by the Garza culture people, and there is some evidence that the interaction was not friendly (Boyd 1997:364).

Fig. 6. House pattern at the Goodwin-Baker site (34RM14), Okla. Photograph by Don Wyckoff, 1972.

The central Texas area is not documented in the historical literature until the late seventeenth century, unless Luis de Moscoso made it to the Balcones Escarpment in the 1540s as Newcomb (1993:5) suggests. The Apachean movement southward, along with the retreat of Indians from Mexico northward in the face of Spanish expansion, combined with the introduction of Old World diseases make it difficult to relate archeological groups to ethnohistorically documented societies (Black 1989:33; Collins 1995:386; Newcomb 1993:2, 12). If Moscoso did make it to central Texas then the people living there were not horticultural. Instead they were hunter-gatherers living in small huts (Newcomb 1993:5). The main subsistence activity appears to be bison and deer hunting (Collins 1995:386).

Toward the end of the period covered here the Dismal River complex came to occupy the area north of the Arkansas River in western Kansas and Nebraska with some occupations occurring south of the river. The complex likely represents one of the Apachean groups (Baugh 1994:285–287; Gunnerson 1987:102–105).

Late in the seventeenth century Apachean occupations in northeastern New Mexico involved contiguous adobe houses, pit houses, pole and earth surface houses, and tepee rings. The rest of the material culture shows a mix of Plains and Southwest characteristics. Possibly horticulture was more important than earlier (Gunnerson 1987:108–109).

Evidence for trade increased greatly during this period. For bison hunters much of their trade activity was with horticulturists, including those in the Southwest, along the Arkansas River in Kansas and Oklahoma, and in northeastern Texas. Horticulturists also traded with one another, but there is limited evidence for trade among bison hunters (Baugh 1994:286; Quigg et al. 1993:468; Spielmann 1991:213–239; Swenson 1986:tables 25 and 26; Vehik 1988; Vehik and Baugh 1994:261–263). Coronado (Winship 1990:151, 198) and others (Hammond and Rey 1927:267, 1953:400, 628, 636, 640, 647, 660, 827, 838–839, 852, 864) documented bison hunter trade with horticulturists.

In sum, with the expansion of bison herds, hunting and gathering adaptations dominated the High Plains. Villages continued to play a role in the settlement strategies of some bison-hunting societies. Trade increased substantially, as did conflict. Early ethnohistoric accounts document the conflict between bison hunters and horticulturists as well as that among bison-hunting groups (Winship 1990:148, 198, 201–202, 214; Hammond and Rey 1953:639, 827, 843, 874–875, 884, 890, 947, 952; cf. Spielmann 1991). The expanding trade, as earlier, is also related to intensification of Plains horticulturist sociopolitical organizations. Specialization in bison hunting, conflict, and intensification of Plains horticulturist political organizations are interrelated.

Conclusion

The warm, dry climate prior to 3000 B.C. provided limited resources in many locations on the Southern Plains. Population levels are uncertain. However, people seem less mobile than earlier, suggesting population numbers did not decline much, if at all.

Subsequent climatic conditions involved an increase in resource availability. Short grass expansion in some parts of the Plains was probably responsible for the increased use of bison. The general increase in resource availability appears to be associated with an increase in human population and decreased mobility. Continuing increases in rainfall were ultimately associated with a westward expansion of tall grasses and a decline in the nutritional value of winter forage. The decline in bison around A.D. 500 probably reflects such conditions. There should also be a decline in xerophyte productivity. This combination of events may be particularly important for the High Plains where the ability to adopt horticulture was limited. It is in this context, supplemented by differences in cultural tradition, that conflict developed. Eastern parts of the Plains may have suffered less from decreased wild resource availability, or declines may have been more easily offset by horticulture. With larger, less mobile populations horticulture to supplement wild resources was likely one strategy, especially in eastern areas. Nonetheless, increasing reliance on resources obtained from smaller spaces increased risk. Risk reduction may have been obtained through the formation of larger sociopolitical organizations.

After A.D. 1000 a change to drier and ultimately cooler conditions, especially after 1200, brought a unique set of conditions to the Southern Plains. The eastward expansion of C_4 short grasses (which prefer drier conditions) and the southward expansion of C_3 grasses (which prefer cooler temperatures) retaining high nutritional values over winter were probably responsible for an increase in and expansion of bison on the Southern Plains. The climatic conditions favoring the expansion of bison may not have been favorable for horticulture in western areas. The productivity of bison hunting may also be such that horticulture was not competitive. Whether nutrition was adequate for those emphasizing bison hunting is a matter for debate. The intensive processing of bison for bone marrow and grease may have offset nutritional losses from any decline in plant use. The transition to a bison-hunting lifeway is associated with physical and, later, documentary evidence for conflict. The documentary evidence suggests conflicts between bison hunters and also between bison hunters and horticulturists. Competition for access to bison herds is likely involved. However, equally important may be control of the trade in nonlocal resources that developed around 1000 and particularly after 1400.

In sum, hunting and gathering societies were present on the Plains from the earliest occupation until historic times. Although this adaptive strategy may have contracted in spatial distribution during the period 1000–1400, there was a subsequent resurgence that coincided with an expansion in the numbers and distribution of bison. This resurgence set the stage for the historic period.

Plains Woodland Tradition

ALFRED E. JOHNSON

From approximately 500 B.C. to A.D. 1000 the river valleys and surrounding grasslands of the Plains supported peoples whose remains are characteristic of the widespread Woodland tradition: subsistence economies based on hunting and gathering (occasionally supplemented by limited horticulture), corner-notched points used with either atlatl darts or arrows, and elongated pottery vessels with straight or slightly flaring rims, slight shoulders, and conoidal bottoms (Willey 1966:267–291). Plains Woodland can be classified using the scheme developed for Eastern Woodland, reflecting the eastern origin of many Plains Woodland features. There are three periods: Early (500 B.C. to A.D. 1), Middle (A.D. 1 to 500), and Late (A.D. 500 to 1000). Following Krause (1969) and Lehmer (1971:32), Woodland archeological complexes are described in terms of variants, each reflecting a relatively uniform cultural tradition. This summary emphasizes the Central Plains variants, about which the most information is available.

Origins

On the basis of formal similarities and temporal priorities, it has long been assumed that technologies such as ceramics and agriculture, which have been used to distinguish the Plains Woodland pattern from earlier Plains Archaic developments, had their origin in eastern North America. It has been assumed that this technological evidence is reflective of a range of social, ceremonial (including mortuary behavior), and perhaps political innovations transferred from the East into the Plains by migration, trade, and the diffusion of ideas (A.E. Johnson 1979).

Similarities in important technologies and adaptation between late Plains Archaic complexes and those of the Plains Woodland pattern suggest that an important component of Plains Woodland origins lies in earlier Plains Archaic developments.

Early Plains Woodland, 500 B.C.–A.D. 1

A series of sites situated along the eastern edge of the Plains provides the earliest evidence of the presence of the Woodland pattern. These sites share thick, stone-tempered pottery with cordmarked surface finish overlaid with textured geometrical designs in the rim area, similar to Early Woodland types of the Midwest, such as Black Sand-Incised (Griffin 1952:98, 128) and Spring Hollow-Incised (Logan 1976), which date between 500 B.C. and A.D. 1.

In the Kansas City locality, evidence for Early Woodland occupation is derived from three sites along the Little Blue River in Jackson County, Missouri. Of the three, the Traff site (Wright 1980) (fig. 1, no. 62) presents the best evidence in the form of Black Sand-Incised–like pottery from a cooking hearth-workshop area with radiocarbon dates of 395 B.C. ± 70 (UGa-2535) and 505 B.C. ± 80 (UGa-2404).

Excavations in northwestern Iowa at two stratified sites, Rainbow (Benn 1981) and MAD (Benn 1980), provide one of the most detailed developmental sequences for Plains Woodland. Its initial ceramic industry, Crawford County ware, is dated as early as 395 B.C. at the MAD site. Crawford County Trailed, one of the constituent types, is similar to Black Sand-Incised.

Early Woodland-like ceramics are found even farther north, in southwestern Minnesota (Wilford 1946; Bonney 1970), in the Fox Lake phase, possibly dating as early as 200 B.C. (Anfison 1982:73–75). Frequently found on islands or peninsulas extending into lakes, Fox Lake phase sites may be warm-season occupations, while cold-season locations are suggested for river valleys. Faunal remains indicate the exploitation of a range of smaller mammals, extensive fishing, and bison hunting.

Middle Plains Woodland, A.D. 1–500

Although Middle Woodland complexes with Hopewellian traits have been excluded from the Plains Woodland tradition (Wedel 1959:table 18), two such complexes situated at the eastern edge of the Central Plains—the Kansas City Hopewell and Cooper variants—seem to have exerted significant influences on more traditional Plains Woodland variants to the west.

Kansas City Hopewell Variant

Archeological sites on the eastern edge of the Central Plains centered about the junction of the Kansas and Missouri rivers in present-day Kansas City, identified in the Midwestern Taxonomic System as components of the Kansas City focus of a westerly aspect of the Hopewell

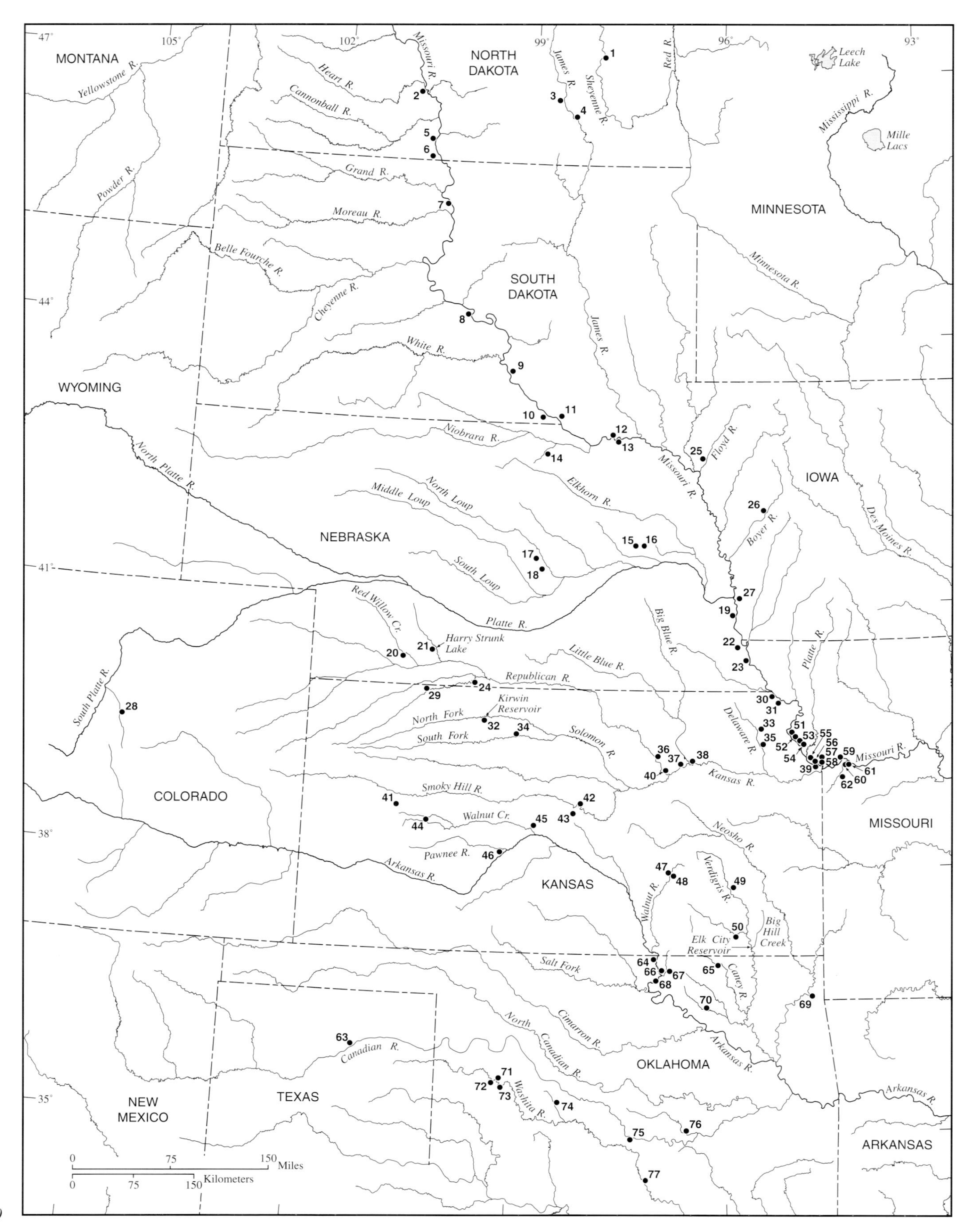

MONTANA
NORTH DAKOTA
SOUTH DAKOTA
MINNESOTA
WYOMING
NEBRASKA
IOWA
COLORADO
KANSAS
MISSOURI
OKLAHOMA
NEW MEXICO
TEXAS
ARKANSAS
Yellowstone R.
Heart R.
Cannonball R.
Missouri R.
James R.
Sheyenne R.
Red R.
Leech Lake
Mississippi R.
Mille Lacs
Powder R.
Grand R.
Moreau R.
Belle Fourche R.
Cheyenne R.
Minnesota R.
White R.
Niobrara R.
Floyd R.
North Platte R.
North Loup
Middle Loup
Elkhorn R.
Boyer R.
Des Moines R.
South Loup
Platte R.
Red Willow Cr.
Harry Strunk Lake
Big Blue R.
Little Blue R.
Republican R.
South Platte R.
Kirwin Reservoir
North Fork
South Fork
Solomon R.
Delaware R.
Kansas R.
Smoky Hill R.
Walnut Cr.
Pawnee R.
Arkansas R.
Neosho R.
Verdigris R.
Walnut R.
Big Hill Creek
Elk City Reservoir
Salt Fork
Caney R.
North Canadian R.
Cimarron R.
Canadian R.
Washita R.
47°
44°
41°
38°
35°
105°
102°
99°
96°
93°
0 75 150 Miles
0 75 150 Kilometers

Fig. 1. Archeological sites of the Plains Woodland tradition. North Dakota: 1, Baldhill (32BA1); 2, Schmidt (32MO20); 3, Naze (32SN246); 4, Beeber (32LM235); 5, Porcupine Creek (32SI6); 6, Alkire (32SI200) and Boundary Mound (32SI1). South Dakota: 7, Swift Bird (39DW233), Grover Hand (39DW240), Stelzer (39DW242), and Arpan (39DW252); 8, La Roche (39ST9); 9, Arp (39BR101) and 39BR102; 10, Scalp Creek (39GR1) and Ellis Creek (39GR2); 11, White Swan Mound (39CH9); 12, Tabor (39BO201). Nebraska: 13, Tramp Deep (25KX204); 14, Eagle Creek (25HT1); 15, Feye (25PT9) and Lawson (25PT12); 16, Bakenhus (25PT2); 17, Schultz (25VY1); 18, Whalen (25SM2); 19, Walker Gilmore (25CC28); 20, Doyle (25RW28); 21, Keith (25FT18) and 25FT70; 22, Leahy (25NH6); 23, Whitten (25NH4); 24, 25HN12. Iowa: 25, Rainbow (13PM91); 26, MAD (13CF101 and 13CF102); 27, Sharp's (13ML42) and Thomas (13ML204). Colorado: 28, Bayou Gulch (5DA265). Kansas: 29, Woodruff Ossuary (14PH4); 30, Kelly (14DP11); 31, Taylor Mound (14DP3); 32, West Island (14PH10); 33, 14AT2; 34, Vohs (14OB401); 35, Teaford (14JF333); 36, Streeter (14CY29); 37, Don Wells (14RY404); 38, Brous (14PO25 and 14PO28); 39, Trowbridge (14 WY1); 40, James Younkin (14GE6); 41, Pottorff (14LA1); 42, 14EW13; 43, Ward (14EW17); 44, Walter (14LA2); 45, Bissell Point Mound (14BT407) and 14BT420; 46, 14PA303, 14PA315, 14PA316, 14PA317, 14PA330, and 14PA333; 47, Snyder (14BU9); 48, Two Deer (14BU55); 49, 14WO203; 50, 14MY305 and 14MY316. Missouri: 51, 23PL44 and 23PL46; 52, 23PL53; 53, 23PL10; 54, 23PL63; 55, Aker (23PL43); 56, Young (23PL4), 23PL61 and 23PL62; 57, Deister (23PL2); 58, Renner (23PL1); 59, Shields (23CL1); 60, 23JA41; 61, Sibley (23JA73); 62, Traff (23JA159). Texas: 63, Lake Creek. Oklahoma: 64, Hammons (34KA20); 65, Weston (34OS99); 66, Von Elm (34KA10); 67, Vickery (34KA41); 68, Hudsonpillar (34KA73); 69, Cooper (34DL49); 70, Big Hawk Shelter (34OS114); 71, Phillips (34CU11); 72, Mouse (32CU25); 73, Goodman I (34CU1); 74, Duncan-Wilson (34CD11); 75, Brewer (34ML3); 76, Roulston-Rogers (34SM20); 77, Pruitt (34MR12).

phase (Wedel 1940:fig. 22), are grouped here to define a Kansas City Hopewell variant.

The best criteria for the designation of Kansas City Hopewell phases are ceramic stylistic changes. Three phases can be characterized: pottery rims decorated with cord-wrapped stick impressions, dentate impressions, or plain-stick impressions and bosses (Trowbridge phase, A.D. 1–250) (fig. 2); pottery rims decorated with cross-hatching and punctates (Kansas City phase, A.D. 250–500); and pottery rims lacking decoration or with crenations (Edwardsville phase, A.D. 500– 750). Stylistic changes in projectile points can probably also be correlated with these ceramic variations (fig. 3) (Heffner 1974; P. Bell 1976:fig. 14).

There are two possible explanations for the Kansas City Hopewell variant. One, it may represent in situ development from the Early Woodland presence in the Kansas City locality. Archeological research in the Illinois River valley has demonstrated a developmental sequence of Early to Middle Woodland phases, with the transition dated to approximately 200 B.C. Two, typological similarities, especially in ceramics, suggest that the earliest Kansas City Hopewell materials should not be equated with the earliest Middle Woodland phases in the Illinois River valley, but rather with the Bedford, Ogden, and Utica phases, which have their beginnings around A.D. 1 (Griffin, Flanders, and Titterington 1970:1–10, table 1). Support for this comes from the earliest dates for Kansas City Hopewell materials, which cluster around A.D. 1. A westward movement of Middle Woodland peoples up the Missouri River to the Kansas City locality at about this time can be suggested.

Within the Kansas City locality, beginning about A.D. 1, Kansas City Hopewell developed an efficient adaptation to the riverine environment about the junction of the Kansas and Missouri rivers, which lasted for at least 750 years.

On the basis of variation in size, location, and duration of occupation, two classes of Kansas City Hopewell occupation sites can be recognized. The first includes large villages, ranging in size from 5 to 10 acres, frequently situated at the bluff line where tributary streams flow into the floodplains of the major rivers. Analyses of data from the large villages suggest occupation during a major portion of each year by sizable groups of people. The second class includes camps with a size range from one-half to two acres, on terraces within the valleys of streams tributary to the Missouri and Kansas rivers. The small size, limited quantity of refuse, and limited variety of artifacts suggest short durations of occupation. These camps may represent seasonally occupied hunting and gathering stations.

U. of Kans., Mus. of Anthr., Lawrence: a, 14WY1 M-1115; b, 14WY1 945-B; c, 14WY1 959-B; d, 14WY1 M-1038; e, 14WY1 M-1245; f, 14WY1 M-149.

Fig. 2. Kansas City Hopewell rim sherds of the Trowbridge phase from the Trowbridge site, Kans.; width of e, 7.5 cm; rest to same scale.

Another class of Kansas City Hopewell site comprises earthen mounds that cover stone-vault tombs, normally on bluff tops in proximity to village sites (Wedel 1943:106–108). Skeletal remains from the mounds indicate a variety of burial types, including primary and secondary inhumation and cremation. Offerings for the dead include both utility items and artifacts manufactured as grave goods.

Kansas City Hopewell subsistence was based on hunting and gathering supplemented by horticulture. Deer were apparently the major source of protein, although both fish and turkeys were taken in quantity (E.M. Johnson 1972:48). Wild nut crops were harvested, as were various types of wild seeds such as amaranth. Horticulture is attested by charred seeds of *Zea mays*, *Cucurbita pepo*, and *Iva annua* from the Trowbridge site (Adair 1984:tables 2, 4).

The easternmost site identified as Kansas City Hopewell is Sibley, near Fort Osage on the eastern edge of Kansas City (fig. 1, no. 61). Initial occupations of Kansas City Hopewell sites to the north, west, and south of Kansas City seem to be somewhat later. Although Kansas City Hopewell pottery has been recovered from the Leahy site near Peru in southern Nebraska (Hill and Kivett 1940:196–199), it is not known whether this indicates a Kansas City Hopewell occupation or represents trade with a contemporaneous but distinct Plains Woodland complex. Hopewell traits, especially pottery, have also been noted along both the Kansas and Arkansas rivers, beyond the most westerly of the Kansas City Hopewell occupation sites.

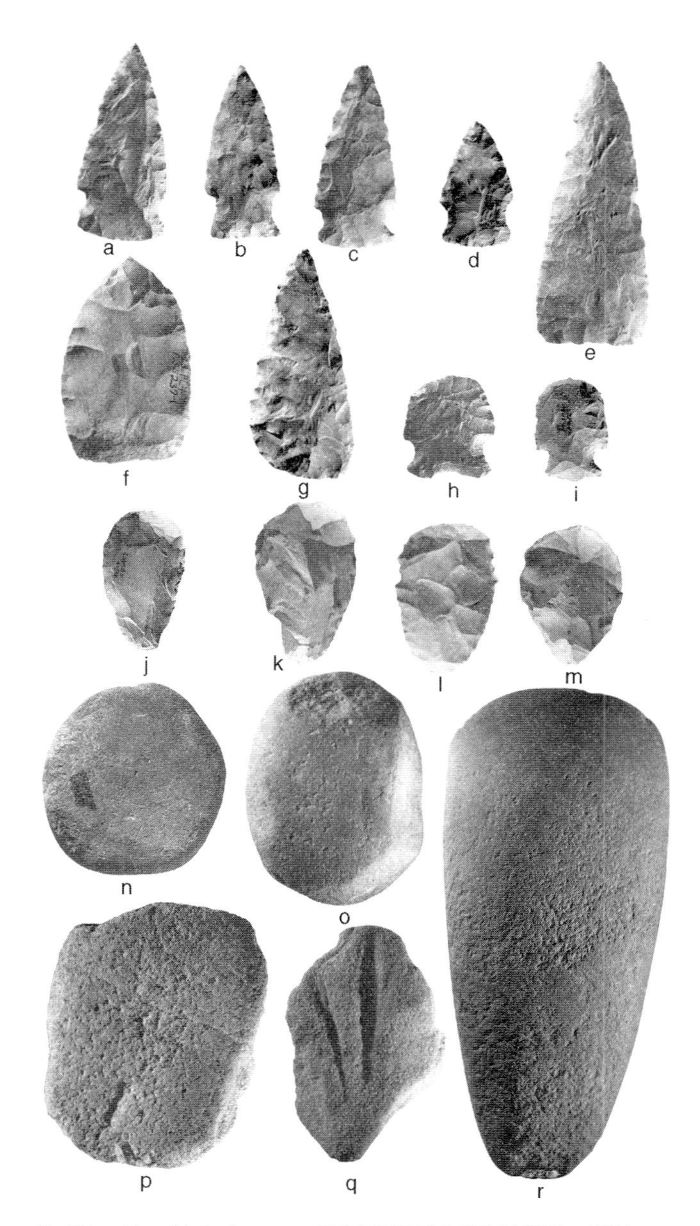

U. of Kans., Mus. of Anthr., Lawrence: a, 23PL4 A54010-1; b, 23PL4 A56134; c, 23PL4 A52206; d, 23PL4 A55919-1; e, 23PL4 A55297; f, 23PL4 A55237-1; g, 23PL4 A56692-1; h, 23PL4 A52206 27-39; i, 23PL4 A81154-1; j, 23PL4 A56452-6; k, 23PL4 55827-1; 1, 23PL4 A57794-1; m, 23PL4 A54011-2; n, 23PL4 A54139-1; o, 23PL4 A54247-3; p, 23PL4 A57364-1; q, 23PL4 A55301-1; r, 23PL4 A56805-1.

Fig. 3. Kansas City Hopewell chipped-stone and ground-stone tools from the Young site, Kans. a–d, Projectile points; e–g, preforms; h–i, hafted scrapers; j–m, end scrapers; n, rubbing stone; o, combination hand milling stone and hammerstone; p, hand milling stone; q, grooved sandstone; r, celt. Length of r, 20 cm; rest to same scale.

Cooper Variant

Data from the Cooper site and similar components along the Grand River, a tributary of the Arkansas in northeastern Oklahoma, were combined to define a Cooper focus of the Woodland pattern (Bell and Baerreis 1951). Investigations along tributaries of the Arkansas in southeastern Kansas (K.L. Brown and M.E. Brown 1986:108–115), southwestern Missouri (R.A. Marshall 1963), northeastern Oklahoma (Bastian 1969), and northwestern Arkansas (Scholtz 1969:55–57) recognized additional Woodland components, which may be combined as the Cooper variant. One local phase known as Cuesta (fig. 4) in southeastern Kansas, has been defined (J.O. Marshall 1972:225–230).

The Cooper site was an extensive village occupied continuously or periodically for a considerable period of time (Baerreis 1950). Bluff shelters and small midden deposits, containing Cooper ceramics, from the vicinity of the Cooper site, indicate the presence of smaller, and perhaps functionally related occupation sites (Baerreis 1950). For the Cuesta phase there are both large occupation sites (14MY305 was estimated to extend over 7 acres) and small ones (Frantz 1964; Weakly 1965:1–4; J.O. Marshall 1972). Cuesta settlements on Big Hill Creek (Brogan 1981) include large nucleated villages along the major drainage and small sites situated on tributaries.

There were no structural remains located within the Cooper site, although small storage pits were present (Bell and Baerreis 1951). A Cuesta phase site in the Elk City Reservoir, Kansas, produced a 13-foot square house with three internal roof supports and wattle-and-daub wall construction. Intramural features included a storage pit and concentrations of burned stones, perhaps a hearth. A midden was nearby (Weakly 1965:1–4; J.O. Marshall

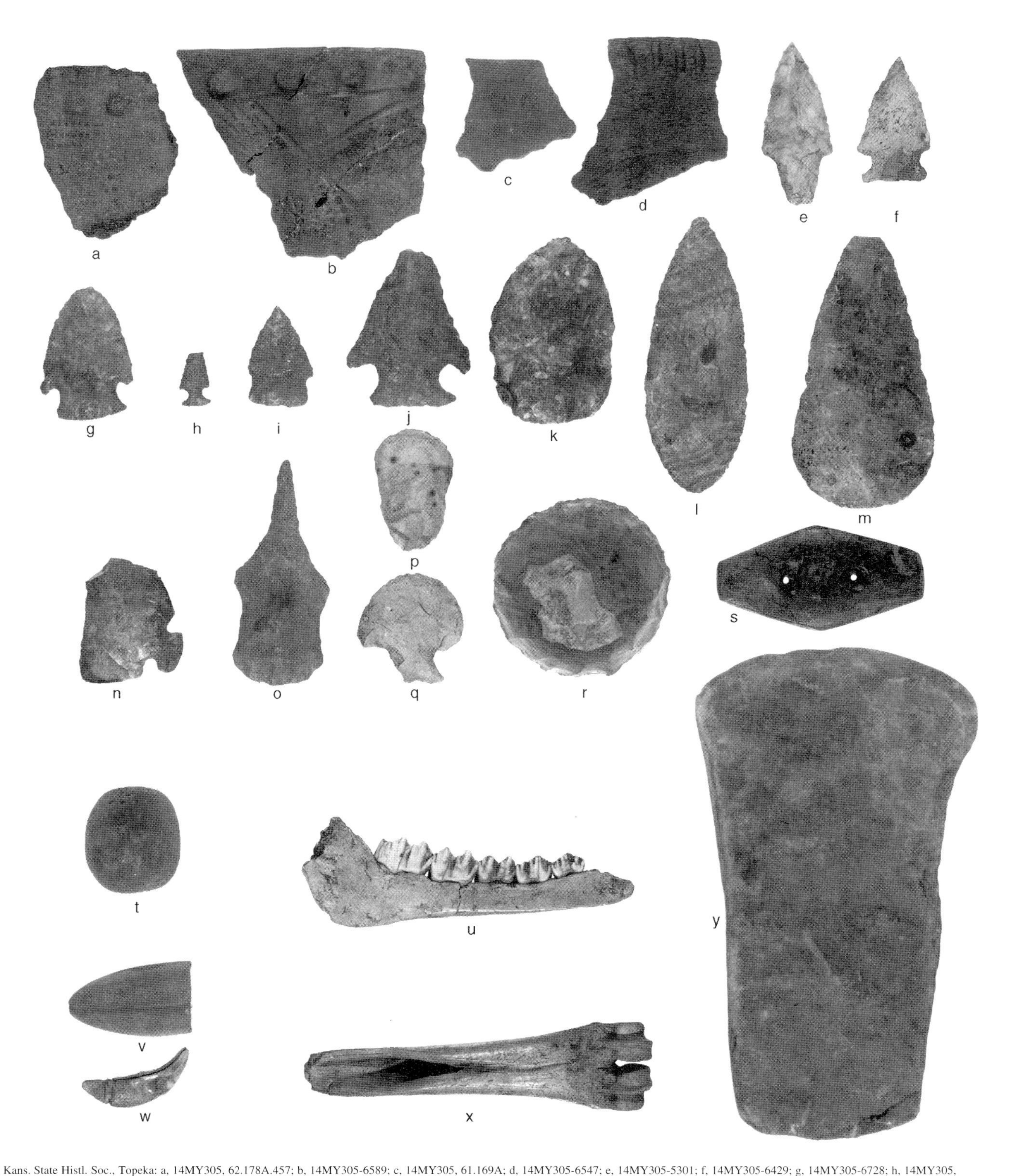

Kans. State Histl. Soc., Topeka: a, 14MY305, 62.178A.457; b, 14MY305-6589; c, 14MY305, 61.169A; d, 14MY305-6547; e, 14MY305-5301; f, 14MY305-6429; g, 14MY305-6728; h, 14MY305, 63.60.608; i, 14MY305-6674; j, 14MY305, 61.168A.262; k, 14MY305-6810; l, 14MY305-6449; m, 14MY305, 61.168A-213; n, 14MY305-7005; o, 14MY305-7006; p, 14MY305, 61.169A.3; q, 14MY305, 61,168; r, 14MY305-5641; s, 14MY305-7009; t, 14MY305-6867; u, 14MY305-7008; v, 14MY305, 64.1376-1248; w, 14MY305-7007; x, 14MY305-6862; y, 14MY305-687 (neg. 14MY305-285).

Fig. 4. Cuesta phase artifacts from the Infinity site, Kans. a, Rim sherd of Havana ware, Naples Stamped, Dentate variety; b, rim sherd of Cuesta ware, Cuesta Decorated, Dentate Stamped variety; c, rim sherd of Cuesta ware, Cuesta Decorated, Cord-Wrapped, Stick Impressed variety; d, rim sherd of Montgomery Cord-Roughened type; e, Gary-type projectile point; f, Enscor-type projectile point; g, Snyder-type projectile point; h, Scallorn-type projectile point; i, Ellis-type projectile point; j, Marcos-type projectile point; k–l, knives; m, combination knife-scraper; n, corner-tanged knife; o, drill; p, end scraper; q, stemmed scraper; r, polyhedral core; s, polished-stone gorget; t, ground conical limestone object; u, modified deer jaw; v, sandstone boatstone fragment; w, incised canine; x, bone flesher; y, siltstone celt. Length of y, 19 cm; rest to same scale.

1972:128–129). Other Cuesta phase sites (J.O. Marshall 1972; Rowlison 1977) contain oval houses measuring 8–12 meters by 11–15 meters, with interior roof supports on the long axis and interior hearths. Extramural features include hearth areas, storage pits, and middens.

Burials were within the Cooper village site (Bell and Baerreis 1951). For the Cuesta phase, infant burials were recorded in a midden (J.O. Marshall 1972:40–41) and in occupation sites (Weakly 1965:61–80).

Cooper variant subsistence was based on hunting and gathering, perhaps supplemented by limited horticulture. Hunting is indicated by the presence, in occupation sites, of the bones of deer and bison as well as smaller animals, turkeys, and turtles. Tools, including numerous projectile points, knives, and scrapers, also indicate hunting. Some reliance was placed on freshwater mussels (J.O. Marshall 1972:42; Frantz 1964). Vegetal foods were also important, as indicated by charred seeds (K.L. Brown and M.E. Brown 1986:tables 12, 24) and grinding stones. The only direct evidence of horticulture is the recovery of a single charred corn kernel (Brogan 1981:70).

Dating of the Cooper variant remains enigmatic. At the Cooper site, a series of traits including pottery rim forms and designs, pottery figurines, and large corner-notched projectile points indicate a Middle Woodland occupation with Hopewellian affiliations. Variability in design elements on ceramics from the Cooper site (Baerreis 1950) suggests a lengthy period of occupation for the site. Similarly, the Cuesta phase has as a characteristic feature plain-surfaced pottery with design elements similar to those associated with the Middle Woodland period in sites to the east (J.O. Marshall 1972; Chapman 1968). On the basis of these similarities, the Cooper variant may be dated about A.D. 1–500, even though radiocarbon dates have not supported this.

Valley Variant

The discussion of the Valley variant (Hill and Kivett 1940; Kivett 1953) is based on 13 components, 7 of which are specialized burial features, and on survey data that indicate the widespread distribution of Valley Cord-Roughened pottery (fig. 5) (Kivett 1949:67–69).

Valley variant sites are most highly concentrated from western Iowa across the Missouri River and along the Platte and its northern tributaries to the eastern edge of the High Plains in western Nebraska, and they occur in both the eastern Prairies and the Prairie-Plains border zones. Valley Cord-Roughened ceramics are found over a much larger range, including Yuma County, Colorado, northwestern North Dakota (Kivett 1949:67–69; Wood 1956), and perhaps central Wyoming (M.E. Miller, Waitkus, and Eckles 1986).

Excavations at the Schultz site on a tributary of the North Loup River in central Nebraska disclosed a village site covering some 30,000 square feet. The depth of the occupation zone suggested an extended occupation or a sequence of reoccupations over a long period. Features included nine probable houses (fig. 6) (Hill and Kivett 1940).

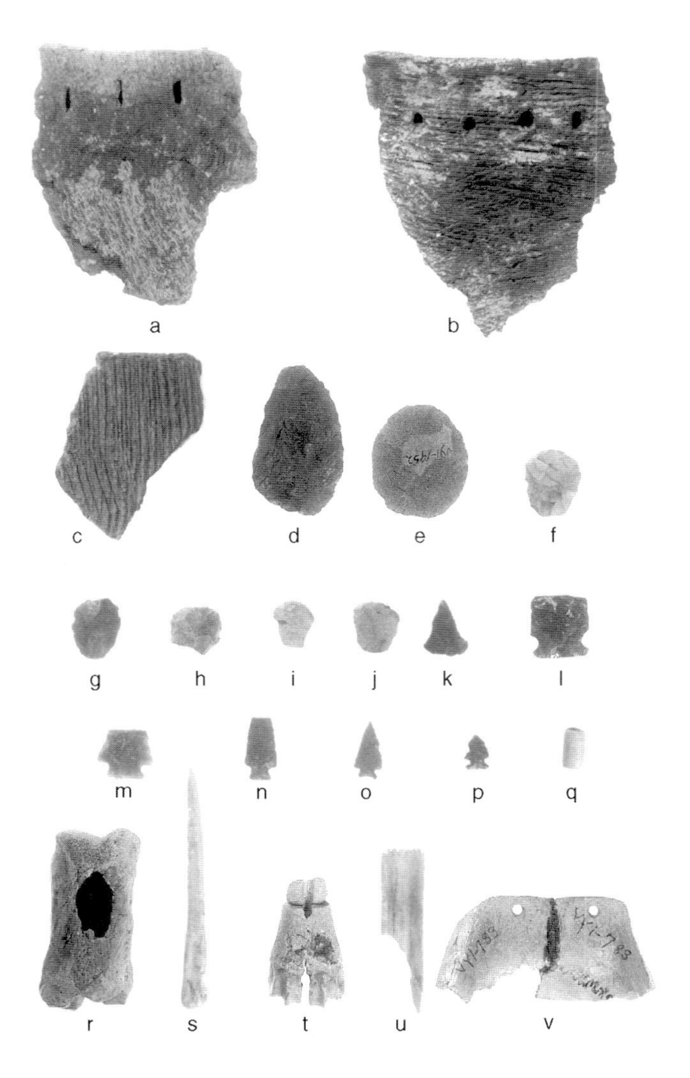

Nebr. State Histl. Soc., Lincoln.

Fig. 5. Valley variant artifacts from the Schultz site, Nebr. a–c, Valley Cord-Roughened type rim sherds; d–e, stone bifaces; f–j, stone scrapers; k, stone drill bit; l–p, stone projectile points; q, tubular bone bead; r, perforated bison phalange; s, bone awl; t, cut deer metapodial; u, fragment of long bone flesher; v, worked section of deer cranium. Length of s, 10 cm; rest to same scale.

Valley variant burial practices are diverse, including a semiflexed adolescent burial at the Schultz site; burial pits, perhaps ossuaries, from near the Bakenhus site and at the Whalen site; and burial mounds (Hill and Kivett 1940:182, 204–215, 219–222; O'Brien 1971).

Data on Valley variant subsistence suggest hunting of bison, deer, small mammals, turtles, and birds (Falk 1981:table 7.8). Freshwater mussel shells and fish bones indicate some reliance on aquatic resources. A lack of grinding tools for the preparation of vegetal foods is notable in the artifact assemblages of the Schultz and

Rainbow sites (Benn 1981:154–179). Wild plant food gathering is suggested at Rainbow by the possible cultural introductions of several wild seed types, while a single kernel of corn (Benn 1981:323) suggests the possibility of agriculture.

The extensive spatial distribution of the Valley variant suggests a long temporal duration. The single radiocarbon date for the Schultz site of 1880 B.C. ± 300 (M-182), from freshwater mussel shell, seems too early when compared with dates for the other Plains Woodland variants.

The association at the Whalen site (Hill and Kivett 1940:219–222) of Valley Cord-Roughened and Harlan Cord-Roughened pottery suggests a partial temporal overlap of the Valley variant and the Late Plains Woodland Keith variant. Radiocarbon dates for the Keith variant indicate a range of A.D. 500 to 1000, and a similar range can be suggested for the Valley variant. Radiocarbon dates from Taylor Mound in northeastern Kansas, A.D. 10 ± 140 (M-2343 and M- 2345) and A.D. 290 ± 140 (M-2344) (O'Brien 1971), extend the temporal range for the Valley variant. Additional support is provided by radiocarbon determinations from the Rainbow site: A.D. 190 ± 125 (GX-6211), A.D. 255 ± 175 (GX-6210), and A.D. 485 ± 135 (GX-6209).

Late Plains Woodland, A.D. 500–1000

For Late Plains Woodland 13 named taxonomic units have been defined. Four are discussed here to suggest the range of variation. The others are: Boyer variant (Benn 1981), Schultz phase (Eyman 1966), Greenwood phase (Calabrese 1967; Jones and Witty 1980; Witty 1982), Butler phase (Grosser 1970; Fulmer 1976; M.E. Brown 1982), Bemis Creek phase (Adair 1982; Adair and Brown 1981), Edwardsville phase (A.E. Johnson 1983), Sperry phase (M.E. Brown 1982; O'Malley 1979; Hassett 1984), Hertha phase (Blakeslee and Rohn 1982–1986), and Wakarusa phase (A.E. Johnson 1969).

Loseke Creek Variant

The Loseke Creek settlement pattern includes villages of extensive temporal duration or frequent reoccupation. In northeastern Nebraska, excavations at the Feye site, an occupation area of 1,791 square yards, disclosed 19 pits for food storage and perhaps pottery vessel supports, five hearths, and post holes suggesting structures (Kivett 1952:43–48). The Lawson site, one-fourth mile west of

Nebr. State Histl. Soc., Archeo. Div., Lincoln: neg. 25VY1-62.

Fig. 6. Houselike structure (Feature 8) at the Schultz site, Nebr. The shallow oval basin is 5.5 m in diameter. Photographed in 1939.

Feye, a village of 3,582 square yards, was nearly completely excavated. Features include shallow basins from four to six feet in diameter, with poorly defined hearth areas, which are probably house floors, and extramural storage pits and hearths (Kivett 1952:43–58). Clusters of structural remains, storage pits, and hearths, at both the Feye and Lawson sites, suggest the sites consisted of from four to eight habitation areas (Kivett 1952:43–58).

Additional evidence for villages in the Loseke Creek variant results from excavations in the area of Lake Francis Case at the Scalp Creek and Ellis Creek sites (Hurt 1952), sites subsequently flooded, and at the Arp site (Hurt 1961; Gant 1967) on the lake shore.

Temporary campsites were probably integral to the settlement pattern of the Loseke Creek variant. Examples are Zone III of the Tramp Deep site, situated on a small intermittent stream (Howard and Gant 1966:16–23); Tabor site in a creek valley at a considerable distance from the Missouri River; and 39BR102, a site exposed in a cut bank of Lake Francis Case, about one-half mile downstream from the Arp site (Hurt 1961).

Patterns of disposal of the dead for the Loseke Creek variant are not well known. At the Eagle Creek site, in northeastern Nebraska, nine earthen mounds covered burial pits containing disarticulated human remains. No diagnostic artifacts were directly associated with the burials, although Loseke Creek pottery styles were found in an occupation area around and under the mounds (R.S. Price 1956:8–88). Additional probable examples of Loseke Creek burial mounds have been noted (Hill and Kivett 1940:240; Hurt 1952; Over and Meleen 1941; Howard 1968).

The Loseke Creek subsistence base included hunting, gathering, and horticulture. Evidence for hunting includes the bones of bison, deer, elk, and antelope, as well as smaller mammals. Hunting and butchering tools are common (fig. 7e–p). Projectile points are small and were probably used to tip arrows. Use of the bow and arrow is also indicated by arrowshaft smoothers. The gathering of wild vegetal foods is indicated by plum pits at the Arp site (Gant 1967) and by handstones and grinding slabs at several sites. Hard evidence for horticulture comes from the Arp (Gant 1967) and Lawson sites (Kivett 1952:43–58), both of which produced corn.

The Loseke Creek variant apparently has an extensive temporal duration. Valley Cord-Roughened pottery is suggested as ancestral to the later Loseke Creek styles, such as Scalp Punctated and Ellis Cord-Wrapped (fig. 8) (Hurt 1952:66–67; L.A. Brown 1968). The two types are similar in exterior cordmarks and decorative bosses or punctations. Scalp Punctated differs in its more rounded vessel form and outflaring rim (Hurt 1952:26) and may have derived from Valley Cord-Roughened between A.D. 400 and 500 (Benn 1980, 1981).

The Loseke Creek variant ends with the appearance of the Initial variant of the Middle Missouri tradition about

Nebr. State Histl. Soc., Lincoln.

Fig. 7. Loseke Creek phase artifacts from the Feye and Lawson sites, Nebr. a–d, Feye Cord-Roughened and Impressed type rim sherds; e, stone biface; f–h, stone scrapers; i–l, stone bifaces and biface fragments; m–n, stone projectile point fragments; o, worked antler tine; p, hammerstone. Length of o, 17.5 cm; rest to same scale.

A.D. 950 (Lehmer 1971:95–96). Similarities between Loseke Creek and the later Initial Middle Missouri and Great Oasis pottery types (R.B. Johnston 1967; Benn 1980:7–8) suggest the possibility of a direct historical relationship.

Sterns Creek Variant

Although detailed information is available only from a single site, Walker Gilmore (D.R. Haas 1982), eight miles south of Plattsmouth, Nebraska, the Sterns Creek variant seems to represent a distinct complex with an extensive range along the Missouri River and its tributaries in eastern Nebraska and western Iowa (Keyes 1949:96–97; L.A. Brown 1967; Tiffany 1977). A northward extension is possible, since the ceramics from White Swan Mound, which was in the spillway of Lake Francis Case in south-central South Dakota, are similar to sherds from the Walker Gilmore site (Neuman 1967:479). Such sherds are also found in Holt County, northwestern Missouri (Wedel 1940:305).

The stratigraphy at Walker Gilmore is complex, involving a series of occupation zones interbedded in the alluvial sequence of two terrace remnants. While earlier investigations recognized three of the occupation zones as Sterns Creek Woodland, D.R. Haas (1982:99–127) identified five. Basic continuities in artifact styles demonstrate reoccupation by the same or closely related social groups.

Best represented in occupation levels 2, 3, and 4, Sterns Creek features include hearths, storage pits, middens, and structural remains (D.R. Haas 1982:182–204). The last suggest elliptical shelters with double or triple walls of

U. of S. Dak., Archaeol. Research Center, Rapid City: neg. A-BR101-15.

Fig. 8. Loseke Creek phase sherds of Ellis Cord-Wrapped Rod-Impressed type from the Arp site, S. Dak. Width of top right, 5.7 cm; rest to same scale.

light, flexible post construction varying in size from 15–20 feet by 1–4 feet. Some burned daubing clay has been recovered as well as preserved reeds and bark segments, which were probably wall and roof covering materials.

The number and variety of features, quantity of artifacts recovered, and evidence of a generalized subsistence procurement system suggest that occupation levels 2–4 represent semipermanent villages. The Thomas site may also be a semipermanent village, while the Sharp's site is a transitory, special use site (D.R. Haas 1982:221–223; Tiffany 1977).

Sterns Creek variant burial features include White Swan Mound (P.L. Cooper 1949; Neuman 1967:479) and the Whitten site in southeastern Nebraska (Hill and Cooper 1938:338–345). White Swan Mound covered a rectanguloid pit, although the only burials found were secondary examples from the fill and at the base of the mound, not in the pit. Accompanying the burials were two small, vertically elongated pots, shell ornaments, perforated canine teeth, and projectile points.

At Whitten, excavations disclosed two concentrations of human remains, including flexed and extended primary burials as well as secondary interments. In addition to ceramic associations that suggest a Sterns Creek affiliation, burial accompaniments included bone armlets and shell beads (Hill and Cooper 1938:338–345).

The subsistence strategy of the Sterns Creek people included hunting, gathering, and at least limited horticulture. Deer, bison, elk, and antelope were hunted, as well as smaller animals and birds. Small, triangular, notched and unnotched projectile points indicate use of the bow and arrow as the principal hunting technique (fig. 9a–e). Freshwater mollusks were obtained from nearby water courses. The gathering of wild vegetal foods is indicated by handstones and by black walnuts, hickory nuts, hazel nuts, ground nuts, and wild beans. Squash and bottle gourd seeds demonstrate the practice of horticulture.

Sterns Creek pottery vessels were elongated with conoidal bases and slightly outflaring rims. While earlier investigators noted cordmarked and brushed-surface finishes (Strong 1935:175–198; Tiffany 1977), D.R. Haas (1982:128–181) identified only plain and simple-stamped finishes. Decoration, limited to the rim area, consists of finger impressions, punctates, or incisions immediately below or across the lip (fig. 9f–h).

Radiocarbon dates of A.D. 525 ± 110 (I-561) from White Swan Mound (Trautman 1963:71) and A.D. 920 ± 150 (M-1129) (Crane and Griffin 1962:193) from Walker Gilmore, as well as ceramic styles and the absence of maize horticulture, suggest an early Late Woodland assignment for the Sterns Creek variant (Tiffany 1978:table 1). Consequently, other dates—A.D. 1116 ± 63 (UGa-2804) to A.D. 1255 ± 63 (UGa-2803) seem surprisingly late, suggesting contemporaneity with the Nebraska variant of the Central Plains tradition (D.R. Haas 1982:175, table 10).

Several sherds from the Walker Gilmore site (D.R. Haas 1982:213–214), which bear horizontal and diagonal cord-impressed decorations on the rim, are reminiscent of the pottery of the Loseke Creek variant and indicate a partial contemporaneity of the two variants. The Loseke variant may also have lasted longer than the Sterns Creek variant, as a Missouri Bluffs Woodland component is in a stratified context above a Sterns Creek component. Based on their close similarity, Keyes's (1949:196–197) Missouri Bluffs Woodland complex may be considered a part of the Loseke Creek variant (Benn 1980).

Grasshopper Falls Phase

The Grasshopper Falls phase (Reynolds 1979) was formulated on data from 124 components along the Delaware River and its tributaries in northeast Kansas, and it has been identified along other nearby drainages in the Kansas Glaciated Region (Reynolds 1981; K.L. Brown and M.E. Brown 1986). Radiocarbon dates of A.D. 600 ± 60 (Beta 10121) and A.D. 760 ± 90 (Gak-1734) support an early Late Plains Woodland placement as suggested by a seriation based on variations in ceramic surface finish (A.E. Johnson 1984:277).

Surface surveys suggest the selection of natural floodplain elevations for site locations, with a tendency for sites to be more frequently placed on secondary drainages (Reynolds 1979:73; Reichart 1974:31). However, Reichart (1974:30) reports the possible remains of Grasshopper Falls phase sites exposed in cut banks along the Delaware River, suggesting that perhaps the major drainages were occupied as intensively as the tributaries but that the sites have either been washed away or buried by alluviation.

Excavations at five sites (Reynolds 1979; T. Barr 1971; B.G. Williams 1986) have uncovered the remains of seven structures, marked by oval post-mold patterns encompassing areas of from 115 to 448 square feet, probably nuclear family dwellings. Superstructures were of light pole construction, covered with wattle-and-daub. The excavated sites each had one or two houses, although clusters of up to 12 houses may be present (Reichart 1974). Basin-shaped pits, presumably for storage purposes, are found both within and without the houses, while hearths are extramural.

Although the recovery of floral and faunal remains from the sites has been minimal (Reynolds 1979:73; Adair and Brown 1981), the artifacts, including hunting and butchering tools and grinding stones, suggest that both hunting and gathering were practiced. The presence of cultigens, including maize, sunflower, and marsh elder, at two sites in Kansas indicates at least some reliance on agriculture (Adair 1999: table 7).

Grasshopper Falls ceramic ware was produced in the form of elongate jars with conoidal bases and slightly outflaring rims. Most were tempered with grit (angular rock fragments) and cordmarked on the exterior, although there is a tendency for the cordmarking to be smoothed over or obliterated. Decoration is rare and consists of brushing or simple textured designs (tool impressions, bosses) in the rim area. Other tools are large corner-notched or contracting-stemmed projectile points, smaller corner- or side-notched arrowpoints, drills, chipped-stone celts, gouges, bifacial knives, and scrapers. Ground-stone axes, celts, and grinding stones are also associated (Reynolds 1979:70–73).

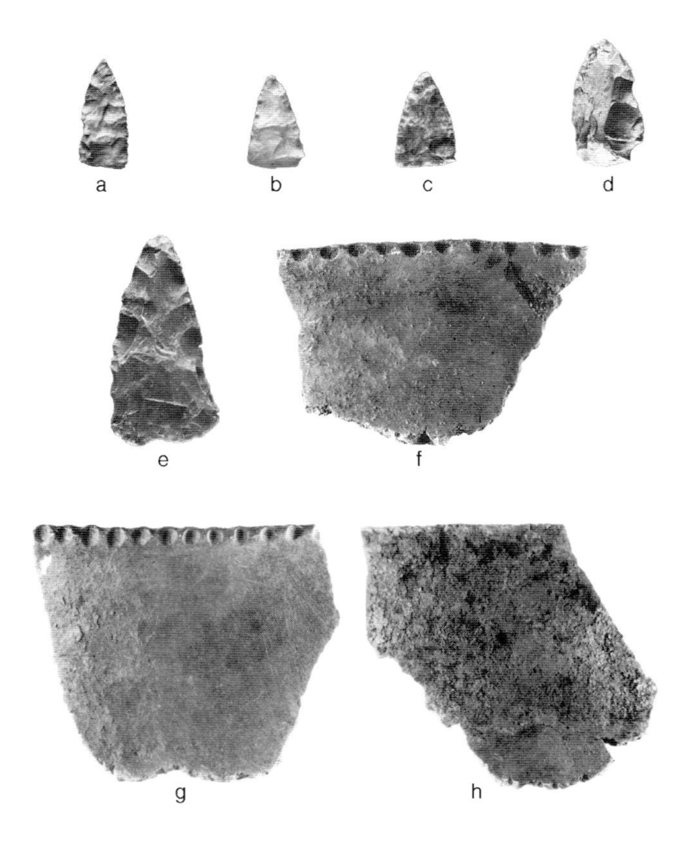

U. of Nebr., Dept. of Anthr., Lincoln: a, 25CC28-939; b, 25CC28-941; c, 25CC28-943; d, 25CC28-945; e, 25CC28-F1724; f, 25CC28-183; g, 25CC28-3 (114); h, 25CC28-1384.

Fig. 9. Sterns Creek phase artifacts from the Walker Gilmore site (25CC28), Nebr. a–e, Sterns Creek points; f–h, Sterns Creek Tool Impressed rim sherds; Length of a, 3.5 cm; rest to same scale.

Burial mounds are present along the Delaware River (Reynolds 1979:74; Bass, McWilliams, and Jones 1967), but it has not been possible to associate them directly with the Grasshopper Falls phase.

Keith Variant

Keith Variant components extend westward from central Kansas and south-central Nebraska to the western portion of these states, and have a north-south distribution from the Platte River to the Arkansas.

Keith variant sites are usually associated with major rivers and smaller tributary streams of the western Plains. The sites are on bluff tops, terrace remnants, or rises in the floodplain itself. Rockshelters were occupied as well as open sites. Most sites are small, often considerably less than one acre, and include extremely limited cultural debris. The presence of animal bone refuse, hunting tools, and grinding implements at most sites, combined with the lack of evidence of any long duration of occupation, suggest hunting and gathering camps as one important settlement type (C.S. Smith 1949:298–299; Witty 1962:55–56; Wedel 1959:381–412; Kivett 1952:24–32).

Villages, of larger size and greater accumulations of refuse, are also present at sites 25FT70 and 25FT18 in the Harry Strunk Reservoir of southwestern Nebraska (Kivett 1949a). Domestic structures in the villages include circular to oval basins, probably house floors, excavated from 12 to 18 inches into sterile soil, with poorly defined fireplaces. Scattered post holes and storage pits suggest extramural work areas.

Variability in Keith settlement patterns suggests that this variant may consist of several spatially or temporally distinct adaptive patterns. Further support for the interpretation that the Keith variant does not represent a homogeneous unit comes from the variability of burial practices, which include primary or secondary inhumations within occupation sites (Kivett 1949a; Bass and Grubbs 1966; Bass, McWilliams, and Jones 1967:475–488), burial mounds (Craine 1956; C.S. Smith 1949:298–299), and ossuaries (Kivett 1953:103–141; Wedel and Kivett 1956:414–415).

Offerings, which frequently occur with Keith variant burials, include pottery vessels, projectile points, knives, scrapers, and grinding stones (Kivett 1953:103–141; Craine 1956), as well as personal ornaments (often in quantity) such as tubular bone beads, shell disk beads, and shell pendants. Although a majority of the shell ornaments are manufactured from freshwater mussel shells, shells from the Gulf of Mexico are also reported (Kivett 1953:103–141).

The subsistence of the Keith variant people was based on hunting and gathering (C.S. Smith 1949:298–299; Witty 1966; Kivett 1949a:278–284; Wedel 1959:381–412). Large mammals were important—deer, bison, and antelope. Smaller mammals were hunted as well. Both indigenous birds and migratory waterfowl are reported as being used. Hunting and butchering tools (projectile points, knives, scrapers), found in quantity at most Keith variant sites, indicate the importance of hunting. Aquatic resources used include freshwater mussels and fish. The exploitation of wild vegetal products is indicated by grinding slabs and handstones. Cultigens have not been recognized from Keith variant sites.

Projectile points from the Keith component of the Walter site, on the south fork of Walnut Creek in Lane County, Kansas (Wedel 1959:416–422), are medium to large corner-notched styles, suggestive of a period prior to the replacement of the atlatl by the bow and arrow (see Neuman 1967a).

A somewhat later period is indicated by several Keith variant sites including the Vohs site (Witty 1969:1–3), 14EW13 (C.S. Smith 1949:298–299), and 25FT70 and 25FT18 (Kivett 1949a:278–284), which have Scallorn-like arrowpoints as the only style (Justice 1987:220–223). Finally, the West Island site, in the Kirwin Reservoir of north-central Kansas, produced Scallorn-like points as well as small triangular points with concave bases, the dominant style in the post-Woodland Plains (Wedel 1961:95).

The single pottery type defined for the Keith variant is Harlan Cord-Roughened (Kivett 1953:131–134). Vessels are elongate jars with conoidal bottoms and straight to slightly out-flaring rims. Decoration is rare, and limited to the rim. Exterior surfaces are vertically cordmarked, while interior rim surfaces occasionally bear horizontal or diagonal cordmarking. Temper is usually ground calcite, although other types of stone tempering occur.

Assignment of the Keith variant to Late Plains Woodland is somewhat debatable, although most of the few radiocarbon dates available are in support. The earliest acceptable date for the Keith variant is A.D. 607 ± 240 (C-928) from the Woodruff Ossuary (W.F. Libby 1955:104). A date of A.D. 828 (M-841) is available from the Harry Strunk Reservoir area (Wedel 1959:619). Three radiocarbon dates on a trash-filled storage pit at site 25HN12 at Harlan County Reservoir, Nebraska—A.D. 700 (UGa-5478), A.D. 730 (DIC-3325), and A.D. 900 (UGa-5482) (Goldstein 1987)—provide further support for a Late Woodland assignment.

Northern, Western, and Southern Plains

Northern Plains, Sonota Variant

On the basis of excavations at the Stelzer habitation site and the Swift Bird, Grover Hand, Arpan, and Boundary burial mound sites, as well as comparative studies, Neuman (1975) outlined a Sonota complex for the Middle Missouri region extending from central South Dakota to central North Dakota. Additional Sonota components include Baldhill (Hewes 1949), Schmidt (Neuman 1975:79), Alkire (D.D. Henning 1965:146–151), the Porcupine Creek component at 32SI6 (Scheans 1957), and a Woodland component at LaRoche (Hoffman 1968). A temporal span of A.D. 1–600, based on 11 radiocarbon and three obsidian hydration dates, places the Sonota variant in the Middle Plains Woodland period. Similarities with the Valley variant have been noted (Hoffman 1968:68).

Cultural debris at the Stelzer site is spread over an area of more than 100 acres, on the first high terrace above the Missouri River, in Dewey County, South Dakota. The largest excavation unit revealed two spatially separated concentrations of features and artifacts identified as work areas where flint-knapping, butchering and hide working, and food preparation occurred. Sonota burial mound sites (three of which—Swift Bird, Arpan, and Grover Hand—are in proximity to Stelzer) include from two to four earthen tumuli, covering from 8 to 50 secondary interments (rarely primary) in subfloor communal pits. Spectacular among the offerings accompanying the burials are complete or partial bison remains, while other artifacts include both utilitarian and ornamental items.

Faunal remains from Sonota components indicate that bison hunting was central to subsistence, an interpretation supported by the artifact assemblage. Although no evidence of horticulture has been found, excavations at the Arp site, a Loseke Creek variant village, indicate that corn had progressed at least this far north by between A.D. 400 and 700 (Gant 1967).

In broader perspective, two characteristics of the Sonota complex—an emphasis on bison hunting and side-notched projectile points—suggest relationships with the contemporaneous Besant complex of the Northwestern Plains ("Hunting and Gathering Tradition: Northern and Central Plains" and "Hunting and Gathering Tradition:-Canadian Plains," this vol.). Burial mounds and some accompanying artifacts seem to indicate ties with Middle Woodland manifestations to the east. Significant in this regard is the discovery in an archeological complex in proximity to deposits of Knife River flint, of artifacts made from marine shells, obsidian, and red pipestone, materials characteristic of the Hopewell Interaction Sphere. Knife River flint is not infrequently found in Middle Woodland sites to the east, suggesting direct trade networks. Much of the marine shell from the Sonota sites is probably from the Pacific coast, while that found within the Hopewell Interaction Sphere is usually from the Gulf, further evidence for trade networks.

Northeastern Plains

Early Woodland expressions in the Northeastern Plains are limited to western Minnesota and northwestern Iowa.

Occupations of the Middle Woodland period, found farther to the west, are exemplified by sites in the James River valley of eastern North Dakota dated as early as 85 B.C. ± 70 (UGa-1398) at the Naze site. Artifact similarities are with the Sonota variant. A possibly later Middle Woodland component from the James Valley is at the Beeber site, which has ceramics similar to the Middle Woodland Laurel complex of the upper Midwest (F.E. Schneider 1982:113–119).

Late Woodland in the Northeastern Plains is recognized by the presence of sites, dating A.D. 600–1700, that have projectile points of a size appropriate for use with the bow and arrow and improved ceramics with thinner vessel walls (Gregg et al. 1986:13–15). Some horticulture was apparently practiced, but this is believed to have been secondary to hunting and gathering. Artifact similarities are with complexes to the east such as Blackduck and Sandy Lake (Gregg et al. 1986:14; L.A. Peterson 1986). Mortuary practices, which are variable within the Northeastern Plains, emphasize mound burial (Syms 1977), with both linear and conical mounds extending as far west as the Missouri valley (Lehmer 1971:61–63).

Western Plains

Within the Western Plains, including the Front Range of the southern Rocky Mountains, the Colorado Piedmont, and portions of the High Plains of western Kansas, Butler (1986:244–250) defined a Colorado Plains Woodland variant that includes a South Platte phase (Reher 1973; J.J. Wood 1967) and suggested the likelihood of a distinctive Arkansas phase along the upper reaches of the Arkansas River.

Woodland peoples in the Western Plains were hunters and gatherers, who moved from the Plains in the winter into the mountains in the spring, and who practiced minimal maize horticulture (Butler 1986:245). Occupation sites were situated near water but away from major drainages. Both rockshelters and open sites were utilized. Occasional bundle burials occur, but the predominant burial form is that of the primary flexed inhumations. Grave goods are limited in quantity and usually consist of tools; ornaments of stone, bone, or shell are somewhat more common with infants and subadults than with adult burials.

This pattern is suggested as continuous from earlier Archaic expressions; pottery, the bow and arrow, and fewer tool types within a functional class, such as scrapers, are the features that allow recognition of a Plains Woodland site (Butler 1986:235–239). Dates for sites assigned to Colorado Plains Woodland range from A.D. 100 to 1150, suggesting that the earliest Woodland influences to reach the Western Plains were during the Plains Middle Woodland period. Continued interaction with eastern Woodland populations is suggested by an analysis of the ceramics from the Bayou Gulch site, dating between A.D. 900 and 1100, which identified similarities with Late Plains Woodland ceramics (Ellwood 1987).

Southern Plains

Few local diagnostics identify the Woodland presence in the Plains south of the Arkansas River (Vehik 1984:175–177, 197). The best example is in northeastern Oklahoma, where the Woodland focus Deleware A, dating from A.D. 1–900, is believed directly descendant from Late Archaic Grove C (Purrington 1971). Deleware A occupations, including both rockshelters and open sites, produce plain and cordmarked grit- and shell-tempered Woodland pottery. Contracting stemmed dart points are frequent. Subsistence was focused on hunting and gathering, evidenced by mammal bones and mussel shells. Deleware B, dating about A.D. 900–1300, is believed to have developed directly from Deleware A. Pottery styles are more varied, including some Caddoan types, and small arrow points predominate. Both floodplain village sites and rockshelter hunting camps are found (Vehik 1984:177–186). The suggestion has been made that Deleware A and B were assimilated by intruding populations of the Cooper variant of Plains Middle Woodland (Purrington 1971:535; Vehik 1984:183).

The greatest concentration of known Woodland sites in the Southern Plains is in north-central Oklahoma, where Vehik (1984:186–192) suggests three Woodland periods approximately dated A.D. 100–300, 300–550, and 550–850. Examples of sites dating to the earliest period are Hammons (Young 1978) and Hudsonpillar (Bastian 1969). Pottery is infrequent but does include sherds with Middle Woodland designs. Site types vary, some with evidence of permanence (burned daubing clay and subsurface features), others short-term camping locations. Hunting was important, and there is evidence of wild plant processing. Cultigens have not been identified with any of the three periods.

Examples of sites from Period 2 include Von Elm (Hartley 1974) and Vickery (Rohrbaugh 1974) in the Kaw Reservoir area. Both are open sites, but rockshelters were occupied as well. Pottery, of more frequent occurrence, is usually plain surfaced and lacks Middle Woodland designs. Both Scallorn arrowpoints and Gary dart points were in use. Subsistence activities included hunting and gathering.

Period 3, represented by Big Hawk Shelter, Level 6 (D.O. Henry 1977), and the Weston site (Howard 1970a), may be transitional to post-Woodland occupations. It is characterized by higher incidences of triangular notched and unnotched arrowpoints and pottery frequently tempered with a variety of nonlithic materials. Open sites and shelters continued in use as bases for hunting and gathering.

A third cluster of Woodland sites, known as the Pruitt complex, is along the Washita and South Canadian rivers in south-central Oklahoma. The Pruitt site was apparently of some permanence as evidences of structural features in the form of post holes were present, as well as a variety of storage and roasting pits. The subsistence economy was based on hunting, gathering, and horticulture, the last evidenced by charred corncobs and stalks.

Projectile point styles include large, contracting-stemmed forms, as well as small corner- and side-notched varieties (fig. 10a–b). Other artifacts include scraping tools, oval knives, drills, choppers, and hammerstones. Handstones and grinding slabs are present, as well as abraders and celts. Bone and shell tools include awls (fig. 10c), flakers, beamers, scrapers, and shell hoes with central perforations. Pottery vessels are globular jars with wide mouths, straight to incurving rims, subconoidal or flat bases, and cordmarked surface finishes (fig. 10d). The Brewer site, on the South Canadian River, about 35 miles north of Pruitt, produced somewhat similar vessels, but with conoidal bottoms, suggesting an earlier period. Two radiocarbon dates from the Pruitt site are A.D. 810 ± 90 (Gak-899). Additional sites of the Pruitt complex are Duncan-Wilson (Lawton 1968) and Roulston-Rogers (Kawecki and Wyckoff 1984:29).

In an area along the Washita River valley, generally to the west of the Pruitt complex, it is possible to see the origin of the Plains Village tradition Custer focus in the Plains Woodland pattern (Buck 1959) ("Plains Village Tradition: Southern," this vol.). The Phillips and Mouse sites have triangular side- and corner-notched arrowpoints and some larger corner-notched points similar to styles characteristic of the Woodland pattern, while the Goodman I site produced a preponderance of small, triangular, unnotched projectile points. Associated ceramics at these sites are the types Stafford Cordmarked and Stafford Plain. Forms are restricted to large conical jars, parallel with the Keith variant type Harlan Cord-Roughened. Phillips and Mouse jars have conoidal bases, straight to flaring rims, and lack appendages, while at Goodman I, the Stafford types have round or flat bases, outflaring rims, and strap handles. The frequency of occurrence of Stafford Cordmarked decreases markedly from the Phillips and Mouse assemblages to that of Goodman I (Buck 1959).

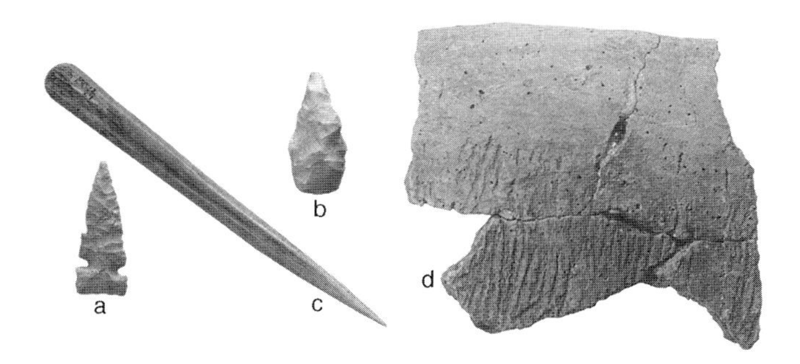

U. of Okla., Sam Noble Okla. Mus. of Nat. Hist., Norman.

Fig. 10. Artifacts from the Pruitt site, Okla. a–b, Projectile points; c, polished bone awl; d, pottery sherd, Pruitt Cordmarked. Length of c, 12 cm; rest to same scale.

In Hutchinson County, in the Texas Panhandle, data derived from a site on Lake Creek, a tributary of the Canadian River, have been used to define a Lake Creek focus (J.T. Hughes 1962). The site contained two components, but only the earlier, which was buried from 18 to 30 inches deep, pertains to the Woodland pattern. An abundance of hunting tools and grinding implements suggests a hunting and gathering camp. Projectile points were corner-notched styles. Pottery was not common. Forty-three of the sherds recovered, which came from cordmarked jars of elongate form with pointed bottoms, can undoubtedly be attributed to the Woodland pattern. The other five sherds bore smoothed surfaces and are similar to brown ware from the middle Pecos River valley of New Mexico, suggesting a date between A.D. 950 and 1300 (J.T. Hughes 1962).

Summary

Into a Late Archaic context a series of new ideas and perhaps peoples moved, apparently from the east. The cumulative effect of this movement over several centuries brought about far-reaching changes on the Plains. The earliest of these influences appeared at the eastern edge of the Plains during the 500 years preceding the time of Christ. The most obvious archeological trace is Early Woodland pottery, recognized in sites from Missouri to Minnesota. The Kansas City locality and southeastern Kansas were subject to intensive social, political, and ceremonial (especially mortuary) influences of the Middle Woodland Hopewell Interaction Sphere during the period A.D. 1–500, while other Plains groups seemingly continued patterns of the Archaic period, with only minimal change (for example, Valley variant). Perhaps reflecting population pressure, important new subsistence-related technological systems, horticulture, and the bow and arrow appeared between about A.D. 500 and 1000, during the Late Plains Woodland period.

The increasing reliance upon horticulture for subsistence, which characterizes both the Archaic and Woodland periods in the eastern United States, seemingly had little effect on Woodland populations in the Plains. While corn, squash, and possibly domesticated marsh elder (*Iva annua*) appear in Middle Woodland Kansas City Hopewell contexts about A.D. 250 (Adair 1984:table 2.4) along the eastern edge of the Plains, their rare occurrence suggests that horticulture was unimportant. To the west, cultigens have not been discovered in Plains Woodland sites until near the end of the Late Plains Woodland period, about A.D. 900, by which time corn, squash, sunflower, and marsh elder co-occur in abundances sufficient to demonstrate significance (Adair 1982:332–333).

Plains Woodland subsistence was primarily based on generalized hunting and gathering (Winterhalder 1981:23).

In the east, 45 species of animals were identified from Plains Middle Woodland Kansas City Hopewell sites (Adair 1977; E.M. Johnson 1975), while a Late Plains Woodland site produced 40 floral taxa (Adair and Brown 1981: table 5.21). In the west the numbers are fewer, although the identification of 23 species of animals at the Late Plains Woodland Doyle site in southwestern Nebraska (Grange 1980) confirms the importance of diversity to the Plains Woodland subsistence strategy.

Across the Central Plains, effective exploitation of a wide diversity of plants and animals, concentrated along the river valleys, made possible varying degrees of residential stability (A.E. Johnson 1979:87; K.L. Brown and A.H. Simmons 1987). Manifested in structural remains of oval or circular houses, specialized facilities including storage pits and hearths, middens and a wide range of artifact types, these more permanent centers of activity were complemented by short-term occupation sites devoted to specialized activities such as hunting and mortuary observances. This pattern of logistical mobility (Binford 1980) is recognizable as a gradient across the Central Plains, with evidences of long-term sedentism in the east (Kansas City Hopewell) diminishing in the west to sedentism of restricted duration. Undoubtedly correlated with this was a decrease in population size from east to west.

Variability in the sizes of Plains Woodland burial mounds supports the interpretation of a population gradient. Excluding Early Plains Woodland, for which burial data are not available, circular mounds of earth and stone covering a chamber designed to contain human remains and burial offerings are probably associated with all Middle and Late Plains Woodland complexes. In the east, Kansas City Hopewell mounds cover rectangular enclosures of dry-laid masonry. On the average, the mounds are 425 square meters. Approximately 100 miles to the west, in the vicinity of Manhattan, Kansas, burial mounds of the Late Plains Woodland Schultz phase (Phenice 1969; O'Brien 1979) average 246 square meters.

While burial mounds represent the prevalent mode of disposal of the dead for Plains Woodland populations, there was occasional disposal in ossuaries within occupation sites or separate from them. Pattern variability is also noticeable in body treatment as primary and secondary inhumations and cremations all occur. Offerings include utilitarian objects and personal ornaments, sometimes present in quantity, as in the case of the thousands of shell disk beads found at the Keith variant Woodruff ossuary (Kivett 1953).

For the Eastern Plains, the presence of large corner-notched projectile points in complexes such as Kansas City Hopewell (A.E. Johnson 1976) until approximately A.D. 500 suggests the atlatl and dart as the principal hunting apparatus. Farther west, small corner-notched points of a size appropriate for use on arrows in sites in the Flint Hills of Kansas (Grosser 1973; Schmits 1978) dating to the Late Archaic (500 B.C–A.D. 1) suggest an earlier adoption of the more efficient bow and arrow (Christenson 1986). Earlier Plains Woodland pottery, with thick vessel walls, copious stone tempering, and conoidal shape, gradually changed so that by Late Plains Woodland times vessel form became more globular, vessel walls thinner, and temper included various nonlithic materials such as bone, grog (sherd), and indurated clay. Surface finish on Plains Woodland vessels is either plain or cordmarked, while decoration is limited to geometrical textured patterns usually concentrated about the rim. The Kansas City and Cooper variants were strongly influenced by Middle Woodland design norms from the east (Illinois and Missouri), and as a consequence they reflect changing styles originating in these eastern centers.

The use of local materials, especially cherts, for the manufacture of a majority of utilitarian artifacts suggests limited intersocietal contact, although the presence of occasional artifacts of obsidian, copper, and marine shell indicates at least limited interregional interaction. Parallels with Woodland complexes of eastern North America, revealed in stylistic changes in pottery and projectile points through time, also suggest ongoing interaction.

In the Plains during the centuries before and after A.D. 1000, far-reaching changes occurred that culminated in the Plains Village pattern. These include shifts to a heavier reliance on horticulture, increased residential stability, and changes in artifact styles. The best argument for continuity between Plains Woodland and Plains Village comes from the Pomona variant of eastern Kansas and western Missouri (K.L. Brown 1985). Similarly, in Iowa and South Dakota, long- suspected continuities between Late Plains Woodland variants such as Loseke Creek and early Plains Village have received strong support from stratigraphic work at the Rainbow and MAD sites (Benn 1980, 1981). In other cases, such as the Central Plains tradition (Wedel 1961), discontinuities seem as apparent as continuities, suggesting the addition of new elements about A.D. 1000. A southern and eastern origin for these elements has been suggested (Wedel 1979a).

Plains Village Tradition: Central

WALDO R. WEDEL

Stretching from the Missouri River to the eastern slopes of the Rocky Mountains, the Central Plains include the states of Nebraska and Kansas, together with adjoining portions of eastern Colorado, southeastern Wyoming, and western Iowa (Wedel 1940, 1961). From roughly A.D. 700 or 800 to the 1400s, and following generally the Woodland occupation, the area was inhabited by semisedentary peoples belonging to several variants of what may be broadly characterized as a small-village semihorticultural way of life for which the term Central Plains tradition has acquired currency (fig. 1) (Wedel 1986:98–133).

The Central Plains tradition is a subarea manifestation of what was previously designated the Plains Village pattern (Lehmer 1954:139), or the Plains Village phase (Hurt 1953:54; Wedel 1959:566). The term *phase* is here used for cultural units elsewhere designated variously as aspects, foci, or variants. Spatial units within the Central Plains tradition include the *locality*, for example, Medicine Creek, Davis Creek, and the *district*, for example, the Loup or Blue River drainage basins or considerable portions thereof. (For discussion of problems of classification and taxonomy see L.A. Brown 1966; Krause 1969; Gradwohl 1969.)

The bearers of the cultural complexes ascribed to the Central Plains tradition seem to have established themselves and their lifeway much more securely than did the earlier Woodland peoples, perhaps among other reasons because they came into possession of improved crop varieties such as the Maiz de Ocho (Galinat and Gunnerson 1963) from the Southwest. The subsistence economy was divided between food-producing and food-collecting and involved the utilization of semipermanent houses and house clusters, or hamlets, that usually contrast sharply with the apparently more transient manifestations attributed to the Woodland hunters and gatherers. The principal and best-known variants are the Nebraska phase along the Missouri River valley in northeastern Kansas, eastern Nebraska, and western Iowa, and the Upper Republican phase in the loess plains of western Kansas and Nebraska. Subsequently defined are the Smoky Hill phase in eastern and north-central Kansas, the Pomona phase in eastern Kansas, and the Steed-Kisker phase on the Missouri River above Kansas City. The probability of a Loup River (Itskari) phase in Nebraska, a Saint Helena phase or subphase in northeastern Nebraska, and of several other units whose suspected distinctiveness awaits support from detailed analyses, must be recognized.

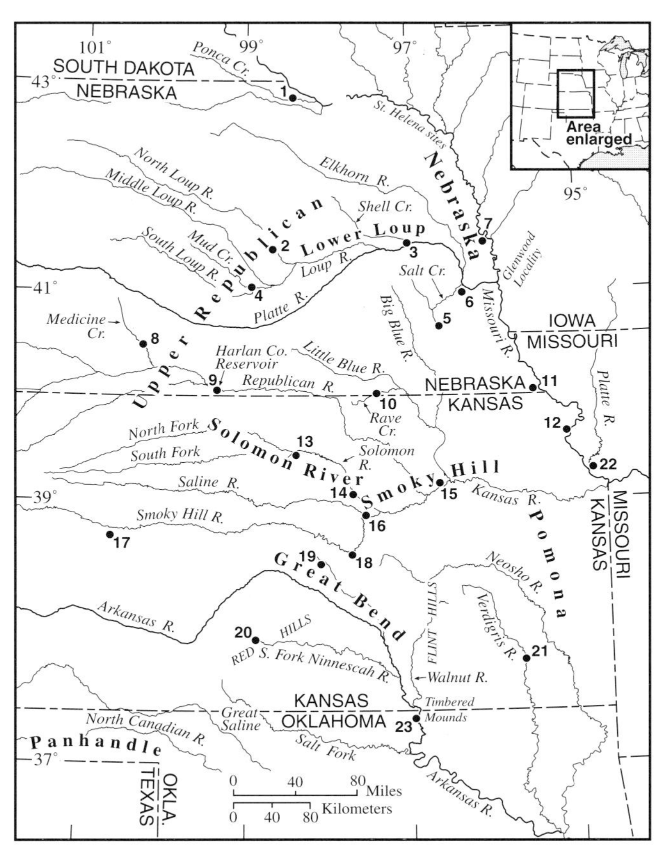

Fig. 1. Archeological sites of the Central Plains. Nebraska: 1, Lynch (25BD1); 2, Coufal (25HW6); 3, Gray (25CX1); 4, Sweetwater (25BF1); 5, Schrader (25LC1); 6, Ashland (25CC1); 7, Renne Farm (25WN5); 8, 25FT13, 25FT28, 25FT35, 25FT70; 9, Graham Ossuary (25HN5), 25HN36, and 25HN44; 10, Lamb (25TY1); 11, Leary (25RH1). Kansas: 12, Doniphan (14DP2); 13, Glen Elder (14ML1); 14, Minneapolis (14OT5); 15, Griffing (14RY21); 16, Whiteford (14SA1); 17, Pottorff (14LA1); 18, Paint Creek (14MP1); 19, Tobias (14RC8); 20, Pratt (14PT1); 21, Neodesha "fort" (14WN1). Missouri: 22, Steed-Kisker (23PL13). Oklahoma: 23, Deer Creek (34KA3).

Material culture traits and trait complexes characteristic of the Central Plains tradition are listed in table 1.

Upper Republican Phase, 1120–1250

Upper Republican materials were first studied and are best known in the Republican River valley of southern

Table 1. Central Plains Tradition Traits

1. A subsistence economy that included maize horticulture, hunting, fishing, and the gathering of wild vegetal products.
2. Semipermanent villages, usually small, unfortified, apparently unplanned as regards internal arrangement.
3. Settlement sometimes on the larger streams, more often on lesser tributaries convenient to arable lands, water, wood, and perhaps to sources of good lithic materials.
4. Houses built on or below the ground surface, the floors sometimes as much as 48 inches deep.
5. Square to rectangular dwellings, with rounded corners, circular floor plans less common; four (rarely 6–12) primary roof supports usually in a quadrilateral pattern around the central unlined fireplace; covered or vestibule entranceway extends from one side of house.
6. Pits for storage, underground, bell-shaped to cylindrical, seldom over 48 inches deep, in and between houses.
7. Burial pattern uncertain; apparently includes single interments and secondary deposition of bones in communal ossuaries after exposure.
8. Pottery grit-tempered, surfaces cord-roughened or smoothed; simple vertical to flared or collared (braced) rims, which are plain or decorated by incising, cord-impressing, or modeling.
9. Projectile points of stone, chipped, small; unnotched, side-notched, or side- and base-notched.
10. Knives bifacially chipped; diamond-shaped with oppositely beveled edges; often ellipsoidal or oblong; much variation in size and form.
11. End and side scrapers, planoconvex, unifacial.
12. Pipes of stone, equal arm or with slightly protruding prow; or of pottery in bent-tubular form; some effigies, and anthropomorphic and zoomorphic decoration.
13. Bison scapula hoes, the head usually modified slightly or not at all; hafting methods uncertain.
14. Awls of split deer metapodial.
15. Arrowshaft wrenches of bone or antler.
16. Fishhooks, bone, curved, unbarbed, one-piece.
17. Fleshing tools, metapodial, smooth-bladed.
18. Milling stones and mullers.
19. Abraders, sandstone, in various sizes and shapes.
20. Celts, chipped and/or ground.
21. Shell work in limited amount and variety; some marine shells.

Nebraska (Strong 1933, 1935; Wedel 1934, 1935a, 1961). The most intensive and informative researches have been on Medicine Creek (fig. 2), where more than 40 house units in several communities were cleared (Kivett 1949a; Wedel 1953, 1970; Wood 1969a). The Loup River basin in central Nebraska is another district of heavy Upper Republican settlement, but with strong cultural influences from the easterly Nebraska phase sites, which make cultural allocation difficult in the absence of full analyses. Particularly important is the Davis Creek locality. Farther south, on the Solomon River, other sites were excavated (Krause 1969, 1970).

In Nebraska, Upper Republican sites are widely scattered on streamside terraces, gentle hillside slopes, or convenient ridge tops along the lesser creeks, and less commonly on larger streams like the Republican. Communities are usually small, consisting of single house units scattered at intervals of a few yards to several hundred feet, or of clusters of two to four or five houses similarly separated from other clusters or single units (fig. 3). Shallow inconspicuous middens may occur just outside the entrances, and cache pits up to three or four feet in depth occur both inside and outside the houses. The houses are typically square to subrectangular in floor plan, with rounded corners, and are characteristically small, floor areas varying from 150 to 1,100 square feet and probably averaging not much more than 500–550 square feet, roughly 20 by 25 feet. It is doubtful that most would have accommodated conveniently more than 6 to 10 individuals, or that settlements often exceeded 50 to 100 persons. Some houses were apparently built on or just below the contemporary ground surface; others were as much as three feet underground, depending in part on whether they were built on flat terrain or into a sloping hillside. Vestibule entrances 8–12 feet in length customarily extended out from one side. Beyond the basic arrangement of the posts within the house as reflected in post molds, there is little solid evidence as to the nature of the superstructure. For some houses, a pole-grass-sod cover comparable to that on historic earthlodges of the Nebraska region may be indicated with flat to peaked roof; for others, a Middle Mississippi style of jacal wall construction has been inferred (Wood 1969a). There are vague hints, too, but no real proof, of aberrant structures that possibly had some ritual function in the community.

The Upper Republican subsistence economy was divided between food producing and food collecting. It included a maize-bean-squash-sunflower hoe-using horticulture, considerable game hunting, some fishing with hooks, and inferentially the gathering of wild plant foods in season. Bison scapula hoes with use-polished blades, and variously hafted, are common. Little is known of the gardening practices, and there is no evidence that fertilizers, irrigation, or other specialized techniques detectable by archeological methods were in use. From analogy with the historic maize-growing Indians of the Plains (see Will and Hyde 1917), it can perhaps be surmised that small gardens, not often exceeding one-half to one acre per family and yielding at a rate of 10–20 bushels of corn per acre, were cultivated in the alluvial soils of nearby creek bottoms. Little is known regarding the crop varieties in use, but charred cobs testify to maize with 6–12 rows of kernels (Kivett 1949a:280); it is not known how these compare with the maize grown earlier in the Eastern Plains by the Middle Woodland–Hopewellian peoples. The sunflower, as represented by achenes large enough to suggest a cultigen, appears in Plains horticulture generally at about this same time. Most of what little is known or can be inferred

Smithsonian, NAA: River Basin Survey. top, 25FT70-7; bottom, 25FT70-11.

Fig. 2. Upper Republican settlement in Medicine Creek Reservoir (Harry Strunk Lake), Nebr. top, Ridge-top house cluster dated about A.D. 1150–1215. bottom, Excavavated houses showing patterns of posts and cache pits. Photographs by Waldo Wedel, 1948.

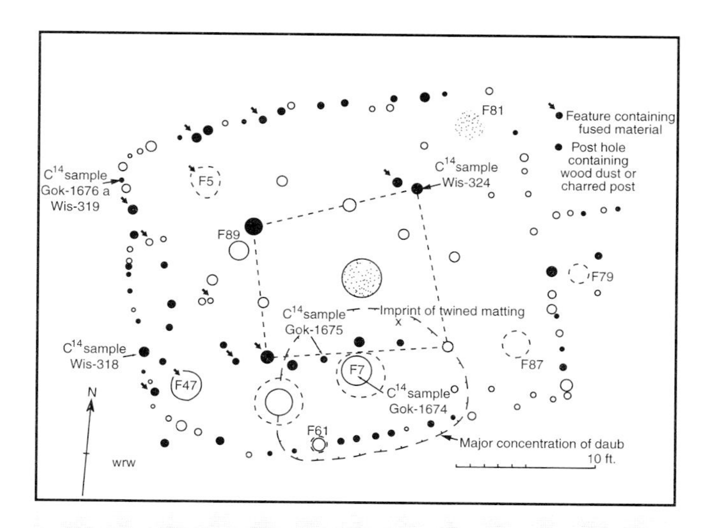

top, after Wood 1969:fig. 4; bottom, U. of Nebr., Dept. of Anthr., Lincoln: 25HN44-1034.

Fig. 3. Upper Republican houses in Harlan County, Nebr. top, Floor plan of Mowry Bluff House I, a 4-post house. Drawn by Roger Thor Roop, 1998. bottom, Harlan County Reservoir house at site 25HN44. Photograph by Jere Moore, 1951.

about the crops grown comes from charred remains in the storage pits, which are usually significantly smaller and fewer in number than those in the prehistoric Lower Loup and central Kansas communities.

Faunal remains from the Upper Republican sites at Medicine Creek represent some 40 species of mammals. Of the larger game animals available, bison and pronghorn, both upland forms, usually lead the lists in abundance. The remains of deer and elk are less common. Among smaller species were the prairie dog, jackrabbit, beaver, cottontail rabbit, woodrat, raccoon, gray fox, mole, woodchuck, pocket gopher, pocket mouse, kangaroo rat, white-footed mouse, grasshopper mouse, prairie vole, muskrat, porcupine, coyote, wolf, swift fox, mink, wolverine, badger, puma, and lynx or bobcat. The dog is the only domestic animal recorded from these sites; it seems to have been mainly a small to medium-sized form contrasting sharply with the large powerful draft or pack animals that have been recorded for protohistoric Pawnee and Wichita sites in the Central Plains (Wedel 1959:233).

Hunting methods can only be inferred. Since the Upper Republican people resided in large part in the heart of the former bison range, they undoubtedly had ready access to the herds—in summer, on the uplands and valley margins and in winter on the sheltered valley bottoms, in the timbered patches, and in the breaks. There is no evidence of mass kills or fire drives; but stalking by solitary hunters with animal skin disguises, ambushing at waterholes and along trails, or stampeding the quarry into boggy or quicksand spots are among the methods that would have been practical to pedestrian hunters (Wedel 1986:125). Since the number of individual bison usually represented by bone refuse seems small in proportion to the probable requirements of the inferred populations, it is likely that there was considerable butchering at the kill sites, with the bones generally discarded away from the home settlements except when wanted for tool-making or to meet ritual requirements. Lack of draft or pack animals, other than small dogs, would have been further incentive to discard useless bones. Surplus meat from the kills was doubtless dried and stored for consumption when the herds were not readily accessible. The smaller animals were presumably taken by individual hunters with bow and arrow, or with snares, deadfalls, and other devices.

Bird bones are relatively scarce. At Medicine Creek, they include chiefly such gallinaceous forms as prairie chicken and sharp-tailed grouse, occasional ducks, geese, and teal, and perhaps less commonly, various raptores and passerine species. It is not apparent that birds were a significant part of the diet; use of the skins, with feet, wings, and head attached, for ceremonial or talismanic purposes, of the wings alone for fans or whiskbrooms, and of appropriate parts for pipe ornamentation, as in historic times, may have been equally important considerations in taking of birds (Ubelaker and Wedel 1975). Almost without known exception, the species identified so far in the bone refuse are forms that were locally resident rather than seasonal migrants.

Fish taken with curved bone hooks also contributed to the diet. More important, perhaps, to judge from Medicine Creek, Davis Creek, and Glen Elder on the Solomon, were shellfish. In the Nebraska localities, some cache pits were nearly filled with large quantities of mussel shells, most of them unburned and many still carrying the periostracum or epidermal layer. At Medicine Creek, the mapleleaf mussel (*Quadrula quadrula*) was predominant in the shell refuse. The indicated extensive use of shellfish and other freshwater fauna by Upper Republican peoples contrasts interestingly with their much more restricted utilization in later times. At Central Plains village sites in protohistoric and historic times, as among the Pawnee and Wichita, mussel shells comprise a much smaller proportion of the food refuse; and the nomadic Indians there as over much of the Plains area seem generally to have avoided such foods.

Very little evidence has been recovered regarding the use of wild vegetal products by Upper Republican peoples, but this undoubtedly reflects in large part the highly perishable nature of these materials where they have not been charred or burned. It seems entirely reasonable to suggest that the leguminous and other edible plants that were native to the Upper Republican habitat and that were so extensively utilized by the historic tribes were also drawn upon by prehistoric groups.

Cultural material from Upper Republican sites is usually much more plentiful and varied than that from most earlier Woodland sites in the subarea. Pottery is usually abundant, almost exclusively grit- or sand-tempered, with cord-roughened exteriors on which the impressions have frequently been all but obliterated. Full-bodied vessels up to 40 centimeters in diameter, occasional bowls, and some miniature pieces are the common forms (fig. 4). Jar rims include both collared and unthickened vertical or outcurved profiles; the relative proportions of these two major form groups may have some undetermined chronological significance, as does the frequency and style of rim ornamentation and its association with rim form (G.F. Carlson 1971). Artifacts of stone include well-made triangular projectile points, commonly side-notched; diamond-shaped bifacially chipped knives with oppositely beveled edges; thin lanceolate to ellipsoidal knives in considerable variety of sizes and shapes; several forms of chipped drill points, including a T-form; abundant chipped celts or axes, commonly made of yellow-brown jasper from the Niobrara Chalk; longitudinally grooved sandstone abraders; pebble pecking stones; ground celts, rare south of Platte River; stone pipe bowls, usually thick-walled and enlarging upward, sometimes with zoomorphic ornamentation; carved human faces; small to medium milling and grinding stones; small stone pendants; and hematite, limonite, and other natural pigments. Among bone tools are bison scapula hoes, with the head of the bone sometimes slightly notched or otherwise modified but not usually detached; several types of split mammal legbone awls; eyed needles; curved barbless fishhooks; edge-slotted knife handles; bison-rib shaft wrenches; pierced toebones of bison; antler clubs and cylinders; bison ulna picks; beamers of bison vertebral spine or occasionally of deer metapoidal; incised bracelets; and deer mandibles with use-polished diastema. The rare shell artifacts include perforated "bear claw" and other pendants, disk beads, and occasional shells with serrate edges.

Raw and processed materials of exotic origin, variously obtained by trade, travel, or otherwise, include wooden disks covered with native copper; shells originating either on the sea coast, such as olivella and conch columellae, or in streams of the eastern United States, such as *Leptoxis* spp.; rare Knife River flint from North Dakota; chalcedony, agates, and other stones from northwestern Nebraska; and Spanish Diggings quartzite from Wyoming. Puebloan or other recognizable Southwestern potsherds are unreported except as occasional surface finds, and there is apparently no Minnesota catlinite. Alibates flint from Texas is rare or absent, and so is the fusulinid Florence flint from the Kay County, Oklahoma, and Cowley County, Kansas, quarries (Wedel 1959:476). Flattop chert from north of Sterling, Colorado, is often present.

There is very little information on the Upper Republican burial practices. These seem to have included secondary deposition of disarticulated skeletons (Strong 1935:103) in large circular pits, which contained also potsherds, worked shell, stone artifacts, and other items identifiable with village site materials. Individual primary interments without diagnostic artifact associations may also belong to this complex. The burial grounds that must have once existed remain undiscovered.

Smithsonian, Dept. of Anthr., Archeol.: A-433658 (92-2678).

Fig. 4. Upper Republican cord-roughened pottery jar from site 25FT70, Medicine Creek Reservoir (Harry Strunk Lake), Nebr.; height 20 cm.

The chronological position of Upper Republican seems fairly well established, at least for the Medicine Creek locality. Here 33 radiocarbon determinations provide the basis for a local chronology. The dates relate mainly to seven sites clustered within three miles of one another around the Medicine Creek dam, and an eighth, 25HN36, in Harlan County reservoir some 80 miles down the Republican. Individual sample means range from the fifth to seventeenth centuries, but when the mean dates for samples from each site represented by more than one reading are averaged, the span of occupation is narrowed to the period A.D. 1120–1250 (Wedel 1986). On the basis of these site averages, it can be suggested that the major occupation of the portion of Medicine Creek represented by the available radiocarbon dates need not have endured much longer than a century, that is, four or five generations.

The Loup River district, including the drainages of the North, Middle, and South Loup, has yielded abundant materials whose basic relationship to the Republican River manifestations has long been recognized but that, in the near absence of adequate site analyses and comparative studies, has not been assigned definite taxonomic status by those most familiar with their nature. The appellation Loup River phase has been proposed by Krause (1969:90) on the basis, apparently, of the archeological characteristics at the Sweetwater site, which has not yet been shown to have more than component significance.

At Sweetwater (Champe 1936), the principal differences from the Medicine Creek–Lost Creek Upper Republican sites are in the prevalence of single-cord impressions on pottery instead of incised or trailed lines on the rim exterior, but retaining the same decorative motifs. The three house floors excavated varied in shape from square with rounded corners to circular, showing rather more variability that would normally be expected from such a limited sample; but there is nothing to indicate whether the variability was due to personal whimsy, a reflection of re-occupancy and change from square to round house floor patterns, or some other factor.

In the Davis Creek locality, the settlement pattern apparently conforms to that in the Republican valley in that houses were not large and tended to show the scattered and variable layouts found in the hamlets to the south and southwest. At the principal site, Coufal, 21 cleared house floors showed some clustering and occasional superpositioning of structures; but it is not clear whether this represents re-occupation of a site that may have been abandoned from time to time or merely the shifting of house units within a continuing community as one structure gave out and had to be replaced (Wedel 1986:105, 225, 232). Square or rectangular house floors predominate but round ones are present; they range in area from about 150 to 960 square feet, averaging slightly more than 400 square feet. The pottery complex there is more varied than at Medicine Creek, including features such as vessel handles that indicate an infusion of elements from the Nebraska phase sites in eastern Nebraska.

The time span for the Davis Creek occupancy is uncertain; the only radiocarbon date—M-835 at A.D. 1130 ± 200 years—is entirely inadequate for a district whose numerous sites and abundant materials are considered by the investigators (Kivett and Metcalf 1997) to imply cultural change through a time period of undetermined but possibly considerable duration. It is unfortunate that for Davis Creek, as for Medicine Creek, insufficient structural wood materials were recovered from the houses to offer hopes for developing an internal tree-ring chronology against which seriation studies could be compared.

Glen Elder Locality

The Solomon River settlements in the Glen Elder locality of north-central Kansas, identified as Upper Republican, are of several kinds (Krause 1969:88, 1970:106). The earliest and most impressive are classified as small farming hamlets of 6 to 10 earthlodges situated on prominent terraces, with a work-storage (cache pit) area along one edge of the community. Dwellings were of substantial construction, the floors rectangular with rounded corners, ranging in area from 500 to 1,000 square feet, and including from two to nine subfloor cache pits each. From 10–15 persons per lodge and 60–120 per community are suggested as reasonable estimates of population. Periodic abandonment, with unfulfilled intent to return, is inferred from caches of raw materials and tools. The subsistence economy was based on "mixed hunting-collecting and gardening, with a surprising emphasis upon collecting" (Krause 1970:107). Walnut-stained stones with small pits for crushing and grinding nuts are present in some numbers, as this locality, unlike Medicine Creek and the Loup district, is in a country of once-fine black walnut stands. There are also "sizable heaps of freshwater musselshells," which, along with the evidence from Medicine Creek and Davis Creek, adds support to the view that shellfish were probably regularly utilized as food by Upper Republican peoples when and as available and were not necessarily a last resort when other protein foods were in short supply. A single excavated burial ground with disarticulated human remains in a large pit, accompanied by two pots and surrounded by smaller pits from which individual (?) primary interments had been removed to the central pit, is believed to indicate a "hitherto unsuspected degree of ceremonial elaboration with an interesting emphasis upon dedicatory reburial" (Krause 1970).

A second and later kind of settlement consisted of three or four households residing in less substantial dwellings located on tributary streams. Floor areas were reportedly (Krause 1969:89) in the neighborhood of 150–250 square feet. Nutting stones and mussel shells were less characteristic, storage pits were smaller, and the artifact inventory sparser and less varied.

A third settlement type, thought to represent seasonal fishing or hunting camps, lacked definable house patterns, had very limited artifact content, and was associated with refuse deposits that included clamshells, potsherds, bone and stone tools, and the like.

That these several settlement types were successive in time—hamlets earliest, followed by the smaller creek-bank communities, and these in turn by seasonal camps—is an inference based on "an inspection of changes in domestic architecture and trends in ceramic change" (Krause 1969:108), plus radiocarbon dates. Seven of the dates suggest an occupation between the ninth and thirteenth centuries for the hamlet peoples, and the complex so represented is termed Solomon River phase (Krause 1969:90). For the later and smaller settlements, a time encompassing the eleventh and fifteenth centuries is regarded as appropriate, and the appellation of Classic Republican phase is proposed. The creek-bank settlements and seasonal camps are said to exhibit a ceramic situation "with close parallels in hunting camps in western Nebraska and eastern Colorado," plus a "domestic architecture . . . more like that in Nebraska sites" (Krause 1970:108), all of which seems to imply that the Solomon valley hamlets preceded the more northerly and westerly Upper Republican communities in Nebraska. As further support for the distinctiveness of Solomon River from Nebraska Upper Republican occupations, Krause (1969:90) cites "nutting stones and large shell heaps." However, the Solomon River shell heaps have their counterpart in the shell-filled cache pits at Medicine Creek and Davis Creek; nutting stones, if such they were, would have been of scant usefulness in localities where nut trees were rare or absent, as at the specified Nebraska districts.

Further light on the archeology of the Glen Elder locality is provided by G.F. Carlson (1971) and by Ludwickson and Steinacher (1972). By seriation of decorative techniques and motifs on vessel rims, Carlson (1971:88) developed a local sequence from which he suggests that rim decoration "appears not only to have become more common through time, but also to have become more varied as new and often more complex decorative motifs appeared." Incised horizontal lines encircling the vessels and diagonal lip incising occur throughout; other motifs have more restricted temporal occurrence. Carlson's findings appear to lend support to Krause's thesis of two phases at Glen Elder, with the later Classic Republican phase more closely resembling the Upper Republican manifestations in southern Nebraska, including Medicine Creek. In two instances, the seriational evidence places excavation units from the same site in different phases, suggesting that the widely discrepant radiocarbon dates may reflect multiple occupations and therefore are possibly valid. Among 14 radiocarbon dates listed by Ludwickson and Steinacher (1972:65), the range of means is from A.D. 624 ± 80 to 1630 ± 90; seven dates precede A.D. 900, one is A.D. 1115 ± 80, and the remaining six range upward from A.D. 1230 ± 90. This distribution contrasts with that for Medicine Creek dates, suggesting in fact that the Glen Elder occupations may have both preceded and followed the Medicine Creek settlements. But how much the later Glen Elder materials differ from the Upper Republican in Nebraska, other than in the seriation rim decoration, is not known, nor is there sufficient evidence to accept the proposed Solomon River and Classic Republican phase as distinct from Upper Republican (Wedel 1986:132).

Nebraska Phase, 1100–1450

The Nebraska phase, long known as the Nebraska culture (Gilder 1926), is represented by numerous sites along the Missouri River in eastern Nebraska, western Iowa, northeastern Kansas, and northwestern Missouri (Gilder 1907; Sterns 1914, 1915; Strong 1933, 1935; Bell and Gilmore 1936; Hill and Cooper 1938; P.L. Cooper 1940; Wedel 1959, 1961; L.A. Brown 1967; Gradwohl 1969). Sites commonly occur on the narrow winding well-drained ridges and bluffs along the Missouri, and less frequently on the bluffs of the lower Platte, Elkhorn, and other tributaries within 30–40 miles of mainstream. House pits are sometimes visible as isolated depressions, in small clusters, or in straggling lines (Sterns 1914); but clustered houses or nucleated settlements may have been more common than was once supposed, since early research was carried out on the basis of visible surface features (Gradwohl 1969:136). The house pits are often large, ranging up to 75 feet or more in diameter before excavation; cleared floors vary greatly in size but tend to be larger than those in western Upper Republican, where timber was scarcer and smaller, with floor areas commonly in the range of 500–1,000 square feet, and not infrequently exceeding 1,500 square feet. They are also deeper, often up to three or four feet, and appear to have been characteristically subsurface when built and used. Cache pits occur inside the houses and possibly also outside. Except in their greater average depth and floor area, the houses generally parallel the Upper Republican style in the predominantly square to rectangular floor with rounded corners, four center posts around a central fireplace, and a long covered vestibule entranceway; but there is great variation in many details. Sterns (1914) reports houses without the entranceway, which were presumably entered through a smokehole in the roof. Circular floors were uncommon (Strong 1935:265; Wedel 1959:105), as are corner entrances and two or more entrances per house from adjoining walls (Strong 1935:155; P.L. Cooper 1940). Occasional oval or elliptical structures with burned and fragmented human bones scattered on the floor may have been charnel houses; other than this, structures identifiable as ceremonial or special-purpose seem to be absent or unreported. Midden heaps in proximity to houses, like those at Medicine Creek, have apparently not been recognized.

Pottery is usually associated with Nebraska phase sites (Strong 1935; Gunnerson 1952; Wedel 1959; L.A. Brown 1967; Sigstad 1969; Gradwohl 1969). It includes varying proportions of sand or crushed granite tempering, or of burned or crushed shell. Surface colors tend more toward browns and buffs than the grays of Upper Republican wares. Globular vessels without the high rounded shoulders of Upper Republican, and with constricted necks from which rise simple unthickened or collared rims, are characteristic; and there are many smaller jars and small deep bowls of various sizes and shapes. Vessel exteriors were sometimes left smooth or else were cord-roughened and then smoothed over, so that even when certainly present the cord impressions are usually much less obvious than in Upper Republican. Flat-strap and loop handles, generally oppositely placed and two per vessel, are common. Incised or trailed body decoration occurs mostly on shell-tempered pieces, often with polished dark surfaces, which probably represent alien influences from Middle Mississippi cultures down the Missouri (Strong 1935:255; Wedel 1943:213). Bent-tubular modified or elbow clay pipes occur to the near exclusion of stone pipes; and they sometimes bear incised or modeled decoration (Gilder 1926:25,28; Strong 1935: pl. 16; P.L. Cooper 1940: pl. 10), including depictions of human faces with exaggerated nose and tear streaks or tattoo (?) lines on the cheeks (fig. 5). Effigy heads of clay, seemingly designed for attachment to pottery vessels or other objects, are also remindful of Middle Mississippi practices.

The nonpottery artifact assemblage generally parallels that of Upper Republican, but with some notable differences. There is more work in shell and greater variety, including perforated hoes (?), "spoons" with handles, fish effigies, beads, and other items (Gilder 1926:23; Strong 1935: pl. 11; P.L. Cooper 1940: pl. 11). Also present and not yet reported from Upper Republican sites are stone pottery anvils, deer-jaw sinew stretchers(?), toggle-head harpoon points of antler (Gilder 1926:26; Strong 1935: pl. 9; Hill and Cooper 1938: pl. 16), and digging tools fashioned from a piece of bison frontal with horn core section attached. Bone artifacts are uncommon at some sites, perhaps because of unfavorable soil conditions.

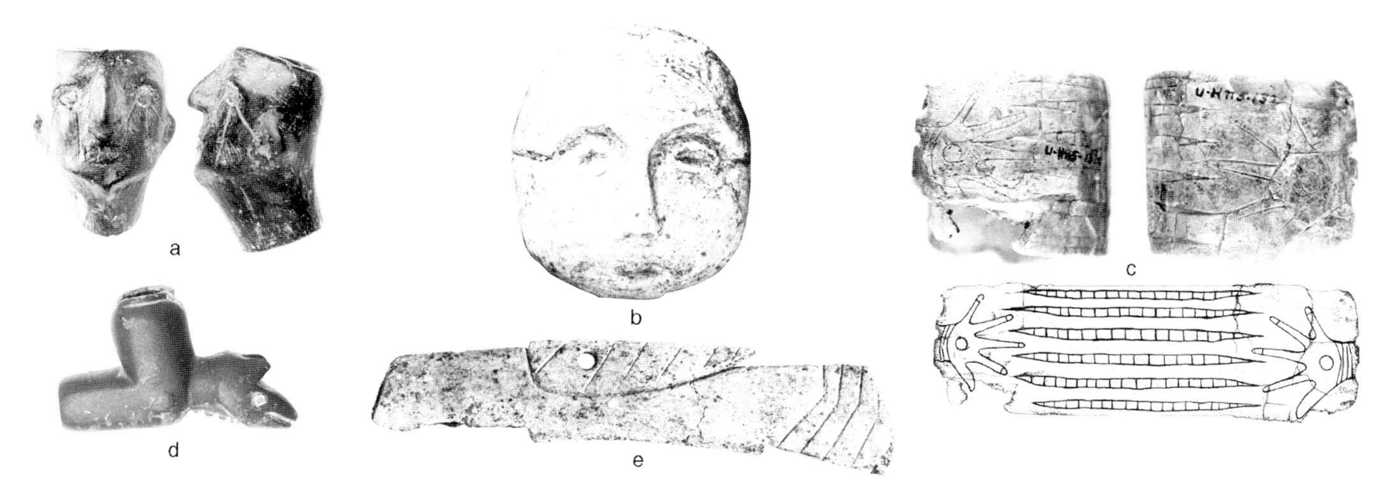

a, Nebr. State Histl. Soc., Archaeol. Div., Lincoln: 25CC1-141; b, Smithsonian, Dept. of Anthr.: 535142 (92-6111); c, U. of Nebr., Dept. of Anthr., Lincoln: UNHN5-132; d, Nebr. State Histl. Soc., Archaeol. Div., Lincoln: 25WN5-228; e, Smithsonian, Dept. of Anthr.: 434133 (92-6112).

Fig. 5. Artifacts from the Nebraska and Upper Republican phases. a, Pottery pipe with molded human face from the Ashland site, Nebraska phase. The incised diagonal lines across the cheeks retain traces of red pigment. b, Carved limestone head from site 25FT13, Upper Republican phase. c, Antler bowguard from the Graham Ossuary site, Nebr., with drawing of the incised design, unrolled, on the bowguard. Drawing by Roger Thor Roop. d, Stone pipe carved in the form of an animal head with shell disks for eyes from Renne Farm, Site W5, Nebraska phase. e, Split rib knife handle carved as a bird effigy from Medicine Creek Reservoir (Harry Strunk Lake) site 25FT28, Upper Republican phase. Height of a 5.7 cm, b and d to same scale; length of c 5.5 cm; length of e 14.2 cm.

The Nebraska phase subsistence economy is much less well-known than the Upper Republican, perhaps owing in part to a more humid environment that is less conducive to long preservation of nonlithic materials. For no locality have faunal remains been recovered to the extent manifested at Medicine Creek. Deer and other woodland and forest margin animals that could be readily hunted by individuals were extensively utilized; bison and pronghorn are much less abundantly represented in the bone refuse, but for bison at least this may well reflect kill-site butchering practices more than actual food preferences or availability. Charred maize has been found, and there are many bison scapula hoes, usually a hallmark of Plains Indian maize horticulturists. The cultivation of beans, squash, and sunflowers can probably be assumed. That these people were any more deeply involved in maize cultivation than the Upper Republican groups has not been established. Wild vegetal foods inferentially included about the same roots, tubers, berries, and fruits that were available farther west, plus an abundance of nuts. The turkey can be added to the list of birds used. To what extent the hunting and food-gathering systems of the Nebraska phase people differed from those of the Upper Republicans is unclear, though it can be supposed that the greater range in kinds and abundance in accord with better growing conditions for most plants would have provided more generous harvests.

Burial practices of the Nebraska phase are somewhat uncertain, though there is evidence of ossuary burial. Little can be added to Strong's (1935:266) conclusion that "these people exposed and dismembered their dead, seem to have kept the skeletal remains in their lodges, perhaps practicing some form of ceremonial cannibalism, and eventually deposited them in mounds natural or otherwise."

From Nebraska phase sites in Nebraska, Iowa, and Kansas, some 40 radiocarbon dates are available. Mean sample dates range from about A.D. 780 ± 120; 29 (75%) of these are between A.D. 1100 and 1450. Site averages, which usually rest on only two or three dates each from a geographic scatter of about 200 miles, run from about A.D. 1050 to 1510—or, adjusted to the bristlecone pine curve, from about 1100 to 1450. They thus begin at about the same time as the Medicine Creek Upper Republican, but about half fall between 1250 and 1450—appreciably later in time than Upper Republican and in a time span when the western portions of the Upper Republican range may no longer have been inhabited by Central Plains tradition people.

That Nebraska phase sites vary in content and probably through time has become increasingly obvious, but the nature of the observed and suspected variations has not been analyzed in sufficient depth and detail to determine their significance. In Mills County, Iowa, A.D. Anderson (1961) outlined a three-phase local chronology based on frequency of collared as against uncollared vessel rims. On a broader scale, L.A. Brown (1967) proposed two subphases but offered no statistical validation that the apparent distinctions are real and meaningful. Krause (1969:91) divided Nebraska culture into two phases: an earlier Doniphan and a later Douglas phase. This sequential ordering is based on the assumptions that Nebraska culture peoples "spread through the region by a process of population growth and adaptation to local environment" and that "through time increasingly intimate ties were established with Upper Republican peoples to the west." Attractive as these propositions seem, given the dearth of radiocarbon or other "precise" dates for most sites, the virtual absence of stratified village deposits, and the lack of seriational or other statistical support, their accuracy remains to be determined.

On the basis of a comprehensive analysis of the Nebraska phase, Blakeslee and Caldwell (1979) have suggested that (1) the southern Missouri River localities around Brownville and Plattsmouth, Nebraska, were occupied first; (2) there may have been two distinct populations working their way upstream and onto some of the tributaries; (3) the proportion of decorated vessel rims increases through time; (4) the use of catlinite is late, mainly after 1250; (5) deer mandible sickles occur frequently after 1250; (6) shell-tempered pottery is an early trait at Missouri River sites, whereas grit tempering appears in late northern sites with shoulder decorations; (7) sites on the western tributaries were radiocarbon dated mainly at 1250–1415, suggesting termination of occupancy later than western Upper Republican.

Smoky Hill Phase, 1000–1350

The complex to which the term Smoky Hill phase is here attached was originally proposed (Wedel 1959:563) as a new taxonomic unit on the basis of evidence from the Minneapolis, Griffing, and Whiteford sites and from others in the lower Smoky Hill drainage that have not been excavated and reported. On the sites named, houses appear to have been loosely clustered or scattered on stream terraces (Wedel 1935a:218, 1959) and to have been erected originally on or but slightly beneath the ground surface so that they are now visible, or were prior to intensive agricultural operations, as low mounds rather than as depressions. The floor areas, straight-sided with rounded corners, ranged from 600 to 2,500 (50 by 50) square feet per house, consistently larger on the average than Upper Republican, but not so deep. This greater size may reflect in part the availability of better building materials, since at Minneapolis, for example, charred center post stubs indicated oak timbers up to 13–14 inches in diameter—probably much larger than anything obtainable, possibly excepting cottonwood, on Medicine Creek or Davis Creek. The associated pottery has grit, bone, and crushed sherd tempering, a more varied range than in Upper Republican; but large jars sometimes show the typical high rounded shoulder characteristic of many western pieces. There is a good deal of worked freshwater shell in the form of perforated "hoes" and other items. In this and in certain other traits, there are interesting similarities to Nebraska phase materials. The Whiteford burial pit near Salina, Kansas, with its massive primary interments and various mortuary accompaniments, provides an important clue to the burial practices of the communities, besides containing ceramic evidence of contacts with prehistoric cultures of eastern Oklahoma and Arkansas. The few radiocarbon dates thought to apply to Smoky Hill are between A.D. 1000 and 1350, too late to be consistent with the suggestion (Wedel 1959:564–565) that Smoky Hill may have been ancestral to the Upper Republican and Nebraska phases.

Pomona Phase, 900–1680

Scattered over the eastern third of Kansas, mainly between the Flint Hills and the Missouri-Kansas state line, are a number of sites classed together as the Pomona focus (Witty 1967, 1978), here considered as of phase status. The traits have been summarized as including: (1) scattered dwellings, often paired, on low streamside terraces, sometimes in large villages; (2) a subsistence economy based on hunting, gathering, and probably small-scale horticulture; (3) lightly framed houses, thatched and clay-daubed, probably oval in floor plan, 25 by 15 feet in size, built on the ground surface, with or without center posts, and usually without interior hearths; (4) projectile points in a variety of shapes and sizes, as well as blades and end scrapers; (5) ground stone including only "a few mullers and grinding slab sections"; (6) bone artifacts scarce, though one scapula hoe is reported; (7) Pomona ware, clay or sherd-tempered, with cord-roughened exteriors that are often smoothed, mostly in the form of globular jars and deep bowls, with rims unthickened, S-shaped in profile, or collared, and with some pieces made in imitation of Middle Mississippi forms.

Except in its reported house form and in the presence of clay rather than gravel pottery tempering, there seems to be little in the foregoing list to distinguish Pomona materials from the Smoky Hill and other contemporary complexes. The indicated absence of interior hearths and the implied light house construction appear inconsistent with year-round occupation of settlements in a region with subfreezing winter temperatures; and, despite the apparently wide distribution of sites, one wonders whether a seasonal variant of some other manifestation is indicated. Seven radiocarbon dates from six sites (Witty 1967) range between A.D. 987 ± 100 and 1560 ± 120 and are of scant help in understanding the significance of the complex in Central Plains prehistory. With their mixed trait inventory, Pomona sites seem peripheral to other defined archeological complexes (Witty 1967:4), spatially between and probably contemporaneous with the more sedentary Central Plains and Mississippian horticulturalists (Marshall 1972:242). Archeological investigation in the Harry Truman Reservoir area of Missouri and other reservoir areas in eastern Kansas has supported the suggestion that Pomona might represent a progenitor of the Central Plains Village tradition (K.L. Brown 1985).

Steed-Kisker Phase, 950–1300

The incised upper-body decoration on some Nebraska phase pottery, along with shell tempering and occasional high exterior surface polish (fig. 6), have been interpreted as influences from Middle Mississippi-related cultures flourishing down the Missouri River and around its junction with the Mississippi. Zoomorphic pottery pipes and anthropomorphic heads set on bowl and pot rims are believed to point in the same direction. Shell tempering appears to be more common in southern Nebraska phase sites, communities that were geographically nearer the Middle Mississippi manifestation represented by the Steed-Kisker complex (Wedel 1943:188, 208). First identified in Platte County, Missouri, Steed-Kisker is a much watered-down version of Middle Mississippi culture, lacking temple mounds, stone hoes, and many other features associated with its classical sites in the Midwest, but it is also based on a semihorticultural and semipermanent way of life. Indeed, the Steed-Kisker site, aside from its pottery, looks much like a Nebraska phase manifestation with regard to its house type, its subsistence complex, and its material culture inventory. The available evidence suggests small villages, a semihorticultural food basis, a Plains Villager lifeway, and burial in community hilltop cemeteries. Radiocarbon dates suggest a time span between A.D. 950 and 1300, more or less contemporary with some Nebraska phase manifestations.

Other Variants

Between those portions of Nebraska and northern Kansas that have usually been assigned to the Nebraska and Upper Republican phases are numerous other sites that share basic pottery, architectural, and other traits with both but cannot on present evidence be readily assigned to either or to any defined unit without some qualifications. They extend from northeastern Nebraska south through the Loess Hills into the Blue River drainage and probably as far south as the lower Smoky Hill–Kansas River country. Included are the sites reported as the Saint Helena focus (P.L. Cooper 1936); probably the Schrader site in Lancaster County, Nebraska (Hill and Cooper 1937a:223); perhaps the Lamb site in Thayer County, Nebraska (Lamb 1932); and other sites mostly unreported in print from the Blue River drainage. Many of these materials have long been loosely categorized as "hybrid" between the Upper Republican and Nebraska phases, with their ultimate allocation to a named unit being deferred until more penetrating analyses were feasible. Some, like materials from the Milford reservoir locality on the Lower Republican, reflect surprisingly strong Middle Mississippi influences, possibly from the Steed-Kisker phase on the Missouri

Smithsonian, Dept. of Anthr.: 381,521 (34086-P).

Fig. 6. Shell-tempered bowl from the Steed-Kisker site, Mo., showing possible bird head and tail effigy lugs. Deaccessioned Oct. 22, 1997, under NAGPRA procedures and conveyed to the Pawnee, Iowa, Ponca, Otoe, and Kansa for joint reburial near Lake Smithville, Mo. Tribal cultural affiliation not established. Diameter 15.2 cm.

above Kansas City (Ludwickson and Steinacher 1972). The time factor is a major unknown; some ceramic and other evidence suggests that Saint Helena may be later than most of the dated Upper Republican and Nebraska phase sites, and a single radiocarbon date for Schrader at A.D. 1415 ± 115 years points in the same direction.

The cultivation of maize on a limited scale has been archeologically attested for the Eastern Plains at least as early as Hopewellian (Wedel 1943:26) and Late Woodland (Kivett 1952:57) times. Representatives of the Central Plains tradition as exemplified by a western variant of Upper Republican appear to have been the first people to undertake serious exploitation of the horticultural possibilities of the trans-Missouri valley bottoms to or beyond the eastern margin of the High Plains. That the region west of 100 or 101° longitude was undependable for climatic reasons (Wedel 1953; Bowman 1972) is suggested by the apparent absence of evidence of maize cultivation and of the permanent four-post earthlodge beyond that somewhat nebulous and inexact line. Related materials including pottery, flints, and other artifacts are widely scattered in western Nebraska, eastern Colorado, and southeastern Wyoming (Wedel 1961:102 and references), but their exact connections with the Upper Republican communities to the east remain somewhat obscure (Wood 1969a, 1971, 1986:124). These sites were not temporary but occupied full-time by hunting-gathering populations having an Upper Republican material culture. This culture did not persist into historic times (Roper 1990).

External Relationships within the Plains

Archeological materials that can be safely assigned to the Upper Republican phase have been examined at least as far south in the Central Plains as the Pottorff site in western Kansas (Wedel 1959), on a southerly tributary of the Smoky Hill. The cord-roughened pottery with typical collared rim form and decoration, bone fishhooks, and four-post earthlodges here all seem much more closely related to Upper Republican to the north than to the pottery-bearing sites south of the Arkansas River. In terms of rim form and decoration, G.F. Carlson (1971:103) found the Pottorff site most closely related to the later or "Classic Republican" phase at Glen Elder. Farther south, in the Red Hills and Cimarron River drainage, the Central Plains tradition is apparently replaced by materials more closely related to the Washita and Custer phases of the Southern Plains Village tradition. Too little intensive work has been carried on in the southern Kansas sectors to provide a sound basis for profitable synthesis (Munsell 1961; Wedel 1959, 1968a).

The Washita and Custer phases of central and western Oklahoma (Bell and Baerreis 1951; Pillaert 1963; Sharrock 1961) are on approximately the same time level as the Central Plains tradition sites. The settlement patterns, square houses with four center posts, and the artifact inventory generally parallel the Central Plains trait lists, but there are differences in type of bone hoe, in presence of bone digging stick heads, and in certain other items (Wedel 1959:567, 1961:139).

Farther west, in the Oklahoma-Texas panhandle district, is another related cultural complex—the Antelope Creek phase, formerly termed the Panhandle aspect (Krieger 1947:71; Gunnerson 1987:87–89). In its sometimes slab-walled house architecture and conjoined rooms in pseudo-Puebloan style, this complex differs markedly from the rectangular pit houses and earthlodges farther east and northeast; but again the artifact inventory resembled Upper Republican (Krieger 1947:55; Wedel 1959:567, 1961:142) and includes items such as transversely scored bison ribs and rib-edge awls, which appear in the Central Plains on a later protohistoric time level. Glaze I Puebloan trade sherds in Antelope Creek sites (Baerreis and Bryson 1966; Crabb 1968), along with a notable series of radiocarbon dates whose site averages fall mainly between A.D. 1200 and 1450, suggest that these Antelope Creek sites are later in time than the western Upper Republican sites in Nebraska and follow, as well, the Washita and Custer phases (Hofman 1978; Lintz 1978).

North of the Central Plains subarea, beyond the Niobrara, the Middle Missouri tradition corresponds culturally and chronologically to the Central Plains tradition, but there are notable differences between the two (Lehmer 1954, 1971; Wedel 1964), despite basic similarities in the lifeway as judged from archeology.

Historical Relationships

The origins and development of the Central Plains Village tradition are still moot. In line with anthropological dogma that views Plains culture history as a somewhat deviant version of Eastern Woodlands prehistory, it has long been thought that the Central Plains tradition was in large measure rooted in older cultures to the east and southeast (Strong 1933; Wedel 1961), with adaptations in response to the changed circumstances of the more westerly environmental setting. Such basic cultural complexes as the maize-bean-squash-sunflower hoe-linked horticultural base, probably house types and settlement patterns, the importance of fishing and shell fishing in the subsistence economy, and perhaps other traits seemed to point generally toward the east rather than, for example, to the southwest. These elements, in essence, could have diffused into the Central Plains by way of the Arkansas River valley and its south-flowing tributaries, as well as up the major westerly tributaries of the Missouri River via the Kansas–Smokey Hill–Republican, and the Platte-Loup-Elkhorn drainage systems.

The relationships of the prehistoric Central Plains tradition peoples to later cultures of the subarea await adequate definition. The suggestion advanced by Strong (1935) of a possible direct connection between historic Siouan-speaking tribes and the Nebraska phase has no direct archeological support, nor does the long-argued development of historic Pawnee culture from Upper Republican via the protohistoric Lower Loup phase. The "clear unbroken line of ceramic and other development" postulated by Strong (1933) has not materialized. Despite the postulated intermediate stage between Upper Republican and Lower Loup, which Ludwickson (1978) called the Loup River phase, the predominantly square to rectangular houses, as well as the artifact assemblage, seem much closer to Upper Republican, and do not provide a transition to the uniformly circular house floors of the Lower Loup phase. "The small, open, undefended villages, prevailingly rectangular pit houses, cord-roughened pottery, and communal ossuary burials of the Upper Republican peoples are consistently in contrast to the large, defensively situated, fortified towns, invariably circular earth lodges, corrugated paddle pottery, and individual flesh interments of the Pawnee" (Wedel 1941:26). The extremely limited and statistically inadequate data of physical anthropology (Bass 1964) likewise fail to show a close similarity between the populations attributable to the Central Plains tradition and those of the historic period in the Eastern Plains.

The end of the Central Plains tradition occupancy of the Kansas-Nebraska region, and the manner in which it took place—whether by drought, by appearance of unfriendly aliens from the west or elsewhere, or for other reasons, is unclear. However, it appears certain that by the mid-sixteenth century, when the first Spanish exploring expedition under Francisco Vásquez de Coronado reached central Kansas, the western territory had long since been abandoned by maize-growing Indians (Wedel 1970a). Their early historic counterparts were by then firmly established in the region.

None of the peoples discussed in the preceding sections of this chapter ever came into direct contact with Europeans. By the time Whites arrived, the widely scattered villages and hamlets throughout the loess plains and the drift hills had long been abandoned, and the Central Plains Indians were living in larger, more compactly arranged clusters of houses east of the 99° longitude meridian. There were two of these groups—the Pawnee tribes in the Platte-Loup district of east-central Nebraska, whose protohistoric remains are known as the Lower Loup phase; and the Wichita tribes in the Arkansas–Smoky Hill district of central Kansas some 200 miles to the south, whose protohistoric remains are known as the Great Bend phase. Both the Lower Loup and Great Bend phases can be dated approximately A.D. 1500–1750.

Great Bend Phase

In central Kansas archeologists have found numerous sites, classified as the Great Bend phase (Wedel 1959:571–589, 630–633). Some of them are large, comprised of circular dome-shaped grass and pole houses, with shallow floors and central fireplaces. Scattered among the houses were great numbers of cache pits, some of them 8 to 10 feet in depth and diameter, usually with a constricted neck (fig. 7). From these have been taken charred maize, beans, squash, sunflower seeds, great numbers of bison and other animal bones, and artifacts in considerable numbers. Milling slabs, hand stones, and bison scapula hoes are abundant. Some triangular unnotched arrowpoints, side and end scrapers, ovate, diamond-shaped, and two-edged side-notched knives, often with oppositely beveled edges, bone fleshing tools, drills, perforators and awls occur in large numbers, suggesting heavy reliance on hunting and well-developed skin-working and bone-working industries. Wedge-shaped pieces of cancellous bone served as paint brushes to decorate articles of hide. Twisted vegetal fiber cordage and shallow coiled basketry are directly indicated.

Other common artifacts include grooved quartzite mauls and hammers; small sandstone disks with or without central perforations; well-made sandstone arrowshaft smoothers, shaped like nail buffers and used in pairs; shaft straighteners or wrenches fashioned of bison ribs; ribs with transverse grooves or notches that have been variously identified as tallies, musical rasps, and pottery-finishing tools; flakers of antler tip; bone tubes and beads; and long, slender, curved strips of bone or antler, pierced at one end and notched at the other. Shell was not extensively used, though there are a few spoons or scrapers and simple ornaments of marine and freshwater forms.

Broken pottery is fairly plentiful on most Great Bend village sites. It is for the most part of mediocre quality, consisting mostly of utility jars of various sizes and shapes (fig. 8). In central Kansas near the Great Bend of the Arkansas River, at sites termed the Little River locality,

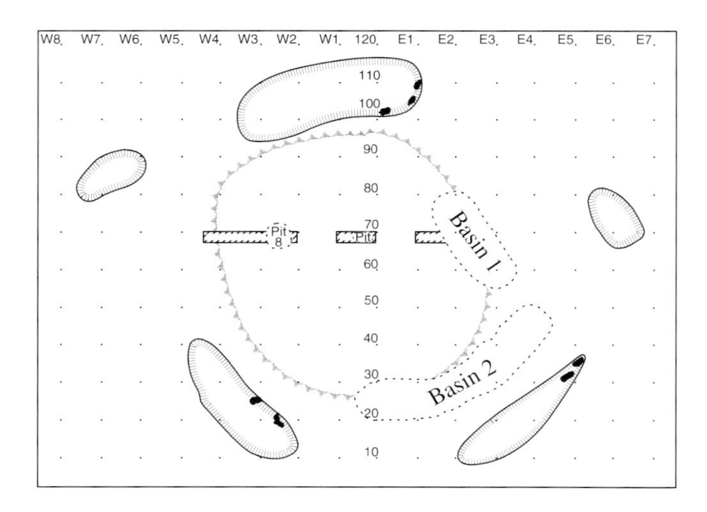

bottom, Smithsonian Lib.: Wedel 1959: pl. 24b.

Fig. 7. Mount 17, Tobias site, Great Bend phase, Kans. top, Site plan showing initial test trench and basins 1 and 2 as excavated, diameter 18.3 m. Drawn by Roger Thor Roop. bottom, Site photograph of the cleared Basin 2 looking northeast. Photograph by Waldo Wedel, 1940.

Smithsonian, Dept. of Anthr., Archeol.: A-388,898 (34713-G).

Fig. 8. Great Bend phase jar, restored, from the Tobias site, Kans.; diameter 23 cm.

pottery is mostly grit or sand tempered; in southern Kansas, farther down the Arkansas near its juncture with the Walnut River, at sites termed the Lower Walnut locality, shell-tempering predominates. Vessel exteriors were unevenly smoothed and seldom polished. Most pottery is plain surfaced, but from 10 to 40 percent shows parallel ridges made by a grooved bone or wood paddle. Incised, trailed, or filleted decoration occasionally occurs on the exterior neck, or rows of small appliqué nodes occur below the vessel rim. Cord-roughened exteriors occur on a small percent of the sherds; red-painted surfaces that rub or wash off easily occur on a few small bowls with lids.

The usual vessel form is a medium to large jar 20 to 40 centimeters tall and slightly less in diameter, with simple vertical or slightly outcurved rim, constricted neck, rounding shoulder, subconical or globular underbody, and rounded or flat base. Flat disk bases are much more common in the south, and so are vessel handles.

Trade or other relationships with people in several directions are indicated by obsidian thought to be from New Mexico or Colorado, by pleasingly banded varicolored and fusulinid Florence chert from quarries on the Kansas-Oklahoma line east of the Arkansas River, and by Minnesota catlinite, used for simple ornaments and for pipes. The pipes include particularly a high-bowled, short-stemmed L-shaped type as well as other forms. At a number of sites, glaze-paint decorated potsherds of types manufactured during the sixteenth and seventeenth centuries on the upper Rio Grande and in the Galisteo Basin have been recognized, indicating direct trade contacts.

A notable feature of several Little River sites is the so-called council circles. Their nature and purpose are unknown. They consist of a circle of four oblong, curved pit houses, with a shallow mound at the center. Within the pit houses, post molds and fireplaces run down the midline and give evidence of occupation. Cache pits are present. Selected ears of corn, pipes, and other carefully kept articles have been recovered from these lodges. There is good evidence that these structures were used as solstice registers by the Indians. Several were used for mass burial of hastily deposited corpses, perhaps the victims of pestilence or violence, and there are clear indications that some were destroyed by conflagration.

Dating of the Great Bend phase is well established by associated glaze-paint decorated Puebloan wares and by repeated finds of chain-mail fragments in or on at least six separate sites in the central Kansas region. Ears of corn, perfectly formed and well filled out, have been found in storage baskets in the council circle structures. In conjunction with the much larger size of the cache pits as compared to those in prehistoric Central Plains tradition sites, they argue strongly for a progressive and highly productive maize-beans-squash-sunflower horticultural economy.

Lower Loup Phase

When Coronado reached the end of Quivira and asked the Indians what lay beyond, they informed him that there was only Harahey, and that it was the same sort of place as Quivira. At Coronado's invitation, the chief of those settlements visited him with 200 armed warriors. The chances seem very good that they were from east-central Nebraska, somewhere within 30 miles of the confluence of the Loup and Platte rivers. Unlike the innumerable hamlets and lodges of prehistoric days, these contact period villages were often along the main streams or on secondary streams just back from the main stream valley. Other sites were located on the Republican and on the Blue River. Pawnee villages were sometimes described as permanent, though few probably were more than 10 years at one place before house and palisade posts began rotting and lodges became insecure and shabby. These sites are in the area where Étienne Venyard, sieur de Bourgmont, exploring the Missouri in 1714, indicated there were 10 villages of Pawnee 30 leagues up the Platte and the Skiri Pawnee were 20 leagues farther up on the Loup River (Norall 1988:109, 123).

These village sites range in size from less than 15 to more than 100 acres, and most are on elevated flood-free terraces or on the bluffs bordering the stream valleys. Before the days of intensive agriculture, house rings and trash heaps abounded along these sections of the Loup and Platte. The Lower Loup communities consisted of numerous medium to large earthlodges from 25 to 50 feet in diameter, always circular in ground plan, and with the floor usually one or two feet below the ground surface. The fireplace was a simple basin in the center, and four to eight large posts about midway between the fireplace and the house wall provided the main roof support. A second series of smaller posts, usually 8 to 16, commonly stood a meter or so inside the wall, and on the stringers connecting their tops rested the outer ends of the rafters. Closely set smaller poles, sometimes planted in the floor at the base of the pit wall and at other times set on the ground surface at the pit edge, formed the frame of the sloping wall closing in the house. The entrance was a long covered passage opening away from the prevailing winds, often but not invariably toward the east. Cache pits were dug into the floor between the fireplace and the beds against the wall; and many of the lodges had an earthen or clay altar platform against the back wall opposite the doorway. On this frequently reposed a bison skull, and above this hung a medicine bundle or a household fetish. Between the hearth and the door stood an upright wooden mortar and billet.

Each house was occupied by 10 to 20 persons. Some villages were fortified with ditches, walls, or stockades. Occasional burials are found in the villages, but most cemeteries were situated on hilltops overlooking the villages.

In most respects, the way of life followed by the Lower Loup people paralleled closely that inferred from the Great Bend remains. Horticulture was important, with a dozen or more kinds of maize, beans, squash, and sunflowers, and the bison-scapula hoe characteristic. Around some of the villages, tillable ground was at a premium, and the women had to walk as far as 10 miles to reach their gardens. The abundance and size of many cache pits suggest a highly productive crop-growing economy and substantial crop surpluses to be cared for.

There is little indication of fishing, but hunting with the bow and arrow was important. There were no domestic animals except the dog, including some large and powerful enough to have served as draft animals.

Stone and bone tools were mostly the same as those in use by the Great Bend villagers, but the Lower Loup craftsmen were perhaps less accomplished flintsmiths and makers of bone artifacts. Hide-working equipment included a wide variety of knives, scrapers, drills, reamers, L-shaped elkhorn fleshing adzes with stone blades, toothed hide fleshers, needles, and bone paint wedges. Catlinite and other suitable stone were used for ornaments and for several kinds of pipes, including some animal effigies. Coarse twined bags were made of vegetal materials and may have been used for storage of maize and other crops. The artifact and tool inventory was generally much more extensive than that for the prehistoric Plains villagers.

Pottery is abundant on virtually all sites. Like that on Great Bend sites, it is grit-tempered, rarely shell-tempered, but is generally superior in manufacture and more varied in vessel forms than the Kansas wares. Many of the vessels have handles, a distinctive feature being the use of many small handles, which give an arcaded or cloistered effect to the vessel rim. Vessel surfaces are commonly treated with a grooved or wrapped paddle to give a corrugated effect. A small percentage of body sherds are cord-roughened. Incised decoration is common on the upper body, often as a series of triangular areas filled with parallel diagonal lines, with the lines in adjacent triangles slanting in opposite directions. Some of this is reminiscent of pottery produced in large quantities on the Missouri River in South Dakota during the fifteenth, sixteenth, and seventeenth centuries. Lower Loup sherds with the typical cloistered rim have been found at the Paint Creek (Great Bend) site near Lindsborg, Kansas; fragments of a large, shell-tempered, flat-bottomed jar undoubtedly made on the Arkansas or Walnut River in central Kansas were recovered from a Lower Loup lodge floor at the Gray site near Schuyler, Nebraska (Udden 1900:fig. 10; Wedel 1959:576).

Plains Village Tradition: Middle Missouri

W. RAYMOND WOOD

A semisedentary, horticultural way of life was introduced into the Northern Plains about A.D. 900–1000 by peoples of the Middle Missouri tradition. This Village way of life was adapted to exploiting, in about equal proportions, large river floodplains for garden crops, and the adjoining upland grasslands for game, especially bison. A distinctive way of life developed there that contrasted sharply with that of the neighboring pedestrian nomads in the northeastern and northwestern Plains. The Village peoples also differed, but to a lesser degree, from contemporary Village peoples in the Central and Southern Plains.

The Village cultures of the Middle Missouri tradition represent a lifeway that developed along the Prairie-Plains border and that was later carried deep into the High Plains along the gallery forest environment provided by the Missouri River and its tributaries in North and South Dakota. This thrust resulted in the development of the northwesternmost effective horticulturists in native North America.

Definition and Age

The Middle Missouri tradition, as defined by Lehmer (1954:140–143, 1971:65–105, 120–128) and redefined by Lehmer and Caldwell (1966:512), consisted of the early horticultural villages of southeastern South Dakota and those along the Missouri River trench as far upstream as west-central North Dakota. The tradition includes at least three additional cultural subunits along the Prairie-Plains border farther east: Mill Creek in northwestern Iowa; Cambria in southwestern Minnesota; and Great Oasis, which was more widespread, found from central South Dakota to northwestern Iowa (D.C. Anderson 1987; Tiffany 1983). This eastern division of the Middle Missouri tradition is described in "Plains Village Tradition: Eastern Periphery and Oneota Tradition," this volume.

There are three variants, or major subdivisions, of the Middle Missouri tradition in the Dakotas, each distinguished by its geographic distribution, age, and cultural content: Initial, A.D. 1000 to 1300; Extended, A.D. 1200 to 1400; and Terminal, A.D. 1400 to 1550 (fig. 1, table 1) (Thiessen 1977).

The Initial variant consists of two geographically separate but closely related divisions of about the same age: the eastern division, in the tall grass prairies of northwestern Iowa and parts of adjoining South Dakota and Minnesota; and the western division, with villages concentrated along the Missouri River trench in south-central South Dakota. A hypothesized late subdivision of the Initial variant in the western division called the Modified Initial Middle Missouri (Lehmer 1971:66) has been identified as components (some of them mixed) of the Initial or Extended variants (A.M. Johnson 1979:157–162). The Extended and Terminal Middle Missouri variants are confined to the Missouri River valley in North and South Dakota.

Cultural Content

Sites of the Middle Missouri tradition are characteristically semipermanent villages, often fortified, of long rectangular houses. These communities were located along major streams near extensive bottomlands suitable for gardening. Villages were usually built on the rims of high terraces, safe from flooding, overlooking the river channel or floodplain. More rarely, they were in defensible positions on steep-sided bluffs or other high points, but in all cases they overlooked the broad valley floors.

The parallel-zoned resources of the river channel, floodplain, terraces, river bluff, and uplands were consequently within easy reach of every community. Villages could therefore have been economically self-sufficient since each had equal access to the same natural resources. There would have been little economic reason to trade between villages, although there was trade with nomadic aliens from outside the valley, as there was in historic times. This trade diffused elements between villagers and nomads but,

Fig. 1. Archeological sites of the Middle Missouri tradition of the Initial, Extended, and Terminal variants, plus one Late Woodland village (4). North Dakota: 1, Grandmother's Lodge (32ME59); 2, Clark's Creek (32ME1); 3, Cross Ranch (32OL14); 4, Menoken (32BL2); 5, Huff (32MO11); 6, Shermer (32EM10); 7, Cadell Homestead (32MO7); 8, Bendish (32MO2); 9, Lower Fort Rice (32MO3); 10, North Cannonball (32MO1); 11, South Cannonball (32SI19); 12, Tony Glas (32EM3); 13, Havens (32EM1); 14, Paul Brave (32SI4); 15, Fire Heart Creek (32SI2). South Dakota: 16, Jake White Bull (39CO6); 17, Helb (39CA208); 18, Smiley-Evans (39BU2); 19, Cheyenne River (39ST1); 20, Fay Tolton (39ST11); 21, Thomas Riggs (39HU1); 22, Dodd (39ST30); 23, Indian Creek (39ST15); 24, Sommers (39ST56); 25, Jiggs Thompson (39LM208); 26, Langdeau (39LM209); 27, Pretty Head (39LM232); 28, Phelps (39CU206); 29, Swanson (39BR16); 30, Johnny (39JK4); 31, King (39LM55).

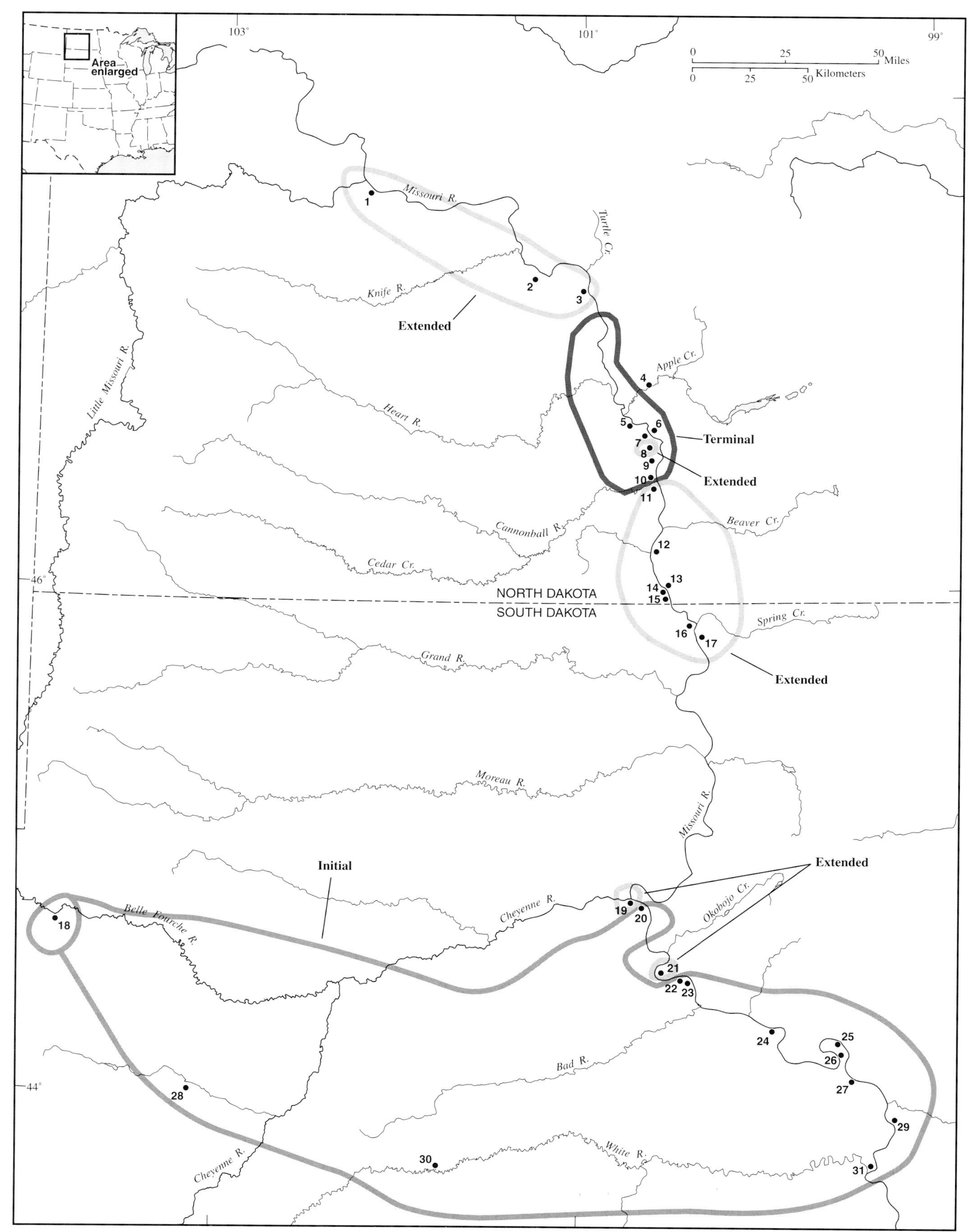
Area enlarged
103°
101°
99°
0 25 50 Miles
0 25 50 Kilometers
Missouri R.
Turtle Cr.
Knife R.
Extended
Apple Cr.
Little Missouri R.
Heart R.
Terminal
Extended
Cannonball R.
Beaver Cr.
Cedar Cr.
46°
NORTH DAKOTA
SOUTH DAKOTA
Spring Cr.
Extended
Grand R.
Moreau R.
Missouri R.
Initial
Extended
Belle Fourche R.
Cheyenne R.
Okobojo Cr.
Bad R.
44°
Cheyenne R.
White R.
1
2
3
4
5
6
7
8
9
10
11
12
13
14
15
16
17
18
19
20
21
22
23
24
25
26
27
28
29
30
31

more important, it intensified the Village way of life and helped stabilize it by concentrating village activities on gardening (Ewers 1954:435).

Subsistence was based on horticulture, and on hunting and gathering, probably in about equal proportions. Corn, beans, squash, and sunflower, known from seeds found preserved in their villages, were doubtless grown in floodplain garden plots, most likely by the women. Tobacco was probably grown by the men, as was the case among historic village groups in the same area (Will and Hyde 1917). These crops suggest an exploitation closely paralleling that of the historic period, but the detailed analysis of plant remains from two Middle Missouri sites (Mitchell and Helb) reveals that a significantly more diverse range of plant resources was utilized in these early sites and that the differences between them and those in the historic sites were as pronounced as the similarities. In these early sites much greater emphasis was placed on the native cultigens sunflowers (*Helianthus* spp.) and marsh elder (*Iva* spp.) as well as on weedy plants and grasses such as goosefoot (*Chenopodium* spp.), knotweeds (*Polygonum* spp.), and wild dock (*Rumex* spp.) (Nickel 1977:55–57).

Most bone refuse from village middens is from bison (Wood 1967:148, 183–186). Lists of other animal species represented by food bone are usually dominated by locally available elk, deer, antelope, domestic dogs, and birds.

Many Missouri valley villages were fortified by means of ditches augmented by vertical post palisades and, on occasion, by palisaded bastions. The plans for and the details of these fortifications vary appreciably in time and space (fig. 2). Dwellings as well as community buildings (or ceremonial lodges) in these towns were rectangular structures about a third again as long as they were wide, with the superstructure supported by a ridgepole along the long axis (fig. 3). Some of them were undoubtedly mantled with earth, like the historic Plains earthlodge, but others may have been covered with less substantial materials, perhaps sheets of bark. A fireplace for cooking and heating was in the house midline near the entry. Deep, undercut and bell-shaped storage pits were common features along house walls and ends (R. Alex 1973; Lehmer, Meston, and Dill 1973; Wood 1967:102–105). The distribution of dwellings within the community sometimes seems random, but in some villages the houses were aligned in irregular rows. The entries to the houses almost invariably were directed to the southwest, especially in the Extended and Terminal variants.

Very little is known of burial customs. There are clues that mound burial may have been practiced at the Mitchell site in South Dakota (Meleen 1938), although there is a strong possibility that these burials were placed in earlier Woodland burial mounds. Along the Missouri River, no cemeteries have been discovered, although occasional human skulls or other skeletal parts, and rare complete or partial burials, occur in some sites. Some of the burial remains may be those of slain enemies. It is therefore probable that platform burial was the preferred way to dispose of the dead. A number of graves accompanied by stone and bone tools (but no pottery) are known along the Missouri River. The grave goods are not distinctive enough to allocate them to any particular variant, although some of them may well include burials of Middle Missouri peoples.

Table 1. Sequence and Subdivisions of the Middle Missouri Tradition, A.D. 1000–1550

Terminal variant	Huff phase	1400–1550
Extended variant	Nailati phase	1200–1400
	Clark's Creek phase	
	Fort Yates phase	
	Thomas Riggs phase	
Initial variant	Anderson phase	1000–1300
	Grand Detour phase	
	Swanson site	

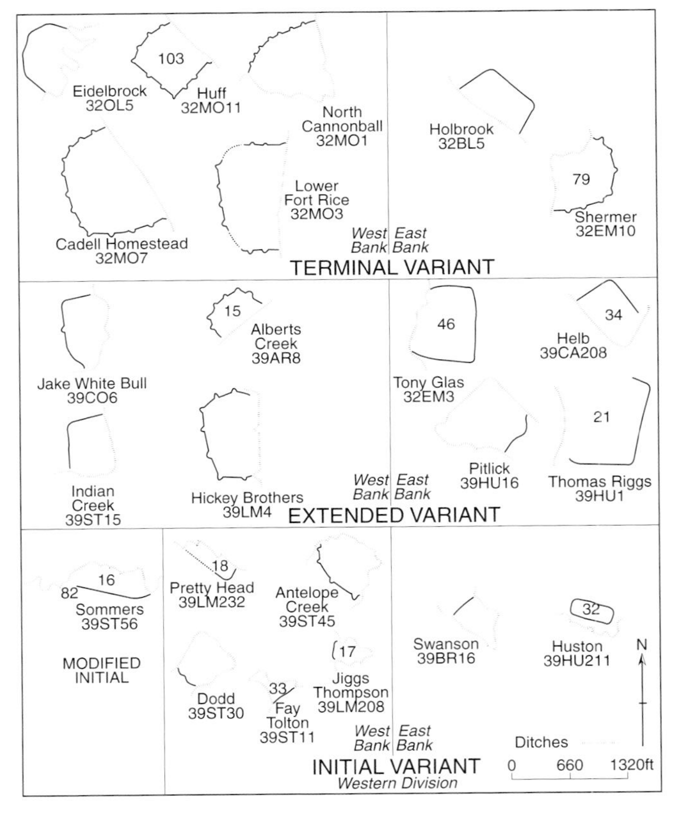

Fig. 2. Fortified Middle Missouri tradition villages. The figure in the center of some sites denotes the probable number of houses in each; all are estimates. East bank and west bank refers to the Missouri River. However, many Initial and Extended variant villages were not fortified. Plans based on 1938 U.S. Dept. of Agriculture aerial photographs. Drawn to the same scale and orientation.

The kinds and proportions of artifacts and utensils reveal that the technology was well adapted to exploit the grassland-deciduous forest biome. Some utensils, particularly pottery, are distinctive to the tradition and its variants. This globular, grit-tempered utilitarian pottery was well made and is common in all sites. Vessels were made by mass modeling local clays and shaped by a paddle and anvil. Shoulders were usually rounded but were occasionally angular. Vessels were sometimes elaborately decorated on the rim and shoulder, but pots more often had relatively simple incised or cord-impressioned decorations on the straight to flared, or recurved (S-shaped or collared) rims (fig. 4).

Triangular chipped-stone side-notched or unnotched projectile points (most of them arrowpoints), plano-convex end scrapers, drills, and bifaces of varying form were common, as were hoes or digging tools made from bison or elk scapulae, scoops fashioned from bison horn cores and frontal bones, perforated rib arrowshaft wrenches, scapula knives, serrated cannon-bone fleshing tools, bone awls, and other bone items. L-shaped elk antler scraper hafts, broad and narrow strip antler bracelets, and mollusk shell beads and other ornaments occur in most sites. Grooved mauls, hammerstones, diorite celts, grooved sandstone shaft abraders, and other groundstone tools were plentiful (fig. 5). Smoking pipes are of such diverse shapes and materials that those in western division sites along the Missouri River, at least, may be imports (Lehmer 1971:81).

Luxury goods imported from great distances occur in small numbers in many sites. They include native copper, apparently from sources near the Great Lakes; whelks (*Busycon* spp.), marginellas (*Marginella* spp.), and olivella from the Gulf or Atlantic coasts; freshwater snails (*Leptoxis* spp.) from rivers in the southeastern United States; steatite from northern Wyoming or Montana; obsidian from the Yellowstone Park area in Wyoming; dentalium from the Pacific coast, and catlinite from southwestern Minnesota or adjoining parts of South Dakota. These goods, especially the Gulf coast items, are plentiful in Initial variant sites in central South Dakota and testify to the wide-ranging trade contacts enjoyed by peoples of the Middle Missouri tradition (Wood 1980).

The degree of homogeneity within the tradition has not been demonstrated. Nevertheless, there is an obvious and striking uniformity and continuity in the tool technologies throughout the tradition, as there seems also to have been in the settlement and subsistence systems. Neither the minor technological innovations within the tradition nor new tools or tool forms introduced from the outside were particularly different from existing ones. Thus, such changes never triggered a major change in pattern or precipitated an appreciable change in structure, in spite of their often high visibility in the archeological record.

Technological change during the tenure of the tradition was minimal, with most of the changes having little obvious adaptive significance. The stability of the material culture inventory is noteworthy in the ceramic and lithic

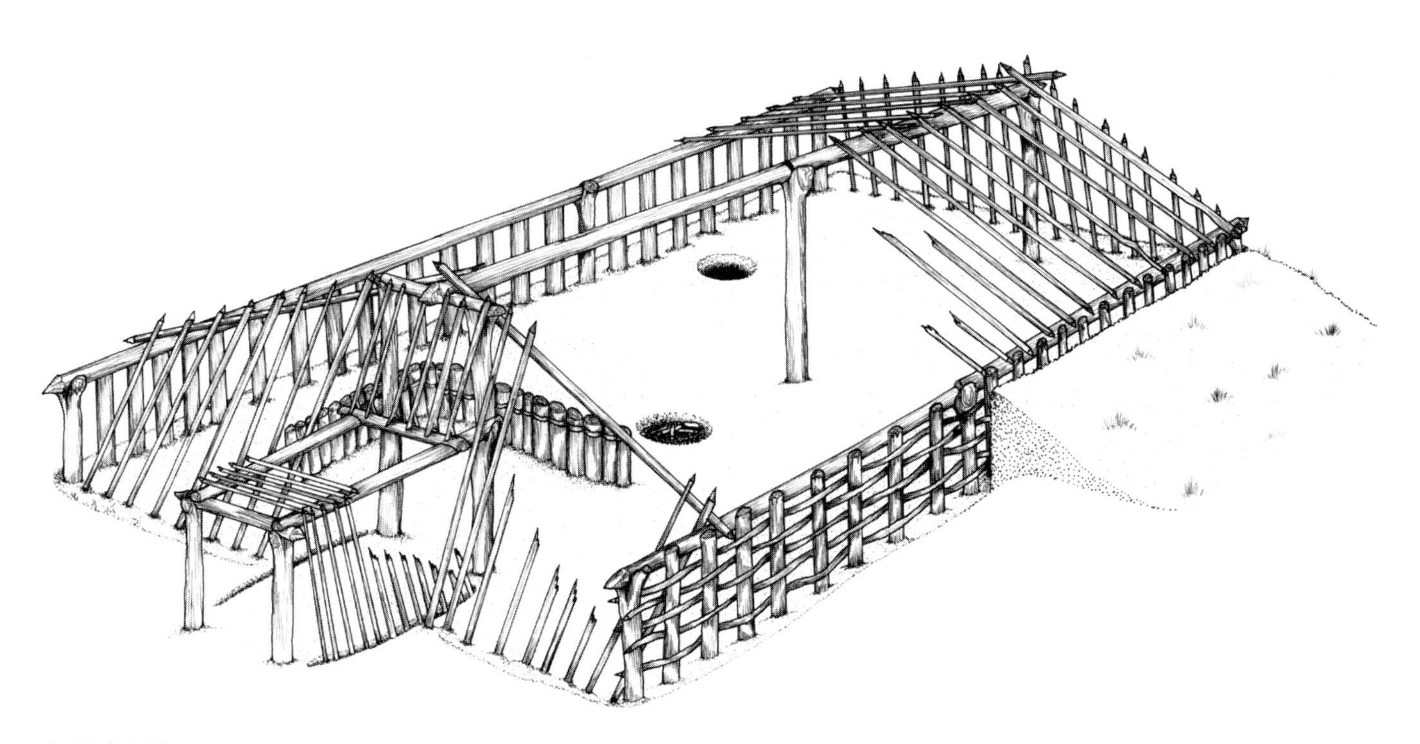

after Wood 1967:fig. 13.

Fig. 3. Speculative reconstruction of a Middle Missouri tradition long-rectangular house at the Terminal variant Huff site, N. Dak. Drawn by Roger Thor Roop.

industries (Calabrese 1972). In sum, the settlement patterns, subsistence systems, and technologies of the tradition were in equilibrium, so there was only minor repatterning and little regional variation in the cultural system during the lifetime of the tradition (Wood 1974).

Origins

No really meaningful assessment of the origins of the Middle Missouri tradition is possible, as no plausible antecedent cultural units for the tradition are known. Radiocarbon dates from Initial variant villages along the Missouri River range from A.D. 1000 to 1300, with tree-ring dates ranging from A.D. 1410 to 1630 (Weakly 1971), although there is widespread suspicion as to the reliability of the later dates. However, there seems to be no doubt that these western division sites were derived from those of the eastern division, although there is little agreement among archeologists concerning the details.

It is surely no accident that the Initial variant makes its appearance on the Prairie-Plains border and High Plains at the time it does. The period A.D. 900 to 1200 has been described as the Neo-Atlantic climatic episode (Bryson and Wendland 1967). This time was a warm period when more moisture was available than previously on the High Plains. The fact that these conditions were conducive to maize horticulture is often, and convincingly, advanced to explain the expansion of horticulturists beyond the Prairie-Plains border (where it is a relatively simple matter to grow corn) deep into the High Plains, where corn growing is a risky pursuit (Lehmer 1970:118). By the time the Neo-Atlantic episode ended, the Missouri River valley was occupied by horticulturists up to the mouth of the Knife River in west-central North Dakota, as far north as it was practical to grow corn even in historic times (Will and Hyde 1917).

Since the beginning dates of the various subunits of the Initial variant are so nearly the same, the tradition may be revealed as a rapid synthesis or recombination of preexisting Late Woodland and, perhaps, early Great Oasis site elements along the Prairie-Plains border in the area where Iowa, Minnesota, and South Dakota meet. Once developed, there must have been a rapid movement west into and across the High Plains to the Missouri valley, first by the Initial variant people, then by bearers of the Extended variant.

Techniques for exploiting the Northern Plains seem to have been much the same as those practiced along the Prairie-Plains border, except for differences engendered by the more abundant timber and bottomland gardening land along the Missouri River. There are, for example, close historic (Lehmer 1963) and prehistoric (Wood 1968) parallels between the hunting patterns of the Prairie-Plains groups and those of historic Plains tribes. Consequently, the village groups who invaded and exploited the valley floor of the Missouri River in the High Plains already possessed a way of life requiring only minor adaptation to this new environment.

left, State Archaeol. Research Center, Rapid City, S. Dak.: 39ST11-21; right, U. of Kans., Mus. of Anthr., Lawrence: 39LM55-1.

Fig. 4. Middle Missouri tradition pottery vessels from the Initial variant, western division. left, Recurved-rim vessel of Foreman ware from the Fay Tolton site, N. Dak. right, Flared-rimmed vessel from the King site, S. Dak. Photographs by Donald J. Lehmer.

Initial and Extended Variants

The history of horticultural peoples in the Missouri valley of North and South Dakota begins with the Initial variant at about A.D. 1000, and with the Extended variant about 1200. These two groups were to remain the pioneer gardeners in the area until the intrusion of peoples of the Initial Coalescent variant about 1400. The Extended variant is *not* believed to be a linear descendant of the Initial variant, as the names imply. Rather, the two variants are distinct cultural and geographic expressions of the Middle Missouri tradition, most likely stemming from common but unknown antecedents. There is, however, a nearly 100-year period between the earliest reliable dates for the Initial and for the Extended variants. Although this raises the possibility that the Extended variant may have developed from the Initial, the two groups coexisted as distinct cultures for the last half of the life span of the Initial variant.

The Initial variant occupied a far greater area than did the Extended or Terminal variants, straddling as it did two physiographic areas. The eastern division is dispersed across much of the Prairie-Plains, along rivers in the tall grass prairies along the western margin of the Prairie Peninsula, whereas the western division is concentrated along the Missouri River trench in the short-grass plains of south-central South Dakota. The midpoints of the two divisions are in fact separated by more than 320 kilometers. The Extended variant, on the other hand, occupied the Missouri River valley upriver from the western division of the Initial variant, in north-central South Dakota and south-central North Dakota (fig. 1).

Several sites are believed to represent camps occupied by historic, as well as by prehistoric Missouri valley Village peoples. The Smiley-Evans site, on the Belle

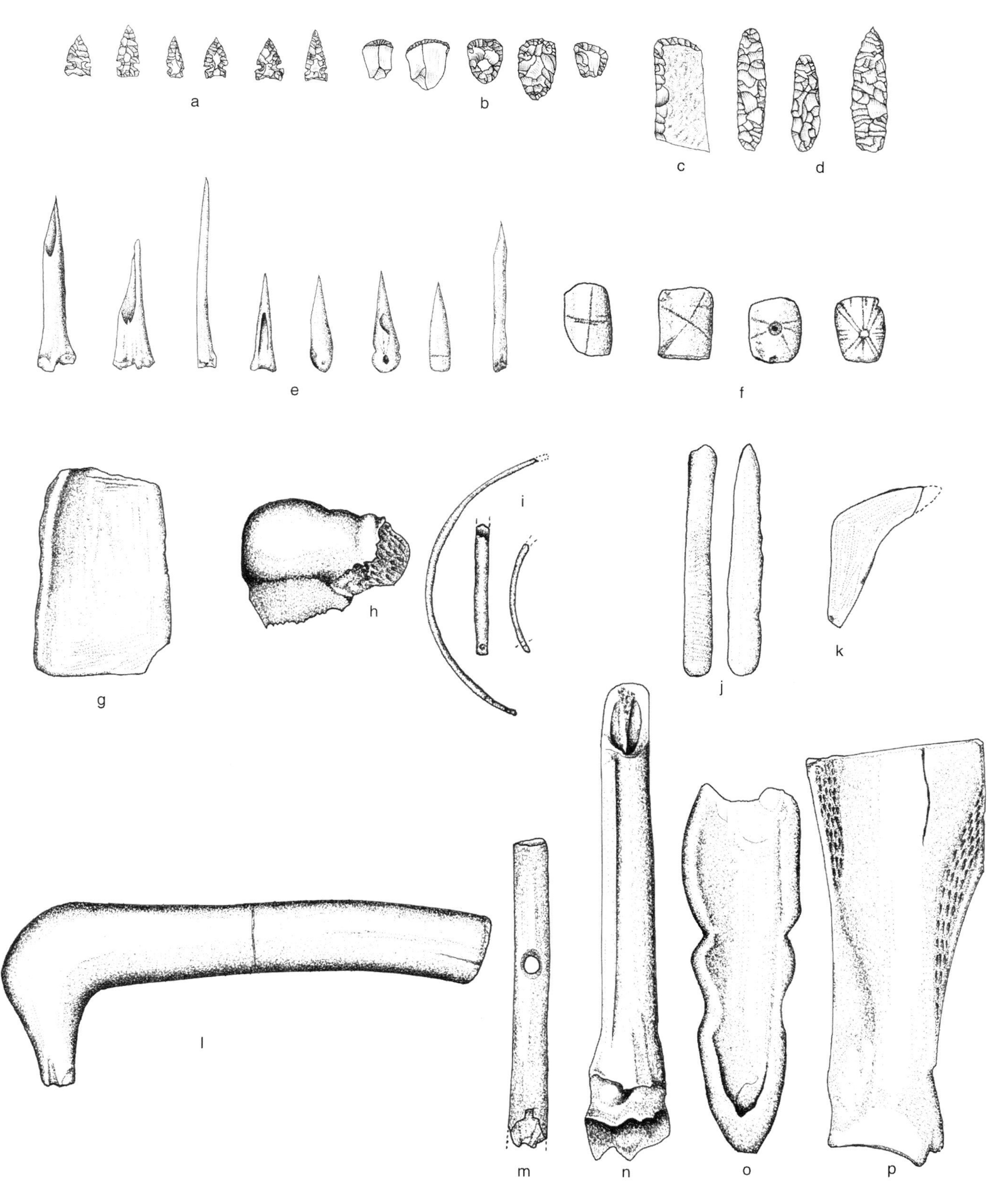

after Wood 1967: figs. 3–11.

Fig. 5. Middle Missouri tradition artifacts from the Terminal variant Huff site, N. Dak. a, Triangular, side-notched arrowpoints with straight and concave bases; b, plano-convex end scrapers; c, plate chalcedony knife; d, narrow, oval, and pointed knives; e, awls of mammal long bones; f, bone embellished game pieces; g, rectangular scapula knife; h, bison humerus abrader; i, narrow bracelets made of antler; j, pottery modeling tools; k, hook-ended scapula knife; l, L-shaped scraper haft; m, embellished arrowshaft wrench; n, cannon bone flesher; o, bison horn core-frontal bone scoop; p, scapula hoe. Drawn by Roger Thor Roop.

Fourche River north of the Black Hills in South Dakota, is one such site. It is fortified by a small ditch and stockade (L.M. Alex 1980:12). There are no dwellings that left tangible remains, but it contains cache or storage pits. The site may be a camp occupied by Initial variant peoples who were hunting bison west of the Missouri River. Certainly, all later village peoples along the Missouri River were hunting in the grasslands west of the river.

Initial Variant, 1000–1300

The Initial variant became established along the Missouri River in south-central South Dakota in the eleventh century (Lehmer 1971:fig. 34). There are about 30 Initial Variant villages set on the terraces overlooking the Missouri River between the mouths of the White and Cheyenne rivers in South Dakota (Lehmer 1971:fig. 38). In the south half of this distribution, villages are on both sides of the Missouri; in the north half, they are confined to the west bank. One-third of the communities are known to have been fortified, usually by a short ditch that isolated the site on a terrace spur, with the other sides protected by steep banks. Fortified sites occupy from less than two to nearly eight acres and contain from about 15 to 50 houses. There is a good deal of variation in fortification systems (fig. 2). The area occupied by unfortified sites is harder to determine, and open villages may have been substantially larger than the fortified ones.

Initial Middle Missouri villages in the Missouri River valley have been assigned to several taxonomic units. The Grand Detour phase is in the Grand Detour (or Big Bend) of the Missouri River about 50 kilometers above the mouth of the White River (Caldwell and Jensen 1969). Two of the sites were fortified, enclosing about 17 structures each. Dwellings were the familiar rectangular structures, set in pits, with entry passages generally directed to the south. There are only minor distinctions between their artifacts and those of the eastern division Initial sites, although all Grand Detour and Anderson phase pottery has cord-roughened bodies (fig. 4). Mill Creek sites farther east often yield high frequencies of smoothed vessels. Shoulders are plain, whereas some eastern division vessels often have complex incised or trailed decorations. By and large, Grand Detour pottery, and that in most other Initial variant sites along the Missouri River, is relatively homogeneous. Nonceramic artifacts are all but indistinguishable from those in other Initial variant villages.

Anderson phase sites are farther north, up the Missouri River from the Grand Detour, near Pierre, South Dakota. They are in the area where Initial sites are confined to the west bank of the river, and in the area of overlap between the Initial and the Extended variants, between the mouth of the Bad and Cheyenne rivers. Dodd and Fay Tolton sites (Lehmer 1954:2–83; Wood 1976) are representative. Some sites, including these two villages, are fortified by a short ditch across the neck of a terrace spur.

One of the earliest (and the easternmost) of the Initial variant sites on the Missouri River seems to be the Swanson site (Hurt 1951), near Chamberlain, South Dakota. The center of occupation by Initial variant peoples after 1100 was in the Grand Detour area (Lehmer 1971:fig. 38), but some groups had moved north along the west bank of the Missouri to the mouth of the Cheyenne River. There, Lehmer suggested, they came into contact with Extended variant peoples moving down from the north. Since many of the Initial and Extended variant sites of the same age (about 1200–1300) in the area between the mouths of the Bad and Cheyenne rivers were fortified, Lehmer (1971:100) posited that they were fortifying their villages against one another.

According to Lehmer (1971), a number of elements were adopted by the Initial variant villagers from Extended variant sources about this time, including the technique of simple stamping on vessel walls using a grooved paddle, and a number of new pottery rim forms. He ascribes this borrowing to the proximity of their villages.

The final disposition of the Initial variant populations of the eastern division is a matter for speculation. None of them appears to be represented in later sites in the Middle Missouri subarea or elsewhere. They disappear from the archeological record, and there is no demonstrable association between them and any historic tribe in the Plains.

Extended Variant, 1200–1400

The Extended variant of the Middle Missouri tradition was localized in two major concentrations; one was along both banks of the Missouri River from just above and below the North Dakota-South Dakota boundary, and along the west bank of the river as far north as the mouth of the Knife River (Lehmer 1971:fig. 39). A second and smaller group was on both sides of the Missouri between the Bad and Cheyenne rivers; there is also a cluster of five sites on the west bank between the Grand and Moreau rivers.

The sites south of the Moreau are called the Thomas Riggs phase (Hurt 1953) and related complexes; those in the northern group downstream from the Heart River are principally of the Fort Yates phase (Lehmer 1966). Those near the mouth of the Knife River are called the Clark's Creek phase and the Nailati phase (Calabrese 1972). Sites in the northern half of the distribution generally date in the last half of the Extended variant.

The Extended variant is somewhat later than most downriver Initial variant sites, but the Extended variant is so ceramically distinctive it cannot represent a simple outgrowth of the Initial variant. On the other hand, its cultural content clearly demonstrates its intimate relationship to the Initial variant, and it probably derives from a common parent stock.

There are about 30 Extended variant villages between the mouths of the Bad and Cheyenne rivers. The majority of Extended variant sites are open, or unfortified. The fortified Extended variant sites (most of them of the Thomas Riggs phase) are principally in the overlap zone with the Initial variant. There are, however, three fortified Extended villages near the North Dakota-South Dakota boundary: Tony Glas (Howard 1962a), Jake White Bull, and Helb. Although Lehmer (1971:122) ascribed all of them to the Terminal variant because they were fortified, they contain ceramic and stone tool inventories characteristic of the Extended variant (Falk and Calabrese 1973).

Extended variant communities are usually small, and villages of more than about 20 houses are rare. One consistent element in community patterning is the orientation of dwellings with entries to the southwest, and the presence of a large ceremonial or community structure facing an open area or plaza (Wood 1967:156). Houses are usually set in irregular rows or arcs. Sometimes they appear to be randomly arranged, but in other instances they are in straight lines, the more regular arrangements often enclosed by defensive ditches (fig. 6). Houses are invariably rectangular structures built over pits of varying depth, and they correspond closely in plan with those of Initial variant dwellings.

Smithsonian, Handbook of North Amer. Ind. Photograph Coll.

Fig. 6. Helb site, S. Dak., a fortified Extended Middle Missouri variant village. The view is to the south; the entire site has since slumped into Lake Oahe because of wave action. Photograph by Donald J. Lehmer, 1966.

The homogeneity among various subunits of the Extended variant is obvious, but there is local variation, especially in community planning, architecture, and ceramics. Pottery is particularly homogeneous, with only minor elements and frequencies characterizing local groups. Three subunits of the variant (Thomas Riggs, Fort Yates, and Nailati phases) can be used to synopsize the geographic diversity of the variant.

The fortified sites of the Thomas Riggs phase, in the overlap zone with the Initial variant, are well illustrated by the type site (Hurt 1953). This bluff-top site, defended by a rectilinear ditch, contained about 21 rectangular houses set over shallow pits, and placed in a rough arc around a plaza southwest of the village. Pottery was stamped with a grooved paddle or was smoothed. Vessels had distinctive designs incised on the shoulder, and incised or cord-impressed patterns embellished the outflaring or collared rims. Except for pottery, material culture was much the same as in the Initial variant sites. In spite of geographic overlap and contemporaneity with the Initial variant, there is little evidence of Initial variant goods in Thomas Riggs sites, although the reverse seems to be true. The Initial response to contact between Extended and Initial communities seems to have been hostility and mutual defensive works; it was not until later that contacts led to material exchange.

Villages of the Fort Yates phase, near the North Dakota-South Dakota border, include the Paul Brave (Wood and Woolworth 1964) and Fire Heart Creek (Lehmer 1966) sites. Communities were generally small and unfortified, although at least one of them, Havens (Sperry 1968), had as many as 56 houses. The principal distinction between the Thomas Riggs phase and the Fort Yates phase is their geographic separation. Furthermore, Fort Yates sites are not visibly fortified, and village plazas, if present, are not obvious community features. Dates for both Thomas Riggs and Fort Yates are about the same, and village architecture approaches identity.

The northernmost well described subunit of the Extended variant is the Nailati phase (Calabrese 1972), defined at the Cross Ranch site. Radiocarbon dates rage from 1300 to 1440; two of the three dates from the related Bagnell site, a few miles upstream, are also in the mid-1400s (Lehmer, Meston, and Dill 1973). The phase is confined to the west bank of the Missouri River near and just below the mouth of the Knife River. Houses at Cross Ranch are set in a row, facing southwest. They differ from other Middle Missouri tradition dwellings in that they were not built over pits but were constructed on or just below the ground surface.

Other differences that set this phase apart from other Extended variant communities are largely found in the pottery. Cross Ranch vessels are simple-stamped and smoothed, like other Extended variant assemblages, but many of them were check-stamped. This technique of finishing vessel surfaces is lacking in Initial variant sites, and it occurs only rarely in Extended (and Terminal) villages. Only in the Nailati phase (and in other sites in its immediate vicinity) is check-stamping a major vessel-shaping technique (Calabrese 1972; Neuman 1963).

A small Extended variant site, represented by a single excavated house, was near the mouth of the Little Missouri River, 113 kilometers upstream from the remainder of the Extended villages. The locale was revered by the Mandan, Hidatsa, and Crow as the home of a supernatural being (Woolworth 1956:4). The house site was preserved due to its associations; traces of other houses may have been obliterated by plowing. The few artifacts found in the house, typical Extended variant forms, were not sufficiently distinctive to assign the site to one of the named subunits of the variant.

In sum, the Extended variant consisted of small, dispersed, and relatively isolated communities, usually open in the north and generally fortified in the south. Only a few of the known 30 Extended villages would have been occupied at a given time during the 200 years the variant persisted. Major evidence for interaction between them and other villagers is found in the Bad-Cheyenne river region, where the fortified Thomas Riggs communities must have been in conflict with Initial variant populations. What happened to all these populations is uncertain, but in the north, the Extended variant sites were the immediate predecessors of the Terminal variant.

Terminal Variant, 1400–1550

The Terminal variant had the shortest temporal span of the Middle Missouri variants and was contained in the smallest area. After 1550, the peoples of the Terminal variant merged into the Postcontact Coalescent variant as the protohistoric and historic Mandan and Hidatsa.

Dramatic social adaptations mark the history of the Terminal variant from first to last. The major changes are related to the appearance, in central South Dakota, of the Extended Coalescent variant. These alien villagers forced the withdrawal of Extended variant populations from the south, and their concentration into large, fortified sites in a small area between the mouths of the Heart and Cannonball rivers (fig. 1). There were concomitant, but minor, changes in artifact inventories, but the dramatic contraction in territory and the adoption of life in large fortified communities are the principal hallmarks of the Terminal variant. The known Terminal sites average more than 100 houses each. Their enemies not only precipitated major changes in territory and community patterning but also were the source for a host of new, albeit minor, ceramic innovations, as well as of a new house type, the four-post circular earthlodge.

One of the most striking differences between the Extended and Terminal variants is the contraction of the area occupied. The Terminal variant consists of about seven villages, scattered along both banks of the Missouri from the mouth of the Cannonball River to a point midway between the Heart and Knife rivers. The Extended variant occupied about 360 kilometers of the Missouri River valley; the Terminal variant, only about 80 kilometers. At the same time, the average size of the Terminal site was more than four times greater than that of the Extended variant communities. The Shermer (Sperry 1968a) and Huff (Wood 1967) sites, for example, had about 80 to 100 dwellings, and there are two other fortified villages (Cadell Homestead and Lower Fort Rice) with enclosed areas twice that of Huff or Shermer (fig. 2).

The Terminal variant, then, is a consequence of the telescoping of the small, scattered Extended variant villages into large, compact redoubts, fortified by rectilinear or curvilinear ditches and palisades, usually reinforced also by regularly set bastions. Shermer and Huff sites (figs. 7–8) are similar enough in content to belong to the same phase.

The changes in community patterning from Extended to Terminal times must have led to marked changes in the social system. An elaborate ceremonial structure, clan organization, and an age-graded society system would not have been so necessary in the Extended variant villages as they were in Terminal ones, and among the historic Mandan (Bruner 1961). The telescoping of villages would also have necessitated changes in political organization, as it brought together leaders from the numerous small and undoubtedly autonomous Extended villages into larger social units.

The continuity in domestic architecture, and in material culture in general, demonstrates that the Terminal variant is a direct outgrowth of the Extended variant. Houses, for example, differ in only minor details of post placement; so the floor plans in both variants require essentially the same superstructure. The rectangular house tradition was shortly to disappear, for in the Postcontact Coalescent sites it was displaced by circular earthlodges. This displacement began during Terminal variant times, for one of the houses at Huff was a subcircular structure supported by four center posts set around the central hearth (fig. 9). This house, so alien to the Middle Missouri tradition, is clearly derived from Coalescent sources downriver (Wood 1967:51–52, 135–136).

The well-executed defensive works in the Terminal variant denote formidable antagonists. There seems little

State Histl. Soc. of N. Dak., Bismarck.

Fig. 7. Aerial photograph of the Terminal Middle Missouri variant Shermer site, N. Dak., during the 1965 excavation. The view is to the northwest. Photograph by James E. Sperry.

Fig. 8. Aerial photograph of the Terminal variant Huff site, N. Dak., during the 1960 excavation. The large structure near the site center faces a plaza. Photograph by James P. Grimstad.

doubt that these antagonists were peoples of the Extended Coalescent variant and that there was a great deal of cultural exchange between them, as evidenced by the adoption of the circular earthlodge, in addition to hostile contacts.

The End of the Tradition

Changes in Terminal variant community patterning are not matched by very extensive changes in the material content of villages. Artifact inventories were modified only slightly by contacts between Terminal variant and Extended Coalescent people. Vessel manufacturing practices and form, for instance, were unchanged, although the high S-rim and braced rims introduced into the Terminal variant became more common; angular S-rims disappeared; and there were minor changes in the mode and frequencies of design elements on pottery rims and shoulders.

Some artifacts simply disappeared from the archeological record: stone axes, picks made from bison radii with socketed proximal ends, hooked bone knives, scapula sickles, and the shell thunderbird silhouettes of the Middle Missouri tradition (Lehmer 1971:162).

In spite of these changes—all rather unimportant ones in terms of the overall cultural inventory—the continuity between the Terminal variant villages and the late prehistoric to early protohistoric Mandan and Hidatsa villages is clear. There is an unbroken sequence of sites, beginning with the Extended variant villages in the northern Missouri valley about 1200, continuing through the Terminal variant redoubts centering on the Heart River, to the historic Mandan and Hidatsa villages in the same area.

The fact the villages of these two tribes were all but indistinguishable in the historic period means that the groups—traditions of separate histories and differences in

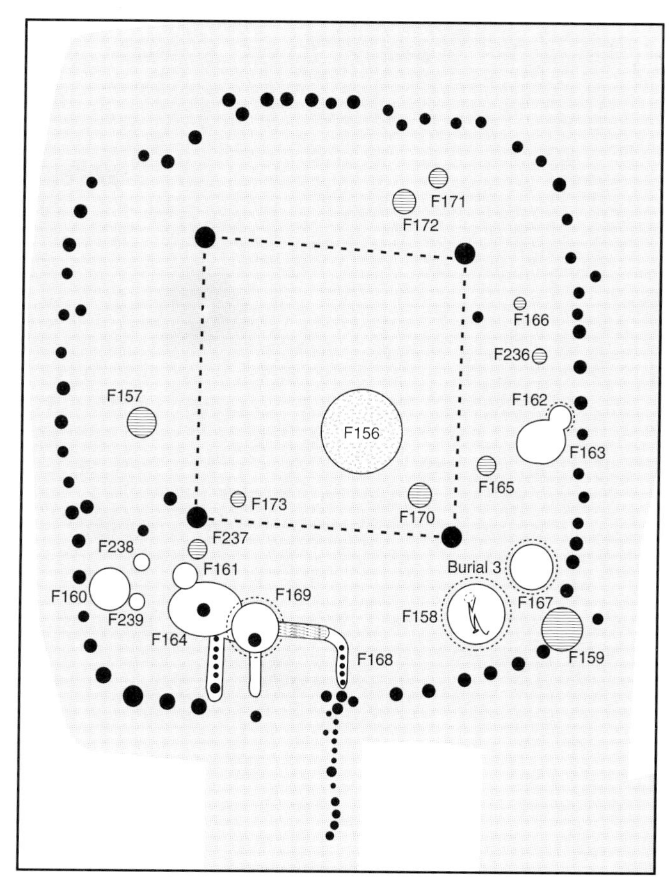

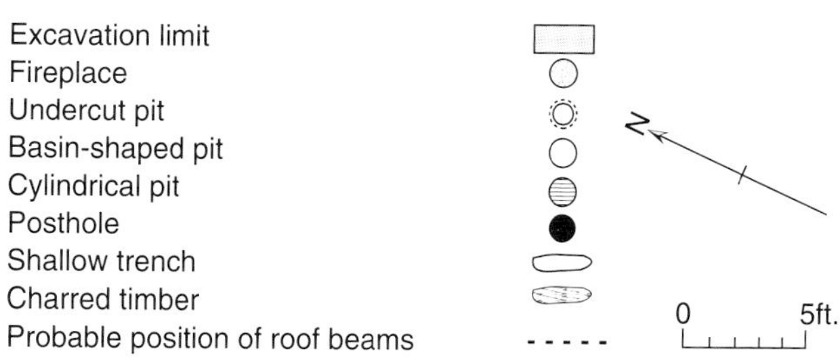

after Wood 1967: map 14.

Fig. 9. House 12 at the Terminal variant Huff site. Such 4-post houses were introduced into the Terminal variant, quickly displacing the older long-rectangular form. Drawn by Roger Thor Roop.

language to the contrary—are very closely related (Wood 1986:13). Distinguishing their individual predecessors in the Middle Missouri tradition has not been accomplished.

The fate of other segments of the Middle Missouri tradition is vague. There are no plausible historic representatives for any of the Initial variant populations that lived between central South Dakota and northwestern Iowa, despite the fact they persisted there well into the sixteenth and, perhaps, even the seventeenth centuries. Their ceramic industry was so distinctive that, had they joined any of the Extended variant populations in the northern part of the Middle Missouri subarea, the merger should be obvious in ceramic inventories. It is not.

Plains Village Tradition: Coalescent

RICHARD A. KRAUSE

The Coalescent tradition represents one adaptation of village-dwelling farmers to the Missouri River valley in South Dakota. In this region, subsistence-settlement strategies required mediation of the tension between the centripetal pull of a linear distribution of tillable soils and the centrifugal force of dispersed reserves of huntable and harvestable natural foods. First defined by Lehmer (1954), the Postcontact variant of the Coalescent tradition is identified as being of mixed Central Plains and Middle Missouri tradition ancestry (Wood 1969:147; Zimmerman 1985:103–104). Prehistorically, the Coalescent is divided into the Initial, about A.D. 1300–1600 (Ahler et al. 1994), and the Extended, about 1450–1650 (C. Johnson 1998), variants (Lehmer 1971:111–120).

Middle Missouri specialists have considered the peoples of the Coalescent tradition's Initial variant to have been intruders, immigrants from the Central Plains who brought with them social, political, and economic practices shaped by centuries of contact with the peoples and natural resources of their heartland. To place this claim in perspective requires a brief examination of the general patterning discernable in the emergence and dispersal of a plains farming lifeway. Peoples identified as bearers of the Central Plains tradition practiced a mixed hunting and farming economy; built isolated homesteads and small hamlets composed of square earthlodges; cultivated maize, beans, squash, gourds, sunflowers, and tobacco; and hunted buffalo, deer, antelope, and smaller, more solitary game animals. They appeared in the central and eastern portions of the Plains by A.D. 900. At about the same time a farming folk identified as carriers of the Initial variant of the Middle Missouri tradition, who lived in moat- and palisade-protected villages composed of long rectangular houses, settled the Missouri River valley and immediate environs in northern Iowa and southern South Dakota (Wedel 1961:164–209; Zimmerman 1985:73–101).

The next millennium was marked by shifts in both population density and distribution. According to Baerreis and Bryson (1965a) at about A.D. 1250 the favorable Neo-Atlantic period of abundant summer rainfall was interrupted by an abrupt change in atmospheric circulation, the introduction of greater amounts of cool dry air, lowered temperatures, and decreased precipitation. Several centuries of modified climatic conditions apparently stimulated: (1) an abandonment of horticultural settlements in western Kansas and Nebraska (Wedel 1961:183); (2) a southwest to northeast shift in the center of population density in the middle reaches of the Central Plains; (3) a northward shift in the center of population density along the eastern margin of the Great Plains and the emergence of small villages along the Missouri River valley in northeast Nebraska (Blakeslee 1978a:139–141); and (4) a northward movement of South Dakota's long rectangular house peoples, at this point identified as representatives of the Extended variant of the Middle Missouri tradition, a movement that left the southern portions of the South Dakota segment of the Missouri River open to colonization (Caldwell 1966a:24; Lehmer 1971:105–107).

It seems, then, that immediately prior to and perhaps during the early years of a Central Plains–derived immigrant population's penetration of the Middle Missouri region, the river bottoms and terrace lands from the Big Bend south to the Nebraska line were abandoned or at least sparsely settled by indigenous long rectangular house peoples of the Extended variant of the Middle Missouri tradition (Caldwell 1966a:24). During the 1400s, the climate seems to have reverted in part to a more favorable character of Neo-Atlantic times, and if Caldwell (1966a:24) and Lehmer (1971:124–126) are correct, the more favorable climatic conditions both intensified a previously established pattern of immigration from the Central Plains and supported attempts on the part of long rectangular house peoples to reclaim their hold on the region. Thus, it is argued, the two groups were brought into contact and conflict. The Crow Creek massacre site, South Dakota, where at least 500 Initial Coalescent villagers were killed and mutilated, bears stark testimony to the seriousness of the military threat (Zimmerman 1985:108).

Initial Coalescent

Initial Coalescent sites were decidedly restricted in space and with one possible exception in time. Most of them lay on flat lofty terrace tops or on bluffs along the Missouri River, six on the west and four on the east bank between the mouth of the White River and the Missouri–Bad River junction, and one to the south along Ponca Creek in Nebraska (fig. 1). These sites, once marked by surface depressions and the detritus of daily life, seem to have been reasonably homogeneous. They were all once composed of subrectangular and oval timber-framed, pole, grass, and earth-covered dwellings, scattered within an

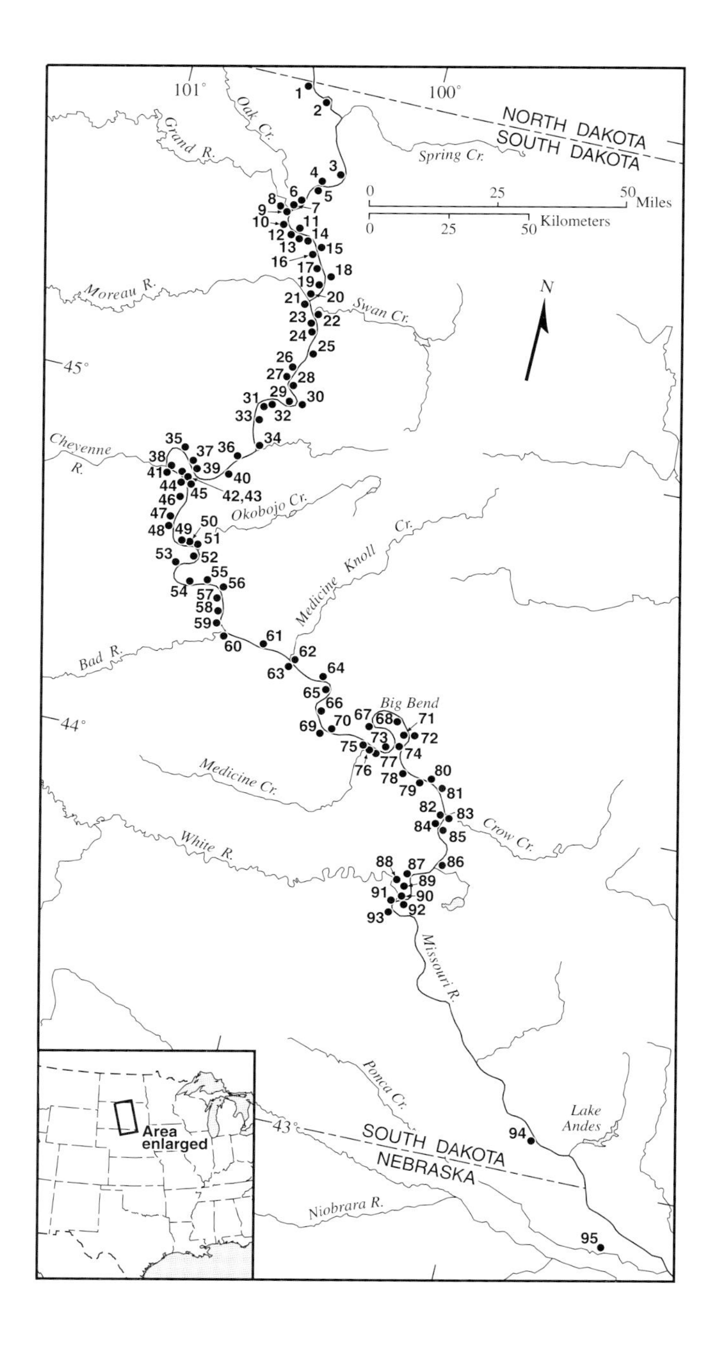

Fig. 1. Archeological sites of the Coalescent Tradition. South Dakota: 1, Demery (39CO1); 2, Ft. Manuel Lisa (39CO5); 3, 39CO8; 4, Leavenworth (39CO9); 5, Anton Rygh (39CA4); 6, Norvold I (39CO31) and 39CO204; 7, Norvold Village (39CO7, 39CO10 and 39CO205); 8, Wilbur's (39CO35); 9, Lower Grand (Davis) (39CO14); 10, Travis (39CO213); 11. Spiry (39WW10); 12, Bells Man (39CO17); 13, 39CO18; 14, Potts (39CO19) and 39CO202; 15, Lake Evarts (39WW8) and Walth Bay (39WW204); 16, Swift Bird (39DW233), Molstad (39DW234) and 39DW236; 17, 39DW228; 18, Bauman's (39WW201) and Payne (39WW302); 19, 39DW302; 19, 39DW218 and 39DW224; 20, Moreau River Village (39DW1) and 39DW254; 21, 39DW217; 22, Swan Creek (39WW7) and 39WW301; 23, 39DW13, 39DW18 and 39DW211; 24, 39DW14, 39DW209 and 39DW210; 25, Latin Draw (39PO201); 26, 39DW15, 39DW16 and 39DW17; 27, Tricia Village (39DW3) and 39DW19; 28, Hosterman (39PO7) and Frank Risen I (39PO8); 29, Cheyenne Agency Village (39DW7); 30, 39PO9 and Forest City Village (39PO11); 31, Gettysburg (39PO209); 32, 39PO14; 33, 39PO13; 34, Moorman (39SL31); 35, 39AR7; 36, 39AR203; 37, No Heart Creek (39AR2) and 39AR4; 38, 39SL8, 39SL24, 39SL30, 39SL36 and 39SL202; 39, Pearman Village (39AR5); 40, Fairbanks (39SL2); 41, Cheyenne River (39ST1) and Meyer (39ST10); 42, 39SL18, 39SL20, 39SL21, 39SL22 and 39SL23; 43, 39SL12, Little Bend (39SL13), 39SL14, 39SL15, 39SL16, 39SL17, 39SL34, 39SL55 and 39SL56; 44, Sand Creek (39ST2), Black Widow (39ST3), 39ST7, Gillette Village (39ST23) and 39ST45; 45, 39SL51; 46, H. P. Thomas (39ST12), 30ST21, Ft. Bennet (39ST26), Lounsbury (39ST42), Hoyt #3 (39ST44) and Ramsey (39ST236); 47, Deep Creek Village (39ST13); 48, Snake Creek (39ST43); 49, Ft. Sully (39SL4) and 39SL40; 50, 39SL26 and 39SL37; 51, Sully School (39SL7), 39SL9, 39SL10 and C. B. Smith (39SL29); 52, 39ST39; 53, 39ST40; 54, Sorenson (39HU28), 39HU44, 39HU46 and 39HU47; 55, Robinson (39HU15), 39HU23, 39HU39 and 39HU45; 56, 39HU29; 57, Leavitt (39ST215); 58, Breeden (39ST16); 59, 39ST18; 60, 39ST49; 61, Arzberger (39HU6) and McClure Ranch (39HU7); 62, Medicine Knoll (39HU202), Howes (39HU203) and Mary Day Sun (39HU208); 63, Buffalo Calf (39ST218), Lame Deer (39ST219), Prairie Owl (39ST222), Ketchen (39ST223) and Cattle Oiler (39ST224); 64, Bowman/East (39HU63), Bowman/West (39HU204), DeGrey (39HU205), Baker-Rhode (39HU206), McKay Ranch (39HU210) and Whistling Elk (39HU242); 65, LaRoche (39ST9) and 39ST231; 66, Three Sisters (39HU219); 67, Gregg (39HU222), Fry (39HU223) and Denny (39HU224); 68, Burnt Prairie (39LM207); 69, 39LM206; 70, Granny Two Hearts (39HU61) and Standing Bull (39HU214); 71, 39LM4 and Black Partizan (39LM218); 72, Aiken (39BF215); 73, Huston Ranch (39HU211); 74, Terrace II (39LM216), 39LM217 and Crazy Bull II (30LM219); 75, Stricker (39LM1), 39LM242 and 39LM243; 76, Medicine Creek (39LM2) and Iron Nation (39LM222); 77, Cable (39LM224); 78, Useful Heart (39LM6); 79, 39LM238; 80, Brother-of-All Spring (39BF205), Lillian-all-Arounds (39BF206) and Farm School (39BF220); 81, Talking Crow (39BF3); 82, Carpenter (39LM25), 39LM82 and 39LM84; 83, Crow Creek (39BF4 and 39BF11); 84, 39LM69 and 39LM70; 85, Brule Flat Village (39BR10); 86, American Crow Creek (39BR11); 87, Bice (39LM31), 39LM60, 39LM85, 39LM86 and 39LM204; 88, Meander (39LM201); 89, 39LM80; 90, Clarkstown (39LM47); 91, Deerfly (39LM39), 39LM64 and 39LM65; 92, Stambaugh (39BR201); 93, Spain (39LM301); 94, Scalp Creek (39GR1). Nebraska: 95, 25BD1.

easily defended area or one bounded by substantial fortifications of complex design (Lehmer 1971:111). Then, too, most of them seem to have been occupied in the relatively brief interval between the fourteenth and sixteenth centuries A.D. Three of the five tested components (the Wolfe Creek component of the Crow Creek site, component B at the Black Partizan site, and the single component Arzberger site), have been assigned calendar dates, either by carbon-14 determinations or through dendrochronological studies. Although there are disturbing discrepancies between carbon-14 and tree-ring determinations from the same components, only two of the 17 calendar assignments fall beyond the A.D. 1400 to 1500 time span posited by Lehmer (1971:114). Further, both the excluded dates can be accommodated by positing a 1300 to 1500 time span (Weakly 1971:31) for the bulk of the Initial variant population. Nevertheless, only one of seven radiometric determinations on charcoal from the Whistling Elk site falls within this range. The Whistling Elk radiocarbon sequence spans the years from the early tenth to the early fourteenth century with the majority of the determinations preceding 1200 (Falk 1984:1A, 45–46). Whistling Elk may, therefore, represent an early and, to judge by the excavated detritus, unsuccessful attempt to colonize the region (Falk 1984:1A, 45–46; Zimmerman 1985:108).

In community plan, Initial Coalescent settlements resembled Central Plains villages, but their fortification systems closely approximated those designed by the long rectangular house people of the Extended variant of the Middle Missouri tradition. At the Arzberger site near Pierre, for instance, fortifications of Middle Missouri tradition style were combined with earthlodges and a village plan reminiscent of late Central Plains tradition complexes. The fortifications formed an ellipse and consisted of a palisade-backed ditch 2.5 kilometers long. The wooden wall and dry ditch enclosed 17.6 hectares and included 24 raised earthen bastions set at enfilade (Spaulding 1956). The 44 house depressions at Arzberger appear to have been strung out along the inner edge of the palisade, but since which of these marked fully contemporaneous dwellings is not known, this tendency may be more apparent than real. Sites resembling Arzberger were also to be found to the south. The Wolfe Creek component at the Crow Creek site (Kivett 1960), the early component of the Talking Crow site (C.S. Smith 1977:152–153), component B at the Black Partizan site (figs. 2–3) (Caldwell 1966), and the Lynch site near the junction of Ponca and Whiskey Creeks in northeastern Nebraska are the best known. All but Lynch were accompanied by carefully engineered defensive perimeters composed of bastions, palisades, and dry moats (Lehmer 1971:113). At Black Partizan, the ditch and palisade system did not extend along the steep terrace edge to the east of the settlement, but this segment of the village defenses may have been destroyed by later erosion (Caldwell 1966). The less than cohesive placement of lodges and their low average density per palisade-enclosed space (about one lodge per half-hectare, have led some to argue that the fortifications were an ad hoc response to warfare that followed the construction of scattered households in areas of high military risk (Lehmer 1971:125; Zimmerman 1985:106–107). Others have viewed this situation as a conscious attempt to retain the basic elements of a Central Plains community in the face of an unfamiliar and potentially hostile social environment (Spaulding 1956:68). Whatever the case, all Initial Coalescent villages were basically the same in size, plan, and, if palisaded, in palisade design.

If the excavated remains at the Arzberger, Black Partizan, Talking Crow, and Lynch sites are good examples, the dwellings within Initial Coalescent villages were substantial structures of wood, grass, and dirt (fig. 4). They must have resembled boxlike or dome-shaped mounds of earth with rectangular tunnellike entrance passages projecting from one side. Both subrectangular and oval or roughly circular floor plans are characteristic. To construct a lodge, sod was removed to form a shallow subrectangular or oval floor. There is no evidence that this floor was plastered. To build the superstructure, four (or sometimes more) roof support posts were set at the corners of a

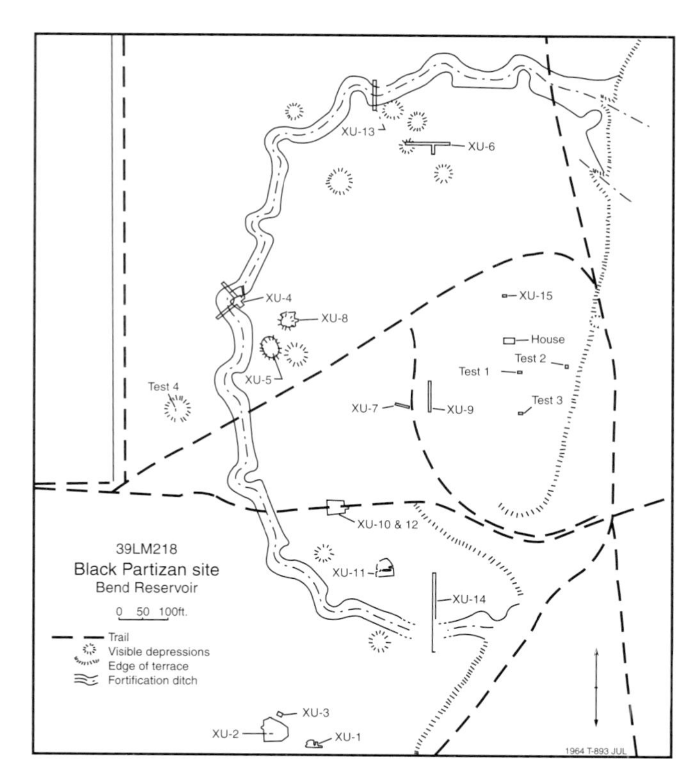

after Caldwell 1966:fig.2.

Fig. 2. Plan map of the Black Partizan site, S. Dak., a typical Initial Coalescent village. Drawn by Roger Thor Roop.

rough square near the center of the lodge floor. These central supports presumably were forked at the top to hold a square of timbers aloft. A circular or subrectangular series (depending upon floor shape) of peripheral roof-wall supports was set about the edge of the lodge basin also presumably used to hold timbers aloft. The entryway frame was built by placing two parallel series of upright posts in the ground at right angles to and projecting outward from the circle or subrectangle of peripheral wall posts. Evidently these uprights were then connected at the top with cross-spars to form a rectangular framework. Details of roof and wall construction may be conjectured by comparison with historic earthlodges. Initial and Extended Coalescent lodges were often provided with one or more cylindrical, undercut, or bell-shaped subfloor storage pits. These too have been traditionally interpreted by analogy with their historically documented counterparts.

Initial Coalescent houses show a basic floor plan generally similar to the Central Plains tradition earthlodges—a centrally located hearth surrounded by a square of centrally located roof support posts—and these in turn surrounded by an outer series of peripheral roof-wall support posts in a subrectangular or circular configuration. Two parallel rows of posts projecting from one side framed the entryways of both Central Plains and Initial Coalescent houses. To be sure, most Central Plains tradition house

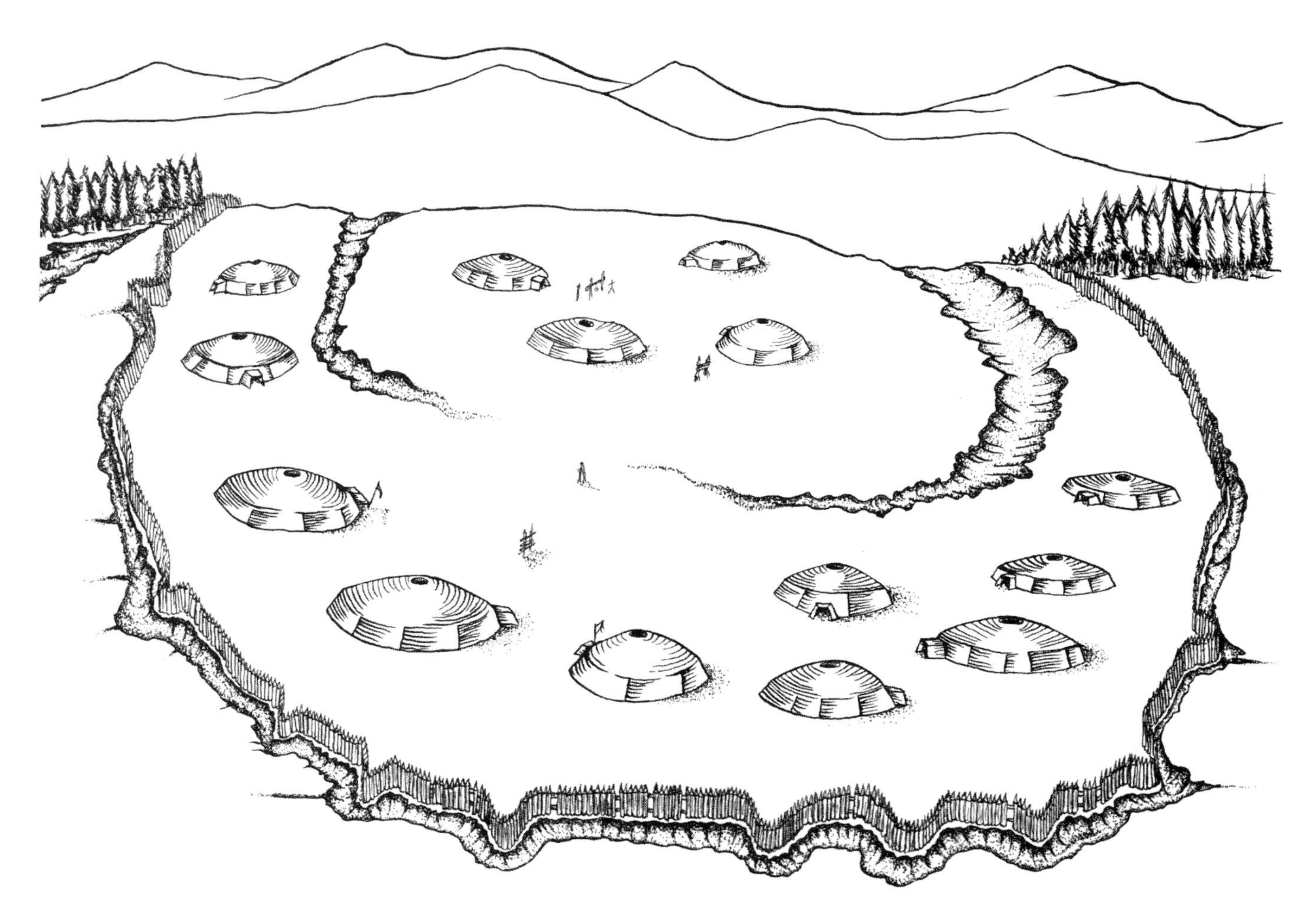

Fig. 3. Artist's reconstruction of Initial Coalescent village at the Black Partizan site, S. Dak. Drawn by Roger Thor Roop.

floors were square or rectangular, but nearly circular houses have been reported by Champe (1936:258) and Wedel (1935:150). Hence, at least some Initial Coalescent structures fall within the accepted range of Central Plains tradition types. Then too, lodges of the subsequent Extended Coalescent variant in both the Dakotas and Nebraska were typically circular in floor plan, leading some to suggest that Initial Coalescent forms were ancestral to both (Spaulding 1956:84; Wedel 1961:183).

The relatively permanent Initial Coalescent settlement was accompanied by a rich and varied assemblage of bone and stone tools. Among them were many that remained virtually unchanged in form or presumably in use despite rather marked shifts in other aspects of Northern Plains village life. These basic forms included: (1) the main gardening and digging tools—bison scapula hoes and frontal-bone diggers; (2) hunting tools and tools for manufacturing hunting implements—notched and unnotched triangular projectile points, drills with narrow bits and broad (or expanding) bases, drills with a narrow bit chipped from an otherwise unmodified flake, groundstone arrowshaft smoothers, and perforated bison-rib arrowshaft wrenches; and (3) tools for skin working and food preparation—snubnose scrapers, flake scrapers, irregular flakes with chipped cutting edges, cleaver-shaped bison scapula knives, bone awls of split mammal rib, bone awls cut from the proximal or distal ends of deer or antelope metapodials, and bone and horn punches fashioned from the tips of antelope horns or tines of deer antler. Multipurpose or composite tools included leaf-shaped and triangular knives of various sizes (some of plate chalcedony), diamond-shaped beveled edge knives, bison rib bone spatulas, knife handles of bison rib or vertebral spine, and pecked and ground three-quarter and full grooved stone mauls. Carved stone tobacco pipes and bone fishhooks complete the list of representative bone and stone artifacts (Lehmer 1971:111–130).

The basic bone and stone tool technologies of the Middle Missouri village-dwelling peoples are remarkably uniform. Coalescent tradition chipped-stone tools are distinctive in that they were made of light-colored varieties of chalcedony, jasper, chert, quartzite, and quartz, whereas Knife River flint predominated in the Middle Missouri tradition (Lehmer 1971:119).

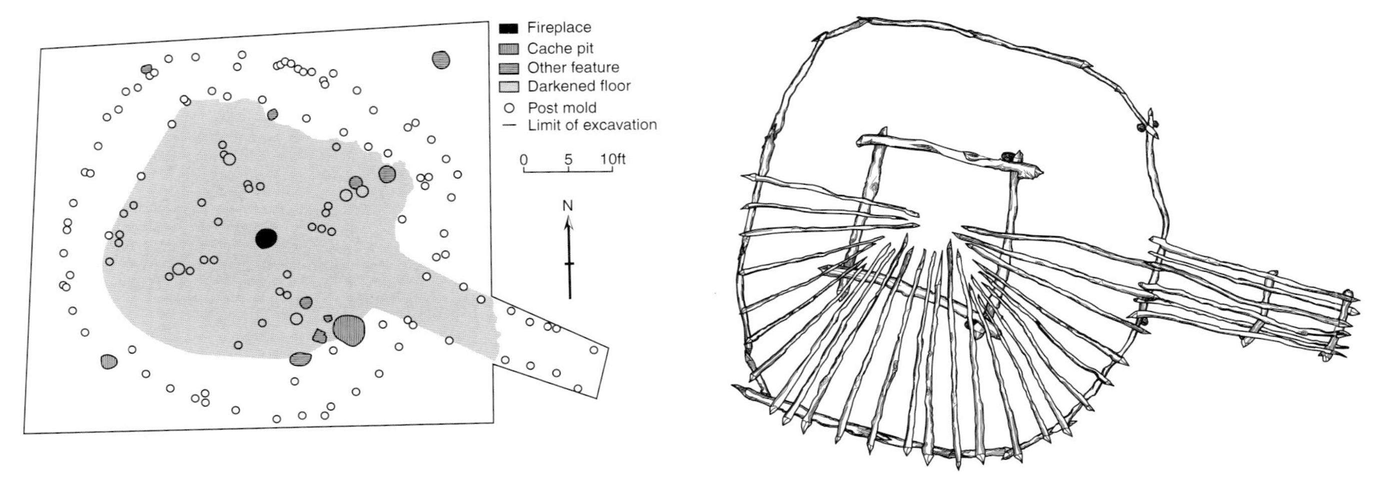

left, after Spaulding 1956:fig.3.

Fig. 4. Typical Initial Coalescent lodge excavated at the Arzberger site, S. Dak. left, Floor plan. right, Artist's reconstruction of the roof frame. Drawn by Roger Thor Roop.

The limiting effects of the material of manufacture together with the physical and morphological requirements set by the uses for which stone and bone tools were intended apparently promoted stability in these technologies. For the Initial variant, only diamond-shaped knives with beveled edges, plate chalcedony knives, carved stone tobacco pipes, full and three-quarter grooved stone mauls and bison skull hoes are distinctive (Lehmer 1971:114). Diamond-shaped knives and carved tobacco pipes are almost certainly derived from the Central Plains tradition; and grooved mauls, knives made from chalcedony, and bison-skull hoe blades were presumably borrowed from the long rectangular house peoples of the Middle Missouri tradition (Lehmer 1971:114).

Initial Coalescent ceramicists lump-modeled their wares from a grit-tempered mass of prepared clay. The artisan punched and excavated a bottom, then pulled, pinched, and scraped the body into shape and formed a rim before compacting the vessel's walls to bring them to their final shape and thickness. For these tasks the potter pressed a flat-sided round or oval stone anvil against the vessel wall's interior surface while pounding its opposing exterior surface with an incised or cord-wrapped wood or bone paddle. The pots thus produced were globular in shape with a rounded or angular shoulder and constricted neck surmounted by a variety of rim and lip forms. There were, for instance, three, perhaps four basic rim shapes: collared, direct, flared, and a form Spaulding (1956:149) designated Hughes beveled, some examples of which seem to be incipient braced rims. To produce a collared rim, the potter added a clay strap to the neck and pulled outward; a second strap was then applied. A small coil was added to form a lip. To produce a direct rim one strap topped by a coil was added. A flared rim was the result of pulling one strap outward and upward such that the vessel lip was of greater diameter than the mouth. To produce a Hughes beveled rim, the potter pulled a single strap addition upward and outward but pressed down against the outer and upper surface of the lip coil, thus beveling it perhaps to provide for decoration.

Initial Coalescent ceramics exhibit six different vessel surface finishes, three of which were mutually exclusive. The mutually exclusive treatments were: simple stamping, check stamping, and cord roughening. The nonexclusive surface treatments were brushing, smoothing, and red filming. The body sherd samples from Initial Coalescent sites all have examples of these treatments. Minute traces of check stamping and a red wash have also been noted on pieces from the Arzberger and Black Partizan sites.

Approximately half the specimens in Initial Coalescent rim sherd samples have plain or smoothed rim exteriors with decoration "most frequently limited to the lips, which are punctated or notched" (C.S. Smith 1959:117). The basic design motifs on sherds with decorated rim exteriors include horizontally incised lines, incised angular rainbows (sometimes called nested chevrons), cross-hatched incised lines, and incised opposed sets of diagonal lines. Cord-impressed designs occur, but they constitute less than five percent of the sample of all decorated rims. All the above decorations may be found on collared rims. Incised parallel horizontal lines and, in fewer instances, opposed sets of parallel incised diagonal lines, are found on direct or flared rims. Tablike lugs, loops, and strap handles (almost always associated with noncollared rims), and modeled knobs or short incisions at the base of collared rims are additional embellishments (fig. 5) (Lehmer 1971:114).

It is with good reason that Plains specialists frequently describe Initial Coalescent ceramics as an amalgam of Central Plains and Middle Missouri elements (Spaulding 1956:87). Simple-stamped and check-stamped body surface finishes, incised angular rainbow rim decoration, and tablike lugs seem to have been derived from the Middle Missouri tradition (Hurt 1953:9–10). Cord-roughened body surface treatment, collared rims with modeled knobs or short incisions at the base, and rim exterior decorations composed of opposed sets of parallel diagonally incised lines were derived from the Central Plains tradition. Although collared rims were indeed present in both Central Plains and Middle Missouri ceramics, in the Middle Missouri they were weakly developed and not usually combined with modeled knobs or short incisions—a combination typical of Central Plains wares (Strong 1935:248).

The mortuary customs of Initial variant peoples and their Extended variant descendants are virtually unknown. No cemeteries have been found, although rare complete or partial cache pit burials occur (C.S. Smith 1977:47). However, these could as well represent slain enemies as the remains of Coalescent tradition dead. Graves have been found along the Missouri River, but the grave goods with them are not distinctive enough to assign the burials to any single tradition let alone a variant thereof. Both individual grave and ossuary burial was practiced by Central Plains tradition folk and cemetery burial in a flexed position characterized the direct descendants of Extended variant peoples. Therefore, it is probable that some form of inhumation was preferred.

In sum, the evidence now available indicates that the authors of the Initial variant of the Coalescent tradition were immigrants from the Central Plains who settled the Big Bend of the Missouri River valley in some numbers between the fourteenth and sixteenth centuries. If so, they represented but one episode in an environmentally stimulated series of population shifts that began in the thirteenth century and had far-reaching effects on Central Plains and Middle Missouri lifeways. According to Caldwell (1966a) and Lehmer (1971) the Big Bend was empty or sparsely settled by Middle Missouri tradition indigenes at the time of the Initial Coalescent penetration; but later, more favorable climatic conditions stimulated Middle Missouri groups from the north to resettle the area and Central Plains groups from the south to intensify their attempts to colonize the region thus bringing the two into contact and conflict. Modifications of social, political, and material life seem to have flowed from both contact and conflict.

Initial Coalescent peoples, for example, built settlements that effected a compromise between the needs for defense in areas of high military risk and a stubborn adherence to a dispersed community plan and other elements of a lifeway developed in the Central Plains. By analogy with historic tribes, Initial Coalescent settlements would have been aggregates of kinsmen organized into extended families, each of which occupied its own dwelling within the fortified community. The co-domiciled, consanguineally related members of the household were most probably the stable units in the fabric of village life. It was to and from these stable units that goods, personnel (affines), and services must have flowed through a network of traditional

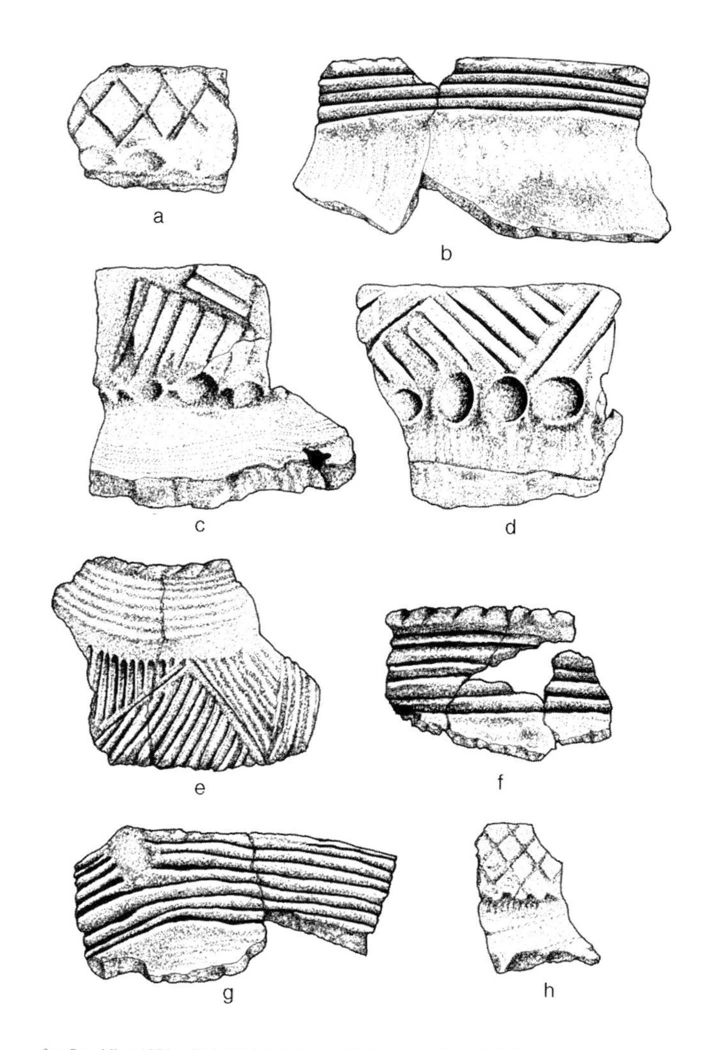

after Spaulding 1956: a,h:Pl. IX c,g: b, e, f, g : Pl. XI m, a, d, j; c, d: Pl. X a, c.

Fig. 5. Cord-wrapped and grooved paddle-stamped rim sherds from the Arzberger site, S. Dak., typical of Initial Coalescent pottery. Drawn by Roger Thor Roop.

social ties that muted the potentially divisive pull of separate domestic group interests and drew domestic groups together in an ongoing social order (Krause 1972:107). In this light, the presence of hostile or potentially hostile Middle Missouri tradition groups can be seen as an external threat intensifying such extrahousehold ties as existed by focusing attention upon communitywide concerns—defense and the preparations for defense among them.

Initial Coalescent village life was, in part at least, shaped by the limitation inhering in floodplain agriculture. One important limitation to the practice of farming was the amount and distribution of land necessary per capita. Villages or population aggregates of any size and permanence must have been positioned near the fields upon which their inhabitants depended, and the heavy use of unimproved land and unmanaged wild faunal and floral resources would invariably be accompanied by declining yields. The nutritional deprivation exhibited by the Initial variant skeletons at the Crow Creek Massacre site may perhaps be taken as a measure of the human cost of maintaining a concentrated population in the face of the natural and social environment of the times (J.B. Gregg and Zimmerman 1986:191–212). When combined with problems of transportation and declining crop yields, the depletion of reserves of wild foods and a decline in the timber supply would force either the periodic relocation of village units or the redistribution of individual households.

Extended Coalescent

Some of the later Initial Coalescent populations in the Big Bend country must have occupied fortified settlements into the third, fourth, and perhaps the fifth decades of the sixteenth century. But others, identified as members of the Extended variant of the Coalescent tradition, began to disperse, in the process building unfortified settlements composed of small clusters or strings of earthlodges scattered along the river's terraces. At a slightly later date (perhaps the late sixteenth century) related groups were building villages along the Missouri River as far north as the Grand River junction (J.J. Hoffman 1967:63; Stephenson 1971:91) and as far south as Lake Andes (Hurt 1952) near the Nebraska–South Dakota border. Like their Big Bend counterparts, these Extended Coalescent villages were straggling affairs with clusters of earthlodges scattered along the river's terraces. In short, an explosive expansion of area occupied and the spreading out of local populations typified Extended Variant settlement practices (fig. 1) (Lehmer 1971:115).

Lehmer (1971:116) and others identified the Extended variant settlement pattern as a reversion to the dispersed community design of Central Plains folk. This community plan was acted upon and "linearized" by the centripetal tug of the region's strip of farmable bottomland soils. There were, for instance, over 100 recorded village sites with a nearly continuous distribution within the 792 kilometers of river bottom between the North Dakota–South Dakota border and the Niobrara River at the Nebraska line (Lehmer 1971:115). Many of these sites were small, containing a dozen or fewer lodge ruins (Wedel 1961:185), and those excavated carried a very thin mantle of debris. Perhaps Lehmer (1971:116) was correct when he observed that "this implies that they were occupied for only short periods of time and that the Extended Coalescent population was generally a rather mobile one." The Extended variant spread may in fact have carried beyond the confines of the Missouri River valley. Extended coalescent pottery has been reported from the Black Hills (Wedel 1947b), the Angostura Reservoir (Wheeler 1957), and the White River Badlands (Nowak et al. 1984). In Montana, Extended Coalescent pottery has been collected from the Nollmeyer site, 30 miles above the confluence of the Yellowstone and Missouri rivers (Krause 1995:19–44) and from the Horse Butte site farther west. On the basis of limited testing Ann M. Johnson (personal communication 1988) identified Nollmeyer as a fortified earthlodge village and Horse Butte as a temporary hunting encampment. This kind of population spread and apparent mobility certainly fits the Central Plains tradition model well. Nevertheless, there were Extended Coalescent sites that contained as many as 100 lodge depressions strung out for two or more kilometers along the high ridges or flat lofty terrace tops that fringed South Dakota's Missouri River floodplains (Wedel 1961:185). Populations of comparable size were not to be found in the Central Plains. It may still be the case, however, that the larger Extended Coalescent sites represented local geographic constraints on the dispersal of rapidly growing populations whose ancestors did indeed prefer and did at first adopt a community design of basic Central Plains type.

Extended Coalescent communities in the Big Bend country were not fortified, but along the expanding frontiers to the north and south fortifications appeared early in the span of settlement. With several exceptions, the fortified strongpoints along the northern and southern frontier of Extended Coalescent settlement did not match the sophistication and complexity of their Initial Coalescent and Middle Missouri tradition prototypes. The fortified areas were smaller; and bastions, when constructed, were not set to provide an enfilade. Instead, they seem to have been mere "gestures to an older tradition" (Caldwell 1964:3). In the southernmost Extended Coalescent site, Scalp Creek, bastions were entirely lacking and reliance was placed upon a ditch and an oval palisade that enclosed the entire village (Hurt 1952). Although Scalp Creek was a true fortified village, the Extended Coalescent fortifications along the northern frontier (with the exception of those at the Payne and Davis sites) seem to have been, as Caldwell (1964:3) suggested, no more than rallying points or redoubts for the peoples from surrounding farming hamlets.

Examples of this redoubt pattern were to be found between the Cheyenne and Grand rivers at the Potts, Molstad, Moreau River, No Heart Creek, and Tricia sites (fig. 6). All these contained strongpoints with oval palisades, one or two loop bastions, fortified gateways, and dry ditches within easy reach of a larger scattered population (R.B. Johnston and J.J. Hoffman 1966:39–65). In the same region fortified strongpoints were also to be found at the Hosterman and Norvold II sites and at sites 39WW204 and 39WW8 (Lehmer 1971:116). In discussing the Hosterman site for example, C.F. Miller (1964:225) noted that "While the main portion of the settlement was surrounded by a palisade and ditch [lacking bastions] . . . other houses together with their trash areas occurred to the east and north of the palisaded area unsurrounded by any protective device."

Although the majority of the fortifications along the northern frontier were small strongpoints serving a larger dispersed population, some sites, like Lower Grand

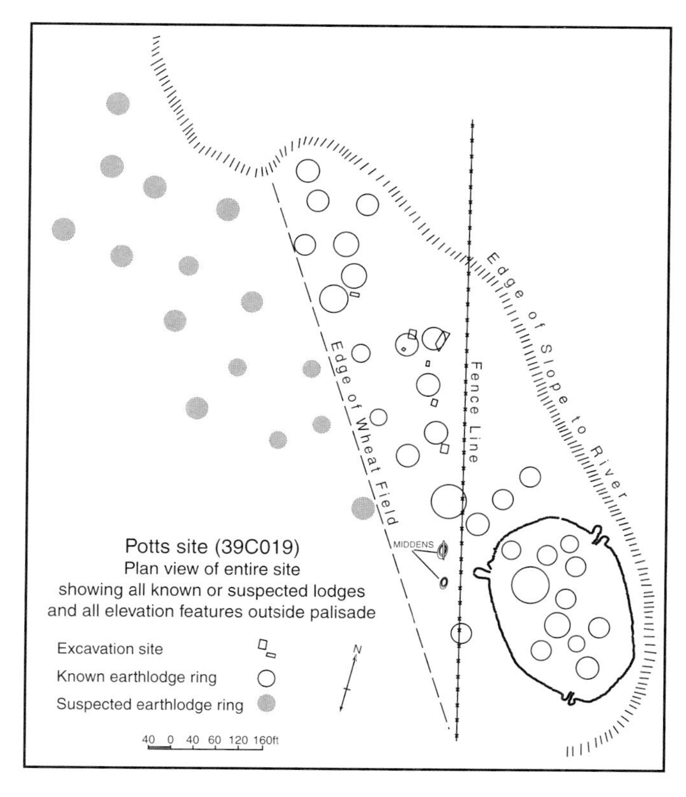

after Stephenson 1971:fig.3.

Fig. 6. Plan map of the Potts site, S. Dak., a typical Extended Coalescent village. Drawn by Roger Thor Roop.

(Davis) and one component at 39WW8, were compact fortified villages surrounded by ditches and by bastioned palisades that were roughly rectangular. These sites were considered late representatives of the Extended variant. If this is indeed the case, the developmental pattern to fortifications along the northern frontier proceeded from small fortified strongpoints serving a dispersed population, to a mixture of dispersed unfortified settlements and fortified villages of some size and permanence. At any single time, then, fortified redoubts or palisade-protected villages may have been constructed along the northern edge of settlement, while unfortified communities flourished in the more secure regions immediately to the south.

The overall patterning to Extended Coalescent settlement practices may be summarized as follows: (1) a Big Bend hearthland characterized by dispersed unfortified settlements that, through population growth, provided the impetus for a northward, southward, and perhaps even westward expansion of area used or occupied; (2) fortified sites along both the northern and southern frontiers of settlement, with fortified villages emerging early in the south and a mixed pattern of redoubts and fortified villages characterizing the pattern of settlement in the north; and (3) a later lapse of fortifications along the southern but not the northern frontier.

Approximate calendrical dates have been tendered for six Extended Coalescent components; three were based on carbon-14 determinations, and the other three were derived from tree-ring studies. Of the sites thus dated, one (Molstad) lay north of the Moreau River junction, two (No Heart Creek and 39SL24) near the Cheyenne-Missouri River confluence, and three (La Roche, Medicine Creek, and Sully) in the Big Bend region. There were four radiocarbon determinations from the Molstad village (A.D. 1475 ± 100, 1565 ± 95, and 1675 ± 85 (Hoffman 1967:45). The excavator discounted the 1675 determination because of putative contamination, then estimated an occupation between 1540 and 1575. Lehmer (1971:119) manipulated two of the four determinations to suggest a 1565 to 1590 range. Seven radiocarbon determinations have been reported from the La Roche site (A.D. 1500 ± 120, 1520 ± 60, 1640 ± 55, 1660 ± 60, 1680 ± 50, 1240 ± 90, 1400 ± 90 (Hoffman 1968:64). The means of these determinations, except the earliest one, which has been discounted, fall into two groups, one centering in the sixteenth and the other in the seventeenth century. The two date clusters support Hoffman's argument for two components at the site, but there are widely disparate determinations on wood from the same structure. A single carbon-14 determination of 1710 ± 80 was reported for 39SL24, but Lehmer (1971:119) considered it too recent. Lehmer (1971:119–120) also refused to use the Stuiver-Suess conversion curve for carbon-14 determinations from Extended Coalescent sites arguing that the "curve throws four of them back into the 15th century, gives five others values between 1510 and 1575, and reduces the latest one to 1645 ± 80. Such a modification makes the group far too early to accord with available dates for the other cultural complexes in the region." Yet the available carbon-14 determinations for the region's "other cultural complexes" had already been so converted (Lehmer 1971:114). Lehmer's calendrical claims must therefore be taken cautiously. The tree ring-derived calendrical dates form a tighter chronological cluster. The Missouri Basin Chronology program produced a bark date of 1556 for No Heart Creek and a 1660 date for Medicine Creek (Lehmer 1971:120). Weakly (1971:29) reported three additional dates for Medicine Creek ranging from 1574 to 1593. He also reported seven dates from the Sully site, which ranged from 1663 to 1694. A 1450 to 1650 span for the variant's major events and processes would seem reasonable.

The lodges built by peoples of the Extended variant resembled their Initial Coalescent ancestors (fig. 7). The ideal lodge was a substantial dwelling of poles, grass, and dirt, which required some effort to build and maintain. The builder must first have cut the sod from a circular area to form a shallow basin-shaped floor. Four roof support posts estimated to be four to four and one-half meters tall, and forked at the top to hold a square of timbers, were set roughly equal distances apart at the corners of a square in the center of the lodge basin. Peripheral roof-wall support posts 1.5 to 1.8 meters tall and forked at the top to hold up stringers were then set in a circle from 1.8 to 3.6 meters apart, 1 to 1.5 meters inside the edge of the lodge basin.

Relying on historic earthlodges for comparison, the walls were constructed by setting poles close together with their bottom ends jammed against the ledge formed by the removal of sod, or stuck in the ground, and their tops secured to the circle of peripheral stringers. The roof was also constructed of poles laid close together, with their bottom ends resting upon the peripheral stringer system and their upper ends supported by the square of beams held by the four center roof-support posts. A pit to hold the fire that provided both heat and light was dug in the center of the area framed by the central roof-support posts, and a small smokehole-skylight was left in the roof directly above. The entryway was constructed by placing two parallel series of upright posts in the ground (extending outward from one wall), connecting them at the top with stringers, and then covering the top and sides of this frame with small, closely set poles. Roof, walls, and entryway were laced together with twigs, over which bundles of coarse grass were laid to hold the final covering of 15 centimeters or so of earth.

The floor plans of excavated lodge ruins indicate that the previously sketched ideal was seldom realized. Peripheral post arrangements approximating circles, rectanguloid shapes, rough ovals, and lopsided ovals have been noted for many sites (Lehmer 1971:115). The evidence of entrance passages was often sketchy. Some lodges may even have had funnellike entranceways extending inward from the peripheral post line (J.J. Hoffman 1968:6). The firepit was often not centered vis à vis the peripheral posts and the primary central supports were frequently difficult to define, leading some to speculate about a two-post alternative for the support of the roof (J.J. Hoffman 1968:15). Then again, Lehmer (1971:115) has suggested that "some Extended Coalescent houses may have had teepee-like pole superstructures." Such houses, lacking vertical outer wall supports, characterize the Demery site (Woolworth and Wood 1964:127–128).

The observed variability in the details of superstructure are interesting and perhaps have significant implications.

after Hoffman 1968: fig. 9.

Fig. 7. Artist's reconstruction of a typical Extended Coalescent lodge. Drawn by Roger Thor Roop.

Lehmer (1971:115–116) described Extended Coalescent houses as giving "the impression of having been hurriedly built," and he suggested that "the builders were struggling with the problem of relating the square of the primary superstructure supports to the circle of the outer wall of the house." From a slightly different perspective, Weakly (1971:41–42) noted a shift from the extensive use of cedar to the use of cottonwood and argued that the concomitant reduction in tensile strength may have forced the reworking of traditional building specifications with an attendant period of experimentation followed by a reduction in overall lodge size. Weakly's claims were lent credibility by work at the La Roche site in which Hoffman (1968) defined an early component characterized by large houses of diffuse pattern followed by a later component with smaller, more regularly constructed dwellings.

Extended Coalescent potters brought aboriginal Plains pottery making to perfection. From the standpoint of Euro-American canons of technical excellence, Extended Coalescent wares were the best to be found throughout the Northern and Central Plains. They were characterized by a hard, grit-tempered, thin-walled globular-shaped utility vessel finished by simple stamping and surmounted by a limited variety of rim forms. Straight rims, either vertical or out-flared and often topped by a small lip fillet that gave them an inverted L- or T-shaped cross-section, were the predominant types. Thus the Initial Coalescent trend toward an incised straight rim ware reached fruition in Extended Coalescent ceramics. Some S-shaped and weakly developed collared rims occurred, but these appeared to be polarities in a minor style continuum (Lehmer 1971:118). Cord-impressed rim decorations occurred but were a distinct minority. Among the more common rim decorations were incised herringbones, horizontal incised lines, diagonal incised lines, and incised triangles. Three combinations of rim form and decoration predominated. These were: horizontal lines with straight rims; horizontal lines with S-rims, and S-rims with incised herringbones or diagonal incised lines arranged around a main element composed of horizontal incised lines (fig. 8). These rim form–decoration combinations encompassed ceramics identified under a plethora of wares and types but that, despite different names, were found at all excavated Extended Coalescent sites.

The bone and stone tools manufactured by Extended Coalescent artisans were, for the most part, duplicates of those produced by their Initial Coalescent predecessors (Lehmer 1971:119). Tobacco pipes were noted more frequently in the samples from Extended than from Initial Coalescent sites, and catlinite was more abundant per site sample than it was previously. Two additional Middle Missouri tradition artifacts, L-shaped elk antler adzes and bison and elk metatarsal fleshers, appeared for the first time in Coalescent tradition assemblages at late Extended Coalescent sites (Lehmer 1971:119)

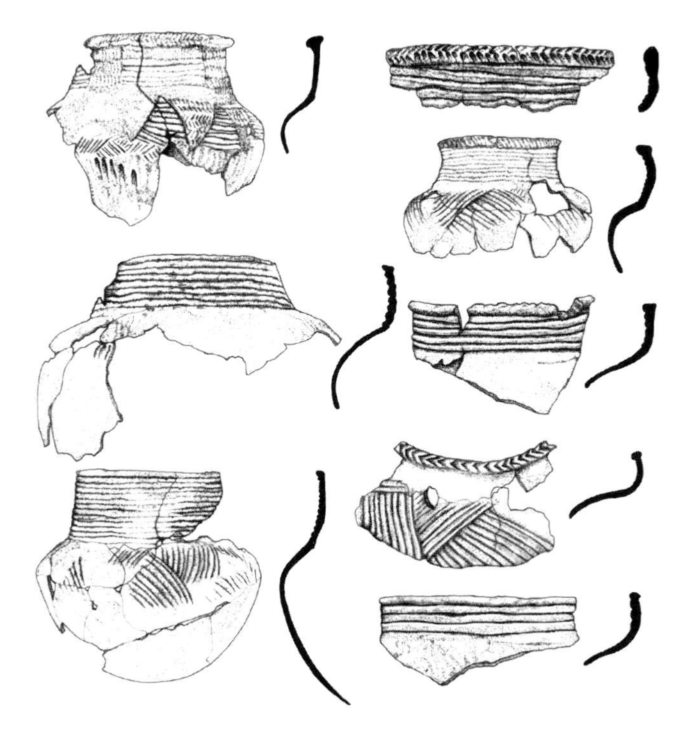

after Hoffman 1968: pl. 12.

Fig. 8. Rim sherds from the LaRoche site, S. Dak., typical of Extended Coalescent pottery. Drawn by Roger Thor Roop.

Conclusion

There can be little doubt that Extended Coalescent peoples were the descendants and cultural heirs of Initial Coalescent immigrants. The continuities in material culture are firm, and the discontinuities in settlement pattern and community design can be seen as adaptive responses to altered social and environmental contexts. By the mid-1500s, for example, the Big Bend country was firmly controlled by Initial Coalescent groups, and matters of defense were not so pressing that palisaded villages were being built. Lehmer (1971:126–127) suggested that a northward withdrawal of Middle Missouri tradition groups removed the military pressure from Coalescent peoples in the southern portions of the Missouri trough, allowing them to readopt a Central Plains pattern of dispersed unpalisaded settlements. Wood (1967:132) argued that disenfranchised Middle Missouri tradition groups moved northward at this time, swelling the village populations of their cultural relatives in North Dakota to produce the Terminal Middle Missouri variant pattern of extremely large, elaborately fortified settlements composed of long rectangular houses.

An abrupt Middle Missouri outmigration is more tenable than it would at first appear. The rapid abandonment of whole regions as they became less habitable does seem to be more typical of Middle Missouri tradition people than does population dispersal or the redistribution of individual households. At any rate, the removal of military threat in the south was accompanied by a rapid expansion of area occupied by Coalescent groups, and there is evidence to suggest the continuation of hostilities along the northern border of Coalescent settlement at the interface of contact between expanding Extended Coalescent and withdrawing Middle Missouri populations. Perhaps this is a striking example of the adaptive value of social practices that permit population dispersal and household mobility in the face of environmental pressure. The period of Middle Missouri relocation and Coalescent expansion and dispersal correlates well with Baerreis and Bryson's (1965a) Neo-Boreal regime—a period of reduced summertime penetration of tropical air and an appreciably cooler and drier climate.

During both the Initial and Extended Coalescent occupations and throughout the Middle Missouri tradition occupation the region-wide population density must have been relatively low. Hence there should have been enough tillable land and bison for all in most locales, not to mention herds of pronghorn antelope and more modest second-line resources—fish, shellfish, and small mammals among them. Nevertheless, in the face of increasing environmental stress the efficient use of these resources seems to have posed different problems for concentrated rather than for dispersed populations. To be sure, horticultural produce and natural foods could be stored against periods of want, and meat could be dried, but a continuing need for fresh meat, skins for blankets, robes, and other clothing, and the even more pressing need for firewood and building materials could not be so easily satisfied. For a reasonably large and concentrated village-dwelling population the effort required in hunting, gathering wild foods, and obtaining firewood and building materials would increase as locally available reserves became depleted. The depletion of local resources would in turn increase the distance one had to go from a village to obtain needed supplies; and transportation might be a problem, especially in the winter months. Thus, if economic and social inducements for the continuation of a concentrated population (trade, warfare, access to improved land or managed resources) were absent, then a spread-out pattern of households would seem to be adaptive. It would minimize the stress on those expendable resources that were slow to renew themselves and maximize the efficiency of hunting and harvesting locally discontinuous reserves of natural foods. In short, a spreading out of the local populace seems to have been advantageous for Extended Coalescent populations. To judge by the archeological record it provided them an edge in their competition with Middle Missouri tradition indigenes.

For Coalescent peoples, population dispersal and household redistribution had ample Central Plains precedents. Thus they may have been pre-adapted to the vicissitudes of climatic fluctuation by virtue of their former Central Plains experience. Population dispersal was obviously adaptive, for it allowed Extended Coalescent groups to consolidate and expand their claims to the territories and resources of the South Dakota portion of the Missouri River valley, and to do so at the expense of Middle Missouri tradition indigenes. For Middle Missouri tradition peoples population dispersal and the redistribution of households apparently lay beyond their range of options. They maintained a tenacious hold on the community design they first brought to the region, settlements typified by the geographic concentration of related households. Such Middle Missouri tradition population movements as occurred, whether realized through population growth and fragmentation or population decline and fusion, seem always to have been fitted to this mold. That Middle Missouri tradition peoples were given to building elaborately fortified villages when they seem to have been the sole inhabitants of the region suggests a penchant for internecine warfare, a propensity to fight their cultural compatriots as well as outsiders, a commitment perhaps to principles of social order that stimulated military action. Coalescent peoples on the other hand seem to have responded, and vigorously so, to the threat of military action by alien groups; but, unlike their Middle Missouri tradition competitors, they readily abandoned an emphasis upon concentrated populations and elaborate village defenses.

The Extended Coalescent settlement pattern of small, dispersed villages occupied for only short durations may also reflect adaptation to less favorable climatic conditions (Lehmer 1971:128). By the mid-eighteenth century, a warming trend improved conditions, allowing for the development of larger, more permanent villages on the Upper Missouri. Many of these were fortified in response to a new pattern of raiding and trading initiated by dislocated groups forced westward as a result of contact and conflict with Euro-Americans. When Europeans arrived on the Upper Missouri during this period they met the three historic village tribes—Mandan, Hidatsa, and Arikara. Archeologically, the Siouan-speaking Mandan and Hidatsa have been directly linked to the Middle Missouri tradition, while the Caddoan-speaking Arikara are seen as the outgrowth of the Extended Coalescent peoples. The three tribes shared a great many cultural similarities, reflecting the convergence between the Middle Missouri and Coalescent traditions during the protohistoric period (Lehmer 1971:136).

Plains Village Tradition: Southern

ROBERT E. BELL AND ROBERT L. BROOKS

Beginning around A.D. 800, societies of farming people began establishing themselves along major river systems on the Southern Plains. They depended on the hunting of bison and other game, gathering of wild plants, and increasingly over time, on the raising of corn, beans, and squash. This distinct cultural expression is referred to as the Plains Village tradition. These people occupied the region until approximately 1500. Villages were placed along the terraces and floodplains of major stream valleys where fertile alluvial soils were especially suitable for farming. Spring floods also tended annually to rejuvenate these lands. In the fall, large-scale bison hunts were organized, which provided the large quantities of meat that served to help carry the villagers through the winter months, usually a period of scarcity. Seasonally available plants and animals were also exploited. Because these Southern Plains Villagers adjusted their society to take full advantage of the diversity in plains habitats, they represent the most successful adaptation to the area in prehistoric times.

The Southern Plains Villagers occupied primarily the central portions of the Southern Plains area in Texas and Oklahoma. While the boundaries are not sharply defined, the area includes the plains region lying south of the Arkansas River in Kansas and extending southward to include most of Oklahoma, northern Texas, parts of eastern New Mexico, and southeastern Colorado. It is an area of rolling prairie grasslands with timbered areas restricted to the stream valleys. The eastern margins are marked by more varied topography and woodlands. Plains Village settlements within the state of Texas were limited to the northern sections, especially along the Red River Valley; regions farther to the south in Texas were occupied by numerous nomadic and foraging groups. The eastern portions of New Mexico, including the valley of the Pecos River, were occupied by some settled villages, but most of these are related to the Southwest culture area.

Despite differences among the groups identified as representing the Southern Plains Villagers, they all shared a way of life that contrasted with that of the inhabitants of the surrounding regions. Their subsistence economy depended upon bison, complemented by the hunting of other game animals, fishing and collection of shellfish, collection of wild plant products, and growing of garden crops. Corn and beans are well documented in the archeological record, but squash, tobacco, and other crops were probably grown as well. These diverse resources contributed to a broader economic base that could mean survival at times when crop failure or a scarcity of shifting bison herds might threaten staple food supplies.

The village sites are variable, although most range in size from one-half to over 20 acres. They are located upon both major streams and tributary creeks close to a reliable water supply and loose sandy soils, which were amenable to cultivation with simple bone, stone, and wood tools. Frequently, several small communities were clustered relatively close together, suggesting a scattered, almost rural, community comprised of several family groups. In other situations, a larger site appeared as the central community with scattered smaller sites located up and down the river valley. Relatively isolated sites also occur, but it appears unlikely that a large number of people occupied any single village. The villages are characterized by the presence of houses, numerous cache or storage pits, scattered sheet middens, and occasional burials or a cemetery area. There are no mounds or evidence of earthworks or fortifications. However, in the Antelope Creek and Washita River phases there are hints of purposeful village planning. Many sites have thick midden accumulations up to three or four feet in depth, indicating a lengthy and apparently continuous occupation.

The artifacts found at these sites vary slightly but tend to represent materials associated with economic pursuits. Articles suggesting marked status differences or ceremonial activities are scarce, implying either a more simple way of life than that found in adjacent areas or social and ritual complexity that was not well reflected in the material culture.

Origins

The origins of the Southern Plains Villagers remain obscure, but it is likely they were derived from poorly documented Plains Woodland groups known to have lived in the region. These groups, identified primarily by the presence of cordmarked pottery, were not yet focused on bison exploitation but were continuing to follow a Woodland economic pattern while venturing onto the Southern Plains. With increasing use of tropical cultigens and exploitation of the bison and the cultural adaptation to use this economic mix of resources within the region, Woodland groups were transformed into various expressions of the Southern Plains villagers, represented by the Custer, Paoli, Antelope Creek, Turkey Creek, and Washita River phases, and the Henrietta, Zimms, Buried City, Bluff Creek, and Pratt complexes. (The closely related Apishapa phase is described in "Plains Village Tradition: Western Periphery," in this vol.)

Cultural Complexes

Custer and Paoli Phases

The best information for the Custer phase is derived from three excavated sites: Linville, Mouse, and Edwards II in the west. Data on Paoli are drawn from Currie, Brewer, and Patton in the south-central area. Radiocarbon dates range between A.D. 800 and 1250 (Drass and Moore 1987; Drass 1997). These sites are situated on a terrace or ridge toe above the floodplain and contain features such as storage and refuse pits, hearths, scattered sheet middens, and occasional houses and burials. They are typically less than five acres in size and seldom contain extensive midden deposits. Thus, it is likely that Custer and Paoli phase sites reflect semipermanent occupations by groups of less than 50 individuals.

Only a few houses have been excavated. Dwellings are made of wall posts with wattle and daub construction outlining a square or rectangular structure ranging from 15 by 20 feet to around 24 feet square. A fireplace area is located at the approximate center of the house, and interior cache pits may or may not be present. The house from the Mouse site lacked any interior roof supports, whereas that from the Currie site has four central roof supports. Because of the small number of structures identified, the most typical form is not known.

Circular or oval cache or storage pits are common in most sites although they do not occur in large numbers. They average three feet in diameter and range from two to three feet in depth. There are also shallower pits, 6–10 feet in diameter.

Information about burials is limited to small samples. The skeletons were placed in a flexed position within oval or rounded grave pits. Grave offerings were present with three or four reported burials and consist of pottery, chipped-stone tools and shell beads although there is no evidence of status differentiation.

Although corn is fairly common at Custer and Paoli phase sites, it is thought that the growing of crops was not so extensively practiced as during later times (e.g., the Washita River and Turkey Creek phases). This suggestion is based on the absence of other cultigens and the limited number of bone tools used for tilling the soil, such as bison scapula and bison skull hoes. Edible wild plants were collected: burgrass, barley, maygrass, chenopodium, amaranth, sunflower, wild mustard, smartweed, and portulaca. In addition, nut crops such as hickory, walnut, and pecan were used for food as well as fuel. Animal remains found at Custer and Paoli phase sites attest to use of a wide variety of large and small game. These include bison, deer, antelope, cottontail and jackrabbit, squirrel, raccoon, gopher, turkey, birds and fish, and considerable quantities of box turtle. Although bison remains are more abundant in Custer sites, it appears that bison was not so extensively hunted as during later Plains Village times.

Artifacts found at the sites are quite similar except for minor differences or changes in frequency, which may reflect time differences. Chipped-stone materials are plentiful including projectile points, scrapers, drills, and knives. Projectile points are represented by small-sized arrowpoints, chiefly simple triangular (Fresno), side-notched triangular (Washita and Harrell), and small corner-notched forms (Scallorn and variants). There is the suggestion that corner-notched forms are dominant early but are gradually replaced through time by side-notched and unnotched forms.

Ground-stone artifacts include manos, grinding basins (both circular and trough-style metates), sandstone abraders, celts, and elbow pipes. Much of the ground stone is made of local sandstone although some red granites from the Wichita Mountains have been used to make large metates. Sandstone abraders have been graded to perform rough-out to finishing tasks.

Bone artifacts are usually made from either deer or bison and include bison scapula hoes, bison tibia digging-stick tips, bone knives or fleshing tools, bone awls or perforators, arrowshaft wrenches, antler flaking tools, antler handles (socketed), notched ribs (musical rasps), deer toe tinklers, and tubular bone beads. Shell artifacts are occasionally found. Mussel shell was used for spoons or scrapers and large disk-shaped beads. Olivella shell beads are also reported.

Clay artifacts include perforated sherd disks, a few fragments of crude human figurines, daub, tripods, and pottery vessels. The pottery is represented by Stafford Plain and Stafford Cordmarked, Lindsay Cordmarked, and occasionally Lee Plain. An important characteristic of these pottery types is the dominance of the cordmarked wares. Particularly in the Custer phase, cordmarked pottery comprises 50–60 percent of the total ceramic assemblage. Typical vessels are small to large conical-shaped jars with a rounded or flattened base and a slightly flaring rim. Attachments or decorations other than cordmarking are rare although handles, small lip tabs, attached clay fillets and nodes, fingernail punctates, and incising occur. Also present are fragments of small thick-walled poorly fired clay cups having a corncob-roughened surface.

Little evidence has been found pointing to extensive trade with other early Plains Village groups. Trade with people to the west may be indicated by the presence of material from the Alibates quarries near Amarillo, Texas, although these pieces may also have been obtained from gravel deposits. Better evidence exists for the use of granites from the Wichita Mountains to the south although it cannot be determined whether this stone was directly procured or obtained through trade.

The Custer and Paoli phases share many characteristics with the Washita River and Turkey Creek phases and Upper Canark cultures to the west, but it appears most closely aligned with the Washita River and Turkey Creek phases. In fact, the Custer and Paoli phases probably served as the developmental base for the Washita River phase culture pattern.

Washita River and Turkey Creek Phases

The Washita River phase is the designation for a series of village sites located along the Washita River in south-central Oklahoma; Turkey Creek phase refers to west-central Oklahoma (Bell 1984a; Bell and Baerreis 1951; Hofman 1978; Brooks 1987; Drass 1997). Additional village sites are found around the peripheries of this region, including the Canadian River valley. The general region appears to extend from the South Canadian River valley on the north to the Wichita and Arbuckle mountain areas on the south. The eastern margins are marked by the Cross Timbers while the western margins abut against or overlap with the short-grass prairies occupied by groups exhibiting characteristics of the Upper Canark variant.

The origins of the Washita River and Turkey Creek people remain somewhat obscure. It is possible that they have dual roots, one associated with late Plains Woodland groups and the other derived from direct historical ties to the preceding Custer and Paoli phases. Radiocarbon and archeomagnetic dates place the range of the Washita River and Turkey Creek phases between A.D. 1250 and 1450 (Drass and Swenson 1986).

Sites consist of small to moderate-sized villages of 5 to 20 houses occurring at relatively regular intervals along the principal river systems and major streams. These villages are often spaced from 1.5 to 2 miles apart along the Washita River proper (Brooks 1983). Over 200 sites have been recorded for western and south-central Oklahoma (fig. 1). Village remains include houses, sheet middens, house middens, storage and refuse pits, hearths, and cemetery areas. Rockshelters were also occupied, either as permanent sites or temporary camps.

Examples of houses are limited but consist of square or rectangular structures made of upright wooden wall posts with wattle-and-daub construction. The best information comes from the Arthur site where five houses were excavated (fig. 2) (Brooks 1987). Four are rectangular, measuring 21 feet by 15 feet, while a fifth house is 20 feet square. All houses have two central support posts, numerous small internal posts for benches and platforms, and a centrally located prepared clay hearth. Most houses at the Arthur site have a large storage or refuse pit in the southeast corner. Based on the studies of the amount of usable floor space available, it has been suggested that these structures each housed from five to eight individuals (Brooks 1987). Houses reported for other villages are similar, although the number of central support posts may range from two to four and internal storage pits may be absent.

Burials are sometimes found as isolated graves within the village area but generally occur as a more formal cemetery area adjacent to the village. The burials are usually single interments placed in a flexed or semiflexed position within a shallow grave pit. The skeletons appear to have been placed with the head to the east (Lopez 1970), and burial offerings, although simple, occur with about 60 percent of the graves. As in the case of the Custer and Paoli phases, little evidence exists to support status differentiation.

Horticultural pursuits probably provided the mainstay of the diet, particularly in the more eastern sites, as suggested by the large number of bone tools such as socketed bison tibia digging sticks, and bison scapula, innominate, and horn-core hoes as well as an abundance of manos and grinding basins. Cultigens included popcorn and 8-, 10-, or 12-row flint corn, squash (or gourd), and beans. Edible wild plants were also collected, including marshelder, smartweed, sunflower, chenopodium, amaranth, persimmons, sand plum, and a variety of nuts (pecan, acorn, walnut, and hickory). In addition to plants used as food, other species such as morning glory, creeping cucumber, and spurge were apparently collected for medicinal and ceremonial uses. In general, plants grown or collected by these people reflect an emphasis on use of the bottomland forest habitat.

Animals hunted were primarily bison, deer, antelope, elk, jackrabbit and cottontail, gopher, prairie dog, fox squirrel, raccoon, and beaver. Bison exploitation appears to have been more intensive than in the Custer and Paoli phases. The ratio of bison to deer remains increases from east to west along the Washita River drainage. These groups also hunted birds, including wild turkey, prairie chicken, and wood duck. Riverine species included box, leatherback, and snapping turtles; catfish, sunfish, drum, and gar; and mussels.

Artifacts of chipped stone include projectile points, scrapers, drills, knives, and a few miscellaneous items. The projectile points are small-sized arrow points (fig. 3a–w), most commonly simple notched or plain triangular forms. There is considerable variation in form, and numerous identified types do occur (e.g., Fresno, Washita, Harrell, Scallorn, Morris, Bonham, Huffaker, and others). Some larger dart points (e.g., Gary, Williams) also occur, but these may have been used as knives. Scrapers (fig. 3x–bb) are also abundant. Drills or perforators (fig. 3cc–dd) are present, as well as chipped-stone knives (fig. 3ee–kk) and numerous retouched flakes apparently also used as knives. Analysis of chert materials from which these tools were made indicates not only utilization of local river and upland gravel resources but

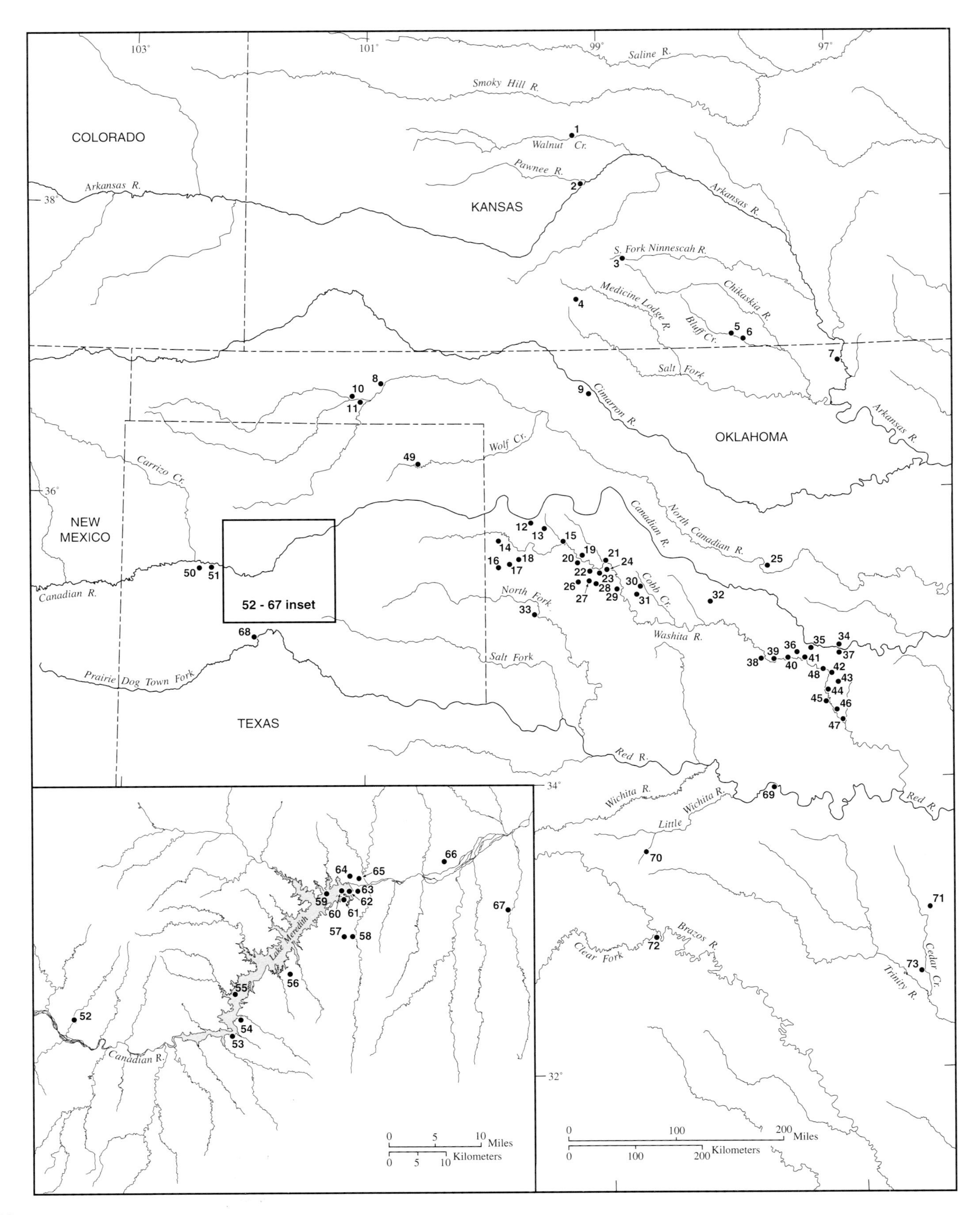

103°
101°
99°
97°
Saline R.
Smoky Hill R.
COLORADO
Walnut Cr.
Pawnee R.
Arkansas R.
38°
KANSAS
Arkansas R.
S. Fork Ninnescah R.
Medicine Lodge R.
Chikaskia R.
Bluff Cr.
Salt Fork
Cimarron R.
OKLAHOMA
Arkansas R.
Wolf Cr.
Carrizo Cr.
36°
NEW MEXICO
Canadian R.
North Canadian R.
Cobb Cr.
North Fork
Washita R.
52 - 67 inset
Salt Fork
Prairie Dog Town Fork
TEXAS
Red R.
34°
Wichita R.
Little Wichita R.
Red R.
Brazos R.
Clear Fork
Cedar Cr.
Trinity R.
32°
Lake Meredith
Canadian R.
0 5 10 Miles
0 5 10 Kilometers
0 100 200 Miles
0 100 200 Kilometers

Fig. 1. Archeological sites of Southern Plains villages, with an inset of sites in the Lake Meredith, Texas area. Kans.: 1, Seuser (14RH301); 2, Larned (14PA307); 3, Pratt (14PT1); 4, Bell (14CM407); 5, Armstrong (14HP5); 6, Buresh (14SR303) and Nulik (14SR305). Okla.: 7, Uncas (34KA172); 8, Roy Smith (34BV14); 9, Hedding (34WD2); 10, McGrath (34TX31) and Two Sisters (34TX32); 11, Stamper (34TX1); 12, Zimms (34RM72) and New Smith (34RM400); 13, Pyeatts #4, (34RM179); 14, Chalfant (34RM294); 15, Hodge (34CU40); 16, Linville (34RM492); 17, Edwards I (34BK2); 18, Hubbard (34BK4); 19, Phillips (34CU11); 20, Mouse (34CU25); 21, Williams (34CU6); 22, Goodman II (34CU2); 23, Goodman I (34CU1); 24, Shahan II (34CU7); 25, Manwell (34OK100); 26, McLaughlin II (34CU5); 27, McLaughlin I (34WCU4); 28, Heerwald (34CU27); 29, Shahan I-(34CU3); 30, Carl McLemore (34WA44); 31, McLemore (34WA5); 32, Duncan-Wilson (34CD11); 33, Edwards II (34BK44); 34, Van Schyver (34PT20); 35, Willingham (34ML5); 36, Lacy (34GV5); 37 Brewer (34ML3); 38, Max Thomas (34GD4); 39, Brown (34GD1); 40, Lee II-(34GV4); 41, Lee I (34GV3); 42, Arthur (34GV32); 43, 34GV1; 44, Wilson (34GV43); 45, Currie (34GV22); 46, Grant (34GV2); 47, Braden (34GV1); 48, Patton (34GV165). Texas: 49, Gould Ruins (41OC00), Handly Ruins (41OC1), Courson B (41OC27) and Kit Courson (41OC43); 50, Landergin Mesa (41OL2); 51, Saddleback (41OL1); 52, Chimney Creek (41HC26); 53, Chicken Creek (41PT45); 54, Coetas Creek Ruin (41PT2); 55, Footprint (41PT25); 56, Alibates 28 (41PT11); 57, Antelope Creek 22 (41HC23); 58, Antelope Creek 24 (41HC24-29); 59, Arrowhead Peak (41HC19); 60, Roper (41HC6); 61, Conner (41HC7); 62, Sanford (41HC3); 63, Pickett; 64, Medford Ranch (41HC10); 65, Spring Canyon (41HC20); 66, Tarbox (41HC2); 67, Jack Allen; 68, Canyon City; 69, Glass (41MU24) and Coyote (41MU28); 70, Onion Creek (41AR4); 71, Pilot Creek (41COL39) and Farmerville (41COL40); 72, M.D. Harrell (41YN1); 73, Ragland (41KF4).

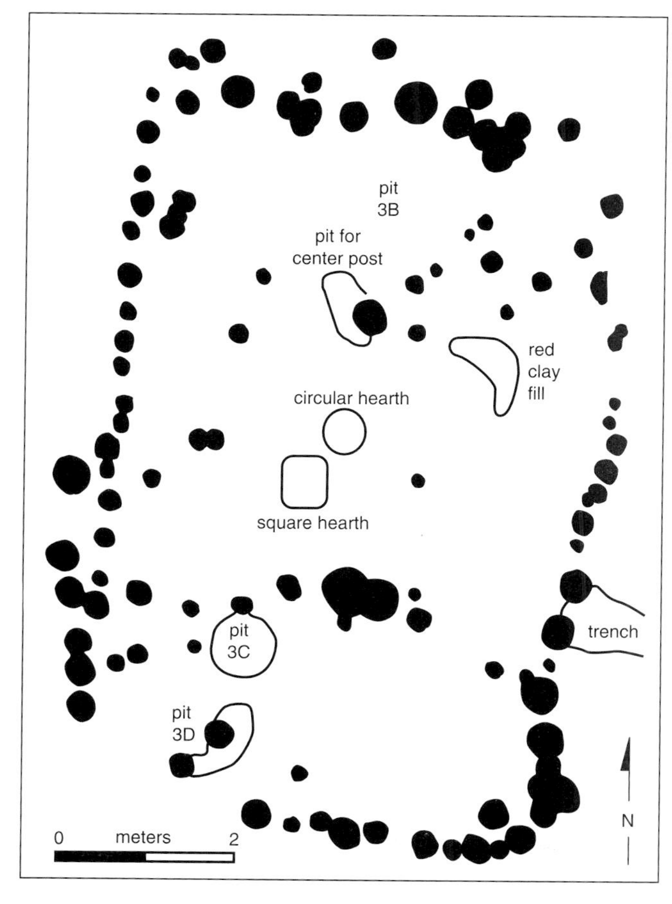

after Brooks 1987:54.

Fig. 2. Floor plan of House 3, Arthur site, Okla., Washita River phase. Drawn by Roger Thor Roop.

also materials derived from sources outside the region: Frisco chert from near north-central Oklahoma, and Alibates from quarries near Amarillo, Texas. Alibates can also be found as river gravel.

Ground-stone artifacts include celts, pipes, sandstone arrowshaft smoothers, awl abraders (fig. 4a–b) and hones, milling basins and metates, mortars, manos and mullers (fig. 4c–d), small stone balls, perforated stone disks, and hammerstones.

Bone artifacts (fig. 5a–p) are similar in range to those from Custer and Paoli phase sites. Bison bone was normally used for agricultural tools, whereas deer and turkey were selected for pins, awls, and other smaller items. Mussel shell beads, pendants, spoons, and scrapers are also found.

Clay was used chiefly for ceramics (fig. 4j–m), although a number of other clay items are found, including human figurines, perforated disks made from pottery sherds (fig. 4g–i), simple elbow-type pipes, thick-walled clay cups having a corncob-roughened exterior, and bell-shaped unidentified objects.

Pottery sherds (fig. 4e–f) are abundant at the village sites. In the eastern part of the region, the most common types are Nocona Plain, Lee Plain, and Lindsay Cordmarked. Stafford Plain and Stafford Cordmarked occur in the more western sites of the Turkey Creek phase.

Trade and contact with neighboring groups is evident from both raw materials and ceramics with major communications extending east and west following the drainage systems. Influences from the Spiro phase peoples of the Caddoan area become reduced as one moves westward along the Washita River valley. There is also evidence that these groups were making replicas of Caddoan pottery, particularly red-slipped (Sanders-type) wares. However, there are increases in Southwest materials as well as Florence A chert from north-central Oklahoma.

Upper Canark Variant

Southern Plains Villages representing the Upper Canark variant are found in the Texas and Oklahoma Panhandle as well as southeastern Colorado and extreme northwestern New Mexico. This cultural pattern has been historically referred to (Krieger 1947; R.G. Campbell 1969; Baerreis and Bryson 1965) as the Panhandle aspect. However, Lintz (1986) redefined the Panhandle aspect as the Upper Canark variant, a unique and reasonably uniform expression distinguishable from other variants of the same tradition by its geographical distribution, age, and material culture.

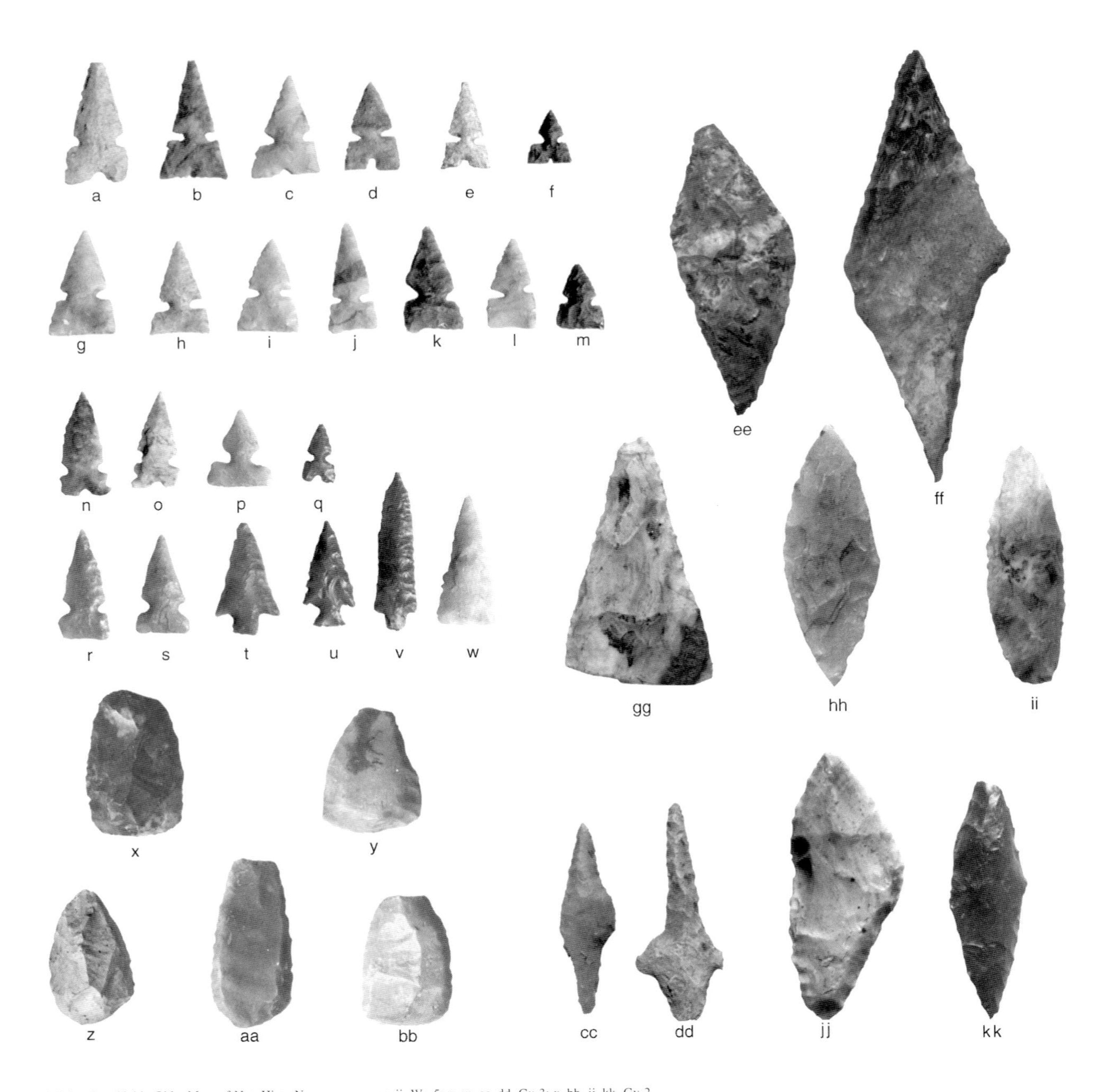

U. of Okla., Sam Noble Okla. Mus. of Nat. Hist., Norman: a–m, ee–ii, Wa-5; n–w, cc–dd, Gv-3; x–bb, jj–kk, Gv-2.

Fig. 3. Chipped-flint artifacts of Washita River phase, Okla. Projectile points from the McLemore site (a–m) and the Lee site #1 (n–w); end scrapers from the Grant site (x–bb); drills from the Lee site #1 (cc–dd); knives from the McLemore site (ee–ii) and the Grant site (jj–kk).

The origins of the Upper Canark variant remain obscure except for roots within older Plains Woodlands populations. Baerreis and Bryson (1965) suggest that it represents a southwestern movement of Upper Republican peoples who were forced to move from the Central Plains because of climatic deterioration. R.G. Campbell (1969) views this cultural expression as arising from local Plains Woodland cultures and a developing Apishapa phase. J.T. Hughes (1968) sees the Upper Canark peoples developing locally out of Plains Woodland and speculates that they eventually abandoned the region to join their Upper Republican relatives, and subsequently, evolved into Lower Loup and Pawnee in Nebraska. However, there is relatively little archeological data to support any of these theories.

Information on the Upper Canark sites shows a wide diversity in architectural features and village patterns. Lintz (1986) attributes variability in architecture to functional differences, engineering constraints, and changes in design over time. Included within this variant are the Antelope Creek phase, the Apishapa phase ("Plains Village Tradition: Western Periphery," this vol.), and the Buried City complex.

U. of Okla., Sam Noble Okla. Mus. of Nat. Hist., Norman: a–c, k–m, Gv-2; d, Cu-25; e–f, Gv-3; g–i, Wa-5; j, Gv-4.

Fig. 4. Pottery and stone artifacts of Washita River phase, Okla. a–b, Sandstone grooved abraders, Grant site; c, circular mano, Grant site; d, oval mano, Mouse site; e–f, decorated pottery rim sherds, Lee site #1; g–i, perforated pottery disks, McLemore site; j, decorated pottery jar with 4 handles, Lee site #2; k–m, pottery bowl and jars, Grant site.

Antelope Creek Phase

The temporal range for Antelope Creek is approximately A.D. 1200 to 1500, placing Antelope Creek somewhat later than the Custer and Paoli phases but contemporaneous with the Washita River and Turkey Creek phases (Lintz 1986; Drass 1997).

Village sites are usually situated on steep terraces or elevated knolls in the floodplain, or occasionally, in the west, on isolated mesas. There seems to be a higher density of sites along principal tributaries of the major rivers than along the primary river systems (Etchieson 1981; Guidry et al. 1979). Hundreds of Antelope Creek phase sites are known for the Texas Panhandle with a few others found in the Oklahoma Panhandle (fig. 1).

Antelope Creek phase sites include temporary camps, isolated farmsteads, hamlets, and villages. Settlements often contain several house units forming a scattered community. A characteristic feature of village dwellings is the use of large stone slabs for wall construction. These were placed vertically to form the wall base and were held in place by adobe mortar. Details of masonry construction vary greatly from site to site, and often from structure to structure. These range in size from less than five meters to large rooms up to 60 square meters, representing single-story pueblos with 30 or more rooms (figs. 6–7). Additional features include passageway entrances, four interior roof support posts, central hearths, floor pits, or other features. Occasionally, rooms have a platform against the west wall, which is thought to have been used for religious or ceremonial purposes. Storage pits are frequently encountered, either within the houses or within the village areas.

Burials generally consist of single interments placed in a shallow pit covered with stone slabs. They frequently occur on hilltops or mesas overlooking the village although they occasionally are found in trash pits, middens, or within the largest house. When they are found within a dwelling, it is usually after it was abandoned (Lintz 1986a). Individuals are usually placed in semiflexed position with no particular orientation to the skull or body. Grave goods typically found with burials are chipped stone tools, bone tools or ornaments, shell necklaces, and domestic pottery. They are rather uniformly distributed within the burial population, suggesting little status differentiation.

The subsistence economy of Antelope Creek phase groups was based on growing cultigens, hunting, and the

U. of Okla., Sam Noble Okla. Mus. of Nat. Hist., Norman: a–e, h–i, o, Wa-5; f–g, k, n, p, Gv-4; j, l–m, Gv-2.

Fig. 5. Bone artifacts of Washita River phase, Okla. a, Decorated arrowshaft wrench and b–e, awls or perforators, McLemore site; f–g, broken arrowshaft wrenches, Lee site #2; h–i, bison tibia digging-stick tips, McLemore site; j, bison scapula blade knife, Grant site; k, bison scapula hoe, Lee site #2; l, bison scapula hoe, Grant site; m, bison horn-core hoe, Grant site; n, bison scapula knife, Lee site #2; o, knife or fleshing tool, McLemore site; p, deer jaw sickle showing wear from lashings, Lee site #2.

collecting of wild plants. In general, dietary practices were similar to those of western groups of the Turkey Creek phase where hunting (particularly of bison) probably played an equal or greater role than horticultural pursuits.

Artifacts manufactured of chipped stone are most commonly made of chert derived from the Alibates quarries north of Amarillo, Texas, and include projectile points, numerous scrapers, knives, drills and perforators, and crude hoes. Arrowpoints are the most plentiful projectile forms although some dart points also occur. Typical arrowpoints are triangular forms with or without side notches (Fresno, Washita, and Harrell types). Some corner-notched and other forms occur, but they are not abundant at most sites. Chert end and side scrapers made from flakes are common and indicate an extensive skin dressing activity. Another characteristic tool in the chipped stone assemblage is the alternatively (diamond) beveled knife.

Implements of ground stone include grinding basins, manos, abraders, hammerstones, ornaments, pipes, and celts. Some of the grinding basins and manos represent Southwest styles. In a few instances, samples of basketry

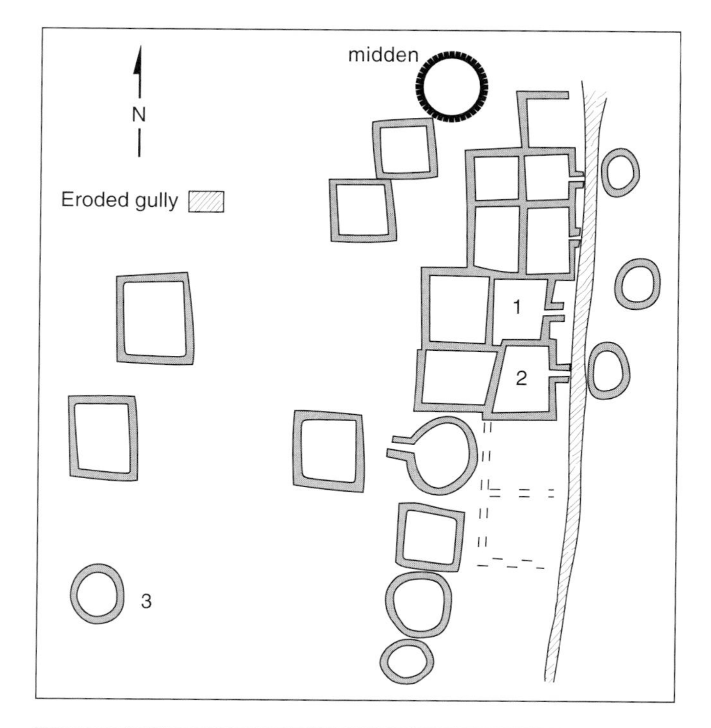

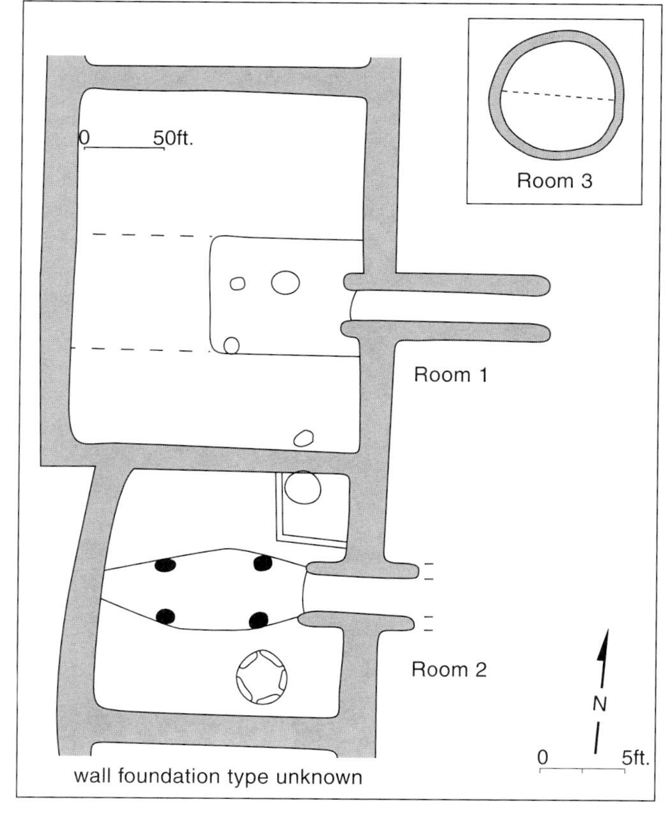

after Lintz 1986a:308,309.

Fig. 6. Antelope Creek phase structures. top, Plan map of Coetas Creek Ruin site, Tex. bottom, Detailed floor plan of rooms 1–3 of the Coetas Creek Ruin site. Drawn by Roger Thor Roop.

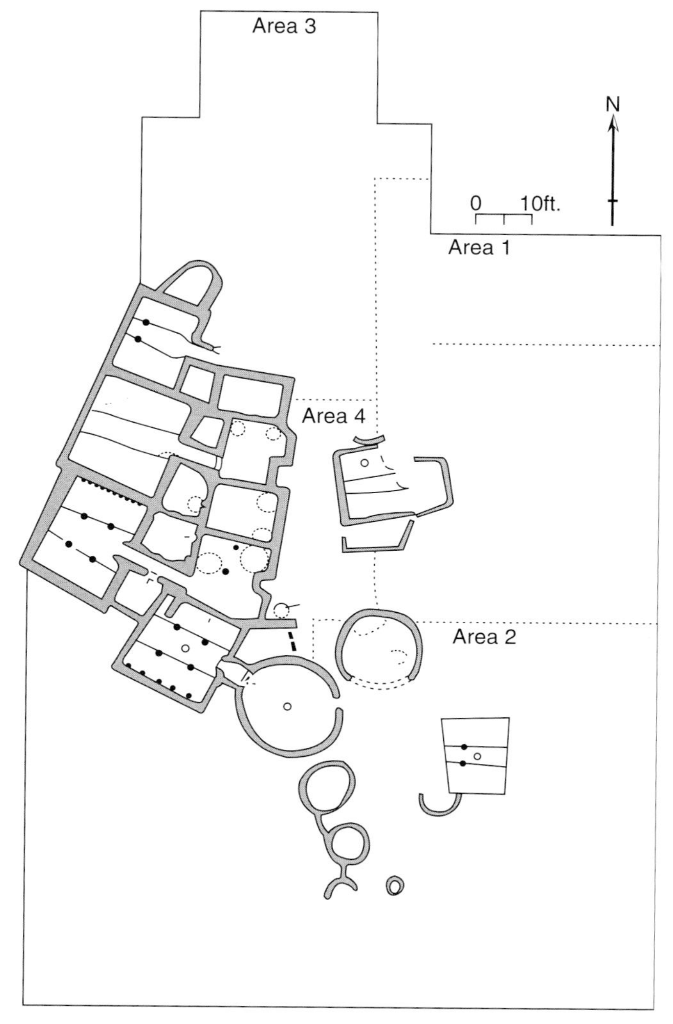

after Lintz 1986a:329.

Fig. 7. Plan map of Alibates Ruin 28, Tex., Antelope Creek phase. Drawn by Roger Thor Roop.

have been recovered. These were manufactured using a plaited, twined, or coiled technique.

Pottery is represented by two types, Borger Cordmarked and Stamper Cordmarked. Vessels are typically globular in form with a rounded base; the rims are straight, either vertical or with a slight outward flare. The bodies are covered with cordmarks, usually placed vertically except in the basal sections of the vessel.

Southwestern pottery trade sherds occur at many of the Antelope Creek sites (Baerreis and Bryson 1966). Other trade materials such as obsidian, turquoise, the tubular pipe, and perhaps olivella shells are also derived from the Southwest. Contacts toward the east are apparently less important, although limited contact may be indicated by the presence of conch shells and stone celts.

In general, the Antelope Creek sites appear as the most divergent of the Southern Plains villages (Lintz 1978, 1984, 1986a). This is largely due to the utilization of stone-slab construction and differences in the ceramics. The proximity to the Southwest and possibility of multiple origins also contribute to this variation.

The Buried City Complex

The Buried City complex refers to a particular expression of the Upper Canark variant found along Wolf Creek, a tributary of the North Canadian (Beaver) River in the northeast of the Texas Panhandle. Additional sites of this complex have been reported for some other portions of the northeast Texas Panhandle. The complex may also extend into Ellis County in western Oklahoma (D.T. Hughes 1985, 1986; Drass and Turner 1989).

Radiocarbon dates from the Courson B site place the temporal range of the Buried City complex from A.D. 1150 to 1330 (D.T. Hughes 1986). Thus, these remains are roughly contemporaneous with the earlier part of the Antelope Creek phase.

With one exception (the Gould Ruin), all structures at Buried City sites represent single units without interior dividing walls. Individual structures consist of four or five houses up to 20 or more dwellings. Most villages appear to be located adjacent to the valley wall, well away from the creek (D.T. Hughes 1986).

The architecture of structures along Wolf Creek is quite similar to Antelope Creek phase houses. Instead of vertical slab walls, boulders of caliche are used as the foundation, a technique reminiscent of some Apishapa phase structures. Other features normally associated with houses include straight-sided refuse-filled storage pits and semicircular or D-shaped rooms attached to the southeast corner of the dwellings.

The little information available on burial practices suggests a pattern of loosely flexed interments with no particular orientation of the body. In contrast to the Antelope Creek phase, burials of the Buried City complex exhibit variety in grave goods. Subsistence practices have not been documented, although the presence of bison tools related to agricultural activities is indicative of the growing of crops. Thus, the subsistence pattern was probably similar to that of the Antelope Creek phase.

The material inventory is also similar to that of the Antelope Creek phase, except in terms of ceramics, which are typically sand tempered with minor amounts of bone, shell, and clay. The most common form is a large globular jar, although occasional rounded forms are also found. Many vessels are thick, poorly fired, and exhibit a soft paste (D.T. Hughes 1986). Unlike Antelope Creek wares, many of the sherds from the Buried City complex exhibit decoration in the form of single, double, and triple rows of fingernail impressions around the vessel neck, chevron designs, and crenulated rims. Ceramics from the Buried City sites seem most similar to pottery found at Upper Republican sites in west-central Kansas (D.T. Hughes 1986).

Zimms Complex

Although its geographic extent is unknown, sites of the Zimms complex are found primarily in Roger Mills County in western Oklahoma. In general, it appears to fall between the Washita River and the North Canadian River drainages. Zimms complex sites are distinguished by an Antelope Creek house floor plan (without stone-slab masonry) and a material inventory analogous to that of the Washita River and Turkey Creek phases.

Origins of the Zimms complex are unclear, but it doubtless stems in part from preceding Woodland developments in the Texas Panhandle and western Oklahoma. The Antelope Creek style house floor plans indicate early contact with Upper Canark variant groups. Summaries of the Zimms complex are presented by Flynn (1984, 1986), M.C. Moore (1984), Drass and Moore (1987), and Brooks, Moore, and Owsley (1992).

Dates from the Zimms site and New Smith site indicate a range for the Zimms complex between A.D. 1265 and 1425, making Zimms complex roughly contemporaneous with the Antelope Creek, Turkey Creek, and Washita River phases.

Settlements consist of small hamlets or isolated homesteads situated on high terraces or ridge toes above principal tributary streams rather than on major river valleys. Documented sites typically contain only one or two houses.

The structures themselves serve to identify the Zimms complex as a distinct cultural expression (fig. 8). A house excavated at the Zimms site is semisubterranean with a central depressed floor channel and a raised floor platform on the west wall. The house is square to rectangular (6 by 6 m) and contains a central hearth and two central support posts. Instead of stone-slab masonry, walls are plastered with daub to a height of 40 centimeters. Except for the absence of the vertically placed stone slabs, this architectural pattern is most like houses found among the Antelope Creek phase.

The only information on Zimms complex burials comes from the two features at the New Smith site. One burial consists of a woman and child placed in a shallow pit in a tightly flexed position with the woman's head facing south. A woven mat was placed over them. An arbor was either constructed over the burial and burned or the individuals were placed under the arbor, which was then burned. A second burial was too badly disturbed to be documented fully, but the pattern is much like the first. The only grave goods were chipped-stone knives. Twelve pits were found around the two burned arbors, each containing expended bison bone tools in the upper level. The only other materials in these pits were turtle bones and carapace fragments. These features are viewed as representing an activity specifically related to a mortuary ceremony (Brooks, Moore, and Owsley 1992).

The subsistence economy of Zimms complex peoples is thought to be similar to that of the Washita River and

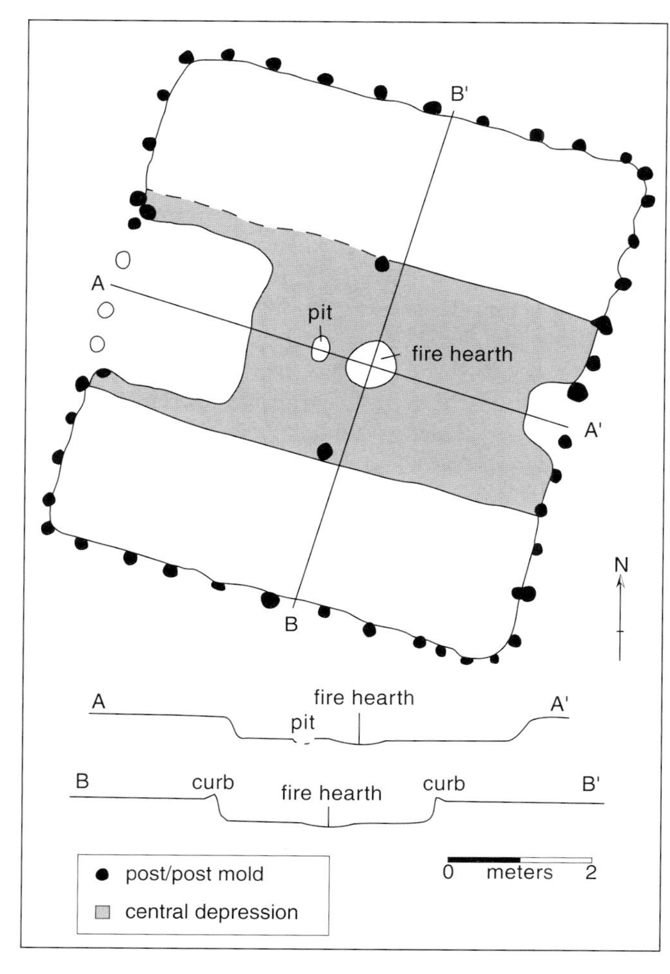

after Flynn 1984:222.

Fig. 8. Floor plan of House 1, Zimms site, Okla., Zimms complex, depicting a semisubterranean structure. Drawn by Roger Thor Roop.

Turkey Creek phases although operating at a less intensive scale. Evidence for horticulture is not extensive. Corn was identified from a refuse pit at the New Smith site, and bison scapula hoes were found at the Zimms site.

There is slightly better evidence for hunting practices. Game animals taken include bison, deer, cottontail, and prairie dog. Box turtle and birds were also exploited. Based on impressions derived from these meager data, the Zimms complex subsistence economy may have focused around hunting and gathering supplemented by gardening.

Ceramics at Zimms complex sites bear strong resemblances to wares found at Washita River phase sites. The dominant pottery type is Quartermaster Plain, a thin compact pottery tempered with shell, limestone, fossiliferous shale, and occasionally grit (M.C. Moore 1984). Vessel forms are not well documented. Other pottery found in small percentages includes Lee Plain and Lindsay Cordmarked.

A few trade items are present. Florence A chert from Kay County occurs in small percentages, and there is some evidence of ceramic trade wares representing contacts with both the Caddoan area to the east and New Mexico.

Henrietta Complex

The Henrietta complex represents the southernmost manifestation of the Southern Plains tradition with all the identified sites located in north-central Texas (Krieger 1947). It was defined largely upon the presence of shell-tempered pottery and other associated traits. Origins for the Henrietta complex remain uncertain, although Lorrain (1969) suggests that it was derived from Plains Woodland cultures such as that represented by the Fish Creek complex in Cooke County, Texas, which she views as transitional between Plains Woodland and early Plains Village tradition.

Henrietta complex villages are located upon sandy knolls or terraces overlooking the river valleys. Most sites are small, ranging from one to five acres, but they frequently have middens of considerable thickness indicating a lengthy occupation. Village features include not only midden deposits but also numerous rock hearths, storage pits, houses, and burials. Fireplaces or rock hearths are common at the Harrell site; they are either flat or shallow dish-shaped hearths often lined with limestone slabs or smaller fire-cracked rocks. Storage pits include simple, irregular-shaped pits as well as larger, more carefully prepared storage pits. Information about houses is scanty. Lorrain (1974) reports a single structure from the Glass site. It is represented by an oval-shaped floor area measuring 6.6 meters by 4.8 meters within a saucerlike depression. There were four post holes irregularly spaced around the margins of the floor area roughly at the sides and ends of the structure. No fireplace was present nor were any peripheral wall support posts noted. It is possible that other architectural elements were destroyed by intrusive cache pits into the house area. However, it is more likely that this is an arborlike structure constructed by later occupants of the site.

The burials occur as flexed or semiflexed skeletons placed within a cemetery area. The graves contain either single or multiple burials, sometimes having stone slabs placed around and over the grave. Burial offerings are not common but sometimes include personal ornaments such as shell beads. R.K. Harris (1945) reports an unusual flexed burial from the Pilot Creek site that contained eight scapula hoes placed upon a bed of mussel shells and charcoal.

Projectile points are the most common chipped-stone artifacts at the Harrell site. Arrowpoints such as Fresno, Washita, Harrell, and Scallorn types are most typical, but Alba, Bonham, and Perdiz types also occur in small numbers. Numerous dart points were also found at the Harrell site, but they probably distinguish an earlier component. Additional chipped-stone implements include knives, scrapers, drills, and unfinished items. Ground-stone artifacts include milling basins, manos, hones and abraders, celts, pipes, and hammerstones.

Bone and antler artifacts are common at the Henrietta village sites, especially those along the Red River. They include gardening tools (hoes and digging sticks), scapula knives and scraping tools (beamers?), rib-edge awls, fishhooks, tubular beads, and bone tubes, some from the Harrell site decorated with incised designs. Deer antler is represented by antler-tip flaking tools and cut antler sections for drifts and tapping tools. Shell items other than whole mussel shells from the middens are scarce in Henrietta complex sites.

The dominant pottery type is Nocona Plain, which is commonly found at eastern Washita River phase sites. Vessel forms are limited to simple bowls and deep jars having a bulging shoulder and outflaring rim; the bases are rounded or flat. Handles appear to be absent and decorations are rare, being limited to small appliquéd nodes applied around the neck section. There are also a few sherds of a thick corncob-roughened ware, similar to the small cylindrical cups found in the Washita River and Turkey Creek phases in Oklahoma.

Occasional trade sherds indicate contacts with the Caddoan area to the east and with the Southwest. Other trade contacts are suggested by the presence of obsidian and Alibates chert.

The Henrietta complex remains one of the poorest documented village complexes in the Southern Plains. J.T. Hughes (1968) suggested that the Henrietta complex represents an early Kitsai occupation, being derived from the Washita River phase in Oklahoma. While this may be plausible, there is other evidence that suggests indigenous Red River valley peoples also contributed to its formation.

Bluff Creek Complex

The Bluff Creek complex refers to a series of villages occurring in southern Kansas adjacent to the Oklahoma border. They exhibit similarities to the Central Plains tradition (e.g., Great Bend phase) and to the Washita and Turkey Creek phases in Oklahoma. Sites belonging to this complex are found along Bluff Creek, a tributary of the Chickaskia River in Hays and Sumner counties, Kansas. This cultural pattern may also extend northward to the Arkansas River drainage in Harvey County (Witty 1978).

Origins of the Bluff Creek complex are unclear. K.L. Brown and A.H. Simmons (1987) attribute its development to the Southern Plains Washita River and Custer phases and to the Central Plains tradition. However, based on radiocarbon dates of around A.D. 1050, these sites appear to be contemporaneous with the Custer and Paoli phases rather than the Washita River pattern. Because these dates reflect relatively early Plains Village developments, origins for Bluff Creek are probably to be found in local Plains Woodland cultures. Reports on the Bluff Creek complex include Witty (1978), P.J. O'Brien (1984), K.L. Brown and A.H. Simmons (1987), and R.R. Gould (1975).

Radiocarbon dates obtained for the Buresh site place Bluff Creek around A.D. 1050 (Witty 1978:63). The settlement pattern consists of small villages or hamlets often situated on high terraces or ridges overlooking the stream valley. As in the case of the Zimms complex, there is a tendency for sites to be located on tributaries rather than in the major river valleys.

Villages characteristically have two or three wattle-and-daub houses. These lodges are usually present as low circular mounds. Based on four structures excavated at the Buresh site, the dwellings are square, oval, or rectangular in shape and may be up to 35 square meters in floor area (Witty 1969). At least one structure had an extended entranceway. Only one house had a central hearth, suggesting that meals may have been prepared outside. Interior features consist of cylindrical-shaped storage pits and large, basin-shaped trash pits. The exterior walls appear to have been partially covered with daub. No burials or cemeteries have been reported.

Agriculture is evidenced by the presence of charred corn cobs and bison scapula hoes. Identification of hunting practices is limited to the knowledge that bison and deer were both utilized.

The chipped-stone tool inventory includes side-notched (Washita) and basally notched (Harrell) arrowpoints, diamond-shaped beveled knives, and unifacial scrapers. Most items are made of Florence A chert from the Flint Hills region of north-central Oklahoma and south-central Kansas.

Bone tools include bison scapula hoes, skull hoes, and tibia digging sticks as well as shaft wenches made from deer tibias (Witty 1978:62–63).

Ceramics from Bluff Creek complex sites have generated considerable discussion (Witty 1969, 1978; K.L. Brown and A.H. Simmons 1987; P.J. O'Brien 1984). The common type is a globular vessel with flattened or slightly concave base and occasional strap handles. Exterior surfaces are generally cord-roughened or sometimes plain. Tempering materials include sand and crushed and burned bone. In some instances, these vessels have collared rims similar to those found in Central Plains villages. A smaller percentage of the pottery consists of shell-tempered wares with smooth exteriors, strap handles, and appliqué strips around the vessel neck. These are thought to represent Lee Plain type vessels traded from Washita River phase sites in south-central or west-central Oklahoma.

Based on the presence of Lee Plain sherds and other items in the material inventory (e.g., Harrell points), Witty (1978:63) suggests that Bluff Creek bears similarities to Southern Plains Village sites. The occurrence of globular cordmarked pottery also points to considerable influence from the Central Plains.

Pratt Complex

The Pratt complex was initially defined by Wedel (1959) on the basis of materials recovered from the Pratt site in Pratt County, Kansas. This complex exhibits similarities to both Central Plains sites and Southern Plains developments (e.g., the Washita River phase). Pratt complex sites appear to be located in the Upper Ninnescah River valley (Witty 1978) and generally between the Medicine Lodge River and the Arkansas and Smoky Hill rivers in south-central and west-central Kansas. The complex is not well documented, with excavated sites recorded for only three Kansas counties: Pratt, Pawnee, and Rush (K.L. Brown and A.H. Simmons 1987). Reviews of the complex are presented in Wedel (1959), Witty (1970), and K.L. Brown and A.H. Simmons (1987).

Origins of the Pratt complex have not been identified. Wedel (1959:510) attributes its development to Central Plains cultures, and potentially, to the Washita River phase in Oklahoma.

No radiocarbon dates are available for the Pratt complex. A date of A.D. 1400–1500 is suggested, based on Southwest trade sherds at Pratt and the presence of a Great Bend variant component overlying the Pratt occupation.

Information on settlement patterns is meager. Pratt complex sites have been found along oxbows (e.g., the Larned site) as well as on terraces. Sites are typically villages of 5–10 earthlodges. No other site types have been reported.

Earthlodges at these villages contain rounded and braced corners, four interior support posts, and a central hearth. Cylindrical storage pits also occur within the houses. Pratt complex structures appear similar in size to those of the Bluff Creek complex, being approximately 20 by 20 feet. No information is available on exterior features, and burials have not been reported at the excavated sites.

The subsistence economy was probably based on agriculture, hunting, and gathering, much like the Bluff Creek sites as well as other Central Plains villages (K.L. Brown and A.H. Simmons 1987).

Characteristic chipped-stone tools consist of notched and unnotched triangular arrowpoints and diamond-shaped beveled knives.

Four indigenous ceramic wares have been described for the Pratt complex (Wedel 1959). The first of these, Ware A, is sand tempered and cordmarked with flaring or excurvate rims. Decoration consists of short diagonal incising or punctations. Ware B is similar except that it is plain surfaced rather than cordmarked. The third ware (Ware C) is much like the previous two except that it is plain surfaced, has a very fine sand temper, and has straight rims. The fourth pottery type (Ware E) differs markedly in being shell tempered with flared rims, and with decoration consisting of diagonal incised lines and appliqué strips around the vessel neck. The fourth ware is thought to bear similarities to Washita River phase pottery such as Lee Plain.

Trade goods were found at Pratt complex sites, including Rio Grande Glaze and Biscuit B (Bandelier Black on Gray) pottery from Pratt and other Southwest sherds from a site in Rush County. Other trade items include turquoise from the Pratt and Larned sites and olivella shell beds from the Larned sites (K.L. Brown and A.H. Simmons 1987).

Wedel (1959:510) suggests that the Pratt complex stands intermediate, temporally and culturally, between the Washita River phase of south-central Oklahoma and the Great Bend variant sites in west-central Kansas.

Other Complexes and Phases

Besides the cultural units discussed here, other village societies undoubtedly existed on the Southern Plains, represented by the Bell site in Comanche County, Kansas, and Manwell (Brooks 1985), Uncas (Galm 1979; Vehik and Flynn 1981; Vehik and Ashworth 1983), and Odessa Yates (34BV100) (Brosowske and Bement 1998) sites in Oklahoma.

Comparative Analysis

The Southern Plains villages exhibit a remarkable homogeneity in cultural expression, especially the material culture, where stylistic attributes of chipped-stone assemblages are maintained over much of the region. This uniformity in lithics can be attributed, in part, to a common focus on bison exploitation. Variability in the ceramic assemblage and the bone-tool industry may be related to internal development from existing Woodland patterns. Despite the impression of a widely shared lifeway, differences also exist, principally in settlement patterns and subsistence practices. The best comparisons in these areas can be drawn among the Antelope Creek, Washita River, and Custer phases and the Zimms, Buried City, and Bluff Creek complexes. The absence of detailed excavation data from the Henrietta and Pratt complexes makes comparative analysis difficult. Some differences among Southern Plains village cultures may be seen as contributing to cultural differences among tribal societies in the region during the historic period.

The greatest differentiation exists in the structuring of Southern Plains village settlements. The stone-slab, multiroom architecture of the Antelope Creek phase and Buried City complex set them apart from other Southern Plains village cultures. The concept of a Southwest style of architecture and construction design was possibly obtained from Puebloan groups in New Mexico. There are also less obvious, although important, differences among the other recognized archeological complexes. The Custer and Paoli phases, earliest of the recognized Southern Plains village manifestations, is characterized by a settlement pattern similar to that of the preceding Plains Woodland period. Hamlets or base camps are generally situated on high terraces or ridge projections above stream valleys. Sites appear to be few and widely separated. This type of settlement pattern is also observed for the Zimms and Bluff Creek complexes. This pattern is in contrast to that of the Washita River phase where numerous, moderate-sized villages are found aggregated on terraces adjacent to principal streams or rivers. In the case of the Washita River phase, this density in settlements is thought to represent population increase as well as shifts in locations selected for settlement. Because the Zimms complex is contemporaneous with the Washita River phase, other cultural and economic forces must have operated to support continuation of the upland settlement strategy in extreme western Oklahoma. One potential explanation is a lowered carrying capacity of the land; alternatively, the Zimms complex may represent a foreign group moving into the area (from the Texas Panhandle?). One conclusion to be drawn from this comparison is that the sociopolitical structure of the Washita River phase was probably much different than that for the more widely dispersed groups such as the Custer, Paoli, Zimms, and Bluff Creek cultures. They may have had a sociopolitical organization similar to Upper Canark groups who maintained similar settlement densities and locational settings.

Contrasts can also be drawn in the nature of the subsistence economies of these groups. This variability is thought to be a function of population dynamics and concomitant expressions in the settlement structure. Although charred cultigens are found at sites of the Custer phase and the Zimms and Bluff Creek complexes, they are not present in large quantities. Thus, it does not appear that these groups practiced intensive agriculture. Furthermore, these groups also lack large numbers of deep storage pits inside residences used to house grain crops and other foodstuffs. And, although digging sticks and hoes are found at these sites, they are not present in large numbers. In contrast, the Washita River and Antelope Creek phase cultures have ample evidence for all these characteristics and can be identified as intensive agriculturalists. The Buried City complex also probably fits this pattern for intensive agriculture although excavated data to support this contention is lacking. The absence of intensive agricultural practices among the Custer phase and the Zimms and Bluff Creek complexes is probably related to the issue of economic need. Cultures with highly dispersed settlements with small populations (two or three houses) would not need to rely on starchy food products so extensively. In fact, this settlement and subsistence system may represent an adaptive strategy to situational constraints each group was locally facing (e.g., lowered carrying capacity).

Perspective

The Southern Plains Village tradition flourished until approximately 1450–1500, when the population appears to have abandoned its former heartland and become more dispersed throughout the Southern Plains region. The reasons for this resettlement are not entirely clear, but it has been suggested that changing climatic conditions ultimately forced these people to move eastward where water supplies were more reliable (Wedel 1961). It is also possible that these later groups, particularly those in south-central and west-central Oklahoma, represent the ancestors of the Wichita and were involved in a north-south movement analogous to that characteristic of their historic descendants (Bell, Jelks, and Newcomb 1974; Bell 1984).

At the same time, agricultural groups along the Pecos River in New Mexico were abandoning their villages to take up bison hunting on the plains (Jelinek 1967). These may represent a group ancestral to the Kiowa. The Apache and related groups were present throughout the western portions of the Southern Plains during the sixteenth century (Schroeder 1962, 1968). There are also some archeological sites in the region that indicate the presence of alien groups between A.D. 1400 and 1600. One of the more prominent is Edwards I in Beckham County, Oklahoma, which consists of a village with a ditch and probably surrounding palisade (Baugh 1982). This has been interpreted as evidence that new peoples, perhaps the Kiowa and Plains Apache, possibly others, were moving into the area previously dominated by Southern Plains Villagers at the time when these latter groups appear to have withdrawn from the region.

It is possible that some of these people moved eastward into the fringes of the Caddoan area where the appearance of Plains Village characteristics has been noted after 1400. It has also been suggested that they are the ancestors of the Great Bend variant located in Kansas along the Arkansas River Valley and who eventually became one of the Wichita groups (Vehik 1992). This aspect contains a number of elements of Southern Plains origin, and there are some known sites in Kansas that may represent a transitional phase or indicate movements northward (Wedel 1959, 1968a).

The Great Bend variant of Kansas was flourishing at the time of Francisco Vásquez de Coronado's entrada in 1541, and it bears some similarities to the Washita River phase of the Southern Plains villagers (Wedel 1968). When it came into existence is unknown, but it could well have been derived from Washita River phase populations moving northward after 1450. Alternatively, J.T. Hughes (1968) has suggested that descendants of the Upper Canark variant migrated northeastward to join their Upper Republican relatives and contributed to the development of Lower Loup Pawnee. The Henrietta complex is less certain in terms of later tribal affinities but may be ancestral to the later Norteño phase or perhaps the historic Tawakoni or Kitsai. Identification of historical continuity for the Bluff Creek and the Zimms complexes is the most problematical. One explanation is that they may have been subsumed under larger tribal entities.

Despite the appearance o f linear continuity between late prehistoric Southern Plains Village societies and their historically recognized relatives, there were significant changes in the social and economic lifeways of groups between A.D. 850–1450 and 1450–1700. Late prehistoric Southern Plains Villagers appear to have been more sedentary, more focused on intensive agriculture, and perhaps less egalitarian. Thus, care should be exercised in drawing too greatly upon analogies to historically identified Southern Plains societies.

Plains Village Tradition: Eastern Periphery and Oneota Tradition

DALE R. HENNING

The Plains Villagers of the Eastern Periphery (fig. 1), the Eastern Initial Middle Missouri tradition, were sedentary groups that directly participated in or influenced events culminating in the Plains Village tradition of the middle Missouri valley. Although there are differences among them, similarities in subsistence patterning, artifacts, and general cultural adaptions suggest development from the same or closely related traditions.

Both Late Woodland and Upper Mississippian (Oneota) peoples were contemporaries and neighbors of the Eastern Periphery Plains Villagers, but they manifested very different cultural traditions. The Upper Mississippian tradition is discussed here because of the proximity of western Oneota villages to Plains Village sites and because Oneota people may have been instrumental in the Plains Villagers' decision to depart from the region. It was Oneota groups who replaced the Plains Villagers in the Eastern Periphery, culminating in the Iowa, Otoe, Omaha, and Kansa occupations at the time of Euro-American contact.

Climate

Understanding the effects of climate on subsistence is vital to reconstructing adaptive patterns in the plains-prairie ecotone. When a broad, generalizing climatic model (Baerreis and Bryson 1967; Bryson and Wendland 1967; Bryson, Baerreis, and Wendland 1970; Wendland 1978) was applied to the Eastern Plains, it was seized upon by most archeologists as an explanatory device for prehistoric culture change (cf. Lehmer 1970). Other studies (H.E. Wright 1982; Anfinson and Wright 1990; Toom 1992; Zalucha 1982) have found little regional data that verifies the climatic generalizations. For the region under consideration there was apparently adequate moisture for intensive gardening from A.D. 1000 into the historic contact period. Judging from the archeological record, for whatever reasons, bison were increasingly available both there and across the Prairie Peninsula.

Initial Middle Missouri Tradition

Taxonomy

Eastern Periphery Plains Villagers lived in the northwestern quarter of Iowa, parts of eastern South Dakota, southern Minnesota, and northeastern Nebraska. Their remains are found in a region that is now the tall-grass prairie/short-grass plains ecotone, which Toom (1992) calls the Southern Northeastern Plains subarea. These villages, dating from 900–1300, are classified as the Eastern Initial Middle Missouri (Toom 1992) Tradition. (For the western division see "Plains Village Tradition: Middle Missouri," this vol.). Within the eastern division there are seven phases: Great Oasis, Big Sioux, Little Sioux, Brandon, Lower James, Cambria (C.M. Johnson 1996:14–15), and Perry Creek (Henning 1996). The Great Oasis, Perry Creek, and Cambria phases readily stand alone, while the Big Sioux and Little Sioux (Mill Creek phases) and the Lower James and the Brandon (Over phases) are closely linked culturally and temporally. Although a Cambria "phase" is named here, Benn's (1992) suggestion that the Cambria phase is part of a broad "Co-Influence Sphere" (Syms 1979) seems applicable.

The arbitrary taxonomic separation of the Over phases in South Dakota from the Mill Creek phases in Iowa is unfortunate. Despite minor cultural differences, they were generally contemporaneous and shared common ancestry and similarity in lifeways. An inclusive taxonomic unit should be defined; in this chapter, it is generalized as Mill Creek-Over.

Time and cultural content determine the differentiation of the Eastern Periphery Initial Middle Missouri phases. The Great Oasis phase appears to be derived from the Late Woodland tradition; it is both antecedent and ancestral to the Mill Creek and Over phases, but it was also contemporaneous with at least some Mill Creek (E. Henning and D.R. Henning 1982) and Over components. The Perry Creek phase (Henning 1996) offers data suggesting the survival of traditional Great Oasis people and their fusion with Mill Creek in northwest Iowa early in the thirteenth century. The Mill Creek and Over phases represent a period of geographic and demographic consolidation, with closely grouped villages or single, fortified locations. They maintained contact with Middle Mississippian, Central Plains, and other peoples to the south and east. The Cambria phase appears to be a late survival of the plains-prairie ecotone adaptation in the Prairie Lakes subarea (Anfinson 1997); it probably is Late Woodland–derived but also contains elements indicative of some shared ancestry with Mill Creek and Over. The developments leading toward definition of the Initial Middle Missouri

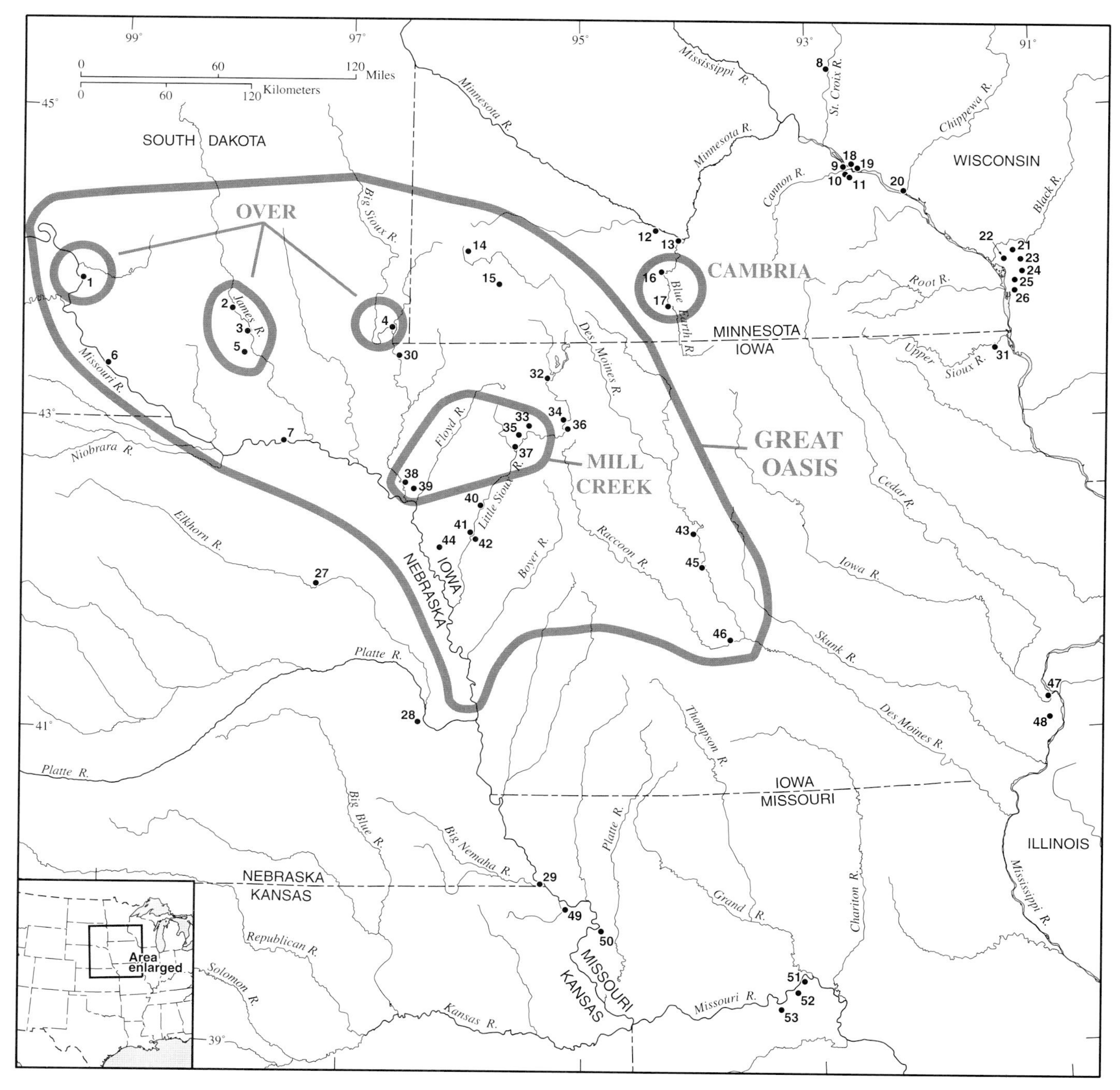

Fig. 1. Archeological sites of the Eastern Periphery. South Dakota: 1, Swanson (39BR16); 2, Mitchell (39DV1, 2, and 3); 3, Ethan or Bloom (39HS1); 4, Brandon (39MH1); 5, Twelve Mile Creek (39HT1); 6, Hitchell (39CH45); 7, Gavin's Point (39YK203). Minnesota: 8, Sheffield (21WA3); 9, Bartron (21GD2); 10, Silvernale (21GD3) and Bryan (21GD4); 11, Energy Park (21GD158); 12, Cambria (21BE2); 13, Price (21BE36); 14, Low Village (21MU2) and Thompson (21MU17); 15, Big Slough (21MU1); 16, Blue Earth (21BE14); 17, Humphrey (21FA1) and Vosburg (21FA2). Wisconsin: 18, Adams (47PI12); 19, Diamond Bluff (47PI2); 20, Armstrong (47PE12); 21, Midway (47LC19) and Ot Cemetery (47LC262); 22, Olson (47LC76) and North Shore (47LC185); 23, Herbert (47LC43) and Sand Lake (47LC44); 24, Valley View (47LC34); 25, State Road Coulee (47LC176); 26, Overhead (47LC20) and Pammel Creek (47LC61). Nebraska: 27, Stanton (25ST1); 28, Ashland (25CC1); 29, Leary (25RH1). Iowa: 30, Blood Run (13LO2); 31, Hartley Fort (13AM103), Lane Enclosure (13AM200), and Grant (1313AM201); 32, Millford (13DK1); 33, Wittrock (13OB4); 34, Gillett Grove (13CY2); 35, Waterman Crossing (13OB3); 36, Harriman (13CY1); 37, Brewster (13CK15), Phipps (13CK21), Bastian (13CK28), and Beals (13CK62); 38, Broken Kettle (13PM1), Kimball (13PM4), and Broken Kettle West (13PM25); 39, Vondrack (13PM51, 56, 62, 80, 98, 103, and 435) and Larson (13PM61); 40, Correctionville (13WD6); 41, Gothier (13WD3); 42, Dixon (13WD8); 43, Gypsum Quarry (13WB1); 44, Linscott; 45, Meehan-Schell (13BN110); 46, West Des Moines Burials (13PK38); 47, KcKinney (13LA1) and Smith (13LA2); 48, Kingston (13DM3). Kansas: 49, Fanning (14DP1). Missouri: 50, King Hill (23BN1); 51, Guthrey (23SA131); 52, Utz (23SA2) and Old Fort (23SA104); 53, Little Osage (23SA3) and Gumbo Point (23SA4).

tradition are summarized by Winham and Calabrese (1998). Toom (1992) argues convincingly for taxonomic separation of his Southern Northeastern Plains subarea from the Middle Missouri subarea, suggesting that the Plains Villager pattern developed in the southern northeastern plains and was subsequently introduced into the Middle Missouri trench by migration.

Characteristics

Eastern Periphery Initial Middle Missouri tradition village sites are composed of rectangular semisubterranean houses, each containing numerous trash or storage pits and a central fireplace. Villages range in size from a few to as many as 25 houses. Burials occur on hilltops surrounding the sites and usually contain few culturally diagnostic grave goods. A tripartite subsistence strategy (Toom 1992) based on bison hunting, horticulture, and general foraging was followed by all Villagers.

The tool assemblage found on most sites is very similar. Chipped-stone artifacts consist of simple triangular and double- and multiple-notched arrowpoints, end scrapers, side scrapers, bifacial knives, perforators, gravers, rough bifaces, choppers, and utilized flakes (fig. 2). Local cherts, Bijou Hills silicified sandstone (J.W. Porter 1962) or Ogallala orthoquartzite (Church 1994), Sioux Quartzite, Knife River Flint, Nehawka flints and, rarely, obsidian were utilized.

Ground-stone tools include manos, metates, hammerstones, grooved mauls, sharpening stones, and shaft abraders of sandstone and scoria or "clinker," thin, flat grinding slabs, polished pebbles, celts, and pipes.

Bone and antler tools are numerous, including bone chisels, awls, punches, needles, fish hooks, projectile points, shaft wrenches, bison scapula hoes, sickles, and squash knives, beaver incisor chisels, and antler "drifts," flaking tools, and arrow points.

Decorative items include ground hematite, disk beads of conch and whelk shell, *Leptoxis* beads, bone beads and pendants, excised strips of bone and antler, bracelets, and deer phalanx tinklers (fig. 3).

Great Oasis Phase

Great Oasis cultural remains were first identified at the Low Village and Big Slough sites in southwestern Minnesota (Wilford 1945, 1955). Archeological investigations have produced similar remains up the Missouri River as far as Chamberlain, South Dakota, in eastern Nebraska, and in the Big Sioux, Little Sioux, and Des Moines River drainages of Iowa (fig. 1). Radiocarbon dates suggest that Great Oasis was an established cultural entity by A.D. 900 and persisted until at least 1200 (Ralph, Michael, and Han 1973; Damon et al. 1974). Great Oasis apparently evolved out of the Late Woodland tradition, perhaps the Loseke (Benn 1990).

Luther College, Decorah, Iowa, Archaeol. Research Center: a, 13PM61-649-24; b, 13PM61-504-4; c, 13PM61-748-7; d, 13PM61-513-35; e, 13PM61-507-41; f, 13PM61-619-45; g, 13PM61-227-32; h, 13PM61-571-34; i, 13PM61-569; j, 13PM61-618-2; k, 13PM61-425.

Fig. 2. Small tools, characteristic of Eastern Periphery Plains villages, from the Great Oasis, Larson site, Iowa. a–c, Arrowpoints; d, arrowpoint reworked into drill; e–f, end scrapers; g, graver on a blade; h, perforator; i, deer antler tine flaking tool; j, bison rib awl; k, bird bone awl.

Great Oasis remains have been studied from the Great Oasis site (Wilford 1941, 1945, 1955), Gypsum Quarry site (Flanders and Hansman 1961), Gavin's Point Dam site (R.L. Hall 1961), West Des Moines Burials (Knauth 1963), Hitchell site (R.B. Johnston 1967), the Meehan-Schell village (B. Mead 1981) in the lower Des Moines River drainage, the Beals site on Mill Creek in the Little Sioux drainage (Henning 1967), and the West Broken Kettle and Perry Creek sites (E. Henning and D.R. Henning 1982). Gradwohl (1969, 1969a), Henning (1967, 1971, 1982, 1991, 1996), E. Henning (1981), E. Henning and D.R. Henning (1982), Tiffany (1991, 1991a), and Williams provide discussions. A documented Omaha cemetery yielded historic materials associated with sherds typical of Great Oasis ceramics (Champe 1949a). In light of the early cluster of dates for Great Oasis elsewhere, the Omaha had apparently included vessels from a Great Oasis site with the burials.

Wilford identified Great Oasis in Minnesota as western Mississippian. Johnston (1967) suggested that the Great Oasis component at the Hitchell site in South Dakota represented an early transitional development that contributed to an emerging Middle Missouri tradition. Johnston also reported partial contemporaneity between Late Woodland and Great Oasis at Hitchell. Great Oasis is fundamental to the Initial Middle Missouri tradition, sharing the early Plains Villager patterns of development while retaining some Woodland characteristics.

Luther College, Decorah, Iowa, Archaeol. Research Center: a, 13PM61-418; b, 13PM61-617; c, 13PM61-412; d, 13PM61-337-1.

Fig. 3. Small ornaments from the Great Oasis, Larson site, Iowa. a, Labret or bead made from human skull fragment; b, olivella shell bead; c, conch shell disk bead; d, conch or whelk columella.

Great Oasis is ancestral to Mill Creek and for a time maintained its cultural integrity as a contemporary. The Mississippian trade network that is evident in Mill Creek–Over sites was apparently initiated by Great Oasis peoples, then expanded in scope by the Mill Creek occupants (E. Henning 1981; E. Henning and D.R. Henning 1982).

The typical Great Oasis village is located on the edge of a first terrace immediately above the floodplain or along a shallow lake and is unfortified. Villages are dotted with basin- and bell-shaped trash or storage pits that average 24 to 30 inches in maximum dimensions and contain an abundance of pottery, stone and bone tools, chipped-stone detritus, faunal materials, and charred flora. Charred corn kernels are generally found, but cobs are rare at Broken Kettle West, Beals, the Low Village, and Larson. Human bone is occasionally found on village sites, and a partial, flexed burial was found in a trash pit at the Low Village in 1971. Gulf and East Coast shell and freshwater shell beads, *Leptoxis* (Turgeon et al. 1988), shell ornaments (probably from the Ohio River drainage) are found in quantity on Great Oasis sites in northwest Iowa.

At Broken Kettle West, four heavily constructed, semisubterranean, rectangular structures with long entrances, characteristic of the Initial Middle Missouri tradition, were excavated (fig. 4). Faunal evidence places major occupation from late fall to early spring (Baerreis 1970); principal food resources were migratory birds, fish, deer, and smaller mammals. The lack of bison bone suggests that they were not locally available when the site was occupied. Stratified and superimposed pits are common and some of the structures were repaired and partially reconstructed, suggesting long-term or repeated village use. Broken Kettle West was the home base of people who apparently spent summers elsewhere, probably hunting bison on the short-grass plains. Corn kernels are common at Broken Kettle West, but cob fragments are rare and digging tools are absent.

The West Des Moines burials (Knauth 1963) can definitely be assigned to Great Oasis. No fewer than 18 individuals were found in single, flexed, and multiple graves in a hilltop cemetery. Associated with the burials were

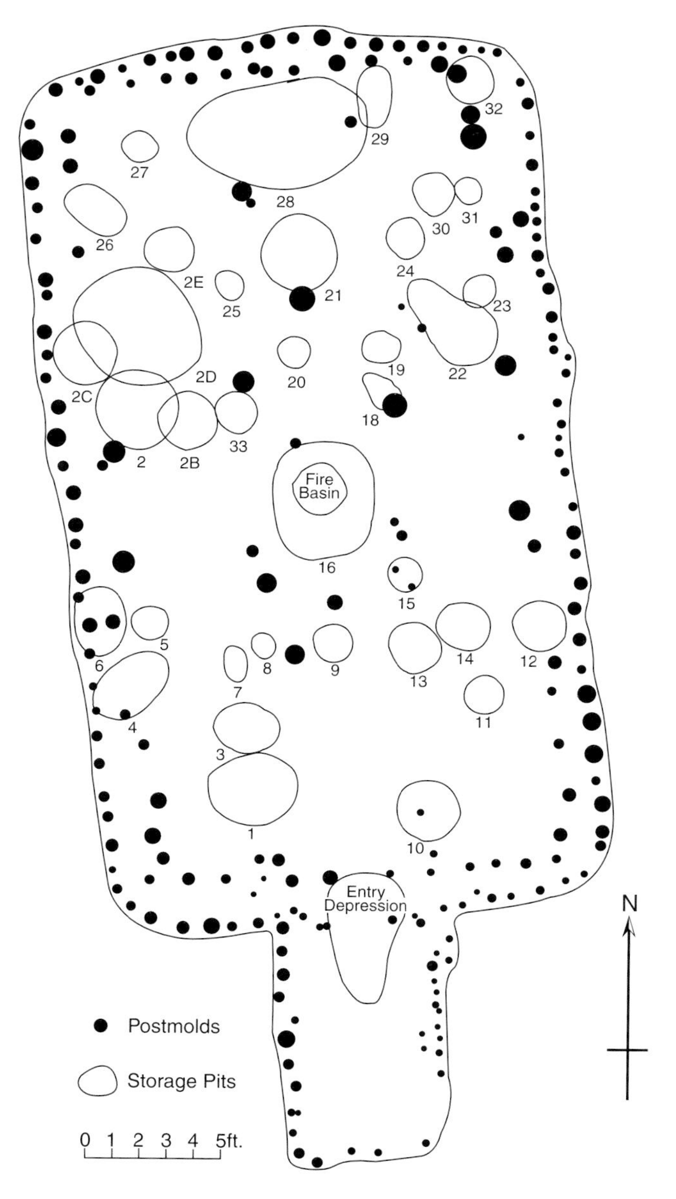

U. of Nebr., Lincoln, Archaeol. Lab.

Fig. 4. Great Oasis house plan at Broken Kettle West site, Iowa. Drawing by Jeff Hoge.

more than eight unique and enigmatic crosses cut out of clam shell, a quantity of *Leptoxis* beads, and typical Great Oasis jars and nonceramic artifacts. Flanders and Hansman (1961) were reticent to assign the mound dug at the Gypsum Quarry site to Great Oasis, but their description suggests that the mound was constructed by Great Oasis peoples, probably for interment. Burials abound on the loess blufftops surrounding the Great Oasis and Mill Creek sites immediately north of Sioux City, Iowa, in the Big Sioux drainage. They include individual flexed burials, ossuaries, and crematoria. Unfortunately, pottery diagnostic of either Great Oasis or Mill Creek is rarely included in burials. Anculosa, conch, and whelk shell beads are often found, supporting their assignment to Great Oasis or Mill Creek peoples, but not allowing for burial differentiation between the two phases.

Great Oasis pottery vessels are globular jars with round bases; exterior surfaces are smoothed-over cordmarked, and interior surfaces are smoothed. The rim most readily identified as Great Oasis is a straight, outflaring form with parallel sides and flattened lip; it is decorated with fine-line rectangular motifs applied on a field of parallel horizontal lines (fig. 5 a–h). Variations on this theme are described by E. Johnson (1969). The other ware grouping is a jar with a low wedge-lip (fig. 5 i–m) occasionally decorated with tool impressions on the lip-rim exterior edge. Until the excavations at Broken Kettle West, wedge-lip ware had been regarded as an item of trade or influence from outside Great Oasis. At Broken Kettle West, wedge-lip ware comprises over 50 percent of the total rim sherd sample.

The Larson site, located along Perry Creek immediately north of Sioux City, Iowa, is the type site for the Perry Creek phase. Excavations (Henning 1982, 1996) yielded the full range of Mill Creek and Great Oasis pottery types with a few pottery fragments of Middle Mississippian derivation. The site, dated at about 1200, also yielded, along with the expected bone and stone tools, a large quantity of trade shell items from the Southeast. These, along with high percentages of exotic stone, including Ogallala orthoquartzite, Nehawka flint, and clinker, suggest that the site functioned as a trade center. Although quantities of charred corn kernels and an occasional cob fragment appear here, the tool inventory includes very few of the bison scapula hoes, manos, or grinding slabs so characteristic of other Eastern Plains Villagers

Luther College, Decorah, Iowa, Archaeol. Research Center: a, 13CK62-19-(103); b, 13CK62-24-(12); c, 13CK 62-15-(385): d, 13CK62-11-(12); e, 13CK62-3-(177); f, 13CK62-2-(128); g, 13PM61-392-2-(177); h, 13PM61-507-(289); i, 13CK62-17-(12); j, 13CK62-4-(461); k, 13CK62-6-(17); l, 13PM61-395-1-(234); m, 13PM61-651-5-(380).

Fig. 5. Great Oasis pottery from the Bastian Village and Larson sites, Iowa. a–h, High rim; i–m, wedge lip.

Mill Creek and Over Phases

Mill Creek sites are by definition restricted to northwest Iowa on the Big and Little Sioux drainages. Mill Creek culture was originally defined (Keyes 1927, 1951) on the basis of excavations in 1934, 1935, and 1939 (Orr 1963; Fugle 1962a ; Ives 1962). Excavations on Mill Creek sites are reported by D.C. Anderson (1969, 1972, 1973a, 1977, 1981, 1985), Baerreis and Bryson (1967 [republished as Henning 1968–1969]), Flanders (1960), and Tiffany (1982). Mill Creek is divided into Big and Little Sioux phases, the latter with two suggested subphases, Little Sioux I (900–1150) and 2 (1150–1400) (D.C. Anderson 1969).

Once thought to have originated from a migration of Mississippian peoples (Griffin 1946; Ives 1962), Mill Creek is now regarded as Great Oasis-derived, and characterized by some interaction with contemporary Mississippian and Nebraska phase groups. While undoubtedly influenced to a degree by both cultural manifestations, Mill Creek is a regional phenomenon; the cultural core is consistently indigenous.

Mill Creek sites are often deep middens consisting of multiple layers of village refuse separated by narrow lenses of sterile soil (Henning, Henning, and Baerreis 1968) or by collapse of earth-covered house walls (Fishel 1996). The middens are riddled with storage or trash pits; some pits are four feet in diameter and up to five feet in depth. Many are bell-shaped. A few villages were heavily fortified by ditches and a stockade and bear evidence of access ramps.

Houses were built on the evolving middens. Orr (1963) located several long-rectangular house post patterns beneath the midden deposits at Broken Kettle and Kimball quite comparable to several house patterns found at the Little Sioux phase Wittrock site. Three superimposed semisubterranean house floors and associated postmolds were identified within the Broken Kettle midden.

Hilltop burials, all culturally indistinguishable, abound around Mill Creek sites. Many have inclusions of exotic shell.

Specific Mill Creek additions to the nonceramic artifact inventory include diamond-shaped "Harahey" knives, strike-a-light pressers, "door-knob" discoidals, stone effigies, calotte bowls, tubular and elbow pipes, bison-skull hoes, deer metatarsus beamers, and quill flatteners. Large numbers of shell items of conch and whelk, *Marginella*, *Olivella*, and *Leptoxis* suggest interaction with groups to the south and east.

Mill Creek ceramics are divided into four or five ware groupings reflecting similarities in paste and rim form; each grouping comprises one or more types. Three wares are indigenously derived: the high-rimmed Chamberlain (fig. 6 a–c), the low-rimmed Sanford (fig. 6 d–e), and the S-rimmed Foreman (fig. 6f). Seed jars (fig. 6g) from Mill Creek components are similar to their counterparts in the

Cahokia region. Mill Creek ware (fig. 6 h–i) includes bottles, bowls, pans, and jars with high, vertical rims, low rims, and rolled lips, combining indigenous traits with characteristics derived from the south and east.

Major sites appear to be clustered around localities where wood was most readily available (Henning, Henning, and Baerreis 1968). Wood was obviously a valuable commodity to people building large and heavily constructed houses surrounded, at some villages, by stockades. Available wood resources may have diminished from about 1150 (Baerreis and Bryson 1967), when wood was needed for fortifications.

Faunal remains are well preserved on most Mill Creek sites and suggest exploitation of a full range of available resources. Gardening was practiced here from 900 into historic times. Bison hunting appears to have fluctuated depending upon the ready availability of those migratory animals. Judging from the data available, bison herds frequented this region from 1100 into the early historic period.

Luther College, Decorah, Iowa, Archaeol. Research Center: a, 13PM61-425-(245); b, 13PM61-477-(263); c, 13PM61-209-3-(106); d, 13PM61-690-(391); e, 13PM61-658-1-(389); f, 13PM61-633; g, 13PM61-144-3; h, 13PM61-178-4; i, 13PM4-SUN.

Fig. 6. Mill Creek pottery from the Larson site, Iowa. a–c, Chamberlain ware; d–e, Sanford ware; f, Foreman ware; g, seed jar; h, polished shell-tempered jar; i, grog-tempered bowl.

When compared with the other Villagers of the Initial Middle Missouri tradition, the Mill Creek groups obtained far more exotic items. Gulf and East coast and freshwater shell objects were brought into the region. Direct contact between Mill Creek and Cahokia-oriented peoples (including those living in the Illinois and Mississippi river drainages) is suggested by a very few vessels. The full range of vessel forms from any one period at Cahokia is not represented on any Mill Creek site; specific forms, especially seed jars, were copied by local potters.

Several authors (R.A. Alex 1981; D.C. Anderson 1987; Tiffany 1991, 1991a) have offered explanatory models for the presence of exotic objects on Mill Creek sites, focusing on the importance of trade with Middle Mississippian people to the south and east, especially Cahokia. These models, focused on the presence of Middle Mississippian exotic objects on Mill Creek sites, have failed to point out how rare some of those objects are in the contexts of masses of indigenous data or to ascertain with any degree of precision the possible derivation of specific items.

Perhaps Mill Creek peoples exchanged meat, hides, and lithic materials for processed goods, including foodstuffs, salt, clothing, and ornaments, but there is no solid evidence for this hypothesized trade. There is very little evidence of direct interaction of any kind with groups occupying the Eastern Periphery from excavated Middle Mississippian sites, although the case has been made for very limited interaction between Cahokia complex occupants and groups over 50 miles away (Pauketat and Emerson 1997). Nonetheless, Southeastern exotic objects are found on Great Oasis and Mill Creek sites, with greatest numbers from the lower Little Sioux and Perry Creek drainages. The stimuli behind their presence may have been social and religious rather than economic. Some form of interaction linking the Middle Missouri region with Mississippian groups was established by Great Oasis peoples, then was variably assumed and developed by Mill Creek and Over groups.

Radiocarbon dates suggest that Mill Creek-Over occupations were contemporaneous with nearby Nebraska phase peoples and early Oneota groups. The interactive network was apparently exclusive; Oneota and Central Plains peoples were not included in the same way. On the other hand, pottery analyses (Henning 1969) suggest some Nebraska phase-Big Sioux phase interrelationships, but not the exchange of exotica that may be Mississippian-derived.

Over was defined (Over and Meleen 1941) to include the Brandon, Mitchell, and Twelve Mile Creek sites. Hurt (1951) suggested inclusion of the Swanson site located north of Chamberlain, South Dakota, and the Ethan (Bloom) site south of Mitchell, South Dakota. However, Toom (1992) assigned Swanson to the Western Initial Middle Missouri in the Big Bend region.

Over and Mill Creek components are sufficiently similar in time and cultural content to be considered as a single broadly defined unit. There is direct correspondence between the two phases in village fortification, house type, size and shape of storage pits, pottery, and bone and stone tool types. Direct evidence for burial practices is limited at the Over sites. Mounds located near Mitchell (Meleen 1938) were probably constructed by Over people, but few diagnostic artifacts have been recovered. Radiocarbon assays suggest Over contemporaneity with both Mill Creek and Great Oasis occupations in northwest Iowa.

The differences between Over and Mill Creek sites are important. Over sites do not exhibit the purposeful midden development seen on many of the Mill Creek components nor are they ever surrounded by a rectangular fortification ditch; they are located in defensible positions with full or partial fortification conforming to typography. Seed jars, high-necked bottles, and the exotic shells often found on Mill Creek sites are rare in the Over phase.

The fate of the Mill Creek-Over phases of the Middle Missouri tradition is not known. Obviously, these people vacated their villages in northwest Iowa and eastern South Dakota during the fourteenth century, but the identifying features of the culture do not subsequently appear elsewhere. The argument (D.C. Anderson 1981:120–124, 1987; Toom 1992) that they moved north and west, merging with the developing tribes of the historic period while undergoing rapid acculturation, seems most tenable.

Cambria Phase

Cambria is best known from the type site located in Blue Earth County, Minnesota. Additional Cambria sites are located in southwestern Minnesota and upstream on the Minnesota and Red rivers (E. Johnson 1971, 1991; Knudson 1967; Watrall 1968).

The Cambria village yielded one long-rectangular house floor. Cambria sites offer a characteristic plains-oriented bone and stone tool inventory. Specific artifacts include chipped-stone arrow points, ovoid scrapers, disks, celts or hoes, and core tools, pecked and ground grooved mauls and pitted manos, bone quill flatteners, beamers, cylinders, barbed points, knife handles, bison scapula hoes, bison radius picks, worked bison horn cores, and an antler scraper handle. Notched mussel shells and mussel shell spoons were also found as well as one copper awl. Faunal remains suggest that the site occupants did extensive hunting and butchering of deer and bison on or very near the site. Horticulture was also important, judging from the number of scapula hoes and the presence of quantities of charred corn. There is no direct evidence for trade to the south and east; *Leptoxis* and Gulf Coast shells are absent.

Detailed analysis of Cambria pottery (fig. 7) (Knudson 1967) defined four types: Linden Everted Rim; Mankato Incised; Judson Composite; and three Rolled Rim varieties. Most vessels are grit-tempered and smoothed-over cordmarked, smoothed or polished on the exterior surface. Cambria ceramics are not directly comparable to Great Oasis or Mill Creek-Over wares, although the Rolled Rim varieties are duplicated in Mill Creek-Over wares, suggesting shared ties to the sources of this style. A few Great Oasis and Oneota sherds were recovered from the type site.

Additional sites assigned to the Cambria phase are found upstream on the Minnesota River, but none is directly comparable to the type site (E. Johnson 1991). The Cambria sites appear to be linked (Benn 1992) by the consistent appearance, sometimes at a high percentage, of "Red River ware" (Knudson's "Linden" types), which is found across a broad region north and east of the Missouri River trench from southern Saskatchewan to the eastern Dakotas and south-central Minnesota. Rather than an example of ceramic unity across vast space, Benn (1990) points out that Red River ware is just one of a number of wares and types that were used by occupants of this extensive ecotonal area, which was probably used by many groups with diverse cultural traditions, even into the historic period (Hickerson 1965). The Cambria type site is unique and offers the remains of simply one of a number of bands that utilized the Minnesota River valley and adjacent environs in the late prehistoric period. The evident interband-intertribal interactions were obviously broad and important to these groups.

U. of Minn., Minneapolis, Archaeol. Lab: a, 21BE2-244-30; b, Jvp 613; c, Jvp 2537; d, 21BE2-244-36; e, 21BE2-244-8; f, 21BE2-567-77; g, 21BE2-184-8.

Fig. 7. Pottery from the Cambria village site, Minn. a, Rolled Rim type; b, Judson Composite; c–e, Linden Everted; f–g, Mankato Incised.

Summary: Plains Village Pattern

The development of the Plains Village pattern along the Eastern Periphery may be due to a combination of climatic and cultural-adaptive factors that culminated shortly before 900 and persisted until nearly 1400. Climatic change was obviously not the only reason for the disappearance of Plains Villagers from the Eastern Periphery. From the number of scapula hoes, manos, and metates that occur on most sites, it seems that gardening continued to be successfully practiced into the historic contact period. Oneota peoples may have made forays there as early as 1200 to procure bison, ultimately establishing villages during the fourteenth century. Perhaps Oneota peoples forced the Mill Creek-Over and Cambria groups to vacate the region.

Drought conditions may have persisted for about four centuries. The Mill Creek peoples left northwest Iowa by no later than 1400. Between 1400 and 1500, Cahokia, the great Mississippian center located near the mouth of the Missouri River, was also vacated and the identifying features of that cultural tradition were dispersed. Peoples of the Central Plains Village tradition also dispersed by this time; all were apparently unable to adapt successfully to the changing cultural environment and maintain their cultural identities.

Oneota

Oneota is a late prehistoric cultural manifestation found in the western Prairie Peninsula. It is part of the Upper Mississippian tradition (T.A. Emerson and J.A. Brown 1992), sharing broadly defined traits with the Fort Ancient tradition (Griffin 1943; Drooker 1997) of Indiana and Ohio. Oneota in its broadest sense (R.L. Hall 1962) may be regarded as a congeries of related traditions (Henning 1998).

The earliest Oneota sites may be those in central Wisconsin (vol. 15:570–572), dating 900–1000. Using pottery as the most available diagnostic, a series of phases has been defined for Oneota; these phases are frequently grouped culturally and spatially, forming "group continuities" (Hall 1962) that suggest technological and probable biological relationship through time within geographically defined areas (Henning 1970:9). Oneota groups were probably attracted to the Eastern Plains periphery as early as 1100 by the bison herds, and by no later than 1300 they established large villages in western Iowa.

Five large prehistoric Oneota sites in northwest Iowa have yielded no historic materials (Fishel 1995; Harvey 1979; Henning 1961, 1970; Tiffany 1979a); four of them are included in the Correctionville phase (Fishel 1995; Henning 1970, 1998). Ceramic similarities suggest some relationship with the Blue Earth components of south-central Minnesota (Dobbs 1984), but it is preferable to separate the two complexes. Generally accepted dates for the Correctionville phase range around A.D. 1350, although some components may be older.

Correctionville phase pottery (fig. 8) (Harvey 1979) is primarily shell-tempered; low, outflaring-rimmed globular jars with broad shoulders and angular shoulder extremities predominate. The vessel lip is generally notched by tool impressions on the lip surface or onto the rim interior; many vessels exhibit trailed-line motifs on the inner rim surface, and on many the rim is so outflaring that its inner surface is nearly horizontal. The shoulder area is broad and flattened; decoration is by rectilinear trailed-line triangular motifs paralleled by tool impressions. Curvilinear motifs are rare. Handles are very small, rounded in cross-section and attached to the lip and upper shoulder area. Bowls occur, but are rare.

Large, often bell-shaped, storage pits found in these Oneota sites are usually filled with village refuse: quantities of bison and other animal bone, charred corn cobs and kernels, large chopping-cutting tools made of Ogallala orthoquartzite (Church 1994), and many grooved mauls. Correctionville phase sites yield many catlinite pipes, cut fragments, and small tablets incised with a variety of motifs (fig. 9). An anthropomorphic figure appears as a motif on catlinite, bone, and antler (D.C. Anderson 1975:66–69).

None of the Correctionville phase sites appears to have been fortified nor are mounds associated. The Dixon site revealed what may be a house structure (Harvey 1979: 63–67) located no less than 24 inches below the surface.

Tiel Sanford Mus., Cherokee, Iowa: a, 13WD6-P10; b, 13WD6-1163-57-M; c, 13WD6-S; d, 13WD6-P10-984-57-M; e, 13WD6-272-57-M-PL; f, 13WD6-M-1290-60-M.

Fig. 8. Oneota pottery from the Correctionville site, Iowa.

No cemetery areas have been located on or near any of these sites; burials are found within the village and occasionally in the pits, but with no discernible pattern of placement.

The Bastian site (Tiffany 1979a; Harvey 1979), located just north of Cherokee, Iowa, on a high terrace overlooking the Little Sioux River, dates later, but bears an attenuated relationship to Correctionville phase sites (Harvey 1979; Henning 1970, 1998). At least a dozen catlinite plaques (R.T. Bray 1963:17–28) and nearly 100 plaque fragments have been recovered from the surface. These compare favorably with other plaques from Oneota sites bearing representations of animals and mythical creatures enhanced with Southern Cult motifs including the forked eye, arrows, and maces. Considering that village refuse is very lightly scattered across the site, which encompasses at least 60 acres, the number of plaque fragments is surprising. Further, even though bison and other animal bone is well represented in the six pits excavated to date, no end scrapers have been found (Harvey 1979:152). No fortification, mounds or other surface features have been reported, and no associated cemetery has been found.

Leary Site

The Leary site (A.T. Hill and W.R. Wedel 1936) is located on the lower Big Nemaha River, near its confluence with the Missouri, in the southeast corner of Nebraska. There is also a Central Plains component at Leary that may suggest some relationship with Oneota.

The Leary site covers at least 120 acres. A group of burial mounds, perhaps associated with the village, is located on a hilltop above the site. Both Correctionville Trailed and Allamakee Trailed–like pottery types are represented (Henning 1970:145). These types are found in different components in Iowa, suggesting that Leary was occupied between 1200 and 1400, perhaps functioning as an exchange center. The site is strategically located to provide access both to the prairie peninsula and the plains. A few glass beads have been recovered from the surface, but no historic component has been identified.

Chariton River Sites

The Chariton River group continuity of north-central Missouri (Henning 1970:142) began about 1350 and evolved rapidly, culminating in the occupations at the Utz site, home of the Missouria tribe (Berry and Chapman 1942). Excavated sites include Guthrey, Dowell (Henning 1970), and Utz (C.H. Chapman 1946, 1952, 1980; C.H. Chapman et al. 1985; R.T. Bray 1963, 1991). Detailed discussions of site excavations are offered by R.T. Bray (1991), C.H. Chapman (1952, 1980), C.H. Chapman et al. (1985) and Henning (1970).

Peripheral Western Oneota Components

The Northwest Periphery (G.E. Gibbon 1995) can be characterized by a distinct Oneota "feel" in the ceramics and other artifacts being recovered from a number of sites in North Dakota (Michlovic and Schneider 1993; C.M. Flynn 1993), probably arising due to movement of people out of western and northern Minnesota into the Red River valley. A similar "feel" of direct Oneota influence is apparent in the Devils Lake–Sourisford burial complex (Syms 1979), where small jars with Oneota-like shoulder decoration, incised stone (often catlinite) tablets, conch-shell mask gorgets, and Gulf Coast columella beads have been recovered. The people of this burial complex must have been involved in an extensive and lively trade network that existed just prior to and into the historic contact period.

A number of sites in South Dakota suggest Oneota or Oneota-influenced interactions with local residents. Such contact is in evidence at the Initial Coalescent (Lehmer 1971) Arzberger site (Spaulding 1956), where some shell-tempered pottery, a few Oneota-like shoulder decorations, a catlinite pipe prow, and a small catlinite tablet have been found. A Sioux Quartzite pitted boulder comparable to those found on the Blood Run site is recorded. Other sites that yield small numbers of potsherds suggestive of Oneota influence or presence are found on the James and Vermillion rivers (L.M. Alex 1994). Some of these Oneota materials probably suggest the presence of bison-hunting parties; artifacts from Blood Run suggest reciprocal visits between its occupants and Initial Coalescent groups to the west.

The Stanton site, near Stanton, Nebraska, has three components, one of which is Oneota. The earliest is Aksarben, then Oneota, and finally historic Omaha, who camped there in the summers of 1869, 1873, and 1876 (D.A. Gunnerson 1949–1956). Oneota pottery from Stanton is distinctive. The rim sherds are very high in proportion to vessel size. The lip-rim juncture is decorated with short tool impressions extending onto the inner rim.

The Ashland site (A.T. Hill and P.L. Cooper 1938:249–278), near Ashland, Nebraska, has at least three components; the latest is Oneota. It is not dated and offers no historic materials. A small pottery sample from the Oneota component is similar to Correctionville Trailed pottery (Henning 1970:146), suggesting a date of about 1350.

There is good evidence for Oneota interaction with late Central Plains tradition groups. Blakeslee (1978a) suggests that both Oneota and Middle Missouri tradition items are found In the St. Helena phase, dating those interactions at about 1200. Billeck (1993) reports Oneota and Oneota-like pottery at the Kullbom site and other late Central Plains tradition sites.

In south-central Nebraska and north-central Kansas is found the White Rock phase (B. Logan 1995). The pottery is less than 50 percent tempered with the characteristic

after R.T. Bray 1963.

Fig. 9. Catlinite plaques from Oneota sites. a, Stiles tablet no. 1, Bastian site, Iowa; b–c, Utz tablet, Utz site, Mo., obverse and reverse; d, Stiles tablet no. 2, Bastian site; e–f, New Albin, Iowa, tablet, obverse and reverse; g, Otoe tablet, northeastern Nebr. Drawn by Roger Thor Roop.

slaked shell and there is some simple-stamping evident on the surfaces; nonetheless, it seems comparable in all respects to many other western Oneota complexes. The pottery (M.K. Rusco 1960) is comparable to that made farther east prior to 1350. A group of Oneota people may have settled in this region at about 1300, maintaining a lively interaction with other Oneota groups to the north and east.

Western Mississippi River Drainage

An important local group continuity has been defined for the La Crosse terrace (Boszhardt 1994); regional definition, including the lower Root and Upper Iowa valleys, has been offered by Sasso (1993). The group continuity appears to have developed out of a Blue Earth-like manifestation and evolved into the Orr phase, probably the contact-period Iowa Indians (Mott 1938; M.M. Wedel 1959, 1981). The horizon styles defined and employed by Boszhardt to mark the phases that characterize this group continuity are used widely.

Blue Earth Region

Sites concentrated in the Blue Earth region are similar to a number of sites across southern Minnesota, northwestern Iowa, and western Wisconsin. Blue Earth sites are considered antecedent and ancestral to components at Red Wing (G.E. Gibbon and C.A. Dobbs 1991) and in western Wisconsin (Boszhardt 1994). The Humphrey and Vosburg sites were described by Wilford (1945, 1955). Survey by Dobbs and Shane (1983) in the region produced over 40 Oneota components. Dobbs (1984:207–220) suggested a long sequence of occupations in the region. No Blue Earth site offers evidence for historic contact.

Red Wing Region

A Red Wing region includes the Energy Park, Bryan, Silvernale, and Bartron sites in Minnesota and the Diamond Bluff and Adams sites in Wisconsin (G.E. Gibbon and C.A. Dobbs 1991; W. Rodell 1991; Green 1997). Initial settlement (perhaps by 1000) was by Blue Earth-related Oneota groups. Contact with Middle Mississippian groups apparently resulted in the unique and short-lived Silvernale phase, 1100–1300, during which many burial and some flat-topped and pyramidal mounds were constructed, large villages were fortified, and the pottery included some excellent local renderings of Mississippian styles. Considering the number of Mississippian-derived pottery vessels, there are very few items (a shell "short-nosed" god mask, some marine shell items, an ear spool) directly linking the sites with Mississippian groups. This small region was must have functioned as an exchange center with Oneota, Mississippian, and Cambria participants.

Central Des Moines Region

A Moingona phase has been proposed (Gradwohl 1969a) for Oneota sites in the central Des Moines River valley (Benn 1984, 1989; Moffat et al. 1990; Osborn 1982). The sites may date between 1175 and 1300. Most sites located to date are villages; some seasonal encampments have been identified (Benn 1984:94). No formal cemeteries have been found; however, the secondary interment in a pit feature associated with a charnel house (Gradwohl 1974) and the ubiquitous human bone fragments on the village sites offer some evidence for the treatment of the dead. These central Des Moines sites may be the earliest found in Iowa, but cultural antecedents to them have not been identified anywhere as yet. They appear to be ancestral to the first occupants of the Wever terrace of the Mississippi Alluvial Plain region (Henning 1995, 1998).

Identification with Historic Tribes

The Oneota tradition has been linked to speakers of the Chiwere Siouan dialect (Griffin 1937; Mott 1938; Berry and Chapman 1942). The Iowa (Mott 1938, M.M. Wedel 1959, 1981) and Missouria (C.H. Chapman 1946, 1952, 1959, 1980) seem most positively identified with the Oneota tradition through historic documentation and archeologically defined ties to their prehistoric material culture traditions.

Three Okoboji phase sites were probably occupied by the Iowa (and, perhaps, Otoe) following their departure from the La Crosse region (which includes the lower Upper Iowa and Root River valleys) late in the seventeenth century (Henning 1998). All yield small trade materials and traditional prehistoric artifacts, including pottery comparable to Allamakee Trailed (Boszhardt 1994), which suggests derivation from the Orr phase. All three sites are likely candidates for occupation by the Iowa during the 1700s (M.M. Wedel 1981; Henning 1998), but none was visited by a European while Indians were present. Most trade materials recovered are small and portable, consisting of brass and copper ornaments (most probably made from kettle fragments, although some may be made of native copper), glass beads, brass rings, iron knives, and a very few axes.

The Milford site has been excavated (D.C. Anderson 1994; Tiffany and Anderson 1993), offering an impressive array of Euro-American trade items including, in addition to the small items listed above, an Apostle spoon fragment, silver Jesuit rings, iron projectile points, fish hooks, a cross, gun barrels, powder cans, gun parts, gun flints, and lead shot. The Gillett Grove site (Henning 1961:32, 1970) once boasted 12 low mounds and a circular enclosed area of about 100 yards diameter with walls 16 feet wide and two feet high. The Harriman site also had 12 low mounds (Henning 1961:32). Both sites offer small historic objects; some turquoise has been recovered from Gillett Grove.

The Utz site is generally linked to the historic Missouria tribe. Utz is a very large site, between 300 and 500 acres, and occupied for three centuries. When first reported (Fowke 1910:86–92), there were some 40 "trash mounds" 16 to 18 inches high that have subsequently been plowed away, leaving the site littered with village refuse. Excavations revealed numerous storage and trash pits and some cemetery areas (R.T. Bray 1963, 1991; C.H. Chapman 1946, 1952, 1959, 1980; C.H. Chapman et al. 1985; Henning 1970). The Old Fort, located near the Utz site, is Oneota (W.R. Wood 1973), probably part of the Utz complex. This enclosure encompasses some 6.2 acres following the hilltop contour.

Pottery from Utz suggests a mixture of Upper Mississippi Valley, Correctionville, and, probably, Blue Earth, providing evidence for trade and continuous interaction among Oneota groups. The evolution of Utz as an exchange center may be tied directly to the demise of Cahokia, since its status as an exchange center may immediately postdate Mississippian efflorescence in the Saint Louis region.

About 1717 the more powerful Little Osage established themselves near the principal Missouria village and took control of the exchange network in the lower Missouri valley (C.H. Chapman 1959:2). Archeological evidence suggests that the Missouria of the early 1700s had retained much of their prehistoric material cultural tradition; the Osage had not, although some of it, particularly pottery manufacture, may have been borrowed from the Missouria.

Four of the Dhegiha-speaking Siouan groups—the Osage, Kansa, Omaha, and Ponca—were apparently late arrivals to the Eastern Plains (Henning 1993). Their linguistic relatives, the Quapaw, probably lived on the Arkansas River when first encountered by Europeans (J.A. Ford 1961), but no documented Quapaw sites have been verified there (M.P. Hoffman 1990). Dhegiha migration legends (Dorsey 1886) generally bear out locational evidence from historic documents and archeology. All excavations at known or suspected Dhegiha villages have yielded historic objects such as brass kettle fragments, glass beads, and brass and copper ornaments; a few also produced guns, gun parts, iron axes, and hoes. Some Dhegiha sites, especially those assigned to the Kansa (W.R. Wedel 1959; Henning 1970, 1998), and the Blood Run site, occupied by the Omaha (M.M. Wedel 1981; Henning 1998), also offer a broad range of traditional Oneota artifacts, including pottery.

The Blood Run site (Henning 1982a, 1998), located in the northwest corner of Iowa and extending across the Big Sioux River onto the South Dakota side, is the largest Oneota site known (well over 1,000 acres); it once boasted over 275 mounds. A large number of boulder outlines, in both circular and ovoid configurations, once were visible; these averaged about 30 feet across and up to 60 feet in length (C. Thomas 1894:38–39). Also described in early accounts of the site is an earthen-enclosed area located in the southern portion, which encompassed about 15 acres (Keyes 1930:219–220; T.H. Lewis 1890). At least eight Sioux Quartzite pitted boulders" are also found on the site. Now, at least 76 mounds can be seen on the surface, but the enclosed area, serpent, and boulder circles are no longer visible. Most professional excavations of mounds at Blood Run (Starr 1889; Keyes 1930: Orr 1963; Harvey 1979) produced burials associated with early historic materials. One mound (Benn 1989) was originally constructed employing prepared soils. Radiocarbon assays and cultural evidence suggest intensive site occupation from the sixteenth century into the early contact period.

Small European trade items were found on the site, including a runtee, blue and green Venetian glass beads, poured multicolored beads, brass kettle fragments, bracelets, rings, and "door spring" earrings, brass tubular beads and bangles, small fragments of iron, and a few knives. No iron axes or gun parts were found on the site. There were many copper items, including long copper serpents and bracelets.

Bison were immediately available to the site occupants. The many articulated long bones, articulated vertebrae, skulls, and skull fragments suggest that many animals were butchered on site, perhaps even killed there. Elk were also common, the elements appearing in the refuse pits as large articulated units. Smaller mammals included dog (many elements of which bear cut marks from butchering), wolf, and bear.

The Blood Run site is probably the Omaha village that was reported by the explorer Pierre-Charles Le Sueur to have been established in the late 1680s on the "River of the Maha," assumed to be the Big Sioux River (M.M. Wedel 1981:9). The Omaha were joined in that vicinity by the Iowa and Otoe about 1699. At this time the Omaha and Ponca probably had not yet separated and the designation "Maha" likely included both groups (Henning 1993). It was at this location, according to legend, that the Omaha made peace with the Cheyenne and Arikara (Fletcher and La Flesche 1911:73–74).

Four Osage sites (C.H. Chapman 1946, 1952, 1959, 1974, 1980; C.H. Chapman et al. 1985) all produced large quantities of historic materials, including guns, gun parts, and related equipment. Chipped-stone and bone or antler tools are rare. Pottery is also rare. The few pieces found are shell-tempered, and most decorative lines were incised into the vessels after they dried, probably using metal knives (Wiegers 1985), a distinctive feature. The ceramic evidence can be interpreted to suggest a relationship between the Osage and western Oneota; that relationship may be assumed to have been derived from the Missouria, their nearest neighbors.

The Kansa may have occupied the Fanning site in eastern Kansas (W.R. Wedel 1959) and King Hill in western Missouri (Ruppert 1974; Raish 1979; Shippee 1967). Both sites offer a full range of traditional Oneota remains and closely related pottery assemblages. The pottery suggests relationships to the historic Missouria and Iowa tribes. European trade items are found at both sites; King Hill yielded large quantities of seed beads in all levels of a deeply stratified site. Pottery from both sites suggests trade relationships with the Pawnee as well as with other Plains and Prairie Peninsula groups. Ceramic indicators of Kansa-Pawnee trade are also found on some Pawnee sites (Grange 1968).

A number of Oneota and Oneota-related pottery vessels have been recovered from contact-period village sites and burial mounds in the Mille Lacs region of central Minnesota (E. Johnson 1969; Lothson 1972), the Ogechie complex. As no regional tradition culminating in the Sioux has been defined, it may be assumed that the pottery technology of the Iowa and perhaps the Otoe was partially assumed by some of the Sioux groups shortly before Euro-American contact.

From the beginning of the eighteenth century, Western European objects replaced native Oneota manufactures. As brass kettles replaced pottery vessels and the gun replaced the bow and arrow, the remains of historic tribes quickly became archeologically indistinguishable.

Plains Village Tradition: Western Periphery

JAMES H. GUNNERSON

The Western Periphery, the short-grass, High Plains that extend east from the Rocky Mountains for 320–560 kilometers was only sparsely occupied during the Plains Village period. During this period the area, with its low and unpredictable precipitation in the rain shadow of the mountains, experienced several major droughts that caused local population displacements; ones in the 1400s were so severe that the entire area was virtually depopulated. With the advent of cool, moist conditions in the 1500s, abundant grass and numerous bison reappeared.

Because strategies for exploiting the resources of the High Plains changed over time, the Western Periphery needs to be viewed as a culturally defined area with the eastern edge changing through time. Between A.D. 1000 and 1400, the eastern edge was roughly 102° west longitude, defined by the locations of the westernmost fixed villages of horticultural complexes (Upper Republican and Antelope Creek phases), which were centered farther east and used the High Plains primarily as hunting territory. Between about 1525 and 1730 the Western Periphery was dominated by Plains Apacheans, bison hunters par excellence, who had just arrived from the north, filling the population void caused by the droughts of the 1400s. By the mid-1600s, the Dismal River Apaches had taken up limited horticulture and had established fixed villages between 99° and 102° west longitude. The locations of the easternmost of these define the eastern edge of the Western Periphery for the protohistoric period, about 240 kilometers farther east than earlier.

The most conspicuous anomaly is the late prehistoric Apishapa phase, which had fixed villages and nearly spanned the territory between the Antelope Creek villages in the Texas Panhandle and the Rocky Mountains in southern Colorado. Throughout most of the Plains Village period there were settlements of horticultural peoples, first Puebloans and later Apacheans, hard against the mountains, mainly in northeastern New Mexico.

Northwestern Plains

There are sites on the Northwestern Plains that may represent the presence of Plains Villagers from the Middle Missouri River area. Most of these are either bison kill or camp sites. However, one, the Hagen site near Glendive in east-central Montana, had evidence of semipermanent habitations (fig. 1). Associated pottery resembles Mandan and Hidatsa wares and has commonly been attributed to the Crow after they separated from the Hidatsa (Mulloy 1942, 1952, 1953, 1958; Wedel 1954, 1961; Frison 1967, 1978; Griffin 1965; A.M. Johnson 1977).

"Crow" pottery with flat-bottomed straight-walled vessels is attributed to an intermountain (Shoshone) tradition (Frison 1976). Although knowledge of the late prehistoric and early historic on the Northwestern Plains is incomplete, the area was at least visited by people of the Plains Village tradition who lived farther east.

Southwestern Plains

Graneros Phase

The Graneros phase (Withers 1954), poorly known and of questionable validity, has not usually been included in the Plains Village tradition because the structures and associated artifacts differ markedly from the general pattern. Also, it apparently dates earlier, between A.D. 450 and 1050 (R.G. Campbell 1976). Bellwood, the type site, which was excavated and did have two quite different structures, yielded a radiocarbon date of 450 ± 55 (Breternitz 1969:118), which would put Graneros in the Plains Woodland period. This phase is potentially very important with regard to the origin of the Central Plains tradition. The ceramics, especially, suggest that it may represent a long-sought transition between the earlier Woodland (Parker) phase and the late prehistoric Upper Republican (Franktown and Buick) phases. R.G. Campbell (1976) considers it ancestral to the Apishapa phase as well. This possibility, plus the location of the Graneros sites near the mountains in southeastern Colorado, leads to another possibility: that some of the new traits found in the Central Plains tradition may have come from the Western Periphery and ultimately from the Southwest.

Apishapa Phase

Sites of the long-enigmatic Apishapa phase are found in southeastern Colorado and perhaps in both northeastern New Mexico and the tip of the Oklahoma Panhandle (Renaud 1931, 1932, 1933, 1942; Chase 1949; Stegler 1949; Gunnerson 1989; R.G. Campbell 1969, 1976; Lintz 1978a, 1985a, 1986; Kingsbury and Nowak 1980; Jones 1984; Nowak and Jones 1986; Nowak and Kantner 1991;

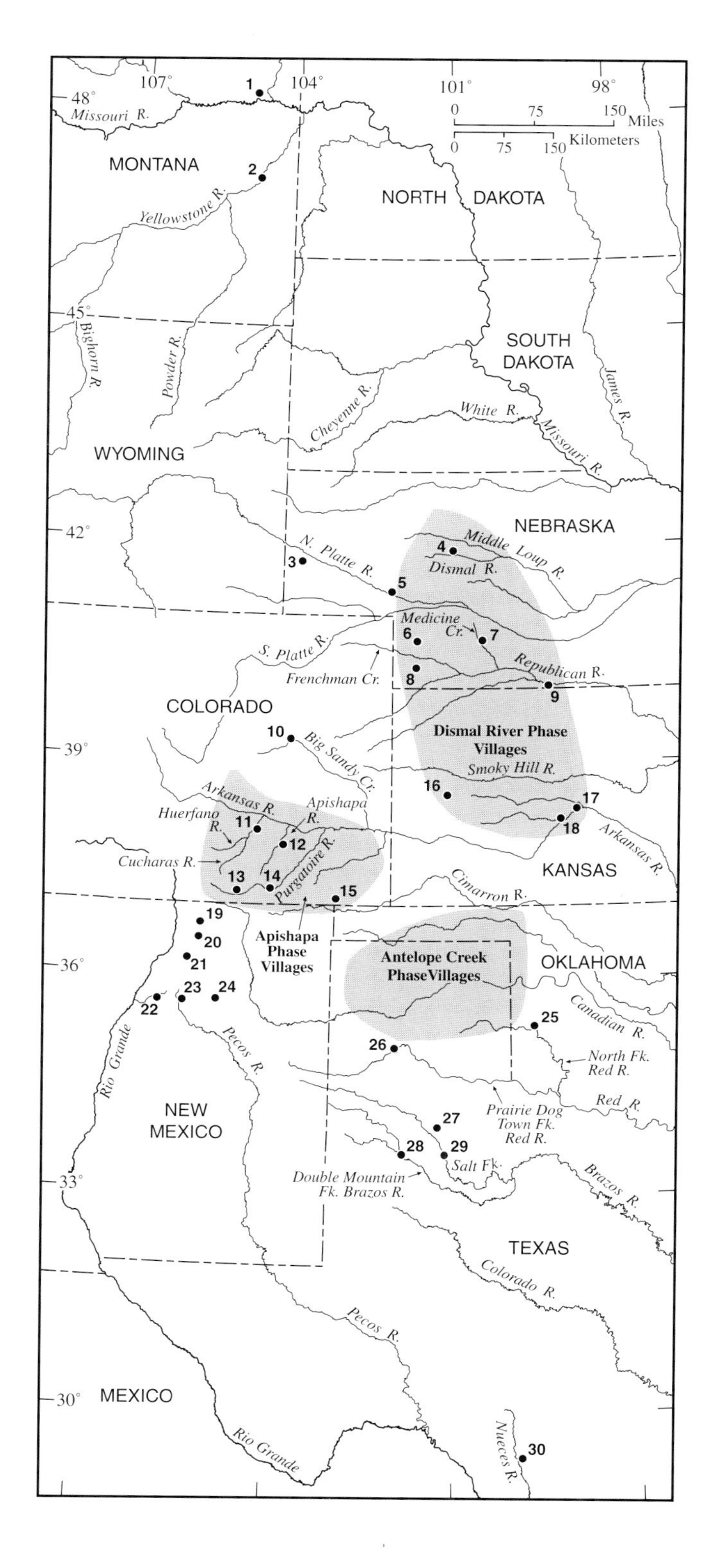

Fig. 1. Archeological sites of the western periphery. Montana: 1, Dune Buggy (24RV1); 2, Hagen (14DW2). Nebraska: 3, Signal Butte (25SF1); 4, Humphery (25HO21); 5, Ash Hollow Cave (25GD2); 6, Lovitt (25CH1); 7, Dick (25FT9); 8, Nichols (25DN1); 9, White Cat Village (25HN37). Colorado: 10, Cedar Point Village (5EL8); 11, Bellwood (Graneros phase); 12, Cramer (5PE484), Canterbury (5PE387), Snake Blakeslee (5LA1247), Juan Baca (5LA1085), and Munsell (5PE797); 13, unnamed Sopris sites (5LA1211, 5LA1416); 14, Pinyon Canyon Maneuver area, central Chaquaqua Plateau; 15, unnamed Carrizo Creek sites (5BA347, 5BA356, 5BA1722, 5BA1725, 5BA2169). Kansas: 16, Coffin (14SC106), Ledbetter (14SC111), and Scott County Pueblo (14SC101); 17, Wells (14BT404); 18, Reed (14PA304). New Mexico: 19, Brewster (29CX73); 20, Chase Bench (29CX59), Sammis (29CX68), and Chase Orchard (29CX78); 21, Glasscock (29MO20); 22, Arroya Hondo (29LA12); 23, Pecos Pueblo (29SM1, 29LA628); 24, Ojo Perdido (29SM32). Oklahoma: 25, Edwards I (39BK2); Texas: 26, Ivy Creek (41AR254); 27, Montgomery (41FL17); 28, Lubbock Lake (41LV1); 29, Pete Creek (41CB1); 30, San Lorenzo Mission (41RF1).

Gutherie et al. 1984; Zier et al. 1988). The Apishapa phase can be assigned to the Plains Village tradition, with which it shares virtually all the distinctive traits, although the relative abundance of some traits varies from phase to phase. The following summary is based primarily on data from the Cramer and Snake Blakeslee sites (Gunnerson 1988b), both of which appear to date from the late part of the Apishapa time span.

• ENVIRONMENT AND SUBSISTENCE The environment of the Apishapa area is harsh. The elevation varies from about 1,370 to 1,830 meters; the sites along the lower Apishapa Canyon are at 1,525 meters. Preferred locations for sites were along the rims of deep canyons dissecting the Chaquaqua Plateau (R.G. Campbell 1976). The soil on the canyon rims and on benches along the streams is very poor, consisting of a thin sandy or gravelly layer over massive Dakota sandstone bedrock. Back away from the nearly level canyon rims are higher ridges of basalt or limestone caprock.

Vegetation consists of cactus, sparse short grass, small shrubs, a few junipers and fewer piñons. Some deciduous trees are to be found in the canyons, but large trees, such as were used farther east for the construction of earthlodges, are absent. The most conspicuous animals are pronghorn, coyotes, rabbits, small burrowing rodents, snakes and lizards; bison were common in early historic times.

Temperatures are extreme and high winds are common. The annual precipitation is about 40 centimeters, with only about 13.8 falling in June, July, and August (Hambridge 1941), far too little for growing dry-land corn. For comparison, the Antelope Creek area receives 50 percent more rain during these three months. The Apishapa people apparently raised five varieties of maize (R.G. Campbell 1969:391), and most Apishapa sites are located along canyons with broad level floors suitable for limited horticulture. The streams, except for the Purgatoire, are intermittent, flowing in the spring and carrying occasional flash floods during the summer, through most of which small pools can be found in the water courses. The volume and quality of the few springs varies greatly.

Hunting and gathering were much more important than horticulture. At the Cramer site some 50,000 pieces of bone were excavated representing nearly 40 taxa of mammals, birds, reptiles, and amphibians; mollusks were rare (Hamblin 1989). All are either present in the area now or were known historically. The bulk came from bison ranging in age from fetal to very old, and all parts of the animals had been brought in. Second in amount of bone recovered was pronghorn. All but the smallest bones of large animals had been crushed for extraction of marrow and grease. This fact, plus their use of many small animals, suggests that the people at the Cramer site were forced to exploit all food resources thoroughly. It is hard to reconcile the poverty and deprivation that this behavior implies with the fact that Cramer and Snake Blakeslee are the richest and most substantial Apishapa sites known, as well as probably the latest. One possible explanation is that people were concentrating near the mouth of Apishapa Canyon to be closer to the bison of the Arkansas valley as horticulture became less dependable. No cultigens were represented in the pollen from the Cramer site, where the pollen profile suggests a climate very much like that of the present time (L.J. Cummings 1989). One small charred corn cob was found at the Snake Blakeslee site. It may be significant in this context that (R.G. Campbell (1969) found very little bison bone at his apparently earlier sites some 80 kilometers to the southeast, where he did find more evidence of corn.

• SITES AND STRUCTURES Apishapa phase sites are numerous, but most are small and appear to have been occupied only briefly (R.G. Campbell 1976:20, 48–50). Many are in rockshelters.

Apishapa sites are commonly situated on rims of canyons 30 meters or more deep. Their location, and the presence at some of what have been interpreted as fortification walls, suggest a concern for defense. If there was conflict, it was probably between neighbors over limited garden spots. Alternatively, site locations could reflect a need to build above canyon floors subject to flash floods or simply a cultural preference for high locations, like that apparently manifested by Upper Republican people. Sites identified as Apishapa have from one to 37 rooms, usually round, but when built against one another, irregular (R.G. Campbell 1976).

The great quantities of large vertically set rock slabs incorporated in the larger structures at Cramer and Snake Blakeslee have attracted much attention and led to fanciful interpretations. However, the slabs are readily available from the Dakota sandstone bedrock, which is everywhere either exposed or only thinly mantled. This caprock often breaks naturally into slabs up to 30 centimeters thick, one to 10 times as wide as thick, and up to two meters or more long. Construction usually involved setting untrimmed slabs on end in a shallow trench so that walls of up to six slabs, one meter thick, were formed. In order to achieve greater wall height, the space between the inner and outer rows of vertical slabs was filled with clay and rubble and intermediate rows of slabs set into the fill. By this procedure a wall two meters high could be constructed. In some structures stone slabs more or less square in cross-section were stacked horizontally, and in some instances vertical slabs were partially supported by leaning them against horizontally stacked slabs. In one instance a slab weighing perhaps half a ton had been set on edge to form a wall. This great variety of approaches to construction techniques suggests that no standard architectural style had been established.

It is not clear whether the smaller rooms had roof supports, but in larger ones, wherever there is evidence, such supports were vertical stone columns, one, two, or four per room depending upon room size. Columns were either wedged into crevices in the bedrock or set in shallow clay-filled basins and braced by setting two or three shorter vertical slabs hard against each side. A few of these roof support columns are still standing and have been variously misinterpreted as phallic symbols, ceremonial features, or astronomical markers. Some room floors were bedrock, but others, where shallow saucer-shaped depressions were excavated into the rocky fill, appeared to have been plastered with clay. Information on entrances is inconclusive. Roofs probably consisted of brush and earth over poles that joined the tops of the roof support columns and the tops of the walls. Smaller rooms may have had a conical arrangement of poles resting on the wall tops and supporting one another in the middle without resort to a central post.

The two largest and richest sites near the mouth of the Apishapa Canyon, 7.2 kilometers apart, differed markedly in their layout. The Snake Blakeslee site had two room blocks: one of three, and one of five or six contiguous rooms on the very edge of the canyon rim, with a half-dozen small outlying single rooms. The Cramer site contained three circular rooms (and probably a fourth, vandalized) joined by a surrounding stone fence or wall forming a roughly circular enclosure 25 meters in diameter and about 25 meters from the canyon rim. The largest room, nine meters in diameter, is the largest reported for Apishapa. It had had four stone roof support columns arranged in a square around a simple central hearth; and walls, one meter thick, were of vertically set stone slabs (fig. 2). It could be viewed as an attempt to construct a Plains earthlodge substituting available stone for unavailable wood wherever possible. The unusual and obviously planned configuration, the oversize main room, and the location at the very mouth of the canyon, with a view for miles (fig. 3), have led to speculations that it may have been a ceremonial center, perhaps analogous to the later "council circles" (Wedel 1967, 1977) of the Great Bend phase of central Kansas.

More typical Apishapa sites consist of one or a few circles of rocks along the canyon rim. For example, the Canterbury site (5PE387), across the canyon from the Cramer site, has two enclosures about four meters in diameter and two meters apart. The walls are made up of stone slabs, few of which are even 50 centimeters in maximum dimension. It is not possible to determine whether they had been placed on end or stacked, but they could not have accounted for a wall much over 50 centimeters high. The

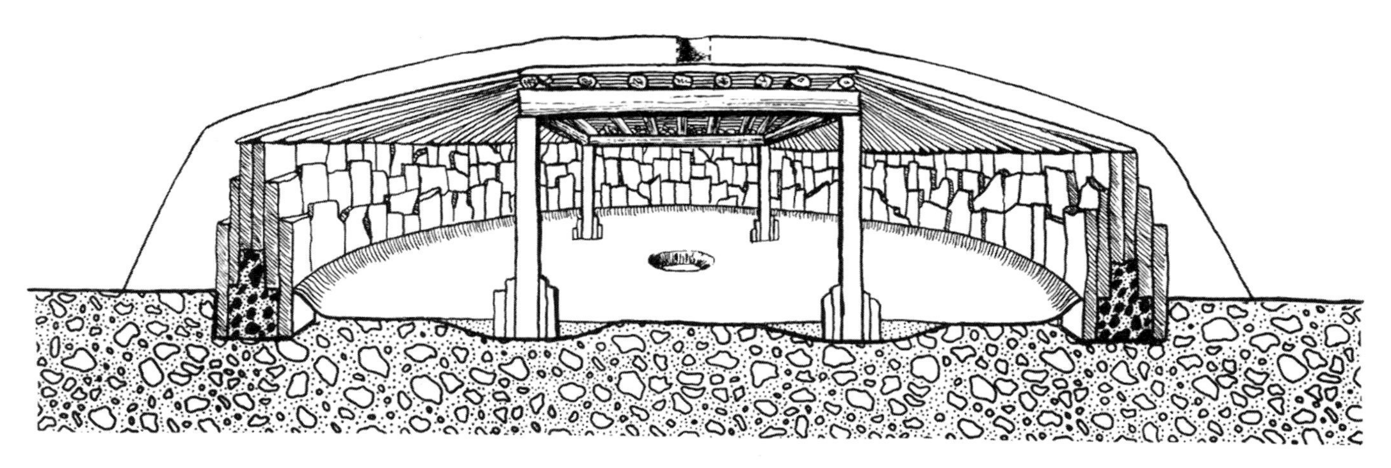

after Gunnerson 1989:fig. 2.

Fig. 2. Reconstruction of an Apishapa phase house based on Room A, the largest room at the Cramer site, Colo. Drawing by Karen Ackoff.

floors had been slightly excavated, but no other evidence of preparation or of interior features could be found. Artifacts (a few sherds, flakes, and bone fragments) were very sparse. However, it is suggested that the sun, viewed from Canterbury site at spring equinox, rises directly over the Cramer site across the canyon. A similar relationship is found at the Great Bend phase council circles.

The Munsell site (5PE797), 0.8 kilometer upstream from Cramer, instead of being on the canyon rim is on the edge of a narrow bench about three-fourths of the way up the canyon wall. It had two sets of two contiguous circular enclosures one meter apart. The rooms were four to five meters in diameter, with walls constructed mainly of vertical rock slabs, many of which had apparently fallen. The walls had probably been less than one meter high, and no evidence of roof supports was found. The most significant artifact recovered was a cord-roughened pottery vessel (fig. 4).

At the Juan Baca site (5LA1085), situated on the tip of a narrow ridge that extends into the Apishapa Canyon four kilometers upstream from Cramer, is what can be interpreted as a defensive wall. Originally there appear to have been five small circular rooms similar to those at the Canterbury site. Part of the stone from two of the rooms had been cannibalized to form a wall joining the remaining parts of these two rooms so as to isolate the top of the ridge. Included in the wall are numerous juniper logs and branches. There were two other rock enclosures on the "mainland" side of the wall. The climb to the tip of the ridge from the canyon floor would be very difficult, but access from the mainland side would be easy if it were not for the barricading wall. Excavations at the site yielded very little material. The four projectile points, all from one of the cannibalized rooms, suggest a date slightly earlier for the rooms than that of the Cramer and Snake Blakeslee sites. Wood from the barricading wall gave a radiocarbon date, with a Stuiver and Pearson (1986) correction, of about A.D. 1640, indicating that the barricaded reoccupation of Juan Baca postdates the Apishapa phase, as well as the rooms.

Pictographs in several geometric and naturalistic styles are common in the area. These often occur in extensive panels on large boulders below Apishapa phase sites with which they were presumably associated.

• AGE On the basis of limited data (R.G. Campbell 1976:62–63, 103–107) dated the Apishapa phase starting about 1000 and terminating before 1400, with a very light occupation after 1300. Eighmy and Wood (1984:286) after reviewing the data, essentially agree that "Apishapa architecture clusters . . . tightly between A.D. 1000 and 1350." Lintz (1986:29) suggests an even shorter span of 1100 to 1350. Evidence from those sites that are most clearly assignable to the Apishapa phase, corrected by the Stuiver and Pearson (1986) calibration of radiocarbon dates, would restrict the Apishapa phase to 1200–1400.

Painted Pueblo sherds from Snake Blakeslee site were identified as Talpa Black-on-white and Rowe Black-on-white, types made in northeastern New Mexico between 1250 and 1400 (Schaafsma 1987). Radiocarbon dates from the Cramer site, with corrections, are 960 to 1210 on wood charcoal and 1410 on bone. Since the charcoal samples were made up of many small pieces, probably from heartwood and perhaps even from wood long dead when used, the last dates seem the likeliest. Moreover, a brief occupation of the Snake Blakeslee and Cramer sites in the late 1300s is consistent with the high percentage of side-notched projectile points as compared with earlier corner-notched forms.

• TECHNOLOGY The pottery from Apishapa sites, classified as Borger Cordmarked by R.G. Campbell (1976), has been described by Gunnerson (1989) as a new type, Munsell Gray (named for the Munsell site), on the basis of 7,000 pottery sherds excavated from the sites along the lower Apishapa Canyon. Some vessels may have been open bowls but most were globular, up to 35 centimeters in diameter, with somewhat constricted necks (fig. 4). Rims were low and from slightly insloping to slightly flaring.

U. of Nebr. State Mus., Lincoln: 5PE484-842.

Fig. 3. Cramer site, Colo. The view is facing the northeast, with the Apishapa River and plains in the background. Two sets of vertical stone slabs brace roof support posts. The room in left foreground is 5.6 m in diameter. Photograph by James Gunnerson.

Most lips are simple, thinned to thickened, and undecorated, but a few resemble the collared rims of Upper Republican Frontier ware (Sigstad 1969), except that the Munsell rims are not so massive. The infrequent decoration is restricted to the rim, primarily to the lip, and consists of simple incisions. Handles are rare. All vessels were probably once cord roughened, although the marks had been obliterated on some sherds. Tempering is grit.

Projectile points from both Cramer and Snake Blakeslee are predominantly small and triangular, and either unnotched or side notched; a few have multiple side notches or a third (basal) notch. Only two percent are of earlier corner-notched types, supporting a relative late date for these two sites. R.G. Campbell (1969) reports a far wider variety of point types with a greater number of corner-notched than side-notched points at most of his sites.

End scrapers are generally small (some very small and very thin) and often crude. Well-chipped straight and expanded-base drills are moderately common; well-chipped bifacial blades, including some alternately beveled and diamond-shaped, are present but exhausted. Utilized flake expediency tools are common. Plains-style sandstone shaft smoothers

U. of Nebr. State Mus., Lincoln: 5PE797-8.

Fig. 4. Apishapa phase pottery vessel from the Munsell site, Colo.; diameter of mouth 20 cm.

are present but rare. Metates, of both bedrock and moveable basin styles, are present along with one-hand manos.

Most chipped-stone artifacts (and nearly all related debitage) are of poor-quality quartzite and basalt locally available. The little high-quality stone, nearly all in the form of projectile points, includes agate, Alibates dolomite (flint) and Republican River jasper. This scarcity of superior stone, as of Pueblo trade sherds, attests to limited external contacts.

Simple bone awls of several types, usually made from splinters, are common as are tools similar but blunt. Bison scapula hoes are apparently absent; bone digging-stick points are present but rare. Pieces of worked or used bone are not uncommon. Most appear to be expediency tools since they do not follow discernible patterns. Tubular bone beads are common, but worked shell ornaments are rare.

• CULTURAL RELATIONSHIPS Strong topological similarities warrant assigning the Apishapa phase to the Central Plains tradition of the Plains Village tradition. Apishapa differs from other Central Plains phases in having stone structures and much less emphasis on horticulture. These variant traits can be explained in terms of environment. Stone structures are also found in sites of the closely related Antelope Creek phase of the Texas Panhandle. In both areas stone suitable for building was readily available while adequate trees were not. Now the Apishapa area is at best marginal for horticulture, but the phase may have flourished during periods of above-normal precipitation, as Bryson, Baerreis, and Wendland (1970) suggested was the case at that time in the Texas Panhandle.

The final abandonment of the area by the Apishapa people was almost certainly prompted by drought conditions of the fifteenth century. Their fate is unclear, but they may have merged with relatives to the east or northeast, perhaps to become a band of the Pawnee who had a tradition, collected before 1889 (Grinnell 1961:224), that their ancestors came from the Southwest where they lived in stone houses.

West Central Plains

Upper Republican Phase

In eastern Colorado north of the Arkansas River, in southeastern Wyoming, and in the Nebraska Panhandle are numerous small sites, often in rockshelters, that have been assigned to one of the foci of the Upper Republican phase, primarily on the basis of ceramics (Withers 1954; J.J. Wood 1967; Wood 1971). Except at Cedar Point, a camp/kill site at the head of the Republican River near Limon, Colorado, the pottery rims do not include the more highly decorated forms (Sigstad 1969) found at classic Upper Republican villages farther east (Wedel 1961, 1986). At none of these western sites, moreover, is there evidence of dwellings, or of artifacts associated with horticulture. Where dated, Upper Republican sites of the Western Periphery fall between 1000 and 1400 (W.B. Butler 1980; Wood 1971; Breternitz 1969; Gunnerson 1987). These sites, once interpreted as camps used by hunting parties and villages to the east, are those of resident Upper Republican hunters and gatherers (Roper 1990).

The Dismal River Phase

The first Indians to occupy the High Plains after the withdrawal of the Upper Republican and Apishapa peoples were apparently the Apacheans. Although the older idea that Apacheans might have arrived in the Southwest as early as 1200 has not been rejected by all authors, most evidence supports an arrival date in the Southwest of about 1525, a time when the Plains were recovering from the severe droughts of the 1400s. No Southern Athapaskan sites, including Navajo and Western Apache, have been dated before this time. Although there were Apacheans on the Plains early in the sixteenth century (D.A. Gunnerson 1956, 1974), the earliest identifiable Plains Apachean archeological sites date from the seventeenth century.

The earliest Plains Apacheans, the dog-nomad, tepee-dwelling Teyas and Querechos encountered by Francisco Vásquez de Coronado (Winship 1896; Hammond and Rey 1940), may have left few if any diagnostic artifacts at their camps. It was not until sometime in the first half of the seventeenth century that Apacheans in what is now western Kansas and Nebraska started living in fixed villages where they made pottery and practiced some horticulture, activities inspired by their Caddoan-speaking neighbors to the east. These Apacheans were known to the Spanish as Palomas and Cuartelejos; the archeological complex that they left has been named the Dismal River phase (Gunnerson and Gunnerson 1971; 1988:1–9) from a stream in Nebraska, where distinctive pottery was found (A.T. Hill and Metcalf 1942a; Strong 1932, 1935; Wedel 1935).

It was not a scarcity of food that caused the Central Plains Apacheans to alter their boundaries eastward into the hunting territory of the Plains Caddoan-speaking villagers in the mid-1600s. Rather, it was a dietary matter—a desire to assure a supply of the corn they had learned to like as supremely successful bison hunters who had been trading their surplus to village dwellers for garden produce. The spur to Apachean horticulture was probably the disruption of this trade brought about when the Apacheans began taking slaves from the Caddoans to sell in the Spanish Southwest.

Dating, based on stratigraphy and dendrochronology and associated Southwestern trade pottery, places Dismal River at about 1675–1725 (Gunnerson 1960, 1968), although documentary evidence indicates that this way of life was established in central Kansas, a least, by 1640 (Wedel 1959:589–599).

• ENVIRONMENT AND SUBSISTENCE Sites yielding Dismal River artifacts are found between the Rocky Mountains and 99° west longitude and from the Black Hills to southern Kansas. The fixed villages, as distinct from mere campsites, are nearly all in the better-watered eastern third of this area, where Apacheans turned farmers were crowding long-established Caddoans such as the Pawnee and Wichita. This proximity has been confirmed in central Kansas where there are both Dismal River and protohistoric Wichita (Great Bend phase) sites near Larned and Great Bend, Kansas, located 40 kilometers apart along the Arkansas River (Gunnerson 1968, 1987a). In Nebraska there is evidence of both Dismal River and protohistoric Pawnee (Lower Loup phase) occupation on Medicine Creek near Curtis, Nebraska.

The average rainfall along the eastern edge of the Dismal River area, where all the major villages are found, is about 50 centimeters with about 43 centimeters falling during the growing season (Hambridge 1941). The western sites were probably occupied intermittently in connection with nonhorticultural activities.

The main resource of the Dismal River area in general was grass that, in turn, provided excellent pasture for the large herds of bison that the Apaches exploited so skillfully. Near all the fixed villages there were bottomlands along small streams that would have provided good garden plots. At the Scott County Pueblo site, there was evidence of irrigation ditches leading from a large spring. Since the Cuartelejo Apaches who lived at this site were in close touch with the Jicarilla Apaches of New Mexico, and with the Pueblo Indians of the Upper Rio Grande, all of whom practiced irrigation, it is entirely possible that these ditches were of Apachean construction.

Subsistence was based primarily on hunting and gathering, with horticulture secondary. Bison was the main animal hunted, but deer, beaver, turtles, and dogs are well represented in the faunal assemblage, while bird bones and mollusks shells are rare (A.T. Hill and Metcalf 1942; Gunnerson 1960; Wedel 1959). Fish remains are absent, perhaps reflecting the pan-Apachean fish taboo. Seeds of wild plums and chokecherries as well as black walnut shells have been recovered. Cultigens included corn and squash or gourds. The low row numbers of the corn recovered (Gunnerson 1968:185) suggest that it was probably of Plains rather than Southwest origin (Galinat and Gunnerson 1963).

• VILLAGES AND STRUCTURES Dismal River fixed villages covered as much as 30 hectares. Houses tended to be grouped in small clusters, perhaps representing extended families. The typical Dismal River house consisted of an unprepared floor, at or just below ground level, and some sort of pole and earth roof. The roof was usually supported by five basic posts (fig. 5) set vertically in a circle three to four meters in diameter. The tops of these were presumably joined by stringers against which small wall poles were leaned so that the resulting framework enclosed an area with a diameter about twice after that defined by the base posts. Two additional posts, usually to the east, framed a doorway (fig. 5). This five-post pattern, unique in the Plains to Dismal River, is possibly related to the five-post pattern of the forked-stick hogan of the Navajo (Mindeleff 1898).

Characteristic of most Dismal River villages are irregular trash-filled pits, perhaps originally borrow pits. Cache pits, common to other Plains village groups, have not been found at Dismal River sites. Baking pits are diagnostic in the Plains of Dismal River and were used until the 1930s by the Jicarilla for cooking green corn. The pits, often heavily burned and about one meter in depth and maximum diameter, constrict at the mouth. At one Dismal River site in Scott County, Kansas, a baking pit contained a burial (Gunnerson 1969a) as did one site in southwestern South Dakota (J.T. Hughes 1949:275). At a Navajo site in northern New Mexico 19 such baking pit burials were found (R.L. Carlson 1965:24–25); one was exposed by flood waters on the Vermejo River in northeastern New Mexico and another was found near Trinchera, Colorado.

• TECHNOLOGY The Dismal River artifact assemblage closely resembles those of other protohistoric complexes of the Central Plains, but the variety of artifact types is not so great. Also, one gets the impression that most Dismal River stone tools, except for projectile points, are not so carefully made as those of contemporary Lower Loup (Pawnee) or Great Bend (Wichita) complexes, for example. A few artifact types diagnostic of Dismal River also occur at Foothills Apache sites in northeastern New Mexico (Gunnerson 1969). Essentially the entire Dismal River inventory can be duplicated, as minority types, from deposits of the historic period at Pecos Pueblo, where the Apachean artifacts stand out as unusual even in the much richer context of the Pueblo assemblage (Kidder 1932). It seems likely that many of these Dismal River style artifacts were left at Pecos by Plains Apacheans who had strong trade relations with the Pecos people. By the mid-1700s Plains Apacheans, including displaced Dismal River people, were living for extended periods at Pecos Pueblo when threatened by Comanches (A.B. Thomas 1935; Gunnerson and Gunnerson 1970; D.A. Gunnerson 1974; Gunnerson 1988).

The most common types of Dismal River pottery, Lovitt Plain and Lovitt Simple Stamped (fig. 6), are actually sherd types, since they are distinguished only on the basis of surface treatment and both can be found on a single vessel (Metcalf 1949). Scott Plain (Wedel 1959:592) is indistinguishable from Lovitt Plain (Gunnerson 1987a). Moreover, Lovitt Mica Tempered (Metcalf 1949) and Scott Micaceous (Wedel 1959:593) are the same. They are found only as minority wares at Dismal River sites and are probably all from Ocate Micaceous vessels made by the Jicarilla of northeastern New Mexico, who were in constant touch with their relatives on the Plains, especially the Cuartelejos, who were nearest (Gunnerson 1969:26–

U. of Nebr., Dept. of Anthr., Lincoln: 25HN37-250.

Fig. 5. Dismal River phase house floor exposed at White Cat Village, Nebr. The 5 interior postholes have been sectioned; the 2 entrance post sockets were cross-sectioned. The hearth is exposed at center. The house was about 4.7 m in diameter. Photograph by John L. Champe.

27). The Lovitt Plain and Lovitt Simple Stamped types have been subsumed under "Dismal River Gray ware" and Ocate Micaceous, along with various other micaceous pottery types from northeastern New Mexico, under "Sangre de Cristo Micaceous ware" (Baugh and Eddy 1987).

Dismal River vessels range from hemispherical bowls to constricted-mouth ollas and are up to about 30 centimeters high. Olla rims are vertical to flaring. Appendages are very rare, and the simple decoration is almost always restricted to vessel lips. Lips may be rounded, slightly flattened, thinned, thickened, or splayed to the outside, inside, or both. Simple stamping, a surface treatment leaving lands and grooves two to four millimeters wide, apparently resulted from malleation with a grooved paddle during the thinning and shaping of the vessel. Paddle marks are often nearly obliterated by smoothing. Gunnerson and Gunnerson (1971) noted that the pottery of individual Apache bands resembled that of their nearest neighbors. In general, simple stamping and lip decoration decrease in frequency from north to south and from east to west across the Dismal River area. This may reflect influence from village tribes to the east where both simple stamping and decoration were more common among the protohistoric Mandan, Arikara, and Pawnee than among the Wichita.

The paste of the majority (nonmicaceous) Dismal River ware is compact. It contains a moderate amount of medium coarse sand and, usually, an abundance of very fine sand. Surface color is black to gray, sometimes shading into reddish buff. Sherd thickness ranges from 3 to 10 millimeters, with an average of about 6 millimeters.

The only other artifacts of clay are tubular smoking pipes that seem to have been patterned after the Pueblo "cloud blowers." In fact, some found at Dismal River sites are apparently imports from New Mexico.

Projectile points are nearly all small, delicately chipped and triangular, either side notched or unnotched, with bases concave to straight. A few points of miscellaneous shapes and sizes may represent items collected by the Apaches. Well-made knives are rare, but rather crude cutting tools, including large choppers, are quite common.

End scrapers are numerous, but crude. Some end scrapers also have graver points. Other combination tools are end scraper–spoke shaves and end-side scrapers. A few flakes were made into gravers or spoke shaves with a minimum of work.

Plain-shafted and expanded base drills, with only the bit portion well worked, are common. The plain-shafted drills tend to be lenticular in cross-section and larger than the expanded-base drills; they often have blunt points at both ends. An uncommon but diagnostic Dismal River artifact is the so-called double-bitted drill, which resembles the plain-shafted variety but has one, two, or four projections near the middle. These, sometimes made of stone too soft for drills, are often found broken.

The most common ground-stone tools are the rectangular sandstone arrowshaft smoothers that were used in pairs. Thin milling slabs with a shallow basin are widespread. Metates of an uncommon but distinctive type have been found at Dismal River sites in western Kansas and Jicarilla sites in northeastern New Mexico (Gunnerson 1969; vol. 9:162–169). They are also known ethnographically for the Jicarilla, and there are some in the tribal museum at Dulce, New Mexico. They are about 30 centimeters long, two to three times as long as wide, relatively thin, rectangular with rounded corners, and finished on all surfaces. The grinding surface is concave along the long axis and slightly convex or flat along the short axis. These distinctive small (portable) metates are thus far unique to the Jicarilla and their closest Plains Apachean relatives.

Awls were usually made from splinters of bone with only the point well finished; however, some were triangular or square in cross-section and carefully finished all over. Tools similar to the latter, but with a blunt end, have been called flakers or punches. Carefully made and well-finished bone projectile points, square in cross-section with a basal tang for hafting, as well as socketed antler projectile points have been found. Bison ribs with holes drilled through them were presumably used for straightening arrowshafts. Serrated bison metapodial fleshers, a time marker for the protohistoric period in the Plains, have been found at most Dismal River villages, as have antler tine flakers and bison scapula hoes or digging tools. What appear to have been curved arm bands or wrist guards, bone whistles, and scored ribs, the ribs possibly musical rasps, have been recovered. Paint was apparently applied with spatulalike bone tools.

• TRADE ITEMS Of the limited amount of aboriginal trade material from the Southwest, Ocate Micaceous (Jicarilla)

Nebr. State Histl. Soc., Lincoln: Ch1-1016.

Fig. 6. Dismal River phase pottery vessel, Lovitt Simple Stamped type, recovered from the Lovitt site, Nebr; height, 20.5 cm.

pottery is most common. Other items found include sherds of Tewa Polychrome, Pueblo cloud-blower pipes, olivella shell beads, obsidian, and turquoise.

Items of European manufacture are rare. An iron trade ax found embedded in a fireplace of a burned house at White Cat Village may have been left by a Pawnee raiding party. A few gun flints, scraps of sheet brass or copper, and conical sheet metal jingles have been found, as well as rusted pieces of iron, some of which may have been awls. The nature and amount of European trade material is compatible with the age and geographical position of Dismal River sites.

• CULTURAL IDENTIFICATION The identification of the Dismal River phase with some of the Plains Apacheans is established (Champe 1949; Wedel 1959; Gunnerson and Gunnerson 1971; D.A. Gunnerson 1974). Documentary, including cartographic, evidence shows Apacheans to have occupied the High Plains over the time span attributed to the Dismal River phase, and both Spanish and French accounts describe an Apachean culture like that suggested by the archeology (D.A. Gunnerson 1974). Specifically, a reconstruction of Juan de Ulibarrí's route from New Mexico to the major village of the Cuartelejo Apaches in 1706 (vol. 9:236–254; Gunnerson 1984) led to the area 12 miles north of Scott City, Kansas, where a Dismal River occupation has been investigated (Wedel 1959; Gunnerson 1968; Witty 1983). This area, as well as the entire route leading to it, matches in detail Ulibarrí's description (A.B. Thomas 1935). Work in northeastern New Mexico (Gunnerson 1969, 1979, 1984; Gunnerson and Gunnerson 1971) shows connections between Apachean sites there and Dismal River Apache sites on the Plains.

One line of evidence used initially as a basis for attributing the Dismal River phase to Apacheans was the association of the seven-room pueblo in Scott County, Kansas, with Dismal River artifacts. The pueblo had been built on top of a Dismal River baking pit (Witty 1975, 1983). The Tewa Polychrome sherds recovered were identified as dating from 1700–1750 (Witty 1933), which is too late for even the 1696 Picuris refugees to transport them there. This evidence, along with the puzzling scarcity of Pueblo artifacts, suggests that the structure may have been built as a Spanish trading post after Ulibarrí brought back the Picuris in 1706. The journal of the French explorer Étienne Venyard, sieur de Bourgmont reveals that Spaniards were trading with the Cuartelejo Apaches (Padouca) as late as 1724 (Margry 1875–1886, 6:398–449). Spaniards commonly traveled with Indian servants, and construction of the building by Pueblo retainers would account for the Pueblo-style fireplaces and corn-grinding bins. That such a trading post, although illegal, may have existed in El Cuartelejo is hinted at in several Spanish documents (A.B. Thomas 1935). This explanation better accounts for all the evidence, especially the post-1706 dates, than does the idea that it was built by seventeenth-century Pueblo refugees. However, there is no doubt that the Scott County site in general was a Cuartelejo Apache village, and specifically the one Ulibarrí visited in 1706 and called Santo Domingo.

Other Plains Apachean Cultures

It is clear from ethnohistorical data that Apacheans were in western Texas and far western Oklahoma in protohistoric times (A.B. Thomas 1935). Edwards I (34BK2), in southwestern Oklahoma, where the occupation appears to be primarily Caddoan (Baugh 1982; Baugh and Terrell 1982), may have had a stockade like the one depicted in the pre-1750 skin painting known as Segesser I (Hotz 1960, 1970, 1991). The collections in the Panhandle Plains Museum at Canyon, Texas, contain small amounts of Apachean pottery, probably all Perdido Plain, from various sites in the Texas Panhandle. The two sites investigated by Spielmann (1983) in that area may have been occupied by Apacheans, but the potsherds recovered do not fit established Apachean types. Sites near Floydada, Texas (Word 1965, 1963); the upper (Garza) level at the Lubbock Lake site, near Lubbock, Texas (E.M. Johnson et al. 1977); and the Pete Creek site, east of Lubbock (M.L. Parsons 1967), have yielded evidence suggestive of Apachean occupation or contact. Several tepee ring sites in extreme southeastern Colorado have also been attributed to Apacheans (Kingsbury and Gabel 1980; R.G. Campbell 1969). Tunnell and Newcomb (1969) reported on the history of the Lipan and the excavation of San Lorenzo, a Lipan Apache mission of the late 1700s, about 144 kilometers west of San Antonio, Texas. A few sherds of pottery plus worked stone and bone, presumably Lipan, were recovered along with much more abundant Spanish (Mexican) artifacts. Since the Lipans practiced horticulture and made pottery, other sites of theirs should exist in western Texas.

Southwestern Foothills Puebloans

In the foothills of the Rocky Mountains near Trinidad, Colorado, are sites of the Sopris phase, a northeastern, attenuated manifestation of Rio Grande Pueblo culture dated at A.D. 1000–1225+ (C.E. Wood and Bair 1980; Ireland 1970). Architecture is highly varied, apparently reflecting the peripheral location of Sopris with regard to Pueblo trade sherds, were a few sherds of cord-roughened pottery, probably from either Apishapa or Panhandle villages. The reverse, however, is not true.

Two of the Sopris phase sites had been reoccupied by Apacheans who left Ocate Micaceous pottery at site 5LA1416 and Cimarron Micaceous at 5LA1211. Thirteen skeletons from sites in the area were all assumed to be those of Sopris people, and among these C.G. Turner (1980) found three with three roots on a first mandibular molar, a trait found statistically diagnostic of Athapaskans. This anomaly has been considered by some to indicate that Athapaskans were on the Park Plateau before 1225. However, the three skeletons in question were from the two sites with evidence of secondary Apachean occupation, and nothing about their locations within the sites would preclude their having been interred well after the end of the Sopris phase occupation. Thus, it is probable that the skeletons do indeed represent Athapaskans, but of protohistoric and historic times.

On the western edge of the Plains in northeastern New Mexico are other Pueblo sites (e.g., Cimarron phase) of the 900–1300 period (Lister 1948; Glassow 1980; Gunnerson 1959). Thus far, no cord-roughened Plains pottery has been reported from these sites, but a few sherds have been found at Pecos Pueblo (Kidder and Shepard 1936:380) and at a large Pueblo site near Santa Fe, New Mexico. Such sherds have been found occasionally on the plains of northeastern New Mexico, presumably left by parties from Plains villages to the east.

Farther south, along the eastern foothills in the middle of New Mexico, were a number of pueblos that had been occupied from perhaps A.D. 1300 until the last of them was abandoned in the 1670s (see vol. 9:201–205, 236–254; Hayes 1981, 1981a). These Salinas villages, along with Pecos Pueblo, were among those settlements on the eastern Pueblo front to which Indians from the Plains came to trade in late prehistoric and early historic times.

Even farther south, along the Middle Pecos River in southern New Mexico, one finds horticultural villages lasting as late as perhaps 1350. Jelinek (1967a:162–163) attributes these sites to the Jornada branch of the Mogollon culture and suggests that late prehistoric sites on the middle Pecos River may have been occupied by Indians ancestral to the Kiowa. Campsites with Pueblo pottery dated in the historic period are also found in the area. Bison procurement along the Middle Pecos in later prehistoric time has been investigated (Speth and Parry 1978, 1980; Speth 1979, 1983; Parry and Speth 1984).

Conclusion

During the Plains Village period, life on the western periphery of the Plains, with its unpredictable climate from year to year and its extended droughts, presented challenges to the various groups that utilized the area (Wedel 1986:39–48). Late prehistoric horticulturalists who had their fixed villages in the better-watered eastern Plains crossed the High Plains on hunting or trading expeditions and left their distinctive pottery to document their presence. During this time the Apishapa phase people, who had cultural affiliations with these horticulturists to the east, established fixed villages in southeastern Colorado. Much labor went into the building of some of their structures, which incorporated great quantities of rock, but these impressive sites were apparently occupied only briefly, as were smaller open sites and rockshelters. Limited evidence of cultigens has been found, but subsistence depended heavily on hunting a great variety of animals and utilizing this food resource completely. Like Plains Villagers farther east, the Apishapa people had abandoned their area by 1400, presumably because of severe drought.

On the far western edge of the Plains, where they meet the mountains abruptly, Pueblo peoples lived in the mouths of the canyons through which flowed permanent streams. In the foothills, from the area around Las Vegas, New Mexico, north to Trinidad, Colorado, where there had been only limited Pueblo occupations before, one finds evidence of substantial populations during the Developmental Pueblo period, which corresponds to the Plains Village period. By about 1200 in the north and 1300 in the south this area was abandoned by Pueblo peoples as were various other peripheries of the Pueblo Southwest. Pueblo peoples continued to occupy the foothills in the middle of New Mexico until the Salinas Pueblos, in the Estancia Valley, were abandoned by about 1670 and Pecos Pueblo in 1838. Their decline was due to a large extent to enemy attacks.

Accounts from the Coronado expedition of 1541 and that of Juan de Oñate in 1601 describe a most successful adaptation to the High Plains for which there is very little archeological evidence. By the mid-1500s the Plains had recovered from the droughts of the 1300s and 1400s that had caused the virtual abandonment of the area. With a change to a cool damp climate in the 1500s, large herds of bison had returned in response to the abundant tall grass that was commented upon by the explorers. Living among the bison were the Teya and Querecho (Plains Apacheans) with large numbers of pack dogs and lightweight sewn skin tents. The Spaniards marveled at this lifeway of the Apacheans who had established themselves as traders of products of the hunt to sedentary villages of the eastern Plains and the Southwest. The dog nomads were reported as wintering with these sedentary neighbors from whom they were to acquire the rudiments of their own semi-sedentary culture before the mid-1600s.

For about a century, from early in the 1600s until about 1730, Cuartelejo and Paloma Apache had fixed villages between about 99° and 102° west longitude, leaving an archeological complex known as the Dismal River phase. Their close relatives, the Jicarilla and Carlana Apache, also lived in fixed villages along the foothills of the Sangre de Cristo Mountains. Ultimately, part of the Dismal River people joined the Jicarilla. Although primarily hunters, the Dismal River people took over the ideas of horticulture, pottery making, and semipermanent villages from their sedentary neighbors to the east as did the Jicarilla from their Pueblo neighbors to the west. Both retained a basic Plainslike assemblage of stone and bone tools with a few unique items. By 1750 the Apacheans, except for the Plains Apache who had joined the Kiowa in the late 1600s, had been forced from the Central Plains by pressure from the Comanche, Pawnee, and French. With the departure of the Apacheans, who had dominated much of the High Plains for about 200 years, came an end to the Plains Village period of the Western Periphery.

Plains Village Tradition: Postcontact

DONALD J. LEHMER

It is impossible to specify a precise date for the beginning of the contact period on the Plains, because 150 years separate the times of the earliest known incursions of European explorers into the southern and northern Plains—Francisco Vásquez de Coronado's entrada into Kansas in 1541 (Hammond and Rey 1940; Bolton 1949) and Henry Kelsey's expedition from Fort Nelson to the Saskatchewan prairies in 1690–1692 (Kelsey 1929). Yet the year 1675 may be generally satisfactory to mark the beginning of the contact period with the groups of the Plains Village tradition, the approximate time for the beginning of significant British and French influences in Canada and the western Great Lakes. Undoubtedly a few horses and other trade items reached some of the villages from the Southwest before that time, but the really significant influx of European traits and the resulting changes in the native culture did not begin until the last quarter of the seventeenth century.

Northern Plains Village tradition archeological sites dating from 1675 until the smallpox epidemics of 1780 are classified as the Post-Coalescent variant; they represent the ancestral Hidatsa, Mandan, and Arikara. Sites of the period from 1780 until the consolidation of the three tribes at Like-a-Fishhook Village in 1862 are termed the Disorganized Coalescent variant (Lehmer 1971). In the Central and Southern Plains the Lower Loup phase appears to have been ancestral to the Pawnee, and the Great Bend phase was ancestral to the Caddoan groups that became the historic Wichita. During the eighteenth century, these five tribes represented what may be considered as the fully developed Plains Village pattern (C.M. Johnson 1998:320–327).

Postcontact Village Populations

One of the most significant aspects of the early postcontact period in the Plains was the explosive increase in total population, largely resulting from the immigration of migratory hunting groups from the west, northeast, and east (Kroeber 1939:79–83). It is possible that there was also an increase in the total number of Plains Villagers during the eighteenth century, but this increase may be more apparent than real, the result of a tendency on the part of the village tribes to concentrate in large villages often clustered in small geographic areas.

The total area occupied by sedentary horticulturalists is extensive (fig. 1), and the loci of the fully developed eighteenth-century village tribes are well known. The Hidatsa were the northernmost of the Plains horticulturalists. Their northernmost village prior to 1780 was on the north bank of the Knife River in North Dakota (fig. 2). They occupied a series of additional villages, mainly on the west side of the Missouri, as far downstream as the badlands area in southern Oliver County known as Square Buttes (Wood 1986:13–16). These villages are considerably larger than earlier ones in the same area, which raises the possibility that village populations from the eastern part of the state moved west to the villages along the Missouri. Such movements could reflect pressures growing out of the emergence of the Sioux as a major power in the Northern Plains (R. White 1978).

The Mandan lived just below the Hidatsa heartland on the Missouri until after 1780. Their villages were built on both sides of the river, although most of them were on the west bank. The southernmost permanent settlement was just a few miles below the mouth of the Heart River.

During the eighteenth century the Missouri valley seems to have lacked permanent settlements in the 85 mile section separating the southernmost Mandan village from the northernmost Arikara village. However, the Arikara did have some semipermanent hunting camps in the lower part of this no-man's land (Lewis and Clark in Moulton 1983–, 3:173–177; Lehmer 1966:67).

Throughout the first three-quarters of the eighteenth century the Arikara established over 60 villages along both banks of the Missouri in South Dakota, scattered from just above the mouth of the Grand River to below the mouth of the White (Lehmer 1971:fig. 82). With the exception of the northernmost sites in this group, they lack the very deep midden deposits found in Hidatsa and Mandan sites, suggesting comparatively short occupations for the individual villages.

Most of Nebraska seems to have lacked village populations during the eighteenth century with the exception of a small section in the central part of the state where a number of villages were clustered near the junction of the Loup and Platte rivers. These are classified as the Lower Loup phase, which has been identified as protohistoric Pawnee (Wedel 1938).

In south-central Kansas there are two groups of villages that appear to have been occupied from the sixteenth century until after 1700. The larger one is located between the Great Bend of the Arkansas and the Smoky Hill River. The

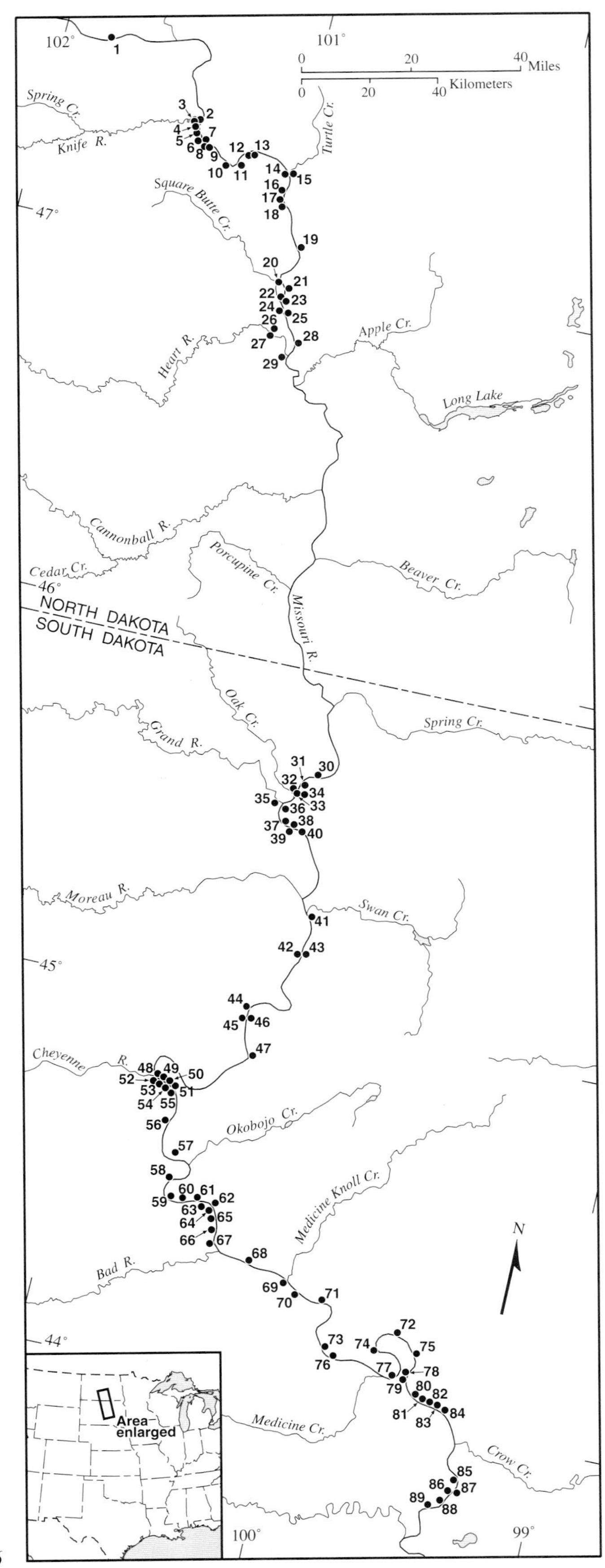

Fig. 1. Postcontact archeological sites. North Dakota: 1, Like-a-Fishhook Village (32ML2); 2, Big Hidatsa (32ME12); 3, Sakakawea (32ME11); 4, Lower Hidatsa (32ME10); 5, Amahami (32ME8); 6, White Buffalo Robe (32ME7); 7, Black Cat (32ML5); 8, Alderin Creek (32ME4); 9, Mitutahank (32ME5); 10, Mahhaha (32OL22); 11, Mandan Lake (32OL21); 12, Dennison (32OL19); 13, Hensler (32OL18); 14, Bagnell (32OL16); 15, Flaming Arrow (32ML4); 16, Upper Sanger (32OL12); 17, Lower Sanger (32OL9); 18, Smith Farm (32OL11); 19, Painted Woods (32BL10); 20, Square Butte Creek (32MO44); 21, Larson (32BL9); 22, Otter Creek (32MO40); 23, Double Ditch (32BL8); 24, Boley (32MO37); 25, Sperry (32BL4); 26, Scattered Village (32MO31); 27, Motsiff (32MO29); 28, Ward (32BL3); 29, Slant (32MO26). South Dakota: 30, Leavenworth (39CO9); 31, Anton Rygh (39CA4); 32, Norvold I (39CO31); 33, Ashley I Village (39CO11); 34, Bamble (39CA6); 35, Red Horse Hawk (39CO34); 36, Mobridge (30WW1); 37, Spiry-Elko (39WW3); 38, Larson (39WW2); 39, Bells Man (39CO17); 40, Blue Jacket I (39WW9); 41, Swan Creek (39WW7); 42, Four Bear (39DW2); 43, Steamboat Creek (39PO1); 44, Stove Creek (39DW239); 45, Pascal Creek (39AR207); 46, Rosa (39PO3); 47, Artichoke Creek Village (39SL1); 48, Madison (39SL19); 49, Coleman's Village (39SL3); 50, Little Bend (39SL13); 51, McNutt (39SL28); 52, Cheyenne River (39ST1); 53, Gillette (39ST23) and Cooper (39ST45); 54, Black Widow Ridge (39ST25) and Duffy Village #2 (39ST50); 55, Fraser (39ST51) and Emilies I Village (39ST25); 56, H.P. Thomas (39ST12); 57, Sully (39SL4); 58, Donovan (39ST5); 59, Oahe Village (39HU2); 60, Spotted Bear (39HU26); 61, 39HU24; 62, Gavitt (39HU22); 63, Buffalo Pasture (39ST6); 64, Dodd (39ST30); 65, Phillips Ranch (39ST14), Indian Creek (39ST15) and Leavitt (39ST215); 66, Johnston (39ST244); 67, 39ST33; 68, Mash Creek (39HU5); 69, Stony Point (39ST235); 70, Ft. George Village (39ST17); 71, Chapelle Creek (39HU60); 72, Cadotte (39HE202); 73, Amos Shields (39HU220); 74, Denny (39HU224); 75, Skunk I (39BF202); 76, Iron Shooter (39HU216); 77, Hawk (39HU238); 78, Peterson (39LM215); 79, Crazy Bull (39LM220); 80, Medicine Crow (39BF2); 81, Two Teeth (39BF204); 82, Pretty Bull (39BF12) and Farm School (39BF220); 83, John Saul (39BF6) and Torn Belly (39BF211); 84, Talking Crow (39BF3); 85, Hass (39LM28) and Fisherman's Gulch (39LM37); 86, Mallory (39LM34); 87, Sanitarium (39BR6); 88, 39LM24; 89, Oacoma (39LM26 and 39LM27).

smaller group was on the Arkansas River where it crosses the Kansas-Oklahoma line. The villages in these two groups have been assigned to the Great Bend phase (Wedel 1959:571–589, 630–634). Archeologists and historians agree that the northern sites are the province of Quivira, visited by Coronado in 1541 and by Juan de Oñate 60 years later. There is also a consensus that the Quivirans were Wichita, southernmost of the Plains village tribes. By 1750, the Wichita were pushing southward into the unoccupied area of Oklahoma and the ecotone between the eastern Plains grasslands and the woodland region of northeast Texas (Bell, Jelks, and Newcomb 1974).

The prehistoric Plains villages seem to have been characteristically small and scattered. While there are differences in village size from one part of the area to another, the pre-contact average appears to lie somewhere between 12 and 20 houses, and settlements with more than 40 houses are very rare.

There are two exceptions to this generalization. A few of the Extended Coalescent (prehistoric Arikara) sites near the mouth of the Grand River in South Dakota are fairly large, and they usually have some sort of fortification. Another group of Terminal Middle Missouri villages (prehistoric Mandan) were consistently large and were fortified with

North Dakota Highway Dept.

Fig. 2. Aerial view of Big Hidatsa village, N. Dak., occupied from prehistoric times to about 1845. Photographed 1964.

ditches and palisades. There are several of these sites in the Missouri valley above the mouth of the Cannonball River (Lehmer 1971:fig. 79) that have a combined area of about 120 acres. House counts from aerial photographs, and projections based on the mean number of houses per acre, have been used to determine the probable number of houses at each site. These range from 68 to 244, with an average of 116 houses per village; the Huff site had at least 103 houses (Wood 1967:map 4). These are the first villages in the Plains known to have attained such sizes, and they set a pattern that was characteristic of most eighteenth-century settlements in the area.

Population figures for the early eighteenth century can be arrived at with varying degrees of confidence for the different village groups. House counts from aerial photographs, site maps made during the early 1900s, and average house densities per acre have been used to estimate population size for the Hidatsa and Mandan. Several villages can be provisionally assigned to the Hidatsa for the period from about 1675 to 1750. They contain a total of over 640 houses. Multiplying this by the average household size of 13 individuals reported by David Thompson in 1797–1798 (Wood and Thiessen 1985:112–119) suggests a total population of over 8,300.

Six sites between Square Buttes and the Heart River can be identified with reasonable assurance as Mandan villages occupied during the same period. They contain some 620 houses, which, applying Thompson's average household size, indicates a Mandan population of over 8,000.

It is more difficult to arrive at an accurate estimate of the Arikara. The more than 60 village sites extending 200 miles along the Missouri valley in South Dakota that date from the late seventeenth century to the end of the eighteenth fall into four geographic groups. One was centered around the mouth of the Grand River, a second lay just below the mouth of the Cheyenne, a third was upstream from the mouth of the Bad River, and the fourth was in the vicinity of the Big Bend of the Missouri (Lehmer 1971:fig. 82).

Although a few of the these villages are extremely large, most are much smaller than the contemporary Mandan and Hidatsa villages, averaging about 40 houses per village. The houses themselves tend to have smaller diameters than those of the Mandan and Hidatsa; the size ratios suggest an average of 10 rather than 13 individuals per household. Estimating that 22 villages may have been occupied at any one time—only about one-third of the 60 known sites—averaging 40 houses per village and 10 individuals per household gives a total of 8,800 Arikaras for the early eighteenth century.

Good archeological data for estimating the early eighteenth-century Pawnee and Wichita populations are not available. What seems to be a reasonable figure for the Pawnee can be extrapolated from the figures given by Mooney (1928), who suggested a combined total of 9,100 Hidatsa, Mandan, and Arikara for the year 1780. This is a reduction of the total figure suggested here for the same three tribes for roughly 1700–1750 by a factor of 2.7. If Mooney's figure of 10,000 Pawnee in 1780 is increased by the same factor, it suggests a population for the early eighteenth-century Pawnee on the order of 27,000. For the Wichita and closely related groups, a conservative estimate for the year 1719 is 15,000, based on historical sources; Mooney's figure for 1780 is 3,200 ("Wichita," this vol.).

If the estimated total of over 60,000 (table 1) is even remotely accurate, it represents a very substantial population block during the first half of the eighteenth century. The geographical distribution of the population is also significant. The eighteenth-century Plains villages were restricted to relatively small sections of some of the larger river valleys. These isolated nuclei of dense population were the heartlands of the village tribes. The interstream grasslands and the unoccupied sections of the stream valleys were hinterlands lacking permanent settlements but heavily exploited for game and other resources.

If only the heartland areas where the people had their homes are considered, the population density for the village clusters is extremely high. For example, the section of the Missouri valley occupied by the Hidatsa around 1700 includes only 110 square miles; the Mandan section of the valley for the same period is 90 square miles. Using the estimated population figures gives densities of 75.4 per square mile for the Hidatsa and 88.9 for the Mandan. Arikara population density is much lower. Because of the scattering of their villages along the Missouri, the overall density was probably no more than about 18.1 per square mile. Population density of the Lower Loup villages was higher than either Hidatsa or Mandan, while the Great Bend–Wichita density may have been somewhat lower.

Table 1. Estimated Populations for the Plains Village Tribes

Tribe	*1700–1750*	*1780 (Mooney1928)*
Hidatsa	8,300	2,500
Mandan	8,000	3,600
Arikara	8,800	3,000
Pawnee	27,000	10,000
Wichita	15,000	3,200
Total	67,100	22,300

Annual Cycle

Each historic Plains village was an integrated, autonomous group of households that could and often did operate completely apart from the physical village as part of the annual round. Although details differed, the functions of the seasonal round of each of the five tribes were the same.

For the village tribes, the Hidatsa and Mandan annual cycle is the best recorded (Wilson 1917; Bowers 1950, 1965; Weitzner 1979). A convenient starting date for the year is the day on which the water rose and the winter ice went out of the Missouri, usually between mid-March and mid-April. This was followed by several busy days of salvaging float carcasses of drowned buffalo, the meat of which was considered a delicacy (Wood and Thiessen 1985:239, 265), as well as large quantities of driftwood for fuel and building materials. More driftwood was dragged ashore during the second period of high water known as the June rise.

The horticultural year began soon after the ice went out of the river. Women tilled the rich loose soil of the floodplain. Sunflowers were planted first, usually in April, with corn planted about a month later. Squash and beans were grown in the same fields as the corn, the squash planted in early June and the beans immediately afterward (Will and Hyde 1917).

The corn was usually knee-high in early June, signaling an abrupt shift from gardening to the summer hunt. A hunt leader had been selected; tepees, riding gear, weapons and other equipment had been put in order; and the gardens had been given their final cultivation. On the appointed day, most of the population moved out of the village, leaving behind only the very old, the sick, and some children.

Mandan and Hidatsa summer hunts were carried out by each village independently. Unlike the High Plains groups, there was no gathering of the entire tribe to resolidify tribal structure, but in other respects the villagers adopted the pattern of the migratory hunting groups. This was their way of life during the summer when they ranged long distances west from their villages. They returned to their villages about mid-August, where the harvesting and processing of crops lasted until after the first heavy frost, sometime between mid-September and early October. During this season, and following the first frost, the women also gathered chokecherries and buffalo berries.

The period from late summer through early winter also included large-scale trade with the High Plains tribes. Assiniboine and Cree brought European trade goods from Canada; and Cheyenne, Crow, and others brought horses, dressed buffalo robes, and other items from the west and southwest (Ewers 1968; Wood 1980). Trading parties also came at other times of the year, but during this period they could count on the availability of ample supplies of garden produce.

A second removal from their primary villages took place during mid-November, when winter set in, and ended in late February or early March when they returned (Maximilian in Thwaites 1904–1907, 23:272). Again, a special leader was selected to choose the site for the winter village, to organize and protect the group while it was moving and after the temporary village had been established, and to oversee the rituals that would call the buffalo into the section of valley where the winter village was established (Bowers 1965:186).

The winter villages consisted of smaller-scale earthlodges, built in heavy stands of timber on the Missouri floodplain, sheltered from winter storms. Many were close to the permanent villages. The trees provided a ready supply of firewood, timber for lodge building, and forage for horses, which ate small twigs and branches when the grass was covered with snow. Since these villages were on the floodplain, it was necessary to abandon them before the river ice went out.

Some winters part of the Hidatsa ranged farther, going on what might be considered a winter hunt far west of their villages into the shelter of the Little Missouri River valley. They lived in tepees and apparently changed campsites throughout the winter.

Less detailed information is available concening the Arikara annual cyle, though it was generally similar to the Hidatsa and Mandan (Hurt 1969; Holder 1970). The Arikara year included a summer hunt, and a return in time to harvest crops. They too were visited by trading parties from the migratory tribes, especially in the fall. Winter villages were built on the floodplain, as reported by Meriwether Lewis and William Clark (Moulton 1983–, 3:147–148). The Spain site (39LM301), located just below the mouth of White River, assignable to the pre-contact Extended Coalescent variant (C.S. Smith and Grange 1958), was apparently an Arikara winter village.

The Pawnee seem to have spent as little time in their villages as any of the northern village tribes. They lived in earthlodges from late February or early March until late June. The gardens were prepared and the first crops planted early in May. The summer hunt lasted from the end of June until late August or early September.

Pawnee hunts of the nineteenth century were far different from those of the northern villagers. Rather than independent village enterprises, they were tribal operations.

Only the sick and the old remained in the villages. The tribal hunt necessitated more planning; a council of village chiefs chose one of their number to take charge of the operation. The tribe moved up the Platte River and crossed over to the hunting grounds along the upper Republican and the headwaters of the Smoky Hill River. The mass hunt provided protection against attack from enemy Cheyenne, Comanche, and Sioux and was apparently a relatively late development that came about as a result of decreased Pawnee population due to epidemics.

After the hunt, each village group returned to its own home. September was the harvest month, with crop preservation extending into October. In early November preparations for the winter hunt were completed. The tribe once again assembled and moved west to the buffalo hunting grounds. The winter hunt may perhaps have been carried on as much to provide forage for the horse herds as to provide meat for the people (Murie 1981, 1:101–114).

The Wichita seem to have spent more of the year in their villages. They did go on a winter hunt beginning in early November and lasting until sometime in March. However, there is no evidence that they went on a mass summer hunt like the other village groups (Newcomb and Field 1967:315; M.M. Wedel 1982:125).

Activity Areas

Since the villagers moved over wide regions of the Plains during the course of a single year, their lifeway embraced a number of different environments, each of which may be considered a major activity area. Five such areas were used by the postcontact villagers: the village; the river on which the village was located; the river floodplain; the adjacent grasslands; and the distant grasslands.

The Village

Village sites were selected with an eye to available resources, especially timber and horticultural land on the floodplain. The primary villages were usually not built in the bottomlands, but on high ground above the level of the worst floods. This placed them in the grasslands biome just outside the floodplain forests. Hidatsa, Mandan, and Arikara villages were typically built on the edge of the first terrace above the Missouri floodplain (fig. 3). The angle between the terrace edge and a deep cut made through the terrace by a small tributary seems to have been considered an ideal location. Pawnee and Wichita also built their villages on high ground near extensive bottomlands. They too used river terraces when they were available; elsewhere they built on ridges and other elevated areas.

Postcontact Hidatsa, Mandan, Arikara, and Pawnee all used essentially the same type of house, a circular dome-shaped earthlodge with a central firepit and an enclosed entrance passage (figs. 4–5). (Wilson 1934). Some groups dug fairly deep pits so the house floor was two feet or more below ground level. In other instances only the sod and loose topsoil were removed. Typically, there were four primary superstructure support posts set at the corners of a rough square around the central firepit. However, Wedel (1936:98) reports that historic Pawnee houses varied from 4 to 11 primary support posts.

According to Wilson (1934:404) it took a group of women working together about a week to build an earthlodge that, with reasonable care, lasted 7 to 10 years. Its deterioration was usually the result of the rotting of the buried portions of the framework posts. Then a new structure was customarily built on the same location.

The Wichita house was an entirely different type of structure. It had a circular floor, usually excavated at least some distance below ground level, and a central firepit. The superstructure consisted of a framework of poles covered with grass thatch (G.A. Dorsey 1904a:4–5).

Other structures in the villages included ramadas made up of a brush roof supported by upright posts and horizontal joists, but without walls. These provided shaded areas used for work activities and lounging. Many villages also contained raised platforms enclosed by railings that were used as drying stages for corn.

Circular storage pits were dug both inside and between houses. Commonly they were undercut to make them wider at the bottom than at the top. Lined with grass and willow shoots, they were used for storing corn and other crops (Wilson 1917:87–93, fig. 25). Later, if they became damp or infested with mice, they served as convenient places for disposing of trash.

Houses were scattered throughout the village area. However, there were tribal differences in village plan. The Mandan had an open plaza near the center, and sizable trash mounds were scattered in and around the village. The Hidatsa, in contrast, lacked defined plazas, and occupants often seem to have raked the village area so that refuse built up in a thick level sheet rather than in mounds. Arikara villages usually contained one unusually large lodge, a ceremonial structure with a low earthen altar against the wall opposite the entrance (Lehmer and Jones 1968:16, 66, figs. 6, 19). In many Arikara villages the occupation area is covered with sheet refuse, but trash mounds occur in those around the mouth of the Grand River.

Fortifications are another variable, related to shifting patterns of warfare (Owsley 1994). The large Hidatsa villages dating from the early eighteenth century do not seem to have been consistently fortified. Those occupied after about 1750 were protected by ditches and palisades of vertical posts inside the ditch. Historic Mandan villages seem to have been consistently fortified, most commonly with a combination of ditch and palisade (Wood 1986:13–21).

Early postcontact Arikara villages seem to have been unfortified with the exception of the ones nearest the northernmost edge of their territory. Like-a-Fishhook, built

Joslyn Art Mus., Omaha, Nebr.: top, NA 118; bottom left, R15; bottom right, Smithsonian, Dept. of Anthr.: 8407.

Fig. 3. Earthlodges and household equipment. top, Interior of a Mandan earthlodge in the village of Mitutahank, Dak. Terr. (Deapolis site; fig. 1, no. 9). Warrior lances, shields and bags, a paddle, gathering basket, backrest, and cooking containers are carefully rendered. Watercolor and ink by Karl Bodmer, 1833–1834. bottom left, View of Mitutahank and Ft. Clark from downriver. Watercolor (detail) by Karl Bodmer, winter 1833–1834. Summer villages were located high on the banks of the river, in easily defended positions. Winter villages, built nearby in heavily timbered bottomland where they were protected from winter winds, were occupied from the end of November until February or March. There was constant traffic between the two villages (Bodmer 1894:284). bottom right, Conical pottery jar showing characteristic cord markings and broad, thick rim. Collected by Charles C. Gray and Washington Matthews at Ft. Stevenson, Dak. Terr., 1867; height, 16.5 cm.

by Hidatsa in 1845, was fortified by palisades but lacked a ditch (fig. 6).

Pawnee villages, and at least some of their Lower Loup predecessors, were also fortified by ditches backed by solid embankments of earth and sod three to four feet high. According to Wedel (1936:55) the Pawnee did not use palisades because of the scarcity of suitable timber.

Wedel (1959:587) categorized the Great Bend phase sites as unfortified. However, at least some historic

top, Amer. Mus. of Nat. Hist., New York: 15981; center, Minn. Histl. Soc., St. Paul, St. Paul *Dispatch-Pioneer Press* Coll.; bottom, Mont. Histl. Soc., Helena: 981-017.

Fig. 4. Construction of earthlodges. top, Framework of an Arikara dance lodge, showing the 4 tall posts in the center that supported the roof. Photograph by Abram J. Gifford, Ft. Berthold, N. Dak., 1887. center, Demonstration of the building of a Mandan earthlodge. A framework of poles around the outer perimeter is then covered with brush and dirt and sod. Photographed at the rededication of the fur trade post on the Upper Missouri River, Ft. Union, Mont.-N. Dak., 1925. bottom, Mandan earthlodge, with storage scaffold on right and log cabin behind it, west bank of Missouri River. A notched-log ladder used to climb up on the earthlodge is next to the entranceway. Photograph by Laton A. Huffman, 1878–1880s.

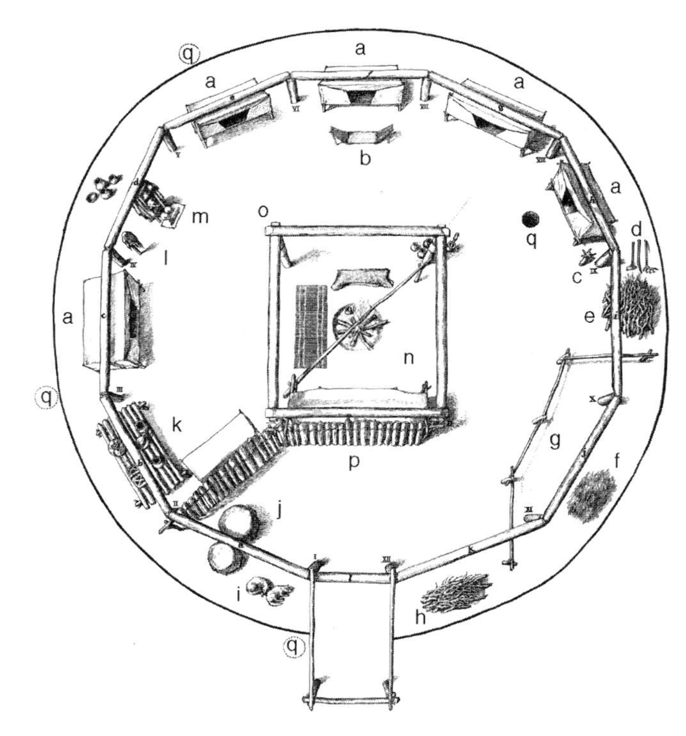

Wilson 1934.

Fig. 5. Sketch of 12-post earthlodge of Small Ankle, father of Buffalo Bird Woman, Ft. Berthold Res., N. Dak., about 1875. a, bed; b, back rest; c, root carrier; d, garden tools; e, firewood; f, feed for horses; g, corral for horses; h, extra firewood; i, dogs; j, bull boats; k, food platform; l, medicine bundle of shrine keeper (on post); m, shrine with Waterbuster clan bundle; n, the cook's place; o, 4 central posts that support the roof; p, fence that deflects drafts from the entranceway; q, caches. Drawing by Frederick Wilson.

Wichita villages in Oklahoma and Texas had palisades around all or part of the occupied area.

Plains villages were the locus of subsistence activities, including the preparation of various kinds of food for storage. Corn was husked in the fields and taken to the village for drying on the elevated stages. Dried corn was shelled by beating with flails in a threshing booth under the drying stage, and the shelled corn was stored in cache pits. Squash was taken to the village as it was picked; some were eaten fresh, others were sliced, dried, and stored in parfleches or cache pits. Sunflowers were also taken to the village for drying and threshing, but beans were dried, threshed, and winnowed in the fields (Will and Hyde 1917).

The enormous quantities of unworked animal bone, especially bison, found in the refuse of postcontact villages are evidence that considerable butchering was done there, presumably the carcasses of animals killed near the village. Much of the meat butchered in the village was presumably used while it was fresh. Surplus beyond immediate needs would have been cut into thin strips, dried, and stored as jerky or pounded into pemmican.

Another fundamental village activity was the manufacture of tools, utensils, weapons, and other articles. Most items used by the villagers were produced by themselves. Each village tribe seems to have had a least some craft specialists who produced particular items, such as arrows, which were used by other members of the group. Other items were made by each household for its own use.

There is very little information regarding the manufacture of many of the important elements of the villagers' technological inventory. Men made weapons, arrow-making tools, pipes, and saddles. Women made pottery (fig. 3), clothing for both sexes, tepee covers, and built the earthlodges with some help from men. Chipped-stone tools were probably made by men—arrow points, grooved stone mauls, bark paddles, and stone balls used as anvils in pottery making. It is uncertain who made the numerous wood, bone, and antler artifacts such as digging sticks and scapula hoes, awls and punches, metatarsal fleshers, and antler fleshing adzes.

Many postcontact villages were the sites of intertribal trade, which was vitally important in disseminating European traits throughout the Plains. During the eighteenth century the Mandan, Hidatsa, and Arikara filled the role of brokers in an intertribal trade network that reached from Hudson Bay to Mexico (Will and Hyde 1917; Mandelbaum 1940; Jablow 1951; Ewers 1968; Wood 1980; vol. 4:351–374). Their villages became warehouses where horses from western tribes were held to be exchanged for guns, ammunition, and other trade goods brought in by northern and eastern tribes such as the Plains Cree, Assiniboine, and the more easterly Sioux groups. The Pawnee and Wichita also obtained European trade goods and horses, but they had to compete with other village-dwelling tribes to the east, such as the Osage, who attempted to prevent direct contact between European traders and the tribes farther west. During the late eighteenth century the Wichita established trade relations with the Comanche, providing them a link with the Southwest trade fairs held at Taos, as well as access to horses, which they in turn traded to the Pawnee for European goods coming from the east (Dunbar 1880a:321–322; Bannon 1964:154).

The introduction of the horse and European trade goods had a profound effect on the technology that related to each of the activity areas of the village tribes. The addition of the horse necessitated some changes in the villages. In many houses an enclosure was added to the right of the inner end of the entrance passage, and valuable horses were kept there at night as a precaution against enemy raiders (fig. 5g) (Wilson 1934:393–394, figs. 25–26). Corrals were also built between the houses, often under the drying stages, to hold less valuable animals.

European trade goods tended to be relatively scarce during the early eighteenth century, especially in the Hidatsa, Mandan, and Arikara villages. They became more common during the late eighteenth century, but the quantities that found their way into the northern villages were still limited by the fact that most of them had to be carried overland from Canada and the Mississippi headwaters (Wood and Thiessen 1985:18–69, figs. 2–3). The same sorts of items tend to be somewhat more common in the early historic Pawnee and Wichita villages, presumably because they could be moved up the Missouri and its tributaries by boat.

Metal tools were by far the most important trade items. Steel axes, adzes, and hatchets were infinitely superior to native stone celts for shaping and fitting the beams and posts of earthlodge frameworks. Steel hatchets and heavy knives also greatly facilitated manufacture of the many kinds of bone tools that continued to be used until well into the late nineteenth century; this is demonstrated by a marked increase in the number of bone tools in postcontact sites.

Chipped-stone tools and arrow points continued to be used until well into the nineteenth century, but metal counterparts were substituted when they could be obtained. European butcher knives and clasp knives were highly prized. In addition, scraps of iron and brass were hafted in slots in the edges of sections of bison rib and vertebral spines—direct counterparts of similar artifacts that had been used with chipped-stone blades for centuries

U. of S. Dak., W.H. Over State Mus., Vermillion: left, N115; right, N114; center, Smithsonian, NAA; 91-13023.

Fig. 6. Like-a-Fishhook Village, Ft. Berthold, N. Dak. Reconstruction of the Mandan and Arikara section of Like-a-Fishhook Village from 3 separate photographs, based on research by Thomas W. Kavanagh. The village palisade is in the foreground. In 1872 the village had 97 log cabins and 78 earthlodges (Matthews 1877:4). Photographs by Stanley J. Morrow, 1870–1872. Background is computer enhanced.

(Lehmer 1971:146, fig. 91). Metal blades were also substituted for chipped-stone ones attached to the L-shaped fleshing adzes made from elk antlers. Occasional metal scraps with notched or serrated edges found in archeological sites appear to be native-made saws. Conical metal tinklers, doubtless hung from the fringes on buckskin garments, and tubular metal beads show that some iron and brass was diverted from purely utilitarian purposes.

Brass and iron kettles are extremely rare in Plains village sites before the late nineteenth century. Prior to that time they were more valuable as raw materials for articles such as arrowpoints and knife blades. Ethnographic evidence from the Hidatsa indicates native cultural preferance for cooking food in pottery vessels; metal pots were said to spoil the taste (Wilson 1908–1918).

In postcontact times Hidatsa, Mandan, and Arikara women practiced an unusual craft—the making of glass pendants from ground and fused trade beads (fig. 7d–f). The Arikara learned the art from a Spanish prisoner (Tabeau 1939:149; Bass, Evans and Jantz 1971:pl. xiii). Meriwether Lewis gave a detailed description of the process, reporting that it had been taught to the Arikara by Shoshone Indian prisoners (Moulton 1983–, 3:313–315).

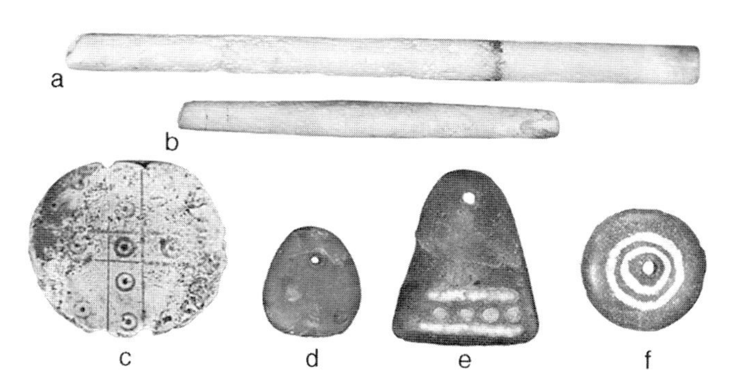

Smithsonian, Dept. of Anthr.: a, 471129; b, 517450; d: AT24428; e–f, 325465; U. of Tenn., Dept. of Anthr., Knoxville: c, F210-B54B.

Fig. 7. Euro-American shell trade objects and native-made glass pendants from Arikara sites of the Postcontact Coalescent. a, Shell hairpipe from the Sully site, S. Dak.; b, shell hairpipe with slightly thickened center from the Leavenworth site, S. Dak.; c, shell disk "runtee" with incised decoration and perforations, from the Larson site, S. Dak.; d, glass pendant made by the fusion of ground glass beads from the Sully site. e–f, Glass pendants from the Leavenworth site. Length of a, 11.0 cm. (Caption based on information from William T. Billeck, 1999).

The River

The Missouri was an important resource for the Hidatsa, Mandan, and Arikara, although rivers were a lesser factor in the lives of the Pawnee and Wichita. For the three northern village groups, the stream along which they lived was also a transportation artery. They used bull boats—bowl-shaped crafts made by stretching a large buffalo hide over a pole framework (Weitzner 1979:247–252). Although used primarily for crossing the Missouri, the Hidatsa, at least, also made long voyages in them. Wilson (1908–1918) recorded a Hidatsa hunting expedition to the Yellowstone River, the party returning down the Missouri in bull boats with the meat and hides, a distance of nearly 200 river miles.

The Hidatsa, Mandan, and Arikara also obtained part of their food supply from the river. The men fished with hook and line or with a double-pointed gorge to which a line was fastened at the middle. They also used circular weirs or traps built in backwaters. Carcasses of drowned buffalo were dragged from the river, as was driftwood, especially during times of high water.

The Missouri also had brief seasonal importance in hunting twice each year. Many antelope herds wintered west of the river and spent the summer in the prairies to the east. They crossed the Missouri at more or less the same places each year. Normally fleet, the animals were at a disadvantage when they were swimming across the river, and Lewis and Clark observed them being killed with sticks and arrows (Moulton 1983–, 3:177).

The Pawnee and Wichita also appear to have relied on salvage from the rivers, but the quantities of material they obtained must have been smaller than those taken from the Missouri. The Pawnee appear to have done some fishing, but the Wichita are reported to have not eaten fish (Bolton 1914, 2:202).

The Floodplain

The floodplains, covered with a dense growth of deciduous forest, were far more important to the villagers than the streams themselves. The trees provided an essential supply of timber for building and firewood, as well as winter fodder for the horses. Many of the forest plants and shrubs were used for food, medicines, and raw materials. The forests were also well stocked with game animals.

Gardening was by far the most important activity carried out on the floodplain. Each household had its own garden plot, ranging up to five acres in extent. These had to be cleared before they could be cultivated. Crops of corn, beans, squash, and sunflowers were planted and tended by women. Old men gave some help in the regular gardens, and theirs was the sole responsibility for the raising of tobacco patches, which were separate from the main gardens.

Crop failures or poor yields due to drought or grasshoppers were extremely serious, but poor years seem to have been relatively rare. The corn yield in good years ranged from 20 to 30 bushels per acre. In those years the fields provided seed for the next year's crop, a major part of the total food supply until the time of the next year's harvest, and usually a healthy surplus for trade (Will and Hyde 1917).

The three northern tribes also carried out one other important activity on the floodplain—buffalo hunting in the timbered sections during extreme cold weather. The timber provided shelter for buffalo during winter storms, when it was possible for the villagers to kill them in large numbers (Maximilian in Thwaites 1904–0907, 23:245–246).

Since the Pawnee and Wichita went on winter hunts far to the west of their villages, the utilization of the floodplain for winter villages and winter hunting was not part of their annual round.

Population size and adaptation were controlled by the availability of timber, the scarcest essential resource of the region. Native tree cover was almost entirely limited to the floodplain forests and occasional "coulee groves"—small clumps of trees that grew in favorable spots in the breaks along major stream valleys. The Arikara were forced to relocate their villages every 5 to 6 years for lack of wood, which was scarcer than farther north in Mandan territory (Tabeau 1939:69–70). However, some historic villages existed for 40 to 50 years through good management of timber resources. This included supplementing local supplies by salvaging driftwood and felling standing timber at increasing distances from the village as nearby tree cover was cut down.

The intertribal trade network forced women to shift their activities from the village to the floodplain. Trading demanded a sizable surplus of garden crops, and this must have substantially increased the time spent in gardening over that necessary for providing household needs. Since dressed hides were one of the items received in exchange for garden crops, it seems likely that as trade increased the women of the village spent less time in dressing hides and more time in gardening.

The Adjacent Grasslands

Many important activities were carried on within a radius from 20 to 40 miles from the village. Wild food plants such as the prairie turnip were gathered there, as was the tall grass used for lining cache pits and as an element in the cover of the earthlodge. After the introduction of the horse, the adjacent grasslands were essential for use as pasture.

The adjacent grasslands also served as places for the disposal of the dead. The Wichita, Pawnee, and Arikara all practiced inhumation. The Wichita seem to have interred their dead in graves distributed around the main area of occupation of the village. Graves contained individual burials with the bodies extended on the back or left side. The Arikara, and apparently also the Pawnee, seem to have selected an elevated area near the village as a cemetery. Again the dead were buried in individual graves, but they were flexed, usually on the back with the knees drawn up against the chest. There is evidence that the Arikara placed a layer of poles or split puncheons above the body before refilling the grave (Lehmer 1971:142; Bass, Evans, and Jantz 1971:99, pl. ix, a). The Mandan and Hidatsa ordinarily disposed of the dead by placing the bodies on elevated wooden platforms clustered a few hundred yards from the village. Scaffold burial seems to have been temporarily abandoned in favor of flexed inhumation on the Arikara pattern during the smallpox epidemics of eighteenth and nineteenth centuries (Strong 1940:362–363).

One of the most important uses of the nearby grasslands was for hunting. A journal written at Fort Clark, provides great detail on the hunting practices of the Mandan village there from 1834 to 1839 (Chardon 1932). In approximately 20 out of every 100 journal entries there were buffalo in the grasslands adjacent to the fort, sometimes in sight, sometimes 15 to 20 miles away. The grasslands near the Mandan and Hidatsa villages were thus a rich hunting ground, exploited by small parties operating for no longer than a day or two at a time. There seem to be no comparable data for the Arikara, Pawnee, and Wichita, but it is likely that they too were able to supplement the mass hunts in the distant grasslands by hunting in the vicinity of the villages.

The Distant Grasslands

All the nineteenth century Plains village tribes went on mass hunting expeditions into the grasslands far to the west of their villages, and there is reason to believe that this was a long-established custom. Whether the party consisted of the population of a single village, as with the Mandan and Hidatsa (Bowers 1965:186–188), or the entire tribe, like the Pawnee (Murie 1981, 1:98–99), the hunts were highly organized in terms of leadership and social control. Throughout the hunt, one group of men acted as police, keeping stragglers up with the line of march, overseeing setting up and breaking camp, and especially preventing any premature action on the part of individuals that might stampede the herd before all the hunters were ready to move on it. This strict organization and control was only present within the villages for a few rare group activities such as building fortifications or cleaning up the village.

Horses were the primary means of transportation after they were acquired, although the villagers seem to have had proportionally fewer of them than most of the High Plains tribes. As a result, dogs dragging travois supplemented horses, especially among the northern villagers (Wilson 1924). The presence of the bones of large dogs in some early village middens suggests that the use of dog traction was an old trait among the villagers.

The Decline of the Plains Villages

By the mid-eighteenth century the Plains Village tribes had reached the peak of their postcontact development. Then, sometime about 1750, the first of a series of disastrous epidemics struck the villagers (Dobyns 1983:15–26). Measles, cholera, malaria, whooping cough, and influenza all appear on the roster, but smallpox was far and away the outstanding item on the list (Stearn and Stearn 1945; Trimble 1985, 1988).

There is no doubt that smallpox struck the northern village tribes at least once between the 1750s and 1775 (Ramenofsky 1987; Trimble 1989). During 1780–1781 a pandemic swept across the western Plains, reaching from New Mexico in the south to the Canadian forests in the north. It devastated the village tribes (Dobyns 1983:15). By 1795 the Arikara were reported to have been reduced to two villages located just below the Cheyenne River (Nasatir 1952, 1:299). The Mandan villages around the mouth of the Heart River were abandoned about 1780 (Moulton 1983–, 3:403), and the survivors moved upstream near the mouth of Knife River where in 1804 Lewis and Clark described them living in two villages near the three Hidatsa villages. Archeological evidence indicates that those villages were themselves remnants of a larger pre-1780 population. There seems to have been another outbreak in 1801–1802, but there is no evidence regarding its effects on the northern village tribes (Dobyns 1983; J.F. Taylor 1977). In 1837 smallpox was introduced from a steamboat sent up the Missouri to supply the fur trade posts (Dollar 1977; Meyer 1977:90–99; Trimble 1986). Mortality rates among the northern villages were 33 percent for the Hidatsa, 98 percent for the Mandan, and 50 percent for the Arikara (Stearn and Stearn 1945:table 1). Another outbreak came from the same source in 1856, and devastated both the Mandan and Hidatsa at Like-a-Fishhook Village and the Arikara living near Fort Clark (Meyer G.H. 1977:105; Smith 1972:17).

There were outbreaks among the Pawnee in 1801, 1831, and 1838 (Stearn and Stearn 1945:76, 79, 86). Mortality rates seem to have been lower than among the northern villages, but the total population seems still to have been materially reduced. In Texas there were outbreaks of cholera, smallpox, and other diseases between 1528 and 1892 (Ewers 1973). The number of Wichita were reduced to a fraction of what they had been. Total population decline for the five village tribes was well over 80 percent by the census of 1890 (U.S. Census Office 1894). There was a corresponding reduction in the total number of villages, and there were so few warriors left that they became easy prey for their enemies.

History of the United States Plains Until 1850

WILLIAM R. SWAGERTY

Protohistory

Europeans entered the Plains from three directions: Texas and New Mexico, the Mississippi River, and the Canadian prairies. For the Southern Plains, the expedition of Álvar Nuñez Cabeza de Vaca and his three companions from 1528 to 1536 across Texas and portions of northern Mexico marks a beginning of sporadic first contact (C.L. Riley 1987:16–17). For the Central Plains, the expedition of Francisco Vásquez de Coronado, 1540–1542, and his contact with Plains peoples of present-day west Texas and Kansas is a similar marker (E. John 1975:20–21; M.M. Wedel 1979; Wedel 1986:137; N.P. Hickerson 1994:23–28). French voyageur-traders active among the Pawnee before 1700 provide a possible second protohistoric encounter on the Central Plains (M.M. Wedel [1979] 1988:9). For the Northern Plains, explorers Pierre Esprit Radisson and Médard Chouart, sieur des Groseilliers, made contact with the Santee Sioux in 1659. Mississippi River explorers Louis Jolliet and Jacques Marquette in 1673 and René-Robert Cavelier, sieur de La Salle in 1682, and continuing French probes past the mouth of the Missouri River by 1700 provide additional intercultural contact (M.M. Wedel [1979] 1988:9; D.R. Russell 1991:50; Swagerty 1991:476–478). This range of dates—1534 to 1700—coincides with a period of poorly documented movements of tribes in all three sections.

The Plains tribes were in a state of demographic flux when Spaniards and Frenchmen met them. By 1700, when historical documentation became more consistent, some tribes had been in the region a very long time; others had recently arrived; still others were yet to come. Some tribes appear to have been attracted to the eastern fringe of the Plains, but most tribes who occupied the Plains in historic times were pushed onto the grassland by other tribes to their east.

The oldest tribes—all horticulturalists—were found on the eastern edges of the Plains. The Caddoan speakers ancestral to the Wichita, Kitsai, Pawnee, and Arikara had moved from the Southeast around A.D. 900, bringing many Mississippian traditions with them as they adapted to the grasslands and tributaries of the lower Missouri and Mississippi river valleys. The ancestors of the Siouan-speaking Mandan and Hidatsa arrived around 1100, settling in earthlodge villages on the Upper Missouri and its tributaries in what is now North and South Dakota. Other speakers of Siouan languages arrived somewhat later from the Ohio Valley. In 1600, the ancestors of the Otoe, Missouria, Iowa, Omaha, Ponca, Kansa, and Osage were all well established in permanent villages with the Missouri River serving as a central and connecting transportation corridor (Holder 1970; L. Fowler 1996, 1(2):2–3).

The second oldest tradition of occupancy was focused in the northwestern subregion of the Plains where the Algonquian-speaking Blackfoot were in Alberta by 1700 (Wissler 1910:16–18; Ewers 1955:16). Like the Blackfoot, the Gros Ventre and Arapaho (also Algonquians) moved out of the woodlands (probably the Red River valley) and onto the plains prior to the early eighteenth century. Pushed southwestward by Assiniboine and Plains Cree from the forks of the Saskatchewan, the Gros Ventre reestablished themselves temporarily between the South Branch and the Missouri, and by 1810 were in present Montana between the Milk and the Missouri rivers (Flannery 1953:2–10). The Arapaho were west of the Black Hills in the 1790s (Nasatir 1952, 2:384), moving south to present eastern Colorado by about 1820 (Hayden 1862:321, Trenholm 1970:33).

Two other Algonquian-speaking groups—Plains Cree and Plains Ojibwa—arrived after 1700 (Mandelbaum 1979; Milloy 1988; D.R. Russell 1991; Peers 1994), as did the Cheyenne, a classic case of woodland-prairie-plains migration and adjustment (Grinnell 1915). When first noted, on a map of 1678–1679 (Winsor 1884–1889, 4:218), the Cheyenne were living in present Minnesota. During the eighteenth century, Sioux expansion pushed them westward to the Sheyenne River, where they built earthlodge villages and cultivated corn, beans, and squash. By the mid-1700s, they were on the move again, pushed by the Plains Cree, Plains Ojibwa, and Assiniboine. The Cheyenne reestablished themselves in the Black Hills region, soon becoming excellent hunters and horsemen, only to be pressured farther west and south by the Teton (Moore 1996:13–29, 79–93). Other tribes who added to the medley of voices and diverse traditions brought by migrants include the Uto-Aztecan-speaking Eastern Shoshone, Comanche, and Ute, and the Kiowa, who all pressed their way from the north in a southeasterly direction into what became their historic homelands in the late eighteenth and nineteenth centuries (Bamforth 1988:85–90).

Disease

No detailed analysis of historical population change and epidemiology of the Plains has been attempted (Kemnitzer 1980; G.R. Campbell 1989). Nevertheless, the variables and principles of disease transmission, as well as the documented chronology of disease episodes, provide an overview of how widespread disease affected demographic trends (Trimble 1979, 1989; Owsley 1992). Several areas, notably the upper reaches of the Missouri River and the southernmost part of the Plains, have received considerable scholarly attention (Lehmer 1971, 1977a; Ewers 1973; Trimble 1994).

Employing the concept of "virgin soil epidemics," defined as "those in which the populations at risk have had no previous contact with the diseases that strike them and are therefore immunologically almost defenseless" (Crosby 1972, 1976:289–290), Dobyns (1983) argued that a pandemic swept northward from the Caribbean and Mexico between 1520 and 1524. While in present-day Texas, the Cabeza de Vaca party described debilitated and dying Indians who "fell sick from the stomach, so that one-half of them died . . ." (Bandelier 1905:68–71). This unspecified disease may be the continuation of Dobyns's postulated hemispheric epidemic or it may be another ailment, possibly influenza or cholera. The Kiowa distinguished cholera from smallpox ('hole sickness') and measles ('pimple sickness') as 'cramp sickness', in nineteenth-century pictorial calendars (Ewers 1973). Disease might also be a contributing factor to movements and disruptions across the Central Plains prior to or contemporaneous with European explorations, although a seventeenth-century disease horizon is far more plausible than one in the sixteenth century, at least for the Middle Missouri River tribes (Ramenofsky 1987).

Although there is no mention of contagious disease in other Southwest chronicles by Spanish explorers until the seventeenth century, some scholars postulate that diseases may have spread along trade and transportation corridors from Mexico and from Spanish colonies in New Mexico and Florida, infecting the Plains with smallpox as early as 1617, again in the 1640s, and after 1671 (Vehik 1989:118–120). This model assumes that germs accompanied trade items carried from the Pueblos to the Southern Plains (Reff 1991) or from the Southeast via the Caddos, whose villages between the Arkansas and Red River valleys underwent precipitous decline prior to 1680 (Perttula 1991, 1992), paralleling the demise of more southerly Coahuiltecans in the area first described by the Cabeza de Vaca party (Ewers 1973:108). The invasiveness of smallpox in its deadlier viral form, *variola major*, is such that a single infected person could transmit the disease through respiratory contact to the entire population, especially in crowded villages or lodges where individuals shared drinking and eating utensils and sleeping environments. Furthermore, smallpox has been known to survive in dried form, only to re-emerge up to a year later, bringing further deaths to already disabled populations in the midst of recovery (Trimble 1979).

The first definite pandemic on the Southern Plains (probably smallpox) dates from 1687 to 1691. The French under La Salle may have witnessed the first virgin soil episode of this disease, which could wipe out 50 percent or more of a population in a matter of a few weeks. Permanent villages such as the Arikara on the Missouri River may well have suffered measles and smallpox as well as endemic tuberculosis early in the eighteenth century (Owsley 1992), a much earlier date than 1780, the well-documented benchmark for the North American smallpox episode thought to have engulfed tribes from Mexico to Canada (Dobyns 1983:15). Prior to the 1780s, smallpox and measles probably moved from Texas to the Great Lakes and up the Missouri River between 1750 and 1752 (Ewers 1973; J.F. Taylor 1977). Another outbreak hit Texas from 1762 to 1766, devastating the Karankawa and halving the Mission Indian population around San Antonio, as well as infecting the Lipan Apache (Bolton 1908a). Plague, cholera, and typhoid have been suggested for the next wave of disease, which struck the area from the Red River south through Texas and Louisiana 1777–1778 (Bolton 1914:231–232). Smallpox recurred 1801–1802, and in 1816 (Ewers 1973:108). In 1828, the biologist Jean Louis Berlandier (1969:84) visited Texas and reported that smallpox occurred among the Indian tribes "every sixteen years, making great ravages for a year at a time."

On the Northern Plains, the earliest documentary record of epidemic disease dates to the 1730s, when smallpox struck the western Cree and probably the western Sioux and Arikara (J.F. Taylor 1977). The earliest postulated date, 1734–1735, is consistent with ceramic sequences found in Arikara village sites (Deetz 1965) and is supported by the journal of trader Jean-Baptiste Truteau, who described the Arikira as once "very large; it counted thirty-two populous villages, now depopulated and almost entirely destroyed by the smallpox, which broke out among them at three different times" (Truteau in Nasatir 1952, 1:299). A recurrence of smallpox is thought to have struck the Arikara around the 1750s (Deetz 1965:101).

For the plains in general, devastating episodes of smallpox are recorded from 1780 to 1782, thought to have spread from Spanish New Mexico (Lehmer 1977a:106) or, more likely, from Louisiana and Spanish Texas (Bolton 1914, 1:27) to the Lipan Apache and then on to the Comanche and the Rio Grande area (Simmons 1966; Ewers 1973) with recurrences almost every decade through the 1850s (Vehik 1989:117). During two disease events that occurred from 1800 to 1803, and from 1806 to 1814, smallpox invaded much of the Northern Plains from the south, while whooping cough, streptococcal infections, and influenza spread southward from Canada (J.F. Taylor 1977:56). Cumulatively, the disease episodes from 1734 to

1800 mark a precipitous population decline across western North America on the magnitude of reductions of between 10 and 50 percent in 1780–1782 alone; some regions suffered a one-third loss in a single generation (Thornton 1987:91–104; Trimble 1989).

On the Missouri, the Mandan-Hidatsa and the Arikara earthlodge villages are thought to have been reduced from a pre-epidemic high of 9,000 Mandan-Hidatsas and 24,000 Arikaras (Bowers 1965:486) to 1,250 Mandans, 2,700 Hidatsas, and 2,000 Arikaras by 1805 (Lewis and Clark 1832:710–711). Of 18 to 23 original Arikara villages, only three were occupied when visited in 1803–1804 by French traders out of Saint Louis (Tabeau 1939:124). Of nine Mandan villages on Heart River occupied when first contacted in 1738 by Pierre Gaultiers de Varennes, sieur de La Vérendrye, all had been abandoned by 1797 in favor of two villages near the mouth of Knife River (Wood 1977). That same year, three distinct Hidatsa subgroups had amalgamated into one village each (Bowers 1965:486) with three other villages consisting of mixed Mandan-Hidatsa populations, interpreted as a survival response following the 1780–1781 epidemic (J.R. Hanson 1983:107–108).

On the western edge, bands of Crow and not yet differentiated Northern and Eastern Shoshone who gathered in large winter villages suffered very high mortality during the 1780–1782 smallpox epidemic, as did their Plateau neighbors, the Kootenai, Flathead, and Nez Perce (Teit 1930:315–316). Tribal groups that wintered in smaller, dispersed family units fared better. Hudson's Bay Company traders based out of Cumberland House on the Saskatchewan River thought that the Blackfoot escaped very high mortality in 1780 due to this factor (Rich 1952:243ff). In reality, at least one division—the Piegan—was hard hit, after attacking a silent Shoshone village whose occupants were sick or dead, and bringing back infected clothing, lodges, and weapons (Tyrrell 1916:336–338; Ewers 1958:28–29).

Epidemic of 1837

Beginning in 1831, smallpox infected the Central Plains and spread north, cutting down many tribes by more than 50 percent in the course of a few months. Then came the High Plains smallpox epidemic of 1837–1838. The infection traveled up the Missouri River on an American Fur Company steamboat, breaking out at Sioux Agency, Fort Pierre, Fort Clark, and Fort Union (fig. 1). By summer's end, traders were reporting mortality approaching 70–80 percent (Chardon in Abel 1932:394–395; Denig 1961:71–72; Larpenteur 1898, 1:131–135). The Mandans lost over 95 percent of their people; the Hidatsa 33 percent; the Arikara 50 percent (E.W. Stearn and A.E. Stearn 1945: table 1; Lehmer 1977a:99–100). No single disease episode since the 1780s left so wide a trail of death (Trimble 1994).

Sociocultural effects among survivor groups beyond 1840 include an increase in suicide, decline in fertility, and the creation of refugee populations that were forced to combine with other remnant or drastically reduced bands or villages (J.F. Taylor 1977). Other diseases that continued to hammer Plains Indian populations up to 1850 include smallpox among the Kiowa (fig. 2), Plains Apache, and Comanche in 1839–1840 (Ewers 1973:108); measles in 1845 among the Arikara, Blackfoot, Plains Cree, Crow, Cheyenne, and some bands of the Sioux; a recurrence in 1847 among the Crow (J.F. Taylor 1977:80–81); cholera beginning in 1848 and spreading widely over the entire culture area by the end of 1849, killing "half the Cheyenne" (Mooney 1898:173, 290–291) and many others (Ewers 1973:108; Vehik 1989:117), including one-fourth of the remaining Pawnee (R. Powers and Leiker 1998:322).

Dogs and Horses

Dogs are found in archeological sites in association with bison kills as far back as 8000 B.C. (Wedel 1986:66). Dogs accompanied pedestrian bands as they established themselves on the Plains between A.D. 500 and 1500 and continued to be an integral part of Plains life after diffusion of the horse in historic times. Long before they used horses, Plains Indians used dogs, and some undoubtedly ate them as a reliable food resource or as a special ceremonial food. Dogs also served as camp guards and, probably, as family pets. The Kiowa credited dogs with helping them move on sledges from the far north to the more hospitable Central Plains (Mooney 1898:153). Dogs, which enabled Plains village horticulturalists to go on seasonal bison hunts hundreds of miles from home, were an integral part of social, ceremonial, and economic life (G.L. Wilson 1924). Among the Pawnee prior to 1700 dogs served as both pack animals and a secondary food source during times of dietary stress (Bozell 1988).

After introduction of the horse, but prior to its full integration, dogs remained essential in seasonal hunts. In 1724, a Kansa hunting party of more than 1,000 people was reported by explorer Étienne Venyard, sieur de Bourgmont to have traveled west on the Kansas plains with more than 300 dogs serving as beasts of burden, dragging and carrying 35–50 pounds of robes, dried meat, and camp gear back and forth 200 miles or so (Margry 1879–1888, 6:414). Scholars are uncertain whether village peoples on the Missouri-Mississippi fringe of the plains used dogs for hunting. Because dogs consume large volumes of meat relative to their weight, some Missouri River tribes may have considered dogs uneconomical (Wedel 1986:124–125). However, communal long-distance hunting was standard among most Plains peoples, giving rise to pemmican production, which in turn fed families and their dogs on the march (Reeves 1990). As late as 1811, each Arikara family owned "thirty or forty" dogs (Brackenridge 1815:141–142).

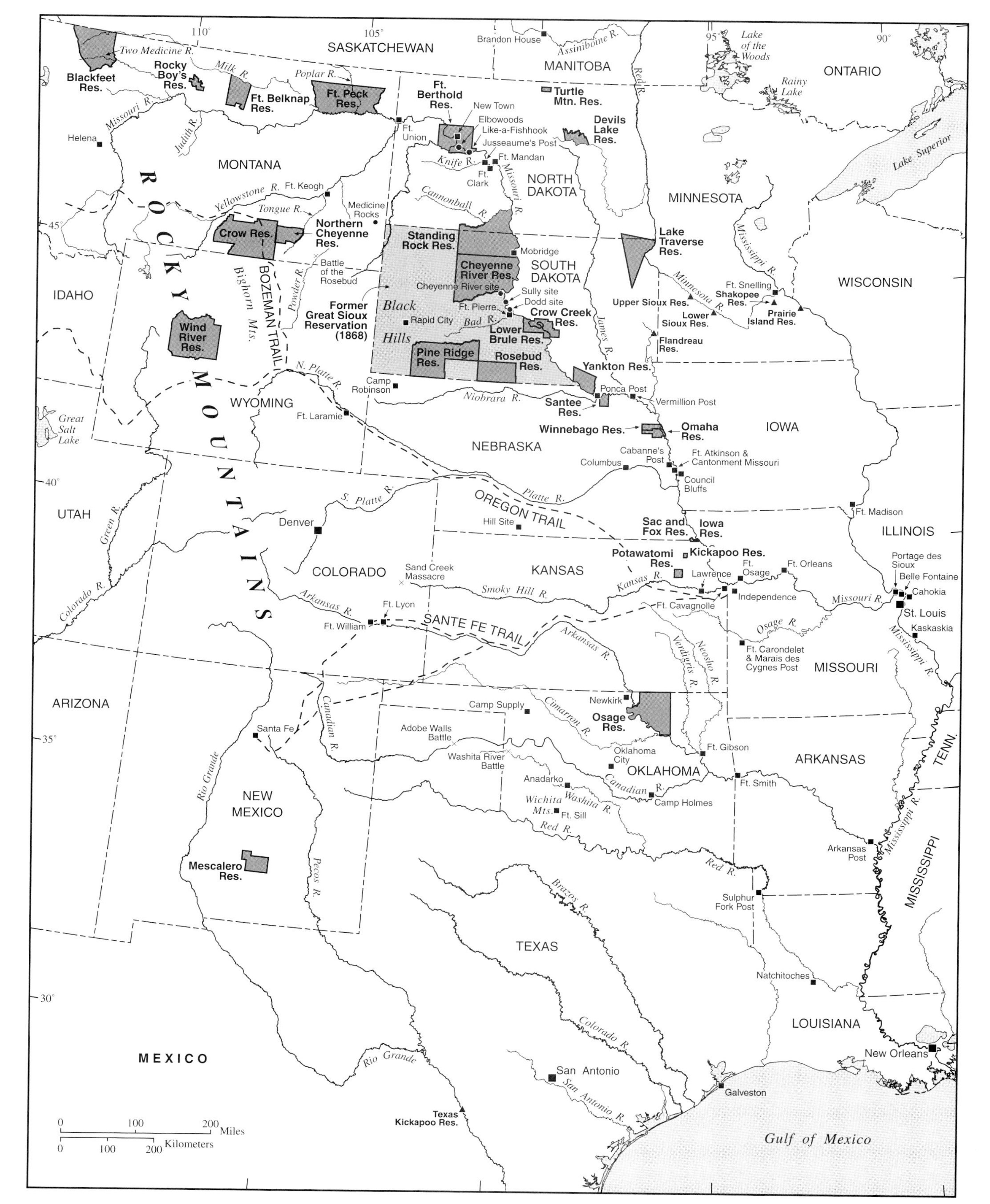

Fig. 1. Historical forts and modern reservations on the Plains.

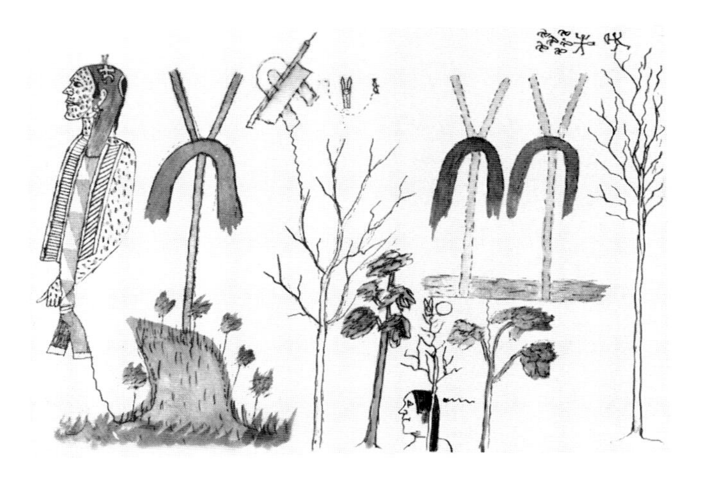

Smithsonian, NAA: ms. 2531:7, neg. 92-11144.

Fig. 2. Kiowa events from 1840–1842 as depicted in pictographs on a "winter count." left to right, Man covered with spots, representing the smallpox epidemic of the summer of 1840, brought to the Kiowa by visiting Osage, which spread throughout the Southern Plains. The forked tree with hanging object depicts a Sun Dance pole, indicating summer. The bare tree indicates winter; the tree with leaves indicates the summer of 1841 when no Sun Dance was held and the 2 forked trees indicate that 2 Sun Dances were held in the summer of 1842. At top right, the figures depict the shooting of Many Bears (Heap of Bears) in the winter of 1842–1843 identified by bear tracks. Watercolor and ink on paper by Haungooah (Silverhorn), Kiowa, 1904.

On the Southern Plains, before the introduction of the horse, Apaches were dog-dependent. Apaches are known to have walked hundreds of miles to the eastern fringe of the Pueblo country to trade. A Spanish account of 1598 described horseless "Indian herdsmen" on foot returning from Picuris and Taos Pueblos, "where they sell meat, hides, tallow, suet, and salt in exchange for cotton blankets, pottery, maize, and some small green stones [turquoise] which they use." For the travois, "the Indians use a medium-sized shaggy dog, which is their substitute for mules. They drive great trains of them. Each, girt round its breast and haunches, and carrying a load of flour [*pinole* or cornmeal] of at least one hundred pounds, travels as fast as his master . . . poles dragging on the ground, nearly all of them snarling in their encounters, traveling one after another on their journey . . . at a steady gait as if they had been trained by means of reins" (Bolton 1916:226–227).

Large dog trains moved slowly, averaging five to six miles per day. Summer travel was often even slower; dogs overheated easily and required water at frequent intervals (Henderson 1994). On the Plains, skeletal remains as well as descriptions in historic times indicate a high degree of interbreeding with wolves. These hybrid canines were capable of carrying burdens of up to 100 pounds (Schwartz 1997:53).

Among the Blackfoot, even owners of a considerable number of horses continued to rely on dogs for transport ("Blackfoot," fig. 2, this vol). Sometimes they transported household items such as arrow-making equipment, pipe-making tools, pemmican mauls, and skin-dressing tools inside rawhide containers on dog travois. Light loads such as these allowed the dogs to keep up with the horses in the moving camp (Ewers 1955:136). As late as the 1850s, artist John Mix Stanley documented the Sioux using dog travois as well as horse travois (Schoolcraft 1851–1857, 6:pl. 30). In addition to the Sioux, the Cheyenne, Blackfoot, Comanche, Plains Cree ("Plains Cree," fig. 5, this vol.), and Pawnee were still using dog travois in the mid-nineteenth century (Schwartz 1997:53). Nevertheless, the arrival of the horse marked the beginning of a revolution, remembered by most tribes as a great event (Mooney 1898:153, 160–161).

The first documented horses appeared on the Plains with Spanish expeditions in the 1540s when Hernando de Soto and his successor, Luis de Moscoso, brought mounted soldiers into Caddoan country on the eastern rim of the Plains. At the same time, Coronado explored the plains of present-day west Texas and Kansas. He met peoples he called Querechos, who were probably Plains Apacheans, and Teyas, who may have been Caddoans (vol. 10:387). Coronado, in 1541, and Juan de Oñate in 1601, visited Quivira, the territory of the Wichita in present-day Kansas (M.M. Wedel 1979). Although both expeditions were well stocked with horses, there is no indication that these earliest contacts resulted in any transfer of horses to Plains peoples.

It is possible that Apaches, accustomed to trade with Taos Pueblo, could have acquired horses as early as 1639 and probably no later than 1659 and could have taken small herds north to trade with other tribes. The real transition occurred during the Pueblo Revolt, 1680–1692, when the Pueblos confiscated several thousand Spanish horses, most of which were transferred to Plains Indians during the 1680s through trade and theft (Haines 1938:117, 1938a:433ff.).

From the Southwest, horses spread to secondary trade centers located in southwestern Wyoming (the Shoshone Rendezvous), along the Missouri River at the Mandan-Hidatsa and Arikara villages, and on the James River where a Sioux trade fair attracted Teton, Yanktonai, Yankton, and Sisseton participation (Ewers 1954, 1955). By the late eighteenth century, several middleman trading cultures functioned as intermediaries: the Ute from the Southwest to the Eastern Shoshone, the Crow from the Eastern Shoshone to the Mandan-Hidatsa villages, the Flathead and Nez Perce to other Plateau tribes, and the western Sioux to the Arikara villages. Direct participation by Plains Cree and Assiniboine in the Mandan and Hidatsa village trade and some direct and some secondary trade by Cheyenne, Arapaho, Kiowa, Plains Apache, and Comanche through the Central Plains completed the trade nexus at the Arikara villages (Ewers 1954). There were secondary and tertiary trading centers of regional importance and a more complex system linking the Middle

Missouri with the Pacific Northwest (Wood 1972, 1980; Picha 1996; vols. 4:352, 12:641–652).

All Plains peoples adopted horse culture by the end of the eighteenth century (figs. 3–4). Some tribes became horse-rich, while others remained horse-poor well into the nineteenth century (Ewers 1955:1–19). Most Plains tribes had acquired their maximum number of horses and hence their relative wealth by 1825, and in some instances by 1800 (Ewers 1955:24–27).

Trade and Its Effects

Some European items made their way through middlemen traders into Plains households. Very little European material culture has been found in Southern and Central Plains sites dating from 1450 to 1750, which otherwise contain ceramic, bone, stone, and shell exotics, evidence of the extensive trade network with the Pueblos (Spielmann 1983, 1991). Glass beads (fig. 5) (vol. 4:367, 399), and, more rarely, lead sprues, musket balls, and gun flints have been found in the Texas panhandle and in southern Oklahoma (Baugh 1986:180ff). Spanish armor in the form of chain mail found within 15 miles along the historic Santa Fe Trail in Kansas may have been from the Coronado or Oñate expeditions to Quivira but could also be from a later period (Wedel 1975a).

A useful distinction has been made between "direct" and "indirect" or second-hand trade. "Middleman trading cultures," which functioned as conduits for biological and material introductions in advance of European traders, are described among the Plains Cree and Assiniboine (Ray 1974, 1978) as well as the Arikara (Orser 1984a; Wood and Thiessen 1985). A hub of trade from sources in all directions, the Arikara received horses from the Spanish southwest and conducted direct trade with the Cheyenne, Arapaho, Comanche, Kiowa, Plains Apache, Plains Cree, and Assiniboine (Jablow 1951; Ewers 1954) in what one scholar has termed the Plains Interband Trade System (Blakeslee 1975), and what another has labeled the Middle Missouri System (Wood 1972, 1980). The villages functioned as a funnel for goods from enemies such as the neighboring Teton Sioux, from historic-period British traders on the Canadian prairies, and from French and Spanish traders out of Saint Louis (Orser and Owsley 1982).

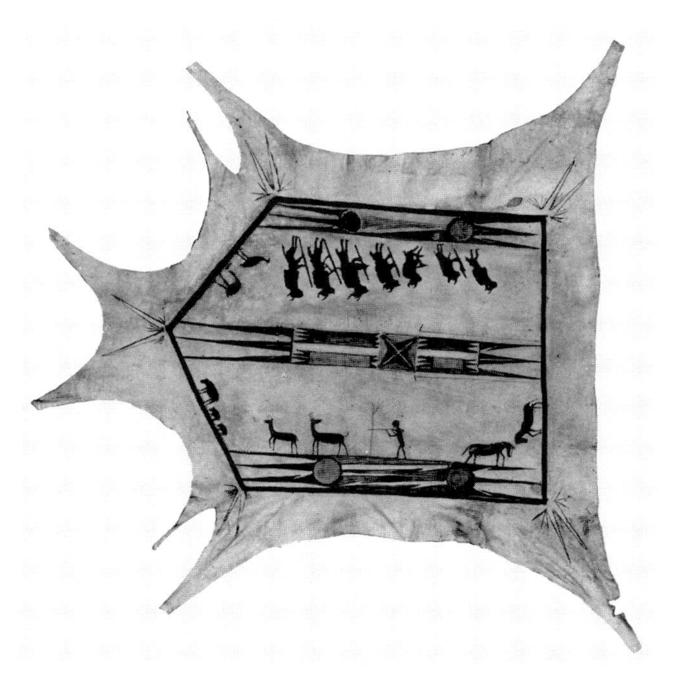

Musée de l'Homme, Paris: C64.2371.493.

Fig. 3. Early evidence for adoption of the horse and gun. Painted robe in red, black, and light blue. The figures on one half depict a deer hunter armed with a gun. Other figures include 2 horses, a bear with 2 cubs, and 2 cranes. The other half features dancers wearing buffalo headdresses or masks. Collected before 1786; length 142.4 cm.

The Middle Missouri trade network served as collector and distributor for all the new goods coming from Euro-American factories, cooperages, and blacksmithing shops before trading posts were built on the plains. Of all of these new items, none accelerated intertribal movement and rivalry more than guns (vol. 4:179). From colonial times through the end of the Plains Indian wars of the nineteenth century, availability and prices for guns and ammunition dictated much of the economic relationship between White traders and Indian clients. Guns accelerated demographic shifts from east to west as woodlands and prairie tribes were pressured by those closer to sources of firearms to move or be pushed aside.

To the north, the Plains Ojibwa pressured the Assiniboine and neighboring Crees, who moved west, becoming suppliers of firearms to tribes on the Missouri and to the Blackfoot (Ray 1974; G.S. Camp 1990a; Peers 1994). The Southwestern Chippewa also confronted the Santee Sioux, who stayed in present-day Minnesota. The western movement of the Teton and Yanktonai Sioux put pressure on other tribes bound for the Missouri (R. White 1978). During the second half of the eighteenth century, an annual trade fair developed on the James River where Sisseton and Yankton brought Euro-American goods that they exchanged with Teton and Yanktonai for furs, hides, and horses (Ewers 1954:431; Wood 1980; Picha 1996). By 1800 the western Sioux engaged other tribes in trade and war as they became more deeply involved in the global marketplace through the fur trade (R. White 1978; Ray 1987), an elaboration of preexisting patterns and processes of the well-established intertribal trade of the trans-Missouri West (vol. 4:351–374).

Guns figured prominently in the trade. Secoy (1953:2) suggested three patterns of firearm adoption. On the Southern Plains, the horse was integrated prior to the gun while on the Northern Plains, the reverse was true for most tribes: guns arrived prior to horses. A third pattern developed in the regions of intersection when the horse frontier and gun frontier met and overlapped.

Joslyn Art Mus., Omaha, Nebr.: left, JAM 1986.49.290; right, Vignette XXVI.

Fig. 4. The importance of guns and the horse. left, Piegan man wearing painted elkhide robe decorated with horseshoe designs, represented by semicircles, indicating horses stolen. Other figures include bows, war hatchets, and guns captured from enemies. Both horses and guns became valued possessions and symbols of status and wealth. This warrior wears a rifle sheath wrapped around his head and carries a ramrod and long-stemmed pipe. Watercolor and pencil by Karl Bodmer, Ft. McKenzie, Mo. Terr., 1833. right, Meeting between Hidatsas and Maximilian, Prince of Wied Neuwied, second from right, and Karl Bodmer, far right, near Ft. Clark, Mo. Terr. Aquatint by Karl Bodmer, 1840s.

Early Euro-American Fur Traders

The Spaniards were first to recognize the potential of furs and hides from the plains. Limited numbers of tanned hides—elk, deer, antelope, and buffalo, some painted—made their way south to Mexico City during colonial times. Most of these had been acquired in trade with Utes, Apaches, and Comanches, then collected by Spanish officials as tribute from the Pueblos (Weber 1971:17–22). In the gateway Pueblos of Pecos, Picuris, and Taos, summer trade fairs predated Spanish colonization (Bolton 1916:226), but grew in volume and significance after the Pueblo Revolt (A.B. Thomas 1935:14). By the 1720s, the Comanche trade had become an important part of New Mexico's economy (Kavanagh 1996:127), so much so that in 1723 the provincial governor proclaimed the summer months a period of truce so that intertribal trade could be conducted at Taos (Hallenbeck 1950:214; Simmons 1991:40–46). When first described in 1726, the Comanche were still on foot, with "a multitude of dogs loaded with their hides and tents," but by the mid-1730s, they were reported as "scattered about, caring for many horses" (Hackett 1931–1946, 3:348). From Taos in 1751, a Spanish official reported a Comanche rancheria of 40 tepees, including 130 men, who "arrived to hold the usual exchange of skins and Indian captives of different nations which they brought from those of the north" (A.B. Thomas 1940:68).

Indian slave trading was an old institution by 1750, but the Comanche took the practice a step further, capturing settlers and exchanging them for ransom (Bailey 1973). The practice so outraged one colonial governor that he violated the Spanish truce with Comanches who came into Taos in 1761, jailing and executing their leaders, killing several hundred of their followers, and enslaving over 400 more. A peace agreement was negotiated in 1762, but the Comanche desired horses and continued to raid Spanish settlements for the next two decades (R.N. Richardson 1933:56–57). In 1779, Spanish lancers, supported by Ute and Jicarilla Apache auxiliaries, tracked the Comanche into present-day southern Colorado. Over 500 Comanche horses were captured at one village, and a powerful Comanche leader known as Cuerno Verde (Green Horn) was killed along with many of his men near a creek now known as Greenhorn (A.B. Thomas 1932:123–139; Sánchez 1997:81–90). In 1785 Comanches under Ecueracapa sued for peace, and in 1786 he was recognized by the Spanish governor at Santa Fe as principal chief of the tribe. The peace was a victory for both sides, providing a respite for the Pueblos as well for the Spanish colonizers (Richardson 1933:62–63; Hoig 1993:78–82; Kavanagh 1996:110–121).

The Peace of 1786 made the plains between Spanish New Mexico and Spanish Texas a safer place and created an atmosphere that promoted the growth of two additional groups that emerged out of the cultural milieu of

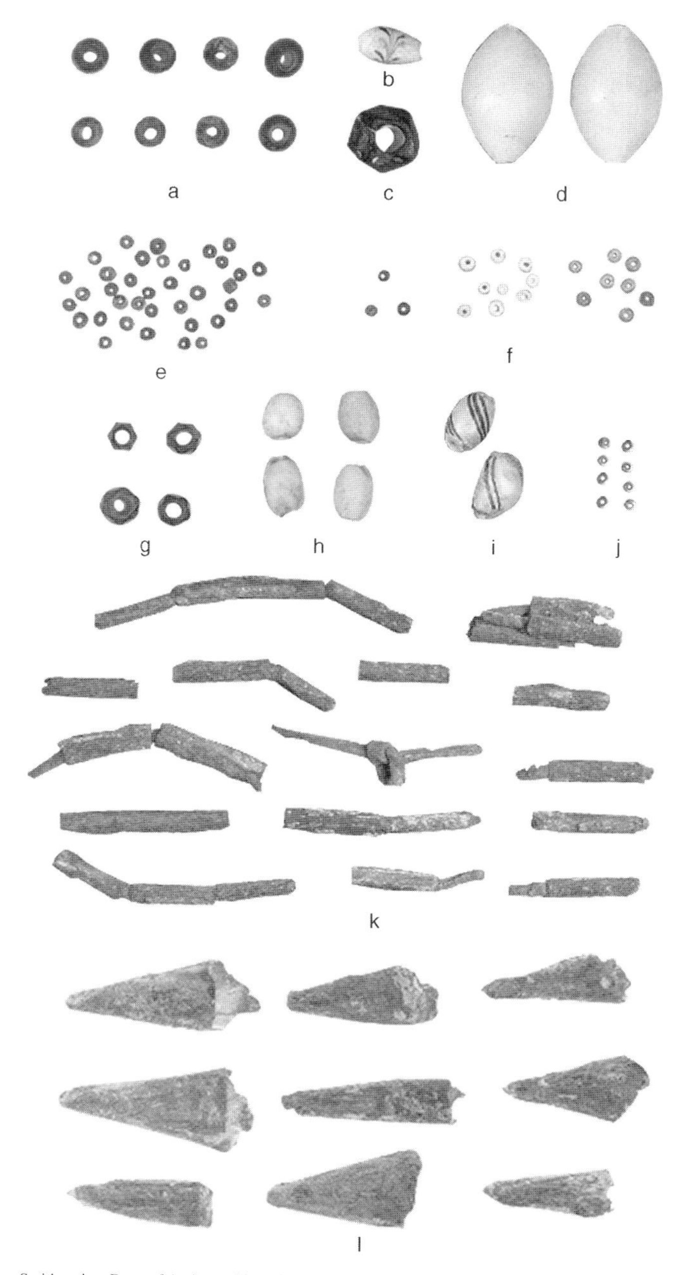

Smithsonian, Dept. of Anthr.: a, 325456; b, 325464; c, 405576; d, 325459; e, 325457; f, 467570; g, 325456; h, 422461; i, 325460; j, 509911; k, AT24362; l, AT24327.

Fig. 5. Glass and metal beads. a, Translucent blue wound (Kidd and Kidd 1970) beads from the vicinity of Mobridge, S. Dak.; b, white mound "Lewis and Clark" bead with color inlay from the vicinity of Mobridge; c, translucent blue press faceted wound bead from the Dodd site, S. Dak.; d, large white wound "pigeon egg" beads from the Leavenworth site, S. Dak.; e, red over translucent green core "Green Heart" pony beads (2–4 mm in diameter) from the vicinity of Mobridge; f, dark purple, white, and blue pony beads from Mobridge; g, translucent blue cut faceted drawn "Russian blue" beads from the vicinity of Mobridge; h, white oval drawn beads from the Cheyenne River site, S. Dak.; i, white oval drawn beads with applied blue stripes from the vicinity of Mobridge; j, light blue seed beads (less than 2 mm in diameter and made from drawn glass) from Lower Brule Agency, S. Dak.; k, Native-made beads of copper or brass on hide strips from the Sully site, S. Dak.; l, Native-made dangles of copper or brass on hide strips from the Sully site. Glass beads c, e, f, h, and i are from sites that date to before 1800 and a, b, d, g, and j from sites that date to after 1800. Diameter of b 7.9 mm, length 14.2 mm, rest to scale. (Caption by William T. Billeck, 1999.)

Plains-Pueblo-Spanish interaction. The first were the Comancheros, known originally as *viajeros* 'travelers', a multiethnic trading culture that ranged from the Pacific to the Gulf during Spanish, and later Mexican times, lasting into the American occupation. After 1786, Comancheros operated openly between colonial suppliers and Indian camps and villages across Comanchería as dealers in arms and ammunition as well as conduits for ransomed captives (Kenner 1969:78–97; Hoig 1993:82; Kavanagh 1996:179). The second group were *ciboleros* 'buffalo hunters', an occupational class composed of Hispanics, mestizos, and Pueblo Indians. Bypassing Indian middlemen, they combed the Southern Plains, especially the Staked Plains (overlapping eastern New Mexico and West Texas), and the Texas panhandle. From late Spanish through Mexican and American-period times, *ciboleros* brought back thousands of buffalo hides and dried meat to their Rio Grande homeland (O.L. Jones 1966; Kenner 1969:98–114; Kavanagh 1996:205).

The volume of trade in hides was significant for such a small population, yet it was never fully developed, in large measure because both resident Pueblos and Spanish invaders distrusted Plains traders, who had a record of stealing back previously bartered items, even during the summer trade fairs. Nevertheless, throughout the Spanish colonial period, the trade network that served in protohistoric times continued to function, albeit under stress from increased raids by better armed and mounted Plains raiders (O.L. Jones 1966; Kenner 1969; A.B. Thomas 1940), and from the possibility that the French had won Indian allegiance.

Spanish fear of the French was not unwarranted. Although few records survive of the contacts made with Plains tribes by French traders in the period 1682–1700, the encounters were of long-term significance. In 1683, La Salle wrote of two Frenchmen who had lived among the Missouri tribes. Two other Frenchmen are reported to have visited the Missouria and Osage during the summer of 1693 (Galloway 1982). In 1698, a French priest, Father St. Cosme, made a trip to the Missouri River region, where he encountered many Indians. A Roman Catholic mission at Cahokia was established in 1699, followed by one among the Kaskaskia (where Saint Louis now stands) in 1700 (Nasatir 1952, 1:4–5). That same year, from bases at Biloxi, and, after 1702, at Mobile, explorers and traders probed the Southeast and Southern Plains beginning with Louis Juchereau de Saint-Denis, who made his way along the Caddo country of the Red River linking the Southeast with the Southwest (Pertulla 1992:30–32).

Simultaneously, news from French voyageurs operating out of the Great Lakes filtered down the Mississippi, giving policy makers some idea of the Pawnee, Missouria, Kansa, Otoe, and Iowa—far to the north of actual French penetration from the south. The French had three goals: to locate and exploit the "mines of New Mexico," alleged to contain vast amounts of wealth; to establish peaceful commercial arrangements with the Spaniards; and, to make alliances of trade and peace with Indians between the Mississippi and the Rio Grande. They also entertained removing certain friendly tribes to the Arkansas River to control trade and to provide additional security against the Spaniards and their Indian allies (Nasatir 1952, 1:5–8; Folmer 1953).

Several official probes were made from 1702–1712, but the extent of these travels and the tribes contacted is unclear. Reports of direct Spanish trade on the Plains and a change of royal attitude spurred the French to a more aggressive approach. In 1712, the French crown granted a 15-year trading monopoly to Antoine Crozat, a merchant. Crozat received exclusive rights to commerce from the Illinois River to the Gulf of Mexico and from the Carolinas to Spanish New Mexico, but his monopoly was rescinded in 1717 due to perceived lack of progress in accomplishing his expected economic goals for France. A commercial oligarchy, the Company of the Indies, took over; New Orleans was established in 1718 to insure control of access to the Mississippi country. Agricultural and commercial expansion soon followed with slavery and plantation agriculture promoted in the delta region and increased commerce with Indians envisioned to the west and north (Usner 1992:24–43).

Three major expeditions entered the Plains under the French flag in 1719. Jean-Baptiste Bénard, sieur de la Harpe, established a post on the Red River among the Nasoni Caddo and then pushed north to the Arkansas where the Tawakoni Wichita lived (M.M. Wedel 1971, 1979; Parks 1993). Claude-Charles Dutisné ascended the Missouri, visiting the Missouria tribe, where he was not allowed to proceed farther, because the Missouria were "jealous that the French go to the home of other nations" (M.M. Wedel 1972, 1973a:87). On a second overland expedition that same year, Dutisné visited the Osage and a Wichita group on the Verdigris River in southeastern Kansas. There he made an alliance and promised French trade goods (E. John 1975:212–218).

Rumors of the French reached New Mexico in 1719, prompting the governor to send a large expedition under Pedro de Villasur in 1720, with 42 Spanish soldiers, a priest, and 70 Pueblo auxiliaries (fig. 6). Only 45 of the force made it back to New Mexico following a disastrous battle with the French-armed Pawnee somewhere on the Loup Fork of the Platte in central Nebraska (A.B. Thomas 1935:26– 39; O.L. Jones 1966:100–102; T.E. Chávez 1994). Three years later, Bourgmont, a trader familiar with the Missouri River tribes, set out on a mission of peacemaking with Southern Plains tribes not already in the French fold. After building Fort Orléans near present-day Kansas City in 1724, Bourgmont pressed on, repeating pledges of friendship and commerce to the Missouria, Osage, Kansa, Otoe, Pawnee, Iowa, and Illinois (Margry 1879–1888, 6:312,398–449).

Peace was short-lived. Once Bourgmont left, his efforts were undermined by New Orleans–based merchants and planters, more interested in human slaves than furs. While the French counted 50,000 skins in the Louisiana trade during 1725 (E. John 1975:220–221), unspecified lots of Apache men, women, and children, supplied primarily by the Pawnee and Osage (R. White 1983:153–154; Din and Nasatir 1983), and secondarily by Kansa middlemen (Haines 1976:82–83; Unrau 1971:60), found ready buyers in French markets. Whereas the goal of direct trade with Spanish New Mexico failed, by 1725, that of making partners of Central and Southern Plains tribes succeeded (Hoig 1998:32–47).

Throughout the eighteenth century, the Missouri, Arkansas, Platte, Red, and sections of the Canadian rivers remained "guardedly friendly" territory for French traders and soldiers. As in other colonial spheres, the French diplomatic formula for making friends rather than enemies of resident tribes rested on several principles, some tested, some new (vol. 4:20–28). First, the French did not attempt to relocate or displace native people whose trade they sought. Instead, they adopted the protocol of trade and social behavior prized by the resident tribes, and they used flexible diplomacy to insure peace and commerce, a pattern well established in French Canada and extended throughout the Great Lakes (Jacobs 1950; Eccles 1969). Second, in this posthorse, pregun era, generous gifts of trade items and firearms to Indian leaders were selectively distributed, making friends of leaders and their families (Secoy 1953). Third, the French acknowledged middlemen trading cultures and relied upon them for protection and for conveyance of trade beyond their own physical operations.

French trading policy intensified rivalries among many tribes while working to the advantage of the French (Holder 1970:79–85). The Pawnee (R. White 1983), Caddo (H.H. Tanner 1972; Gregory 1986; Pertulla 1994), and Osage (Loomis and Nasatir 1967; Bailey 1973; Rollings 1992) stood out as middlemen upon whom the French became increasingly dependent to achieve economic and diplomatic goals. These three tribes exemplify the complicated fur trade web whereby Indian tribes initially controlled terms and conditions, only to have the balance of control shift toward equal need, and in time, to dominance by the outside trading partner.

French-Osage relations illustrate the dependency shift. Exports flowing toward New Orleans from the Illinois country could, in theory, bypass the Osage, but traffic up the Missouri and overland to the elusive but highly desired trade with Spanish New Mexico could not. In 1739, the brothers Pierre-Antoine and Paul Mallet crossed the plains to Santa Fe via the Platte, returning along the Arkansas with the good news that the Spaniards would trade silver specie in exchange for French textiles, metal goods, and exotic spices, a policy often not honored in decades to come (Bolton 1917; Folmer 1953; Loomis and Nasatir 1967:54–61). In 1741, as the French were building Fort

Mus. of N. Mex., Santa Fe: 149804.

Fig. 6. Detail from a hide painting depicting the 1720 defeat of Spanish troops over Pedro de Villasur at the confluence of the Platte and Loup rivers, near the present Columbus, Nebr. Sent from Santa Fe to investigate French activity on the Plains, the Spanish troops were defeated by a combined force of Pawnee, Otoe, and French soldiers (Hotz 1970:158, 228). The Indians, adorned with extensive body painting, carry arrows, quivers, spears, and tomahawks; the soldiers are armed with flintlock guns. A priest carrying a cross is in the center. Painting on hide about 1720–1729 by unknown Spaniard. Collected by H.A. Von Segesser von Brunegg; painting about 574 cm long.

Cavagnolle on the Kansas River (with the intent of serving the Kansa, Osage, and Missouria trade with one post and as a staging ground for the interior trade), the Osage showed their displeasure by blocking an expedition bound for New Mexico. The French acceded, reliant upon Osage traders for transshipment of slaves, deer and bear skins, as well as beaver, river otter, and other small furs. By 1750, the Osage and their allies, the Missouria, were supplying the French with an annual average of 80 packs of deer and bear skins (Nasatir 1952, 1:50).

After 1763, the relationship continued with the Spaniards in Louisiana, but soured in the 1790s when Spanish authorities sought to direct all Osage affairs and trade to the west as well as toward Upper Louisiana. A short war with the Osage was followed in 1795 by the building of Fort Carondelet near their villages on the Osage River and the placing of all trade privileges with the Osage in the hands of the Chouteau family of Saint Louis (Chapman 1974b). A workable compromise left the Osage controlling trade and traffic to their west. While satisfying Spanish policy makers in New Orleans, the partnership had its cost: the Osage became irreversibly caught in the market economy of the fur trade. In exchange for highly desired cloth, metal, guns, and other European goods, the Osage taxed their environment heavily, supplying 950 packs of skins annually by 1800 and 1,240 packs two years later (Rollings 1992:192). Their world was one bound by political, social, and economic ties with French aristocrats such as the Chouteaus (Lecompte 1972a; Foley and Rice 1983; Thorne 1984), who worked the clan system to control Osage trade (Rollings 1992:191–192), a pattern found in many other parts of North America where the French were active in the fur trade (Giraud 1945; J.C. Peterson and J.S.H. Brown 1985; J.C. Peterson 1990).

On the Northern Plains, initial French reconnaissance in the 1730s by the La Vérendrye family might have produced a parallel history to that of the combined efforts of La Harpe, Du Tisné, and Bourgmont to the south, but it did not. After building a number of posts for France from Rainy Lake and Winnipeg in the Subarctic to the Saskatchewan River country, La Vérendrye and his two sons undertook a new mission: the search for the "western sea" and potential sites for additional posts in the western interior. In 1738 they joined an Assiniboine trading party to the Mandan-Hidatsa villages. Expeditions in 1741–1742 and 1742–1743 by the sons revealed the full extent of the trade network linking the Central and Northern Plains. Crow and possibly Shoshone traders guided them as far as the Bighorn Mountains, but there was little follow-up (vol. 4:28, 9–10).

During the French and Indian War, 1756–1763, most western tribes remained loyal to the French, but problems of unlicensed traders (coureurs de bois), hunters, and itinerant peddlers heightened tensions, as did inconsistencies on the part of French officials in the granting of trade licenses to individuals of good standing. In 1763, Maxent, Laclède, and Company received the exclusive right to trade in the three most lucrative districts of the territory: Illinois, Natchitoches, and Opelousas (present Louisiana). This was rescinded within a year, but as a concession, Laclède was granted a trading monopoly from the mouth of the Missouri north to as far as the Minnesota River. With transfer of political sovereignty of Louisiana from France to Spain by the Treaty of Paris in 1763, Spanish attention turned to protecting its interests from the English, while maintaining good commercial and political alliances with resident Indian tribes. Toward this end, French commandants at the frontier posts were retained, French traders were allowed to apply for trading privileges, and, most important, the French policy of distributing presents to "chiefly authorities," as well as to their families and friends, continued (Kinnaird 1946–1949; Ewers 1974b). Chiefs' coats, medallions, batons, and other symbols of high office were distributed (figs. 7–8), as were annuities of food, blankets, ammunition, and ornaments. All these were ceremoniously distributed in Saint Louis, which served the Mississippi and Missouri Districts, represented by 23 tribes, and at two other locales—the Arkansas Post ("Quapaw," fig. 3, this vol.), and Natchitoches—which served the lower Missouri tribes and the Red River tribes and the Red River district, especially the Caddo (Bolton 1914). Before 1776, when the Spanish internal provinces were reorganized, annual gifts for "friendship" to the Indians accounted for less than 5 percent of the total yearly annual expenses. After 1776, they accounted for 10–40 percent of the yearly budget (Pertulla 1994:77–81) and were an essential element of the Spanish strategy to pacify sedentary tribes, while simultaneously reducing or exterminating the horse nomads who refused to settle in one place or accept missionaries, especially the Apache (A.B. Thomas 1941).

That task was given to Teodoro de Croix, the *comandante general* of the northern provinces of New Spain, headquartered in Chihuahua City. His work was interrupted by Spain's entry into the American Revolution, which brought yet another shift in policy, ultimately producing the Peace of 1786 with the Comanche, who teamed up with Spaniards and Wichitas to defeat a large group of Lipan Apaches near San Antonio in 1790 (Hoig 1993:87–90).

While Spanish officials placated Indian leaders, expecting to stimulate commerce and the growth of the Indian trade, merchants and investors were less confident in the risky business of sending men and materiel into the interior without posts, military garrisons, or the backing of the Spanish state. Following the formation of Maxent, Laclède and Company, the only other fur trade concern of scale was the Upper Missouri Company, formed in 1794. All other Spanish efforts at trade were small-scale entrepreneurial ventures where individuals with licenses brought furs to Saint Louis and then on to New Orleans without agents, credit systems, or capital in reserve. The system

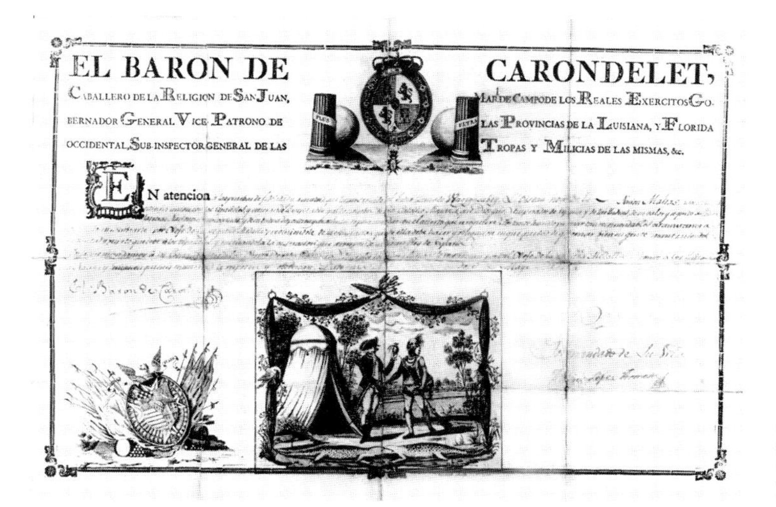
EL BARON DE CARONDELET,
CABALLERO DE LA RELIGION DE SAN JUAN, MARISCAL DE CAMPO DE LOS REALES EXERCITOS GO-
BERNADOR GENERAL VICE PATRONO DE LAS PROVINCIAS DE LA LUISIANA, Y FLORIDA
OCCIDENTAL, SUB INSPECTOR GENERAL DE LAS TROPAS Y MILICIAS DE LAS MISMAS, &c.
EN atencion

Nebr. State Histl. Soc., Mus. of Nebr. Hist., Lincoln: cat. no. 1568.

Fig. 7. Certificate given with a small medal to Blackbird (L'Oiseau Noir), an Omaha chief, in 1796 by the Spanish governor of La., Francisco de Carondelet. Spanish authorities routinely presented certificates to Indian allies. Compare this depiction of a medal ceremony with the British ceremony (vol. 4:11). Length 46.7 cm. right, Detail.

was inefficient and expensive at both ends: traders paid high prices for goods, often of inferior quality in comparison to those manufactured in England or France, had little or no credit on account with vendors and suppliers, and often had to pay surcharges to Spanish officials in order to maintain trade licenses and territories (Trudeau in Nasatir 1952, 1:175–180). This opened the door for British- and French-Canadian-backed traders and larger companies, who saw opportunity on the Plains, especially along the Upper Missouri.

Changing Alliances on the Northern Plains, 1738–1803

During their extensive travels from 1738 through 1742, La Vérendrye and sons witnessed political environments of increased intertribal rivalry, attributable to the spread and integration of the horse, as well as to the success of riverine horticulturalists providing themselves and outsiders with surpluses of garden produce, especially corn. Warfare was typified by the singular mobile raid, in which horses and people (especially women and children) were captured. Combat between individual males was limited, but bloody, with women warriors occasionally participating as well (Robarchek 1994; Ewers 1994). These "hit and run" tactics, often deep within an enemy's hunting territory, confused Europeans who were accustomed to longer campaigns resulting in victory or defeat and ultimately, a transfer of sovereignty or territory (McGinnis 1990:1–5). La Vérendrye dismissed the idea of expanding the string of French posts into the Missouri River country as long as internecine warfare among tribes persisted. In 1744 he concluded: "It will take a long time to pacify all these tribes who from time immemorial have been deadly enemies" (Burpee 1927:455).

Although many French Canadians and French Americans entered the Plains as traders, voyageurs, and settlers in generations to follow, La Verendreye's departure marked the end of official French presence above the lands of the Osage on the Missouri. The vacuum was slowly filled by others. In 1743, James Isham, a factor (trader) with the Hudson's Bay Company, suggested brokering peace between the Blackfoot and their enemies, the Cree and Assiniboine, whose animosities were "a hinderance to their Coming to the English Setlements to trade" (Isham in E.E. Rich 1949:113–114). In 1754, the Hudson's Bay Company sent Anthony Henday south to the Red Deer River, where he met Assiniboines and "Archithinue Natives" (Blackfoot and possibly Gros Ventre) eager to acquire guns, hatchets, kettles, and knives (Ewers

Nebr. State Histl. Soc., Archaeol. Div., Lincoln: cat. no. 25WT1-496.

Fig. 8. Spanish medal improvised around a peso set in the middle and bearing the profile of Charles IV, dated 1797. The hand-engraved medallion was excavated from a Pawnee grave at the Hill site, Nebr., in 1925. It was repatriated to the Pawnee Tribe in 1995. Diameter 109 cm.

1955:24–26). Henday noted the presence of horses and commented on the many "fine Girls who were captives" but neither he nor other Hudson's Bay traders in the next three decades pursued peacemaking or fort building south of the Saskatchewan River (Hendry in Burpee 1907:335ff, at 351).

In the meantime, guns as well as horses trickled into the interior, changing further the balance of power between rival Plains tribes. Mounted Shoshone held sway over all other tribes in the 1740s: "They are not friendly with any tribe. It is said that in 1741 they had entirely ruined seventeen villages, killed all the men and the old women, made slaves of the young women and sold them on the coast for horses and merchandise" (La Vérendrye in Burpee 1927:412). That "merchandise" did not include guns. A generation later, their stone war clubs and rawhide shields were no match for English muskets, provided in trade through the Assiniboine to the Blackfoot, as well as to the Gros Ventre and Sarcee. By 1800, lacking a supplier of guns from the south, the Shoshone were driven off the Northern Plains into less contentious areas of the central Rockies and northern Great Basin (McGinnis 1990:7–11; Madsen and Rhode 1994).

Tribes that ascended in power and prestige demanded the finest firearms manufactured in England. These "Northwest guns" were preferred by Indian hunters because of their strength, reliability, and a unique trigger guard, which was large enough to permit firing while wearing gloves or mittens. A smoothbore, .58 caliber octagonal barrel of 30 to 48 inches allowed single- or multiple-shot loading and could be filed down for easier use on horseback. Cut-off or worn-out barrels as well as the brass buttplate were often converted into hide scrapers or fleshers (vol. 4:400). Broken stocks or wrists were easily repaired with wet rawhide, and stocks could be personalized with decorative brass tacks or carved designs identifying the owner. Easily recognized by a brass sea serpent or dragon-shaped sideplate, these guns were supplied by both the North West Company and the Hudson's Bay Company after 1777. American and Belgian gunmakers replicated the guns, which were the most popular Indian trade guns on the Plains to 1875 (C.E. Hanson 1955; Garavaglia and Worman 1998:345–346).

As guns spread on the Northern Plains, the record of European activities from 1744 to 1790 and of intertribal shifts and specific histories is fragmentary. Northern Plains history during this period can be constructed only from sporadic accounts that bear the bias of fur traders' personal interests. These traders continued to probe on their own as "tenant traders" or as "residenters," living among specific Indian groups, often intermarrying. At least 14, including Toussaint Charbonneau, are known to have reached the Mandan-Hidatsa villages from the late 1770s to the early 1800s. In 1790 Jacques D'Église, the first Spanish-licensed trader to enter the Mandan-Hidatsa villages after the transfer from France in 1763, found a trader named Ménard living with his Indian wife and family. Ménard appears to have arrived some time between 1778 and 1783, supplied on credit by the Hudson's Bay Company from Brandon House. Traveling with a group of Hidatsas to their Crow relatives' camps in eastern Montana, he represented a prototype of the French-Canadian or Métis cultural broker (Wood and Thiessen 1985:27, 42–47).

Alarmed by D'Église's reports of British-backed trade, Spanish authorities encouraged Saint Louis merchant-traders to risk capital. In 1794, the Company of Explorers of the Upper Missouri was chartered to develop the Indian trade. Jean-Baptiste Truteau, a French-Canadian who had lived among the Yankton and Pawnee, was selected leader of field operations (Nasatir in Hafen 1965–1972, 4:381–397). Truteau slipped by the Omaha and Ponca at night, but the Teton discovered his boats and helped themselves to his merchandise, essentially exacting a "toll" for passage through their section of the river, a practice other Euro-Americans would experience in the decade to come. Truteau cached his remaining goods and entrenched for the winter of 1794–1795 at Ponca Post in present-day South Dakota. The following year, he returned upriver as far as the Arikara, but the goal of reaching the strategic Mandan-Hidatsa center eluded him. Still, he persuaded Ménard and another residenter, René Jusseaume, to temporarily switch allegiances from the British to Spaniards, promising goods and a post for their Mandan clients. Truteau also made friends with Cheyenne traders who visited the Arikara villages and sent presents back with these middlemen to the Kiowa and Arapaho (Nasatir 1952, 1:84–93).

Several expeditions cordelled their way up the Missouri between 1795 and 1803 but were ineffective in channeling much of the Mandan-Hidatsa-Arikara trade away from Hudson's Bay Company traders based at Brandon House, and down the Missouri into Spanish warehouses. That of John T. Evans, a Welshman, and his partner James Mackay to the Mandan villages in 1796 has been described as the single most important expedition to ascend the Missouri River in the decade before Lewis and Clark (Wood and Thiessen 1985:28). Evans and Mackay confiscated posts and equipment of North West Company and Hudson's Bay Company men, including Jusseaume's Post at the mouth of Knife River. They gave official notice to both companies at their posts along the Assiniboine River that they were trespassing on Spanish territory, stimulating the North West Company to send David Thompson to the Mandans in 1797 to determine the boundary by astronomical observation (Wood 1977; Alwin 1979; Wood and Thiessen 1985:93–128). Despite these pressures, the Upper Missouri tribes remained oriented toward the north and west into the nineteenth century, with the village trade influenced more by communication with Canadian traders than with those from Saint Louis or from posts along the Mississippi

River (Provo 1984; Wood and Thiessen 1985:42–52). By 1803, the trade of the Northern Plains still had not been won by any North American power (Nasatir 1952, 1:93–115; Hafen 1965–1972, 1:35–37; Alwin 1979).

American Entry on the Plains, 1803–1822

In 1800, a reoccurrence of smallpox hit the Northern Plains. Estimates of mortality range from 33 percent to as high as 66 percent, but few eyewitnesses documented the scourge (Vehik 1989:119). The Omaha were particularly hard hit, losing their head chief, Blackbird, as well as some 400 others (G. H. Smith 1974:64–66; O'Shea and Ludwickson 1992:30–31). In the spring of 1801, Spanish officials attempted to quarantine the Omaha, Iowa, Otoe, and Ponca in order to keep the disease from spreading, but it reached the Brule (Mallery 1893:313) and other interior tribes later that year (Nasatir 1952, 2:631), as well as the Caddo and Kiowa to the south (Mooney 1898:168, 1928:12; Ewers 1973:108).

Disease made it easier for Euro-American policy makers to dominate tribes closest to permanent White settlement. For example, in 1802, during the waning days of Spanish claims over their lands, the Osage split into factions, compromising traditional social structure (Bailey 1973). For years, French, Spaniards, British, and Americans to the east had appointed chiefs when convenient and advantageous for White goals. Traders and agents assigned to specific tribes or geographic areas sought cooperative leaders and created new chiefs, disregarding native systems of political succession. Having been the leading contact between the Osage and the White economy, during the 1790s the Chouteau family of Saint Louis used their influence to displace the hereditary chief Claremore (Clermont) with White Hair. In 1802, Osage trade was divided between the Chouteaus and Manuel Lisa. One group, the Little Osage under White Hair, remained on the Missouri, with Lisa as trader-agent, but around one-half of the Grand Osage were persuaded by Pierre Chouteau to join Claremore in the buffalo-hunting country of present-day eastern Oklahoma (Lecompte 1972a; Din and Nasatir 1983). Following American takeover, Chouteau was named Indian agent for Upper Louisiana, in which capacity he attempted to reunite all the Osage under White Hair. Those under Claremore resisted.

The Meriwether Lewis and William Clark expedition marked the beginning of official or "public" policy by the United States on the Plains. The expedition entered the Plains in 1804 with the mission of impressing Indians with the serious intent of the United States to honor peace in order to promote trade and to determine the potential of the land (T. Jefferson 1803 in D.D. Jackson 1978, 1:61–66). Throughout the expedition, Lewis and Clark used a precise formula in their formal Indian policy. At Council Bluffs among the Iowa, influential headmen met with the Americans and received presents and symbols of office as a courtesy for their cooperation. These presents included flags, hats, chiefs' coats, and most important, presidential peace medals, the first of 87 medallions given to head chiefs from 1804 to 1806 (Prucha 1971; vol. 4:39, 239–241). The expedition leaders also admonished their Indian hosts to cease warring against their neighbors and to acknowledge the United States as their new ally. Overall, this policy succeeded because Lewis and Clark needed Indian cooperation more than the Indians needed them or their goods (Ronda 1997). During the winter at Fort Mandan, Lewis and Clark (1832) prepared a statistical report on the tribes of the Missouri River and Northern Plains, giving Plains Indian populations, locations, and economic relationships.

The expedition's two major negative encounters on the Plains were with the region's strongest military powers—the Teton and the Piegan Blackfoot. The Teton in 1805 attempted to block the expedition's boats. Accustomed to being paid for passage through their section of the Missouri, and described by Clark as "miscreants" who "view with contempt the merchants of the Missouri," these enemies of the Mandan-Hidatsa envisioned Lewis and Clark dispensing guns to their foes (Moulton 1983–, 3:418).

The only fatal encounter took place with a band of Piegan, who were interested in stealing guns as well as horses. Two Piegans died at the hands of Lewis and his party on the Two Medicine River in present-day Montana (Moulton 1983–, 8:133–136; Ronda 1984:238–244). The Blackfoot blamed all Whites for this act (Tyrrell 1916:375). Immediately after Lewis and Clark's return, as White trappers began entering the Northern Plains and Rockies in larger numbers, intersocietal relations on the Upper Missouri—and especially the Blackfoot country—were tense and hostile (D. Smyth 1984; Judy 1987), but this single incident may be less significant than the widespread perception among the Blackfoot that American traders were potential arms merchants to their traditional enemies (Josephy 1965:651–653; Ronda 1984:243–244).

Shifting Tribal Balances of Power, 1806–1830

Weakened by losses from disease, traditional trade centers became vulnerable to loss of power and position. On the Missouri, the Teton Sioux continued to hold an annual summer rendezvous. Mounted Tetons began making greater inroads on the Arikara and pushed their way south and west becoming the dominant force on the Central Plains by 1810 (R. White 1978; Ronda 1984).

Through the 1820s, the Arikara struggled to hold on to their former position as middlemen, only to have to confront Sioux raiders and American trappers and soldiers (Orser 1984a; Nichols 1963). The Mandan-Hidatsa villages remained important hubs to Indians and to Whites alike up to 1837 when the High Plains smallpox epidemic spread, killing an estimated 95 percent of the Mandan and 50 percent of the Hidatsa (Meyer 1977:95–97). A similar scenario occurred at the trade center of Pecos on the Southern Plains. Continued demographic decline and Apache raiding sapped Pecos. Trade fairs ceased after 1815, and the Pueblo was abandoned in 1838 (Kessell 1979:401ff.).

While these traditional trade centers underwent decline, other shifts in power and alignments were taking place. Blackfoot territorial expansion was challenged after 1806. In 1810, a party of 150 Flatheads, armed with 20 muskets, met a band of Piegans, killing seven and wounding at least 13 more. Thereafter, the Piegan remained on the defensive, but consolidated interests with the Blackfoot, Blood, and Gros Ventre, in order to strengthen their military and trading powers and to police their territory in the wars for furs, horses, and guns (O. Lewis 1942; Ewers 1955; Haines 1976:120–134).

From about 1805 to the 1830s the Crow rebounded from earlier population losses and were able to hold their own against their major enemies, the Blackfoot and the Assiniboine (Hoxie 1995:31ff, at 47). As they became rich in horses, strong leaders emerged whose exploits of warfare and raiding or as medicine bundle owners were noticed by traders and remembered years later by admiring descendants. Among these, Long Hair (also known as Red Plume) of the Mountain Crow and Arapoosh or Rotten Belly of the River Crow stand out (Bradley 1896–1923:200; Hoxie 1995:48–56, 75–76). The Crow were seriously challenged in the 1830s by the Teton and by continued, protracted war with the Blackfoot, accelerated by dynamics of the fur trade (Hoxie 1995).

At this time, the Cheyenne, who lived around the Black Hills and hunted in a large area from the North Platte to Powder and Tongue rivers of present-day Montana, were also developing into a major force. In 1805, they were described by Clark as "ancient enemies of the Sioux," but "well disposed towards the whites," a people whose trade "may be made valuable" (Clark in Moulton 1983–, 3:421). In 1811, the Cheyenne were met in the Dakotas by the Overland Astorians, heading for the mouth of the Columbia River to establish a trading post. They were depicted in the traders' journals as still reeling from warfare with the Sioux, who continued to push them south and west. Between 1825 and 1830, they split into two divisions; the southern branch relocated on the Arkansas River in southern Colorado. The Northern and Southern Cheyenne each enjoyed substantial trade and military power (Grinnell 1915, 1923a:68–69; Jablow 1951:60–65; Berthrong 1963; Hoig 1993).

United States Indian Policy, 1806–1835

Between 1806 and 1834, the most serious challenges that faced Plains Indians were twofold: coping with an equestrian-based world with changing boundaries and more competitors; and confronting United States public policy makers and private citizens who assumed that Plains people would be eager to engage in commerce and open to negotiation for egress and land cessions. Official policy was designed to regulate Whites entering and leaving Indian country. The reality was a system that provided little regulation of White activities. From 1790 to 1834, a loosely defined "Indian department" consisting of superintendents, agents, subagents, interpreters, clerks, and mechanics managed United States Indian affairs as political appointees or hired employees of the War Department. Their major frontier institution was the "factory" or government trading house from 1796 to 1822 (vol. 4:354; Peake 1954; Prucha 1962). In 1805, a new factory was opened at Belle Fontaine on the Missouri River just north of Saint Louis. It was replaced in 1808 by Fort Osage, farther west on the Missouri, and Fort Madison on the Mississippi. Four additional government factories served some Southern Plains tribes: Natchitoches on the Red River in Louisiana (1805–1818), replaced by Sulphur Fork (1818–1822) farther upriver; the Arkansas Post (1805–1810) and Spadra Bluffs (1818–1822) on the Arkansas River; and, Marais des Cygnes (1821–1822) in western Missouri. Each of these trading houses was designed to have a military fort nearby to aid the government factors, enhance their prestige in the eyes of the Indians, maintain the premises, and to provide labor for transportation of goods and packing of furs (Prucha 1984, 1:120–125, 1990:55).

Few military posts were actually built prior to the end of the factory system in 1822. The most significant for Plains Indian–United States relations were garrisons attached to the factory at Fort Osage and to Fort Atkinson above Council Bluffs, established in 1819. Since 1816, William Clark and others had advocated building more forts on the northwestern frontier to extinguish British influence among Indians and to oversee western commerce. In 1818, Secretary of War John Calhoun authorized three expeditions. One, under Col. Henry Leavenworth, built Fort Snelling in 1819 to police traffic between the Canadian prairies and the upper Midwest. The second ended by establishing Fort Atkinson. The third, or Scientific Expedition, led by Maj. Stephen H. Long, 1819–1820, crossed the Plains on horses, collected botanical and faunal samples, and met with the Pawnee en route to the Rocky Mountains (fig. 9), returning by way of the Canadian River with an unfavorable image of the "Great Desert" (Ronda 1997:64–68; Kane, Holmquist, and Gilman 1978).

From the beginning, the factory-post system was hampered by the tension between civilian and military affairs. In 1806 Congress created the Office of Indian Trade and named a superintendent to administer the factories, to carry on "a liberal trade with the several Indian nations, within the United States, or their territories," and to separate some responsibilities for Indian affairs from the Department of War. The new law built upon the Intercourse Act of 1802 (revised in 1834), which required posting of bonds by traders, forfeiture of goods and bonds upon violation of the law, and a fine and imprisonment structure for serious offenders. Noncitizens were forbidden to enter Indian country; horse trading was discouraged; squatters were prohibited to settle on Indian lands under threat of eviction; and, any White convicted of murdering "an Indian or Indians, belonging to any nation or tribe of Indians, in amity with the United States" was subject to the death penalty (Washburn 1973, 3:2154–2163). "Factors" or managers were to "purchase and take charge of all goods intended for trade with the Indian nations" and to accept only skins and furs, to be publicly auctioned. A system of heavy fines and penalties, designed to keep agents honest and nonlicensed traders out of Indian country, was prescribed. A credit system was established "with caution to principal chiefs of good character," and liquor was strictly prohibited. Between 1808 and 1812, the Office of Indian Trade made a profit on furs and skins collected at the factories from Indian hunters (Prucha 1984, 1:121–122).

The factory system was also used for the distribution of presents and annuities, which required annual review by the War Department, a bureaucratic snarl that hampered the Indian Office, whose agents reported to the Department of the Treasury. Nevertheless, the system was fairly efficient and had the potential of regulating Whites as well as keeping the peace with Indian tribes. In 1816, Thomas McKenney became superintendent of Indian trade. His goals of keeping private traders out of Indian country and "civilization programs" incorporated in the trading houses to train Indians in agriculture and domestic arts met keen opposition among American capitalists and their supporters in Congress (Viola 1974). John Jacob Astor's American Fur Company and other private concerns were eager to build their own trading posts in Indian country with minimal government interference or inspection.

When the factory system was abolished in 1822 the Office of Indian Trade was replaced by creation of the Bureau of Indian Affairs, which was known within months as the Office of Indian Affairs (S.L. Tyler 1973:51–69; E.E. Hill 1974). McKenney was appointed the first superintendent of Indian affairs.

Southern and Central Plains Indians were affected directly by relocations of eastern Indians on their hunting grounds and by land cessions beginning in 1808 (vol. 4:43–46). In the first decade of the nineteenth century, Northeast and Southeast Indians began moving into Osage country, soon outnumbering them. Potawatomis,

Yale U., Beinecke Rare Book and Manuscript Lib.

Fig. 9. Council between the Pawnee and the expedition under Maj. Stephen H. Long, Oct. 7, 1819. Watercolor by Samuel Seymour.

Chickasaws, Delawares, Choctaws, and Cherokees, as well as American squatters, established camps in Osage territory. The Osage fought back. Meriwether Lewis, newly appointed governor of Louisiana Territory, restricted the sale of gunpowder to the Osage and colluded with William Clark and Saint Louis merchants to pressure the Osage into a land cession by treaty in 1808 (Kappler 1904–1941, 2:95–99). Backed by federal dragoons, Clark called upon the Osage to establish a line separating themselves from the United States to insure peace. One faction agreed to allow hunting in a tract of their homeland; another to a legitimate cession in exchange for safety near Fort Osage, a blacksmith, grain mill, plows, log houses, and a trading post; still others not present contested the treaty and considered it a bargain struck in bad faith (Washburn 1973, 4:2332–2338; Rollings 1992:220–230). This was a paradigm of misunderstandings in the treaty-making process on the Plains for the next 50 years, where Indians and Whites had different purposes and expectations (DeMallie 1980).

In 1816, Congress passed two acts that affected Indians of the upper Midwest and Northern Plains. The first provided that "licenses to trade with the Indians within the territorial limits of the United States shall not be granted to any but citizens of the United States, unless by the express direction of the President . . . ." The second, the Tariff of 1816, imposed a duty of up to 30 percent on hats or caps of wool, fur, leather." Blankets, textiles, gunpowder, distilled spirits, and iron goods were also targeted to protect American manufacturers from British suppliers (Phillips 1961, 2:158–163). Indians accustomed to high-quality British goods faced potentially diminishing supplies at a time when demand was on the rise. Further complicating their lives, they faced treaty commissions hoping to gain their allegiance, while breaking their bond with the Canadian traders.

Two styles of treaties were constructed in an attempt to better regulate Indians and Whites on the frontier (Prucha 1994). The first is exemplified in the Treaty with the Teton in 1815, signed at the Portage des Sioux with William Clark, one of three American commissioners, and nine Teton chiefs. Desirous of "re-establishing peace and friendship," all parties agreed to forgive and forget "every injury, or act of hostility, committed by one or either of the contracting parties against the other." A second article declared, "perpetual peace and friendship" between the citizens of the United States and the individuals of the Teton tribe. A final article stated that "The undersigned chiefs and warriors, for themselves and their said tribe, do hereby acknowledge themselves and the aforesaid tribe to be under the protection of the United States of America, and of no other nation, power, or sovereign, whatsoever" (Kappler 1904–1941, 2:112–113). Identical treaties were signed with the Yankton and "Sioux of St. Peter's River" as well as the Iowa during the same proceedings and with the Osage and Kansa later that year (Kappler 1904–1941, 2:114, 115, 119–120, 122–124). Additional treaties of friendship with the Santee Sioux in 1816, the Otoe in 1817, and four branches of the Pawnee and the Quapaw in 1818, each incorporated language specific to the situation (Kappler 1904–1941, 2:128–130, 139–140, 158–161). For example, in the Treaty with the Grand Pawnee, 1818, in addition to affirmation of loyalty and friendship, the Pawnee were asked to "oblige themselves to deliver up" their own tribal members who might defect to any foreign power other than the United States (Kappler 1904–1941, 2:156–157). No lands changed hands; no annuities or special favors were promised, but the language was that of expectation that the Pawnee might become allies, in the event of confrontation with Spain (Washburn 1973, 4:2360–2361).

Similar concerns and an interest in protecting trade with Mexico on the Santa Fe Trail led federal dragoons into the Southwest in 1834. After a long and arduous march, during which many troops died of cholera, 19 Comanche and several Wichita headmen met American representatives to wipe the slate of past depredations and to reduce attacks on other Indians and White traders (Hoig 1998:159–190). In the Camp Holmes Treaty, both tribes retained their right "to hunt and trap in the Great Prairie west of the Cross Timber, to the western limits of the United States," and were encouraged to continue in their "friendly relations with the Republic of Mexico, where they all frequently hunt and the Comanche nation principally inhabit" (Kappler 1904–1941, 2:435–439). In short, the Comanche gave up nothing, but the United States had nothing to lose in courting Comanche cooperation (Kavanagh 1996:236–242).

A second, more intrusive style of treaty became standard between 1818 and 1830. Its principal architect for Plains tribes was William Clark, who as governor of Missouri Territory, 1813–1821, and superintendent of Indian affairs, 1822–1838, became an advocate for the policy of removing Eastern Indians to Indian lands west of Saint Louis. Government reports by Zebulon M. Pike of 1805–1806, released in 1810; Lewis and Clark of 1804–1806, published in 1814; and, Stephen H. Long from 1819–1820, available in part by 1822, reenforced the image of the plains as a "Great Desert" unsuited for White settlement, where Indians might subsist as long as buffalo were plentiful (Ronda 1997). In the middle of this grassland, in 1825, Congress created an Indian Territory as a permanent home for native peoples, bounded by the Platte River to the north, the Red River to the south, Spanish territory to the west, and Arkansas Territory to the east. The resident Osage, Kansa, Otoe, Missouria, Quapaw, Pawnee, and Ponca were pressured to cede portions of their domain and to move onto smaller parcels away from the Missouri, where Americans seeking farms were pushing westward and where emigrant Eastern Indians were relocating prior to final settlement in their respective portions of Indian Territory. Treaties concluded by William Clark in 1818 with the Quapaw and Osage (Kappler 1904–1941, 2:160–162, 167–168), and in 1825 with the Osage and the Kansa (Kappler 1904–1941, 2:217–225, 246– 250) liquidated all lands of resident tribes in the state of Missouri and most in Arkansas Territory. These treaties were designed to ease tension between the emigrant Indians and the resident lower Missouri tribes (Washburn 1973, 4:2362–2365, 2395–2405). The Osage were promised a $7,000 annuity for 20 years, as well as one-time purchases of $6,000 in merchandise and $2,600 in "horses and equipage." Debts owed at the United States trading houses were forgiven, and the government agreed to pay tribal debts to private traders, as well as $1,000 to be paid to the Delaware for Osage depredations (Kappler 1904–1941, 2:218–220; Washburn 1973, 4:2395–2401; Prucha 1994:139–140).

The 1825 treaties did not accomplish their goal. Increasingly, emigrant Eastern Indians became a problem for Plains Indians (Foreman 1930). Traditional sites had to be abandoned in favor of locations that made the Osage and Kansa, in particular, vulnerable to attacks by the better-mounted Pawnee, Arapaho, Southern Cheyenne, Kiowa, and Comanche (Unrah 1979:22– 23). The Osage had other enemies too. The first group of Cherokee emigrants settled to their east in Arkansas where they numbered around 6,000 in 1816. Blocked and harassed by the Osage, the Cherokee complained to William Clark in 1817 that "the rivers are red with the Blood of Cherokees." The Cherokee vowed to retaliate, surprising the Osage under Claremore, killing a reported 14 men, 69 women, children, and boys, and taking "just over a hundred captive" (Hoig 1993:118–125). The government responded by building Fort Smith to separate the two tribes in 1817, and by holding a peace summit in 1818 where the Osage agreed to make peace with the Cherokee, Delaware, and Shawnee, and to allow the Cherokee to hunt in the west in exchange for the return of all captives. The peace was short-lived and was violated immediately by Cherokees who stole 40 horses and killed four Osages as they left the peace council. Raids and murders continued for the next decade. Peace conferences held in 1830 and finalized in 1831 at Fort Gibson (established in 1824) brought an end to the conflict, but by the end of the decade, the Osage were weakened and vulnerable—surrounded by strangers, economically dependent on White traders, and internally disunited (Rollings 1992:238–245, 279–285).

On the Middle Missouri, a more aggressive approach was taken. Rather than building posts and inviting Indian nations into treaty and peace parlays, the government went to the Indian nations in their own lands. For this purpose, Gen. William H. Atkinson and Indian agent Benjamin O'Fallon were appointed treaty commissioners in 1825 by President John Quincy Adams. During that summer, they traveled up the Missouri, accompanied by a military escort of 476 men. This was deemed necessary in the wake of a confrontation between private fur traders and the Arikara two years previously, which was brought on by Whites attempting to circumvent the Arikara as middlemen traders, and ended in the death of 14 White trappers and the wounding of nine others, all employed by entrepreneur William H. Ashley (D.L. Morgan 1964:25–29, 44–45). A retaliatory campaign, intended to "chastize the Arricaras & inforce respect among the other Tribes in that Section of Country," was organized under Col. Henry Leavenworth and consisted, according to William Clark, of a combined force of "220 Regular Troops and about 80 men of the Trading Companies and to be joined by a party of Seioux to releave Gen. Ashley and the upper Traders" (D.L. Morgan 1964:45–46). The Leavenworth expedition drove the outnumbered and outgunned Arikara from their villages to seek refuge farther up the Missouri River near the Mandan and Hidatsa (Nichols 1984).

Under this guarded diplomatic atmosphere, separate treaties were signed with the Ponca, Teton, Yankton, Yanktonai, Cheyenne, Arikara, Hidatsa, Mandan, and Crow in 1825 (Kappler 1904–1941, 2:225–246). The commission intended to negotiate additional treaties with the Blackfoot and the Assiniboine, but word of hostilities against Whites in the Yellowstone country discouraged further travel inland. Upon returning downriver, the commission held additional councils in the fall with the Pawnee, Otoe-Missouria, and Omaha (Kappler 1904–1941, 2:256–269; Prucha 1994:143–144). At each treaty proceeding, presents were given out, troops paraded in review, cannon were fired, and speeches were made. Article one of each treaty opened with the assertion that the Indian nation in question "admitted . . . that they reside within the territorial limits of the United States, acknowledge their supremacy, and claim their protection," admitting "the right of the United States to regulate all trade and intercourse with them." For its part, in article two, the United States agreed to receive Indians "into their friendship, and under their protection, and to extend to them, from time to time, such benefits and acts of kindness as may be convenient, and seem just to the President of the United States. Only licensed traders holding American citizenship would be allowed to conduct business with the Indians under "mild and equitable regulations" in exchange for which the chiefs were "to exert themselves to recover stolen property," to refrain from buying guns from any power hostile to the United States, and to apprehend and deliver to a United States military post any unlicensed or foreign persons attempting to trade with their people. They also pledged to "give safe conduct to all persons who may be legally authorized by the United States to pass through their country" and to avoid taking "private revenge" or asserting tribal customs in punishing outsiders accused of injuring their own people. These were to be the personal responsibility of the "said Chiefs," who were to deliver up such persons so that they might "be punished agreeably to the laws of the United States" for such crimes as robbery, violence, or murder (Washburn 1973, 4:2406–2409).

These treaties were supplemented in 1830 with major cessions by all divisions of the Santee Sioux, Omaha, Iowa, and Otoe-Missouria (Kappler 1904–1941, 2:305–310) and further cessions by the Pawnee, Quapaw, and Otoe-Missouria in 1833 (Kappler 1904–1941, 2:395–397, 400–401, 416–417). In 1835, the Caddo ceded land in the United States and portions of the contested borderland between Louisiana and Texas (Kappler 1904–1941, 2:432–434). Their neighbors to the west, the Comanche and Wichita, parlayed with federal dragoons at the Camp Holmes Treaty of 1835, but did not give up hunting rights, a precursor to treaties of the 1850s, which guaranteed the right to hunt and fish in "usual and accustomed places" (Kappler 1904–1941, 2:435–439).

Fifteen additional treaties with Plains Indians were ratified by the United States Senate from 1836 to 1851. In addition to reducing land base, these treaties rewarded cooperative chiefs with special provisions for presents and annuity payments; often provided land for mixed-blood relatives of Whites intermarried into tribes; supplied a "farmer" and agricultural implements, where appropriate; and promised to pay "full indemnification" for horses or other property stolen from them by other tribes or by Whites. Land cessions and new living situations within oddly shaped reserves, often bordered by enemies or total strangers from the east, created crisis and factionalism in many of the treaty tribes.

Beginning in 1819, Congress provided a limited appropriation to subsidize missionaries among the emigrant Indians bound for new homes in the West (vol. 4:438–440). Christian groups quarreled among themselves over jurisdictional areas for their missionaries (Lutz 1906; Foreman

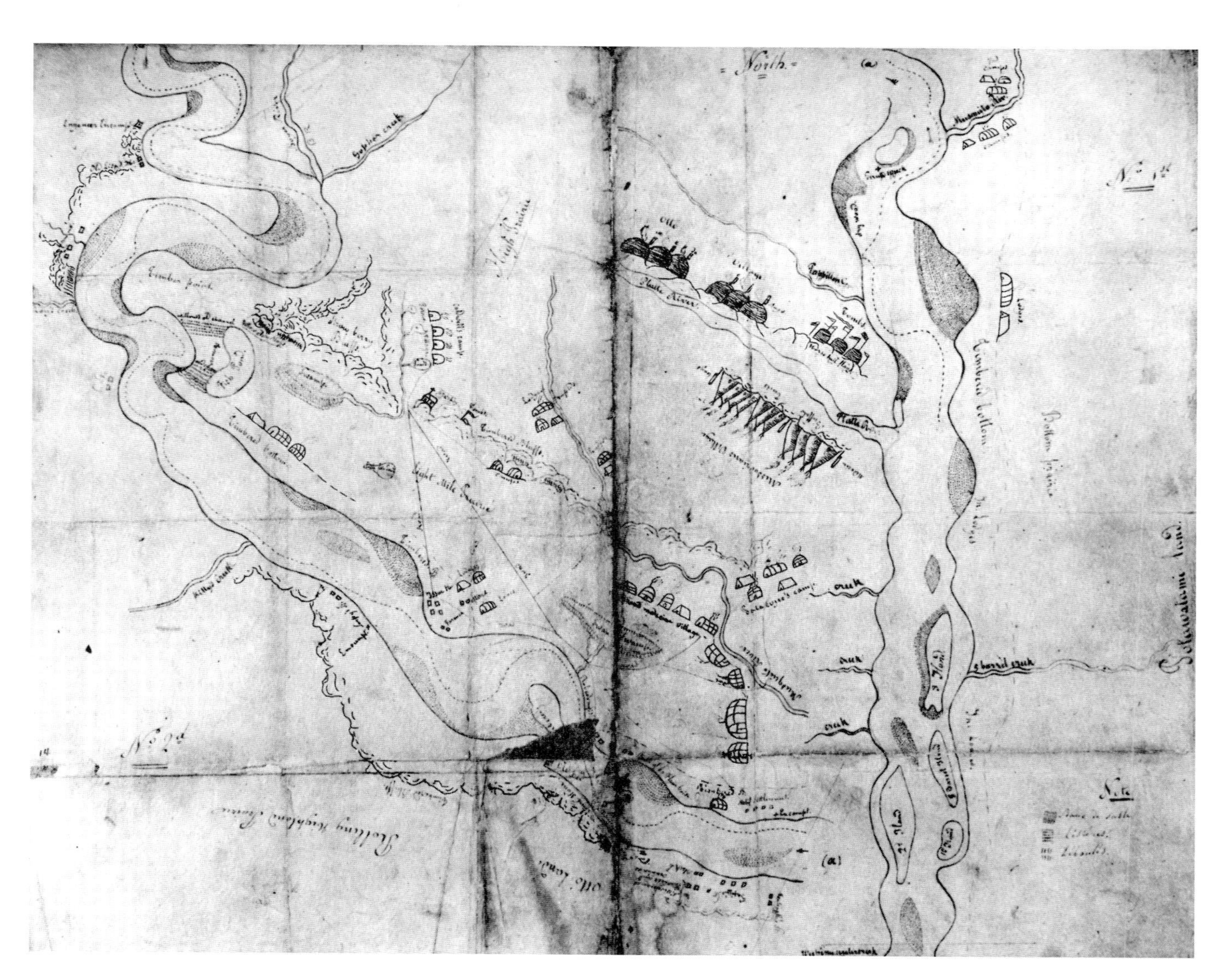

Midwest Jesuit Arch., St. Louis:IX C8-11B, side 1.

Fig. 10. Map of the Missouri River from the Boyer River (top left) to Weeping Water Creek (bottom right), showing earthlodges, grass lodges, and buffalo-hide tepees. Villages and camps (computer enhanced) of the Otoe and Missouria tribes are labeled as Grand Medicine, Missourians, Otto, and Patacuyee's; a Potawatomi village is labeled as Caldwell's camp. Ink on paper by Pierre-Jean de Smet, about 1840.

1930:80–89; Berkhofer 1965). Within a year, the United Foreign Missionary Society established Union Mission for the Osage under Claremore in present-day Oklahoma. In 1821, 20 additional missionaries (mostly Presbyterians) arrived to serve the Missouri Osage at Harmony Mission near the Grand Osage village on the Marais des Cygnes. Both would last until 1836 and would be expanded with a branch at Neosho in 1824, the first mission and school in what is now Kansas (Barry 1972:95, 96, 117).

Soon other denominations were active. One Baptist faction led by Isaac McCoy, an ardent champion of removal since the 1820s, advocated a separate Indian state in 1840 (McCoy 1840; Schultz 1972; vol. 4:47). Reaction of the nontreaty resident tribes in Indian Territory was one of alarm, especially in light of increased competition for buffalo range and trading privileges. The Kiowa, Comanche, Jicarilla Apache, Southern Cheyenne, and Arapaho were to face challenges in their own intertribal relations as a result of these shifts beyond the 1820s (Hoig 1993:118–135). All felt the demographic strain as Indians from the Northeast and Southeast took up residence in the Indian Territory.

Those within or near the Texas border felt general anti-Indian sentiments in Texas under Mexico. In 1826, advanced parties of Cherokees living in Texas were persuaded by impresario Stephen F. Austin to help pacify or eradicate several tribes at war with Mexico. A protracted war between resident Tawakonis and Wacos against American immigrants, Western Cherokees, and Tejanos (old Spanish and Mexican families) engulfed central Texas for the next several years with scalpings and atrocities committed by all parties (Hoig 1993:124–129). Texas remained contested ground for the next 30 years. Comanches bore the brunt of hostile attitudes and actions. By the early 1840s, the Texas Rangers (organized in 1836 to protect Texans from Indians) had killed or pushed most Indians (including Cherokees) out of the republic making central Texas an unsafe home for any Indian tribe. Because Texas entered the union as a republic, the public domain remained state land. In 1854, the state of Texas donated lands on the Brazos River for the establishment of two reservations to honor treaty obligations with the United States. Continued antagonisms by Whites and depredations by Indians made this untenable. In 1859, the remaining reservation Indians of Texas were removed north across the Red River into Indian Territory.

Fur Trade, 1806–1850

As Lewis and Clark descended the Missouri in 1806 to report their findings, they met 11 separate groups of American traders headed upriver—all private parties—indicative of the many unlicensed traders on the frontier at the time. Five methods of fur trading on the Plains were employed from 1806 to 1850. Each required Indian cooperation and each inadvertently resulted in varied levels of conflict (Wishart 1976).

Arch. de la Compagnie de Jesus, Saint-Jérôme, Que.

Fig. 11. Trade relations between Euro-Americans and Plains Indians. In the upper sketch an Indian, on the right, wearing a chief's coat and holding a liquor jug and small kettle, gestures toward the trader, who offers a large kettle. In the lower sketch the Indian, on left, wearing fringed garments and face paint and holding a liquor jug, is receiving something from a seated White man. The 4-legged animal at the very top and the bird sketch at left may designate personal names. Drawing by a Blackfoot artist, Camp Ft. Lewis, near Ft. Benton, Mont., 1846.

The first was the itinerant peddler who traveled periodically to specific villages on his own or on behalf of a fur company. Between 1785 and 1812, these peddlers were active between the Canadian posts and the Mandan and Hidatsa villages (Anfinson 1987). Sometimes called North Traders, they generally traveled on foot with Indian middlemen as conductors. They carried small items such as firearms and gun accessories, knives, tobacco, blankets, ornaments, and glass beads and often had records from their home base of Indians who had been given credit at the Canadian posts in advance of receipt of furs or robes (Wood 1990:5–6). This type of trading, known as *en dérouine*, was well established in Canada and became important on the Plains, especially as traders' goods changed from luxuries to necessities (Wood and Thiessen 1985:12; Ray 1987:23–24). Buffalo robes, wolf and fox pelts, beaver pelts, and a few otter pelts and bear skins were primary items in demand by the North Traders, but they also accepted dogs, Indian corn, and slave women, and they expected horses or mules as part of their payment in order to transport the heavy robes and furs back to Canada (Wood and Thiessen 1985:9–11).

A second type of fur trade was a continuation of placing "residenters" or "tenant traders" among Indians, with expectations that their integration into Indian society would produce diplomatic and economic alliances beneficial to both trading cultures. French traders who lived among the Teton from 1800 to 1817 were particularly successful in finding resident Indian hosts (Nasatir 1952, 1:75–115), as were British and French-Canadians, many of them deserters from the large fur companies. Many of these men integrated into Indian society by intermarriage, remaining with their Indian families once reservations were established (H.H. Anderson 1973; Swagerty 1980).

A third approach, the "Rocky Mountain system," placed White trappers in direct competition with Indian hunters and bypassed middlemen (Chittenden 1902, 1:247–308; Wishart 1979:115–204). In 1807, Manuel Lisa organized a party of trappers and tested Indian protocol. Lisa's original strategy was to funnel furs out of the Middle Missouri trade network via a string of trading posts from the Mandan down to the Omaha villages near Council Bluffs. These posts would not infringe on Indian hunters and trappers but would protect company interests in the relatively hostile Teton and Arikara country. Most trappers would operate in large groups beyond the Yellowstone, collecting furs and depositing them at depots and defensive redoubts in friendly tribes' domains. Lisa's scheme of placing trappers in the beaver-rich Yellowstone country was the first of a series of efforts by Whites to circumvent the Indian trade system of the trans-Mississippi West (Oglesby 1963).

Naively, Lisa believed that his own employees could operate on the Plains and in the Rocky Mountains independent of Indian approval or cooperation. The result was a predictable conflict with the Arikara, Teton, and especially the Blackfoot, who considered American beaver trappers trespassers (vol.4:362). From 1807 to 1831, the Upper Missouri and especially Blackfoot country was dangerous for any White trapper or trader. Dozens of trappers were slain in the region beyond the Yellowstone, and thousands of dollars in trade goods, packs of furs, and horses fell into Indian hands (Chittenden 1902, 2:850–854; Dunwiddie 1974).

In 1822, as the United States factory system began closing its trading and collecting posts, William H. Ashley and seasoned trader Andrew Henry gathered over 100 White trappers and obtained a license to "trade with the Indians of the Missouri River" (D.L. Morgan 1964:1–2). Ashley's initial losses at the Arikara Villages in 1823 did not deter him. In 1824 he crossed the Plains with a license to trade "with the Blackfoot and Crow tribes, within and west of the Rocky Mountains" (D.L. Morgan 1964:21) and sent brigades of trappers in several directions with instructions to meet at the Shoshone Rendezvous the following summer in Wyoming's Green River country (Ewers 1954). For 15 summers, these rendezvous included participation by some Plateau peoples, especially Nez Perce and Flathead, and some Eastern Indians, especially Iroquois, active as free trappers or engagés of British and American companies. However, the major Plains tribes in whose usage areas the Whites trapped were seldom present, and they benefited little from a White-centered production system. Resentment of Whites was widespread; the Blackfoot, Gros Ventre, and Teton were the most successful in defending their lands and streams. This pattern of "free trapping" without benefit of fur posts continued into the 1840s but was always a risky enterprise, even for brigades of trappers who worked in large groups for mutual protection (Utley 1996). Relations with Plains Indians suffered during the peak years of the Rocky Mountain system, which waned after 1833 due to a decline in the price of beaver and a surplus of furs on world markets (Wishart 1979:146–147).

A fourth approach depended on Indian producers and used fur-trading posts. By the time fur companies began building forts on the plains, the system had been well tested by the Hudson's Bay Company and North West Company throughout the Canadian plains and to a lesser degree by French and Spanish traders on the Missouri (Nasatir 1952; A.R. Woolworth 1960). Its principal American architects were John Jacob Astor, owner of the American Fur Company, founded in 1808; Kenneth McKenzie, a Scot who formed the Columbia Fur Company with other former North West Company managers in 1822; and Pierre Chouteau, Jr., whose Pratte, Chouteau and Company allied with Astor in 1822, absorbing Columbia Fur Company posts under a new Western Department of the American Fur Company (Chittenden 1902; Lecompte 1972a). The organization was broken into "outfits." The largest and most important for Plains Indians was the Upper Missouri Outfit, formed in 1827, and active until 1865, when the company was sold to the Minnesota-based firm of Hubbell and Hawley (Lass 1994).

The methods employed by the Western Department were a synthesis of various Euro-American and Euro-Canadian fur trade systems, modified by Native American protocol and priorities. Posts served company personnel and an extensive Indian clientele and were only successful if resident tribes wanted them built in their respective hunting territories or adjacent to their villages on major rivers. Whites and their families (mostly mixed-bloods) lived year-round at the posts. Indians were encouraged to hunt and trap on their own and to trade with company representatives using products of the chase as barter for Euro-American trade goods. Three depots served entire districts: on the Missouri River, Fort Union (1829) among the Assiniboine (E.N. Thompson 1968) and Fort Pierre (1831) between the Teton and the Arikara (Schuler 1990) served as anchors; on the Platte River, Fort Laramie (1834) connected the lower Missouri posts with the trade of the Plains proper (vol. 4:372–373), especially that of the

Brule and the Cheyenne (Hafen and Young 1938). Other posts of secondary importance included Vermillion Post (1822), Cabanne's Post (1826), and Fort Clark (1830) ("Plains Village Tradition: Postcontact," fig. 3, this vol.) (Dill 1990). "Wintering houses" completed the system. These cabins or lodges lacked palisades and were occupied from late fall through early spring to serve bands encamped at favorite, well-sheltered sites where trees provided fuel and protection from wind for the long winter. In addition, some company traders lived and moved with their assigned tribes as they followed the buffalo during annual migration (Chittenden 1902, 1:309–395; Wishart 1979:41ff.; vol. 4:369–371).

At the posts, a select number of Indian males were employed as "fort soldiers." These liaisons encouraged fellow tribesmen to trade there, kept order among them, and minimized Indian thefts from Whites (Ewers 1972:17, 1976a:17–18). Nearly all those on salary were Whites or mixed-bloods, most of French ancestry (Swagerty 1994). Some of this class, most of the craftsmen, and nearly all traders wed or cohabited with Indian women if they stayed in the trade more than a season (Swagerty 1980). Traders able to afford marrying into prominent families could expect to make larger profits (Kurz 1937:156).

From the Indian point of view, the trading posts were more than general stores stocked with useful and ornamental articles. A post was a social center and a "bank" where the Indian obtained credit for his winter's hunt in advance (Ewers 1972:6–7). Whites worked as day laborers, but never in competition with Indians, who were given the prerogative and the incentive to become productive trappers and hunters as well as partners (Wishart 1976). Overall, the system was a mixed success for Indians and Whites (Lehmer 1977). Side effects included the widespread provision of alcohol in order to secure trade (O. Lewis 1942; Wishart 1979; Unrau 1996); the abandonment of Indian women attached to fort personnel when their husbands left the country or changed their positions; and the proliferation of a class of fort Indians, dependent on White wages or largess in order to survive (Catlin 1844, 2:120; Ray 1974).

As the building of posts proliferated from 1822 to 1850, the American Fur Company grew in power and in stature among the Indians of the region. Beginning in 1831, company steamboats entered the Missouri, enabling traffic to move much faster upriver (Chittenden 1903). Artists George Catlin (fig. 12) (vol. 4:629), Karl Bodmer, and James John Audubon were among many in the 1830s and 1840s who recorded firsthand the Missouri River tribes (Catlin 1844; Maximilian in Thwaites 1904–1907, 22–24; Bodmer in D.C. Hunt et al. 1984; Audubon 1900).

From the beginning, the key to the entire system was the buffalo robe, not the beaver pelt. One trader estimated that only one-quarter of the total bison kill was for the purposes of the fur trade. Most was consumed for meat and leather. The production of robes was limited not by the number of animals that could be killed by male hunters, but by the number of hides Plains women could process. Twenty-five to 30 robes per woman was considered "an excellent winter's work," with the average at "about 18 to 20 each" (Denig 1930:541). A Crow elder recalled a time when his people never dressed more robes than they needed for themselves, but after the White traders arrived, "every lodge had from sixteen to eighteen robes to sell" (Bradley 1896–1923:200).

There had always been specialization of labor and commodities in the Indian-centered trade on the plains. However, the White-directed exchanges forced alterations in the division of labor, in gender roles, and in some cases in social organization, as men, women, and children killed, skinned, cured, and marketed animal products (Albers and Medicine 1983). Women in horse-rich societies such as the Blackfoot and the Crow may have increased their political and economic status during the nineteenth century (Lowie 1935:60–61, 1954:80–81; Ewers 1955:315). In nearly all Plains societies, women owned lodges, horses, and household items and retained these when they divorced or remarried (C.F. Taylor 1994:93–94). Female work groups were critical not only to survival of the family and the band but also in accumulating surpluses (A.B. Kehoe 1992:313). In the 1850s, one trader wrote that women have "a share in the dressed skins, which they exchange for clothes, ornaments, and dainty tidbits" (Kurz 1937:176). Another observed: "When buffalo are plenty, anyone can kill. The raw hide of the animal has no value. It is the labor of putting it in the form of a robe or skin fit for sale or use that makes its worth. Women therefore are the greatest wealth an Indian [man] possesses next to his horses" (Denig 1930:506). Other analysis suggests that trade benefited males at the expense of Indian women. Within once egalitarian buffalo-hunting cultures, the power, wealth, and prestige associated with the trade flowed mainly to men, eroding, rather than improving, the position of women (Klein 1980:134, 1983, 1993; J.H. Moore 1974, 1987; A.B. Kehoe 1995).

By 1850, Indians across the Plains had become integrated into the capitalist economy. Indian-produced furs, robes, pemmican, and other commodities of the hunt were fed into staple industries in the United States and abroad. As the economies of the tribes became inextricably linked to the fur trade, changes in social organization resulted. When the production of buffalo robes increased to an average of 100,000 robes annually for the 1850s (Sunder 1965:17), the demand for hides far outstripped Indian ability to supply them. The result, it has been hypothesized, was an increase in multiple marriages, which intensified intertribal warfare and interband raiding for wives, whose victims in turn left widows available for remarriage (O. Lewis 1942:38ff; Ewers 1958:134ff; Albers 1993). The demand for wives also increased the cost of bride purchase and heightened the necessity for a family to accumulate bridewealth (Flannery 1953:171–194). The new dynamics of trade also resulted in an increase in the num-

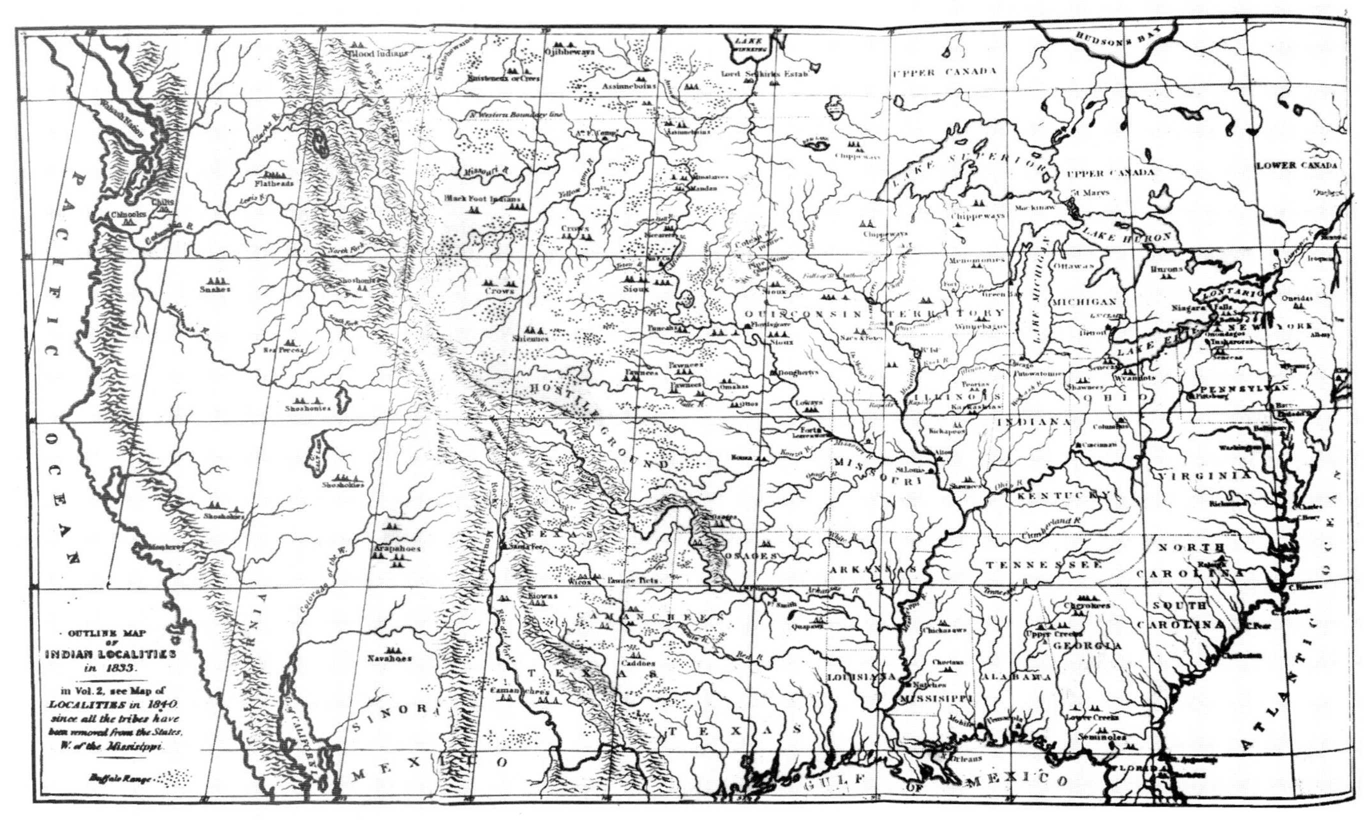

Smithsonian Lib., Catlin 1866: neg. no. 99-196.

Fig. 12. "Outline Map of Indian Localities in 1833." This map, which first appeared in the 1841 edition of Catlin's *Letters*, shows a few Euro-American place-names as well as the buffalo range. It was the most accurate for tribal locations, prior to 1850. Drawn by George Catlin. Computer enhanced.

bers of women and children taken captive (McGinnis 1990; Hoig 1993).

The Central Plains exemplifies a fifth type of fur trade activity—that of the itinerant robe-traders on international caravan routes. From the opening of the Santa Fe Trail in 1821 to 1850, tribes on the route from Missouri to New Mexico faced increased traffic by Whites and increased demands for robes (Foreman 1933; Hoig 1998:191–211). As early as 1828 Charles and William Bent operated Fort William on the boundary between Mexico and the United States. By 1833, it was replaced by Bent's Fort, an adobe structure built by Bent, St. Vrain and Company that served as a hostelry for Santa Fe and Missouri bound traders, as a resupply point for mountain men active in the southern Rocky Mountain fur trade, as an observation post for those in Congress eager to acquire portions of Mexico, and as a collecting and resupply point for the Indian robe and fur trade with Central and Southern Plains tribes (Grinnell 1923a; Lavender 1954; Comer 1996). Trade out of Bent's Fort included Kiowas, Comanches, and Arapahos, but it was the resident Southern Cheyenne upon whom traders depended for protection and for the majority of their commerce (Jablow 1951). And it was through Pawnee country that the robes and trade goods had to pass (Wishart 1979). While the Southern Cheyenne and Pawnee were initially friendly to Whites and eager to trade, by 1850, both groups experienced pressures on habitat, especially diminishing resources, as traders and settlers crossed their lands. Simultaneously, intertribal warfare escalated.

For the Pawnee, dependency and dispossession intersected. From their strong position as middlemen traders during early historic times, Pawnee power and options eroded rapidly as Whites and other Indian nations pressed them for their strategically desired habitat (R. White 1983). Following treaties of commerce and friendship with the United States in 1818, 1825, and 1833, the Pawnee land base was progressively reduced. By 1839, the Pawnee had splintered into two village clusters, one on the Loup River, the other on the Platte. Those on the Loup faced depredations from the Sioux, who annually raided their villages, killing men, capturing women, and stealing large numbers of horses (Wishart 1994:80). Promises of protection from the United States were not honored. Those on the Platte came in conflict with emigrants bound for Oregon, who rapidly depleted timber, grass, and game.

Jesuit Mo. Prov. Arch., St. Louis.

Fig. 13. Intertribal relations and Christianity. Written on the bottom of this sketch is "A Blackfoot chief, after having seen the Catholic ladder that Ambroise, Chief of the Flatheads explained to him, asked to be incorporated, together with his 28 lodges, into the Flathead people." Although the Flathead and Blackfoot were at war with each other during the 19th century, the Small Robes band of Blackfoot joined the Flathead to learn Christianity, demonstrated here by the mnemonic Roman Catholic ladder, which the 2 discuss through sign language. Most of the Small Robes died in a battle with the Crow (J. Peterson and L. Peers 1993:108). Ink on paper sketch by Father Nicolas Point, 1841–1847 (cropped).

By the 1840s, the Pawnee were a dislocated society. The traditional mixed economy of horticulture and buffalo hunting no longer fed them; Oglala and Brule warrior parties continued to harass them regularly; Cheyenne and other neighbors, especially the Iowa, also made inroads and took Pawnee scalps; and, their annuities from the 1833 treaty had run out after 1845, starving them for staples (Hyde 1951:225–227). By 1848, the agent of those on the Platte saw his charges "in a miserable condition; their crops this season have almost been an entire failure, owing to the drought." He reported that "these three bands seem more than willing to move; they say they cannot make corn on their present place, and they cannot get timber to rebuild their lodges." More importantly, "they wanted the Great Father to make the grand Pawnee band cross over [the Platte] with them [so that] they would be better able to defend themselves against the Sioux" (J. Miller in ARCIA 1848:466). The Pawnee ceded yet more land in 1848 in exchange for $2,000 (Kappler 1904–1941, 2:571–572). They further consolidated their villages and defended themselves against Whites and other Indians as best they could into the 1850s, but their numbers continued to decline (Hyde [1951] 1974:Appendix E, p. 364).

The annual reports of the commissioners of Indian affairs reflect the dilemmas facing Indians and Whites (Kvasnicka and Viola 1979). In 1850, Commissioner Luke Lea (ARCIA 1850:41) wrote:

> It is much to be regretted that no appropriation was made at the last session of Congress for negotiating treaties with the wild tribes of the great western prairies. These Indians have long held undisputed possession of this extensive region, and, regarding it as their own, they consider themselves entitled to compensation, not only for the right of way through their territory, but for the great and injurious destruction of the game, grass, and timber, committed by our troops and emigrants. They have hitherto been kept quiet and peaceable by reiterated promises that the government would act generously towards them, and considerations of economy, justice, and humanity require that these promises should be promptly fulfilled. They would, doubtless, be contented with a very moderate remuneration, which should be made in goods, stock animals, agricultural implements, and other useful articles.

From 1840 to 1848, an estimated 18,847 emigrants crossed the Plains on trails and wagon roads, traveling through many Plains Indian hunting grounds (Unrah 1979:119). In 1850 almost 100,000 emigrants crossed the Plains bound for California, Oregon, and Utah (Unrah 1979:119–120). The stage was set for the great treaty councils beginning in 1851 near Fort Laramie, which established new reservations, thought by government officials as the solution for the Indians, an "alternative to extinction" (Trennert 1975).

History of the United States Plains Since 1850

LORETTA FOWLER

By the mid-nineteenth century, Plains peoples faced a serious challenge from the citizenry of the United States, whose settlement of the West resulted in the destruction of the bison herds, brought epidemic diseases, and provoked wars that led to native peoples' confinement on reservations. Directed by a federal policy of assimilation, the reservation system worked to destroy native social institutions and cultural orientations, though native accommodations to reservation life incorporated social and cultural continuities, as well as change. In the second half of the twentieth century, federal policy shifted to an emphasis on self-determination for native peoples; in response, Plains peoples have worked to regain control of their communities and strengthen or build cultural traditions that they associate with their histories.

Westward Expansion and Reservation Settlement

Opportunities in agriculture, mining, and trade drew emigrants from the eastern United States west along two main routes in the 1840s and, in greater numbers, in the 1850s. The Oregon Trail to California and Oregon went along the Platte River through the hunting territory of some of the village groups, particularly the Pawnee, and through the territory of the nomadic Teton Sioux, Cheyenne, and Arapaho. The Santa Fe Trail linked the border towns of Westport and Independence with settlements in New Mexico and presented both an opportunity for raiding and a threat to the trading position of Comanche and Kiowa. As emigrants moved west, pockets of settlement appeared, particularly in Kansas and Nebraska territories and in the foothills of the Colorado Rockies where gold had been discovered.

The federal government hoped to facilitate westward expansion by preventing clashes between Indians and the emigrants and settlers. In 1851 Congress implemented a policy of concentration of Indians on reservations away from settlements and emigrant highways and appropriated funds to negotiate treaties with Plains groups. A departure from "removal" policy, the reservation system would encourage native peoples to become "civilized" and allow at least some to remain in their homelands (A.M. Gibson 1980:354; P.H. Carlson 1998:137; R. White 1991:85–118)). By a series of treaties and land cessions, the government tried to restrict native peoples to their assigned territories and obtain their promise to forgo raids on settlers and travelers. In return, tribes received the promise of compensation in the form of supplies and protection from the depredations of Americans.

The Treaty of Traverse des Sioux, made in 1851 (vol. 4:50), guaranteed reservations on the upper Minnesota River to the four divisions of the Santee Sioux (Kappler 1904–1941, 2:588–590). The Fort Laramie Treaty of 1851 was signed by the nomadic Arapaho, Cheyenne, Teton Sioux, Crow, and some Assiniboine, and representatives from the allied Mandan, Hidatsa, and Arikara (Kappler 1904–1941, 2:594:596). At this treaty council the federal officials also promoted the selection of spokesmen or intermediary chiefs who would represent the interests of their people in dealings with the federal government and with United States citizens in some circumstances. The Treaty of 1853 at Fort Atkinson was made with several bands of Comanche, Kiowa, and their Plains Apache allies (Kappler 1904–1941, 2:600–602). In 1855 on the Judith River, the allied Blackfoot and Gros Ventre agreed to a treaty (Kappler 1904–1941, 2:736–740). Treaties also were made with the villagers on the lower Missouri River: in 1853 Commissioner of Indian Affairs George Manypenny made treaties with several Plains peoples in the northern sector of Indian Territory, including Omaha, Iowa, Otoe, and Missouria, in order to make room for settlers who had already trespassed on their preexisting reservations. The village peoples faced famine on a regular basis; food and annuity goods from the federal government offered hope for their survival (A.M. Gibson 1980:359; Wishart 1994:102). The Yankton, whose territory had been extensively settled already, occupied a small reservation on the Missouri River in 1858 (Hoover 1988:30–31).

In 1854 Congress passed the Kansas-Nebraska Act, which created the Kansas and Nebraska Territories from the northern section of Indian Territory. The village peoples, who already had been pressured to sell much of their land for less than market value, had accepted small reservations there, where they tried to maintain their communities despite attacks by Teton Sioux and other nomadic groups, competition from eastern tribes who had emigrated west of the Missouri River, and depredations from American settlers living in proximity to the reservations. The United States failed to provide agreed-upon protections, and drought in the 1860s undermined the village peoples' farming efforts. Gradually more Indian land in Kansas and Nebraska was ceded in the face of continued incursions (vol. 4:215) (Wishart 1994:105–137).

In Nebraska, the Omaha fared the best. They produced sufficient crops and, compared to the other tribes, had considerable assistance from the federal government. Less threatened by the Brule Sioux than others, they continued to hunt. The allied Otoe and Missouria faced attacks from Teton Sioux and Cheyenne but did not cease their hunts. They did not do so well in farming and received less federal aid than the Omaha. The Pawnee and Ponca fared the worst. The Pawnees' crops failed and, under constant attack from Sioux, their hunts failed. They experienced devastating economic decline and population loss. The Ponca also led a marginal existence and lost population. Their land was poor and they received little assistance from the federal government, either with farming or with defense against Brule attacks. Under these conditions, leaders had difficulty mobilizing support; nonetheless, social and ceremonial life underwent reorganization along lines that were culturally meaningful (Wishart 1994:144–185).

In 1865 the Osage ceded part of their reservation on the southern border of Kansas. Still, settlers trespassed on the reduced reservation, and Osage hunters were challenged by the Cheyenne when they went on their buffalo hunts. Also under pressure, the Kansa sold part of their small reservation in Kansas in 1859 (Bailey 1973: 69–70).

Ultimately unable to subsist under extremely adverse conditions, the native peoples in Kansas and Nebraska decided or were forced to remove to the southern section of Indian Territory. Referred to as a second "trail of tears" by one historian, these relocations contributed to further loss of population (A.M. Gibson 1980:403–406). In the 1870s in Nebraska, native people had to choose between accepting individual allotments of land (and ceding more land to settlers) or selling their reservations and moving south. The bison hunts ended in the 1870s and economic assistance from the federal government hinged on cooperation in ceding or selling land. The Pawnee, with the support of the chiefs and religious leaders, sold their reservation and moved to Indian Territory between 1873 and 1875. They hoped that, after reimbursing the government for their relocation and the purchase of land in Indian Territory from the Creek and Cherokee, they could reestablish their community and improve their economic circumstances. The Otoe and Missouria peoples also decided to move to Indian Territory to improve their circumstances. They sold some land in 1876 and the remainder in 1881 and removed to Indian Territory in 1880 and 1881. The Ponca refused to move, preferring to stay in their homeland in Nebraska. They were forced by troops to leave in 1877, despite Congress's promise that they would not be relocated without their consent. Congress appropriated money to buy land from the Cherokee in Indian Territory where Ponca settled. A splinter group returned to Nebraska in 1880 and, with the assistance of prominent eastern reformers sympathetic to their plight, obtained allotments there. The Omaha, taking advantage of their successful efforts to farm and otherwise demonstrate commitment to "civilization" and of the support from prominent advocates allied with Omaha families, sold some land in 1874 but obtained allotments on their reservation in Nebraska (Wishart 1994:188–238; Boughter 1998).

The Osage agreed to sell their reservation in Kansas in 1870. They bought land from the Cherokee in Indian Territory and moved there between 1871 and 1874. Osage bands settled in five areas, corresponding to the five villages to which they had belonged in Kansas. The Osage sold acreage in the northwest corner of the reservation in Indian Territory to the Kansa, and the Kansa sold their land in Kansas in 1872 and moved to Indian Territory in 1873 (Bailey 1973:71–73, 78).

On the Upper Missouri, the Mandan and Hidatsa were farther removed from the emigration routes than the villagers in Indian Territory and were not subject to pressure from local settlers for the cession of their village lands. Seeking strength in unity, in 1845 they had combined to form a new village, Like-a-Fishhook, in North Dakota, and in 1862 the Arikara joined them there. In 1870 President Ulysses Grant by executive order created a reservation out of a portion of the lands assigned to them in 1851; the reservation included the village. Plagued by raids from Sioux, the village economy deteriorated, but the agency provided rations and wage work, including work for a large number of men who became scouts at nearby military posts. Even after the end of the Indian wars, scouts (primarily Arikara) worked as mail carriers, herders, guards, and couriers. The Mandan, Hidatsa, and Arikara shared the village, each occupying a separate section, and a group of families headed by French-Canadian men occupied another separate section. By the time these peoples had settled at Like-a-Fishhook, epidemics had reduced their populations significantly and, as a result, some of the Hidatsa and Mandan matrilineal clans became extinct, moiety exogamy was discontinued, and rules for medicine bundle transmissions changed to accommodate the new circumstances. Mandan and Hidatsa clans and societies consolidated; members selected one medicine bundle as the primary bundle and ceased to transfer duplicate bundles. Intermarriage with other peoples helped to augment their numbers but the in-marrying spouses accepted the village cultural orientation. These adjustments helped perpetuate the ceremonial life of these villagers in their difficult new circumstances. Dissidents (the Crow Flies High band of Hidatsas, joined by one-fourth of the Mandans) left the village and lived a nomadic hunting life until 1894, when they were forced back to the reservation (Bruner 1961:230–231, 235, 236, 240, 244, 247–248).

Some of the Wichita and their Caddo allies resided in the Wichita Mountains region in Indian Territory and some settled on a reservation in 1854 on the Brazos River in western Texas. In Texas, the Caddo farmed successfully and hunted, but they were subject to attack by Comanches and by Texans, despite their efforts to maintain peace and mediate between Texans and hostile Plains groups. Wichita groups (Taovaya, Tawakoni, Waco, and Wichita proper) and the related Kitsai vacillated from peaceful relations to raids. The hostility of settlers in Texas led to the removal of native peoples on the Brazos reservation to Indian Territory in 1859, where the combined groups were relocated on the Washita River on an old Kitsai village site in the vicinity of the Wichita Mountains (A.M. Gibson 1980:347–348; F.T. Smith 1995:149, 151, 160–163, 166–168). In 1872 a reservation was established for them there. The Caddo groups met in a council in 1874 and agreed to unite as the Caddo tribe under one chief; they and the Wichita retained distinct social identities, remaining socially and politically separate. They continued to farm under adverse conditions, including raids on their stock from Texans (F.T. Smith 1996:105, 110).

The more easterly villages had little choice but to accommodate to American designs, at times allying militarily in order to defend themselves against nomadic groups and to make their residence in their homeland more secure. Beginning in the late 1850s, men from the villages served as scouts for the U.S. Army. For example, Osage men scouted against the Cheyenne, and Pawnees, Arikaras, and Hidatsas assisted the army against the Teton Sioux. In Indian Territory, Pawnees, Caddoes, and Wichitas scouted against Comanches and others. Yanktons, closely allied with traders, aided the army against the Tetons (Dunlay 1982).

For nomadic groups farther removed from the emigration process, the 1850s also were generally a time of accommodation, when these groups tried to continue to hunt and, at the same time, coexist with the United States and its citizens. Hostilities did break out between the army and several Sioux divisions in 1854–1855, after the Brule were provoked by an army attack. Peace was negotiated in 1856. The 1860s brought an increase in Indian-White conflict. The rapid settlement of Minnesota and the failure of the United States government to abide by treaty provisions resulted in the Sioux Conflict of 1862 (vol. 4:169), in which Santee Sioux could not prevail against the U.S. Army. Subsequently, many fled to join other Plains peoples west of the Missouri River (W.B. Anderson 1984). In the mid-1860s, the Civil War brought about an increase in Indian-White hostilities along the major roads and near the areas of American settlement.

During the Civil War both the North and South sought aid from Plains peoples. The Confederacy tried to control the Plains region to develop the West independent of the United States and to create a continuous land corridor across Texas, Indian Territory, New Mexico, and California. The South also planned to use the Indian Territory as a source of supplies. Promising that their reservations would be inviolate, Confederate agents recruited among some Plains tribes, particularly the Caddo and Wichita and other tribes at Wichita Agency, which made them subject to attack from Union forces. Native warriors served the Confederacy mostly as scouts, but an Indian Cavalry Brigade, including an Osage Battalion, raided into Union territory. Confederates negotiated with Comanches to encourage raids against Union settlements in Kansas, and Comanche and Kiowa raids on freight trains led to retaliation by Union troops near Adobe Walls in 1864 ("History of the United States Plains Until 1850," fig. 1, this vol.). After the war the groups associated with the Confederacy faced punitive measures. Kansa men were impressed into the Union army and some Osage men also fought on the Union side, but their loyalty did not help them retain their lands in Kansas (A.M. Gibson 1980:367–375; Bailey 1973:70–71).

Generally the Civil War encouraged the formation of volunteer infantry and cavalry regiments in the western territories after U.S. troops withdrew. These volunteers provoked clashes with nomadic native peoples and contributed to the military conflicts of the 1860s. During 1864–1865 the Southern Cheyenne and Arapaho fought a war, often assisted by some Sioux bands and Comanches and Kiowas, to retaliate against the miners and settlers who attacked them and disturbed the buffalo grounds in Colorado Territory. The Sand Creek Massacre, in which volunteer militia attacked peaceful Southern Cheyennes and Arapahos in November 1864, precipitated the war, which eventually was brought to a close by a peace treaty in 1867 (vol. 4:201), at Medicine Lodge Creek (Hoig 1961; D.C. Jones 1966). There, the Southern Cheyenne and Arapaho and the Kiowa, Comanche, and Plains Apache agreed to settle on reservations in Indian Territory, where they would be protected from hostile settlers and allowed to hunt bison (Kappler 1904–1941, 2:982–989).

When gold was discovered in Montana, traffic on the Bozeman Trail disrupted the ability of Teton Sioux bands and their Northern Cheyenne and Arapaho allies to hunt in the Powder River country. The army engaged these tribes but was unsuccessful in getting them to withdraw. The U.S. negotiated a treaty in 1868 at Fort Laramie (vol. 4:54, 372–373) that provided for peace but closed the Powder River country to forts and other development. This treaty also created the Great Sioux Reservation, where many of the northern bands agreed to settle (Kappler 1904–1941, 2:998–1007, 1012–1015). The Crow also participated in a council at Fort Laramie and accepted a reservation in their homeland and agreed to relinquish other areas of their territory (fig. 1) (Kappler 1904–1941, 2:1008–1011).

Nomadic groups who were not in the immediate path of the emigrants avoided hostile encounters with Americans, and in the case of those groups threatened by the Sioux, men fought with the U.S. Army against "hostile" bands. Scouts and auxiliaries had flexible enlistments that allowed men to return to their bands periodically. Indian scouts ("Pawnee," fig. 4, this vol.; vol. 4:173) provided services including reconnaissance, location and assessment of the enemy, and instruction on how troops could adapt to the terrain and to Indian military tactics. By

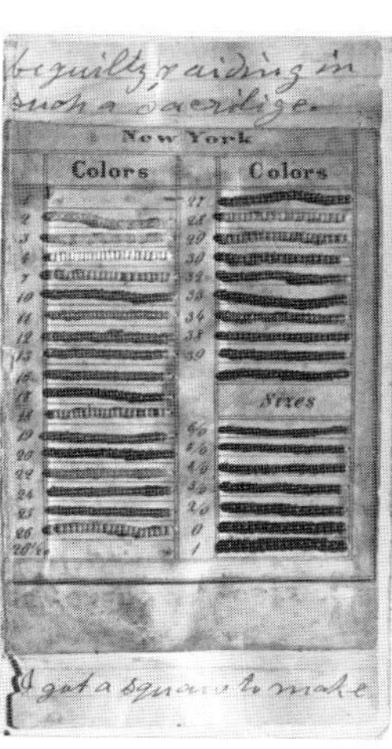

top, Smithsonian, NAA: 3434a; bottom left, Mont. Histl. Soc., Helena:955-778; Smithsonian, Dept. of Anthr.: bottom center, 154,329, neg. 41933-D; bottom right, 211312, neg. 79-5068;

Fig. 1. Euro-American influence. top, Ft. Parker, south of the Yellowstone River, near Livingston, Mont. It was the first Crow agency, built in 1869 as a result of the Ft. Laramie Treaty of 1868. The agency served as an administrative center from which annuity goods promised by the treaty could be distributed to the Crow. Photograph by William H. Jackson, 1871. bottom left, Crow children mounted on horseback. Horse gear includes beaded head mask, collar, saddle, saddle blanket, and crupper decorated with metal spoons. Photograph by Fred Miller, 1898–1910. bottom center, Brass trade kettle and beaded hide carrying cover. Height about 13 cm, collected by W.J. Hoffman, Crow Agency, Mont., 1892. bottom right, Seed bead sample card from a New York firm containing beads in nearly 30 colors and a range of sizes. These cards were sent to Indian traders, who ordered merchandise to suit the preferences of their local customers. Used at Ft. Keogh, Mont., by Rev. Lindesmith, who ordered beads for a cradleboard, 1882.

scouting, Plains warriors defended their territory against more powerful native groups, earned prestige by their exploits, and provided provisions and supplies to their relatives (Dunlay 1982; Fowler 1996).

In Montana, the Gros Ventre and Crow made alliances with the United States and each other to strengthen their resistance against the Sioux. Crow men also served as scouts for the army in campaigns against the Northern Cheyenne and Arapaho. The Blackfeet generally avoided conflict with the army, as well. Several bands withdrew north to Canada rather than come into conflict with Americans. Baker's Massacre, an army attack on a Southern Piegan camp in 1869, did not provoke a war (Wooster 1988; Ewers 1958:236–253). The Blackfeet realized they could not fight both the United States and their numerous Sioux enemies. In 1878, the Blackfeet bands, Gros Ventre, and westernmost Assiniboine bands agreed to settle on reservations in Montana (Blackfeet and Fort Belknap), north of the area being settled by Americans. The eastern Assiniboine, allied with Yanktonai bands and some Santee and Teton who would not join in fighting the army, obtained permission in 1872 for a reservation in Montana, Fort Peck.

On the Southern Plains, conditions worsened for the Cheyenne, Arapaho, Kiowa, Comanche, and Plains Apache in the 1870s because settlers continued to come into conflict with them and because the army pursued bands who left the reservations to hunt. Several clashes between the army and the southern tribes, particularly the Cheyenne, occurred in the late 1860s, until finally in 1869 by executive order a reservation south of the emigrant roads was established for the Southern Cheyenne and Arapaho on the North Canadian River. The Comanche and Kiowa continued to periodically leave their reservation near Fort Sill to hunt or raid. In the 1870s the army engaged Kiowa, Comanche, and Cheyenne in retaliation for raids against Americans. After several skirmishes during 1874–1875, known as the Red River War, all the bands surrendered and remained on the reservations (Chalfant 1997; Wooster 1988). Representatives of the United States sent several military leaders to prison, most to Fort Marion, Florida.

On the Northern Plains in the 1870s, trespassers in the area of the Black Hills, which, as a major buffalo ground, previously had been reserved by treaty to the Teton Sioux (and some absorbed Santee, Yanktonai, and Yankton) and Northern Cheyenne and Arapaho, provoked clashes that led to a major offensive against these tribes. Although allied tribes initially turned back troops (notably those under Gen. George Custer in 1876; see Hatch 1997), by 1878, after the army's winter campaigns destroyed their provisions, most of the hostile bands agreed to a peace and to reservation settlement. Although the Northern Cheyenne and Arapaho had agreed in the 1868 treaty to settle on the Great Sioux Reservation or in the Indian Territory, they preferred to remain in their own northern country. Arapaho and Cheyenne men scouted for the army and eventually were able to use these connections to help facilitate settlement on reservations in Wyoming and Montana. The Arapaho were moved to the Shoshone Reservation in 1878, where they eventually were allotted. In 1877 several bands of Northern Cheyenne arrived at the Cheyenne-Arapaho agency in Indian Territory but, unwilling to remain in the south, 300 fled the reservation in 1878. Eventually, after large casualties, they settled with other Northern Cheyenne in Montana. Bands of Cheyenne began settling at Fort Keogh in Montana in 1877; a reservation was created for them by executive order in 1884. Sioux bands gradually moved onto the Great Sioux Reservation until all but those who settled on Fort Peck Reservation and those who fled to Canada had taken up residence on the reservation. Demonstrating their "friendly" intent, Teton Sioux men served as scouts once their families settled on reservations; they helped the army subdue off-reservation Tetons. In 1881 Sitting Bull brought his followers back from Canada to the Great Sioux Reservation (vol. 4:179), where separate agencies had been created for the different Sioux divisions (Fowler 1982; Svingen 1993; DeMallie 1986; on the peace and war divisions among the Teton, see C. Price 1996).

The Reservation System and Assimilation Policy

In the post–Civil War years, federal officials attempted to confine their charges on reservations and force them to accept Euro-American lifeways. In reality, assimilation policy as it was put into practice, focused less on the belief that Indians could be transformed into mainstream Americans, and more on the idea that Indians were inherently inferior and peripheral to American society. The rising power of politicians from the western states helped mold the assimilation program into a means to escalate the opening up of more Indian land for the benefit of the majority society. After 1899, under the direction of Commissioners William Jones, Francis Leupp, Robert Valentine, and Cato Sells, the pace of allotment and land sales accelerated (vol. 4:68, 227, 683). Plains reservations bore the brunt of these developments. New rules for selling and leasing land facilitated non-Indian access to Indian land in order to foster regional economic growth. The new policies brought about the loss of a large portion of Indian-owned land (vol. 4:212, 225), and this left a legacy of inadequate resources for an agricultural economy and, in general, inadequate experience for economic development (Hoxie 1984:150–152, 158–159, 200, 235–237, 1996; Prucha 1984, 1:562–581, 589; Hagan 1993:134; P.H. Carlson 1998:175; Gibson 1980:409).

Forced Americanization

Federal officials insisted that male heads of households farm (even though on some reservations farming was impractical) (fig. 2) (vol. 4:51). For peoples with a horticultural tradition and land that could be successfully farmed, accommodation to the agents' demands was possible (for example, see F.T. Smith 1996 on the Wichita agency). On reservations on the Northern Plains, hay could be grown but livestock offered a better means of subsistence (see Samek 1987 on the Blackfeet agency). Until non-Indian stockmen objected to the competition, the raising of livestock was eagerly pursued on some reservations (see Fowler 1987 on the Fort Belknap Reservation). Reservation superintendents encouraged manual labor and discouraged group cooperative labor. They pressured allottees to live on their allotments, apart from extended family clusters or bands. Rations and other supplies were withheld from individuals whom the agent viewed as unwilling to work. Agency jobs—as herders, laborers, domestic workers, for example—provided wages for some, who were influenced to conform to agents' standards in order to retain these positions. Although the wages fell below what non-Indians received for the same work, these jobs helped offset the loss of rations, cut off for all but the elderly and infirm as early as 1875 on some reservations.

Plains peoples adopted various strategies to accommodate themselves to these developments, often finding ways to influence economic practices to make them more culturally acceptable. Among the Pawnee, Teton Sioux, and Cheyenne-Arapaho, opportunities to transport supplies provided income. For example, at the Cheyenne-Arapaho agency, the agent issued wagons to bands that formed freight trains headed by the band headman, and the bands hauled freight to the agency from depots. For several years, these bands maintained camp life and headmen continued to retain authority; at the same time, the agent could demonstrate that the Cheyenne-Arapaho were industrious workers. On many Plains reservations, band members took allotments in clusters; bands could farm cooperatively on large fields and the members share in the produce (P.H.

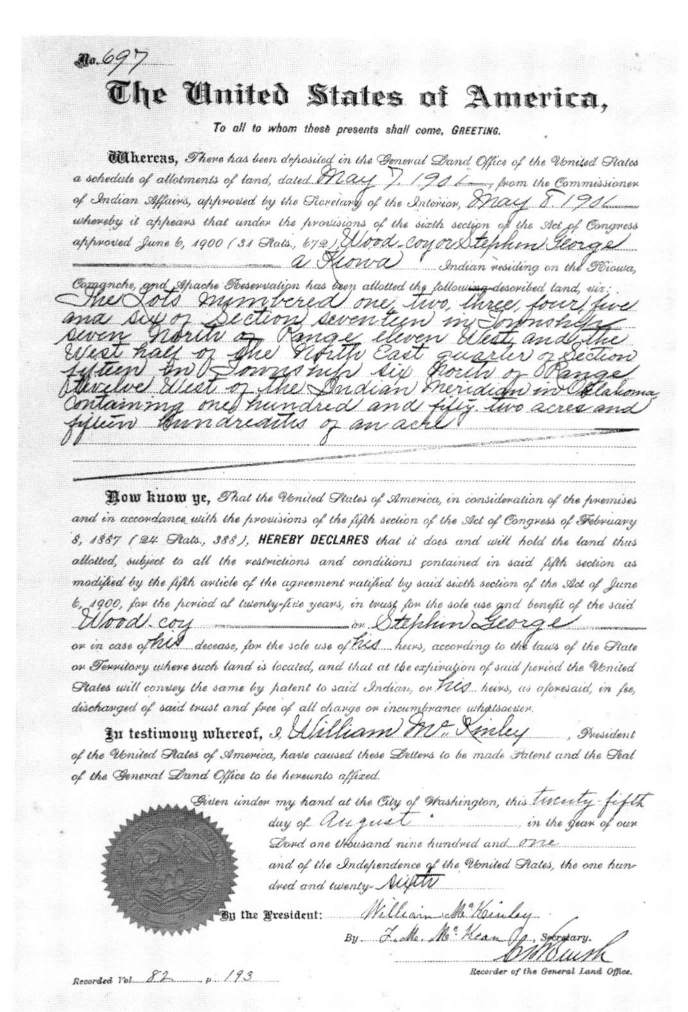

No. 697

The United States of America,

To all to whom these presents shall come, GREETING.

Whereas, There has been deposited in the General Land Office of the United States a schedule of allotments of land, dated May 7. 1901, from the Commissioner of Indian Affairs, approved by the Secretary of the Interior, May 8. 1901 whereby it appears that under the provisions of the sixth section of the Act of Congress approved June 6, 1900 (31 Stats., 672) Wood-coy or Stephen George a Kiowa Indian residing on the Kiowa, Comanche, and Apache Reservation has been allotted the following-described land, viz: The Lots numbered one, two, three, four, five and six of Section seventeen in Township seven North of Range eleven West and the West half of the North East quarter of Section fifteen in Township six North of Range twelve West of the Indian Meridian in Oklahoma containing one hundred and fifty two acres and fifteen hundredths of an acre

Now know ye, That the United States of America, in consideration of the premises and in accordance with the provisions of the fifth section of the Act of Congress of February 8, 1887 (24 Stats., 388), **HEREBY DECLARES** that it does and will hold the land thus allotted, subject to all the restrictions and conditions contained in said fifth section as modified by the fifth article of the agreement ratified by said sixth section of the Act of June 6, 1900, for the period of twenty-five years, in trust for the sole use and benefit of the said Wood-coy or Stephen George or in case of his decease, for the sole use of his heirs, according to the laws of the State or Territory where such land is located, and that at the expiration of said period the United States will convey the same by patent to said Indian, or his heirs, as aforesaid, in fee, discharged of said trust and free of all charge or incumbrance whatsoever.

In testimony whereof, I, William McKinley, President of the United States of America, have caused these Letters to be made Patent and the Seal of the General Land Office to be hereunto affixed.

Given under my hand at the City of Washington, this twenty-fifth day of August, in the year of our Lord one thousand nine hundred and one and of the Independence of the United States, the one hundred and twenty-sixth

By the President: William McKinley

By F. M. McKean Jr., Secretary.

[signature] Recorder of the General Land Office.

Recorded Vol. 82 p. 193

left, Vanessa P. Jennings, Ft. Cobb, Okla.; top right, Natl. Arch., Seattle Branch; inset, Smithsonian, Dept. of Anthr.: 431024, neg. 91-19245; bottom right, Mont. Histl. Soc., Helena.

Fig. 2. Allotments and farming. left, Allotment certificate issued to Wood-coy or Stephen George, Kiowa, on Aug. 25, 1901, for slightly more than 152 acres on the Kiowa, Comanche, and Apache Reservation, Okla. top right, Fish Guts, Assiniboine, at age 76, with some of the potatoes he raised on his allotment. Photographed at Ft. Belknap Res., Mont., 1925. inset, Top of a metal Indian land allotment stake from Ft. Berthold II, Garrison Reservoir, N. Dak. Taken from Like-a-Fishhook Village and transferred from the Missouri River Basin Survey, 1959. Length 91.5 cm. bottom right, Crow farmers from the Black Lodge district, Two Medicine Rocks, Mont.: Pretty Horse, Louise Bompard, and Top of the Moccasin sitting on the mower that cut the hay. The Bompard family farm was one of the most successful on the Crow reservation, whose crops, barn, and outbuildings were praised by the agent (Hoxie 1995:279–280). Photographed about 1910–1915.

Carlson 1998:172; Fowler 1982; Hoxie 1995:18, 272). Often, economic transformations took place in a context that made change culturally acceptable and, thereby, reaffirmed native values; for example, Crow leader Plenty Coups validated his people's transition to cattle ranching by a vision experience (Linderman 1962:64). Ultimately, though, the success or lack thereof of a transition to an economy based on agriculture rested less on cultural orientations and more on the kinds of resources available to Indians for the transition.

Federal agents also tried to encourage "thrift" by supervising the patterns of consumption of their charges. Even the reduction of rations was justified on the grounds that Indians would work and stop sharing with others or they would starve. In fact, malnutrition contributed to significant population loss during the late nineteenth and early twentieth centuries. Not only did the government require income from allotted land to be managed by the reservation superintendent, but also the superintendent could determine prices for leasing and sale of land (often determined below market value). In 1904 superintendents received authority to limit withdrawals from Individual Indian Money accounts to 10 dollars a month. Individuals who wished access to more than 10 dollars from their account had to obtain permission from the agent for a specific purchase (such as a plow or wagon). On many Plains reservations, individuals devised all sorts of schemes to convince the agent to release funds by requesting money for approved-of purchases, only to sell or mortgage the property or purchase something else. Often ceremonial duties intended to be screened from the superintendent's view were funded from these transactions. Although agents strove to discourage sharing among members of a community, these efforts failed. As large camps gave way to smaller, scattered households, people pooled food and supplies and continued to find ways to participate in gift exchange.

Federal agents also set out to undermine native leaders, in part to encourage individuals to separate themselves from the tribe. Although at first rations and supplies were issued to leaders who distributed the goods to followers, gradually the agents stripped leaders of these duties, which had helped them maintain authority. The agents began issuing supplies to heads of households rather than leaders, and whereas beef initially was issued "on the hoof" (vol. 4:262), agents began to issue it already butchered (on the block) (fig. 3) so that leaders would not be able to direct the distribution of the meat.

Congress authorized the organization of Indian Police in 1878 (fig. 4) (vol. 4:58). These men acted as couriers, butchers, census takers, laborers, scouts, and guards at the agency, and posses to turn back intruders or arrest horse thieves. The agents expected them to enforce assimilation policy, given expression in a series of regulations in the 1880s that prohibited various native activities. Police returned truants to government schools, helped to quash dances and curing ceremonies, reported cases of polygamy, gambling, and wearing traditional hair and clothing styles (see Hagan 1966). Violations of regulations could be punished by loss of rations and other supplies or by incarceration. On most reservations the agent appointed a Court of Indian Offenses, authorized by Congress in 1883, to enforce regulations. The activities of the Indian Police and the courts potentially worked to undercut the authority of chiefs and religious leaders. In 1885 Congress adopted the Major Crimes Act (23 U.S. Stat. 385), which gave states and territories jurisdiction over certain crimes in Indian communities; this action was intended to counter the Supreme Court decision *Ex Parte Crow Dog* in 1883 (109 U.S. 556; see Harring 1994) that held that the United States did not have criminal jurisdiction over sovereign Indian tribes. After Crow Dog shot Spotted Tail (both Teton Sioux), the Dakota territory courts convicted him of murder, and the case was appealed to the Supreme Court.

As time distanced federal officials from memories of the Indian wars, they were less willing to meet with and negotiate with tribal leaders; in fact, Congress's decision in 1871 to stop making treaties with tribes undermined the role of intermediary leaders or chiefs. Gradually, federal officials discouraged leaders from coming to Washington as delegates if they could not speak English, which worked to undermine the ability of many respected headmen to maintain the support of their peoples (P.H. Carlson 1998:165; Prucha 1984, 1:598, Hagan 1993).

Native leaders generally worked to reassure federal officials that they would cooperate with the Americanization program while, at the same time, trying to address the concerns of their people. Often on their own volition, native communities organized "Business Committees" to act for them. Such "elected" committees suggested a departure from traditional leadership but, in fact, chiefs often furnished the membership of the committees (for example, see Fowler 1982, 1987; Hoxie 1985, 1995) and religious leaders exerted great influence in the selection process (Fowler 1982). These business committees tried to pursue the agendas of native communities more often than those of non-Indians. Similarly, on some reservations, the Indian Police's loyalty to native leaders was stronger than to the agent (Fowler 1982; Svingen 1993:66). In some cases, however, federal officials imposed a political structure, usually to undermine a native leadership that resisted particular federal demands (see Bailey 1973:83 and T.P. Wilson 1985:30, 42, on the Osage case).

The agents worked diligently to stop native religious ceremonies in the late nineteenth century: in particular, the Sun Dance, the Ghost Dance, and Peyote ceremonies. They also tried to prohibit gatherings and gift exchange. Agents used agency employees or missionaries to learn about ceremonies held in secret, and transgressions were punished by the withholding of rations. Sun Dance ceremonies often did take place in secret or, particularly during the twentieth century, were presented to the agent as harmless social or patriotic events, their religious purpose being de-emphasized or disguised (for example, by being renamed "Willow Dance" among Arapahos and Cheyennes).

New religions emerged and helped Plains peoples cope with their changing world, often in ways that escaped the repression directed by agents. The Grass Dance spread from Poncas, Omahas, and Pawnees west, particularly to Teton Sioux groups, who passed it on to other Plains tribes in the late nineteenth century. These ceremonies could be represented as harmless social dances, but they served to restore community solidarity and provide an outlet for individual ambitions (see Fowler 1987). The Ghost Dance spread across the Plains in the 1890s (Mooney 1896). Initially federal officials perceived it as a threat, particularly because it took on a militant cast among some Teton Sioux (Utley 1963), but it was reoriented in many communities as the Ghost Dance Hand Game, in which form it thrived well into the twentieth century (see Lesser 1978).

The Peyote religion—which helped individuals adjust to the disappointments and transformations in their social world without rejecting native religious ideas—spread northward to Nebraska, Montana, Wyoming, and South Dakota from the Southern Plains; local variations developed (see O.C. Stewart 1987). In 1908 Quanah Parker, a Comanche chief, lobbied the Oklahoma legislature to repeal a 1898 statute banning peyote (fig. 5), and in 1911 the Native American Church received a state charter (P.H.

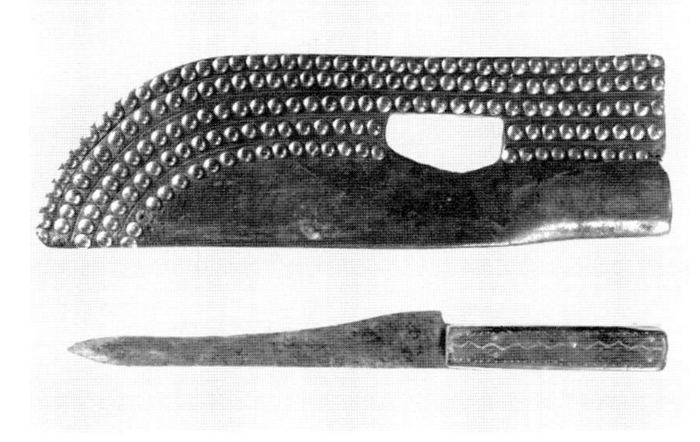

(5-160.) Beef.

Weekly Rations.

3 Qr, 1904

Band ...

Family No. 16

Men ---- 1

Women -- 1

Boys ----

Girls ----

Total -- 2

Or.............. Rations.

Name of Family: ...

top, Mus. of N. Mex., Santa Fe:14283; center left, Joe Swallwell, Topeka, Kans.; center right, Smithsonian, Dept. of Anthr.: 385,908, neg. MNH-1566; bottom left, State Histl. Soc. of N. Dak., Bismarck:SHSND 603.L; Denver Public Lib., Western Hist. Dept., Colo.: F8839.

Fig. 3. Subsistence through rations. top, Arapahos receiving rations at Camp Supply, Indian Terr. Established in 1868 by the U.S. Army and renamed Fort Supply in 1878, it was a military post until 1894, when it was turned over to the Interior Dept. Photograph by Jos. Hitchins, 1869. center left, Comanches butchering meat. On the reservation cattle were killed by agency employees, and the carcasses issued to families. The animal was placed on a layer of brush, skinned, eviscerated, and quartered, primarily by women. The sinew along the spine was saved for sewing. Dogs ate the remains. Photograph by W.J. Lenny and Sawyers, 1890s. center right, Knife and sheath, Comanche. This Green River knife with heavily worn blade and incised handle was manufactured by J. Russell and Company, perhaps as early as the 1840s (J.A. Hanson 1975:51). The sheath of commercial leather adorned with brass upholstery tacks dates to the reservation era. Both were given to Maj. James D. Glennan on Christmas, 1894, by White Wolf, a Comanche leader, who said that he had used the knife for many years. Length of sheath, 36 cm. bottom left, Ration card for the family of Sioux Woman, a Hidatsa, to receive beef at Independence, Ft. Berthold Res., N. Dak. bottom right, Rations distribution to the Teton Sioux at Pine Ridge Agency, S. Dak. Photograph by Clarence Grant Morledge, 1891.

Carlson 1998:169). Similar developments occurred in other states.

Missionaries learned native languages, introduced orthographies for them, and initiated newspapers and other publications in native languages, particularly in Sioux communities (vol. 17:451). As Indians became lay leaders in Christian congregations, they indigenized Christianity (fig. 6). In general, native peoples of the Plains drew on all these religious traditions, often at the same time, to try to cope with their circumstances (DeMallie and Parks 1987).

top, U. of Wyo., Amer. Heritage Center, Laramie; center, State Histl. Soc. of N. Dak., Bismarck: 239-15.

Fig. 4. Indian police and veterans. top, Crow tribal police. standing, Big Medicine; on horseback, from left, White Arm and Bear Claw; other 4 unidentified. Photograph by Richard Throssel, Crow Res., Mont., 1905–1911. center, Three Affiliated Tribes veterans of World War I at Elbowoods American Legion Post #253, Joseph Younghawk Post, N. Dak. left to right, Martin Levings, Daniel Hopkins, John Bearstail, Ernest Fox, Charles Grady (with U.S. flag), John Smith, Mark Necklace, Joe Wheeler (with American Legion flag), David Packineau, Frank Birdsbill, Charley Fox, and William Deane. Photographed about 1935–1938. bottom, Comanche Vietnam veterans. Members of a contemporary warrior society, they participate as color guards for special occasions. left to right, back row: Charles Kerchee, Ernest Tate, James Garrett, and Mike Blackstar; front row: James Johnson, Melvin Kerchee, and Fred J. Allison. Photograph by Lynn Ivory, Red Earth Powwow, Okla. City, June 1996.

New kinds of gatherings appeared in the twentieth century (fig. 7), which also helped perpetuate native values and create social bonds within and between native communities. The Crow Fair ("Crow," fig. 10, this vol.), Hays Fair (Ft. Belknap) (Fowler 1987), and Anadarko Fair (Kiowa and Comanche) all worked to address local stereotypes, bring income into the community, symbolize community identity, and create new avenues for leadership in the twentieth century. Among many tribes, sodalities evolved into social clubs with new functions.

Education was central to assimilation policy (fig. 8). Carlisle Indian School, operated by Capt. Richard Pratt, which opened in 1879 in Pennsylvania, served as a model for Indian education. Haskell in Lawrence, Kansas; Chilocco in Newkirk, Indian Territory; Hampton in Virginia; and Rapid City, South Dakota, boarding schools accepted students from Plains communities and others in the 1880s. The schools emphasized vocational rather than academic training, so that students were prepared mainly for trades. Government and mission (at first, subsidized by the government) boarding schools, and also day schools in local communities advanced a curriculum that, in addition to teaching trades, farming, and domestic work, demeaned native institutions. Children typically spent half the day working in the school fields, kitchen, laundry, or doing other chores. The children were kept away from their communities as much as possible and punished for speaking their native language. Upon entering school, children commonly received an English name, including the surname of their fathers. (Fathers received an English given name and surname when they were put on the allotment or census rolls.) On some reservations, where denominations competed with each other for students and with the government school, community leaders frequently tried to play them off against each other to mitigate the repressive elements of the educational program or obtain resources. Plains headmen often sent their children to boarding schools, along with orphans, to demonstrate their friendship and loyalty to the United States. Children returned home, sometimes with skills such as literacy that were used to help older leaders pursue tribal goals, and sometimes with

top, Minn. Histl. Soc., St. Paul: E99.4/p02; bottom, Ft. Sill Mus., Ft. Sill, Okla.: P1350.

Fig. 5. Challenges to government administration. top, Crow Indian prisoners captured and chained for participation in Sword Bearer's disturbance. When young men led by Sword Bearer celebrated a successful horsestealing raid against the Piegan by riding into the agency compound and firing guns in the air, the military at nearby Ft. Custer demanded Sword Bearer's surrender. In the ensuing skirmish, Sword Bearer was shot and killed by the Crow Indian Police. The other young men who had taken part in the gun play surrendered. Deaf Bull, second from left, is one of the leaders who had urged them to resist federal authorities. They were all sent to prison at Ft. Snelling, Minn. (Hoxie 1995:154–164). Photographed on the Crow Reservation shortly after the death of Sword Bearer on November 5, 1887. bottom, Southern Plains Peyotists, lead by Quanah Parker, and the medical committee who met before the Oklahoma Constitutional Convention to debate the legality of peyote in Oklahoma. The Peyotists are left to right, front row: Tennyson Berry, Plains Apache; Codsy, Kiowa; Apache John, Plains Apache; Otto Wells, Comanche; Quanah Parker, Comanche; Apeatone, Kiowa; Little Bird, Cheyenne; and Young Calf, Cheyenne. second row: Ned Brace, Kiowa; far right, Joseph Blackbear, Cheyenne, and Leonard Tyler, Cheyenne. The others are not identified. Photographed in 1907.

vocational skills that they could not use in their home communities. Sometimes, returned students found it difficult to reenter community life. Some children ran away from boarding schools; others formed friendships with children from other tribes at the off-reservation boarding schools and these associations formed the basis for

Fig. 6. St. Stephen's Indian Mission 100th anniversary, Aug. 1984. Northern Arapahoe tribal elders, William Samuel C'Hair, Sr., far left, and Ernest Sun Rhodes, Sr., far right, hold up burning cedar as a cleansing offering during a mass of celebration. Father Joseph Damhorst, S.J., of St. Stephen's, Father Provincial David Fleming, S.J., of St. Louis, and Father John Padberg, S.J., offer the sacrament. Photograph by Dianna Troyer, Wind River Res., Wyo.

cultural borrowings and political alliances. Even in the early twentieth century, reservation schools rarely went beyond the sixth grade (Hagan 1993:152–154; Riney 1999; Lomawaima 1994; C. Ellis 1996).

Land Policies and their Social Consequences

The federal government continued to press Plains peoples for land cessions after their settlement on reservations in the late 1870s. In the 1880s cessions were secured in Montana from the Blackfeet; the Gros Ventre and Assiniboine on Fort Belknap Reservation; the Crow; and the Assiniboine, Yanktonai, and Santee at Fort Peck; in the 1890s, from Crow, Yankton, Blackfeet, and others. Major land cessions also occurred in the first part of the twentieth century, including those at the Rosebud (1904), Crow (1905), Wind River (1905), Yankton (1929), Standing Rock (1908), and Cheyenne River (1908) reservations (vol. 4:215–216) (Hoxie 1984:152–165). The Northern Cheyenne were unusual in obtaining an increase in the size of their reservation in 1900 (Svingen 1993:151) and the Osage in mineral rights (T.P. Wilson 1985).

Despite protests by native peoples—for example, an intertribal council in Indian Territory and lobbying in Washington by prominent Plains leaders, such as Sitting Bull and Lone Wolf (who appealed to the Supreme Court)—and the efforts of other opponents, including anthropologist James Mooney, the Dawes Severalty Act (24 U.S. Stat. 338) passed in 1887 (P.H. Carlson 1998:177; A.M. Gibson 1980:496). This act provided that individuals would receive allotments (usually of 160 acres), the title to which would remain inalienable for 25 years and that reservation lands remaining after individuals received their allotments could be sold and, in this way, more

State Histl. Soc. of N. Dak., Bismarck:C21.

Fig. 7. Three Affiliated Tribes team from Elbowoods, Ft. Berthold Res., N. Dak. Baseball created social bonds within the community and was an outlet for competition between communities. left to right, front row: Frank Birdsbill, Hidatsa, and Joseph Young Hawk, Arikara; center row: Burton B. Bell, Arikara; Claire Everett, Arikara; Arthur Old Mouse, Mandan; Joseph Packineau, Hidatsa; back row: John Two Crow, Hidatsa; Earl Bateman, Arikara; Albert Simpson, Arikara; Charles Goodbird, Mandan; Reuben Duckett, Arikara. Photograph by Fred Olson, Elbowoods Fairgrounds, 1911–1917.

Indian land become available to non-Indians. Other legislation worked to force Indians into leasing their land for less than market value and selling their allotments. In 1891 Congress passed a statute that permitted tribal leaders and individuals to lease land to non-Indians. After 1902, as allottees died the government encouraged their heirs to sell the inherited land by the Dead Indian Land Act. The Burke Act of 1906 gave the secretary of the interior the power to allow certain allottees deemed "competent" by their agent to receive a fee patent, which permitted them to sell their land and made the land taxable. In 1907 Congress gave the commissioner of Indian affairs the power to authorize the sale of allotments of "noncompetent" Indians who were unable to "develop" their allotments (Hoxie 1984:165–166). Patents were issued indiscriminantly, without Indian consent, and lands sold far below their market value. Indians went into debt for purchases or illegal local taxes on trust property, and this situation encouraged them to sell land.

Commissioner of Indian Affairs Robert Valentine (1909–1912) established competency commissions to speed up the issue of fee patents to allottees, whether they consented or not. Allottees were expected to sell what they could not cultivate. The Omnibus Act of 1910 also allowed for competent Indians to receive their portion of tribal monies held in the treasury. Under Commissioner Cato Sells (1913–1921), federal "competency commissions" ordered the issue of fee patents to Indians of less than one-half Indian blood or to "educated" Indians (arbitrarily defined), despite the protests of the recipients, who would then be liable for state and local taxes on the lands. Again, allottees were forced into selling land.

As allotments were inherited, increasingly large numbers of heirs owned shares in the allotments, which made it difficult for the land to be farmed or otherwise used by Indians. Instead, the fractionated allotments were sold or leased to non-Indians and the money divided among the heirs. Even single owners found it difficult to acquire enough capital to make their land productive; they too leased land in increasing numbers. The federal government actively encouraged leasing to non-Indians, who often were charged less than market value or were allowed to renege on payments.

Allotments were protested by Plains leaders, including Sitting Bull and Lone Wolf. In 1902 the Supreme Court (*Lone Wolf* v. *Hitchcock*; see B. Clark 1994) ruled that Congress could overturn treaties through the doctrine of plenary power. Lands were increasingly withdrawn from Indian control by the government's preference for leasing to commercial interests and by the inclusion of tribal lands in federal conservation and irrigation projects despite the protests of the tribes. American sugar beet companies were encouraged with long-term leases; Indians were to labor in the fields for low wages. In 1908 Congress authorized Commissioner Francis Leupp to negotiate long-term agricultural leases for Fort Belknap and Wind River reservations. Irrigation projects, appealing to Western interests, were also implemented on reservations (fig. 9) (as on Blackfeet in 1906 and Wind River in 1905), and Congress could use money derived from the sale of surplus lands for these irrigation systems. Allottees had to demonstrate that they were using the water in order to have access; without the means to farm they were pressured to sell or lease their land. Despite the guarantee of water rights in 1908 (*Winters* v. *United States*) lands on Fort Berthold were flooded by the construction of the Garrison Dam; water control projects disrupted the economies and social life of other native communities (see Lawson 1982). In the second decade of the century, leasing Indian lands for mineral exploitation (often below market value) was a major interest of the government (Hoxie 1984:167–171; T.P. Wilson 1985). In some cases—for example, Northern Arapahoe and Osage—mineral leases generated income for all tribal members, for the mineral rights were held by the tribal members in common. Elsewhere, wealth differentials followed mineral development.

Although Congress made Indians citizens in 1924 (vol. 4:232–233) (in large part in response to pressure from groups sympathetic to the contributions of Native Americans in World War I), the federal government subsequently continued to act as trustee and to exercise control over Indian land and income from that land. Indians were "protected" from exploitation by limitations on their freedoms, on the one hand, and their resources were transferred to non-Indians considered more qualified to use them, on the other.

The effect of these new policies on Indian communities varied. Reservations not very desirable for farming and

Smithsonian, NAA: Photo Lot 81-12, top left, neg. 1043; top center, neg. 848; bottom left and right, Eastern Wash. State Histl. Soc., Cheney Cowles Mus., Spokane.

Fig. 8. Schools and pupils. top left, Rosy White Thunder, Brule Sioux, as she entered Carlisle Industrial School, Pa., Nov. 1883 (see vol. 4:399); and top center, 6 months later. She left Carlisle in June 1887. top left, Photograph by John A. Choate. top right, Jacket of Ft. Berthold Community College, New Town, N. Dak. Founded in 1973 the college is run by the Three Affiliated Tribes for the purposes of training tribal members and retaining tribal culture. Courses include the teaching of Mandan, Arikara, and Hidatsa languages. Accredited since 1988, it is one of 29 tribal colleges granted 1994 land-grant institution status. Photograph by Ilka Hartmann, Ft. Berthold powwow, 1989. bottom left, Baking bread at Willow Creek School, Blackfeet Res., Mont. Photograph by J.H. Sherburne, about 1907. bottom right, Pawnee Training School, Okla. Maintaining the school buildings was part of the vocational education. Photographed about 1898–1910.

those coveted by cattlemen generally were allotted later than others (Hagan 1976). Allotment was disastrous for the Cheyenne and Arapaho in western Oklahoma. After allotment in 1892 the Cheyenne-Arapaho reservation was opened to settlement. Non-Indians then outnumbered Indians nine to one. The non-Indian neighbors systematically defrauded the Cheyenne and Arapaho of their property, as well as their land. The money from the sale of the tribes' surplus land was paid per capita and tribal members bought agricultural equipment and stock, much of which was stolen by non-Indians or mortgaged to creditors who foreclosed, even though it was illegal to purchase property bought with trust funds. Property was mortgaged for less than its value, so merchants profited greatly from foreclosure. Local officials collected taxes on personal property that was in trust status, though this was also illegal. When Cheyennes and Arapahos leased land, they often were not paid full value. Legal representatives of the federal government did not defend Indian interests, and local courts discriminated against Indians (Berthrong 1976). The Dead Indian Land Act freed allotments of deceased Indians from trust status and heirs were encouraged to sell. The agent allowed land to be sold for less than market value; merchants inflated prices so that Indians actually received little benefit from the sale of land (Berthrong 1985). Land sales took on momentum with the passage of the Burke Act; when Indians received a fee patent, their land was taxed, which resulted in the loss of land to non-Indians when the Indian owner was unable to pay the tax. In 1917 the commissioner of Indian affairs, through the competency

Smithsonian, NAA:56813.

Fig. 9. Irrigation project. Four Eagles, Sioux, and Bad Hawk, Assiniboine, excavating Poplar River East Canal "C" on the Ft. Peck Res., Mont. In the period 1910–1911 approximately 7,500 acres were supplied with ditches for irrigation. Photograph by Harry T. Cory, 1913.

commission, classified many Cheyennes and Arapahos as competent, despite their lack of much formal education, and they received fee patents. Local businessmen loaned poverty-stricken Indians money on the partial value of the land, then foreclosed. By 1928, 63 percent of the land had been sold (Berthrong 1976).

In Oklahoma, the competency commissions were very active. The Osage sold 70 percent of their land; other tribes sold almost as much. On the Northern Plains, the competency commissions were most active in the Dakotas. The Sioux sold up to 40 percent of their land. Some reservations (for example, Northern Cheyenne and Fort Belknap) retained most of their lands (G.D. Taylor 1980).

The new land policies had important social consequences. On the Sioux reservations in the Dakotas, the sale of land set the stage for subsequent conflict between landless mixed bloods and the full bloods who retained their allotments (G.D. Taylor 1980). At Lower Brule reservation, the Brule began collecting at ecologically favored areas and reviving collective ceremonies; the settlement pattern became more compact. Six native "towns" were established (Schusky 1975:159–161).

Among the Cheyenne and Arapaho, over time, land ownership was concentrated in the hands of the elderly. Only those born before 1893 were allotted. Between 1917 and 1922, 58 percent of the Arapaho in their thirties and forties had land; 100 percent of the elderly did. Among the population under the age of 21, 53 percent were landless. Elderly Cheyennes and Arapahos provided the major, most stable part of family income because there was a lack of regular employment for younger people. Their economic position gave the elderly considerable influence within the household. But the loss of the land base, the main source of income, contributed to the gradual undermining of the authority of Arapaho chiefs. Land loss led to a gradual outmigration to larger towns in Oklahoma, and attendance at tribal religious ceremonies declined. The result was the decline of the authority of leaders of Arapaho religious rituals (Fowler 1990:162–164).

Among the Comanche, after the allotment of land and the settlement of homesteaders on the "surplus" land, non-Indians outnumbered the Indians 33 to one. As the Comanche lost their land, they settled in multifamily households or "bunches." These communities held their own gatherings, rather than attending tribal ceremonies, since transportation was difficult because of fences and roads. Churches built in these communities were led by non-Indian pastors but had Comanche members, usually young people. Local missionaries were employed as farmers and matrons, individuals who controlled funds and could give recommendations for aid of various kinds. Landless young Comanches began to participate in church activities in large part to have access to the resources controlled by these non-Indians. The result was the division of the Comanche into a Peyote faction of older people and a church faction of younger people (Foster 1991:116–123). The heirship policy put in place by the federal government made it possible for women to inherit from their husbands, hitherto unlikely. Among the Gros Ventre this resulted in new ritual roles for women (Flannery 1947).

The social and economic problems that stemmed from allotment were a major focus of a congressional investigation in 1928 (Meriam 1928). The publicity from this and the activities of various reform groups, such as the Indian Defense Association, laid the groundwork for the Indian New Deal, a reversal of the policy of assimilation.

The Indian New Deal

With the election of Franklin D. Roosevelt to the presidency, the Bureau of Indian Affairs (BIA) made an unprecedented effort to provide tribes with a degree of political autonomy and assistance in economic development. Spearheaded by Commissioner of Indian Affairs John Collier, the Indian Reorganization Act (IRA) was passed in 1934. The act ended allotment, allowed for the restoration of surplus reservation lands to tribal ownership and for the purchase of land to augment tribal holdings, and set up credit programs for individuals and tribal corporations. The act also provided for the establishment of tribal governments empowered to prevent the sale or lease of tribal land, employ legal counsel, and preserve cultural institutions. An educational loan fund was established and new criteria for employment in the Bureau were adopted that made it easier for Indians to be employed. The bill, as amended in 1935, required a simple majority vote of those tribal members voting in order for reorganization to go into effect. Bureau staff prepared a model constitution and worked with tribal leaders to tailor it to local needs. A tribe could qualify for loans after its members ratified a corporate charter (G.D. Taylor 1980; Philp 1977).

On the Plains the tribal governments established under the act were reservation-wide, even where there was more than one tribe on the reservation. In Montana, Wyoming, North Dakota, and South Dakota, 11 reservations accepted and seven rejected the Indian Reorganization Act. Several of the reservations that rejected the act subsequently enacted constitutional governments modeled after the IRA governments. The Crow and Northern Arapahoe retained a form of government in which tribal members at large had important decision-making powers in general councils. Oklahoma Indians were excluded from the Indian Reorganization Act, but in 1936 the similar Oklahoma Indian Welfare Act was passed by Congress, and six Plains tribes elected to be "reorganized" under its provisions; nine did not, in general retaining some form of chieftainship. Tribal councils or business committees were widespread on the Plains before the IRA, some elected, some chosen by elders, and some selected by the local BIA representative. In Oklahoma, chieftainship was more common; some chiefs' councils were elected and some hereditary. In general, the groups that accepted this legislation saw it as a chance to improve rather desperate economic circumstances.

The reasons for rejection of the legislation varied from tribe to tribe. The Northern Arapahoe and the affiliated Kiowa, Comanche, and Plains Apache felt frustrated by the federal government's refusal to distribute tribal funds in per capita payments (Fowler 1982; Foster 1991). Mistrust of the government undermined Collier's efforts with these peoples.

The consequences of the Indian New Deal have been a subject of some controversy, some scholars arguing that the proposed reforms eventually failed and even exacerbated problems on some reservations. On the other hand, the legislation set in motion a host of changes that eventually helped transform federal-Indian relations.

One of the first things that Collier did was to obtain emergency relief funds to establish the Indian Emergency Conservation Works program, which provided jobs for Indians in their own communities. He also convinced other agencies to fund Indian projects. The Depression did not affect Indians so harshly as it did other Americans. Few Plains Indians were involved in the commercial economy. However, agricultural prices collapsed and lands deteriorated due to droughts and other ecological problems, all of which made the lands less valuable to lessees and resulted in reduced incomes for allottees. Therefore, Indians were very interested in the proposed loan programs, as well as the wage work opportunities.

In the short term, several Plains reservations benefited greatly from the funding of projects to build roads, dams, wells, fences, fire breaks, and community halls, and to start canning projects and communal gardens. The BIA promoted cooperatives using the revolving credit fund, especially livestock cooperatives. At Northern Cheyenne Reservation a tribal cattle herd was established in 1937 with the largest single loan from the revolving credit fund. Livestock cooperatives managed the herd and the tribal corporation marketed it (G.D. Taylor 1980). A tribally owned cattle ranch was established for the Northern Arapahoe on the Wind River Reservation, partly with rehabilitation funds (Fowler 1982). Most loans went to individuals, however; over 50 percent were for less than $1,000. As of 1945 less than one percent of the loans were in default and 95 percent had been repaid (G.D. Taylor 1980:110). On the Plains, most loans were to purchase livestock. On the Yankton (Hoover 1988), Pine Ridge, and Rosebud reservations several communities were established for landless families; funds were provided for livestock, irrigated gardens, and housing (Biolsi 1992). The trust status of Indian lands was extended indefinitely. The Blackfeet, Cheyenne River Sioux, and others borrowed money to buy land. While some tribes increased their land holdings, the amount of land returned to Indian ownership was smaller than originally planned and the heirship problem was not effectively addressed.

Shortly after the implementation of the IRA tribal governments, disillusionment set in. When Collier met with representatives of the Northern Plains tribes in Rapid City, South Dakota, in March 1934 (fig. 10), he stressed the powers tribal governments would have over tribal funds, reservation budgets, and hiring of BIA employees. Later Congress eliminated many of these powers. In actuality, tribal wishes were usually ignored (G.D. Taylor 1980). On several occasions, the BIA rejected constitutions that tribal representatives had prepared because they deviated from the model constitution. The Pawnee, however, established a chiefs' council as one of two governing bodies. The eight elected Pawnee chiefs could not be members of the eight-member business council. Only chiefs, with inherited rights of chieftainship, were eligible, and they had the right of review of business council actions concerned with tribal membership and treaty claims (Lesser 1978:xii). Once a tribe had accepted the Indian Reorganization Act they could not rescind their action. Moreover, adding to the disillusionment of the IRA tribes, Congress did not fully fund programs. The land purchase program was deliberately underfunded because it alarmed Congressmen from the western states. After 1940, no new projects were begun, for the war occupied the attention of the government. Under pressure, Collier resigned in 1945.

The new tribal governments had limited constitutional powers. They could negotiate with federal, state, and local governments; review federal appropriation requests; regulate the domestic relations of tribal members; cultivate native arts and crafts; and employ legal counsel. However, the choice of counsel and the counsel fees were subject to review by the secretary of the interior. In fact, all other "powers" were subject to the secretary's approval: civil and criminal codes, levying taxes on tribal members and nonmembers, issuance of permits for hunting and fishing, appropriation of tribal funds not under the control of

top, Mont. Histl. Soc., Helena: 900–905; bottom, Ft. Belknap College, Harlem, Mont.

Fig. 10. Indian organizations. top, Delegates to the Indian Protective Association, Helena, Mont., Nov. 2–3, 1925. The group discussed the failure of U.S. Indian policies and the Bureau of Indian Affairs and sent a letter to President Calvin Coolidge demanding the removal of Commissioner of Indian Affairs Charles H. Burke. 1, Wolf Plume, Blackfeet; 2, A.A. Grorud, attorney; 3, Sadie King Travies; 4, Joshua Wetsit, Assiniboine, Ft. Peck; 5, Frank Kirkpatrick; 6, Ida Henry, stenographer and reporter; 7, Albert Lemery, adopted into the Flathead; 8, Russell White Bear, Crow; 9, Rides at the Door, Blackfeet; 10, Jim White Calf, Blackfeet; 11, Robert J. Hamilton, Blackfeet; 12, Jim Denny, Blackfeet, Plains Cree, and French from Rocky Boy's; 13, Thomas Burland, Flathead; 14, Caville Dupuis, Flathead; 15, Day Child, Chippewa or Plains Cree from Rocky Boy's; 16, Joseph Spanish, Blackfeet; 17, Peter Kennewash, Chippewa or Plains Cree from Rocky Boy's. Photograph by Art-Kraft Studio, Helena. bottom, Gros Ventre and Assiniboine delegation from Ft. Belknap Res., Mont., to the Congress of Plains Indians, Rapid City, S. Dak., March 1934. left to right, standing: John Buckman, Gros Ventre; James Kirkaldie, Assiniboine; Frank Ohlerking, Assiniboine; William Bigby, Assiniboine; Commissioner John Collier; Charlie Bear, Assiniboine; August Moccasin, Assiniboine; Clarence Brockie, Gros Ventre; William Crasco, Assiniboine. seated or kneeling: George Cochran, Gros Ventre; Tom Main, Gros Ventre; Victor Brockie, Gros Ventre; The Boy, Gros Ventre; Richard King, Assiniboine; Rex Flying, Assiniboine; Talks Different, Assiniboine. At this meeting Collier first presented the ideas for the Indian Reorganization Act. The Gros Ventre and Assiniboine were the first Plains tribes to accept the Act although they mistakenly believed that they were going to be allowed to organize as separate tribes. Photograph by Carl H. Rise.

Congress, revision of tribal membership rolls, electoral procedures, and land transactions—in short, "all the powers that could have consequence in the regulation of the economic and political affairs of the tribes" (G.D. Taylor 1980:103). Constituents understood that their council could not act independently, and this hurt the credibility of the councils, particularly when the councils were unable to accomplish the goals of the constituents (Fowler 1987). This situation encouraged a resignation to political and economic dependence on the federal government (see Biolsi 1992).

A consequence of reorganization probably not anticipated by Collier was that factionalism was exacerbated, if not instigated, by the introduction of the new councils. On the Pine Ridge and Rosebud reservations, a conflict between mixed bloods and full bloods (cultural, not biological categories) carried over into a new arena. Two rival councils eventually formed, although each had its full blood and mixed blood supporters. The Treaty Council continued to operate the way earlier councils had—by the "three-fourths rule." The concept of three-fourths rule was based on an "indigenous Lakota reading of treaty law," which had become accepted by the Teton Sioux as the traditional method of tribal decision making. Councilmen selected as delegates expressed the wishes of people of their districts; they did not act as representatives empowered to make decisions for their constituents (Biolsi 1992:34, 45–46). On the Blackfeet Reservation, the IRA constitution allowed the council to distribute royalties from the tribe's oil lease money. A full blood minority came into conflict with the council, which was dominated by mixed bloods who wanted to use the money for economic development projects that would favor mixed bloods rather than for per capita payments. At Northern Cheyenne Reservation, full bloods used the reorganization of tribal government to displace mixed bloods from the business council (G.D. Taylor 1980). On several Sioux reservations Indians who still had their allotments resented landless Indians who shared in IRA benefits.

IRA constitutions varied but generally all had provisions for recall and referendum, electoral districting, and decision making by majority vote. Recall petitions and elections eventually came to be used so frequently on some reservations that the ability of the tribal government to conduct business was undermined and the costs of holding the recall elections siphoned money from other projects. Because these tribal councils had a role in managing reservation resources they were open to charges of corruption and favoritism, a situation exacerbated by scarce resources generally and by the fact that the constitutions lacked provisions for checks and balances on the business council. The secretary of the interior or his representatives could intervene on behalf of constituents (although they seldom did) but these constitutions contained no bill of rights or any way to protect civil liberties or deal effectively with misconduct of tribal officials, and the tribal courts did not have the power to test the constitutionality of council actions (see Biolsi 1992:104; Farber 1970).

With few exceptions (for example, the Pawnee), the reorganized governments allowed women to vote and hold office. However, it was not until the 1960s, and later on some reservations, that women began to be elected in any significant numbers.

Despite the problems and disappointments that followed implementation of the IRA, Collier's reforms set in motion a new set of expectations among tribal leaders and provided them with experience in administering credit and other programs (Deloria and Lytle 1984). Those tribes that rejected the IRA continued to receive economic aid, and the BIA accepted the legitimacy of their tribal governments. Collier's efforts established a new political, economic, and social status for "tribes" in the United States (Washburn 1984). The New Deal stimulated a pan-Indian political movement, with considerable participation from Plains leaders, a by-product of the idea of Indian self-determination instigated by Collier's reforms (G.D. Taylor 1980).

Collier also directed that Indian religion and ceremonial life not be interfered with, and he attempted to phase out boarding schools and replace them with day schools and, with passage of the Johnson-O'Malley Act in 1934, to make public schools more responsive to the needs of Indian students. The acceptance of Indian culture promulgated by Collier had repercussions for ritual life and for the arts. In 1935 the Indian Arts and Crafts Board was established to encourage the arts and expand the market for the sale of Indian art. Funds were provided for arts and crafts clubs and cooperatives. On the Yankton Reservation a star quilt business was established (Hoover 1988:61). The Museum of the Plains Indian, on the Blackfeet Reservation, Browning, Montana, was established through the Public Works Administration in 1941. A craft shop and Sioux Indian Museum in Rapid City, an arts and crafts center at Fort Sill Indian School in Oklahoma, and the Southern Plains Indian Museum in Anadarko, Oklahoma, were established (Schrader 1983). On the Crow Reservation, Robert Yellowtail, a Crow Indian and the new superintendent of the agency, helped introduce the Shoshone Sun Dance, which became institutionalized, and otherwise assisted Crow ritual life (Voget 1984). On the other hand, on the Fort Belknap Reservation the BIA representative pressured the business council to take over the sponsorship of tribal ceremonies that had been organized by ceremonial moieties; this was an important factor in the declining participation in these rituals (Fowler 1987).

World War II and the Relocation Program

The entry of the United States into World War II in December 1941 set in motion a series of social changes in Plains Indian communities. The participation of communities and individuals in the war effort eroded the BIA's exclusive control over tribes. Collier was unsuccessful in promoting an All-Indian division administered by the BIA or in administering the draft in Indian communities. Indian servicemen and women were integrated into White units. Military pay and benefits raised the living standards of dependents. Pro-Nazi agitators' efforts to encourage draft resistance among Native Americans, which focused on Plains Indians, were unsuccessful. The percentage of Indian men in the military ranged from 33 to 70 percent in Plains communities. Among Plains tribes, volunteers exceeded draftees by a two to one margin. The army recruited Comanches for Signal Corps work because their language was regarded as difficult to decode. Plains Indians also worked in defense plants and the airplane industries in Los Angeles, Denver, Albuquerque, Tulsa, and Oklahoma City (Bernstein 1991:22–26, 38–46).

Many veterans (fig. 4) returned to their home communities determined to obtain equal rights at the state level. Veterans and other activists sought eligibility for social security and access to state relief funds, an end to the prohibition of the sale of liquor to Indians, and rights to the same benefits non-Indian veterans obtained. Their efforts dovetailed with a shift in Congress away from support of Collier's programs toward assimilation. The National Congress of American Indians was established in 1944 (vol. 4:312); its members, a large portion of whom were Plains Indians who had participated in the war effort and IRA programs, joined in the struggle to attain both civil and tribal rights. Indian leaders began to espouse an ideology of self-determination on their own terms, not those of the BIA (Bernstein 1991:94–95, 112–117).

Among the Northern Cheyenne and Northern Arapahoe, for example, veterans who returned to their communities assumed new political roles, serving on business councils in increasing numbers (Weist 1970; Fowler 1982). American Legion chapters were organized among many tribes, and these organizations took on new ritual roles. Indian women organized War Mothers groups, as well ("Otoe and Missouria," fig. 12, this vol.). In Oklahoma, veterans and War Mothers groups were especially important in helping to revitalize ceremonies associated with warfare.

The postwar era brought a return to the trend of land loss and loss of control over reservation resources. Veterans were unable to get loans and found it difficult to get jobs on reservations or in their home communities, even though they were eligible for the GI Bill of Rights. Thus land sales increased. During the war the BIA had increased the leasing of tribal land to non-Indian oil and gas operators in order to aid the war effort (Bernstein 1991:65, 141–143).

Federal policy in the 1950s focused on ending the federal trust responsibility (vol. 4:77). The Indian Claims Commission was established by Congress in 1946. Pursuit of claims against the federal government for treaty violations and other injustices occupied the interest of Plains tribes and their representatives. Virtually all Plains tribes filed claims against the government, and the work of the commission did not end until 1978. The National Congress of American Indians vigorously supported the settlement of these claims. For Congress the goal was ultimately to end federal responsibilities, to "get out of the Indian business" (Fixico 1986:26–27); it was proposed that settlements could be used for economic development, thereby decreasing the need for federal assistance. However, most of the judgment funds were distributed per capita. In some cases, per capita distribution encouraged a trend toward individualism and a rejection of business council efforts to develop tribally owned enterprises (Fowler 1987). The distribution of claims and the IRA constitutions also encouraged the establishment of "blood" criteria for tribal membership that generally were foreign to the way Plains tribes defined cultural identity (fig. 11). The result was social conflict. In the case of the Quapaw, the problem of the distribution of their claim settlement led in 1956 to the replacement of the chieftainship and the formation of a business committee empowered to distribute the award. The struggle to win this claim helped revitalize Quapaw culture (Baird 1989).

The termination policy, as expressed in House Concurrent Resolution 108, resulted in other legislation. Public Law 280 in 1953 provided for the transfer of responsibility for Indian affairs to state governments, although it did not apply to the Plains states, with the exception of Nebraska. Nonetheless, beginning in the postwar years Indians applied for state services generally. Congress set out to end the trust status of tribal land and property, identifying those tribes able to manage their own property (Fixico 1986:96–99, 101, 111, 122, 163). The Osage, Iowa, Quapaw, and a few other Plains tribes were threatened but staved off the termination process. Only the Northern Ponca Tribe was terminated, in 1966, and it was restored in 1990 (Grobsmith and Ritter 1992). Several Indian schools were closed, and responsibility for Indian health care was transferred from the BIA to the Public Health Service (the Indian Health Service). In 1953 the poorly enforced prohibition against selling liquor and firearms to Indians was lifted (O'Brien 1989:84), although the restriction continued later in some places. In general the Plains tribes opposed the termination policy and organized to resist its implementation, fearing that without federal protection they would face severe local and state discrimination.

Rejecting the New Deal argument that a better future for Indians lay in the development of their land, Commissioner Dillon S. Myer launched a program of training and placement assistance or relocation off the reservations.

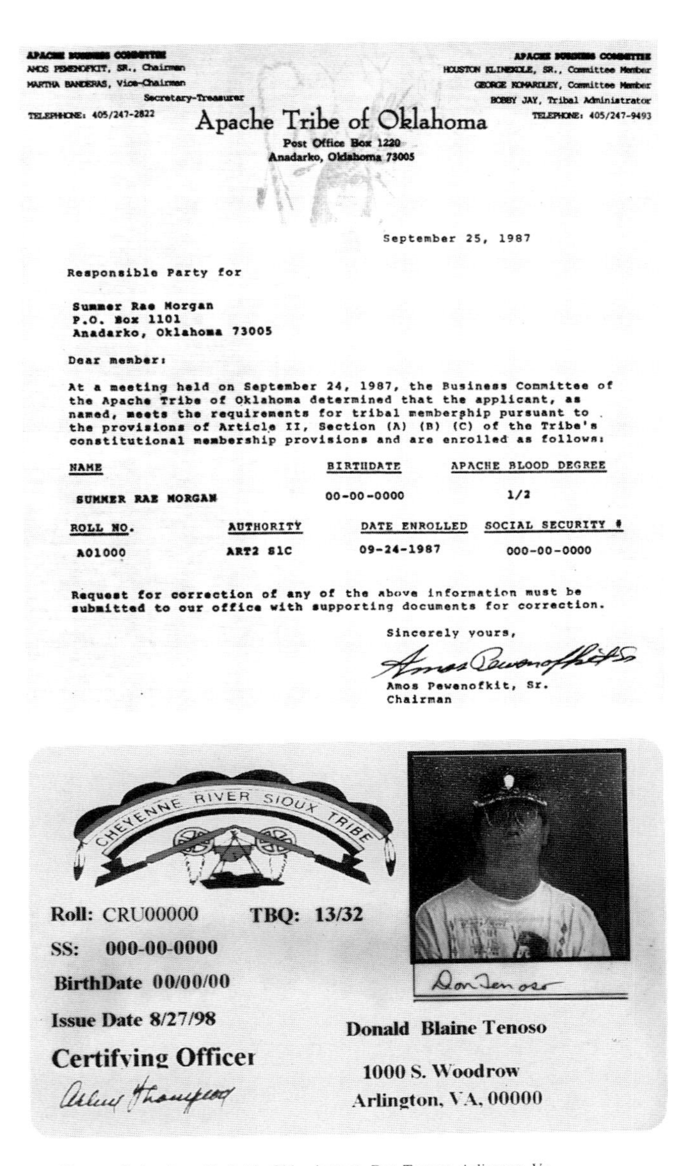

APACHE BUSINESS COMMITTEE
AMOS PEWENOFKIT, SR., Chairman
MARTHA BANDERAS, Vice-Chairman
Secretary-Treasurer
TELEPHONE: 405/247-2822

APACHE BUSINESS COMMITTEE
HOUSTON KLINEKOLE, SR., Committee Member
GEORGE KOMARDLEY, Committee Member
BOBBY JAY, Tribal Administrator
TELEPHONE: 405/247-9493

Apache Tribe of Oklahoma
Post Office Box 1220
Anadarko, Oklahoma 73005

September 25, 1987

Responsible Party for

Summer Rae Morgan
P.O. Box 1101
Anadarko, Oklahoma 73005

Dear member:

At a meeting held on September 24, 1987, the Business Committee of the Apache Tribe of Oklahoma determined that the applicant, as named, meets the requirements for tribal membership pursuant to the provisions of Article II, Section (A) (B) (C) of the Tribe's constitutional membership provisions and are enrolled as follows:

NAME		BIRTHDATE	APACHE BLOOD DEGREE
SUMMER RAE MORGAN		00-00-0000	1/2
ROLL NO.	AUTHORITY	DATE ENROLLED	SOCIAL SECURITY #
A01000	ART2 S1C	09-24-1987	000-00-0000

Request for correction of any of the above information must be submitted to our office with supporting documents for correction.

Sincerely yours,

Amos Pewenofkit, Sr.
Chairman

CHEYENNE RIVER SIOUX TRIBE

Roll: CRU00000 TBQ: 13/32
SS: 000-00-0000
BirthDate 00/00/00
Issue Date 8/27/98
Certifying Officer

Donald Blaine Tenoso
1000 S. Woodrow
Arlington, VA, 00000

top, Vanessa P. Jennings, Ft. Cobb, Okla.; bottom, Don Tenoso, Arlington, Va.

Fig. 11. Tribal certifications of "blood" quantum fractions (other identifying numbers altered). top, Letter of Sept. 25, 1987, certifying Summer Rae Morgan as a half-blood of the Plains Apache tribe. bottom, Cheyenne River Sioux tribal identification card showing Don Tenoso as having a "tribal blood quantum" (TBQ) of 13/32.

The plan was that once Indians adjusted to living in cities they would not return to the reservations. The government furnished transportation, helped find jobs and housing, and provided vocational training. In fact, a growing Indian population was putting a strain on reservation economies. Between 1954 and 1957 the incidence of tuberculosis nationwide dropped 40 percent among Indians; there was a 12 percent drop in infant mortality. The Indian population was growing at a much greater rate than the general population, and postwar expectations and aspirations were increasing, as well. Large numbers of Indians relocated without federal assistance. Fifty-four percent of the relocatees were from the Plains area alone. However, once in the cities, low wages and poor housing were the norm and the percentage of returnees varied from 30 to 75 percent. Those who remained in cities, for short or long periods of time, became active in the establishment of Indian centers (Fixico 1986:67, 138, 148–150, 169).

The developments of the 1950s had important effects in Plains communities. Almost half the population of the Lower Brule Reservation left. Among the migrants, intermarriage with non-Indians and others increased dramatically (Schusky 1975). Half the Comanche left their community in southwest Oklahoma. After the war, veterans were able to take advantage of job preference policies to obtain employment in Oklahoma hitherto denied them. During and after the war years, powwows (periodic intertribal dances usually held on weekends) increased in importance, for they enabled people living in cities to return to the Comanche community for these ceremonies, and in so doing to renew social ties and reaffirm cultural identity. Kinship obligations were weakened due to geographical distance, and "adoptive" relationships between coparticipants in local Comanche social gatherings assumed greater importance (Foster 1991:131–143). In general, many of the children of Plains Indians who relocated to cities grew up without much social contact with home communities; from these young people came much of the leadership for social change in the 1960s.

The War on Poverty and Tribal Sovereignty Policies

In the mid-1960s, War on Poverty and civil rights legislation transformed American society (R. White 1991:577–588, 600–601). Commissioner of Indian Affairs Philleo Nash (1961–1966) persuaded Congress to approve the eligibility of Indian reservations for War on Poverty funds. Nash encouraged the tribes to apply for federal grants for housing, education, manpower training, and economic development. Agencies with funds often dealt directly with tribal governments, which expanded their responsibilities and powers. With the passage of the Indian Civil Rights Act in 1968, the consent of tribes was required before state governments could extend control over tribal affairs, effectively reversing an important component of the termination policy.

These developments had a major impact on the Plains, as elsewhere. Before 1960 the BIA had no housing program; in 1965 the Department of Housing and Urban Development began a homebuilding program in Indian communities with funds from the Indian Health Service for water and sanitation. The Elementary and Secondary Indian Education Act of 1972 funded bilingual and bicultural programs and required the participation of Indians in the planning of projects. In addition, Indian communities could operate their own elementary and secondary schools. Several community colleges were established—for example, on the Fort Belknap, Fort Peck, Fort Berthold (fig. 8), Crow, Cheyenne River, Rosebud, and Pine Ridge reservations. Because Vietnam veterans could obtain federal funds to attend college, increasing numbers of Native Americans attained higher education. The Economic Opportunity Act of 1964 funded Headstart and several job programs, as well as the construction of community halls and tribal government complexes. In 1976 the Indian Health Care Improvements Act funded a number of programs, including the hiring of Native American health care workers. Nonreservation Indian communities in Oklahoma eventually became eligible to participate in these programs, as well (O'Brien 1989; Castile 1998).

Building on the policy of self-determination without termination, promoted by the administrations of Lyndon B. Johnson and Richard M. Nixon, in 1975 Congress passed the Indian Self-Determination and Education Assistance Act and amended it in 1988 and 1994 to facilitate the contracting process. This act allowed for the transfer of partial responsibility for the administration of programs for Indians, along with federal funding, to tribal governments. Tribes could contract for programs formerly run by the BIA. The Indian Child Welfare Act was passed in 1978, which allowed Indian tribes to determine the custody of Indian children (Castile 1998).

By the 1980s tribal (or multitribal) governments were committed to controlling their own resources and making their own decisions. Tribal and intertribal courts (e.g., the Intertribal Appeals Court of South Dakota) replaced BIA courts in many communities (vol. 4:234). There were many tribally owned businesses established, including the Blackfeet Indian Writing Company, which manufactured pens and pencils; WCD Enterprises, a Wichita, Caddo, and Delaware hat factory; Devils Lake Sioux Manufacturing Company, which made camouflage netting; and numerous gaming (largely bingo) enterprises and tobacco retail stores. Subsequent to a Supreme Court decision (*Merriam* v. *Jicarilla Apache Tribe*) tribes were able to collect a severance tax on resources removed from tribal land (i.e., minerals); thus, tribes with oil or other minerals (which includes a large number of Plains tribes) had a large source of income separate from the federal monies that were subject to fluctuation. In the 1990s tribes contested the states' right to collect severance tax on these same resources. Tribes issued automobile license plates (fig. 12), required taverns to buy a tribal liquor license (e.g., Wind River Reservation), and levied an excise and sales tax on goods sold on tribal land. Smoke shops and bingo enterprises brought large amounts of income under the control of tribal governments (O'Brien 1989). Like the claim settlements in the past, the question of how to distribute these monies (in the form of investment or development or per capita payments) was a source of controversy in reservation communities.

These wide-reaching changes since the 1960s have had a variety of social consequences. In the area of housing, there is no doubt that in many communities, living conditions improved. Prior to these programs most families

Fig. 12. Economic pursuits and tribally owned businesses. top, Comanche (except as noted) firefighters. In Florida for 21 days, they were assigned to the Jacksonville complex, Ocala Forest, and Withlacoochee fires. left to right, top row: Erwin Palmer; Richard A. Camarena; Kendall Jirtle; Mike Makos (non-Indian); Tim Klukas, crew boss (non-Indian); middle row: Donnell Big Bear Heminokeky; Kathleen L. Pappan; Michael Tiddark; Daniel E. Roundface; Bruce McCarthy; Heath Morrison; Ernest Frank Komalty; Greg Cable; Shane Grant Schartzer; bottom row: Lendy Koassechony; Linda Carson; Terry Pueblo; Morgan Tosee; Theodore Round Face; George Brown, Laguna. Photograph by Lynn Ivory, Ft. Bragg, Fl., 1998. center, Howard Brown, Northern Arapahoe, calling numbers during a bingo game on the Wind River Res., Wyo. Photograph by Tom Stromme, 1984. bottom, License plate issued by the Pawnee tribe. Photograph by William Meadows, Denver March Powwow, 1997.

lived without electricity or indoor plumbing. On the other hand, housing was still inadequate. For example, on Rosebud, there was poor coordination between phases of the building projects; some homes were never hooked up to sewer systems. Poor-quality materials were used and there was no maintenance or insurance program to help homeowners or renters with upkeep. In addition, because of different criteria for ownership among types of housing and a sliding scale of rent, occupants incurred different costs, and this precipitated resentment and accusations of favoritism. Tribal government bore the brunt of the criticism, although the federal government may have made the policy and determined the amount of funding (Grobsmith 1981:21–27). Some housing was built on land owned by extended families; other projects were built on tribal land, drawing together people not related by kinship. Without kinship bonds, quarrels often went unresolved or escalated into situations that jeopardized the safety of the community.

Education levels rose dramatically, and 87 percent of BIA jobs were held by Indians (*Indian News* 1992). However, unemployment was much higher than in the society at large, especially in reservation communities.

In general, social changes starting in the 1960s—especially a significant increase in available jobs and housing—drew relocatees back to the reservation or Indian community and reversed the trend toward outmigration. The new opportunities drew women into the labor force and into tribal government (M.N. Powers 1986). On the one hand, tribal governments had vastly extended responsibilities and powers; on the other hand, they were under constant pressures from constituents to solve community problems and provide jobs and other resources to a growing population. The newly established courts were often used by constituents to contest the actions of the tribal government or to contest election results. Since these tribal courts were often under the jurisdiction of the elected officials, they were sometimes perceived as biased in favor of tribal officials.

In addition to economic and political revitalization, the post-1960s changes had vast repercussions in ritual life. Native American Studies programs and positive media

Smithsonian, Office of Repatriation.

Fig. 13. Repatriation of skeletal remains. left, Northern Cheyenne repatriation of the remains of 17 individuals killed near Ft. Robinson, Neb., in 1879. The remains were returned to Busby, Mont., 1993. Photograph by Jane Beck. right, Lynn Rice, Pawnee, smudging and praying over the remains of 6 Pawnee military scouts, 5 other historic period Pawnees, and 11 sets of ancient remains affiliated with Northern Caddoan materials at a repatriation ceremony. Photograph by Jane Beck, Ft. McNair, Washington, D.C., 1995.

attention, as well as the increased income that makes participation in rituals more feasible, led to a widespread cultural revival. Beginning in the 1980s new ceremonies borrowed from other tribes were reinterpreted to conform to local cultural orientations; ceremonies not performed in decades were revived, with reinterpretation (Fowler 1987). The civil rights movement promoted a spirit of activism (fig. 13) and cultural revival in Indian communities in general and precipitated the organization of the American Indian Movement in 1968, which attained considerable influence on some Plains reservations, at least for a brief period of time. American Indian Movement members and other urban relocatees introduced features in ritual that reflected their participation in the civil rights struggles (Grobsmith 1981:107–108). For example, participation in the Sun Dance on Sioux reservations no longer centered exclusively on a quest for power but also included the desire for recognition as an Indian and the desire to recover from alcoholism (Medicine 1987). After the Native American Graves Protection and Repatriation Act became law in 1990, Plains people obtained ceremonial objects from museums and incorporated them in tribal rituals.

History of the Canadian Plains Until 1870

JENNIFER S.H. BROWN

In 1870, a substantial portion of the northern plains became part of the new nation of Canada. Situated in present-day southern Manitoba, Saskatchewan, and Alberta, this region already had a 200-year history as the southwestern quadrant of the territory granted to the Hudson's Bay Company on 2 May 1670 by Charles II of England as "one of our Plantacions or Colonyes in America" (Mackay 1936:39). Canada's creation of the province of Manitoba and of a huge jurisdiction known as the Northwest Territories, stretching from Manitoba and 49° north latitude to British Columbia and the Arctic Ocean, brought the area under an expansionist government whose home (Ottawa, Ontario) lay far to the east. The Northern Plains, however, were entirely distinct from Canada as it was defined until 1870. Before that time, they were part of Rupert's Land, a vast area defined by the flow of its waterways into the Arctic Ocean through Hudson Bay (fig. 1).

Waterways were crucial transport arteries to both Native peoples and European newcomers, and the English and French defined their early North American land claims in terms of the heights of land dividing them. When the Hudson's Bay Company received its royal charter in 1670, it gained rights to the "whole trade of all those seas, streights and bays, lakes, creeks and sounds . . . within the streights commonly called Hudson's Streights" and to all the inland regions (largely unknown to Europeans) whose waters drained into Hudson Bay (Mackay 1936:38). Twelve years later, René-Robert Cavelier, sieur de La Salle, claimed the entire drainage of the Mississippi River for France, thereby establishing the territory of Louisiana as the southern neighbor to Rupert's Land. The height of land between them, although largely unmapped, was the de facto boundary until the Convention of 1818 established 49° north latitude as the northern limit of the United States from Lake of the Woods, Ontario, to the Rocky Mountains. However, this line was not surveyed on the ground until the Boundary Commission did its work in the 1870s. The shift in 1818 from a watershed to a latitudinal border definition had little import for most Native people until much later, particularly as the boundary was scarcely operational before 1870. Indian and Métis people either ignored the boundary, or later, made use of it to claim refuge, resources, or recognition from whichever governmental authority presented an immediate threat or opportunity.

The plains portion of this territory includes the watersheds of the Saskatchewan River, up to the banks of the North Saskatchewan, and of the Assiniboine and Red rivers (the last two known in fur trade sources as the Upper and Lower Red River respectively), all of which flow through Lake Winnipeg to the Nelson and Hayes rivers, which enter Hudson Bay near York Factory (Ray 1974:fig. 1). Until 1818, Rupert's Land, owing to the flow patterns of the Red and Souris (Mouse) rivers, encompassed a substantial portion of what became Minnesota and North Dakota. In turn, Louisiana's boundary followed the height of land into a corner of southwestern Saskatchewan and southeastern Alberta.

The Seventeenth Century

News of Europeans would certainly have reached Indians of the northern plains by the mid-1600s. In 1659–1660, Pierre-Esprit Radisson and Médard Chouart, sieur des Groseilliers wintered along the south shore of Lake Superior where they joined "Eighte[e]n severall nations" in a celebration of the Feast of the Dead, a ceremony held periodically to memorialize those who had recently died. On this occasion, their Ojibwa and Ottawa hosts brought several hundred people together for exchanges of honors and gifts. The visitors included Sioux and Crees. Since the Crees' relations with the other groups were uneasy, Radisson declared them to be "our brethren," protected by the French, and announced his intent to "conclude a generall peace," to help foster trade and extend French influence (G. Warkentin 1996:60–63). The two Frenchmen, intent on impressing the people they met, distributed quantities of European goods as gifts and in exchange for furs. However, they did not return, and their subsequent conflicts with the authorities in New France led them to England in 1666 where they played key roles in the founding of the Hudson's Bay Company.

The westernmost guests at this gathering ranged only to the edges of the plains. Ojibwa parties traveled seasonally inland southwest of Lake Superior. The Woods Cree groups occupied much of the area north of Lake Superior, their southern limits approximating the present international boundary as far as the Rainy Lake area. (The differentiation of the Plains Cree from the other Cree groups does not become clear until the end of the eighteenth century.) In the region west and south of present-day Duluth,

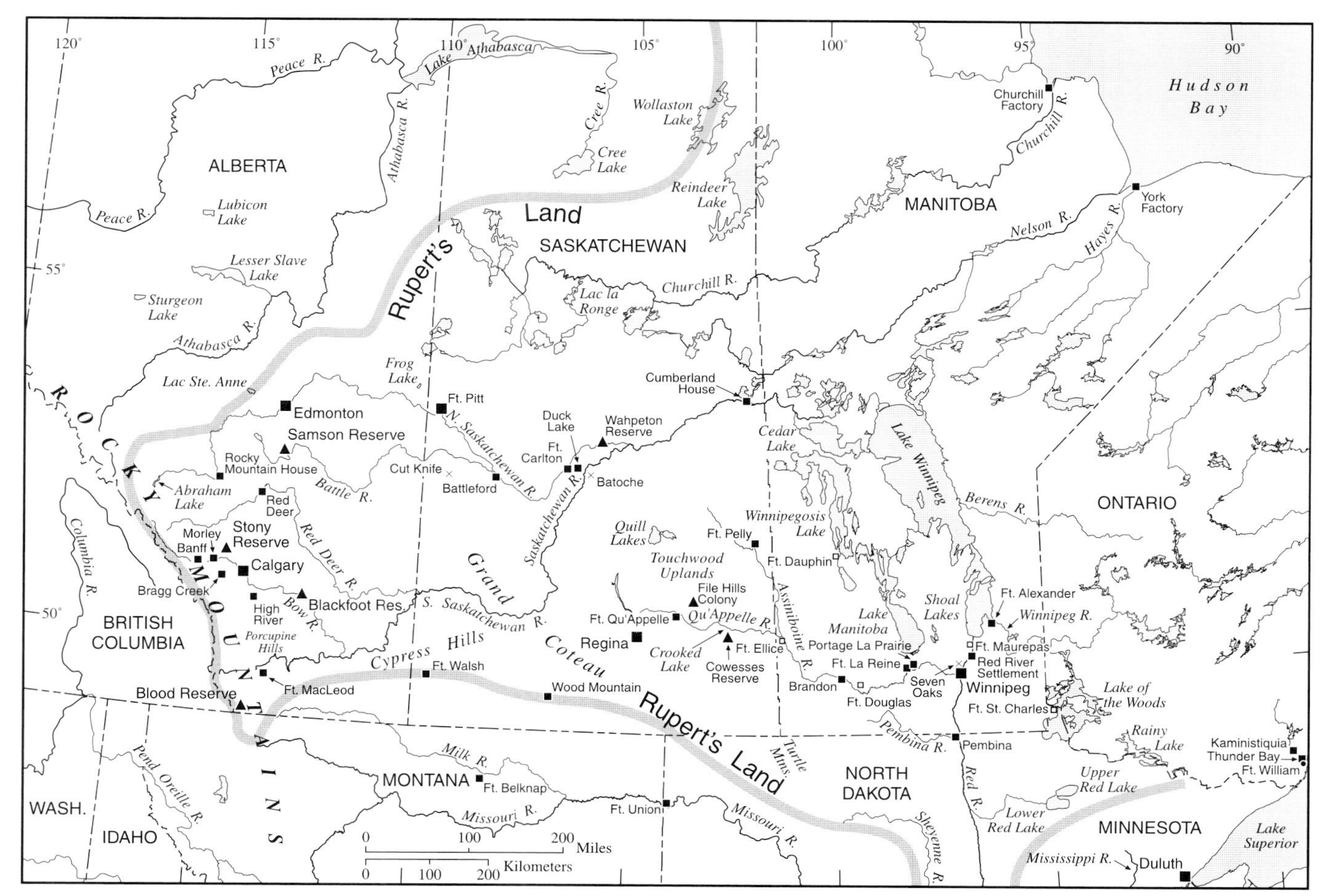

Fig. 1. Rupert's Land, 1670–1869, set by royal charter as the height of land surrounding the Hudson Bay watershed. In 1818, 49° north latitude became the southern boundary of Rupert's Land, placing most of the Red River watershed and its inhabitants in the U.S. Reserves shown were established under treaties in the 1870s. Trading posts were founded beginning in the 1700s.

Minnesota, the Sioux, whom the two Frenchmen visited for a time, hunted seasonally in a state of warfare or uneasy peace with their Algonquian neighbors to the north and south. Not met by Radisson were the Assiniboine, also Siouan speakers, who then resided from Lake of the Woods, Ontario, to the plains around the lower Red and Assiniboine rivers and Lakes Winnipeg and Manitoba (Harris and Matthews 1987, 1: pl. 37). In the late 1660s, the Jesuit priest Jean Claude Allouez reported that they regularly visited the north shore of Lake Superior as far as Lake Nipigon; they were already important suppliers of furs to the Ottawa-Ojibwa middlemen trading with the French (Ray 1974:11). Their own role as traders became critical during the next century.

By 1700, the English had founded three posts on James Bay and one (York Factory) near the mouths of the Nelson and Hayes rivers. To counter Hudson's Bay Company expansion, French explorer Daniel Greysolon Dulhut worked to negotiate peace with Algonquian and Siouan groups around western Lake Superior in 1679 and built posts on Lake Nipigon and at Kaministiquia (present-day Thunder Bay, Ontario) in 1684 (Zoltvany 1969:262–263). These contending establishments, although remote from one another, generated the first major European trade rivalry in the region. French-English strife became most intense on Hudson Bay itself; the French occupied the English posts in James Bay from 1686 to 1693, and after losing them, seized and held York Factory from 1697 to 1714. The conflict was not settled until the Treaty of Utrecht in 1713 awarded the Hudson Bay watershed to England.

The Ojibwa, Cree, and Assiniboine traded in growing numbers with the newcomers, whether French or English. In the 1670s, the western Cree and Assiniboine became middlemen like the Ojibwa before them, trading the furs of more distant groups to the Europeans and returning inland with trade goods on which they made ample profits. The Native traders were the ones who carried the trade into new areas (Ray 1993:121). Long distances were no impediment; the Assiniboine, in particular, regularly undertook return trips of 2,000–2,400 kilometers by canoe, traveling for three to six months. Travel for them was not an opportunity cost; rather, it "was something they liked to do" (Ray 1993:114, 121). This point provides a useful perspective on Hudson's Bay Company Englishman Henry Kelsey's travels with the Cree and Assiniboine from York Factory onto the plains in 1690–1692. For historians, Kelsey stands out as the first European to visit this region and to write about its peoples and characteristics. For his Native companions, he was surely a supernumerary on long canoe trips they regarded as usual, though his connections, his access to new resources, and perhaps his exoticism presented attractions.

Hudson's Bay Company Gov. George Geyer concisely outlined Kelsey's mission: "I sent up *Henry Kelsey* (who chearfully undertook the Journey) up into the Country of the *Assinae Poets*, with the Captain of that Nation, to call, encourage, and invite, the remoter Indians to a Trade with us" (Doughty and Martin 1929:xx). Kelsey named five inland groups on his travels: the Nayhaythaway (western Cree); the Stone (Assiniboine); the Eagles brich Indians (unidentified band in east-central Saskatchewan); the Mountain Poets (thought to be an Assiniboine band near the Manitoba Escarpment); and the unidentified Naywatame Poets who are "the most intriguing problem of all because those Indians were the goal of Kelsey's travels" (J. Warkentin 1994:ix).

Kelsey's meetings with the "Naywatame Poets" and others brought him and his Assiniboine companions to the edge of a major trade network that predated the arrival of Europeans in the interior of western North America. The Mandan-Hidatsa villages on the Knife and Upper Missouri rivers and the Arikara villages farther downstream (northern South Dakota) were two major exchange centers in "a self-sufficient and surplus-abundant trading system as elaborate as that of the Southwest" (vol. 4:352–353). Before the advent of European goods, these river horticulturalists were trading corn and other produce and Knife River flint for dried meat, deer and buffalo hides, and other items brought by the Crow, Sioux, and others; Assiniboine traders also probably traveled to the Mandan-Hidatsa center by the mid-1600s. Cree-Assiniboine relations with the "Naywatame Poets" were uneasy, however, and Kelsey, like other Europeans before and after him, tried with mixed success to make peace for the benefit of trade (J. Warkentin 1994:xv).

After Kelsey's return to York Factory in 1692, the Hudson's Bay Company sent no travelers to the plains for over 60 years. The reasons were various: a glut of coat beaver in the mid- to late 1690s and early 1700s, conflicts with the French at Hudson Bay until 1714, a scarcity of men like Kelsey who learned Native languages and would undertake such travel, and particularly, the fact that the Cree and Assiniboine trading captains and their followers effectively dominated the Native middleman system with the aid of guns and ammunition obtained at the Hudson's Bay Company posts (Ray and Freeman 1978:43). The French too went through a period of retrenchment, although it was shorter. Beaver gluts and an expensive war with the Iroquois in the east led the French government to order closure of inland posts in 1697; French trade to the interior did not begin to recover until 1717 (Harris and Matthews 1987: pl. 39).

Northern Plains Indians, French, and English to 1781

Siouans, Algonquians, and French Traders to the 1750s

In 1717, Zacharie Robutel de La Noue was sent west of Lake Superior in search of an inland route to the elusive Western Sea that the French long hoped to find (Voisine 1969:581). He spent four years establishing posts at Kaministiquia and Rainy Lake, building ties with the Sioux who dominated much of the Boundary Waters area at the time, and encouraging their warfare against the Cree and Assiniboine trading to Hudson Bay. As a result, the York Factory trade suffered and the Cree-Assiniboine middlemen endured numerous casualties although, being well armed, they were not deterred from trading by the coureurs de bois or by Sioux attacks. Those Assiniboine living in the region did move west, however. In the early 1730s, Lake of the Woods was still called Lake of the Assiniboine, but when explorer Pierre Gaultier de Varennes, sieur de La Vérendrye got there in 1733, he found very few Assiniboines (Ray 1974:14, 16, 1978:44).

French and Dakota hostility to the Assiniboine in the 1720s also probably reinforced the Assiniboine-Cree connection, which began sometime in the 1600s. Pierre-Charles Le Sueur wrote in 1700 that their alliance originated after the Cree began to get arms from the Hudson's Bay Company and "continually waged war against the Assinipoils, who were their nearest neighbors. The latter finding themselves weak asked for peace; and to render it more firm, allied themselves to the Christinaux [Cree], taking their women to wife" (Sharrock 1974:107). The scale of this alliance is difficult to judge. Neither the Assiniboine nor the Cree was a unitary "tribe"; the Assiniboine consist of multiple linguistic subgroups in two divisions (Stoney and Assiniboine) whose dialects have diverged considerably, suggesting separations over a considerable period (Parks and DeMallie 1992). Outsiders who encountered only one or two local bands could easily take them as representative of a whole people. In any case, it is clear that some Cree and Assiniboine were bilingual, intermarried, and lived and traveled in the same bands, constituting a force that required the attention of both French and English traders.

La Vérendrye was the first French explorer to record substantial information about the northern plains. Native news of a westward-flowing river (the Winnipeg River), and of large waters lying beyond, along with concerns to extend French influence and trade, led La Vérendrye and his sons and nephew to establish a chain of posts west of Lake Superior. Fort Saint-Charles, founded on Lake of the Woods in 1732, was the headquarters for the building of

Fort Maurepas on the Red River in 1734, and Fort La Reine (at present-day Portage La Prairie, Manitoba) in 1738. French movements into these regions necessitated the friendship of the Cree and Assiniboine, which in turn provoked Sioux hostility and their killing of 20 Frenchmen on Lake of the Woods in June 1736. In October 1738, La Vérendrye led a five-month expedition from Fort La Reine to the Mandans, arriving with 600 Assiniboines in their main village on 3 December with "drums beating and flags flying" (Zoltvany 1974:249–252). Sons of La Vérendrye led two trips to the Upper Missouri, in 1741 and again in 1742–1743, when they reached either the Bighorn Mountains, Wyoming, or the Black Hills of South Dakota (Wood and Thiessen 1985:298).

In the early 1740s, the La Vérendryes turned their efforts northward to the building of Fort Dauphin (Winnipegosis, Manitoba) in 1741–1743, and two other posts in Subarctic Woods Cree country northwest of Lake Winnipeg (Zoltvany 1974: 252). Diverting furs from the Hudson's Bay Company was one concern. When La Vérendrye resigned his military position in 1744, he requested recognition for two other contributions to New France: "the great number of people my enterprise provides with a living [and] the slaves it procures to the colony." The number of slaves he sent eastward is unknown, but one dispatch of 1742 mentioned a battle in which his Cree and Assiniboine allies routed the Sioux, killed 70 men, and "captured such a large number of slaves that they made a line four *arpents* [perhaps 800–1,000 feet] long" (Zoltvany 1974:252).

From La Vérendrye's time until they were obliged to retrench during the Seven Years' War (1756–1763), the French focused their trade incursions into Rupert's Land on the lower Saskatchewan River, which flows for some 470 kilometers through boreal forest into northwestern Lake Winnipeg (Meyer and Thistle 1995:405). Although French records after La Vérendrye are few, some reports survive from Joseph La France, son of a French trader and an Ojibwa woman. During his travels in the 1740s, La France met Sioux who were living southwest of Lake Winnipeg. He distinguished two categories of Assiniboine: those of the woods in the north, and those of the prairies or meadows living to the west of Lake Winnipeg and Lake Winnipegosis. South of the Assiniboine and north of the Sioux lived the "Nation of Beaux Hommes," possibly a reference to the Siouan-speaking Crow (for a full discussion of their identity, consult "Enigmatic Groups," this vol.).

Archithinue and the Hudson's Bay Company, 1750–1770s

In 1754–1755, the year-long travels of Hudson's Bay Company man Anthony Henday initiated significant recorded contacts with Indians of the Northern Plains. The new French posts along the Saskatchewan River had hurt the York Factory returns, and James Isham, in charge at York, hoped to extend direct trade ties beyond the Cree and Assiniboine who were supplying furs to both the Hudson's Bay Company and its rivals. Henday was sent to contact groups whom he and Isham knew only as "Earchethinues" or "Archithinues," their spellings of *a·ya·hciðiniw*, a Woods Cree term signifying 'stranger' that they applied to the Blackfoot and also sometimes to the Gros Ventre, Sarcee, and Eastern Shoshone (Rich 1949:113; Ewers 1958:25). All these distant groups were receiving European goods indirectly from 1750 to the 1760s (Ray and Freeman 1978:48–49). In September 1754, Henday became the first European to see Native horsemen in Rupert's Land, and in October, he met with an Archithinue (evidently Blackfoot) chief in a camp of 200 tents near present-day Red Deer, Alberta (G. Williams 1978:45). In May 1755, he and his Cree and Assiniboine companions filled their 60 canoes with furs traded at a Blackfoot camp of more than 277 tents. Metal goods were the main attraction; Henday noted that afterward there was "scarce a Gun, Kettle, Hatchet or Knife amongst us" (Ray 1974:90).

Several Hudson's Bay men traveled inland in the next two decades leading up to the founding of their company's first major inland post, Cumberland House on the lower Saskatchewan, in 1774. Matthew Cocking reached the Blackfoot country in 1772–1773 and recorded names of several groups he encountered. Besides the "Powestic-Athinuewuck (i.e.) Water-fall Indians" (Gros Ventre) whose buffalo pound he described, Cocking also named "four Tribes or Nations more," all equestrian: "Mithco-Athinuwuck or Bloody Indians, Koskitow-Wathesitock or Blackfooted Indians, Pegonow or Muddy-water Indians, and Sassewuck or Woody Country Indians" (Rich 1949:313), Woods Cree names for the allied groups better known as Blood, Blackfoot, Piegan, and the Athapaskan-speaking Sarcee (Ewers 1958:27–28). Andrew Graham, writing from Hudson Bay in 1775, summarized the lifeway of what he called the "Archithinue Nation": having plenty of buffalo, they "never eat beaver or fish or fowl; and know nothing about managing a canoe," hence their lack of interest in bringing furs to Hudson Bay themselves. They traded quantities of wolf pelts to the Plains Cree for metal goods. Most impressive were their "fine horses which they . . . manage with amazing dexterity." Every March, they rode "from their pleasant country towards the NE as far as their horses can permit; where they are met by our traders, and where several of the Company's servants have seen above three hundred brave men mounted on light horses of various colours" (G. Williams 1969:202–203).

Horses and Guns

The Spaniards had brought horses to the Southwest in the 1500s, and Native traders introduced them to the northern plains by about 1720. An unusual earthlodge site, Cluny near Blackfoot Crossing on the Bow River (Alberta), contained a few horse bones; they likely date to the 1730s (L.

Bryan 1991:173–179). The Cluny people probably were migrants from the Missouri River farming villages to the southeast; horses would have aided their long-distance travel.

Hudson's Bay Company explorer David Thompson also alluded to the 1730s as the period in which horses reached the northwestern plains. In 1787–1788, while helping to establish Hudson's Bay Company posts on the upper Saskatchewan River, Thompson wintered in a Piegan camp in the foothills of the Rockies. His host was Saukamapee, a Cree aged about 80, whom the Piegan had adopted as a young man. Saukamapee recounted how, sometime in the 1730s, the Piegan asked him and some other Cree and Assiniboine to help them in a pitched battle against the Eastern Shoshone Indians. Because he and his companions had 10 guns, the Piegan considered them "the strength of the battle," and so it proved. Their enemies on this occasion lacked horses; but the Piegan had told them of being attacked by some Eastern Shoshones who had these animals, "on which they rode, swift as the Deer, on which they dashed at the Peegans, and with their stone Pukamoggan [Plains Cree *pakama·kan* 'club'] knocked them on the head. . . . This news we did not well comprehend and it alarmed us, for we had no idea of Horses and could not make out what they were." That fall, while Saukamapee was hunting with the Piegan on the edge of Eastern Shoshone country, he and his companions saw their first horse, an Eastern Shoshone's mount killed by an arrow: "we all admired him, he put us in mind of a Stag that had lost his horns; and we did not know what name to give him. But as he was slave to Man, like the dog, which carried our things; he was named the Big Dog," Plains Cree *mistatim* (Thompson in G. Warkentin 1996:235–238).

According to Saukamapee, guns and metal goods transformed warfare: "The terror of that battle and of our guns has prevented any more general battles, and our wars have since been carried by ambuscade and surprize, of small camps, in which we have greatly the advantage, from the Guns, arrow shods of iron, long knives, flat bayonets and axes from the Traders" (G. Warkentin 1996:238). But he also made clear that guns of that period compared poorly to bows and arrows with respect to range, accuracy, complications of reloading, and ammunition requirements. Further, it was difficult to confirm each warrior's claim to the scalps of those slain by gunfire, since bullets, unlike arrows, bore no personal marks of their possessors. Because the souls of dead enemies were to serve the deceased relatives of those who held their scalps, deaths by gunfire complicated the assigning of those rights (G. Warkentin 1996:237).

Horses from the south and guns from the east quickly became valued possessions that affected mobility, warfare, social organization, and gender roles. The Blackfoot and their allies expanded westward and southward, pushing the Kootenai and Flathead across the Rocky Mountains, while the Eastern Shoshone in the 1730s to 1750s withdrew to the headwaters of the Missouri River; behind the Blackfoot, the Gros Ventre moved west from the lower South Saskatchewan to the Red Deer River region (O. Lewis 1970:148–152). Horses aided the buffalo hunt and thereby increased the need for women's hide- and meat-processing labors; and as brideprice wealth, they enabled men to acquire more wives, widening social distinctions between the wealthy and those with few or no horses. Successful horse raids brought prestige to those who mastered "stealth horsemanship," an art form in itself, though overall horses "enhanced a preexisting way of life" rather than bringing radical change (Kipp 1996:257).

Smallpox, Fur Trade Rivalries, and Expansion, 1781–1800

To the Europeans involved, the conquest of New France by the British in 1763 was the end of an era; however, 17 years later, Indians of Rupert's Land faced a cataclysm of far greater immediacy. A smallpox epidemic that began in Mexico in 1779 reached the northern plains with deadly effect in 1780–1781. The trading and agricultural villages of the Mandan and Hidatsa shrank from about 24 communities with a population of from 9,000 to 11,500 residents, to five villages totaling under 4,000 people (Wood and Thiessen 1985:71). Horse travelers spread the disease widely, to the Blackfoot, Gros Ventre, and Assiniboine, and northward to the Plains Cree by the end of 1781 (Ray 1974:105–107). Saukamapee told David Thompson how the Piegan were infected. On approaching a strangely quiet Eastern Shoshone camp, "with our sharp flat daggers and knives, [we] cut through the tents and entered for the fight; but our war whoop instantly stopt, our eyes were appalled with terror; there was no one to fight with but the dead and the dying." They took some tents and other goods, whereupon "this dreadful disease broke out in our camp, and spread from one tent to another as if the Bad Spirit carried it" (Thompson in G. Warkentin 1996:239). Saukamapee believed the Piegan lost half their population. Reportedly, adult men died more than women and children, "for unable to bear the heat of the fever they rushed into the Rivers and Lakes to cool themselves, and the greater part thus perished" (Ray 1974:106). One-half century later, to the east, Ojibwa historian William Warren heard a story of a Cree-Assiniboine-Ojibwa war party from the lower Red River that attacked a Gros Ventre village on the Upper Missouri. Mystified at its feeble resistance, they discovered "lodges filled with dead bodies" and retreated with the scalps of those they had killed. Only four men survived the trip home, bringing smallpox to the great Western Woods Cree village at Netley Creek near Lake Winnipeg with deadly results; Ojibwa refugees then carried the smallpox to Rainy Lake, Ontario, and beyond

(W.W. Warren 1984:261–262).

This disaster struck just when the fur trade was poised for renewal. Smallpox losses briefly curbed its expansion, but new entrepreneurs from Canada brought fresh energy and capital into Rupert's Land and beyond, forging ties with more distant Native groups, and also with plains people who not only replaced those who had died but also took on new economic roles. In 1779–1784, a loose partnership of Montreal fur trade merchants of largely Highland Scottish origin coalesced into the North West Company, which competed vigorously with the Hudson's Bay Company until the two firms merged in 1821. The Nor'Westers built on the explorations of Peter Pond and others into the upper Churchill and Athabaska river drainages, trading with Athapaskans previously unreached by Europeans. Inland posts proliferated even though many were temporary; by 1774, the Montreal-based traders had built 10 and the Hudson's Bay men had seven (Harris and Matthews 1987:144–145). The 1780s also saw the renewal of trips from the Red River region to the Mandan-Hidatsa villages. In the years 1780–1800, 23 trips by North West Company men or other Canadian traders are on record; Hudson's Bay men made nine trips in that period (Wood and Thiessen 1985: appendix, table 1). All this activity reduced the formerly central roles of the Cree-Assiniboine middlemen.

Another development that impinged on Plains Indian groups was the hiring from the 1790s into the early 1800s of hundreds of Iroquois and other eastern Indians by the North West Company and its short-lived rival, the XY Company (1798–1804). Battling with each other and with the Hudson's Bay Company for furs that proved increasingly scarce in many areas, the Canadians equipped these men with steel traps and castoreum. Their aggressive trapping temporarily raised returns, but conflicts arose with some of the peoples into whose lands they intruded, notably with the Gros Ventre. Many Iroquois remained in the West after their company service and married into Métis and other Native commmunities as the most competitive years of the fur trade ended (Nicks 1980; vol. 15:544–546).

The growing numbers of newcomers who traveled from Lake Winnipeg to Athabaska fueled a new plains industry. Needing to cover vast distances while waterways were ice-free, traders' canoe brigades could not stop to hunt for fresh provisions if furs and trade goods were to reach their destinations on time. Plains people were drawn into the production, largely by women, of pemmican (Plains Cree *pimihka·n*), a mix of fat and pounded dried meat (Ens 1996:42) that from the 1780s on served as a nourishing, compact, and durable "trail food." As Cree and Assiniboine survivors of the smallpox shifted from middleman trading to provisioning the new posts and the voyageurs, they faced more direct competition with other groups and with some new neighbors on the plains (Ray 1974:102, 104).

New Peoples on the Plains:
Ojibwa and Métis, 1790s to 1820

William Warren's reference to Red River Ojibwa who transmitted smallpox to Rainy Lake is one of few sources mentioning Ojibwa on the plains by 1781. The earliest clear reference to Ojibwa west of Lake Winnipeg dates from January 1778 at Cumberland House (Peers 1994:30, 219). To the south, Ojibwa Chief Peguis (d. 1864) recalled how some of his people, decimated by smallpox, left the woodlands "and entered on the plains of Red River." They met with some Crees and Assiniboines at the Pembina Mountain, "and after smoking and feasting for two or three days . . . were formally invited to dwell on the plains—to eat out of the same dish, to warm themselves at the same fire, and to make common cause with them against their enemies the Sioux" (Donald Gunn quoted in Peers 1994:21). Soon after 1800, the band to which Peguis belonged settled near the mouth of the Red River at Netley Creek, which the Cree had abandoned after the smallpox of 1781 (Peers 1994: 89).

Ojibwa groups had other reasons to move west. They were evidently keener beaver hunters than the Western Woods Cree (Ray 1974:102). They had long trade experience with the French and their North West Company successors, and the rapid expansion of rival posts onto the northern plains, especially after 1790 (Harris and Matthews 1987: pl. 61), assured the availability of goods that they valued (fig. 2). They had growing interest in horses, although their ongoing movement between the plains and wooded areas and their focus on water travel made them less reliant on horsemanship than were the Assiniboine and Cree. Kin and familial ties ramified westward as small groups traveled back and forth to the plains and eventually joined relatives in the west. The narrative of John Tanner, the Kentucky boy who lived 30 years with the Ottawa and Ojibwa from the 1790s through the 1820s, vividly documents these far-reaching movements and connections (James 1830).

Ojibwa ties with the traders themselves contributed to migration. Both Hudson's Bay men and their Canadian counterparts, moving west without wives or families, found that Native groups regularly sought to secure mutual trust and a stable exchange relationship through idioms of kinship (J.S.H. Brown 1980). Adoption and marriage served to place the newcomers in a complex web of reciprocities and obligations, in hopes of assuring predictability and continuity of relationships. Although few traders fully understood these claims, they recognized that they too needed allies, and the economic, travel, and linguistic skills offered by Native kin.

Nor'Wester Duncan Cameron and his family exemplify the joint westerly movements of traders and their Native relatives. From 1796 to 1807, Cameron was in charge of the Lake Nipigon department, trading among the Central and Northern Ojibwa to the north and west of Lake Superior.

left, U.S. Military Academy, West Point Mus. Coll., N.Y.: no. 557; right, Amer. Mus. of Nat. Hist., New York: 50.1/7369-A.

Fig. 2. Trade goods used by Plains Ojibwa. left, Family with dog travois. The man holds a flintlock and pipe tomahawk. The woman and girl wear stroud dresses. There is an ax with a metal head on the dog travois at the left, and a brass kettle (vol. 4:340) on a dog at the right. Watercolor by Peter Rindisbacher, 1821–1823. right, Woman's stroud dress. Trade cloth dresses became popular in the late 19th century, most made simply by folding the cloth over at the shoulder and slitting the material for the wearer's head. The dresses lacked sleeves and side gussets characteristic of T-shaped dresses elsewhere on the Northern Plains (Hail 1980:90). These distinctive dresses represent a continuation of the Woodlands strap dress, which was made by sewing together two skins or by sewing shut the open edge of a single folded skin. Sleeves were separate, tied at the back of the wearer's neck. Collected by A. Skinner at Cowessess Res., Sask., 1913. Length, 113 cm.

By the early 1800s, he had an Ojibwa wife of the Loon clan and was writing perceptively about Ojibwa kinship, marriage, and customs. When in 1807 he moved to take charge of the Lake Winnipeg department, she and perhaps several relatives went too. At Bas de la Rivière (Fort Alexander, Manitoba) in the fall of 1807, Cameron arranged for one of his wife's cousins to marry his clerk, George Nelson, who was trading with Ojibwas lately established on the west side of Lake Winnipeg. These "marriages according to the custom of the country" contributed much to traders' success, but understandings of their meaning and status varied widely. Indian marriages diverged from European custom in their informality and in the flexibility with which either party could end the relationship. What the Ojibwa or Cree defined as marriage might be seen by a fur trader as casual and lacking legitimacy, or it might become lifelong. Cameron's Ojibwa union ended by 1817 and he married a woman of Upper Canada in 1820. Nelson, in contrast, married his Ojibwa wife in a church ceremony in Lower Canada in 1825, having settled her and their eight children there some years before (J.S.H. Brown 1988a; J.S.H. Brown and Brightman 1988:20).

Whatever forms they took, unions with Native women were almost universal for men who stayed in the fur trade for any length of time (fig. 3). The demographic implications were far-reaching. A reconstruction of 176 Hudson's Bay Company and North West Company officers' Native families, based on often spotty records, traced a minimum of three to four children per completed family before 1821, and over seven per family in 1821–1850 (fig. 4) (J.S.H. Brown 1980:154). "Country marriages" became common around the Great Lakes by the mid-1700s; several thousand children of mixed European-Indian parentage had probably been born in that region and in Rupert's Land by the 1820s. They did not all become Métis, a sociocultural and ethnic category that is not entirely biologically determined, but occupied diverse social and economic niches. Unknown numbers passed into their mothers' Indian communities, where their descendants left a legacy of French surnames from Canada, and Scottish names, notably from the Highlands (where many Nor'Westers originated) or from the Orkney Islands (the principal source of Hudson's Bay Company recruits by the late 1700s). Some took on their British or other patrilineal identities.

Around Red River and westward, however, a "new people" was forming by 1816, assuming distinctive economic roles and cultural attributes (Peterson and J.S.H. Brown 1985). The Red River Métis (or "Half-breeds" to use the English term then common) became dominant in buffalo hunting and pemmican manufacture, sometimes competing with Plains Cree and Ojibwa or Sioux for resources, but also often cooperating and intermarrying. They also overlapped with another social category known as *gens libres* or "freemen" (Canadian-born or part-Indian) who had left their fur trade employers and settled, usually near Native

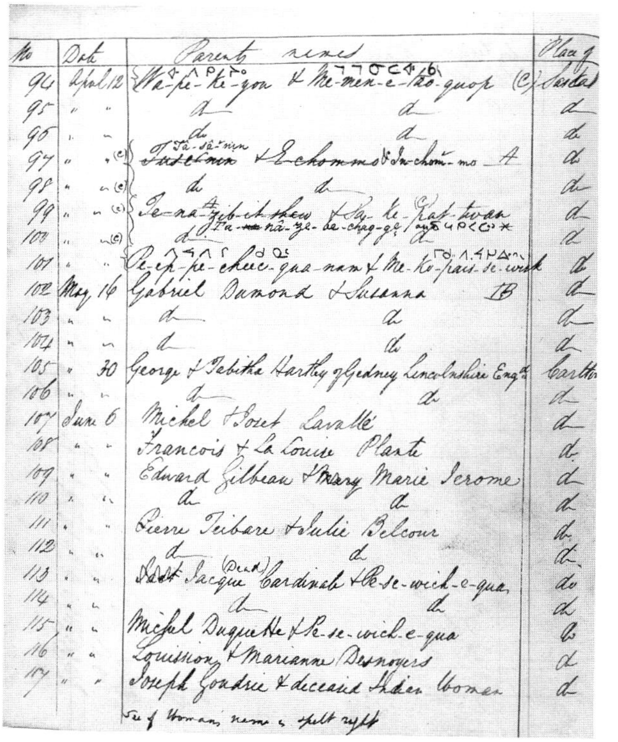

No	Date		Parents names	Place
94	April 12		Wa-pe-ke-yow & Me-men-e-ko-quop (C)	Sask
95	"	"	do do	do
96	"	"	do do	do
97	"	" (C)	Ta-sa-win & E-chom-mo & In-chom-mo A	do
98	"	" (C)	do do	do
99	"	" (C)	Pe-na-zib-it-shew & Sa-ke-Kah-twan	do
100	"	" (C)	do Ta-na-na-ye-ba-chag-ge	do
101	"		Pe-ep-pe-cheec-qua-nam & Me-ke-pais-se-wish	do
102	May 16		Gabriel Damond & Susanna IB	do
103	"	"	do do	do
104	"	"	do do	do
105	"	30	George & Tebitha Harthy of Gedney Lincolnshire Eng^d	Carlton
106	"	"	do do	do
107	June 6		Michel & Soset Lavallé	do
108	"	"	Francois & La Louise Plante	do
109	"	"	Edward Gilbeau & Mary Marie Jerome	do
110	"	"	do do	do
111	"	"	Pierre Teibare & Julie Belcour	do
112	"	"	do do	do
113	"	"	(Dead) Jacque Cardinal & Ke-se-wich-e-qua	do
114	"	"	do do	do
115	"	"	Michel Duquette & Ke-se-wich-e-qua	do
116	"	"	Louison & Marianne Desnoyers	do
117	"	"	Joseph Gondrie & deceased Indian Woman	do

See if Woman's name is spelt right

Glenbow-Alberta Inst., Calgary: NA-2371-2.

Fig. 3. Baptismal records, Apr. 12–June 6, 1841. The facing page (not illustrated) indicates that nos. 96–101 are baptisms from Plains Cree and Assiniboine camps in Sask., nos. 102–104 are from Ft. Edmonton, Alta., and nos. 105–117 are from Ft. Carlton, Sask. Children baptized ranged from a few days old to 12 years. Several were from marriages of French men and Native women. Some Indian names are respelled in dictionary phonetics or Cree syllabics. Manuscript page by Robert T. Rundle, a Methodist missionary for the Hudson's Bay Company, who traveled throughout the Sask. district.

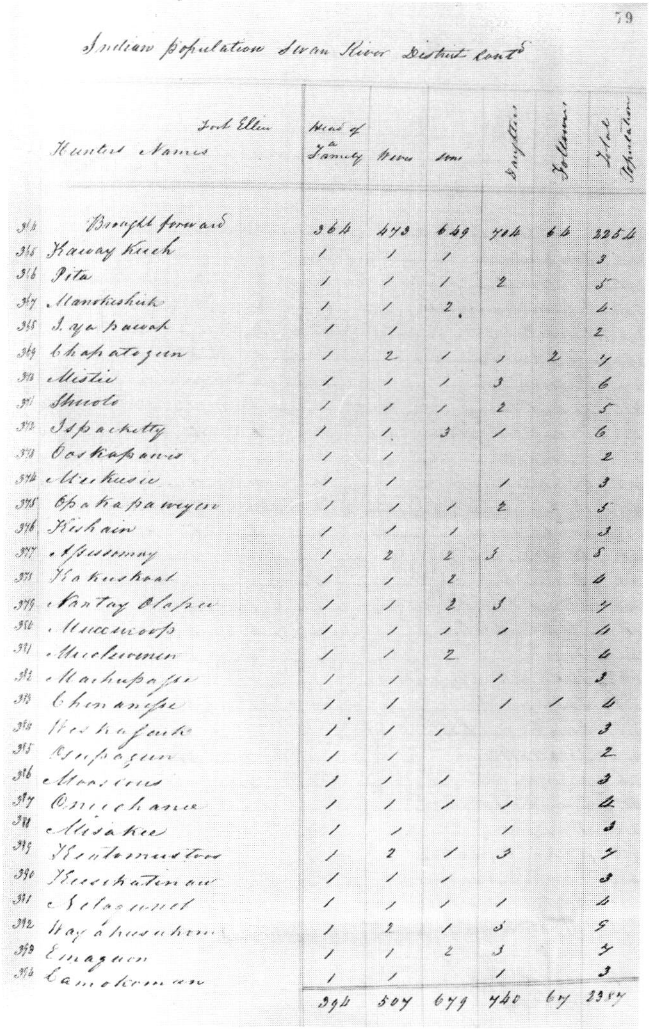

79

Indian population Swan River District cont^d

	Fort Ellice Hunters Names	Head of a Family	Wives	Sons	Daughters	Followers	Total Population
364	Brought forward	364	473	649	704	64	2254
365	Kaway Kuch	1	1	1			3
366	Pita	1	1	1	2		5
367	Manokeshuk	1	1	2			4
368	I.ya pawak	1	1				2
369	Chapatogun	1	2	1	1	2	7
370	Mistie	1	1	1	3		6
371	Shuolo	1	1	1	2		5
372	Ispacketty	1	1	3	1		6
373	Ooskapawis	1	1				2
374	Mukusie	1	1		1		3
375	Opakapawegun	1	1	1	2		5
376	Kishain	1	1	1			3
377	Apussomay	1	2	2	3		8
378	Kakuskoat	1	1	2			4
379	Nantay Olaspe	1	1	2	3		7
380	Muccewoop	1	1	1	1		4
381	Muckewenen	1	1	2			4
382	Machupasse	1	1		1		3
383	Chenanisse	1	1		1	1	4
384	Weskaisauk	1	1	1			3
385	Osupaguen	1	1				2
386	Moosicus	1	1	1			3
387	Onichance	1	1	1	1		4
388	Misakee	1	1		1		3
389	Kentomustoo	1	2	1	3		7
390	Kusikatinau	1	1	1			3
391	Nelasunit	1	1	1	1		4
392	Hay ahusuhom	1	2	1	5		9
393	Emaguen	1	1	2	3		7
394	Camokoman	1	1		1		3
		394	507	679	740	67	2387

Hudson's Bay Company Lib., Winnipeg, Man.:B239/z/p.79.

Fig. 4. Page from Hudson's Bay Company census of 1838 from the Swan River District, Ft. Ellice area. Hunters apparently from Plains Cree and Assiniboine local groups are listed by name, and tabulation shows head of family, wives, sons, daughters, followers, and total population.

relatives, as trappers, provisioners, guides, and interpreters ("Plains Métis," this vol.).

The rise of the colony of Red River around the Forks of the Red and Assiniboine rivers propelled the Plains Métis toward greater ethnic distinctiveness than their American kin of mixed descent ever acquired. In 1811, Thomas Douglas, earl of Selkirk, received about 116,000 square miles of land (known as Assiniboia) from the Hudson's Bay Company to found a colony for Scottish migrants; the company favored the settlement because it offered livelihoods, farmland, and other amenities for the growing numbers of Hudson's Bay Company traders and their Native families for whom Rupert's Land was the only home they knew. The colony began amid bitter competition between the Hudson's Bay and North West companies, as both expanded their trade toward the Athabaska and Mackenzie watersheds, and toward the Upper Missouri. Because Red River was at the heart of the North West Company's pemmican-producing country, the Nor'Westers and their Métis employees, led mainly by Cuthbert Grant, Jr., of Scots and Algonquian descent, were angered at their rival's colonial incursion. In 1814, colony Gov. Miles Macdonell moved to secure his settlers' survival by forbidding the export of pemmican and other provisions from Assiniboia for one year. Another proclamation prohibited hunting buffalo with horses, a measure that affected the Métis more than it did the neighboring Ojibwa, who still largely lacked horses (A.S. Morton 1973:561, 568). The conflict peaked on 19 June 1816 when colony Gov. William Semple and 19 others were killed by Métis Nor'Westers under Grant at Seven Oaks, just north of the Forks. Hostilities continued in Assiniboia, Athabaska, and elsewhere until the North West and Huson's Bay companies merged in 1821.

In July 1817, the first Indian treaty in the region was signed between Lord Selkirk and five Cree and Ojibwa chiefs, among them Peguis, whose assistance had been crucial to the first colonists (fig. 5). In European terms, land extending for the most part two miles on each side of the Assiniboine River to a point above Portage la Prairie, and along the Red River "to the mouth of the river going to Red Lake," was ceded in return for annuities of 100 pounds of tobacco to the two signing nations. Peguis and the other chiefs (fig. 6) doubtless saw the transaction as one of alliance and renewal where Selkirk saw surrender of land title. Peguis later often criticized the agreement, particularly as Métis and European dominance of the area cast his people into increasingly disadvantaged positions. Ojibwa concerns about it helped motivate the 1871 negotiation of Treaty No. 1 with the government of Canada (Peers 1994:92; Morris 1880:15, 25–26). In 1818, the fixing of the American border at 49° north latitude diminished the size of Assiniboia by one-third. The resultant bisecting of the Red River watershed placed the Ojibwa living between Pembina, North Dakota, and Red Lake River, Minnesota, under American jurisdiction one year after signing a British treaty (Morris 1880:15, 298).

In 1819–1820, measles reached the Red River and Lake Winnipeg region, initiating a new era in the disease history of Rupert's Land. Probably endemic by then in New York, Philadelphia, and Baltimore, it was carried westward by travel and contact as eastern populations grew. There were two paths of entry: from Sault Sainte Marie to Fort William (Thunder Bay, Ontario) and beyond on North West Company transport routes, and from the Mandan villages to Brandon House (near Brandon, Manitoba) and on to Red River. Whooping cough accompanied it in many instances, and influenza and scarlet fever came in subsequent years (F.J.P. Hackett 1991:10, 23, 136). Then smallpox revisited the northern plains in 1837–1838, sweeping up from Fort Union in the Missouri country (Trimble 1994:81–88). Its effects were deadly among the Blackfoot and their allies, and the Assiniboine lost up to three-quarters of their people. The Saskatchewan Cree largely escaped through the vaccination efforts of Hudson's Bay Company doctor William Todd at Fort Pelly on the upper Assiniboine River (Ray 1974: 188). In sum, even while many traders' Native families were multiplying in the early to mid-1800s, recurring epidemic disasters swept Plains Indian communities despite the probable speed with which populations recovered after each episode (Herring 1992:159).

Shifting Trade and Power Relations, 1821–1870

The merger of the Hudson's Bay and North West companies brought relative peace to the trade and fueled the growth of Red River as both the Métis and large numbers of Hudson's Bay Company families made it their home, many having lost employment in postmerger cutbacks. As well, in the early 1820s, the Hudson's Bay Company applied pressure to move the growing Métis settlement at Pembina

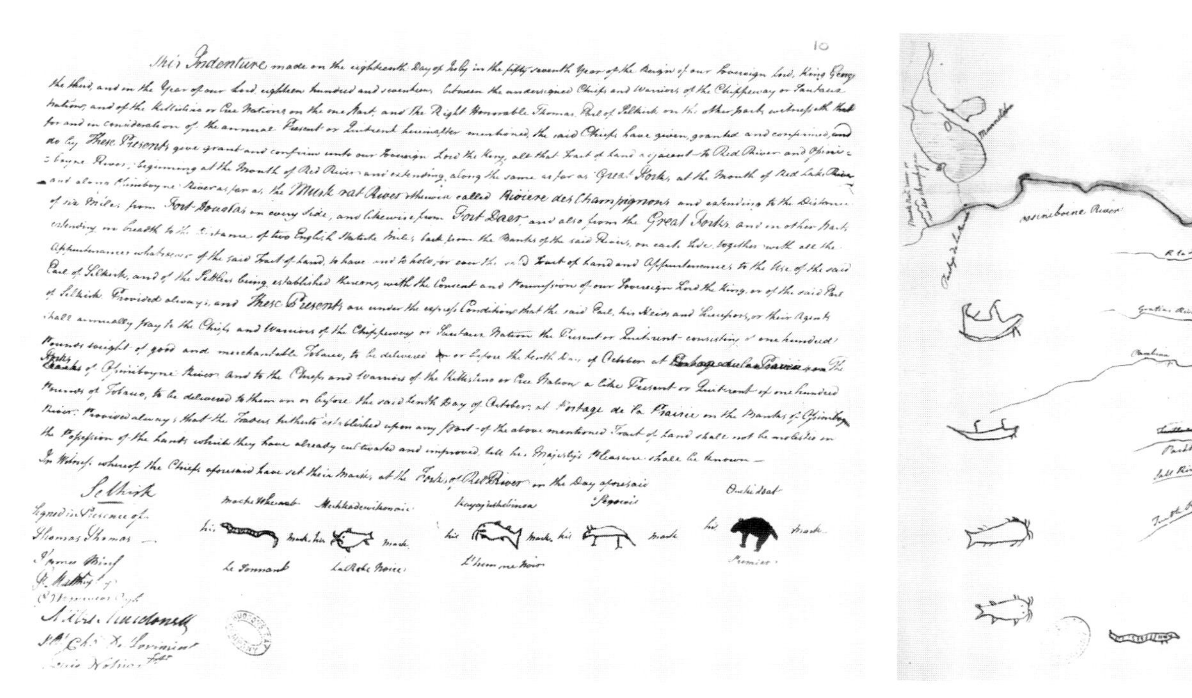

10

This Indenture made on the eighteenth Day of July in the fifty seventh Year of the Reign of our Sovereign Lord, King George the third, and in the Year of our Lord eighteen hundred and seventeen, between the undersigned Chiefs and Warriors of the Chippeway or Saulteaux Nation, and of the Killistine or Cree Nation, on the one Part, and the Right Honorable Thomas Earl of Selkirk on the other part, witnesseth that for and in consideration of the annual Present or Quitrent hereinafter mentioned, the said Chiefs have given, granted and confirmed, and do by These Presents give grant and confirm unto our Sovereign Lord the King, all that tract of land adjacent to Red River and Assiniboyne River, beginning at the Mouth of Red River and extending along the same as far as Great Forks at the Mouth of Red Lake River and along Assiniboyne River as far as the Musk rat River otherwise called Riviere des Champignons and extending to the Distance of six Miles from Fort Douglas on every Side, and likewise from Fort Daer, and also from the Great Forks and in other Parts extending in breadth to the Distance of two English Statute Miles back from the Banks of the said Rivers, on each Side, together with all the Appurtenances whatsoever of the said Tract of Land, to have and to hold for ever the said Tract of Land and Appurtenances to the Use of the said Earl of Selkirk, and of the Settlers being established thereon, with the Consent and Permission of our Sovereign Lord the King, or of the said Earl of Selkirk. Provided always, and These Presents are under the express Condition that the said Earl, his Heirs and Successors, or their Agents shall annually pay to the Chiefs and Warriors of the Chippeway or Saulteaux Nation the Present or Quitrent consisting of one hundred Pounds weight of good and merchantable Tobacco, to be delivered on or before the tenth Day of October at ~~Portage de la Prairie on the~~ Forks of Assiniboyne River. And to the Chiefs and Warriors of the Killistine or Cree Nation a like Present or Quitrent of one hundred Pounds of Tobacco, to be delivered to them on or before the said tenth Day of October at Portage de la Prairie on the Banks of Assiniboyne River. Provided always that the Traders hitherto established upon any Part of the above mentioned Tract of Land shall not be molested in the Possession of the Lands which they have already cultivated and improved, till his Majesty's Pleasure shall be known —

In Witness whereof the Chiefs aforesaid have set their Marks, at the Forks of Red River on the Day aforesaid

Selkirk

Signed in Presence of

Thomas Thomas

Miles Macdonell

Mache Wheseab his mark, Le Sonnant

Mechkaddewikonaie his mark, La Robe Noire

Kayajieskebinoa his mark, L'homme Noir

Pegowis his mark

Ouckidoat his mark, Premier

Hudson's Bay Company Arch., Winnipeg, Man.: left, E. 8/1, fos. 9d, 10; right, E. 8/1, fo. ll.

Fig. 5. Treaty between Lord Selkirk and Plains Cree and Plains Ojibwa chiefs. Names of Indian chiefs with their pictographs, left to right: Mache Wheseab (Le Sonnant), a marten; Mechkadewikonaié (La Robe Noire), catfish; Kayajieskebinoa (L'homme Noir), sturgeon; Pegowis (Peguis), otter; Ouckidoat (Le Premier), bear. right, Map showing the lands adjoining the Red and Assiniboine rivers that the chiefs were conveying to the British, July 18, 1817. The pictographs apparently represented the relative locations of each chief's band.

McGill U., McCord Mus., Montreal: M965.9.

Fig. 6. *Captain Bulger, Governor of Ossiniboia, and the Chiefs & Warriors of the Chippewa Tribe, of Red Lake, In Council, in the Colony House, in Fort Douglas, May 22nd 1823.* Chief Peguis, Plains Ojibwa, is thanking Andrew Bulger for the flag and medal presented to him. Watercolor, ink, sepia ink on paper by Peter Rindisbacher, 1823.

to Red River because of fears that their buffalo-hunting would provoke Sioux attacks and that they would use their base just south of the international boundary to challenge the Hudson's Bay Company's new monopoly (Ens 1996:51; A.S. Morton 1973:650). From the 1820s to 1870, Red River grew to a population of over 10,000, of which nine-tenths were of part-Indian descent (fig. 7). Dominated by the Hudson's Bay Company, it maintained a mixed economy based on trade, agriculture, and the buffalo hunt. However, farmers endured frequent floods, droughts, plagues of locusts, and early frosts, and lacked access to markets and hybrid varieties of wheat and other grains.

Summer buffalo hunting on horseback was a mainstay for many. Yet its very success eliminated the herds from the Red River area by 1862. The Hudson's Bay Company pemmican trade shifted westward, first to Brandon House, and after 1830, to Fort Ellice (Saskatchewan) at the confluence of the Qu'Appelle and Assiniboine rivers; a still more westerly base was needed after 1852 (Milloy 1988:105). By 1840, Métis hunters began wintering regularly in the region of the Qu'Appelle and Saskatchewan rivers, and around Pembina, Turtle Mountain, Wood Mountain, and the Touchwood and Cypress hills, in order to profit from the rising buffalo robe trade, which demanded prime skins with the winter hair intact (Ens 1996:75). These communities of up to 200 families were the settings in which Mitchif, a structured combination of Plains Cree verbs, French nouns, and other elements arose, becoming fixed as a unique language by the 1840s (Bakker 1997:173).

The Métis winterers entered a plains world shadowed by increased resource pressures, rivalry, and warfare despite the best peacemaking efforts of leaders such as the Plains Cree chief Maskepetoon (Broken Arm). The Plains Cree became dominant over a wide area, aided by a flexible and adaptable band structure; and trade and horse transport allowed enrichment of material culture. Yet they and their Assiniboine allies suffered recurring shortages of both horses and buffalo, while their Blackfoot enemies to the west enjoyed relative abundance (Milloy 1988:105). However, the Blackfoot Confederacy had its own troubles. About one-third of the Piegan and Blood population had been lost to measles in 1819–1820, and conflicts with their western and southern neighbors, the horse-rich Crow, Flathead, Eastern Shoshone, and Kootenai were endemic (Milloy 1988:86–87).

As for trade, the Hudson's Bay Company in the 1830s and 1840s saw its monopoly claims eroded across the plains. In Red River, the Métis developed their own profitable trade to Saint Paul, Minnesota, and to the west, using hundreds of their trademark two-wheeled Red River carts (Ens 1996:80–81). In 1849, public pressures for free trade kept the company from punishing the Red River Métis Guillaume Sayer despite his being convicted of trading independently (A.S. Morton 1973:815). Farther west, new American competition undercut old trade relationships. Since the 1780s, the Blackfoot and their allies had traded with the Hudson's Bay Company and its Canadian rivals; in the early 1800s, trade centered at Fort Edmonton and Rocky Mountain House on the North Saskatachewan River. Hostile encounters with the United States exploring expedition under Meriwether Lewis and William Clark in 1806 and with Missouri Fur Company traders long precluded American trade with the Blackfoot Confederacy. However, in the 1820s, the dynamics of the American fur business changed drastically with the advent of John Jacob Astor's American Fur Company. In 1827, former Nor'Wester Kenneth McKenzie took charge of the American Fur Company's Upper Missouri Outfit, founding Fort Union (vol. 4:370) (fig. 8) soon thereafter at the junction of the Yellowstone and Missouri rivers (D. Smyth 1984:4–5, 9–10). By 1832, aided especially by Jemmy Jock Bird, a Cree-English son of Hudson's Bay Company chief factor James Bird strongly connected to the Piegan, McKenzie cut severely into the returns of the Hudson's Bay Company Saskatchewan District. The use of large keelboats and steamers on the Missouri River permitted transport of trade goods at low cost and bulk shipping of buffalo robes for a growing American market: about 70,000 annually in 1833–1843, compared to at most, 10,000 a year traded to the Hudson's Bay Company. Guns traded to the Blackfoot and their allies strengthened them in their battles against the Flathead and others, although internal strife between the Piegan and Blood also surfaced (D. Smyth 1984:11–13; Milloy 1988:93, 95).

American Fur Company prices and diplomacy attracted other groups to Fort Union. In 1831, four chiefs of the Plains Cree, Assiniboine, Yanktonai Sioux, and Plains Ojibwa trading at Fort Union were invited to visit President Andrew Jackson in Washington, D.C., to foster peace with

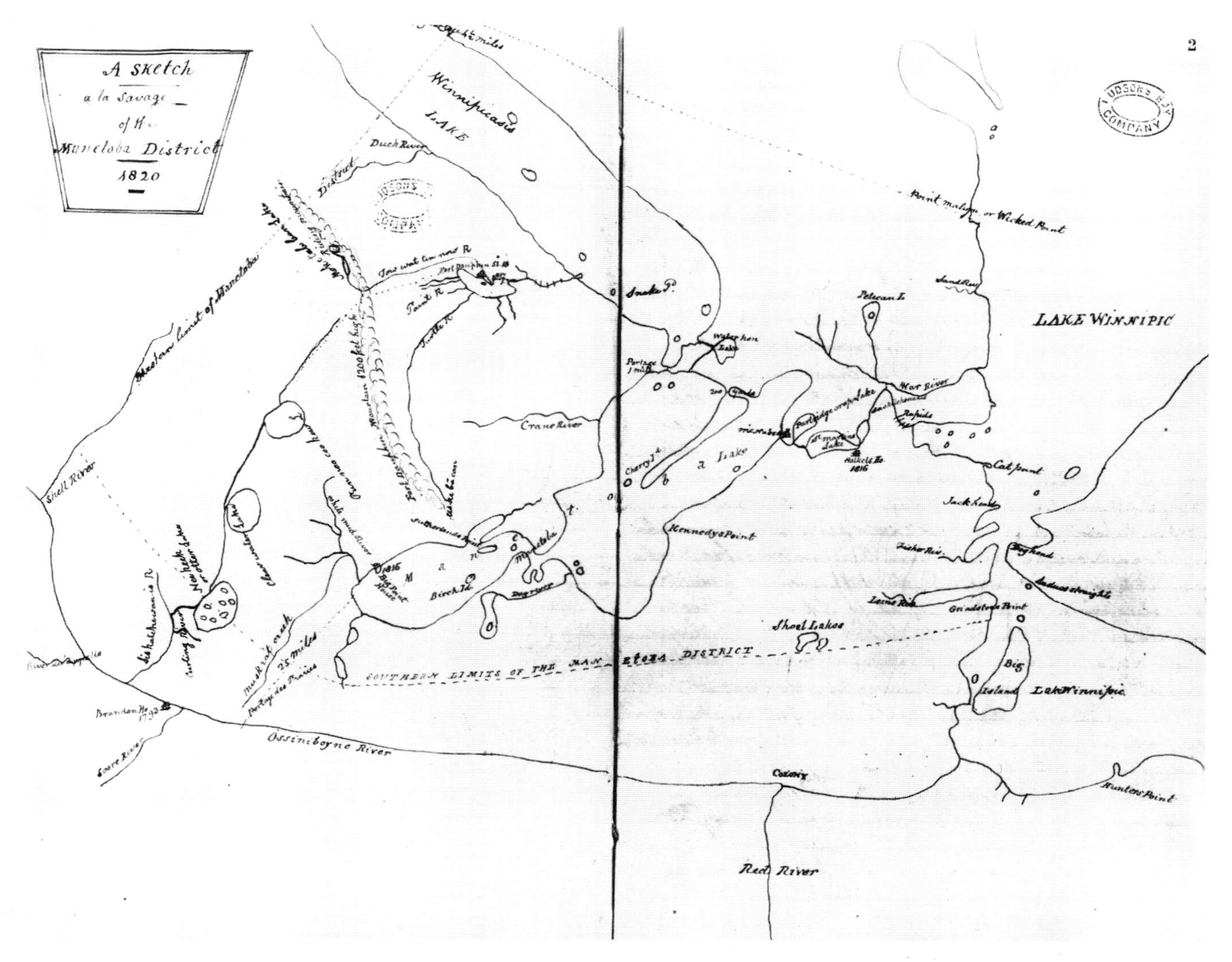

Hudson's Bay Company Arch., Winnipeg, Man.: B.51/e/1 fols. Id-2 (N3196).

Fig. 7. *A Sketch a la Savage of the Manetoba District 1820*, the last of many important maps attributed to Hudson's Bay Company cartographer Peter Fidler. It includes information from several individuals, possibly Plains Métis. Drawn during Fidler's posting at Ft. Dauphin, Man., this map may have accompanied his first district report (Ruggles 1991:67).

the western tribes. The Plains Cree chief, Maskepetoon, later became known for his efforts to make peace with the Blackfoot, and was killed in 1869 during one such attempt (Dempsey 1976:537). Temporary peace agreements were common but usually short-lived among mobile peoples competing for buffalo, horses, trade, and increasingly, land on which to live undisturbed. Métis incursions across the unmarked international boundary and into Sioux lands also fostered ongoing conflict, manifested most dramatically in the Red River Métis buffalo hunters' defeat of a large Sioux force on the Grand Coteau of the Missouri in July 1851 (M.A. MacLeod and W.L. Morton 1974:144–149). Farther west, Father Pierre-Jean de Smet in 1846 described how shortages of buffalo were bringing different groups into hostile proximity: "The Crees, Assiniboines, the Snakes [Eastern Shoshone], the Bannocks, the Crows, the Blackfeet, the Aricaras and the Sioux are drawing near to these plains each year; whenever they meet, it is war to the death" (quoted in Milloy 1988:99).

Missions, Schools, and Cultural Change to 1870

In 1818, Father Joseph-Norbert Provencher was sent from Quebec to serve the Red River Métis; the priests who followed not only worked in the Roman Catholic parishes but also traveled on the Métis buffalo hunts, being present, for example, at the Battle of Grand Coteau in 1851 to offer support and record the event (M.A. MacLeod and W.L. Morton 1974:146–148). In 1820, the Hudson's Bay Company brought the first Church of England clergyman, John West, to minister to its current and former employees

Joslyn Art Mus., Omaha, Nebr.

Fig. 8. Pasesick-Kaskutau, Assiniboine man of the Stone band. He wears a coat made from buffalo hide but cut in Euro-American style, mittens, and a badger skin hood. He carries a gun, powder horn, ramrod, and ammunition bag, all trade goods. The name Prince Maximilian used for him is Plains Cree *pisisik-kaskite·w* 'nothing but gunpowder'. Watercolor and pencil by Karl Bodmer, Ft. Union, Mo. Terr., 1833.

and their families and to Native communities. West married numerous couples previously united according to the "custom of the country" and established a small boarding school for Indian students drawn from a wide area, in hopes that they would become converts and teachers to their people (A.S. Morton 1973:634–635). Some did so; the most interesting Plains Indian graduate of the 1820s was Charles Pratt (Askenootow), a *ne·hiyawi-pwa·t* (Cree-Assiniboine) whose preaching career reveals motifs of hardship and discrimination common to Native clergy, along with a faithful connection to his own people that is covertly expressed in his writings but vigorously alive in familial oral traditions about him (Stevenson 1996).

Native people had long heard about Christianity from conversations with fur traders and sometimes freely incorporated its ideas and explanations into their own thought. Missionaries were seen as potential allies and powerful helpers; Peguis and his people at Red River, for example, saw their charity as "a slender but important new resource for the Ojibwa to harvest." The fact that the churchmen expected Indians to settle into European-style farming and gender roles and set aside all but one wife generated debate and resistance. Peguis did not convert until 1840, 20 years after the first Anglican mission began (Peers 1994:130–131, 160–161).

By the 1850s, Red River was unique in Rupert's Land both for its growing size and for its high per capita ratio of clergy. Alexander Ross recorded that this "snug little flock" was cared for by "one English Bishop and five Church of England missionaries, who are equally balanced by one Catholic Bishop and five French priests" (quoted in Pannekoek 1991:33). Elsewhere, the mobility and warfare of plains people were not conducive to missions except at a few major posts. In 1840, several British Wesleyan Methodist missionaries from Canada settled at strategic points; Robert T. Rundle (fig. 3) was their plains emissary at Fort Edmonton. A Roman Catholic priest, Jean-Baptiste Thibault, arrived two years later and succeeded better than Rundle with the local Métis and Cree; however, Rundle did better with the Stoneys. Their best-known successors were Father Albert Lacombe (vol. 6:149) and the Methodist father and son, George and John C. McDougall. Anglicans and Presbyterians arrived on the western prairies somewhat later. All sought to encourage agriculture and schooling. They did best with the groups who had been involved longest in the fur trade; none made progress with the Blackfoot until after 1870, although Lacombe made friendly contacts. The buffalo-based way of life of the holdouts was blamed, and its demise welcomed by the missionaries (Grant 1984:145–148, 157). The clergy were less aware, however, of the extent to which even their Plains converts and catechists, especially if still retaining their language and connections with their people, also retained Native identities and world views, while often satisfying outsiders with "a yes that means no," or appropriating Christian ideas and practices "on terms consonant with native modes of thought and relevant to perceived needs" (Grant 1984:238, 263).

In the 1850s and 1860s, explorers with new agendas came to the Northern Plains. Two scientific expeditions that arose from British and Canadian interest in the resources and settlement potential of Rupert's Land had particular significance. In 1857–1859, the British Colonial Office and the Royal Geographical Society supported an expedition across the west led by John Palliser; it found the Red River and north Saskatchewan promising for agricultural development, though warning of water and wood shortages in southern Saskatchewan (the semi-arid "Palliser Triangle") (Spry 1973:10–11, 283–284). In summer 1858, Henry Youle Hind of the University of Toronto conducted scientific exploration of the Red, Assiniboine, and South Saskatchewan river valleys and agreed with some of Palliser's findings, though as a Canadian annexationist, he was "more anxious to find the country fertile than Captain Palliser," and placed the semi-arid zone farther west (A.S. Morton 1973:835).

Canadians' perceptions of Rupert's Land as a rich, empty hinterland to be cultivated for their own purposes contributed to troubles in 1869–1870. Red River Métis leader Louis Riel and many followers, frustrated that the Hudson's Bay Company sold its territory to Great Britain for transfer to Canada without consultation, and without confirming residents' land titles, resented the arrival of land surveyors and of a new Canadian governor in the fall of 1869 before the transfer was even completed. The governor was stopped at the border at Pembina, and Riel established a provisional government that negotiated the formation of the province of Manitoba and its entry into the Canadian confederation in 1870 ("Plains Métis," this vol.).

Parallel to rising Métis tensions, Indian groups on both sides of the border grew increasingly concerned about proposals for telegraph and rail lines, the disappearance of the buffalo, and losses of their lands to newcomers. The 1862 Sioux Conflict, provoked by the rapid White settlement of Minnesota, propelled many Sioux refugees westward and into Rupert's Land in search of assistance and supplies; their visits, notably that of Little Crow and 80 Mdewakanton Sioux followers to Red River in May 1863 (G.C. Anderson 1986:174–175), were the best known of many Sioux trips across the border to seek allies and munitions before those of Sitting Bull and his band in the 1870s. Their movements and requests taxed the diplomatic skills not only of the British and American officials involved, but also of the Métis and Ojibwa concerned by their presence.

The stresses of the 1860s were harbingers of enormous changes in the following decade. By 1880, Canadian Plains Indians had signed seven major treaties ceding the great majority of their land, leaving them with only scattered reserves, and they were subject to increasingly restrictive governmental legislation and control. The buffalo were gone, and rail and telegraph lines were becoming a reality, along with steamships and commercial fishing on major waterways. Canadian and European settlers were flooding in to claim newly surveyed homesteads. Northern plains people were rapidly and dramatically affected by the transition from Rupert's Land to Canada. For them, 1870 was genuinely the end of an era.

History of the Canadian Plains Since 1870

DAVID McCRADY

Rupert's Land and the North-Western Territory, the vast territorial holdings of the Hudson's Bay Company, were transferred to the Dominion of Canada in 1870. During the next three decades, the Canadian government took steps to integrate this immense area into the new state.

The Conservative government of John A. Macdonald was careful to retain control over its new possessions. Manitoba was made a province in 1870 and Saskatchewan and Alberta in 1905 under the Canadian federal-provincial model, which granted certain powers to each level of government (L.H. Thomas 1978). The Canadian constitution grants jurisdiction over land and natural resources to the provinces, but in the case of the prairie provinces the federal government usurped control until 1930. The federal government also administered law and order in the Northwest Territories, establishing the North West Mounted Police in 1873. Controlling land and bringing law to the frontier contributed to Ottawa's three-part "national policy" to promote and colonize the West while developing the entire nation. A protective tariff would promote Canadian industry, western settlement would provide a market, and a transcontinental railway would send people and goods west while returning grain eastward.

An unspoken fourth pillar of the national policy was that aboriginal peoples would be brought under Canadian administration and not allowed to obstruct western development. The Manitoba and Northwest superintendencies, established soon after the transfer of Rupert's Land to Canada, were replaced by the eastern model of Indian agencies and agents. The Indian policy of the older Province of Canada was "generalized" across the new Dominion after confederation (Upton 1973:51). Before 1867, the primary goals of Indian policy were to protect, christianize, and assimilate Native peoples. These remained the basis of policy after confederation, but the Canadian government later employed more coercive strategies, which it embodied in the Act to Amend and Consolidate the Laws Respecting Indians, or, as it was short-titled, the Indian Act, first passed in 1876 (Tobias 1976). Despite the increasingly restrictive nature of its administration, Canada nonetheless prided itself on its "humane" Indian policy.

Aboriginal societies on the plains moved from independence to dependence after 1870. Canadian Indian policy promoted Christianity, agriculture, and European-style education over the objections of Native peoples, and the Indian Act and its amendments gave increasing power to government.

Transfer and Treaties

The Canadian government's hope that it would peacefully acquire Rupert's Land backfired at the outset. The inhabitants of the territory—Indians, Métis, and Europeans—were not consulted about the transfer, and the Red River Métis, whose land titles were directly threatened by the arrival of Canadian surveyors in 1869, even before the transfer was complete, responded by establishing a provisional government under the leadership of Louis Riel ("Plains Métis," fig. 2, this vol.). An expeditionary force under Gen. Garnet Wolseley arrived from Canada in August 1870, and Riel's resistance was crushed.

The events at Red River were restricted to the Métis and European residents of the Red River Settlement, although some commentators feared that the resistance would spread beyond the settlement, or that the Indians might be incited to take up arms. Newspapers in Saint Paul, Minnesota, for example, reported in late 1869 that Santee Sioux refugees from Minnesota who had arrived in Rupert's Land in 1862 following the Sioux Conflict were being recruited to fight the Métis by William McDougall, the Canadian governor, and Col. J.S. Dennis, the leader of the Canadian surveyors. A delegation of Santee Sioux from Portage la Prairie did arrive in the settlement on 31 December 1869 and met a number of Métis, including Louis Riel, but they had only come to find out what was happening (W.L. Morton 1956:72–73, 246–249).

Knowledge of the sale of Rupert's Land and the arrival in Red River of soldiers traveled across the northern plains and made aboriginal leaders in the region wary of Canadian intentions toward them and their lands. Mistawasis, a Plains Cree leader from Battle River, heard that "the white man was coming to take their lands, that the white braves [soldiers] were coming to the country," and he asked William Butler, a member of Wolseley's expedition, during the winter of 1870–1871 to tell him whether this was true (W.F. Butler 1891:237, 360). An Assiniboine leader, apparently from the Carlton district, disclosed to Methodist missionary George McDougall in October 1875 that "foolish men have told us that the Great Chief [the lieutenant governor] would send his young men to our country until they outnumbered us, and that then he would laugh at us" (A. Morris 1991:174), and Roman Catholic missionary Constantine Scollen reported in 1876 that the Blackfoot were fearful that "this country will be gradually taken from them without any ceremony" (A. Morris 1991:249). Even the Teton and Yanktonai Sioux who lived along the Missouri River in American territory were said to be aggrieved "by the state of matters in the province consequent on the transference of this country to Canada" (M.L. West et al. 1873).

Native peoples, who saw it as visible proof that the Whites had stolen their land, were alarmed when the Hudson's Bay Company began surveying the land around each of its trading posts, an action permitted under the terms of the transfer. At the negotiations for Treaty No. 4 in September 1874 the issue of surveys consumed two days of talks. Plains Ojibwa spokesman Pasquah, who saw that the Hudson's Bay Company had proceeded to survey the land before the aboriginal title had been extinguished, on this basis argued that the £300,000 paid to the company by Canada belonged, in fact, to the Indians (A. Morris 1991:106). As far as the Indians were concerned, the Hudson's Bay Company was present on aboriginal lands only because they had given the company their permission.

Between 1871 and 1877, the Canadian government negotiated seven treaties with the aboriginal peoples of the southern part of the Northwest Territories. Five of these (Treaties No. 1, 2, 4, 6, 7) involved Plains Indians (fig. 1). To what degree native leaders and government commissioners held the same understanding of the concepts embodied in these European documents has long been a matter of debate.

Canadian historians have generally agreed that the numbered treaties were fraught with misunderstanding: the cultural distance between native and newcomer was sufficient to preclude a mutual understanding of the treaties' terms (Archer 1980:61; Chalmers 1977:25; Dempsey 1972:105–7; J.R. Miller 1991:164–5; Spry 1991:88). Native and non-native leaders viewed treaties and treaty rights "within two different systems of knowledge and perceptions of reality" (Price 1987:ix), and the difference between these two systems, remarked Stoney Chief John Snow, "is like day and night" (J. Snow 1985:44).

While the Canadian government clearly saw the treaties as instruments for the extinguishment of aboriginal title, native peoples were apt to view them quite differently. The context in which aboriginal leaders probably viewed western treaty making was undoubtedly set before 1870 in the fur-trade period. Aboriginal people in Rupert's Land had long before established the custom of meeting annually with representatives of fur trade companies, notably the Hudson's Bay Company, to renew and renegotiate their political and economic relations, and the rituals associated with these agreements appeared during negotiations with Canadian treaty commissioners (J.E. Foster 1987:181–200; Tobias 1986:241–252). However, agreements between Indians and fur traders were used to facilitate the fur and provision trade, not to buy and sell land. With the legal transfer of Rupert's Land from the Hudson's Bay

left, Glenbow-Alberta Inst., Calgary: NB-16-114; right, Prov. Mus. of Alta., Edmonton: Ethnology Dept: H86.49.1.

Fig. 1. Treaty medals, issued to the chief of each tribe who signed Treaties No. 1–8. left, Chief Yellow Horse, Blackfoot, wearing a Treaty No. 7 medal (with ribbon) issued in 1877. He did not sign the treaty; the medal was probably inherited in 1903 when he became head chief of the tribe. A second medal is the Assembly of Indian Tribes medal issued in 1901 to commemorate a visit of the Duke and Duchess of Cornwall and York to Calgary. He also wears a beaded buffalo effigy figure on his lapel. The band of his top hat says "Head chief." His wife, Double Cutting Woman, and grandson, David Yellow Horse, are at right. Harry Lawson Webster Levy, Lord Burnham, Chairman of the Imperial Press Association, at left, had been made a "chief" and given an Indian name, and for the occasion he wore a buckskin shirt and feather bonnet and held a pipe and tobacco pouch. Photographed at Gleichen, Blackfoot Res., Alta., fairgrounds, Aug. 1920. right, Obverse of Treaty No. 8 silver medal (Jamieson 1936:53; for reverse side, vol. 6:274). Diameter 7.6 cm.

Company to Canada, aboriginal nations, knowing that Canadian treaty commissioners were not fur traders and that their intentions were very different, adapted their own strategies in their effort to create an effective working relationship with the new government.

Native peoples held a diverse range of beliefs about treaties. In some cases they saw treaties as agreements to share the land with Whites, while in others they viewed them as agreements to relinquish only limited rights or simply as pacts of friendship and peace (Saskatchewan [1974–1975]:134; Tarasoff 1980:178–179; Friesen 1986:48–49; Price 1987; Treaty 7 Tribal Council 1996). It is probable that groups like the Blackfoot saw the treaties as an opportunity to obtain allies against American whisky traders arriving from the south, with whom they had had considerable destructive contact (McCrady 1993). At least some Indian leaders understood that the treaties involved the sale of enormous tracts of land and that, in exchange for that land, Indian negotiators expected to obtain economic security from the Canadian government (Friesen 1986:43–45, 49–50). The demands made at the treaty negotiations indicate that the Indians wanted the Canadians to guarantee the same level of economic security that the land itself had provided. At the negotiations for Treaty No. 6, for example, the Plains Cree made clear their desire to learn more about farming. They indicated that they wanted agricultural implements, cattle, seed, tools, schools, missionaries, and a ban on the sale of liquor. They expected to be allowed to hunt as formerly, wanted free medicines, and hoped to extract a promise from the government that it would provide them with emergency rations if such became necessary during the transitional period (A. Morris 1991:212–215).

The Food Crisis

The disappearance of the buffalo from the Canadian plains in the late 1870s occurred at virtually the same time as treaty making. The bison's range had been shrinking to the south and southwest by the 1820s and 1830s (Ray 1974:182–183). Nevertheless, they remained numerous as late as 1874 in the Milk River region of what became southern Alberta (Graspointner 1980:34–35). This abundance, however, proved transitory. By the close of 1879 the bison was all but extinct in Canada, and the last remnants of the northern herd in the United States failed as an exploitable resource for Indians and hide-hunters alike by 1883 (Spry 1976a:26).

Native peoples observed the dwindling herds and understood the phenomenon in ways that differed from those of Europeans. Nineteenth-century Western Woods Cree did not possess any western-style concept of scarcity. The Cree believed that as long as religious observances regarding the hunt were observed, animals that were hunted were reborn either as young animals or adults. Such religious precepts encouraged, rather than discouraged, harvesting (Brightman 1993:chap. 9). Plains Cree and Plains Ojibwa had close ties to their woodland kin and subscribed to similar beliefs. Moreover, some aboriginal leaders viewed the arrival in the winter of 1876–1877 of some 3,000 Teton Sioux refugees in the Cypress Hills and at Wood Mountain in the southern part of the Northwest Territories as a factor contributing to the food shortage. Crowfoot, a Blackfoot leader, blamed the crisis on the Teton Sioux, telling Edgar Dewdney, the Indian commissioner for Manitoba and the Northwest Territories, at their first meeting in July 1879, "If you drive away the Sioux and make a hole so that the buffalo may come in, we will not trouble you for food; if you don't do that, you must feed us or show us how to live" (Canada 1880:78–79). Dewdney commented in 1881, after the majority of the Teton Sioux had returned to the United States, that knowledge of their surrender led the Plains Cree to believe that the buffalo would be able to move north (Canada 1882:37).

The government of Canada took advantage of the food crisis to coerce Plains peoples into surrendering their lands and submitting to its authority. In the fall of 1879, Commissioner Dewdney announced that rations would be given only to those who took treaty, save the sick, aged, and orphans. Many leaders, among them Big Bear (vol. 4:348) and Little Pine of the Saskatchewan River Cree and Piapot of the Plains Cree and Assiniboine of the region south of the Qu'Appelle River, refused, preferring to wait to see how faithful the government would be in honoring the treaties. In response, Dewdney employed an old Hudson's Bay Company practice: he would recognize any adult male Cree as chief of a new band if 100 or more people acknowledged him as leader. Dewdney expected the starving Cree to abandon their leaders and adopt new ones in order to get rations and, in part, his plan worked. Little Pine's people persuaded him to take treaty in 1879, and when Big Bear refused to take treaty, almost half his following left him, joining Lucky Man and Thunderchild to form new bands and to receive rations. Taking treaty to avoid starvation was not, however, an acceptance of the treaty terms. Those leaders who took treaty continued to meet to discuss treaty terms and issues (Tobias 1983).

The government's solution to the food crisis was the introduction of a reserve-based agricultural program. The government began surveying aboriginal reserves and appointed 12 farming instructors to teach European-style farming to the Indians of the Northwest Territories. European-style agriculture, it was expected, would provide a long-term economic base for Plains Indians (in fact, for all Indians in Canada who took up agriculture) and eliminate the need for government rationing. However, the program was a failure. Euro-Canadians had no knowledge of the climate or soil types of the region; nor did they understand how to farm the prairies (N. Dyck 1991). As European agriculture was based on grains, and not on the potatoes, squash, and corn familiar to some Plains Ojibwa or Saulteaux bands (Moodie and Kaye

1982), Euro-Canadians were unable to provide seed grain and plant stocks acclimatized to the region. Attempts to import European-style farming were also hampered by the lack of reliable and efficient means of transportation from Ontario to the West, which caused seed and equipment to arrive late, and by the poor quality of what was delivered. Heavy rains, such as those in the spring of 1877, washed out existing trails and prevented the delivery of seed (Laird 1877). Farming instructors were political appointees, and thus the level of farming instruction they were able to impart was limited.

Plains Cree leaders from Carlton and Battleford, Saskatchewan, including Big Bear, Mistawasis, and Attackakoop, made a comprehensive list of the inadequacies of the agricultural program during a council held at Duck Lake, Saskatchewan, in August 1884. The cattle and horses that the government had supplied under the treaty terms were insufficient for them to make a livelihood and many were wild. Indian Agent J.A. Macrae, who attended this meeting, noted, "This was bad faith on the part of the government, as the Commissioners who made the treaty promised them well broken beasts." They had been given poor quality wagons, and none of the promised clothing or medical supplies. They were in dire need of food assistance; when the treaty was being negotiated they had been promised "that when they were destitute liberal assistance would be given to them." Agent Macrae noted the "sweet promises" made by the government in order to get the country from the Indians, and the Indians' growing fear that the goverment would now cheat them (Macrae 1884).

Despite the difficulties, many Plains peoples attempted to farm. Plains Cree bands in Treaty No. 6 and the Plains Ojibwa and Assiniboine bands in the eastern part of Treaty No. 4 were initially receptive to the agricultural program. The Plains Cree leader Poundmaker settled on a reserve in 1879, and in the following two years he and his band made substantial progress in breaking land and constructing buildings. They were "working like Trojans," their farm instructor reported (Canada 1880:84). In 1880 over 11,000 Indians settled on reserves, erected houses and broke some 4,600 acres of land for cultivation. The harvest that year yielded modest quantities of wheat, oats, barley, and potatoes. Indian Commissioner Dewdney, repeating a report on the harvest at the Red Pheasant Reserve near Battleford, observed that the crop there had been "magnificent," with heavy yields of potatoes, turnips, and beets; the wheat and barley had matured and the Indians of this band were said to have demonstrated themselves to be "intelligent, peacefully inclined and good workers" (Canada 1880:83).

Farmers were supported in their efforts by their leaders, who both farmed and used their relationship with the Canadian government to lobby for their people. Crowfoot had taken a co-operative approach to his relations with Canadian officials since the signing of Treaty No. 7 in 1877 (Dempsey 1972). While his followers were generally willing in principle to take up farming, he insisted that sufficient rations be provided to allow them to commit themselves fully to agricultural pursuits. Accordingly, the Blackfoot did not settle on reserves until 1881. Mahpiyahdinape, a Dakota leader in western Manitoba, planted test crops and was one of the earliest to plant Red Fife wheat (Elias 1988:73). On the Pasquah Reserve, farmers broke 30 acres of virgin prairie without draft animals and resorted to eating their dogs as they could not feed themselves while breaking new land. Pasquah went to Winnipeg to ask the lieutenant governor of Manitoba, Joseph Cauchon, for seed, draft oxen, and food. All he got was a small amount of provisions (S. Carter 1990:76).

Those who did not take up farming in the 1870s and early 1880s went after the remaining buffalo herds in Montana. By the autumn of 1879, officials noted that hunting parties of Plains Cree, Assiniboine, Blood, Blackfoot, and Peigan had all left for the United States (Canada 1880:2, 81, 97). Dewdney estimated that these groups numbered somewhere between 7,000 and 8,000 people (Canada 1880:81). That large numbers were involved was also indicated by Norman T. Macleod, the Indian agent for Treaty No. 7, who wrote that "only the old and helpless" remained behind in the Blackfoot camp near Fort Macleod (Canada 1880:97). Some of the Plains Cree and about half of the Blood returned to Canada during the summer of 1880 to receive their annuities, but the Plains Cree immediately returned to the south when they heard that bison had been moving into the area around Fort Belknap on the American side of the Milk River (Canada 1880:93). Many Indians returned during the summer of 1881, but 4,000 remained in the United States (Canada 1882:54).

The presence of so many "British" Indians on American territory produced friction between the Canadian and American governments, especially as Native peoples from Canada sometimes traveled south with tacit Canadian approval. Dewdney encouraged Plains Cree bands and most of the Blood, Blackfoot, Peigan, and Sarcee to hunt on American territory when it became clear that the Canadian government could not provide sufficient rations (Jobson 1985; Samek 1987:40). To keep this fact from American authorities, who did not want "British" Indians depriving American Indians of their own food supply, the Indian Department directed Indian Commissioner Dewdney "to notify all Agents or other employés of the Department who are likely to come in contact with the officials of the American Gov[t] or officers of the American Army to enter into no discussion with or express any opinion to them in regard to Canadian Indians crossing the American line" (Canada. Deputy Superintendent General of Indian Affairs 1881). Relations between the two governments were already strained by the presence in Canada of Teton Sioux under Sitting Bull, Big Road, Spotted Eagle and others who had crossed into Canada following their victory over American troops at the Battle of the Little Bighorn in the summer of 1876 (Manzione 1991; Utley 1993). In the midst of a food shortage of cataclysmic proportions, the migration of so many people back and forth across the boundary gave both governments an opportunity to vent their frustration over their inability to respond to the crisis.

Not wanting disputes over reserves with Native peoples to obstruct its plans for western settlement, or for its difficulties with the American government to escalate, the Canadian government tried to force Native peoples to select reserves farther north, closer to the North Saskatchewan River. This brought federal officials into conflict with Plains Cree and Assiniboine leaders. When confronted by requests to remove to the north, Native leaders politely, but firmly, refused. Not only did they want to remain in the south because this would position them closer to the remaining herds, but claiming reserves in close proximity to one another in and around the Cypress Hills would concentrate their numbers and help them to preserve their autonomy (Tobias 1983).

Nevertheless, the federal government refused to accept reserves Native peoples had chosen in the south. Instead, Indian Affairs and North West Mounted Police officials used starvation to compel Indians to leave the boundary area and go to reserves in the north. North West Mounted Police Commissioner A.G. Irvine announced in the spring of 1882 that he was "fully determined to starve them out" if they remained in the Cypress Hills at Fort Walsh (Irvine 1882). Later that year, Indian Agent A. McDonald reported that the aboriginal peoples then camped at Fort Walsh "look very bad. I know they are not getting enough flour but I like to punish them a little" (A. McDonald 1882). Government attempts to starve the Plains Cree, Assiniboine, and others into leaving the borderlands resulted only in making it even more necessary to stay in the south where they were closer to the remaining herds. Only when the herds failed in Montana were Native peoples compelled to leave the Cypress Hills and to migrate to reserves along the North Saskatchewan River.

The Northwest Rebellion of 1885

The money spent on rations for western Indians was an embarrassment to the Canadian government and fodder for its opponents. Government support of needy individuals and communities was almost unknown in nineteenth-century Canada and was morally repugnant in the neomercantilist economic ideologies favored by most parliamentarians (N. Dyck 1991:61). Thus, the government took pains to reduce the Indian Affairs budget at every opportunity. Spending on rations between 1882 and 1884 was reduced by 15 percent (N. Dyck 1986:128), sparking several near-fatal incidents on reserves. The farming instructor at Fort Pitt, in Treaty No. 6, was threatened at knifepoint when he refused rations to an Indian who had just returned from an unsuccessful hunting trip. A band from the Crooked Lakes district in Treaty No. 4 seized a government storehouse and distributed its contents to band members. The police officer sent to investigate the incident recorded the explanation offered by their leader, Yellow Calf: "When they stole the provisions their women and children were starving . . . and that they were well-armed and might just as well die as to be starved by the Government" (I. Andrews 1975).

Other incidents, and reports that Big Bear and other leaders were planning meetings throughout the region in 1884, were insufficient to convince officials in Ottawa to modify their approach. Although ration levels were increased very slightly in 1884, the government strengthened the North West Mounted Police and redoubled its efforts to enforce the Indian Department's "no work, no food" rule. All those who received rations, except the aged and the ill, were to provide some work in exchange for it. The inadequacy of this response was quickly demonstrated when a police patrol tried to arrest Piapot, the chief organizer of an Indian council held in the southern part of the prairies. The patrol was surrounded by armed warriors, and the Thirst Dance and political council it was sent to prevent proceeded as planned. The police chose to withdraw from the situation (Tobias 1983:534–535).

The Northwest Rebellion, which lasted only a little over two months in the spring of 1885, marked a turning point in the history of the region. The defeat of the Métis at Batoche by Canadian military forces that had been speeded to the Northwest by the Canadian Pacific Railway marked the end of any serious threat to the government's authority within the region. The most remarkable aspect of Indian involvement in the rebellion was that it was so limited (Stonechild and Waiser 1997). Dissident members of Big Bear's band under Wandering Spirit and Imases killed Indian Agent Thomas Quinn and eight other men at Frog Lake, and two farming instructors in the Battleford district in Treaty No. 6 were also murdered in a settling of personal scores (Tobias 1983:543–546). The only military action that involved substantial numbers of Indians was the engagement at Cut Knife Hill, at which government forces attacked a group of Indians that had gathered around Poundmaker. Poundmaker and other Plains Cree chiefs exercised tremendous restraint in preventing their followers from destroying the government force (Stanley 1960:367). Small numbers of Indians, mostly Plains Cree and White Cap's Santee Sioux, joined Métis forces. Elsewhere in the Northwest several bands left their reserves and slaughtered for food cattle that the government had provided as draft animals.

Government officials—especially Edgar Dewdney—chose to interpret the limited involvement of Indian peoples as an attempted "insurrection" by rebel Indians. Privately Dewdney acknowledged that the actions of the Plains Cree were those of a starving, desperate people, but publicly he accused them of involvement, and used this charge to crack down on them. He ordered the arrest of Plains Cree leaders involved in protests against the government, notwithstanding ample evidence of the efforts made by most of these leaders to prevent violence. In addition to eight Indians who were tried, convicted, and hanged for murder, Big Bear and Poundmaker (vol. 4:91–92) were sentenced to three-year terms at Stony Mountain Penitentiary in Manitoba. Neither served his full term, and both died shortly after their release (Bingaman 1975; Beal and Macleod 1994:306–333).

The Department of Indian Affairs was transformed by the rebellion. To forestall aboriginal resistance to Canadian hegemony or to the Canadian program to "civilize" and christianize them, the department adopted a forceful approach to dealings with Indians. In a memorandum on the future management of Indian affairs in the west, Assistant Indian Commissioner Hayter Reed argued that Indian agents needed to make "rebel" Indians understand that they had forfeited all claims to treaty rights. "Loyal" Indians should, he argued, be rewarded with the blankets, cattle, and ponies confiscated from "rebel" Indians (Titley 1993:117–118). Consequently, a list of "rebel" and "loyal" Indians and bands was drawn up by senior departmental officials, and the practice of distributing resources not on the basis of rights or needs but as a reward for compliance with departmental authority was begun. After the rebellion, the department—following Reed's direction—also introduced a system of travel passes designed to prevent Native peoples from moving off their reserves to attend Thirst Dances or political meetings without the permission of their Indian agent. This prohibition, which the North West Mounted Police recognized to be of dubious legality, was practiced albeit inconsistently, as late as World War II (S. Carter 1985; Barron 1988).

Amendments to the Indian Act followed the rebellion. Attendance at residential schools was made compulsory in 1894, and nonattenders were treated as juvenile delinquents. Changes made in 1895 strengthened the government's efforts to end aboriginal ceremonials. Both the Sun or Thirst dances on the Plains and the potlatch on the Northwest Coast were outlawed, not least because the government suspected that these gatherings might be used by Indians for political purposes (Pettipas 1994).

Aboriginal Affairs, 1890–1945

Missions

Roman Catholic, Anglican, Methodist, and Presbyterian missionaries entered the Canadian Plains relatively late. The Roman Catholics established a mission at Red River in 1818, but as late as the 1870s missions on the Canadian Plains were restricted to the parkland and to well-watered river valleys like the Qu'Appelle. Plains Indians quickly adopted the new faith. Some individuals converted to cement trading relationships with Europeans; others, to obtain food and other aid from missionaries. Crises in native communities occasioned by alcoholism and tuberculosis prompted conversions. Many people adopted Christianity for purely spiritual reasons. By 1899, more than 70 percent of the native population in Canada adhered to a Christian denomination (fig. 2) (J.W. Grant 1984:190).

Scholars have repeatedly shown that aboriginal peoples who adopted Christianity did not necessarily abandon older beliefs and worldviews. On the contrary, indigenous

left, Glenbow-Alberta Inst., Calgary: NB-11-2; right, Prov. Arch. of Alta., The Edmonton Journal Coll.: J 849/2.

Fig. 2. Christianity. left, First mission among the Peigan, at the foot of the Porcupine Hills west of the Old Man River, Alta. It was built in 1881 by Oblate of Mary Immaculate missionaries Leon Doucet and Emile Legal. Photographed by McDermid Studio, 1880s. right, Pilgrimage to Lac Ste. Anne, Alta., shrine. The first Roman Catholic mission was established there in 1844 at a sacred lake then renamed Lac Ste. Anne. Photographed in 1972.

beliefs often coexisted alongside Christian ones, and traditional ceremonies persisted. The Plains Cree and Plains Ojibwa in the Qu'Appelle Valley, for example, held rain dances, smoking tepees, and sweats in the early twentieth century, while also attending Christian churches (Tarasoff 1980).

Education

Each treaty included a clause promising that the Canadian government would establish and maintain schools on reserves as soon as the Indians settled and asked for them. The government handed this responsibility over to missionaries, who slowly established schools with funds provided by the government. In 1879, the government gave $100 for the erection of a schoolhouse on each reserve in the Northwest Territories, if the band was prepared to send its children to school. By 1885, 44 day schools were in operation with around 1,300 students.

Anticipating the creation of off-reserve residential schools, the government sent Nicholas Flood Davin, a Conservative member of Parliament, to study industrial schools in the United States in 1879. Upon his return, Davin recommended that similar schools be established in the Canadian West to teach husbandry and mechanical skills to boys and home economics to girls in addition to reading and writing English and other elementary subjects. The first industrial schools in the West, at Battleford, Qu'Appelle (fig. 3), and High River, were opened in 1884 (J.R. Miller 1996:101–103).

To combat poor attendance at day schools, the government built boarding schools—five by 1887. Eventually these schools, which were intended to serve as feeders for the industrial schools, were merged with industrial schools and called residential schools (Canada 1967:18–20). Only a minority of Native children attended residential schools, but the effects of these institutions are difficult to overestimate. The Department of Indian Affairs viewed the removal of Native children to off-reserve industrial and residential schools as an essential part of the civilizing and assimilating process. They prepared students for careers as farm or domestic laborers by prohibiting them from speaking their native languages and subjecting them to harsh disciplinary regimes. Children were separated from their families for up to 10 months each year, and their aboriginal cultures were denigrated. This constant pressure, along with other forms of abuse experienced in schools, became a factor in the intergenerational divisions that surfaced when students returned either temporarily or permanently to their reserve communities (J.R. Miller 1996; Milloy 1999).

Agriculture

The involvement of the Canadian government in Native agriculture, sporadic before the rebellion, began in earnest after 1885.

Despite the enthusiasm of Plains farmers, Plains Indian agriculture failed. On the basis of stereotypes, Euro-Canadians blamed Indians for this failure: the nonagricultural nomad was without the capacity or inclination to farm; farming upset the traditional spiritual beliefs of Native peoples: the Blackfoot did not like agriculture because it would mean turning Mother Earth "wrong side up" (Samek 1987:57). But the idea that Plains Indian agriculture failed because they did not want to farm is wrong. Native leaders had asked for farming instructors, seeds, and implements during treaty negotiations with Canadian representatives. Farming was a tool Native peoples could use to provide themselves with economic security. The reason aboriginal farming failed was because the government implemented policies that, in essence, ensured that it would fail (S. Carter 1990).

By the end of the 1880s, non-Native farmers began to complain about "unfair" competition from Native peoples. Euro-Canadian farmers had more expenses: they had to buy land, seed, stock, tools, and houses, while Indians had these things bought for them. Moreover, Indians were given rations while they waited for their first crops to ripen while Whites had to buy their own food during this time. Euro-Canadian farmers did not understand that all the things that Indians received had not been free, but had been purchased with the land.

Euro-Canadian settlers had votes while Indians did not. In 1889 the government responded to the pressure brought by Euro-Canadians by introducing the "peasant agriculture" policy. Each aboriginal family was restricted to a single acre of wheat, a plot of vegetables, and a cow for meat and dairy products. All farm work was to be done manually: seeds were to be sown by hand, wheat was to be cut with scythes, bound with straw, threshed with flails, and ground into flour with hand mills. Native farmers were not allowed to pool their resources to buy labor-saving devices. Nor could they buy farm machinery on credit from a bank, as their lands could not be used as collateral. This was the official Indian policy at a time when surrounding White farmers were mechanizing and participating in the commercial farming boom of the 1890s. Indians would no longer be dependent on the government, as they would be raising their own food, but neither would they be able to compete with Euro-Canadians. Given the backward and restrictive nature of the peasant policy, the number of acres of land being farmed by Native peoples had fallen by the middle of the 1890s to about half of what it had been before the policy was adopted (S. Carter 1990).

By the twentieth century, Native farmers had fallen behind in technology and training (fig. 4). This, combined with government restrictions and the loss of land, meant that they could not catch up or compete with Euro-Canadian farmers. Successful on-reserve farming operations were often the product of large capital investments and considerable Euro-Canadian labor, which were atypical for farming operations in general. For example, in the

top, Natl. Arch. of Canada, Ottawa: PA 118765; bottom, Prov. Arch. of Alta., Edmonton: left, B-9511; right, B9513.

Fig. 3. Schools and Indian students. top, Staff and students, many probably Plains Cree, at Ft. Qu'Appelle Industrial School, Sask. Photograph by Otto B. Buell, 1885. bottom, Student classes at St. Albert's Industrial School, Edmonton, Alta. Established by the Grey Nuns of Alberta in 1863 as a mission school, students, of Assiniboine, Plains Cree, Plains Métis, Sarcee, and Blackfoot tribes as well as non-Plains Chipewyans and Iroquois, were instructed in religion, French, English, arithmetic, and later, manual labor. bottom left, Girls' knitting and spinning classes. bottom right, Boys with tools for the trades of saddle making, tailoring, shoe production, and rug sewing. bottom, Photographs by Charles W. Mathers, 1898.

early 1900s, Indian Agent W.A. Markle sold parts of the Blackfoot Reserve to raise the capital needed to build roads, fences, houses, and barns and to pay for farming instructors and equipment operators. The four paid instructors made all decisions about planting and harvesting, and they supervised all operations and did all the bookkeeping. In the fall, machines took off the crops and professional stockmen removed cattle. The farm operation was run by Whites: the Blackfoot learned nothing about farming. In 1938, Blackfoot farmers were seeding fields of 40 acres, while neighboring White farmers needed 640 acres to make a profit. The reserve farms bore no relation to surrounding Euro-Canadian farms (Hanks and Hanks 1950:xiv; Buckley 1992:62–65).

The File Hills Colony was another example of successful reserve farming. It was the product of excessive paternalistism. The colony was established in 1901 on 19,000 acres on the Peepeeksis Reserve in the Qu'Appelle Agency, a special project of Indian Agent W.M. Graham. Eighty acres of farm land was allotted to each individual, while additional lands were reserved for hunting and pasture. In this model village, virtually every element of peoples' lives, including visits between homes, gatherings and even marriage partners, was controlled by the Department

Glenbow-Alberta Inst., Calgary: ND-8-404.

Fig. 4. Indian plowing, Stoney Indian Res., Alta. Photograph by William J. Oliver, about 1920s.

Whyte Mus. of the Canadian Rockies, Banff, Alta.: V469.

Fig. 5. Marketing using the Indian image. Many products bore Indian names or showed stereotypical Plains Indians in their advertising. Such was the romantic image of the Indians that association with them in products was considered a positive economic package. Hector Crawler, Stoney chief, promotes, the "Big Chief" banjo for the Ludwig Banjo Company, about 1925. Photograph by George Noble, Banff, Alta.

of Indian Affairs. The farming operations were successful, but the colony was not cost-effective and the Department of Indian Affairs never repeated the experiment (S. Carter 1991; Brass 1987).

With government regulations and restrictions came a greater disinclination on the part of Native farmers to take up or continue agricultural pursuits. Their "idleness" provided a basis for federal officials like Clifford Sifton, the minister of Indian affairs from 1896 to 1905, to seek to cajole or coerce bands into selling choice portions of their reserve lands (D.J. Hall 1977:127–51). The Department of Indian Affairs told Indians that in exchange for giving up reserve lands, they would be paid large sums that would be more than enough to develop those parts of the reserves that remained. The Peigan gave up almost one-third of their reserve in 1909, and the Blackfoot lost about half of theirs, some 115,000 acres, between 1911 and 1917. Of the Blackfoot peoples, only the Blood resisted all attempts to give up any of theirs. The proceeds of land sales were placed in a trust fund used by the department to defray the costs of reserve development projects (Hanks and Hanks 1950:35–36).

Government officials were oblivious to their role in reducing agriculture on reserves. To them, Native peoples made inefficient use of their lands, if they made any use of them at all. Alienating reserve land was, in their estimation, a sound policy choice. This attitude was summed up by David Laird, the Indian commissioner between 1898 and 1909, who noted, "The locking up of vast tracts which the Indians could not make any use of was neither in their own nor in the public interest. Yet the Indians were in many cases averse to parting with any [reserve lands]" (quoted in Dickason 1992:323). In such cases, the government might choose to expropriate reserve lands or force bands to lease land to non-Natives. This second avenue is exemplified by the Canadian government's Greater Production Campaign, initiated during World War I. Based on the pretext that arable land must not lie idle during wartime, 62,128 acres of reserve lands that were not worked by Native peoples were leased, without band consent, to non-Indians, who used them to raise wheat and cattle. Native complaints went unheeded by the government (Dempsey 1986:50–52).

Since 1945

Native peoples supported Canada's involvement in the two world wars of the twentieth century to a degree far greater than other minority groups. Between 3,500 and 4,000 Canadian Indians served in the Canadian Expeditionary Force during World War I, some 35 percent of those who were of the eligible age for service (fig. 6). Moreover, they raised considerable sums of money for the Red Cross (L.J.

Dempsey 1989). During World War II, some 6,000 Indians enlisted in the Canadian army, a higher proportion than any other ethnic group (Pitsula 1994:131). Of these, 762 (including 29 women) were from the prairies. This is about the same percentage as in World War I (Canada 1967:23). Virtually all aboriginal recruits became infantrymen, and suffered higher casualties than the forces as a whole. Their loyalty was not for the Indian Department, but for the British Crown, with whom their ancestors had made treaties. One Cree in Saskatchewan told a British journalist that he enlisted because his great-grandfather, Mistawasis, had an alliance with Queen Victoria in the 1870s (J.H. Thompson 1998:142–143).

Native communities in the 1940s remained subject to poverty, illness, and intergenerational divisions. Among the Blackfoot, for example, the mortality rate was high, especially among infants, and the life expectancy was less than half that of the national norm. Children who were sent to residential schools returned home lacking not only the skills needed to participate in the Euro-Canadian economy but also the traditional language and culture to give them continuity with their communities. Elders wore braids and spoke Blackfoot; young people dressed in European clothes, spoke English, and tried to find work on or near the reserves (Dempsey 1995:408–409). Traditional leading families that owned horses validated their positions by purchasing medicine bundles or memberships in societies with horses, but younger people—those more likely to have participated in wheat farming or wage labor—were excluded (Goldfrank 1945:31–8).

Sask. Arch. Board, Regina: R-A 2151(3).

Fig. 6. Indian soldiers on their way to fight in Europe, 1915–1918, with their parents and friends from File Hills Colony, Sask., before their departure for England. Photograph probably by Edgar C. Rossie, Regina, Sask., 1915. back row, left to right: David Bird; Joe McKay; Joseph Peters, Standing Buffalo Band, Sioux, Ft. Qu'Appelle, Sask. (killed in action 4/9/17); and Ed Sanderson. second row from back: L. Harry Stonechild; Leonard Creely; Jack Walker; Alex Brass; Ernest Gofroth. seated third row from back: Moostatik; Feather; William Morris Graham, Indian agencies supervisor responsible for the File Hills Colony; Pimotat (Earth Walker); Kee wisk. seated on floor: Jos McNab; Shavetail; Day Walker; Jack Fisher (Young Man). All except Peters were Plains Cree.

Political Organization

Participation in the two world wars did give Native peoples opportunities to obtain a greater awareness of national and international events and of the power of united forces to shape those events. This knowledge contributed to the formation of a pan-Indian political consciousness in Canada. The forerunner of aboriginal political organizations in Canada was the League of Indians of Canada, founded in Sault Sainte Marie in 1919 by F.O. Loft, a Mohawk who had risen to the rank of captain in the Canadian army during service in France. The league held its first western meeting in 1920, and a new, western-based organization, the League of Indians of Western Canada, was formed in 1929 (Titley 1986:107). In 1944, Andrew Paull, a Squamish from British Columbia, invited members of the League of Indians of Western Canada to attend a meeting in Ottawa for the purpose of forming a national Indian organization. This led to the creation of the North American Indian Brotherhood, and the Saskatchewan Section of this organization, based in the Treaty No. 6 area. The Protective Association for the Indians and Their Treaties was started after World War I by members of the Pasquah, Piapot, and Muscowpetung bands to fight the seizure of lands under the Soldier Settlement Act and was based in Treaty No. 4. Provincial aboriginal associations were founded during the 1940s, the Indian Association of Alberta in 1939, and the Union of Saskatchewan Indians, a merger of the Association of Indians of Saskatchewan, the Protective Association for Indians and Their Treaties, and the North American Indian Brotherhood, Saskatchewan Section, in 1946 (Pitsula 1994:131, 133–135). Early leaders of these organizations, men like Mike Mountain Horse of the Blood and Edward Ahenakew and John Tootoosis of the Plains Cree, were often Christians and graduates of residential schools (J.R. Miller 1991:217–9).

The growth of aboriginal political organizations and challenges to the Canadian government's hegemony over Indian affairs were hallmarks of the period after 1945. No longer content to be wards of the state, Native peoples questioned the status quo and forced themselves onto the Canadian political stage.

When Native soldiers returned home at the close of World War II, one Indian Department official noted, "These returned Indian soldiers are subject to the provisions of the Indian Act and are in the same position as they were before enlisting" (quoted in L.J. Dempsey 1989:5, 6). Not only Native peoples, but Euro-Canadians as well, saw the fundamental need to alter the way Indians were treated. An Alberta member of parliament noted, "the Canadian people as a whole are interested in the problem of Indians. . . . they are anxious to remedy our shortcomings.

Parliament and the country is [*sic*] 'human rights' conscious" (quoted in J.R. Miller 1991:221). Calls for reform resulted in the appointment of a Joint Committee of the Senate and House of Commons to examine all aspects of Indian Affairs.

The Joint Committee of the Senate and House of Commons on Indian Affairs held hearings between 1946 and 1949. Native witnesses from the prairies were primarily concerned about treaty rights (fig. 7) and self-government. These were central concerns, for example, of the Indian Association of Alberta and the Union of Saskatchewan Indians. On behalf of the Union, John Tootoosis, John Gambler, Joseph Dreaver, and the Rev. Ahab Spence went to Ottawa in May 1947 to present a brief to the committee. They pointed out that at the time of the treaty negotiations, Canada had treated Native nations as sovereign; afterward, Canada had treated them like children. The treaties, they asserted, had been abrogated by the Indian Act and the way it was administered. They asked for amendments to the act that would restore the spirit of the treaties. In particular, they requested that the powers of Indian agents be limited, that Native peoples' right to self-government be recognized, that bands, not the Indian Department, be granted the right to determine membership, that bands be allowed to choose chiefs and councillors as they saw fit, not according to the system imposed by the act, and that bands be allowed to spend money from their trust funds without departmental consent. Their brief also asked for the closing of the church-run industrial schools and addressed needs in the areas of health, social assistance, housing, veterans' aid, and economic development (Pitsula 1994:143; Barron 1997:87–92).

Glenbow-Alberta Inst., Calgary: NA 1954-1.

Fig. 7. Plains Crees and Ojibwas meeting at Rocky Mountain House, Alta., at Adhesion to Treaty No. 6 negotiations. Two bands living in the foothills of the Rocky Mountains had not signed a treaty with the Canadian government until the 1940s, when fur trader Henry Stelfox was hired to negotiate with the groups. One band of Plains Cree under Sunchild signed in 1944. The second group, Plains Ojibwas under John O'Chiese, split, half signing the adhesion in 1950 and getting a reserve, while the other half refused to sign and remained non-treaty Indians in 1999. left to right, standing: Jim Yellow Eyes (Sunchild), Norman Legrelle (Sunchild), Pete Beaver (O'Chiese), Okimaw Yellowface (O'Chiese), Tom Bremner (O'Chiese), Jim Whitford (Sunchild), Joseph Bremner (O'Chiese), George Daychief, Joe Strawberry's mother (O'Chiese), Sam Strawberry (O'Chiese), Maggie Yellowface (Sunchild), William Bremner (O'Chiese). Daychief sisters, unidentified officer, and Joe Strawberry (O'Chiese). seated, left to right: Desjarlais, Plains Ojibwa interpreter; Henry Stelfox; Malcolm McCrimmon; George H. Gooderham; and W.B. Skead. Photograph by Farthing Studio, Red Deer, Alta., May 1947.

Led by James Gladstone of the Blood (fig. 8; vol. 4:94) (named Canada's first native senator in 1958), Native peoples rejected the proposals finally made by the Joint Committee, claiming that they took away all that was good in the Indian Act and replaced it with provisions better designed for concentration camps than reserves. Faced with such criticisms, the government agreed to revise its draft (Dickason 1992:329).

The final report of the Joint Committee led to a number of amendments to the Indian Act in 1951. These removed some of the most criticized features, such as compulsory enfranchisement, the prohibition of the Sun Dance, and the ban on raising money for political purposes, but did not alter the assimilationist goal of the legislation. The new Act allowed bands to incorporate as municipalities (a measure far short of self-government), introduced the secret ballot, and enfranchised women in band elections.

The amended Indian Act of 1951 favored assimilation without coercion, and, in that, it reflected the political thought developing among White Canadian politicians since the 1930s. This philosophy underlay the Indian policy of the Co-operative Commonwealth Federation (CCF), first elected to provincial government in Saskatchewan in 1944 under the leadership of T.C. Douglas. The CCF supported the idea that Native peoples be integrated into mainstream society and insisted that this could happen "without curtailing the Indians' traditional rights or reducing in any way the welfare and security they now enjoy." The CCF did not support the abolition of the Indian Act: "The rights and privileges and traditional securities provided in the Act and the Treaties must be preserved as an irreducible minimum" (quoted in Pitsula 1997:50). The CCF also supported aboriginal treaty rights, while maintaining that treaties did not serve as the foundation for the separate development of Indians but conferred only minor advantages that were compatible with integration. CCF Indian policy revolved around three initiatives: granting the franchise to Native peoples, removing restrictions on the sale of alcohol to Indians, and transferring responsibility for Indian affairs from the federal to provincial governments. These initiatives were based on the belief that equality of citizenship required the removal of legal distinctions and uniformity in the ways citizens related to the government (Pitsula 1997:52–54).

Although the CCF was unique in being the first (and at the time, only) democratic socialist government elected in North America, its position on Indian affairs was not unlike those of other parties. Ross Thatcher's Liberals, who replaced Saskatchewan's CCF government in 1964, were equally in favor of assimilation (which they

left, Natl. Arch. of Canada, Natl. Film Board, Ottawa: PA 114835; center, Prov. Arch. of Alta., The Edmonton Journal Coll.: J 1089/2; right, *The Globe and Mail*, Toronto, Ont.: L7125.

Fig. 8. 20th-century Indian activism. left, left to right: Sen. James Gladstone, Blood (b. 1887, d. 1971); George Callinglast, Blood; and Howard Hindman, Blood. Gladstone helped to found the Indian Assoc. of Alta. in 1939 and was instrumental in getting Canadian Treaty Indians the right to vote in national elections in 1960 (Malinowski 1995:165–166). Photograph by Gar Lunney, Blood Indian Res., Alta., 1958 (computer enhanced). center, Dedication of a copper tepee monument to Stoney Indians at Banff National Park, Alta., to promote and take pride in Indian heritage. Taking part are Premier of Alberta Peter Longheed and Stoney Chief John Snow. The photograph on the monument is of Silas Abraham, Stoney. Photographed near Abraham Lake, Kootenay Plains, Alta., 1973. right, Harold Cardinal, Plains Cree from Sucker Creek Cree Res., in foreground, and his assistant Tony Mercredi, Chipewyan. Cardinal is the author of *The Unjust Society* (1969), an appeal to Canadians to let Treaty Indians control their future. He was elected president of the Canadian Indian Youth Council in 1966–1967 and president of the Indian Assoc. of Alta. in 1968. In the late 1990s he worked with Saskatchewan elders, collecting oral histories, especially as they related to Indian understandings of treaties. Photograph by Rudy Platiel, Cold Lake, Alta., 1970.

expressed as integration). The Liberals viewed the separate legal status of Indians and the existence of a separate branch for service delivery to Indians as a barrier to integration. Thatcher, like his CCF predecessors, recommended that the Canadian constitution be amended so as to transfer control over Indian affairs from Ottawa to the provinces. His government also proposed that Indian reserves be amalgamated with local authorities (school districts and municipalities) (Pitsula 1996).

The federal Liberal party reaffirmed its commitment to the assimilation of aboriginal peoples in 1969 when it introduced the White Paper on Indian Affairs, its blueprint for the future of Indian policy under the government of Pierre Elliot Trudeau. In most respects, the White Paper embodied the principles established by the CCF government in Saskatchewan (Pitsula 1994a:23). It also resembled the termination policy in the United States, which had intended in the 1950s to end the paternalism of the Bureau of Indian Affairs by giving aboriginal peoples status as equal citizens and handing service delivery over to state agencies (Barron 1997:212–213; Pitsula 1997:53; Jorgensen 1986:6–7).

Minister of Indian Affairs Jean Chrétien released the controversial White Paper in June 1969, outlining how status Indians were to be fully integrated into Canadian social, economic, and political life by 1975 (vol. 4:281–282). The constitution would be amended to terminate the legal distinction between Indians and non-Indians, the Indian Act would be repealed, aboriginal peoples would take control of their reserves (subject to provincial laws) and the Department of Indian Affairs would be phased out. Services provided by the federal government would be transferred to the federal and provincial agencies that served the general public. Taken together, these measures were intended "to enable the Indian people to be free—free to develop Indian cultures in an environment of legal, social and economic equality with other Canadians" (Canada 1969:3). Indians would remain a part of Canada's ethnic mosaic, but they would disappear as a legal group.

The White Paper did not, however, recognize aboriginal rights and it challenged the need and importance of the treaties Canada had entered into with aboriginal peoples. "A plain reading of the words," opined the authors of the White Paper, "reveals the limited and minimal promises which were included in them. . . . The significance of the treaties in meeting the economic, educational, health, and welfare needs of the Indian people has always been limited and will continue to decline. . . . once Indian lands are securely within Indian control, the anomaly of treaties between groups in a society and the government of that society will require that these treaties be reviewed to see how they can be equitably ended" (Canada 1969). Believing so fully that one segment of society should not have a treaty with another segment, the government did not foresee the opposition of Native peoples to the abrogation of the instruments that guaranteed aboriginal rights.

Aboriginal denunciation of the White Paper was swift and uncompromising. Immediately, in 1969, David Ahenakew, chief of the Federation of Saskatchewan Indians (the successor of the Union of Saskatchewan Indians), denounced the White Paper as contrary to the treaties. The response of the Indian Association of Alberta to the White Paper was the book, *Citizens Plus* (1970), known as the Red Paper. It rejected wardship and espoused special status as defined by treaty. Native responses countered the White Paper's arguments and forced the federal government to withdraw the document.

Economy

When the reserves were established in the nineteenth century, the Canadian government had expected Native peoples to become self-supporting by pursuing agriculture. By the middle of the twentieth century, however, agriculture had been transformed. No longer a small-scale, family-run business, farming was a corporate enterprise (J.H. Thompson 1998). Lacking capital and subject to numerous restrictive regulations, Native communities rarely participated in modern agriculture unless it was by leasing their lands to non-Natives (Buckley 1992:101).

As agriculture continued to decline as a means of supporting Native communities during the 1950s and 1960s, little beyond social assistance took its place. Opportunities ended, and Native peoples' level of education was too low for all but the most casual of work. Wage labor on non-Native farms dried up as White farmers mechanized and turned to commercial farming, and the demand for men to work in construction and on road building was also disappearing. The smaller Plains Cree reserves in Saskatchewan tended, in particular, to lack a sufficient economic base. Wage labor, for example, remained significant only for Native communities located close to urban areas (Ray 1996:262). In many areas, people often resorted to taking the low paying, unskilled work non-Natives refused to do (Buckley 1992).

Economic development and diversification, therefore, have been of central concern to aboriginal peoples and government alike in the postwar years. The efforts of the Department of Indian Affairs to introduce new industries to reserves have gravitated toward "economic-development techniques used in the Third World," thus revealing its "obsession with 'backwardness'" (Buckley 1992:102–103). New enterprises have generally proven to be only moderately successful.

Petroleum and natural gas have provided revenue for some reserves (fig. 9). In 1950, one of nine wells on the Stoney Reserve, Alberta, was brought into production. By the next year, there were 16 productive oil wells on the reserve. In 1952, oil was obtained from wells on the Sturgeon Lake, Samson, and Blood reserves in Alberta; and leases were granted for exploration on several reserves in Saskatchewan and Manitoba. There were 90 producing wells on Alberta reserves in 1959 (Canada 1967:22, 24). Oil produced revenue for only a few bands, and little employment.

Unemployment, poverty, and social problems (alcohol and drug abuse, school absenteeism, and high dropout rates, for example) persisted for aboriginal peoples both on and off-reserve. However, younger people, those first to graduate from integrated provincial schools, did begin moving into professional careers in the 1960s. Increasingly, band managers, welfare officers, public-works staff, police, and teachers were aboriginal (Buckley 1992:101; Dempsey 1995:408–409).

top, Glenbow-Alberta Inst., Calgary: ND-8-400; bottom, Prov. Arch. of Alta., Edmonton: BL 116/3.

Fig. 9. Participation in the Euro-Canadian cash economy. top, Stoney Indians receiving payments for oil lease rights on the Morley Reserve, Alta. of $10 per person per year. Photograph by William J. Oliver, July 1929. bottom, Plains Cree probably from Stony Plain Res. receiving treaty money at Winterburn, near Edmonton, Alta. The man seated in center is Indian Agent George Laight of the Edmonton Indian Agency. Stony Plain Res. residents were descendants of employees of the Hudson's Bay Company, mostly Plains Cree, Plains Métis, and Subarctic Cree. Photograph by Alfred Blythe, 1932.

Cultural Persistence

Although it was a commonplace among European observers in the nineteenth and the first half of the twentieth centuries to view aboriginal populations as "vanishing," Native populations did not disappear and instead grew significantly after 1945. The Native population increased by 91 percent between 1945 and 1967, when 91,246 Status Indians and 113,500 Métis resided in Manitoba, Saskatchewan, and Alberta. About half of Canada's Status Indians lived in the Prairie provinces in 1981, making about 6 percent of the population there (compared with 3% nationwide), and by 1996, Status Indians comprised 11 percent of the population of Saskatchewan and Manitoba (J.H. Thompson 1998:164, 180).

Native peoples not only on the Plains but throughout Canada sought to preserve and revive traditional cultures ("Plains Métis," fig. 10, this vol.). This was not easy in the face of residential schooling, missionization, and the influence of television. Central to the preservation of culture and identity was the maintenance of language. Although rates of language retention varied among reserves, Blackfoot, Cree, Saulteaux, and Assiniboine were all viable in Canada (Norris 1998).

Cultural persistence in Canada was stronger in some cases than on neighboring American reservations. An excellent example is that of the Ghost Dance, which disappeared from Sioux reserves in the United States after the Wounded Knee Massacre but survived on the Wahpeton Reserve in Saskatchewan into the 1960s (A.B. Kehoe 1989). As a result of government prohibitions, traditional ceremonies fared poorly in the twentieth century. The Sun Dance, for example, virtually disappeared from most reserves. However, since the 1980s, Sun Dances have been practiced by the Assinboine, Plains Cree, and Blackfoot peoples. Modern ceremonies, such as the powwow (fig. 10, "Plains Ojibwa," fig. 5, this vol.), fostered Native pride and were widely adopted.

Education was also a key to the preservation and promotion of culture. The majority of aboriginal students in 1999 were educated in provincial schools, but the Department of Indian Affairs had agreed in 1972 to Native control of education as a principle, and most reserves had facilities for teaching elementary ("Blackfoot," fig. 10, this vol.), high-school, and language courses. Many bands and tribal councils established postsecondary institutions or made arrangements with non-Native schools to offer Native studies. The Bloods operated Red Crow College, affiliated with Lethbridge Community College, Alberta; and the Blackfoot operated Old Sun College, affiliated with Mount Royal College and the University of Calgary. The University of Lethbridge Native Studies program was directed toward the Blood and Peigan. The Saskatchewan Indian Federated College, Regina, began offering courses in Assiniboine history, culture, and language in the mid-1980s. The Cree language was taught at the Saskatchewan

Glenbow-Alberta Inst., Calgary: top left, NB-16-577; top right, NA-446-111.

Fig. 10. Activities at tribal events. top left, Tug-of-war between Sarcees and Stoneys. The man in chaps with arms raised is Jack Water; the umpire, in business suit, is Col. James Walker. William J. Oliver, the photographer, is at far left. Photographed probably at the Calgary Stampede, 1920s. top right, Pete Bruised Head, Blood, with the Will Rogers trophy for calf roping won at the Calgary Stampede. Photograph by William J. Oliver, 1927. bottom left, Arthur A. Youngman, Blackfoot elder and Anglican minister during a break in activities at a Tribal Day sponsored by Luxton Mus., Banff, Alta., 1997. bottom center, Ronnie Small Legs, from Brocket, in a Peigan traditional dance at Tsuu T'ina Nation Powwow (Sarcee), Bragg Creek, Alta., July 1998; bottom right, Charity Red Gun, Blackfoot, Calgary Stampede princess, 1998. bottom left and right, Photographs by Rob McKinley. bottom center, Photograph by Paul Melting Tallow.

Indian Federated College, the University of Alberta, Edmonton, and the University of Manitoba, Winnipeg.

The economies of the reserves in the 1990s remained predominantly rural, and unemployment continued to plague native communities, although reserves made efforts to diversify. Many provided retail services. The tribal offices on the Blackfoot Reserve, for example, share a building with a shopping mall. Businesses operated on-reserve by Native peoples included supermarkets, cafeterias, video stores, laundromats, service stations, banks, and craft shops. Working for the band became a major part of the reserve economy. Larger bands employed several hundred people, including administrators, office staff, teachers, and social workers (Buckley 1992:126).

Beginning in the 1960s, Native communities exercised increasing control over band government. All reserves were virtually self-governing in the 1990s. No Indian Affairs or federal official resided on reserve (the last Indian agent departed in 1969), and the majority of band employees were Native. Reserves assumed responsibility for education, social welfare, and the administration of justice. By the end of the 1980s, some bands administered all services, and most administered at least half (Buckley 1992:126). Although decisions of the tribal councils still must be approved by the government, this was usually a formality (Dempsey 1995:409–411).

Prairie Native leaders were involved in shaping the National Indian Brotherhood into the Assembly of First Nations in 1980. Their role in this process was pivotal as 300,000 of the 375,000 Native peoples represented by the Assembly of First Nations in the 1980s lived between the Great Lakes and the Pacific. Prairie bands were "remarkably cohesive, well-developed at the community level, and relatively likely to retain the use of native languages" (Gerber 1979). The Assembly of First Nations lobbied successfully to have aboriginal rights recognized in the Canadian constitution in 1982 and set self-government as a goal.

Hidatsa

FRANK HENDERSON STEWART

Language and Territory

The Hidatsa (hĭˈdätsu) are first mentioned in the historical sources toward the end of the eighteenth century, when they were living in three earthlodge villages at the mouth of the Knife River (fig. 1). According to Hidatsa and Crow traditions, the two tribes once constituted a single group, and this is borne out by linguistic evidence. Both tribes speak Siouan languages that, though not quite mutually intelligible, are close enough for speakers of one easily to learn the other* (Lowie 1935:3).

The Hidatsa consisted of three divisions, in descending order of size the Hidatsa proper, the Awatixa, and the Awaxawi. The divisions (also referred to as village groups or subtribes) differed slightly from each other in culture and preferred when possible to occupy separate villages. Each spoke a distinct dialect, and this confirms their own traditions, which indicate that the divisions were not always geographically as close to one another as they were in the late eighteenth century.

According to these traditions the Awatixa had always resided on the Missouri. The site of what appears to be their oldest village on Knife River, Lower Hidatsa, is only a few hundred yards from Sakakawea, their early nineteenth-century village site (Bowers 1965:17–21, 474). Lower Hidatsa was already occupied in the early sixteenth century (Ahler, Theissen, and Trimble 1991:90). The Awatixa themselves probably reached the middle Missouri before then, since their myths link them to village sites farther downstream, in the Painted Woods area; one can be dated about 1100 (Ahler, Theissen, and Trimble 1991:29). Tradition asserts that the Awaxawi and the Hidatsa proper arrived successively from the east. All this fits with the fact that of the three divisions, the Awatixa most resembled the Mandan in culture, while the Hidatsa proper resembled them least.

*The phonemes of Hidatsa are: (voiceless lax unaspirated stops and affricate) *p*, *t*, *c*, *k*, *ʔ*; (voiceless aspirated stops and affricate) *pʰ*, *tʰ*, *cʰ*, *kʰ*; (voiceless preaspirated stops and affricate *hp*, *ht*, *hc*, *hk*; (voiceless spirants) *š*, *x*, *h*; (voiceless preaspirated spirants *hš*, *hx*; (resonants) *w*, *r*; (short vowels) *i*, *e*, *a*, *o*, *u*; (long vowels) *i·*, *e·*, *a·*, *o·*, *u·*; (primary stress) v́, (secondary stress) v̀. In word-initial position, and in syllable-initial position in slow speech, *w* is [m] and *r* is [n]. The preaspirated stops vary between preaspirated and geminate stops; *hš* is either [hš] or [š·], and *hx* is [hx] or [x·]. This phonemic inventory follows the analysis of A. Wesley Jones (1979).

History, 1781–1886

In 1781 the Hidatsa suffered from the smallpox epidemic that swept the northern Plains. The survivors numbered about 2,000, probably no more than half the pre-epidemic population.

After this the sedentary peoples of the Middle Missouri were much more vulnerable than before to their nomadic enemies, notably the Sioux and Assiniboine, possibly because the nomadic tribes suffered less from the disease. Both the Sioux and Assiniboine made massive attacks on the Hidatsa and other river tribes (Henry in Coues 1897:358ff.; cf. Bowers 1965:256; Bruner 1961:210; White 1978). The surviving villagers moved closer to each other. The only pre-1781 Mandan or Hidatsa village site that continued to be occupied for more than a very short time after the epidemic was Big Hidatsa, where the Hidatsa proper lived. By the end of the eighteenth century they had drawn to their immediate vicinity not only the two smaller Hidatsa divisions, the Awatixa and Awaxawi, but also the surviving Mandans. The Hidatsa and Mandan were probably on good terms even before the 1781 epidemic; thereafter they were in alliance, neither making war or peace without the consent of the other. There were exceptions, and relations between them were sometimes tense, as the more numerous Hidatsa tried to keep the upper hand (Henry in Coues 1897:372). In 1812 some Hidatsas even killed the Mandan chief Big White (Luttig 1920:82ff.; cf. Brackenridge 1814:77).

The first third of the nineteenth century was a period of relative stability for the two tribes. The five villages near the mouth of the Knife—three Hidatsa and two Mandan—were for many years able to defend their existence, and none of the Hidatsa ones even changed its location (Stewart 1974). Some Hidatsa proper are said to have broken away from their main village for a few years early in the nineteenth century, when they formed a village near the mouth of Cherry Creek; but major change came only in 1834, when a Sioux attack destroyed the villages of the Awatixa and Awaxawi. They were never rebuilt. The survivors—at least at first—moved in with the Mandan (Stewart 1974:296). Later the Awatixa built a village close to Big Hidatsa (Ahler, Theissen, and Trimble 1991:97).

From about 1600 important changes began in Hidatsa life as a result of European influence, in particular because of the growth of trade and the introduction of horses and of new manufactured goods, notably metal implements and firearms

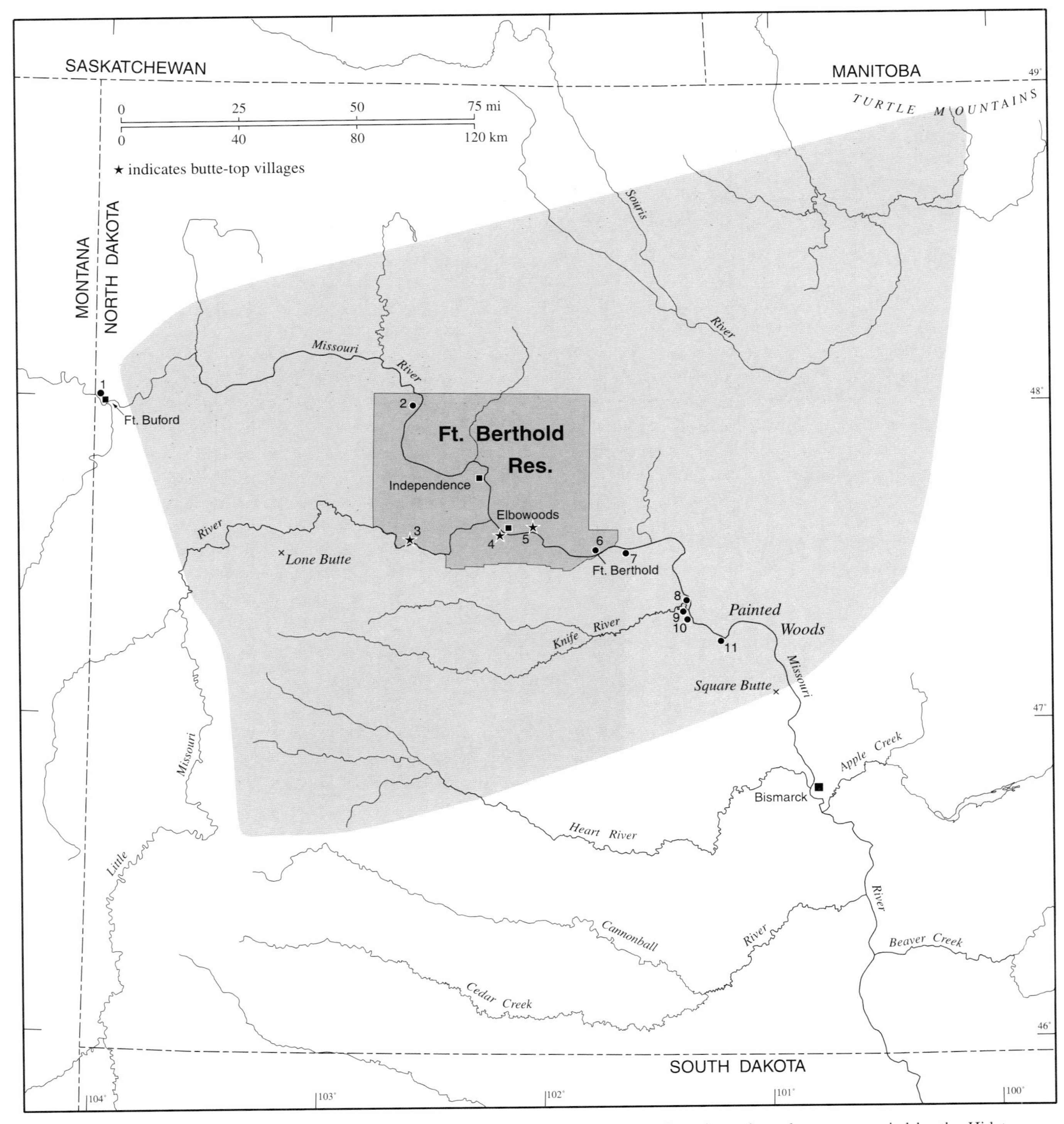

Fig. 1. Hidatsa territory, showing summer villages, 1781–1894. The sites noted may not have been the only ones occupied by the Hidatsa during this period. 1, Badland village, Crow Flies High band, about 1870–1884 (Wilson 1928:109, 115ff.; Meyer 1977:140); Garden Coulee site (32WI18), next to the military post of Ft. Buford (1866–1895) (Remele 1987). 2, Crow Flies High village (32MZ1), Crow Flies High band, about 1870–1894; neither this site nor Badland village was continuously occupied (Malouf 1963:155). 3, Nightwalker's Village (32DU1), some Hidatsa proper, early 19th century, probably the group led by Strong Jaw, father of Walks-at-Dusk (Nightwalker) (Bowers 1965:392, 412ff.); also called Jacobsen, Little Swallow, or Nightwalker's Butte in the Badlands. 4, Midipadi Butte (32DU2), probably Hidatsa proper, late 18th or early 19th century (Kuehn, Falk, and Drybred 1982). 5, Nightwalker's Butte (32ML39), probably Hidatsa proper, late 18th or early 19th century. 6, Like-a-Fishhook (Ft. Berthold) (32ML2), Hidatsa, Mandan, and after 1862 Arikara, 1845–about 1886. 7, Rock Village (32ME15), Awatixa and some Hidatsa proper, about 1781–1797. 8, Big Hidatsa (32ME12), Hidatsa proper, about 1600–about 1844 (Ahler, Thiessen, and Trimble 1991:85). 9, Sakakawea (32ME11), Awatixa, about 1798–1834. 10, Amahami (32ME8), Awaxawi, about 1786–1834. 11, Mahhaha (32OL22), Awaxawi, about 1781–1786. Sources: Stewart 1974, 1975c; Bowers 1965:12.

(Ahler, Theissen, and Trimble 1991:64–68, 71). After 1781 there was almost always at least one fur trader living among or near the Hidatsa. As a result of the Louisiana Purchase the tribe passed in 1803 from the nominal control of Spain and France to the nominal control of the United States; Meriwether Lewis and William Clark distributed a few medals to the chiefs in 1804, and the first treaty with the United States was signed in 1825 (Kappler 1904–1941, 2:239). From then on an official agent visited the tribe most years, though very briefly; but for all practical purposes the Hidatsa were left to manage their own affairs.

In 1837 the tribe was again struck by a devastating smallpox epidemic. The Hidatsa, though apparently less hard hit than the Mandan (Bowers 1965:36, 287; cf. Chardon 1932:126, 145), probably lost about two-thirds of their population of about 2,100. Most of the survivors drew more closely together and moved northward. They tried to augment their numbers by capturing and adopting the women and children of their enemies (Bowers 1965:95, 256). Some Hidatsa joined the River Crow, but the rest, together with a group of Mandans, in 1845 founded a new village, Like-a-Fishhook (Bowers 1965:29, 35–40, 464–466, 472). At the same time the adjacent fur trading post of Fort Berthold was established (G.H. Smith 1972:5fc.; Meyer 1977:100).

During the first two decades in Like-a-Fishhook Village, White influence seems to have altered Hidatsa culture very little. In 1851 the Hidatsa signed the Fort Laramie treaty, which defined the boundaries of Hidatsa, Mandan, and Arikara territory; from 1853 onward the tribes received an annuity from the government agent who visited them for a day or two every year. Roman Catholic missionaries appeared from time to time and baptized children, but the church did not succeed in establishing a mission (Pfaller 1950).

The most significant changes in Hidatsa life in these years were those that arose from the move to Like-a-Fishhook Village. The Hidatsa and Mandan retained their separate social and ceremonial organizations and occupied separate quarters of the village (cf. Medicus 1951:4). But there was almost certainly a joint village council, and the influence of the two tribes on each other was even greater than it had been in the preceding period. The Hidatsa, for instance, came to adopt the Mandan practice of having a special lodge for ceremonies, instead of simply using an ordinary residence (Bowers 1965:402, 39, 352, 383, 419; Malouf 1963; cf. Bowers 1965:488; Wilson 1934:410).

An equally important effect of the move to Like-a-Fishhook Village was that the three Hidatsa divisions abandoned their separate social and ceremonial organizations and formed themselves into a single community. This unification was by no means easily achieved, and a variety of problems arising from it existed for many years (Bowers 1965).

In the 1860s White influence on the tribe began to grow much more rapidly (Matthews 1877:30ff.). Troops were permanently stationed in the area from 1864 onward, a resident Indian agent appeared in 1868, a day school was opened in 1870, and a resident missionary arrived in 1876 (Meyer 1977; Bruner 1961:233). In 1879 the main religious ceremony of the tribe, the Naxpike, was performed for the last time (Bowers 1965:309); and in the early 1880s the buffalo, materially and symbolically a central feature of Hidatsa life, disappeared.

The size of the territory allotted to the three tribes (Mandan, Hidatsa, and Arikara) was several times reduced in these years, and in the 1880s the federal government began parceling out the tribal lands to individual Indians in the form of allotments. This destroyed the traditional pattern of settlement. Like-a-Fishhook Village, which had long suffered from the lack of grazing and wood in its vicinity, was virtually abandoned by 1886, its people dispersed in individual homesteads or small settlements throughout the reservation.

One group of Hidatsa was not directly affected by the abandonment of Like-a-Fishhook. About 1870 conflicts within the Hidatsa community led a number of families, known after the name of their leader (fig. 2) as the Crow

Smithsonian, NAA: 55956.

Fig. 2. Crow Flies High (d. 1900), leader of a band that broke away from the other Hidatsa about 1870 (Malouf 1963:158). He wears a quill-decorated buckskin shirt and a feather bonnet and holds a nonregulation Army sword. Photograph probably by David F. Barry, Bismarck, N. Dak., 1881.

Flies High band, began to move out of Like-a-Fishhook and set up their own villages (Bowers 1965:42–45, 185, 225, 240–251). The band refused to accept government annuities and remained outside the reservation until 1894. Their return marked the extinction of the last independent Hidatsa community.

Culture in the Early Nineteenth Century

Political Organization

A Hidatsa village was a clearly defined and socially very important entity. Its inhabitants did not usually marry outsiders (Bowers 1965:77). In the early nineteenth century the three villages, each consisting almost exclusively of the members of a single division, clustered together within sight of one another at the mouth of the Knife River.

The villages varied considerably in size but were similar in appearance. Each consisted of a number of large round structures built of sod on a strong wooden framework. These earthlodges were closely packed together in no particular order. In at least the Big Hidatsa village there was an open space used for ceremonial purposes, though in contrast to the Mandan, the Hidatsa did not consider the village plaza to be sacred (Bowers 1965:39, 488).

Each village had a council of elders to deal with matters that involved the village as a whole (Bowers 1965:33, 39, 186)—relations with other tribes (and Whites), movements out of the village, and the organization of religious ceremonies. The time and purpose of each meeting were formally announced in advance so that every household might have the opportunity to put forward its views, and after the meeting any decisions were also formally proclaimed. The council avoided making decisions that would arouse serious opposition, since a dissident group might simply break away from the village.

There were two types of chief. The war chief was the elder who had the best reputation as a warrior. There seems generally to have been only one war chief in a village, but probably at times there were more. The peace chief was the elder with the highest ritual status. Among the Hidatsa proper and the Awaxawi this meant the owner of the Earthnaming bundle, of which there was one in each of these divisions. These bundles, and hence the office, generally passed from father to son. In Awatixa village there were two peace chiefs, the keepers of the bundles that belonged to the Waterbuster and Knife clans (Bowers 1965:38, 473–474).

A chief's power lay in his influence and reputation. The war chiefs were military experts, and the peace chiefs ritual experts, but there was no clear division of authority. Originally, and perhaps still during the earlier part of the nineteenth century, the peace chief was considered the more important, but as a result of the increasing military pressure from the nomadic tribes he lost this position to the war chief (Bowers 1965:58, 32, 281).

Before the 1781 epidemic there seem to have been no pantribal institutions, but soon after, as a result of the need to unite against their nomadic enemies, a tribal council consisting of about a dozen men, mostly leading warriors, was established. It dealt mainly with matters of war and peace, and the maintenance of good relations among the three villages (Bowers 1965:27–29).

Annual Cycle

The tribe followed a well-marked annual round. In April and May respectively sunflowers and corn were planted (Wilson 1917:16, 22). Like all horticultural activities, these were mainly women's tasks. The summer was the most active time of the year in every sphere: horticulture, hunting, ceremonial life, and war. In July and August there would be a great buffalo hunt undertaken by the whole village together (cf. Boller 1959:96). The council chose someone—usually a man who had not hitherto acted as a chief—to be the hunt leader, and during the hunt the war and peace chiefs apparently lost their special authority (Bowers 1965:51, 56). People lived in tepees, which were formed into a camp circle (Bowers 1965:53). The villagers returned home after three or four weeks (Boller 1959:98) and harvested their crops. In the fall many people would form small groups that scattered over a wide area, where they lived in camps on traditionally established sites. They hunted game and trapped eagles, the feathers of which were highly valued (Densmore 1923:60–80; Wilson 1928; Bowers 1950: 206–254). These groups returned to the area of the summer village before the river froze over, an event that usually occurred in the second half of November (Bowers 1950:250, 252, 1965:57).

Around mid-November the people left their villages and moved into winter camps, usually not more than a few miles away from the summer villages, where they built smaller and less carefully constructed earthlodges (fig. 3) (Wilson 1934:395). The inhabitants remained in one place throughout the winter but did not in general return to the same location the following winter. There seems to have been some tendency for the people of a single summer village to split into several winter camps if the threat of enemies was not severe (Bowers 1965:34, 45, 215, cf. 1950:250ff.), but in the early 1830s, at least, all the inhabitants of a summer village moved into a single winter camp. After Like-a-Fishhook was founded, the three divisions each established a separate winter camp (Bowers 1965:39; Boller 1959:192ff.; cf. Matthews 1877:6ff.). The main reason for leaving the summer village was that in the course of time all the wood in its vicinity would have been depleted; winter camps were located in densely wooded river bottoms, partly to provide shelter from the weather, partly to supply fuel, and partly to provide fodder for the horses (McKenzie

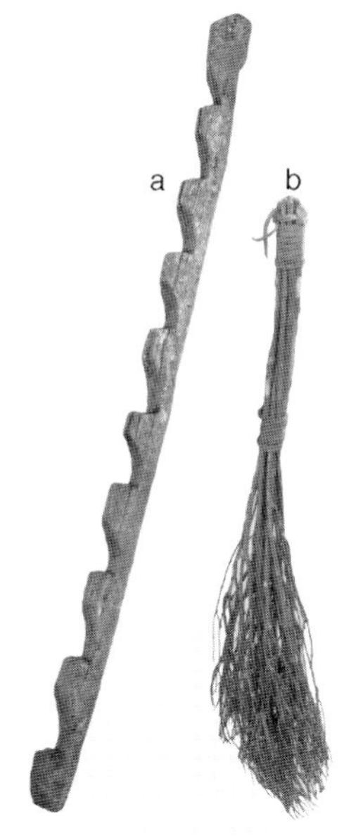

Minn. Histl. Soc., St. Paul: top left, 41318; bottom left, 9462-A; b, 7059.47 (neg. 09050-6); a, Smithsonian, Natl. Mus. of the Amer. Ind.: 1/3885; Amer. Mus. of Nat. Hist., New York: bottom center, 286481, bottom right, 286482.

Fig. 3. Earthlodges and household equipment. top left, Edward Goodbird at the hunting lodge built by Owl Woman. This type of small earthlodge had a wooden entryway. Photographed in 1918. bottom left, Interior of Hairy Coat's earthlodge with sleeping platform, storage area, and fireplace with heavy metal chain and hook to hang kettles. Photographed in 1912. a, Carved wooden ladder, the type commonly used by the Arikara, Hidatsa, and Mandan for climbing scaffolds. Collected by Gilbert L. Wilson, Ft. Berthold Res., N. Dak., 1907; length 762.9 cm. b, Buckbrush broom tied with leather strips. Such brooms were used to sweep out the earthlodges. Daily use meant it lasted only about 20 days (Gilman and Schneider 1987:39). Collected by Gilbert L. Wilson, Ft. Berthold Res., N. Dak., probably before 1918; length 88.5 cm. bottom center, Wolf Chief making a skin door. bottom right, The door installed. Photographs by Gilbert L. Wilson, Independence, N. Dak., 1910.

in Wood and Thiessen 1985:239ff.; Boller 1959:204ff.). The buffalo, the main source of food in the winter, also tended to shelter in the timber at this time of year. The council chose a special leader—again usually someone who had not hitherto acted as a chief—to be in charge of the winter camp (Bowers 1950:251).

In late February or early March (Maximilian in Thwaites 1904–1907, 23:272) the winter camp would break up. Some groups of people would follow the buffalo for a while, setting up small spring camps (Bowers 1965:61ff.), but soon all members of each division would be back in their summer villages.

Clans, Phratries, and Moieties

The Hidatsa had seven named matrilineal exogamous clans, representatives of all of which were to be found in each village. Three of them constituted the Three Clans moiety, and the remainder belonged to the Four Clans moiety (table 1). There was also one clan, the *xú·ra*, said to be of exogenous origin, and found only in Awatixa; and another, Speckled Eagle, whose members were said to be of Mandan origin, found mainly in Awaxawi (Bowers 1965:65–69, 293). Both belonged to the Four Clans moiety, which therefore actually contained six clans. Moiety affiliation did not

Table 1. Hidatsa Clans

Three Clans (*rá·kira·wi*) moiety	
waxó·xatì	Alkalai Lodge
wé?ec^{h}iro·ka	Knife People
ap^{h}úhkawika·	Low Cap
Four Clans (*rá·kito·pa*) moiety	
Unnamed phratry	
cí·ckaruxpà·ka	Prairie Chicken People[a]
awahéra·wihta·	Three Hills Sliding Down (?)
Unnamed phratry	
wiripa·ti	Waterbuster
xú·ra	[no translation][b]
ihtíšuhka	Wide Hill

Sources: Bowers 1965:65–69; Curtis 1904–1930, 4:183. Modern phonemic retranscriptions and translations by A. Wesley Jones.

[a]Hidatsa members of the Mandan Speckled Eagle clan were assimilated into the Prairie Chicken clan.

[b]Bowers (1965, 1966) says the name is derived from the noise of the cicada. In the 20th century this clan functioned as a lineage of the Waterbuster clan.

affect marriage, nor apparently were the moieties of much significance in any other sphere (though see Lowie 1917:21–22). The Four Clans moiety was divided into two phratries; in certain special contexts members of different clans in the same phratry treated each other as if they were members of the same clan (Bowers 1965:68, 97).

The clan was an important unit. Unlike the Mandan clan, it does not seem to have had a leader, but its members had many important obligations to each other. Old people and orphans were the responsibility of their clan, and if a man was killed, it was the duty of his clansmen to exact revenge. The clan was one of the main institutions to make people behave as they should: for instance, if a woman was suspected of stealing from the gardens of others, then women from her clan would lie in wait for her and, if their suspicions proved to be justified, beat her. A man's clansmen supported him in his career, particularly by helping him when he needed property for ceremonies.

Wealth and Trade

Hidatsa society was not one in which wealth was accumulated and retained, nor was wealth a measure of status: "those highest in the regard of the group were likely to be relatively poor because of their numerous social obligations" (Bowers 1965:289, 427; cf. Boller 1959:55ff.). However, there were prosperous households and poor ones: a lodge with a high proportion of hardworking women and good hunters fared better than one with many unproductive mouths to feed. It helped a young man to come from a prosperous household: he would then have the wealth to join an age-society, to buy his father's bundles at an early age, and to pay the horses that might be demanded as bride-price (Bowers 1965:136, 152, 158).

The Hidatsa could produce all their own necessities but increased their wealth by trade, especially with their nomadic neighbors. Their main export was their horticultural produce, though they also offered some other items, notably eagle feathers (Bowers 1950:207). In exchange they received mainly horses and buffalo robes (McKenzie in Wood and Thiessen 1985:236, 246; Matthews 1877:27). In the early nineteenth century, at least, they were also reexporting large quantities of goods that they had received from White traders in exchange for beaver skins (McKenzie in Wood and Thiessen 1985:246; cf. Ahler, Thiessen, and Trimble 1991:66). Trade was not simply a matter of business: it was rather part of a complex of relations that found formal expression in a man from one tribe adopting a man from another as his son (McKenzie in Wood and Thiessen 1985:244; Wilson 1928:140ff.; Bowers 1965:47–50, 91ff.). Relations with other tribes were also facilitated by the presence among the Hidatsa of a number of non-Hidatsas—often fugitives from their own tribes—who served as interpreters and emissaries. The Hidatsa treated such outsiders well (McKenzie in Wood and Thiessen 1985:259; cf. Bowers 1965:95, 218), and indeed even prisoners of war were kindly dealt with (Maximilian in Thwaites 1904–1907, 23:351).

Age-Groups

The Hidatsa had a complicated and unusual system of age-groups, resembling, in all essential features, that of the Mandan (for a detailed account see Stewart 1977). Most males, except the very young and the very old, belonged to an age-group, that is, a group of coevals. Each group drew its membership from a single village; at any one time there might be half a dozen such groups in the village. In a variety of circumstances, for example, in the accumulation of the large quantities of property needed for certain religious ceremonies, a man could turn to the other members of his age-group for help. Each group bought successively, usually but not always from the immediately senior group, a sequence of age-societies (table 2). An age-society consisted of a collection of rights, in particular the rights to sing certain songs, perform certain dances, and wear certain costumes. After a time, usually some years, the age-group would sell the society to a junior age-group. A single age-group might at a given moment own more than one society.

The age-group would generally meet several times a year in the lodge of one of its members. It might also parade through the village, and dance out of doors both in the village and in neighboring villages, whether Mandan or Hidatsa. The ceremonies were, with minor exceptions, secular in nature. Though the members might display their military honors at meetings, the societies as such took no part in warfare.

Only one of the age-societies, the Black Mouths, was of major significance in the life of the tribe. It was owned by men who were just below the age at which they might join

Table 2. Hidatsa Men's Age-Societies, Youngest to Oldest

Hidatsa	*English*
wíˀwaˀu·paki	Stone Hammer Owners
wa·cawé·	Hot Dance
wiráraxxùxi	Scraped Wood
wašúkakarìšta	Little Dogs
wašúkawa·ra·xi	Crazy Dogs
wiráxiši,[a] also *wiráˀicìhkita*	Lumpwood, Tree Root
hérero·ka ihkè·[b] also *pe·rická ihkè·*	Crow Indian Society, Raven Society
iixúhka ihkè·	Kit Fox Society
cú·takirakšú·ki	Half Shorn
wa·ˀihá· ihkè·, also *í·šipihe·*	Enemy Society, Blackened Mouths
wašúka ihkè·	Dog Society
kí·rapi ihkè·	Bull Society

SOURCES: Bowers 1965:175; Maximilian in Stewart 1977; Curtis 1907–1930, 4:182; Lowie 1913:227. Phonemic retranscriptions and translations by A. Wesley Jones.

NOTE: The literature is inconsistent concerning the names and relative rankings of Hidatsa men's age-societies. Bowers (1965:175) lists 12 societies, not all of which were found in all three Hidatsa divisions.

[a]This form may literally mean 'red wood', a reference to a type of club that served as an insignia for this society (Densmore 1923:108–109).

[b]The initial element is based on Maximilian's recording and is borrowed from Mandan *hreró·ka* 'Crow'.

the village council. In addition to the usual age-society rights, they had the often onerous duty of ensuring that the decisions of the council were carried out. If necessary they could use force. Their responsibility was limited to matters that involved the village as a whole; ordinary disputes—arising, say, from theft or adultery—were not their province (Bowers 1965:185). Their executive duties meant that they met far more frequently than the other societies—often every few days, or even daily—and for entirely practical purposes.

Women had an age organization similar to the men's, though with fewer societies. Of the four recorded women's societies, at least two, and perhaps three, were of Mandan origin. The two junior societies were the Skunks (aged about 15 to 20) and the Enemies (young married women). Their ceremonies were an important part of the celebrations that accompanied the return of successful war parties.

The two senior women's societies had considerably more religious elements than did the men's societies (Lowie 1919:415). The Goose Society (aged around 30 to 40) was concerned with rites for ensuring good crops, while the White Buffalo Calf Society performed rites for bringing buffalo to the village in winter.

Religion

Religion permeated every aspect of Hidatsa life, from agriculture, warfare, and hunting, to trapping fish and building an earthlodge. Frequent and elaborate religious ceremonies took up a large part of the people's attention.

The Hidatsa believed that whatever a man achieved, he achieved by virtue of the supernatural power he possessed (Bowers 1965:243). Power was viewed as a commodity, which was depleted by participating in any difficult or dangerous undertaking.

All power derived from supernatural beings, many of which were identified with animals. Power could either be acquired directly from a spirit, or indirectly by transfer from someone who already possessed it.

In order to acquire power directly a man had to suffer by fasting, by self-torture, or by a combination of the two. In some instances it may have been thought that this would lead a spirit to take pity on the sufferer. In other instances, acts of self-torture, for example, the cutting off of a finger, were carried out as an offering to a particular spirit (Bowers 1965:322, 333).

Self-inflicted suffering always brought about an increase in power (Bowers 1965:285). If the individual was fortunate, he also received a vision in which, characteristically, an animal would appear and promise him, for example, success in hunting or warfare. The animal would also instruct him in some kind of ritual, probably including a song. When a man received such a vision, he put together a (personal) bundle, that is, a collection of small objects associated with his vision and wrapped up together. He would take the bundle with him to war in order to enjoy the protection of the guardian, and he would perform rituals to it. In many instances he would have to follow various special rules in his daily life (cf. Maximilian in Thwaites 1904–1907, 23:383).

The most prominent bundles were those whose origins went back to mythical antiquity. In such cases there would be a tale of the circumstances under which a spirit (again, usually an animal) had given to a member of the tribe instructions on how to make up the bundle, sing the accompanying song, and perform the rites (Bowers 1965:361). Bundles of this sort are known as tribal bundles, in contrast to the personal bundles. A tribal bundle and its rite was, like a personal bundle, essentially a channel by which supernatural power could be tapped.

Both tribal and personal bundles could be transferred to other individuals, but in the case of personal bundles such transfers were rare (the bundle usually being left with its owner's corpse), whereas tribal bundles were normally handed down from generation to generation. Most tribal bundles passed from father to son, but a certain number of the bundles in Awatixa—among them the most important ones—were owned by particular clans and usually kept by some eminent representative of the clan. One or two Awaxawi bundles also passed on in female lines (Bowers 1965:31, 32, 296, 350, 381, 473, 391, 1950:227).

The method by which a bundle passed from one person to another is usually referred to as purchase. In the case of an important bundle this was a lengthy process, culminating in an extended and elaborate ceremony. The process began when the son (or in the case of an Awatixa clan bundle, junior member of the clan) of a bundle owner had a dream or vision, often in the course of fasting and self-torture, in which he was instructed by the spirit to take over the bundle of his father (or senior clansman). Without such a dream he could not purchase it. The purchaser then had to collect the large amounts of property needed for the ceremony. In the case of major bundles this usually took a year (Bowers 1965:286, 310, 437). The purchaser would receive goods from many sources, among them his own clan, his father's clan, and his age-group. A member of the father's clan would instruct the purchaser in the myths and rituals of the bundle he was to purchase; the instructor was in turn instructed by some well-informed person. These people, and many others, were given property in the course of the ceremony, although neither they nor the seller actually retained what they were given but instead distributed it to others. Those who participated in the ceremony thereby sanctioned the transfer, and certain of them invoked their own spirits to favor the purchaser. Often enough the father was dead by the time the son was ready to purchase, but his bundle would have been kept in abeyance, and the father's role in the ceremony was not of great importance (Bowers 1965:171, 308, 311, 362, 368, 385, 415, 427, 407, 432).

The owner of a tribal bundle could in principle sell it four times. For this purpose duplicate bundles were produced. The rule was that the first three purchasers would each be given a new bundle, while the last one obtained the original. It was apparently only with the fourth sale that the seller lost all the advantages conferred on him by ownership, though possibly each sale involved some diminution of power. In practice there were many bundles of which there was no recollection that they had ever been duplicated (Bowers 1965:308, 332, 418, 445, 309).

Tribal bundles were a source of benefit not only for their owners but also for the village at large. The major religious ceremonies were almost all either bundle purchases or feasts for bundles (see Bowers 1965:451–463). A feast could be given for a bundle either by its owner or his son (in which case it is what Bowers calls a bundle renewal feast) or by someone else. The person would promise the feast long in advance, in exchange for supernatural benefits either received or desired. So, for instance, a young man would promise a feast to the spirit called Old Woman Who Never Dies if she would help him to scalp an enemy; she was represented by one tribal bundle in each village, and the young man would make his pledge to the owner of a bundle to whom he stood in the relationship of son (there were many such men, including all members of his father's clan). Having got a scalp, the young man would collect, by his own efforts and from relatives and age-mates, as much property as possible (in the case of an important bundle the amount would be immense). He would then invite the owner of the Old Woman Who Never Dies bundle to a feast; the owner would bring his bundle, the property would be distributed to him (and others), and the young man would decorate the bundle with the scalp. For his part, the bundle owner would pray for the young man and would give him an object from the bundle for his own use; it was not uncommon for objects to be removed from bundles in this way (Bowers 1965:109, 332, 347).

A ceremony like this involved and benefited only a limited number of people, but others served all the people, for instance by bringing buffalo or by causing rain. The most prominent tribal ceremony was the Naxpike 'hide-beating' of the Hidatsa proper and Awatixa. Among the Awaxawi the annual Tying the Pots ceremony had a similar status. The Naxpike was a bundle transfer that had many features in common with the Sun Dance of other tribes. There were a number of Naxpike bundles, and the ceremony was probably held once in most summers (Bowers 1965:389, 308, 312). It was believed to benefit the community in a general way. The purchaser would be a mature man who had shown both his courage in war and his ability to undergo the suffering needed to acquire power.

Like other rituals, the Naxpike was seen as a dramatization of the bundle's origin myth (Bowers 1965:308, 344, 1950:107, 341). In the case of the Naxpike bundle the myth involved Long Arm, leader of the People Above, directing the torture of a man called Spring Boy. The purchaser of the Naxpike bundle represented Spring Boy, while the owner of the Long Arm bundle represented Long Arm; a good many other people also had special roles.

With great ceremony a lodge would be built for the occasion, the main events of which took place over a period of four days in the presence of the whole community. There was much singing and dancing, but the most striking feature of the rites was that any men who wished to do so would fast and subject themselves to torture. In an 1805 ceremony, a group of young men had wooden pins fixed under the flesh on their backs; to each such pin was attached a cord eight yards long, at the end of which were seven or more buffalo skulls. The men dragged the skulls to the lodge. When they arrived the skulls were passed over a high beam, serving as a counterweight to suspend the men in the air. While they were in this position the Long Arm bundle owner at their request removed slices of their flesh, cut off parts of their fingers, and branded them with red-hot irons (McKenzie in Wood and Thiessen 1985:253–56). Maximilian (in Thwaites 1904–1907, 23:378) remarked that the Hidatsa men were much more scarred from self-torture than were the Mandan.

After being released from the buffalo skulls, a man "took his stripes of flesh and his finger joint, placed them into a neat little bag with which he hastened to the outside of the village (Singing a lamentable dirge as he went) to deposit as an offering to his God" (McKenzie in Wood and Thiessen 1985:256). The notion of making flesh offerings was quite general, but many spirits were content with buffalo hides (Bowers 1965:370; Maximilian in Thwaites 1904–1907, 23:371ff.), kettles, blankets (Maximilian in Thwaites 1904–1907, 23:339), calicoes (Bowers 1950:387), eagle feathers, knives, and food (Bowers 1965:436, 370). Offerings could be made in various ways. Some were placed on poles in or near a summer village; others left near stone effigies of certain animals (turtles, snakes, birds) that were to be found in various parts of Hidatsa territory; yet others were thrown into the Missouri (Bowers 1965:436, 370, pl. 6, 373; Maximilian in Thwaites 1904–1907, 23:339).

The variety of religious practices that might be connected with a bundle can be illustrated by the famous Waterbuster clan bundle (Pepper and Wilson 1908; Gilmore 1926; Lowie 1939:231–239; Bowers 1965:467–73; Gilman and Schneider 1987:296–301, 315). The bundle, which was stored in its keeper's lodge on a special stand, consisted of two human skulls, a medicine pipe, a buffalo skull, a turtle shell, and an eagle wing fan. The origin myth explains that the human skulls are those of two eagles who assumed human form; when the second of them was dying, he told the people how to use the various objects in the bundle. For example, if enemies menaced the tribe, the keeper of the bundle was to roll the medicine pipe toward them, singing a special song; if drought threatened, the keeper was to take down the human skulls, put certain herbs on them, and sprinkle them with water.

These practices are exemplified by an event that took place in about 1867. A group of men came to Small Ankles, the keeper of the bundle, with guns, blankets, and other gifts, and asked him to be their winter camp chief and to pray that they should have many buffalo. In accordance with the instructions handed down from the eagle man, Small Ankles took out the medicine pipe, anointed it with buffalo fat, laid it on top of the two human skulls, and spent the night singing the song that was to bring buffalo. The next morning he announced that he had had a vision that buffalo would arrive within four days—as indeed they did (Pepper and Wilson 1908:295).

Women had less need of power than men, since they did not hunt or fight (Bowers 1965:284). They did not mutilate themselves to gain power (Gilman and Schneider 1987:196; Bowers 1965:138), though they might fast (Bowers 1965:290). They rarely had personal bundles, and only in exceptional cases did they have some rights in tribal bundles (Bowers 1965:290, 381, cf. 474, 1950:249). Nevertheless, a woman might gain considerable supernatural status; whether in this case she was viewed as having power in exactly the same sense as a man might have power is not clear. A number of the older women, together with the berdaches, constituted the Holy Women Society. They were an important group, in fact the only people who had the right to participate in every tribal ceremony. Though the Holy Women did not have bundles, each one transmitted her rights exactly as one would a bundle (Bowers 1965:324, 326). A woman apparently also gained supernatural status from participation in ceremonies relating to bundles owned by her husband, and perhaps also from "walking" (having sexual intercourse) with a senior man (this was believed to transmit power from the senior man to the woman's husband) (Bowers 1965:462). An unmarried man could not purchase a tribal bundle (Bowers 1965:307), and a woman who took part in many ceremonies with her husband became very knowledgeable and was "viewed as sacred and therefore dangerous" (Bowers 1965:157). For this reason she would not usually remarry after her husband's death, unless to one of his brothers or to a man with the same ceremonial rights as her deceased husband (Bowers 1965:157, 320, 351).

Death in the prime of life, and indeed almost any kind of misfortune, tended to be ascribed to lack of supernatural power, the result, for instance, of an error in ritual or of failing (perhaps inadvertently) to obey instructions given in a vision. A young man might also die because he had "spoken unkindly to or mistreated someone possessing unrevealed supernatural powers" (Bowers 1965:164, 283), but accusations of sorcery were not characteristic of the culture. Leaders were held responsible for mishaps that occurred to those in their charge: for instance, if someone accidentally broke a limb in the winter camp, or if someone died prematurely, the chief would be blamed. Such an event would indicate that the chief lacked power, and he would try to increase it by the usual means; he would also attempt to appease the victim or his relatives with feasts and gifts (Bowers 1965:34, 57, 61, 63, 186).

Mythology

Two extended myths, referred to by Bowers (1965) as the First Creator (or Exodus) myth and the Sacred Arrows myth, accounted for the beginning of the world and the origin of the Hidatsa people. These myths, with motifs that are found throughout the Plains, are ones that the Hidatsa linked to their origins. The myths covered two series of events thought of as having taken place simultaneously.

The First Creator myth begins with an earth diver motif, the story of how a diving bird brought up mud from below the waters and how First Creator fashioned the land from this mud. Spirits corresponding to human beings already existed but were living in the underworld. First Creator caused some of them to come to the surface, and then scattered them across the land as different tribes. In the versions of the myth recorded in the nineteenth century First Creator is the only creator, but by the 1930s a second creator, Lone Man, had been introduced, apparently as a result of Mandan influence. Lone Man and First Creator brought into being many animals and the spirits that correspond to them; but the females of these animals and spirits were created by another spirit, Village Old Woman. The First Creator myth tells of many events and deals with the movements of the Hidatsa proper and Awaxawi until they reached the Missouri (Bowers 1965:290, 297, 323).

The history of the Awatixa is given in the Sacred Arrows myth, which takes place entirely on the Missouri (Bowers 1965:291, 303). It starts with the story of Charred Body, who lived in the heavens. Hearing the bellowing of buffaloes, he looked through a hole in the sky and discovered the earth below. Liking what he saw, he descended to earth in the form of an arrow at a place near Painted Woods. Here he set up 13 earth lodges, and to populate them he brought down 13 young couples from the sky. They founded the 13 original clans (of which six later went back to the sky). The myth tells of events through which the twin sons of Charred Body's sister, Lodge Boy and Spring Boy—who were torn prematurely from their mother's womb by an evil spirit—used the power of the sacred arrows to subdue the evil spirits menacing the people.

The First Creator myth and the Sacred Arrows myth converge when the Hidatsa proper and Awaxawi settle on the Missouri. A single, joint myth takes up the tale of legendary events from that time on.

In general, each episode in these tribal myths recounts the origins of a particular tribal bundle (for the exceptions, see Bowers 1965:303). A bundle owner would know the episode relating to his own bundle and know which episodes preceded and followed it, but not necessarily much more, for the tribal myths were knowledge of a very esoteric kind. Apart from the bundle owner himself, a particular episode would also be known to certain other bundle owners whose spirits played some part in that episode. These owners were the major participants at ceremonies relating to the bundle, whether sales or feasts. Furthermore, by giving feasts to a bundle, it was possible to purchase knowledge of its myth without purchasing the bundle itself, and important people would gain extensive knowledge of the tribal myths in this way (Bowers 1965:304, 329, 392, 295, 464).

The Household

Women were closely identified with the household. The earthlodge, which was largely built by women, belonged to the line of mothers and daughters that lived in it, as did its gardens, domestic equipment, and sometimes some of its horses (Bowers 1965:114, 138, 157; on the acquisition of horses see 115, 138, 172). A husband usually slept in the home of his wife (cf. Hanson 1983). The oldest sister was supposed to marry first, and all else being equal the younger sisters would marry the same man as they came of age (Matthews 1877:53; Wilson 1917:9; Bowers 1965:107, 114, 159). They would all live in the same household. If a man subsequently married a woman from a different lodge, she often remained in her home, and he divided his attention between two (or more) households. If a younger sister married someone other than the oldest sister's husband, then she normally went to live with her husband; even in this case the notion of the line of women asserted itself, for if the marriage lasted long enough, the wife would assume the place of a daughter to her husband's mother (Bowers 1965:155, 105, 114, 119).

A married man hunted for his wife's household, but his horses were cared for by the younger members of his mother's household, most of his property was kept there, and he returned to it often for meals. He was forbidden even to talk to his wife's mothers, that is, the senior women in her lodge; only with the passage of time, and after he had brought his mothers-in-law a scalp, was the taboo set aside (Bowers 1965:106, 121). Although it was desirable for a household to have a man to hunt for it, it was by no means essential: "households were known which had had no adult male for a decade or more and in which the members lived very well by exchanging garden produce for other necessities" (Bowers 1965:107, 1950:82).

The ties that bound the successive generations of women who formed the core of the household were often not only familial, but also ritual and, so to speak, professional. Certain skills were passed on from generation to generation, and these skills were not simply taught but had to be purchased in a religious ceremony. The rights in male skills, such as making arrows, making bullboats (fig. 4), trapping eagles, and certain kinds of doctoring, were linked to particular bundles (Bowers 1965:120, 166, 357, 372, 1950:206, 374). The rights in female skills, such as potting (fig. 5), basketmaking, setting up the four central supports of the earthlodge, building the chimney and fireplace of a log cabin, and certain kinds of doctoring, were either also linked, in some fashion not entirely clear, to bundles, or else were passed on in much the same way as bundles. Thus "basketmaking was practiced by those with Holy Women rights" (Bowers 1965:120, 161; Wilson 1934, 1977). Because bundles generally passed from father to son, tribal bundles tended to move from lodge to lodge; female skills, in contrast, tended to remain in the same house.

Life Cycle

• BIRTH The Hidatsa believed that human beings, like animals, exist in both an actual and a spiritual form and that every infant originated as a spirit that entered its mother's body. These spirits were generally thought to inhabit certain known hills in the tribal territory.

A woman customarily gave birth to her first child in her mother's lodge, and it was the maternal grandmother's responsibility to dispose of the placenta and care for the newborn infant. The child was often named by the maternal grandfather; and ceremony introduced the child to his father's clan. The name given was one associated with a bundle belonging to the name-giver, and the name-giver would pray to the spirit associated with the bundle to bless the child (Bowers 1965:128–129).

• CHILDHOOD A sharp distinction was made between male and female: children were, for instance, discouraged

Amer. Mus. of Nat. Hist., New York: top, 286496; center, 288251; bottom, Smithsonian, Dept. of Anthr.: 9785 (neg. 71-3064).

Fig. 4. Bullboats, often made by women and sometimes used to bring firewood to the village (Gilman and Schneider 1987:53). Bullboat-making rites were inherited with the Missouri River bundles, and those who wanted to make a bullboat paid the bundle owner for the right to do so (Bowers 1965:372). The vessels were paddled by 1 or 2 individuals kneeling in the boat (Gilman and Schneider 1987:184). top, Construction of boat probably by Owl Woman and Many Growths, Hidatsa-Mandan, binding the bent lower ribs with rawhide strips. Photographed in 1912. center, Method of carrying a boat for a long distance. Photographed in 1909. Photographs by Gilbert L. Wilson, Independence, N. Dak. bottom, Bullboat constructed of buffalo or cowhide stretched taut over a circular frame of saplings. A paddle with a triangular hole in the blade is in the boat. Collected by Dr. Charles C. Gray and Dr. Washington Matthews, Ft. Buford, Dak. Terr., 1870. Diameter 157 cm.

from playing with toys characteristic of the opposite sex (Bowers 1965:130). This foreshadowed the differences of adulthood: except under special circumstances, almost the only tasks performed by both sexes were butchering and retrieving wood from the river (Bowers 1965:52, 132; cf. 374).

A boy was disciplined largely by members of his own clan; his father neither scolded nor punished him (Bowers 1965:72, 111, 129). However, the father was responsible for the boy's ritual activities. A boy of no more than six or seven years old might be induced by his father to fast for several days and then allow himself to be suspended from sharpened sticks passed through his back (Maximilian in Thwaites 1904–1907, 23:378; cf. Bowers 1965:73, 135, 284).

• MARRIAGE A man was considered ready to marry at the age of 18 (Wilson 1910:231). A woman normally married soon after puberty (Bowers 1965:138; Wilson 1910:226, 231), sometimes to a young man of her own choice, sometimes to one selected by her father or by her maternal relatives (Gilman and Schneider 1987:108; Bowers 1965:158). The most prestigious form of marriage was one in which a bride-price (mainly horses) was paid, and this was preferred for a girl's first marriage (Lowie 1917:46; Bowers 1965:139). More commonly, no bride-price was paid (Wilson 1979:278). Either spouse could easily divorce the other, and in the early stages of marriage, especially when there were no children, divorce was very common (Bowers 1965:111, 142; cf. Matthews 1877:53). Because so many men were killed in war, the survivors often had more than one wife. Jealous husbands were laughed at: an example of true savoir faire was a man who knew that the two youngest and prettiest of his four wives "sometimes met other men . . . but thought nothing of it as long as they attended to their work and did not cause too much gossip" (Bowers 1965:153, 155, 248). As one Hidatsa remarked, "We did not think it right for men to get jealous and fight about women" (Wilson 1911:203). If a husband beat his faithless wife, her brothers, otherwise quick to protect her, would not intervene (Bowers 1965:115).

• DEATH The aged were highly respected and well cared for; Hidatsa households even took in elderly women from neighboring nomadic tribes who might otherwise have been abandoned (Bowers 1965:164, 218). People who had in their earlier years acquired much ritual and other knowledge prospered in old age from the sale of this information to the younger generation (Bowers 1965:120, 289). Giving feasts for the older people is frequently mentioned as part of the way to power (Bowers 1965:232). When an old person's power was completely exhausted, death ensued (Bowers 1965:282).

Those no longer young made careful preparations for death: they set aside fine clothes in which to die, and gave a particular person instructions as to how their body was to be dressed, decorated, and disposed of. Some were placed on scaffolds or in trees, others laid on the ground, while in

Amer. Mus. of Nat. Hist., New York: left, 288261; right top, 286473. bottom right, Minn. Histl. Soc., St. Paul: 7059.123.

Fig. 5. Pottery making, a secret and sacred activity. Rights to make pottery were inherited and purchased in the female line (Bowers 1965:165, 373). left, Hairy Coat's wife making a pot, 1911. top right, Sioux Woman putting hay into a pot being fired, 1910. "For firing, the pots were covered with coals made by burning dry bark; then they were coated with liquid made from boiling pounded corn" (Gilman and Schneider 1987:118). Photographs by Gilbert L. Wilson, Independence, N. Dak. bottom right, Grooved pot paddle carved from cottonwood, used during pottery manufacture to thin and strengthen vessel walls. The impressions made by the grooves and ridges were often left as decoration. Collected by Gilbert L. Wilson, probably before 1918; length 25.4 cm.

the course of the nineteenth century underground burial became common (Wilson 1979:287). Personal property was disposed of according to the wishes of the dying person; a few items were placed with the body. Mourning was intense, and any woman who had been given horses by a man would cut off part of a finger on his death. (Usually a man gave horses only to his mother and his sisters.) Members of the deceased's father's clan were in charge of the obsequies, and for this they received payment in food, horses, and other property from the deceased's own clan (Bowers 1965:75, 116, 168–173).

The Hidatsa thought that life in the afterworld was much like life on earth, and a dying person was often given messages to take to those who had gone before. However, there were considerable differences of opinion as to the details of the afterlife (Bowers 1965:75, 173–174). Many believed that the dead rejoined the spirit people left behind in the underworld (as related in the First Creator myth). To reach them, it is reported, the dead have to cross a narrow bridge across a river; those who in their life have been useful to their people pass over with ease, while the others fall off and are swept away (James in Thwaites 1904–1907, 15:65). Other Hidatsas considered that those descended from any of the 13 couples mentioned in the Sacred Arrows myth would rejoin the spirits in the sky. One man told of two villages of the dead—a small one for the wicked or cowardly, and a larger one for the good or brave (Maximilian in Thwaites 1904–1907, 23:374).

Clothing and Adornment

By far the most highly developed visual art among the Mandan and Hidatsa was personal adornment, especially of men. Many men were extensively tattooed on their bodies (but not faces); in addition they painted themselves in varying and individual ways, depending on the occasion (fig. 6). They wore their hair long, and glued on extra hair (often from dead enemies) to lengthen their own. There was a great variety of head ornaments. Men's clothing consisted of moccasins, leggings, breechcloth, and buffalo robe (buckskin shirts were uncommon). All these items (except the breechcloth) were often beautifully decorated, most attention being paid to the buffalo robe. Most of a man's adornments had significance: they indicated his achievements in war and the gifts he had given on ceremonial occasions (Mallery 1893:437–440). The decorated buffalo robes of the Crow and Hidatsa were known to be the finest of all the tribes in the region of the Missouri (Maximilian in Thwaites 1904–1907, 23:102, 264; see Vatter 1927; Hotz 1935, 1937; Krickeberg 1954; Hartmann 1968).

Division of Labor

In the summer, young men spent much of their time, day and night, on the large flat roofs of the lodges, keeping watch, talking, singing love songs, or sleeping in the sun (Henry in Coues 1897:327, 351); an older man's day might

Joslyn Art Mus., Omaha, Nebr.

Fig. 6. Roadmaker (*ari hiris*, written by Maximilian as Addih-Hiddisch), a war chief in the village of Awaxawi and a member of the tribal council. He died after 1837 (Bowers 1965:380). He has extensive tattooing on arms, hands, and breast. He wears moccasins and leggings decorated with beadwork and an elaborate necklace with a peace medal incorporated into it. A coup feather is attached to his hat, and he holds a tomahawk with scalp locks. Watercolor by Karl Bodmer, 1833.

State Histl. Soc. of N. Dak., Bismarck: 39–48.

Fig. 7. Yellow Wolf. He wears a brass bead bandolier, multiple clamshell necklaces, bead necklace and hair decorations probably made of hairpipes (thin tubes made of animal bone), fur, and brass beads. Photograph by Monroe Killey, Elbowoods, N. Dak., 1942.

largely be spent sitting in his lodge, where he "receives his friends, smokes, and chats the time away with the greatest dignity" (Henry in Coues 1897:339). The women of the household, meanwhile, were busy from morning to night, not just with light tasks, but also with heavy work such as bringing in, often from a considerable distance, the great bundles of firewood that were consumed every day of the year (Boller 1959:200; Maximilian in Thwaites 1904–1907, 23:272). The men hunted and fought, performed elaborate ceremonies, and participated in a variety of sports and games. Some, for instance, shinny (fig. 9), were also played by women. Racing, both on foot and on horseback; swimming; archery and shooting; and hoop and pole (fig. 10) all enlivened the day and gave the opportunity to gamble (Boller 1959:201, 287).

Story telling was highly developed (Beckwith 1938; Parks, Jones, and Hollow 1978). Oral traditions ranged from solemn and esoteric myths connected with important bundles to light-hearted folk tales recounted purely as entertainment. Men also told stories of their own war and hunting exploits and those of great figures of the past (Boller 1959:201). In many cases payment had to be made for the right to tell a tale, and a few people—men and sometimes women—became specialists as storytellers and could recoup their costs through the many invitations they received to be feasted and tell their tales (Matthews 1877:63; Bowers 1950:93, 1965:296).

Warfare

The central activities of a man's life were the acquisition and deployment of power, activities carried on in a highly competitive environment. A man might decide to concentrate his energies on warfare and hunting, or he might devote himself primarily to ritual (Bowers 1965:136, 138, 278). But though a man's standing did not necessarily depend mainly on his military achievements, every man was intensively trained as a warrior from his earliest youth, and cowardice was the worst of all faults (Bowers 1965:281, 125, 327). A boy first went to war at the age of 14 or 15 and was expected to have won some war honors before he

Smithsonian, NAA: 56,597

Fig. 8. Women's clothing. Cloth wing dresses were common in the Plains at this period, as were dentalium necklaces and ear ornaments. The woman on the left is wearing a brass bead bandolier. Both women wear plain hightop moccasins. Photograph by David F. Barry, 1890s.

married (Maximilian in Thwaites 1904–1907, 23:353; Bowers 1965:222, 271).

The village would from time to time send out war parties consisting of anything from a handful to dozens of men. The usual aims of a party were either to capture horses or to take scalps or both. If it achieved its objective without casualties, it would return home, even if this meant neglecting a clear opportunity for further gains (Bowers 1965:224, 232). This was consistent with the religious ideas that permeated every aspect of warfare. The starting point of the expedition was always a vision. A man would be promised, for example, that if he went in a certain direction he would get a certain number of horses of a particular kind, or the scalp of a man or woman fitting a particular description; this indicated that the man had the power to get these things, and also gave him the right to them, whoever in the party might actually capture the horse or kill the victim. Once the promise had been fulfilled, there would be no point in continuing the expedition. An old man who had had a vision of this kind, and who had not acted on it, could sell his power and his rights to a younger one. These visions, like those relating to tribal bundles, were subject to interpretation by the senior men, who tried to hold in check the tendency of eager young men to set out on expeditions that might lead to unnecessary loss of life or to conflict with neighboring tribes with whom the Hidatsa were at peace.

To lead a war party called for much power and was undertaken only by those who had rights in tribal bundles, had suffered much, and had given many feasts. In the course of the expedition the leader would pray to his particular spirit and perhaps subject himself to self-torture. The fact that he would be held responsible for deaths and injuries to members of his party (like a winter camp chief)

top, Minn. Histl. Soc., St. Paul: 42133; bottom, Smithsonian, Natl. Mus. of the Amer. Ind.: 13/2820.

Fig. 9. Shinny, a woman's game widespread in North America (Culin 1907:641), played with a hide-covered ball and sticks. The aim of the game was for team members to get the ball past goal markers. top, Photograph by Gilbert L. Wilson, Independence, N. Dak., 1916. bottom, Quilled ball. Collected by Melvin Gilmore, Ft. Berthold Res., N. Dak., 1924. Circumference 575 cm.

is another reason why he would bring it back as soon as it had achieved its narrowly defined aim. When on one expedition six men were killed, its leader, running home with his men, stripped himself naked, cut off all his hair, cut himself in many places, and amputated the tips of his two fingers (Bowers 1965:234). These were acts of mourning but may also have been intended to gain power.

There were three sets of tribal bundles that were principally related to warfare. All were connected with wolves, and in a secondary way with coyotes. These animals also gave their names to the men in the war party, each of whom had a particular role. The leader and his deputies were Old Wolves, the scouts were Coyotes, and the other members, who were assigned various tasks, were Young Wolves (Bowers 1965:224, 393).

There was an elaborate system of symbols to record a man's military achievements: for instance, if several men together killed an enemy, "the first to strike painted one side of his shirt and leggings in black, wore one coyote tail, and one eagle tail feather. The second dressed in the same manner except that he painted one red band on the eagle tail. The third and fourth to strike painted only the leggings black; the third wore a feather with two stripes and the fourth wore a feather with three stripes" (Bowers 1965:279; cf. Maximilian in Thwaites 1904–1907, 23:375).

Joking Relatives

Even the most important men would find that any tendency to arrogance or other unacceptable behavior was quickly checked by their joking relatives, that is, by certain classes of relative (notably those whose fathers came from the same clan as their own fathers) who had the right

Mus. of Fine Arts, Boston: 50-3932.

Fig. 10. Hoop and pole game. The pole is thrown toward a hoop rolling along the ground. The pole "has four markings indicated with leather and at the end a pad made of leather strips, scraps of cloth, or, for want of something better, even bunches of grass. The winner starts the hoop, both players run along beside it and throw their wands, the flight of which is retarded by the pads, called *idi* by the Herantsa, so that they do not take too wide a range over the smooth course. . . . According to that mark on the cue or wand on which the hoop in falling rests, they reckon the game." Wagers on the outcome included bows, arrows, knives, moccasins, buffalo robes, guns, horses, tents, and even their older wives (Kurz 1937:147–148). The 2 figures at the left, presumably spectators, hold an eagle-wing fan and a gunstock war club. Pen and wash by Rudolph Friedrich Kurz, 1851.

to tease or criticize them, often in an exceedingly direct fashion. "The importance of the joking relative cannot be overemphasized" (Bowers 1965:125).

Berdaches

Some youths, always sons of women in the Holy Women society or of men with rights in one of the Women Above bundles, started dreaming, in their late teens, of a spirit called Village-Old-Woman or of symbols connected with her. This was interpreted as an instruction to become a berdache, and such a person would henceforth wear women's clothing and take up women's work. The berdache would set up a household with a man and adopt children. There might be as many as one or two dozen berdaches in the village. They were pitied, and adults were reluctant to see their sons accept this role. Yet at the same time berdaches were seen as especially close to the supernatural, and they took a more active part in village rituals than even the most distinguished men. "There was an atmosphere of mystery about them . . . people tended to fear, respect, and avoid them" (Bowers 1965:167–168).

Population

The Hidatsa population probably reached its high point in the fifteenth century. It then suffered a catastrophic decline, mainly as a result of diseases introduced by Europeans (Ahler, Theissen, and Trimble 1991:52–57). Bowers (1965:486) suggests that there were about 4,000 Hidatsas before the epidemic of 1781. Figures from primary sources suggest a total population of 1,730 in 1797–1798 (Stewart 1975:78–80, 1975a), 2,700 in 1804–1805 (Lewis and Clark 1806:26, 1814, 1:130), and 2,100–2,200 in 1832–1833, when the proportion of warriors in the populations was about 1:6 among the Hidatsa, as opposed to about 1:4 among the Mandan (Maximilian in Thwaites 1904–1907, 23:255; Maximilian 1819–1849, 2:212; Stewart 1974:295). This accords with Catlin's (1841, 1:187) statement about the Hidatsa that "they, unlike the Mandan, are continually carrying war into their enemies' country" (cf. Henry in Coues 1897:373). Bowers (1965:110, 1950:82) assumes "nearly three [adult] females to each [adult] male."

Estimates for 1837–1886 come mostly from the annual reports of the commissioner of Indian affairs, which are inconsistent. The first figures after the 1837 epidemic are 300 men and 800 souls (ARCIA 1842:433). This seems to be reliable, as does an 1850 estimate of 700 souls (Culbertson 1952:137).

After the 1860s the populations may have declined further (Matthews 1877:17), as a result of disease, emigration to the Crow, and fierce warfare (Bowers 1965:267). Bowers (1965:67) traced 377 Hidatsa living in Like-a-Fishhook Village in 1872. After 1876 the ARCIA-figures suggest a population of about 350–400. There were in addition some 100–150 Hidatsas in the Crow Flies High band. The

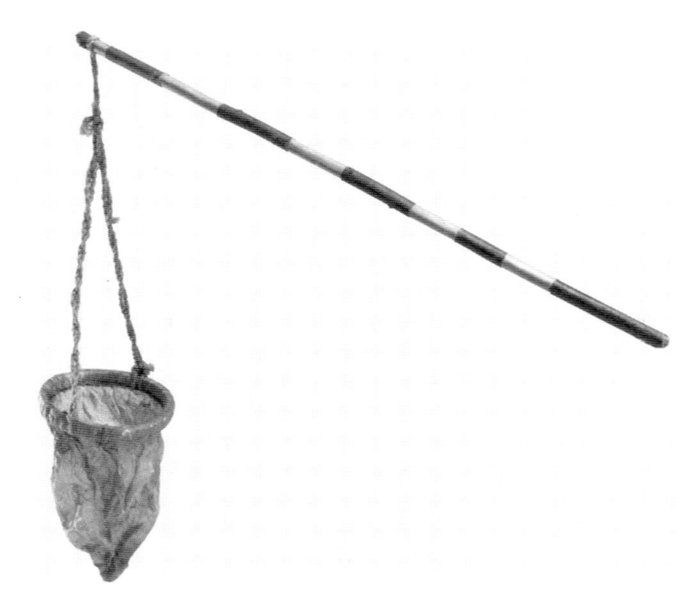

Minn. Histl. Soc., St. Paul: 7059.67a (neg no. 09014-4).

Fig. 11. Heart skin bucket constructed from the outer membrane of a buffalo or cow heart attached to a wood rim and tied to a willow handle by braided sinew strings. Containers of this sort were most commonly used to carry water. This one is of the type used to carry water for a war party. The 4 unpeeled and 5 peeled sections on the handle represent the 9 occasions on which the maker spied either enemies or their tents. Collected by Gilbert L. Wilson, 1916. Length of stick, 49.4 cm.

1910 census counted 547 Hidatsas (U.S. Bureau of the Census 1915:18). Two decades later, the popultion had risen to 681 (ARCIA 1931:51). In 1950, 933 Hidatsas resided on the Fort Berthold Reservation (U.S. Congress. House. Committee on Interior and Insular Affairs 1953:817). Subsequent figures were combined with those of the Arikara and Mandan as the Three Affiliated Tribes.

Synonymy†

Historically the three groups that comprise the Hidatsa—the Hidatsa proper (*hirá·ca*), the Awaxawi (*awaxáʔwi*), and the Awatixa (*awatixá·*)—were known either by their individual village names or by the designations Gros Ventre, Minitari, Willow Indians, Fall Indians, Soulier or "Shoe Indians," and Wattasoons; only in the mid to late nineteenth century, after the three divisions combined into a single village, did Hidatsa come into use as their tribal name. Of these various designations, Hidatsa and Gros Ventre continue to be used synonymously on the Fort Berthold Reservation during the twentieth century, even though the tribe is officially known as Hidatsa; Minitari and the other designations have long ceased to be used.

†This synonymy, like the others in this volume, was written by Douglas R. Parks to ensure consistency of style and comparability of scope and detail. For that reason, this synonymy replaces an earlier synonymy of high quality authored by Frank H. Stewart, who was not offered the opportunity to revise his synonymy.

Hidatsa proper

Hidatsa (*hirá·ca*) was formerly the name of the largest social division. The earliest recording of the name appears in two forms, Ena-sa and E-na-ta, the former cited as the Hidatsa name for themselves and the latter given as the Crow form of the word for this division, 1805 (McKenzie in Wood and Thiessen 1985:249). Other nineteenth-century examples of the name are Eláh-Sá (Maximilian 1843:178); Herantsa, 1851–1852 (Kurz 1937); Hedanza, 1867 (de Trobriand in Kane 1951:51); E-năt´-zä (Morgan 1871:47); Hidhatsa (Dorsey 1882a:829); Hedatse (Hamilton 1885, 1:75); and Hidatsa, its modern spelling (Matthews 1877:35).

Although the name has no recognizable etymology (formerly it was simply the designation of a division, and now the tribe) in the nineteenth century it was reputed to be an obsolete word meaning 'willows' (Matthews 1877:148) or 'red willow village' (W.P. Clark 1885:194). Popularly it was thought to derive from the name *wirahacitatí* 'willow tree houses, willow village' (Lowie 1939:178), first recorded in the treaty of 1825, in which the tribe is named Belantse-Etea (or Belantse-Etoa) or Minitaree (Kappler 1904–1941, 2:239). In 1833 Biddahátsi-Awatiss (*wiraháci awátiš* 'willow village') was recorded as the Hidatsas' name for themselves, with the note that the American designation of the tribe as Bellantsiä was incorrect (Maximilian 1839–1841, 2:211, 213). Recorded in the early twentieth century as Midahátsi-atíush or Willow Village, the name was remembered in myth as the largest of the former Hidatsa villages (Curtis 1907–1930, 4:131). For this reason, then, the Hidatsa—sometimes the Hidatsa proper and the closely related Awatixa, and sometimes these two divisions together with the Awaxawi—were known as the Willow Indians, 1805 (D. Thompson in Wood and Thiessen 1985:111; Matthews 1877:35) and Osier tribe or People of the Willows, 1843–1851 (de Smet 1905, 2:651, 4:1381).

One common early name for the Hidatsa was Gros Ventre, the designation given them by French and English fur traders (Maximilian in Thwaites 1904–1907, 23:367). In its French form the name occurs as Gros Ventres, 1795–1796 (Truteau in Parks 1992; Tabeau 1939:157), Gross Ventre and Gross Vintres (Lewis and Clark in Moulton 1983–, 3:310, 404), and Grovan (Bonner 1856:162). In English translation it appears as Great Belly Indians, 1786 (Anonymous 1794, 3:24), Big bellied (Mackenzie 1801:lxiv), Big bellies (Lewis and Clark in Moulton 1983–, 3:404), and Bigbellys (Gass 1807:76). During the Spanish period in Louisiana the name was Ventrudos, 1804 (Loisel in Nasatir 1952, 2:739).

The designation Gros Ventre or Big Belly, which was used to denote the Hidatsa, was also a name used by French and other Canadian traders for the Atsina (called Gros Ventre in the *Handbook*), who in the late eighteenth century were erroneously thought to be related to the Hidatsa. To avoid confusion of these two linguistically and socially unrelated tribes, early writers sometimes differentiated them by specifying the Hidatsa as Gros Ventres of the Missouri (Hale 1846:220; de Smet 1905, 2:651) or as Gross Ventres proper (Schoolcraft 1851–1857, 1:259).

Sometimes, too, the designation Fall Indians, another common name for the Gros Ventre (Atsina), was also used for the Hidatsa, 1797 (D. Thompson in Wood and Thiessen 1985:111). The Hidatsa were sometimes differentiated by qualifiers like the Missouri Fall Indians, 1810 (Biddle in Jackson 1962:525) and flying Fall Indians (D. Thompson in Wood and Thiessen 1985:111).

Another common early name for the Hidatsa is Minitari, which comes from the Mandan designation *wrį́tari* (pronounced [m^{i}nį́tari]), which is itself a borrowing into Mandan of the Hidatsa word *miríta·ri* 'crosses the water' (Hollow 1970:305; Jones 1979; Parks 1991). The name occurs in many variant spellings: Mönnitarris or Mennitarris (Maximilian 1839–1841, 2:211); Munitarees, 1796 (Evans in Nasatir 1952, 2:496); Manitarres, Menitares, and Me-ne-tar-re (Lewis and Clark in Moulton 1983–, 3:241, 310, 404); Minetarees, 1809–1811 (Bradbury in Thwaites 1904–1907, 5:127); Minnitarees (Hayden 1862:420); and Minitari and Miditadi (Matthews 1877:34). Other variants are in Hodge (1907–1910, 1:548–549).

Parallel to the use of the name Gros Ventre to designate both Hidatsa and Atsina is the occasional use of Minitari to designate both tribes as well. To differentiate them, designations for the Hidatsa were often modified as Minnitarees of the Willows (Lewis and Clark in Coues 1893, 1:199); Mennetarries at the mouth of Knife R. (Lewis and Clark in Thwaites 1904–1905, 1:271); and Stationary Minetares (Gallatin 1836:125).

Although Maximilian used the name Mönnitarris for the entire tribe, other writers have cited it either for only the Hidatsa proper or for the Hidatsa proper and the closely related Awatixa (Maximilian 1839–1841, 2:212; Bowers 1965:15). Lewis and Clark and later Hayden, for example, differentiated the Hidatsa division from the Awatixa by referring to the former as the Minnitarees proper and the latter as Minnitarees Metaharta, or Minnitarees of the Willows (Moulton 1983–, 3:404; Hayden 1862:422).

The association of the Hidatsa with water in the preceding name perhaps accounts for the Pawnee designation *pi·takícaha·ru?*, literally 'marsh man', which refers to the entire tribe and not just the Hidatsa proper (Parks 1965–1990). The cognate Arikara name for the Hidatsa, *wi·tatshá·nu?*, has been interpreted both as 'marsh man' (or 'people at the water') and as 'well-dressed man' (Hayden 1862:357; Matthews 1877:36; Parks 1970–1990); both translations would be correct, but Pawnee shows that it is the first one that is historically valid.

The earthlodge domicile of the Hidatsa has provided another source of names for the tribe. The Crow designation is *awašê·*, literally 'lodges made of earth' (Medicine Horse 1987:15; Curtis 1907–1930, 4:180), first recorded as A-me-she′ (Hayden 1862:402). The Blackfoot name, which is used to denote the Mandan and Arikara as well, is *ksáókò·yi·wa*, literally 'he has an earthlodge' (Allan R. Taylor, personal communication 1987).

Related to these names referring to the Hidatsa earth lodge are two names denoting their sedentary villages. One is the Arapaho designation wa-nuk′-e-ye′-na 'lodges planted together' (Hayden 1862:326), and the cognate Gros Ventre name Wuhnókayăn (Curtis 1907–1930, 5:154). The recorded Ojibwa names A-gutch-a-ninne (pl. A-gutch-a-ninne-wug), supposedly 'the settled people' (Tanner 1830:58), and Gi-aucth-in-in-e-wug or Gi-aucth-in-ne-wug, supposedly 'men of olden time' (Warren 1885:178), cannot be etymologized.

The Cheyenne name is *mOhonooneo?o*, reputed to mean 'scouting all over ones' (Glenmore and Leman 1985:201), although older sources do not give an etymology for it. Other recordings are Honúhn (Maximilian in Thwaites 1904–1907, 24:222); M'onón-éo (sg. M'onón), interpreted as 'spreading tepees' (Mooney 1907:423); Homónoneo (Curtis 1907–1930, 6:158); and Mononeo (pl.) (Petter 1913–1915:582).

The Sioux name in the Teton, Yankton, and Yanktonai dialects is *xewáktokta* (Curtis 1907–1930, 3:141; Cook 1880–1882:184), although one source translates the term as Arikara (Buechel 1970:193); in Assiniboine it is *xewáktukta* (Curtis 1907–1930, 3:141), first cited as Saiwahtoukta, 1809, where it is glossed 'Mandan' (Henry in Gough 1988–1992, 2:393). The corresponding Santee form is *xewáktokto* (Matthews 1877:36), which is also translated as Arickaree Indians (Riggs 1890:164). The identification of this name with Arikara, however, seems to be a confusion since the common Sioux and Assiniboine designation of Arikara is *p^haláni* or one of its dialectal variants. Despite the doubtful suggestion that the common Sioux and Assiniboine name might mean 'dwellers on a ridge' (Matthews 1877:36), no plausible etymology for the name has been given, probably because it is a borrowing.

An anomalous name for the Hidatsa is Kiowa *hénó·gɔ́*, which has no known etymology (Laurel Watkins, personal communication 1979).

In the Plains sign language there were several gestures denoting the Hidatsa. Most common was the sign for 'big belly', made by passing the hands (or just the right hand), flat and extended, from the top of the chest downward, outward, and inward toward the groin (Mallery 1881:469; Scott 1912–1934). Use of the gesture 'corn shellers', the sign denoting the Arikara, was common for the Hidatsa as well as the Mandan, since the three horticultural tribes were frequently confused with one another, especially after they settled together in Like-a-Fishhook Village. Similarly, the sign for 'earthlodges' was frequently used to designate all three tribes (W.P. Clark 1885:193; Scott 1912–1934).

One sign designating the Hidatsa was recorded as a usage of the Sioux, but perhaps by only one particular Sioux band, since the sign for 'big belly' is reported as used by that tribe, too. A composite form, the gesture signifies them as "the Indians who went to the mountains to kill their enemies" (Mallery 1881:469). Another sign, reported to be used by the Hidatsa to denote themselves, represents something being bitten off or cut off, and is the same sign used for the Oglala Cut-Off band at Pine Ridge (W.P. Clark 1885:193).

Awatixa

In the nineteenth century the name of the Awatixa (*awatixá·*), a formerly independent group by then closely associated with the Hidatsa proper, was recorded as Awatichai (Maximilian 1839–1841, 2:212–213) and Amatiha (Matthews 1877:35, 38). In the twentieth century it has been anglicized as Amatiha (Meyer 1977) and Awatixa (Bowers 1965). Its literal meaning, 'high village', has been given variously as 'short earthlodge village' (Lowie 1939:178), 'village on the hill' (Maximilian 1839–1841, 2:212), and 'earthlodge on top' (Curtis 1907–1930, 4:131).

The Mandan name for this division was its village name *wį́?tixa·re* 'village spread out' (Robert C. Hollow, personal communication 1985), cited by Bowers (1965:14) as mitixata. The Cheyenne borrowed the Hidatsa name as Amatsichá (Maximilian in Thwaites 1904–1907, 24:222). In the early nineteenth century the French were said to call it the Petit Village (Maximilian 1839–1841, 2:212), while Lewis and Clark referred to it as the Little Menetarre village, in contrast to the Grand Village of the Minetarrees, which was the village of the Hidatsa proper (Moulton 1983–, 3:209, 318–319). Lewis and Clark also designated the village as Me-ne-tar-re Me-te-har-tar (Moulton 1983–, 3:209, 211), later rendered Minnitarees Metaharta (Hayden 1862:422), incorporating the Mandan name (Lewis and Clark in Moulton 1983–, 3:206). The name was also recorded as Mahantas, 1757 (Bougainville 1908:188) and Míhtichare (Maximilian 1839–1841, 2:214).

Awaxawi

In the nineteenth century this independent social division, which was recognized to be more distant from both the Hidatsa proper and the Awatixa, was distinguished by several designations. A common one was its native name, *awaxá?wi*, examples of nineteenth-century English renditions of which are Ah na ha wa's, Ahwahharways, and Ahwâh-hâ-way (Lewis and Clark in Moulton 1983–, 23: 193, 362, 403), Ahahaways and Ahahawa (Schoolcraft 1851–1857, 3:250, 522), Awacháhwi (Maximilian 1839–1841, 2:212), A-wa-ha-was (Schermerhorn 1814:35), Annahawas (Gallatin 1836:125); and Amahami (Matthews 1877:15). In the twentieth century it has been anglicized as Amahami (Meyer 1977) and Awaxawi (Bowers 1965). Although the etymology of *awaxá?wi* is not entirely transparent, the name is related to, but distinct from, *awaxá·wi* 'mountain' (A. Wesley Jones, personal communication 1991). Translations of it have been given as 'rough hill village' (Lowie 1939:178), 'village on the mountains' (Maximilian 1839–1841, 2:212), and 'people whose village is on a hill' (Lewis and Clark in Thwaites 1904–1905, 1:271).

The Mandan name for this division is *wąxá·xa*, literally 'spread out place', a village name, which has been recorded as Máchahä (Maximilian 1839–1841, 2:214); Mahaha, Mahawha, and Mah-har-ha (Lewis and Clark 1814, 1:130); and Maxaxa (Bowers 1965:302).

French Canadian traders referred to this group as the Gens des Soulier (Lewis and Clark in Thwaites 1904–1905, 1:208), Soulier or les souliers, 1804 (Larocque in Wood and Thiessen 1985:145; A. Henry 1806 in Gough 1988–1992, 1:216; Lewis and Clark in Moulton 1983–, 3:402; Maximilian 1839–1841, 2:212), and les souliers noirs or Soulier Noir (Maximilian 1839–1841, 2:212; Biddle notes from Lewis and Clark in Jackson 1962:539). This name has also been rendered in English translation as Shoe nation, Mocassin, and Shoes Men (Lewis and Clark in Moulton 1983–, 3:256 403). In Spanish it was given as Zapatos, 1804 (Loisel in Nasatir 1952, 2:739). In the early nineteenth century the name was said to derive from that of a previous chief, Black Moccasins (Maximilian 1839–1841, 2:212).

In the late eighteenth and early nineteenth centuries, still another name designating this division is Wattason, 1810 (Biddle in Jackson 1962:525), Weter soon (Lewis and Clark in Thwaites 1904–1905, 1:208), and Wattasoons and Wattassoons, 1795–1796 (McKay and Evans in Nasatir 1952, 2:492, 496), a name said to derive from the Mandan designation for the group (Hayden 1862:422), but which is, in fact, an early rendition of the Arikara name *wi·tatshá·nu?*. Although among explorers on the upper Missouri during this period the name is used only for the Awaxawi, in contrast to the other divisions, which are designated Minitari (for example, McKay and Evans in Nasatir 1952, 2:492, 496), there is no recorded evidence suggesting the Arikara ever had separate names for any of the divisions of the tribe.

In the sign language the gesture denoting the Mandan, 'dwellers on a cut bluff', was also sometimes used for the Awaxawi (Scott 1912–1934), undoubtedly because they were closely associated with that tribe in the early nineteenth century, 1810 (Biddle in Jackson 1962:524).

Sources

The literature on the Hidatsa is remarkably rich for so small a tribe; Meyer (1977), Gilman and Schneider (1987), and Human Relations Area Files electronic data all offer extensive bibliographies. Wood (1986a) is the best guide to the archeological literature.

The earliest mention of the tribe relates to a visit in 1787 by the fur trader James Mackay (1952), and the first extended description is by Thompson, 10 years later (1916). Thompson's original journals and excellent annotated editions of the accounts of several other early visitors to the village tribes, are in Wood and Thiessen (1985). Lewis and Clark were among the Hidatsa in 1804 and 1806 (Thwaites 1904–1905; cf. Stewart 1976) and Alexander Henry in 1806 (Coues 1897). James (Thwaites 1904–1907, 15:57–66, 127–129, 17:290–298, 304) presents data dating from before 1820, perhaps from John Dougherty (see Mattes 1971).

Catlin visited the Knife River villages in 1832 but recorded little useful information on the Hidatsa (1973: letters 23 and 24; this is the best edition, since it reproduces the originals of the paintings). Maximilian (1839–1841) spent the winter of 1833–1834 in the area, and his book, together with Bodmer's pictures, is the most important nineteenth-century source on the Hidatsa. The English translation of Maximilian (in Thwaites 1904–1907, 22–24) is neither accurate nor complete; his original journals, preserved in the Joslyn Art Museum, Omaha, Nebraska, have not been published, though some brief excerpts are given in Maximilian (1976), which reproduces Bodmer's watercolors (Bodmer 1984).

Henry A. Boller, a fur trader who lived in the post next to Like-a-Fishhook Village from 1858 to 1861, left an informative book about his experiences (Boller 1959 with useful notes and introduction by Milo M. Quaife). Washington Matthews, an army surgeon who was in the area from 1865 to 1872, wrote the first book exclusively devoted to the tribe (1877); the ethnographic part of it was reprinted in 1969. It is reliable but brief, and very little survives of Matthews's manuscript materials on the Hidatsa (Wheelwright Museum of the American Indian 1985).

Twentieth-century authors attempted to reconstruct the old culture. Curtis (1907–1930, 4) is a good general account, and Lowie wrote important studies of particular topics: age-groups (1913), kinship system (1917a), social organization (1917), Naxpike (1919), and myths (1942). Beckwith (1937) recorded mythology. Wilson concentrated mainly on economy and material culture (1917, 1924, 1928, 1934, 1977, 1979). He also edited two autobiographies (1914, 1921). The Minnesota Historical Society, Saint Paul, has copies of his field notes and reports, made between 1906 and 1918. Available on microfilm, they are extensively cited in Gilman and Schneider (1987). The American Museum of Natural History, New York, also has unpublished material of Wilson's. Incomparably the most important study of the Hidatsa is Bowers (1965), which reports on fieldwork carried out mainly in 1932–1933; there is also a good deal about the Hidatsa in Bowers (1950). Meyers (1977) offers a well-documented history of the tribe. Ahler, Theissen, and Trimble (1991) is an account of Hidatsa prehistory. Schneider (1989) is a brief ethnography.

Chafe (1976:36–37) surveys the literature on the Hidatsa language. The first extensive grammatical sketch and vocabulary is Matthews (1877). Robinett (1955) is a descriptive grammatical study, while G.H. Matthews (1965) is a transformational grammar. Lowie (1939) presents a collection of Hidatsa texts as does Jones in Parks, Jones, and Hollow (1978). Jones (1979) is a basic Hidatsa vocabulary in a modern phonemic orthography.

Among the major artifact collections are those of the American Museum of Natural History, the Minnesota Historical Society, and the National Museum of the American Indian, Smithsonian. Gilman and Schneider (1987) contains many fine photographs from these and other sources. Maximilian's small but important collection is mostly in the Linden-Museum, Stuttgart (Schulze-Thulin 1976 is a complete catalog, with numerous illustrations); some other items from it are in the Museum für Völkerkunde, Berlin.

Mandan

W. RAYMOND WOOD AND LEE IRWIN

Language and Territory

The Siouan-speaking Mandan* (ˈmăn͵dăn) lived in villages on the middle Missouri River where they developed a way of life that combined horticulture and buffalo hunting. Aggressive pressure from other village and nomadic tribes in the Central Plains forced the Mandan to consolidate; by the early 1700s they were well established in strongly fortified villages along both sides of the Missouri River near the mouth of the Heart River (Lehmer 1971:203–205; Wood 1986:13).

The Mandan and the Hidatsa, also a Siouan-speaking people, originated in the Post-Coalescent variant of the Plains Village tradition, dating to the middle seventeenth century (see "Plains Village Tradition: Postcontact," this vol.). The settlement patterns, subsistence, and technology of the two tribes were all but identical, and only historical documentation provides a means for identifying the tribal affiliation of village sites. The Mandan habitat included not only their permanent villages along the Missouri River but also a large area to the west (fig. 1) over which they ranged in the fall on annual bison hunts and eagle-trapping expeditions. In historic times it is impossible to separate clearly their hunting territory from that of the Hidatsa, who lived upstream near the mouth of the Knife River.

External Relations

Historically, the Mandan were in close contact with two of the Hidatsa divisions, the Awatixa and Awaxawi. They were also on generally friendly terms with the Caddoan-speaking Arikara, who lived farther down the Missouri and who contributed a great deal to Mandan culture, especially in late prehistoric times. Mandan relations with nearby nomadic tribes, especially the Sioux, were usually hostile, although many of the nomadic tribes came to the Mandan villages to trade for corn and other garden surplus. Their enemies included the Blackfoot, Plains Ojibwa, Sioux, Assiniboine, Cheyenne, and Plains Cree. They were at peace with the Crow (Maximilian in Thwaites 1904–1907, 23:353–354; Wood and Thiessen 1985:21).

History

Eighteenth Century

The Mandan villages, like those of the Hidatsa and Arikara, were all important trade centers. In the fall, many tribes would come to trade for corn and other garden produce. From tribes living to the west, with contacts as distant as the Pacific coast, the Mandan received dressed skins, shells, and other native goods; from tribes to the east they received guns and other Euro-American goods. In the late eighteenth century, according to the fur trader Pierre-Antoine Tabeau, more than 20 different peoples, including the Assiniboine, Teton Sioux, Cheyenne, and Crow went to the Mandan villages to trade (Tabeau 1939:161; Ewers 1954; Wood 1974, 1980, 1986:13–21).

The first European explorer to visit the Mandan and write about them was Pierre Gaultier de Varennes, sieur de La Vérendrye, in 1738, who was drawn to their villages because of their importance as trade centers. In return, the Mandan began to send trading expeditions to European posts on the Assiniboine River. By 1776 European traders lived in the Mandan and Hidatsa villages, either intermittently or permanently, and had Indian wives and children (La Vérendrye 1927; Wood and Thiessen 1985:21, 42).

Before the 1781 smallpox epidemic, the Mandan were variously reported to be living in six to nine villages, and in 1834 Maximilian recorded the names of eight villages from the pre-epidemic period (table 1). According to tradition there were four Mandan social divisions (referred to by Bowers 1950:24 as bands), speaking three dialects, whose distinctness broke down during the period in which they lived at Heart River. The Ruptare division had its villages on the east bank of the Missouri River and a separate dialect. The Nuweta and Istope divisions both spoke the Nuweta dialect, which had by far the largest number of

*The phonemes of Mandan are: (voiceless unaspirated stops) *p*, *t*, *k*, ʔ; (voiceless spirants) *s*, *š*, *x*, *h*; (resonants) *w*, *r*; (short oral vowels) *i*, *e*, *a*, *o*, *u*; (long oral vowels) *i·*, *e·*, *a·*, *o·*, *u·*; (short nasal vowels) *į*, *ą*, *ų*; (long nasal vowels) *į·*, *ą·*, *ų·*; (stress) v́. The resonants *w* and *r* are pronounced [m] and [n], respectively, before nasal vowels. Initial *r* is pronounced [ⁿd]. A predictable anaptyctic vowel is inserted between a consonant and *r*. For example, in accordance with these phonetic rules *wrį́s-* 'horse; (archaic) dog' (in compounds) is pronounced [mįnį́s].

This phonemic inventory follows the analysis of Mauricio Mixco, who transcribed most Mandan words cited into this orthography (communication to editors, 1998), except that intervocalic ʔ is written. Other words were transcribed by Robert C. Hollow (communication to editors 1975; Hollow 1970), whose system does not mark the distinction of vowel length.

speakers, and had their villages west of the Missouri (with one probable exception), the Istope being some distance farther upstream. The Awikaxa (*awíkaxa*), the smallest division but with its own dialect, was closely associated with the Arikara in the eighteenth century and later lived near or with the Istope, eventually becoming incorporated into the Nuweta (Bowers 1950:24–25, 1965:484–485; Stewart 1974:289–290). Differences between the Ruptare and Nuweta dialects were illustrated in a comparative vocabulary recorded by Maximilian in 1833–1834 (Thwaites 1904–1907, 24:259–261). A possible fifth division was a Nuweta group called Mananare 'those who quarreled', but this name may have been a general designation for any group that, as a result of a quarrel, separated from their village (Bowers 1950:24–25, 116).

The smallpox epidemic of 1781 reduced the Mandan to two villages. Harrassed by the Sioux and unable to defend themselves, they moved north to settle near the Hidatsa at the mouth of Knife River. Living in such close proximity led to increased contact and cultural exchange, reinforcing the close ties between the two tribes. The diminished population meant that substantial changes took place in social and political organization as survivors of different villages sought positions in the new communities. Skills and values were lost as key individuals died. For example, after the epidemic the pottery in both Mandan and Hidatsa village sites became different from and markedly inferior to that made earlier, perhaps reflecting the death of pottery-making specialists.

Early European visitors to the Mandan reported that these Indians commonly had light skins, silvery gray hair, and sometimes blue eyes. These characteristics gave rise to a theory of Welsh origin perpetuated by Catlin ([1841] 1973, 1:94, 206–207, 2:259–260; McLaird 1988). In fact, physically, the Mandan resembled most of their Siouan neighbors in the Northern Plains although there seems to have been an unusually high incidence, perhaps as much as 10 percent, of premature graying of the hair (achromotrichia). This condition was known in other tribes, particularly the Cheyenne. These features were most likely the result of genetic variability in pigmentation, perhaps augmented by intermarriages with non-Indians (Newman 1950).

Table 1. Mandan Villages Before 1781

1.	míh-tutta-hangkusch *wį́ʔti ų́tahąkt*	'southern village' 'East Village'
2.	míhti-ochtä *wį́ʔtioxté*	'largest village' 'Large Village'
3.	míhti-cháde *wį́ʔtixá·re*	'scattered village' 'Spread Out Village'
4.	míhti-sangasch *wį́ʔtisą́kas*	'smallest village' 'Small Village'
5.	ruhptáre *rúpta·re*	'those who turn themselves around' Ruptare
6.	míhti-ahgi *wį́ʔtiá·ki*	'upper village' 'Above Village'
7.	macháhhä *wąxá·xa*[a]	'village of the people who spread their legs' 'Spread Out Place'
8.	históppä *istópe*[b]	'those who tattoo their faces' 'Tattoo'

SOURCES: Maximilian (1839–1841, 2:165) for the first line in each entry; phonemic transcription by Mauricio Mixco (communication to editors 1998) and translation by Douglas R. Parks based on Hollow (1970) for the second.

[a]A predominantly Hidatsa village.

[b]Recorded in the 20th century as *istópe ta wį́ʔti* 'Tattooed Face's Village' (Hollow 1970:94).

Nineteenth Century

The Mandan continued to live near the mouth of the Knife River through 1845 (fig. 1). In 1804–1805, when Meriwether Lewis and William Clark visited the two Mandan villages (Moulton 1983–, 3:199–332), the Nuweta and remnants of other divisions lived on the southwest side of the Missouri in a village called Mitutahank (East Village, a name that apparently memorializes an earlier location), identified archeologically as the Deapolis site, while the Ruptare lived in a village upriver on the northeast side called Ruptare, also known as Black Cat, after the village chief (the site of which was later destroyed by the action of the river). During this period Charles MacKenzie and Alexander Henry visited the Mandan as representatives of the North West Company to trade with them. Alexander Mackenzie (Masson 1960, 1:330) recorded that in 1806 over 130 Mandans died of whooping cough, while Alexander Henry (Gough 1988–1992, 1:233–234) left a vivid description of a Mandan village. By 1822 the Ruptare had abandoned the northeast bank of the Missouri and built their village at the Deapolis site, while East Village had moved a few miles downstream, near which the American Fur Company built Fort Clark trading post in 1830 (Stewart 1974:297–299).

In 1832 George Catlin visited the Mandan and was the first to witness and record the Okipa ceremony and many other aspects of Mandan life (Catlin 1844, 1:66–184). He was followed by Maximilian, Prince of Wied, and the artist Karl Bodmer, who spent the fall and winter of 1833–1834 at Fort Clark. With the aid of resident traders, Maximilian recorded a detailed account of Mandan culture while Bodmer preserved a pictorial record (Maximilian in Thwaites 1904–1907, 23:252–366; Meyer 1977:36–58; Bodmer 1984; Stewart 1996).

The first deaths in the 1837 smallpox epidemic occurred on July 14, following the arrival of the steamboat *St. Peters* on June 19 at Fort Clark (Trimble 1985). There was a mortality rate of about 90 percent, leaving a group

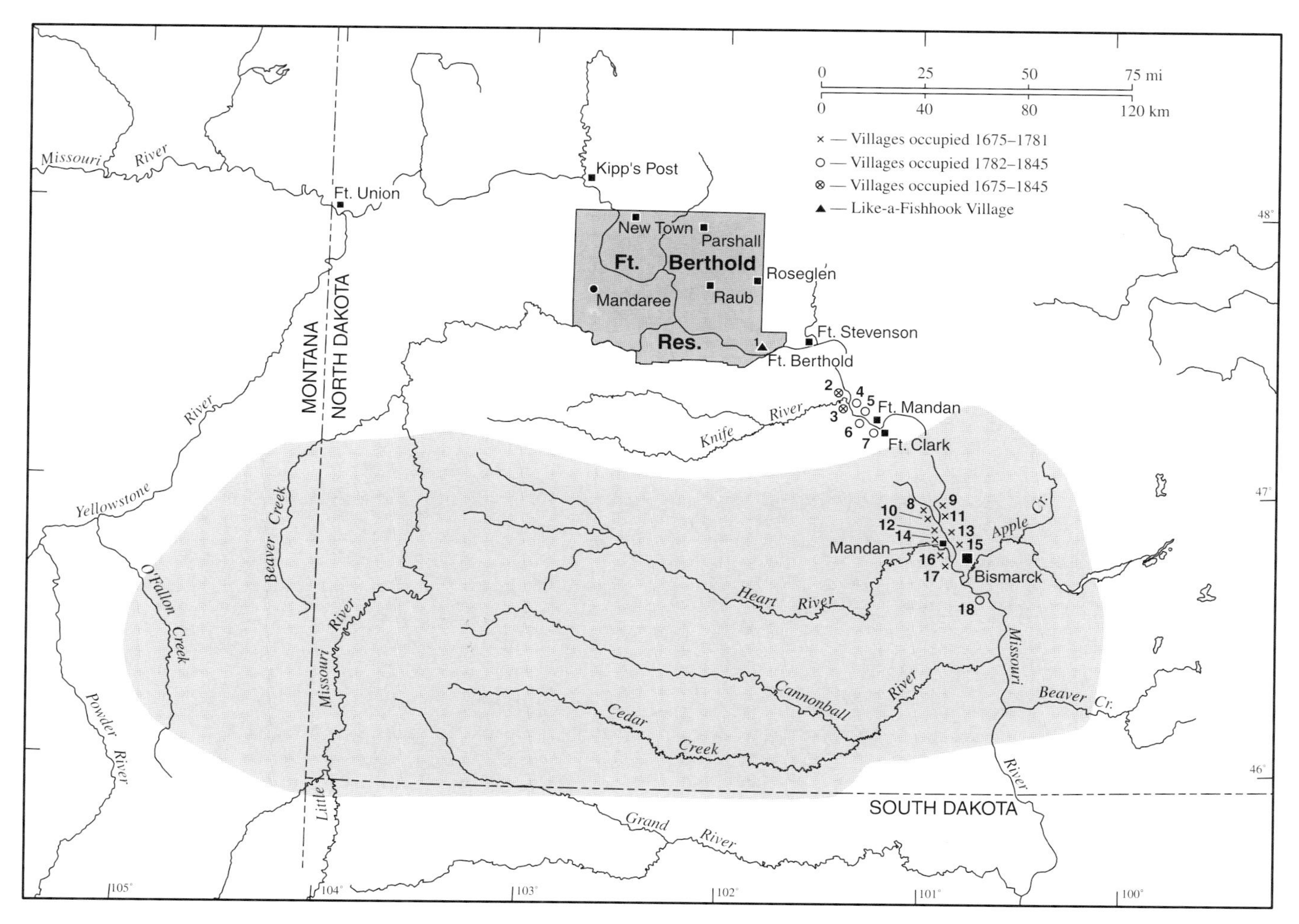

Fig. 1. Mandan territory, about 1780, showing principal villages to 1885 (after Lehmer 1971; Wood and Thiessen 1985), historic trading posts, military forts, and 20th-century towns. Not all villages listed for an individual time period were necessarily occupied at the same time. 1, Like-a-Fishhook; 2, Big Hidatsa (Hidatsa village shared with the Mandan); 3, Sakakawea (shared with Hidatsa); 4, name unavailable; 5, Black Cat (Ruptare); 6, Deapolis (Mitutahank); 7, Ft. Clark village (Mitutahank); 8, Square Butte Creek; 9, Larson; 10, Otter Creek; 11, Double Ditch; 12, Boley; 13, Sperry; 14, Scattered village; 15, Ward; 16, Motsiff; 17, Slant; 18, Eagle Nose. Numbers 8–17 bear the names of archeological sites; their correlation with the traditional villages on table 1 has not been established.

scarcely large enough to maintain itself. In consequence, the Mandan recruited individuals from other tribes to build up their numbers (Dorsey and Thomas 1907a:798; Bruner 1961:213, 231–232; Champagne 1994:164; Berman 1996:353; Swagerty 1997).

After the epidemic Mandan moved to their winter village in August 1737, it was taken by the Arikara, who occupied it until 1861. Some Mandan lived there also (Wood 1993:544, 551). Most of the Mandan from the Fort Clark village later moved up the Missouri and joined the Hidatsa villages on the Knife River. The Ruptare chose to remain in their village below the Knife River, a few miles above the Arikara; there they maintained friendly relations with the Yanktonai Sioux, with whom they intermarried (Bowers 1965:36, 343). In 1845, the Knife River Mandan and Hidatsa moved about 45 miles farther up the Missouri and founded Like-a-Fishhook Village in an easily defended bend of the river. In the same year, the trading post of Fort Berthold was built adjoining the village. By about 1860 the Ruptare, the last independent Mandan village, had joined their relatives at Like-a-Fishhook. In 1862 the Arikara also joined the consolidated village and together with the Mandan and Hidatsa came to be known as the Three Affiliated Tribes (Meyer 1977:97–101; Stewart 1974:298–299).

After 1864, a military garrison was established near the trading post of Fort Berthold, and contact with American settlers and miners on their way to the Montana goldfields increased dramatically (Matthews 1877:31). In 1867 Fort Stevenson was built about 18 miles below Fort Berthold on land ceded by the Three Affiliated Tribes. An Indian agent and staff maintained quarters at Fort Berthold after 1868. In 1867 a Congregationalist mission was established as a consequence of President Ulysses Grant's Peace Policy, and by 1880 a school had been constructed (Meyer 1977:110–133).

The Treaty of Fort Laramie in 1851 assigned the Mandan, Hidatsa, and Arikara a large territory west and south of the Missouri River, extending as far as the Black Hills (Kappler 1904–1941, 2:594–595). The reservation was reduced several times, until its permanent boundaries were established in 1886 (fig. 1). Members of the Three Affiliated Tribes began to move out of Like-a-Fishhook Village onto individual allotments, and by 1886 the village was reported to be deserted and "rapidly decaying" (ARCIA 1886:63).

Population

The Mandan population in 1750 seems to have been about 9,000 individuals. Donald J. Lehmer (personal communication 1974) believed there was a reduction in the number of their villages some time between 1750 and 1780 and consequent decline in the population to about 4,400. The 1781 smallpox epidemic left only 1,000–1,500 individuals. Mandan were further reduced by smallpox in 1837, from which fewer than 150 survived (Hayden 1862:433; Chardon 1932:138).

Mandan population for the rest of the nineteenth century has been estimated between 250 and 420 (Dorsey and Thomas 1907a:798; Will and Spinden 1906:101; Hayden 1862:427; ARCIA 1855:575, 1886:361, 1877:290, 1886:614). The numbers at Like-a-Fishhook are unknown, since the inhabitants believed that a census taken before the 1837 epidemic was linked to that disaster and subsequently thwarted efforts at another count (Matthews 1877:16).

After reaching a low in 1910 with 209 individuals identifying themselves as Mandan (U.S. Bureau of the Census 1915:18), the Mandan population began to increase from 263 in 1921 (ARCIA 1921:45) to 351 in 1939 (U.S. Department of the Interior 1939:11), and 387 in 1945 (U.S. Congress. House. Committee on Interior and Insular Affairs 1953:817). In subsequent reservation counts the Three Affiliated Tribes on the Fort Berthold Reservation were counted as a unit. Nevertheless, the ethnic awareness that marked Indian life during the second half of the twentieth century fostered the maintenance of tribal identity, and in the 1990 census 1,207 Indians identified themselves as Mandan (U.S. Bureau of the Census 1992:35; Hirshfelder and de Montaño 1993:89).

Culture in the Early Nineteenth Century

The Village

Villages were built on high terraces ("Plains Village Tradition: Postcontact," fig. 3, this vol.) overlooking the Missouri River floodplain or river channel, in order to be near water and firewood. Gardens were planted in the rich soil of the floodplains. Village locations, chosen for defense, were protected by high palisades, sometimes reinforced by bastions or architectural strong points, and reportedly by a ditch on the inner side, though in prehistoric times the ditch was on the outside.

The earthlodges were arranged around a plaza, some 150 feet in diameter, which was used for ceremonies and dances. This plaza might be located either at the edge of the village or in the center (Bowers 1950:112). Erected in the plaza was the "retreat of the waters," a sacred red-painted cedar post surrounded by a circular wall of cottonwood planks. A water willow or cottonwood sapling, woven around the planks, represented the highwater mark of an ancient flood. The shrine memorialized the culture hero Lone Man (*rų̨wą̨́ʔk wxą̨́rą̨*), symbolized by the cedar, who saved the people from the flood by building a wall around the village (Bowers 1950:162, 351). Offerings were frequently made to the cedar post both by individuals and by the age-societies, entreating the aid of Lone Man (Catlin 1844, 1:158; Curtis 1907–1930, 5:24–25; Bowers 1950:116). These goods were later distributed to the old men and women of the Waxikena clan.

On the north side of the plaza was the ceremonial lodge used for the Okipa ceremony (*okípa* '(buffalo) impersonation'); although Catlin (1867:49) stated the lodge was unoccupied except during the Okipa ceremony, other accounts report that it was the home of a leader of the Waxikena clan. Effigy figures were tied to the tops of four 20-foot poles erected in front of the ceremonial lodge; other lodges might have similiar poles before them (Maximilian in Thwaites 1904–1907, 23:269, 324; Bowers 1950:112–113; Curtis 1907–1930, 5:27; Will and Spinden 1906:106).

Those earthlodges immediately surrounding the plaza were occupied by members of the Okipa religious society and by other important men who owned tribal bundles. Lodge openings around the plaza faced the sacred cedar post, the symbol of village unity (Bowers 1950:24, 36). Other lodges in the village were placed in no particular order, although kinsmen tended to build homes near one another. The lodges were circular, earth-covered structures, averaging 30 feet in diameter and sunk into the earth, with a four-post central support and a covered entryway ("Plains Village Tradition: Postcontact," this vol.). During the notching of the center posts an old woman would be called upon to sing and ask for blessings on the inhabitants of the lodge. The lodge was constructed by clan members with help from a clan of the opposite moiety. In the construction of the ceremonial lodge, corn was placed in each of the postholes on the east and buffalo hair in those on the west; the lodge was constructed by the collective efforts of representatives of every clan, each moiety assuming responsibility for half the lodge (Bowers 1950:27, 29).

The interior of the earthlodge was divided into sleeping quarters around the perimeter, a windbreak across the entrance, a central fire pit with seats and cooking arrangements (vol. 4:629), and a section for favorite horses to protect them from theft (Maximilian in Thwaites 1904–1907, 23:270–271). A rectangular altar was built of raised earth opposite the entrance upon which was placed the various sacred items of the household. These lodges were virtually identical to those of the Hidatsa (Wilson 1934).

Lodges were built close together. The spaces between were occupied with scaffolds for drying corn, beans, and meat and were honeycombed with underground, bell-shaped storage pits. Cemeteries of scaffold burials were located near the village, outside the palisade, as well as tall poles from which offerings were hung, sacred effigy poles, and shrines consisting of buffalo and human skulls (Maximilian in Thwaites 1904–1907, 23:273, 340, 360–361).

During the winter, the permanent villages were abandoned and the inhabitants built temporary villages of smaller earthlodges (fig. 2) in heavily wooded bottomlands (Maximilian in Thwaites 1904–1907, 23:272).

Prior to 1781 each village consisted of 75 to 130 lodges, with an estimated 10 persons to the lodge, so that the larger villages contained more than 1,000 individuals (La Vérendrye 1927:339–340). In the period 1781–1837, the largest village had only 68 lodges. Each of these villages was economically, politically, and ceremonially independent, but they were integrated by social and ceremonial ties, and by their common language and customs (Bowers 1950:8–13).

Clothing and Adornment

Everyday dress was minimal. In 1738 Mandan men frequently wore no breechcloth and were otherwise naked except for a casually worn buffalo robe; women always wore a narrow breechcloth about a foot in length, and some wore a two-piece buckskin dress described as a "petticoat" and a "jacket" (La Vérendyre 1927:319, 341–342). A century later, men wore only breechcloths, leggings, and buffalo robes, even in winter. Women wore long fringed buckskin dresses with open sleeves, as well as leggings, earrings, and necklaces (Maximilian in Thwaites 1904–1907, 23:262, 265).

In the 1830s, men's ceremonial dress included porcupine-quilled deerskin shirts and painted buffalo robes (fig. 3); quilled moccasins; elk teeth and bear claw necklaces; and elaborate eagle, hawk, or raven feather headdresses representing membership in men's societies. White weasel and ermine were particularly valued for ceremonial dress. Men wore their hair long, hanging to the thighs or knees and separated into strands, each strand stuck with colored clay every two or three inches, with strips of beaver skin or enemy scalps attached. One short lock of hair hung down over the forehead. In everyday dress the hair was knotted into a tuft.

Both men and women bathed daily and rubbed their faces with red paint mixed with pleasant-smelling castoreum, and men frequently rubbed the scented paint into their hair. Face and body painting, which was sometimes very elaborate, reflected a man's war deeds. Black face paint signified a brave deed (fig. 3), while white signified mourning. Tattooing was generally restricted to parallel stripes on the left half of the breast and left upper arm (Maximilian in Thwaites 1904–1907, 23:260–266).

Technology

River travel was by means of the bullboat, a circular craft made of bent willows and covered with a whole bison hide, capable of carrying very large loads, although barely

left, Glenbow-Alberta Inst., Calgary: NA-1533-19.

Fig. 2. Structures. left, Snow-covered earthlodge with covered tunnel-entrance leading to main living section. A bullboat or coracle, leaning against the entrance way, is made of bison hide sewn to a willow frame. Photographed in 1870s. right, Eagle-trapping site lodge made of bark and tree limbs with cloth-covered entrance on right. Occupied only by men, it was built in a thicket of timber near running water (Bowers 1950:233). Bear on the Flat and Crows Heart, consultants to Alfred Bowers on the social and ceremonial life of the Mandan, are standing in front of the lodge. Photograph by Alfred Bowers, Ft. Berthold Res., N. Dak., 1930–1931.

maneuverable (fig. 2) (Maximilian in Thwaites 1904–1907, 23:279).

Men manufactured bows from elm or ash, and sometimes from horn or bone with sinew backing and a twisted sinew string. Arrows were made with hawk or eagle feathers glued on in a spiral fashion and a red spiral line, representing lightning, was carved or painted down the shaft to the barb. Quivers were made of whole mountain lion or wolf skins (Maximilian in Thwaites 1904–1907, 23:279, 354–358; Will and Spinden 1906:112).

Women manufactured earthenware pottery in great quantities and many shapes and sizes. Made of tough black

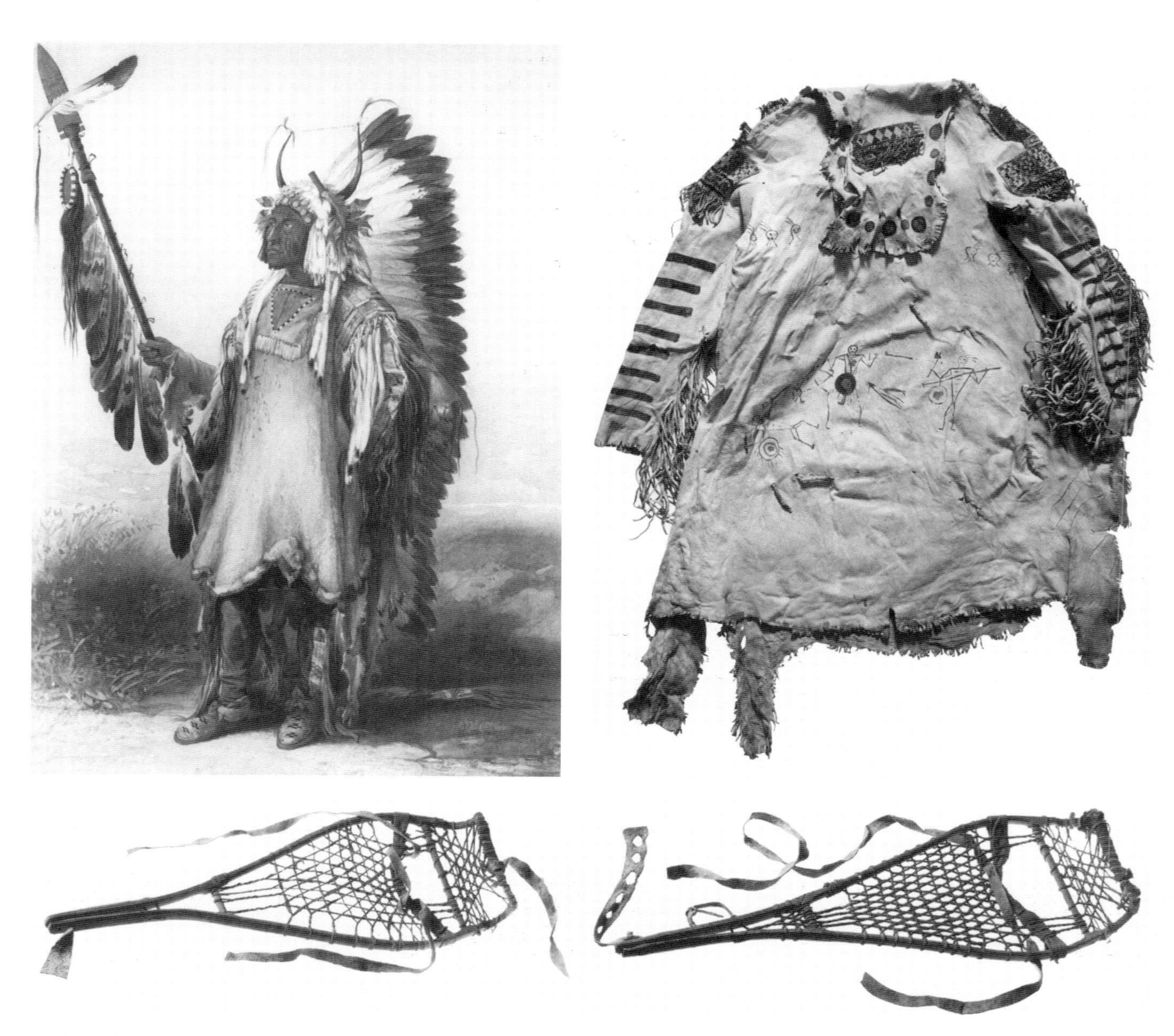

top left, Joslyn Art Museum, Omaha, Nebr.; top right, Smithsonian, Dept. of Anthr.: 386506, neg. 81-11336; bottom, Mus. für Völkerkunde, Berlin: IV B144 a,b.

Fig. 3. Men's clothing. top left, Mato-tope or Four Bears (d.1837), one of the chiefs respected for his many war successes. According to Maximilian (Thwaites 1904–1907, 24:72) the chief had many outfits and wore different clothes almost every time he visited him. He wears an antelope-horned headdress decorated with ermine tails and eagle feathers, which also has a red-painted carved wooden knife attached. Such a headdress was worn only by the most outstanding leaders. Bead-outlined porcupine quills decorate his bighorn sheepskin shirt, and quills decorate his leggings and moccasins. On the shoulders of the shirt he has painted symbols of his war deeds. The splatter marks on the front of the shirt were red, recalling old wounds (Bodmer 1984:308). He holds a lance, the head covered with a red-painted sheath to which a single eagle feather is attached. The lance is embellished with a scalp lock and feathers (Thwaites 1904–1907, 24:79). His face is painted with red and black lines. Watercolor by Karl Bodmer, Ft. Clark, April 1834. top right, Man's shirt with quilled, fringed epaulets, quilled strip on left arm and neck flap, black stripes painted on arms, and pictographs of warrior's activities probably added by the collector. Collected by George Catlin, upper Missouri River, about 1832. Length 60 cm. bottom, Pair of snowshoes. Each snowshoe has a 2-part wooden frame, with a blunt upward-curving front and weave of rawhide strips. The foot is held in place by the hide straps while the toes are inserted through the opening at the front. Collected by Prince Maximilian of Wied, 1834. Length 79 cm.

clay, tempered with coarse sand made by burning and pulverizing granite, pots were smoothed and sometimes polished on the surface and then decorated with designs cordmarked on the rim and neck, or incised on the shoulder. After firing with dried buffalo dung, the clay sometimes turned dull orange or red. Pipe bowls were reportedly also made of clay, although catlinite pipes were obtained from the Sioux (Maximilian in Thwaites 1904–1907, 23:279; Will and Spinden 1906:115, 173–179).

Women used quills and beads to decorate clothing and implements (fig. 4).

Like the Arikara and Hidatsa, the Mandan manufactured large colored glass beads. The glass was obtained from traders and each color was pounded to powder and washed; then the wet, ground glass was molded around slender baked clay rods and placed on a clay platter over hot coals under a special clay pot. Dry wood was placed around the pot and burned until the beads were red hot; after they cooled the clay was picked out of the beads with a bone awl (Moulton 1983–, 3:314–315).

top, Smithsonian, NAA: 56,831; bottom, Smithsonian, Dept. of Anthr.: 8437, neg. 43795-B.

Fig. 4. Bead and quill decoration. top, Eagle Woman sewing quill designs on hide. Such designs were frequently used to decorate men's shirts and other items of hide clothing, including moccasins as well as pipe bags and other flat-surfaced items. Photographer and date not recorded. bottom, Beaded case for holding awl used in quill working. Collected by Dr. Charles C. Gray and Dr. Washington Matthews, Ft. Berthold, Dak. Terr., 1869. Length of case 18 cm.

Subsistence

Women planted corn, beans, squash, and sunflowers in small bottomland gardens, which they supplemented by gathering wild plant foods. Each family cultivated three to five acres. Narrow trenches were planted with seed corn, and sunflowers were planted between the rows, which were cultivated three or four times over the summer.

Planting took place when the waterbirds returned north. An individual who had dreamed of the gardens during the winter sponsored a feast for the owner of one of the corn bundles, the women's Goose age-society, all those owning garden medicine power, and the men's Black Mouth age-society. A sweatlodge was constructed and the bundle was opened; sacred songs and dances promoted growth of the crops (Maximilian in Thwaites 1904–1907, 23:276, 335; Bowers 1950:192).

During the ceremony of "cleansing the seeds," which the owner of a Corn bundle held on the roof of his lodge, special seeds were sanctified through the singing of songs, and two seeds of each kind of plant were given to each woman for planting with her own seeds. When this ceremony was held by the owner of the Sacred Robe bundle, he displayed the robe depicting the migration of the ancestral Corn people, which was believed to have the power to bring rain (Will and Hyde 1917:262–263; Bowers 1950:184).

Throughout the summer, the Corn bundle owner observed numerous restrictions to insure the success of the crop. When the weather was too hot or cold, payments of robes and other clothing were made to him, and in return, he sang ritual songs in the gardens. When corn was sold to other tribes, the owner of the Corn bundle ritually "called back" the corn spirits. He also blessed and purified the storage pits (Bowers 1950:192–194).

Seven types of corn were cultivated, and several varieties of beans and squash. All members of the village helped during the October harvest, after which the produce was dried and shelled. Care was taken that no grains were left scattered on the ground, and the stalks were not to be touched with a metal knife (Will and Hyde 1917:204).

Men grew tobacco, which they dried and mixed with red willow bark and sometimes with bearberry leaves for smoking; it was stored in the earthlodge caches (Maximilian in Thwaites 1904–1907, 23:274–275).

Bison was by far the most important game animal, with deer, antelope, elk, and smaller game, including wildfowl, as important supplements. Antelope were taken by driving a herd between two converging brushwood drive lines, one or two miles in length, over a sharp drop and into a pole corral (Maximilian in Thwaites 1904–1907, 23:347).

The importance of fishing is attested to by the large quantities of catfish bones found in Heart River village sites. A fish trap was used with appropriate ceremonies by men, though women made the traps and cleaned the fish (Bowers 1950:27).

Anyone dreaming of the buffalo might sponsor one of the Snow Owl bundle ceremonies or the Red Stick ceremony, which were buffalo-calling rites. These were held during the winter when buffalo were scarce to lure them near the small winter encampments. Rituals performed by the women's White Buffalo Cow Society were also meant to attract buffalo to the vicinity of the winter camp (Bowers 1950:282, 315, 325). In the spring, especially after a rigorous winter, drowned bison floating past the villages were gathered from among the drift ice and provided an important source of food, especially during periods of starvation (Maximilian in Thwaites 1904–1907, 23:346).

A hunt leader, a man who had a buffalo skull as part of his sacred bundle, was chosen by the village council. All those with buffalo power also assisted the leader who sent out scouts to find the herds. Order was maintained by the Black Mouth Society. At sites selected in advance, tepees were set up in a camp circle with the leader's tepee located on the east side of the entrance. Ropes were tied between the tepees to form a corral within the camp circle for the horses. These late summer communal hunts, which ascended the Knife and Heart rivers, sometimes ranging into eastern Montana, provided buffalo meat for winter consumption. In earlier times, dogs were used to transport goods when traveling; they were replaced by horses (Bowers 1950:87–90; Maximilian in Thwaites 1904–1907, 23:273).

Before the hunters charged on the herd, prayers were given and offerings of sage and eagle feathers were tied to the horns of a nearby buffalo skull. Meat was shared equally among all families, and quarrels over its division were unknown. If any injuries were received in the hunt, the leader forfeited his right to lead future hunts. The hunt was concluded and the surplus meat carried back to the village before the corn was fully ripe.

In the fall, eagle trapping expeditions set out to the hills along the upper Missouri, Yellowstone, and Little Missouri rivers (fig. 2). There pits were dug for hunters to hide under a cover of brush on which a dead rabbit or other bait was placed, and sometimes a live eagle was tethered nearby as a decoy. When an eagle alighted, the hunter seized it by the legs and pulled it into the pit, breaking its neck. Eagle trapping parties were led by owners of special sacred bundles to obtain feathers for religious purposes and for trade. Sweatbaths, self-torture, vision questing, and other religious rituals were integral to eagle trapping. These expeditions also served as supplementary hunting parties for buffalo meat and hides (Bowers 1950:206–254; Maximilian in Thwaites 1904–1907, 23:348).

Mythology

Myths recorded tribal origins and history, explained the origin of sacred bundles, and provided the context for ceremonial performances. They were considered to be sacred, and knowledge of them was transferred with sacred bundles. Tribal origin traditions told of the migration of the ancestral Corn People up the Mississippi and Missouri rivers, and of the creation of the ancestral Buffalo People in the primordial homeland near Heart River (Bowers 1950:25–26, 117).

According to one myth, the ancestral Corn People emerged from beneath the earth near a body of water, sometimes identified with the mouth of the Mississippi River (Bowers 1950:156, 183). There they came to the earth's surface by climbing a grape vine until it broke under the weight of a pregnant woman, leaving some of the people within the earth. Led by Good Furred Robe, the son of the Corn Father who had been left underground, they gradually moved north, eventually migrating up the Missouri River (Harrod 1995:36–37).

At the death of Good Furred Robe, two bundles were made: the Sacred Robe bundle containing the robe depicting the migration up the Missouri and a special wooden stone-lined pipe in the form of a goose head that was used in weather-related garden ceremonies. A second bundle, the Skull bundle, owned by the Awikaxa division, contained the skulls of Good Furred Robe and his two brothers, Corn Husk Earrings and Uses His Head for a Rattle. These two bundles were loosely associated with the Old Woman Who Never Dies bundles, and all were used in Corn ceremonies. Old Woman Who Never Dies was the spirit inhabiting all plant life and was identified with the Corn spirits and their related ceremonies. The white-tailed deer and the elk guarded the maize fields for her, together with the blackbirds (Maximilian in Thwaites 1904–1907, 23:304–317, 337; Beckwith 1937:1–18; Bowers 1950:156–163, 183–196; Curtis 1907–1930, 5:39–48).

According to other origin traditions, the ancestral Buffalo People were created near the Mandan's historic location on the middle Missouri River (Bowers 1950:347–361). First Creator (*kirųwą́ʔkši* 'Became a Chief', identified with Coyote) made the earth out of mud brought to him from below the waters by an aquatic bird. While wandering on this primordial island, he met Lone Man; after a contest of power, First Creator demonstrated that he was the elder because of his ability to renew his youth (Maximilian in Thwaites 1904–1907, 23:305–306). Then the two finished the creation of the land. The Mandan conceived of their world as comprising four horizontal levels, of which the surface of the earth was the uppermost, surmounted by four semicircular hemispheres in the shape of an earthlodge roof supported by four posts (Bowers 1950:272, 298; Maximilian in Thwaites 1904–1907, 23:312; Harrod 1995:35–36).

At the mouth of the Heart River First Creator and Lone Man made the first sacred pipes, which they offered to the animals (Maximilian in Thwaites 1904–1907, 23:307). Tobacco was the gift of the buffalo who taught Lone Man how to smoke it. Then Lone Man created the ancestral Mandan Buffalo People, taking the lower ribs from each side of his body, making men from the right rib and women from the left (Curtis 1907–1930, 5:20–23, 41–42; Bowers 1950:159).

Lone Man was subsequently born to a Mandan woman of the Waxikena clan and grew rapidly to manhood. At this time the people were accustomed to make offerings of white buffalo robes to Hoita (*hoʔíta* 'speckled eagle'), a powerful man who lived among them. Coveting a white robe for himself, Lone Man managed to steal Hoita's best one. In anger, Hoita withdrew to Dogden Butte where he shut in all the animals and performed the first Okipa ceremony. As famine threatened the people, Lone Man tricked Hoita into believing that one of the villagers was Hoita's own son, and Hoita therefore released the animals to end the famine. Subsequently the people performed the Okipa ceremony, imitating the buffalo dance held inside Dogden Butte and enacting the release of the animals and other episodes from the origin narratives. Lone Man made the three sacred Turtle Drums for the ceremony, which were believed to have the power to attract buffalo and were considered to be the most sacred tribal possessions. Later, Lone Man protected the people from a flood by building around the village a wall surrounded by a band of water willow, which prevented the waters from rising any higher. When the waters subsided, the people built a shrine consisting of a cedar post representing Lone Man, surrounded by an enclosure of planks around which a water willow was woven to represent the high water mark. When Lone Man finally left the people, he became identified with the life-giving South Wind (Bowers 1950:118–122, 347–365).

Other sacred beings important to the Mandan included the People Above: Old Woman Above; her two sons, the Sun (a cannibal figure associated with war) and the Moon; and their three sisters, Morning Star, Above Woman, and Evening Star, collectively known as the Holy Women. These celestial beings were considered to be dangerous powers who brought to the world miscarriage, insanity, paralysis, drought, and death; the People Above ceremony was performed to appease them. However, they might be regarded as beneficial to those who owned Holy Women bundles, giving them the power to heal the afflictions they sent. These powers were so feared that individuals treated the knowledge transferred with the bundles with such secrecy that little was recorded about them. If a son of the owner of one of these bundles dreamt of Old Woman Above, it was taken as direction to dress as a woman and become a berdache; these individuals did not go to war and were deeply involved in religious and ceremonial life (Maximilian in Thwaites 1904–1907, 23:302–303; Bowers 1950:296–307).

Religion

Mandan men were vitally concerned with the acquisition of *xóprį* 'power', which could be obtained either through the vision quest or through the purchase of an inherited tribal bundle or other types of personal bundles. All aspects of the natural world, including animals and various mythic beings, possessed power. Ritual fasting away from the village, a common practice for gaining power, might last 4–10 days. At this time a finger joint might be sacrificed (Maximilian in Thwaites 1904–1907, 23:318). Power, which could be given by any of the various spirits as well as by a deceased warrior or shaman, was communicated through a vision. Power was lost slowly in leading war parties and was exhausted by the fourth expedition. Any hazardous activity resulted in a loss of power. Power could be renewed through fasting and through acts of kindness and generosity to elders. An elder man could transfer power to a younger man through ritual intercourse with his wife, although this diminished the elder's power (Bowers 1950:335–337; Curtis 1907–1930, 5:16–20). If he had the requisite dream, a shaman might elect to transfer some of his power to a "medicine son." This was a formal adoption ceremony involving a gift exchange and the presentation of a pipe that the medicine son must then care for (Maximilian in Thwaites 1904–1907, 23:320; Bowers 1950:324–331; Irwin 1994:99–100, 110–111).

Personal bundles were assembled as tangible evidence of visionary contact with a specific spirit, though if its power was deemed inadequate a bundle might be disposed of and another vision sought. An individual might also be "adopted" by one of the sacred powers and become highly successful without owning a bundle. Each bundle had sacred songs and specific procedures for opening. Women's bundles granted them long life and the power to heal. A woman could also receive power by holding a bundle to her breast during ceremonies; this power was subsequently transfered to her family and particularly to her husband. Power allowed an individual to see into the future and forecast the outcome of war expeditions. It also granted healing ability and the power to call the Thunder-beings to bring rain and to give success in life. These bundles were rarely inherited, but a successful man might sell his personal bundle to his son (Bowers 1950:335–336, 343).

Tribal bundles were inherited, some from the mother's brother, others from the father (the latter perhaps reflecting Hidatsa influence). The normal pattern was for the sons and daughters of a household to purchase their parents' bundle, then designate one of their number to be its keeper. This was usually the eldest son but might be a daughter or a son-in-law. Tribal bundles were believed to have originated in the earliest times and each had a sacred myth explaining its origin, ceremonies, and powers. The myths established patterns of social interaction and related the Mandan people to the sacred world through an extension of the kinship system, the various powers being designated by specific kin terms (Bowers 1950:341–343). The foremost tribal bundles were those of the Corn ceremonies and of the Okipa. Secondary bundles were also made; before the 1837 epidemic, each Mandan village contained two such bundles (Bowers 1950:118).

The Okipa (fig. 5), which had many parallels with the Sun Dance, was a four-day ceremony held during the summer by the Waxikena clan bundle owner who impersonated

top, Smithsonian, Natl. Mus. of Amer. Art:1985:66.505; bottom left, British Mus., Mus. of Mankind, London: 034-169/5; bottom center, Smithsonian, Dept. of Anthr.: 8431, neg. 78-3023; bottom right, Minn. Histl. Soc., St. Paul: 9613-A.

Fig. 5. Okipa ceremony. top, Performance of the Bull Dance in the village. In the center is the sacred ark (the barrel-shaped shrine made of planks surrounding the sacred cedar), and on the 4 poles are cloth offerings. Eight men in buffalo skins are dancing with green willow boughs tied on their backs (for more detail about the ceremonial clothing see Truettner 1979:290). At far left is The Foolish One, painted black and carrying a long staff tipped with a red ball of buffalo hair. Oil on canvas by George Catlin, 1832. bottom left, The Foolish One, with his staff and phallus raised, held in check by Lone Man's medicine pipe being wielded by the Okipa Maker, who is painted with yellow clay covered with designs. Watercolor sketch by George Catlin, 1864–1865. bottom center, Buffalo head headdress worn by the leading members of the Bull Society during the Bull Dance. Collected by Dr. Charles C. Gray and Dr. Washington Matthews, Ft. Berthold, Dak. Terr., 1869; length 106 cm. bottom right, Wolf Chief at the sacred ark of the Mandan, which has cloth offerings draped around it. Photograph by Gilbert Wilson, 1909.

Lone Man (Bowers 1950:118). It was a ritual of renewal that evoked tribal unity through dramatization of the origin myth. The ceremony was held in the Okipa lodge each time a man had four successive dreams of the Okipa songs sung by the Buffalo dancers. It was given to ensure the reproductive success of the buffalo, the crops, and the people themselves; it also served as an initiation ceremony for young men. During the ceremony, a sacred feast was held for all tribal bundles (Catlin 1844, 1:155–177; Curtis 1907–1930, 5:25–38; Bowers 1950:111–163; Harrod 1995:47–52).

The principal leaders of the Okipa were those who impersonated Lone Man and Hoita, as well as the sponsor of the ceremony (Okipa Maker; *okípa kosíka* 'he who hires for the Okipa') and the principal singers (Bowers 1950:118). Hoita directed the ceremony within the ceremonial lodge, enacting the imprisonment of the animals in Dogden Butte as told in the origin narrative, and supervised the painting of the various participants and the timing of their appearance. Lone Man supervised the use of the Turtle Drums, rites performed at the sacred cedar post, and the reenactment of the flood story. Only the bravest and wealthiest of men could sponsor the dance, as he was required to give many feasts for members of the Okipa society while he received instructions. The sponsor's wives, assisted by clan members, had to assemble more than 100 articles of clothing as well as other goods, which were required to be given away.

The interior of the Okipa lodge was entirely painted by those owning rites in the Women Above bundles; the west half was painted black, the east half red. During each day of the ceremony the participants fasted and danced, both within the ceremonial lodge and outside in the main plaza around the cedar post, in order to receive good dreams. The Turtle Drums were brought into the ceremonial lodge on the second day; if the drums were heavy, that meant the buffalo would be abundant. On the second day, fasters were pierced with skewers through the skin over the chest or back muscles and pulled aloft by rawhide ropes thrown over the main support beams of the lodge. They hung there until losing consciousness, when they were lowered to the ground and left undisturbed since it was at this time that the most powerful visions would be received.

On the third day many of the dancers dressed to represent the various sacred powers associated with the bundles, as well as mythological characters from the creation story. Included among the dancers was The Foolish One (*oxį́ hré*), a male clown painted black covered with small white circles and other designs and wearing oversized genitalia, including a carved wooden phallus, who represented those who did not respect sacred things. When The Foolish One approached the sacred cedar post, he was fended off by the pipe of Lone Man after imitating the behavior of a buffalo bull during mating season (C. Taylor 1996). He was then driven from the village by the women. Fasters were pierced and attached to the long pole set up next to the cedar post where they danced for a time until they were cut free and replaced by others.

On the final day, four outstanding warriors performed a Bull Dance after the completion of the piercing of the young men. Hoita then led the way out of the lodge carrying the pipe of Lone Man, symbolizing the release of all the animals from Dogden Butte. The four Bull dancers then called the buffalo, one in each of the four directions representing the four seasons.

The Okipa was performed until 1889, although the aspects of bodily sacrifice were discontinued under Christian missionary pressures at Like-a-Fishhook Village.

Social and Political Organization

According to the origin tradition of the Okipa, Mandan society consisted of 13 exogamous matrilineal clans grouped into east and west moieties (table 2), each clan composed of one or more lineages. The west-side moiety, comprising six clans (only 4 of which are recorded), was established by Lone Man and was symbolically associated with the buffalo; it represented peace. The east-side moiety, comprising seven clans, was established by Clay on the Face and was symbolically associated with corn; it represented war. The west-side Waxikena clan was the dominant leadership clan because it held the rites to the Okipa. Other clans also held rites to various ceremonies, and each clan was the custodian of a specific type of corn (Bowers 1950:30–31, 113–115). Other traditions give eight or nine as the original number of clans (Curtis 1907–1930, 5:145).

Residence was matrilocal, and lineages were intimately tied to "lodge groups," matrilineally related families who owned the lodge and its associated goods. It seems unlikely that clans were linked with residence in older villages, though this may have been the case in some instances. After the 1837 smallpox epidemic only four clans survived, grouped into two unnamed moieties: Waxikena and Tamisik from the west side, Prairie Chicken and Spotted Eagle from the east side. Moiety exogomy was no longer practiced (Bowers 1950:29–30, 37, 114; Hanson 1986:63).

The Mandan kinship system was of the Crow type. Father's brothers were classified with father and mother's sisters with mother. Father's sister was designated by a term that included all her female descendants and all other females of her clan. A separate term designated the mother's brother; his wife was a sister-in-law. All husbands of the women of the father's lineage were grandfathers; all sons of "father's sisters" were fathers, and their children were called siblings and classified according to age and gender. Kinship extended to the limits of the tribe and determined social behavior within the village (Bowers 1950:37–57).

Table 2. Mandan Clans

East Side Moiety	
Prairie Chicken People	*sipų́ška rųwą́ʔka·ki*
Spotted Eagle People	*xtaxtáhe rųwą́ʔka·ki*
Bear People[a]	*wątó rųwą́ʔka·ki*
Little Red Butte People[a b]	*wąséksuk rųwą́ʔka·ki*
Crow People[a]	hoxexaka[c] *rųwą́ʔka·ki*
Badger People[a]	*wąxték rųwą́ʔka·ki*
Clump of Wood People[a]	*wą́·rą kaštúk rųwą́ʔka·ki*
West Side Moiety	
Waxikena	*waxíkirą́*
Tamisik	*taxįsike*
Bad Pack Strap	*tawį kaxík*
Charcoal People[d]	*wára rašų́t rųwą́ʔka·ki*

SOURCES: Bowers (1950:29, 113); Curtis (1907–1930, 5:145). Phonemicizations by Mauricio Mixco (communication to editors 1998).

[a]Extinct in the 20th century.

[b]Also Red Butte People, *wąsé rųwą́ʔka·ki*.

[c]Given as [xóxexaka] (Curtis 1907–1930, 5:145), [hoxexaka] (Bowers 1950:113), and [hokíxaka] 'crow' (Hayden 1862:440), all normalized.

[d]Moiety unrecorded.

All village leaders were part of a decision-making council of headmen who owned important bundles. Two of these were elected as leaders because of their success in hunting or warfare and because of their generosity to elders, as it was a responsibility of clan leaders to care for those who had no living blood relatives (Bowers 1950:31). An outstanding warrior was elected chief of the east-side moiety, and a peace chief who owned an important ceremonial bundle and who had performed many rites for the benefit of the village was elected as head of the west-side moiety. Peace chiefs were expected to give many feasts, maintain relations with other tribes, and settle village quarrels. A successful chief was a highly skilled orator whose authority rested on his ability to hold a consensus in decision making; a leader in one activity might have a subordinate role in other activities. Lodge groups could change villages at will if they disapproved of village leadership. Clan affiliation extended through all villages and several were later equated with Hidatsa clans (Bowers 1950:33–36).

A distinctive aspect of Mandan social organization, which parallels the Hidatsa, was their system of age-societies (table 3). A group of boys from the ages of 10 to 15 joined the first society by buying the rights to it from the current members. Each of the members established a father-son relationship with one or more of the initiates, which served as the means by which a man advanced from society to society. When an age-group purchased subsequent societies, the men brought their wives to assist in the transfer by having ritual intercourse with their husbands' ceremonial fathers. The custom was an essential means for the transfer of power from older to younger men (Maximilian in Thwaites 1904–1907, 23:291–292; Bowers 1950:48, 62–63, 84, 1965:180–182; Kehoe 1970).

Table 3. Mandan Age-Societies

Boys' Societies, younger to older	
Cheyenne Society[a]	*šóta óxate*
Swift Fox Society[a b]	*ó·xa óxate*
Men's Societies, youngest to oldest	
Little Dog Society	*wrįs rįk óxate*
Crazy Dog Society[c]	*wrįs óxka (óxate)*
Crow Indian Society	*hreró·ka óxate*
Half-Shaved-Head Society	*išą́he kakóš óxate*
Soldier Society[d]	*xrák óxate*
Dog Society	*wrįs óxate*
Old Dog Society	*wrįs xįhe óxate*
Buffalo Bull Society	*wrók óxate*
Black-tailed Deer Society	*šų́psi óxate*
Women's Societies, youngest to oldest	
Gun Woman Society	*írupa wį·h óxate*
Skunk Society[a]	*šų́xte óxate*
Creek Woman Society	*pasą́h wį·h óxate*
Hay Woman Society	*xą́h wį·h óxate*
Cheyenne Woman Society[a]	*šóta wį·h óxate*
Goose Society[a]	*wí·ha óxate*
White Buffalo Cow Society	*ptį ták óxate*

SOURCES: Maximilian (in Thwaites 1904–1907, 23:291–298); Lowie (1913:295, 323); and Curtis (1907–1930, 5:144–145). Phonemic transcriptions and translations by Douglas R. Parks based on Hollow (1970).

[a]Probably introduced after 1837 and consolidation with the Hidatsa.

[b]The eponymous species is the swift fox (*Vulpes velox*), locally called the kit fox.

[c]'The foolish dogs or the dogs whose name is not known' (Maximilian in Thwaites 1904–1907, 23:291); translated 'bronco, wild horse' in the 20th century.

[d]Also called Kau'a Karakáchka by Maximilian, and *íhepsihre óxate* 'Black Mouth Society' (Lowie 1913:295).

The exact number of age-societies is not known, reflecting differences among villages, historical changes, and the fact that a single group of age-mates might own two or more societies at the same time. Each society had its own leaders, dances, songs, and distinctive regalia. The Black Mouths consisted of the most prominent warriors who vowed never to retreat before the enemy and who were responsible for maintaining village order and punishing those guilty of violating social norms. The Black-tailed Deer Society consisted of respected men over 50. Elderly men passed out of the age-society system altogether (Maximilian in Thwaites 1904–1907, 23:293–295; Stewart 1977:286–293).

Women had four age-societies paralleling those of the men, though sources do not agree on their names, in part reflecting Hidatsa influence (fig. 6) during the second half of the nineteenth century. Women joined the highest society, the White Buffalo Cows, after menopause. The members were reputed to be highly knowledgeable with regard to healing and herbal medicine (Maximilian in Thwaites 1904–1907, 23:297; Bowers 1950:95–96, 324–328; Berman 1996).

Life Cycle

A woman gave birth in her mother's lodge, with the mother attending. If labor was prolonged, a drink was prepared by the father's sister using herbs from her brother's medicine bundle in which she also had rights. On the tenth day after birth a naming ceremony was held, and gifts were distributed by the family of the child. Upon acquiring a name, usually associated with a particular bundle, the child received recognized clan and household affliations. Belief in reincarnation was common, and the child was often believed to have chosen its mother (Bowers 1950:58–60).

Children were socialized according to gender. Females were instructed primarily by the elder women of the lodge in horticultural and household skills, curing of meat and hides, food preparation, and the making of clothing. Some women specialized in the making of pottery and in lodge construction. Males were instructed by their fathers and other elder men of the lodge in hunting, fishing, warrior skills, manufacturing of weapons and ceremonial articles, and tobacco planting. Males might learn special skills such as singing, painting, or storytelling. Skills learned from parents or relatives were purchased through gift giving. Preadolescent males and females were encouraged to join age-societies where they contributed their labor to society projects and established new father-son and mother-daughter relationships (Bowers 1950:60–62).

Boys, taught to fast when eight or nine years old, increased their duration until they were able to fast for the entire four days of the Okipa ceremony. Fasting was believed to assist the individual in recalling instructions received by the sacred powers before birth and to obtain power for warfare or healing through dreams and visions. Mother's brothers would supervise the fasting and vision seeking rites of their adolescent nephews, which took place away from the village in special brush lodges (Bowers 1950:63–64).

Such fasting was common during the summer hunt when the buffalo were believed to be likely to give their power. Young men might be pierced through the chest or back muscles and hang from a limb of a tree over the river, or drag buffalo skulls. Men also fasted at the human skull shrines that were dedicated to various celestial powers (Maximilian in Thwaites 1904–1907, 23:340; Catlin 1973, 1:90; Bowers 1950:90,168). A young woman fasted for a vision at least once in her lifetime, either at her garden or on the corn-drying scaffolds. Women also fasted, while doing quill work, and when praying for the success of their brothers while they were on war expeditions (Bowers 1950:65).

Marriages were arranged by the relatives of a young couple. Families owning important tribal bundles generally selected marriage partners from the families of other tribal bundle owners because of the high degree of formal training given to those who were to inherit the bundle rights. Such families displayed as much wealth as possible during the marriage ceremonies. A son-in-law was selected and invited to the lodge where a tanned white buffalo hide was placed over the shoulders of the couple. Horses were given by the brothers of the bride. The prospective groom would return to his father's lodge with the buffalo robe, which he gave to his father's sisters for temporary care. The Okipa lodge was used for the marriage ceremony, during which the white buffalo robe was painted with designs of one of the sacred societies, to which it was then given, or it was left as an offering to the sacred powers of that society. The couple gave gifts to older bundle owners, who reciprocated by offering prayers and by presenting them with small objects from their own sacred bundles. Through this ceremony, the wife was considered to be married to the husband's bundle.

right, Amer. Mus. of Nat. Hist., N.Y.: 50.1/4312.

Fig. 6. Goose Society. left, Dance of the Goose Society, the next to oldest women's society. Members of this age-society were felt to have supernatural powers over agriculture and hunting. Ceremonies, held March to Oct., were thought to ensure rains and good growing conditions for the garden (Bowers 1950:95–96, 108). Photograph by Alfred Bowers, Ft. Berthold Res., N. Dak., 1930–1931. right, Headband. Used by a Hidatsa Goose Society woman, it is very similar to those used by the Mandan Goose Society. It is made of the head, beak, and neck feathers of a duck, sewn onto a cloth band. Collected by Robert Lowie, Ft. Berthold Res., N. Dak., 1910. Circumference 54 cm.

Marriages between members of less prominent families involved the exchange of horses, after which the bride's family provided a feast at the groom's lodge. The couple lived for a time with the husband's family; then the wife's father would present his son-in-law with a horse and invite the couple to live in his lodge. Residence after marriage was normally matrilocal, and matrilineally related women were co-owners of the lodge and its property. Marriage included all the younger sisters of the bride as they came of age. If a woman did not wish to marry her sister's husband, she might elect to marry without the consent of her parents (Bowers 1950:74–79; Maximilian in Thwaites 1904–1907, 23:279–282).

Illness was attributed to a loss of power through improperly performed rites, the breaking of social prohibitions, quarreling, or witchcraft. A person on the verge of death was dressed in his or her finest clothes and painted. Individuals might indicate preference for interment or scaffold burial. Tribal tradition asserts that interment was a common choice in early times, though by the nineteenth century scaffold burial was more common (Lehmer 1971:142; Maximilian in Thwaites 1904–1907, 23:360–361). Relatives mourned for four days, the women slashing their arms and legs or cutting off the first joint of a finger. Close relatives mourned for one year, dressing poorly and keeping their hair cut short. Property was divided among the brothers and sisters of the deceased, or by other clan members if there were no brothers and sisters living (Bowers 1950:95–101).

A person was believed to have four souls. The principal soul was often seen as a shooting star. After death the soul became a star or went to the sun (Maximilian in Thwaites 1904–1907, 23:304, 360–362; Bowers 1950:97–101).

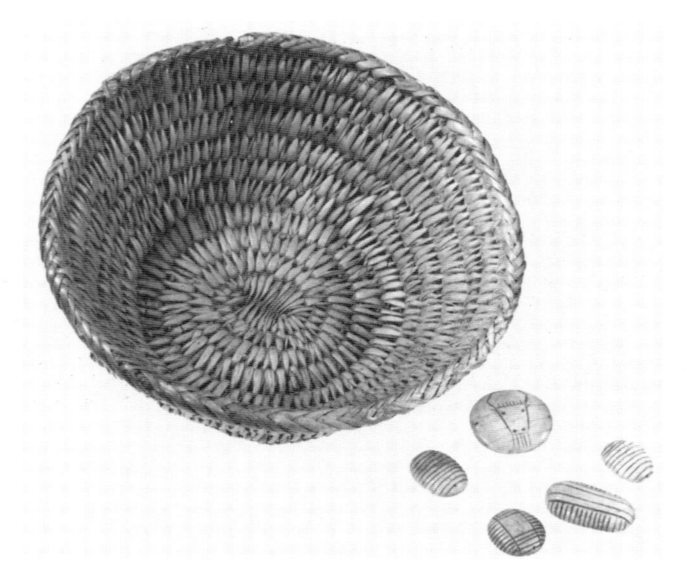

Smithsonian, Dept. of Anthro.: 8427, neg. 88-14682.

Fig. 7. Basket and bone dice for playing a game of chance. The dice are incised on one side and filled with red paint; the basket is made of split willow-shoots. The game is played by tossing the dice in the basket and scoring points according to how the dice fall. Collected by Dr. Charles C. Gray and Dr. Washington Matthews, Ft. Berthold, Dak. Terr., 1869. Diameter of basket 19 cm.

Warfare

As male social status was largely determined by success in war, young men sought to join war parties as soon as they had received an appropriate vision. The Shell Robe bundle ceremony was held for war party leaders, and articles from the bundle were carried on the expeditions to ensure success (Bowers 1950:308). Raids were led by war leaders, referred to as Old Wolves, who selected the scouts and scout leader, the warriors or Young Wolves, and the camp tenders or young men on their first expedition. Scouts were young men who had not yet attained warrior status but who were being trained in proper warfare techniques. The first capture of a horse or the striking of an enemy was a special cause for celebration, and a young man's reputation was tied to the generosity of his relatives in giving away gifts on his successful return. At such times, young unmarried women were frequently offered in marriage to successful warriors (Bowers 1950:66–68).

War honors gave men the right to specific body paint and special symbols. Women also qualified for such honors if they had fought an enemy during a raid on the camp. Captured children were adopted into the tribe (Bowers 1950:70–74). Scalps were preserved by painting them red and stretching them on small hoops. Locks of hair from enemy scalps were attached to men's clothing as a sign of prowess in war (fig. 3). When warriors returned from a successful raid, women usually performed a scalp dance for four nights. After the dance, the leaders of the war party were expected to share the booty with the villagers (Maximilian in Thwaites 1904–1907, 23:348–353).

When returning from an unsuccessful raid, the leader was expected to mourn and fast for any member of his party who was killed. The relatives of the deceased usually opposed any attempt by the unsuccessful leader to advance his status until a sufficient number of gifts had been distributed by his clan and age-society. If the gifts were rejected, a respected elder would be asked to offer a sacred pipe to the relatives, a gesture that was rarely refused. Gifts were then distributed and the war leader was socially reaccepted, though his status as a war leader was diminished. A second unsuccessful raid would terminate his role as a war leader (Bowers 1950:66–67).

Synonymy†

The name Mandan is a borrowing based upon the common Sioux designation for the tribe (Maximilian in Thwaites 1904–1907, 23:253; Matthews 1877:14): Teton *miwátąni* (Riggs 1890:317; Buechel 1970:337); Yanktonai *miwátani* (Curtis 1907–1930, 3:141); Yankton *mawátani* or

†This synonymy was written by Douglas R. Parks.

mąwátanį (Williamson 1902:104; Cook 1880–1882:184); Santee *mawátąna* and *mawátadą* (Riggs 1890:309); Assiniboine *mayátana* and *mayátani* (Curtis 1907–1930, 3:141; Parks and DeMallie 1988). The same term occurs in Omaha-Ponca as *mąwádanį* (Fletcher and LaFlesche 1911:102; Howard 1965:134) and *mąwádąðį* (Dorsey 1890:432; both terms phonemicized). Hayden's (1862:426) form Mi-aħ'ta-nēs, translated as 'people on the river bank' and given as the Mandan name for themselves, is perhaps only a folk-etymology. Variant names that may reflect the Sioux forms directly include Huatanis (Rafinesque in Marshall 1824, 1:28), Mandani (Capellini 1867:226), and Wahtani (Keane in Stanford 1878–1885, 1:520).

Most forms in eighteenth- and nineteenth-century historical sources cite the name Mandan either in its modern spelling or as obvious variants of it: Mantannes, 1738 (La Vérendrye 1927:313, passim); Mantons, 1755 (M. Bellen in Winchell 1911:47; Neill 1858:173); Mendanne and Mandanne (Truteau in Parks 1992); Mandians (Janson 1807:233); Maw-dân (Sibley in American State Papers 1832–1834, 1:710); and Meandans (Gale 1867:182). The form les Mandals is attributed to the French Canadians (Maximilian in Thwaites 1904–1907, 23:253) but is not corroborated by the historical literature.

Several names have been used by the Mandans for themselves. Their inclusive self-designation before 1837 was *rųwą́ʔka·ki* 'men, people', recorded as Numakaki (Matthews 1877:14) and Numangkake (Maximilian in Thwaites 1904–1907, 23:253). Later in the nineteenth century the former village name *wį́ʔti ų́tahąkt* 'East Village' was used inclusively; recordings were Metutahanke and Mitutahankish (Matthews 1877:14), and Me-too'-ta-häk 'south villagers' (Morgan 1871:285). The use of Numakshi (*rųwą́ʔkši* 'chief') as a tribal name (Maximilian in Hodge 1907–1910, 1:799) was found in a myth but not otherwise attested (Maximilian in Thwaites 1904–1907, 23:308). The modern Mandan designation for themselves is *rų́ʔeta*, a name restricted in the early nineteenth century to the west bank division. First recorded in 1877 as a name of tribal identity, the term is said to mean 'ourselves' or 'our people' (Matthews 1877:14; Curtis 1907–1930, 5:148; Bowers 1950:25), but subsequent recordings do not offer an etymology for it (Hollow 1970:191; Parks 1987). In the late nineteenth century the name was sometimes generalized to include the Hidatsa (Matthews 1877:14).

The history of these names suggests that the Mandan formerly used *rųwą́ʔka·ki* 'men, people' when speaking of themselves as members of a larger tribal entity but used village or division names when being more specific (Maximilian in Thwaites 1904–1907, 23:253). Use of this tribal designation apparently died out during the late nineteenth century, when it was replaced by two division names, Nuweta and Ruptare. Of these, *rų́ʔeta* survived into the twentieth century, when it became generalized as the tribal name.

Apparently borrowed from the Sioux name but no longer in use in the late twentieth century is Cheyenne wíhwatann (Maximilian in Thwaites 1904–1907, 24:222); Mevatan (pl. Mevataneo) (Petter 1913–1915:582; Mooney 1907:422); and Mivátaneo (Curtis 1907–1930, 6:158). Another Cheyenne form, mo-no'-ni-o, recorded as designating the Mandan (Hayden 1862:290) but which Petter (1913–1915: 582) says designates the Hidatsa, is apparently a conflation with *ónoneoʔO* 'Arikara' (Glenmore and Leman 1985: 202), since it is not uncommon for other tribes, particularly those at a distance, to confuse or lump into one the names for the three horticultural tribes (Arikara, Hidatsa, and Mandan) after they settled together at Like-a-Fishhook Village.

A name of northern Caddoan provenience that designates the Mandan occurs in Arikara as *kánIt* 'stone' (Parks 1986:39; Curtis 1907–1930, 5:148), recorded a century earlier as Wil.tâ.câ.riqua (Wilkinson 1805) (*wi·takarí·tuʔ* 'stone man' or its locative form *wi·takarítkAt*), and in Pawnee as *pi·takari·tuʔ* 'stone man' (Parks 1965–1990). The Pawnee name is reflected in an eighteenth-century designation used by traders, Pitacaricó, given also in Spanish as Higadosduros 'hard livers'. The form was cited by the Spanish governor-general in 1785 for a tribe living "along the Missouri higher up than the Arricaras" (Miró in Nasatir 1952, 1:127), who are to be identified as the Mandan. Apparently borrowed from the Arikara form is the Arapaho name *kó·ne·ní·t* (Ives Goddard, personal communication 1990), which has no known etymology in Arapaho.

The Hidatsa name for Mandan is *aráxpakua* 'at the confluence' or 'toward the mouth of the creek' (Curtis 1907–1930, 4:186; Parks 1987). In 1805 the same name for the Mandan was cited as common to both the Hidatsa and Crow—Arrach bugja wrach baga in Hidatsa and Annach bogu minnach baga in Crow—differing only dialectally in form and composed of Hidatsa *aráxpakua* followed by *ruxpá·ka* 'people' (McKenzie in Wood and Thiessen 1985:249; Jones 1979:61). In the twentieth century the Crow name was replaced by *assahkašé*, literally 'lodge at the edge' or 'lodge at the extreme end' (Curtis 1907–1930, 4:180; Medicine Horse 1987:15; Randolph Graczyk, personal communication 1987).

Perhaps related to the Crow name is the Kiowa designation *tòhóngɔ̀*, literally 'last camp' (Laurel Watkins, personal communication 1979).

Two names refer to the earthlodges that typified Mandan life: Blackfoot *ksáókò·yi·wa*, literally 'earthlodge dwellers' (Allan R. Taylor, personal communication 1987); and Cheyenne *tséhešeʔemAheónesE*, literally 'those who have earthen houses' (Glenmore and Leman 1985:201). The last is attested only in the late twentieth century.

An early Algonquian designation for the Mandan was Koüathéatte, 1736, garbled as Courtchouattea, 1739 (La Vérendrye 1927:215, 298), recorded as Ottawa Kwowahtewug (Tanner 1830:316). An Ojibwa name, learned from the

Monsoni, was ouachipouanne, that is, *wa·ši-pwa·n* 'cave Sioux' (La Vérendrye 1927:107, 298), a reference to their living in earthlodges.

There are several variants for Mandan in the sign language. The most common one is to make a scratching motion from the lower lip to the chin, as if painting vertical stripes there, a sign that denotes the tattooing of the chin practiced by the Mandan and reflected in the name of one division, Istope—*istópe* 'tattoo' (Hadley 1893:111; Clark 1885:238; Hollow 1970:94). The Crow sign for the tribe was to form two circles with the thumbs and index fingers and hold them beside the ears, indicating big holes in the ears that were made for wearing earrings (Clark 1885:238), a designation that is found in the current Crow name for the Arikara, *ahparro·pisé·* 'big ear holes' (Medicine Horse 1987:15). The Sioux, in contrast, knew the Mandan as the people wearing a scarlet sash with a train, signed by the first and second fingers of the right hand—extended, separated, backs outward—being drawn from the left shoulder in front of the body to the right hip (Mallery 1881:471). The sign for the Arikara, which indicates shelling corn, was often used for the Mandan as well (Clark 1885:238).

Divisions

Although the Mandan formerly comprised four to five social divisions, each in turn composed of one or more villages, only two of those groupings survived into and were important throughout the nineteenth century: the east bank and the west bank divisions.

The east bank division was denoted by the name *rúpta·re* (Ruptare), also pronounced *rúpta·* and *rų́pta·re*, and also used as a village name (Maximilian 1839–1841, 2:165). It occurs in numerous variant forms; for example, Roop-tar-hee, Roop-tar ha (Lewis and Clark in Moulton 1983–, 3:211, 401); Ruhptare (Maximilian in Thwaites 1904–1907, 23:254); Rùptari, Nuptadi (Matthews 1877:14). The name has been anglicized as Nuptadi (Bowers 1950), but Ruptare is a more appropriate rendering.

The name of the west bank division, *rų́ˀeta* (Hollow 1970:191), occurs in variant forms, for example, Núweta (Matthews 1877:14) and Nú^{n}ěta (Curtis 1907–1930, 5:148). Although it has been anglicized as Nuitadi (Bowers 1950), the form Nuweta is closer to its actual pronunciation in Mandan. This social unit is represented by several former divisions and villages, the most prominent of which is *wį́ˀti ų́tahąkt* 'East Village'. The name for East Village, Mitutahank, has been rendered in several variant forms: Matootonha, Ma-too-ton-ka, Mar-too-ton-ha (Lewis and Clark in Moulton 1983–, 3:203, 209, 211); Mih-Tutta-Hangkusch (Maximilian 1839–1841, 2:165); Métutahanke, Mitutahankish (Matthews 1877:14); and Mitutanka (Bowers 1950:186). Mitutanka is a form followed by some writers (Meyer 1977:37), but a more appropriate anglicization is Mitutahank.

Another name, Mahna-Narra, translated as 'the sulky', is given as a name for the Mandan tribe when it first "separated from the rest of its nation, and went higher up the Missouri" (Maximilian in Thwaites 1904–1907, 23:253–254). In the twentieth century it was identified as a division name, Mananare (Bowers 1950:25).

Sources

The basic descriptive source for the Mandan is Bowers (1950), whose strength is a reconstruction of nineteenth-century Mandan culture based primarily on fieldwork in 1930–1931. Information on the Mandan is found in Bowers (1965), which focuses on the Hidatsa. The primary historical study of the Three Affiliated Tribes is Meyer (1977). Bruner (1961) is a succinct but insightful synopsis of Mandan culture and history. Stewart (1974) traces the movements of Mandan villages through time.

Useful historical accounts include those of the visits by explorers Pierre Gaultier de Varennes, sieur de La Vérendrye, in 1738 (La Vérendrye 1927), David Thompson in 1797–1798 (Thompson 1916), Lewis and Clark in 1804–1805 (Moulton 1983–, 3), and Alexander Henry the Younger in 1806 (Gough 1988–1992; Coues 1897 is a bowlderized version). Other historical accounts of the Mandan in the early fur trade era are printed in Wood and Thiessen (1985).

Two classics of western exploration devote a great deal of attention to the Mandan: the works of George Catlin (1841, 1867), and Alexander Philipp Maximilian, Prince of Wied (Maximilian in Thwaites 1904–1907, 23–24), who visited them in 1832 and in 1833–1834, respectively. Both Catlin and Karl Bodmer, who accompanied Maximilian, left numerous drawings and paintings of the Mandan and their neighbors. Henry Boller (1868) provides certain historical details, and Matthews (1877) includes some information on the Mandan in his account of the Hidatsa.

Will and Spinden (1906) compile material on archeology, culture, and language. Curtis (1907–1930, 5) presents a brief cultural summary focused primarily on religion and mythology. Lowie (1913, 1917) describes social organization and age-societies; Stewart (1977) is the most thorough study of Mandan and Hidatsa age-societies; Beckwith (1938) includes a collection of mythology and information on ceremonialism; Densmore (1923) is a study of Mandan and Hidatsa music. Kennard (1936) is a grammatical sketch of Mandan, Hollow (1970) includes a description of Mandan phonology and morphology as well as an extensive dictionary, and Parks, Jones, and Hollow (1978:79–118) include Mandan linguistic texts recorded and translated by Hollow.

Pre-salvage archeology syntheses include those of Will and Spinden (1906), Strong (1940), and Will and Hecker (1944). These accounts, while historically useful, are superseded by Wood (1967), Lehmer (1971), and G.H. Smith (1972).

Arikara

DOUGLAS R. PARKS

Although the twentieth-century Arikara (əˈrĭkəˌrä, əˈrĭkəˌru) formed a single tribal entity, in the eighteenth century their ancestors were an aggregate of Caddoan-speaking bands or villages. Some may have been loosely united politically, like the subdivisions of the related Skiri Pawnee (Murie 1981, 1:7–8, 32); but some were apparently autonomous, like other Pawnee groups of that period. In fact, some of the groups that became the Arikara were related more closely to the Pawnee than to the other Arikara bands.

Territory

After the devastating smallpox epidemics of the late eighteenth century, the surviving Arikara consolidated into two villages in the area of the confluence of the Cheyenne and Missouri rivers in South Dakota (fig. 1). Over the next century they continued a general northward movement along the Missouri that ended with their settlement in 1862 on the Fort Berthold Reservation, North Dakota. They share the reservation with the Siouan-speaking Mandan and Hidatsa, with whom they have been in more or less close association for at least two centuries and with whom they share a common horticultural tradition as well as many cultural similarities.

During the first decade of the nineteenth century, the Arikara were said to claim only the land near their villages and gardens at the mouth of the Grand River; the aggressive and more numerous Teton Sioux claimed the country around them (Lewis and Clark in Moulton 1983–, 3:401). Three decades later, just after they had abandoned the Grand River villages, the Moreau River was recognized as the southern boundary of their territory and by implication extended north to the area of the Cannon Ball River, which marked the southern boundary of Mandan territory (Maximilian in Thwaites 1904–1907, 22:335; 339). After 1837 the locus of Arikara territory shifted northward to their village at Fort Clark near the mouth of the Knife River and to the country west of it where they hunted game and trapped eagles.

Although in the period before the epidemics of the late eighteenth century the Arikara engaged in large communal buffalo hunts that undoubtedly extended their territory westward onto the plains, throughout the historic period the combined pressures of population loss and warfare forced them to concentrate their activities on horticulture and trading in the vicinity of their villages. In the nineteenth century, communal hunting parties generally traveled no more than 40 miles from their permanent villages, although smaller parties would venture farther west—earlier, as far as the Black Hills and, later, the badlands of the western Dakotas.

Language

Arikara, the northernmost member of the Caddoan language family, has been considered a divergent dialect of Pawnee (Lesser and Weltfish 1932; Taylor 1963a); however, in the twentieth century it and Pawnee were no longer mutually intelligible (Parks 1979:202).* In the late eighteenth and even into the nineteenth century, each village had its own dialect. Those dialects formed two major groups, one closer to Pawnee and another that diverged more sharply and closely resembled twentieth-century Arikara speech (Tabeau 1939:125–126). After surviving members of previously separate villages combined into fewer, larger villages, the former dialectal diversity gradually leveled. In the twentieth century only vestiges of it survived.

Although commonly asserted to be a historical outgrowth of the Skiri dialect of Pawnee, Arikara speech actually diverged from Pawnee preceding the split of the Pawnee into the Skiri and South Band dialects. Thus twentieth-century Arikara shared as many distinctive traits in common with the South Band dialect as it did with the Skiri dialect (Parks 1979).

*The phonemes of Arikara are: (voiceless unaspirated stops and affricate) *p, t, č, k, ˀ*; (voiceless spirants) *s, š, x, h*; (resonants) *w, n, r*; (short voiced vowels) *i, e, a, o, u*; (short voiceless vowels) *I, A, U*; (long voiced vowels) *i·, e·, a·, o·, u·*; (stress) v́. The resonants are ordinarily voiced, but voiceless when immediately preceding a voiceless vowel. The occurrence of the voiceless vowels is almost entirely predictable from the phonemic environment, but vowels fail to devoice in some words in what would usually be devoicing contexts. Arikara words cited in the *Handbook* were transcribed by Douglas R. Parks, with orthographic substitutions made to conform to the technical alphabet.

In the Arikara orthography established in 1975 for the bilingual education program in the White Shield School, Roseglen, N. Dak. (Parks 1986, 1991), these segments are written as follows: p, t, č, k, '; s, š, x, h; w, n, r (W, N, R when voiceless); i, e, a, o, u; I, A, U; ii, ee, aa, oo, uu; (stress) v́, vv́. This orthography also marks the underlying |i| that is elided in prefixes between *t* and *n* as superscript ^{i}; this vowel is rarely pronounced.

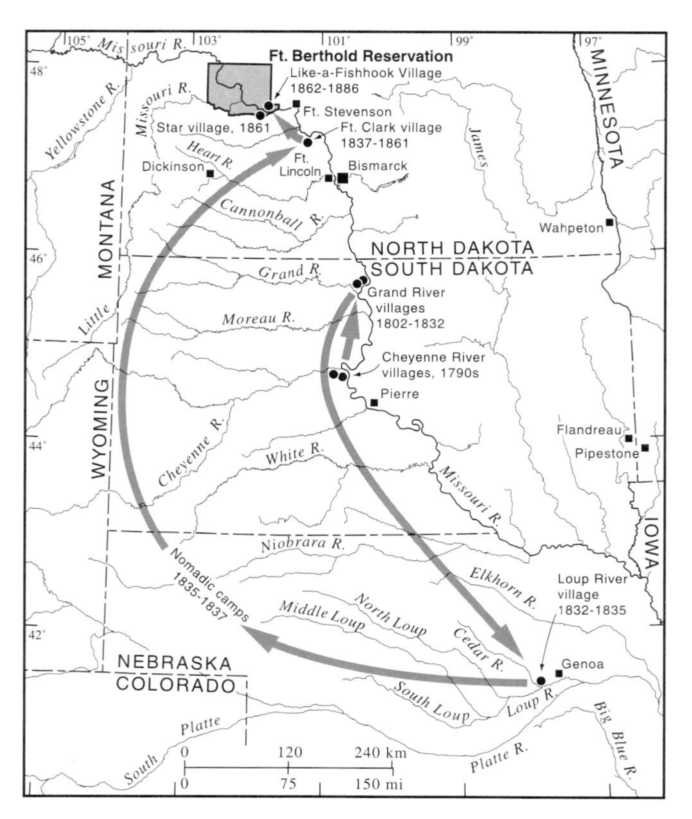

Fig. 1. Villages, and movements of the Arikara from the late 18th to late 19th centuries. For details of the Fort Berthold Res. see fig. 1 in "Three Affiliated Tribes" (this vol.).

Prehistory

Both the Arikara and Pawnee have been traced to the Upper Republican phase of the Central Plains Village tradition that was located in Kansas and Nebraska and that may date as late as the fifteenth century (Grange 1979:134). These ancestors of the Arikara and Pawnee lived in small scattered hamlets during this period and even later, when the ancestral Arikara groups began moving northward and merged with the Middle Missouri Village tradition peoples then living in the Dakotas to become part of a new Coalescent Village tradition. In the eighteenth century, as a result of the combined effects of warfare with mounted nomads and, later, epidemic disease, the small settlements gave way to fewer larger, compactly arranged, fortified villages.

History

The earliest historical references to the Arikara, based on reports rather than observation, are scant and generally provide little information beyond designating locations and enumerating villages. Among the earliest of these is the report of Étienne Venyard, sieur de Bourgmont, who in 1714 placed three villages of Arikaras on the west bank of the Missouri River above the Niobrara River and 40 villages still farther upriver on both banks. They were said to be a very numerous people engaged in the fur trade (Villiers 1925:62). In 1719 Jean-Baptiste Bénard de La Harpe reported that the Arikara formed part of 45 villages of Pawnee (Margry 1876–1886, 6:293). In 1723 they were recorded as 10 leagues from the Omaha, with whom they were allied (Renaudière in Margry 1876–1886, 6:395).

Perhaps the earliest reference to European contact with the Arikara is a 1734 letter documenting a visit to the tribe by a Frenchman who had been living with the Skiri Pawnee; he claimed that these people had never seen the French before and that there were several silver mines in the region where they lived (Bienville in Margry 1876–1886, 6:455). In 1738, when Pierre Gaultier de Varennes, sieur de La Vérendrye, the French fur trader from Montreal, visited the Mandan along the Missouri in North Dakota during his search for a route to the Pacific Ocean, he was told that the villages of the Panaux were a day's journey away, and beyond them were the Pananis (Burpee 1927:335), both of which were undoubtedly separate Arikara divisions. On another expedition in 1743, La Vérendrye's sons visited a group they called the Little Cherry People, apparently an Arikara band living along the Missouri near the mouth of the Bad River (Burpee 1927:424; Gilmore 1927:345).

By the end of the eighteenth century traders from Saint Louis began providing more definite information on the Arikara. In a 1785 report enumerating tribes living along the Missouri, Gov.-Gen. of Spanish Louisiana Esteban Rodriguez Miró placed seven Arikara villages on the Missouri below the Cheyenne River (Nasatir 1952, 1:123, 126–127). Jean-Baptiste Truteau led a trading expedition up the Missouri and lived a year among the tribe in 1795–1796. Although other traders from Saint Louis had previously traded at the Arikara villages, Truteau's visit was the first sustained contact these people had with Europeans and represented their entry into the fur trade. Truteau stated that before three smallpox epidemics the tribe had comprised 32 large villages, but during his visit most of the surviving Arikara were living in two large consolidated villages on the west bank of the Missouri just below the Cheyenne River. In addition to them, one small group had gone north to reside with the Mandan below the mouth of the Knife River, and another group had traveled south to visit the Skiri Pawnee. Truteau's stay was cut short in 1796 when the Arikara anticipated a major Sioux onslaught and abandoned their two villages, one group going north to be near the Mandan and the others moving west to be near the Cheyenne (Parks 1993).

For a year in 1803–1804 Pierre-Antoine Tabeau, another Saint Louis trader, resided among the Arikara, who were again living on the Missouri, at that time in three villages just above the Grand River, one on modern Ashley Island above the mouth of Rampart Creek and the other two villages four miles north on the west bank of the river. Tabeau (1939:123–124) reported that these three villages were the remainder of 18 that had embodied 10 divisions. Meriwether Lewis and William Clark, who visited the tribe while Tabeau was living with them, also stated that these villages were composed of the remnants of 8 or 10 former tribes (Moulton 1983–, 3:400–401).

The island village was abandoned prior to 1811 (Bradbury in Thwaites 1904–1907, 5:127; Brackenridge in Thwaites 1904–1907, 6:111), but the two upper villages on Cottonwood Creek were occupied continuously until spring 1823, when hostilities broke out between a group of Arikara and a fur trade party under William Ashley that was ascending the Missouri. The incident, which resulted in the deaths of as many as 15 members of Ashley's party, prompted the government to send a punitive expedition of United States Army troops under Col. Henry Leavenworth against the Arikara. The American force of 275 men was joined by 750 Sioux, and over several days the troops shelled the Arikara villages. After peace negotiations collapsed, the Arikara slipped away under cover of night and fled upriver to the Mandan and Hidatsa villages (D.L. Morgan 1964; Nichols 1984).

The Leavenworth campaign epitomized a turning point in Arikara relations with traders traversing the middle Missouri region. Prior to it, traders and travelers had described the friendly disposition of the Arikara toward Whites (Truteau in Parks 1993; Lewis and Clark in Moulton 1983–, 3:163), but as fur traders established posts and direct trading relations with other tribes throughout the region, upsetting old trade patterns in which the Arikara were middlemen, and other abuses occurred, erstwhile friendly relationships between traders and the Arikara deteriorated and resulted in hostilities and sometimes murders on both sides (Catlin 1848, 1:204–205). After the Ashley affair, which infuriated the traders and further antagonized the Arikara, the tribe acquired a reputation for being hostile and treacherous to Whites, a reputation that was dogma in the trading community and was often repeated by travelers throughout the mid-nineteenth century and that was sustained by periodic incidents (Maximilian in Thwaites 1904–1907, 23:386; Denig in Ewers 1961:42). Certainly that reputation was disproved after the collapse of the fur trade in the late nineteenth century, when the Arikara proved to be one of the tribes most cooperative with the United States government.

After fleeing north, the tribe resided near the Mandan villages for a year and in spring 1824 returned to reoccupy the Cottonwood Creek villages near the Grand River, where in 1825 they signed a treaty of peace and friendship that at the same time recognized the right of the federal government to regulate trade with the tribe (Kappler 1904–1941, 2:1052–1056). In 1832 they were still living there (Catlin 1848, 1:204), but the following year they abandoned their villages. Maximilian (in Thwaites 1904–1907, 22:335–336) attributed the abandonment to a combination of reasons: fear of the Sioux, further harassment by the Americans in the aftermath of the Leavenworth campaign, crop failure because of drought, and scarcity of bison.

When the Arikara left the Missouri River area, they moved south to take up residence near the Skiri Pawnee on the Loup River in east-central Nebraska. The entire tribe seems to have removed there, where they remained until summer 1835 when friction between them and the Skiri broke out. The Arikara departed from the area when they learned that troops under Col. Henry Dodge were coming to the villages to investigate the discord. They moved into western Nebraska and South Dakota, where they lived for two years as nomadic hunters (Dodge 1861:133).

In 1837, continuing their gradual northwestward movement upriver, groups of Arikara began returning to the Missouri to settle at Fort Clark, the American Fur Company post, where the Mandan lived. Shortly after taking up residence there, a major smallpox epidemic broke out among the horticultural tribes of the middle Missouri River that lasted nearly a year and resulted in the loss of almost half the Arikara population. The Mandan, who suffered an even greater loss from the epidemic, abandoned their village, and many moved upstream to join the Hidatsa. Later, after a fire destroyed the old Mandan lodges, the Arikara built a new village there and remained until the abandonment and destruction of Fort Clark in 1861.

Then the Arikara, too, moved upriver and in 1862 built two villages on the south bank of the Missouri opposite Like-a-Fishhook Village. However, because of harassment by the Sioux they moved across the river before a year had passed and united with the Hidatsa and Mandan in Like-a-Fishhook, which had been founded by the Hidatsa in 1845. The newly combined village was created for self-protection, and within it each tribe had its own section, where at first each tried to recreate its former lifeways. By 1872 the Arikara section comprised 43 earthlodges and 28 log cabins (W. Matthews 1877:4). The three tribes remained there until the mid-1880s when individual families were moved out of the village and onto tracts of land that they began to farm. By 1886 all the Arikaras had left Like-a-Fishhook.

Throughout the two decades preceding the abandonment of Like-a-Fishhook, life for the Arikara and their allies was characterized by Sioux harassment and, more important, by increasing contact with the federal government and the advancing White population. The Fort Laramie treaty of 1851, although never ratified by the United States Senate, first defined the territory of the Arikara, Hidatsa, and Mandan. An 1866 treaty agreement, also never ratified, established peaceful relations between the Arikara and the United States, gave the government the right to construct roads through Arikara territory, prohibited the introduction and use of liquor among them, and provided annuities for the tribe. However, it was not until 1868 that the three tribes had their own resident agent and there was a concerted effort to bring them within the agency system. In 1870 their territorial boundaries were revised when the Fort

Berthold Reservation was established by executive order (Kappler 1904–1941, 1:883). During this period, when the military was attempting to subdue the Sioux, the Arikara provided the United States Army with mail carriers, hunters, and scouts. Noteworthy was the service of Arikara scouts on Lt. Col. George A. Custer's 1874 exploring expedition to the Black Hills and subsequently on his 1876 military expedition against the Sioux in southeastern Montana (Libby 1920).

Missionary contact with the Arikara began in 1840, when the Jesuit Pierre-Jean de Smet began an intermittent ministry to the three tribes that continued through the 1860s. His activity was primarily restricted to helping the tribes by pleading their cause with fur traders, military officers, and government officials. In 1876 the Rev. Charles L. Hall, a Congregational minister, arrived at Fort Berthold, under President Ulysses Grant's Peace Policy, whereby reservations were alloted to different religious bodies. His missionary work included the operation of a boarding school and complemented government efforts at acculturation through education, which had begun in 1870. Roman Catholic missionary work, which also included a boarding school, commenced again in 1889.

Culture in the Late Eighteenth and the Early Nineteenth Centuries

Structures

Set on a high terrace overlooking the Missouri River, a typical Arikara village was a collection of earthlodges surrounded by a ditch with an earthen embankment. In the embankment was a vertical post palisade, four to five feet in height and sometimes reinforced by bastions. The number of lodges in a village varied from 30 to as many as several hundred, and each dwelling housed approximately 20 individuals. There was no order in the arrangement of the lodges, but there was always an open area or plaza in the center of the village. Here was the medicine lodge, much larger than the individual dwellings and always facing toward the southeast. Accommodating 400–500 people, it was the ceremonial center around which village religious life focused. Near this central area were the larger dwellings of the leading families. Radiating from them were the smaller lodges of the commoner families, and on the periphery of the village lived the poor.

The earthlodge was a circular structure, generally about 40 feet, but sometimes as many as 60 feet, in diameter. Like the Mandan and Hidatsa lodges, it was set on a four-post foundation. The interior of the lodge consisted of a central area framed by the four central roof-support posts and an outer area along the periphery of the lodge. The central area was used for domestic activities as well as social and ceremonial gatherings. A sunken fireplace that served for cooking, heat, and light was in the center. Driven into the floor beside it were sticks for suspending pots over the fire; and farther away, sunk into the floor, was a wooden mortar used for grinding corn. In the roof above the fireplace was a smokehole-skylight that during inclement weather was covered by a bullboat. The outer area along the wall of the lodge provided sleeping quarters and space for food and implement storage. Built between pairs of posts along the outer circle were sleeping chambers, each partitioned by curtains of dressed elkskin and containing a bed on a 12-inch high platform of willows. In the back of the lodge, directly opposite the doorway, was a raised earthen altar. On it were one or more painted buffalo skulls, and above the altar hung a sacred bundle, if the family possessed one, or such other sacred objects as bird or animal skins, shields, and arrows. Cache pits for food storage were dug between the sleeping areas and near the edge of the central area of the floor. At night during the cold winter months, a family's horses were also kept in the lodge in a corral set up near the door on the left side (Truteau in Parks 1993; Tabeau 1939:146–148; Brackenridge in Thwaites 1904–1907, 6:115; Culbertson 1952:97).

Settlement Pattern

Spacing between lodges in the village varied from narrow to as many as 15–20 feet, and interspersed in these areas were scaffolds (fig. 2) used for drying meat, corn, and squash and for dressing robes. Cache pits were located outside the lodges as well as within them; they were also placed along the terrace edge.

On the surrounding prairie beyond the village, herds of horses grazed. In one area on the prairie, often a mile in length, were the mounded graves of the village cemetery, where the Arikara buried their dead rather than scaffolding them as the surrounding tribes did. Also on the prairie outside the village were occasional shrines, typical of which was a line of 14 buffalo skulls, each filled with sage and intended to be a propitiatory offering to the spirits of buffalo that had been killed (Bradbury in Thwaites 1904–1907, 5:140–141; Morgan 1963:134). In the rich alluvial bottom lands near the village, frequently extending a mile from it, were the cultivated gardens. Each female head of a household had her own plot, which ranged in size from one-half to one and one-half acres and was surrounded by a brush fence (Brackenridge in Thwaites 1904–1907, 6:116; Denig in Ewers 1961:44).

Although the Arikara lived in these permanent villages throughout the spring and summer, in late October or November they generally moved into the bottomlands of the Missouri River, where they built impermanent winter villages for the coldest months. Most of these villages were identical in form to the ones on higher ground, even surrounded by a palisade, but the lodges were smaller and more roughly constructed, often of only dried grass and wood, and placed closely together for protection from the bitter winter winds (Truteau in Parks 1993; Lewis and Clark in Moulton 1983–, 3:149; Morgan 1963:135). Other

left, Denver Public Lib., Western Hist. Dept., Colo.: F33935; top right, Smithsonian, Natl. Mus. of the Amer. Ind.: 10/3016; bottom right, Smithsonian, Dept. of Anthr.: 167,141.

Fig. 2. Storage scaffold and containers. left, Earthlodges and 2-tier storage scaffolds at Like-a-Fishhook Village, Ft. Berthold Res., N. Dak. In the foreground is Badger, an Arikara scout holding a saber, and an unidentified man. Photograph by Stanley J. Morrow, about 1870. top right, Burden basket constructed of bark strips plaited on a willow wood frame. Patterns were produced by plaiting strips of black willow and box elder bark. Such baskets were used to gather and carry corn, vegetables, and fruits. Collected by Melvin R. Gilmore, Ft. Berthold Res., N. Dak., 1923. Diameter of rim 42 cm. bottom right, Pottery bowl used to prepare and serve food. Collected at Ft. Buford, Dak. Terr., 1870s. Diameter 18.4 cm.

winter villages, reflecting an alternate adaptational strategy, were encampments of tepees (Denig in Ewers 1961:48). In the bottomlands the Arikara were not only better protected from the severe weather but also closer to an abundant supply of firewood and feed for their horses; in all but the coldest weather they traveled on communal buffalo hunts (Truteau in Parks 1993; Culbertson 1952:99).

Subsistence

• HORTICULTURE For Arikara corn was their most important crop. They grew as many as 11 varieties, including variously colored types of flint and flour corn (Will and Hyde 1917:299–300). They also cultivated several varieties of squash and beans, a small variety of watermelon, sunflowers, and native tobacco (*Nicotiana quadrivalvis*) (Truteau in Parks 1993; Will 1934:6).

Planting began in the spring as soon as the frost was out of the ground, generally in mid-April or early May so that they could have a crop as early as possible. For corn the proper time to plant was said to be when the buckbrush (*Symphoricarpos occidentalis*) began showing new leaves; for squash and beans it was when the wild plums blossomed. There were also late plantings of corn so that the green corn period could be extended until shortly before the first frost of autumn.

The entire horticultural process—planting, cultivating, and harvesting—was the work of women, who were the owners of their gardens and the produce from them. Like the Mandan and Hidatsa, they had four tools for their work: a dibble made of ash; a buffalo scapula hoe bound to a crooked stick; a rake made of five pieces of ash or willow bent over at the end, the pieces separated from each other by interlaced rods, and all tied to a handle; and an antler fork. These tools continued in use through the early nineteenth century, but by 1833 they had generally been replaced by metal tools from European traders (Tabeau 1939:149; Bradbury in Thwaites 1904–1907, 5:175, Maximilian in Thwaites 1904–1907, 23:276; Curtis 1907–1930, 5:148).

When clearing garden areas, which were always on the floodplain of the river, where the soil was an alluvial sandy loam, women cut the brush close to the ground with axes, gathered it together to dry, and burned it. They removed roots from the ground with digging sticks. For planting corn they dug hills with their hoes and worked the soil to a fine texture with their hands. The hills, arranged in rows, were approximately a cubit (about 18 inches) in diameter and spaced two steps apart. Nine grains of corn were planted in each hill, the first four in a square, one in the center, and then each of the remaining four interspersed among the four outer kernels. The pattern was said to replicate the pillars, wall posts, and fireplace of an earth lodge. Squash and beans were later planted in rows of hills between the rows of corn, but the seeds were not placed in the ground in the same pattern as the corn (Gilmore 1920–1930).

After the crops were planted and the fields cultivated, the village left on its annual summer buffalo hunt. When the people returned in early August, the crops were ready for harvesting, and roasting and drying for storage. The usual yield of corn was 20 bushels to an acre (Denig in Ewers 1961:45).

While still green, a portion of the corn crop was boiled and then dried and shelled. Called sweet corn, it could be boiled for eating at any time and retained the taste of corn fresh from the stalk (Denig in Ewers 1961:45). An alternative Arikara method of preserving corn, not shared by the Mandan and Hidatsa, was to lay ears of corn still in the husk on a bed of burning willows. After the ears were roasted, they were husked, dried, and shelled (Wilson 1917:41). Seed corn was dried in the husk and the husks braided together. Squash was sliced into rings that were dried and then strung together. The corn and squash, like beans and sunflower seeds, were dried on scaffolds beside the earthlodges.

After drying, loose corn and beans were put into sacks, and they together with braided corn and strings of squash were stored in cache pits for use throughout the year. The caches were generally cellars that were dug into the ground, with a narrow neck at the top and a wide interior. Their depth ranged from two to eight feet, their diameter from two to six feet. Floors were usually covered with wooden slabs, grass, or twigs, and walls were lined with bundles of dry grass secured with wooden pins to protect the stored vegetables; when covered with two bull-hide lids with puncheons between them, and grass and earth over them, these caches were not only impervious to rain but also undetectable to any but those who knew their location (Morgan 1963:130; Wilson 1917:87–97; Krause 1972:24–48).

The most common method of cooking dried corn was to boil it with fat or marrow; beans were frequently cooked with corn. Hominy was also made by bruising corn in a mortar and soaking it for a long period in warm water with lye. A common dish was boiled hominy or dried sweet corn and dried buffalo meat. Another favorite food was corn balls, which were made by mixing finely pounded corn with tallow or kidney fat. Molded into balls, corn in this form did not need to be cooked and consequently was taken by people when traveling, especially men on war parties, to sustain them over periods when cooking was not feasible. Squash was also cooked by boiling (Thwaites 1904–1907, 5:131, 172, 6:116–117; Denig in Ewers 1961:50).

• INTERTRIBAL TRADE Horticulture provided a large surplus for trade. In a moderately wet year in the mid-nineteenth century the Arikara produced from 2,000 to 3,000 bushels of grain (Denig in Ewers 1961:45). In a prosperous year they were said to raise a superabundance of it and other vegetables; in 1853, for example, they traded 5,000 bushels of corn in addition to what they consumed (Saxton 1855:265). In 1855, a combination of drought and early frost reduced their crop by two-thirds, but still they had an abundance for their own consumption (ARCIA 1855:72–73).

In the late eighteenth and early nineteenth centuries the Arikara were one of the primary intermediaries in a far-flung intertribal trading network that had its center among the riverine villages of the Arikara in South Dakota and the Mandan and Hidatsa in North Dakota. Although after White contact this commercialism also included the bartering of furs and articles of European manufacture, it primarily involved perishables and commodities whose sources were east and west of the Missouri area. At annual late-summer trade fairs in the Arikara villages during the late eighteenth century, the Oglala and Saone divisions of the Teton Sioux and the Yanktonai Sioux traded to the Arikara dried meat, dressed hides, bows and arrows, and objects of European manufacture such as guns, ammunition, and knives. At an earlier annual spring trade fair the trade goods had been obtained by the western Sioux for beaver and other peltries from the Yankton and Santee Sioux, who in turn had traded for them from the English traders on the Minnesota and Des Moines rivers. The western Sioux traded these items for Arikara corn, squash, and beans as well as tobacco and sometimes horses. At another fair at their villages the Arikara traded more horticultural produce and newly obtained objects of European origin from the east to high plains nomadic groups south and west of them for hides, meat, and horses. In the late eighteenth century these western tribes were the Cheyenne, Arapaho, Kiowa, Plains Apache, and several groups whose identity is no longer known (Truteau in Parks 1993; Lewis and Clark in Moulton 1983–, 3:135–136).

As middlemen in this trade, the Arikara concentrated more of their time on horticulture and became less dependent on hunting by procuring from the nomadic tribes the hides, meat, and clothing they needed, as well as the objects of European manufacture that they desired and also traded to others. The Arikara played an important role in the diffusion of horses, obtaining them in trade from the nomadic tribes to the south and west and then trading most of them to tribes north and east of them, keeping few of the animals for themselves. They were similarly instrumental in the spread of the gun from tribes in the northeast to those southwest of them (Denig in Ewers 1961:48; Ewers 1955:8–14, 23–28).

Although by the mid-nineteenth century some of the participants in this trade had changed, the pattern remained the same. Trade with the nomadic groups west of them ceased, but it continued with western Sioux bands who were at peace with the Arikara; the Sioux still brought to them buffalo robes, pelts, meat, dried fruit, and prairie turnips (*Psoralea esculenta*) in exchange for corn. The Arikara kept the robes, meat, and commodities for themselves, but traded the skins and pelts at Fort Clark or to other traders for the cloth and domestic and cooking utensils wanted by the women and for guns, ammunition, and horses needed by the men. Frequently, a group of Sioux camped a few miles from the Arikara village for the entire winter, carrying on a constant trade. At other times, when the Sioux had procured neither meat nor skins and suffered from hunger, they forced the Arikara to provide them with corn, and relations between the two tribes were typically tense (Tabeau 1939:130–134; Denig in Ewers 1961:47). Nevertheless, these visits for trade afforded both groups opportunities for social interaction that included feasting, dancing, horse racing, gambling, courting, and storytelling.

Meanwhile, an important new market that developed for the Arikara was the traders themselves, especially those at Fort Clark, to whom in a favorable season they traded 500–800 bushels of corn. This bartering was conducted entirely by the women, who as owners of their fields and producers of their crops, were entitled to the profits accruing from them, and they used those profits to provide their families with the trade articles that made their lives more comfortable (Denig in Ewers 1961:46–47).

• HUNTING AND FISHING Although the earlier pattern of extended communal buffalo hunts changed in the late eighteenth and early nineteenth centuries, after epidemic diseases and warfare forced them to concentrate upon gardening and trading for their livelihood, the tribe left its permanent villages twice a year in pursuit of buffalo. These hunts, each generally lasting one to two months and involving everyone in the villages but the older people and the incapacitated, occurred in early summer after the crops had been planted and again in late fall and early winter before the severest cold weather. During these periods the people lived in tepees and other types of temporary dwellings (Truteau in Parks 1993). In the nineteenth century the communal summer hunt waned as the aggressive Sioux restricted the lives of the Arikara to the immediate vicinities of their villages. Nevertheless, throughout the year smaller groups also hunted not only near their villages but often at quite a distance from them. While buffalo was the most important game animal, notable supplements were antelope, deer, elk, and smaller prey, such as rabbits. Coyotes, wolves, and wildcats, which were not normally hunted, were consumed during periods of want (Curtis 1907–1930, 5:148). Dog meat, prepared by boiling, was also considered a delicacy (Gilmore 1933).

After a hunt most of the meat was preserved by slicing it thin and drying it, either in the sun or partly roasted over a fire. However, the backbone, neck, and ribs with their meat were cooked and eaten immediately; so also were the heart, liver, kidneys, and tripe. Tripe was boiled. The tail was used for soup (Gilmore 1920–1930a). Dried meat was prepared for eating by boiling, roasting, or pounding fine into pemmican.

In addition to hunting bison, the Arikara collected the carcasses of buffalo that floated down the Missouri River during the breakup of the ice in the spring. Termed *hu·hú·nu?*, they were animals that had tried to cross the river in the fall before the ice was sufficiently strong to hold them, fell through it, and drowned. Noted as good swimmers, Arikaras went out onto the floating cakes of ice and brought the drowned animals to shore or collected the flesh from those that drifted along the bank. Frequently, the flesh was so putrefied that it did not stick together and was eaten raw with spoons; when the meat had not fully rotted, it was boiled (Denig in Ewers 1961:49).

During the summer fishing provided another food source. Arikaras liked catfish in particular. The most common technique for catching fish was to plant willow pens, shaped round to symbolize the earth lodge, in eddies or backwaters in the Missouri and lure the fish into the traps with small pieces of meat, particularly maggoty ones. Once a sufficient number of fish entered a trap, the door was closed and the fishermen would jump into the pen and throw the fish out into a pit on the sandy bank. The most common method of cooking fish was to boil them in water, the viscera removed but the heads left on, until they disintegrated and formed a thick soup. Alternatively, after the viscera were removed, fish were coated with mud and put into a fire, covered over with coals. After the coating became red hot, it was allowed to cool, then was cracked, exposing a well-baked fish (Denig in Ewers 1961:50–51; Gilmore 1924).

• GATHERING Among the most commonly utilized wild fruits were the June berry and chokecherry, which were both collected by Arikara women and procured in trade from the Sioux. The fruits were dried; the chokecherries were pounded into pulp (fig. 3) and formed into cakes to dry (Gilmore 1929:90–91). Other fruits and berries that were collected included buffalo berries, plums, red haws, sand cherries, grapes, gooseberries, and raspberries (Curtis 1907–1930, 5:172).

Integral to the Arikara diet was the ground bean (*Falcata comosa*), which in late fall was gathered and stored in caches by the bean mouse or meadow vole (*Microtus pennsylvanicus*). Arikara women, like those of most Plains tribes, sought out these stores and gathered the beans, which were boiled. The prairie turnip, an important tuber in the Arikara diet, was gathered in July, peeled, braided in strings, and dried for later use in soups or pounded and made into a gruel. Braided turnips were also obtained in trade from the Sioux (Gilmore 1929:89–90, 192–195; Brackenridge in Thwaites 1904–1907, 6:116). Wild onions were collected as well (Curtis 1907–1930, 5:172).

State Histl. Soc. of N. Dak., Bismarck: left, A-2231; right, 39-29.

Fig. 3. Food processing. left, Maude Gillette (b. 1870, d. 1935) pounding chokecherries on a stone mortar. Photograph by Russell Reid, Nishu (formerly Armstrong), Ft. Berthold Res., N. Dak., 1930. right, Weasel Woman (b. 1862, d. 1956), a Crow-Sioux married to Andrew Little Crow, Arikara, using a wooden mortar and pestle for grinding corn. Photograph by Monroe Killy, Elbowoods, Ft. Berthold Res., N. Dak., 1942.

Technology

Until replacing them in the nineteenth century with trade utensils, Arikara women made a variety of earthen pots of various sizes and shapes in which food was cooked, water stored, and corn pounded. The most common vessel was a globular cooking pot with constricted neck (fig. 2). These pots, for which the Arikara were noted among surrounding tribes, were generally heavy, thick, and coarse. They were made of clay tempered with roasted and pulverized granite and fired over a hollowed-out bed of elm wood coals. After cooling, the fired pots were often rubbed with grease in order to give them a glossy black appearance; commonly, they were dull gray, tan, or terra cotta in color. Most rims were braced and frequently bore lugs, knobs, and even spouts. Most pottery also bore cordmarked or incised decorations built up from sets of straight parallel lines that were applied to the shoulders and exterior necks and rims (Denig in Ewers 1961:51; Gilmore 1924; Will 1934:7; Krause 1972:86–105).

For pounding corn and other dried food the Arikara also used wooden and stone mortars. More common were wooden ones, made from ash logs anchored in the ground inside the lodge. Pestles were made of hickory sticks that were reduced at one end to form a handle and were blunted at the other end to crush the dried food (Morgan 1963:128–129).

The Arikara were also noted for their basketry, the manufacturing technique of which was an old Caddoan one that they introduced to the Mandan and Hidatsa (Curtis 1907–1930, 5:61). Baskets were made from black willow and box elder bark (fig. 2). The former turns dull reddish brown after exposure to the air but was sometimes dyed black by burying it in black mud; the box elder bark was white. Baskets were generally woven in two shapes and sizes: a large work basket (*satwá*), which was a standard measure of quantity for trading commodities; and a small fancy basket (*satčiripásIt*), in which trinkets and household articles were kept. Seven patterns of plaiting were utilized by combining the colored and uncolored bark (Gilmore 1925; Will 1934:7). In addition, the Arikara wove a small flat basket (*kaˀístš*), which was used in the plum seed game and served as a tray in the Calumet ceremony (Curtis 1907–1930, 5:149; Will 1934:34, 37).

Distinctive decorative objects manufactured by the Arikara as well as other tribes of the middle Missouri were blue glass beads and pendants. As early as the beginning of the nineteenth century, the Arikara pulverized glass trade beads and moistened, shaped, and fired the glass paste on copper plates to create new beads more to their liking. Most were a solid, translucent turquoise-blue, but a few were cloudy white or black. The shape of smaller beads was oval, while that of larger ones was ellipsoidal and globular. Also made were flat ornaments, some of which were triangular with rounded points and others circular. This bead-making process was said to have been introduced to the Arikara in the eighteenth century by either an Eastern Shoshone or a Spanish prisoner; the widespread distribution of the technique suggests that the Arikara introduced it to other northern Plains tribes (Lewis and Clark in Moulton 1983–, 3:313–315; Tabeau 1939:149; Stirling 1947; Howard 1972; Ubelaker and Bass 1970).

Clothing and Adornment

Men generally went naked in the summer, but occasionally wore over their shoulders a lightweight buffalo robe or deerskin. Since men usually carried weapons at all times, a quiver and bow hung over the left shoulder. In the mid-nineteenth century, use of the breechcloth, which was made of thin buffalo skin procured in the summer, tanned and smoked to render it soft, became more common as everyday wear. In the winter and when going to war or on the hunt men wore an antelope skin shirt decorated with porcupine quills as well as a pair of leggings that extended from their moccasins to their waist. During cold weather they covered themselves with a buffalo robe (fig. 4) with the hair left on, which also served as a bed cover. Formerly, men wore their hair long, ordinarily loose and disheveled; some wore it in braids, often with strips of buffalo fur or otter skin plaited in them, that hung in front of the shoulders. Sometimes the braids were matted at intervals with white clay; occasionally they were rolled up into a ball and fixed on top of the head. Men always wore feathers, the most esteemed of which was the black eagle.

When dressing for special occasions, especially dances, men wore quilled shirts (fig. 5) and robes that were painted or decorated with quilled strips. Young men in particular adorned their heads with feathers of various kinds and daubed their faces and bodies with red, black, and white paint. All wore little coiled brass wire earrings as well as necklaces and bracelets of brass wire. Blue clamshell earrings were also popular. Older men frequently wore bear claw necklaces. Men often fastened fox tails to their moccasins and suspended deer hooves from their leggings to create a rattling sound.

Throughout the year women wore a lightweight dress made of two pieces of deer or antelope skin, attached at the shoulder and sewed down the sides to the bottom, which was fringed and reached the ankles. It had two sleeves, each made from half a hide unsewn along the underside. Skirts were frequently decorated with porcupine quills, blue beads, and copper bells. Sometimes rattles of mountain sheep hooves hung from the shoulders. Antelope skin leggings that extended from below the knees to the moccasins were also worn. In winter women wore a buffalo robe as well. They parted their hair in the middle and braided it (fig. 6); the braids were wrapped with deerskin thongs, which were sometimes decorated with porcupine quills. At an earlier period girls and young women rolled the braids around a wad of hide attached behind the ear and covered the wad with a band of cloth or hide decorated with blue beads. For festive occasions women also painted their faces with vermillion and wore both the brass wire and clamshell earrings favored by men (Truteau in Parks 1993; Tabeau 1939:174–177, 181; Thwaites 1904–1907, 6:120–121, 5:173; Curtis 1907–1930, 5:148).

Joslyn Art. Mus., Omaha, Nebr.

Fig. 4. Pachtüwa-Chtä wearing moccasins with bear-paw motif, a painted buffalo robe, and painted decorations on his body representing gunshot wounds. He carries a gunstock club with a metal blade. He lived among the Mandan and was a member of a war party that attacked and killed 3 traders near the Heart River in 1830 (Bodmer 1984:283, Maximilian in Thwaites 1904–1907, 24:73). Watercolor by Karl Bodmer, 1834.

Political Organization

The basic unit of Arikara political organization was the village or band. As a political entity the Arikara were a loose confederacy of bands, each originally embodying at least one village but some bands apparently consisting of two or more villages. Estimates of the number of these social divisions prior to the smallpox epidemics of the late eighteenth century vary widely. Some estimates are for groups designated *naciones*, nations, or tribes, the number of which has generally been given as between 7 and 12 (table 1) but as many as 17; in contrast, the number of villages has been reported to range from 18 to 42 (Tabeau 1939:123; Parks 1993; Brackenridge in Thwaites 1904–1907, 6:122; Troike 1964).

Each village had a separate political organization and was a distinct, ideally endogamous social entity whose

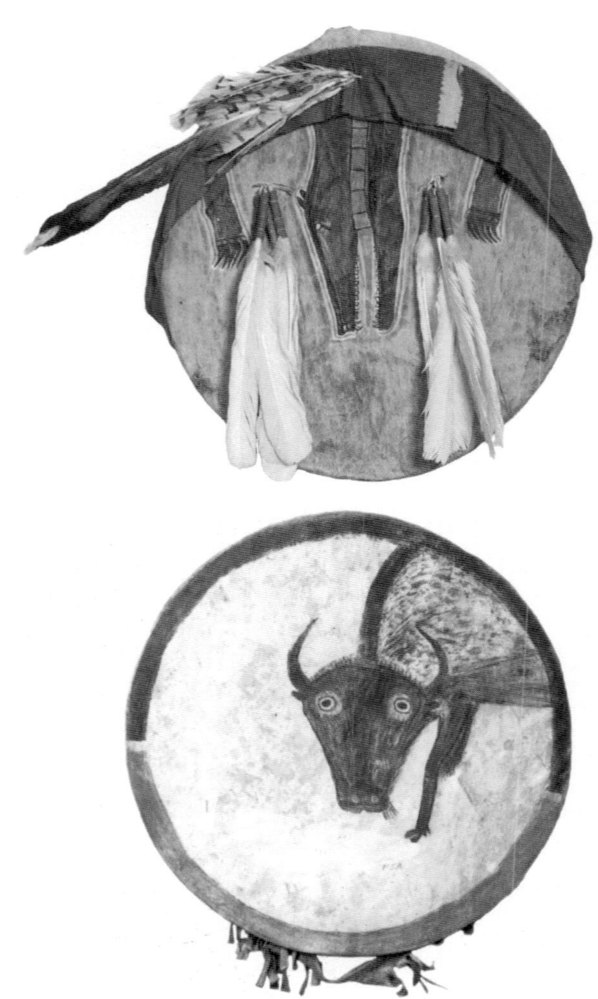

left, State Histl. Soc. of N. Dak., Bismarck: A-182; top right, Smithsonian, Natl. Mus. of the Amer. Ind.: 15/5624 (neg. 31499); bottom right, Smithsonian, Dept. of Anthr.: 6349.

Fig. 5. Warrior and paraphernalia. left, Soldier (b. 1831, d. 1921), who served as a scout for Fts. Stevenson and Abraham Lincoln and accompanied Lt. Col. George Armstrong Custer on his 1876 expedition against the Sioux on the Little Bighorn River. In 1904 Soldier was made a chief. Here he is wearing a headdress of magpie feathers and a typical quill-decorated war shirt. In his hands is a catlinite pipe. Photographed about 1912. top right, Painted shield cover of deerskin depicting a bear's head and front paws, decorated with feathers. Collected by Melvin R. Gilmore, Ft. Berthold Res., N. Dak., 1915. Diameter 53.3 cm. bottom right, Shield cover made of deerskin, painted with black and green margin and black head of a buffalo. Collected at Ft. Stevenson, Dak. Terr., 1868. Diameter, 50.8 cm.

members conceived of themselves as a large extended family, the head of which was a hereditary chief. Symbolically the village was distinguished by a sacred bundle—a religious shrine that was a sacred charter of the village, sanctioning its political and economic organization and serving as the focus of its religious life. As such it was central to the maintenance of traditional social order, at the head of which was the chief, who was ostensibly a descendant of the original bundle owner (Holder 1970:42–46).

Although each village was politically autonomous and governed its own affairs, at least in the nineteenth century, after the formerly separate villages had amalgamated, all of them were organized into a confederacy for united and cooperative action. For such joint tribal affairs, secular as well as ceremonial, the 12 recognized bands were subdivided into four groups of three each. For example, when the people gathered in the medicine lodge for public functions, they seated themselves in one of the four semicardinal quarters designated to members of the village group to which they belonged. One village was the leader of each group of three. Over the confederacy there was a head chief and four subchiefs. After consolidation into a tribe in the nineteenth century the head chief came from the Awahu band (Gilmore 1927).

Social Organization

Arikara society was stratified, with distinct, if somewhat fluid, social groupings. At the top was a small group of

Smithsonian, NAA: 76-6241.

Fig. 6. Annie Red Star wearing a late-reservation-style dress made of stroud, based on traditional dresses made of skins. The yoke is ornamented with dentalium shells. German silver disks or conchos and a beaded knifecase are on the belt. She has a commercial blanket over her arms. Photograph by Gerhard sisters, St. Louis, 1904.

leading families whose rank was assured by religious sanctions and reinforced by economic position. From these families came the chiefs and priests, whose positions were patrilineally inherited. The chief, who owned the village sacred bundle, was not only a political leader but a religious figure as well; however, only the priest knew the mysteries of the bundle and its rituals. In addition, the hereditary leaders chose subchiefs, men usually from prominent families for whom a high social position was generally assured. Together these individuals and their families comprised the power structure.

Below them, but holding high status, were the doctors, especially the leaders of the doctors' societies. Although they did not necessarily occupy hereditary positions, their offices tended to remain among a privileged group because of a propensity for class endogamy and because the structure of the economic system maintained wealth among the high-ranking families. Furthermore, the doctors, because of their knowledge and power, were both respected and feared. Similarly sharing high status were the families of prominent warriors who had achieved notable position. Two other positions that carried modest but highly respected status were those of the errand man and the crier. Both individuals assisted chiefs, priests, and doctors in political and ceremonial functions.

The bulk of the population was commoners, who by personal achievement might raise their status, although generally they would not be able to work their way to a position at the very top. A man from a commoner family, for example, might become a prominent warrior and even a chief by success in war and by making certain sacrifices to the deities, but his children would not inherit his status (Holder 1958, 1970:43–56).

• SOCIETIES Cross-cutting band and village organization were the secular societies (*na·níšuʔ*), many of which were influential in village sociopolitical affairs (table 2). In contrast with the Mandan and Hidatsa, Arikara societies were not age-graded, despite early references to the existence of identical organizational principles among the three tribes (Brackenridge in Thwaites 1904–1907, 6:123; Clark 1885:44–45). Although among some Arikara societies there was an emphasis on members' age, there existed an older conception of societies as coordinate units, like their Pawnee counterparts. The Crow Shin Society, for example, was comprised exclusively of boys, but most organizations had adult members of all ages and individuals were free to leave one society to join another whenever they wished. At any one time a man could not belong to more than one society (Curtis 1907–1930, 5:150; Lowie 1915:654).

The men's societies were both military and social organizations. Members of each society had their distinctive dress, which was not always the same for all members, as well as sometimes a special style of wearing their hair or painting themselves. Distinctive of each society was a staff or lance, which was its insignia. Each society also had its individual musical instruments as well as its own dances and songs. On war parties men grouped themselves into their societies, which rivaled each other in battle and marched together in formation on triumphal returns to the village. On communal hunts one of the societies was chosen to act as the camp police. In some villages the Black Mouth Society fulfilled this function.

Within the village the societies met frequently to sing and at times to parade through the village dancing. Although all the men's organizations had military functions, certain ones like the Taroxpa were noted for their bravery in battle. Some societies also acted as benevolent organizations that achieved prestige through the performance of voluntary services, for example, distributing food to the needy, and as such they afforded status to their members.

Table 1. Arikara Band and Village Names

	1790 *7 naciónes* *(Troike 1964)*	*1803–1804* *10 villages* *(Tabeau 1939:125)*	*1903* *7 bundles* *(Murie 1981)*	*1909* *10 bands* *(Curtis 1907–1930, 5:149)*	*1920s* *12 villages* *(Gilmore 1927: 344–345)*	*1970s* *10 bundles* *(Parks 1970–1990)*
1.	Astaray	Rhtarahé		Ḣtadhahé 'concave 'foot'		*AxtárAhi* 'Concave Foot'[b]
2.	Aquajere	Sawa-haini	Awahiri			
3.		Waho-erha		Wahúkḣá 'Hill in water'		*wa·hukAxá* 'Sides Of Head Shaved'[b]
4.		Awahaux	Awaho 'People Who Came Out of Ground Last and Left Behind'	Awáhu 'Abandoned'	Awáhu 'Left behind'	*awá·hu* 'Left Behind'
5.		Toucatacaux	Tuchkataku 'Village Upon the Prairie'	Itukátaku 'Village at foot of hill'	Tukátuk 'Village at foot of hill'	*tUhka·tákUx* 'Village Against A Hill'
6.	Turucatuqu	Touno-catacaux				*tu·nu·ka·tákUx* 'Village On Creek Bank'[b]
7.	Naucat	Laocata		Nhukát 'River-bank'	Hokát 'Stake at the shore'	*nAhu·ká·tA* 'By The Water'
8.		Tchinantacaux	Chiriruttaku 'An Opening Up on a Tree'	Chinhnátáku 'Ash on hilltop'	Tšinina'ták' 'Ash woods'	*činIhna·htákUx* 'Ash Wood on Hill'
9.	Tucastinao	Toucoustahane	Tuchkatstaharu 'Village on Buffalo Grass Land'	Itukstánu 'Turf Village'	Tukstánu 'Sod house village'	*tUhkAsthá·nu?* 'Buffalo Sod Village'
10.	Acarica	Narh-karicas	Nakariek 'Horn on Tree'		Nakarik'	*na·karíkA, ha·karíkA* 'Tree With Branch Sticking Out'
11.			Hokawirat 'From the East'	Hukawidhát 'East'	Hukáwirat 'East'	*hu·ka·wirát* 'Eastern'
12.				Wadhíḣķá	Waríhka 'Horn log'	*warihká?*
13.				Shitĭnishapĭsht	Nišap[st] 'Broken arrow'	*šitni·šáplt* 'They Broke The Arrow'
14.					Wítauh 'Long-hair people'	*wi·ta?ú·xU* 'Long Haired Man'
15.					Nakanústš 'Small Cherries'	[*naka·nústš* 'Small Chokecherry']
16.					Sciriháuḣ 'Coyote fat'	
17.	Alicara[c]					

[a]Informants stated that there were originally 12 bundles but were able to remember only 10 names.
[b]Linguistically recognized form but not remembered as a bundle name.
[c]The name Arikara, which in the 20th century is not recognized as a native term.

Table 2. Arikara Societies

Maximilian 1839–1841, 2:240–242	*Curtis 1907–1930, 5:150*	*Lowie 1915*	*Parks 1970–1990*
	Men's Societies		
	Chĭsht-ḳáḳa 'Shin Raven'		*čištItká·ka?* 'Crow Shin'
	Kaȟkawís	káxkawīs 'Hopping Society'	
Háhtschti-Sakkahúhn 'Crazy Dogs'	Ḣósakhúnu 'Foolish Dog'	xō'sak hō'nu 'Crazy Horse'	*xo·sakhú·nu?* 'Crazy horse; Crazy Dog'
	Nansh-húkus̜ 'Buffalo Bull Society'	nancu'kos 'Buffalo Society'	*na·nIšukós* 'Buffalo Bull Society'
	Nansh-paȟtéhat 'Straight-head Society'	nānc^{px}tē'hat 'Straight Head Society'	*na·nIšpAxté·hAt* 'Straight Head Society'
	Ḣachi-pidhínu 'Young Dog'	xā'tcipirī'nu 'Young Dogs'	*xa·čipirí·nu?* 'Young Dog'
Náhni-Schahía 'White Earth Dance'	Nan-shahíya 'Chippewa Society'	nānc chiá 'Chippewa Society'	*na·nIššíAhí?A* 'Chippewa Society'
	Nansh-ḳáḳa 'Raven Society'	nānc kā'ka 'Crow Society'	*na·nIšká·ka?* 'Crow Society'
	Ṗanĭshúk 'Cut-throats'	pā'ncū'k 'Cut Throat Society'	*pa·nIšúkAt* 'Cut Throat Society'
	Suȟḳáṭĭt 'Black Mouth'	s^{xu}kátit 'Black Mouths'	*sUxkátit* 'Black Mouth'
Tirúh-Pahí 'Soldiers'	Tadhóȟpa	Taro'xpà	*taróxpa* 'Taroxpa'
	Tawádhĭsht 'Speckled'		*tawárIt* 'Speckled'[a]
	Natshaká		
Titschiwáhn 'Foxes'		nānc tciwáku 'Fox Society'	*na·nIščiwáku?* 'Fox Society'
		hānāni''t 'Grass Dance'	*ha·nUhna·níhtA* 'Grass Tied At The Waist'
		sakhū'nu 'Foolish People'	*sakhu·nu?* 'Foolish One'
		'Young Buffalo'	
Wichkatítt 'Hot Dance' (lit. 'black arm')		kawen'hó 'Hot Dance'	*wihkatít* 'Black Arm'
Kúhnuch-Tiranehúh 'Band of Bears'			*kú·nUx tira·nIhú·?U* 'Many Bears'[a]
Stiri-Sakkahúhn 'Crazy Wolves'			*sčiri·sakhu·nu?* 'Crazy Wolf'[a]
Okóss-Sakkahúhn 'Crazy Bulls'			*hukosIsakhú·nu?* 'Crazy Bull'[a]
Nánisch-Táhka 'Kit Fox Society'			*na·nIštá·hka* 'Kit Fox Society'[a]
Naníschta 'Ghost Dance'			
Tschiri-Wakáh 'Outstretched Robe Dance'[b]			
Hunúchka 'Bird Egg Dance'[b]			
Cáwita 'Youngest Child Dance'[b]			*ka·wítA* 'Youngest Child'[a]
	Women's Societies		
	Stanshciṭap̣át 'Otter Society'		
	Stanshkó 'Goose Society'	sdānc gō$^{'hat}$ 'Goose Society'	*sta·nIškó·hAt* 'Women's Goose Society'
	Stansáhnĭni 'Creek Society'	sdāns hā'nini 'River Snake Society'	*sta·nIšshá·hnini?* 'Women's Creek Society'

[a]A linguistically recognized form but not remembered as a society name in the late 20th century.
[b]Apparently the names of dances and not societies.

Although not mentioned in nineteenth-century sources, at least three women's societies, parallel in name to similar organizations among the Mandan and Hidatsa, were recorded early in the twentieth century (Curtis 1907–1930, 5:150; Lowie 1915:676–678). The Creek society was noted for aiding men's societies, while the Goose society, which comprised older women who strove for outstanding gardens, focused its activites on horticulture, although it too aided male organizations. The Goose society was exceptional among all societies in that membership was inherited (Lowie 1915:676).

• KINSHIP Although the village was conceived to be a large kin group, the basic unit was the extended family that lived in an earthlodge and usually consisted of 15 to 20 persons. At its head was an older woman, who had built the lodge, and her husband. Since sororal polygyny was common, her younger sisters might reside there as well. The next generation included unmarried sons and one or more daughters, together with their spouses if they were married; and finally a third generation, their children. The most common postmarital residence pattern was matrilocal, although occasionally a couple would set up its own household or even more infrequently a woman would join the household of her husband's family. Whatever the residence pattern, the lodge was considered the property of its women.

The Arikara kinship system was bilateral and generational. Conceptually a father's brother was a father, a mother's sister was a mother, a man's brother's child was his child, a woman's sister's child was also her child, and finally children of siblings of like sex were siblings to each other. All these features were extended to all collateral lines. Although a father's sister was termed a mother, a mother's brother was called uncle. In addition, some Arikaras had several usages of a lineal, Crow-type classification, apparently borrowed from the Mandan and Hidatsa systems. Thus, for these individuals a mother's brother's children were termed children, while the father's sister's children were called mother and father.

Patterned social behavior between relatives involved either a respect or joking relationship. Respect obtained between children and their parents, as well as other individuals to whom the parental and child kin terms were extended. Among siblings close ties were highly valued, although a man could not remain alone with his sister and generally spoke only briefly with her. Brothers, who were expected to maintain the family's honor, had a close relationship in which there was a lifelong respect for seniority. Brothers-in-law were also closest of friends. A relationship analogous to that between younger and older brother was the one between nephew and maternal uncle. At puberty a boy would go to live in the lodge of either uncle or older brother and there be instructed in the arts of manhood. The wife of the older brother or uncle initiated the youth in sexual relations.

A strict taboo against communication between son-in-law and mother-in-law obtained. The restriction could be removed if the son-in-law gave the woman either an enemy scalp that he had taken or horses that he had captured.

Between grandparents and their grandchildren relations were relaxed, and joking was obligatory. Grandparents, in fact, were frequently more involved in the childrearing process than were the parents (Curtis 1907–1930, 5:62; Lesser 1979; Schmitt and Schmitt 1951).

Life Cycle

When a woman was pregnant she and her husband abstained from sexual relations; they did not resume until the thirtieth day after delivery. The woman retired to a small willow lodge when she was about to give birth and was assisted with the delivery by one or more old women, usually midwives who had medicine. The mother's confinement generally lasted no more than two days. If the village was traveling on a hunt, a woman gave birth along the trail, wrapped the newborn child in a piece of buffalo robe, tied it to a small board about three feet long, and caught up with the party after it stopped to camp (Truteau in Parks 1993).

Shortly after birth an older relative or perhaps the midwife would bestow a name on the baby that would generally last through most of its childhood. If the child had bad fortune or ill health, the name was usually changed. The name might be dreamed by the relative, it might come from a set of names associated with a bundle if the family had one, or it might derive from the medicine of the midwife.

Children nursed until they were two or three years old but might nurse until four or five years of age. Weaning was generally accomplished by separating the child from its mother. A child's worn-out moccasins and other clothes were ordinarily saved until the child attained the age of reason, when the moccasins were strung together or tied into a bundle with the clothes and thrown into the Missouri (Hilger 1951:69). This custom was thought to bring the child good fortune.

When a boy killed his first bird, his father gave a feast to celebrate the deed, ceremonially presented the dead bird to a priest or doctor, and distributed presents to the guests who attended. The recipient of the bird was obliged to eat it whole in the course of his meal (Tabeau 1939:209). Another public ceremony, given when a family wished to honor its son or daughter, was the piercing of the child's ears. After a father amassed food and goods, he invited people to the medicine lodge, where he distributed the presents to the guests in attendance, chose a distinguished person to pierce his child's ears, and later feasted the crowd. Sometimes a father invited a distinguished man in another village or another tribe to come to his village and dance the Calumet over the heads of his children. During the dance the hosts and visitors liberally exchanged presents; at its end the invited guest pierced the children's ears and received many presents (Tabeau 1939:214–215).

Smithsonian, Natl. Mus. of the Amer. Ind.: 12/2946.

Fig. 7. Sled made of animal ribs and hide. Sledding was a popular winter activity for children. The child sat astride the sled with his feet up, and gripped the rawhide thong for balance while sliding downhill. Collected by Melvin R. Gilmore, Ft. Berthold Res., N. Dak., 1923. Length 50 cm.

Similar to the ear-piercing ceremony was the Calumet ceremony (*pi·reškáni?* 'many-handed child') (fig. 8), an important adoption ceremony that functioned to establish bonds between families in two tribes or bands, often to create peace between social groups when there had been war or hostility. It was the Arikara form of the Pawnee Hako, and it was introduced by the Arikara to the Sioux, Mandan, and Hidatsa. In it a man invited a distinguished person in the other village or band to come "dance the pipe" over his children. Again, presents were liberally distributed between hosts and guests, and afterward bonds of kinship were established between the two families (Tabeau 1939:215–216; Curtis 1907–1930, 5:150). In the late nineteenth and early twentieth centuries this dance was performed by parents who wished to honor their children by having them named publicly; it was a puberty ritual that symbolized the children's entrance into a new period of life, and its performance was thought to bring good fortune to the children throughout their lives (Will 1934:33–39).

When a young man wished to marry a certain woman, his family sent an old man to the lodge of the other family to ask for the daughter. The following day the young woman's father consulted with her brothers and uncles. If these male relatives favored the union, they responded to the other family, who then accumulated gifts of horses, robes, and other goods that they gave to the girl's family. The following day the young woman's family reciprocated by taking gifts to the lodge of the young man's family. Afterward the young man was invited to his bride's lodge, where he was feasted and allowed to sleep with his new wife. During the night the wife's brothers took the young husband from his bed, washed him ceremonially, clothed him in a magnificent outfit, and gave him presents of weapons. The young man then lived in the lodge of his wife's family, generally until he had one or more children, when he and his wife were free to establish a separate household (Truteau in Parks 1993).

It was rare, however, for a man to live long with his first wife, since by the age of 30 a man had generally had as many as 10 wives. After that age couples tended to remain together, especially when they had children. If a man was killed his younger brother customarily married the widow (Truteau in Parks 1993). An adulterous woman usually received a beating or was abandoned, while the guilty male, if known, might have his best horse shot but he was rarely injured bodily (Curtis 1907–1930, 5:63).

Shortly after death the corpse, dressed and painted red by relatives, was wrapped in a skin or robe and then placed, head facing east, in a natural depression or in a shallow hole dug by an old woman paid by the family. If the deceased was a male, his weapons and other possessions might be placed in the grave with the body; if a woman, the tools she had used. The grave was first covered with poles and then with rocks and earth. Relatives and friends mourned at the grave until sunset; women cut their hair and gashed their legs while a man cut off the tips of his braids to place them in the robe with the corpse. On the fourth day, food and water were placed beside the grave to feed the spirit of the deceased on the journey to the afterworld (Curtis 1907–1930, 5:63, 151). The period of mourning generally lasted until someone brought back an enemy scalp to the village; until that time mourners covered their faces and bodies with white clay (Truteau in Parks 1993).

Religion and Healing

The Arikara had an elaborate system of religious ritual that was distinct from an equally notable shamanistic system. A basic dichotomy was thus made between priests (*na·wi·nAhčitawí?u?*), who were concerned with group or tribal welfare and general thanksgiving; and doctors (*kuná·?u?*), who were generally members of animal lodges that were concerned with the mysteries of disease and curing and who ministered to personal destiny. Together these two groups formed the single most powerful element in the tribe. Symbolically they were united in the medicine lodge, in which both priests and doctors met for their rituals as well as civic activities.

• PRIESTS AND RELIGIOUS RITUALS The Arikara account of their origin relates that human beings, who were created by the Chief Above, first lived underground. Through the intercession of Mother Corn and the help of various animals and birds, the people came up out of the ground and then traveled a path beset by various obstacles that they were helped to overcome. In this tribal journey each band had its place in the sequence, and at the end of their travels the people were taught, among other things, horticulture and the bundle ceremonies of thanksgiving that they were to perform (Dorsey 1904:12–35).

The sacred bundle was a shrine that symbolized the history of a particular band within the total history of the tribe. Physically it was a collection of objects that

State Histl. Soc. of N. Dak., Bismarck.: top, 200-4x5-C-647; bottom, 200-4x5-C-637.

Fig. 8. Calumet ceremony, called locally the Baptismal ceremony, performed in the Council House, Armstrong, N. Dak. top, a Procession led by 2 men holding the feathered pipe stems; immediately behind them are men beating hand drums. bottom, Little Crow and Little Sioux, officiating priests. Photographs by Russell Reid, Ft. Berthold Res., N. Dak., 1922.

mnemonically represented that history. Some three to four feet long and nearly one and one-half feet wide, it was wrapped in a dressed hide and had five large gourd rattles attached to the binding (fig. 9). Among the contents there were always four perfect ears of corn, a calumet pipe, and braids of sweetgrass as well as the skins of various birds. The bundles were in the custody of a keeper who was not necessarily the priest, but only the priest knew its ritual and was able to perform it. Both offices, custodian and priest, were hereditary and normally remained in families, being passed on to a son or other male relative deemed fit for the position. Becoming a priest and learning the ritual was a long, arduous, and expensive procedure; and assuming the office necessitated, in addition to a religious disposition, adherence to certain ethical vows, including benevolence and work for tribal welfare and refraining from quarrels, fighting, anger, and envy. The ritual opening of a sacred bundle took place at the altar in the medicine lodge. There

Smithsonian, NAA: 75-11683.

Fig. 9. Three village sacred bundles, with gourd rattles attached, hanging from rafters at the west end of an earthlodge. On the raised earth altar below are a pipe and 2 hand drums. Photograph by Edward S. Curtis, Beaver Creek, N. Dak., © 1908.

the contents were spread out, and the history of the band and the moral teachings given by Mother Corn were recited. A bundle was normally opened yearly for renewal of its contents; and one or more bundles had to be opened preceding any of the tribal ceremonies during the ritual calendar (Gilmore 1929a, 1931).

In the Arikara world view there was a supreme power denoted by several terms, the Chief Above (*ne·šá·nuʔ tnačitákux*), Our Father Above (*atíʔAx tnačitákUx*), and the Great Holy One (*še·ni·wa·rUxtinIhú·nU*). He was characterized as an amorphous power overhead in the heavens (some Arikaras, in fact, said he was the heavens) and the ultimate source of the world and everything in it. He was a neutral force who did not intervene directly in human affairs. Mother Corn, in contrast, was his intermediary on earth, sent down from the heavens to lead the people out of the primeval underworld, to give them their cultural institutions, and to come to them in times of need. Below, and including, the Chief Above and Mother Corn was a host of powers, all subsumed under a general term *awa·háxuʔ* that refers to the animate and inanimate elements of the universe believed to have supernatural power. Some Arikaras distinguished between the heavenly powers, such as Sun, Moon, and various stars, and earthly powers like animals, rocks, and rivers. All of these powers could be malevolent or benevolent (Parks 1991, 3:91–93).

Early in the spring before the planting season, the ritual calendar began with the corn planting ceremony. In the medicine lodge the priest opened the village sacred bundle and laid out on the raised altar its articles of mythological significance, which included ears of corn representing Mother Corn and the skins of the animals that had aided the people to emerge from the underworld early in their history. In front of the altar there was a framework on which lay three bows and arrows; under it were three ears of corn, and behind it were three buffalo-scapula hoes. After the priest recited the genesis myth and men took meat offerings on red osier sticks to plant in the ground outside the lodge, there was a dramatic enactment of the planting process intended to bring success to the coming season's activities. With the bows men pantomimed their duty to protect the crops from the enemy, while with the hoes women went through the motions of hoeing the ground. Following this enactment there was a dramatic prayer for bountiful crops and success against the enemy as well as a ritualized distribution of corn mush (Curtis 1907–1930, 5:70–73; Tabeau 1939:216–218). Subsequent to this initial ceremony, and lasting until the summer hunt, a sequence of rituals was performed at different stages during the planting and growth of the corn crop (Ewers 1961:45).

Still remembered in the early twentieth century was the Mother Corn ceremony (fig. 10), a thanksgiving rite, which historically involved the sacrifice of a consecrated animal as an offering of thanks (Will 1934:27–33). The Cedar Tree ceremony (fig. 11), another thanksgiving ritual, preceded the opening of the medicine lodge for the doctors' ceremonies in late summer. Immediately before each of these rites, the Sage Dance, a purification ritual, was performed (Will 1934:19–21).

During the nineteenth century the Arikara had, in addition, a Sun Dance. Since its existence among them is not recorded in the preceding century and its practice did not survive into the twentieth, it was apparently a short-lived borrowing from surrounding tribes that never became an integral feature of Arikara religious life. Although similar to the Sun Dance of other tribes, it differed considerably in details. Its two general purposes were personal supplication for spiritual strength and promotion of virtue in women (Curtis 1907–1930, 5:76–80).

• DOCTORS' SOCIETIES AND RITUALS Doctors were medical practitioners. They comprised two classes, those who were members of the older, established societies and those who did not belong to any society but had medicine for special purposes. Members of both classes, however, specialized in the cure of certain diseases, wounds, or ailments. Each of the established societies had its assigned place in the medicine lodge, where its members sat whenever they met for their rituals or there was a public function in the lodge. Ranged along the wall from left to right, the societies were the *tuwá·sA* or Ghost (*ne·ksá·nuʔ*); Stag (*arikará·nuʔ*) or Black-Tailed Deer (*ta·katít*); Shedding Buffalo (*kiwí·kuʔ*); Cormorant (*kohnít*); Duck (*AxwahAtkúsuʔ*); Moon (*pah*) or Owl (*wAhúruʔ*); Din Of Birds (*waka·nawíʔuʔ*), Mother Night (*atina·kAxá·nuʔ*), or Sioux (*sá·nat*); and Bear (*kú·nUx*). The altar, with four societies flanking it on either side, was at the back of the lodge opposite the door. It was an elevated earthen platform, six or seven feet square. Behind it sat the leading

State Histl. Soc. of N. Dak., Bismarck: 200-4x5-C-675.

Fig. 10. Mother Corn ceremony. Members of 2 medicine societies dance facing one another. Photograph by Russell Reid, Ft. Berthold Res., N. Dak., about 1926.

doctor and his three assistants who, by virtue of having mastered the secrets of all the societies, led ceremonies. Each society had its own ritual, a bundle containing objects associated with that ritual, and its distinctive dress.

Every year, beginning in mid-August, the doctors' societies had a protracted ceremonial schedule that in the late eighteenth century lasted two to three weeks but by the mid-nineteenth century lasted two months. During this period the doctors of all the societies virtually lived in the medicine lodge. Both day and night were filled with ritual activity: the day with singing and dancing that was closed to the public; and the evening with public performances of singing, dancing, and magic. Each society had its distinctive sleight-of-hand (*IšUhu·na·wa·núx*) that was in some way connected with the diseases in which it specialized. The feats of magic performed were many and varied, each designed to demonstrate to the people the powers that the doctors possessed. For example, a man's head would seemingly be cut off, paraded around the lodge and perhaps outside it, and then reattached to the body, whereupon the man would be well again; or a man would be shot, die, and then revived. Alternatively, a doctor would beat his sides

State Histl. Soc. of N. Dak., Bismarck: left, 200-5x7-681; right, 200-5x7-691.

Fig. 11. Cedar Tree ceremony, performed at Nishu, Ft. Berthold Res., N. Dak. left, Tree at the front of the dance lodge. right, Priests painted with white clay performing a ceremony before the tree. Photographs by Russell Reid, 1930.

with his hands and a jackrabbit would leap into his hand from his mouth. Arikara doctors were adept at such legerdemain and were noted among tribes on the northern Plains for their mysterious power. Even skeptical White observers frequently marveled at the performances that they witnessed (Truteau in Parks 1993; Tabeau 1939:187–189; Curtis 1907–1930, 5:70; Will 1934:41–48).

• POWER ACQUISITION The priesthood and the doctors' societies provided an institutionalized means of access to the supernatural. In the case of priests, it was a path that was restricted to the male members of certain families. In the case of doctors, admittance was not solely a hereditary matter, but by and large it did depend on wealth and status. In addition to these formal organizations an individual could also solicit supernatural power through the vision quest. Men would retire to the top of a hill or go to the burial ground, where they made themselves pitiable by fasting and crying; alternatively they would torture themselves by cutting off fingers, driving blades into the arms or legs, or piercing themselves and dragging buffalo skulls through the village. By such means they sought blessings from supernatural spirits, generally animals but often celestial beings as well. If a man were successful, he was granted special powers by his guardian—be it power for curing, success in war, hunting, or whatever. He was instructed in a special ritual and songs; and afterwards he would put together a personal medicine bundle that contained the physical objects associated with his vision. The bundle then represented his power and afforded him the protection that accrued from it.

Alternatively, an individual might not have a vision himself, but could still have access to power by acquiring the "medicine" of another person by purchasing it from a willing owner and learning the ritual and secrets associated with it. Frequently a man's wife served as the intermediary, obtaining a doctor's power through sexual intercourse and learning his secrets, which were then passed on to the husband. By such means a man could procure more and more power and thereby increase his social standing. At the same time, particularly efficacious medicine was transferred and maintained within the community rather than being restricted to the individual who had originally received it. The medicine of the doctors' societies was of this kind, since it had become part of the repertoire of an institutionalized group.

• BUNDLES Bundles symbolized each of the levels in the Arikara religious and curing systems. All were mnemonic collections of objects associated with a bundle's origin in a supernatural experience and with the prescribed ritual that derived from it. By far the most important were the band or village bundles. Concerned with group welfare and history, they were symbolic of the relationship of the band to the heavenly beings; were intimately tied up with success in horticulture, hunting, and war; and were the authority for moral teachings. The bundles of the medicine societies represented another level, subordinate to the preceding but representing powerful, organized groups whose purposes were complementary to those of the priests: the doctors were curers of individual ailments. Finally, there were personal bundles, which represented no corporate interests. Their power and status were transitory and depended on the experience and success of a particular individual and his medicine. The kinds of personal bundles varied: some were for curing, some for success in war, and some for good fortune in hunting. These three types of bundles—band, medicine society, and personal—thus represented the three major divisions in Arikara religion and their hierarchical arrangement.

Oral Traditions

The Arikara classified their oral traditions into two fundamental categories, true stories and tales (*na·ʔi·káwIš*). True stories, which for Arikaras were their history, covered a wide range of narrative types. One general class comprised sacred stories that told about mysterious events in the "holy period" before the earth had taken its present form, before or just at the time human institutions were developing, and included the genesis tradition. Such myths were set in a period when animals were actors in dramas, when deities came down to earth from the heavens, and when animals killed humans and buffalo ate people rather than the reverse. Related to these myths were other sacred stories that told of legendary events, which occurred more recently in time. Some of these were etiological narratives—dream or vision stories that related an encounter between a human and some animal or other supernatural agent who taught an Arikara a ritual for the benefit of his people. Other legendary accounts—actually the most popular type among Arikara oral traditions—were dream stories in which an animal or some other supernatural agent pitied a poor boy or young man and endowed him with supernatural powers for hunting, warfare, or healing. Still other legendary stories recounted a supernatural occurrence, as when a priest pouted and turned into stone.

Contrasting with sacred stories were nonsacred ones that described events more recent in time and did not have a predominant supernatural component. They constituted what from a Western perspective is oral history: war stories, accounts of events in the recent past, and personal anecdotes.

In contrast to true stories were tales, which were fictional and were told for amusement, generally to evoke laughter or to entertain children. The most common were trickster stories that told of Coyote's antics. Arikaras did not put Coyote into the role of a divine being; although he had mysterious power, he was always portrayed as a tricky, deceitful character who tried to outwit others but invariably bungled and generally died through his own folly. Only secondarily was he a transformer. Another fictional character was Stuwi, a sexually loose, meddlesome woman who was something of a clown. Other tales, many of them shared with other tribes, were more like European Mother Goose stories; they were more serious, often frightening, and generally had a human cast of characters (Parks 1991, 3:44–58).

Crosscutting these types of narratives were stories of Scalped Man, a ubiquitous character unique to Arikara and Pawnee oral tradition. He was based on men who were scalped in battle but survived and were then forced to shun human society because they were believed to be spirits. Many stories of scalped men were historical accounts, some simply about encounters with them but others describing them as malevolent spirits who stole possessions from people and abducted women and children. More frequently, the character was a legendary one who bestowed supernatural power on men, generally lone hunters. Sometimes, too, Scalped Man appeared in myths and in tales. In tales he was a comic character taking on the attributes of a trickster much like Coyote (Parks 1984, 1991, 3:51).

Warfare

Warfare was a dominant feature of Arikara life. Defensive and offensive attacks and raids were almost constant enterprises, since warfare among all Plains tribes enabled men to achieve renown and glory and thereby raise their status in society as well as to acquire wealth, primarily in the form of horses. Contributing to the maintenance of warfare was also the implacable hatred borne toward enemies that was constantly fueled by the desire for revenge. When an individual was killed by someone from another tribe, no matter the reason, it was cause for retribution—for killing any member in the responsible group. Parents and grandparents inculcated a hatred of enemies and the desire for revenge in their children and grandchildren. In the eighteenth and nineteenth centuries the enemies of the Arikaras included most of the Sioux bands, Chippewa, Assiniboine, Blackfoot, Crow, and Eastern Shoshone. Relations with the Mandan, Hidatsa, Omaha, Ponca, and the Oglala, Saone, and Tacowa bands of the Teton Sioux alternated between hostility and friendship.

Although a war party could be formed by anyone, large parties were organized only by war chiefs, men who had achieved distinction through bravery, exploits, and experience in leading many previously successful expeditions and who thereby attracted most of the warriors of the village to their enterprises. Smaller parties, usually organized by men of less renown, were comprised primarily of a leader's relatives and young men seeking adventure. For war chiefs, the decision to undertake an expedition was often a personal one, precipitated perhaps by a transgression against the village or band, but as often in acquiescence to the supplication of someone who had lost a relative and wanted revenge.

Preceding a large war expedition, the war chief gave a feast to which he invited the principal chiefs and influential men to announce his plans and gain their approval. Similar feasts, primarily of dog meat, were subsequently given by the warriors who wished to join the party. Then there was a final feast in the war chief's lodge, where all the warriors were present and a ritual was performed with the war bundle and calumet that the leader would take with him. The objects in the bundle were ones the leader used in rituals on the journey and that he wore as part of his insignia as leader. The insignia included a hawk skin and an ear of white corn that were attached to the ends of a cord worn around his neck, with the two objects hanging over his back. On the journey the leader kept the war bundle and carried the calumet in his hand constantly.

Before daybreak on the morning after the final feast, the party set out. All parties, in fact, set out before dawn and ordinarily traveled on foot since they expected to return on horses they captured. The war party comprised the leader, who on large expeditions was often assisted by one or two other leaders; the leader's assistant, who carried his weapons and performed the services of a retainer; the warriors, young and old; young men who traveled with the party as errand men (*taro·síhUx*), building shelters at night during inclement weather, gathering wood, building fires, cooking food, and fetching water; and scouts (*čiriče·ríšu?*), who traveled ahead of the party watching for the enemy.

The goal of a large party was to attack an enemy village and kill as many inhabitants as possible, especially all males over 15 years of age. After successfully overcoming the enemy, the attackers scalped the dead and gathered all the enemy horses and belongings, chopping up and burning what they were not able to carry off. Then they fled home to their village, marching day and night. During the return the members of the expedition stopped to give the booty to the leader, who had claim on all spoils; he kept what he wished and divided the remainder among members of the party, giving the better articles and horses to the most courageous and the older men.

A day before arriving home, the party lit fires on hills to signal their successful return to the village, and then when nearing the village they made a triumphal march into it. Old women took the poles from which the scalps were hung and danced with them through the village; then the trophies were taken to the medicine lodge and the warriors distributed much of their booty as presents to their closest kin. The following day the females of the village prepared for the victory dance (*čiwIhákUx*), while the war chief and his party assembled in the medicine lodge to recount the expedition. After their recital, the party, preceded by the priests and followed by the women, marched outside the village and formed a circle in the midst of which the priests performed rituals. Then the scalps were given to women who danced in the middle of the circle; this dance was followed by celebratory dances throughout the village that lasted at least several days and sometimes months.

At the conclusion of the victory celebrations the priests cut hair from the scalps, attached tufts of it to sticks painted red, and planted the sticks on hills near the village. The war chief then incensed the scalps and placed them in war bundles.

In contrast to the goals of these large war expeditions, small parties did not openly attack villages but lay in wait outside them either to kill and scalp lone individuals who happened to come out of the village or to capture horses in the village at night. There were the same celebrations for such small parties returning with a single scalp as for large parties returning with many; but for a party that brought back only horses there were no festivities (Truteau in Parks 1993).

History and Culture Since 1885

Resettlement

Land allotment, which moved the Arikara out of Like-a-Fishhook Village and onto individual farmsteads between 1884 and 1886, represented the most profound change in the tribe's history and culture, ending the community mode of life. At the same time the Arikara religious and curing practices symbolized by the Medicine Lodge ceased being celebrated. The Indian agent at Fort Berthold was able to suppress those ceremonies at the same time that families were taking up their allotments. The last ceremonial lodge, built in 1888, was in ruins by 1900 (Meyer 1977:155–156).

The Arikara settled on farmsteads on the eastern portion of Fort Berthold Reservation. Four settlements developed: *AxtárAhi* 'Concave Foot', the easternmost district; *xa·čipirí·nu?* 'Young Dog', located west of *AxtárAhi*; *čitákA nihwá?A* 'Muskrat Eaters', located along the east side of Six Mile Creek; and *wIso·wikUxíhAt* 'Kicks The Stomach', on the west side of Six Mile Creek. These settlement patterns were based on earlier social divisions, and during the late nineteenth and early twentieth centuries members of the communities rivaled each other in competitions, such as footraces, horse races, and bronc riding (Parks 1979a:223, 1970–1990).

Education

The Congregational missionary school was only moderately successful in its early years, but by the late 1880s the school enrolled 30 to 40 students. Fort Stevenson served as a boarding school for the reservation, 1883–1894. In 1889 Roman Catholics built Saint Edward's School (Meyer 1977:142–145).

The first day school was opened in 1895 in the Arikara settlement near the site of old Fort Berthold. Both the school and the settlement were named Armstrong. Shortly afterward schools were built at Independence, a Mandan and Hidatsa settlement west of the Missouri, and at Elbowoods and Shell Creek, Hidatsa settlements. In addition to communities that developed around schools and became seats of reservation districts, several other district communities took form: Beaver Creek, an Arikara community on the south side of the Missouri River; and Red Butte (now Twin Buttes), Little Missouri (or Short River), and Santee (later Lucky Mound), all primarily Hidatsa and Mandan settlements. In addition to the schools in four of them, the initial core of each community was a dance hall and generally a trading post or store. Later, churches were built in Armstrong (renamed Nishu), Red Butte, Independence, and Little Missouri (later called Charging Eagle); and a post office, in addition to the one in Elbowoods, was opened in Armstrong.

During the last decade of the nineteenth and the first half of the twentieth centuries, Arikara life was dominated by efforts to implement government Indian policy: to educate youth, primarily by teaching them trade skills, and to train them to become farmers or livestock ranchers. The goal was to merge Arikaras into rural American society. In 1878, as part of Office of Indian Affairs policy to establish off-reservation boarding schools that would separate children from their families and reservation communities and teach them useful trades, the first group of Fort Berthold youth, half of them Arikaras, went to Hampton Normal and Agricultural Institute in Virginia, a school for Blacks that developed a three-year program for Indians. Beginning in the 1880s Arikara children went to boarding schools at Genoa and Santee, Nebraska, as well as to Carlisle Indian School in Carlisle, Pennsylvania. After 1900 they attended schools in Flandreau and Pierre, South Dakota; in Bismarck and Wahpeton, North Dakota; and in Pipestone, Minnesota.

Religion

The most successful missionary was Hall, who received the first converts among the Arikara beginning in 1887. He oversaw construction of the first Congregational church at Armstrong in 1900 and trained native lay readers and ministers. The Congregational church was a dominant force in the Arikara community throughout the twentieth century. Episcopal and Roman Catholic missionaries established smaller, but equally enduring, congregations. In the twentieth century each of these churches held a summer convocation or congress to which local members and members from other reservations, particularly Standing Rock, came for three days of camping and church activities. Each church, moreover, had a women's club that sponsored sewing bees. The early groups made patchwork quilts, but before World War II Edith Badger introduced the star design to the Arikara community and subsequently the star quilt became the favorite of quilters throughout the reservation. These clubs died out after World War II began and women moved into the workforce.

Economy

Despite periods of drought during the first decades after resettlement, the Arikara persevered in raising gardens for subsistence and increased wheat production and built up herds of horses and cattle. Most Arikaras took their excess grain to Minot and, later, to Garrison to sell. To supplement the generally meager income of these activities in the late nineteenth century, they gathered old buffalo bones and hauled them to Minot to sell, and during the early twentieth century they cut posts that they took to Roseglen to trade for groceries. Arikaras in the Beaver Creek district took their grain and posts to Dickinson. Men hunted small game and deer to provide meat in the diet, and families dug coal and cut wood to provide fuel for winter (Parks 1970–1990).

Housing

When families first moved onto allotments after leaving Like-a-Fishhook Village, they built log houses, which generally comprised two rooms, one about 20 feet square and the other about half that size, both with dirt floors. The larger room was the men's sitting and sleeping quarters. The other room served as kitchen, pantry, storeroom, women's quarters, and nursery. Beginning in the 1890s many of these cabins were replaced by frame houses, but log houses continued in use during the first half of the twentieth century (Missouri River Basin Investigations Staff 1949:194; Meyer 1977:155).

Cultural Survivals

Around 1900 there were attempts in the Beaver Creek district to revive Arikara religious traditions. Two ritual leaders living there, Crow Ghost and Red Star, had dreams in which each was given Grass Dance songs. Crow Ghost tried to revive older ceremonies, and Winnie Enemy Heart had a vision in which she was told that Arikaras should return to their former way of life (Parks 1991, 3:18, 323–324). In 1907, with permission from the agent, Edward S. Curtis arranged a revival of the Medicine Lodge so that he could photograph and describe its rituals (Curtis 1907–1930, 5:59–100). That reenactment and two others in the 1920s fueled a revival of Medicine Lodge rituals that continued sporadically until the early 1930s.

The Grass Dance represented a more enduring survival of traditional culture among the Arikara. When it was introduced about 1870 from the south, it gained vast popularity on the northern Plains and replaced other men's societies. The Pawnee Grass Dance was brought to the Arikara by Pawnee Tom, who helped Enemy Heart, an influential Arikara, inaugurate the dance among his people. Another form of the dance was sold to the Arikara by visiting Santees from the Devils Lake Reservation. The Arikara in turn took it to the Crow, to whom they sold it, and then reformed it for a short period as the Baby Grass dance (*ha·nUtpi·ráʔuʔ*). From the late nineteenth century until the late 1920s, the Big Grass Society (*ha·nUtkúsuʔ*) was the dominant group in Arikara social and political life. In 1918 a group of younger men on the north side of the Missouri River built a dance hall at Nishu and formed the Dead Grass Society, which was patterned after the Big Grass organization and later replaced it. The Dead Grass Society continued until World War II (Parks 1991, 3: 323–324, 1970–1990).

In the 1940s and 1950s there were revivals of rituals. In 1948 Wilbur Howard, an Arikara who taught music in Ohio schools, arranged a partial reenactment of the Medicine Lodge in order to record the songs of each of the societies. In 1952 Howard's grandparents sponsored his ceremonial induction into the Bear Society, long defunct but many of its rituals and songs remembered, so that Howard would know the songs (Howard and Woolworth 1954). At the same time, other ritual practices continued without interruption until the end of the century. One of the most fundamental was the mourning feast, a ritual meal prepared for the spirit of a departed individual on the evening of the fourth day after death. Another enduring practice was the ritual bestowal on an individual of an Arikara name. Until World War II, in addition to their legal English name, all Arikaras received an Indian name that was used in most social contexts. Servicemen, in particular, took Arikara names, which were used in ritual contexts and at dances when those individuals were honored by their relatives. In the late twentieth century many families still had names bestowed on their children.

Recreation

During the first half of the century, Arikara social life focused around dances, church activities, and stockmen's association activities. The Big Grass and Dead Grass societies sponsored two or three dances a year. Other major celebrations included a dance on Memorial Day, and a three-day camp on the Fourth of July, marked by dances, footraces, horse races, moccasin games, and a rodeo. Preceding the Depression, there was a fair each August in Elbowoods, patterned after county fairs, where families brought their garden produce, cooking, and sewing for display. The fairs included a dance and rodeo. In late summer each district on the reservation also sponsored a rodeo.

In 1912 the surviving scouts who had served under Lt. Col. George A. Custer formed a society, the U.S. Volunteer Indian Scouts, whose members were active in community affairs and who sponsored a dance and other activities on Decoration Day. After their fathers passed away, the sons of the scouts continued the society until it dissolved after World War II began. In the 1970s their descendants re-formed it as the Old Scouts Society, membership in which was open to any Arikara, male or female. It, too, sponsored dances.

An important feature of Arikara social life, before and after the reservation period, was intertribal visiting. In the late nineteenth and early twentieth centuries, they exchanged regular visits with two groups, the Sioux on the

Devils Lake Reservation and the Yanktonai Sioux living at Cannon Ball on the Standing Rock Reservation. Occasionally they also visited Teton groups on the southern part of Standing Rock Reservation and on the Cheyenne River Reservation. Individual Arikaras and Pawnees also exchanged visits during this same period.

Kinship

The Arikara kinship system, with its patterned behavior among relatives and in-laws, continued to shape family relationships throughout the twentieth century, although late in the century, younger generations failed to learn the system. Nonetheless, historical patterns of kin behavior, including respect, avoidance, and joking relationships, persisted, even though the kin terms themselves might be in English. Kinship obligations remained central to Arikara society throughout the twentieth century.

Post-Dam Communities

At the time of construction of Garrison Dam and the flooding of the Missouri River trench on the reservation in 1953, most Arikara families living on the north side of the Missouri chose to relocate to the upland prairie north of Nishu in what became the Eastern Segment of the reservation. In 1954 the Bureau of Indian Affairs built a combined elementary and secondary school for the Eastern Segment population in the present White Shield ("Three Affiliated Tribes," fig. 1, this vol.). The school, together with its housing for teachers and administrators, a community hall, and three churches, made up the nucleus of the community. In the early 1970s, the Bureau of Indian Affairs constructed housing in the White Shield area that enlarged its population as Arikaras returned to a community mode of life. In the late twentieth century, White Shield identified itself as the Arikara community on the Fort Berthold Reservation.

Arikaras living in the Beaver Creek area moved to what became the Southern Segment, comprising the populations of the Beaver Creek, Red Butte, and Little Missouri communities. There the Bureau of Indian Affairs built the Twin Buttes elementary school, and subsequently the school, a community hall, churches, and Bureau of Indian Affairs housing constituted the Twin Buttes community, which identified itself as Mandan on the reservation. Arikaras living in Elbowoods and Lucky Mound, as well as some families living in Nishu and Beaver Creek, moved to Parshall, a White community in the Northeastern Segment of the reservation, and to New Town, a community built in the Northern Segment to succeed Elbowoods as the administative center for the reservation, housing both Bureau of Indian Affairs and Fort Berthold tribal government offices. The Indian population in both Parshall and New Town was predominantly Hidatsa.

Beginning in the 1960s each community sponsored an annual summer celebration, or powwow. The first White Shield celebration was held in 1962, while the first Twin Buttes powwow was in the 1950s. The White Shield celebration was held on the second weekend in July, and the Twin Buttes celebration in August. Each year at the end of the celebration a new committee would be selected to raise money during the coming year for the next powwow. Fundraising activities, which included Warbonnet Dances, socials, and bingo, were held throughout the year. No less important, the White Shield powwow provided a focus of Arikara identity.

Population

Estimates of Arikara population are given in table 3. The primary cause for the declines was disease. Because of their highly concentrated populations in fixed villages, the Arikara were especially prone to epidemics. Smallpox struck the tribe on at least seven occasions: three times during 1771–1781, in 1837–1838, 1855, 1861, and 1866. There was an outbreak of measles in 1846 and a cholera attack in 1851. In addition, tuberculosis became rampant among the tribe during the late 1800s and continued to take a toll on the population until about 1915. Warfare was not a significant factor in population decline, although harassment by the Sioux did contribute to brief periods of starvation and deaths from chronic raids.

The earliest population estimate is given by Truteau (Parks 1993), who related that prior to the smallpox epidemics during 1771–1781 the Arikara numbered 4,000

Table 3. Arikara Population, 1795–1950

Date	*Estimated Number*	*Source*
1795	500 warriors	Truteau (Parks 1993)
1802	500 warriors	Tabeau (1939:123–124)
1804	2,000 or 3,000; 500 warriors	Lewis and Clark (Moulton 1983–, 3:400)
1834	2,200	Allis (Dunbar and Allis 1918:701)
1842	1,200	ARCIA 1842:432–433
1850	1,500	Culbertson (1952:137)
	600 warriors	Kurz (1937:165)
1855	600	Denig (Ewers 1961:60)
	840 (60 lodges, 14 to a lodge)	ARCIA 1855:393
1866	1,500	Kane (1951:278)
1875	900	ARCIA 1875:106
1885	529	ARCIA 1885:29
1895	420	ARCIA 1895:233
1905	379	ARCIA 1905:283
1915	409	ARCIA 1915:71
1921	418	ARCIA 1921:45
1931	480	ARCIA 1931:51
1950	682	U.S. Congress. House. Committee on Interior and Insular Affairs 1953:817

warriors. Assuming his estimate is roughly accurate, the preepidemic Arikara population would then have been approximately 16,000—or at least 10,000 and possibly as high as 20,000 individuals.

Synonymy

The source of the name Arikara is unknown. It has been attributed by one source to a Pawnee designation *arikará·ru?* 'elk, stag' (Lesser and Weltfish 1932:8), apparently because of the similarity in form of the two words. A similar, less plausible explanation derives the name from a Pawnee form *ariki* 'horn' plus an unknown suffix and attributes to it a reference to a former custom of wearing two pieces of bone standing upright in the hair like horns, one on either side of the crest (J.B. Dunbar 1880:245–246; Hodge 1907–1910, 1:83).

In 1795 Spanish officials in San Antonio, Texas, recorded the Skiri Pawnee name for an Arikara band, or *nación*, as Alicara (Troike 1964:385), indicating that the name Arikara was in use among the Pawnee in the eighteenth century. In the nineteenth century the Arikara were also said to be called Riks, an abbreviation of Arikaras used by traders, 1851 (Kurz 1937:72). Whether the origin of the name is in the Pawnee or Arikara languages is unclear. The late nineteenth and twentieth century Mandan name for the Arikara is the same form, *aríkra*, which is a loanword in that language (Curtis 1907–1930, 5:147; Hollow 1970:59). Similar to it, and apparently also a borrowing, is the Hidatsa designation *arakárahu* (A.W. Jones 1979:8; W. Matthews 1877:125). A-rĭk′-a-hŭ, an incorrect form of the Hidatsa name, said to mean 'people of the flowing hair', is erroneously cited as the source of the name Arikara and is said to have been borrowed into Mandan as Ai-dĭk-a-da-hu (Hoffman 1886:294; Hodge 1907–1910, 1:86); the last, in fact, represents the Hidatsa form, which has no known etymology.

Throughout the eighteenth and nineteenth centuries the most common designation in European and American sources is the name Arikara, which occurs in two forms, those with a final syllable ra and those with a final syllable ree or ri. Examples of variants of the former are Aricaras, 1720 (Beaurain in Margry 1876–1886, 6:289), Arricara, 1719 (La Harpe in Margry 1876–1886, 6:293), Arricaras, 1785 (Miró in Nasatir 1952, 1:126), Arickara (Secretary of War 1829:99), Arikkaras (Maximilian 1843:143), and Auricara (Kappler 1904–1941, 2:236). Other variants lack the initial vowel, for example, Ricara (Renaudière in Margry 1876–1886, 6:395; Truteau 1795–1796 in Parks 1993); Ricora (Boudinot 1816:128), Rikaras (Irving 1868:236), Rikkara (Maximilian 1843, 2:237); and Re-ke-rahs and Re-ka-ras (Bonner 1856:162, 255).

Examples of variants with syllable final ree or ri are Arickarees (Morgan 1871:30), Aracaris (Gass 1810:400), Ariccarees, 1850 (Culbertson 1952:96), Aurickarees (Schoolcraft 1851–1857, 1:523), Archarees (Morgan 1869:493), and Arikari, 1861 (Burton 1963:42). Many of these variants also lack the initial vowel of the name, for example, Ricrerees and rickeries, 1804–1805 (Lewis and Clark in Moulton 1983–, 3:135, 143); Riccari, 1805 (Wilkinson in Jackson 1978, 1:272–274); Rickarees, Rickerees, and Ricaris (Gass 1810:48, 53, 82); Riccarree, 1833 (Catlin 1848, 1:204); and Ricaries (Domenech 1860, 1:443).

French Canadian traders shortened Arikaree to Ree (Lewis and Clark 1804–1805 in Moulton 1983–, 3:400), a designation that continued into the late twentieth century to be commonly used on the Fort Berthold Reservation. Other examples of this abbreviated form are Riis, 1785 (Miró in Nasatir 1952, 1:126), Rih's or Ris (Maximilian 1843, 2:237), and Rhea (Hallam in Beach 1877:134).

Less obvious renditions of Arikara, many of which are apparent misprints, include Ankora (ARCIA 1851:63), Aricas (Hodge 1907–1910, 1:86); Arichards (Secretary of War 1832:63), Biccarees (Domenech 1860, 1:431), Caricara, 1714 (Giraud 1958:17), Pucaras (Alegre 1841, 1:336), Kees (Secretary of War 1869, 1:35), and Rice Indians (Franchère 1854:54).

The Arikara designation for themselves is *sáhniš* 'human being, people' (Parks 1986:2), which has been rendered as Tsa′nish (Hoffman 1886:294) and sanish or tanish (Hayden 1862:356). Another commonly used self-referential term is *natara·kó·čɪ* 'ourselves', parallel to the same usage in Pawnee. When an Arikara asks someone if he or she is Arikara, the question is *ka kunatará·kɪt* 'are you one of us?' and if the answer is affirmative it is *kutatará·kɪt* 'I am one of us'.

In the eighteenth and early nineteenth centuries the Arikara were frequently referred to as Pawnees, beginning with the Vermale map of 1717, where they are designated as Panis; this usage reflects information then current in lower Louisiana that the Arikara and Pawnee were a single group speaking the same language (M.M. Wedel 1973:208). Traders and travelers occasionally also referred to them as Panis, 1800–1801, and Pawnees, 1806 (Henry in Gough 1988–1992, 1:90, 211, 222, 225, 277) or as the Ricara band of Panies, 1804 (Moulton 1983–, 3:126), illustrating local use of this designation as late as the early nineteenth century. Other examples of the designation Pawnee qualified by a form of Arikara are Panis ricaras (Jefferys 1761, 1:143; Truteau 1795–1796 in Parks 1993), Pawnee-Rikasrees, 1819 (Nuttall 1980:92), and Pawnee Hocá, 1795 (Nasatir 1952, 1:332).

In the early nineteenth century, and presumably earlier, the designation of the Arikara as Pawnee was current among the Mandan, who at that time referred to all Arikara bands as Pawnee (Moulton 1983–, 3:251). The Sioux name for the Arikara also designates the Pawnee: Santee, Yankton, and Yanktonai *pʰadáni*; Teton *pʰaláni*; and Assiniboine *pʰanáni* (Williamson 1886:112; Curtis 1907–30, 5:141; Hoffman 1886:295; Scott 1912–1934).

The last form is undoubtedly one or both of the Assiniboine names Panana and Panani recorded by La Vérendrye (Burpee 1927:335–337). A Yankton name Wazíyata Padáni^{n} distinguishes the Arikara as 'northern Pawnee' (J.W. Cook 1880–1882:184).

Dhegiha and Chiwere Siouan speakers designate the Arikara as 'sand Pawnee': Omaha-Ponca *páðį piza* (Fletcher and La Flesche 1911:102, retranscribed), Ioway-Otoe Pányi púça, apparently *pánʸi puða* (Dorsey 1879). The last was the source of French spellings such as Paniboucha, 1700 (Tonti in Delanglez 1939:232); Panigoucha, 1701 (Delisle in M.M. Wedel 1973:207); and Panibousa, 1703 (Delisle in Tucker 1942:pl. 13).

In the late nineteenth and twentieth centuries some Sioux speakers apparently neutralized the distinction between Hidatsa and Arikara by using the name for the Hidatsa, *xewáktokta*, for both tribes; thus Santee ȟe-wá-kto-kto and Teton *xewáktokta* (Riggs 1890:164; Buechel 1970:733, retranscribed).

The Blackfoot refer to the Arikara, as well as the Mandan and Hidatsa, as *ksáókò·yi·wa*, literally 'one who has an earthlodge' (Allan R. Taylor, personal communication 1987). The Cree use a similar designation, *o·taski·wikamikwe·w* 'earthlodge dweller' (A. Cuthand and H.C. Wolfart, personal communication 1975). Many distant tribes also used the sign language designation for earthlodge to refer to the Arikara as well as the Mandan and Hidatsa (W.P. Clark 1885:44).

The Kiowa name for the Arikara is *k̓ɔ̂·tʰà* (pl. *k̓ɔ̂·tʰàgɔ̀*). It is said to mean 'biters' (Mooney 1898:410) or 'flint (or knife) nick' (Laurel Watkins, personal communication 1979). The former meaning is related to the Kiowa sign language designation for Arikara, an imitation of the motion of biting or twisting off something held in the mouth, said to refer originally to the gnawing of corn, since the Arikara were noted for corn cultivation (Mooney 1898:410). The other meaning represents a variant sign signifying 'corn sheller'. Another form of the Kiowa name is k̓ɔl-k̓ʸa 'Arikara man' (Harrington 1928:96, normalized).

Similar in meaning to the Kiowa designation is the Cheyenne *ónoneoʔO* (sg. *ónonE*), translated literally as 'taking off with the teeth' (Mooney 1907:423; Petter 1913–1915:582; Glenmore and Leman 1985:202) and 'shellers' (Curtis 1907–1930, 6:158), recorded also as Óhnunnu (Maximilian in Thwaites 1904–1907, 24:222) and O-no′-ni-o (Hayden 1862:326). Related to it in meaning is the Arapaho designation ká-nan-in, translated as 'people whose jaws break in pieces' (Hayden 1862:326).

The Pawnee name for the Arikara is *astárahi*, which was cited as the Arikara name for themselves (Lewis and Clark in Thwaites 1904–1907, 6:89), the "primitive" name of the tribe (Bradbury 1817:128), and the name of the largest of the 10 eighteenth-century Arikara villages, 1804 (Tabeau 1939:125). It survived among the Arikara into the early twentieth century as a district name on the Fort Berthold Reservation (Parks 1979a).

The Crow designation is *ahpanno·pisé·*, literally 'large ear holes' (Medicine Horse 1987:15; Curtis 1907–1930, 4:180; Hayden 1862:402), a name related to one of the sign language designations for the Arikara.

An anomalous name with no known etymology is Salish s'quiestshi (Hoffman 1886:371).

Divisions

Although the precise number and identity of the various divisions of the Arikara are not known, many names appear repeatedly in the early historical literature. Table 1 correlates six lists of these names, termed *naciones* in late eighteenth century Spanish sources, and villages or bands in the nineteenth and twentieth centuries. Many names were also remembered in the twentieth century as village sacred bundles.

Characterized as the original name of the Arikara, the *AxtárAhi* division was also said to be the largest (Tabeau 1939:124–125). Examples of its occurrence, in addition to those in table 1, are Star rah he, 1804–1805 (Lewis and Clark in Moulton 1983–, 3:400), Es. ter. râ. hê (Wilkinson 1805), Starrahe and Stăr-ră-hĕ, 1811 (Bradbury in Thwaites 1904–1907, 5:128); Satrahe (Balbi 1826:54).

The name *wa·húkAxa*, which translates both as 'hill in the water' and 'sides of the head shaved', occurs less frequently, although it, too, was one of the larger Arikara villages (Tabeau 1939:124–125). Another occurrence is Wâ. hôô. kâ (Wilkinson 1805).

Examples of the name of the *nAhuuká·tA* division, which was an independent village as late as 1832, are La ho catt (Moulton 1983–, 3:143) and Nahokáhta, 1833 (Bodmer 1984:282).

The name *na·karíkA*, which has a dialectal variant *ha·karíka*, occurs as Nâ. câ. rê kâ (Wilkinson 1805).

Additional recordings of the name *hu·ka·wirát* are Hóhka-Wirátt, 1833 (Bodmer 1984:282) and village of the Easterners (Libby 1920:179).

Sign Language

In the Plains sign language several variant gestures designated the Arikara, the earliest and most prevalent referring to them as corn people. Most widespread is the gesture that signifies 'cornshellers'; it symbolizes the shelling of corn by holding the left hand stationary and making shelling movements with the right hand (W.P. Clark 1885:43–44; Scott 1912–1934; Mallery 1881:461). Until 1875 only the Arikara were known by that sign, but subsequently it was often generalized to designate the Mandan and Hidatsa as well (Scott 1912–1934).

On the southern Plains a variant sign was to bring the closed right hand to the mouth, as if holding an ear of corn, and then rotate it forward and downward, imitating a person gnawing corn on a cob. A variant of this sign is to make, in accompaniment to the gnawing gesture, chewing movements with the jaw (Scott 1912–1934). Both variants designate the Arikara as eaters of corn, wherefrom the name Corn Eaters (Culbertson 1851:130).

Of more limited provenience is a gesture used by the Crow and Hidatsa that indicates a big earring hanging from the ear. It is made with the right hand closed, with the thumb and index finger curved and tips joined, forming a circle, placed below and touching the lobe of the ear (Mallery 1881:461). Although reportedly used to designate the Mandan also (W.P. Clark 1885:238), the sign is a reflection of the Crow name for the Arikara.

An obsolete sign, reputedly used by Arikara to designate themselves previous to their adoption of the sign for corn eater, is one in which the fingers and thumb of the right hand are brought together to a point and then moved toward the upper portion of the cheek in a dotting motion (Mallery 1881:461). The sign represents tattooing the upper cheek and was perhaps the former practice of an Arikara band.

Beginning in the late nineteenth century, the sign for an earthlodge was sometimes used to designate the Arikara, as well as the Mandan and Hidatsa. This usage represents, especially among more distant tribes, a relatively recent conflation of the identities of all three tribes living on the Fort Berthold Reservation and sharing the distinctive earthlodge domicile (W.P. Clark 1885:44; Scott 1912–1934).

Sources

Two early, indispensible accounts by fur traders provide extensive information on Arikara culture when it was first observed during the late eighteenth and early nineteenth centuries: Jean-Baptiste Truteau (Parks 1993), who lived with them in 1795–1796, and Pierre-Antoine Tabeau (1939), who lived among them in 1804–1805. A later account is provided by Edwin T. Denig (Ewers 1961:41–62), who lived among the tribes of the Upper Missouri between 1833 and 1858. Additional useful information is to be gleaned from the journals of Meriwether Lewis and William Clark (Moulton 1983–), Prince Maximilian (Thwaites 1904–1907, 22–24), John Bradbury (Thwaites 1904–1907, 5), Henry M. Brackenridge (Thwaites 1904–1907, 6), and Thaddeus Culbertson (1952). Hayden's (1862:351–363) short description of the Arikara is in large part copied from Denig. Paintings that illustrate Arikara life were done in 1832 by George Catlin (1848) and in 1833 by Karl Bodmer (1984).

Modern ethnographic accounts begin with an extensive collection of mythology recorded by James R. Murie (G.A. Dorsey 1904). Curtis (1907–1930, 5:59–100, 148–152, 178–180) describes Arikara ceremonies and presents a general ethnographic sketch as well as a vocabulary and six short biographies of prominent Arikara men. Lowie (1915) describes Arikara societies. From 1924 through 1933 the ethnobotanist Melvin Gilmore published numerous articles on ethnographic topics, the most important of which describe Arikara religion and tribal organization (1926, 1927, 1929a, 1931). George Will (1934) provides an ethnographic sketch and descriptions of several ceremonies that he witnessed in the 1920s. Preston Holder discusses Arikara social stratification (1958) and contrasts Plains horticultural and nomadic groups (1970); the latter deals only generally with the Arikara, but offers a fine overview of northern Caddoan culture. The Buffalo doctors' society bundle and its contents are described by James H. Howard (1974).

The most succinct chronological summaries of Arikara history are by Wedel (1955:77–84) and Parks (1991, 3:10–22). An overview of Arikara culture history appears in Deetz (1965:5–37). DeLand (1906) brings together original historical and ethnographic materials but makes no attempt at synthesis. Macgowan (1942) is a similar, though far less ambitious, endeavor. Hyde's (1951–1952) study of Arikara history is extensive but unreliable. Libby (1920) records the reminiscences of the surviving Arikara scouts who served under Custer in 1874 and 1876; he includes short biographies of nine scouts.

The Arikara language is described by Parks, Beltran, and Waters (1979), while aspects of Arikara syntax are examined by Merlan (1975). Parks (1991) presents an extensive collection of Arikara oral traditions in interlinear Arikara-English and free English translation. Small collections of Arikara texts are also presented by Parks and Taylor (in Parks 1977:1–19, 20–26). Parks (1986) is a short English-Arikara dictionary. The relationship of Arikara to other northern Caddoan languages is portrayed in Parks (1979).

The Field Museum of Natural History in Chicago has an extensive collection of Arikara material culture objects purchased by Murie and Dorsey during the first decade of the twentieth century. Other institutions having smaller but significant holdings are the Four Bears Museum in New Town, North Dakota; the State Historical Society of North Dakota in Bismarck; the Museum of Anthropology at the University of Colorado, Boulder; and the Museum of Anthropology at the University of Michigan, Ann Arbor.

Three Affiliated Tribes

MARY JANE SCHNEIDER

The Three Affiliated Tribes of Fort Berthold Indian Reservation has been since 1936 the official name of the Mandan, Hidatsa, and Arikara, three culturally and linguistically different tribes who once lived in earthlodge villages on or near the Missouri River. Even though they abandoned the old villages and moved northward to congregate in Like-a-Fishhook Village and then separated again into tribal communities, they continued to live on the Missouri, but in the 1950s a dam turned the river into Lake Sakakawea, flooding the bottomland communities and changing the geography of the reservation. Despite these and numerous other historical changes, the distinct tribal identities survived and in 1998 each tribe had its own cultural "heart" in a separate district of the reservation (fig. 1).

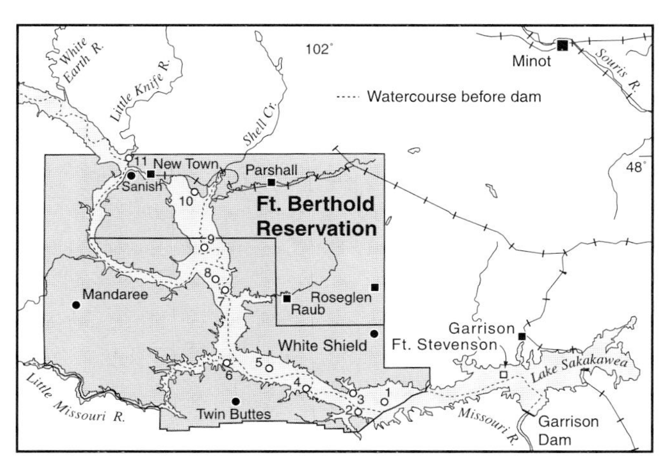

Fig. 1. Ft. Berthold Res., N. Dak. Dashed line indicates watercourse before Garrison Dam. The northeast segment (indicated by a line), opened for settlement in 1912, was returned to the reservation in 1970. Towns inundated by Garrison Dam: 1, Like-a-Fishhook Village; 2, Beaver Creek; 3, Nishu (Armstrong); 4, Red Butte; 5, Elbowoods; 6, Charging Eagle; 7, Lucky Mound (Santee); 8, Independence; 9, Shell Creek; 10, Van Hook; 11, Sanish.

The political unity of the three tribes began in 1866, four years after the Arikara joined the Mandan and Hidatsa in Like-a-Fishhook Village. The village, established by Mandan and Hidatsa leaders around 1845 (fig. 2) for survivors of a devastating smallpox epidemic, was small at first, but it soon became home to most of the Mandan and Hidatsa. Its size and location attracted numerous fur traders, military men, government officials, missionaries, and visitors, making it one of the best documented transitional Native American communities in North America (Meyer 1977:111). Despite living in the same village, the three tribes gathered in separate enclaves that maintained distinctive tribal cultures and languages. Before the Arikara joined them, the Mandan and Hidatsa part of the village consisted of randomly scattered earthlodges and a few log houses. The Mandan had a large ceremonial lodge with an open space holding a shrine in front, but the Hidatsa did not. The Arikara occupied the north side of the village ("Plains Village Tradition: Postcontact," fig. 6, this vol.), removing some of the stockade to make room for their lodges (Smith 1972:25–30, 54).

A few years after the Arikara moved to Like-a-Fishhook, commissioners representing the United States arrived to make a treaty with them. In the Treaty of Fort Berthold in 1866, signed by White Shield and 23 others, the Arikara agreed to maintain peaceful relations, abide by the laws of the United States, refrain from using alcohol, and allow the construction of roads and telegraphs through their territory. An addendum to the treaty included the Mandan and Hidatsa (the latter then known as the Gros Ventres) in the treaty and got them to cede lands south of the reservation for use in constructing a stage line. The new agreement was signed by Arikara, Hidatsa, and Mandan leaders (Kappler 1904–1941, 2:1052–1056). The 1866 treaty was never ratified and the tribes were left with no specifically designated reservation until 1870, when President Ulysses S. Grant signed an executive order setting aside 7.8 million acres as Fort Berthold Reservation. With no official treaty guaranteeing rations and annuities the three tribes felt they were ignored and the leaders complained that the government treated the tribes who fought against it better than those that did not take up arms, but the peaceful relationships between the tribes and outsiders continued (Tappan in ARCIA 1872:264). In 1880, an executive order by President Rutherford B. Hayes reduced the reservation to 1.2 million acres (Meyer 1977:112–114; Gilman and Schneider 1987:272–273). Following the mandate of the Dawes Severalty Act that lands not awarded to individual tribal members be opened for sale to the public, the tribe agreed to another reduction of the reservation in 1891 (Kappler 1904–1941, 1:425–428), but by then the tribes had abandoned Like-a-Fishhook.

Treaties brought agents and other employees of the federal government to Fort Berthold to carry out the government's obligations to the Indians and to push the adoption of non-Indian culture. The agents, instructed to get Indian

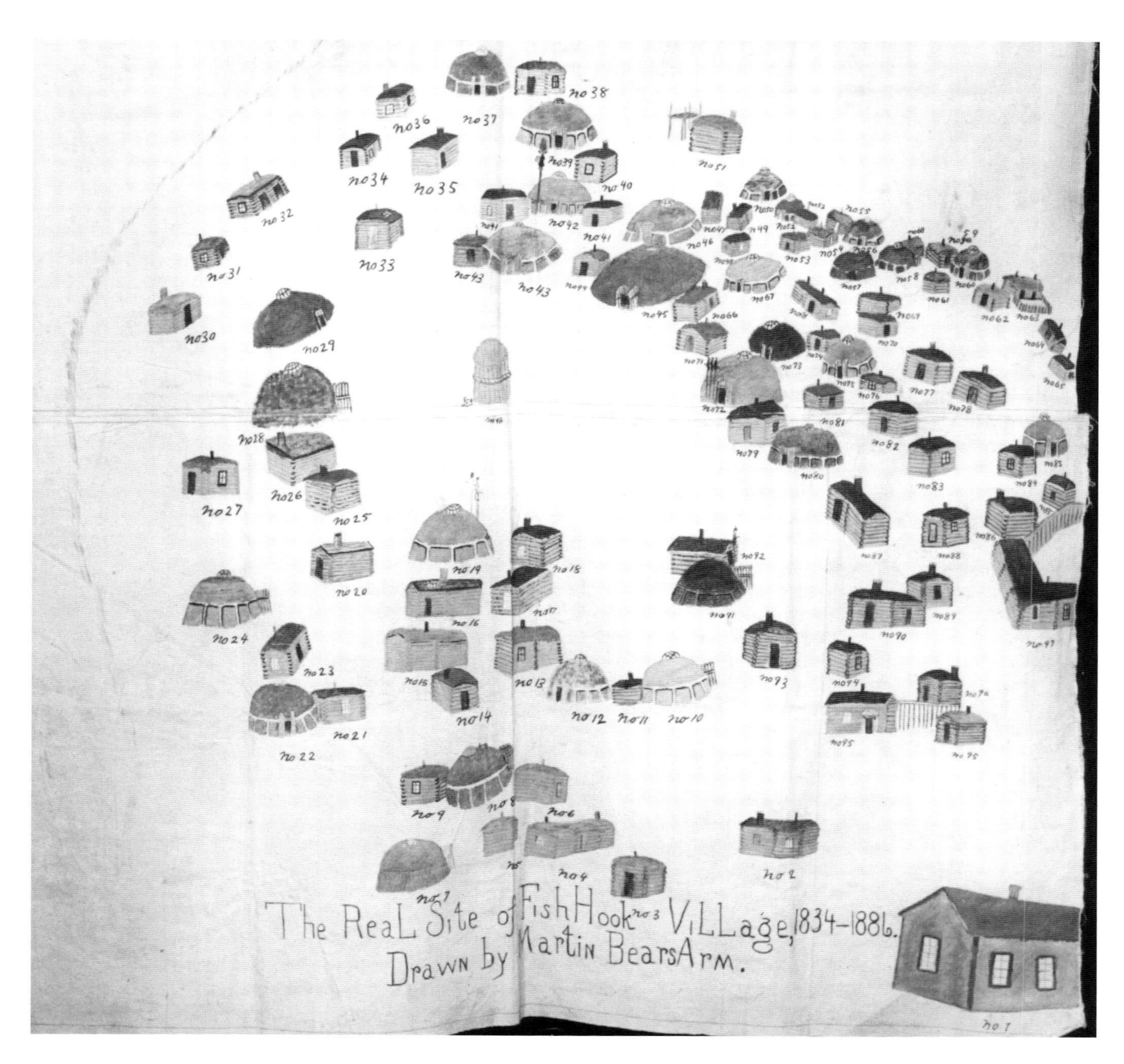

State Histl. Soc. of N. Dak., Bismarck: 799, neg. no. B-93.

Fig. 2. Pictograph of part of Like-a-Fishhook Village, Ft. Berthold Res., N. Dak., by Martin Bears Arm, Mandan, showing the Mandan and Hidatsa area of the village and the Missouri River bank, the hatched line on the left. No.1 on the lower right, government commissary, is probably a warehouse for supplies; no. 97 is the Cosier &-Shaw store and no. 98 "Lone Man Stocket [stockade] Standing on Fasting Ground" is the site of the Okipa ceremony ("Mandan," fig. 5, this vol.). The 95 numbered earthlodges and log cabins around the central plaza are residences belonging to: 2, Black Horn; 3, Wolf Ghost; 4, Big Foot Bull; 5, Buffalo Paunch; 6, Foolish Wolf; 7, Twelve; 8, Two chief; 9, Frank White Calf; 10, Bear on the water; 11, Bear on the Flat; 12, Raven Chest; 13, Water Chief; 14, Leggings; 15, Lie Pheasant; 16, Poor Wolf; 17, Spotted Bear; 18, Moccasins Carrier; 19, Bears Looks Out; 20, Scattered Village; 21, Knife; 22, Bull Against Wind; 23, Good Bear; 24, Little Shield; 25, Good Assinoboine; 26, Belly Up; 27, Gun Guarding House; 28, Crows Heart; 29, Clam; 30, Frank Tail; 31, Hawk's Blacksmith shop; 32, Hawk; 33, Goes Along Good; 34, Hard Horn; 35, Mrs. Fred Huber; 36, Joseph Packineau; 37, Bad Gun; 38, Moving Woman; 39, Cedar Wood Feather; 40, Layed Yellow; 41, Wounded Face; 42, Young Man Chief; 43, Woman in the Water House; 44, Arthur Mandan; 45, Good Worker; 46, Blue Bug; 47, Spotted Horn; 48, Bear's Necklace; 49, Bear's Tail; 50, No Milk in Breast; 51, Stands Blossom; 52, Plain Tail; 53, Foolish Heart; 54, Bad Shirt; 55, Walking Chief; 56, Jerry Black; 57, Red Cow; 58, Big Turtle; 59, Bears Ghost; 60, Foolish Chief; 61, Bears Teeth; 62, Old Bear; 63, Mrs. John Nagle; 64, Little Bull; 65, White Face; 66, Seven Bear; 67, Hairy Coat; 68, Afraid to be Chief; 69, William Belle; 70, Little Bear; 71, Son of Star; 72, Thin Shin; 73, Wolf Eyes; 74, Red Feather; 75, Dance Flag; 76, John Smith; 77, Old White Man; 78, Old Wolf; 79, Snake Cane; 80, Strikes on Back; 81, Spirit Bird; 82, Deposits his Hair; 83, Little Crow; 84, Woman Ghost; 85, Peter, an Indian Interpreter; 86, Sitting Elk; 87, Crow Breast; 88, Rabbit Head; 89, Plenty Walks; 90, Pine; 91, Moves Slowly; 92, Holding Eagle; 93, Bad Bull; 94, Mrs. Henry Weidman; 95, Charles Manouri; and 96, Beaver Head. The founding date 1834 in the caption of the drawing is a decade too early. Pencil, blue-black ink, and water-based pigments on canvas, painted at Elbowoods, N. Dak., 1912. Size 220.7 cm by 175.3 cm.

men to work for wages or to become farmers, opened small plots for the men to plant oats, corn, potatoes, beans and squashes, but getting the men to perform work that was normally done by women was difficult (Kauffman in ARCIA 1880:32). Numerous crop failures discouraged even the most willing.

Indians liked the idea of education and supported the establishment of day schools on the reservation. Indians wanted to be able to read the treaties and other documents and the government fostered schools to encourage assimilation. In 1876, Charles L. Hall, representing the American Board of Commissioners for Foreign Missions and supported by the Congregational church, arrived to begin missionary work among the three tribes. With the approval of tribal leaders, Son of the Star (Arikara), Crows Breast (Mandan), and Red Cow (Hidatsa), he built a mission house, church, and school a little way from the village. The school was well attended, but conversion was slow (Case and Case 1977; Meyer 1977:142–143).

Despite the best efforts of the agents and missionaries, the three tribes maintained their traditional languages and religious customs. In 1880 Agent Jacob Kauffman (ARCIA 1880:32–33) reported that the Indians still lived in earthlodges, used scaffold burials, and held Sun Dances. Traditional medicine was more popular than that offered by the agency physician (Cock in U.S. Census Office 1894:517), yet some leaders felt that changes were coming too fast.

Either a conflict over tribal leadership or the heavy-handed actions of agents caused Crow Flies High, a dissatisfied Hidatsa man with a distinguished war record, and his followers to leave the reservation and establish a village at Fort Buford, a U.S. Army post built in 1866 at the confluence of the Missouri and Yellowstone rivers to control the Sioux and other western tribes. The Crow Flies High band, by hunting, gardening, cutting wood for steamboats, and working for the military as scouts, messengers, and hunters, maintained a separate existence for more than 25 years and served as an escape mechanism for people who had trouble adjusting to reservation life (Malouf 1963:154).

Leaving Like-a-Fishhook

By the early 1880s Like-a-Fishhook was overcrowded, the wood supply exhausted, more room was needed for gardens and fields, and the lodges and houses needed serious repairs. The Plains tribes had been settled on reservations and the agent was able to convince the people to leave the protection of the village and take up lands in different parts of the reservation. Related families moved together to their chosen locations. The Arikara stayed in the vicinity of Like-a-Fishhook Village, establishing the community of Nishu, sometimes called Armstrong. Some Hidatsas moved to scattered farms on the east side of the Missouri, but many crossed the river, settling a community that became known as Independence. Charging Eagle and Red Butte, located south of the junction of the Little Missouri with the Missouri, were Mandan communities. By 1886 Like-a-Fishhook was deserted and the agents began agitating for a new administrative center more centrally located to the dispersed tribes, but not until a fire in 1891 burned most of the agency buildings was permission given and building started at a site called Elbowoods. A few years later the Congregational Mission moved there, too (Meyer 1977:149).

Leaving Like-a-Fishhook fit into the federal government's plans to encourage farming and ranching by dividing the reservation. In 1887 Congress passed the Dawes Severalty Act, which required that reservation lands be divided into allotments and given to individual Indians and families. Under the Act, a male head of household got 160 acres, later 320; women and orphans got smaller lots. Any land that was not given to Indians was opened for sale to non-Indians. Allotment proceeded slowly at Fort Berthold. A federal commission that visited the reservation in 1886 obtained the three tribes' agreement to reduction of the reservation and allotment of the remaining portion, but not until 1891 did Congress approve the agreement. Unlike other tribes whose unallotted lands were opened for sale to non-Indians, the agreement at Fort Berthold allowed the tribes to retain unallotted lands for 25 years in order to provide them to children born after the first distribution (Kappler 1904–1941,1:425–428). When surveying began in 1892, it was learned that Elbowoods was outside the reservation boundaries, so President Benjamin Harrison issued an executive order returning a small segment to the reservation (Meyer 1977:137). Whenever they could, people took allotments where they were living and this, accompanied by federal assistance in building houses, barns, schools, and other buildings, made the communities permanent and helped to maintain tribal distinctions. In 1894, Crow Flies High and his followers returned to the reservation and accepted allotments near Shell Creek. Because they had avoided education and other changes, the Crow Flies High band retained more of the traditional ways and served as a reservoir of knowledge for years to come. In the 1990s their descendants, known as the Little Shell people, sponsored an annual powwow and other events.

Allotment pushed the assimilation process by forcing the men to become farmers and ranchers (I.C. McLaughlin 1993). Although the lots were too small and the weather too uncertain for really successful operations, Mandan, Hidatsa, and Arikara men tried to do as the government wished. Other men, forced by the agent to find work, accepted employment as Indian police, hauled goods for the agency, and cut wood for the steamboats. Women planted home gardens and dried their produce as they had for generations.

1900 to 1934

Between 1900 and 1934 the Arikara, Hidatsa, and Mandan took on more and more outward attributes of the non-Indian culture that surrounded them. A number of children had been educated in community or mission schools and gone on to boarding schools. On their return, these people obtained jobs with the Bureau of Indian Affairs; Charles Hoffman, an Arikara, became an agent and others held other positions. Some used their knowledge to challenge the federal government's plans for selling tribal lands.

In 1902, Special Agent James McLaughlin, former Indian agent at Devils Lake and Standing Rock, arrived at Fort Berthold to negotiate the sale of 315,000 acres of unallotted land. He met stiff resistance, but, pointing out that the mood in Congress was to reduce all reservations and that the tribes had little protection, he finally got the agreement. It was never ratified and so in 1909 a new agreement, ceding most of the northeastern corner of the reservation, was made. The new agreement was ratified in June 1910, but not until 1914 was there any noticeable settlement of non-Indians on the reservation. As soon as the railroad line was set the towns of Parshall, Van Hook, and Sanish developed rapidly (Meyer 1977:160–165).

In addition to diminishing the reservation by cession, allotment made it possible for Indians to sell their lots. The Dawes Act gave allottees 25 years to become successful farmers. At the end of this time, the allottee would receive title to the land, called a fee patent, and could dispose of the land as he wished. New legislation gave Indian agents, or superintendents as they were called, authority to issue fee patents before 25 years had passed. By the time the process ended, 63,510 acres inside the reservation had passed into non-Indian ownership (Meyer 1977:168–169).

Life on the reservation combined Indian and non-Indian elements (fig. 3). Wealthier people lived in two-story frame houses, while the poor and elderly occupied log cabins. Both types of houses were furnished with goods issued by the federal government or purchased from local shops or mail order catalogs. Men wore cowboy hats, cotton shirts and pants, while women made themselves cotton dresses. Kinship relations structured social life. Even though several generations had attended school, native languages continued to be strong.

The Congregational Mission maintained a church and boarding school at Elbowoods and smaller churches in the Indian communities. The first permanent Roman Catholic mission was established in 1889 when Father Francis M. Craft built a school and church at Elbowoods. The non-Indian settlers brought other denominations, including Lutheran, Fundamentalist, and Mormonism to the reservation. Christian Indians also participated in traditional religious ceremonies.

Although the agents and missionaries opposed tribal customs and ceremonies, young people continued to attend Indian dances sponsored by societies of relatives, and non-Indian celebrations incorporated Indian traditions. Fourth of July became a time for powwows as well as an opportunity to celebrate returning veterans. Christmas took on an Indian style as people held giveaways in place of gift exchanges. Cars and improved roads made it easier for people to attend off-reservation fairs, circuses, and other non-Indian functions (Gilman and Schneider 1987).

Although they maintained distinctive languages and cultural traditions, the three tribes had shared a political identity since the Treaty of Fort Berthold in 1866. In 1910 the three tribes united in a representative form of government by members elected from the tribal communities. Called the tribal business committee in order to distinguish it from the older tribal council form of government it was supposed to act as an advisor to the agent, but lacking any substantial governing power, the committee served no real purpose (Meyer 1977:180). The presence of such a committee and familiarity with the electing process paved the way for the adoption of the Indian Reorganization Act in 1934.

Organizing the Three Affiliated Tribes

In June 1934 Congress passed the Indian Reorganization Act, ending allotment and giving tribes the opportunity to form constitutional representative governments similar to those in small non-Indian communities. At Fort Berthold, people voted 477 to 139 to accept the act and set about drawing up their constitution (T.H. Haas 1947). The Bureau of Indian Affairs provided assistance and models, but the work took more than a year. Following much discussion and revision the constitution was approved in 1936. In their new constitution, the three tribes adopted the name of The Three Affiliated Tribes of the Fort Berthold Indian Reservation. The Indian Reorganization Act also gave accepting tribes the right to incorporate themselves, and the Three Affiliated Tribes took advantage of the opportunity and drew up a charter establishing the Three Affiliated Tribes Business Council as the governing body. The charter was approved in 1937 (Meyer 1977:195–196).

Despite changes in the government, tribal life continued much as before. The federal government built more day schools, some in the older communities and new ones near other centers of population; these became community centers where people worked and socialized. World War II brought additional changes as people went off to war or participated in various war activities. Tribal members also left the reservation for jobs vacated by non-Indian men (Meyer 1977:203).

Secured by their relationship to the Missouri River, the three tribes survived migrations, smallpox epidemics, attacks by unfriendly tribes, land reduction, and federal policies aimed at assimilation, never imagining that they could lose the river, too. Beginning in the 1930s, the Army Corps of Engineers proposed flood control schemes for the Missouri and Mississippi rivers, but not until 1943 did floods and droughts raise congressional interest. Two men, Col. Lewis A. Pick of the Army Corps of Engineers and W. Glenn Sloan of the Federal Bureau of Reclamation, one oriented toward flood control and the other toward irrigation, devised plans for the Missouri. Congress, meanwhile,

top left, Minn. Histl. Soc., St. Paul: 9757-A; top right, State Histl. Soc. of N. Dak., Bismarck: C115; center left, Smithsonian, NAA: River Basin Survey 32ML41-1; center right, Marquette U. Arch., Milwaukee, Wis.

Fig. 3. Ft. Berthold during the early 20th century. top left, Mrs. Goodbird hanging meat to dry, and making "marrow butter," which is the fat from the boiled bones skimmed off. Photograph by Gilbert Wilson, 1910. top right, Group traveling to the Stark County Fair, N. Dak., 1924. Photographer not recorded. center left, Dance House, Santee Hall, between Elbowoods and Sanish, N. Dak. Although called a dance hall, it was used for many other community activities; it was last used in 1946 and was flooded by the Garrison Reservoir in 1954 (Hartle 1963:128). Photograph by George Metcalf, 1950. center right, Roman Catholic Indian Congress, Shell Creek, near Elbowoods, N. Dak. Photograph by Rev. William Hughes, 1922. bottom left, Feast at a giveaway in the Independence Congregational Church. Ruth White Owl Charging, Hidatsa (originally from the Shell Creek District), preparing to distribute food. bottom right, Pete Hale, Mandan and Hidatsa; Francis Charging, Hidatsa; Rev. H.W. Case, pastor 1922–1965; and John Goodbird, Hidatsa, at the Independence Congregational Church, N. Dak. This location was also inundated by the flooding from the Garrison Dam. bottom right and left, Photographs by Edward M. Bruner, 1951–1953.

discussed the idea of a flood control plan similar to the one in the Tennessee Valley. To forestall the third option, Pick and Sloan combined their ideas and presented their proposal to Congress, which passed it in the Flood Control Act of 1944 (Meyer 1977:211–212).

As soon as people heard of the plan to dam the Missouri, the Three Affiliated Tribes Business Council opposed it and that opposition grew. The tribe hired lawyers and asked the Bureau of Indian Affairs to help them overturn the legislation, but in 1945 the planning for restructuring the reservation began. The dam would flood most of the bottomland of the reservation, necessitating moving almost all the Indian homes, building new roads and sanitation systems, and moving or building schools, bridges, and other structures. Anthropologists found a mix of traditional and western cultures (Bruner 1953, 1955, 1956). Most people spoke both English and their ancestral language, and native values of generosity and kinship continued strong. People were very closely tied to the resources of the bottomland. Many people still lived in log cabins that they heated with wood or coal from lignite outcroppings. Women planted small household gardens, collected berries and wild plants, and men supplemented family income by hunting deer in the wooded terraces of the river. Tribal members were ill prepared for any move out of the bottomlands; they could not imagine a life away from the river (Macgregor 1949:53–55).

The protests and obvious difficulties associated with moving people and facilities resulted in 1948 in Public Law 296, which contained provisions for a payment of more than five million dollars as long as the tribe would negotiate and accept a contract to allow construction of the dam. Having done this, the tribe asked for additional compensation, and another seven million dollars was awarded in Public Law 437 (Meyer 1977:216–218). The 12 million dollars appropriated by Congress fell far short of the sum estimated by an outside consultant as appropriate (Lawson 1982:61).

The construction of Garrison Dam and the subsequent formation of Lake Sakakawea cost the Three Affiliated Tribes everything they held dear, their livelihood, homes, sacred sites, even the river itself (vol. 4:428). Ninety percent of the homes were moved out of the bottomlands into the rough tracts away from the river and many miles of water separated the sharing, cooperating relatives. Elbowoods, the reservation tribal center, combined with the non-Indian communities of Sanish and Van Hook to become New Town, tribal and agency headquarters. Due to the lack of reservation land, New Town was established off the reservation and became essentially a non-Indian town, a source of grievance for many Indian people (Meyer 1977:219–228). In 1970 the northeastern segment containing New Town was returned to the reservation, but the tribe had already built a new tribal administrative center on the reservation.

The New Reservation

After the dam was constructed, the three tribes adjusted to their new homes in various ways. Three new Indian communities, White Shield for the Arikara, Mandaree for the Hidatsa, and Twin Buttes for the Mandan, replaced those lost to the dam. These had schools, medical clinics, and community centers, but people still missed their old homes. Economically the people appeared to be worse off. A study conducted for the Economic Development Administration of the Department of Commerce reported that the major source of income was part-time employment on ranches and farms. The income was so low that more than half the population received some support from the federal government, either as welfare or by employment in government-funded work projects (Boise Cascade Center for Community Development 1972:105). The construction of Four Bears Motel and Resort complex and the development of oil and coal resources were believed to have the most potential for economic improvement.

If people were suffering socially and economically, legally they were making great strides. The skills learned fighting Garrison Dam were put to use in prosecuting claims for lands taken by the federal government, in seeking return of the northeast segment, and asserting legal rights in state and federal courts (Meyer 1977:254–255). The treaty claims resulted in financial awards, some of which were used for economic development, and the return of the northeast segment gave the tribe much-needed room for expansion as well as jurisdiction over residents in the area. At first, the non-Indians in the area opposed tribal control, but since the late 1970s, opposition has disappeared and more and more Indian people have moved into New Town and Parshall. Much earlier than most tribes, the Hidatsa at Mandaree took control of the school operated by the Bureau of Indian Affairs (Meyer 1977:256). Local control of the schools meant that the curriculum could include more Native history and culture.

In the early 1990s the reservation population was about 6,000, of whom nearly two-thirds were Indian, mainly members of the Arikara, Mandan, and Hidatsa tribes (U.S. Bureau of the Census 1993:25; Bureau of Indian Affairs 1991:table 3/1). A tribal enrollment of 8,750 in 1998 indicated that most Indian people lived off the reservation (table 1). The tribal population clustered around three small, rural, Indian communities, although others lived in non-Indian communities of New Town and Parshall or on farms and ranches scattered across the reservation. Tribal housing programs provided modern ranch-style homes, many with satellite dishes, for most tribal members. Good transportation was a necessity as many people drove long distances to conduct business at the tribal offices or to larger shopping centers in Bismarck and Minot. Children attended tribal, federally funded, and state-supported public schools. Depending on interest and availability of teachers, the community schools offered classes on ancestral

Table 1. Population at Fort Berthold Reservation, 1880–1998

Date	*Population*	*Source*
1880	1,252	ARCIA 1880:32
1890	1,183	ARCIA 1890:30
1910	1,200	U.S. Bureau of the Census 1915:15
1939	1,767	U.S. Department of the Interior 1939:5
1950	1,958	U.S. Congress. House. Committee on Interior and Insular Affairs 1953:817
1958	3,134[a]	U.S. Department of Health, Education, and Welfare, 1959:5
1972	2,750[b]	U.S. Department of Commerce 1974:427
1974	5,200[a]	Cash and Wolff 1974:87
1983	3,081[a]	Bureau of Indian Affairs 1983:table 3/1
1991	3,776[b]	Bureau of Indian Affairs 1991:table 3/1
1996	8,500[a]	Tiller 1996:491
1998	8,750[a]	John Charging, communication to editors 1998

[a]Tribal enrollment.
[b]Resident Indian population.

languages and Indian culture. The Fort Berthold Community College, New Town, offered a wide variety of vocational and academic courses aimed at preparing people for local employment or higher education. According to the 1990 federal census, the reservation had a higher percentage of college graduates living on the reservation than any other North Dakota reservation. The graduates were employed as teachers, tribal and federal administrators, lawyers, doctors, and nurses (U.S. Bureau of the Census 1993:25).

Traditional cultures and attitudes were seen more vividly in the powwows (fig. 4) and tribal ceremonies held in New Town, White Shield, Mandaree, and Twin Buttes. Each community had a group, often called a clan, but no longer strictly kinship based, that worked all year to raise money to sponsor a summer powwow. Fund-raising events were bake sales, bingo games, auctions, and special celebrations called War Bonnet Dances in which families gave away war bonnets, quilts, shawls, yard goods, money, and other items in honor of the clan members who had been chosen as officials of the powwow committee. At the ceremony, the officials, some of whom are children, wear war bonnets in the special dances that honor them and then gifts are given to friends and to the sponsoring committee and other fund-raising groups for eventual auction. The money from the auctions is used to underwrite the great expense of the summer powwow.

All four Indian communities had permanent powwow grounds where the dances were held. These grounds included an arbor or arena and places for people to camp. Some of the communities also held traditional powwows, that is without the dance competitions, but in order to attract dancers from all over the northern plains, competitions with cash prizes were held. In addition, the large powwows provided food to all the campers.

Fig. 4. Ft. Berthold Res., N. Dak. top, Indian veterans at the Flag ceremony during a powwow. front row, left to right: Ron Rabbithead, Darcy Medicine Stone, Melvin Rabbithead, Bert Flynn, Kenneth Charging, William Bell, Sr., and Dominic Silletti, from Italy married into tribe; back row, Emery Goodbird, Sr., wearing sunglasses. center, Three Tribes Museum and Arts and Craft Shop. bottom, Giveaway at a powwow. Photographs by Ilka Hartmann, 1989.

Giveaways can be held at any time, but many families choose the large summer powwows to honor someone for an accomplishment or a special event like receiving an Indian name (Parks 1991:642). During a break in the dancing the family will bring in blankets filled with gifts and, following an announcement describing the reason for the ceremony, the honored person, family, friends and relatives all circle the arena in a dance. After the dance some gifts will be given to friends and others will be given to strangers in the honoree's name.

For many Arikara, Hidatsa, and Mandan, religion is the real essence of tribal culture. Some ancient beliefs and practices like the vision quest, the sweatlodge, the use of sacred bundles and offerings to the Mandan shrine or "Ark" survived, but some bundles and the knowledge necessary to perform most ceremonies were lost. Therefore, the Three Tribes, like many others around the country, adopted the Teton Sioux–style Sun Dance (Irwin and Liebert 1996:101–102, 114).

Economically, the tribe struggled. After the dam, agriculture and ranching declined dramatically (McLaughlin 1993:484–505). The Four Bears Resort, which never really prospered, was closed and reopened as the Four Bears Casino for high-stakes gaming. Continuing economic problems formed the basis for a request to Congress for more than 140 million dollars in additional compensation for damages from the dam. The land received in exchange for the riverside land, especially that on the west side of the reservoir, had not proven good for agriculture and many of the promised compensations, such as all-weather roads, low-cost electricity, irrigation to offset poor conditions, and adequate rural and municipal water did not arrive in the 30 years following dam closure. After years of discussion, public hearings, and negotiations, in 1992 Congress awarded the Three Affiliated Tribes the interest on more than 140 million dollars to be used for economic development. Following the time-tested procedures that have enabled the three tribes to operate as a unit while maintaining distinct identities, the Joint Tribal Advisory Committee, created by the tribal Business Council, held meetings in each reservation community to determine how the money should be spent (*Mandan, Hidatsa, Arikara Times* 1997).

In adopting the name, The Three Affiliated Tribes of Fort Berthold Reservation, the Mandan, Hidatsa, and Arikara recognized the importance of maintaining separate tribal identities, even as they united for political strength. Keeping the languages and cultures alive was not easy. Intermarriage smoothed differences for some people, and the modern world offered access to non-Indian ideas that attracted many. Some of the old ways were gone forever, but others, like the sweatlodge and Sun Dance, were revived, while others, like quillworking, were increasing in popularity. By sharing administrative and political history, while maintaining separate languages, cultures, and residences, The Three Affiliated Tribes continued to flourish.

Sources

The history of the Manda, Hidatsa, and Arikara to 1975 has been summarized by Meyer (1977), but this work omits Lowie (1939), Will (1934), and Wilson (1914, 1926), cultural studies containing materials relating to the reservation period. Schneider (1989) is a brief, general history of the Hidatsa. Ladner's (1984) biography of William de la Montagne Cary includes a photograph of his oil painting *Fire Canoe at Fort Berthold* made in 1874, while Stewart, Ketner II, and Miller (1991) reproduce numerous drawings made by Carl Wimar in 1858.

Cultural studies include Hanson (1980, 1983) on kinship and residence patterns, Gilman and Schneider (1987) on the Goodbird family, Schneider (1981) on Mandan-Hidatsa giveaways, and McLaughlin (1993) on ranching. Parks's (1991) introduction to his collection of Arikara narratives describes life on the reservation and some of the stories refer to historical events and tribal life. Case and Case (1977) and Haynes (1987) describe the Congregational Mission and its role on the reservation, while Maxfield (1986) is a biography of missionaries Harold and Eva Case. Lawson's (1982) book on the impact of dams along the Missouri includes some references to Garrison Dam and Fort Berthold. A more personal view of reservation life and Garrison Dam is presented by tribal member Louis Two Ravens Irwin (Irwin and Liebert 1996).

Omaha

MARGOT P. LIBERTY, W. RAYMOND WOOD, AND LEE IRWIN

The Omaha (ˈōmə͵hä), together with the Ponca, speak a language of the Dhegiha branch of the Siouan language family.*

Origins

Oral traditions suggest that the ancestors of the Dhegiha speakers once lived on the lower Ohio River (Dorsey 1884, 1886; Fontenelle 1885; Fletcher and La Flesche 1911:37–38, 70–82). According to an Omaha migration legend, after separating from the Quapaw at the mouth of the Ohio, the remaining Dhegiha speakers traveled up the west bank of the Missouri River, following the west bank of the Mississippi. They ascended the Mississippi to the Missouri, to a peninsula marked by a high bluff where they lived together for some time. At the mouth of the Osage River the people separated into three distinct groups: the Kansa continued up the Missouri; the Osage traveled west on the Osage River; and the Omaha-Ponca crossed the Missouri where they were joined by the Iowa and together they moved toward the northwest, following the tributaries of the Des Moines River, until they reached the vicinity of the red pipestone quarry, in southwestern Minnesota (Dorsey 1884:211–212, 1886:218).

According to another version of the migration tradition, when their ancestors arrived at the mouth of the Ohio River, the Osage and Iowa crossed the Mississippi in skin boats; then a heavy fog blew over the river and the Omaha-Ponca and the Quapaw remained on the east side. The Omaha-Ponca turned north and crossed the Mississippi at the mouth of the Des Moines, while the Quapaw turned south to the Arkansas River. An Osage tradition relates that the separation of the Omaha-Ponca from the Osage and Iowa resulted from a conflict over the discovery of rich hunting grounds to the northwest of the Missouri (La Flesche 1917:460–461).

Continuing to move westward from the pipestone quarry, the Omaha-Ponca and Iowa built a fortified earthlodge village on the Big Sioux River where they lived a long time before being forced out by the Yankton Sioux. They then moved west and south to a lake near the head of Chouteau Creek, believed by some Omahas to be Lake Andes.

Eventually the Omaha-Ponca moved downriver, the Ponca (probably to this point an Omaha clan) separating as a distinct tribe and building a village near the mouth of Niobrara, while the others continued south, the Omaha building Bad Village at Bow Creek (fig. 1) and the Iowa at Aowa Creek (Dorsey 1884:212–214; Fletcher and La Flesche 1911:78–81; O'Shea and Ludwickson 1992:20–21).

History, 1673–1882

The Omaha enter written history through the explorations of Jacques Marquette and Louis Jolliet, appearing on Marquette's 1673–1674 map as the Maha (Tucker 1942:pl. V). In 1700 they were reported to be living on the banks of the Missouri River (Margry 1876–1886, 6:91). On a 1703 map they are shown northeast of the Missouri on the lower reaches of the Big Sioux or another nearby tributary (Paullin and Wright 1932:pl. 23A), as they are in 1718 (Tucker 1942:pl. XV).

When French trade expanded beyond the Great Lakes in the late eighteenth century, it initiated a century of strong Euro-American influence on Omaha life. An economy of hunting for trade as well as for subsistence developed in response to the desire for trade goods. By 1758 the Omaha were well known to French (after 1762, Spanish) traders from Saint Louis (Kerlérec in Nasatir 1952, 1:52; Smith 1974:35–37). New wealth standards prevailed, and polygyny increased in response to the need for preparing robes and skins for trade (Fletcher and La Flesche 1911:614–615). This was a period of cultural expansion, accelerated by the mid-eighteenth-century acquisition of horses, which

*The phonemes of Omaha-Ponca are: (glottal stop) ʔ; (voiced stops and affricate) *b, d, ǯ, g*; (voiceless aspirated stops and affricate) p^h, t^h, $\check{c}^h$, k^h; (voiceless tense stops and affricate) *pp, tt, čč, kk*; (glottalized stops and affricate) *ṗ, ṫ, ċ*; (voiceless spirants) *s, š, x, h*; (voiced spirants) *z, ž, γ*; (glottalized spirants) *ṡ, ṧ*; (nasals) *m, n*; (resonants) *w, ð* (retroflex and lateralized, resembling [l̩]; (oral vowels) *i, e, a, u* ([o]~[u]); (nasal vowels) *į, ą* ([ạ]~[ə̣]~[ɔ̣]~[ə]); (high pitch preceding fall) v́. Tense stops are long intervocalically and tense with a following raised pitch word-initially. This phonemic inventory follows the analysis of John E. Koontz, and words in this orthography have been phonemicized by him; unitalicized words could not be phonemicized.

In the Omaha-Ponca orthography used by Francis La Flesche, an Omaha speaker (Fletcher and La Flesche 1911), the consonant phonemes are written as follows: (glottal stop) ʼ; (voiced) b, d, j, g; (voiceless aspirated) p, t, ch, k; (voiceless tense) p (rarely bp; later p̣), t (later ṭ), ch (later c̣h), k (rarely gk; later ḳ); (glottalized) pʼ (p̣ʼ), tʼ (ṭʼ), kʼ (ḳʼ); (voiceless spirants) ç (representing dialectal [θ]), sh, x, h; (voiced spirants) ç (probably representing dialectal [ð]), zh, x; (nasals) m, n; (resonants) w, th; (oral vowels) i, e, a, u; (nasal vowels) i^n, o^n.

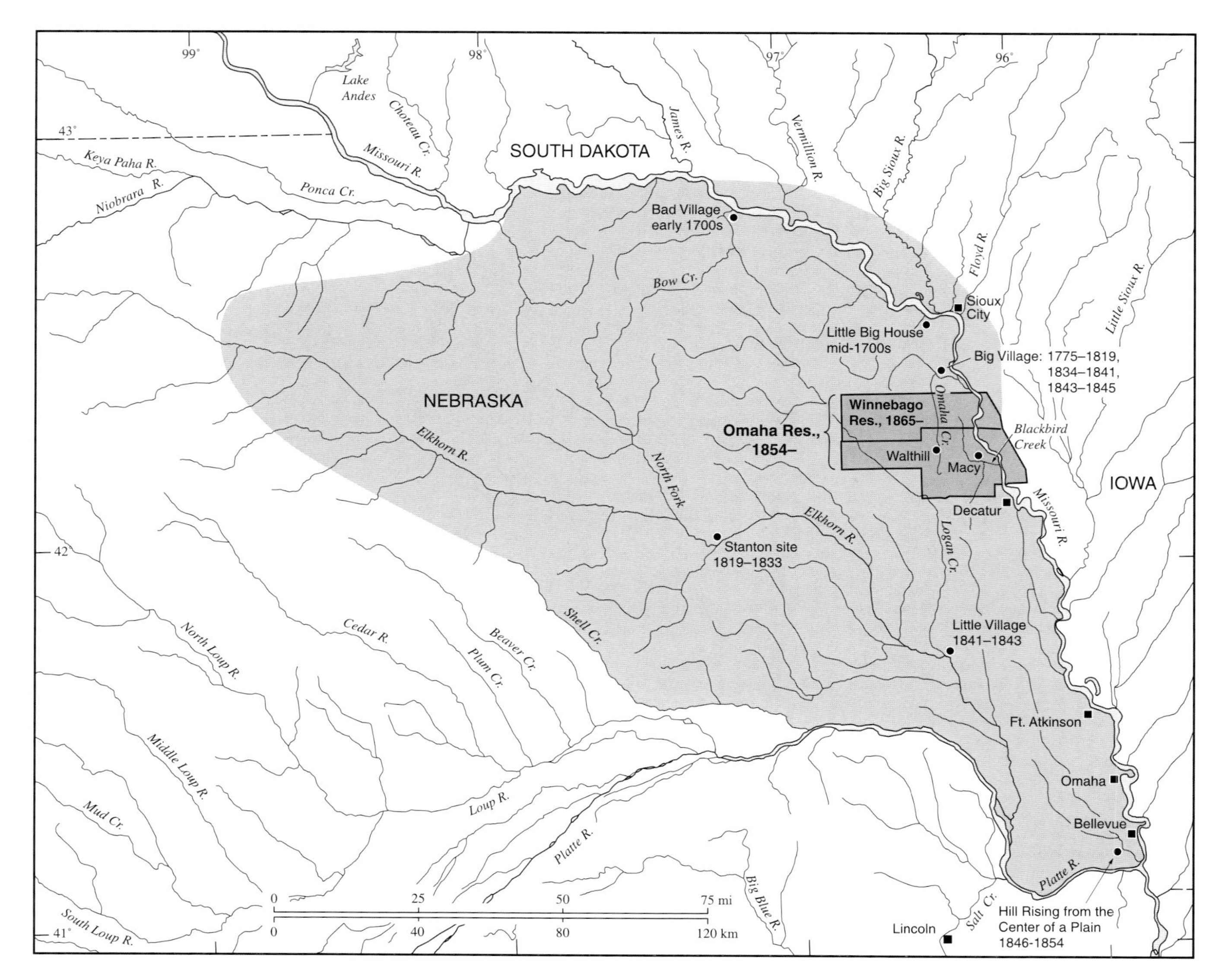

Fig. 1. Omaha territory, early 18th century to mid-19th centuries. The Winnebago Reservation was part of the Omaha Reservation until 1865.

permitted greatly increased access to the bison and an improved standard of living.

Following a series of village moves, in the early 1770s the main body of Omaha established Big Village, on Omaha Creek (fig. 1). Under the leadership of Blackbird (*wažįga sabe*), mentioned in Spanish sources in 1777 as principal chief, the Omaha successfully fought the Padoucas (Plains Apache) and the Ponca, then in the 1790s defeated both the Skiri and Kitkahahki Pawnee before themselves being defeated by the Kansa (Kinnaird 1949, 1:228; Houck 1909, 1:138–144; Long in Thwaites 1904–1907, 15:87–91). During this period Blackbird gained dictatorial control over his people, using arsenic obtained from French traders to poison his political rivals (Truteau in Parks 1992; Fontenelle 1885:78; Fletcher and La Flesche 1911:82). Prior to 1800 Blackbird failed in an attempt to poison a rival chief, Little Bow, who subsequently led over 200 followers to reoccupy the old Omaha village on Bow Creek, farther up the Missouri. In 1800–1801 the Omaha were struck by smallpox and many died, including Blackbird (Long in Thwaites 1904–1907, 14:318–319; Truteau in Parks 1992; Ludwickson 1995; Thorne 1993).

With the 1803 Louisiana Purchase, Omaha territory became part of the United States. Although Meriwether Lewis and William Clark did not meet the Omaha on their 1804 expedition up the Missouri, they visited Blackbird's grave, a landmark on the river, and described the abandoned Omaha earthlodge village sites on the Missouri (G.H. Smith 1974:89–92). At that time, according to Lewis and Clark, the surviving Omahas were living year round in tepees and hunting on the Niobrara River (Moulton 1983–, 3:399). However, they soon reestablished themselves at Big Village.

In 1814, the trader Manuel Lisa, appointed United States government subagent to the upper Missouri tribes, established Fort Hunt and married the daughter of a prominent Omaha family. As a result of this liaison, Lisa was instrumental in bringing an Omaha delegation to Portage des Sioux for a peace conference where, on July 20, 1815, the Omaha and representatives of 19 other Plains tribes signed their first treaty with the United States (James in Thwaites 1904–1907, 15:27; O'Shea and Ludwickson 1992:35; G.H. Smith 1974:102–104; Kappler 1904–1941, 2:115–116).

By 1820, divided by internal conflicts and pressured by hostilities from the Sauk and Iowa, the Omaha moved to the Elkhorn River and constructed an earthlodge village where they remained until 1833 (G.H. Smith 1974:107, 116–117; O'Shea and Ludwickson 1992:37–41). In 1821 the Omaha signed a treaty with the federal government by which they ceded an area of 15 square miles for the construction of Fort Atkinson; there in 1825 they signed another treaty of peace and friendship with the United States (G.H. Smith 1974:79–82; O'Shea and Ludwickson 1992:38–39; Kappler 1904–1941, 2:260–262). With the termination of the Black Hawk War of 1832, the Omaha under the leadership of Big Elk reestablished themselves at the Big Village site, where they lived in relative peace until they were driven out by the Teton Sioux in 1841, beginning a period of warfare of 25–30 years. In spring 1843 the Omaha returned to Big Village but in 1845 were again driven away by the Sioux, this time permanently.

The Omaha then moved their village to a site west of the Indian agency at Bellevue, Nebraska, near the mouth of the Platte River. There they remained until signing the treaty of 1854 (O'Shea and Ludwickson 1992:51).

A Baptist mission was initiated in 1837 but was unsuccessful and was withdrawn by 1839. A Presbyterian mission and school were established at Bellevue in 1845, and the first Omaha agency was established there in 1856. Under the 1854 treaty the Omaha relinquished claim to all their lands, reserving 300,000 acres about 85 miles north of Bellevue along the Missouri River. The Presbyterian mission and boarding school constructed on the reservation in 1857 had, in 1858, 31 boys and 7 girls in residence, among them Francis, Susan, and Susette La Flesche (Hoxie 1996:325–327; Diffendal 1994). By a treaty of March 1865, the Omaha sold the north part of their reservation for use as the Winnebago reservation (Fletcher and La Flesche 1911:623–627; G.H. Smith 1974:110–114; N.K. Green 1967:272–276, 280; Kappler 1904–1941, 2:611–614, 872–873).

The Omaha made a rapid adjustment to reservation life, although they continued their annual summer buffalo hunt to the west, with varying success, until 1876. During this period, three distinct Omaha communities were formed on the reservation: the Earthlodge Dwellers (*bik*^{h}*úde*) on Blackbird Creek near present-day Macy; the Make-Believe White Men (*wįjáge*), near the Presbyterian mission on a terrace above the Missouri River; and Wood Eaters (*žaδát*^{h}*e*), near the town of Decatur. The village of Make-Believe White Men was so named because its residents, under the leadership of Joseph La Flesche, began in 1857 to build houses. The name Wood Eaters apparently referred to the cutting of firewood for sale to steamboats. Although Indian agent T.T. Gillingham claimed in 1876 that these villages had been deserted, they appear to have survived until 1930 (Dorsey 1896:270–271; Fletcher and La Flesche 1911:629–633; Bureau of Indian Affairs 1967:97; Mead 1932:33; N.K. Green 1969:25).

Mus. für Völkerkunde, Berlin: A 1688.

Fig. 2. Dance, probably of a men's society, described by the artist as follows: "The head-dress was always the same, namely: a great plume of feathers; but there was scarcely two lines of a paint alike, in the whole party, consisting of thirty men. . . . placed in a semicircle, and every one took in his right hand a kind of rattle, consisting of an elegantly-cut stick, with a number of claws fastened to it, with which they accompanied the beating of the drum by four elderly warriors . . ." (Möllhausen 1858, 1:256–257). Watercolor by Heinrich Balduin Möllhausen, Bellevue, near modern-day Omaha, Nebr., 1852.

In the early 1880s a government-run industrial boarding school for boys was established. A missionary day school for girls was opened at the same time, which continued until 1894; the school was run by Margaret Wade. Wade helped to establish the Thaw Fellowship at the Peabody Museum, Harvard University, which supported Alice C. Fletcher's (vol. 4:644) anthropological studies among the Omaha (N.K. Green 1967:282).

The Omaha were deeply concerned over the security of their title to reservation lands. Although the 1865 treaty called for allotment, an 1869 attempt proved abortive (ARCIA 1869:344). With Fletcher's energetic support, congressional legislation was passed on August 7, 1882, by which every individual Omaha was to be allotted a parcel of land; this was the prototype for the Dawes Severalty Act of 1887. Each head of a family received 160 acres, those unmarried or orphans received 80 acres, and those under 18, 40 acres. In assigning allotments, Fletcher also registered each household by name and kin relationship. After 25 years the land was to be released under fee patents to individuals (Kappler 1904–1941, 1:213; Fletcher 1885b:661; Fletcher and La Flesche 1911:636–641; N.K. Green 1969:56–81; Mark 1988:38–39).

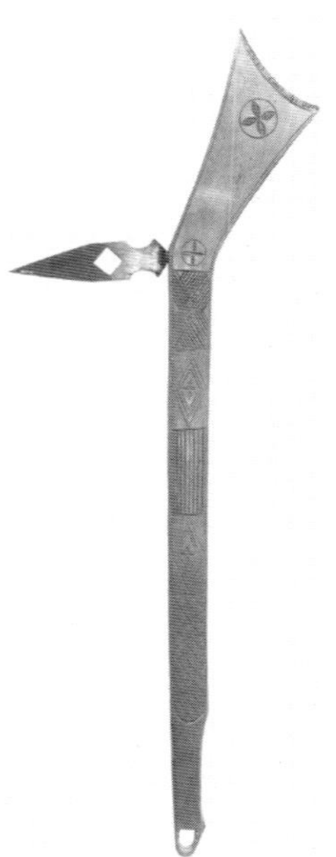

left, Rochester Mus. and Science Center, N.Y.: 66.132.16; right, Smithsonian, Dept. of Anthr.: 23729.

Fig. 3. Omaha leaders. left, Part of the delegation of 1852. back row, Louis Sanssoucci, mixed-blood interpreter, and 2 wives of Yellow Smoke. The men in the front row are unidentified, but the complete list of delegation members is given by Scherer (1997:119). Three men in the front row wear fingerwoven turbans. The man, third from left, with the upright feather headdress also wears multiple brass neck rings (O'Shea and Ludwickson 1992:190) and holds a gunstock warclub.

The delegation left Council Bluffs in Sept. 1851, supporting themselves by putting on exhibitions in cities on the way (R.D. Johnson 1961:156–173). They reached Washington on Jan. 21, 1852, met with President Millard Fillmore on Feb. 2, and returned home in March (Wheeling and Johnson 1852). Their purposes were to request federal help against raids by other tribes and to obtain agricultural assistance. Daguerreotype possibly made in Washington, Feb. 1852, one of the earliest known images of the Omahas. right, Gunstock warclub. Handle is made of wood and painted in zigzag lines. The head contains a painted blade of steel, from which a square portion has been cut out. Collected by Paul Beckwith, 1876. Length 79 cm.

Although land allotment was designed to effect assimilation of the Indians with their non-Indian neighbors, it failed for a number of reasons. In a communally based society, it was unacceptable for families to live on individual allotments isolated from one another. For Omaha men, whose only previous horticultural labor had been helping women relatives clear small patches of bottomland for gardens, breaking the tough prairie sod was decidedly distasteful. Moreover, the capital required to finance rapidly modernizing farming methods was never available. The early allottees quickly discovered that leasing land to non-Indian settlers was much more attractive than attempting to work it themselves.

Culture in the Nineteenth Century

Omaha life changed sharply after the summer bison hunts ended in 1876. Ethnologists began in the 1870s and 1880s to record Omaha recollections of their traditions (Dorsey 1884, 1890; Fletcher and La Flesche 1911). The material they published characterizes the period from about 1800, when the Omaha reached their peak as traders on the Missouri, to 1854, when White settlers began to impinge on the Omaha home country.

Structures

The dual adaptation to gardening and bison hunting was clearly reflected in the three kinds of Omaha housing: earthlodges, characteristic of Plains village peoples; bark- or mat-covered lodges, which were sometimes constructed during the summer; and buffalo-hide tepees, constructed on a four-pole foundation, used during the buffalo hunts when the camp circle was formally arranged to reflect moiety and clan membership (Dorsey 1896:269–273).

Earthlodges (fig. 4) were circular, earth-covered structures supported by posts set around a central hearth with a covered entryway projecting toward the east. These were constructed by both men and women, the men marking out the site and cutting the logs. The sod was stripped off, the floor tamped and flooded with water, then dried grass was burned on it to harden the surface. Women owned the earthlodge and its furnishings (James in Thwaites 1904–1907, 14:306). Each lodge had an underground cache for food, pelts, and extra clothing. These earthlodges lacked the complex symbolism of the Arikara or Pawnee, from whom the technology of building them was borrowed (Dorsey 1896:269; Fletcher and La Flesche 1911:75, 97–98; O'Shea and Ludwickson 1992:71–74).

Smithsonian, NAA: 4039.

Fig. 4. Section of a village with earthlodge, tepees, and storage racks in view. Typical prairie landscape is evident in the foreground (Kinsey 1996:70). Photograph by William H. Jackson, 1868.

Earthlodges were the preferred dwellings until about 1830, when they were in part replaced by tepees, which were displaced by log cabins and frame houses during the reservation period. Earthlodges were used only in the spring and fall, when activity in the gardens was at its height. A few survived as late as World War I (Welsch 1981:5).

Subsistence

The subsistence pattern of the Omaha followed an annual cycle, alternating between hunting and gardening. In April, the people returned to the earthlodge village from their winter hunting trips. In May, they planted crops and tanned winter robes and skins for trade. In late June, nearly everyone cached important possessions and abandoned the village and its gardens for the summer hunt. In September they returned to harvest green corn, and other crops were harvested into October. After caching garden surplus, the village was abandoned again, people scattering to trade and hunt game locally. About the beginning of January they returned to the village to procure supplies from their caches, then departed on the tribal winter hunt for bison robes, returning to the village in April (James in Thwaites 1904–1907, 14:289–312).

Hunting thus served two economic ends: subsistence and trade. Both included dependence on a variety of game. Deer, elk, antelope, and bear were killed throughout the year. Both men and women participated in fishing using various methods, including spears and willow weir traps (Fletcher and La Flesche 1911:312). Bison provided the staple food and were stalked by individual hunters during the fall and winter. The communal hunts were under the direction of four men, one of whom was appointed the *waðą́* 'hunt leader', a position of high honor. The hunt leader's religious duties included eating little, living apart from his family, and continual prayer for the success of the hunt; he also led the council at the time of the hunt and assigned various tasks. He directed the journey to the herd, selected camping places, and dispatched runners to find the buffalo.

Every able-bodied person participated in the communal hunts. After locating the buffalo, conformity was enforced by the *waną́še* 'soldiers' appointed by the principal chiefs. The herd was approached in four stages under the direction of the keeper of the White Buffalo Hide and the hunt leader. Prayers and smoke offerings were made for success. The hunters were led to the buffalo by two young men, one carrying the pipestem and the other the ceremonial staff (*wašábe*) of the White Buffalo Hide tepee, a crooked staff with a banner of feathers. After these two had ritually circled the herd the hunt began, and the two young men were required to gather 20 hearts and tongues to be used in a ceremony that honored both the buffalo and the corn (Dorsey 1884:286–293; Fletcher and La Flesche 1911:155, 276–283).

Gardening was carried out cooperatively by men and women. Plots ranged from one-half acre to two or three acres. The principal subsistence crop was corn, which was ritually referred to as "mother" because it nourished the people. Gardens along stream bottoms were planted in separate mounds of corn, beans, squash, and melon. Crop mounds were hoed and then weeded by hand until the corn was a foot high, when they were hoed again. The gardens were usually abandoned between the second hoeing and harvest time. Ritual surrounding the crops included the distribution of sacred kernels of red seed corn by certain members of the Black Shoulder clan to the women of each lodge and the singing of a corn ritual. The Omaha may have first obtained corn from the Arikara, whose corn origin legend was preserved by the Omaha. Corn was a staple food but apparently became less important after large-scale bison hunting began, with its heavy demands upon female labor for tanning (Fletcher and La Flesche 1911:76–78, 261–270). In years of poor bison hunting, other foods were gathered, stolen, or bought, including Mormon cattle in 1846–1847 and supplies obtained through a $5,000 annuity established in 1852 (Ludwickson 1988).

Peabody Mus. of Salem, Mass.: E53449, neg. A6943.

Fig. 5. Quilled buckskin pouch with animal motifs in orange, black, yellow, and white dyed porcupine quills. Design and technique of manufacture are typical of those in the late 18th and early 19th centuries. The pouch was decorated with three Underwater Panthers, powerful mythological creatures (Maurer 1977:155). Collected in Nebr.; length 23.5 cm.

Technology

Material culture was heavily influenced by European trade in the nineteenth century. Native manufacture of many items was abandoned: pottery, for example, was not made after about 1800. Stone and bone tools became less important, except for ceremonial use; porcupine quill ornamentation (fig. 5) gave way to beadwork; and cloth was used in place of hides for clothing. Canvas tepee covers appeared about 1850. Despite innovations, Omaha material culture retained many native items for years, especially those used in religious contexts and transportation (fig. 6). Pipes used in ceremonies were of three types: sacred pipes, including the two tribal pipes used for making peace (fig. 7 top) and the two war pipes; the two adoption pipes or calumets used in the *wáwą* ceremony (fig. 7 bottom); and the seven pipes representing the clans. Catlinite pipes and metal hatchet pipes, acquired through trade, were used for ordinary smoking (Dorsey 1896:279–280; Fletcher 1885a:616). Plain and sinew-backed bows, arrows with metal tips, war clubs, shields, and musical instruments were all produced during the nineteenth century (Dorsey 1896:269–288; Fletcher and La Flesche 1911:612–617).

Nearly all precontact needs could be made from raw materials available from nearby sources. However, expeditions were made to obtain salt along Salt Creek, near present-day Lincoln, Nebraska, and pipestone from the catlinite quarries in southwestern Minnesota (Fletcher and La Flesche 1911:342). Traditional clothing, made of buckskin, included men's leggings and shirts; women's tunics, in early historical times reaching below the knees, but later shortened and worn over a skirt; and soft-soled moccasins and robes, which were worn by both sexes (Fletcher and La Flesche 1911:354–360).

Social Organization

Omaha society was structured into moieties, each composed of five patrilineal clans (*ttą́wągδą* 'villages'). The Sky moiety was symbolically male, while the Earth moiety was symbolically female (table 1). During the summer, tepees were pitched to reflect this social order in the camp circle (*húδuga*), which opened in the direction of tribal movement. When moving eastward and during tribal ceremonies, the north half of the circle consisted of the sky clans, while the south half consisted of the earth clans. Each clan was divided into subclans, and the clans of each moiety were linked by mythical association to founding ancestors. The four subclans of the *δáttada* clan were particularly well developed, had their own assigned places in the camp circle, and were comparable in the size to the other clans (Dorsey 1884:220, 1897:226–228; Fletcher 1896:458; Fletcher and La Flesche 1911:134–141; Barnes 1984:74–77).

The duality of Omaha social organization was further symbolized by two sacred tribal pipes. Both were flat stemmed with red stone bowls; one stem was plain with seven woodpecker heads representing the seven chiefs of the governing council; the other stem was decorated with porcupine quillwork and had one woodpecker head representing the unified authority of the chiefs' council (Fletcher and La Flesche 1911:135, 207).

left, Nebr. State Histl. Soc., Lincoln: I394-156; right, Smithsonian, Natl. Mus. of the Amer. Ind.: 20/1381.

Fig. 6. Horse transportation and equipment. left, Woman with horse travois set up to carry a small child. The horse has a decorated rawhide case and fringed, beaded knife scabbard visible. The woman, wearing a skirt with ribbonwork hem, holds a blanket with floral beadwork designs. Her blouse also has ribbonwork and beaded decorations. Photograph by Nathaniel Lee Dewell, probably Omaha, Nebr., 1922. right, Crupper decorated with brass buttons and tacks, red strouding, and blue, white, and black beads. Collected by De Cost Smith before 1939; length 73 cm.

Functions of the clans included exogamous marriage regulation and specific religious and ceremonial functions. Each clan had a stock of personal names used for clan members, and each had taboos on the consumption or use of specific clan-related items (Fortune 1932:16). For example, many of the names of the Elk clan related to the elk, such as Dark Breasted and Standing Elk. Members could not eat the flesh of the bull elk or wear elkskin moccasins.

Within each clan, three classes of men were recognized: the chiefs (*nįkkagahi*), the leaders who made all important decisions affecting the entire tribe; the soldiers or braves (*wanąše*), mature men who acted as police during the buffalo hunts and were messengers for the chiefs; and the commoners (*šénužįga* 'young men'), those who had not distinguished themselves (Dorsey 1884:216–217).

Political Organization

A man who became a chief had a record of success in warfare and of generosity. He made prescribed gifts to the highest-ranking chiefs, which they used in turn to fulfill the obligations of generosity expected of chiefs. A man was first elected to the ranks of lesser (*xúde* 'brown') chiefs; when a vacancy occurred by death or retirement, he might be elevated to the rank of *šábe* 'dark' chief, a term that signified a silhouetted image raised above others as seen against the skyline. A chief inducted into either grade accepted the office for life unless he resigned (Fletcher and La Flesche 1911:202–206). The induction ceremony culminated in the ritual tattooing of a virgin female relative of the new chief, bestowing on her "the mark of honor," a small round spot on the forehead representing the sun and a larger four-pointed star on the chest, just below the throat. Such women were honored throughout life (Fletcher 1893:449; Fletcher and La Flesche 1911:503–509). O'Shea and Ludwickson (1992a) have demonstrated that chieftainship was hereditary.

There were chiefs in every clan, but there was no clan council of chiefs, nor did clans act independently of one another except for an occasional buffalo hunt. Authority within the clan belonged to those chiefs who had given the greatest number of gifts, were in charge of sacred rites, or who had acted as soldiers during the communal hunts. Chiefs of the lower division could be elected to lead a buffalo hunt; they also had the authority to approve war parties, to hold adoption ceremonies, to use the sacred pipes to stop tribal conflicts, and to send out scouts in cases of danger (Dorsey 1884:362).

Chiefs of the upper division were required to pass through seven grades represented by seven specific gifts before being eligible to join the council of seven chiefs. Members of the council served for life or until voluntary retirement. According to Omaha tradition, this council dated back to the time when the sacred pole was acquired and involved the giving of seven pipes, one each to seven of the 10 clans. By the late nineteenth century, only two of these pipes were recognized and were in the care of the Pipe Keeper subclan of the Black Shoulder clan. These two pipes represented the two principal chiefs, the highest office, consisting of two outstanding chiefs chosen from the council of seven (Fletcher and La Flesche 1911:202–209; O'Shea and Ludwickson 1992a).

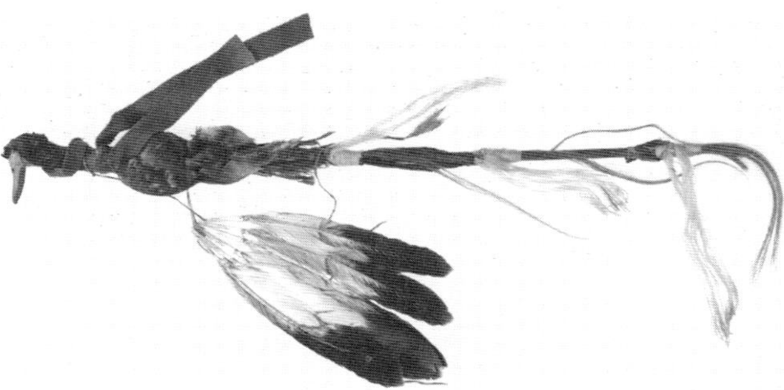

top, Harvard U., Peabody Mus., Cambridge, Mass: N711; bottom, Smithsonian, Dept. of Anthr.: 358698, neg. 88-14677.

Fig. 7. Ceremonial pipestems. top, George Miller (left) and unidentified man demonstrating manner in which the Omaha pipes of fellowship would have been used. These sacred items were returned to the Omaha in 1989. Photograph probably by Pembrooke Marshall and Francis T. Gilling, Washington, D.C., 1886–1887. bottom, One of the 2 ceremonial adoption pipestems used in the *wáwą* ceremony, which encouraged peaceful relations between unrelated groups by establishing a ceremonial tie equivalent to that between a father and a son. This pipestem, which was not functional as a smoking pipe, was made from a bored length of ash and decorated with owl, eagle, and duck feathers, bands of buckskin, and horsehair streamers. On the end of the stem was stretched the head, neck, and breast of a mallard. Collected by Victor J. Evans before 1931; length 91.4 cm.

The two principal chiefs, one from each moiety, were sanctified in their office by the sacredness of the pipes. The council of seven was the highest governing body among the Omaha. Joining them in council in an advisory capacity were the keeper of the two sacred pipes, the keeper of the

Table 1. Omaha Social Divisions

Earth moiety *hą́gašenu* 'leader boys'
wéžįšte 'angry ones' (Elk clan)
įk^h*ésabe* 'black shoulder(ed)' (a Buffalo clan)
hą́ga 'leader' (a Buffalo clan)
δáttada 'on the left (side)'
wasábehit^h*aži* 'they don't touch black bear hides' (Bear people)
wažį́ga δat^h*áži* 'they don't eat (small) birds' (Bird people)
tteppá' it^h*aži* 'they don't touch buffalo heads' (Eagle people)
kké?į 'carrying a turtle on their backs' (Turtle people)
khą́ze 'Kansa' (Wind clan)
Sky moiety *įštásąda* 'flashing eyes'
mąδį́kkagaγe 'earth lodge maker' (Coyote and Wolf clan)
ttesį́de 'buffalo tail' (a Buffalo Calf clan)
ttappá 'deer head' (referring to the Pleiades; Deer clan)
įgδéžide 'red dung' (a Buffalo Calf clan)
įštásąda 'flashing eyes' (Reptile and Thunder clan)

NOTE: Sources differ in detail on clan names and subdivisions. Dorsey (1884:219–251) is followed here; cf. Fletcher and La Flesche (1911:134–198) and Barnes (1984:50–67). Phonemic retranscriptions are from Dorsey and retranslations by John Koontz.

Nebr. State Histl. Soc., Lincoln: I394-165.

Fig. 8. Woman with baby in hammock. Photograph by Nathaniel Lee Dewell, probably 1922.

pipe-filling ritual, and the keepers of the three sacred tepees. These were the highest ceremonial positions (Fletcher 1893:444–449; Fletcher and La Flesche 1911:208).

The powers of the chiefs' council included the right to order soldiers to punish disobedience, to appoint public heralds, to appoint those worthy of the honor of serving at feasts, to determine membership in the upper division of chiefs, and to elect those qualified to join the chiefs' council (Dorsey 1884:362). Decisions made by the council had to be unanimous. Their unity was symbolized by the sacred pole, and decisions were regarded as having religious authority because they were ratified by making smoke offerings with the two tribal pipes. The most important function of all chiefs was to maintain tribal harmony and peace. An individual who defied the authority of the chiefs could be executed by being stabbed with a poisoned ironwood staff kept in the Sacred War tepee, if so decided by the chiefs' council. Chiefs also punished theft, adultery, and murder (Fletcher and La Flesche 1911:209–216).

Life Cycle

• BIRTH A ceremony was performed for both male and female infants on the eighth day after birth, when a priest of the Flashing Eyes clan consecrated the child to the tribe. A prayer was addressed to the powers of the heavens, air, and earth, which sought protection for the child's journey through life. A baby name was given to the child by an elder male of his clan, who chose a name not presently used by any living person (Fletcher and La Flesche 1911:115–116; Fletcher 1897:254–255). After a child could walk, at three or four years of age, a second ceremony was held known as Turning the Child, which was also conducted by members of the Flashing Eyes clan. This ceremony took place in a consecrated tepee where the child was lifted and turned to the four directions, and was given new moccasins. The child's baby name was discarded in favor of a name belonging to his clan, which he alone used during his lifetime (Fletcher and La Flesche 1911:117–122). Later, in the Hair Cutting ceremony, dedicated to war, a boy was consecrated to the Thunder and had his hair cut in the distinctive symbolic pattern of his clan (fig. 9) until he was seven or eight years old (Fletcher and La Flesche 1911:122–129; Fletcher 1888:116–117).

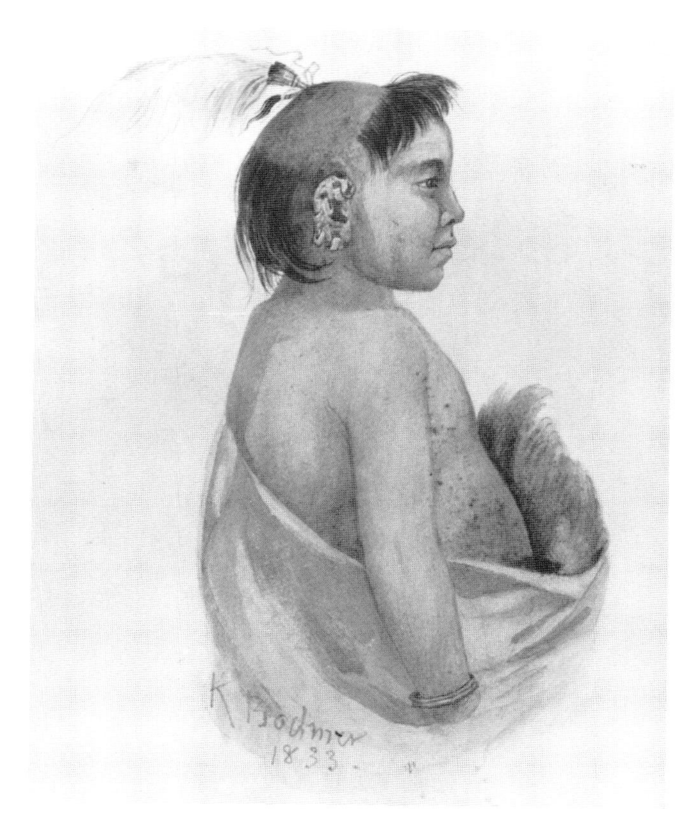

Newberry Lib., Chicago.

Fig. 9. Young boy with hair cut in style that identified his kin group. From ages 2–8 such hairstyles were worn by the male children. The boy's face was painted with vermillion by his father for this portrait. He wears multiple metal earrings. Watercolor by Karl Bodmer, near Bellevue near modern-day Omaha, Nebr., May 4, 1833.

• PUBERTY At puberty, boys (and sometimes girls) engaged in the vision quest, called *nąžį́žą* 'to stand sleeping'. Four days and nights of solitary fasting and prayer were expected, during which time a vision was sought. The faster, with clay on his head, hands raised, and shedding tears, prayed for aid and guidance. The successful supplicant received a vision with an accompanying song or animal call. After returning to the village, the vision seeker spoke and ate very little for four days. Then he sought out an elder known to have had a similar vision, told him of his experience, and received instructions on how to use the power given to him (Fletcher and La Flesche 1911:128–132).

Some visions were considered lucky: the hawk gave aid in warfare; the bear, recuperative power. Visions obtained at puberty conferred a life-long personal relation with sacred powers. Hunting and war power were frequently granted, but doctoring power was considered the most prestigious because it brought long life, immunity from sickness, and wealth in curing fees. There were three degrees of power based on the type of vision: animals gave protection from danger; a cloud or human being with eagle wings gave the additional ability to foresee future events; and a voice alone, with no physical form, gave both of the preceding together with the ability to foretell the coming of death (La Flesche 1889:3). Sometimes a vision carried predictive power: for example, dreaming of a woman's burden strap meant that a boy was to become a transvestite. Membership in many religious societies depended upon a vision of a particular object, animal, or type of power. A man could transfer his vision power to his son by verbal instruction, but this transfer divested the original visionary of all protection and was believed to precipitate his death (Fletcher and La Flesche 1911:128–133; Fortune 1932:37–43).

• MARRIAGE Marriage and family life were closely bound up with the clan system. Clan exogamy was practiced, and marriages between moieties were considered ideal, although many marriages took place within the moiety (Fletcher and La Flesche 1911:135; Fortune 1932:14 Barnes 1984:187). Polygyny was practiced, although few men had more than two wives (Fletcher and La Flesche 1911:326). Marriage to the brother or sister of a deceased spouse was obligatory. Formal courtship generally took place in the spring. While chastity for women before marriage was highly honored, it was not rigidly enforced. Some marriages were arranged formally, usually between a young woman and an established older man. After the family of the bride received valuable gifts, they dressed her in her best clothing, mounted her on a pony, and four elder men of her clan escorted her to the lodge of the groom. Most marriages took place through elopement, which was confirmed when the couple returned to the lodge of the husband's father, where a feast was held and gifts were exchanged between the two families. The couple then returned to the lodge of the wife's mother, where the new husband was expected to work for his father-in-law for a year or two. All cohabitation constituted marriage and adultery was a punishable offense. Divorce was common, and the children, as well as the home with its property, remained with the wife (James in Thwaites 1904–1907, 15:11–14; Dorsey 1884:259–261; Fletcher and La Flesche 1911:313, 318–327).

• DEATH After a death, relatives expressed their grief in loud wailing. The immediate family stripped themselves of all adornments and cut their hair short; older women gashed their legs. The corpse was dressed and painted according to social position or rank. A society member's sacred objects would be placed in his hands. When a highly respected individual died, young men performed a piercing ceremony in which willow sticks were thrust through the skin of their upper arms to express their sympathy for the mourners.

After several days, the body was taken in an informal procession to a shallow grave, where it was interred facing the east. A man's weapons and a woman's work bag were placed with the body. A split log or bark roof, supported at either end by two crotched poles, was built over the grave; the whole was covered with grass, tamped earth, and sod, forming a burial mound. Society insignia were suspended from a pole at the head of the grave, and a favorite horse might be strangled over the mound. By the late nineteenth century, interment was generally replaced by scaffold burial.

Mourning might continue for a year, and a wife might give away most of her possessions and live alone. Both men and women might go out at night to mourn with others on the outskirts of the village (La Flesche 1889:8–10; Fletcher and La Flesche 1911:592–594; Morgan 1959:88, 91; James in Thwaites 1904–1907, 15:26, 66–68).

Kinship

Omaha kinship terminology was fitted to the patrilineal descent groups. Terms for father and mother were extended to father's brothers and mother's sisters, while father's sisters and mother's brothers were called aunt and uncle. Parallel cousins were called brother and sister; but patrilateral cross cousins were grouped with nephews and nieces, while matrilateral cross cousins were grouped with mothers and uncles. The children of anyone called uncle were in turn called uncle and mother, continuing through the descending generations, even though the individuals so classified were considerably younger than the speaker. The effect was to organize relationships according to lineage and clan, rather than age and generation (Barnes 1984:124–154).

Religion

Religion permeated Omaha life. The world was seen as being guided by Wakanda (*wakką́da*), the powerful, mysterious and invisible reality to whom prayers were offered and from whom power and guidance were sought. The term *wakką́da* was also used for any new, strange or excessive demonstration of ability and as a general form of address to both individual sacred powers and to all powers together, as well as to elder shamans. The term *xubé* 'holy' referred to individuals or objects that were believed to be endowed with sacred power or properties in contrast to those with little or no such power. This term was most frequently used when referring to medicine bundles and the objects within them (James in Thwaites 1904–1907, 15:51; Dorsey 1894:366–367, 372; Fletcher and La Flesche 1911:597–599; Fletcher 1912). Other general concepts of the sacred included nonka 'supernatural punishment for the infraction of ceremonial rules or for improper behavior'; and *bδą́* 'odor', a supernatural power emanating from all sacred things and persons, whose influence might be for good or evil (Fortune 1932:29–34).

There was a dual division of the above and below powers. The above was masculine and associated with the sacred powers of day, sky, and sun. The below power was feminine and associated with sacred powers of night, earth, and moon. Human beings were first created from the union of earth and sky. A tradition of the Pebble society was that human beings were once spirits that first tried to live on the sun and moon, but as neither of these was a good home, they descended to earth. Other prominent powers were the Four-Headed Horses, messengers of the Sun; the Four Winds, whose messengers were the Thunderbird or eagle; and the Morning Star. All the sacred powers were addressed in morning prayers (Dorsey 1894:372; Fletcher and La Flesche 1911:134–135, 570; Fortune 1932: 48–49).

Omaha cosmology was encoded in the duties and rights of the moiety. The five Earth clans of the southern half of the tribal circle were responsible for those rites related to the provision of food, shelter, and protection from enemies. The five Sky clans of the northern half were responsible for the rites associated with the celestial powers pertaining to the stages of life. The Earth and Sky cosmology was also expressed in the complex symbolism of the adoption pipes used in the *wáwą* ceremony (Fletcher and La Flesche 1911:194–198, 376–377).

Sacred bundles were central to Omaha religious life. Some were personal bundles, received by an individual in a vision; some belonged to the secret societies; and others belonged to the individual clans. The most prominent of the clan bundles were those housed in the three sacred tepees, whose efficacy worked for the good of the entire tribe; they were the visible symbols of Omaha religion, especially during the summer hunt when these lodges were pitched within the tribal camp circle. The sacred tepees were objects of fear, and anyone who accidentally touched one of them was required to be ritually purified to forestall disaster. Society and clan bundles were cared for by keepers, who knew their rites, songs, and prohibitions. Keepers were members of designated lineages within each clan. All bundles were fed and renewed in the spring at the first sound of thunder (Dorsey 1894:413–416; Fletcher and La Flesche 1911:221, 595; Fortune 1932:164–165).

The Sacred War tepee held the most important of the five war bundles (*waʔį́waxube* 'sacred bundle'), only three of which were preserved into the late nineteenth century. All were used to insure success in warfare. The bundle of the Sacred War tepee, cared for by the Elk clan, contained two round-stemmed war pipes. The Sacred War tepee also housed a sacred cedar pole associated with the war power of Thunder, who was said to live in a forest of cedars and whose manifestation was lightning. This pole served as the prototype of the pole kept in the Sacred Pole tepee. The bundles received their power from Thunder as represented by the bird skins kept within them (Dorsey 1884:319–320; Fletcher and La Flesche 1911:218–219, 229, 403–416, 452–458).

The White Buffalo Hide tepee was one of the two sacred tepees of the *hą́ga* clan, each in the care of a family from different subclans. Keepers of the White Buffalo Hide bundle (*ttesą́ha* 'white buffalo skin') were responsible for the construction and care of the *wašábe* staff that symbolized the office of the hunt leader. Two White Buffalo Hide bundles were said to have existed in the early nineteenth century, made from male and female buffalo hides. Songs of the bundles memorialized the creation of the buffalo, the gift of the sacred disk pipe used for prayer offerings, and the 12 stages of a successful buffalo hunt. The rites were carried out to insure that the buffalo would perpetuate themselves (Fletcher and La Flesche 1911:154–155, 276, 284–309).

The second of the *hą́ga* clan sacred tepees was that of the Sacred Pole (*waxðéγe* 'that which is marked'), which contained the pole first made during the period of tribal reorganization. This pole, similar in construction to the cedar pole in the Sacred War tepee, was made of cottonwood and a small piece of ash. In form it represented a man and symbolized tribal unity and the authority of the council of seven chiefs. The pole was topped by a human scalp. The Sacred Pole bundle, containing a long-stemmed keel pipe, was opened for the Anointing the Pole ceremony, held after the fourth successful buffalo hunt of the summer. A very large semicircular tepee was constructed, and the Sacred Pole was propped up while songs were sung and a symbolic altar was prepared by cutting into the earth and removing the sod. Four grass images of men, representing the enemy, were charged at and captured by the warriors, who then enacted their brave deeds in battle (Dorsey 1884:234–235; Fletcher 1896a; Fletcher and La Flesche 1911:217–251).

The *hédewač^hi*, the Omaha equivalent of the Sun Dance, followed the ceremonies of the Sacred Pole. This four-day rite, which celebrated the successful hunt as well as the growth of the corn, was sponsored by a man who wished to increase his social standing and candidacy for chief. Under the direction of the keeper of the rite, who was a member of the Black Shoulder clan, a woman bearing the mark of honor tattoos ritually struck a cottonwood tree, which was then cut down and brought to the camp, painted with red and black bands signifying day and night, and planted upright, usually in the center of the camp circle. On the final day of the ceremony, the two sacred tribal pipes were carried around the center pole in a dance of thanksgiving (Fletcher and La Flesche 1911:251–260).

The *wáwą* 'to sing for someone' ceremony focused upon peacemaking, one man ceremonially adopting another from a different clan or tribe. The four-day ceremony culminated in a procession to the lodge of the man being adopted where the *wáwą* bundle, wrapped in a wildcat skin, was opened and the two feathered pipestems and two ears of corn were removed. These ritual objects involved complex symbolism representing sky and earth, male and female. The pipestems were danced and waved over the head of a child selected by the man being adopted; both this man and the child became ritual sons to the "father" who adopted them. A lavish gift exchange concluded the ceremony. The pipes were also used to end quarrels (Dorsey 1884:276–282; Fletcher 1893:449–454; Fletcher and La Flesche 1911:376–401).

Warfare

The culture hero *ištínik^he*, the trickster, was believed to have taught the Omaha their war-related rites and practices. Two types of warfare were recognized: *ttíadi* 'at the dwellings' or *waʔų́ʔattaðišą* 'tending to women', referred to defensive actions taken against an attacking enemy, and *núʔattaðišą* 'tending to men', referred to the aggressive actions of a war party away from the village.

Because chiefs were bound to use their influence for peace, they could not initiate war parties. It was generally a younger man who did so by going to one of the keepers of a war bundle, usually to the keeper of the Sacred War tepee, to invite him to a ceremonial feast. This was repeated four times while the keeper instructed those making up the war party in the proper behavior. Obtaining the authority of a war bundle keeper relieved the leader of responsibility should a member of the party be killed. There were two classes of aggressive war parties, those undertaken to secure goods and horses, and the more highly esteemed revenge parties.

left, Histl. Mus. Bern, Switzerland: neg. 1190C15; right, The British Mus., Mus. of Mankind, London: 5205.

Fig. 10. Warrior-hunters and their weapons. left, Young Elk (left) carrying a quiver and bow. Man on right wears a decorated buffalo robe depicting 3 scenes: a warrior using his lance to knock down an enemy's tomahawk, an Indian dancer representing a dead warrior, and a warrior's lance penetrating his enemy's chest. Ink and pencil drawing by Rudolph F. Kurz, May 5, 1851. The artist paid each of his Omaha subjects 50¢ to be allowed to draw their portrait (Kurz 1937:61). right, Bow set composed of bow, bowcase, painted hide quiver, and arrows. Case shows traces of painted lines and further designs with feather pendant, possibly crow. Collected by Duke Paul Wilhelm, 1823; length of bowcase, 119.4 cm.

War parties consisting of 10–20 men left under the cover of night so as not to attract unwanted warriors. When returning from a raid or battle, the war party kindled a fire near the village to signify success. If any of the party were killed, a herald was selected to approach the village and call out the names of the casualties. The warriors then made a mounted charge on the village, carrying scalps and other trophies. Six grades of war honors were recognized, and a man's right to appropriate insignia was validated by a ritual involving the war bundles. During the Scalp Dance celebrating victory over the enemy, women carried the scalps on poles or carried other objects taken from the enemy to honor the deeds of their warrior relatives (Dorsey 1884:312–333; Fletcher and La Flesche 1911:402–458).

Men's Societies

There were secret men's societies collectively called *xubé wačʰi* 'mystery dance'. These were nonkin groups in which membership was supposed to be obtained through appropriate dreams or visions. Members practiced sorcery, conjuring, and healing. After the initial vision, members could obtain more advanced knowledge of herbal and other types of healing through various degrees of initiation, each of which required payments in gifts to elder members.

The Grizzly Bear and Rattlesnake Society treated swelling of the limbs, rheumatism, and abdominal complaints through the method of sucking out the cause of the disease from the affected part of the body. The Buffalo Society healed wounds through the use of herbally treated water, and the Ghost Society treated delirium, fainting, and strokes (believed to have been caused by ghosts) through songs and water-sprinkling rites. Ghost Society members could predict and forestall death and prevent rain. Members of the Thunder Society practiced weather control and engaged in conjuring contests with other shamans.

The *wašíška aðį* 'shell owners' society, whose membership was constituted by chiefs, and the *įkkugði aðį* 'translucent pebble owners' society, whose membership was constituted by shamans, were closely allied. Both were related to the widespread Midewiwin society, which originated in the Northeast. The Pebble Society practiced doctoring through the use of herbs, magic, and song, whereas the Shell Society focused around ritual performances. Both regarded *wakką́dagi* 'water monster' as the sacred power that taught the secret of shooting an object into a victim, thereby causing illness or death (Fletcher and La Flesche 1911:486–493; La Flesche 1890:221; Fortune 1932:58–102).

In addition to the secret societies, there were societies associated with warfare as well as societies of a purely social nature. The *hą́he wač^hi* 'Night Dance' was an honoring society for those who had accomplished 100 or more charitable deeds but who were not necessarily members of the chiefs' council. There were also feasting societies for men of different ages. The *heδúška* was the largest and most important warriors' society. The *ppúgδą* was a society for chiefs, and the *kkikhúneδe* 'gather together to build a fire' was an informal society for leading men. These societies were later overshadowed by the secret societies, which were a major force in nineteenth-century social organization (Fletcher 1892; Fletcher and La Flesche 1911:459–486; Fortune 1932:4, 146–158; Mead 1932:97–98).

History, 1883–1980s

Lands were allotted to individual heads of families in 1883, and in 1899 virtually all remaining land on the reservation was allotted to women and to children born since the first allotment (Kappler 1904–1941, 1:486; Fletcher and La Flesche 1911:639–640). The money provided by leasing much of their land to Whites for farming was the Omahas' main economic support for some years. A final complication of the land issue lay in the laws regarding inheritance of those who died intestate. The children of anyone who had retained ownership of land inherited it equally at his death, which led to increasingly impractical subdivision as generations passed. In 1902, legislation permitted the heirs of deceased allottees to sell their land to outsiders (ARCIA 1902:238). Ultimately, the Omaha lost over 90 percent of their reservation land (Green 1969:122–161).

The Indian agent in charge of the Omahas was located on the adjacent Winnebago Reservation. As late as 1900 no physician served the Omahas except the doctor at the Omaha boarding school (ARCIA 1902:239). In 1904, an independent Omaha Agency was established (ARCIA 1904:235).

From the 1890s through the first decade of the twentieth century, the Indian agents complained of the troubles caused by bootleggers, who traded illicit intoxicants to the Omahas. In 1896 an Omaha Indian police force of six men was arresting bootleggers. In 1906 a Court of Indian Offenses comprised of three Omaha judges was established (ARCIA 1896:198, 1906:265).

Omaha ethnic identity was strengthened through both religious and secular developments. In 1894 "war, medicine, and other dances" concerned the Indian agent in his annual report, and a year later he noted the continued practice of polygyny and the ritual tattooing of privileged young girls (ARCIA 1894:190, 1895:200). Social songs and dances became increasingly important, and dance halls were constructed on the reservation.

Despite cultural conservatism, the Omahas embraced education. Throughout the 1890s some 70 students annually attended the boarding school, others attended district day schools, and a large number attended off-reservation boarding schools. In 1906, when the boarding school was closed, the agent reported that 80 students were attending day schools and 150 were at off-reservation boarding schools (ARCIA 1906:266).

During this period the Omahas developed as farmers, although the agents reported that the ease with which land could be leased was a detriment to Omaha agriculture. Omahas had good houses, were well fed and clothed, and were respectful of the law. Most complaints of legal infractions involved the Omahas' reluctance to accept United States marriage laws, and the continued detrimental effects of the whiskey trade (ARCIA 1901:272, 1904:235, 1905:249).

In the winter of 1906–1907, peyote was first introduced among the Omaha by Cyrus Phillips who was seeking a cure for alcoholism from the leaders of the mescal societies of the Winnebago and Otoe (Gilmore 1919a:163; Howard 1956:432). The ceremonial use of peyote spread rapidly among the Omaha and became a means of stressing Indian values formerly associated with sacred artifacts (Fortune 1932:159–162). Many rituals had been discontinued with the deaths of the bundle keepers and priests.

In 1930, toward the close of the allotment era, the reservation population was described as demoralized and disorganized (Mead 1932; Fortune 1932). On June 18, 1934, the sale of land to outsiders ceased under the Indian Reorganization Act. On February 15, 1936, the Omaha tribe ratified a new constitution and a charter of incorporation on August 22.

During the World War II period, as a result of military service and urban migration, many Omahas left the reservation. Under the Indian Claims Commission Act of August 1946, the Omaha were able to seek legal redress for tribal lands lost under the 1854 treaty. Settlements were received in 1961 of $2.9 million and in 1964 of $1.75 million. However, the termination era of national Indian policy, from 1953 to 1975, encouraged a new species of assimilation, urban rather than rural, by encouraging relocation to cities. By the 1970s approximately half the 2,600 enrolled Omaha tribal members had moved to cities, mostly to Omaha and Lincoln, Nebraska (Liberty 1973a).

Reservation Life, 1960s–1980s

The Omaha Reservation, in 1967, consisted of 27,403 acres. About one-fourth (6,778 acres) was held by the tribe, and the rest was allotted to individuals. Allotments were greatly subdivided by inheritance, creating complex economic and administrative problems: many of the original 80-acre tracts had 10 or more owners by the 1980s. The sale of land to non-Indians produced a pattern of "checkerboarding" of interspersed Indian and White land, which characterized most of the reservation (Bureau of Indian Affairs 1967:2–4; Mead 1932:34–35).

Omahas living on the reservation elected at large the seven members of the tribal council. A tribal judge presided over a Court of Indian Offenses dealing with many crimes committed on the reservation, although major crimes were tried in federal courts. The Bureau of Indian Affairs retained major administrative functions on the reservation.

In 1965, the annual income of 273 Omaha families averaged $1,653, with an average per capita income of $551. Only three families received more than $5,000 per year. Of a labor force of 618, more than half were unemployed during the summer, and 95 percent during the winter (Bureau of Indian Affairs 1967:6, 13). Assistance was provided through state and federal welfare programs. Few reservation Omahas in the 1960s had completed high school (Bureau of Indian Affairs 1967:16), but in 1972 high school facilities were established in Macy. The reservation people, by the early 1970s, were concentrated in the town of Macy, although some remained on allotted farms. Macy was a small town, having a few stores, a post office, mission churches, and schools. Bureau of Indian Affairs offices serving it were off the reservation at Winnebago Agency, 10 miles north of Macy.

Lib. of Congress: Amer. Folklife Center: FCP/O/-CF-214061-2-3.

Fig. 11. Clown with apron poking fun at the Bureau of Indian Affairs (BIA). Photograph by Carl Fleischhauer, Macy, Nebr., Aug. 14, 1983.

Although radical changes in Omaha society took place during the three centuries of contact with Whites, loss of tribal identity did not occur. In 1998 the Omaha language was still alive, although it was spoken fluently only by some of those over the age of 55, amounting to an estimated 70 speakers (Mark Awakuni-Swetland, communication to editors 1998). Vestiges of the clan system survived, although by 1985 most Omahas recognized only seven distinct clans. In daily practice, the structure of kin terminology shifted toward the general American usage, although the old system was still used by elders (John E. Koontz, personal communication 1992). Traditional Omaha religion largely vanished, but the Native American Church continued to have widespread membership and influence. Strong interest in Omaha traditions was also demonstrated in the continuation of music and dance: the Omaha believed that "The Original Omaha Powwow," held at Macy, Nebraska, following the first full moon of August, was the oldest such celebration in existence (the 1981 celebration was advertised as the 115th) (fig. 12). The Omaha influence on powwow dancing has been so extensive that the name Omaha dance is a synonym for war dance, the major event for men at contemporary powwows.

A revival of interest in cultural tradition was led by the reintegration in 1983 of historic Omaha music into the summer powwow by means of wax cylinder recordings made by Fletcher and La Flesche at the end of the nineteenth century and preserved in the collections of the Library of Congress (Lee and La Vigna 1985). In 1989 the Sacred Pole bundle was repatriated to the Omaha tribe by the Peabody Museum of Harvard University, where it had been deposited by its last keeper a century before (fig. 13). It was brought to the summer powwow where it was displayed as a symbol of tribal unity and as the focus for spiritual renewal (Ridington and Hastings 1997).

A museum of Omaha reservation history, the Susan Picotte Center, opened in Walthill in 1988. Picotte, the daughter of Joseph La Flesche, was the first Indian woman to become a medical doctor.

Population

In historic times the Omaha probably never numbered above 3,000. After the smallpox epidemics of the middle and late 1700s, they mostly banded together in the single village (Fletcher and La Flesche 1911:135).

The estimated number of 2,800 individuals in 1780 (table 2) was soon drastically reduced by disease. Three epidemics were devastating—smallpox in 1800–1801, 1831, and 1835. There were also heavy losses from smallpox and cholera in 1851. Severe attacks of measles occurred in 1874, 1888, and 1889.

In spite of such losses, Omaha population began to recover dramatically after 1860. An extremely high birth rate, plus declining mortality from disease, was largely responsible (Mooney 1907a; Liberty 1973a).

Nebr. State Histl. Soc., Lincoln: top, 1394-167; bottom left, 1394-150; bottom right, Lib. of Congress: Amer. Folklife Center: FCP/O/-CF-214061-6-5.

Fig. 12. Powwows. top, Line of women participants, many dressed in robes with ribbon appliqué and silver ornamentation. One woman wears a warbonnet and another a hairpipe breastplate. bottom left, Drummers at rest. top and bottom left, Photographs by Nathaniel Lee Dewell, Macy, Nebr., Sept. 1922. bottom right, Competitor in men's traditional dance, wearing feather bustle and porcupine hair roach. Photograph by Carl Fleischhauer, Macy, Nebr., Aug. 1983.

Synonymy†

The name Omaha comes from their designation for themselves, *umą́hą* (John E. Koontz, personal communication 1987), earlier written as Uma^{n}ha^{n} (Dorsey 1884:211) and umo^{n}′ho^{n} (Fletcher and La Flesche 1911:36). The name has been said to mean 'upstream, against the flow', because of its similarity to the Omaha word *kkimą́hą* 'upstream' and related forms in other Dhegiha languages, all derived from an apparent root *mą́hą* (Dorsey 1884:211; John E. Koontz, personal communication 1992).

The Omaha were known to all other Siouan tribes by variants of their name: Ponca *umą́hą* (Parks 1988; Howard 1965:134); Kansa *omáha* (Dorsey 1883, retranscribed) and *ǫmǫ́hǫ*; Osage *omąhą* (Robert L. Rankin, personal communication 1990), recorded as Omahá (Maximilian in Thwaites 1904–1907, 24:299); Iowa *umą́hą* (Parks 1988); Winnebago *homąhą́* (Kenneth

†This synonymy was written by Douglas R. Parks.

Fig. 13. The return of the Sacred Pole at the annual Omaha powwow, Aug. 14, 1989. It is being publicly displayed so the people may see and pray with it. According to Dennis Hastings, the tribal historian, Omaha tradition said God talked to the Omaha through the sacred pole and that is why it is so important to the tribe. The pole is held by Tribal Chairman Dorrin Morris, whose great-grandfather Yellow Smoke was the last keeper of the pole. In 1897 it was given on extended loan to the Peabody Museum, Harvard, for safekeeping. Photograph by Ilka Hartmann, Macy, Nebr.

Miner, personal communication 1987), recorded also as Ho′mă^n-hă^n (Dorsey 1886). An Otoe recording ’uma:ha is said to designate the Ponca as well as the Omaha (Harrington 1940). The form Oma′ha has been recorded for each of the Sioux dialects: Yankton (Williamson 1902:120), Santee (Riggs 1890:373), Teton (Curtis 1907–1930, 3:141; Buechel 1970:394), and Assiniboine (Curtis 1907–1930, 3:141). In Yankton Sioux it has also been recorded with a nasalized vowel in the second syllable, O-maŋ-ha (Cook 1880–1882:184). In Yankton the name also occurs with the common derivational suffixes *-xca* and *-xcaka* ‘real’, as in O-maŋ-ha-ħca ‘true Omaha’ (Cook 1880–1882:184) and Omahaħcaka (*Iapi Oaye* 1884, 13:33). Mandan recordings are Óhmaha (Maximilian in Thwaites 1904–1907, 24:249) and *ówahą* (Hollow 1970:132).

Among Caddoan languages the same name has been borrowed into Pawnee as *uwá·ha* (Parks 1965–1990) and into Caddo as *ímaha·* (Wallace L. Chafe, personal communication 1998). In Kiowa it occurs as *ómɔ̀hɔ̀·gɔ̀*, pl. (Laurel Watkins, personal communication 1979). Among Plains Algonquian languages the form has been borrowed into Arapaho as *howóho·nóʔ* (Ives Goddard, personal communication 1990) and into Cheyenne as *onéhaoʔO* (Glenmore and Leman 1985:201), cited also as Onī́haeo (Curtis 1907–1930, 6:158) and Oneha and Onehao (Petter 1913–1915:582). In both languages the name designates the Ponca as well as the Omaha. The Cheyenne form has become associated with two Cheyenne words, *onéhavóʔE* ‘drum’ and the verb ‘to sit down to beg’ (Mooney 1907:424), which are said to be derived from them (Petter 1913–1915:582). The form Omaha has also been recorded as an alternate Cheyenne designation for the tribe (Petter 1913–1915:582). The name appears in one Eastern Algonquian language, Shawnee, recorded in its plural form as mahági (Gatschet 1879), undoubtedly *maha·ki* (Ives Goddard, personal communication 1992), which implies singular *maha*.

In recordings from the seventeenth through the nineteenth centuries the name occurs most commonly as Maha, 1673 (Marquette autograph map in Tucker 1942:pl. 5) or Mahas, 1701 (Iberville in Margry 1876–1886, 4:587; Bourgmont 1714 in Norall 1988:109; Miró, 1785 in Nasatir 1952, 1:120; Truteau 1795 in Parks 1992). Other renditions of this variant are Mahan, 1794 (d’Église in Nasatir 1952, 1:234), Des Machas, 1794 (Zenon Trudeau in Nasatir 1952, 1:208), and Mahar (Lewis and Clark in Moulton 1983–, 3:65, 398). The shortened form of the name used by the French Creoles was *les ma*, rendered La Mar (Lewis and Clark in Moulton 1983–, 3:398).

Prior to the nineteenth century the full form of the name Omaha occurs sporadically, for example, Omouhoa, 1681

Table 2. Omaha Population, 1780–1998

Year	*Population*	*Source*
1702	1,200 families	LeSueur in M.M. Wedel 1981:9
1758	800 men	Kerlérec in Nasatir 1952, 1:52
1780	2,800	Mooney 1928:13
1796	1,100	J.B. Truteau in Nasatir 1952, 2:384
1798	600 men	Z. Trudeau in Nasatir 1952, 2:539
1804	150 warriors	Lewis and Clark in Thwaites 1904–1905, 6:87–88
1812	800	Schermerhorn 1814:33
1829	1,900	P.B. Porter in Schoolcraft 1851–1857, 3:594
1834	1,400	ARCIA 1835:297
1849	1,300	ARCIA 1849:140
1855	800	ARCIA 1855:86
1871	984	ARCIA 1871:610
1883	1,226	J.O. Dorsey 1892
1891	1,153	J.O. Dorsey 1892
1910	1,105	U.S. Bureau of the Census 1915:19
1931	1,576	ARCIA 1931:48
1950	2,006	U.S. Congress. House. Committee on Interior and Insular Affairs 1953:880
1969	2,660[a]	U.S. Department of Commerce 1971:203
1984	2,188[b]	Bureau of Indian Affairs 1985:2
1998	4,950[c]	Gaile Bertucci, communication to editors 1998

NOTES:

[a]Total tribal enrollment; includes 1,357 reservation residents and 1,293 off-reservation residents.

[b]Reservation residents only.

[c]Total tribal enrollment; includes 3,800 reservation residents and 1,150 off-reservation residents.

(La Salle in Margry 1876–1886, 2:134); Omans (Jefferys 1761, 1:135); Ohah, 1767 (Carver in Parker 1976:100); Omaha, 1797 (MacKay in Nasatir 1952, 2:489), but during the nineteenth century its usage increased. While it sometimes occurs in its modern spelling (Maximilian 1839–1841, 1:301; in Thwaites 1904–1907, 22:274), it frequently appears in some variant form, such as Oh Mar-ha (Lewis and Clark in Moulton 1983–, 3:398), Omawhaw (Schoolcraft 1821:309), Oo-ma-ha (Brackenridge 1814:76), Omau′-hau (M'Coy 1838:84), and Omahahs (Treaty of Prairie du Chien 1830 in Kappler 1904–1941, 2:309).

The Sioux also referred to the Omaha as *oyáte nųpa*, 'two peoples', reputedly because the Omaha sometimes camped in two concentric circles (Dorsey 1884:319; Buechel 1970:733).

There is no designation recorded for the Omaha in the Plains sign language.

Sources

The literature on nineteenth-century Omaha culture is much richer than that for later periods, although annual reports of the commissioner of Indian affairs are important sources. See also the observations of trader John Dougherty prior to 1819 (James in Thwaites 1904–1907, 14–17). The Indian Claims Commission report by G. Hubert Smith (1974, see also the 1973 summary) is a compendium of historical sources, and O'Shea and Ludwickson provide a narrative of Omaha ethnohistory in the prereservation period (1992), and an ethnohistorical study of Omaha chieftanship in the nineteenth century (1992a). Boughter (1998) covers Omaha history from 1790 to 1916.

Dorsey wrote on Omaha sociology (1884, 1891), religion (1883a, 1894), and technology (1896), published collections of texts in the Dhegiha language (1890, 1891a), and compiled an unpublished dictionary (1880a). Fletcher and La Flesche (vol. 17:58) published numerous separate studies of the Omaha, in addition to co-authoring a comprehensive historical and ethnographic study (1911) that is an idealized account of traditional culture. La Flesche (1900) gives autobiographical insight into conditions on the reservation in the 1860s. Fletcher (1893, 1896, 1897) records many details of traditional Omaha life, including music (with La Flesche 1893).

Fortune (1932) reported on Omaha secret societies, religion, and social organization. Mead (1932) described the reservation in 1930, focusing on the role of women among the rapidly acculturating Omaha (disguised as the "Antlers" in this study). This is an important description of the 1930 reservation.

Norma K. Green (1969) gives material on the early reservation period. An Omaha view of this same time is given by Stabler (1943). Liberty (1973, 1973a) compared Omaha families on the reservation with those in Lincoln, Nebraska. For an annotated bibliography of the Omaha tribe see M.L. Tate (1991). Ridington and Hastings (1997) present a thorough history of the return of the Sacred Pole to the Omaha.

There are several fine collections of Omaha material culture. Fletcher and La Flesche placed many Omaha artifacts in the Peabody Museum at Harvard University. Other Omaha collections are in the National Museum of the American Indian, New York and Washington; the National Museum of Natural History, Washington; the Nebraska State Historical Society, Museum of Nebraska History, Lincoln; and the University of Nebraska State Museum, Lincoln (see, for example, Myers 1992).

Ponca

DONALD N. BROWN AND LEE IRWIN

The Ponca (ˈpäŋku) separated from the Omaha to become an independent tribe by the late seventeenth or early eighteenth century. Because they spoke a single Dhegiha Siouan language, Omaha-Ponca,* and shared common social and cultural characteristics, historic and ethnographic records have tended to conflate the two tribes. Nonetheless, distinctive linguistic and cultural differences existed. Following the 1877 Ponca removal the tribe was split into two divisions. The main part of the tribe settled in Oklahoma and became known as the *mą̨šté ppą́kka* 'warm Ponca' (Southern Ponca), while a smaller group returned to northeastern Nebraska and became known as the *usnį́ ppą́kka* 'cold Ponca' (Northern Ponca).

Prehistory

It seems probable that the Ponca were a distinct group within the Omaha tribe before their actual separation from them (Jablow 1974:6–17). Other Dhegiha peoples—Osage, Kansa, and Quapaw—included a "Ponca" clan as an integral part of their social organization. The absence of such a clan among the Omaha suggests the origin of the Ponca tribe from an ancestral "Ponca" clan among the Omaha (Fletcher and La Flesche 1911:38–39). The separation of the Ponca from the Omaha may date to about 1715 (Howard 1965:15). The 1718 Guillaume Delisle map depicts the Maha (Omaha) village on the Big Sioux River but also shows a group of Wandering Maha (presumably the Ponca) farther north (Tucker 1942:pl. XV; Wood 1965:128).

According to tradition, the Ponca followed the Missouri upriver to a place where they could "step over the waters," then turned southward. While hunting buffalo on the high plains they met the Padouca (Plains Apache), who were armed with stone axes and rode horses shielded with heavy rawhide. These were the first horses seen by the Ponca. After many battles, peace was agreed upon, the Ponca trading bows and arrows for Padouca horses. Having mastered the skills of riding, continued horse raids by the Ponca against the Padouca led to a new outbreak of war and the Padouca were driven south of the Platte River. The Ponca followed the Platte back to the Missouri and rejoined the Omaha (Fletcher and La Flesche 1911:49, 79–80; Dorsey 1886:219).

*For the spelling of Omaha-Ponca words in the *Handbook*, see the orthographic footnote in "Omaha," this vol.

The final separation of the Ponca from the Omaha occurred about 1735, possibly at the site of Bad Village located on Bow Creek in northeastern Nebraska (Wood 1965:128). The Ponca then settled in their historic homeland in the valley of Ponca Creek near the mouth of the Niobrara River (Howard 1970:119).

At the time of European contact, the Ponca hunting territory was bounded on the north by the White River, on the south by the Niobrara River and extended from the west side of the Missouri River to the Black Hills (fig. 1) (Howard 1965:130–133; Jablow 1974:92–93). Tribes with whom the Ponca fought included the Sioux, Cheyenne, Arikara, Pawnee, and, on several occasions, the Omaha (Dorsey 1890:368–383; James in Thwaites 1904–1907, 15:88–89; Fletcher and La Flesche 1911:87–89).

History, 1785–1848

Historical documents first identify the Ponca by name in 1785, when they probably were living on Bazile Creek, a tributary of the Missouri just below the mouth of the Niobrara (Miró in Nasatir 1952, 1:126; Jablow 1974:73–74). From 1790 through 1800, the Ponca may have occupied a site on Ponca Creek, a tributary of the Missouri River just above the Niobrara, referred to as *ną́za* 'barricade', known as the Ponca Fort. This site contained a fortified village surrounded by an oval ditch with a six-foot interior earth wall, topped with a defensive post palisade. The remains included Euro-American goods as well as a type of pottery (Stanley ware) generally associated with the Arikara, suggesting close contact between the Arikara and Ponca either through trade or intermarriage (Dorsey 1884:313–314; Wood 1959:3, 1960).

The first European trader known to have contacted the Ponca was Jean Munier, in 1789. The Ponca chief gave him a peace pipe to be presented to the Spanish authorities with a request that traders be sent to them every year (Nasatir 1952, 1:194–196). In 1793, Munier requested exclusive trade rights with the Ponca from the newly formed Missouri Company in Saint Louis. During 1794–1795, Jean-Baptiste Truteau's Missouri Company expedition wintered upstream from the Ponca, with whom they traded in the spring at what came to be known as the Ponca House (Diller 1949; Truteau in Nasatir 1952, 1:279,

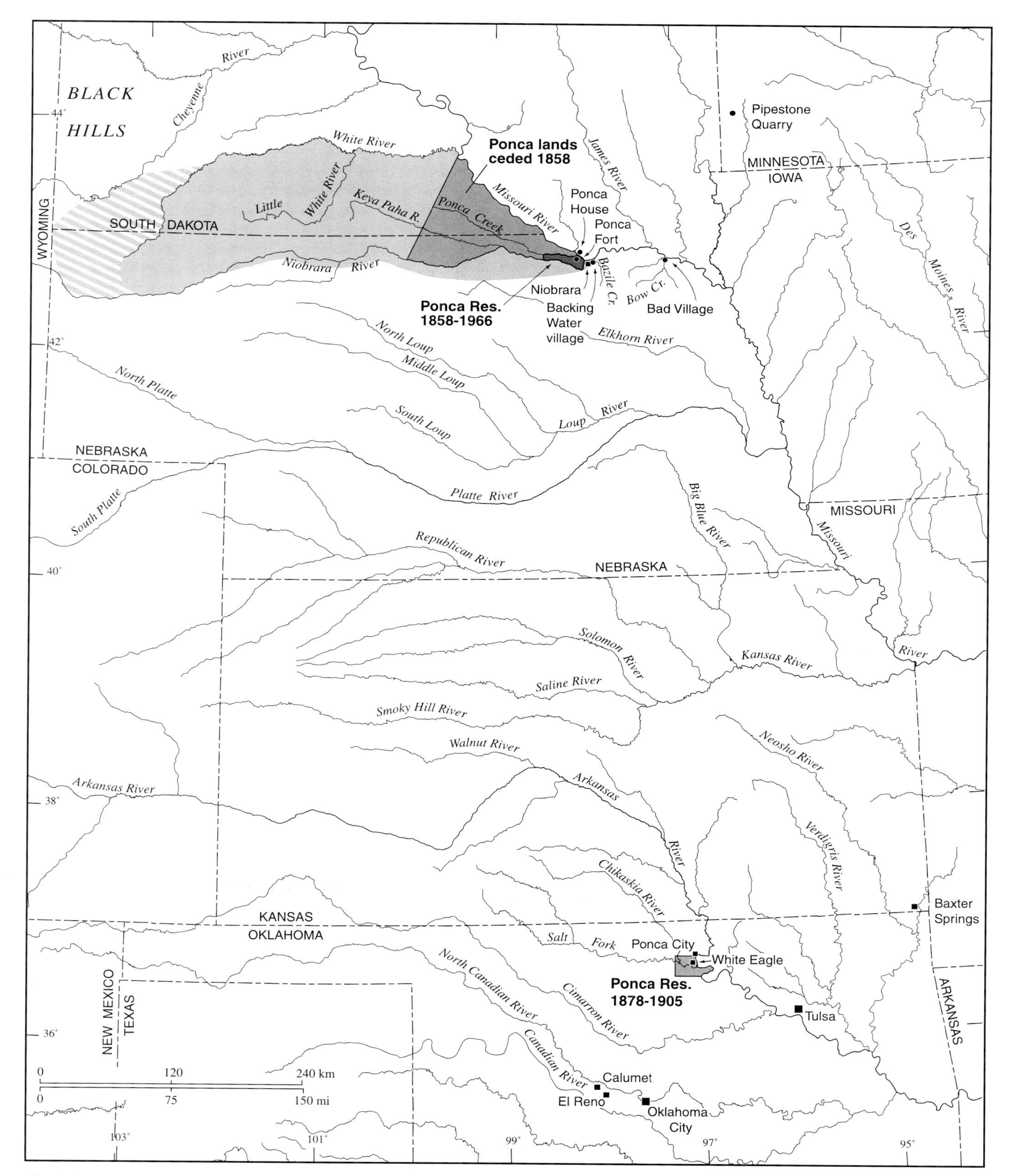

Fig. 1. Ponca territory during the late 18th century, with subsequent land transfers and reservations.

290–293; Wood 1959:7). The Ponca often confiscated goods from traders ascending the Missouri to prevent weapons from reaching their enemies upstream, the Sioux and Arikara (Tabeau 1939:100–101; Jablow 1974:128). During the late eighteenth century the Ponca were controlled by the Omaha chief, Blackbird, who demanded hides and other goods from them in return for protection from their mutual enemies (Nasatir 1952, 1:283, 293; 1931:455).

In 1801, armed with guns and powder supplied by British traders from the north, the Ponca and Omaha were reported to be disrupting the trade from Louisiana up the Missouri River. Aggression was heightened that year by a smallpox epidemic transmitted to the Ponca by the Omaha who attacked them during this period of starvation and sickness (Dorsey 1890:401; Jablow 1974:141). According to the fur trader Pierre-Antoine Tabeau (1939:100), in 1804 there remained only 40 Ponca warriors, more than half of whom were killed the next spring in an attack by the Brule Sioux. To protect themselves from the Sioux, the Ponca took refuge among the Omaha. These two events drastically reduced the Ponca population. Hostilities with the Sioux continued, and in 1824 a party of 30 Poncas returning from a friendly visit to the Oglala Sioux were attacked by a group of Teton Sioux, who killed 18 men, including the Ponca chiefs (H.H. Anderson 1961:253–254).

In 1817, Ponca chiefs and warriors journeyed to Saint Louis where, on June 25, they signed their first "peace and friendship" treaty acknowledging the protection of the United States government (Kappler 1904–1941, 2:140; Jablow 1974:161, 176). A second treaty was concluded with the Ponca on June 9, 1825, at the Ponca Village on Bazile (White Paint) Creek, in an attempt to bring peace to the warring tribes of the upper Missouri. This treaty regulated trade on the Missouri and designated the mouth of the Niobrara River as the specific place for the Ponca to trade (Kappler 1904–1941, 2:225–227; Jablow 1974:196, 200–201).

Competition resulting from the 1830 federal policy removing eastern Indians west of the Mississippi exacerbated intertribal warfare and contributed to the diminishing animal resources needed for subsistence and trade (Catlin 1926, 1:212; Jablow 1974:210). By the mid-nineteenth century, extensive fur trade was being carried out by the Ponca. While traders placed an increasing emphasis on the value of buffalo robes, thereby diminishing the buffalo herds, the Ponca became increasingly dependent upon Euro-American goods (Jablow 1974:253–262).

The Teton Sioux movement into the Black Hills area reduced much of the western hunting territory of the Ponca, and pressure from the Sioux was so intense that it became difficult for the Ponca to maintain their fields. Caught between the constantly warring Sioux and Pawnee, the Ponca were forced for a time to abandon their horticultural practices and live a more nomadic life (Maximilian in Thwaites 1904–1907, 22:289). However, during times of decreased warfare, horticulture was again emphasized (Jablow 1974:234–235). During the winter of 1846, 200 Mormon settlers encamped at the mouth of the Niobrara, where they formed an alliance with the Ponca to provide mutual protection from hostile tribes (Jablow 1974:279–280). By 1848, the buffalo were so diminished that the Ponca were forced to hunt in Sioux territory (de Smet 1905, 3:1187–1189).

Thirty Ponca village sites centering around the Niobrara River from the late eighteenth through the late nineteenth centuries have been recorded. One of the best known is Backing Water Village on Bazile Creek, which was occupied from the late eighteenth century until at least 1858 and was the primary Ponca settlement during the historic period (Howard 1970:110, 128–129).

Culture in the Nineteenth Century

Subsistence

Hunting, horticulture, and gathering of wild plants were the foundation of Ponca subsistence. The annual cycle included cultivation of gardens near the village in the spring, the tribal buffalo hunt in mid-summer for meat and hides for tepee covers, and a return to the village to harvest crops in the early fall. Individuals or small groups hunted informally during the late fall and winter for meat and for the thickly furred winter hides used for robes and for trade (Jablow 1974:74–75).

The principal crops grown in the Ponca gardens were corn, beans, squash, pumpkins, gourds, and tobacco. Gardening was a woman's activity, although men assisted with the harvest. Corn and squash were planted together in mounds. Seed corn was planted in ritually made buffalo tracks; this method of planting represented the origins of the four different types (colors) of corn, which the Ponca attributed to seven sacred buffalo (Howard 1965:20–21, 44–46). Produce was dried on scaffolds and cached in underground pits for winter consumption. Tobacco for smoking was generally mixed with the inner bark of the dogwood and red willow (Dorsey 1884:309; Howard 1965:47).

Many wild plants, fruits, berries, and nuts were gathered by women, including wild rice, onions, Indian potatoes, sweetpeas, and prairie turnips. Crabapples, strawberries, raspberries, plums, sand cherries, chokecherries, grapes, buffalo berries, groundberries, elderberries, hickory nuts, black walnuts, hazelnuts, hackberries, and acorns were also collected (Howard 1965:43–44).

Fish and turtles were hunted with specially made arrows and barbed spears, and, when abundant, they were caught by hand. Hooks were made from bird claws or obtained through trade with Europeans; twisted horse-hair lines were staked to the shore below the water line and left overnight. A successful catch was distributed among the old people as was other surplus from the hunt (Dorsey 1884:301–302; Fletcher and La Flesche 1911:312; Howard 1965:43).

Hunting was considered the most prestigious subsistence activity and provided the primary source of food. During the historic period, the Ponca were occasionally forced by their enemies to rely entirely upon hunting and gathering and to trade meat to the Omaha and Pawnee for corn (Dorsey 1884:274; Maximilian in Thwaites 1904–1907, 22:285; Jablow 1974:41). The most highly valued game animals were buffalo, deer, elk, bear, and rabbit. Beaver and otter were trapped throughout the winter for trade (Dorsey 1884:283–284; Fletcher and La Flesche 1911:44, 207).

The mid-summer buffalo hunt lasted about two months and was initiated after the corn was about a foot high. The hunt was under the direction of the *wašábe* clan who appointed the hunt leader and the *mą́kką* clan who supervised the Feast of Soldiers. A highly respected man was chosen as the hunt leader (*nudą́hąga* 'war leader') (Howard 1965:92; Fletcher and La Flesche 1911:48; Skinner 1915:795 reports that two men were chosen). Men with recognized war honors were selected from the men's societies to act as hunt police or "soldiers" (*waną́še*). Hunt leaders and police appealed to the sacred powers of the crow and the wolf for a successful hunt (Fletcher and La Flesche 1911:44–45, 442–445; Howard 1965:92).

About 40 young men were honored by being selected as buffalo scouts and were divided into four groups, each sent out in one of the four cardinal directions. The hunt leader determined when and where the camp should move, when the scouts should be sent out, and other details related to the hunt. When buffalo were discovered, the successful scout would return to camp and ritually announce the location of the herd, kicking over a pile of dried buffalo dung arranged before the lodge of the hunt leader as an oath attesting to the truth of his report. Thereafter no individuals were allowed to leave the camp, and the tribe moved toward the buffalo (Skinner 1915:794–797).

When the hunters reached the buffalo, the hunt police ensured that all acted together to surround the herd so that as many animals as possible were killed. Any man who disobeyed the hunt leader and hunted on his own was punished by the hunt police, who would destroy his property and beat him. The next day the offender would be brought to the lodge of the hunt police where he was given gifts to compensate for his losses (Skinner 1915:796–797).

Upon completion of a successful hunt, the Feast of Soldiers was held in honor of deceased chiefs. During this ceremony soup made from buffalo meat was dripped into small depressions as offerings to deceased leaders, and to the crow and the wolf. Chiefs, although long dead, were regarded as still caring for the people; this offering of food recognized their continued guidance and help (Fletcher and La Flesche 1911:309–312).

Technology

Ponca material culture blended both Eastern and Prairie Plains traditions. Mortars were used to grind corn and prepare herbal medicines. Willow rod backrests with chokecherry braces and carved cradleboards attested to woodworking skills. Men made bows of seasoned ash or Osage orange, rabbit-leg warclubs, and war shields from thick buffalo bull hide. Each man made his arrows with clan and individual markings while arrowheads were made by specialists. Basketmaking, using nettle, elmbark fiber, and peeled sandbar willow, was moderately developed as well as mat-weaving techniques for seats and floor coverings (Gilmore 1919:73; Howard 1965:51–55).

Structures

Ponca villages comprised round earthlodges (*mąδítti* 'earth dwelling') arranged in no specified manner. The construction of an earthlodge began with setting four main elmwood posts into the earth, forming a tall central square. Each post had a crotch in the top across which connecting logs were laid to form the main supports for the roof. Rafter poles connected a shorter outer post wall to the center posts, and the roof was then covered with brush, red sloughgrass, and tamped earth. The entrance usually faced east. Men set the large central posts while the rest of the lodge was completed by women who were also responsible for repairing them each autumn. Cache pits were dug into the floor in the four directions, the first to the south of the central fire (Howard 1965:56, 59).

Less permanent structures in the Central Algonquian wigwam style were constructed using bent frame construction consisting of opposing pairs of green saplings driven into the earth, the tops bent over and tied together. Smaller saplings or vines were woven horizontally to complete the frame. The entire structure was usually covered with hides rather than bark. Two types were made—

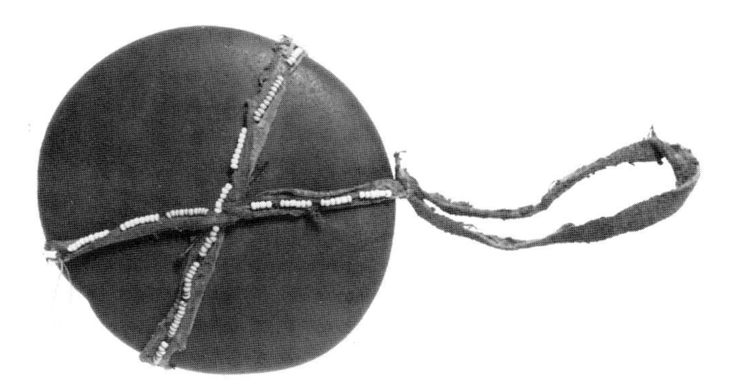

Smithsonian, Dept. of Anthr.: 166551.

Fig. 2. Whetstone, used to sharpen tools and weapons. Strands of dressed skin with turquoise and white beading are attached to a loop, which may have been used as a carrying device. Collected by Albert S. Gatschet; diameter 9 cm.

smaller, round structures (*ttiúðippu*) and larger, elongated lodges (*ttiúðippu snéde* 'long lodge') up to 40 feet in length (Howard 1965:56–57). These served as temporary houses and for ritual use. Small bent-frame menstrual huts were constructed on the outskirts of the village, and similarly constructed sweatlodges were used for purification rites (Howard 1965:59).

The Ponca tepee (*ttí* 'dwelling') had a three-pole foundation using 12–30 poles. The buffalo hide cover had wind flaps to regulate the draft of the center fire. The front was laced with wood pins, and wood stakes held the cover to the ground. Tepees, often painted with clan and personal symbols (Skinner 1915:779), were used when hunting away from the permanent village site (Howard 1965:57).

Clothing

Men's summer clothing consisted of a well-tanned breechcloth, leggings, moccasins, and a belt. Soft-soled moccasins were used during the first half of the nineteenth century (fig. 3), then were displaced by the hard-soled Plains style. In winter, hide shirts and fur caps might be added. Women's dress was the typical Plains deer or elk skin garment worn with knee-length leggings, a wide belt, and high-topped moccasins. A black dye was made from walnuts to dye buckskin, and other colors were produced through smoking over fires made with various types of wood (Maximilian in Thwaites 1904–1907, 22:285; Howard 1965:52). Buffalo robes were worn by all during cold weather. Skinner (1915:779) also mentions a woman's garment of Central Algonquian style composed of a two-piece open skirt and notes that soft-soled moccasins were worn only by women who had been tattooed, a symbol of social prestige indicating that their fathers or husbands had been admitted to the Night Dance society. On special ceremonial or feast days, men wore otterskin bandoliers and porcupine or deerhair roaches and carried quilled pipe bags (fig. 4) and eagle-feather fans; bone breastplates were worn by both men and women. Finger-woven sashes, turbans, and knee bands were also made (Howard 1965:52, 61–62, 113).

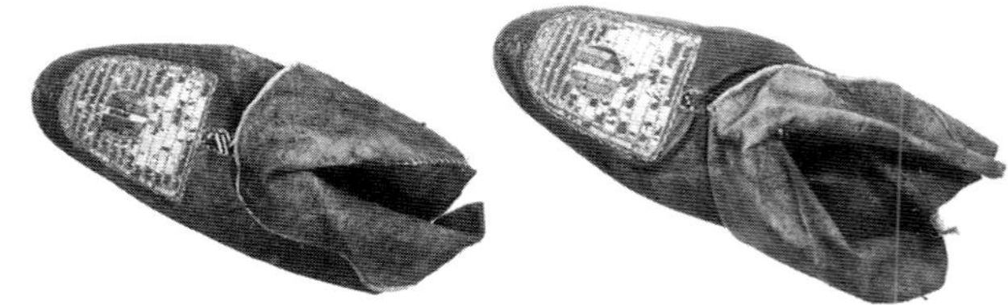

top, Smithsonian, Natl. Mus. of Amer. Art: 1985.66.97; bottom, Linden-Mus., Stuttgart: 36077.

Fig. 3. Soft-soled moccasins. top, Great Chief, son of Smoke. He wears a trade blanket, decorated soft-soled moccasins, multiple shell earrings and necklaces, a wrist band of trade silver and holds an eagle wing fan. A quiver full of arrows hangs over his back. Oil on canvas by George Catlin, Ponca village, Nebr., 1832. bottom, Moccasins with quill embroidery decoration. Collected by Maximilian, Prince of Wied, 1832–1834; length 28 cm.

Social Organization

The Ponca, like the Omaha, were divided into patrilineal clans based on mythical associations with founding ancestors. Position in Ponca society depended on clan affiliation, the family position in the clan, and the inherited rights passed down through kinship relations (Howard 1965:81–82). The kinship system was of the Omaha type, reflecting the patrilineal clan organization, and was identical with that of the Omaha tribe.

Clan affiliation was visibly expressed in the camp circle (*húðuga*), consisting of a set arrangement of tepees by clan that was used on ritual occasions and during the summer

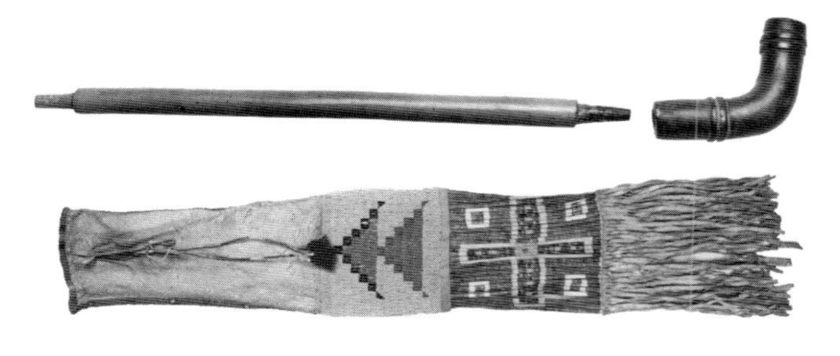

top, Field Mus., Chicago: 67352 (neg. A-111785); bottom, Smithsonian, Natl. Mus. of the Amer. Ind.: 3/6738 (neg. 30960).

Fig. 4. Smoking equipment. top, Pipe and stem made of catlinite and wood. Collected by H.R. Voth, Ponca Res., Okla., 1889; length 49.0 cm. bottom, Pipe bag with quilled and beaded decoration. Collected by M.R. Harrington before 1914; length 91.4 cm.

buffalo hunts. In enumerating positions within the circle, the entrance facing east, Dorsey (1897:228–229) listed eight clans divided equally between two moieties, the southern called *ččížu* (no known meaning) and the northern called *wažáže* ('Osage'). Each moiety was divided into two unnamed phratries. The moiety and phratry organization apparently fell into disuse by the time the tribe was split in 1877, since later studies of Ponca social organization do not mention them (Fletcher and La Flesche 1911:41–47; Howard 1965:87–90).

The following presentation describes the tribal structure as recorded by Dorsey (1897:228–229) and incorporates material from later writers (Fletcher and La Flesche 1911:41–47; Skinner 1915:799; Howard 1965:87–90).

The *hísada* 'stiff legs', first of the *ččížu* clans, camped on the south side of the entrance of the tribal circle. They were the keepers of the sacred songs used in the spring at the first sound of thunder in a bundle renewal rite directed by *hísada* thunder shamans, called "eagles," whose voices after death were heard in the thunderstorms. Because their rites were associated with war, the *hísada* did not own one of the seven tribal peace-making pipes, as did each of the other seven clans. The association of the clan with thunder power was retained into the mid-twentieth century when certain clan members were believed to have rainmaking ability. Fletcher and La Flesche list the *hísada* as a subclan of the *wašábe* clan, though all other sources give it as an independent clan.

The *wasábe* 'black bear', the clan to the southeast in the camp circle, apparently died out in the late nineteenth century. Dorsey (1894:382) recorded a brief *wasábe* prayer directed to the first spring thunder.

The *δíγida* clan, on the south side of the circle, consisted of two subclans; one lineage was responsible for the sacred puma skin bundle containing the *wáwą* pipestems used for establishing peaceful relations with other tribes. The tepee of this bundle keeper was painted with a blue and green pipe on one side and a puma on the other side. Also within this clan were two war honor bundles, whose keepers were responsible for testing the truthfulness of exploits claimed by warriors during battle and for assigning war honors in the form of symbolic paint and feathers. One of these bundle keepers represented the preeminent war powers, those of thunder and wolf. The clan owned one of the seven sacred pipes, which symbolized the right to take charge of the council that elected chiefs. Clan members were believed to have the ability to call game through hunting rituals.

The *nįkkappašna* 'no hair' (said to refer to the exposure of the skull by scalping) camped on the southwest side of the circle and consisted of at least three subclans. They owned the sacred ball and its associated ceremonies. One lineage cared for a powerful war bundle containing a pipe that conveyed the authority to preside over war councils and to direct war parties. Certain members of one subclan had the right to direct all elk and deer hunting.

The first clan of the *wažáže* moiety on the west was *mąkką* 'medicine', also called *ttesįde it^{h}áži* 'does not touch buffalo tails', consisting of two subclans. The clan possessed valuable knowledge of herbal medicine and healing practices. One of the two principal chiefs was elected from this clan. One lineage of the *ppąkkaxti* 'real Ponca' subclan was responsible for the most sacred of the seven pipes, the chief's pipe. The principal chief from this clan used the pipe to punish tribal offenders through a rite, involving the ashes from the pipe, which was believed to cause death. The bundle and its keeper received power from the Thunder. They were responsible for various aspects of the buffalo hunt as well as the Feast of Soldiers and the Turning the Child rites.

The *wašábe* 'dark buffalo' clan camped to the northwest of the circle and had two subclans. This clan had the right to provide the second principal chief. At the corn harvest, special ears were gathered by clan members for preservation and ceremonial use in the coming year (Dorsey 1884:302). Dorsey (1884:359–360) recorded several traditions of the induction of new chiefs in which a *wašábe* shaman possessed a bundle containing six of the seven sacred clan pipes. Clan ownership involved a specific pipe in this bundle and the right to handle it in appropriate ceremonial circumstances. Tribal unity was strongly symbolized by the six pipes being kept together, while the seventh pipe was the pipe under the care of the *mąkką* clan. The *wašábe* also had duties connected with the buffalo hunt and the right to appoint the camp police.

To the northeast of the circle were camped the *wažáže*, with three subclans, who were believed to be an archaic remnant of the Osage and were associated with snake power. Members were believed to be able to cause and cure snake bites. This clan owned the sacred pipe with a round stem (the others were flat stemmed) that had highly revered ability to mediate quarrels and conflicts within the tribe. Tribal heralds were appointed from this clan and members were believed to be expert at tracking.

Just north of the entrance camped the *núxe* 'reddish yellow buffalo' (according to Dorsey; translated 'ice' in other sources), who had power related to winter, hail, and the upper world. Hailstones were graphically represented on men's leggings and other objects as a form of protection.

It is clear that this structure is an idealized one. The earliest historical mention of Ponca clans was a list of eight names recorded in 1862 (Morgan 1959:147); in 1880, the Ponca chiefs visiting Washington, D.C., confirmed that there had been eight clans in the past but that one had recently become extinct and three subclans had developed into clans, bringing the total to 10. In the 1880s, Joseph La Flesche recognized only seven clans (Dorsey 1884:215). Later accounts also list seven clans, Fletcher and La Flesche omitting the *hísada* and classifying it as a subclan of the *wasábe*, Skinner omitting the *wašábe*, and Howard omitting the *wasábe*. Howard added an eighth clan in addition to those in the camp circle, the *wáxežiga* 'White men's sons', composed of the descendants of White traders married to Ponca women. Morgan's 1862 list gives eight clans, omitting the *hísada* and adding wáh-ga, which may represent the *wáxežiga*; Dorsey (1884:359) noted that a representative of the "half-breed band" played a role in the inauguration of chiefs.

Political Organization

Two classes of chiefs were recognized: "big" chiefs of the higher rank, usually consisting of older men who were descended from other big chiefs, and "little" chiefs of the second rank, consisting of accomplished warriors and other outstanding men who might be elected by retiring chiefs. Each of the clans recognized a hereditary chief. The number of chiefs of higher rank was limited to seven or eight, apparently corresponding to the number of clans (though it was not the case that at any time every clan was represented among the big chiefs), and these men made most of the decisions affecting tribal life (Howard 1965:91–92; Fletcher and La Flesche 1911:51).

The highest positions within the chiefs' council were held by the two principal chiefs, one from the *wašábe* clan and the other from the *mą́kką* (Fletcher and La Flesche 1911:48). The chiefs' council was responsible for decisions affecting the entire tribe, and decisions were implemented by the camp police. Chiefs were expected to be generous, to avoid war and warfare activities unless the village was attacked, and to promote peace and tribal welfare. Special face and body paint, otter skin cap, and a pipe and pipe bag were the traditional symbols of the chief's position (Dorsey 1884:217, 359; Howard 1965:92–93).

A man succeeded to the position of big chief when his father resigned or died. Although inherited position made accession to leadership roles probable, individuals needed to demonstrate qualities of courage and generosity that earned the respect of other warriors and tribal leaders. Those who did not inherit a position of leadership might attain chiefly rank by joining many of the men's societies and by demonstrating notable leadership qualities, including generosity with gifts and feasts (Skinner 1915:783). A chief could voluntarily pass his office to another in recognition of a service done for him, such as revenging a son's death (Fletcher and La Flesche 1911:49–50).

Life Cycle

In the late nineteenth century, girls married at the age of 15, though in earlier times they were said to have waited until reaching 20 (Dorsey 1884:259). A young man gave horses and buffalo robes to the family of his prospective wife, sometimes while she was preadolescent. Accepting the gifts signified approval. A less direct approach was to request an intermediary to talk to the girl's parents. If the parents did not object within four days, gifts would then be given. After a marriage feast, gifts of equal worth were presented by the parents of the wife to the new couple. There was no specified rule for residence after marriage (Howard 1965:83, 147).

If a man mistreated his wife, she could divorce him with the help of her mother or elder brother. However, a man could give his wife away at a *heδúška* dance; the woman had no choice but to return to her parents' lodge. Sororal polygyny was practiced by men wealthy enough to support two or more sisters. Both the sororate and levirate were practiced (Skinner 1915:784–785; Whitman 1937:41; Howard 1965:148; Dorsey 1884:258).

An important ceremony for all Ponca children was the Turning the Child rite given each spring by a member of the *mą́kką* clan in which the child was led into a tent and his feet were placed on a sacred stone symbolizing long life. The child was then turned toward each of the four directions, representing the power of the winds, and was given a traditional clan name. The hair of male children was then cut symbolically to denote clan identity. As the children grew older, they learned the privileges and prohibitions of their clan (Dorsey 1894:411–412; Fletcher and La Flesche 1911:44–45; Whitman 1939:182–183; Howard 1965:144–146).

At adolescence, a boy went on a vision quest to seek power that could help him throughout his lifetime. His face blackened with charcoal or earth, he spent four days in a secluded spot fasting and praying to the sacred beings to pity him. Power received could not be refused without risk, and to do so might result in death. Later in life a man might gain additional power through another vision quest, participation in the Sun Dance, or by purchase from a shaman. An elderly man might tell his visions to a grandson but only after receiving an appropriate gift (Howard 1965:99–100; Fletcher 1907:441–442; Whitman 1939:184–185).

A girl's puberty might be commemorated by the gift of a finely appointed horse with appropriate speeches by an elder. During menstrual periods a woman moved without explanation to a small lodge apart from her family where she lived alone, making a new fire each day and cooking for herself (Dorsey 1884:267; Howard 1965:146).

Old age was respected and elders were provided with food, shelter, and firewood when hunting parties left the camp. It was considered dangerous to abandon elders because the sacred powers would punish anyone who did so (Dorsey 1884:274–275, 1890:29).

Illness was attributed to two causes: either natural or supernatural. The first type was treated with herbal remedies and such other traditional methods as splints for broken limbs. The second type required the help of a powerful shaman. Most remedies combined both techniques (Howard 1965:150–153).

Some Poncas believed that death was caused by malevolent spirits and that all possessions of the survivors must be given away to prevent the spirits' return (Dorsey 1894:374). The ghost of the dead might hover about causing mischief and accidents or it might give power to a vision seeker who came to the grave immediately after burial (Fletcher and La Flesche 1911:216). Relatives cut off their hair and gashed their arms and legs in mourning. The dead were dressed in their best clothes and painted according to their clan affiliation. Burial was either in a log structure covered with earth or on scaffolds or trees. Following burial, a giveaway accompanied the mourning feast. After death an individual's soul (*wanáγi*) was believed to join those already dead. Deceased chiefs were believed to watch over the people and help them during times of trouble. Shamans were believed to be able to predict their own death, and some claimed to be reincarnated (Dorsey 1888:73, 1894:419; Fletcher and La Flesche 1911:310; Skinner 1915:801; Whitman 1939:193; Howard 1965:153–155).

Religion and Mythology

Central to Ponca religion was the concept of *wakkąda* 'sacred power', which referred to anything mysterious or uncanny, to various types of spirit beings, to natural phenomena, and to a supreme power. The personal, immediate manifestation of sacred power was *xubé* or *waxúbe* and anyone able to control that power was called a *xubé*, that is, a shaman. Typical manifestations of power were curing ability, luck in gambling, success in love or war, and other types of good fortune. However, curing ability alone did not secure the status of *xubé* as the candidate must be one whose visions and abilities were truly remarkable. All chiefs were considered to be *xubé* because they worked for the good of the people (Dorsey 1894:366–368; Whitman 1939:180–181; Howard 1965:99).

Such power could be obtained through the vision quest, inheritance, or purchase. Medicine bundles were made by visionaries to hold sacred objects revealed in the vision. These objects manifested the specific power of the vision such as the eagle down worn by shamans that made them invulnerable in battle (McGee 1898:157). Smaller bundles were individually owned while larger ones were society or clan bundles under the care of a bundle keeper. Clan bundles contained pipes and other objects that were considered extremely powerful and required handling with great care (Fletcher and La Flesche 1911:42–48; Howard 1965:100–102).

Day and night were regarded as two primary sacred powers in Ponca cosmology. Men who gained admittance to the Night Dance society or who became recognized chiefs had their wives or daughters tattooed on the hand or forehead with symbols that represented the conjoined powers of the day and night by which human life was created and maintained (Fletcher and La Flesche 1911:507; Skinner 1915:798; Howard 1965:113). According to a Ponca creation story symbolized by the Sun Dance altar, a primal fireplace or sun contained the four sacred colors. Then a buffalo bull came out of the earth carrying a pipe and ceremonial paint; he offered himself to the people (G.A. Dorsey 1905:87–88). An alternative creation narrative referred to the gift of a bow, a dog, and a kernel of corn by *wakkąda* (Fletcher and La Flesche 1911:49), while yet another narrative attributes the gift of corn to the buffalo (Howard 1965:20–21). Prayers were offered to the powers through the use of a pipe or by burning cedar needles (Dorsey 1894:373).

The sun, moon, winds, and stars were all sacred powers. Some boys dreamt of the moon presenting a bow and arrows in one hand and a woman's pack strap in the other; if the boy were tricked into taking the pack strap he became *mįxuga*, a berdache, and thereafter dressed and acted as a woman (Dorsey 1894:378–379). Thunder (*įgδą́*) was a great war power and played an important role in the Sun Dance as the center pole supported its nest (G.A. Dorsey 1905:69). There were numerous other sacred creatures, including water monsters (*wakkąđagi*) that inhabited the Missouri River; trickster (*ištínįkʰe*) who was both a helpful and harmful figure in a cycle of humorous tales (Skinner 1915:779); deer women (*ttáxti waʔú*) who attracted young men with their sexual power and could cause sicknesses and death; and *įdáδįge*, a very powerful long-haired creature that haunted the woods, hooted like an owl, and was threatening to children (Dorsey 1885a:105–108, 1894:386–387; Howard 1965:75–78).

Voluntary Societies

Dancing or medicine societies were prevalent in Ponca social life and consisted of three types: those open to all members of the tribe; those associated with war honors; and sacred societies open only to those initiated into shamanistic practices. Each society had its own dress, songs, and oral traditions as well as a certain number of official positions that must be filled at all times (Dorsey 1884:342; Howard 1965:114–115).

The *heδúška* men's society originated in the visionary experience of a woman. The society sponsored dances in which warriors wore insignia representing their war honors and acted out their brave deeds. It also helped people mourn the dead and provided gifts for the poor. After 1880 this dance became more religious in character, and long prayers were offered in the place of warriors narrating their deeds (Skinner 1915:784–785; Howard 1965:106–107).

The *ṫé gáγe* 'make to die' men's society was led by four spear holders who in battle stuck their spears into the ground, vowing not to flee unless rescued by another warrior (Skinner 1915:785–786).

The *iskáʔiyuha* society included four leaders who carried crooked spears and who, like the *ṫé gáγe* spear holders, could not flee in war. They would make donations during dances, as well as request presents from wealthy men by dancing in front of their lodges (Skinner 1915:786–787).

Other men's societies included the t^h*okála*, consisting of young warriors who were rivals of the *mąwádaδi*, a society of older and more experienced warriors. Both groups practiced competitive wife-stealing; a man who found his wife guilty of illicit sexual intercourse would publicly give her away at the next society dance (Skinner 1915:788).

Two less formal groups were the *heyóka* who, as the result of certain dreams, used backward speech and took food from boiling pots with their bare hands; and the *δanį́xaδa*, who were looked upon as clowns and fun-makers (Skinner 1915:789).

Three women's societies were recorded. The Tattooed Women was the highest ranking, consisting of the tattooed daughters of chiefs and wealthy men. The *nudą́* 'war' society danced to war songs and gave aid to poor tribal members, the elderly and blind, as well as feasts for the entire tribe. They also led the women's scalp dance to celebrate the return of a victorious war party. The Medal Dance society performed a dance in which the women wore silver chief's medals (Dorsey 1884:355; Skinner 1915:790–791).

In addition to dancing societies four sacred societies were recorded. The Bear Dance ceremony was held in a lodge with a cedar tree placed in the center, the society members demonstrating their shamanistic powers through magical performances; the Buffalo Dance members specialized in the healing of wounds; the Medicine Lodge or White Shell Owners, the largest and most important sacred society, held ceremonies in which initiates were magically shot with sacred cowrie shells to prolong life and to demonstrate power; and the Mescal Bean society involved secret rites held in a tepee where bundles were opened and mescal bean tea was consumed, inducing visions of the future (Skinner 1915:792–793, 1920:306–308; Howard 1957:83–84, 1965:119–124).

Shamans typically demonstrated a variety of supernatural abilities, including foretelling the future, calling game animals during the hunt, and magical feats of invulnerability (Dorsey 1888:73, 1894:417). Esoteric knowledge, vision songs, or power objects could be purchased as they were considered the personal property of the shaman.

Ceremonies

The most sacred tribal ceremony was the Sun Dance (fig. 5), called the "sun watching dance," the name referring to the belief that the sun witnessed the ceremony (G.A. Dorsey 1905:69). The Sun Dance was directed by Thunder shamans, men who had learned the ritual by dancing in four previous ceremonies. Held annually in mid-summer when the corn was in silk, the ceremony included four days and nights of fasting and prayer. Four sacred tepees were erected, each containing a dry painting altar. On the last day the dancers were fastened to the forked center pole of the dance lodge by rawhide thongs attached to their chest muscles and danced gazing at the Thunderbird nest at the top of the pole. Blowing eagle-bone whistles and holding sage-wrapped hoops, they danced until the thongs were pulled free (G.A. Dorsey 1905; Howard 1965:103–104).

The Sacred Pipe Dance (*wáwą*) was another important tribal ceremony that involved the redistribution of wealth. It was initiated by a tribal member giving a small bag of tobacco to a selected individual as potential sponsor; if the bag was accepted, the ceremony was performed and gifts were distributed. Two feathered pipestems painted to represent dawn and the sky (only one pipestem according to other accounts) and a large gourd rattle were removed from their puma or lynx skin bundle and used to imitate the flight of the eagle. An honored child of the sponsor, usually female, would then be "captured" and adopted by a ceremonial grandfather. The ceremony was also used to establish peaceful relations with other tribes (Whitman 1937:121–125; Howard 1965:105–106).

Warfare

The Ponca attitude toward war was generally defensive. However, incursion into Ponca territory by other tribes was strongly resisted. War parties were led by men who had not yet attained the status of chief, since chiefs were forbidden to participate in warlike activities. Such leaders were considered solely responsible for the welfare of all participants. Borrowing a sacred war bundle, a party of men set off with the leader in advance. He slept away from the war party and, although cooking was done for him, he was only allowed to eat four bites. Scouts were sent out in the four directions and the lead scout left an arrow marking the direction of travel. When an enemy was sighted, the war bundle was opened, after which it was imperative that the enemy be killed (Skinner 1915:797).

Failure of a war party or the death of a member was regarded as reflecting a lack of sacred power, and the leader might be severely whipped by the camp police (Whitman 1939:180). Protracted warfare involving large numbers of men was not common for the Ponca. Ordinarily, only if attacked in their village did they fight as a group and in such instances women joined in the fighting. Men gave scalps taken in raids to their female relatives who stretched them on willow hoops and carried them on poles in the Scalp Dance (Dorsey 1884:312, 317–319; Howard 1965:135–141).

History, 1849–1990

The Ponca Removal

In the mid-nineteenth century competition between tribes over territory for buffalo hunting intensified. The Ponca fought with the Sioux to the north and the Pawnee to the south for access to buffalo. In 1855 a large group of Ponca hunters encountered a Pawnee hunting party and

top, Okla. Histl. Soc., Oklahoma City:2100A; bottom left, Lib. of Congress: 3858; bottom right, Field Mus., Chicago: Anthr. 1636.

Fig. 5. Southern Ponca Sun Dance. top, Camp with cloth offerings on left, Sun Dance lodge on right, and 2 tepees on either side of the dance lodge. Photograph by Fred S. Barde, possibly with Southern Cheyenne, at Calumet, Okla., 1905–1906. bottom left, Women's dance. Cloth offerings include one made to resemble an American flag. Photograph by Thomas Croft, Ponca Res., Indian Terr., 1894. bottom right, Sixth group of dancers on the third day of the Sun Dance. "The grandfather and three dancers wore a bandoleer of crow feathers, the last dancer wearing a bandoleer of hawk feathers. All the dancers carried in their right hands a large sage ring, to which was attached eight eagle breath feathers. The grandfather in his right hand carried a black handkerchief to which was attached a bell. . . . The bodies of all were painted yellow. The faces were surrounded by small white dots. On the breast, back, and arms were marks made by applying the fingers when the paint was wet" (G.A. Dorsey 1905:84). Photograph by George A. Dorsey, Ponca Res., Okla. Terr., 1902.

annihilated them. However, that summer's hunt was the last successful one for the Ponca; in subsequent years their hunts were interfered with by Sioux war parties, and at a time when horticultural produce was essential to their survival, pressure from the Sioux prevented the Ponca from cultivating fields away from the protection of their village. Moreover, the bottomland available for horticulture was rapidly being occupied by illegal White settlers (Howard 1965:30–31).

Attempting to alleviate pressure from settlers and to obtain government protection from their enemies, on March 12, 1858, a Ponca delegation in Washington signed their third treaty with the United States, ceding most of their hunting lands for a reservation on the Niobrara River (Kappler 1904–1941, 2:772–795). Although an agency was established for the Ponca in 1859, the government proved incapable of protecting them from the Sioux. That summer a war party of Sioux and Cheyenne attacked the Ponca while on their summer hunt at the headwaters of the Elkhorn River, killing 15 men (including two chiefs) and capturing three children. The Sioux sent word to the Ponca that the attack was punishment for their having sold lands to the Whites (Howard 1965:31; Jablow 1974:323–343).

In 1861 the Ponca agent, John B. Hoffman, recruited 50 men to constitute the first agency police force and the next year established the first school. The Sioux continued to attack. The Sioux treaty of 1868 complicated the situation by mistakenly ceding the Ponca reservation land to the Sioux (Kappler 1904–1941, 2:998; Prucha 1990:110–114). When this administrative blunder was discovered, the United States government chose the practical solution of removing the Ponca to Indian Territory. Despite their protest, under military escort the Ponca removal began in the spring of 1877, only 36 individuals choosing to remain in the north with the Omaha. The trek—remembered as the Ponca trail of tears—took two months, during which they suffered sickness and deaths. When they reached their new home near Baxter Springs, Kansas, on lands reserved for the Quapaw, they found that no preparations had been made for them.

Dissatisfied with the location, the Ponca were allowed to move in 1878 to north-central Oklahoma where an agency was established on the Salt Fork River, two miles above its confluence with the Arkansas. For two summers, 1877 and 1878, the Ponca were unable to plant crops. In 1878 they were struck by a malaria epidemic that, in combination with the lack of food and unaccustomed climate, resulted in many deaths (Foreman 1946:247–252; Howard 1965:31–36).

The Northern Ponca

When his eldest son died in 1878, Standing Bear (figs. 6–7), a Ponca chief, decided to return north to bury him in traditional Ponca territory. Accompanied by 65 people, Standing Bear made his way to Nebraska where he was intercepted and taken into custody by the army. Public sympathy was aroused and a writ of habeas corpus was filed on his behalf in federal court in Omaha. Standing Bear's remarkable orations during the ensuing trial attracted national interest and resulted in a landmark decision by which the protection of the rights of individual American Indians was recognized under the United States constitution (King 1969). Standing Bear's party was allowed to continue their journey to their old reservation on the Niobrara. This journey resulted in the formation of separate Northern and Southern Ponca groups (Foreman 1946:252–253; Tibbles 1957:193–235, 1972; Howard 1965:36–37).

Aided by newspaperman Thomas H. Tibbles and Susette (Bright Eyes) La Flesche, an Omaha woman who Tibbles later married, Standing Bear toured the country speaking on the mistreatment of the Ponca. The case became a national scandal, and in 1880 a federal commission was appointed to investigate it. As a result of their investigations, an agreement was negotiated with the Sioux to return to the Ponca a portion of their former Niobrara reservation in Knox County, Nebraska, to be alloted in severalty (Foreman 1946:254–256; Cash and Wolff 1975:58–60).

Following Standing Bear's example, the Northern Ponca discontinued many traditional activities and

left, Smithsonian, NAA: 4244-C; right, Smithsonian, Dept. of Anthr.: 357905.

Fig. 6. Men's clothing. left, Delegation in Washington to request that the Ponca be allowed to leave Indian Terr. and return to their traditional lands on White River in Dakota Terr. back row, left to right: Big Snake; Baptiste Barnaby, interpreter; White Eagle, the last hereditary chief of the Ponca; Charles LeClair, interpreter; The Chief or Big Chief. front row, left to right: Black Crow, Big Elk, Standing Bear, Standing Buffalo Bull, White Swan, and Smoke Maker. reclining, in front: Hairy Grizzly Bear. Big Snake, the younger brother of Standing Bear, was killed by U.S. cavalry in 1879, while being arrested at the Ponca Agency. Photograph by Charles M. Bell, Washington, D.C., 1877. right, Pair of leggings made of dressed skin, dyed green. Wide beaded strips run along the outside of the leggings; the back edges have pieces of fur, locks of human hair, and feathers attached by thongs, the tops of which are wrapped in porcupine quills. Collected by Victor J. Evans; length 104.1 cm.

Smithsonian, NAA: 54,538.

Fig. 7. Residence of Standing Bear, Niobrara Res., Nebr., typical of the reservation period. A small frame house, a tepee, a brush arbor, wagon frames, and a mowing machine are visible. The first frame houses were constructed for the Northern Ponca about 1885. They consisted of 2 rooms and measured about 12 by 24 feet. Photograph possibly by George LeRoy Brown, 1882–1889.

attempted to assimilate into the surrounding non-Indian society, although some Northern Ponca participated in traditional activities by visiting other tribes. In the first decade of the twentieth century both Southern Ponca and the Winnebago John Rave introduced the Peyote religion to the Northern Ponca; they largely discontinued its use by 1950 (Howard 1965:125). The last recorded Northern Ponca *heδúška* dance was performed in the 1930s, by which time many other religious ceremonies had also been discontinued. Intermarriage with the Santee and Yankton Sioux, as well as with non-Indians, was common. However, history and sacred narratives were strongly maintained because the many geographic features of the environment were directly linked to oral tradition.

Among the small Northern Ponca population, already greatly mixed with White parentage and White culture, there grew a desire for complete assimilation. At the request of the tribal council, Congress passed an act (76 U.S. Stat. 429) in 1962 to terminate the federal trust relationship with the Northern Ponca (Howard 1965:38–39). When the act was implemented in 1966 the 834 acres of reservation land were removed from federal trust status and the 442 enrolled members of the tribe lost their eligibility to participate in federal programs for Indians. Many of the Northern Ponca continued to live in the vicinity of the former reservation as well as on the nearby Yankton Sioux and Santee Sioux reservations. After termination there was a decline in their health, economic status, and cultural activities. Consequently, in 1971, the Ponca Tribe reincorporated and began to seek restoration of federal status (Grobsmith and Ritter 1992). On April 8, 1988, the Nebraska state legislature extended recognition to the Ponca Tribe of Nebraska and expressed support for federal recognition, which was granted on October 31, 1990 (Grobsmith and Ritter 1994; Tiller 1996:409–410).

The Southern Ponca

After arriving at the new agency on the Salt Fork in the summer of 1878, the Indian agent attempted to induce the Ponca to spread out over the reservation. Soon the "half-breed band" formed a separate community eight miles from the agency at the mouth of Chikaskia River. In 1881, as a result of the government investigation into the Ponca removal, $165,000 was awarded to the Southern Ponca to help establish themselves in Indian Territory. By 1883 they had built 70 log homes; purchased cattle, horses, and wagons; and cultivated 350 acres. An industrial boarding school was attended by 65 Ponca children (Foreman 1946:252–255). In 1882, for administrative purposes, the Ponca were consolidated with the Pawnee and Otoe into a single agency.

To provide income for the tribe, the Ponca leased most of their reservation lands to White stock raisers. In 1890 a presidential order required the Poncas to take individual allotments; most opposed allotment, and traditionalists formed a strong antiallotment faction that fractured the tribe. Nonetheless, in 1892, 300 Poncas were induced to take allotments. By 1907, when Oklahoma became a state, all the reservation land had been allotted. As the original allottees died, the Miller Brothers 101 Ranch purchased their allotments as they came up for sale. The land became more valuable with the discovery of oil (Foreman 1946:257–258; Cash and Wolff 1975:62–67).

In 1902, during this period of internal strife and external pressure, the Peyote religion was introduced to the Ponca by Robert Buffalohead, who had learned the ritual from the Cheyenne, though another Ponca tradition credits the Tonkawa. It spread rapidly among the Southern Ponca, who introduced it to their Northern relatives. In 1916, the superintendent of the Ponca Agency in Oklahoma reported that one-half the population of 630 was involved with the new religion. Among the leaders of the Peyote religion who met in El Reno, Oklahoma, in 1918 to establish the Native American Church were two Poncas, Frank Eagle, who was elected the first president of the main church, and Louis McDonald, who was elected treasurer (Stewart 1987:116–117, 173–174, 224).

In addition to the Native American Church, five Christian churches were associated with the Ponca in Oklahoma: the Ponca Indian Methodist Church, the Phil Deschner Methodist Church, the Ponca Indian Nazarene Church, the Ponca Indian Baptist Church, and the Ponca Full Gospel Church.

Many Southern Poncas maintained their traditional activities during the twentieth century. Octagonal wooden dance halls (called round houses), replicating the general form of the earthlodge, were constructed along the Arkansas River where, during the winter months, many Ponca families camped in the cover of the brush. These were in use until the 1920s (Howard 1965:56; D.N. Brown 1979–1989). The Sun Dance was conducted each summer until the first decade of the twentieth century. The tribal pipe and its bundle was kept and treated with ceremonial respect (Howard 1965:102). Winter camps along the Arkansas River continued until pollution of the river by oil operations and sewage from Ponca City killed the fish and made the water unsafe to drink (D.N. Brown 1979–1989).

In 1950, under the Oklahoma Indian Welfare Act of 1936, the Ponca organized an elective tribal government. The new constitution identified tribal membership and defined a seven-member governing body elected for two-year terms as the Tribal Business Committee, which was legally empowered to act on behalf of the tribe. A tribal roll was also established as well as by-laws for conducting business (Ponca Tribe of Oklahoma 1975).

Twenty-six Ponca men served in the United States Army during World War I, and all returned home. In 1919, the Ponca veterans organized American Legion Post #38, the Buffalo Post, and the wives and mothers formed an auxiliary. Of the many Ponca men and women who served in World War II six men lost their lives. One Ponca man was also lost in the Korean War and another killed in the Vietnam War. The veterans' groups conducted the Memorial Day ceremony at the Ponca Indian cemetery, funeral ceremonies for deceased veterans, and sponsored dances on Armed Forces Day and other occasions (D.N. Brown 1979–1989).

In the 1960s the Ponca Housing Authority was formed and new homes replaced the older frame houses. A community developed at White Eagle with subsidized houses and rental duplexes for the elderly. A health clinic was built by the tribe and leased to the Indian Health Service. The former school at White Eagle was renovated and became the Tribal Affairs Building. A cultural center with cooking facilities and a gymnasium was constructed. In 1961 Ponca activist Clyde Warrior helped cofound the National Indian Youth Council and was a leader in Indian nationalism.

Factionalism and disharmony characterized Ponca tribal government in the 1970s and 1980s. As the Tribal Business Committee assumed responsibilities for management of federally funded programs, accusations of mismanagement and dishonesty led to several recall elections. Elections for the seven members of the Business Committee were acrimonious, and frequent changes in the composition of the committee made continuity in tribal programs difficult (D.N. Brown 1979–1989).

In 1980 the tribe received 2.3 million dollars to administer 16 federally funded programs, including health, nutrition, food distribution, alcohol and drug abuse, child welfare, law and order, legal services, higher education and adult education, training and employment, and rehabilitation of housing. The Ponca in association with the other tribes of north-central Oklahoma, the Pawnee, Otoe-Missouria, Kansa, and Tonkawa, established a Court of Indian Offenses. The Comprehensive Employment and Training Act program was especially important because it provided funding for many staff members involved with tribal operations (D.N. Brown 1979–1989). Of the 325 Poncas who were in the labor force in 1979, 310 worked; an additional 152 individuals were not in the labor force. However, many were underemployed since only 155 Poncas worked 40 or more weeks during the year. According to the 1980 U.S. Census, only 215 individuals were working. The majority of the jobs were provided by the tribe (40%), the federal government (18%), and the state government (12%) (U.S. Bureau of the Census 1986:1006, 1026).

With the reduction of federal funding for programs in the early 1980s, the Business Committee searched for other sources of revenue. Regularly scheduled bingo games sponsored by the Business Committee generated over one million dollars in 1983 for tribal operations and programs and provided employment for a few Poncas (D.N. Brown 1979–1989).

Although the Southern Ponca retained strong tribal identity, by 1990 the Omaha-Ponca language was spoken by only a small number of elders. Clan membership continued to be important, with eight clans being recognized: Thee-xee-dah (Blood), Mau-Kau (Medicine), Nu-xay (Ice), Wah-sha-bay (Buffalo), Heh-sah-dah (Rain), Wah-ja-jay (Osage or Snake), Neh-kah-pah-shnu (No Hair or Bald Head), and Wah-xay-hay-bay (Half Breed) (D.N. Brown 1979–1989).

Many traditional cultural activities continued. The Ponca Indian War Dance Society, formed in the 1950s as a

left, The Glass Negative, Ponca City, Okla.

Fig. 8. Dancers in costumes characteristic of the Southern Plains. left, Fancy Dancers at the White Eagle Res., Okla. left to right, Unidentified, Paul Little Voice, Dana Knight or Big Buffalo, unidentified man wearing a Plains upright war bonnet, Newman Little Walker, Perry Crazy Bear, Gus McDonald (who started the fancy dance), Walt Rowe (Cherokee), unidentified man, Jimmy Clark, Andrew Snake, and an unidentified man. Photograph by Jerry Drake, 1920s. right, War Dancers at the annual Ponca powwow. The leggings and breechcloth of the straight dancer, on the left, are decorated with matching ribbonwork. He also wears a wide beaded belt, ribbon shirt, and deerhair roach headdress with an eagle feather. The fancy dancer, on the right, wears feather bustles on his back, a deer hair roach headdress with 2 eagle feathers, and angora anklets. Both dancers wear the Southern Plains hard-sole moccasin. Among the Ponca the fancy dance style of contest dancing and dress began in the early 1920s. In the 1990s the feather dance or fancy dance costume could be seen at powwows throughout the United States among many other tribes. Women dancers wearing shawls are in the center. Photograph by Donald N. Brown, 1975.

revival of the *heðúška* society, sponsored a spring and fall dance each year. Membership included a number of non-Indians as well as nonveterans. At each dance a meal was served and groceries distributed to elderly tribal members, and clan songs were performed. As part of a Mother's Day dance in 1983 the Ponca Indian Women's Society revived the Scalp Dance, which had not been held since the end of World War II. Special dances were held throughout the year, and the Wah-ja-jay clan also sponsored two dances each year.

A chapter of the Gold Star Mothers was prominent, and men continued to participate in American Legion Post #38 as well as in Wah-Shu-Shay, the Veterans of Foreign Wars Post 9145, which drew its membership from tribes throughout north-central Oklahoma (D.N. Brown 1979–1989).

In the late 1970s Wah-Hun-Thing-Gay was formed, an organization of Ponca elders that is often invited to attend special events. For four consecutive Sundays each spring the shinny game (*ttabégasi*) was played at White Eagle, under the direction of a family of the Neh-kah-pah-shnu clan (Howard 1971; D.N. Brown 1979–1989).

The Southern Ponca were very active in the powwow circuit and served as singers and dancers at celebrations throughout the United States, helping to develop a pan-tribal Oklahoma style, including the fancy dance style of powwow dancing (fig. 8). The Ponca held their annual powwow (fig. 9) in late August, which in the 1980s included dance contests for both men and women and drew dancers from many tribes. The powwow also provided an opportunity to hear the Ponca war dance songs. A number of Ponca singers gained wide recognition and were invited to sing at dances throughout the United States (D.N. Brown 1979–1989).

Fig. 9. Powwows. top, Honoring Dance. Antoine LeClair (center) leads Rosette Le Clair, an unidentified dancer, Tina Youker, and Antoinette LeClair in the dance. Those honored follow with a giveaway of blankets, shawls, cash, and other property to guests. Photograph by Donald N. Brown, 1980. bottom, First annual youth powwow, at tribal powwow grounds, near Niobrara, Nebr. Photograph by Dion Zephier, 1996.

Population

The first estimate of Ponca numbers was "eighty fighting men" in 1785 (Miró in Kinnaird 1946–1949, 4:166; cf. Mooney 1928:13). In 1804–1805 the population had fallen to 200 as a consequence of smallpox and constant fighting with the Sioux (table 1). In the same period Pierre Chouteau estimated their numbers at 250 (Nasatir 1952, 2:759).

In 1978, of the 2,020 enrolled members of the Ponca Tribe in Oklahoma, only 24 individuals were listed as of full Ponca inheritance, 18 males with a median age of 67.6 years and 6 females with a median age of 62.2 years. Names of 23 additional tribes were included by those who listed multiple

Table 1. Ponca Population, 1780–1998

Date	*Total*	*Northern Ponca*	*Southern Ponca*	*Source*
1780	800			Mooney 1928:13
1804–1805	200			Lewis 1832:709
1820	750/1,250			Morse 1822:251, 366
1836	900			Cass in Schoolcraft 1851–1857, 3:611
1846	2,000			Bent 1850:185
1847	1,600			Matlock in Schoolcraft 1851–1857, 6:696
1852	800			Mitchell in Schoolcraft 1851–1857, 6:695
1862	1,054			ARCIA 1862:356
1876	730			ARCIA 1876:32, 208
1880	825	225	600	Dorsey and Thomas 1910:279
1892	775	208	567	Dorsey 1892
1910	875[a]	193	619	U.S. Bureau of the Census 1915:20
1939	1,237	395	842	U.S. Department of the Interior 1939:9, 12
1950s	1,350	350	1,000	Howard 1965:10
1960	1,258	400	858	U.S. Department of the Interior 1961:22, 27
1983		[b]	2,221	Bureau of Indian Affairs 1983:5
1989	3,277	890	2,387	Grobsmith and Ritter 1994:459; Bureau of Indian Affairs 1989:5
1998	4,387	1,895[c]	2,492[d]	Stan Taylor, communication to editors 1998; Marcella Hudson, communication to editors 1998

[a]Includes 42 Poncas in Kans., 18 in S. Dak., 3 in Pa.
[b]No official figure available during termination.
[c]Lineal descendants.
[d]Tribal enrollment.

Fig. 10. Activities of the 1990s. left, Trade mission in Beijing, China. left to right, Tony Raimondo, Chairman of Nebr. Economic Development Committee; Nebr. Gov. E. Benjamin Nelson; Li Lanqing, Vice Premier of China; and Northern Ponca Tribal Chairman Fred LeRoy. A poster of one of 8 murals in the Nebr. State capitol by Stephen Cornelius Roberts, dedicated in 1966, is being presented to the vice premier. The mural, *The Ideal of Freedom*, depicts the 1879 trial of the Ponca Chief Standing Bear, which established Native Americans as "persons" in the eyes of the law (Howard 1965:36–37). Photograph by David Beaver, 1997. right, Northern Ponca tribal council at the dedication of the Ponca Health and Wellness Center. left to right, Alex Taylor, James LaPointe, Secretary John (Andy) Tate, Chairman Fred LeRoy, Treasurer Rick Wright, Donna Wendzilla, Linda Stolle, and David Zephier. Marion Peniska is vice-chairman. Photograph by Kim Kuhle, 1998.

tribal inheritance. Eighty-five percent of the enrolled members lived within 100 miles of White Eagle. The Oklahoma Ponca were a young population with 41 percent of the enrolled members under 20 years and only 6 percent over 60 years (D.N. Brown 1979).

Synonymy†

The Poncas' name for themselves is *ppą́kka*, an etymologically obscure form that is the source of most other tribal designations for them as well as their official name. The same form is used by the other Dhegiha Siouans, the Omaha, Osage, Quapaw, and Kansa; a variant *ppǫ́kka* is also recorded in Osage and Quapaw (Fletcher and La Flesche 1911:101; La Flesche 1932:129; Dorsey and Thomas 1910; John E. Koontz and Robert L. Rankin, personal communications 1988). The Chiwere Siouans—Iowa and Otoe—use *p*^{h}*ą́ką*; an Otoe variant *p*^{h}*ą́ka* is also recorded (Dorsey and Thomas 1910; Parks 1988; Louanna Furbee, personal communication 1990). A Winnebago variant Kañ′ka^{n} has been recorded, but it may be a misreading of Pañ′ka^{n} (Dorsey and Thomas 1910). Other tribal designations based on this name are Santee and Yankton Sioux *pą́ka* (Riggs 1881; Cook 1880–1882; Williamson 1902:146; Deloria 1935), Comanche *pɔ́nkɨ* (Jean Charney, personal communication 1990), and Caddo *pankah* (Chafe 1979).

European and American renditions of the name for the Ponca have been variations of the same name. The earliest citation occurs in a 1785 Spanish report in which the name is Poncas, the form that occurs throughout the Spanish period in French Louisiana (Miró in Nasatir 1952, 1:123, also, for example, Tabeau 1939:86, 99–101). In addition to this more common form, Lewis and Clark cite a variant La Pong and Les Pongs, which is attributed to French traders (Moulton 1983–, 3:399; Coues 1893, 1:108); a similar form, Pons, is attributed to the French by Maximilian in Thwaites (1904–1907, 22:284). Lewis and Clark's own renditions include Ponca, Poncaras, Poncarars, Porncases, Ponckais, and Ponkas (Lewis and Clark in Moulton 1983–, 2:195, 438; 3:26, 27, 493). Other nineteenth-century variants are Poncârs and Poniars (Lewis 1832:709, 711), Ponsars (Farnham 1843:31), Puncaw (Long in James 1823, 1:343), Ponkaws and Pongkaws (Gale 1867:183), Punchas (Domenech 1860, 2:306), and Punchaws (Biddle 1820:4).

Occasionally in early documents and on several maps Panas or Panias, the name of the Pawnees, is mistakenly given for the Poncas. Lewis and Clark, for example, erroneously cite Panis and Panias where they mean Poncas (Moulton 1983–, 3:46, 47). The name Pana on the 1673 Marquette map (Tucker 1942:pl. 5) has erroneously been considered to designate the Ponca (Dorsey and Thomas 1910).

The Ponca name of one of their clans, *δíγida*, is the source of their designation by the Northern Caddoan tribes: Pawnee *rí·hita*, Arikara *ní·hitA*, and Wichita *ni·hit* (Parks 1976:101, 1965–1990, 1988). The Kitsai name Mooney (1893) recorded for Otoe, Dehit, is actually the term for Ponca, and the term he recorded for Ponca, Âraho, is the name for the Kansa. Unrelated to these terms is a Caddo name, Tchiáχ sokush, recorded by Gatschet (Dorsey and Thomas 1910).

The Kiowa and Plains Apache names for the Ponca refer to the hairstyle of Ponca men: Kiowa *ɔ́lt*^{h}*ǫ́ɔ̀lk*^{h}*ɔyk̓ìhà·gɔ̀* 'oval head hair' (Laurel J. Watkins, personal communication 1979), and Plains-Apache kxàdé·cìts'ìcį́ 'hair cut in the center' (Bittle 1952–1953).

The Cheyenne and Arapaho do not distinguish the Ponca from the Omaha. The Cheyenne name for both tribes is *onéhaoʔO* (Glenmore and Leman 1985:201; Mooney 1907:423–424); the Arapaho term is *howóho·nóʔ* (Ives Goddard, personal communication 1990). Both terms are borrowings that derive from the name Omaha itself.

A common Sioux name for the Ponca is *oyáte yámni* 'three peoples', reputedly coined because the Ponca sometimes camped in three concentric circles (Riggs 1890:397; Williamson 1902:146; Buechel 1970:733).

In the Plains sign language there was no standard sign for the Ponca. Two sources give the designation for them as 'cut-throat', the same sign that generally denotes the Sioux, indicated by drawing the right hand, open and palm facing downward, across the throat (Hadley 1893:151; Howard 1965:6). Another source cites three unrelated designations: the Arapaho sign, which was to tap the forehead with the right hand fixed; and two others, the signs for 'sitting down soldier' and 'shaved heads', neither of which was attributed to specific tribes (W.P. Clark 1885:305).

†This synonymy was written by Douglas R. Parks.

Sources

The Ponca have been the subject of relatively little historical or anthropological study. Howard (1965) presents the most comprehensive overview of history and culture while Jablow (1974) provides a detailed chronology to 1858 prepared for the Indian Claims Commission. Grobsmith and Ritter (1992) detail the restoration of federal recognition to the Northern Ponca. The fullest source of Ponca historical ethnography is the many publications of James Owen Dorsey (1884, 1894, 1897), though it is often conflated with material on the Omaha. George A. Dorsey (1905) gives a brief account of the 1902 Ponca Sun Dance. Fletcher and La Flesche (1911) include ethnographic information on Ponca in their encyclopedic study of the Omaha. Skinner (1915, 1920) describes Ponca dances and societies and provides other cultural detail. Tibbles (1972) gives a contemporary account of the trial of Standing Bear. Whitman (1939) presents an autobiography of a Ponca man. Tiller (1996:409–410, 528–529) gives economic profiles of the Ponca Tribe of Nebraska and the Ponca Tribe of Oklahoma.

Iowa

MILDRED MOTT WEDEL

Language and Territory

The Iowa (ˈīōu, earlier ˈīōā) are a Siouan-speaking group. They, the Otoe, and the Missouria spoke dialects of the Chiwere language,* whose closest linguistic relative is Winnebago (Chafe 1973:1181–1182).

According to oral tradition (Dorsey 1886:213), the Iowa split off in the distant past from an ancestral group located between the Mississippi River and the western side of Lake Michigan, probably in the general region of Green Bay, where the Winnebago remained. The Iowa migrated west toward the Mississippi. Their proto- and early historic village sites on the Upper Iowa River are identified as the Orr focus (see "Plains Village Tradition: Eastern Periphery and Oneota Tradition," this vol.). In the late seventeenth century the Iowa lived also along Bear Creek, a north tributary of the Upper Iowa, and Riceford Creek, a south tributary of Root River in southern Minnesota, as well as along the south fork of Root River, having perhaps spread in that direction from the Upper Iowa (fig. 1) (Withrow and Rodell 1984). Analysis of these remains (M.M. Wedel 1976:18–21, 1986:49) suggests that the Iowa may have lived in two villages concurrently.

Environment

During the seventeenth century the Iowa lived on elevated terraces along the lower reaches of the Upper Iowa River, where they fished and gathered mollusks, and grew gardens in the floodplain below. Above were unglaciated hills wooded largely with hickory, walnut, maple, birch, and oak. The Iowa foraged for fruits, nuts, roots, and edible leaf plants near their villages, where individuals or family groups also hunted deer and other small mammals, as well as wild fowl. The tribe hunted bison, elk, and deer in village parties on the tall grass prairie to the northwest, at the head of the Upper Iowa, the Iowa, and Des Moines rivers, and possibly the Blue Earth River. The situation, which thus included river valley, upland forest, and prairie, made possible a diversified economy.

Culture in the Seventeenth and Eighteenth Centuries

Iowa culture integrated elements from a mixed heritage (Whitman 1937:xiv). From their Siouan-speaking progenitors the Iowa inherited horticulture and a sharply defined class system; from contact with early or Proto-Central Algonquians they borrowed their social structure, including patrilineal descent, clans, and kinship system (Callender 1962:69; Murdock 1965:28–29). From association with Plains cultures they adopted summer village bison hunts and many material items, such as skin-working tools (fig. 2) and arrowshaft wrenches; and from the Santee Sioux they obtained certain traditional tales (Skinner 1920:189–261, 1925:425).

Seventeenth- and eighteenth-century European accounts provide some direct observations of Iowa social and cultural patterns. The first European to write about the Iowa was the Jesuit Louis André who met them at a Winnebago village in 1676 (M.M. Wedel 1986:14–19). Later, Michel Accault and Nicolas Perrot traded at the Upper Iowa River villages of the Iowa, Accault in 1678–1679 seeking bison hides and Perrot in 1685–1686 searching for beaver furs (M.M. Wedel 1986:30–32, 38–46).

Large-scale hunting on foot of bison, elk, and deer (Bacqueville de la Potherie 1722, 2:184), using bows and arrows with chipped-stone points, took place during the summer while the gardens matured, and for a briefer period in the winter (Mott 1938; M.M. Wedel 1986:39–40).

Perrot described the Iowa wailing ritual he witnessed in 1685, performed as part of a welcoming ceremony, when tears mixed with nose excrement were spread on heads, faces, and garments of Frenchmen, a ritual shared by many Siouans and some Caddoans into early contact times (Friederici 1906; M.M. Wedel 1974:170–171, 1986:40–41). Perrot wrote of being carried on a bison hide to the Iowa head chief's lodge after the initial meeting, a rite soon after discontinued. Upon his approach to the Iowa, he noted that the women fled raising their hands to the sun to seek supernatural protection. At the feasting ritual he, as honored guest, was hand-fed his first bites. Of

*Chiwere (Iowa-Otoe) consonants are: (voiced or voiceless stops and affricate) *b*, *d*, *ǰ*, *g*, ˀ; (aspirated stops) p^h, t^h, $\check{c}^h$, k^h; (glottalized stops and affricate) *p̓*, *t̓*, *č̓*, *k̓*; (voiceless spirants) *θ*, *s*, *x*, *h*; (voiced spirants) *δ*, *y*; (glottalized spirants) *θ̓*, *s̓*, *x̓*; (nasals) *m*, *n*, n^y, *ŋ*; (resonants) *w*, *r* ([r], [l]); (short oral vowels) *i*, *e*, *a*, *o*, *u*; (short nasal vowels) *į*, *ą*, *ų*; (long oral vowels) *i·*, *e·*, *a·*, *o·*, *u·*; (long nasalized vowels) *į·*, *ą·*, *ų·*. Stress (marked by an acute accent) is also phonemic. The resonant *r* has several phonetic realizations: [r, δ, l, d, y, n]. For some speakers *s* is [s] varying with [š] and *y* is [y] varying with [ž]. The phonemic orthography used in the citation of Iowa and Otoe terms follows the tentative analysis of Robert L. Rankin (communications to editors 1991, 1998), based on Whitman (1947) and his own work.

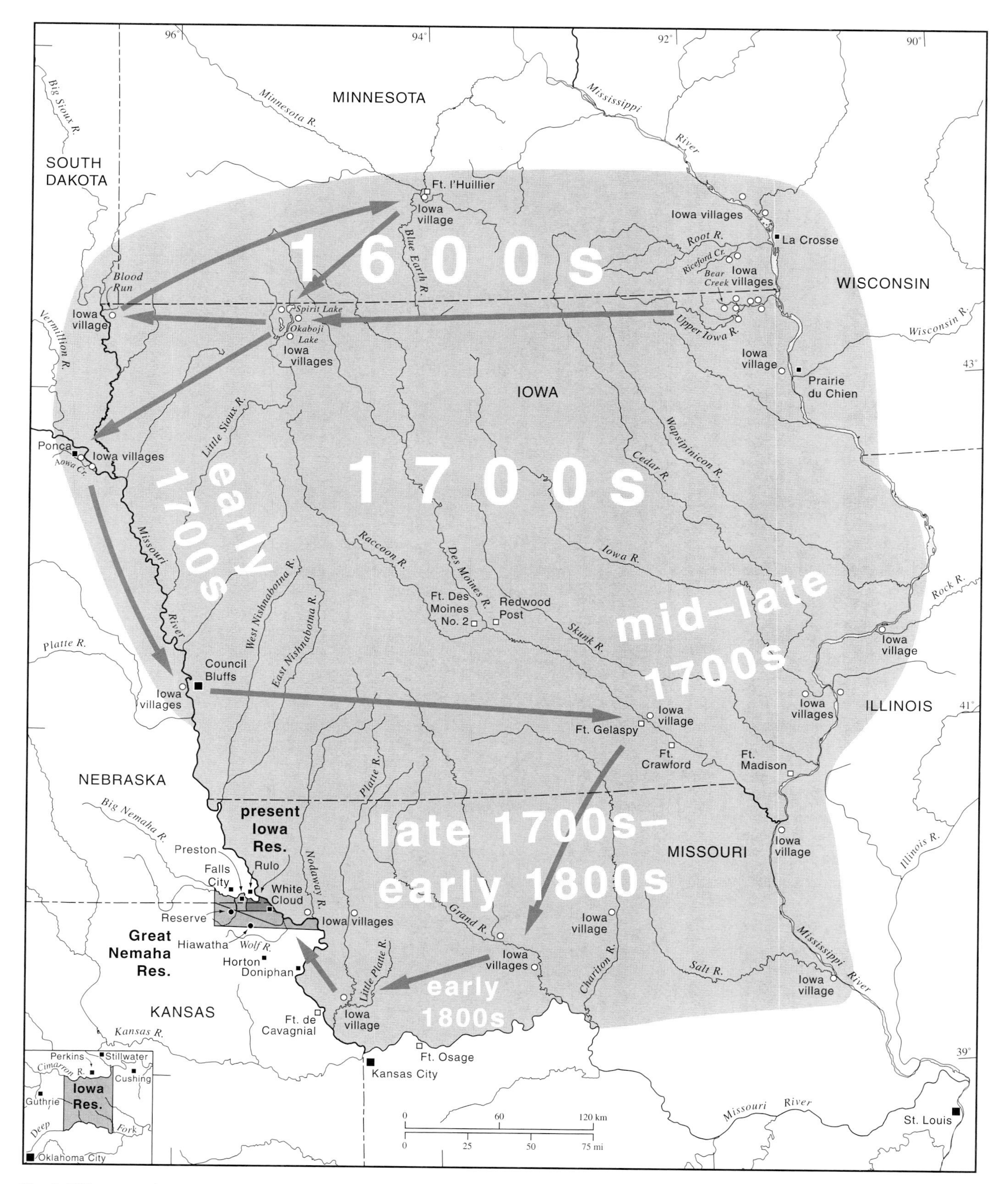

Fig. 1. Villages, territory, and movements of the Iowa (Schoolcraft 1851–1857, 3: Tucker 1942; Wedel 1959; Jackson 1966; Blaine 1979). Dates label areas of major population concentrations; additional villages were outside these areas at various times. The villages at the mouths of the Rock and Salt rivers are traditional locations (Schoolcraft 1851–1857, 3:257). The Iowa portion of the Great Nemaha Reservation (1837–1890), shared with the Missouri River Sauks, was at first north of the diagonal line (1837–1854), later north of the horizontal line (1854–1861), and lastly in the northeast corner. The inset illustrates the area of the executive order reservation in Ind. Terr. for the Iowa between 1883 and 1891.

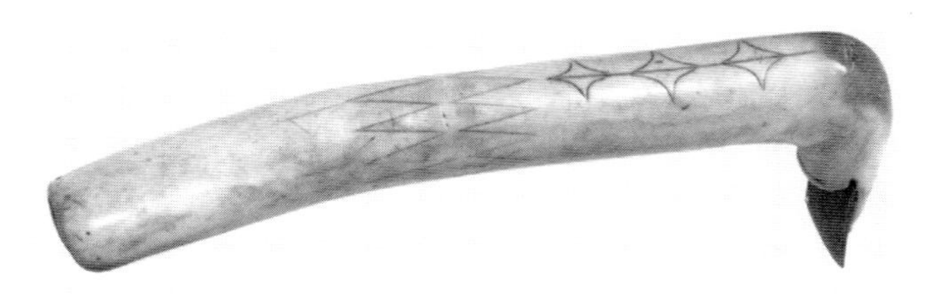

Milwaukee Public Mus., Wis.: 30160/7287.

Fig. 2. Hide scraper, elkbone handle with metal blade. Iowa scraper handles were often decorated with incised and colored lines, sometimes with symbolic meaning; these are apparently decorative (Skinner 1926:292). Collected by Alanson B. Skinner, Great Nemaha, Nebr., 1922–1923; length 32 cm.

special interest, Perrot described elements of the Calumet ceremony, performed to make him an honorary chief of the Iowa, thereby confirming an alliance between the Iowa and the French (M.M. Wedel 1974:43–45).

History, 1686–1837

Migrations, 1686–1765

In 1686 Perrot found the Iowa and the Sioux to be on generally friendly terms with one another. He made alliances and set up trading arrangements with them (Bacqueville de la Potherie 1722, 2:216), which angered the Algonquian tribes to the east (Illinois, Fox, Potawatomi, Sauk, certain Miami, Prairie Kickapoo) who cherished their dominance over more western tribes that had few if any firearms. Consequently, they and the western Mascouten made frequent, persistent attacks upon the less numerous Iowa who decided that to survive they must move farther west. They established villages somewhere on the shore of Spirit Lake in Dickinson County, Iowa, in the late 1680s (Franquelin 1697:map; M.M. Wedel 1981:5–7).

During the following decade warfare was common between the allied Iowa-Sioux and the Illinois groups, especially the Miami and Piankashaw. The western Mascouten may have continued to attack the Iowa even at their new villages (M.M. Wedel 1986:47). In the summer of 1700 the Sioux were apparently beginning to move onto what the French called the "Little Prairie," in southeastern Minnesota, impelled no doubt by their enemies in the Illinois country, and the Spirit Lake village was found to be deserted (M.M. Wedel 1986:23; Delisle 1702:55). Later the Iowa were living near the Omaha, who were then either on the Big Sioux River or its tributary, Blood Run, in Lyon County, Iowa (M.M. Wedel 1981:7–8). They were persuaded to join other tribes gathering around Fort l'Huillier on the Blue Earth River where they would be protected and could obtain European trade goods. This they did in 1701; but when the French could not protect them from their enemies, they fled west again.

For over four decades after 1701–1702 the Iowa lived in far northwest Iowa. Documentation for this period is sparse. Although Iowas were still on a friendly basis of accommodation with the Sioux at the turn of the century, the Sioux were beginning to take control of the Little Prairie (Franquelin 1699:map). Upon leaving Fort l'Huillier, the Iowa may have chosen to live along the Little Sioux River below Spirit and Okaboji lakes (Henning 1961:32–33). They hunted to the south and southeast along the Little Sioux and east into the Des Moines River valley, where they were reported in 1714 by Étienne Venyard, sieur de Bourgmont (Norall 1988:109).

In 1724 Bourgmont thwarted an alliance between the Iowa and the Fox, which he attributed to the fact that only one trader had reached the Iowa in recent years, causing them to seek trade goods through Fox middlemen. To his camp at a Kansa Indian village near present Doniphan, Kansas, Bourgmont invited representatives of nearby tribes. Six Iowa "chiefs" came from the north on October 5, flourishing their peace calumets. After speechmaking, feasting, and presentation of gifts, Bourgmont chose three Iowas to join his party. However, when the journey was delayed, they apparently returned home and were not recalled (Norall 1988:143–147).

Just when the Iowa left their villages in the Little Sioux area to move farther west is unknown. Fletcher and La Flesche (1911:86, 91) were told by Omahas that the Iowa lived at one time across the Missouri River on Aowa Creek in Dixon County, just south of Ponca, Nebraska, compelled to move there because of Sioux hostilities. They may have moved southward out of Omaha territory along the Missouri River in the 1740s, and have lived briefly, possibly with the Otoe, above the mouth of the Platte in Otoe territory (Chouteau 1816). Again they moved, crossing the Missouri to its eastern side where Meriwether Lewis and William Clark saw the remains of an "old" Iowa village on the site of modern Council Bluffs, Iowa (Moulton 1983–, 2:424; M.M. Wedel 1986:70–71). This would have put them within easy reach of the French Fort de Cavagnial established in 1744 (Hoffhaus 1964; M.M. Wedel 1981a:41), thereby providing the coveted opportunity to trade furs and hides for European merchandise. In this period the Iowa may have acquired horses in some number, perhaps through Otoe and Pawnee middlemen. Hunting was probably in the modern region of western Iowa and east into the drainage of the Des Moines. Here they came into conflict with the Osage to the south and French coureurs de bois to the east (IHC 29:102–103, 443; WHC 18:195).

When in 1757 two Iowas killed two Frenchmen on the Des Moines River, the tribe sent 10 representatives, including the guilty persons, to Montreal to appear before Pierre de Rigaud, marquis Vaudreuil-Cavagnal, governor-general of New France (WHC 18:195–196; Neill 1892), to ask mercy for the murderers. This was the first visit of Iowas to Montreal. The two were pardoned in an impressive ceremony in which the entire Iowa contingent—their roach hairstyle conspicuous—performed a high-stepping dance wearing bells on their legs and shouting words, unintelligible to the onlookers, in time with their movements (Blaine 1979:39). Afterward these Iowas accompanied Gen. Louis-Joseph de Montcalm in his successful attack on Fort William Henry, New York. According to Chouteau (1816), in 1765 and the years immediately following, the Iowa, having received assurance that traders would be sent to them, moved east near the mouth of the Des Moines River.

On the Des Moines River, 1765–1837

In their location on the Des Moines River, the Iowa found trade more accessible, both through Spaniards from Saint Louis and from British traders representing the North West Company (Fitzpatrick 1931:32; Thomas 1894:110–111). The Iowa also went to Prairie du Chien and Mackinac to receive British trade items. They served as middlemen between the British and the Otoes living on the Missouri River (Nasatir 1952, 1:125). With trade goods becoming more available in this period, manufactured goods replaced many handmade articles that had required much labor and time in preparation.

A 1778 map (Hutchins, in Tucker 1942:pl. 29) depicted Iowa villages on the east side of the Mississippi, one below the mouth of the Des Moines and one below that of the Iowa River on its west bank. An acceptable interpretation of these occupancies has not been made, nor have the sites been identified.

The Iowa hunted westward through the headwaters of the Grand and Chariton rivers and northwest up the Des Moines River. Game was still plentiful in the mid-eighteenth century. The women continued to garden successfully. In their leisure they played games, usually associated with gambling, that reflected both Northeast (lacrosse, women's shinny) and Plains (hoop and javelin, moccasin) influences (Lowie 1954:121–122). The young men still sought to gain war honors by killing and scalping enemies; and they stole horses from White settlers and from other Indians, the animals having become a prestige item (Nasatir 1952, 1:160, 184–185).

The Iowa became pawns in the competition between the Spaniards and British for trade and tribal control in the Mississippi valley. However, in 1803–1804, Saint Louis passed from Spanish domination to French and then to American. In 1808 the United States established trading posts, called factories, where the Iowa could trade with Americans at Fort Madison at the rapids of the Des Moines River and at Fort Osage near present-day Kansas City (Gregg 1937). The Iowa became involved in American-British competition. Traditional chiefs sided with the British traders, influenced no doubt by Winnebago allegiance to them. By the turn of the century North West Company traders had set up regular trading posts on the middle Des Moines (Redwoods, Fort Gelaspie, Fort Crawford) to which the Iowa went. By 1804 the Des Moines River basin was divided between the Sioux and the Iowa, the Iowa controlling the lower half.

A written treaty of peace between the Osage and certain Midwestern tribes, including the Iowa, was concluded on October 18, 1805, under the guidance of Governors James Wilkinson and William Henry Harrison (Carter 1934–1962, 13:245–247), a form of alliance that contrasted with the Calumet ceremony. In 1806 some Iowas, accompanied by representatives of other tribes, went to Washington for the first time in order to meet the president and be shown the power of Americans (Ewers 1966).

Although the main tribal village on the Des Moines continued, other settlements are recorded before the War of 1812: one about 10 miles up the Iowa River (Pike 1810:43), and one near Prairie du Chien where Iowas in 1811 were involved in mining lead (Boilvin 1811). The old-style summer tribal hunts were apparently disappearing with hunting limited more to procuring meat for subsistence (Boilvin 1811). The federal government appointed Hard Heart to be chief of the Iowa. When the War of 1812 split the tribe, Hard Heart and his followers joined the American-allied Otoe. At the end of hostilities the Iowa participated in another treaty of peace, this one with the Americans, their representatives placing their marks on the documents September 16, 1815 (Kappler 1904–1941, 2:122–123).

The period between the War of 1812 and the Iowas' move to a reservation in 1837 was beset with difficulties for them. For those Iowas inclined toward the British, the years were characterized by village movements back and forth between the Des Moines and Missouri rivers, and southwest to the Chariton, Grand, and other Missouri tributaries along which they hunted. The westward migrations were forced by the Sauk especially, and by the Fox, pressing west from the Mississippi, and return migrations eastward by the Otoe and Omaha, who were disinclined to share their hunting grounds east of the Missouri where game was disappearing (Ketchum 1827; Dougherty 1831). The Sioux were sporadic enemies. Apparently Hard Heart and his followers continued to live with the Otoe for a time, but when the Des Moines River Iowa attempted to join the Otoe in 1819, they were not accepted (O'Fallon 1820). Finding it no longer possible to maintain a single stable tribal village on the Des Moines, they moved to a site 70 miles up the Chariton River, then in 1822 to the Grand River, perhaps on the north fork.

Land claimed by the Iowa that lay along the lower Missouri was given by the federal government to American veterans of the War of 1812. These settlers raised a great clamor whenever Iowa warriors stole their horses or were involved in other hostilities against them, and even when they came near with peaceful intent. These confrontations were often the result of overreaction, lack of understanding, and fear, as was the settlers' constant denigration of the Iowa and the frequently expressed wish for their extermination (Caldwell 1970).

In 1822 an acting subagent and interpreter was appointed for the Iowa in order to keep them in a single village, to encourage peace, and to provide necessary goods and services. In 1825 the Iowa were parties to the Treaty of Prairie du Chien (Kappler 1904–1941, 2:250–255). After 1825 regular subagents were appointed (Hill 1974:81–82). The harried Iowa benefitted in some ways, but at times subagents were in league with traders and untrustworthy interpreters, to the detriment of the Indians.

By 1827 most of the tribe was settled on the Little Platte River in northwest Missouri, on high land near Robidoux's trading house (Clark 1828; Thwaites 1904–1907, 22:257). The Iowa were described as being "mild, friendly, well-disposed" at this time (Bean 1839), but problems soon arose attributable to nearby traders who urged whiskey upon them, an encompassing term for alcohol to which was added varying lethal ingredients (Bean 1839).

In three land cession treaties (August 4, 1824; July 15, 1830; September 17, 1836), the Iowa released claim to all territory in Missouri and Iowa (Kappler 1904–1941, 2:208–209, 305–310, 468–470; Royce 1899:706, 726, 760). In 1834 White Cloud became principal chief (fig. 3). In 1837 the Iowa moved onto a 200-section reservation west of the Missouri River and south of the Great Nemaha River, straddling the Nebraska-Kansas border, administered by the Great Nemaha Subagency (fig. 1) (Hughes 1837; Hill 1974:69–70).

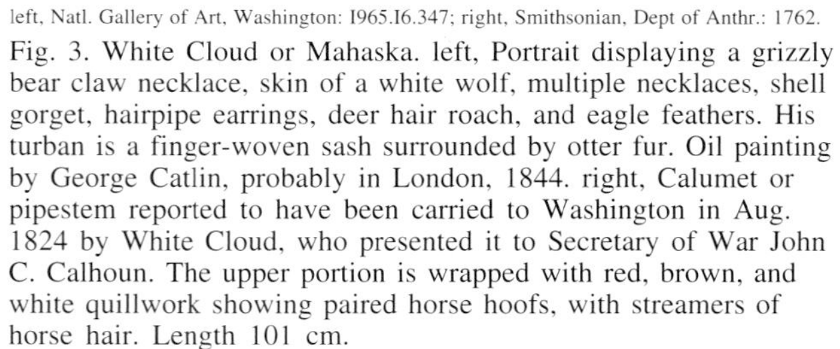

left, Natl. Gallery of Art, Washington: 1965.16.347; right, Smithsonian, Dept of Anthr.: 1762.

Fig. 3. White Cloud or Mahaska. left, Portrait displaying a grizzly bear claw necklace, skin of a white wolf, multiple necklaces, shell gorget, hairpipe earrings, deer hair roach, and eagle feathers. His turban is a finger-woven sash surrounded by otter fur. Oil painting by George Catlin, probably in London, 1844. right, Calumet or pipestem reported to have been carried to Washington in Aug. 1824 by White Cloud, who presented it to Secretary of War John C. Calhoun. The upper portion is wrapped with red, brown, and white quillwork showing paired horse hoofs, with streamers of horse hair. Length 101 cm.

Culture in the Early Nineteenth Century

Structures

Iowa villages were composed of lodges built with a pole framework and covered with elm or walnut bark slabs or woven rush mats (fig. 4). The larger rectangular lodges were bark covered, approximately 20 by 30–40 feet, and each housed an extended family. They were lived in during the summer and were also used for ceremonies. The smaller oval mat or bark-covered lodges were 10 by 14–20 feet, and each housed a nuclear family. They, as well as tepees, were lived in during the winter, situated in protected locations. Earthlodges were apparently used only temporarily when the Iowa lived near the Otoe in the early nineteenth century (Skinner 1926:273–277; M.M. Wedel 1986:58–61).

Subsistence

The women raised maize, beans, and probably squash or pumpkins in small garden patches (M.M. Wedel 1981:4). The men planted tobacco and sacred maize for ceremonial use (M.M. Wedel 1986:55–57). Storage caches, lined with bark, woven mats, or grasses, were dug into the lodge floors.

Technology

Articles of everyday use, as well as ceremonial objects, were made from bone, wood, stone, pottery, and hides; reed mats and natural-fiber bags were also woven (M.M. Wedel 1959; Skinner 1926). Log mortars, with one end burnt and scraped to form a bowl, were set into the earth and used to grind corn and medicinal plants. Earthenware jars made of pounded clay and burnt stone or fibers were used for storage. Small rawhide boxes were distinctively painted with geometric designs (fig. 5). Transportation on foot involved the use of the head strap for heavy loads carried on the back. The dog, and later the horse, travois was commonly used. Little children and household goods were transported in rawhide boxes attached to the poles (Skinner 1926:277–287).

Social Organization

The Iowa tribe was a confederation of exogamous patrilineal clans whose names related to their mythical origins. Kinship terminology followed the Omaha system (Skinner 1915:735–738; Hamilton and Irvin 1848:vii; Morgan 1871:293–382), which emphasized relationships by clan. The names of 10 different clans were recorded, eight of which Morgan reported as existing in 1859. In the twentieth century, the Iowa considered their tribe to comprise seven clans, each of which consisted of four subclans. During the nineteenth century, the clans were grouped in two unnamed moieties (table 1), but in the twentieth century

top and bottom left, Denver Public Lib., Western Hist. Dept., Colo.: F40584 and F40586; bottom right, Mildred Wedel.

Fig. 4. Houses. top, Rectangular bark house with poles used to hold bark down and an attached arbor for working. The peaked roof shows Euro-American influence. Two girls and one boy all have decorated horse blankets. The boy (at left on horseback) has haircut in a clan style, and the man on the far right holds a feather fan. Probably by J.J. Hargrave, Guthrie, Ind. Terr., May 1890. bottom left, Rectangular bark house with curved roof and arbor working area covered with bark. The split board walls show Euro-American influence. Photographed about 1900. bottom right, Elm bark house on Kansas Res.; drying rack for corn at right. Photographed about 1900.

moiety organization was no longer reported. Tribal leadership was divided on a semiannual basis, with the head chief of the Buffalo clan in charge during the spring and summer. The head chief of the Black Bear clan presided over the hunt and other village activities in the autumn and winter (Morgan 1959:67; Dorsey 1897:238–239; Skinner 1915:729–732, 1926:193–201).

A clan chief was the eldest male lineal descendant of any of the four subclan ancestors, the eldest brother's son being most likely to inherit the position. If there were no sons, his daughter's son or niece's son would be chosen. Each clan had its own sacred pipe (fig. 6), a war bundle, and a tattoo bundle. Seven pipes were the traditional number representing the clans, although in fact there were probably a larger number of pipes (Skinner 1915:685, 729, 1926:215ff.; Miner 1911:45–47). War chiefs were in charge of war bundles, and clan chiefs cared for their sacred pipe bundles. The Thunder clan was the keeper of the "Ghost bundle," which was used to test oaths when conflict arose over counting coups (Skinner 1915:734–735, 1926:199).

Each clan had customary responsibilities within the tribe. For example, no gardening preparations were to take place until the chiefs of the Buffalo clan performed a ritual asking for supernatural help in producing a good crop, planted some kernels themselves, then sponsored a feast (Skinner 1915:685–686, 1926:201). Each clan was also characterized by personal names and distinctive clan hairstyles for boys (Dorsey 1879:9–10; Skinner 1915:683, 730, 1926:198–201; Lowie 1954:93–94). The tattoo bundle keeper was responsible for tattooing those male clan members who had distinguished themselves or the women who were daughters of distinguished men. Two pipe bundle owners were required to be present to offer pipes that sanctified the tattooing rites. Tattoos were made around

Milwaukee Public Mus., Wis.: top, 31447/7557; bottom, 30608/7322.

Fig. 5. Small trunks made from pieces of cut, folded, and sewn rawhide. The square to rectangular end pieces are sewed to the rest with sinew and rawhide thongs. They are painted in red, yellow, blue, and green on a natural white background. The design was laid out in black before the color was filled in. Collected by Alanson B. Skinner, Perkins, Okla., 1922–1923. Length of top, 34 cm; length of bottom 49 cm.

Table 1. Clan names, late 19th century

First moiety clans	
Tu′-na^{n}-p'i^{n}	Black bear
Mi-tci′-ra-tce	Wolf
Tce′-xi-ta	Eagle and Thunder-being
Qo′-ta-tci	Elk
Pa′-qça	Beaver
Second moiety clans	
Ru′-tce (*rú·hǰe*)	Pigeon
A′-ru-qwa	Buffalo
Wa-ka^{n}′ (*wakhą́*)	Snake
Mañ′-ko-ke (*mąkhóge*)	Owl

Sources: Dorsey 1897:238–239; phonemic retranscriptions have been provided by Robert L. Rankin.

the wrists of warriors and, in earlier times, on the breast. They were placed on the forehead of women between the eyes, on the hands and breasts, and formerly on the neck, abdomen, and lips (Skinner 1926:221–222, 264–265).

Milwaukee Public Mus., Wis.: 30137/7322.

Fig. 6. Red catlinite raccoon effigy pipe associated with the Pigeon clan. Formerly a "keel" was on the upper surface of the pipe, but it has broken off. Collected by Alanson B. Skinner, 1923, Perkins, Okla.; length 12 cm.

Activities, such as village hunting and warfare for personal status or family revenge, were carried out according to rigidly prescribed rituals that included songs, opening of medicine bundles, feasting, and dances such as the Buffalo, Bear, and Scalp (Dorsey 1879a:1–12).

Cutting across clan lineages were two relatively small and for the most part endogamous prestige classes (Skinner 1915:683–684, 1926:190, 206–207). One was composed of clan chiefs who filled the inherited leadership roles in the tribe. They and their families were affluent by tribal standards and the men's rank and that of their daughters was symbolized by distinctive tattoos. Chiefs often had several wives, frequently sisters, to help with their many social and ceremonial obligations. The chiefs kept the clan sacred pipes in bundles that hung near their houses (Irvin 1871:8; Skinner 1926:215). The use of these pipes in council regulated interclan quarrels. Within the tribe, the clan chief symbolized peace. As head of a clan, he was responsible for the welfare of its members. Certain dances, such as the Night Dance, were performed only by chiefs and their relatives as a kind of thanksgiving ceremony and to bring health and longevity to the tribe and themselves (Skinner 1915:704, 1926:241).

The second prestige class was composed of titled warriors and their families. In the seventeenth and eighteenth centuries, the French called these warriors *les braves*, the brave ones. There were several kinds of war exploits that could make a warrior eligible for the class of braves. These included a war bundle owner who led a successful war party, a hunt leader whose party fought off the enemy, or anyone who killed or scalped an enemy (Skinner 1926:205). A brave might wear a deer-tail roach with an eagle feather (Dorsey 1879a:7); he also had the right to wear a crow feather bustle. Braves might acquire distinguishing tattoo marks, and only they participated in certain dances, such as the Braves Dance (Skinner 1915:700, 1926:239).

The rest of the population had more limited rights in society, were more often observers than participants in ceremonies, and were poorer. For them monogamy was the rule. There was little opportunity to move into the upper classes, although it is reported that occasionally a commoner became a brave.

Life Cycle

Formal rituals marked the individual's life cycle. Names were given at birth and after war or raiding exploits, and teasing nicknames were often given by an uncle. Fasting for varying periods was required of young boys and girls until puberty, at which time the males would undertake a four-day vision quest. Youths were told to pray to the celestial powers such as Sun or Thunder and to reject powers that might come out of the water or earth (Skinner 1926:249).

Marriage rituals differed according to class affiliation. Among clan chiefs and other wealthy men, a young girl selected by the groom's parents would be brought to their lodge and dressed in beautiful clothes, then sent back to her parents with 15–20 horses and other gifts. After the marriage feast, the couple returned to the lodge of the groom with equivalent wealth in gifts from the parents of the bride. Marriages among the majority of the population involved fewer gifts, depending on available wealth. In divorce, children were given into the care of grandparents. Both mother-in-law and father-in-law avoidance were practiced (Dorsey 1879a:33–35; Skinner 1926:251–252).

At death, the body was painted by the oldest male member of the deceased's clan. It was placed on the ground in a small shelter outside the lodge. An all-night, ritual recitation of coups was held, and at dawn the body was buried with grave goods. Scaffold burial was practiced in an earlier period. At the grave, mourners lacerated or pierced themselves, cut off hair, and fasted. Over the grave, a favorite horse was sometimes strangled. The dead were believed to follow the Milky Way to a spirit village in the west where there was plenty of food. Feasts were given to feed the dead over a four-year period (Skinner 1926:254–256; Dorsey 1879a:38–40; Morgan 1848–1852).

Religion

Sources on precontact Iowa religious concepts are conflicting and often superficial. The Presbyterian missionary, William Hamilton, who lived with the Iowa between 1837 and 1853, wrote that the Iowa used a term that meant 'creator of the earth' (Dorsey 1890:423). According to Skinner, the Iowa recognized an upper realm of *mą́ʔų* 'earthmaker', who created the world, and a lower realm of *ixčéxe* 'horned water panther', who on occasion took human form. Thunder powers were also associated with Earthmaker as well as the eagles that returned each spring to renew the earth and fight against the water panthers (Skinner 1926:252–253). Earthmaker appears in the origin myth of the Medicine Dance, the "principal religious ceremony" of the Iowa, which they borrowed in the distant past from the Central Algonquian Indians (Skinner 1915, 1920:189, 693). Earthmaker provided the people with tobacco, corn and squash and showed them how to build the medicine lodge and make pottery. Each of the four quarters of the world was guarded by sacred powers, two male and two female, who could give visions or dreams. According to myth, these four had sought the power of life, and failing to find it instructed the Iowa to make food offerings to Earthmaker and to pour out grease offerings to the earth to receive spiritual benefits. A twentieth-century tradition, reflecting missionary influence, identified Earthmaker as *wakʰą́da*, the Great Spirit (Skinner 1920:189ff., 1926:252–254); Hamilton wrote in the mid-nineteenth century that he had never heard the term Great Spirit used by the Iowa (Dorsey 1890:423).

Hamilton (in Morgan 1848–1852) and Samuel M. Irvin (1841–1849, 1871:1, 3, 7–8, 12), also a Presbyterian missionary between 1837 and 1853, made much of the reverence shown toward inherited medicine bundles, which he called bags, that were believed to have great power. Some contained individual clan pipes (Skinner 1926:215–218); others were carried by war chiefs and thought to aid in achieving victory (Skinner 1926:201, 207–208, 247). There were also bundles owned by doctors for use in healing ceremonies (Skinner 1926:242–243, 248), and by tattooing practitioners (Skinner 1926:220). The sacred quality of medicine bundles was repeatedly compared by the Iowa to the Bibles of the Christians.

The missionaries observed frequent Iowa rites of propitiation: gestures of gratitude to Sun, pipe smoke blown to the heavens, gifts offered to the earth (Irvin 1841–1849; Morgan 1848–1852). When asked what deities they worshiped, the Iowa named the Sun, Moon, Evening Star, North Star, "Big Star," Thunder especially, and Wind. They attributed spirits to almost all natural objects in the environment. Over a 16-year period, the missionaries were unable to make a single conversion to Christianity (ARCIA 1853:333).

Societies and Ceremonies

The ranking men had always given much of their time and effort to ceremonialism. Guidance of tribal and clan religious ceremonies was the prerogative of chiefs, society membership or direction was sometimes restricted to them and titled warriors, and expensive gift-giving was often involved. The ceremonial structure as a whole, in all its mystical, fun, or status-giving aspects, was an important integrating force for the entire Iowa tribe. It gave significance to the life of the individual, and particularly it offered a means of establishing a personal identity as an Iowa.

Ceremonies were connected with warfare, or linked to social, military, and medicine societies. Some of the societies and dances originated among the Iowa, but a number were borrowed from Northeast or Plains Indians. Many had become extinct by the early 1900s.

War dances were part of the rituals associated with clan war bundles, or with preparations for warfare, or with victory celebrations, including Scalp Dances in which women participated (Skinner 1926:201–204, 207–214). They were not organized by particular societies.

The Calumet ceremony established a kinship alliance by the ritual adoption of the child of a prominent and wealthy member of another tribe. Lavish exchange of gifts occurred. The long calumets, symbolic pipe stems lacking bowls, decorated with duck heads and eagle and owl feathers, were wielded as wands in a dance performed by two members of the tribe giving the ceremony (Skinner 1915:706–709, 1926:241).

Societies were not age-graded, and a man could belong to many different societies at the same time. Each society had its own ritual songs, painting, dances, hairstyles, and required dress. Military societies included the Heloska, the Acting Dead Society, and the Tukala and Mawatani societies, which were rivals, each striving to outdo the other in war and in social performances. Wife stealing between the two was common, though not sanctioned by the society leaders. The Fire Dance Society was an organization of contraries whose members demonstrated their power by plunging their arms into boiling water to retrieve meat, which was distributed to guests. The Heloska society also fostered generosity to the poor and those in mourning (Skinner 1915:692–701).

Societies with fundamentally social functions included one that performed the Braves Dance to welcome visitors. Another performed the Bone Dance when visiting a friendly tribe (Skinner 1915:700–701, 703).

Medicine men were looked upon with awe. They danced, sang, and used objects from their medicine bundles to try to cure ailments. Medicine dances of a strictly religious nature were commonly performed and usually centered around a sacred bundle. Like the warrior societies, these societies originated in the visionary experience of the founder and consisted of a ceremonial opening of the bundle, an imitative dance in which the members dressed to represent their sacred powers, and songs sung for the healing of the sick, though war powers could also be invoked this way.

Unique among these societies was the Medicine Dance, which consisted of four groups that, unlike the Central Algonquian Midewiwin, were coequal rather than progressively ranked. The society was basically religious and esoteric, emphasizing humanity's place in the world and the means of achieving immortality during an elaborate initiation. Men and women sought membership by giving gifts to one of the four leaders of the dance. During the four-day initiation, candidates fasted, gave a series of feasts, and each night took a sweat bath. On the fifth day the candidates were dressed and painted, then, using otterskin medicine bags, they were ceremonially "shot," subsequently coughing up sacred cowrie shells that were believed to have entered their bodies (Skinner 1920:237, 239). Members of the Medicine Dance Society also sought to cure illnesses by ceremonies that included songs, dances, and the ritual opening of sacred bundles. The use of herbs and roots was believed to have been taught by the Thunder powers.

One of the most important societies, which was open to both men and women, was the Buffalo Society, a loosely organized group of doctors who specialized in healing broken bones and wounds. Membership required the candidate to have the appropriate dreams. Within the Buffalo Society was a group of Grizzly Bear doctors—originally a separate society—who had their own bundle, and who performed curing rites, controlled the weather, and practiced conjuring. Buffalo Society members accompanied war parties with their bundle to attend the wounded. The Buffalo Tail Society performed rites for the propagation of the herds. The Red Bean Society made a medicine drink from roasted and ground mescal beans, drunk during an all-night ceremony, which induced vomiting and ritually cleansed the society members (Skinner 1926:242–245).

By the mid-nineteenth century many of these ceremonies had been shortened and altered in emphasis (Skinner 1920:205, 1926:255–256). Those dances named and described during that period by Catlin (1844), Hamilton (in Dorsey 1879a), and Morgan (1959:68) probably were remnants of longer rituals.

History, 1837–1988

Great Nemaha Reservation, 1837–1854

Two settlements were laid out on the new reservation (fig. 1) where the Iowa lived as they had in prereservation times in bark- or mat-covered lodges or tepees, according to the season (Dougherty 1838; Richardson 1842, 1843). The women's small gardens, which included potatoes and cabbages, totaled less than 200 acres (Richardson 1843a; Irvin and Hamilton 1847). For 25 years of reservation life a form of the traditional economic cycle of gardening and hunting was pursued. Native dress (figs. 7–8) and hairstyles persisted. Well into reservation days, Iowa life continued to be enriched by the performance of ceremonies.

In the 1840s, some Iowas journeyed to Washington, D.C., and some were taken overseas to Great Britain and France by G.H.C. Melody, where they performed dances and ceremonies for the public under George Catlin's direction (fig. 9) (Catlin 1844, 1845).

In 1846 a manual labor boarding school was established for the Iowa where instruction took place both in Iowa and English (Irvin 1846; Irvin and Hamilton 1847; Blaine 1979:216–218), but pupils were absent for long periods during hunting and gardening seasons. The Iowa themselves instructed their children in the tribal heritage and recounted to them traditional tales (ARCIA 1859; Skinner 1925, 1926). Parents sympathized with their children's rebellion against school confinement and were angered by the teachers' use of corporal punishment (Dorsey 1879a:35; ARCIA 1855).

Young men continued to leave the reservation to win war honors by attacks on enemy tribes such as the Omaha and Pawnee until the late 1850s. In the 1860s, 46 Iowas served on the Union side in the Civil War. The custom of intertribal visiting, most often with the Otoe, attended by feasting and gift exchange, continued to afford an opportunity for the Iowa to strengthen cultural bonds and, at times, to reinforce resistance to acculturation (Blaine 1982:113).

Early reservation life was severely complicated by traders, resident across the Missouri River in Holt County, who victimized the Iowa in order to get a substantial part of Iowa annuities resulting from land cessions. Through the sale of whiskey the traders urged the Iowa to resist acculturation, hoping to keep them under their control (ARCIA 1848). Tribal factionalism developed between the privileged classes and impoverished commoners (Richardson 1843a; Irvin 1846; Irvin and Hamilton 1847; ARCIA 1862). The former succumbed particularly to alcohol and insisted upon controlling distribution of those annuity moneys the traders did not take, while showing less tribal paternalism than traditionally (Kurz 1937:50). A population decrease of 300 reportedly occurred between 1837 and 1853 at the Great Nemaha Subagency (Hamilton 1885:64). In the 1850s and 1860s, while No Heart of Fear (fig. 10) was chief, the tribe took enforcement of temperance into its own hands through generally effective tribal regulations and establishment of its own police force.

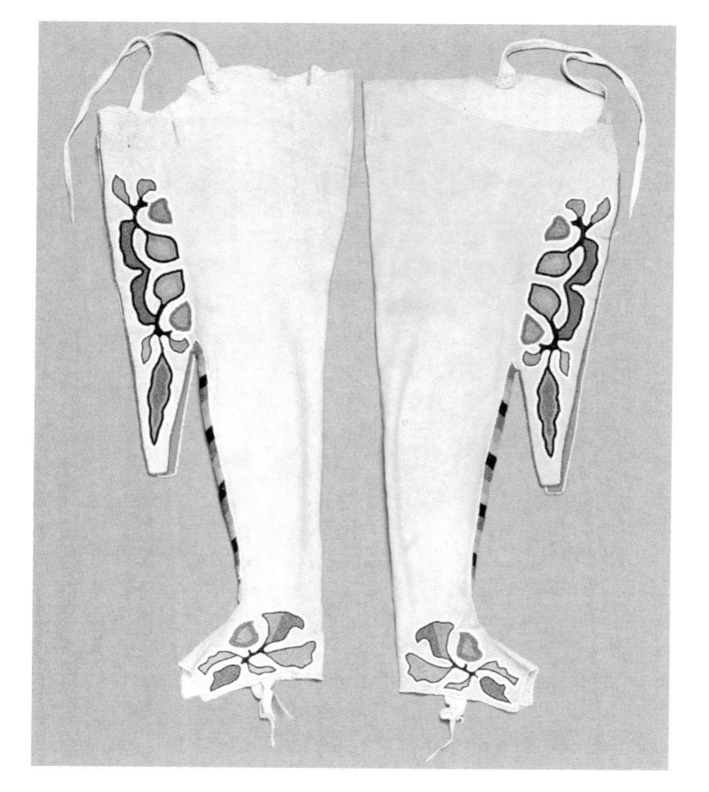

Detroit Inst. of Arts: top, 81.543.1–2; bottom, 81.775.1.

Fig. 7. Men's beaded clothing. top, Late 19th-century front-seam leggings (shown in side view). The bottom tabs have been tailored to fit the top of the wearer's feet; belt ties and instep ties held the leggings in place. Collected by M.G. Chandler; length 90.2 cm. bottom, Mid-19th-century moccasins with asymmetrical floral designs. Collected by M.G. Chandler; length 27.3 cm.

Milwaukee Public Mus., Wis.: 30562/7322.

Fig. 8. Hand-sewn woman's silk appliqué skirt on blue trade cloth base, with small sequins, metallic fringes, and hawk bells. Collected by Alanson B. Skinner, Perkins, Okla., 1922; length of vertical, 79 cm.

In 1851 two bands of Winnebago, some 300 individuals, left Minnesota to join the Iowa for a nine-year stay (ARCIA 1851, 1860). Then about 1863 over 100 other Winnebagos came to the Iowa from South Dakota, staying for five years (ARCIA 1864–1868).

Iowa Reservation, 1854–1878

In 1854 the Great Nemaha Reservation was condensed into the smaller (32,800-acre) Iowa Reservation (fig. 1) (Kappler 1904–1941, 2:628–631). Afterward, individual farms began to replace the village community pattern, a development completed in the 1860s (ARCIA 1861, 1862).

In the early years of reservation life, most of the Iowa, the half-bloods especially, had changed in many respects, and by 1878 they were fairly well acculturated and being assimilated somewhat into neighboring communities. Many full-bloods, fewer in number, were discontented and talking of moving south to Indian Territory.

The last large-scale Iowa hunt occurred in 1863. With the diminution of game both east and immediately west of the

left, The British Mus., Mus. of Mankind, London: 248994; right, Smithsonian, Natl. Mus. of Amer. Art: 1985.66.505.

Fig. 9. Iowa Indians during a visit to London and Paris, 1844–1845. left, Engraving made after a daguerreotype (Truettner 1979:47). Probable identifications based on George Catlin's sketch (Blaine 1979:231) and comparison with individual portraits painted by Catlin during this visit (Truettner 1979:295–296), left to right: Se-non-ty-yah (Blister Feet), a medicine man wearing a George III medal inherited from his father; Oke-we-me (Female Bear that walks on the back of another), wife of Little Wolf; Shon-ta-yi-ga (Little Wolf) wearing necklace of bear claws, 2 peace medals, and skin cloak over his shoulders; Wa-tan-ye (One always foremost); Ruton-we-me (Pigeon on the Wing); Wash-ka-mon-ya (Fast Dancer); Koon-za-ya-me (Female War Eagle Sailing); Neu-mon-ya (Walking Rain); Wa-ta-we-bu-ka-na (Commanding General), the 10-year-old son of Walking Rain; No-ho-mun-ya (One who gives no attention); Ruton-ye-we-ma (Strutting Pigeon), White Cloud's wife; Ta-pa-ta-me (Sophia), the 2-year-old daughter of White Cloud; Jeffrey Dorion (Deroin), husband of White Cloud's niece, and the interpreter; and G.H.C. Melody, who accompanied the group. right, Female War Eagle Sailing, wearing skin dress decorated with porcupine quillwork and hairpipe necklaces, and multiple earrings along the edges of her ears. Her hairstyle, parted in the center, was traditional for women. Oil painting by George Catlin, 1844.

Missouri River, Iowa men began to farm and raise cattle and hogs. The crop roster had expanded to include wheat when seed was available, oats, barley, and onions (ARCIA 1863, 1872, 1874). Some young Indian men were working for non-Indians by 1876. Provided with horse-drawn wagons, some hauled stone and wood to nearby villages to obtain money to purchase food items, such as sugar (ARCIA 1865). "Citizen" clothing was worn by many Iowa, but women still carried babies on cradleboards (ARCIA 1863, 1872). Some Iowa were beginning to build houses of logs and to install stoves (ARCIA 1861, 1866, 1872).

By 1873 many half-blood Iowas were becoming proficient in speaking English, some in reading it (ARCIA 1874). The Society of Friends undertook to provide missionaries in 1869. They established the Iowa Industrial Home for orphans in 1871, and a related day school, which were flourishing in 1880. By 1874 drunkenness had almost disappeared; three years later the authority of chiefs was reported to be very much diminished (ARCIA 1874, 1877). Indian agents were deploring the annual intertribal visits because of concomitant neglect of agricultural duties, but their words had little effect (ARCIA 1860, 1881).

Iowa doctors used herbs, roots, and other natural materials to make salves or remedial potions to drink. Evidence that they and medicine men were losing their prestige is an 1864 petition signed by four chiefs (Iowa Chiefs 1864) that asked permission to obtain medicine and help from a druggist at White Cloud, with the charges being paid out of annuities.

Two Reservations, 1878–1988

Between 1878 and 1881 those Iowas, mostly full bloods, who identified more closely with the old ways and who opposed allotment in severalty began to move to Indian Territory. In 1883 a reservation was designated for them between Deep Fork of the Canadian River and the Cimarron River (fig. 1, inset) (Chapman 1943). The rest, mostly mixed-bloods, successfully resisted removal (Acts of 3/3/1885, 1/26/1887; Kappler 1904–1941, 1:228–229, 245), with 143 of them receiving land allotments in fee simple, under trust, in 1894. On May 20, 1890, even the Iowa in Oklahoma Territory agreed to 80-acre allotments (Chapman 1936). The next year land patents under trust, mostly in Payne County, Oklahoma, were issued to 109 Iowas.

The Ghost Dance was introduced in the 1890s to the Oklahoma Iowa by Pawnee leaders (Blaine 1979:309–310). Those few society dances that persisted in the early twentieth century were replaced by the Peyote religion (fig. 12) to which the Oklahoma Iowa were especially receptive for a time. In 1898, the Drum Dance religion was introduced to the Iowa by the Kickapoo of Kansas; it was a form of worship using the drum, blending Indian and Christian symbols, that is said to have originated

Newberry Lib., Chicago.

Fig. 10. No Heart of Fear or Natchininga (*nąhje nįge* 'heartless') (b. 1797, d. 1862), member of the Bear clan and uncle of White Cloud. He became principal chief of the Iowa in 1852. He is wearing a calico shirt, trade blanket, shell ear ornaments, and a beaded choker. He holds a half-stock Northwest trade gun. Daguerreotype by Thomas M. Easterly, 1846–1847.

among the Santee Sioux during the late ninteenth century and spread to several midwestern tribes ("Intertribal Religious Movements," this vol.) (Skinner 1915:720–724).

The Iowa were subjected to land exploitation by non-Indians in the early decades of the twentieth century. A period of land leasing by a substantial part of the Iowa followed allotment in both areas, which led to economic losses. Land released from trust was sold. In the 1930s less than 10 percent remained of the original 1894 allotments in the Kansas-Nebraska reservation. (For per capita payments in the early 1900s of principal in the United States Treasury remaining from land treaties, see U.S. Congress. House. Committee on Interior and Insular Affairs 1950:347–350.) In 1936, under the Oklahoma Indian Welfare Act, the reservation land belonging to the Oklahoma Iowa was ceded by them to the government (Chapman 1936). This was followed by allotment of the same land to individuals. Although the locality is still spoken of as a reservation at times, this is inaccurate.

The Kansas-Nebraska Iowa adopted a constitution and bylaws in 1937, with credit advantages one of the main attractions. The corporate charter was ratified June 19 of the same year. The Iowa tribe of Oklahoma also adopted a constitution and bylaws in 1937, ratifying a corporate charter February 5, 1938, but in both cases by only a small majority.

Through Indian Claims Commission judgments, by 1972 the Iowa had been awarded almost eight million dollars on land claims in western Iowa and Missouri and over $11,000 on accounting claims (Indian Claims Commission Dockets nos. 79, 79A, 135, 138, 153, 158, 209, 231; see also Ross 1973).

Denver Public Lib., Western Hist. Dept., Colo.: F40588.

Fig. 11. White Cloud's house with some of the principal men of the tribe. The man seated on the left wears a bear-claw necklace. The other men wear native made finger-woven shawls around their heads. Probably by J.J. Hargrave, Guthrie, Ind. Terr., May 1890.

The Iowa in 1988†

In 1988 the Iowa comprised two groups, one identified as the Iowa of Kansas and Nebraska, and the other as the Iowa of Oklahoma.

The Executive Committee of the former group had its headquarters in White Cloud, Kansas. Their reservation, located in Kansas and Nebraska, was served by the Horton Agency, located at Horton, Kansas. Approximately 475 enrolled Iowas lived on the reservation that consisted of about 1,000 acres, while others lived in the adjacent towns of Rulo, Preston, and Falls City, Nebraska; and White Cloud, Reserve, and Hiawatha, Kansas, or in other towns. The Executive Committee, composed of five elected members, managed tribal affairs with technical assistance provided by the Horton Agency upon tribal request. Tribal land that was farmed was worked by the Iowa themselves.

Housing projects were completed with financial assistance from the federal Department of Housing and Urban Development. The tribe sponsored a profitable bingo operation, the returns from which helped the tribe to develop other projects. It built a filling station and a fire station. The tribe sponsored an annual rodeo and, less regularly, a powwow was held at White Cloud.

Two of the 2,089 Kansas-Nebraska Iowas on the roll were full-bloods; only a few more were half-bloods, some were one quarter-blood, whereas many were one-eighth or less. Many Iowas were farmers or laborers; a number achieved important professional positions.

The Business Committee of the Iowa of Oklahoma, or tribal council, had its headquarters in a building three miles south of Perkins, Oklahoma. These Iowa were served by the Shawnee Agency headquartered in Shawnee, Oklahoma, near Oklahoma City. Most (225) lived on individually owned land (about 1,300 acres) between the Cimarron River and Deep Fork in northern Lincoln, southern Payne, and Logan counties, Oklahoma. Much of their land was of poor quality and was surface-leased to non-Indians for pasture or farming. In addition to rental revenues, most of the Oklahoma Iowas supported themselves by working in nearby towns such as Stillwater and Cushing. Oil and gas leases benefited 52 landowners. The tribe held 20.5 acres of land in trust in several locations around Perkins. Some tribal members lived in Oklahoma City, Tulsa, and other cities.

The tribe was establishing an industrial development corporation to handle commercial enterprises. A non-Indian dentist ran a denture business in Perkins, renting his building from the tribe, where other dentists came to receive a month's training in making dentures for which they each paid a fee of $250 to the Iowa. The tribe maintained an Indian court to handle civil cases. The tribe sponsored an annual powwow near Perkins, and its members participated in numerous powwows in the Oklahoma area. It ran a very successful bingo operation.

There were at least nine full-blood Iowas listed on the tribal roll of 366 Oklahoma Iowas, which included Iowas with only a one-eighth blood requirement.

Both units of the Iowas published newsletters.

In the 1980s, under the Iowa Living History Farms Project, an early eighteenth-century Iowa village was recreated near Des Moines, Iowa. For a description of the Iowa reservations in Kansas and Nebraska, and Oklahoma see Tiller (1996:343–344, 518–519).

†This section was assembled in 1988 with data from Irvin Santiago, Harvey Frederick, Janice Krug, Carol Kaulaity, Ed Herndon, Larry Scrivner, Marjorie M. Schwietzer, and Lance Foster.

Howard Springer, Perkins, Okla.

Fig. 12. Native American Church members, near Perkins, Okla., May 1911. left to right, back row: 2 unidentified girls, unidentified woman, Emma Sines with unidentified girl, unidentified woman, Julia Small, Mrs. Wooten, Jack Lincoln, Henry Black (Otoe), Battiste Jones (Otoe), Joe Springer wearing decorated collar and blanket robe, Robert Roubideaux, and Tom Lincoln; front row: Wooten boy, Quaker Rev. Wooten holding rattle, Robert Koshiway Small holding rattle and feather fan, Jake Dole, John Springer holding rattle and peyote staff, Charley Tohee, Blaine Kent holding rattle and feathers, and Frank Kent.

Population

Population figures before 1837 are basically guesses. A total population of at least 1,000 Iowas is suggested for the 1700s (M.M. Wedel 1986:50). In 1837, when reservation life began, Hamilton (1885:64) estimated that about 800 lived there, but in the next decade and a half more than one-third of the tribe died. In later reservation times available figures (table 2) reflect Iowa migrations, changing concepts of jurisdiction, and at times census inaccuracy. By the end of the 1880s, some Iowas had moved to Indian Territory, leaving the majority near the Great Nemaha.

The first recorded smallpox epidemic among the Iowa was about 1800 (Dorsey 1894:426; Stearn and Stearn 1945:78). Others occurred during the years up to 1870. The first recorded tribal vaccination program was in 1839. Diseases reported to have caused notable mortality have been smallpox, tuberculosis, malaria, cholera acquired in 1849 from western migrants, heart disease, and cancer. Infant mortality decreased in the late nineteenth century.

Table 2. Iowa Population, 1805–1996

Year	Population	Source
1805	about 800	Lewis and Clark in Moulton 1983–, 3:405
1814	1,400	Schermerhorn 1814:39, 44
1848	669	Vaughan 1848:482
1858	498	ARCIA 1858:105
1861	305	ARCIA 1861:53
1875	219	ARCIA 1875:176
1880	222[a]	ARCIA 1880:244, 246
1890	267[b]	ARCIA 1890:546, 549
1899	318[c]	ARCIA 1899, 1:566, 574
1910	353[d]	ARCIA 1910:62, 64
1920	417[e]	ARCIA 1920:67, 70
1931	575[f]	ARCIA 1931:47, 51
1940	649[g]	Haas 1947:25, 28
1961	348[h]	Bureau of Indian Affairs 1961: 18, 22, 27
1983	541[i]	Bureau of Indian Affairs 1983: 5, 6
1991	896[j]	Bureau of Indian Affairs 1991: Table 3
1996	2,608[k]	Tiller 1996: 343, 518

NOTES:

[a]176 in Nebr. and 46 in Ind. Terr.

[b]165 in Kans. and 102 in Okla.

[c]230 in Kans. and 88 in Okla.

[d]273 in Kans. and 80 in Okla.

[e]339 in Kans. and 78 in Okla.

[f]471 in Kans. and 104 in Okla.

[g]539 in Kans. and Nebr., and 110 in Okla.

[h]70 in Kans., 41 in Nebr., and 237 in Okla.

[i]275 in Kans., 56 in Nebr., and 210 in Okla.

[h]357 in Kans., 132 in Nebr., and 407 in Okla.

[k]Total tribal enrollments: 2,147 in Kans., and 461 in Okla.

Figures refer to the tribal population on or near reservations; they do not reflect total tribal enrollment.

Synonymy‡

The name Iowa derives from a designation in Sioux and several Algonquian languages. In Sioux it occurs in two dialectal forms, Santee and Yankton *ayúxba* and Teton *ayúxwa* (Riggs 1890:60; Williamson 1885:106). Although the term has been interpreted to mean literally 'sleepy ones' (Riggs 1890:60; Dorsey and Thomas in Hodge 1907–1910, 2:612) and 'dusty heads' (Foster 1876–1877, 1:1), in addition to other less plausible interpretations (Aldrich in Brower 1897:179–180; Miner 1911; Gerard 1900), all are folk etymologies that have no linguistic basis.

The name occurs in several of the Algonquian languages spoken by tribes living east of the Iowa: Fox *a·yaho·we·wa* (Voorhis 1971:65) and *a·yohowe·we* (Ives Goddard, personal communication 1998); Kickapoo *aayohoea* (Paul Voorhis, personal communication 1971); Shawnee *ha·yawʔhowe* (Voegelin 1938–1940, 10:443); Menonimee *ayo·ho·wɛ·w* (Bloomfield 1962:248); and Ottawa ioewaig (Tanner 1830:316). The name has no etymology in any of these languages. Although it has been suggested that it spread to the Algonquian languages from Sioux (M.M. Wedel 1978:51, 58), there is no compelling evidence to support the actual direction of borrowing of the term.

In the nineteenth and twentieth centuries the name was recorded twice as a self-designation for the Iowa, first as ah-e-o-war (Lewis and Clark in Moulton 1983–, 3:405) and later as ai'yue or ai'yuwe (Skinner 1926:191). At least one nineteenth-century visitor to the tribe denied that the Iowa ever called themselves Ioways but insisted that they used the name Pa-ha-cae, 1800 (Carleton 1943:66). Although not the primary Kansa name for the tribe, áyowa has been recorded as a Kansa usage (Gatschet 1878:27). In Caddo the name appears as *ʔáyuway* (Chafe 1979), apparently a recent borrowing from English.

From the late seventeenth century the tribe has been designated most commonly by a variant of the name Iowa. Its earliest use is attributed to French explorers traveling from settlements on the lower Saint Lawrence River into the Upper Mississippi valley, where they adopted the name used by Algonquian tribes, probably Chippewa or Ottawa (M.M. Wedel 1978:59–60). Examples of its occurrence in the seventeenth and early eighteenth centuries are Aiaoüa, 1676 (André 1695 in JR 60:202), Ayoës, 1689 (Perrot 1864:63), Ayouez, 1695 (Lamothe Cadillace in Margry 1876–1886, 5:124), Ayaoues, 1702 (d'Iberville in M.M. Wedel 1978:73), Ayowest, 1714 (De Bourgmont in Giraud 1958:16), Ayovois and Ayoois, 1724 (De Bourgmont in Margry 1876–1886, 6:407, 396), ayoüais, 1734 (Beauharnois and Hocquart in Thwaites 1906:206), Aïouez, 1723 (Charlevoix 1966), and Aiaouez, 1697 (Franquelin 1697; Jefferys 1761, 1:139). Some citations of the name have g in place of y in the second syllable, presumably reflecting a scriptographic error, for example, Agouais, 1726 (De Ligney in Whittlesey 1855:22) and Agoual and Agoues, 1736 (Chauvignerie and Hutchins in Schoolcraft 1851–1857, 3:557). Other citations have j in the second syllable, again perhaps reflecting a scriptographic error: Ajaouez (Jeffreys 1776:map 5), Ajouas (de Smet 1848:108), and Anjoues (Buchanan 1824, 1:138).

Late eighteenth and early nineteenth-century renditions show similar variation in spelling. Many writers, continuing French orthographic practice, cite the name with initial Ai or Ay: for example, Ayauwais (Lewis and Clark in Moulton 1983–, 3:405), Aowias, 1802 (Vilemont in Nasatir 1952, 2:694), Ayuwas, 1811 (Brackenridge in Thwaites 1904–1907, 6:89), Ayowäs (Maximilian in Thwaites 1904–1907, 24:313), Aijoues (Schoolcraft 1851–1857, 3:522), and Ayouahs (Domenech 1860, 2:34). Spanish renditions are exemplified by Ayoas, 1793 (Zenon Trudeau in Nasatir 1952, 1:180) and Hayuas, 1777 (Cruzat in Houck 1909, 1:145). Other renditions use initial I, when, following English orthographic usage in which the letter i is written for the diphthong ai, this letter becomes more prevalent: Iawa, 1806 (Dearborn in Carter 1934–1962, 13:488), Ihowais (La Roche and Chevalier in Carter 1934–1962, 14:654), and Iowas, 1808 (Jefferson in Carter 1934–1962, 14:221). Several citations

‡This synonymy was written by Douglas R. Parks, based in part on M.M. Wedel (1978).

have initial J, for example, Jowas, 1807 (Pike in Coues 1895, 1:2) and Joways (Schermerhorn 1814:39, 44).

In contrast to the preceding designation is the Iowa name for themselves, *páxoǰe*, which has been cited by many early writers: pahódje (Maximilian in Thwaites 1904–1907, 24:313), pa-ha-cae, 1847 (Carleton 1943:66), pa-ho-cha (Hamilton 1885, 1:47), Pá-qo-tce (Dorsey 1880h:[7]; McGee 1897:162), and Pa′-qu-tse (Dorsey 1888:[2]). The same name is used by other Chiwere Siouan groups: *pa·xóǰe* in Otoe (Parks 1988; Louanna Furbee, personal communication 1990) and *wa·xóč* in Winnebago (Kenneth Miner, personal communication 1987). Although some Otoe speakers in the twentieth century interpret the name as 'gray nose', there is no substantiation for this etymology.

The Dhegiha Siouan tribes designate the Iowa with the same name: Osage *páxoce*, *hpáxoce* (Robert L. Rankin, communication to editors 1998; La Flesche 1932:25, 126, phonemicized); Kansa *ppáxoǰe*, *ppáxocce* (Robert L. Rankin, communication to editors 1998; J.O. Dorsey 1882, retranscribed); and Omaha and Ponca *máxude* (Fletcher and LaFlesche 1911:102, retranscribed; Parks 1988). In Caddoan languages the same name for the Iowa occurs as a borrowing in Pawnee *páhkuta* (Parks 1965–1990) and Kitsai Wăqkotsi (Mooney 1893). Recordings of pashóhan as the Arikara and Pawnee terms for the Iowa are probably confusions of the Iowa with the Otoe (Gatschet 1878).

For a short period in the late seventeenth and early eighteenth centuries there occurs a less frequently used French designation for the Iowa that is based on the preceding Siouan name. The form is exemplified by Pah8tet, 1673–1674 (Marquette in Tucker 1942:pl. 5), Paoté, 1681 (La Salle in Margry 1876–1886, 2:215), Paoutaoüa, 1703 (Delisle map in Tucker 1942:plate 13), Paouté, 1700 (Marest in Villiers du Terrage 1925:34), and Paoutez, 1718 (Delisle map in Tucker 1942:plate 15).

In the late seventeenth century, some French sources use a designation for the Iowa, possibly also including the Otoe, that is apparently derived from Ottawa and means 'little-prairie Sioux' (M.M. Wedel 1978:57): Mascotens nadouesiou, 1684 (Franquelin map in JR 63), Mascouteins nadoessi, 1676 (André in JR 60:202), Maskoutens Nadouessioux, 1681 (La Salle in Margry 1876–1886, 2:215), and Nadouessi maskoutens (Perrot 1864:237).

Finally, a designation for the Iowa that appears only twice in the early historical literature is the French form of 'pierced nose', given as ne persa (Lewis and Clark in Moulton 1893–, 3:405) and Ne Perce, 1810 (Pike in Coues 1895, 1:346), which is said to be based on a confusion of the name *páxoǰe* with the Iowa word pa-o-ja 'pierced nose' (Long in Thwaites 1904–1907, 15:131).

There is no recorded sign for the Iowa in the Plains sign language.

Sources

The major source on the Iowa is the historical study by Blaine (1979). See also Miner (1911), Fulton (1882), Dorsey and Thomas (in Hodge 1907–1910, 1:612–614), Meyer (1962), Anderson (1973), and M.M. Wedel (1961, 1976, 1978, 1981, 1986).

Louis André's remarks about the Iowa occur in the *Jesuit Relations* (JR 60:202, 204). Michel Accault's activities among the Iowa are described by René Robert Cavelier, sieur de La Salle (1876–1886, 1876–1886a, 1876–1886b) on the basis of Accault's letters to him (M.M. Wedel 1986:30–32). Perrot's information on the Iowa appears in Bacqueville de la Potherie (1722, 2), which probably incorporates information given to La Potherie both orally and in writing (Pouliot 1969:422–423). A translation appears in Blair (1911–1912, 2), but with some errors (M.M. Wedel 1986:39 n. 19, 41n. 21). Pierre-Charles Le Sueur recorded facts about the Iowa that were acquired by his men when in 1701 he built Fort l'Huillier (Delisle 1702; M.M. Wedel 1981). For correlations between archeology and the Iowa, see Mott (1938), and on Upper Iowa River archeology, see M.M. Wedel (1959).

A detailed anthropological study of the Iowa was made by Skinner (1915, 1920, 1925, 1926) between 1914 and 1923 based on interviews conducted on both Iowa reservations. Validity of the information is subject to the limitations of oral history (cf. Whitman 1937 and Radin 1923).

Other sources present fragmentary material only. See Dorsey (1881, 1881a, 1881b, 1891, 1894, 1897) for data obtained in 1880 from Hamilton and from Iowas in Washington in 1882. See also Irvin and Hamilton's 1848 reply to the Schoolcraft questionnaire (1851–1857, 3:259–276), Irvin's description of a sacred bundle (1871), Irvin's intermittent diary 1841–1849, Hamilton's autobiography (1885), excerpts taken by L. H. Morgan from a Hamilton manuscript covering 1848–1852, Dorsey (1881a, 1879a); and Dorsey's copy of Hamilton's letters published in a Presbyterian newspaper about 1848 (Dorsey 1879b). Subagent reports in the annual reports of the commissioner of Indian affairs are useful.

On the Iowa language, see Hamilton and Irvin's pioneering grammatical studies, hymns, and Bible translations (1843a, 1843, 1846–1847, 1848, 1849; Hamilton 1854). See McMurtrie and Allen (1930, 1930a) for early printing in the Iowa language. Dorsey's Iowa language studies (1879, 1881b, 1881c) remain unpublished. Whitman (1947:233–248), based on 1936 fieldwork, is the best modern grammatical study. Wistrand-Robinson (1972, 1977, 1978) presents pedagogical materials on vocabulary and grammar. Good Tracks (1992) is a dictionary of the Iowa and Otoe-Missouria dialects of Chiwere.

Iowa material culture is represented in the Milwaukee Public Museum (Skinner 1922, 1923, 1926); in the Museum of the American Indian, Washington (war bundles); the American Museum of Natural History, New York; Saint Joseph Museum, Saint Joseph, Missouri; National Museum of Natural History, Smithsonian Institution, Washington; Oklahoma Historical Society, Oklahoma City; and Denver Art Museum.

Otoe and Missouria

MARJORIE M. SCHWEITZER

The Otoe (ˈōtō) and Missouria (mĭˈzo͞orēu), along with the closely related Iowa tribe, spoke mutually intelligible dialects of the Chiwere language;* together with Winnebago, they form the Chiwere-Winnebago subdivision of the Siouan family. Tribal legends, recorded in the nineteenth century and recounted throughout the twentieth century, place the prehistoric origins of the Chiwere people as bands of a single tribe living north of the Great Lakes (Maximilian in Thwaites 1904–1907, 24:313–314; Long in Thwaites 1904–1907, 15:131–132; Gallatin 1836:126).

By the 1990s, use of the Otoe dialect was primarily restricted to ceremonial contexts, often in prayer; even elderly native speakers spoke almost exclusively in English. The Missouria dialect was extinct (Chafe 1973:1178; Wolff 1950:63).

Although officially recognized as the Otoe-Missouria tribe, the name Otoe is commonly used to refer to the tribe and its members. Unless otherwise indicated, the name Otoe refers to the consolidated group.

History, 1673–1804

The first known historical reference to the Otoe and the Missouria appears on Father Jacques Marquette's autograph map of 1673–1674, which placed them vaguely in separate locations west of the middle Mississippi, apparently in the area of the Iowa-Minnesota border and in Missouri (Tucker 1942:pl. 5). The first recorded contact with Europeans was in 1680, when two Otoes visited Fort Crèvecoeur, René-Robert Cavelier, sieur de La Salle's post near Lake Peoria (M.M. Wedel 1986:19). The 1703 De Lisle map, drawing on information from Pierre-Charles Le Sueur's account of 1700, locates the Otoe near the Blue Earth River (M.M. Wedel 1974:45). A document attributed to Étienne Venyard, sieur de Bourgmont, and thought to date from 1714, cites the first evidence of the Otoe farther west, at a village on Salt Creek about 10 leagues from the mouth of the Platte River (Norall 1988:94–95, 108–109). There are no references to Otoe villages east of the Missouri River after this time, although they continued to hunt east of the Missouri as well as south of the Platte. Traders and explorers reported Otoe villages in various locations near the Platte River until the mid-1800s (Strong 1935:13–14; Villiers du Terrage 1925:61; Mott 1938:259–269; Gallatin in M.M. Wedel 1974:50; Shea 1902:101–106; Thwaites 1908:178, 358–363; Thwaites 1904–1907, 14:221, 15:130–135; Nasatir 1952, 1:51–52, 125–126, 262–264, 2:384, 539, 694; M.M. Wedel 1974:47). The Yutan site, in Saunder County, Nebraska, is believed to be a late eighteenth- to early nineteenth-century Otoe village (fig. 1) (Grange 1968).

After France's entry into the Missouri River area following 1700, conflict between various tribes became a concern to traders. Bourgmont was dispatched to the region to counsel the Otoe, Missouria, and other tribes to live in peace and to trade with each other as well as with the French. From 1712 Bourgmont lived at the Missouria village for several years with his Missouria wife. To impress the tribes with France's power, Bourgmont chose several tribal leaders, including two Missouria chiefs and one Otoe chief, to accompany him on a trip to Paris in 1725 (Norall 1988:17, 81–87; Woolworth 1956:14, 23; Nasatir 1952, 1:12–22; Sheldon 1923:9–10).

In 1720, when a Spanish expedition led by Pedro de Villasur arrived in Nebraska, the Otoe affirmed their loyalty to the French by joining the Pawnee in the attack; the Indians killed Villasur and nearly half his group of more than 100 men, driving the survivors south (Hotz 1991:191–196).

Most documents that mention the Otoe and Missouria during the seventeenth and eighteenth centuries focus on their role as middlemen between French and Spanish traders and other tribes farther up the Missouri River (Nasatir 1952, 1:351–354).

The Missouria village remained on the Missouri River near the mouth of the Grand River throughout the eighteenth century. Archeological evidence for their pre-1724 village is found at the Utz site south of the Missouri River in Saline County, Missouri; the Gumbo Point site to the south and west, on the south bank of the Missouri, is believed to be a late eighteenth-century Missouria village (C.H. Chapman 1946, 1959). Several times during the century the Missouria

*The phonemes of Chiwere are: (plain, voiced or voiceless stops) *b, d, ǰ, g, ʔ*; (aspirated stops) *pʰ, tʰ, čʰ, kʰ*; (glottalized stops) *ṗ, ṫ, č̇, k̇*; (voiceless spirants) *θ, s, x, h*; (voiced spirants) *δ, y*; (glottalized spirants) *θ̇, ṡ, ẋ*; (nasals) *m, n, nʸ, ŋ*; and (resonants) *w, r*; (oral vowels) *i, e, a, o, u*; (nasal vowels) *į, ą, ų*. Stress (marked by an acute accent) and vowel length (marked by a raised dot, v·) are also phonemic. The resonant *r* has several phonetic variants: [r, δ, l, d, y, n]; *s* varies between [s] and [š].

The phonemic orthography used in the citation of Otoe terms follows the tentative analysis of Robert L. Rankin (communication to editors 1991, 1998), based on Whitman (1947) and his own work.

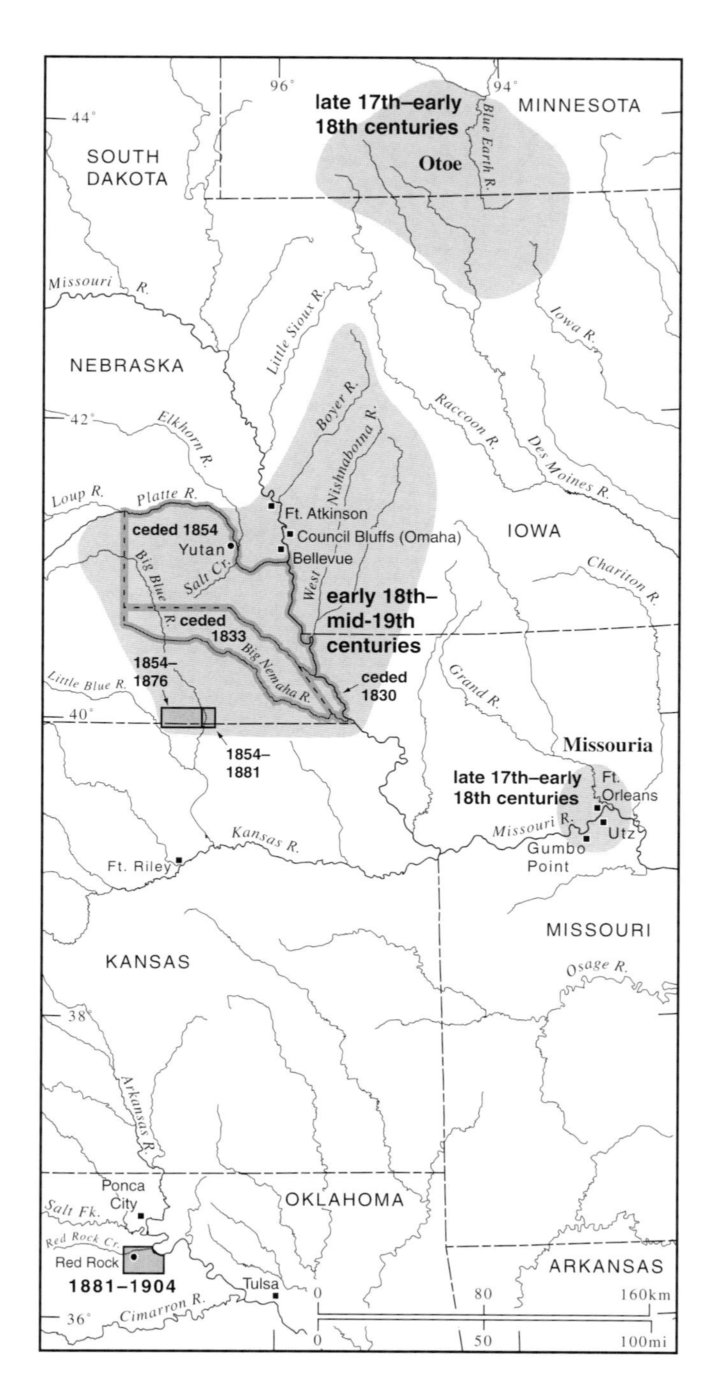

Fig. 1. Late 17th- to mid-19th-century territories, selected villages, land transfers, and reservations of the Otoe-Missouria.

suffered losses at the hands of the Sauk and Fox and other enemy tribes and from smallpox; by 1794 they were reported to have been almost destroyed. Some survivors joined the Little Osage band and the Kansa, while the largest group, numbering about 80, joined the Otoe on the Platte River. Although the Otoe and Missouria lived together as one social, political, and economic unit, during the 1800s the Missouria retained their clan chiefs and customs in an effort to maintain their cultural distinctiveness (Thwaites 1904–1950, 1:47–49; Milner 1982:121; Nasatir 1952, 1:261).

Culture, Eighteenth to Mid-Nineteenth Centuries

Subsistence

The Otoe and Missouria were sedentary village horticulturalists who also depended on the hunting of bison and the gathering of wild plants. The basic horticultural products were corn, beans, squash, and pumpkins. Each family had its own creek bed garden, tended primarily by women with help from the men. The harvest, gathered by the entire family, was owned by the women. Seed corn was considered to be sacred, and children were prohibited from touching it. No planting rituals were recorded, but the Red Bean Medicine Lodge gave a feast before the green corn was harvested (Whitman 1937:5).

Although they remained sedentary village dwellers along the timbered waterways of the Missouri River drainage, the introduction of the horse (probably by 1730) was instrumental in the adoption of traits that were characteristic of High Plains tribes (Shea 1902:101–106; Whitman 1937:1–2, 5–7; Haines 1938:430, 433).

Increased wealth obtained through trade in buffalo hides led to greater emphasis on hunting. The Otoe developed a biannual buffalo hunt, led each spring by the Buffalo clan and each fall by the Bear clan. A ritual leader was chosen who had recognized sacred power to ensure a successful hunt. Social control was maintained by four outstanding warriors who were wholly responsible to the hunt leader, while additional men were chosen to help regulate the charge on the herd. On the hunt, the people lived in tepees, arranged in a camp circle (*hóraga*) with the opening to the east. Each morning scouts were sent out, and if the buffalo were sighted the hunt leader spread tobacco on the ground and prayed to the buffalo for success. The meat from the hunt was shared communally (Whitman 1937:7–8).

Women cared for the lodge and children, though men might help carry wood and water. Wives owned all family property other than the personal belongings of the men, including all game brought home by their husbands.

Smithsonian, Dept. of Anthr.: 22414, 22415.

Fig. 2. Stone maul and fire-hardened wooden wedges used to split dry wood for kindling. The maul was also used to open bones to extract the marrow. Collected by Jesse W. Griest before 1876; length of wedges, 28 cm; maul same scale.

Structures

Otoe and Missouria villages contained from 40 to 70 earthlodges. In 1810 Bradbury described a village with about 54 circular lodges. Each was about 40 feet in diameter, the floor dug into the earth to a depth of three feet, with seven-foot peripheral posts and four 20-foot-high central posts around a circular fire pit in the center of the lodge dug an additional two feet into the earth. The entrance was an inclined plane about 10–12 feet in length, the whole lodge covered with sod layered over rafter poles (Thwaites 1904–1905, 5:78–79). The mythic origin of the earthlodge was attributed to beaver (Whitman 1938:189). Each earthlodge housed several related families, while a tepee housed only a couple with their children and perhaps a few other relatives. The Otoe also constructed bark lodges typical of the Winnebago and the Iowa (Whitman 1937:1–2).

Social and Political Organization

The kinship system of the Otoe and Missouria was organized lineally, with Omaha-type kin terminology and patrilineal exogamous clans. Individuals identified strongly with both clan and lineage, but the basic social group was the extended family. Family prestige and prerogatives permeated all activities. Children were socialized by the extended family, especially grandparents, and if growing children did not heed those teachings, the family itself was considered at fault (Whitman 1937:40, 42–43, 70).

The clan system prescribed marriage partners and ceremonial duties. The structure of clans differed between the two tribes in the nineteenth century (Dorsey 1897:240), but the details of clan organization were not recorded until the twentieth century (Whitman 1937:15–35). By that time they had coalesced into a single system traditionally said to comprise seven clans, each associated with a chief and a sacred pipe. However, 10 clan names were recorded, perhaps reflecting the incomplete merger of the clan systems of the two tribes (table 1).

Each clan had its own sacred origin legends, rituals, privileges, rights, and duties. Each also had its own naming ceremonies, using names derived from events in the origin legends.

The Bear clan was the largest and most powerful, providing leadership for the fall buffalo hunt and other fall and winter activities. The Buffalo clan provided leadership in the spring and summer and was associated with the origin of corn. In addition to control of spring and summer by the Buffalo clan and fall and winter by the Bear clan, Pigeon and Owl clans were active in the spring and summer and Beaver and Elk clans were active in the fall and winter. The Eagle clan was called upon in any season but was also associated with spring and summer (Waters 1984:47–56). Cutting across the clans and thereby countering potential divisiveness were voluntary associations that included the secret societies, dance groups, and benevolent societies (Whitman 1937:15).

Based on the association of the clans in the origin legends, Whitman (1937:15) suggested that the Otoe and

Table 1. Clans

19th-century Otoe clans (Dorsey 1897:240)	*19th-century Missouria clans (Dorsey 1897:240)*	*20th-century Otoe-Missouria clans (Whitman 1937:17–18)*
Beaver (Pa-ça′)		Beaver
Black bear (Tuna^{n}′pʔi^{n}) or Wolf (Mŭ^{n}-tci′-ra-tce)	Black bear (Tu-na^{n}′pʔi^{n})	Bear
Buffalo (A-rú-qwa)		Buffalo
Pigeon (Ru′-qtca)		Pigeon
Owl (Ma-ka′-tce)		Hoot Owl
Eagle, Thunderbird, etc. (Tce′-xi-ta)	Eagle, Thunderbird, etc. (Tce-xi′-ta) subclans:[a] Thunderbird (Wa-kan′-ta) Eagle (Qra) Hawk (Gre′-ta^{n})[c] A-people-who-eat-no-small-birds-which-have-been-killed-by-larger-ones (a recent addition) (Mo′-mi)	Eagle subclan Tcɛxita[b]
	Elk (Ho-ma′ or Ho-ta′-tci)	Elk
Snake (Wa-ka^{n}′)		Snake (extinct)
		Coyote (extinct)

NOTES:

[a]Whitman (1937:18) reports the tradition that all clans originally had 4 subclans.

[b]Actually the name of the Eagle clan (Furbee and Hopkins 1990).

[c]Dorsey's turned K, a phonetic symbol for a lenis stop, is here transcribed as G′.

Missouria may in the past have had a moiety system designated as Earth and Sky, parallel to that of the Omaha, Osage, and other Siouan tribes. Bear came from underground to the earth's surface and joined Beaver (who brought the pipe stem), Elk (who brought fire), and Eagle. Buffalo (who had their own pipe and a tattoo bundle) descended from the sky and was associated with Pigeon and Hoot Owl (who brought the holy pipe bundle). However, in the twentieth century the Otoe themselves did not recognize such a moiety division.

Hereditary clan chiefs met as a tribal governing council, with the primary chief selected from the Bear clan, the largest and most powerful. A qualified son, a brother's son, or a grandson through the female line inherited the position. An Otoe chief owned a clan peace pipe with which he could settle intertribal and extratribal conflicts. His dwelling was recognized as a sanctuary. He elected two warriors to serve him and maintain order on special occasions. Although the powers of the clan heads were limited and there was little they could do to enforce their authority, a chief was nevertheless expected to care for the aged, sick, and orphans and to offer help wherever it was needed, even to those in other clans. He was considered to be the head of his family; as keeper of the clan pipe of peace he would not fight unless it were in self-defense (Whitman 1937:35–38). The chief and the warriors maintained social control in situations involving murder or endangering the success of the bison hunts. The family maintained control over individuals who did not follow society's norms (Whitman 1937:15, 20, 35–41).

Otoe-Missouria society was organized by rank. The chiefs comprised the most prestigious and affluent group. Warriors invested with secular or supernatural power and their families comprised the second class status. The powers of these groups were hereditary, and thus it was not easy for a person to move from one group to another. The common people—those who were poorer in material wealth and who had limited rights in ceremonies—comprised the third class. Families controlled the inheritance of power (a man could pass his vision power to his son, a brother's son or a grandson) as well as membership in secret societies, benevolent societies, and dance societies (Whitman 1937:15, 35–36, 85).

Games

The Otoe-Missouria shared certain games with the Algonquians of the Northeast as well as with other Siouans. Men played stick ball (lacrosse), a sacred game believed to have healing powers, and hoop and javelin; women played shinny and a gambling game using seven dice and a wooden bowl (Whitman 1937:12–13).

Religion

Fundamental to the Otoe and Missouria world view was Wakanda (*wakʰą́da* 'sacred power'), which permeated all nature and was manifested through dreams, visions and supernatural encounters. This power was symbolized by the circle with its center and the four directions. East was associated with birth, sunrise, the east wind, and the source of life for people, plants, and animals. South was associated with adolescence, summer, and the south wind. After death the body was laid with the head to the north, enabling the individual to see both the sunrise and sunset. South was also linked to the seven stars of the Pleiades, which represented each of the seven clan chiefs. West was associated with middle age, autumn, danger, storms, the west wind, and the spirit world of the dead. North had associations with old age, winter, good, pleasure, cold, and the snow and moisture brought by the north wind. Associated with the center of the circle was the cottonwood tree and water. The sacred circle and the four directions were expressed in the culture through a grouping of the seasons into spring-summer and fall-winter and the association of each division with different clans. The significance of the number four was expressed in other ways such as in "the four stages of life," the four subdivisions of each clan, performing tasks four times, and praying to the four directions (Whitman 1937:84; Waters 1984:47–56, 65–66; Schweitzer 1974–1998).

Mythology

As each clan had its own origin narrative, the mythic structure of Otoe belief was highly diverse. Each clan guarded its legendary origin narratives, and no outsiders were permitted to hear them. Each narrative was the property of a particular family, and ownership implied a blessing from the sacred powers that could be transferred to others. All accounts begin in mythological time with the earth already established and four animal brothers who seek a place to live. The brothers named objects and events, providing traditional sacred knowledge passed down through clan lines. Ceremonies were initiated that became the inherited rites of the clan or subclan or referred to the collective rituals of the tribe, such as the distribution of buffalo meat, tattooing rites, and the use of the pipe (Whitman 1938:173–175). Mythological figures included the tricksters *isčįkʰe*, who created food for the people from his own body, and *mįsčįŋe* 'rabbit', who also helped the people in time of trouble. Both Earth and Day were personifed as central characters as well as animals. Sacred stories were narrated only during the winter (Waters 1984:242ff.).

Life Cycle

Ceremonies connected with the life cycle celebrated a baby's arrival and recognized an individual's final rite of passage. A separate tepee or grass lodge was constructed for childbirth, during which the mother was attended by experienced women. After birth, the mother remained in seclusion for 15 days if the child were female, 30 days if male. The newborn infant was rubbed with tallow and was wrapped and tied to a cradleboard. An ear-piercing ceremony was soon held, and gifts were distributed in the child's honor. Children were also honored at the time of namegiving, when they first walked, and when they wore their first pair of moccasins. Ceremonies for a girl were held at the first menses, when she talked to her first suitor, and when she was tattooed. The oldest daughter of a chief would be painted and given instructions by a respected tattooer; she was then tattooed on the forehead, breast, and back of the hands and was blessed with a sprinkling of fresh earth. Tattoo bundles were inherited through the lineages. Adoptions and marriages were also marked with ceremonies. The emphasis on the individual, especially the child's place in the family and clan, provided identity with a large social group without losing a sense of the importance of the person (Whitman 1937:64–67, 73–79, 83).

Name giving (vol. 17:204–205) was meant to insure the blessings of a long and successful life. There were sacred and secular names as well as nicknames. A name might be given on the fourth day after birth; the first two children received sacred names selected from the father's clan origin legend. Each name had a song that became the property of the owner. The naming ceremony, including a feast and the giving of gifts, was the official initiation of the child into the clan and further evidence of the individual's place within the group (Schweitzer 1985). An adult could take a new name based on a vision or a deed.

The nickname, considered to be a lucky name, was given by the mother's brother. Such names were obscene or uncomplimentary and derived from disparaging remarks made about the uncle, heard by the niece or nephew, and reported back to the uncle. He would give the name to his niece or nephew at a public event, at the same time bestowing a gift. The use of nicknames was said to act as a social deterrent to keep people from talking unkindly about others (Whitman 1937:67–68).

At puberty a boy was sent on a vision quest. His face painted with charcoal, carrying only a buffalo robe, the boy would fast and cry to Wakanda. The emphasis, however, was on the appeal for power rather than on an actual vision experience. Inheritance was the expected way to obtain power. Ideally, the youth would receive a blessing that would make him worthy of inheriting his father's powers. Supernatural powers were considered dangerous and potentially deceitful, demanding recompense for their gift, such as the death of a relative. The validation of a gift of power was assured by the exchange of tangible goods. Visions proved their validity through the individual's success in life. Women were not supposed to practice artistic techniques, presumably porcupine quillwork, until they had been authorized to do so by a particular vision. Designs on tepee covers might be inherited through an ancestor's vision experience (Whitman 1937:81–88).

Ideally marriages were formally arranged between families of equal status, although elopments also occurred. The boy's family was expected to give horses and other gifts to the girl's family. Later, return gifts of goods and horses of equal value were given to the groom's family. The teachings of the elders stressed monogamy but polygyny was also practiced; co-wives usually were sisters. Although matrilocal residence was initially observed, after the birth of the first child, couples more often chose patrilocal residence. If the wife bore no children, the husband might take one of her classificatory sisters as a second wife. In divorce, a man returned to his parents' lodge for six months to a year, after which time either could remarry (Whitman 1937:50–53, 55).

When a person died, the entire village mourned and all activity ceased. Mourning by the villagers lasted four days, after which the fireplaces of the lodges were cleaned and relit. Close relatives continued mourning and might slash their shins, pierce their ears, and cut off their hair. The mourning period for a spouse usually lasted four years. A variety of mourning ceremonies, held either before or after burial, included piercing the flesh of the forearm (*aráhį waxróge*) to honor a dead chief, holding contests in the deceased's favorite activity such as horse racing, and the giveaway contest (*wegráwe*), with points for gifts given in the past. Each clan had its own customs for preparation of the body; in general, the body was dressed in the finest clothes and the face painted in a distinctive clan pattern. The body was laid out in a tepee or lodge with burial usually on the second or third day. The dead were placed high in trees or, more commonly, the body was set upright in a grave, facing north, and covered with logs and earth. The deceased's horse might be strangled and left near the grave. Spirits were believed to journey north to the spirit world where they lived a life similar to that on earth (Whitman 1937:58–63, 100; Curtis 1907–1930, 19:157).

Medicine Societies

Secret societies helped to solidify the group and worked for the common good. The two most important were the Buffalo Doctors' Lodge, primarily associated with curing and the cultivation of corn, and the Medicine Lodge, a group related to the Algonquian Midewiwin society and similar to the Iowa and Winnebago forms. The Medicine Lodge was open to chiefs and their families, warriors, priests and the wealthy; both men and women were eligible. The blessings that membership gave were long life and perpetuation of the family. The society also served to institutionalize antisocial behavior and the expression of aggression through the practice of sorcery (Whitman 1937:105, 111–113).

Members of the Buffalo Doctors' Lodge effectively treated wounds, broken bones, and other illnesses. They used a special curing technique in which they chewed herbs, known only to them, which they sprayed over the patient's wound. There were six or eight leaders, each with a sacred bundle (fig. 3). The leaders handed on their power to younger followers eager to pay for it (Whitman 1937:105–106).

Warfare

Duties of warriors included carrying out orders of the clan chief and punishing offenders through institutionalized "soldier killing" (for example, whipping those who disobeyed the hunt leader). The Otoe were organized for peace, not for war, and valued skill in hunting more than skill in war. Nonetheless, the Otoe validated ceremonial life through warrior status and trained young boys for war. A warrior was held in high esteem and was expected to look after the people and help them in times of trouble. Intertribal hostilities in the 1830s and 1840s and pressures by White encroachment exaggerated warfare in the lives of the Otoe.

Before acquiring the horse, the Otoe waged war on foot with the war club (fig. 4), wearing black charcoal paint marked with streaks (fig. 5). Warriors carried war bundles (in which their power resided) with them into battle. Individual warriors owned war bundles as did clans and societies. Warriors counted coup on the fallen enemy, and the man dealing the death blow claimed the scalp. He took the scalp to his mother-in-law or his sister-in-law who danced with it. Later he tied it to a war bundle. At war dances celebrating their return, warriors recounted their war deeds while "striking the post," a ceremony that obligated them to be truthful. After intertribal wars subsided, ceremonies that had been validated by acts of bravery were validated by acts of giving (Whitman 1937:10–12, 36).

Milwaukee Public Mus., Wis.: 30703.

Fig. 3. Sweetgrass necklace from a Buffalo Doctor's bundle. One length of sweetgrass braid is looped and braided with a second length. The composite length was then looped into a double strand. Collected by Alanson Skinner, Red Rock, Okla., 1922; length of loop 54 cm.

History Since 1804

Treaties and Land Cessions

The period from 1804 to 1854 can be characterized as years of change, treaties, and land cessions. Meriwether Lewis and William Clark, the first Americans officially to record the location of the Otoe-Missouria villages on the south bank of the Platte River near the confluence of the Elkhorn River, estimated the tribes to contain 200 men, two-thirds of

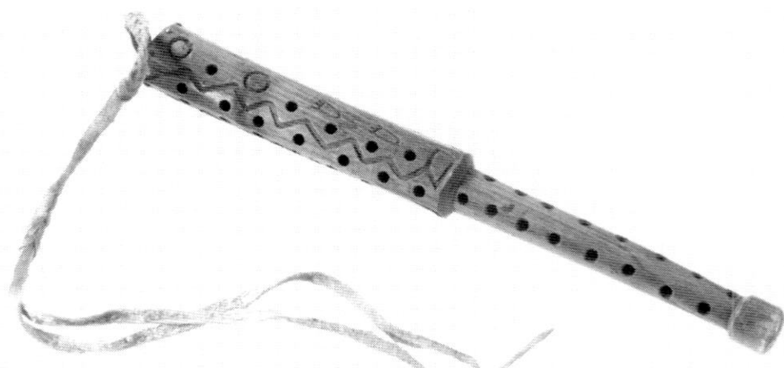

Smithsonian, top, NAA: 3889-a; bottom, Dept. of Anthr.: 22418.

Fig. 4. War paraphernalia. top, left to right: Iron Eyes (Insta-muntha) holding a mirror in wooden frame, Little Thunder (Ko-inga) holding an 1861 rifled musket, Walking Elk (Op-po-hom-mon-ne) holding a pipe, and Blackbird (E'en-brick-to) holding a Remington revolver (W.H. Jackson 1877:59; Dorsey 1880d). Photograph probably by William H. Jackson, Omaha, Neb., 1868–1869. bottom, Whip and war club carved with the owner's war record. The whip is made of plaited strips of buckskin; the wooden club has holes that indicate the number of battles; other marks indicate the number of scalps taken. Bear tracks and zigzag lightning indicate the qualities of fierceness and quickness in the owner. Collected by Jesse W. Griest, Nebr., before 1876; length 54 cm.

Mus. für Völkerkunde, Berlin: A1690.

Fig. 5. *Otoe Hunting Party in the Snow.* The artist described Wakitamone (far left) as "a man of gigantic height . . . his hair was cut rather short, and, by great pains bestowed on it, made to stand straight upright, except the plaited scalp lock at the top of his head, which hung low down his back. His face was decorated with black stripes. . . . he was one of the most distinguished warriors of the Ottoes, and . . . a great medicine man" (Möllhausen 1858: 1:149). The party has both bows and arrows and guns. Watercolor by Heinrich Balduin Möllhausen, 1852.

them Otoe and one-third Missouria (table 2). Otoe and Missouria chiefs met with the explorers at Council Bluffs (on the west side of the Missouri). The tribe was then still hunting south of the Platte and on their old hunting grounds east of the Missouri River. Their first treaty with the United States in 1817 formally acknowledged the protection of and allegiance to the United States (Thwaites 1904–1905, 1:87–90; Kappler 1904–1941, 2:139; Allen 1915, 1:14–26).

In 1819 half the Iowa tribe, sympathetic with the Americans during the War of 1812, joined the Otoe-Missouria (fig. 6). When the Otoe-Missouria-Iowa village was burned by the Sauk in 1820, they were forced to move downstream and the Iowa soon returned to their own village. Rivalries between tribal members and a quarrel between two Otoe leaders caused the two most powerful bands to occupy separate villages. Hostilities between the Otoe and the Sioux, Sauk, Fox, and Comanche and the advancing frontier of American settlement put additional pressures on all Missouri River tribes (Morse 1822:204; Thwaites 1904–1905, 14:239, 15:34–35, 17:150).

Although the 1825 Treaty of Prairie du Chien left the Otoe-Missouria claim to their hunting territory in Iowa intact, the 1830 Treaty of Prairie du Chien resulted in the cession of land in Minnesota, Missouri, and the western third of Iowa. Game was becoming increasingly scarce and when the Treaty of 1833 was concluded, the Otoe and Missouria ceded even more land; the United States agreed to provide money and livestock if the tribe would abandon the hunt and become wholly agricultural (Kappler 1904–1941, 2:256–258, 305–310, 400–401).

Table 2. Population, 1758–1998

Year	*Total*	*Source*
1758	150 Missouria men; 100 Otoe men	Kerlérec in Nasatir 1952, 1:52
1777	200 Missouria warriors; 100 Otoe warriors	Houck 1909, 1:142–143
1798	400 men	Trudeau in Nasatir 1952, 2:539
1804	200 men	Moulton 1983–, 3:393–394
1809–1811	130–140 warriors	Bradbury in Thwaites 1904–1905, 5:80
1829	1,200 Otoe; 80 Missouria	P.B. Porter in Schoolcraft 1851–1857, 3:593
1830	1,500	B.B. Chapman 1965:16
1835	964	B.B. Chapman 1965:16
1855	600	B.B. Chapman 1974:95
1866	513	A.L. Green 1930:181
1867	430	Hayden 1873:33
1878	459	Milner 1982:145
1881	473	B.B. Chapman 1965:139
1890	358	U.S. Census 1894:528
1911	416	B.B. Chapman 1965:349
1919	529	B.B. Chapman 1965:349
1939	814	B.B. Chapman 1965:349
1945	886	B.B. Chapman 1965:349
1959	1,009	B.B. Chapman 1965:349
1979	1,385	The Otoe-Missouria Tribe 1979: fig. 13
1989	1,553	Schweitzer 1974–1998
1994	1,561	Bureau of Indian Affairs 1994:2
1998	1,520	Schweitzer 1974–1998

Academy of Nat. Sciences, Lib., Philadelphia: Lawson Coll. 79.

Fig. 6. Council of Otoe, Missouria, and Iowa meeting with Maj. Benjamin O'Fallon, Oct. 4, 1819. There were about 100 Otoes, 70 Missourias, and 50–60 Iowas present. O'Fallon urged the tribes to stop all warfare and encouraged the Iowa living with the Otoe-Missouria to become more friendly to the United States. The Otoe-Missouria reacted favorably, and speeches were given by Shonga-tonga and the Crenier, the only 2 recognized as chiefs. At the end of the council a celebration took place, which included dancing and giving of gifts. O'Fallon gave blankets, kettles, strouding, tobacco, guns, powder and ball. The Crenier was given a large medal in exchange for a smaller one he possessed (Thwaites 1904–1907, 14:236–239). Watercolor by Samuel Seymour, 1820–1822.

Nationalmuseet, Dept. of Ethnography, Copenhagen.

Fig. 7. Ietan (d. 1837), also called Shaumonekusse or Prairie Wolf, a leader of the Otoes during the 1820s–1830s. He wears a bear-claw necklace along with necklaces of shells, a peace medal on a ribbon, and multiple earrings. His headdress includes buffalo horns and scarlet horse hair. In 1821 Ietan and his wife, Eagle of Delight, traveled to the East with Maj. Benjamin O'Fallon's delegation. They met with President James Monroe and other government officials and had their portraits painted (Viola 1976:24–31, 119). Oil painting by Charles Bird King, Washington, D.C., 1822.

In 1833 Rev. Moses Merrill established a Baptist Mission at Bellevue on the Missouri River among the Otoe, Omaha, and Pawnee. He convinced the Otoe-Missouria to relocate to the north bank of the Platte, and by 1836 half the tribe was living six miles west of Bellevue. Although the new location put the tribe nearer the agency with its blacksmith shop and trading post, the tribe was also more vulnerable to attacks from the Sioux. Hunting was poor, American settlers were pressuring for Indian land, and excessive drinking exacerbated tribal disorganization. By the Treaty of Bellevue of 1836, the Otoe, Missouria, Omaha, and Yankton and Santee Sioux ceded title to land between the Missouri River and the state of Missouri (McCoy 1840:405, 464–466; Merrill 1892:175–176, 182; Anderson 1919:75–77; Kappler 1904–1941, 2:479–481). These lands were known as the Platte Purchase.

In 1837, when the Otoe chief Ietan (fig. 7) was killed by a fellow tribesman, the Otoe and Missouria divided into quarreling factions. In 1839 the Missouria left the village and moved south of the Platte. In 1841 the Otoe set fire to the village on the north bank because they felt it harbored an evil spirit, and by 1842 they and the Missouria were living in five small villages on the south side of the Platte from the Missouri River to the mouth of the Elkhorn (McCoy 1840:562–563; Merrill 1892:182, 185, 189; ARCIA 1842:430–431).

The 1840s and early years of the 1850s did not see much improvement in the condition of the Otoe-Missouria. Not satisfied with the land already gained, settlers poured into the Platte region making demands on grazing land, timber, and whatever game was available. In 1843 the tribe expressed the desire to sell their land for annuity money, but it was not till 1854 that a treaty was concluded in which the Otoe-Missouria ceded all their lands west of the Missouri (almost two million acres) except for a strip 10 miles wide and 25 miles long in the valley of the Big Blue River on the Nebraska-Kansas border (fig. 1) (Kappler 1904–1941, 2:608–611). By this time the two groups totaled only about 600 people, having lost one-third of their population in the smallpox and cholera epidemics of 1851 (B.B. Chapman 1974:95).

The Big Blue Reservation

In 1855 the Otoe-Missouria moved to the Big Blue Reservation in Nebraska and Kansas. There the government built a house for the agent, erected saw and grist mills, and hired farmers to teach the Indians by example. Several mixed-blood families settled on the eastern end of the reservation and established small farms (Edmunds

1976:53–56), but most of the Otoes did not become farmers, even though the land was fertile and well-watered, with valuable stands of hardwood. By 1869, when the first Quaker agent, Albert Green, arrived as a result of President Grant's Peace Policy, he found fewer than 450 people living in 30 earthlodges and a few bark houses in a 25-acre village. The Otoe continued to rely on their traditional garden horticulture and some hunting.

The Quaker agents came with good intentions, but they failed to understand the organization of the tribe and succeeded in disrupting the leadership pattern, contributing to factionalism. The faction known as the Coyote band (not related to the Coyote clan) or Wild Bunch was led by Medicine Horse and other traditional chiefs. Medicine Horse was an articulate spokesman for his people and was determined to preserve tribal traditions. The more acculturated faction, known as the Quaker band, was led by chiefs appointed by the agent. Factionalism existed before the arrival of the Quaker agents, but their actions and sympathies exacerbated the situation. The key issue was whether or not to sell the Big Blue Reservation and remove to Indian Territory (fig. 8).

In addition to the uncertainty over where and how they were to live, the lives of the Otoe and Missouria during their 26-year stay on the Big Blue were beset by environmental difficulties as well as the continuing pressures exerted by the expanding White frontier. Grasshoppers and drought destroyed their crops, and they could not hunt because of Sioux raiders; many children died. Whites stole their horses and timber and settled on the reservation as squatters.

In 1876 Congress approved the Quaker plan to sell 120,000 acres in 160-acre tracts. The Quaker agent wanted the Otoe to farm the remaining few thousand acres. Whites immediately began to settle on the land even though in 1877 when they marked off their claims, cut timber, put up their homes, and formed vigilance committees, the land had not yet been appraised or opened for settlement.

In December 1876 Big Elk and others of the Quaker faction approved the sale, and in 1878 tribal members sent a

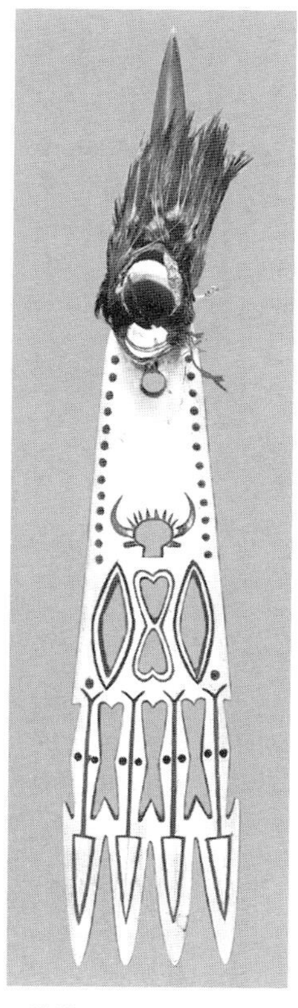

left, Smithsonian, NAA: 3822-b; center, The British Mus., Mus. of Mankind, London: 5216.

Fig. 8. Hair roach and spreader. left, Big Bear (Mŭntcehŭntce), also known as Joseph Powell, a Missouria. He wears a bear claw necklace, hair roach, and multiple ball and cone earrings. Big Bear was one of 5 chiefs who traveled to Washington, D.C., in Oct. 1873 to meet with Commissioner of Indian Affairs Edward P. Smith to request the sale of Big Blue Res. The commissioner's refusal led to increased factionalism on the reservation, where Big Bear was the only one of the 5 chiefs who did not join the Coyote band (Milner 1982:128). Photograph by John K. Hillers or Charles M. Bell, Washington, D.C., before 1884. center, Elk antler spreader for use with a roach headdress, with a bone socket for a feather ornamented with an ivory-billed woodpecker bill and red- and black-dyed woodpecker scalp feathers (Gibbs 1982:60). The carved designs are outlined in red and black paint. Collected by Friedrich Paul Wilhelm, 1823; length 22.9 cm. right, Diagram of how a spreader is used. It is fastened to the head by looping the scalplock through the large hole in the base of the roach and spreader and pinning it with a short stick. After men began wearing short hair, roaches were attached by a thong from the front of the roach and spreader down to the chin. The back of the roach and spreader are secured by a thong tied to the back of a headband or, in modern times, around the chin. The spreader fans out the dyed deerhair, porcupine hair, or turkey beards. Drawing by Donald B. Tenoso.

petition to the commissioner of Indian affairs requesting removal to Indian Territory. The vote was narrowly in favor of removal and was swung by the Coyote band, whose members hoped to retain a traditional hunting lifeway. In February 1880 families of the Coyote faction left to settle on the Sac and Fox reservation. By March 1881, when Congress passed an act for the sale of the remainder of the Big Blue Reservation, 238 of the Coyote band were already in Indian Territory. The Quaker band, numbering 234, moved to their own reservation on Red Rock Creek in Indian Territory in October 1881. Gradually members of the Coyote faction joined the Quaker band, but it was several decades before the tribe was totally reunited (Milner 1982:117–152; Hopkins 1980).

Red Rock Reservation

The Otoe-Missouria reservation of 129,113 acres, located in north-central Indian Territory, bordered the Ponca and Pawnee reservations (fig. 1) (B.B. Chapman 1965:134). Soon after the tribe's arrival, agency buildings, a school, laundry, and cottages were built near Red Rock Creek.

By 1890 the Otoe lived in frame houses as well as brush houses, tents, earth lodges, and dugouts. About 100 farmed, and some had a few cattle and hogs as well as teams of horses for farmwork and transportation. Most Otoes raised subsistence gardens. Ninety children attended the boarding school. Tribal members took advantage of both Indian doctors and a White physician who lived on the reservation. Most of the Otoe were bilingual but preferred to converse in their own language. They had their own reservation court system; a dozen mounted policemen helped patrol the reservation and Otoe judges held court (U.S. Census Office. 11th Census 1894:553–555; Edmunds 1976:71).

In the 1890s a vision of William FawFaw (Wawnoshe) developed into a religion practiced among the Otoe. The religion called for a ceremony and the wearing of clothing decorated with symbols FawFaw saw in his vision (fig. 9).

Allotments

In 1890 authority was granted to allot the reservation. The Otoe resisted for over a decade, and during the long process of making individual allotments they steadfastly opposed the process; however, by 1899, 64,936.05 acres had been divided into 441 allotments. The Otoe then requested that all children born since the original division be given allotments and that the remaining land be divided among all tribal members. In 1907, 514 tribal members received additional land bringing each person's total acreage to 280–290 acres. Thus the entire reservation was divided among the Otoe-Missouria and not opened for settlement to Whites. Unallotted land held in common for the use of the tribe amounted to 640 acres, with 720 acres held for school and administrative purposes (B.B. Chapman 1948:143–158).

left, State Histl. Soc. of Wis., Madison: WHi(X3) 44154; center and right, Denver Art Mus., Colo.: 1938.79.

Fig. 9. Faw Faw coats. left, White Horse, wearing a wool coat decorated in beaded designs associated with the religious revitalization movement of William Faw Faw of the early 1890s. While ill, Faw Faw dreamed that he visited the dwelling of the gods where he was given details of a new dance and ceremony, including the wearing of clothing embroidered with specific beaded designs (Fletcher and La Flesche 1895; Wooley and Waters 1988). White Horse also holds an eagle-wing fan. Photograph by Thomas F. Croft, Oklahoma City, Okla. Terr., 1896–1904. center and right, Front and back of man's wool coat with beaded designs characteristic of the Otoe-Missouria: curvilinear florals and outlining of forms with rows of white beads. The figures associated with the Faw Faw religion include uprooted cedar trees, symbolic of the trees ritually planted in the earthlodge during the ceremony, as well as stars, bison heads, human figures, and horses. Made before 1896, length 97 cm.

Under the 1906 Burke Act, the secretary of the interior issued patents in fee simple whenever it was thought appropriate rather than waiting for a petition from the allottee. By 1910, 78 original allotments had already been sold (B.B. Chapman 1948:158). Between 1917 and 1921 agents of the federally funded Competency Commission visited Otoes at their homes and forced patents on several individuals who did not want them. By 1919, 42 patents had been awarded as a result. Those who retained their lands favored leasing to White farmers, especially when holding part of an allotment through undivided heirship.

Many Otoes left the community during the 1930s and 1940s, some for cities during the Depression and others overseas as members of the armed forces. After World War II over 100 tribesmen, including many veterans, formed the Otoe Indian Credit Association with funds from the Department of Interior. They loaned this money to tribal members at low rates with little or no collateral (Edmunds 1976:81–83).

In 1947 the tribe sent nine claims to the Indian Court of Claims. The Otoe-Missouria land claims case was the first award made by the Indian Claims Commission on the basis of aboriginal use and occupancy commonly known as Indian Title. The Indian Claims Commission awarded the Otoe-Missouria monetary settlements in 1964 and 1967 for lands ceded in 1830, 1833, and 1854. The money was distributed in per capita payments although there was much sentiment in the tribe for the settlement to be held in common for the use of the tribe as a whole.

The 1980s

The 1970s and 1980s were an era of building and economic development. The tribe constructed houses in Red Rock and, in 1977, with a community block grant, constructed 50 single-family dwellings southeast of the agency grounds. New tribal buildings included the Otoe-Missouria Cultural Center with offices and a multipurpose room used for dances, hand games, funerals, and other large gatherings; the senior citizens' building used for lunch and activity programs for the elders; and the tribal enterprises building. The Otoe-Missouria tribe was one of the first to establish income-generating bingo. It also built and operated a gas station and store just south of the Cultural Center. The Otoes' elected tribal council, with a constitution and bylaws adopted in the 1980s, oversaw Otoe housing, a child welfare program, summer programs for children, the senior citizens' program, and the economic enterprises, although

Smithsonian, NAA: 53496.

Fig. 10. Otoe men and women in ceremonial dress. left to right, back row: Pearl Art; Miriam Dent; Josephine Atkins; William Atkins; Hoke S. Dent, chief of Otoes; and Charley Duncan. The boys are Harvey Atkins (b. 1904) and Amos Black (b. 1904, d. 1978). The women wear ceremonial clothes including blouses decorated with buttons and skirts with ribbonwork appliqué. Photograph by Fred R. Lambrecht, about 1909.

political factionalism typical of the nineteenth century continued into the 1980s.

As a result of long contact with missionaries, many Otoes were members of the Baptist Indian Church and the Assembly of God Church. A large percentage of the tribe were members of the Native American Church (introduced to the Otoe in the late 1890s) and the Church of the First Born, a Peyote church chartered in 1914 and founded by an Otoe–Sac and Fox (fig. 11) (La Barre 1969:167–168).

The Otoe-Missouria tribe held a yearly four-day encampment at the dance ground on Red Rock Creek and one-day dances and hand games in the Cultural Center throughout the year. Although Otoes denied playing the hand game in the past (Whitman 1937:13), the game was played in the 1980s, held to honor an individual, as a benefit to raise money, and simply as a social event. The person chosen as "guesser," one from each side, took turns trying to guess in which hands the "buttons" (beaded bone tubes) were held by two members of the opposite side. One person from each side, in charge of the counting sticks, kept score. At the beginning of the game, each side had five sticks; one game was over when all 10 sticks were on one side. Usually five games were played, interspersed with giveaway songs, during which people danced and gave money to the honoree or organization sponsoring the hand game. The Otoe did not gamble, but the person sponsoring the hand game usually put money up for each side ($10 or 20), and the person guessing the most games received the money. The Otoe always fed the participants before the game began.

The values and beliefs that remained an integral feature of Otoe life found expression in activities such as the funeral ritual and feast, the "paying the way" ceremony for a young boy or girl to dance in the arena, praying to Wakanda and to the four directions, the sacredness of the dance circle, the drum as messenger from the people to Wakanda, reverence for the elders, the sacred circle as represented by the dance ground and the drum, and the prime importance of water (it is always served first at a feast). These sacred rituals and secular gatherings continued to integrate the members of the community and to nurture an enduring sense of Otoe identity (Schweitzer 1983, 1983a). Clan affiliations were maintained, and elders were still reluctant to divulge clan secrets.

As in the past, Otoe people interacted with friends from other Oklahoma tribes through gourd dancing, war dancing and singing. The Otoe maintained an especially strong friendship with the Kiowa from whom they received the Gourd Dance between 1927 and 1930. Traditional men's dance costumes were revived, and women wore skirts and

Okla. Histl. Soc., Oklahoma City: 797.

Fig. 11. Otoe men and women dressed for Peyote meeting. left to right, back row: Frances English, Hoke Dent, Reuben English, Mrs. Frances English, Miriam Dent, Sally Diamond; front row: George Washington Dailey, Moses Harragarra, Bert Diamond, John Hudson, holding staff, cedar bags, and feather fans used in Peyote meetings. Photographed near Red Rock, Okla., 1915.

shawls decorated with Otoe ribbonwork and Otoe-style moccasins. The tobacco ceremony (a ritual offering of tobacco to Wakanda to ask for blessing) was revived for the 1981 centennial celebration; giveaways and other forms of sharing occurred on every occasion. The naming ceremony and the memorial feast to release the mourners were conducted in the 1980s.

The oral tradition so important in ceremonial and secular traditional events remained a vital part of all Otoe functions, affirming the strong emphasis the Otoe placed on social relationships. The family social structure and kin classification (including reciprocal obligations) continued, although the matrilineal line was sometimes substituted for the patrilineal one in cases of intermarriage with non-Indians or with members of other tribes.

The Otoe-Missouria chapter of the American War Mothers, the first all-Indian chapter, organized in 1942, served and honored the servicemen and women of the tribe and remained one of the most active in the state (fig. 12). In addition to monthly chapter meetings, the Otoe women held state and national offices and attended conventions. The most important functions of the war mothers were to provide services, including gifts, money, and supplies, to Otoe disabled veterans, retired veterans, and to servicemen and women home on leave and to honor them with dances, hand games, special songs, and giveaways. Other aid included providing the meal for one evening's services at a veteran's or war mother's funeral vigil and at the ceremony officially releasing the relatives of a deceased veteran or war mother from their period of mourning. The War Mothers' activities illustrate the network of sharing basic to Otoe interaction within the tribe: they received gifts from relatives and friends, which they in turn gave to others.

Fig. 12. Members of the Otoe-Missouria chapter of the American War Mothers. left to right, back row: Vena Deroin, Lorena Deroin, Zelda Yeahquo, Priscilla Arkeketa, Pat Little Crow, Dorcas Tohee, Vera Cleghorn, Minnie Moore, Frances Little Crow; front row: Lucy White Cloud, Lizzie Harper, Grace Kihega, Genevieve Bassett, Fannie Gant. Photograph by Marjorie Schweitzer, Otoe-Missouria Cultural Center, near Red Rock, Okla., June 7, 1984.

The blankets and shawls worn by the war mothers when they danced, decorated with Otoe-style ribbonwork, beadwork, and quillwork as well as symbols of the American War Mothers association, represented the integration of Otoe and non-Indian culture traits as the Otoe adapted a White organization to Otoe beliefs and values. The War Mothers, a highly respected group of women who reflected the high prestige of modern-day warriors, exemplified the Otoes' ability to adapt to culture change (Schweitzer 1981).

Otoe people who made careers in the armed forces or worked at jobs throughout Oklahoma or other states frequently returned to the Oklahoma community after retirement to be more involved with family and friends in tribal activities. These activities often took place as part of the intertribal network of north-central Oklahoma involving members of neighboring tribes—Osage, Pawnee, Ponca, Tonkawa, Sac and Fox, and Iowa—and with members of southwestern Oklahoma tribes—Kiowa and Comanche. Some Otoes married members of these tribes. In 1989, of the 1,553 enrolled members, approximately 800 resided in the vicinity of the reservation in Red Rock, Ponca City, and other small towns. Others lived in Tulsa and Oklahoma City and in cities on the west coast.

On October 22–24, 1981, the Otoe-Missouria commemorated their arrival in Indian Territory with a centennial celebration. The tobacco ceremony, offered to bless the celebration, and the flag-raising just after dawn each day, took place in the campground along Red Rock Creek where the Otoe first camped. On the afternoon of the 23d, exactly 100 years from the day of their arrival, the tribe dedicated a historical marker honoring the event. Other ceremonies dedicated the tribal housing complex of 50 new homes and the senior citizens' center.

Speeches by visiting Bureau of Indian Affairs and government officials and tribal members noted the achievements of the past 100 years, and a publication (The Otoe-Missouria Tribe 1981) honored the ancestors who made the move as well as their direct descendants, the elders. Afternoon dancing featured clan songs for members of the seven clans, followed in the evenings by war dancing. A traditional feast was served on the grounds of the old school.

The Otoe-Missouria people maintained a strong sense of tribal identity in spite of the many changes that have taken place in material culture and loss of land. Especially important in their adapting to change has been the example set by the elders of the tribe who recognized that change was inevitable and taught their young people to prepare for the future (The Otoe-Missouria Tribe 1981:56).

Synonymy†

Of the names used to designate the Otoe, the earliest one in its full form is recorded in several variants that differ

†This synonymy was written by Douglas R. Parks.

primarily in their initial syllable, which may be O-, Wa-, or Ma-. Most common are forms with initial O-, exemplified by Otoutanta, 1682 (La Salle in Margry 1876–1886, 2:215); Otoctatas, 1700 (Le Sueur in Margry 1876–1886, 6:82; also Truteau in Parks 1992); Autocdatás, 1785 (Miró in Nasatir 1952, 1:120); Octoctatas, 1702 (Iberville in Margry 1876–1886, 4:598; also Clamorgan in Nasatir 1952, 2:632; Tabeau 1939:100); Octotata, 1718 (Delisle map in Tucker 1942:pl. 15); and Othocatatas and Othoctatas, 1795 (Mackay in Nasatir 1952, 1:357). Other variant spellings are Otontanta, 1673 (Marquette map in Shea 1903; Tucker 1942:pl. 5), Ototenta, 1688 (de Tonti in Pease and Werner 1934:277), Anthoutantas, 1680 (Membré in Shea 1903:154), Autantas, 1700 (Marest in Villiers du Terrage 1925:33–34), Autocdata, 1769 (in Houck 1909, 1:44), Attotactoes, 1795–1796 (McKay in Nasatir 1952, 2:494), and Otoetata (Keating 1824, 2:320).

Early recordings with initial Wa- are illustrated by Wâd-doké-tâh-tâh and War-doke-tar-tar (Lewis and Clark 1806:14; Moulton 1983–, 3:393); Wa-dook-to-da (Brackenridge 1815:75); Wah-tok-ta-ta, Wah-tooh[-]tah-tah, Wah-toh-ta-na, and Wa-do-tan (Say in James 1823, 1:338, 2:lxxx, 363); and Wagh-toch-tat-ta (Maximilian in Thwaites 1904–1907, 24:313). All these forms are said to be the Otoe term for themselves; Say noted that various individual Otoes, when questioned, gave the four forms he recorded as different ways the name was thought properly to be said. In the nineteenth and twentieth centuries, Otoes have associated the name with the verb *watúhtaną* 'to copulate' (Marsh 1936), which it resembles in form; hence their name has commonly been explained as meaning 'those who will copulate' (James 1823, 2:338), and translated variously as 'aphrodisian' (McGee 1897:162) and 'lechers' (Hodge 1907–1910, 2:164). This folk etymology is reinforced by popular stories like a "love scrape between an Otoe chief's son and an Iowa chief's daughter, Watota" (Hamilton 1885, 1:75). The actual origin of the name is obscure, especially since Otoe speakers do not agree on the precise form of the word.

In the late nineteenth century this name was recorded in Otoe as Watóta (Dorsey 1879), rendered *watótta* (Robert L. Rankin, personal communication 1991). The longer form is preserved in several Siouan languages: Osage wadochtáta (Maximilian in Thwaites 1904–1907, 24:299); Kansa *wadóttatta* and *wadóttadą* (Dorsey 1882 as retranscribed); Omaha and Ponca *waδúttada* (Dorsey 1890:334; Fletcher and La Flesche 1911; Parks 1988; retranscribed); and Santee Sioux Watóȟtata (Riggs 1890:539).

Historical forms with an initial M- are Matoutenta, 1682 (La Salle in Margry 1876–1886, 1:487), Motantees, 1682 (La Métairie in French 1875, 2:25), Metotantes, 1698 (Hennepin 1903, 2:443), Maquetantala, 1714 (Bourgmont in Giraud 1958:16), Mactotatas, 1761 (Charlevoix 1966, 2:224), and Malatantes (McKenney and Hall 1854–1858, 3:82). Forms in Algonquian languages with an initial *m-* are: Fox *mato·htata* (Gatschet 1882–1889, phonemicized), Shawnee *matoʔkata* (Voegelin 1938–1940, 9:354), and presumably Menominee *meto·htat* (Bloomfield 1975:128).

The modern form of the name Otoe (also spelled Oto) derives from the first two syllables of the longer variant with initial syllable *o* illustrated above. Its usage dates to the early eighteenth century, exemplified by Otho, 1723 (Bourgmont in Margry 1876–1886, 6:402; Mackay in Nasatir 1952, 1:351), Hotos (Bourgmont in Margry 1876–1886, 6:396; Miró in Nasatir 1952, 1:125), Othouez, 1758 (Le Page du Pratz 1947:59), Othoves (Alcedo 1786–1789, 3:410), Autos, 1794–1796 (Truteau in Parks 1992), Otto's and Ottoos (Schermerhorn 1814:10, 32); Otoe (Irving 1835:10), and Ottoes (Lewis and Clark in Moulton 1983–, 3:393; McKay in Nasatir 1952, 2:494). Frequently the same source uses one of these shorter forms interchangeably with one of the longer forms above (for example, Truteau in Parks 1992). Les Ottoe (also la Zoto) was the form used among French Canadian traders (Lewis and Clark in Moulton 1983–, 3:393). The Mandan name for the tribe was Óhto (Maximilian in Thwaites 1904–1907, 24:249).

A name of self-designation in use among the Otoe and the Iowa since the late nineteenth century is *ǰiwére* (Hamilton 1885:75; Curtis 1907–1930, 19:228; Furbee and Hopkins 1990; Parks 1988), *ǰíwere* (Whitman 1947:240; Robert L. Rankin, communication to editors 1999). The word, a composite of deitic particles meaning 'from here, i.e., this place', has no significance for Otoe speakers other than being an ethnonym (Dorsey 1885:1; Whitman 1937:xi; Marsh 1936).

Another name designating the Otoe, and perhaps formerly the Missouria as well, is Pawnee *pasu·hara* (Parks 1965–1990) and Wichita *wasó·harah* (David S. Rood, personal communication 1987), both of which are borrowings of the name Missouria itself. Borrowings, too, are Arapaho *wosóu·hinénnoʔ* (Ives Goddard, personal communication 1990) and Cheyenne Masohan (pl. Masohanan) (Petter 1913–1915:582). The Cheyenne name, no longer current in the mid-twentieth century, also designated the Missouria (Mooney 1907:425). In the twentieth century the Arapaho name is said to mean 'people having a mole (on the face)', but this interpretation is a modern folk etymology. Both Arapaho and Cheyenne designations are related to the Caddoan names and may derive either from them or from the Dhegiha usages below.

During the twentieth century the Osage name for the Otoe has been *wažóxδa* (Robert L. Rankin, personal communication 1990), and an equivalent Kansa name *wažóxla* is also found (Dorsey 1882; Gatschet 1878:27; retranscribed). In Quapaw *wažóxda* is the name for the Missouria and possibly for the Otoe as well (Robert L. Rankin, personal communication 1987). These Dhegiha Siouan forms are the same as the preceding Caddoan and Algonquian names.

An anomalous designation is Kiowa *á·k̓ɔ̀pʰà·gɔ̀*, literally 'wood(land) Osage' (La Barre 1935, phonemicized).

There is no known sign for the Otoe in the Plains sign language.

The name Missouri is ultimately derived from Illinois misouri 'dugout canoe' (Gravier 1700); from this was formed the Illinois name for the Missouria, rendered Emessourita 'people having dugout canoes' (Le Sueur in Delisle 1702). Early examples of the original and shortened forms of the name are 8emess8rit, 1673 (Marquette map in Shea 1903; Tucker 1942:pl. 5), 8missouri, 1681 (Thevenot in Shea 1903:268), Emissourita, 1684 (de Tonti in Margry 1876–1886, 1:595), Massourites and Messorites, 1698 (Hennepin 1903, 1:map facing p. 23, 207), Missiouris (Harris 1705, 2:map), Missouris, 1687 (Joutel in Margry 1876–1886, 3:432), Missoury, 1720 (La Harpe in Margry 1876–1886, 6:293), Misuris (Barcia Carballido y Zuñiga 1723:298; Miró in Nasatir 1952, 1:120), and Missouria, 1797 (MacKay in Nasatir 1952, 2:487).

The Missouria name for themselves was Ni-ú-t′a-tcí (Dorsey 1897:240), *nʸút⁾ačʰi* (Furbee and Hopkins 1990; Robert L. Rankin, personal communication 1991), recorded in various forms, for example, New-dar-cha (Lewis and Clark in Moulton 1983–, 3:394), Ne-o-ta-cha or Ne-o-ge-he (James 1823, 1:339), Neu-ta-che (Maximilian in Thwaites 1904–1907, 24:313), Ne-u-cha-ta, Ne-u-tach, or Ne-yu-ta-ca (Hamilton 1885, 1:47, 48), and Nutáchi (Curtis 1907–1930, 19:228). The Ioway form is *yút⁾ačʰi* (Marsh 1936). Although the name was said to mean 'those who build a town at the entrance of a river' (James 1823, 1:339) or 'those that arrive at the mouth' (Maximilian in Thwaites 1904–1907, 24:313), its etymology is obscure. The Omaha and Ponca designation for the Missouria, Ni-út̓-ati′ (*nįút̓atʰi*), is a borrowing of this name (Dorsey 1878, retranscribed).

The Quapaw name for the Missouria is *wažóxda*. The related forms in Osage and Kansa, *wažóxδa* and *wažóxla* respectively, which in the twentieth century designate the Otoe, probably formerly designated the Missouria. Like the Cheyenne name, the Pawnee, Wichita, and Arapaho names above may also have designated the Missouria since there is no recorded name for this tribe in any of these languages.

The Kansa are also reported to have applied to the Missouria their name for the Missouri River, Nicúdje (*nišóje*), literally 'roiled water' (Dorsey 1882, retranscribed), but this may have been a misunderstanding.

There is no sign recorded for the Missouria in the Plains sign language.

Sources

The primary ethnographic source on the Otoe-Missouria is Whitman (1937, 1938, 1947).

Eighteenth- and nineteenth-century writings concerning the Otoe-Missouria include: Davis (1890), Dorsey (1880, 1880a, 1880b, 1880c, 1880d, 1880e, 1880f, 1880g, 1880–1881, 1884, 1885a, 1885, 1886, 1891, 1894, 1897), A.L. Green (1930), T.L. Green (1954), Gallatin (1836), Hamilton (1856), Hayden (1873), Irving (1955), Jackson (1960, 1966), Jefferys (1760), Kercheval (1893), Long (in Thwaites 1904–1907), Maximilian (in Thwaites 1904–1907), McCoy (1840), McKenney and Hall (1854–1858), Merrill (1892), Morgan (1871, 1959), Nasatir (1952), Skinner (1925), Thwaites (1904–1905), Wilhelm (1973), and Yarrow (1881).

Ethnographic studies from the twentieth century include M.R. Harrington (1913, 1920), Howard (1956), Shunatona (1922), and Skinner (1925). Waters (1984) is a discussion and comprehensive presentation of oral narratives. Ethnographic information for the 1970s, 1980s, and 1990s is drawn from fieldwork by Schweitzer (1974–1998).

B.B. Chapman (1965, 1974) included much of his findings as expert witness in the Otoe-Missouria's Indian Court of Claims case. Woolworth (1956) summarizes history to 1854, Small (1958) presents Missouria history; Edmunds (1976) provides a brief historical synopsis to the 1970s; Milner (1982) and Hopkins (1980) summarize the Big Blue era; and Wright (1967) presents biographical information on Moses Harragarra.

Otoe-Missouria language is recorded in the manuscripts of the 1880s by Dorsey and in J.P. Harrington (1940). Wistrand-Robinson (1978) presents language lessons. Lieberkühn (1888) is a Christian religious tract in the Chiwere language. Good Tracks (1992) compiled a dictionary of the Iowa and Otoe-Missouria dialects of Chiwere. L. Stanley (1993) related the life history of Truman Dailey, one of the last fluent speakers of the Chiwere language.

Major museum collections of Otoe-Missouria material items are found at the Milwaukee Public Museum and the National Museum of the American Indian, Smithsonian. Smaller collections are found at the National Museum of Natural History, Smithsonian Institution, and at the Philbrook Museum of Art, Tulsa, Oklahoma.

Kansa

GARRICK A. BAILEY AND GLORIA A. YOUNG

The Kansa (ˈkănzu) (more commonly called the Kaw [kô]), spoke a language of the Dhegiha branch of the Siouan family, whose other members were Osage, Omaha-Ponca, and Quapaw. The Kansa considered themselves to be most closely related to the Osage, who stated that the differences between the Kansa* and Osage languages were no greater than the dialect differences that previously existed between Osage bands. It is possible that some degree of linguistic convergence occurred, reflecting the close association and degree of intermarriage between the two tribes that began in the late nineteenth century.

Origins

The Kansa shared with other Dhegiha tribes the tradition of originating from a single tribe living along the Ohio and, perhaps, Wabash rivers. At the mouth of the Ohio, the Quapaw proceeded south while the remainder ascended the Mississippi River to its junction with the Missouri. From there, the people who became the Kansa and Osage migrated slowly west up the Missouri River (McGee 1897:191; La Flesche 1921:459; Dorsey 1886:211–213). According to tradition, the Osage and Kansa became separate groups only after they separated from the other Dhegiha people.

A connection between shell artifacts in nineteenth-century Kansa medicine bags and Mississippian-style gorgets of Oneota cultures has been considered (Howard 1956a). However, the Pomona variant found in eastern Kansas and western Missouri may be a more likely candidate to be ancestral to the Kansa (Johnson 1991).

History, 1673–1800

The Kansa were first noted by Europeans in the 1670s, when Father Jacques Marquette and Louis Jolliet located them on the lower Missouri River upstream from the Missouria Indians (fig. 1) (Young and Hoffman 1993: illustration 27; Baughman 1961:12). Contact was not made until French traders penetrated the Missouri valley in the 1680s. At that time, the Kansa probably occupied a small area in present-day northeastern Kansas and northwestern Missouri along both sides of the Missouri River. The tribe probably controlled territory eastward to the Grand River, after the decline of the Missouria tribe.

Trade rapidly developed as the French exchanged guns, metal knives, axes, and other items for slaves, horses, buffalo wool, deerskins, and smaller pelts. The trade in slaves resulted in large-scale warfare, the Kansa raiding both the Pawnee and the Padouca (Plains Apache) for slaves to trade with the French. Initially, trade with coureurs de bois from Canada at the settlements along the Mississippi was irregular. Then, in 1723, the government of Louisiana established Fort Orleans at the junction of the Grand and Missouri rivers. Although still far from the principal Kansa village, which was reported to consist of 150 lodges, Fort Orleans did bring greater contact between the Kansa and French traders until it was destroyed in 1725 or 1726 (Nasatir 1952, 1:52; Margry 1876–1886, 6:393; Wedel 1946:10).

In 1724, the French regent commissioned Étienne Venyard, sieur de Bourgmont, to lead an expedition to establish peace with the Plains Apache and to initiate trade with the Spaniards to the southwest of Louisiana. Proceeding up the Missouri River from Fort Orleans in July, Bourgmont found the principal Kansa village on the west bank of the Missouri north of Independence Creek in Doniphan County, Kansas. Bourgmont and his party of French, Osages, and Missourias were met by the head chief of the Kansa and six war chiefs "with calumet held high and with great rejoicing." After inviting the Frenchmen to smoke, they spread out the sacred bundle and offered a feast (Norall 1988:126). Bourgmont made the Kansa village the staging area for his expedition to the Plains Apache.

The Kansa were at this time staunch allies of the French and desirous of continuing trade. They had 30 Plains Apache slaves and several horses to trade to Bourgmont. Knowing that the French expedition to the Plains Apache depended on their horses, the Kansa demanded more than what Bourgmont offered in trade, claiming that they had received twice what Bourgmont offered from Frenchmen the preceding year as well as from the Illinois Indians.

*The phonemes of Kansa are: (lax voiced stops) *b*, *d*, *ǯ*, *g*; (tense voiceless stops) *pp*, *tt*, *čč*, *kk*, ʔ; (aspirated stops) p^h, t^h, c^h, k^h; (glottalized stops) *ṗ*, *ċ*, *k̇*; (voiceless spirants) *s*, *š*, *x*, *h*; (voiced spirants) *z*, *ž*, *γ*; (nasals) *m*, *n*; (resonants) *w*, *l*, *y*; (oral vowels) *i*, *e*, *a*, *o*, *ü*; and (nasal vowels) *į*, *ą*, *ǫ*. Vowel length (v·) and stress accent (primary: v́; secondary, in compounds: v̀) are also phonemic, but their analysis and marking are tentative.

This phonemic analysis of Kansa follows Robert L. Rankin, who has also provided phonemic transcriptions of Kansa words (communications to editors 1990–1991).

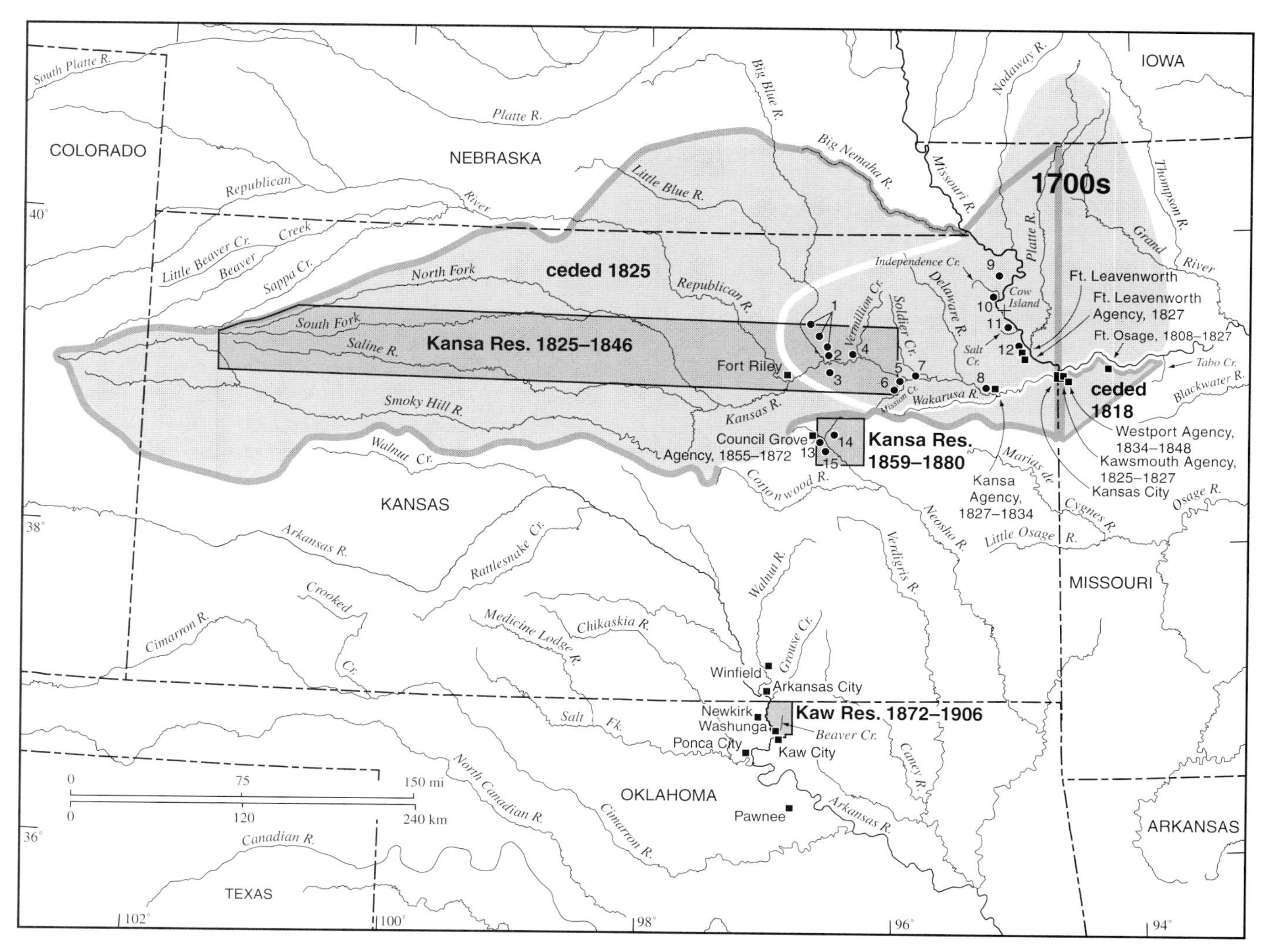

Fig. 1. Kansa lands in the 18th and 19th centuries, reservations 1825–1906, and prominent villages: 1, villages about 1718; 2, Blue Earth Village, about 1800–1830; 3, village about 1795; 4, Hard Chief's village, 1834–1848; 5, Hard Chief's village, 1831–1834; 6, American Chief's village, 1831–1848; 7, Fool Chief's village, 1831–1848; 8, White Plume's village and settlement, 1828; 9, approximate location of Ft. Cavagnial and the Grand Village of the Kansas, 1750s; 10, Kansa village, 1724; 11, Grand Village of the Kansas, 1723; 12, Kansa village, 1750s; 13, Fool Chief's village, 1848–1873; 14, Big John's Village, 1848–1873; 15, Hard Chief's village, 1848–1873.

Only after Bourgmont forbade his men to trade with the Kansa for a day was an agreement reached and a reconciliation made by means of a calumet ceremony.

Most of the Kansa tribe accompanied Bourgmont on a trek of several days westward, traversing the transitional prairie zone characterized by heavily wooded sections along riverbottoms and streams, with open grasslands between the valleys. While Bourgmont was attempting to contact the Plains Apache, the Kansa were actually on the way to the Plains for their annual summer bison hunt. Their numbers included two great chiefs (*Grands Chefs*), 14 war chiefs, 300 warriors, about 300 women, and 500 children. There were also at least 300 dogs, most dragging travois loaded with household equipment and with the tepee covers, each tepee big enough to sleep 10–12 persons. Some loads weighed as much as 300 pounds. The women also carried loads reported to weigh up to 100 pounds. Kansa hunters provided deer as the main food source for the expedition (Norall 1988:127–137; Reichart 1979).

Bourgmont was "ill with a fever" as were many of the Indians who had been with his party for some time. When Bourgmont and his followers turned back after six days, two Kansa chiefs returned to their village while the rest of the tribe continued west three or four more days to carry out the bison hunt. In early October, Bourgmont brought together chiefs of the Iowa, Otoe, and Missouria at the Kansa village to pledge peace with the head chief of the Skiri Pawnee and a Plains Apache chief. Later that month, accompanied by Kansa, Iowa, Otoe, and Missouria chiefs, Bourgmont made the trek west to reaffirm the peace in the country of the Plains Apache (Norall 1988:64–75, 143–158).

The French returned in 1739 or 1740 to build Fort de Cavagnial next to the Kansa village, then near the mouth of

Salt Creek. Trade in beaver, deer, bear, and other pelts was regularized, with French officers barring both unlicensed traders and British traders from the Kansa village. Seeking better trade opportunities, in 1752 the Kansa moved their village to the Kansas River near its confluence with the Missouri (Unrau 1971:66–67; Wedel 1946:10).

External Relations

Throughout the 1700s, the Kansa were usually at peace with their Siouan relatives—the other Dhegiha tribes and the Iowa, Otoe, and Missouria of the Missouri valley. Visiting between tribes was common, and intermarriage with Otoe and Missouria was noted (Thwaites 1904–1905, 6:84). Warfare did break out between the Kansa and Osage in 1794 and continued intermittently until a peace settlement was arranged in 1806 by Zebulon Pike (Pike 1810, Pt. 2 [Appendix]:144; Unrau 1971:33). Following the settlement, combined Kansa-Osage hunting and war parties were not uncommon. In 1811, they attacked the Iowa, and from 1813 to 1816 hostilities existed with the Otoe (Unrau 1971:91, 94, 99, 102). Intermarriage occurred between Kansa and Osage.

Relations with the tribes to the west, whom the Kansa raided for slaves, were extremely hostile. These peoples included the Plains Apache, with whom peace was made, and the Pawnee, who remained enemies even after 1766, when slave raids were stopped (Pike 1810, Pt. 2 [Appendix]:17). The Kansa continued to raid for horses because of the presence of British traders operating illegally in Louisiana. In the late 1700s, the Pawnee villages to the west of the Kansa disintegrated, and their inhabitants moved north. This gave the Kansa greater access to the Plains and large herds of bison as a food source. Thus, the Kansa sometimes hunted in the territory of the Cheyenne and Arapaho, but they tried to avoid contact with these tribes since they were usually hostile.

Contact with the Sauk and Fox had been irregular, and usually peaceful, though not openly friendly, until the last half of the eighteenth century. Then, pressured by the settlements of Europeans in the Ohio valley, these tribes began moving west across the Mississippi. The Kansa were resentful of encroachment on their hunting territory and occasionally raided other tribes' hunting camps. Conflict soon developed. Attacks by tribes to the east plus the lure of the bison herds on the Plains resulted in a westward movement by the Kansa. By 1800, they had established Blue Earth Village on the Kansas River.

Culture in the Nineteenth Century

Subsistence

When the Kansa established Blue Earth Village, their economy was based on horticulture, bison hunting, and fur trading. In the spring, small fields were cleared along the river bottoms near the village where corn, beans, squash, and other cultigens were planted (Brackenridge in Thwaites 1904–1907, 6:84). Not long after planting was completed, the tribe left on the summer bison hunt. They hunted to the west along the Smokey Hill River unless Pawnee or Comanche were in that region, in which case they traveled south to join the Osage hunting along the Arkansas and Salt Fork rivers. Bison hunting was only for subsistence as there was no market for hides and a very limited market for robes. The hunt was organized by three band chiefs who appointed a hunt leader each summer. The leader appointed 20 *ákkida* 'soldiers' who maintained order on the hunt and who had the authority to beat or whip transgressors (Skinner 1915:747).

In late summer, they returned to Blue Earth Village and remained there until their crops were harvested. After the harvest, they prepared for the winter hunt. Once again, they went onto the Plains to hunt bison, but at the end of the hunt they did not return to the village. Instead, they scattered into the prairie region to spend the winter hunting deer and trapping small fur-bearing animals, such as beaver and otter, for pelts to trade. Pike (1810, Pt. 2 [Appendix]: facing p. 53) reported that on one trip to Saint Louis, Kansa traded 250 bundles of deerskin, 15 of beaver, and 100 of otter worth $8,000.

European and American visitors were served fresh venison, dried bison meat, corn, hominy, and a sweet corn soup made with bison meat, grease, and beans, seasoned with rock salt procured near the Arkansas River. In the 1840s, Tixier (1940:201) was fed boiled buffalo meat, dried pumpkin mixed with beans, and a drink of roasted acorns sweetened with maple syrup. The Kansa were reported to eat corn on the cob, boiled pumpkins, muskmelons, and watermelons (James in Thwaites 1904–1907, 14:191).

After 1825, the Kansa became partially dependent on the annuities received from the federal government, although the subsistence cycle remained the same. In 1850, the Kansa were still conducting an annual bison hunt and were raiding Pawnee and Omaha villages for horses (Barnes 1967:372).

Adornment and Clothing

In personal appearance, the Kansa were similar to most prairie tribes. The men plucked all their facial hair, including eyebrows. The hair on their heads was cut leaving only a small scalplock toward the back (fig. 2 right). Their ears were pierced in several places around the edge, and ornaments of bone, shell, and metal were attached. In addition, leading warriors were tattooed on the chest (James in Thwaites 1904–1907, 14:196–198; Catlin [1841] 1973, 2:23; Skinner 1915:753–754).

The basic male attire for warm weather was quite simple, consisting only of moccasins, leggings, and a breechcloth. These items were made of deerskin and decorated with quills, quail bone, and bead work (Morehouse 1904:209).

Kans. State. Histl. Soc., Topeka: left, E99-K2-*I and center, E99-K2.I REE *I; right, Smithsonian, NAA 4251-a.

Fig. 2. Clothing and body decoration. left, Unidentified woman wearing silver brooches on a cloth blouse, ball and cone earrings, bead necklaces, a ribbon appliqué skirt, a yarn sash, and beaded leggings and moccasins. Photograph by Hezekiah Beck, Winfield, Kan., 1882–1894. center, Josiah Reece and his wife. She is wearing a cloth blouse with a silver brooch, and her skirt is decorated with ribbon appliqué and smaller silver brooches. His clothing is decorated with buttons and beads; he wears garters with a floral pattern. Photograph by Van's, Newkirk, Okla. Terr., 1900–1907. right, Pi-sing. He is wearing a beaded octopus bag, which was a popular accessory for men. The octopus bag, while ornamental here, was originally a firebag used to carry flint, steel, and tinder or shot. His hair is cropped close except for the scalplock. Photograph by A. Zeno Shindler, Washington, D.C., 1868.

During the nineteenth century, red or blue broadcloth leggings and breechcloths slowly replaced deerskin. With the change to cloth, ribbon appliqué work became a popular form of decoration. Men carried turkey feather fans during warm weather. During cold weather, men added a trade blanket (fig. 3) or a buffalo robe, painted or decorated with beaded strips (James in Thwaites 1904–1907, 14:197).

For formal or ceremonial occasions, men added a wide variety of items to their attire. A dyed deer-tail roach, usually crowned with an eagle feather, was attached to the scalplock. Older and more important members of the tribe commonly wore a flat otterskin hat (fig. 4), with feather and silver brooches and bison horns occasionally attached. Finger-woven sashes made from commercial yarn were worn as belts or, occasionally, wrapped around the head, giving the effect of a turban. Formal dress was usually completed by a number of necklaces made of shell, porcelain trade beads, bear claws, and elk teeth (James in Thwaites 1904–1907, 14:196; Catlin [1841] 1973, 2:23–24). De Smet (in Thwaites 1904–1907, 27:200) reported in 1841 that the Kansa painted their faces in red, black, and white and wore ornaments of silver, copper, tin, and brass.

Kansa women parted their hair in the middle (the part sometimes painted red), hanging loose down the back or in two braids. Like the men, their ears were pierced. The wives of tattooed warriors were also tattooed with designs on the chest, arms, and calves, and a round spot on the forehead between the eyes. Women's basic clothing consisted of moccasins, leggings, sashes, a wraparound skirt, and a loose-fitting blouse, also decorated by ribbon appliqué and silver ornaments (fig. 2). Sometimes leggings and belts of blue or red cloth were added (James in Thwaites 1904–1907, 14:197; Morehouse 1904:210; Skinner 1915:754).

Structures

The Kansa had five distinct house structures: three permanent types of lodges and two mobile types used by hunting parties. Still present in the nineteenth century were rectangular wigwams about 60 by 25 feet, covered with bark, skins, and mats (Brooks 1965:174–175; Bushnell 1922:97). The most common dwelling in the permanent village was the earthlodge.

A third type, uniquely Kansa, was a circular structure, 30–60 feet in diameter, with walls four to five feet high and a gradually sloping roof, covered with bark, hides, or reed mats (fig. 5). A village of 120 such houses, probably covered with reed mats and "destitute of any regularity of arrangement," looked like haystacks to the members of an 1819–1820 American expedition as they approached it (Thwaites 1904–1907, 14:188). Descriptions of the interior beams indicated that the construction was the same as that of an earthlodge, but with no earth covering. Nonetheless, people were "atop the lodges" to watch the visitors' approach. The interior floor of a lodge was excavated one to three feet. The entire circumference of the

top, Kans. State. Histl. Soc., Topeka: E99-K2.I-EP-*I; bottom, Smithsonian, Dept. of Anthr.: 127621.

Fig. 3. War paraphernalia. top, Eagle Plume wearing a horned war bonnet, ball and cone earrings, and beaded choker and holding a pipe tomahawk. Photographer and date not recorded. bottom, "Missouri war hatchet" with pierced blade decorations. The handle is wrapped in white-edged red trade cloth. This style of tomahawk was popular on the eastern Plains 1810–1830 (Peterson 1965:23). It was treasured as an heirloom or for ceremonial use. Collected by James Owen Dorsey, 1882; length 56 cm.

circular interior wall was lined with reed mats woven with bark cord, to which cylindrical medicine bags were attached. In a permanent lodge, a bench circling the inside wall, raised about two feet off the ground, served as a seat, bed, and storage place. Both the bench and the floor were covered with robes and woven mats. A central fireplace in a shallow cavity was equipped with "an upright and a projecting arm" from which kettles were suspended. A house sheltered 30–40 people, with the largest (that of the principal chief) serving as a council house (James in Thwaites 1904–1907, 14:188–190; de Smet in Thwaites 1904–1907, 27:198).

Kans. State Histl. Soc., Topeka: E99-K2-*5.

Fig. 4. left to right, Albert Taylor, William Jones, Toney Butler (non-Indian), Roy Monroe, Elmer Franklin (mixed-blood), Forrest Chouteau, Jesse Mehoja. Monroe is wearing a flat otterskin hat with beaded decorations and holds pipe tomahawk and beaded bag. He, Butler, and Franklin wear beaded breechcloths. Photographed in 1873.

Descriptions of portable Kansa hunting lodges were vague, but Tixier (1940:200–201) noted two types. One type consisted of frames covered with painted skins, "with semicylindrical roofs, raised in the middle in the shape of a tent" a variation of the typical prairie hunting lodge; the frames of these structures were usually left standing at frequently used camp sites so that only the hide covers had to be transported (Morehouse 1904:209). Tixier's second type, "real tents," probably refers to tepees (fig. 6).

Technology

Everyday utensils used by the Kansa included wooden and bison horn spoons and wooden bowls. Pottery, not mentioned by early European visitors, had probably been replaced very early, as it had among the Osage, by brass kettles. In the 1820s iron pots were in use, and both men and women carried "in the girdle of the breech cloth behind" a large knife used for eating and defense (James in Thwaites 1904–1907, 14:190). Skinner (1915:753) mentioned a butcher knife. During the nineteenth century, painted parfleches (fig. 7) were used for storage.

Kansa warriors usually carried lances, as well as guns, and often had round, painted shields "from which hung any prized scalps they possessed" (Morehouse 1904:211). Pike (1810, Pt. 2, [Appendix]:facing p. 53) reported 450 guns for 465 warriors in 1806–1807. The use of short bows was primarily confined to bison hunting. Metal tomahawks were valued possessions (fig. 3).

Musical instruments consisted of drums of green bison hide stretched over wooden frames or the open end of a keg (Skinner 1915:708), flutes carved out of wood, and

Southern Methodist U., DeGolyer Lib., Dallas, Tex.: Ag82.152.2.

Fig. 5. Circular bark house of Nopauwoi on Beaver Creek, Kansa Res. Photograph by Thomas Croft, 1896–1898.

rattles made of gourds or animal bladders filled with small stones or shot, or of a string of dried deer hoofs (James in Thwaites 1904–1907, 14:209).

Kansa bullboats were described as "made of buffalo skins, stretched, while recent, over a light frame work of wood, the seams sewed with sinews" (Townsend 1839:33).

Gaming equipment was reported (Skinner 1915:773–774) for the hoop and javelin, hand game (played in later times with a bell as a hider), bowl and dice, and moccasin game.

Life Cycle

The birth of a Kansa child was not surrounded by elaborate activity. The child was born in isolation, according to the only description (Unrau 1971:35). Mother and child were washed immediately with cold water and the baby was bound onto a cradleboard (James in Thwaites 1904–1907, 14:198). Soon after birth, the child was given a name that was the property of the clan. Naming took place in a ceremony conducted by a tattooed warrior (Skinner 1915:753). The name a child received reflected both clan membership and birth order within the family. Each clan had five to seven names that were assigned according to birth order (Skinner 1915: 766–769). Additional names referring to some deed of valor might be assumed during an individual's life, but these did not replace the original clan name. A tattooed warrior was hired to pierce the ears of the young child (Skinner 1915:754).

Treatment of children varied with the sex of the child. Female children were trained to be obedient and, even while young, were expected to help in the household. While girls at a young age were performing menial tasks, young boys were obstinate and aggressive. Aggressiveness on the part of boys was considered a desirable trait; Kansa boys were rarely physically punished (James in Thwaites 1904–1907, 14:193; Unrau 1971:35–36).

At about age 12 or 13, a boy would begin dream fasting. Going to an isolated spot, he would fast and pray for up to four days. It was hoped that he would be contacted by the ghosts of his ancestors or an animal or other supernatural spirit. His contacts with the supernatural world would prophesy his future. Designs associated with the vision were later painted on his shield and tepee. At puberty, girls also underwent a period of fasting, but their dreams were seldom considered important; usually they concerned their brothers' success in war (Skinner 1915:769–770).

Girls were considered ready for marriage shortly after puberty at around 12 to 14 years. To announce her readiness, a girl was dressed in her finest clothes and paraded through the village by either her mother or another relative (Spencer 1908:374; Tixier 1940:203). Marriage negotiations were initiated by the groom's family, who had a tattooed warrior act as their intermediary (Skinner 1915:753).

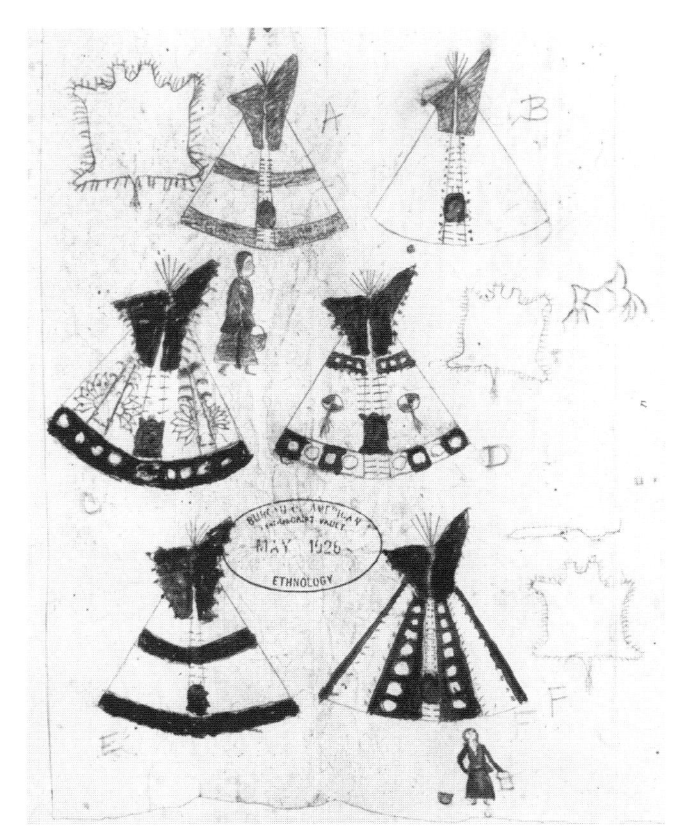

Smithsonian, NAA: 92-2478.

Fig. 6. Camp scene showing painted tepees and skins stretched to dry on the ground. The painted design of tepee C shows that the owner had, during a vision quest, communicated with an eagle who gave him some feathers; he had also danced the pipe dance; at the base of this tent on each side of the entrance are peace pipes. At the back are a black bear and a turtle. Tepee D shows the design of a man who had danced 3 pipe dances; feathers are shown hanging from the 2 painted shields, and stars are depicted on the border and on a strip below the flap of the tepee. Buffalo tails are fastened around the smokehole flap. Feathers, shields, and stars are on the back of the tepee. Tepee F belonged to a man who had danced the pipe dance 4 times. The owner probably also had a vision. Stars are also depicted (Dorsey 1894:405–406). Drawings in pencil and watercolor by Stephen Stubbs, Kansa, about 1882.

Smithsonian, Natl. Mus. of the Amer. Ind.: 2/7465 (neg. 30691).

Fig. 7. Parfleche, painted in a bold geometric pattern in red, light and dark blue, yellow, and black. Collected before 1910 by M.R. Harrington; length 132 cm.

Visits and presents such as horses and blankets were exchanged between the two families, after which the girl's parents dressed her in her best attire and led her on horseback through the village to the groom's home. The groom's parents then removed the bride's clothes and redressed her in fine clothing of their own making. After presenting her with horses and other gifts, they returned her to her parents. A feast was then held in the wife's home. Spencer (1908:374) stated that if the wife was not of mature age she became "one of the family of the groom until she [was] old enough to take charge of her own house." Although Skinner (1915:771) inferred from this that postmarital residence was patrilocal, elsewhere it has been noted that the eldest daughter, when married, assumed control of the domestic affairs of her parent's household ("her own house") and the couple took up residence with the wife's family. When this occurred, her new husband assumed the role of the head of the household, and the bride's parents and younger sisters became subservient to him. The husband of the eldest daughter had the right to marry all her younger sisters as they came of age. This uxorilocal residence pattern conforms with the Osage practice. In the 1820s men had as many as four or five wives, not necessarily all from the same family, but sisters were preferred. Mechanisms for divorce were present (James in Thwaites 1904–1905, 14:191–193; Skinner 1915:770–772).

At death, the responsibility for burial rested with the female members of the deceased's clan. The face of the deceased was painted, and the body wrapped in bark and robes. After an elderly man had given instructions to the deceased on traveling to the land of the dead, the body was placed in a shallow grave and covered with stones. Graves were usually located on some prominence near the village or along a well-used hunting trail. The individual was buried in either a sitting position facing the setting sun, with arms crossed and knees flexed, or in a horizontal position with the head to the east. The deceased's personal property was usually buried with the body, and, in the case of a warrior, his horse might be killed and left at the grave (Unrau 1971:47–48; Skinner 1915:772–773). Dorsey (1885b:670–671) reported an elaborate mourning ceremony preparatory to a revenge war expedition.

After the death of a married man, his widow went into mourning for one year. During this time she fasted, sometimes mutilated herself, covered herself with clay, and wore only her poorest clothes (Dorsey 1885b:672–680). At the end of mourning, she automatically became the wife of one of her husband's brothers (James in Thwaites 1904–1907, 14:193). The period of mourning for a widower varied; some extended it for as long as 18 months. During this time, a man's actions paralleled those of a widow (Dorsey 1885b). For at least two weeks after burial, the grave was regularly visited by mourners who could neither eat nor communicate with others. Wealthy families hired others to perform their ritualized mourning for them (Skinner 1915:773; Unrau 1971:48–49). Men allowed their hair to grow long as a sign of mourning (de Smet in Thwaites 1904–1907, 27:205).

The death of a prominent individual would usually precipitate a raid on an enemy tribe. A member of the deceased's clan who was a sacred bundle owner called a council. Four soldiers were selected to lead the raiding party. Then, two warriors would pledge themselves to kill an enemy or die in the attempt. After a mourning party had left the village, the group would not return until an enemy had been killed (Skinner 1915:749–752). By 1885, the mourning party at the death of a man named Hosasage killed five prairie chickens to satisfy the requirement of appeasing death with death (Dorsey 1885b:677).

Religion

Although the creation story told to Thomas Say (Thwaites 1904–1907, 14:194–195) may have been the Kansa version of Roman Catholic creed, it included a statement that the voice of the creator (*wakką́da*), was often heard in thunder. Slain warriors were "taken up by thunder" and men often wore a shell necklace (gorget) to represent the Master of Life. The term *wakką́da* also referred to lesser sacred powers, a venerable man or powerful shaman, or any object regarded as sacred (Dorsey 1885b:675).

Two sacred bundles (*waxóbe*) apparently belonged to the tribe collectively. Dorsey (1885b:673–675) reported that one contained a sacred clamshell "brought from the east by the ancestors of the Kansa," and the other contained a sacred pipe. Dorsey observed them used in funeral rites. Both had five symbolic wrappings around them. Skinner (1915:758) described war bundles, one in each clan, with outer wrappings of reed matwork patterned with angular designs apparently ressembling the black designs mentioned by James (in Thwaites 1904–1907, 14:189) on the mats suspended on the interior house walls. The bundles were not only war talismans but also protectors of the lodge and of health.

Ceremonies and Dances

Kansa ceremonies and dances were first listed in 1859 (Morgan 1959:35). Pictographic charts were used to direct sacred dances (Dorsey 1885b:675). Many dances were

Yale U., Beinecke Rare Book and Manuscript Lib., Western Americana Coll.

Fig. 8. *War Dance in the interior of a Konza lodge.* According to records of the event the dancers burst in on the expedition members carrying lances, bows, and arrows, which caused some strained moments until the Kansa hosts started to dance for the entertainment of their guests. In addition to their weapons the dancers had "rattles made of strings of deer's hoofs, some part of the intestines of an animal inflated, and inclosing a few small stones, which produced a sound like pebbles in a gourd shell" (McDermott 1950:500). Watercolor by Samuel Seymour, at Blue Earth Village above Ft. Osage, Stephen H. Long expedition, 1819.

related to war (fig. 8) (James in Thwaites 1904–1907, 14:209; Dorsey 1885b:678–679). De Smet (in Thwaites 1904–1907, 27:205) reported that the major motivation for war was revenge, possibly because he noted warfare occurring as part of the ritual after death. Just before going to war in warm weather, the *wašábe wačʰį* 'dark-colored object dance' (the name referring to a flag carried by the village crier during the dance) was performed for four days by men going around the village, half in one direction, half in another. On returning from war, men danced the iloshka (*íloška*) and women danced the scalp dance. From its name, it is probable that the iloshka was the warrior society dance the Kansa took to the Osage in 1884. Skinner (1915:755–757) described it as a Sioux grass dance that the Kansa had received from the Ponca.

The Calumet dance (*mą́kką wačʰį* 'sacred dance') was used to adopt another individual or tribe into the Kansa kinship network. The two calumets used in the ceremony were about a yard long. One was ornamented with white eagle feathers and was symbolically male; the other, with black eagle feathers, was symbolically female. Two men danced with the calumets during the ceremony, which was believed to confer long life and good fortune (Spencer 1908:380–381; Skinner 1915:755–760).

Unilineal Descent Groups

The Kansa were divided into patrilineal clans (*oníkkašįga* 'clan, people') (table 1). Clans were ranked in relation to one another with the Earth, Sun Carrier, Big *hą́ga*, Elk, and Deer clans being the highest. Each clan had both specified privileges and taboos. For example, Deer clan members were not allowed to eat venison, and Thunder clan members were in charge of controlling the weather. Each clan owned its own sacred bundle and a set of personal names, usually associated with the clan totemic symbols, which could be used only by clan members (Skinner 1915:762–764).

Table 1. Kansa Clans

1. *mąyį́kka* 'earth' or *mąyį́kka gá·γe* 'earth maker'
2. *tta* 'deer' or *wažáže* 'Osage'
3. *ppą́kka* 'Ponca'
4. *kką́·ze* 'Kansa' or *čči háši* 'last lodge'
5. *wasábe* 'black bear'
6. *wanąγe* 'ghost'
7. *kke kį* 'turtle carrier'
8. *mi kį* 'sun carrier'
9. *ópʰą* 'elk'
10. *xüyá* 'eagle'
11. *hą* 'night'
12. *íbačʰe* 'kindle' or *hą́ga žį́ga* 'small *hą́ga*'
13. *hą́ga ttą́ga* 'big *hą́ga*' or *hą́ga ottánąže* '*hą́ga* between' or *tta sį́že xaga* 'deer-tail roach'
14. *ččedóga* 'buffalo bull' or *si ttą́ga* 'big foot'
15. *ččížo waštáge* 'gentle *ččížo*, peacemaker'
16. *ló oníkkašįga* 'thunder clan' or *ledą́ oníkkašįga* 'hawk clan'

SOURCE: Dorsey 1897:230–232.

NOTE: Skinner (1915:760–761) listed 15 clans (lacking Dorsey's no. 12), while Fletcher and La Flesche (1911:67) listed 12 (Dorsey's nos. 1–4, 7–12, plus *wažíga* 'bird' and *čče* 'buffalo cow').

Dorsey (1897:230–232) reported that the Kansa camped in a circle, each clan having a specific position; however, he may have assumed the circular form because of its prevalence among other Siouan tribes. Skinner (1915:747) reported that the Kansa camped in "two rows on the prairie" and that there was no clan order to their camps except that the Earth clan pitched their lodges first. In 1724, while traveling with Bourgmont, the Kansa arranged the camp as follows: "The Kansa chief ordered his camp master to place the French camp on the right, with the Missouris next, and their tribes (the Kansas?) in two lines, with the head of our camp facing west and the rear facing east" (Norall 1988:135). Dorsey reported that the 16 clans were grouped into moieties of eight clans each, with *yátta* 'left' clans on the left side of the clan circle and the *ištóga* 'right' clans on the right side. If camps actually were arranged in two lines, there would be left and right lines rather than left and right sides of a circle, corresponding to the Osage village arrangement in two lines on either side of an east-west street. In contrast to other Dhegiha tribes, no special clan paintings or hair cuts were reported for the Kansa (Skinner 1915:764).

In addition, Kansa clans were grouped into six phatries (*wáyǫmįdą* 'those who sing together'), which cut across the moiety lines. The number of clans in a phratry varied between two and three, and one clan had no phratry affiliation. Dorsey (1897:230–232) reported that each clan was divided into two subclans, but Skinner (1915:764–766) believed that the reported names were clan names for individuals rather than for subclans.

Kinship terminology was of the Omaha type (Skinner 1915:766–769).

Political Organization

In the nineteenth century the Kansa were divided into three bands: Kahola (*gaxólį* 'they live by the creek'), whose chief was Nopauwoi (possibly *nóppewaye* 'inspires fear'); Rock Creek (*mą́hazolį* 'they live by the yellow cutbank'), whose chief was *alį́kˀawàho*, and Picayune (*bígiu* 'nickel' from the French *picaillon*, so named because this band was the first to obtain five-cent pieces), whose chief was Washunga (*wašǫ́ge*). These three bands probably corresponded to the three villages—Hard Chief's, Fool Chief's, and American Chief's—which were founded about 35 miles east of Blue Earth Village at the time of its disintegration in 1831 (Unrau 1971:113; Wedel 1946:14). A fourth band, primarily mixed-blood, was led by White Plume.

By the end of the nineteenth century village chiefs and hereditary chiefs formed two levels of Kansa political structure. The three village chiefs were elected by a council consisting of all the village. From these three, a tribal chief was elected. The right to fill the positions of the five hereditary chiefs was held by the five highest ranking clans. On the death of a hereditary chief, the position was assumed by his eldest son. If the deceased chief had no son, the position was filled by his brother or by his eldest daughter, since Kansa chiefs were sometimes female. The main difference between village and hereditary chiefs was that the power of hereditary chiefs was limited to internal civil problems (Skinner 1915:746).

Civil and military distinction could arise from bravery or generosity. Outstanding warriors or leaders who had no hereditary rights could be elected to the chief's council after which their children could inherit the position. Most disputes were decided among the parties involved rather than by a chief (Thwaites 1904–1907, 14:191).

History, 1800–1873

The First Reservations, 1800–1873

The acquisition of Louisiana by the United States in 1803 had no immediate consequence for the Kansa. In 1808, Pierre Chouteau built Fort Osage on the Missouri, which became the nearest trading post to the Kansa. Over 1,000 Kansas made the long journey to initiate trade but complained to head factor George Sibley about the distance to the post and the lack of traders at the Kansa village (Unrau 1971:86–88). In 1815, the Kansa signed their first formal peace and friendship treaty with the United States (Kappler 1904–1941, 2:123–124). In 1819, the Yellowstone Expedition, under Maj. Stephen H. Long, met with 150 Kansa warriors and chiefs at Cow Island, up the Missouri from Fort Osage (fig. 8). There Indian agent Benjamin O'Fallon warned them that military force would be used against them if they did not cease their "insults and depredations upon whites" (James in Thwaites 1904–1907, 14:176–178).

Besides providing lands for American settlers, one of the purposes of the purchase of Louisiana was to provide a place to resettle Indians removed from east of the Mississippi River. Thus, land cession treaties were signed with the original tribes of the region. In June 1825, facing rapid encroachment upon their lands by White settlement in the new state of Missouri, some Kansas ceded all their territory except a reservation (fig. 1) (Kappler 1904–1941: 2:222–225). In August other Kansa leaders granted the government the right to mark a roadway through the reservation from Missouri to New Mexico. This became the Santa Fe Trail (Finney 1957–1958:416). The Kansa were to receive $70,000 in annuities over the ensuing 20 years. In addition, some of the ceded land was sold and the funds made available for missionaries to the Kansa. The years following 1825 saw groups of Roman Catholic, Methodist, Baptist, and Presbyterian missionaries arriving to educate and christianize. Christianization apparently failed, as not one convert was reported. Kansa lifeways did change, as the government insisted that the Kansa adapt to agriculture and as free and unmolested passage through the heart of the Kansa reservation was promised Santa Fe Trail traders (Unrau 1979:106–110, 117–137).

Forced change apparently exacerbated an ambiguity in Kansa political structure that seems to have long been present. In 1724, Bourgmont reported both "chiefs" and "war chiefs" among the Kansa. In 1811, George Sibley noted "jealousies . . . of the warriors and minor chiefs" toward the head chief, whose office was in general hereditary (Brooks 1965:176–177). Again, in 1819, Fool Chief was the principal hereditary chief, with 10 to 12 "inferior chieftains," and he observed a dispute among chiefs coming to meet Major Long's expedition "respecting rank, in consequence of which ten or twelve of them returned to the village" (James in Thwaites 1904–1907, 14:188, 191).

In 1825, this ambiguity developed into factionalism. White Plume (fig. 9), son of the Osage chief Pawhuska and a Kansa woman, who had been characterized (Thwaites 1904–1907, 14:177) as "rising rapidly in importance, and apparently destined to become the leader of the nation," was recognized by the federal government as the principal Kansa chief. He agreed to the inclusion in the treaty of a land cession to provide 640-acre plots in fee simple for 23 mixed-bloods, including four of his grandchildren. This created a rift between him and Fool Chief, American Chief, and Hard Chief, and the three full-blood bands moved to the upper Kansas and Neosho river valleys (Unrau 1971:109, 118–119).

In 1830, reflecting village factionalism, the full bloods left Blue Earth Village and separated into three distinct villages where they remained until 1845. A village of 20 lodges under American Chief settled on the west side of Mission Creek where Frederick Chouteau established the principal trading house for the Kansa. About a mile away near the Kansas River was the village of Hard Chief, consisting of 100 lodges; the largest Kansa village, that of Fool Chief, was on the north bank of the Kansas River (Adams 1904:425, 432; Wilmeth 1960:155–157; Unrau 1971:118). In 1831, these villages were visited by George Catlin ([1841] 1973, 2:23) who painted portraits of a number of leading Kansa chiefs.

In 1846, one year after the annuity payments of the 1825 treaty stopped, the Kansa signed a new treaty with the federal government (Kappler 1904–1941, 2:552–554). Under its terms, the reservation in the Kansas valley was ceded for a small reservation, some 20 by 20 miles, in the Neosho valley, centering around Council Grove. As a bonus, the Kansa were to receive $202,000 in annuities paid over 30 years. In the Neosho valley, the Kansa came into close contact with White settlers for the first time. The town of Council Grove had been established before the government had agreed to assign the area to the Kansa. The White citizens there refused to leave, and an illegal town continued to grow. Pressure from White settlers forced the negotiation of a new treaty. In 1859, another

The White House.

Fig. 9. White Plume or Monchousia. He is wearing a finger-woven turban, hair roach, multiple earrings including one with hairpipes, and a peace medal. In addition to painting official portraits for Thomas L. McKenney, the first superintendent of the Bureau of Indian Affairs, the artist painted a portrait of each member of the 1822 delegation to Washington, including White Plume, which he gave to the subjects to take home with them (Viola 1976:41). Oil painting by Charles Bird King, 1822.

treaty was signed by which the Kansa ceded over two-thirds of the reservation. Only 80,000 acres in the southwestern portion of the reservation were retained (Kappler 1904–1941, 2:800–803; Unrau 1971:161–163, 187).

Like other tribes the Kansa had been plagued by European diseases since contact. Records of smallpox epidemics in the 1750s and in 1827 and 1828 suggest heavy tolls on the Kansa; in 1831 as many as 300 may have died and again in 1839 nearly 100 (Unrau 1971:41, 132). Conditions at the Council Grove reservation led to population decline. By 1873, the Kansa were plagued by measles, whooping cough, and respiratory and digestive disorders (table 2) (Unrau 1976:3–4).

Houses contracted for the tribe were constructed so poorly that they were unfit for habitation during the winter. The Kansa used them for stables and lived in lodges of their own construction. By the time of the Civil War, it had become evident that the Kansa would have to move again. At this time, the four bands were conducting their political affairs separately, with the mixed-blood band predominating (Miner and Unrau 1978:79, 102).

Indian Territory, 1873–1902

Following the Civil War, pressure increased for removing the remaining tribes from the state of Kansas. In 1873, the Kansa agreed to sell what remained of their reservation and to buy 100,000 acres from the Osage along the Arkansas River in Indian Territory. When they moved that year to the new reservation, they found only a few government cabins where Beaver Creek emptied into the Arkansas River. The Kansa went on their last bison hunt, returning with pack horses laden with bison hides, meat, and tallow (Finney 1957–1958:47).

Table 2. Kansa Population, 1702–1998

Year	*Full bloods*	*Mixed bloods*	*Total*	*Source*
1702			1,500	Iberville in Nasatir 1952, 1:8
1806			1,565	Pike 1810, Pt. 2 [Appendix]:53
1837			1,471	ARCIA-1837:647
1841			1,606	ARCIA-1841:268
1853			1,375	ARCIA 1853:255
1860			803	ARCIA 1860:337
1870			574	ARCIA 1870:333
1880		50	300+	ARCIA 1880:76
1890			198	ARCIA 1890:458
1900	97	120	217	ARCIA 1900:337
1910	71	167	238	U.S. Bureau of the Census 1915
1924	77	343	420	Chapman 1947:350
1945			544	ARCIA 1945:10
1971	15		900	Tom Dennison, personal communication 1971
1983			527	Bureau of Indian Affairs 1983:5
1990			673	Bureau of the Census 1991:25
1995			1,866	Kaw Tribe in Tiller 1996:519
1998			2,333	Freda Lane, communication to editors 1998

The Kaw subagency was placed under the jurisdiction of the Osage agency. A stone subagency building, boarding school, agent's house, barn, wooden employees' houses, a small trader's establishment, a sawmill and a gristmill were constructed. In an 1883 report, an inspector stated that the Kansa "possess the cream of the original Osage reservation. With an abundance of choice bottomland along the Arkansas and Beaver rivers and choice grazing land between these streams they have the most desirable reservation in the Territory" (Bureau of Indian Affairs 1883). However, it was a physically devastated tribe that settled there. The inspector continued: "their disease has become constitutional, no healthy children being born. . . . Two thirds of all the children of school age are in the school, mostly boys, they claim only 12 girls of school age in the tribe" (Bureau of Indian Affairs 1883). A doctor was assigned to the Kaw subagency and his medical care began to deal with the problems of disease and malnutrition. The tribal population bottomed out in 1887 at 193 individuals (140 full bloods and 53 mixed bloods) (ARCIA 1888:416). As the population of the tribe as a whole increased, the number of full-blood members continued to decline.

As the Kansa struggled to recover, government agents and inspectors praised their progress. In 1883 (Bureau of Indian Affairs 1883) more than 3,500 bushels of corn were raised on the two agency farms, making the Kaw the only agency in Indian Territory able to feed their beef cattle. Some individual Kansa had earned money by selling surplus corn, and a few had small herds of cattle.

In 1884 some 414 acres were reported to be under cultivation. Forty-seven non-Kansa Indians, including Sioux and Citizens' band Potawatomi, lived on the reservation, some of them listed among the more prosperous farmers. The reservation sawmill provided cottonwood planks for the many houses that were built in the 1880s. These houses were not warm enough for winter, either, and during cold weather most families abandoned their houses and moved "into the timber with their lodges" (Bureau of Indian Affairs 1884).

Besides health, the financial situation of the tribe presented problems. The Kansa were unable to pay the $70,096.12 owed for their land on the Osage reservation until 1881, when they finally received payment for their reservation in Kansas (B.B. Chapman 1947:338). Revenue also began to come from land leases, for both grazing and farming. A government patterned on the Osage system was formed to serve the tribe in leasing. At a meeting of the four bands, a council was elected comprised of a principal chief and four councilors. Kebothliku was the first principal chief, succeeded in 1885 by Washunga. In 1887 the inspector complained that although the Kansa had $200,000 on deposit in the U.S. Treasury at 5 percent interest, producing an annual revenue of $10,000, they received annuity payments amounting to only $3,750 (Finney 1957–1958:419–420; Bureau of Indian Affairs 1887).

In 1893, the nearby Cherokee Strip was opened to White homesteaders, and settlers began looking at the Kansa reservation. By the late 1880s, government officials were complaining that few Kansa were interested in farming, but wished to raise horses and cattle and hold giveaway dances sometimes called "pony smokes" and that they were spending "a good deal of their time visiting other Indians and dancing" (Bureau of Indian Affairs 1887; Finney 1956–1958:417–420). The 1880s and 1890s brought to Indian Territory a florescence of intertribal interaction in which the Kansa participated (Skinner 1915:458–475). It included both the spread of men's society dances such as the iloshka and of the Ghost Dance and Peyote religion. With a drastic decline in population, tribal ceremonies that would require specific participation by members of every clan might decline in favor of intertribal ceremonies. Also, participation in giveaways at intertribal events closely approximated a return to the profession of trading practiced in former times and followed the precept of the Ghost Dance and Peyote religion in reviving traditional lifeways.

When the Cherokee Commission visited in 1893 to persuade the Kansa to accept allotment of the reservation, the Indians declined. With the Kansa, especially the full-blood bands, not interested in farming, they preferred to lease the land as a tribe. Because they had acquired title to the reservation by purchase, as had the Osage, Otoe, Ponca, and Missouria, they were under no obligation to allot. Land continued to be held in common by the tribe; however, the influence of the mixed-blood band was increasing, and by 1900 they were leading the way for allotment.

Allotment and Outmigration, 1902–1958

A dominant force behind allotment was Charles Curtis, a Kansa mixed blood descended through his mother from White Plume. Curtis served as a representative in Congress from Kansas and was vice-president of the United States under Herbert Hoover (1929–1933) (Unrau 1929–1933). He drew up the allotment agreement, which was signed in Washington in 1902 by Washunga, one full-blood councilman, and four mixed-blood councilmen. One-hundred-sixty-acre homesteads, nontaxable and inalienable for 25 years from January 1, 1903, were chosen by 89 full-blood and 154 mixed-blood individuals. The government was granted 160 acres for an agency and school (fig. 10), and 80 acres were set aside for a township surveyed into lots to be sold at public auction. Twenty acres were set aside for a cemetery. The remaining acreage of the reservation was divided among the tribe, giving each person about 405 acres (Finney 1957–1958:422; B.B. Chapman 1947:345–348).

No principal chief was elected at the death of Washunga in 1908 and the tribe was without political structure. In 1920, the agent characterized the tribe as "mainly mixed bloods . . . . many of them, in the various industries. Some are teaming for oil companies, others drillers, tooldressers, pipeline men, truck drivers, garage mechanics, clerks, baggagemen, expressmen, bookkeepers, [and] county officials." There was very little cattle raising in the 1920s, especially

Kan. State Histl. Soc., Topeka: E99-K2-C5 *1.

Fig. 10. Boys at Kaw Agency school, Washungah, Okla. Terr. (ARCIA 1906:306–307). The agency school was built following the 1902 act of Congress that provided for allotment of tribal land to the enrolled tribal members and for the termination the Kaw Tribe as a legal entity (Unrau 1975:74–77). The school was closed in 1908. Photographed 1902–1907.

after oil well leases began to bring in revenue (Bureau of Indian Affiars 1920; Unrau 1976:5; Finney 1957–1958:421).

In 1922, Lucy Tayiah Eads, Washunga's adopted daughter, was elected principal chief, together with eight councilmen. A claim was pressed against the government for a balance alleged due from the land sales in Kansas and for acknowledgment that oil and gas rights were owned communally by the tribe. There were 62 oil leases on allotments but most of the producing oil wells were on surplus lands sold to Whites (Bureau of Indian Affairs 1922; Finney 1957–1958:423). This bid for tribal control by the full-blood bands apparently failed. When restrictions on homesteads expired and the Kansas agency was abolished in 1928, its jurisdiction was transferred to the Central Agency at Pawnee, Oklahoma (Finney 1957–1958:423; Bureau of Indian Affairs 1930).

Throughout the 1920s and 1930s the tribe maintained its separate identity. They continued to hold their annual iloshka dance to which they invited other tribes and maintained their own encampment when attending the dances of other tribes. The Depression dispersed the Kansa as they migrated to surrounding cities to find work. The iloshka dances were discontinued, and the Kansa ceased to attend other tribes' functions as a group. In 1934 Ernest E. Thompson was the last elected chief. In 1935 the tribal council was dissolved (Wright 1951:163).

In 1932, there were 341 tribal members said to be residing in the jurisdiction and in 1934, 92 allotments were still held in trust by the government. By 1945, 85 percent of the original reservation was alienated, leaving 13,261 acres. There was said to be no tribal organization and very little money on deposit with the United States treasury (Bureau of Indian Affairs 1934; B.B. Chapman 1947:351).

Tribal and Cultural Revival, 1958–1990s

A Kaw Cemetery Association may have functioned uninterrupted during the periods devoid of tribal government. The tribe also held an abandoned meeting house and 1/100 of an acre as a Kaw place of worship after the government sold the school and agency buildings in 1955. In 1958, the mixed-blood-dominated Cemetery Association led the way in drawing up a tribal constitution, and Cemetery Association member Tom Dennison was elected chairman of a business committee. Claims then were filed against the government pertaining to article 6 of the 1825 treaty (lands alloted to mixed-bloods). At this modern assertion of mixed-blood band members for legal control of the tribe, members of the three full-blood bands (Kahola, Rock Creek, and Picayune) united to represent their portion of the claims (Unrau 1976:6).

Tribal issues intensified with the construction of Kaw Dam in the 1970s. Kaw Reservoir inundated much of the reservation. Kaw City was relocated. Members of the Kahola band, led by the Mehojah family, established the Kaw Protective Association to represent full-blood interests and began to hold regular meetings. They questioned Dennison's qualification as to blood quantum to hold the office of chairman. The Kaw constitution, modeled after that of the Creek tribe, required business committee chairmen to be of one-quarter blood quantum. A lawsuit, *Pepper v. Dennison*, resulted, and in 1975 Dennison was ruled ineligible for office. The next business committee elected included members of the Kahola band (Unrau 1976:4–6).

In the 1980s the tribe acquired, by grant and purchase, 1,095 acres. The tribe prospered financially, establishing business and social programs. In 1990 the tribe adopted a new constitution and bylaws under the Oklahoma Indian Welfare Act of 1936 (Tilles 1996:519). The Kanza Museum, at tribal headquarters in Kaw City, was dedicated in 1995. Language classes were provided, and tribal culture records were maintained.

Synonymy†

The Kansa name for themselves is *kką́·ze*, which is also the name of one of their clans. It is the form by which the tribe was known to most other Plains Indian peoples as well as to Europeans and Americans.

The surrounding Siouan-speaking tribes knew the Kansa by this name, with variations in its form reflecting sound differences among the languages. The Omaha, Ponca, and Osage terms are *kką́ze* (John Koontz, personal communication 1987; Parks 1988; Robert Rankin, personal communication 1990); the Quapaw form is *kką́se* (Robert Rankin, personal communication 1987). In Otoe the name is *kʰą́·ðee* (Louanna Furbee, personal communication 1990; Parks 1988); in Iowa it was recorded as Kantha (Hamilton 1885:73), which is likely identical in form to the Otoe. In Santee and Yankton Sioux the name is *kʰą́ze*, cited as Káŋ-ze (Riggs 1890:261) and káŋze (Williamson

†This synonymy was written by Douglas R. Parks.

1902:95); an alternate Yankton form is kahaŋze (i.e., *kʰahą́ze*) (Williamson 1902:95). The same name was borrowed into Kiowa as *kʰɔ̀sɔ́·gɔ̀*, with inverse suffix *-gɔ̀* 'plural' (Laurel Watkins, personal communication 1979).

The same form is found in Central and Eastern Algonquian languages, in which it was apparently borrowed from Siouan speakers. In Miami-Illinois the term for Kansa was recorded as kansa (Marquette in Tucker 1942:pl. 5), káⁿze, káⁿsä, káⁿza, and kánsa (Gatschet 1895, 1895a, 1895b), reflecting two forms, *ka·nse* and *ka·nsa*, the former a direct borrowing and the latter normalized to the regular animate noun pattern of Miami-Illinois (David Costa, personal communication 1991). In Fox the name is *aka·sa* (Michelson 1925:382, phonemicized), earlier *oka·sa*, recorded as Úkasa (Gatschet 1882–1889:4); in Shawnee it is *ka·θa* (Voegelin 1938–1940, 8:299); and in Unami it is *ká·nsiya* (Ives Goddard, personal communication 1992).

From the earliest citations in the eighteenth century until the twentieth century, European and American designations have been variants of this same term. Many renditions closely approximate the full form of the name, differing only in an *s* or *z* in the second syllable: Kansé, 1722 (La Harpe 1722 in Margry 1876–1886, 6:365); Kancas (Bacqueville de la Potherie 1753:271); Kansæ (Coxe 1741:11); Kancès (Perrin du Lac 1805:vi); Kanzies and Kanzas, 1804–1805, (Lewis and Clark in Moulton 1983–, 3:27, 392); Kants (de Smet 1847:161). Many variants have an initial *c* rather than *k*; for example, Canchez and Canzez (Le Page du Pratz 1758, 1:324, 2:251), Canses (W. Smith 1766:70), and Cauzes (Trumbull 1851:185). Some citations have the vowel *o* in the initial syllable: Konzas (Maximilian in Thwaites 1904–1907, 22:251; James 1823, 1:111). Renditions occasionally lack the nasalization in the first syllable: Kaw′-ză (Morgan 1877:156) and Kasas (Schoolcraft 1851–1857, 2:37). A form Okanis (Schoolcraft 1851–1857, 3:557) may be a rendition from an Algonquian language (see Fox form above).

A shortened form of the name comprising only the first syllable is a common variant. Attributed to French traders, some of these forms reflect nasalization of the vowel in the native term: Cans (Maximilian in Thwaites 1904–1907, 22:251) and Quans, 1723 (Bourgmont in Margry 1876–1886, 6:393). More common are variants that do not indicate nasalization, written with either an initial *c* or *k*; for example, Caw (Farnham 1843:14), Kah, 1804–1805 (Lewis and Clark in Moulton 1983–, 3:392), and Kaws (Gregg 1844, 1:41). In Oklahoma in the twentieth century the tribe was generally known by this form, written as Kaw.

For the similar but distinct name Cancy used in French sources for various Plains Apache groups see volume 10:390.

Guaes, or Guas, a name recorded in the Castañeda narrative from the Coronado expedition in 1540–1542 (Winship 1896:503, 529), was identified as Kansa (Bolton 1949:233; Hammond and Rey 1940:234; M.M. Wedel 1982:121). However, this identification is unlikely, since the Kansa were not an independent group at that early date and since the linguistic similarity between the two names seems entirely adventitious (Hodge 1907–1910, 1:508–509). The form probably derives from a variant of the Osage self-designation.

The ethnonym Escanjaques, spelled variously in sixteenth-and seventeenth-century Spanish sources, has been identified as a Spanish rendition of the name Kansa (Hodge 1907–1910, 1:655), but the name has been more properly attributed to an as yet unidentified nomadic group, perhaps a Wichita group (Thomas 1935:8; M.M. Wedel 1982:121; D.A. Gunnerson 1974:55, 65, 107; Hammond and Rey 1953, 2:841).

Another name for the Kansa that occurs among several Plains tribes is represented by Pawnee *árahu* (Parks 1965–90), first recorded in 1795 as Arau or Arauju (Troike 1964:384–388). It occurs in Cheyenne as Anahō (Petter 1913–15:582), where it is said to designate the Quapaw as well; and it is attributed to the Kiowa as Alähó, and the Arapaho as Ánahú, the name designating both the Kansa and the Quapaw (Mooney 1898:300, 394; Hodge 1907–1910, 1:655). The Kitsai form Ăraho, recorded as the name for Ponca, apparently actually designates the Kansa (Mooney 1893:93). Swanton (1952:293) gives a cognate form, Anahou as a name used by the French in the seventeenth and early eighteenth centuries for the Osage, illustrated by Annaho, 1687 (Joutel in Margry 1876–1886, 3:410) and Anahous, also misprinted as Anahons, 1719 (La Harpe in Margry 1876–1886, 6:261, 284). The distribution of the form does suggest a Caddoan provenience, although the Caddo and Wichita names for the Kansa have never been recorded.

A Comanche name for Kansa, recorded in the nineteenth century but not attested in the twentieth century, is rendered as Mo′'tawâs and Móhtawas (ten Kate 1884:9, 1885a:383).

Another, perhaps recent, Cheyenne name for the Osage, *oo?kóhtAxétaneo?O* 'cut hair people', is said to refer to the Kansa and Quapaw as well (Glenmore and Leman 1985:201; Mooney 1907:425).

No sign language designation has been recorded for the Kansa.

Sources

The only substantive study of the Kansa is a history covering the tribe from 1673 until their removal to Oklahoma in 1873 (Unrau 1971). Unrau (1975) summarizes tribal history to the mid-1970s. Information on Kansa ethnography is presented in Dorsey (1885b, 1890, 1897), Skinner (1915), and Connelley (1918). Kansa archeology is discussed by Wedel (1946, 1959) and A.E. Johnson (1991). The life of Charles B. Curtis and the role of mixed bloods in the tribal allotment period is covered by Unrau (1989). Tiller (1996:519–520) gives an economic profile of the Kaw Tribe of Oklahoma in the 1990s.

Osage

GARRICK A. BAILEY

Origins

Culturally and linguistically the Osage (ˈōˌsāj) are closely related to the Quapaw, Kansa, Omaha, and Ponca, the tribes of the Dhegiha branch of the Siouan language family.* When French explorers arrived in 1673, the Osage were living in a number of villages along the Osage River and its tributaries in southwestern Missouri (fig. 1). Osage mythology describes a migration from a more easterly location, which some scholars interpreted as meaning the Ohio River valley (McGee 1897:191; La Flesche 1917; Dorsey 1884:211–213). The thesis that this migration occurred during the protohistoric period, just prior to French contact (Hyde 1951:32), has not been verified archeologically since prehistoric and protohistoric Osage sites have not been identified.

Because historic Osage sites contain a preponderance of items of European manufacture, knowledge of precontact Osage material culture is extremely limited. Early Osage pottery, projectile points, and pipes are Oneotalike in appearance, which suggests a more northern origin (Chapman and Chapman 1964:94–97). However, the Osage may actually have been descended from some of the small prehistoric groups who occupied the northern margins of the Ozark Plateau and who were culturally associated with the Neosho focus and marginal Mississippian peoples. The "Oneota" character of some artifacts has been interpreted as the result of late prehistoric influence on the already resident Osage population (Chapman 1974:30–31; Wedel 1936:288).

History to 1871

At the time of contact with the French in the late seventeenth century, the Osage were a typical prairie tribe. They lived in permanent villages of mat- or bark-covered wigwams. Their economy was mixed, combining hunting, gathering, and horticulture. Crops of corn, beans, and squash were planted near the villages along the Osage River. Hunting expeditions for bison, elk, and deer were short, seasonal, and limited to the adjacent woodlands and prairies of southwestern Missouri (Bailey 1973:4).

Horses were first acquired by the Osage in the 1680s (Mathews 1961:27; Bailey 1973:36), at the same time trade with the French was being established. Initially the trade was more important to the Osage than horses. Although quickly altering the lives of more westerly tribes, horses had little effect on the Osage, who hunted bison but did not have access to the vast herds farther west. Thus the horse had only limited value in Osage subsistence and failed to revolutionize Osage culture.

The French trade quickly produced far-reaching changes. Initially the trade involved a wide range of goods such as robes, pelts, skins, tallow, horses, and Indian slaves, which the Osage either produced or acquired to exchange for French guns, knives, axes, brass kettles, and other metal goods (Lahontan 1703, 1:259; Defoe 1720:59; Nasatir 1952, 1:50; Chapman and Chapman 1964:96, 100; Bailey 1973:33–34). However, as French settlements developed in Louisiana during the early eighteenth century, Indian slaves and horses became the items most eagerly sought by the traders from the Osage (Hyde 1951:15, 56).

Armed with French guns and metal axes and knives, the Osage found the poorly armed Pawnee and Wichita peoples of the Arkansas valley to be easy prey for their horse- and slave-raiding parties. As trade with the French increased during the early decades of the eighteenth century, the level and intensity of warfare between the Osage and Caddoan peoples escalated. The Osage also tried to prevent French traders from visiting the Caddoan villages to deny them access to guns (Din and Nasatir 1983:37–47; Bailey 1973:35–37). During the 1730s and 1740s many

*The phonemes of the Osage are: (voiceless lax unaspirated stops and affricate) *p, t, c, k,* ˀ; (voiceless aspirated stops and affricate) p^{h}, t^{h}, c^{h}, k^{h}; (voiceless tense stops and affricate) *pp, tt, cc, kk*; (glottalized stops and affricate) *ṗ, ċ, k̇*; (voiceless spirants) *s, š, x, h*; (voiced spirants) *z, ž, γ*; (nasals) *m, n*; (resonants) *w, l, δ*; (oral vowels) *i, e, a, o, ü*; (nasal vowels) *į, ą, ǫ*; (stress) v́. The lax stops are voiced by some speakers following nasal vowels. Aspirated stops have a strongly velarized release [p^{x}, t^{x}, k^{x}] before non-front vowels, and an assibilated release [$p^{\check{s}}$, $t^{\check{s}}$ ~ $t^{\check{s}}$, $k^{\check{s}}$] before front vowels. Tense stops are either long or preaspirated and are alternatively written with *h*; e.g., *šáppe* (or *šahpe*) 'six' is [šáp·e] or [šáhpe]. Some Osage speakers at the end of the 20th century had reportedly lost the opposition between tense and lax stops in initial position. This phonemic inventory follows the analysis of Robert Rankin.

In the Osage orthography used by Francis La Flesche (1932), an Omaha speaker, the consonant phonemes are written as follows: (lax) b, d, ds, g; (aspirated) p (psh), t (tsh), ts, k (ksh); (tense) p̣, ṭ, ṭs, ḳ; (glottalized) p̣', ṭs', ḳ'; (voiceless spirants) ç, sh, x, h; (voiced spirants) ç, zh, x; (nasals) m, n; (resonants) w, gth, th. (The writing of gth for *l* may represent an older pronunciation, as this segment reflects the common Dhegiha cluster **kδ*.) In La Flesche's writing of the vowels, *i, e,* and *a* are written ⟨i⟩, ⟨e⟩, and ⟨a⟩; *o* is written as both ⟨o⟩ and ⟨u⟩; *ü* is represented as ⟨u⟩, ⟨iu⟩, or ⟨i⟩; *į* is ⟨i^{n}⟩; and both *ą* and *ǫ* are written ⟨o^{n}⟩.

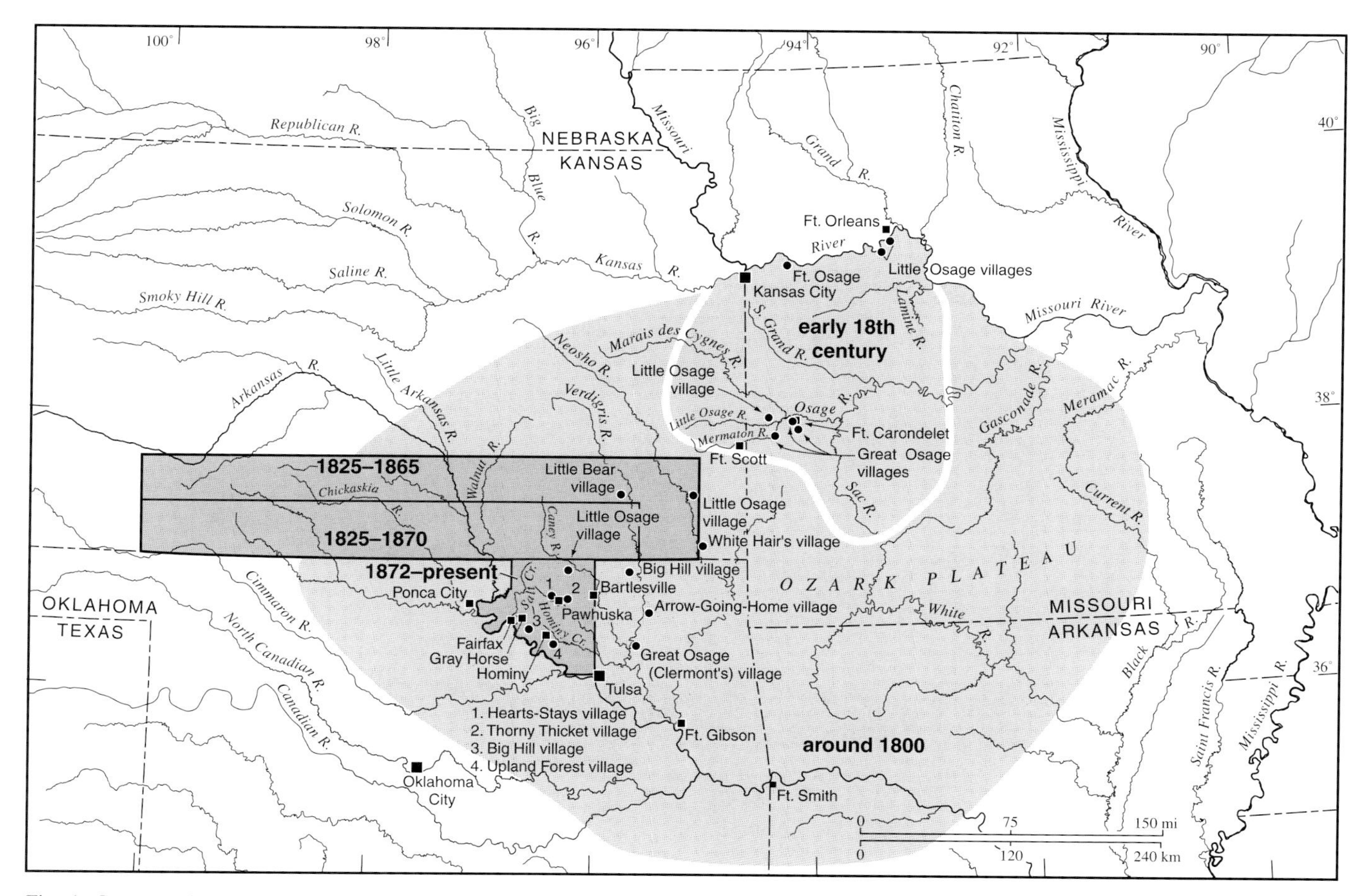

Fig. 1. Osage territory during the late 18th century, with 19th-century and modern reservations and villages.

Caddoan groups fled south of the Red River seeking security as well as trade with the French (Hyde 1951:54–55).

Spanish occupation of Louisiana in the 1760s transformed the nature of the Osage trade. The Spaniards abolished Indian slavery, thus ending the slave trade (Kinnaird 1946–1949, 2:126–127), and also severely curtailed the trade in guns to most Indian groups (Harper 1953b:182–183). However, fearing an intrusion of English traders, authorities did not restrict the trade in guns to the Osage (Bailey 1973:39; Din and Nasatir 1983:387). As pelts and skins became the focus of the new trade, the Osage embarked on a war of territorial expansion against the already weakened Caddoan peoples. Shortly after 1770 the last Caddoan villages in the Arkansas valley were abandoned (Hyde 1951:59–60, 63). The Osage had gained almost complete control over the game-rich Ozark Plateau and Arkansas valley, as well as access to the vast herds of bison on the plains west of the Arkansas. A new seasonal economic cycle soon emerged. The Osage retained their permanent villages in the prairie region, where they planted their crops of corn, beans, and squash. Twice a year they moved west onto the plains to hunt bison for hides and for tallow and meat for their own use. In the winter they scattered east and south, into the Ozarks and Arkansas valley, to hunt and trap beaver, otter, bear, deer, and other animals whose skins and pelts had become their principal trade goods (Bailey 1973:42–43).

Toward the end of the eighteenth century, the Osage began to feel pressure from tribes along their eastern boundaries. Exhaustion of game resources east of the Mississippi and displacement by White settlers forced many tribes to seek new lands west of the Mississippi. As a result the Osage found Algonquian-speaking peoples (Sauk and Fox, Delaware, Kickapoo, Ottawa, Potawatomi, Shawnee, Peoria, Miami, and Kaskaskia) from the Ohio and upper Mississippi valleys to be increasingly infringing on their hunting territories (Bailey 1973:49–52; Din and Nasatir 1983:87–356). After the Louisiana Purchase in 1803, these pressures mounted as the United States government encouraged the resettlement of other eastern tribes on lands west of the Mississippi. Under treaties signed in 1808, 1818, and 1825, the Osage ceded all their lands in present-day Missouri, Arkansas, and Oklahoma, retaining only their lands in southern Kansas as a reservation (fig. 1). Although these treaties cleared the way for the relocation of the eastern tribes, they allowed the Osage to continue to hunt in these areas. However, many Osage refused to recognize the treaties and to move their villages to the reserved areas; they considered the eastern Indians to be hostile invaders who were competing with them for hunting and trapping areas. The Osage resisted by attacking small parties of eastern hunters and in turn suffered retaliatory raids on their hunting camps. After the government gave the Chickamauga Cherokee a tract of land in Pope County, Arkansas, in 1808 (Woodward 1963:131), the level of warfare quickly escalated. In 1817 a Cherokee war party attacked an Osage village, Claremore Mound, on the Verdigris River while the men were away on a bison hunt. Some 53 old men, women, and children were killed in the raid and more than 100 captives were taken. In 1821 the Cherokee again attacked the Osage village on the Verdigris. In order to separate the warring parties, the United States government established Fort Gibson in 1824 (Foreman 1936, 1936a; Beares and Gibson 1969:8–9; Din and Nasatir 1983:357–354).

In the decade following the passage of the Indian Removal Act of 1830, the problems of the Osage increased. Over 60,000 eastern Indians were resettled in portions of what had been the Osage hunting territory, while larger areas were appropriated by White settlers (Foreman 1933:7, 15). These newcomers quickly exhausted the game resources— beaver, otter, bear, and deer— on which the Osage trade depended. Their situation was made more precarious because the Osage were also at war with several neighboring plains tribes, the Kiowa, Comanche, and Cheyenne, which limited their access to the bison herds on the plains. Short of both food and trade items, they were surrounded and greatly outnumbered by hostile neighbors (Bailey 1973:57–59). In 1839 the last off-reservation Osage villages were finally forced to move to the reservation in Kansas (Foreman 1936:266).

Fortunately, the situation improved quickly for the Osage. In the late 1830s and early 1840s, a market developed for buffalo robes, which replaced pelts and hides as the primary trade item (O. Lewis 1942:29). At almost the same time, in the late 1830s, the Comanche and Kiowa became involved in a war with the Texans, who had been their major source of trade. The Osage promptly made peace with the Comanche and Kiowa, and established themselves as middlemen, supplying the Comanche and Kiowa with guns, powder, blankets, and metal goods in exchange for horses and buffalo robes. Peace with these tribes also gave the Osage greater and more secure access to the bison herds, and a period of relative prosperity and security for the Osage continued until the mid-1850s (Bailey 1973:66–67).

In the early 1840s the United States government initiated programs to "civilize" the Osage. At first they tried to alter the Osage economy by distributing livestock such as pigs and cattle, and farm implements such as plows and axes, in the hope that they would become settled farmers. Most Osage leaders responded by either killing and eating their livestock or taking the animals and farm implements to local traders. In 1847 Jesuit missionaries, with government sponsorship, established the Osage Mission and Manual Labor School on the reservation (Bailey 1973:67–68; Wilson 1985:10). In the 1830s Baptist missionaries published a primer to teach reading (vol. 17:31).

In the mid-1850s the government began opening many reservations in Kansas to White settlement, and for the first time the Osage came into direct contact and conflict with White farmers and settlers. It was not long until the White settlers started to lobby for the removal of the Osage and the opening of their reservation (Hagan 1961:97–99; Bailey 1973:70). The Civil War temporarily diverted the attention of local Whites, who were divided in their loyalties. For the most part, the Osage remained aloof from the small but bloody battles that were fought in southeastern Kansas (Mathews 1961:632–649).

At the war's close, tens of thousands of veterans, spurred by the Homestead Act of 1862, migrated west in search of new lands. In 1865 the Osage ceded the easternmost 30-mile and northernmost 20-mile portions of their reservation. White squatters quickly moved onto the diminished reservation, occupying the best land. They burned some of the villages, fenced Osage fields, and stole Osage horses. Government Indian agents were unable to stop the intruders or protect Osage property. In 1870 the Osage signed a treaty that allowed the government to sell their remaining reservation lands in Kansas to farmers for $1.25 per acre. Part of the money from this sale was to be used to purchase a new reservation in Indian Territory (Oklahoma) to be selected by Osage leaders. The remaining funds were to be held in trust by the federal government, the interest to be used for the benefit of the tribe (Wilson 1985:11–16; Bailey 1973:71–73).

Osage leaders selected a 1,500,000-acre portion of the Cherokee Outlet for their new reservation (fig. 1), for which the Cherokee were paid 50 cents an acre. Although the land was in Indian Territory, it bordered the Kansas reservation on the south. In 1871, all the Osage full bloods and most Osage mixed bloods moved south to Indian Territory (Wilson 1985:14–16).

Culture in the Early Nineteenth Century

The first general descriptions of Osage culture did not appear until the early nineteenth century. By this time, 150 years of European contact had either directly or indirectly altered Osage culture. Stone and bone implements had already been replaced by metal tools and clay pots by brass kettles. Horses, guns, and trade with Europeans had become important elements in the Osage economy. Warfare had wrought changes in Osage political and family structure. While hereditary chiefs and religious leaders were still present, their influence was rapidly waning and being usurped by war leaders and the younger warriors. Within the family, postmarital residence had shifted from patrilocal to matrilocal. The following description of Osage culture applies only to the early nineteenth century with some known historic changes in Osage culture noted.

Structures

Osage house structures were of three basic types. The most common was the rectangular wigwam, covered with bark, woven mats, or hides. The average size was about 40 to 50 feet in length by about 20 feet in width, but wigwams as long as 100 feet were reported. Less frequently the Osage constructed smaller, circular dome-shaped lodges that were also covered with bark, mats, or hides. They used both types of structures in their permanent villages and in hunting camps in the forest (Tixier 1940:117, 134; Farnham in Thwaites 1904–1907, 28:132).

When hunting bison on the plains or when traveling, the Osage lived in skin tents, made of hides placed over a rectangular pole framework, which was about 15 feet long and seven feet wide. The result was a long tent open at both ends (Tixier 1940:159–160; J. Gregg 1954:419). The Osage never adopted Plains-style tepees.

In permanent villages and in village hunting camps, dwellings were located along either side of a main east-west street, arranged according to moiety and clan membership of the families (fig. 2). Each moiety had a chief's house that served as place of refuge; these were the only houses with two doors, facing east and west. Each village also had a fire house where firebrands could be obtained. Sacred lodges (*ccí wakkątaki*) were constructed for rituals (La Flesche 1921:62). Villages were sometimes fortified by means of log stockades.

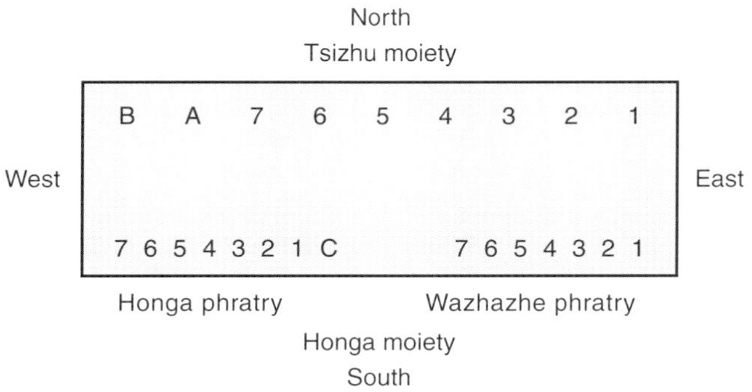

North
Tsizhu moiety
B A 7 6 5 4 3 2 1
West East
7 6 5 4 3 2 1 C 7 6 5 4 3 2 1
Honga phratry Wazhazhe phratry
Honga moiety
South

Fig. 2. Symbolic organization of the Osage (La Flesche 1921:51–53). The Tsizhu moiety consists of the *ccížo* phraty: 1, *ccížo wanǫ* 'elder Tsizhu' 2, *sį̨ce ale* 'tail wearers', 3, *ppét*^{h}*ą ttąka žoikaδe* 'big crane people', 4, *ccetóka įce* 'buffalo bull face', 5, *mik̓į wanǫ* 'elder sun and moon carriers', 6, *hą́ žoikaδe* 'night people', 7, *ccižo oδohake* 'last Tsizhu'; and *c*^{h}*í haši* 'last to arrive' clans: A, *níkka wakkątaki* 'mysterious men', B, *δóγe* 'yellow buffalo'. The Honga moiety consists of the *hǫ́ka* 'sacred ones' (Honga) phratry: 1, *wasápettǫ* 'black bear owners', 2, *įlǫ́ka* 'mountain lion', 3, *óp*^{h}*ą* 'elk', 4, *mǫ́įkkakaγe* 'earth makers', 5, *hǫ́ka leže* 'mottled Honga', 6, *xüδá* 'eagle', 7, *hǫ́ka žįka* 'little Honga'; C, *hǫ́ka ottanǫci* 'lying between Honga'; and the *wažáže* 'Osage' (Wazhazhe) phratry: 1, *wažáže ska* 'white Osage', 2, *kkék̓į* 'turtle carrier', 3, *mikkéδescece* 'cattail', 4, *wáccec*^{h}*i* 'star arrives', 5, *ozókaγe* 'they who clear the way', 6, *ttaδáγį* 'deer lungs', 7, *hó inikkašika* 'fish people'. The town layout is a physical reflection of tribal organization, which in turn is a reflection of the universe (Bailey 1995:27-45).

Subsistence

Osage economy was based on hunting, horticulture, gathering, and trading. Hunting was by far the most important economic activity since game provided the major source of subsistence as well as trade items. Bison, deer, and elk were the major game animals. Bears were hunted mainly for their skins, although the meat was eaten. Otters, beavers, skunks, rabbits, raccoons, and opossums were primarily hunted for their pelts, but they also provided variety in the Osage diet.

Although horticulture was of secondary importance, it did play a critical role in their economy. Corn, beans, and squash, dried and stored, served as the major food source during the late winter and early spring when hunting was poor (Bailey 1973:26).

The Osage gathered wild foods. Cherries, plums, pawpaws, blackberries, hackberries, dewberries, and pecans (Bailey 1973:25) were particularly relied on. There are even reports that they collected maple sap (Perrin du Lac 1807:59; Cortambert 1837:36). The most valued and important of these wild foods were pomme blanche (prairie turnips, *Psoralea esculenta*), persimmons, and water chinquapins. Large quantities of the roots and fruits of these plants were gathered and dried for winter use (La Flesche 1925:104–107, 1932:38).

Trade was critical. Guns, traps, knives, axes, kettles, and other metal tools were by this time an integral part of the technology. Although Osages still made and wore leather moccasins, trade goods had replaced leather for much of their clothing. Men usually wore cloth breechcloths and even leggings. Women's clothing consisted of blouses, skirts, and leggings of trade cloth. These garments, similar to twentieth-century styles, were decorated with either bright ribbonwork (fig. 3) or with beadwork and ornaments of German silver. Finger-woven belts and bags, which had formerly been made from bison hair, were woven with brightly colored trade yarns. Even buffalo robes were being replaced by trade blankets (Tixier 1940:120; Nuttall 1980:216).

The Osage year began in April or May when they cleared fields and planted their crops along the river and creek bottoms near their permanent villages (Morse 1822:205). Horticulture was an individual or household activity carried out primarily by women (Tixier 1940:171; Graves 1916:148). The fields were tended only until the plants had grown large enough not to be choked out by weeds. In June, after the plants were established, preparations began for the summer bison hunt.

Both the summer and fall hunts were planned at the tribal level, by all the village chiefs meeting in council. There were three main hunting areas, the Cimarron valley, the Great Salt Plains, and the great bend of the Arkansas River. The village leaders reached an agreement upon the areas in which the different villages would hunt so that they would not compete or interfere with one another. Frequently two or more villages would agree to a joint hunt (see Tixier 1940:140–144).

Careful preparations were made before they left the permanent villages. The houses were stripped of their coverings, which were cached. Only the pole frameworks were left standing. All valuable items, such as extra kettles, axes, and furs, that were to be left behind were secretly buried by their owners near the village. Only invalids, the

U. of Pa., U. Mus., Philadelphia: 13631.

Fig. 3. Young woman wearing traditional blanket decorated with ribbonwork and bells. She wears ornaments of German silver around her neck along with multiple bead necklaces. A Peyote house is in the background. Photograph by Girda Sebbelov, Gray Horse, Okla., 1911.

aged, women with young children, and individuals too poor to have the necessary tents and horses remained behind (Tixier 1940:154). Some of these individuals stayed in the villages, while others kept out of sight in small camps.

The bison hunts were under the control of the village chiefs and the soldiers appointed by them. Security was a major concern because these hunting areas were commonly frequented by hostile parties of Pawnee, Comanche, Kiowa, and Cheyenne. A series of well-defined trails led from the villages to the plains, and along these trails, at one day intervals, were campsites with tent frameworks that were used and repaired over and over again (Burns 1984:98–101).

Not all families and individuals stayed with the main party on the return trip. Small groups of young warriors would break away to search for enemy camps to raid for horses. Some families would leave to hunt deer in the wooded areas along the eastern margins of the plains. They frequently used fire drives for deer hunting; fires were set in such a manner as to drive the deer toward a river where hunters, waiting in ambush, could kill them (Ponziglione 1882:164).

By about the middle of August, all the families had returned to the permanent villages to harvest their crops and prepare for the fall hunt. Crops were dried and stored in family caches built in the woods some distance from the villages to avoid discovery by enemy raiders. These caches usually consisted of several small lodges that were guarded by old men and women, girls, and the infirm (de Mun 1928:193–195).

In September the villagers left on the fall bison hunt. The major objective was to secure hides for robes. They returned to the permanent villages in December and remained there until February or March, when most families left the villages and moved to small hunting camps scattered from the Saint Francis River in Missouri to the Arkansas valley in Oklahoma and Arkansas. From these camps, they hunted deer and bear and trapped beaver, otter and other small game animals whose pelts were sought by European traders (Morse 1822:203–205). In April they returned to the villages to plant their crops and begin the cycle anew.

Religion and Social Organization

Osage religious rituals, as well as tribal social and political organization, were modeled after their concept of the universe, which was seen in terms of a creative and controlling power called Wakanda (*wakką́ta*). All living things were manifestations of this mysterious power. Wakanda created through thought the bodily forms of all that existed on earth. The four major manifestations of Wakanda were earth and sky, night and day. All living things existed on the surface of the earth, the meeting place between the sky above and the earth below. Night and day were the endless cycles through which all living things passed. Night was death, mystery, and the female power of the moon and stars symbolized by the black hawk and the sacred bow. Day was life and the vital male power of the sun symbolized by the red hawk and the sacred arrow. Prayers were addressed to the evening and morning stars, the four winds, and to the rising sun, which symbolized the birth of human beings and the revitalization of all living things (La Flesche 1921:47–50, 1930:566–570).

Human beings were not a single manifestation of Wakanda, but the product of numerous manifestations. There was a duality between those humans associated with the sky and those who were of the earth. Earth people and sky people were further divided on the basis of their closeness to a particular set of "life symbols" (*žóikaðe*). These groupings of people were the 24 patrilineal clans (*ttą́wąlą*), which were the basic units of social and ceremonial organization (fig. 2). Each clan possessed its own set of "life symbols," and the clan name was taken from the most important of these. Thus each clan had a unique relationship to particular sacred powers and could influence or control only that part of the supernatural world. Important rituals were divided into 24 parts, which consisted of clan-owned ceremonial prayers (*wíkie*), ritual equipment or sacred bundles, and the authority to make particular items or perform specific ritual acts.

The clans were grouped into exogamous moieties. Nine clans, symbolic of the sky and peace, formed the Tsizhu (*ccížo* 'household') moiety, while the Honga (*hǫ́ka* 'sacred ones') moiety consisted of 15 clans, symbolic of the earth and war. The Osage explain this division by stating that the tribe was formed by the joining together of two peoples; the Tsizhu who came to earth from the sky and the Honga who were already on earth (La Flesche 1921:59–60). The unity of the sky and earth peoples was symbolized in the form of a perfect man who faced east in times of peace and west in times of war.

The village plan was a model of the Osage universe (fig. 2). The east to west street represented the surface of the earth, the place of interaction between the earth and sky. It also symbolized the daily course of the sun and the passage of life from birth to death. In many Osage rites, the turning of the perfect man represented the cooperative unity of the two divisions (La Flesche 1920, 1930:577–578).

The Honga moiety was divided into two phratries, each comprising seven clans, *wažáže*, water people, and *hǫka*, land people. One Honga clan belonged to neither phratry, thus its name, *hǫ́ka ottanǫci* 'Honga lying between'. The Tsizhu moiety consisted of only one phratry of seven clans called *ccížo*. In addition, there were two other clans called *cʰí haši* 'arrive last'. According to tradition, these were the last two clans to join the Osage; in order to maintain the dual ritual division they were grouped with the Tsizhu (La Flesche 1921:60–62, 65).

Clans were divided into two to five named subclans and into lineages, each of which also had its own sacred associations. Subclans, unlike clans, were hierarchically ranked. The ritual specialists of the clan were members of the highest ranking subclan. Members of the lowest ranking subclan in each clan, called the *šókka* subclan, acted as the ceremonial messengers for the clan's ritual leaders and carried messages to leaders of other clans (La Flesche 1932:132). Some tribal political offices were filled by members of particular named lineages (La Flesche 1921:123).

Clans were neither economic nor political units. Economic activities were carried out at either the household or the village level. There was no single head of the clan. Within every clan there were a number of *nǫ́hǫžįka* 'little old men' who served as its religious leaders and whose responsibility was to remember all the sacred rites and prayers and to pass them on to younger members who showed a reverence for sacred traditions.

The Little Old Men were the only individuals within the clan who had the authority to recite the prayers and perform ritual acts associated with the bundle. The process of becoming a member of the Little Old Men was long, arduous, and very expensive. Those young boys who were selected had to learn to recite the long and complex ritual prayers verbatim. The instruction had to be paid for with specific animal skins as well as with other gifts, including blankets and horses (La Flesche 1921:146–147; 1930:543–544). Within every clan there was a sequence of seven stages or hierarchically ranked degrees of training. Each degree required the learning of a particular body of ritual knowledge, and initiation in a degree conferred upon the individual the authority to use this knowledge. Most men took only one degree, although some took the seventh, called *níkkiwaðǫ* 'singing with men', which required mastery of the knowledge found in all the other degrees and thus conferred upon the individual the authority to perform any ritual act associated with the clan's bundle (La Flesche 1921:152–153). Only these individuals could be appointed a *totą́ hǫka* 'ritual leader' (La Flesche 1939:93).

From among the Little Old Men who had been initiated into their clan's bundle were chosen the custodians of the two tribal bundles; the *waxópe ttąka* 'big sacred bundle' and the *mąkką́ ttąka* 'great medicine bundle'. Custodians of the great sacred bundles were also the *ttǫwą atkpe* 'village overseer' and were responsible for having village rituals performed. In addition they performed the tattooing ritual for both men and women (La Flesche 1921:73–74, 146–147, 254). Warriors who had achieved 13 *otą* 'war honors' were tattooed with the design of a pipe, a knife, and 13 sun rays, one for each war honor. Their wives could also be tattooed with elaborate designs on the forehead, upper body, and limbs, representing sky and earth powers, and with spider designs on their hands, representing the surface of the earth where people live until released by death. Into the twentieth century tattooing (fig. 4) was associated with fecundity, long life, and an unbroken chain of descendants (La Flesche 1919:111–113).

Bands and Political Organization

The Osage were divided into five named bands: Little Osage (*ücétta* 'at below'), Big Hill (*ppasuolį* 'hilltop dwellers'), Hearts Stay (*ną́ce waspe* 'peaceful hearts'), Thorny Thicket (*waxákaolį* 'thorny plant dwellers') and Upland Forest (*ząćeolį* 'upland forest dwellers'). According to tradition, each band occupied its own separate village, so that at one time band and village were synonymous. Each band had its own chiefs and a complete representation of clans and Little Old Men. This meant that the bands were ceremonially independent of one another. There is even evidence that at one time bands may have had their own hunting territories. It was reported in the early 1700s that the Little Osage hunting territory was separated from that of the Great Osage—comprising the other four bands—by the Lamine River (Nasatir 1930:532).

Each of the five bands had two chiefs (*kahíke*), one from each moiety. The band was thus a single political unit with two heads, the two chiefs having identical authority. The two chiefs of the Upland Forest band were sometimes called the grand chiefs and treated as tribal chiefs as well as band chiefs. It is open to question whether the Upland Forest chiefs had any actual authority over the chiefs of the other four bands (see Bailey 1973:19).

The office of chief was hereditary within specific clans and lineages. The Tsizhu chief came from the *ppétʰą ttąka žoikaðe* clan, while the Honga chiefs came from the *wáccecʰi* clan. To assist them, the chiefs chose 10 soldiers (*ákkita*) from a group of 10 specific Tsizhu and Honga clans. Individuals were chosen on the basis of personal war honors as well as their friendship with the chief. On the death of a chief, the new chief was chosen by the five soldiers of the deceased chief (La Flesche 1921:68).

left, Amer. Mus. of Natl. Hist., New York: 316873; center and right, Smithsonian, Dept. of Anthr.: 263122.

Fig. 4. Tattooing. left, Heska Molah (Walking Horn or White Horn Walks, d. 1914), of the Little Honga clan. His face is painted, probably black, and he has traditional tattooing on his shoulders and chest. His hair is cut close to the scalp, leaving only a roach. He wears a shell or bead breastplate, metal arm bands, and a peace medal and holds a song tally stick in his hand. Photograph by Joseph Dixon, Osage Res., Pawhuska, Okla., 1913. center and right, Tattooing bundle owned by Wa-çe′-to^{n}-zhin-ga. center, Beaded tape of brown wool used to contain the tattooing implements. right, Buffalo hair wallet and implements: a, mussel shell to hold the coloring matter; b, package of feathers wrapped in cotton; c, tin tubes worn on the fingers of the tattooer to guide the instruments; d, steel needles fastened to wood shafts, covered with buffalo hair to protect them from rust, the left 3 shafts with feathers and bells attached, the right 3 shafts with rattles made of pelican or eagle quills (La Flesche 1921:72). Collected by Francis La Flesche, Pawhuska, Okla., 1911. Length of needle on right, 34 cm, others to scale.

Osage chiefs were peace chiefs; their primary duties were to lead the people on hunts and maintain harmonious relations among the families. They also settled disputes between individuals. When it was necessary to keep peace within the band, they could call upon the soldiers to expel a particularly troublesome person or in extreme cases to execute the individual (see La Flesche 1921:67).

The chiefs were in charge of the seasonal hunting expeditions of the band. During bison hunts, the two chiefs alternated on a daily basis in assuming responsibility. They chose the routes to be taken and determined when and where the band would camp, and the soldiers saw to it that their orders were carried out (La Flesche 1921:67). Some sources contend that the chiefs owned all the animals taken on the hunts and distributed them among the families; others allege that the chiefs were entitled to a part of all animals taken by the hunters (Tixier 1940:174). In any case, the chiefs were well supplied with food, which they in turn used to support the poorer members of the band (Ponziglione 1883:297, 1889:75–76). The chiefs were also responsible for the safety of the hunting party and property of the families. If an enemy attacked the party and killed some people or took their horses, the chief in charge that day had to reimburse the families for their losses (Tixier 1940:174–175).

The office of chief was a secular rather than a ritual position, and as such carried limited power and authority. There were, however, some sacred qualities associated with the office of chief. The houses of the chiefs were considered to be sacred places. Anyone, Osage or non-Osage, could take sanctuary in the houses of the moiety chiefs. The chiefs were also thought to have the power to cure illness (La Flesche 1921:69–71).

The real power within the tribe and the bands was held by the Little Old Men, by their control of the ceremonies necessary to the well-being of the Osage. However, their power and authority went much farther than the simple performance of ceremonies. The Little Old Men within the band or village constituted a council that met almost every morning at the home of one of their members. This man could belong to any of the clans, and he was given the title *nǫhǫžįka waðį* 'keeper of the Little Old Men'. He served as host and presiding officer but had no greater authority than any of the others. To be chosen keeper was a great honor since it meant that the man was considered to possess the highest character (La Flesche 1939:3–4).

Some gatherings of the Little Old Men were formal meetings, called for the discussion of a particular problem. However, most of the time they had informal gatherings in which they discussed any practices they thought harmful to the people; acts of generosity and kindness were also recognized (La Flesche 1939:3–4). Osage mythology described the Little Old Men as having changed the organizational structure of the tribe in the past to meet new problems. The dual chieftainships together with the war organization were said to have been their creations (La Flesche 1921:59–67). The major concern of these men was the total well-being of their village, band, and tribe in regard to both the natural and supernatural worlds.

Warfare

Warfare was under the control of the Little Old Men, not the chiefs and their soldiers. The Osage distinguished two types of war organization: raids carried out by a clan and war in which the tribe as a whole was involved.

Kans. State Histl. Soc., Topeka: E99 08 *3.

Fig. 5. Band chiefs and leaders at the time of removal in 1871: left to right, Strike Axe, Chetopah, Governor Joe (Big Hill Joe), Big Chief, and Hard Rope. Governor Joe was the principal chief from 1869 to 1881. Hard Rope was the leader of the Osage scouts who fought with the U.S. Army, under George Armstrong Custer at the Battle of the Washita in 1868. Photograph by Thomas M. Concannon, Osage Agency, Okla., 1876.

Each of the 24 clans had its own war medicine bundle—the *waxópe žįka* 'little sacred bundle'—and thus could, with the approval of their own Little Old Men, undertake raids against their enemies without the consent or approval of any other clan. There were two types of clan raiding parties. The first, *waxópe okkǫci* 'lone war bundle' party, could include men from only one clan. The second,

top, Henry Francis du Pont Winterthur Mus., Winterthur, Del.: 54.19.3H; bottom, Smithsonian, Dept. of Anthr.: 364541, 364542 (neg. 91-8618).

Fig. 6. Warriors and deerhair roaches. Among many Prairie Plains tribes, the hair roach was the insigne of a warrior. Since the late 19th century, it has been a standard headdress for the iloshka, War, and Grass dances. top, Warrior with red-dyed roach and multicolored headband. The area around his ear is painted with green stripes, and he wears ear ornaments. His silver armband bears an eagle holding the seal of the United States. Watercolor based on a physiognotrace outline by Charles B.F. de Saint-Memin, 1804–1807 (E.G. Miles 1988). bottom, Roach of red-dyed horsehair and black turkey beard with German silver spreader. Collected by Tom Baconrind, Pawhuska, Okla., 1932. Length of roach 27 cm.

ccíkaγa totą 'house making war', a raiding party organized outside the sacred lodge, could include men from two or more clans, as long as they were from the same moiety. Raiding parties organized at the clan or moiety level were led by warriors or war leaders, and did not require the long and tedious ceremonies that accompanied the formation of a tribal war party (La Flesche 1921:66).

Actual tribal warfare was controlled by the Little Old Men collectively and was far more complex in organization. An Osage war party was as much a religious ceremony as it was a military operation, and it was associated with the sacred power of the red hawk and its bundle. The Little Old Men alone determined if a war party was to be organized. Neither the chiefs nor their appointed soldiers in their official capacities played any part in decisions and operations. A ritual leader was selected from among the Little Old Men to oversee the war party. A sacred pipe, representing tribal unity, was sanctified by the leaders of the sky and earth moieties and given to the ritual leader. This pipe, with a human face representing all the Osage men carved in the black stone of the bowl, had shell beads representing each of the clans on the ties that attached the bowl to the stem. After a ceremonial sweatbath, the ritual leader offered the pipe to Wakanda (La Flesche 1920:68, 71–72, 1939:4–5).

The ritual leader of the war party fasted and prayed for four to seven days in quest of a vision. This vigil was followed by seven days of rituals and dances. Eight additional leaders were chosen to head the actual attack, and all clan bundles were prepared. The ritual activities leading up to and accompanying the actual battle were considered more important to success than the conduct of the warriors (see La Flesche 1939:3–143 for a description of the war ceremony). Due to the time-consuming nature of the required ritual preparations, tribal war parties were not common.

As a result of the encroachment of enemy tribes and the general escalation of warfare during the eighteenth and early nineteenth centuries, political structure began to change. Clan-organized war parties were designed to attack enemy camps, not to defend the Osage villages. Similarly, tribal war parties were better suited for attacks than defense. The band chiefs, on the other hand, were selected on the basis of heredity, and not on war records or their ability to act as war leaders.

In response to external threats, traditional villages began to fragment, and separate villages were formed around successful war leaders. The first of these new leaders was Black Dog. An aggressive warrior, reputedly seven feet tall, he was also an effective war leader. Although he had no claim to be a chief, he developed a following of warriors, and in 1803 he broke away and established his own village (see Bailey 1973:60). In 1839, Tixier (1940:126–129) reported eight Osage villages, and by the 1850s the Osage had fragmented into 17 villages (Ponziglione 1890:171–177).

As the war leaders increased in authority and prestige, the younger warriors also began asserting their influence.

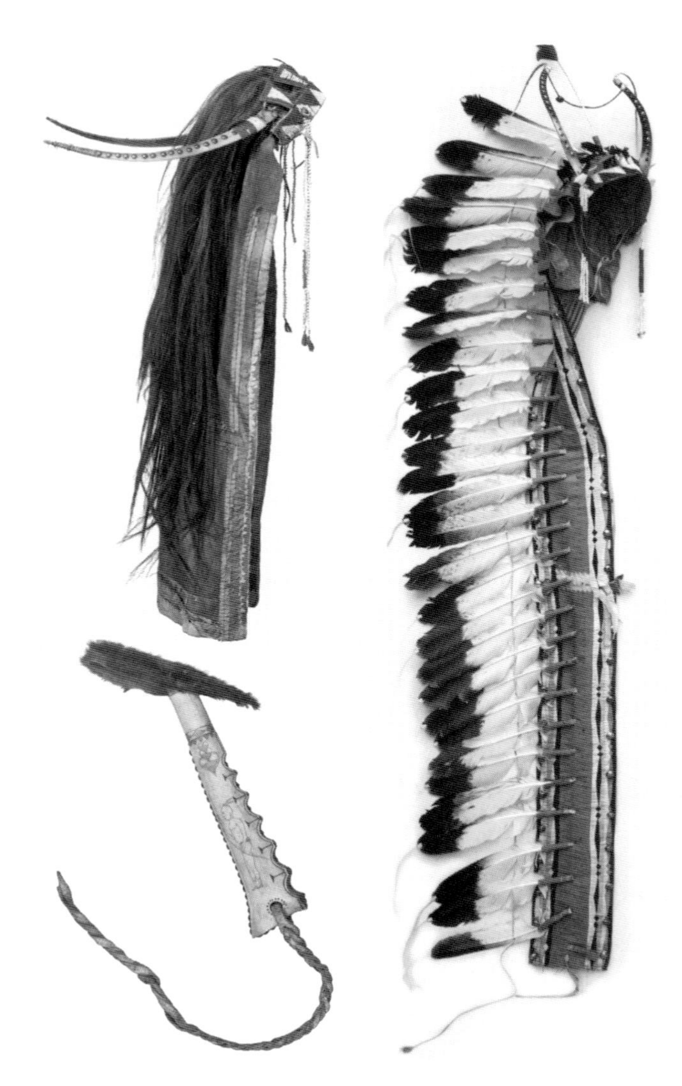

Field Mus., Chicago: top left, 57513, and right, 59254; Linden-Mus., Stuttgart: bottom left, 36113.

Fig. 7. Warrior paraphernalia. top left, Split horn headdress, with purple dyed horse-tail scalp. The cap and trailer are of red trade cloth lined with calico and edged with ribbonwork. The brow band is of red, white, blue, and green pony beads. Collected by C.C. Auger in Okla., 1870–1880; length 81.7 cm. right, Single trailer split horn headdress of 30 eagle tail feathers tipped with yellow horsehair, and a stripped quill central plume. The brow band and dangles are of blue and white pony beads. The cap is on a leather base; the trailer is of red trade cloth lined with bed-ticking, and edged with ribbonwork and hawk bells. Collected by George A. Dorsey, 1901; length 177 cm. bottom left, Elk antler quirt, studded with brass tacks. The lash is of buffalo rawhide; the wrist strap is probably of elk fur. The engraving depicts an Osage warrior wearing a roached hair cut and carrying a bow; on the other side is a warrior holding a lance and a scalp, and a running dog. Collected by Maximilian Prince of Wied, about 1830; length of handle 37.5 cm.

Tixier (1940:143) mentioned the presence of "councils" of warriors, and stated that they even chose the village leader.

Life Cycle

The ideal marriage was arranged by families. A boy was considered eligible for marriage in his late teens or early twenties, while girls were considered marriageable at puberty. Many girls were married by 14 years of age. Frequently a boy's family would arrange a marriage without his consent or even knowledge. Many families considered it preferable that the bride and groom did not know each other, and marriages between individuals from different villages were common. A girl was selected because of "her family, her interest in her work, and her physical strength" (Tixier 1940:182). The relative social statuses of the families were also important considerations. However, the most important factors were the clan and moiety affiliations of the couple. Since Osage moieties were exogamous, every marriage symbolized a reuniting of the Tsizhu and Honga peoples. In addition, individuals could not marry someone who belonged to any of their four grandparental clans (Nett 1952:181). After the boy's parents had selected an eligible girl, the family sent gifts to the girl's parents. If the girl's family decided to accept the boy, they kept the gifts; otherwise they returned them.

On the first day of the marriage, the groom and his family visited the home of the bride carrying gifts that they distributed to her relatives. On the second day, the bride, dressed in special wedding clothes (fig. 8), mounted a horse and traveled to the home of the groom, followed by her relatives on foot. Her family then presented gifts to the groom's relatives. The bride remained with the groom and his family that night. On the third day, the bride and groom led a procession of the groom's relatives back to the bride's home.

Postmarital residence constitutes a problem in the reconstruction of early Osage social organization. The presence of patrilineal clans, together with the fact that most southern Siouan tribes had patrilocal residence, suggests that the Osage were patrilocal and they are so described (Nett 1952). However, the Osage practiced matrilocal residence during the late nineteenth and early twentieth centuries, and early nineteenth century sources also describe matrilocal residence (Vissier 1827:57). Tixier (1940:143), writing of the 1840 period, reported that White Hair had married a girl of the Little Osage band and therefore could not be home to establish his claim to be chief of his village. Thus both patrilocal and matrilocal residence are reported for the Osage. This apparent contradiction in residence pattern is probably the result of a shift from patrilocal to matrilocal residence sometime during the early historic period (Bailey 1973). During most of the nineteenth century, the predominant household type was a matrilocal extended family. Tixier (1940:124) stated that heads of such extended families were called "lodge chiefs."

Polygyny was usually of the sororal form. The husband of the oldest daughter of a family had marriage claims on all the younger sisters (Tixier 1940:183). Once married, a man had some degree of control over his wife and could kill an unfaithful spouse. However, a man who murdered his wife for no apparent reason was himself executed by the "warriors" (Ponziglione 1890:277–279). A divorce could take place only when both parties consented, and the husband was entitled to take back the gifts he had given his father-in-law (Tixier 1940:183). If the husband died, it was expected that the widow would marry her deceased husband's brother (Ponziglione 1889:74).

The formal naming of a child was an extremely important ritual, which conferred both clan and tribal membership (La Flesche 1928:122–164). Personal names were owned by the clan and reflected its sacred associations. The name given in this ritual to a boy was considered to be only a child's name; he would later receive an adult clan name. In addition, men were frequently given nicknames based upon some exploit or personal characteristic. A girl retained the name received at this time throughout life.

Names for both males and females were also bestowed on the basis of birth order. Distinctive "sky names" were given to the three oldest sons and daughters in each family based on birth order; all younger children were given "earth names" (see La Flesche 1928:124–164).

At death the body was washed, ornamented and painted according to clan affiliation, and wrapped in a good robe. A member of the opposite moiety was chosen to sing over the body. On noon of the fourth day the body, with personal possessions and food for the journey, was buried in a sitting position, covered with a rock mound. For important personages, there was frequently a mourning rite that involved, among other things, the killing and scalping of an enemy by a designated group of men. In this way the deceased would be provided with a companion on the path of the dead. The Osage had no idea what happened to the spirit after death (La Flesche 1939:86–145)

Kinship

Osage kinship terminology was of the Omaha type. Mother and mother's sisters were called mother. Father and father's brothers were called father. A separate term 'aunt' was used for father's sisters, and a separate term 'uncle' for mother's brothers. Sibling terms were extended to include parallel cousins as well. Maternal cross cousins were called 'mother' if a female or 'uncle' if a male. Patrilineal cross cousins were termed 'son' or 'daughter' in the case of a woman or 'niece' and 'nephew' by a man. Given the social importance of relative birth order, not surprisingly their sibling terms distinguished between 'older' and 'younger' brothers and sisters (Nett 1952).

History Since 1871

The removal to Oklahoma in 1871 signaled the beginning of a new era in Osage culture history. The Osage who moved to Oklahoma were in fact two very distinct populations. Of the 3,956 individuals, 3,679 belonged to what their agent called the "full-blood" bands. The remaining 277 individuals were

Osage Tribal Mus., Pawhuska, Okla.: top left, P-1205-B, bottom left, P-1205-D; Smithsonian, Natl. Mus. of the Amer. Ind.: right, 23/7300(g) and 23/7300(a).

Fig. 8. Weddings. top left and bottom left, Wedding of John Bates Yellowhorse and Anna Collum Others. top left, The bride, with a handkerchief over her mouth, being led out of the house. Her coat is based on a 19th-century military officer's dress coat, with gold epaulets and brass buttons, Osage ribbonwork, finger weaving, and beadwork plus silver medallions and buckles. Around the waist of the coat is a finger woven sash. The coat was a valued heirloom. The hat, being carried, has large downfeather pompoms and is covered with ribbonwork (Callahan 1990:115–116). bottom left, Horse and buggy transporting the bride's party. The horse blanket bears appliqued hands, a common Osage design. Photographs by Vince Dillon, 1917. right, Outfit worn by Mary Redeagle at her marriage to Paul Beartrack. The black hat is decorated with a band of red-dyed rooster hackle feathers, a German silver hatband, and 6 red, blue, and green hackle plumes. The blue broadcloth coat is machine sewn with embroidered red silk cuffs, lapels, shoulder and pocket facings, and with military-style buttons and epaulettes. The outfit also includes a blue silk blouse, sash, leggings, moccasins, and a ribbonwork shawl. Collected 1966; length of coat 120.65 cm.

grouped together in what was called the "mixed-blood band" (ARCIA 1872:246). Though categorized in terms of ancestry, this division was more social and cultural than biological. The mixed-bloods were primarily of French-Osage ancestry. Most were Roman Catholics, and in culture little distinguished them from the White settlers in Kansas. They lived in houses and dressed in "citizen" clothes. Most were small farmers or ranchers, and some were traders. While many still spoke Osage, their social identity was White, not Osage. Many had moved south from Kansas only because of the hostility of White settlers who looked upon them as "Indians" (Wilson 1985:17–18).

In contrast, the members of the full-blood bands, some of whom were also of mixed Osage-French ancestry, retained a traditional lifeway. While some spoke fluent English and were literate, having been educated by the Jesuits, overt White cultural influences were limited. They lived in wigwams; dressed in traditional clothing; depended upon hunting, horticulture, and gathering for their subsistence; and retained traditional religious practices and beliefs.

The Osage quickly re-established their communities after arriving at their new reservation. Most of the mixed bloods settled along the Caney River on scattered farms in the bottomlands. The full bloods settled in small villages or camps according to band affiliation. The Big Hill people settled along Salt Creek. The Upland Forest people established their camps along Hominy Creek (fig. 10). The Little Osage settled near the mixed-bloods on the Caney River, while the Thorny Thicket and Hearts Stay bands settled along Bird Creek near the new agency at Pawhuska (Bailey 1973:78).

Wyandotte Co. Histl. Soc. and Mus., Bonner Springs, Kans.: 1963-28.

Fig. 9. Studio portrait of Hlu-ah-to-me and her daughter Magella Whitehorn (b. 1894), who has a deer clan haircut. Photographed 1895.

With the loss of the buffalo and the last hunt in 1876, the full bloods had to turn to the agency for rations in order to survive (Bailey 1973:79–80). Fortunately for the Osage the sale of the Kansas reservation provided a new economic base. By 1880 the Osage tribe had almost $2,000,000 in funds deposited in the United States Treasury, and that year $90,000 was earned in interest. Ten years later the tribal fund had grown to over $8,000,000 (Wright 1951: 196). Initially the government used part of the interest income to purchase rations. In 1879, they changed this policy and began making quarterly per capita cash payments to the Osage. During the 1880s, every Osage man, woman, and child received about $160 annually.

By the 1880s, these funds together with the value of reservation land led Special Agent E.E. White (1965:202) to conclude that, per capita, the Osage were "the richest people in the world." Control of the quarterly payments gave the agents tremendous leverage, while control of undistributed income gave them the resources. As part of the attempt to break up village life, farms were established and assigned to each family. Houses were built for the full bloods, and livestock was distributed (Bailey 1973:81–82).

The Osage political structure had virtually disintegrated by the 1870s. With the support and strong encouragement of the agency, an Osage National Council, complete with a constitution, was created in 1881. Supported by both full-blood and mixed-blood leaders, the Council consisted of an elected chief, assistant chief, and 15 legislators. The constitution also provided for a judiciary and sheriffs, who were elected for each of five districts (Wilson 1985:31–34).

The Quaker agents assigned to the new reservation blocked the attempts of the Jesuits to re-establish schools for the Osage in Oklahoma. Instead, a new agency school was established in 1872 (Bailey 1973:52). Due to the reluctance of many parents to enroll their children in school, the National Council passed a law in 1884 that empowered the agent to stop the quarterly payment to any family who kept its children from attending school (Wilson 1985:78). In 1887 the Roman Catholic church was allowed to establish Saint Louis's School for girls and Saint John's School for boys on the reservation.

In spite of increased education and pressures for change, the full bloods appeared to be culturally conservative. Disease and other factors were causing a major decline in the full-blood population, which created havoc in their religious rituals. By the 1880s some of the clans had lost all their Little Old Men. In order to carry out necessary tribal ceremonies, uninitiated males from these clans literally stood with the Little Old Men, so that all 24 clans would be physically represented. The clan's actual part in the ceremony was deleted. By the 1890s one clan had been reduced to a single elderly woman, and rituals could no longer be performed. With the extinction of major tribal rituals a void was created in Osage society and culture (Bailey 1973:102).

Wyandotte Co. Histl. Soc. and Mus., Bonner Springs, Kans.: 1963-28.

Fig. 10. Black Dog's camp near Hominy, Okla., showing dome-shaped lodges covered with canvas. Photographer and date not recorded; copyright Jan. 1906.

In 1889 Oklahoma Territory was created, and the nonreservation lands in central Oklahoma were opened for homesteading. Ignoring the reservation status of Osage lands, many settlers illegally occupied land within the reservation. Still others became tenant farmers, working for Osages, and thus legalizing their presence. By the late 1880s the Osage had been reduced to a minority population on their own reservation (Wilson 1985:45–73).

While the full-blood population was suffering a rapid decline, the mixed-bloods were undergoing a population explosion. This growth was partially attributable to better health conditions and natural increase, but it was also the result of an influx of nonresident "Osage" families who had discovered the economic advantages of being Osage. Some of these "new" mixed bloods were individuals of mixed Osage-White ancestry who had remained behind in Kansas and Missouri. Others, lacking Osage ancestry, bribed officials to have their names placed on the roll (Bailey 1972).

In 1884 the Kansa tribe brought the iloshka (*įloška*) dance to the Thorny Thicket band at Pawhuska (fig. 11). Later the Kansa gave another iloshka drum to the Upland Forest band at Hominy. Still later, the Ponca gave a third iloshka drum to the Big Hill band at Gray Horse. The iloshka quickly became popular, and large round dance houses were built at Pawhuska, Hominy, and Gray Horse. Few details are known about the early iloshka other than it was a religious ceremony and helped fill the void left by the extinction of traditional Osage rituals.

In 1891–1892 the Ghost Dance was brought to the Osage by John Wilson, known as Moonhead, a Delaware-Caddo. It was danced once by the Big Hill people and once by the Upland Forest band and then dropped (Bailey 1973:88).

About 1897 John Wilson returned and brought to the Osage the Big Moon Peyote ceremony, which combined Christian and Indian religious beliefs and practices. For example, the altar included the symbolic grave of Christ. Wilson preached that the old ways must be abandoned and forgotten, and that medicine bundles should be put away or destroyed. By the time of his death in 1901, Wilson had established three Peyote churches among the Upland Forest band and had authorized four men, two Osages and two Quapaws, to carry on his work after his death (Bailey 1968–1989; D.C. Swan 1998).

Allotment and Oil

In 1893 the Cherokee Commission arrived at the Osage Agency for the purpose of securing an agreement from the Osage National Council to allot their reservation. The Council, however, refused the request. The full bloods, who controlled the Council, were adamant in their opposition to allotment. Only the mixed bloods supported allotting the reservation. In the middle and late 1890s the pressures on the Osage to allot their lands and open the reservation to settlement increased. Frustrated by the failure to persuade the Council to allot, the federal Indian Service unilaterally dissolved the Osage National Council in 1900 (Wilson 1985:37–42).

By 1900 the mixed bloods had become the majority. In 1904 the agency created the Osage Business Committee and held elections for chief and eight councilmen. The pro-allotment mixed-blood faction won control of the Business Committee. In 1906, with the approval of the Business Committee, the Osage Allotment Act was passed by Congress (Wilson 1985:74–92). By July 1907, 2,229 individuals had been enrolled.

Oil had been found on the reservation in 1897, and this discovery as well as the Osage tribe's actual title to reservation land resulted in a unique system for dividing tribal properties. In contrast to other reservations, there would be no "surplus" lands for homesteaders. Town sites, railroad right of ways, agency buildings, three Indian village sites, and Roman Catholic school lands were to be withheld. The titles to these tracts were to be sold, given away, or retained by the tribe. All other land on the reservation was equally divided among the 2,229 enrolled members of the tribe. As a result every man, woman, and child received approximately 658 acres of land, usually in four or more separate tracts (Wilson 1985:89–98; Bureau of Indian Affairs 1953:14–15).

The title to all minerals, oil, natural gas, sand, and gravel was retained by the tribe as a whole (vol. 4:683). Future income from mineral leases and royalties was to be distributed on the basis of "headrights." Each allottee received one headright. Headrights were individual property that entitled each owner to 1/2,229th of the tribal income, less expenses. Headrights could be sold, given away, inherited, and even divided. All Osages born after the allotment roll was closed could acquire headrights only through purchase, gift, or inheritance (Wilson 1985:93).

The Osage Allotment Act created a new Osage Tribal Council to manage the tribal mineral estate. This council consisted of a chief, an assistant chief, and eight councilmen who were elected at large by all adult male headright owners (Bureau of Indian Affairs 1953:14).

The Osage Allotment Act did not dissolve the Osage Reservation; the act only allotted the land and made it legal for Whites to acquire land. Technically the Osage Reservation remained in existence in 1998. When Oklahoma became a state in 1907, the Osage Reservation was incorporated as Osage County. Following allotment and statehood, White farmers and ranchers hurried onto the reservation. Many Osage quickly sold portions of their allotments. The majority chose to lease their land for grazing or farming. Merchants followed, establishing Pawhuska, Hominy, and Fairfax as trade centers. Between 1907 and 1910, the population of the county grew from 15,332 to 20,101. Oil played only a minor role in this initial growth. Exploration was limited, and production remained low until World War I. It was during the war and the early 1920s that the real oil boom hit.

top, Okla. Histl. Soc., Oklahoma City: 3191.

Fig. 11. Iloshka dance. top, Performers in front of a round house. The ceremony, performed annually in June, honored the eldest son who was chosen to be drumkeeper for a year (Callahan 1990:19–107). The drum is in the center. Photograph by George W. Parsons, Pawhuska, Okla. Terr., 1890–1895. bottom left and bottom right, Parade during the "paying for the drum." On the first day of the dance a new drumkeeper sponsors a giveaway. Items given away include wedding outfits (bottom left). This is the only use made of these outfits since the 1930s. Photographs by Garrick Bailey, Pawhuska, Okla., 1990.

The growth of the oil industry in the early twentieth century is best reflected in the yearly headright incomes. In 1907 a headright paid $345, and throughout the early 1910s payments were usually in the range of $300–500. In 1917 they suddenly jumped to $2,719. By 1920 they had increased to $8,090, and in 1923, at the very height of the boom, a headright yielded $12,400 (Bureau of Indian Affairs 1953:16–18).

Exploration for and production of oil led to a population explosion. By 1920 the county's population had risen to 36,536, and by the mid-1920s, when oil exploration peaked, its population was probably in excess of 50,000. As late as 1930 the county had a population of over 47,000. Most mixed-blood Osage blended into the general White population. It was the full-blood families who remained culturally distinct and socially aloof.

Early Twentieth Century

During allotment a special roll was kept for members of the full-blood bands, totaling 874 individuals. It was these individuals and their descendants, full bloods and mixed bloods, who constituted what, from this period on, is called the Osage "Indian community." For the period from about 1906 until 1940, this community numbered between 800 and 1,000 individuals (Bailey 1968–1989).

During the 1910s–1920s, the Peyote religion became the dominant force within the Osage Indian community. From only three churches among the Upland Forest people in 1901, it spread to the Big Hills at Gray Horse and to the Hearts Stays, Thorny Thickets, and Little Osage in and around Pawhuska. Over 30 churches were established during this period (fig. 12). At its height, during the 1920s, the Peyote religion had the vast majority of full bloods as adherents. The Peyote church espoused the idea of acculturation and assimilation. The church taught that the Osage could and should become like other Americans. Though it varied from family to family, Osage Peyotists generally discouraged the use of the Osage language among their children and encouraged them to attend school and become Roman Catholics, Baptists, or Quakers (Bailey 1968–1989).

The iloshka dance was retained and supported, but the Peyotists forced the elimination of all its overt religious elements. Thus the iloshka dance and societies were retained, but primarily as social events and organizations. While Osages dropped numerous traditional cultural practices during the 1920s, they borrowed many others from different tribes. The Omaha brought them the Soldier dance, and three women's Soldier dance societies were organized. From the Otoe and Cheyenne they acquired the hand game, which became a very popular social activity. Osage-sponsored powwows became commonplace (Bailey 1968–1989).

Although some families still arranged marriages for their children, these became increasingly rare. At the same time marriages between full-blood Osages and either Whites or members of other tribes become common. In most cases the non-Osage spouses were integrated into the Osage community.

During the economic Depression of the 1930s oil prices collapsed. In 1932 a headright earned only $585 (Bureau of Indian Affairs 1953:19). The Depression brought to an end the era of extreme Osage economic prosperity.

The 1970s and 1980s

In 1990 the Osage tribe continued to be composed of two distinct groups. The majority of tribal members were socially and culturally White, and the Osage Indian community was a minority population within the tribe. Osage blood quantum statistics alone are misleading as indicators of ancestry. Culturally White mixed bloods tend to marry Whites; members of the Osage Indian community tend to marry Indians from other tribes. Many individuals who are only one-half or one-quarter degree Osage are in fact full-blood or near full-blood Indians in ancestry. In the 1980s the Osage Indian community, including non-Osage spouses (Indian and White) who participated in Osage community activities, probably numbered 3,000 or more individuals.

Members of the Osage Indian community were geographically dispersed. Probably half resided on the reservation, with a large number in Tulsa, Bartlesville, Ponca City, and Oklahoma City. Smaller concentrations are found in Arizona, New Mexico, Texas, Colorado, California, and Washington, D.C.

In 1986, out of the 2,229 headrights, 1,667 were owned by individuals of Osage ancestry. The remainder were owned by Whites or Indians from other tribes. These 1,667

Smithsonian, NAA: left, 90-7259, right, 90-7260.

Fig. 12. The Peyote ritual. left, House where Peyote ceremony was performed. Photograph by Vince Dillon, Fairfax, Okla., 1910–1921. right, Black Dog's West Moon Peyote altar near Hominy, Okla. This altar was built about 1898–1899. Photograph probably by Francis La Flesche, 1910–1929.

U. of Pa., U. Mus., Philadelphia: 13640.

Fig. 13. Mourning Dance, sometimes called a "war dance," the last of the traditional dances to survive. The mourning party would ride west to kill and scalp an enemy whose scalp would then be placed on the grave. The man with light blanket around his waist is one of the drummers. Photograph by Girda Sebbelov, Pawhuska, Okla., 1911.

headrights were owned by a total of 2,835 Osages. The majority of Osage headright owners had less than one-half a headright share. A small number of Osages owned between two and five headrights.

Income from headrights reached $34,580 in 1981; by the mid-1980s, it declined to $9,000–$10,000 a year. Few Osage families depended upon headright income for their total support. Most families earned salaries or business income.

The Osage Tribal Council was based on the provisions of the Osage Allotment Act of 1906 with only minor revisions. Beginning in 1942, women headright owners were allowed to vote and run for office. Only individuals of Osage ancestry voted for the Council, and their votes were weighted according to headright ownership. Thus an individual with one-tenth headright had one-tenth vote, while an individual with three headrights had three votes. Under this system, most adult Osages, regardless of degree of ancestry, have no voice in tribal government.

Natl. Arch.: 75-BK-85A; inset, Smithsonian, Dept. of Anthr.: 364522.

Fig. 14. 20 Osages at the White House, Jan. 12, 1928. The Osage Council and their families traveled almost yearly to Washington in the 1920s to discuss tribal issues and to see the sights. left to right, Charles Curtis (Kansa mixed blood, at this time Congressman from Kansas), Francis Revard, Mo-sah-mun-pah, Mrs. George Pitts, George Pitts, Francis Wheeler, Edgar McCarthy, Mrs. Hunkahoppy, Hunkahoppy, Mrs. Roanhorse, Lizzie Baconrind, Roanhorse Baconrind, President Calvin Coolidge, Joe Abbott, Fred Lookout, Mrs. Lookout, Newalla, Henry Pratt, Dick Petsemoie, John Abbott, and Virginia Logan. Photograph by Frank R. Scherer. inset, Otter fur turban, lined with blue trade cloth and red velvet, and edged with white seed beads. The central medallion is made of translucent and blue cut beads. Given to the Smithsonian by Tom Bacon Rind, 1932. Height of crown 12.45 cm.

In 1962 the Osage Nation Organization was organized to challenge the legality of the Osage Tribal Council. Between 1962 and the early 1980s, the organization fought both in Congress and in the federal courts to have the vote extended to nonheadright owners, but to no avail. Responding to a finding by a federal court that the 1881 Osage constitution had never been invalidated, in 1986 a group of younger Osages proceeded to hold elections and re-establish the Osage National Council. This council sought unsuccessfully to be recognized by the Bureau of Indian Affairs as the legal government of the Osage tribe.

By the late 1980s, the Osage language was verging on extinction, with only a few dozen older speakers. Osage children attended public schools both on and off reservation. Most middle-aged and young adult Osages attended college, and many held degrees in law, medicine, engineering, business, and education. The majority of families, both on the reservation and in nearby cities, lived what is best characterized as a middle-class American life-style.

The majority of Osages were Roman Catholics, with smaller numbers being Baptists and Quakers. In the 1980s there were three active Big Moon Peyote houses. In addition, two men occasionally held Little Moon or "tepee" meetings in the county. About 150 Osages were active Peyotists in the early 1980s (Wilson 1985:200).

The community as a social unit was delineated by support of and participation in a number of events defined as "Osage," including dances, dinners, hand games, namings, and funeral feasts. These events defined and reinforced social solidarity as well as publicly expressed Osage cultural beliefs and practices.

The iloshka societies and their associated dances were the key institution in defining the community. There were three iloshka societies, Pawhuska, Hominy, and Gray Horse, each with its own dance committee, membership, dance ground, and arbor. In June each society held a four-day dance, acting as host to the members of the other two societies. The three weeks during which these dances took place were the highpoint in the Osage year. Nonresident families returned home to take part in the dances, to have children receive Osage names and be formally initiated into the dance, to visit relatives and friends, and to participate in the giveaways that serve to acknowledge publicly their continuing social obligations.

The iloshka dance itself is the "straight dance" performed to the accompaniment of iloshka dance songs. On the fourth day "individual" songs are sung, in honor of particular individuals and their families. Following the song, descendants or relatives of the honored individual gave gifts to other families and individuals who assisted them during the year.

The iloshka dances were elaborate and expensive. The host society must feed their visitors, usually 1,000 or more over the four-day period. Osage clothes cost from $2,000–$5,000 for each male dancer. Giveaways by the family required Pendleton blankets, shawls, groceries, and cash.

As of the mid-1980s, 300 to 350 male dancers took part in each four-day dance, while women dancers numbered 200 or more. During the three dances in June, possibly as many as 700 different men participated as dancers, while as many as 2,000 other individuals took part as cooks, hosts for family dinners, and other supportive roles.

Other organizations and events throughout the year involved smaller segments of the community, such as dances sponsored by War Mothers societies, the Gourd clan, and the Catholic Indian Women's society.

Hand games were the most common form of social activity, used as a benefit to raise money for dances or special projects. Individual families sponsored them for school graduations, marriages, returning servicemen, or merely as a way of honoring a family member for some special accomplishment.

Osage names, which are required for induction into the iloshka societies, are given to children in Peyote meetings and at special naming dinners. Although clan names are still given, determination of a clan affiliation is a problem because many children have a non-Osage father. In such instances, older relatives or family friends are simply asked to give an Osage name to children. Sometimes a name from the child's mother's clan is given. In other cases the namer bestows a name from his or her clan on the child, which constitutes an adoption into the namer's clan. In all cases, only adult names are given, and birth order is rarely considered.

Death, burial, and mourning were marked by Osage events. Following a death, members of the community stayed with the family and the corpse, night and day. Burial is at noon on the fourth day. The individual is buried with a blanket, a feather or fan, and a box of food. Following the burial the community has a funeral feast. Mourners rub themselves with cedar smoke to be purified, prayers are said, those in attendance are fed, and the family of the deceased has a giveaway.

Periodically the Catholic Indian Women's society hosts a memorial breakfast for the families of Osage who have recently died. It is not unusual for families to hold a memorial breakfast a year after the death of a member to announce the end of mourning.

The Osage Indian community demonstrates few overt traits that can be shown to be derived from historical Osage culture. Osage organizations and events are for the most part of late nineteenth and twentieth-century adoption, either from other tribes or from the White community. Regardless of their history or origin, the Osage have remodeled these organizations and events to meet Osage social and cultural needs.

Population

In 1701, it was estimated that the Crevas, assumed to be the Osage, numbered 1,200 to 1,500 families (Margry 1876–1886, 4:599). In 1754 the French governor of Louisiana calculated that the Osages numbered about 950 warriors (Din and Nasatir 1983:49). In 1800 James Flint

left, Smithsonian, NAA: 57,116; right, Smithsonian, Dept. of Anthr.: 358849 (neg. 91-19229).

Fig. 15. Cradles. left, Cradleboard makers Harold Redcorn and his wife Louise Redcorn at the Smithsonian Folklife Festival. He made the boards, and she made the finger-woven coverings. Both were important in Osage economic enterprises. Louise and her sisters organized the Red Man store in 1957, which was instrumental in revitalizing and preserving Osage crafts. Photograph by Dick Ferrar, Washington, July 1970. right, Cradle. The carved and painted triangles on the panel are highlighted with hot-file burn decorations and outlined with brass tacks. The bow is covered with machine-sewn ribbonwork, selvedge trade cloth, and hawk bells. The tie is loom-woven beadwork in white, blue, and red seed beads. This cradle was first owned by Shah-Ke-Wahpe (*šáke wapį* 'bloody hand') and his wife in 1884. Collected by V.J. Evans before 1931; length 107 cm.

(Thwaites 1904–1907, 9:249) reported that they had 1,800 warriors. In 1842, 4,102 Osages were counted (Bailey 1973:110), certainly a minimum number, but there is some question as to the number not counted. A census in 1872 enumerated 3,679 full bloods and 277 mixed bloods, totaling 3,956 (ARCIA 1872:246).

The Osage population slowly declined during the early nineteenth century. Mooney (1928) estimated 6,200 for 1780, but a more realistic estimate would probably be about 7,000. By the 1850s their population was about 5,000 (Bailey 1973:109–110).

Following their removal to Oklahoma in 1871, the Osage population declined sharply. Between 1872 and 1880 their population dropped from 3,956 to 2,008. In 1889 their population reached its lowest level with the agency reporting 1,496 individuals. By 1900 their population had risen to 1,783 and was growing (Bailey 1973:111). This growth was in the number of mixed bloods and was primarily the result of previously nonresident mixed bloods being placed on the tribal roll, the Osage ancestry of many of them questionable (see Bailey 1972). In contrast the full-blood population had declined to 1,170 by 1885. By 1900 there were only 866 full bloods (Bailey 1973:111–112). The special 1910 census of Indians recorded an Osage population of 1,373, of whom 591 were counted as full bloods (U.S. Bureau of the Census 1915:145).

The 1952 census gave a total population of 5,307 of whom 478 were full-bloods (Bureau of Indian Affairs 1953:27). An unofficial census made in 1968 reported a total of 8,513 of whom 352 were full-bloods. A 1976 unofficial census reported a total population of 8,842 of whom 151 were full-bloods. A breakdown of the 1976 census by blood quantum showed that over 40 percent of the population was less than 1/32 Osage in ancestry. In the 1990 census, some 9,527 respondents identified themselves as Osage (U.S. Bureau of the Cenus 1992:39). Tiller (1996:522) reported a tribal enrollment of 12,000.

Synonymy†

The Osage name for themselves, *wažáže*, anglicized as Wazhazhe, is also the name of a tribal phratry and, in modified form as White Osage (*wažáže ska*), the name of a clan within that phratry; it is as well a personal name belonging to the *wáccecʰi* clan. The etymology and significance of the name are obscure (La Flesche 1932:209–210).

The Osage are known to most Plains tribes by their own name. All Dhegiha groups use that name: Omaha and Ponca *wažáže* (J.H. Howard 1965:134; John Koontz, personal communication 1987; Parks 1988), cited for Omaha as Wajáje (Dorsey 1890:652) and Wazházhe (Fletcher and La Flesche 1911:86); Kansa *wažáže* (Robert L. Rankin, personal communication 1987); Quapaw *wažáže* (Dorsey 1891b, retranscribed). The Chiwere languages use cognate forms: *wará·ye* (Louanna Furbee, personal communication 1990; Parks 1988), cited also as Wálaye (Curtis 1907–1930, 19:228); and Winnebago *waráš* (Kenneth Miner, personal communication 1987). The same name is used by the different divisions of the Sioux: Santee, Yankton, and

†This synonymy was written by Douglas R. Parks.

Teton *wažáža* (S.R. Riggs in Hodge 1907–1910, 2:158; J.P. Williamson 1902:123; Dorsey 1897:219); among the Blackfeet tribe of the Teton, it occurs as a band name, *wažáže* (Dorsey 1897:220). In Buechel's Teton dictionary (1970: 590), the form *wítapaha(tu)* is erroneously translated as both Osage and Kiowa; Buechel's (1910–1954) files give *wažáže* only as an Oglala band name.

Caddoan languages have borrowed the same name for the Osage: Arikara *wašá·ši* (Parks 1970–1990); Pawnee *pasa·si* (Parks 1965–1990); Kitsai Washăsh (Mooney 1893:93); Wichita *wasá·s* (David S. Rood, personal communication 1988); and Caddo *wášaš* (Chafe 1979). Two Plains Algonquian languages have also borrowed the form: Arapaho *wosô·sí·* (sg. *wóso·s*) (Ives Goddard, personal communication 1990), given also as Wássash (Gatschet in Hodge 1907–1910, 2:158); and Cheyenne Vasāsan (sg. Vasās) (Petter 1913–1915:582) and W'sásä'n (sg. Wasás)-(Mooney 1907:425). The same name also occurs in Comanche as *wasási* (Jean Charney, personal communication 1987) and *waʔsá·siʔ* (Robinson and Armagost 1990:209).

Other tribes living to the east and south of the Osage have borrowed the name: Fox *waša·ša* and later *aša·ša* (Ives Goddard, personal communication 1998); Kickapoo *wasaasa* (Voorhis 1998:129); Unami Delaware *wəšá·ši* (Ives Goddard, personal communication 1990); Shawnee *hoša·ši* (Voegelin 1938–1940, 5:449), Miami wašaši (Voegelin 1938–1940, 5:418), Cherokee *ani·hwsa·si* or *ani·wahsa·si* (Floyd Lounsbury, personal communication 1977); and Creek wûsasĭ (Grayson 1885:184).

An early French reference to the Osage is pasosé, 1683 (La Salle in M.M. Wedel 1988:58), which apparently reflects the Pawnee form *pasa·si* that La Salle obtained from his Pana captive. That form was rendered pasoso on Franquelin's 1684 and 1686 maps (M.M. Wedel 1988:58).

Most early European references to the Osage are seventeenth- and early eighteenth-century renditions, generally French, of the modern form Osage or a close variant of it, based on *wažáže* but with an initial syllable o probably reflecting transmission through an Algonquian language in which *o-* characterized tribal names. Examples include Osage, Ozages, and Ozanges (Hennepin 1698, 1:141, 2:47); Osages, 1703 (De Lisle map in Tucker 1942:pl. 13); Huzzau, 1719 (Pénigaut in B.F. French 1869, 1:151); Huzaas, Huz-zaws and O-saw-ses, apparently based on Pénigaut (E. James 1823, 2:244, 311); Ouchage, 1673 (Marquette map in Tucker 1942:pl. 5); Ouasoys, 1759 (Croghan in Rupp 1846:146), and Ousasoys, 1759 (Croghan in T. Jefferson 1825:145); Ousasons (Boudinot 1816:128); and Ausages or Ausage, 1714 (Bourgmont in Giraud 1958:15; also Soulard map 1795 in W.R. Wood 1983: pl. 2). As was common practice among the French Creoles, some French references to the Osage use only the initial syllable of the name (Nicollet 1838–1839); examples are Ous, 1719 (Pénigaut in B.F. French 1869, 1:151), Ose (anonymous French map ca. 1797 in W.R. Wood 1983:pl. 6), and Os in Petits Os, 1802 (Perrin du Lac in W.R. Wood 1983:pl. 9). Eighteenth- and nineteenth-century American renditions of the French form of the name include Orages (Coxe 1741:15); Osayes (Morse 1776:map); Osarge (Lewis and Clark in Moulton 1983–, 3:390); Ossage, 1812 (Schermerhorn 1814:31); and Ozas (*American Pioneer* 1843, 2:190).

More common renditions of the name during the American period of the nineteenth century are variants of *wažáže* with renditions of the initial syllable *wa*. Examples are Wasashe (Brackenridge 1814:72), Wassashsha (S.R. Brown 1817:193), Waw-sash-e (E. James 1823, 1:328), Wasagè (Hunter 1823:18), Huashashas and Wahashas (Rafinesque in H. Marshall 1824, 1:28, 30), Wasas, 1830 (Berlandier 1969:111), Wos-sosh-e (McCoy 1835–1838, 2:17), Wausashe (Gallatin 1836:126), Washbashaws (Schoolcraft 1851–1857, 6:689), and Wahsash (Keane in Stanford 1878–1885, 6:542). Sometimes the initial syllable is omitted, for example, Zages (map in Harris 1705, 1:685).

Spanish recordings, which are also based on *wažáže*, indicate the initial syllable by hua or gua. Examples are Huasas (Castañeda 1936–1958, 5:119ff.), Guasas, 1795 (Troike 1964:384; Prieto 1873:137), Guasers (Bolton 1914, 1:270), and Guazas (Texas State Archives, Nov. 15, 1785; erroneously identified as a misprint for Kiowa in Hodge 1907–1910, 2:700, 1:510).

A different term sometimes attributed to the French as a usage for the Osage in the late seventeenth and early eighteenth centuries is the name, apparently Caddoan in origin, that for many tribes in the nineteenth century designates the Kansa: Annaho, 1687 (Joutel in Margry 1876–1886, 3:410), and Anahons and misprinted Anahous, 1719 (La Harpe in Margry 1876–1886, 6:261, 284).

In the Plains sign language the Osage are indicated by one of several variant gestures that signify removal of the hair from the sides of the head, leaving a roach extending from the forehead to the occiput. One variant is to pass the flat hand, back up, back and forth one to two inches above the head (Hadley 1893:124); another is to "bring [the] backs of [the] extended hands, fingers pointing to [the] rear and slightly upwards, alongside of [the] head; move [the] hands downwards, as though cutting [the] hair with [the] lower edges of [the] hands," repeating the motion (W.P. Clark 1885:274); and yet another, attributed to the Comanche, is to pass the flat, extended right hand backward over the right side of the head, moving the index against the second finger in imitation of cutting with a pair of scissors (Mallery 1881:472). A different sign, cited to the Sauk, Fox, and Kickapoo as well as the Osage themselves, is to "pull at the eyebrows over the left eye with the thumb and forefinger of the left hand" (Mallery 1881:472).

The sign language designation of a head with the sides shaved is reflected in two tribal names. The Kiowa term for Osage is *k̓ɔ́p*^{h}*àttɔ̀*, literally 'roached hair' (La Barre 1935; Laurel Watkins, personal communication 1979). A

Cheyenne name is *oo?kóhtAxétaneo?O*, literally 'cut-hair people' (Glenmore and Leman 1985:201), cited variously as Oóhthítaneo 'shorn men' (Curtis 1907–1930, 6:158) and Hooxtxetan (pl. Hooxtxetaneo) 'cut hair people' (Petter 1913–1915:582). In the early twentieth century this Cheyenne name was said to designate the Kansa and Quapaw as well as the Osage (Petter 1913–1915:582), but in the late twentieth century its meaning narrowed to the Osage specifically and the term replaced the borrowing from Sioux.

Two other tribal names recorded for Osage are Tonkawa *he·topow*, perhaps meaning 'cut-throats' (Hoijer 1949:57) and Plains Apache tsi·γiłʒé·cí, which has no known etymology (Bittle 1952–1953). An anomalous Blackfoot name, apparently a calque, is *ka·ksimí·yitsitapi·wa* 'sage people' (Allan R. Taylor, personal communication 1974).

Divisions

The Grand Osage division, which comprises most of the Osage bands, is designated in Osage as *ppaxáci*, which has been explained as 'campers at the mountain top' (Dorsey in Hodge 1907–1910, 2:184; Dorsey 1883) but may refer to the distinctive hairstyle of Osage men (La Flesche 1932:126). This name occurs in several historical sources as Bar-har-cha, 1719 (Pénigaut in B.F. French 1869, 1:151), Pa-ha-sca (Schoolcraft 1851–1857, 6:540), and perhaps A-ba-chae (Hamilton in Schoolcraft 1851–1857, 4:406). French references to the division include Grand Eaux (Boudinot 1816:126), Grandes Eaux (W. Smith 1776:70), and Grands Osages, 1794 (Clamorgan and Trudeau in Nasatir 1952, 1:210). Based on French usage are several American references: Grand Osâge and Grand Zo (Lewis and Clark 1806:11); Grand Zue, 1759 (Croghan in Rupp 1846:146) and Grand Tuc, a misprint for the preceding, 1759 (Croghan in Jefferson 1825:145). Other American references to the division are exemplified by Great Ozages (Jefferys 1776: map 5), Great Osage (Lewis and Clark in Moulton 1983–, 3:437), Great Ossage (Schermerhorn 1814:31), Grand Osarge (Lewis and Clark in Moulton 1983–, 3:390), and Elder Osages (Dorsey 1884b:114). Spanish references are translations of the same—Grandes Osage (De Mézières in Bolton 1914, 1:74) translated as Big Osages (Nasatir 1952, 2:426).

The Osage name for the Little Osage, composed of only the Little Osage band, is *ücétta* 'at the base of a hill' (Dorsey 1894:30, retranscribed). It occurs as Oo′-zâ-tâu (Lewis and Clark 1806:13) and U-dse′-ṭa (La Flesche 1932:167). European and American references to the Little Osage parallel those for the Grand. French examples are Petits Osage and Petits Eaux, 1794 (Clamorgan and Trudeau in Nasatir 1952, 1:210), and Petits Os, 1805 (du Lac in Wood 1983:pl. 9); based on the French forms are, for example, Petit Zo (Lewis and Clark 1806:13) and Teat Saws (Featherstonhaugh 1844:71). American designations include Lesser Osage (Fisher 1812:250) and Little Osage (Kappler 1904–1941, 2:878). Similarly, the Spanish designation is Osages Pequeños (De Mézières in Bolton 1914, 1:74), translated as Little Osages (Nasatir 1952, 1:120).

The Arkansas Osage, a group that originally split off from the Grand Osage, comprised one of the three largest Osage divisions in the nineteenth century. Its name, *zạcéolị* 'upland forest dwellers' (La Flesche 1932:32, retranscribed), has been rendered Sanze-Ougrin (de Smet 1863:355), Santsĕ pasü 'point of a timbered highland' (Dorsey 1883), and Santsukhdhin (Hodge 1907–1910, 2:462). Among French traders they were known as the Osages des Chênes, and among nineteenth-century American travelers as the Osages of the Oaks (Long in Thwaites 1904–1907, 16:266, 280). Other examples of this designation are Chancers (Sibley in Long in Thwaites 1904–1907, 16:274), Chanier's band (Brackenridge in Thwaites 1904–1907, 6:191–192), Chaneers (Long in James 1823, 2:244), and Chêniers (de Smet 1863:355).

Because they were sometimes located on the Arkansas River they were also known as the Arkansaw band (William Clark in D.D. Jackson 1962:509), Arkansaw Osage (Z.M. Pike 1811:173), and Arkansa band (McGee 1897:162). They were also referred to by the name Clermont, one of the two early nineteenth-century chiefs under whom the division separated from the Grand Osage; hence Clermont's band (Long in Thwaites 1904–1907, 16:280) or Clermo's band (Long in E. James 1823, 2:244) and Clamore (Keane in Stanford 1878–1885, 6:470). In at least one instance they were also designated by the other early nineteenth-century chief's name, Big Track (Schermerhorn 1814:31).

Sources

Tixier (1940) accompanied the Osage on their summer bison hunt in 1840 and wrote an excellent general description of Osage culture. Paul M. Ponziglione, S.J., a missionary teacher at the Osage Mission and Manual Labor school in Kansas, wrote a year-by-year account of the mission and the Osage and published short descriptions of Osage culture and history (1878, 1882, 1883, 1889).

The most important sources of Osage cultural data are the works of La Flesche (1921, 1925a, 1930, 1932, 1939, 1995), presenting detailed accounts of ritual, political structure, clan and mythology, as well as an Osage dictionary. For an account of La Flesche's life see Liberty (1978). The best general description of Osage life and culture is by Mathews (1961), an Oxford educated Osage mixed blood (b. 1894, d. 1979), who based his study on published sources as well as on extensive interviews and firsthand observations. Unfortunately, since he did not document his sources, his account is difficult to evaluate. His novel (Mathews 1934) portrays the struggles of a young Osage attempting to adjust to life during the early decades of the twentieth century. For accounts of Mathews's life see Bailey (1978) and Wilson (1981).

Additional studies of Osage culture are limited. Nett (1952) published the only data available on Osage kinship. Using ethnohistoric data Bailey (1973) focused on changes through time in Osage social organization. Wilson (1982) provided a valuable study of the changing role of women in Osage society.

There are two excellent studies of particular periods in Osage history. Din and Nasatir (1983) is a political history of the Osage during the Spanish period; Wilson (1985) concentrates on Osage political and economic change from 1871 to the 1980s. For a bibliography of the Osage see Wilson (1985a). Rollings (1992) is an ethnohistorical study of Osage hegemony on the Prairie Plains during the eighteenth century, up to its demise in the late 1830s.

Quapaw

GLORIA A. YOUNG AND MICHAEL P. HOFFMAN

Origins

The Quapaw (ˈkwôˌpô) were the only representative of the Dhegiha-speaking Siouan* peoples in the Lower Mississippi Valley. According to oral tradition, the ancestors of the Dhegiha lived as a single group near the mouth of the Ohio River. Those who moved up the Mississippi and Missouri rivers became known as the Omaha (*omáha* 'upstream'), while the group that moved down the river became the Quapaw (*okáxpa*, interpreted as 'downstream') (Dorsey 1884:211; Fletcher and La Flesche 1917:36; La Flesche 1915; Dickinson 1984:201; Robert L. Rankin, personal communication 1988).

The date of the earliest Quapaw presence in the Lower Mississippi Valley is a topic of archeological debate. The Menard-Hodges site near the mouth of the Arkansas River has been identified as the late seventeenth-century Quapaw village of Osotouy (fig. 1), and the late Mississippian material there as the protohistoric Quapaw phase (Ford 1961). Ceramics of this phase (and the closely related Carden Bottoms phase) are found on the Arkansas above its mouth for 200 miles and on both sides of the Mississippi above the mouth of the Arkansas. They are also found sporadically on the lower Little Red and the White River. Since these ceramics seem related to earlier Mississippian ceramics in the area, many archeologists interpreted this to mean that the Quapaw had long been residents of the area (Morse and Morse 1983; House and McKelway 1982; Davis 1973; McGimsey 1964). However, the distribution of Quapaw phase sites corresponds very poorly with the locations of seventeenth-century Quapaw villages (Hoffman 1985, 1985a). Also, no site excavated shows strong evidence of the characteristic Quapaw bark-covered longhouse. Since the ceramics resemble those from protohistoric northwest Mississippi identified as Tunica (Brain 1988), and the Tunica were known to have been on the Arkansas in the sixteenth and seventeenth centuries (Hudson 1985; Jeter 1989), most archeological material on the lower Arkansas may in fact represent the Tunica (Hoffman 1986).

*The phonemes of Quapaw are: (plain stops) *p*, *t*, *k*, *ʔ*; (tense stops) *pp*, *tt*, *kk*; (aspirated stops) *pʰ*, *tʰ*, *kʰ*; glottalized stops *ṫ*, *k̇*; (voiceless spirants) *s*, *š*, *x*, *h*; (voiced spirants) *z*, *ž*, *γ*; (glottalized spirants) *ṡ*, *ṧ*, *ẋ*; (voiced nasals) *m*, *n*; (approximants) *w*, *d*; (oral vowels) *i*, *e*, *a*, *o* ([u] ~ [o]); (nasal vowels) *į*, *ą*, *ǫ*; (stress) v́. The phonemic orthography used in the citation of Quapaw terms follows the analysis of Robert L. Rankin.

A related issue is whether the Quapaw were residents in 1541–1543 of Pacaha, an Indian town in northeastern Arkansas mentioned in the narratives of the Hernando de Soto expedition. Some scholars support an early identification as Quapaw (Fletcher and La Flesche 1911:186; Thomas 1910:333; Morse and Morse 1983), while others, including most modern anthropologists, reject it on varying grounds (Swanton 1985; Phillips, Ford, and Griffin 1951; Hoffman 1977; Hathcock 1983; Robert L. Rankin, personal communication 1988). Pacaha and its inhabitants appear to be Tunican (Young and Hoffman 1993:213–230). If there was a Quapaw presence in the Southeast this early, it must have been temporary hunting camps. The Quapaw believe that when they arrived above the Arkansas River, they drove out the Tunica residing there (Bizzell 1981:72).

History, 1673–1804

Relations with Other Tribes

At the time of European contact, the Quapaw were generally hostile toward most of their Southeast neighbors as territorial competitors. Their enemies, at least during colonial times, included the Chickasaw, Natchez, Tunica, and Koroa. Their early relations with the Caddo were hostile to ambivalent. In 1707 they were "generally at war with the nations to the westward of them as far as the Rio Bravo" (Pittman 1906:83). They appear to have maintained a closer relationship with the Osage, a related group of Siouan speakers to the northwest, except for a few incidents of hostility in the late eighteenth and early nineteenth centuries. They were also allied with the Illinois tribes up the Mississippi River, at least throughout the colonial period. In the late seventeenth century they also maintained a weak and somewhat ambivalent alliance with the Taensa of the Lower Mississippi Valley (Sabo 1989:3–7).

Relations with Europeans

The first recorded contact between the Quapaw and Europeans occurred on July 16, 1673, when Jacques Marquette and Louis Jolliet, sailing down the Mississippi River with a party of Illinois Indians, arrived at the Quapaw villages on the banks of the Mississippi about 20 miles upstream from its confluence with the Arkansas River. Marquette displayed a calumet as a sign of peace,

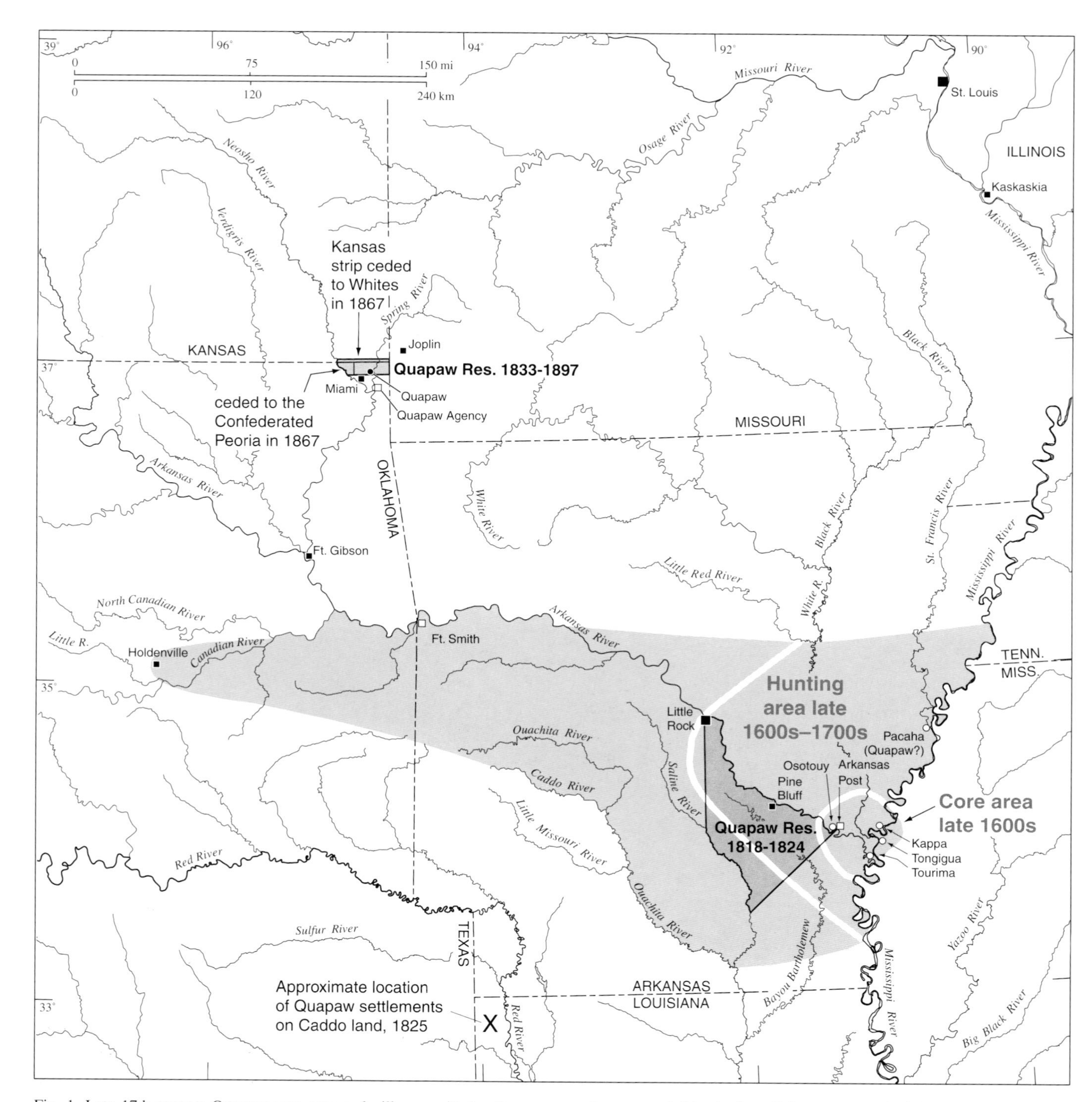

Fig. 1. Late 17th-century Quapaw core area and villages, with hunting areas as they expanded in the late 18th century, and 19th-century reservations.

and his party was met by Quapaws in two canoes, offering tobacco and food. In the village, sitting under the chief's arbor on mats of woven river cane, they sealed a pact of friendship by smoking the calumet and sharing a meal. The Quapaw never broke these vows of friendship and loyalty to the French (JR 59:152–161).

In March 1680 a party of Quapaws journeyed to Fort Crèvecoeur near modern Peoria, Illinois, to trade for axes (Hennepin 1880:186). They were again visited by the French on March 12, 1682, when the expedition of René-Robert Cavelier, sieur de La Salle, arrived at the Quapaw villages. Hearing drums and cries through the fog, and fearing that preparations were being made for war, the French hastily built a redoubt on the east side of the Mississippi. As a party of Indians crossed the river, Henri de Tonti, La Salle's second in command, called out in Illinois asking who was approaching. An Illinois in the party answered, "Akansa" (Tonti 1898:72), their name for the Quapaw.

The Indians came ashore and smoked the calumet with the French and later six tribal elders crossed the river, again smoked the calumet, and received presents. They invited the French to their village, called Kappa, where the Quapaw greeted them ceremoniously, built them a lodge, and brought wood and food. The next day the French erected in the village a large cross and a post on which had been painted the coat of arms of Louis XIV. The Quapaw listened intently as the French explained the Christian mysteries, fired a volley, and shouted, "Vive le Roi!" The Quapaw danced through the night and rubbed the column with their hands which they then passed over their own bodies to transfer the power from the post to themselves. Later, they erected a palisade around the cross and post (Tonti 1898:73–74; Margry 1876–1886, 2:181–189, 207; Falconer 1844:64).

La Salle's party recorded four Quapaw villages—Kappa, Tongigua and Tourima on the Mississippi and Osotouy on the lower Arkansas—each apparently a corporate unit with its own government (La Salle 1898:21). Shortly thereafter, Tourima moved to a site on the Arkansas River, perhaps combining with Osotouy (Joutel 1714).

By 1699, the Quapaw had been ravaged by smallpox (Shea 1861:72). Kappa and Tongigua combined into a single village on the west bank of the Mississippi River. Within a year, the remaining inhabitants of Tourima moved from the Arkansas River to Kappa. With the Quapaw concentrated in only two villages, the church in 1701 sent a priest, Nicolas Foucault, to establish a mission. Foucault was killed by Koroa warriors near Natchez in 1702, leaving only a few coureurs de bois trading in the area (Faye 1943:646, 669).

Tonti had established a trading post named Aux Arcs on on his third visit to the Quapaw in 1686 (Murphy 1941:39; Faye 1943:636). The Quapaw already had bison and deer hides to trade and were taught to trap beaver (Baird 1980:26). When the priest Anastase Douay visited the Quapaw in 1687, he reported that they had "prodigious quantities of beaver and otter hides," and at Tonti's post at Osotouy (called Aux Arcs or Arkansas Post) the supply of peltries was so abundant that the Indians burned them in great heaps (Shea 1852:219). The Quapaw had French arms, utensils, and other merchandise that they had received in trade (Murphy 1941:37–38).

By this time, the British had pushed their trading efforts from the Carolinas to the Chickasaw villages on the east bank of the Mississippi River (Baird 1980:27–28), and the Quapaw were approached by British traders seeking slaves. In response, the Quapaw raided a Muskogean-speaking village on the upper Yazoo River in order to capture slaves to trade for British goods. Usually, the Quapaw traded bear, deer, and bison hides; beaver pelts; bear grease; and bison suet for guns, utensils, metal tools, and alcoholic beverages (Faye 1943:669).

By 1721, the French realized the importance of the Quapaw in retaining a hold on the route between New Orleans and Kaskaskia by serving as a bulwark against Chickasaw expansion. Soldiers were sent to garrison Arkansas Post on the Arkansas River, and 80 French colonists were sent to the area by the French government (Arnold 1991:9–17). By this time, the Quapaw once again had three villages, all located on the Arkansas River. The colonization scheme soon failed, and when another priest, Paul du Poisson, arrived in 1727, he found few Europeans (JR 67:319). Between 1732 and 1749, some 300 Quapaw warriors aided the French soldiers in making sporadic attacks on the Chickasaw (Arnold 1991:31–32, 101). By this time, Arkansas Post itself was often the victim of Osage raids from the west, and the Quapaw were its only real hope of defense (Faye 1943:673–674).

In anticipation of war with Britain, France decided to strengthen its military posture on the Mississippi. Marine captain Jean-Bernard Bossu, sent to inspect Arkansas Post in 1751, found the facility in decay, garrisoned by only seven French soldiers. The Quapaw had again been ravaged by disease (Faye 1943:709). Moreover, by this time the Quapaw were somewhat disillusioned with their alliance with the French, stemming primarily from their dissatisfaction with trade goods, which were usually of poor quality at high prices. Twenty deerskins would buy only one and one-half yards of stroud cloth; it took 60 hides to procure a gun. One hide bought only 10 bullets (McDowell 1958:1970, 2:415). There is much evidence that the Quapaw were shrewd traders.

In 1762 the century of French-Quapaw alliance came to an abrupt close when France ceded Louisiana to Spain. The Spaniards rebuilt the fort at the mouth of the Arkansas in 1769, renamed it Fort Carlos III, and garrisoned it with 50 men. The continued importance of the Quapaw in their strategic location is evidenced by the fact that they received 16 percent of all the goods distributed to Indians in New Spain. As early as 1768 the British had established a trading post called Ozark on the Mississippi across from the mouth of the White River, where the goods were better and the prices cheaper (Arnold 1991:108–111). Around 1774 the Quapaw sought an alliance with Britain, but since it would have been a diplomatic affront to Spain, the British were forced to refuse the offer (Baird 1980:42–43).

Following the Louisiana Purchase, the Quapaw remained on about the same footing with the United States as they had with France and Spain. Presents continued to be distributed, and Jefferson peace medals were given in the place of French or Spanish ones. The United States manned Arkansas Post under the name of Fort Madison.

Culture in the Seventeenth and Eighteenth Centuries

Although the Quapaw maintained their political independence, over the 150 years of European and American colonial rule, their culture changed greatly. When Marquette arrived in July 1673, he was met by Quapaw men who were naked save strings of beads in their noses and ears, and who had designs painted on their bodies (Joutel 1714:158). Besides European beads, the Quapaw already had procured hatchets and knives of European manufacture (JR 59:155; Hennepin 1880:186; Shea 1861:73). By the time Arkansas became United States territory, young Quapaw men were dressed in "blazing" calico shirts, scarlet blankets, feathers, and silver pendants, some with handkerchiefs on their heads like turbans (Nuttall 1980:89). Most were employed by the Europeans as warriors, hunters, guides, and boatmen. They were well armed with European firearms.

Subsistence

At the time of French contact the Quapaw were intensive cultivators who also gathered wild plants, hunted, and fished. The sexual division of labor followed the general pattern of the farming peoples in the Southeast. In 1723 the men hunted and the women did all the other work, including the dressing and painting of buffalo hides; "these skins are very highly praised among the other nations" (Mereness 1961:58). Bossu (1777:104–106) described the activities of women in 1751 as cooking, housekeeping, caring for children, transporting game animals, dressing hides, making clothing, and cultivating gardens. Men hunted, engaged in warfare, and held political and religious positions.

Marquette noted that the Quapaw had "an abundance of Indian corn" (JR 59:157). Beans and squash were other native cultigens. Tonti (1898:75) reported in 1683 that the Quapaw had already obtained chickens and peaches. Joutel (1714:154) mentioned persimmons, and both he and Douay agreed that they were served "watermelons." La Salle (1898:21–22) was given dried fruits and a drink made of crushed grapes. Bossu (1777:115) observed that flour was made from southern wild rice (*Zizaniopsis miliacea*). An 1819 visitor indicated that the nut of the water chinquapin was used in a soup and that wild potatoes were eaten (Nuttall 1980:106). Le Page du Pratz (1774:158) mentioned pawpaws. Meals were served on oval wooden platters or in clay pots.

The lowland riverine environment offered abundant resources for hunting and fishing. Mobility was great because of the use of dugout canoes, called by the French *pettyaugres*, made from cypress or poplar logs, to move over the territory easily traversed by water (Tonti 1898:75; Le Page du Pratz 1774:158). Joutel (1714:154) remarked in 1686 that they did not "want for fish of all sorts." Bossu (1777:106) described fish spearing in a slough from a dugout canoe. Waterfowl were present in great numbers in the autumn and were taken with the aid of live decoys by men who swam underwater and grabbed them from below. Ducks and geese were kept in pens until they were eaten (Bossu 1777:107). Bear and deer were important game animals and were sometimes hunted with the aid of dogs (Bossu 1771:99).

Bison, which abounded in the nearby Grand Prairie and the Saint Francis River area to the north (Le Page du Pratz 1774:155–157), were an important part of Quapaw subsistence until the end of the nineteenth century. One of the greatest changes in Quapaw hunting practices was the result of the introduction of horses. In 1751 Bossu (1982:47) described Quapaw bison hunting techniques: "Some Indians were armed with a strong lance. Others carried a long pole at the end of which was a very sharp crescent-shaped iron blade. Spurring his horse in pursuit of these animals the hunter reaches out and cuts the buffalo's hamstring with this instrument. Immediately Indians who follow on foot kill the fallen buffalo with blows of an axe or club." Quapaw made extensive use of the bison. Meat was smoked for later use, and suet was melted to form tallow cakes, a frequent item of European trade. Bedding, moccasins, and winter clothing were made from the hides; and buffalo wool was spun into thread used to make men's breechcloths and woven bags. Horns were used for spoons and powder horns, bones for punches and awls, and sinews for sewing and for making bowstrings. Storage vessels were gourds or cane basketry.

Seventeenth and eighteenth-century sources did not mention great seasonal hunts that took many people away from villages for extended periods of time; only small hunting parties were absent for long periods. But by November 1805 government trader John Treat (Carter 1934–1962, 13:280) wrote that the men of a village were hunting and would not be back until spring, probably reflecting increased presence of White men, participation in the fur trade, and local depletion of game.

Social Organization

An Omaha-type kin terminology, the common pattern for Dhegiha groups, was recorded (J.O. Dorsey in Riggs 1893:xx). During the late nineteenth century, the names of 21 patrilineal clans extant or remembered by the Quapaw were recorded, as well as the name of one larger grouping (*hą́ka*), which by analogy with the Omaha was apparently a moiety (table 1). Fletcher and La Flesche (1911:38, 68, 141) listed 14 Quapaw clan names (all of which were included in Dorsey's list) but also mentioned earth-maker and Kansa or wind clans, as well as an ice subclan; they concurred that the Quapaw were divided into moieties.

Structures

The Quapaw lived in cypress-bark-covered longhouses, some of which may have been round. Burning reeds furnished indoor light (Joutel 1714:155; Arnold 1991:14–15, 189). Council houses (probably also used for religious purposes) were located in the central part of each village. These were larger versions of the bark-covered longhouses and could hold several hundred people. Chiefs' structures were open-sided flat-roofed arbors or shades with floors

Table 1. Quapaw Social Divisions and Clan Names

Ancestral (*hą́ka*) Clans	
mą́ška, also *hą́ka ttą́ka*	Crawfish, also Big Hanga
wažį́ka	Small Bird
tte, also *hą́ka žíka*	Buffalo, also Little Hanga
ǫ́pʰą, *ǫ́pʰǫ*	Elk
xidá	Eagle
toxe	Reddish-yellow Buffalo
šǫ́ke, *šą́ke*	Dog (or Wolf)
Opposite Side Clans	
ho	Fish
níkiáta	(Unidentified)
kke	Turtle
ttížo	Tizho (matching Osage *ccížo*, a tribal division)
Other Clans	
ną́pątta	Deer
wasá	Black Bear
mątʰó	Grizzly Bear
žáwe	Beaver
mikkáxe	Star
ppétʰą	Crane
wakką́ta	Thunder Being
ttą́dą, also *ttą́ną*	Panther
wešá	Serpent
mi	Sun

Source: Dorsey 1897:229–230.

covered with fine rush mats (JR 59:153–154). The form and composition of Quapaw villages apparently remained the same throughout the colonial period, but the number and size of villages changed periodically, in part due to population decline caused by epidemic disease.

Clothing and Adornment

Men plucked their body hair and fashioned the hair on the head into scalplocks in which they intertwined rings, feathers, and beads. Women, before marriage, braided their hair into two plaits, which they wound around each ear. After marriage, they wore their hair in a single lock down the back.

Men wore hide robes, the women hide skirts. For ceremonial occasions, they colored their faces with red and black paint and wore feathers, as well as pendants of beads on ears and nose (Baird 1980:11–12; Joutel 1714:159–160).

Political Organization

One result of the shrinking population (table 2) was a change in the structure of authority. In the 1600s there were at least four chiefs, one in each village, who acted together only when national interests required it. Du Breuil (1943:55) recorded two chiefs in each of the three villages in 1783. Some time after 1721, the French elevated one chief to the position of principal chief or "medal chief" by giving him a peace medal (Smith 1951:350; Pittman 1906:83; Carter 1934–1962, 15:180). Henceforth, French governmental authorities conducted all business with the medal chief, who then was recognized by the Quapaw as their principal chief. The position soon merited special prerogatives (Baird 1980:37) and was inherited patrilineally.

Chiefs presided at tribal and war councils, were hosts to visitors, sponsored feasts, and were ritual leaders. Joutel (1714:158) related that the chief of Tourima had seven or eight attendants always with him. Chiefs were sometimes represented by orators (Bossu 1777:96). Each village also had a council consisting of male elders (Joutel 1714:157). Council seating was arranged by rank, with the chiefs and elders constituting the highest rank, the warriors next, and finally the common people (JR 59:155).

Warfare

The Quapaw participated in the general Southeast and Plains patterns of warfare. Warfare was fueled by revenge and retaliation for hostile acts against them and by the demands of the alliance with France. A war chief was mentioned by Bossu (1982:39). When going to war, after a feast, a council was called, presided over by a village

Table 2. Quapaw Population, 1682–1996

Year	*Population*	*Source*
1682	6,000	Faye 1943:636
1764	2,000[a]	H. Bouquet in Schoolcraft 1851–1857, 3:559
1780	2,500	Mooney 1928:9
1814	600[b]	Schermerhorn 1814:28
1829	500	P.B. Porter in Schoolcraft 1851–1857, 3:594
1834	476[c]	ARCIA 1835:296
1853	314[d]	ARCIA 1855:256
1871	225	ARCIA 1871:684
1883	205	J.O. Dorsey 1892
1891	204	J.O. Dorsey 1892
1910	231	U.S. Bureau of the Census 1915:15
1931	513	ARCIA 1931:51
1939	570	U.S. Department of the Interior. Bureau of Indian Affairs 1939:[12]
1950	720	U.S. Congress. House. Committee on Interior and Insular Affairs 1953:935
1956	1,190[e]	Baird 1980:210
1961	1,199	Baird 1994:523
1983	1,241[f]	Bureau of Indian Affairs 1983:13
1992	2,329[g]	Mary Moss, communication to editors 1992
1996	2,510[g]	Tiller 1996:529

Notes: [a]Identified as "Arkanses".
[b]Identified as "Arkensas, or Ozark".
[c]Includes 176 removed to Indian Territory and 300 temporarily with the Caddo on Red River.
[d]Those residing "West of Arkansas".
[e]Those who could trace ancestry to the 1890 roll.
[f]Residing on or adjacent to the former Quapaw Reservation.
[g]Tribal enrollment.

chief (Bossu 1771:99). The chief made a speech urging participation and obtained commitments to join the raid from those assembled by distributing rods, which probably promised the payment of a horse or other gift. A war club was painted red, the color of war, a feast was held to enlist allies, and a war dance was held. Women, eager to avenge lost kin, helped recruit warriors. Each volunteer consulted his guardian spirit, and the chief fasted to obtain propitious signs. By 1751, weapons used in warfare included not only wooden clubs, hatchets, and bows and arrows but also guns (Bossu 1771:103–104). Quapaw warriors first fired a volley with their guns, then threw them aside and charged with clubs (Nuttall 1980:96). Scalps and prisoners were taken. In early times, prisoners were adopted into families who had lost members in warfare, or they were tortured and burned to death (Bossu 1771:106). In later times they were traded as slaves.

Trade with Europeans

It was the enthusiastic entry into the trading economy that most changed Quapaw culture. Warfare became a service to the Europeans in trade for the annual distribution of presents. The object of hunting and raiding came to be the acquisition of hides, horses, and captives for trade. By 1769, Quapaws were bringing in both captives and horses from the "Cadodaquias, Paneise and Podoquias" (Caddos, Wichitas, and Plains Apaches) (Pittman 1906:83). They were also trading meat and crops to the soldiers garrisoned at the post and to settlers. The Quapaw enjoyed a virtual monopoly on all these trade items. Also, more and more in colonial times, the Quapaw turned to service as guides and boatmen. This service, which aided in European exploration and in the transportation of goods, was apparently acknowledged at the annual distribution of goods (Nuttall 1980:106).

Religion

European contact failed to induce significant change in Quapaw religion (Baird 1980:38). Although early Quapaw religious beliefs are not well known, Ouakantaque (*wakądake* 'Great Spirit') was the sacred dynamic force of the universe (JR 67:323; Bossu 1777:99). Other deities mentioned in early accounts included the sun (Bossu 1771:107), the moon (Mereness 1961:57; Bossu 1771:106), and thunder (Bossu 1771:107). Animal guardian-spirits included the eagle (Thompson 1982:29), whose feathers were considered sacred, as well as snake (Bossu 1771:107, Smith 1951:350, Nieberding 1976:132; Nuttal 1980:98)), buffalo, owl, and raven (Nuttal 1980:98). Medicine bundles at both the individual and village levels probably existed among the Quapaw (Carter 1934–1962, 20:30; Bizzel 1981:72).

Religious practitioners included both priests and shamans. The priests, like those of the Southeast tribes and the Pawnee, may have been associated with the celestial deities and with rites surrounding cultivation. In 1806 the Quapaw had four major seasonal festivals, each of which included prayer, thanksgiving, feasting, singing, and dancing (Ashe 1808:306–308). A dog sacrifice and feast were held at the time of corn planting (Nuttall 1980:106), then various harvest feasts and dances led up to the major Green Corn feast. Quapaw priestly religion differed from most of their seventeenth-century Lower Mississippi neighbors in that fire did not appear to be a major spiritual force. There was no special "temple" where a sacred fire or bones of the elite were kept (Swanton 1911:166); however, at least one large bark-covered structure was denoted a "sacred cabin" and was a place of sanctuary. Religious paraphernalia in the form of hide masks and "conic pelt caps" were kept in the largest of three bark-covered structures found in a village in 1819 (Nuttall 1980:246–247). Black drink, widely used by Southeast Indians, is mentioned only once in early literature, and then in a nonritual context (Bossu 1777:96).

The shamans were curers (Mereness 1961:57). Several curing societies to which shamans belonged were remembered in the late nineteenth century, including the Buffalo, Grizzly Bear, Panther, and Beaver societies (Dorsey 1894:393–394). As in other Siouan tribes, shamans were probably connected with animal guardian-spirits and were masters of conjury. Life-crisis rites were also a part of the ritual repertoire of the priests and shamans. The naming of children from a stock of names possessed by a priest and a small gift exchange at marriage were important ceremonies (Nuttall 1980:97), as were funeral rites and mourning, which lasted four days (Thompson 1982:65).

Music and dance were an important part of the ceremonial realm. Musical instruments included a drum made of a pottery vessel with a skin head stretched across its mouth, rattles, and wood and reed flutes (fig. 2). In 1687 Joutel (1714:160) noted that Quapaw dances were much the same as those of the Caddo whose villages he had passed through, but that some Quapaw warriors wore bison horn headdresses. Bossu (1771:97) wrote: "They have religious, physical, merry, ceremonious, warlike, pacific, nuptial, funeral, playful, hunting and lewd dances."

Calumet Dance

The Calumet Dance was mentioned much more frequently in the early colonial literature than in later chronicles (Bossu 1771:96, 108, 1777:94; La Salle 1898:19; Shea 1861:220; Joutel 1714:155–156). It was actually a lengthy ceremony that incorporated several dances relating to warfare, including the War Dance, the Discovery Dance, and the recounting of former deeds of valor (Strike-the-stick Dance). It was a ceremony of alliance (often in preparation for war) which incorporated fictive kinship as the basis for the alliance. One person was usually adopted as the "child" of another person from a different social group (clan, tribe, or, as in the case of the French, nationality). From the

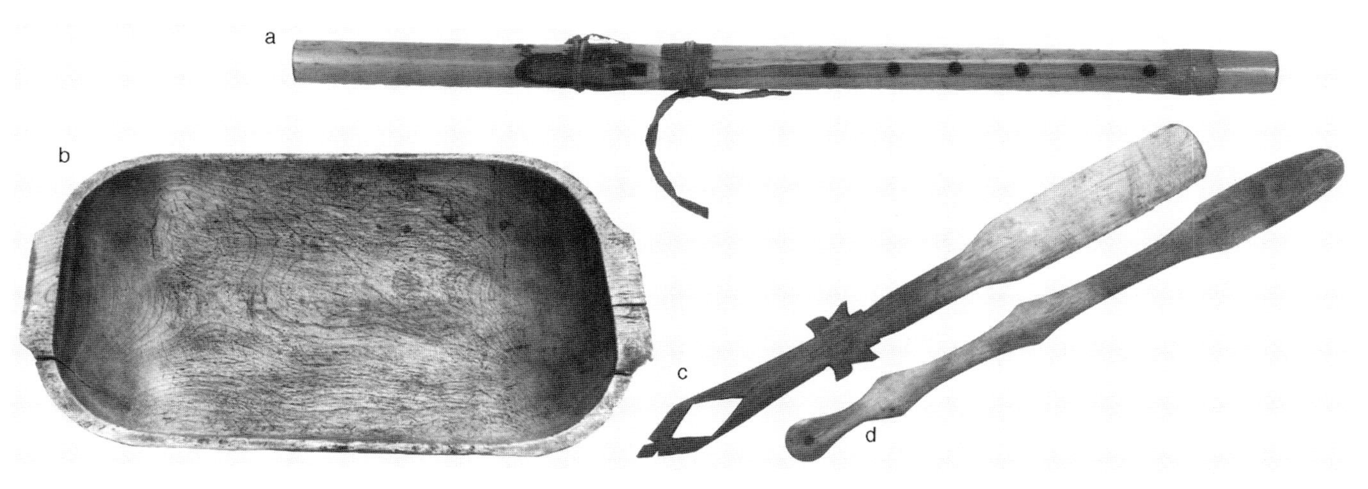

Smithsonian, Natl. Mus. of the Amer. Ind.: a, 10/2921; c, 16/9286 d, 1/9869; b, Ark. State U. Mus., State University: 563.

Fig. 2. Wooden objects. a, Flute. Collected by W.C. Barnard, Quapaw, Okla. before 1920; length 105 cm. b, Dough bowl made about 1880 and used by several generations of Quapaw families. Collected by Frances Baker, Quapaw, Okla., 1963–1965; length 48 cm. c, Perforated stirring paddle. Collected by W.C. Bernard, Quapaw, Okla., before 1930; length 52 cm. d, Stirring paddle. Collected by M.R. Harrington, Quapaw, Okla., before 1908; length 54 cm.

recorded words of both the French and Quapaw it is apparent that the early Calumet ceremonies established the French (especially in the identities of God, king, and the missionary priests) as fathers and the Quapaw as children. In this relationship, the Quapaws asked for goods in return for their loyalty. Basic to the alliance established by the Calumet ceremony was reciprocity expressed in gifts or service. Service might be required when, because they had become fictive kinsmen, individuals were obliged to participate in acts of revenge against their fictive kin's enemies.

With the arrival of Father Poisson in 1727 the ideal of reciprocity with Europeans began to break down somewhat because the priest, complaining that the Quapaw were interested only in receiving material goods rather than learning about Christianity, refused to participate in an entire Calumet ceremony. He allowed only the Discovery Dance, which he felt would require fewer gifts (JR 68:248–263). Nonetheless, when Poisson was killed by the Natchez in 1729, the Quapaw avenged his death as they would have that of a kinsman. By this time, the French had themselves instigated a ceremony to take the place of the Calumet Dance as a pledge of alliance. This was the presentation of peace medals to principal chiefs. Quapaw leaders were invited to visit the governor in New Orleans where the presentation was made (Faye 1943:712). The Quapaw accepted the new ceremony and maintained their allegiance to the French. When the Spaniards traded their medals for the French ones, the Quapaw, albeit reluctantly, shifted their allegiance to Spain.

History, 1804–1893

When the United States took control of Louisiana Territory in 1804, the Quapaw were residing in three villages on the Arkansas River (fig. 3). A fourth village located on the Mississippi at the mouth of the Arkansas was made up of Choctaw who had intermarried with the Quapaw. Each village had a chief, and one principal chief, Wapatesah, presided over the entire tribe (Nuttall 1980:101; Baird 1980:51). In 1805 a government "factory" (trading post) was established near the Quapaw villages, but it could not always stock the silver items, rifles, and scarlet cloth desired by the Quapaw, who in any case showed a preference for traders of French descent (Baird 1980:52).

The Quapaw were significant to the United States because of government plans to use their aboriginal lands to create reservations for other tribes, especially the Cherokee, Creek, and Choctaw, who were to be removed from their homelands east of the Mississippi.

Treaties of 1818 and 1824

The United States recognized the Quapaw claim to all the territory west of the Mississippi bounded by the Arkansas and Canadian rivers on the north and the Red River on the south, westward to an undetermined point. The Quapaw were quick to recognize the value of this land to the United States. In 1818, headed by Heckaton, then principal chief, the Quapaw entered into a treaty with the federal government (fig. 4), ceding 13 million acres of land and reserving two million acres for themselves (Kappler 1904–1941, 2:160–161) (fig. 1). The government granted the Quapaw perpetual right to hunt in the relinquished territory, made a gift of manufactured items valued at $4,000, and promised a perpetual annuity of $1,000 in goods and merchandise (Nuttall 1980:104). It was a good treaty for the Quapaw. They would stay in their homeland and be allowed to hunt in the large territory to which they had claimed ownership only for hunting purposes in the first place. The annuity demonstrated government commitment to perpetuate a reciprocal alliance (Baird 1980:56–60).

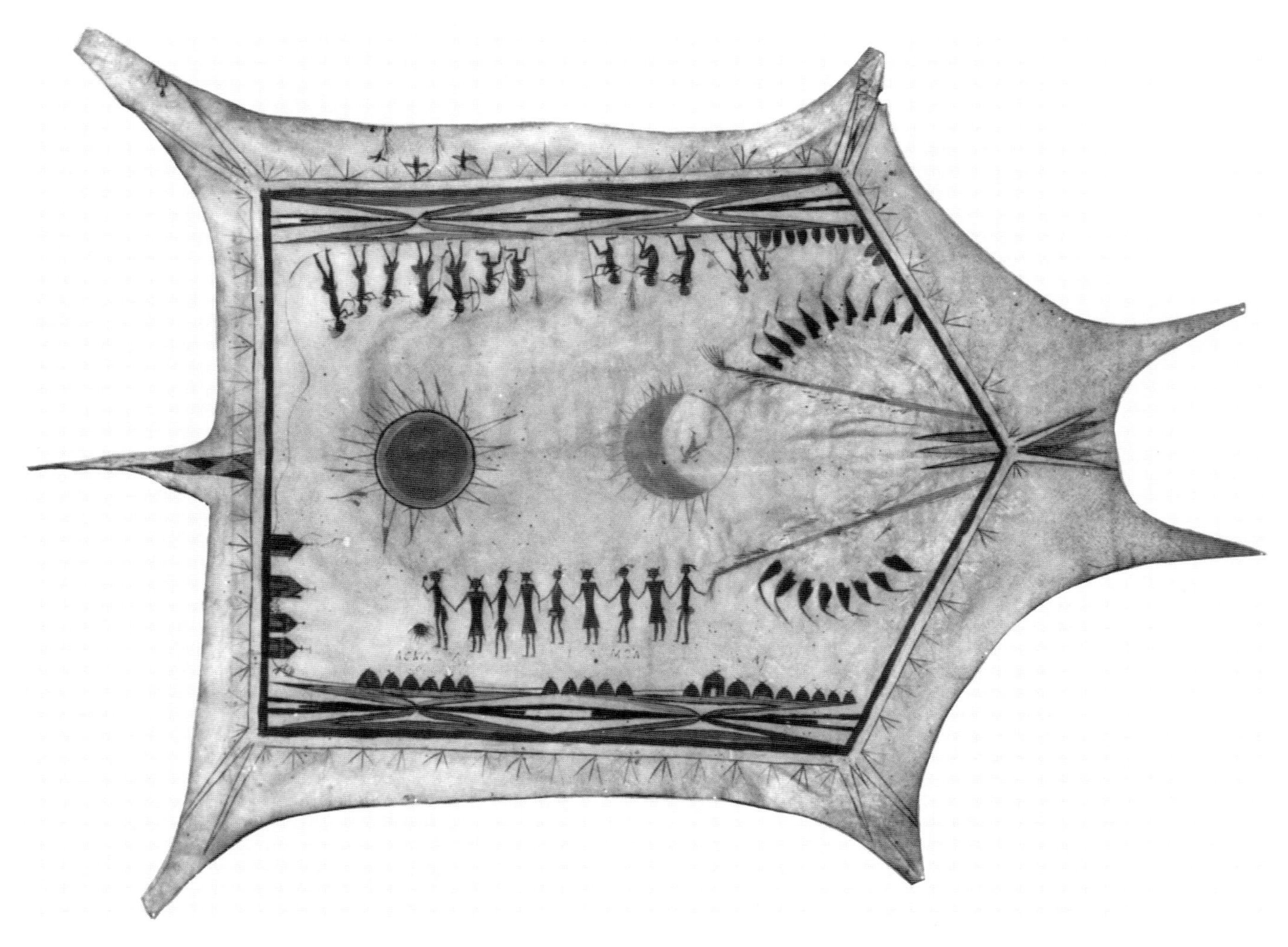

Musée de l'Homme, Paris: MH 34.33.7.

Fig. 3. Painted hide robe. The origin is established by the 4 words above the 3 sets of lodges: Ackansas, the French name for the Quapaw, and 3 Quapaw village names—Ouzoutouoüi (Osotouy), Touarimon (Tourima), and Ouqappa (Kappa) (Robert L. Rankin, communication to editors 1998) (Horse Capture 1993:56, 136). Dancers were placed over the villages; their leader holds a rattle, and a scalp is at their feet. A line connects the 2 groups on either side of the robe. The figures have black and red face paint, while in the middle of the robe are 2 feathered calumets, which were important in both war and peace (Arnold 1994; cf. Horse Capture 1993:54–56). French buildings at Arkansas Post, about 1730s–1740s, are pictured at the tail end of the robe (Arnold 1994:125, 1998). Collector unknown, probably acquired before 1789; length 189.4 cm.

On July 4, 1819, the new governor of Missouri Territory arrived on the Arkansas with a keelboat of presents for the first annual distribution. The Quapaw danced a Calumet Dance in return (Nieberding 1976:65). But what at first seemed to be a successful partnership much like that of the Quapaw and the French was soon to dissolve. In 1819 Arkansas Territory, with the capitol at Arkansas Post, was carved out of the Missouri Territory. White settlers flooded into the area, laying claim to lands the government had originally intended to use for Indian reservations. The government was persuaded to look farther westward for lands to be reserved for Indians.

Arkansas Territory White residents persuaded the government that the Quapaw wished to remove to the Red River and join the Caddo. In fact, neither tribe had any knowledge of the plan. To their surprise and dismay, the government asked the Quapaw in 1824 to sign a new treaty giving up all of the land they still held under the 1818 treaty and to join the Caddo. This turn of events was entirely illogical to the Quapaw. They had placed themselves in the kin position of children to a father in Washington, only to be betrayed by him. Proud of the Quapaw reputation of never having shed the blood of a White man, the chiefs relied on the sanctity of the original ceremonies of alliance, signed the new treaty on November 24, 1824, and threw their tribe on the mercy of the government (Kappler 1904–1941, 2:210–211). The plea for just treatment made by Chief Heckaton on this occasion was an eloquent one (Anonymous 1824; Baird 1980:67–68).

Quapaw "Trail of Tears"

In January 1826 the entire Quapaw tribe, consisting of 455 individuals, made the terrible winter march from Arkansas

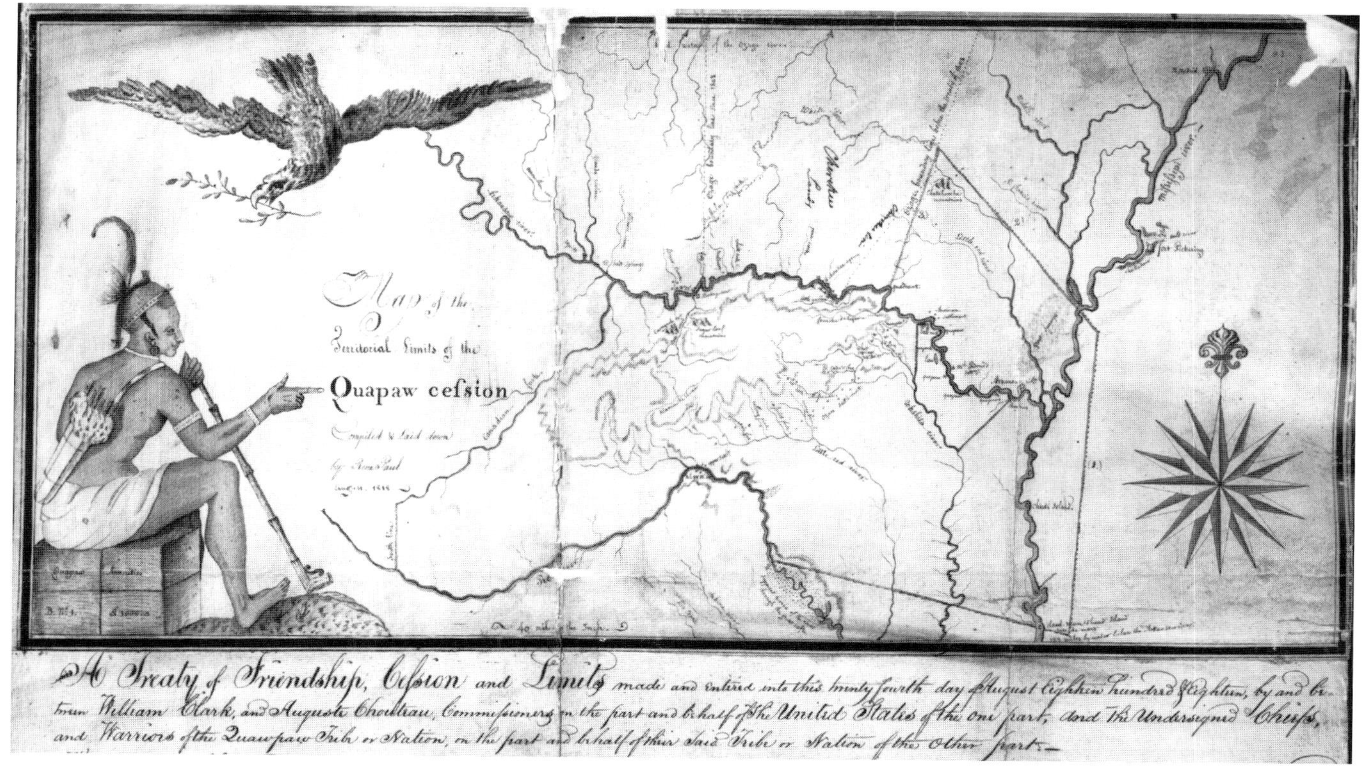

Nat. Arch.: Record Group II; Indian Treaty No. 96, M668:5.

Fig. 4. Map of the territorial limits of the Quapaw showing former hunting lands south of the Arkansas River, east to the Mississippi River, and west to the Canadian River. This map decorates the treaty of 1818 (Baird 1980:58). The Quapaw cessions were based on negotiations by William Clark and Auguste Chouteau, commissioners for the United States. Compiled and drawn by René Paul on the Quapaw–United States Treaty, August 24, 1818.

to the Caddo lands on the Red River in northwestern Lousiana, traveling in misery by day and dancing at night (Thompson 1982:29). This was the last time the entire tribe acted as a unit. After suffering from floods and epidemics, one-quarter of the Quapaws followed the half-French chief, Sarasin, back to lands in Arkansas that had been granted to 12 Quapaw individuals by virtue of their French ancestry. By October 1830 most of the Quapaw had moved back to Arkansas, living as squatters and foregoing their treaty annuities. The last 40 Quapaws left on the Red River, under Chief Heckaton, were finally unable to endure the floods to which their homes and fields were subjected and also returned to Arkansas. In December 1830 Heckaton traveled to Washington, where he proposed that the Quapaw buy land for themselves in Arkansas and send their young men to school. As Sarasin had requested three years before, Heckaton asked that the Quapaw be granted United States citizenship. In order to remain in their homeland, the Quapaw were prepared to assimilate into territorial society, cultivating small fields or hiring out as hunters or cotton pickers (Baird 1980:72–74).

Although Heckaton gained permission for the Quapaw to remain on the Arkansas land where they were squatting, two $1,000 warrants of annuity money never reached them there. For many years, what little money had actually reached the Quapaw had neither paid their debts nor supplied their needs, and they had often lived in destitution. So, when news came in 1833 that some of their earlier annuity money was in the hands of the Caddo agent on the Red River, 300 Quapaws under Sarasin trekked back to Caddo country. Only 50 of these rejoined the portion of the tribe that finally moved to the new reservation (Baird 1980:74–79).

Quapaw Reservation in Indian Territory

In September 1834 the 161 Quapaws led by Heckaton moved to a reservation in northeastern Indian Territory near the Shawnee and Seneca lands (fig. 1). Under a new treaty signed in 1833, the government paid the removal expenses and provided subsistence for one year; granted the Quapaw livestock, agricultural equipment, and firearms; authorized the employment of a farmer and a blacksmith for the benefit of the tribe; and allocated $1,000 per year for educational purposes. While the perpetual and limited annuities of earlier treaties were commuted to pay the tribe's debts, a new $2,000 annuity was authorized for 20 years (Kappler 1904–1941, 2:210–211).

In Indian Territory, the Quapaw once again established themselves in traditional villages and, the following spring, planted common fields of corn and pumpkins. They were joined by more than 100 Quapaws from the Red River when the first $2,000 annuity was paid (Baird 1980:78–83).

Two years later the Quapaw were forced to move again when it was discovered that they had been placed on the wrong land. After this move, they were not allowed to resettle in villages but were placed on individual homesteads. This caused some 100 members of Sarasin's band, representing one of the traditional villages, to leave once again (Farnham in Thwaites 1904–1907, 28:133). Although Sarasin himself returned to Arkansas, his band finally found a home on the western frontier on lands recently settled by the Creek tribe. By 1842, there were 250 Quapaws living where Little River empties into the Canadian River near present Holdenville, Oklahoma. They lived in small log cabins and sustained themselves by fishing and trapping for furs. They also hunted bison on the Plains and served the Creek Nation by providing a warrior buffer between them and the Comanche, Pawnee, and other western tribes (Baird 1980:85).

The Quapaw who remained on the reservation in northeast Indian Territory hunted bear, beaver, deer, and raccoon and also made an annual trek westward for bison hunts. They melted lead from outcroppings on the reservation into shot for their firearms (Nieberding 1976:90). Although settled in cabins on arable homestead acreages since 1839, Quapaw men did not want to farm (Baird 1980:86–87), an occupation traditionally perceived as women's work.

The tribe preserved the social units that corresponded to villages. Each was led by a chief, with one as principal chief. At Heckaton's death in 1842, Warteshe became principal chief (Baird 1980:89). Annuity payments were a time of festive tribal reunion when members of the Canadian River band returned to the reservation. In 1846, 264 Quapaws gathered at annuity times; in 1852, 314 were paid. By this time the agent reported that they were "wearing pantaloon, shoes, etc., in place of their former rude apparel" (Baird 1980:87–88). Another annual get-together was the Green Corn feast held in August. Aboriginal religious beliefs appear to have been strong, although there were some converts as soon as Roman Catholic priests begin to work among the Indians in Kansas and opened schools there. The Quapaw had long valued education, and they sent children to school whenever one was available.

During the 20 years after the move to Indian Territory, when the annuity was distributed, the divided tribe at least had annual reunions. After that time, more moved to the freer life on the Canadian River and soon less than half the tribe was actually in residence at their agency. This "home band," under Warteshe, was faced with the problem of maintaining themselves without an annuity. Experience had proven that their most valuable trade asset was land. By 1853, they were willing to sell the reservation and move westward once again where they could sustain themselves by hunting bison (Baird 1980:93–94). When this plan failed, Warteshe and seven others signed a treaty to sell all the reservation except an 80-acre homestead for each individual and 12 sections of common property; in return the government would make a $3,000 payment for noncompliance with former treaties. Although it was approved by the secretary of the interior, this treaty was never submitted to Congress for ratification.

Next, finding that some of the reservation was actually in Kansas, they offered to sell that land plus the eastern portion of the reservation. The Quapaw wanted to create a tribal capital fund out of which annuities could be paid. By 1859, the reservation again housed around 350 of the 400 members of the tribe in anticipation of the success of one of their attempts to raise a cash payment for distribution. In 1860, when the government presented them with a scheme by which the whole reservation would be preserved by allotting it to individuals, the Quapaw rejected it (Baird 1980:94–96).

Destitution and Economic Recovery

Quapaw tribal life was disrupted by the Civil War. After initially signing an agreement with the Confederacy, the Quapaw found themselves forced to flee to Kansas. Quapaw men then fought for the Union while the women and children suffered in refugee camps. The reservation in Indian Territory was devastated by troops from both sides of the conflict, and the end of the war found the Quapaw once more a destitute people. When they finally were able to sell their land in Kansas, they also sold the western portion of their reservation in Indian Territory to the Peoria tribe. The money was to have gone into a capital fund, but when it was finally paid in 1872, it was distributed, around $100 per capita (Baird 1980:107–110).

With the death of Warteshe in January 1865, Kihecahteda succeeded to the position of principal chief. After his death in autumn 1874 Tallchief (Louis Angel or *kahíkašte*) became the last hereditary chief of the tribe. In 1874, President Ulysses Grant's Peace Policy placed the Quapaw reservation in the charge of Quakers; in response, Tallchief abandoned the reservation to settle with many of his band among the Roman Catholic Osage (Baird 1980:102, 114–116). By 1876, half the tribe (115 individuals) were among the Osage and by 1877, two-thirds of the Quapaw, representing two of the traditional village units, were on the Osage reservation. In 1883, a federal inspector reported that "the [154] Quapaws have intermarried with the Osages, live in comfortable houses, cultivate small patches and are making a living" (Anonymous 1883).

Those left on the Quapaw reservation had a more difficult time. In 1879, there were only 38 Quapaws holding a reservation of 56,685 acres. Despite government schemes to settle other Indian tribes on the Quapaw reservation, the home band refused to give up the land without adequate compensation. By the 1880s, around 600 acres were leased to White agriculturalists. Many more were used as grazing land, for which the Quapaw charged a tax, for cattle driven up the Texas Trail to the railhead in Kansas (Baird 1980:123). The bison had been exterminated from the southern Plains by the mid-1870s, and the younger generation had given up most subsistence hunting.

Allotment

In their attempt to retain their reservation lands, the home band sent Alphonsus Valliere to Arkansas in 1883 to invite Quapaw descendents there to relocate to the reservation. Several families did so, and the reservation population nearly doubled (Baird 1980:128–129). They also began the practice of adopting "homeless" members of other tribes. The addition of several people of Miami, Cherokee, Peoria, "New York Indian" (Seneca, Tuscarora, Oneida, St. Regis, Onondaga, Cayuga, Stockbridge, Brotherton, or Munsee), and Wyandot descent further swelled the reservation population. Seeing, by this move, the determination of the home band to retain the reservation, and valuing their Quapaw citizenship, a number of Quapaw began to return from the Osage reservation. By 1889, a tribal roll of those living on the reservation who could receive grazing per capita payments included 116 names. The roll swelled to 193 in 1890 and 215 by 1893. The return to the reservation was precipitated, in part, by the passage of the Dawes Severalty Act of 1887, according to which the government proposed to allot Indian land, 80 acres per person. Remaining Indian lands were to be opened to homesteaders or sold. Realizing the real value of their land and, by this time, not wishing to relinquish any of it, the Quapaw tribal council meeting of March 23, 1893, was attended by all but four adult members of the tribe. In a move unprecedented by any other tribe, they voted to allot their land among themselves before the government did it arbitrarily. Each enrolled member chose 200 acres for an allotment and, in 1894, each received an additional 40 acres so that the entire reservation would be allotted. The move was ratified by Congress in 1895, and 236 fee patents to the land were issued in 1897 (Baird 1980:140–145).

Culture, 1870s–1990s

During the 1870s and 1880s the Quapaw maintained their ritual calendar, including their annual Green Corn ceremony, Stomp Dances, and other celebrations (Anonymous 1883a; McCoontz 1937). For Stomp Dances, men went hunting on Friday and Saturday and women cooked the meat all night "in great iron kettles" for a feast on Sunday. The dance itself took place on Sunday night (Valliere and Valliere 1937:34; Brotherton 1937:395). Another kind of Stomp Dance was held in connection with the Peyote religion (fig. 5).

George Lane (Watesha) was the "tribal doctor," a shaman who cured the sick. Tallchief, spiritual leader of the tribe, claimed the hereditary right to preside at weddings and funerals and to bestow upon children their Quapaw names (Nieberding 1976:125). Tallchief returned from Osage country periodically to perform these ceremonies (Baird 1980:130).

Okla. Histl. Soc., Oklahoma City: 7481.

Fig. 5. Stomp Dance, held in the morning after a Peyote meeting. Photograph by Joseph Andrew Shuck, Seneca, Mo., about 1903.

Religion

By 1894 "all Quapaws by blood" were nominally Roman Catholic (Nieberding 1976:134). However, shortly after 1895, the Peyote religion was introduced to the Quapaw by John Wilson (Moonhead), a member of the Caddo tribe of Caddo, Delaware, and French descent. Wilson was a shaman and had been a successful Ghost Dance leader. His version of Peyote rites was based on a vision during a trance in which he believed he was transported to the moon. Wilson's Big Moon Peyote ceremony was adopted by many Quapaws, who built a permanent round house for ritual use. Quapaw Peyotism (fig. 6) developed into a unique version of the religion. The round house altar was a concrete slab with an outer apron raised into a crescent moon that opened to the west, the altar representing the grave of Jesus Christ. A straight west-east line represented the road Wilson had traveled when transported by peyote to the moon. The line pierced three hearts reflecting Roman Catholic influence: the "heart of the world," the "heart of Jesus," and the "heart of goodness." Peyote was placed on the "heart of goodness" during a meeting. Around the "heart of Jesus" was a circle representing the sun, a messenger to God. The road was intersected near the top with another line representing the "road across the world," thus forming a cross. On the apron of the altar were seven lines representing seven magic star groups (or the seven days of the week) and five lines which, when added to the seven, symbolized the 12 appearances of the moon in a year. Representations of the footprints of Jesus (sometimes also considered footprints of Wilson) were located on either

left, Okla. Histl. Soc., Oklahoma City:1989; Smithsonian, Natl. Mus. of the Amer. Ind.: top right, 1/9965, bottom right, 1/9855.

Fig. 6. Peyotism. left, Church at Devil's Promenade (now the tribal grounds) near Quapaw, Okla., about 1920s. Photographer not recorded. top right, Decorated feather worn in the hair; length 35 cm. bottom right, Gourd rattle with beaded handle; length of handle 14 cm. Both items were used in the rituals of the Peyote religion. Collected by M.R. Harrington, Quapaw Agency, Okla., before 1908.

side of the "heart of goodness." The ritual consisted of a sweatbath, an all-night meeting incorporating the consumption of an infusion or "tea" made from peyote buttons, smoking, speeches, singing and drumming, and a feast at noon of the next day (C.V. Wilson 1978:14–15, 23–30).

The first Quapaw convert and disciple of the Peyote religion, which became formalized in Oklahoma as the Native American Church, was Victor Griffin. From the 1920s to the 1940s he and John Quapaw led a congregation made up, for the most part, of the full bloods of the tribe.

It is probable that John Wilson also brought the Ghost Dance when he introduced the Peyote ritual. Both the Ghost Dance and the Peyote religion emphasized traditional customs, such as men wearing their hair in braids. Shirts for the Ghost Dance were made of flour sacks sewn with sinew, and the dance was at first preceded by smoking ceremonies, and later, by a Peyote meeting (Nieberding 1976:146–148).

Economy

At allotment, the full-blood Quapaws, those least likely to wish to farm, had been granted allotments of prairie land in the western part of the reservation, while the mixed-blood and adopted Quapaws had taken the rich farmland near the Spring River on the east. The full bloods had been able to sustain themselves through cattle leases. However, the factor that had motivated the Quapaw to divide their land in severalty was knowledge of the existence of rich quantities of lead and zinc ore on the reservation. Nearby Joplin, Missouri, had been a mining center since 1874 (Baird 1980:149). In 1897, lead deposits were discovered on the western portion of the reservation. These ore veins were located on the allotments of full bloods, who then became the wealthiest members of the tribe. By 1914 five million dollars worth of lead and zinc concentrates had been mined on the reservation. From 1923 to 1943 royalties from mining totaled $14,689,599, peaking in 1926 with a one-year total of $1,679,863 (Baird 1980:183).

Because of their participation in the Native American Church, the full-blood Quapaws were able to make a cultural adjustment to wealth that conformed to the prevailing standards of White conduct while they remained internally true to Indian tradition. The Native American Church emphasized generosity (Lanternari 1963:82), making it the responsibility of the more fortunate Quapaws to share with others. They made "loans" to the unfortunate, and their homes were always open to those in need. They hosted elaborate funerals, memorial gatherings, and holiday celebrations, paying for all food, prizes, and expenses.

Mining royalties were paid by the private mining companies that leased Quapaw allotments. During the 1930s, some mines were closed due to a reduction in the amount of ore found and to the Depression. Both mining royalties and Quapaw income from other rental property decreased. By the late 1930s, both the federal government and the state of Oklahoma were allowed to impose taxes on Quapaw income. Although some additional income was secured by the federal government through suits against mining companies for unpaid royalties and noncompliance with leasing agreements on restricted allotments, by the mid-1950s, the heyday of the wealthy full-blood families was over. Royalty income from lead and zinc mining totaled only $280,972 in 1956, and by 1960, there was none (Baird 1980:211).

In 1956, a tribal Business Committee was elected to distribute over $927,000 received from a suit for recompense for lands ceded in 1818. The money was distributed to the 1,190 Quapaws by blood who could trace their ancestry to the 1890 rolls (Baird 1980:210). The tribal Business Committee took over tribal economic affairs, including lands and leases, from the Bureau of Indian Affairs. It assumed responsibility for 528 acres purchased in the tribe's name in 1937, leasing some as agricultural land and improving the 40-acre tract set aside as the council ground (Baird 1980:211). In the 1980s, a business manager and staff were employed to handle tribal financial affairs. General revenue was generated by a tribally owned bingo operation and a convenience store east of Miami, Oklahoma.

Tribal Government

Although Tallchief had become hereditary chief in 1874, he had moved to Osage country that same year (Baird 1980:114). In an effort to persuade all Quapaws to abandon the reservation and assimilate with the Osage, in 1878 the agent declared Tallchief to be principal chief of the tribe. The home band at that time, led by John Hotel, refused to accept Tallchief as principal chief (Baird 1980:118). The government acquiesced and continued to deal with the chief of the home band, first John Hotel, then Charley Quapaw. On July 19, 1892, the tribe assembled and elected John Medicine as chief, creating a position of second chief for Charley Quapaw. With the election of Peter Clabber in 1894, leadership shifted to those Quapaws who had once resided among the Osage, although a member of the home band, John Quapaw, was selected second chief. This shift was also reflected in four tribal positions called councilors (Baird 1980:137, 142).

During the 1880s the tribal council had spoken for all the tribe; but after allotment, and with the rise of cohesiveness among full-blood participants in the Native American Church and the election of Peter Clabber (a full-blood Quapaw), the council began to mirror the wishes of the full bloods. Since Tallchief had no son, the position of hereditary chief did not continue after his death in 1918, although his daughter, Maude Supernaw, continued to confer Quapaw names until her death in 1972. Thus, after 1918, both political and religious leadership rested in the hands of the elected chief. Under Peter Clabber, support of Roman Catholicism continued, but after his death in 1926, an anti-Catholic sentiment emerged. The next two chiefs, John Quapaw (1927–1928) and Victor Griffin (1929–1958), both full bloods, were Peyote leaders. This traditional chief and council system was strong enough to resist tribal government reorganization under the Oklahoma Indian Welfare Act of 1936. It continued to work in the interest of the wealthy full bloods through the 1940s. When a judgment regarding who was eligible for the recompense payment was to be made in 1956, the legal authority of Chief Griffin was challenged by members of the tribe with less than one sixty-fourth Quapaw blood. Finding no written record empowering the traditional leadership to speak for the tribe, the Bureau of Indian Affairs ruled that the Quapaws were without a recognized governing body. A Business Committee consisting of chairman, vice-chairman, secretary-treasurer, and four council members was elected to conduct tribal affairs, with Robert Whitebird, a full blood, as chairman (Baird 1980:209–210). The committee was able to reject termination of the tribe and, in 1970, extend the favorable prerogatives on restricted allotments until 1996.

During the 1970s and 1980s, the Business Committee contracted directly for several federal programs previously administered by the Bureau of Indian Affairs. They also ran grant-related social service and educational enterprises. Following Whitebird's retirement in 1968, chairmen were elected for two-year terms. Elections and annual general tribal council (Business Committee) meetings, open to any member of the tribe, were held at the Fourth of July powwow.

Change and Persistence

During the upheaval of the removals, starting in the 1820s, most of the Quapaw lifeways that had been practiced in the villages on the Arkansas River were lost. The introduction of Peyotism led to the setting aside of still more aspects of culture considered antithetical to that religion. It is probable that the Green Corn ceremony was abandoned at that time. By 1891, a yearly homecoming picnic, held in June or July, had replaced the Green Corn ceremony as a time of tribal integration. In the 1920s, the rich full-blood

The Thomas Gilcrease Inst. of Amer. Hist. and Art, Tulsa, Okla.: 9637.33.

Fig. 7. Cornhusk doll with dried cornsilk hair. Made by Anna Mae Quapaw McKibbin for her granddaughter in 1959. Height 15.2 cm.

Native American Church members made this celebration, by then called a powwow, a time of lavish hospitality. In 1927, 2,000 Quapaws and visiting Indians camped at the powwow. Alex Beaver spent $5,000 "running a table" where anyone could eat free of charge. There were war and stomp dances, a "buffalo hunt," horse and mule races, foot races, and the traditional football game formerly played at the Green Corn ceremony (Nieberding 1976:12). Long after the Quapaw lost their incomes from mining royalties, the Fourth of July three-day powwow remained one of the major summer events among the tribes of northeast Oklahoma. A Powwow Committee planned throughout the year for the event which included a meeting of the general council, intertribal dancing (fig. 8), giveaways, communal meals, and sometimes rodeos, Indian ball games, and golf tournaments. Hundreds of participants and thousands of spectators filled the Beaver Springs Park tribal grounds to capacity each year.

At least since colonial times, amalgamation of other Indians and non-Indians into the tribe through adoption and marriage has been a fact of Quapaw history. By the 1800s, some tribal members were of recorded or unrecorded Michigamea, Choctaw, Caddo, Osage, or French ancestry. Adoptions at the time of allotment and intermarriage with members of other nearby groups such as the Cherokee and Ponca accounted for a continuing decrease in percentage of Quapaw ancestry. By 1961, only 20 percent of tribal members were more than one-quarter Quapaw. In 1999 only one "pureblood" Quapaw survived. There were no Quapaw speakers. About one-quarter of the approximately 2,000 members of the tribe lived within 30 miles of Quapaw, Oklahoma (Henry Ellick, personal communication 1989).

Relations with the Osage remained close, but Quapaw and Osage culture and cultural activities always remained distinct, as, for example, the distinctive Peyote rituals of the two tribes. Both tribes, along with the Seneca-Cayuga and Shawnee, came under the jurisdiction of the Neosho Agency in 1851. In 1871, the Quapaw Agency was established, eventually including the Quapaw, Miami, Peoria, Ottawa, Wyandot, Modoc, and Seneca-Cayuga. These small tribes offered mutual support for cultural activities, even though these usually remained distinct by tribe. Quapaw support of the tribal ceremonies of the Shawnee and Seneca-Cayuga, often by clan, continued through the 1990s.

In 1985, Pine Bluff, Arkansas, and the Arkansas Endowment for the Humanities sponsored a Quapaw symposium in which over 50 members of the tribe discussed and demonstrated traditional beliefs and arts. Quapaw religious belief and ritual continued strong in the observance of funerals and mourning feasts. The tribe designated an official to respond to the Native American Graves Protection and Repatriation Act of 1990 (fig. 9).

Synonymy†

The Quapaw designation for themselves and the source of their modern name is *okáxpa*, which in the late twentieth century was pronounced [ogáxpa] and [ugáxpa] (Robert L.

†This synonymy was written by Douglas R. Parks.

left, U. of Okla. Lib.: Western Hist. Coll., Norman; right, U. of Ark., U. Mus., Fayetteville: 850023.

Fig. 8. Powwows. Annual Quapaw powwow at Devil's Promenade, Quapaw, Okla. Prize money drew dancers from many tribes. left, 1949 Fancy Dance or War Dance contest winners Charles Chibitty (Comanche, a World War II "Code Talker"), first prize winner, and his daughter Pam, and Tehi Secundine (Shawnee), Chibitty's brother-in-law, winner of the second prize. The beaded harnesses and breechcloths as well as feather crests and bustles were standard costume in Okla. in this era. right, Women elders. front row, left to right: Maude Supernaw, Mary Redeagle, Anna Quapaw McKibben, Alice Gilmore, Fanny Goodeagle Richards, and unidentified. Photographed probably 1965.

top, Office of the Secretary of State, State of Ark.; U. of Ark., U. Mus., Fayetteville, center and bottom.

Fig. 9. Late 20th century. top, Presenting the Quapaw flag to be flown at the state capitol for the 150th anniversary of the state of Arkansas. left to right, Tribal princess Deana Rae Hughey, Chief Jess McKibben, Gov. William J. Clinton, tribal representative Carrie V. Wilson, and Secretary of State William McCuen. The Quapaw representative to Arkansas requests tuition waivers for Quapaws at state universities, organizes events pertaining to the tribe, presents programs about the tribe to institutions and organizations, and is the tribal official handling activities for the Native American Grave Protection and Repatriation Act (NAGPRA). Photograph by Hubert Smith, 1986. center and bottom, Participants and audience during a lecture relating to NAGPRA. center, left to right: Edna McKibben Wilson, Maude Quapaw Smith, Carrie V. Wilson, Judge Morris Sheppard Arnold, United States Court of Appeals, Eighth Circuit, James Imbeau, Olin Gokey. bottom, Audience, including James Moore and Mary Harpy, listening to Judge Arnold lecture on "The Quapaw and the Old World Newcomers, 1673–1804." center and bottom, Photographs by Sara Clinard, tribal headquarters near Quapaw, Okla., 1998.

Rankin, personal communication 1990). The name is generally said to mean 'downstream', a reference to the location of the Quapaw relative to the other Dhegiha tribes (Hodge 1907–1910, 2:333), and at the end of the nineteenth century it was said to be associated perhaps with a questionable term *káxpa* 'south wind' (Dorsey 1891b). It is not certain that the name derives from forms with either meaning; its etymology, in fact, is obscure (Robert L. Rankin, personal communication 1990).

During the seventeenth and eighteenth centuries these people were most commonly designated as the Akansas or Arkansas, but were also frequently known by one of their village names, sometimes termed nations, indicating their former autonomy. After 1800, Quapaw, the name of one village, became the predominant tribal designation.

Quapaw

In the seventeenth and early eighteenth centuries, the French used this name to designate one of four Quapaw villages, recording it variously as Kappa, 1687 (Joutel in Margry 1876–1886, 3:451), Kapaha, 1682 (Le Métairie in French 1875:21), Kappas, 1721 and 1774 (Charlevoix 1761, 2:246; Le Page du Pratz 1774:304), Kappa Akansea, 1700 (Gravier in Shea 1861:125), Cappas, 1700 (Pénigaut in French 1869:62), Capas, 1713 (Bourgmont in Norall 1988:105), Ougapa, 1722 (La Harpe in Margry 1876–1886, 6:365), and Ogojpas, 1783 (Du Breuil in 1943:55).

Later renditions in the nineteenth century, when the name began to be used for the more inclusive tribal designation, occur in two variants: those like the contemporary tribal name that lack the initial vowel of the native Quapaw form, as in most of the earlier French examples; and those that reflect the initial vowel of the Quapaw word. Exemplifying the former are Gappa, 1827 (cited in Hodge 1907–1910, 2:336), Kappaws (Lynd 1864:58), and Kwapa (Powell 1881:xvii). Many of these examples, which date to the first half of the nineteenth century or earlier, reflect the modern spelling with an initial qu: Quawpas, 1700 (Iberville in French 1869:62), Qawpaw (Pike 1811:map), Quapaws, 1821 (Nuttall 1980:70; Schoolcraft 1851–1857, 3:537), Quappas (Gallatin 1836:126; Schoolcraft 1851–1857, 4:310), Quapois (Whipple 1856:16), Quppas (Schoolcraft 1851–1857, 5:98), Querphas (NYCD 1853–1887, 7:641), and Quappaws (Shea 1861:76). Examples that are clearly misprints of these forms are Wiapes and Wyapes (Jefferys 1761, 1:143, 144) and Gnapaws (Keane in Stanford 1878–1885, 6:513).

Examples of renditions that retain the initial vowel of the native form are Ocapa (Sibley 1806:85); O-guah-pa

(Nuttall 1980:94); O-guah-pah (Balbi 1826:56); Oo-yapes, Oo-gwapes, and Ouguapas (Shea 1855:447, 449); O-qua-pas (Gale 1867:202); and Ogoh pæ (Fontenelle 1885:77). A misprint of these variants is Onyapes (McKenney and Hall 1848–1850, 3:81). At least two recorded examples have an initial a rather than an o: Aquahpa and Aquahpah (Adair 1775:269, 320); and A-qua-pas (Hadley 1882). Moreover, several early linguistic recordings have an initial u (a phoentic variant of the phoneme *o*): Ugakhpa (Dorsey 1878–1880:129), U-gá-qpa-qti and Ukaqpaqti 'real Quapaw' (Dorsey 1883b, 1891b), and Ugaχ-páχti (Gatschet 1884–1888, 1:30). The forms that translate as 'real Quapaws' are nineteenth-century designations apparently used after all the Quapaw villages coalesced to distinguish either the descendants of the original village of that name or perhaps those Quapaws who did not unite with other tribal groups.

Various tribal designations for the Quapaw are based on the Quapaw name for themselves. In the closely related Dhegiha languages the name is Osage *okáxpa* (Robert L. Rankin, personal communication 1990), Kansa *ogáxpa* (Dorsey 1883c, retranscribed), Omaha *ugáxpa* (Dorsey 1880a; Fletcher and La Flesche 1911:101; retranscribed), and Ponca *ugáxpa* ([ukáxpa]) (Parks 1988) and *ugáxpe* (Howard 1965:134). In these languages the name is generally interpreted to mean 'downstream people', a folk etymology based on its partial similarity to the word *kaxá* 'stream'; however, the name has no known etymology (Robert L. Rankin, personal communication 1988).

Among Caddoan languages Pawnee *ú·kahpa* and Caddo *ukwáhpah* are borrowings of the same name (Parks 1965–1990; Wallace L. Chafe, personal communication 1992). So also are examples in various Algonquian languages, for example, Shawnee *hoka?pa* (Voegelin 1938–1940, 10:447), Delaware *úkahpa* (Ives Goddard, personal communication 1992), and Peoria *ka·hpa* (David Costa, personal communication 1991). The same form also occurs in Muskogean languages, for example, Choctaw Okahpa (Byington 1915:293) and Creek Ŭ-kăh-pû (Grayson 1885).

Arkansas

During the seventeenth and eighteenth centuries the French, and later in the eighteenth century the Spaniards, knew the Quapaw by forms of the modern name Arkansas, cited sometimes as a village name and also as the name of the river upon which it was located (Pénigaut in McWilliams 1953:34; Iberville 1702 in Nasatir 1952, 1:8). Although the native form of the name—if in fact it was a Quapaw name—was not recorded in the late nineteenth or twentieth centuries, it is Siouan in origin and related to the Kansa name for themselves, *kką́·ze*, a tribe with whom the Quapaw were frequently associated. The form written variously as Akansa and Arkansa apparently represents a borrowing by the French of the Illinois form akansa, presumably *aka·nsa*, which is itself a borrowing from Siouan and has added to it the standard *a-* formative of Illinois and Fox that occurs in tribal names (Ives Goddard, personal communication 1992).

There are two nearly identical variants of the earliest renditions of the name. Most common are ones lacking an r in the initial syllable, examples of which are Akansas, 1682 and 1721 (La Salle in French 1875:21; Charlevoix 1761, 2:249), Acansas, 1699 (Iberville in Margry 1876–1886, 4:121), Accanceas, 1687 (Joutel in French 1846–1853, 1:176), Akansea, 1673 (Marquette autograph map in Tucker 1942:pl. 5), Akanscas and Acanseas, 1699 (St. Cosme in Shea 1861:47, 65), Akanzas (Bossu 1771:70), Acanssa and Accanssa, 1714 (Bourgmont in Norall 1988:105), Akancas (Tonti in French 1846–1853, 1:60), A Kancea and Accances (Bacqueville de la Potherie 1753, 1:map, 2:222), Akamsians (Boudinot 1816:125), and Akinsaws (Trumbull 1851:185). Variants with r in the initial syllable are exemplified by Arkansas, 1700 (Pénigaut in Margry 1876–1886, 5:402; Le Page du Pratz 1774:304), Alkansas and Atcansas, 1720 (La Harpe in Margry 1876–1886, 6:241, 311; the latter form probably a transcriptional error), Arcanças (de Montigny Dumont 1753, 1:134), Arkensas and Arcansa (Sibley 1806:85, 138), Arkensas (Schermerhorn 1814:28), and Arkansaws (Pike 1811:168).

The abbreviation of this name in Mississippi Valley French was Arks, which sometimes occurs as Arc Indians and, in English translation of French *arc* 'bow', Bow Indians (Schoolcraft 1851–1857, 3:537). The French expression "les Montagnes aux Arks," meaning the Mountains of the Arkansas [Indians], was interpreted in English as Ozark Mountains (Nicollet 1839), and by extension the name Osark or Ozark was cited as a tribal designation of the Quapaw (Nuttall 1980:94; Schermerhorn 1814:28).

An anomalous historical form, Savansa, was recorded in 1684 as an alternate for Akansa, perhaps a transcriptional error (Tonti in Margry 1876–1886, 1:616).

Other village names

• TOURIMA A second eighteenth-century village name also used as a tribal designation appears as Tourimans or Tourimas, 1700 (Iberville in French 1869:62; Pénigaut in McWilliams 1953:34), Torima and Torimas, 1714 and 1721 (Bourgmont in Norall 1988:105; Charlevoix in 1761, 2:246), Tualinsori, 1783 (Du Breuil 1943:55), Imahans, 1718 (La Harpe in Margry 1876–1886, 6:261). In the nineteenth century the name was recorded phonetically as Tí-u-á-d¢i-ma^{n} (Dorsey 1897:229), and retranscribed *ttí oádimą*. Although *ttí* means 'lodge', the etymology of the remainder of the form is unknown (Robert L. Rankin, personal communication 1990). I'ma, recorded as the Caddo and Yatasi name for the Quapaw, is apparently derived from this village designation (Gatschet 1884:82).

• OSOTOUY The name of a third seventeenth- and eighteenth-century village, Osotouy, occurs in the following forms, which probably reflect at least two dialectal variants: Atotchasi, 1673–1674 (Marquette autograph map in Tucker 1942:pl. V); Osotonoy, Assotoué, Ozotoues, and Ossoztoues, 1687 (Tonti in French 1846–1853, 1:60, 71, 82, 83); Otsoté, Otsotchaué, and Otsotchove, 1687 (Joutel in Margry 1876–1886, 3:444, 463; in French 1846–1853, 1:176); Ossoteoez (Hennepin 1698, 2:44); Souchitiony and Aesetooue, 1702 (Iberville in Margry 1876–1886, 4:429, 601); Sittëoüi, 1700 (Gravier in Shea 1861:131); Zautooüys and Zautoouys, 1721 (La Harpe in Margry 1876–1886, 6:357, 365); and Sotouis and Sothouis (Jefferys 1761, 1:134, 144); Southois, Otsotchoué, and Ossotteoez (Charlevoix 1763:307, 1866–1872, 4:108); and Osutuys, 1783 (Du Breuil 1943:55). Renditions in the nineteenth century are illustrated by Ossotoues, Ozotheoa, and Sothoues (McKenney and Hall 1848–1850, 3:81, 82). In the late nineteenth century the name was recorded phonetically in two forms: U-zu′-ti-u′-hi (Dorsey 1883b) and U-zu′-ti-u′-wĕ (Dorsey 1897:229), which in modern retranscription are *ozóttióhi* and *ozóttiowé*, respectively. Both variants, perhaps reflecting obsolete final positional elements, mean 'they dwell in a tree-covered bottomland'.

• TONGIGUA The fourth village name of the seventeenth and eighteenth centuries appears as Tongenga, 1688 (Tonti in French 1846–1853, 1:71); Tongigua, Tonguinga, 1687 (Joutel in Margry 1876–1886, 3:457); Tonginga, Tonningua, 1687 (French 1846–1853, 1:179); Touginga, 1722 (La Harpe in Margry 1876–1886, 6:365); Topingas, 1721 (Charlevoix 1761, 2:246); Dogenga (McKenney and Hall 1848–1850, 3:81); and Thonges (Hamilton 1885:48). In the late nineteenth century this name was recorded phonetically as Ta^{n}-wa^{n}-jiʞa (Dorsey 1883b) and Ta^{n}wa^{n}zhika (Gatschet 1884–1888, 1:30), which in modern transcription is *ttą́wą žíka* 'little village'.

The name Papikaha, which appears on the 1673–1674 Marquette autograph map, has been identified as a Quapaw village, but there is no corroborating evidence for it (Hodge 1907–1910, 2:336).

Other Designations

Another tribal designation for the Quapaw is Kiowa *áláhô·gɔ́*, pl. (Laurel Watkins, personal communication 1979); Mooney (1898:436) has the singular, Ä′läho′. The name also occurs in Cheyenne as Anahō and designates the Kansa as well as the Quapaw (Petter 1913–1915:582).

Some designations for the Quapaw, as well as the closely related Kansa and Osage, refer to the distinctive men's roached hairstyle. In Cheyenne all three tribes are designated O-óqt-qitä′n-eo (sg. O-óqt-qitä′n-) 'shaved hair people' (Mooney 1907:425), rendered also as hooxtxetan 'cut-hair people' (Petter 1913–1915:582); the modern recording, *ooʔkótAxétaneoʔO*, is said to designate Osage and Kansa (Glenmore and Leman 1985:201). The Yankton Sioux name, used only for the Quapaw, is *p*^{h}*éša* 'deer-hair roach' (Williamson 1902:162, retranscribed).

An anomalous name is Wyandot Utsúshuat 'wild apple' (Gatschet 1881).

Based upon an early statement that the Akansas, because of their reputation for being the handsomest Indians of the continent, were called "Les beaux hommes" (Charlevoix 1761:248), several later writers attributed to them the French designation Handsome Men (Jefferys 1761, 1:44) and Beaux Hommes (Gallatin 1836:130).

There are no recorded designations for the Quapaw in the Plains sign language.

Sources

Two major historical overviews chronicle the Quapaw from earliest European contact through the late twentieth century: Baird (1980), written by a historian, is based on documentary research; Nieberding (1976), written by a journalist, is anecdotal and derived from long familiarity with the Quapaw.

The best early accounts of the Arkansas River Quapaw are the Jesuit Relations (JR) and the narratives of French travelers of the La Salle-Tonti era (Falconer 1844; Tonti 1898; Margry 1876–1886; Hennepin 1880; Joutel 1714). Spirited, but sometimes questionable, descriptions during the late eighteenth century were contributed by the letters of Bossu (1771, 1777, 1982), a French naval officer who lived briefly among the Quapaw and passed through their domain several times. During the early nineteenth century the Arkansas River Quapaw were described by the naturalist Nuttall (1980). Another useful account from that era, including the first Quapaw vocabulary, was provided by Arkansas Territorial Gov. George Izard (Bizzell 1981).

Archeological investigation of Quapaw prehistory was pioneered by C.B. Moore (1908) on the lower Arkansas River and adjacent territory. Attempts to link the tribe with specific archeological complexes were made by Dickinson and Dellinger (1941), Phillips, Ford, and Griffin (1951), Ford (1961), Hoffman (1977, 1985, 1986), Morse and Morse (1983), and Hathcock (1983).

No ethnographies of the Quapaw have been published. James Owen Dorsey visited them in 1890–1891 and 1894 and recorded language, mythology, social organization, and settlement but published little of this material (Dorsey 1894, 1897); his field notes are in the National Anthropological Archives, Smithsonian Institution. Rankin (1982, 1985) compiled a dictionary, working with the last speakers and utilizing the Dorsey manuscripts and other historical materials.

The Oklahoma Historical Society, Oklahoma City, recorded interviews with several Quapaw people in 1937, which provide useful historical and ethnographic information (Valliere and Valliere 1937; Brotherton 1937; Haynes 1937); other interviews were made in 1938. In 1976 the Oklahoma Indian Affairs Commission recorded 30 hours of interviews with 20 senior tribal members; the resulting publication (Oklahoma Indian Affairs Commission 1977) consists only of excerpts and the entirety of the interviews has not been transcribed. In 1978, Carrie Wilson, an anthropologist who is a Quapaw tribal member, wrote a study of the Peyote religion among the Quapaw based on interviews; it remains unpublished. Videotaped interviews of Quapaw elders from the 1980s are housed at the tribal headquarters at Quapaw, Oklahoma, and at the University of Arkansas, Fayetteville. Tribal publications may be found in the Periodicals of Native Americans Collection, University of Arkansas at Little Rock.

Collections of Quapaw artifacts are held by the Museum of the American Indian and the Museum of Natural History, Smithsonian; Peabody Museum at Harvard University; and Woolaroc Museum, Bartlesville, Oklahoma. Musée de l'Homme, Paris, holds eighteenth-century painted buffalo hides that depict Quapaw history.

Pawnee

DOUGLAS R. PARKS

The Pawnee (pô'nē) were a semisedentary Caddoan-speaking people who lived in east-central Nebraska until the late nineteenth century, when they relocated to a reservation in Oklahoma. Although they have formed a single tribal entity since the mid-nineteenth century, they are an aggregate of four historical groups, usually designated bands, that previously had been politically autonomous tribes. The bands did not have a unitary name for themselves as Pawnee, but rather designated themselves and each other by separate names that reflected their status as independent political entities. The identity of the four bands was maintained through the end of the twentieth century.

Territory

From the earliest historical references to the Pawnee in the mid-sixteenth century until their removal to Indian Territory in 1876, the four divisions occupied semipermanent earthlodge villages in a crescent-shaped area of Nebraska that begins at present Yutan, 15 miles below Fremont along the Platte and Loup rivers (fig. 1) and extends 120 miles upstream to Central City and to St. Paul. Most historical villages were located along the central Platte and lower Loup rivers. Other Pawnee villages were located for periods on the Big Blue River near present Beatrice, Nebraska, and on the middle Republican River (Wedel 1986:152).

The northernmost group was the Skiri (Panimaha or Loup), who formerly comprised numerous villages or bands living along the Loup River, most of which were politically and socially united (table 1). The Skiri spoke a distinct dialect that contrasted with the speech of the other three bands, whom they designated *tuha·wit* 'East Village(s),' a reference to the geographical position of those bands in relation to the Skiri. East and south of the Skiri were the Chawi (Grand), the Kitkahahki (Republican), and the Pitahawirata (Tappage), each of which generally comprised a single village. The Chawi lived in several locations on the south side of the Platte River between the mouths of the Loup River and Skull Creek. In the eighteenth century the Kitkahahki lived at two different sites on the middle Republican River, but in the early nineteenth century they moved north to the area on the south side of the Platte near the other bands. The Pitahawirata, as a distinct social group, do not appear in historical references until the mid-eighteenth century, when they were living near the Chawi and Kitkahahki. In the twentieth century those three groups were commonly designated the South Band Pawnee.

Throughout the eighteenth and early nineteenth centuries, the hunting grounds of the Skiri generally extended along the north side of the Platte River as far as the Forks, while those of the other bands were along the south side of the Platte River and along the Republican River. There is no evidence of hunting north of the South Loup River or

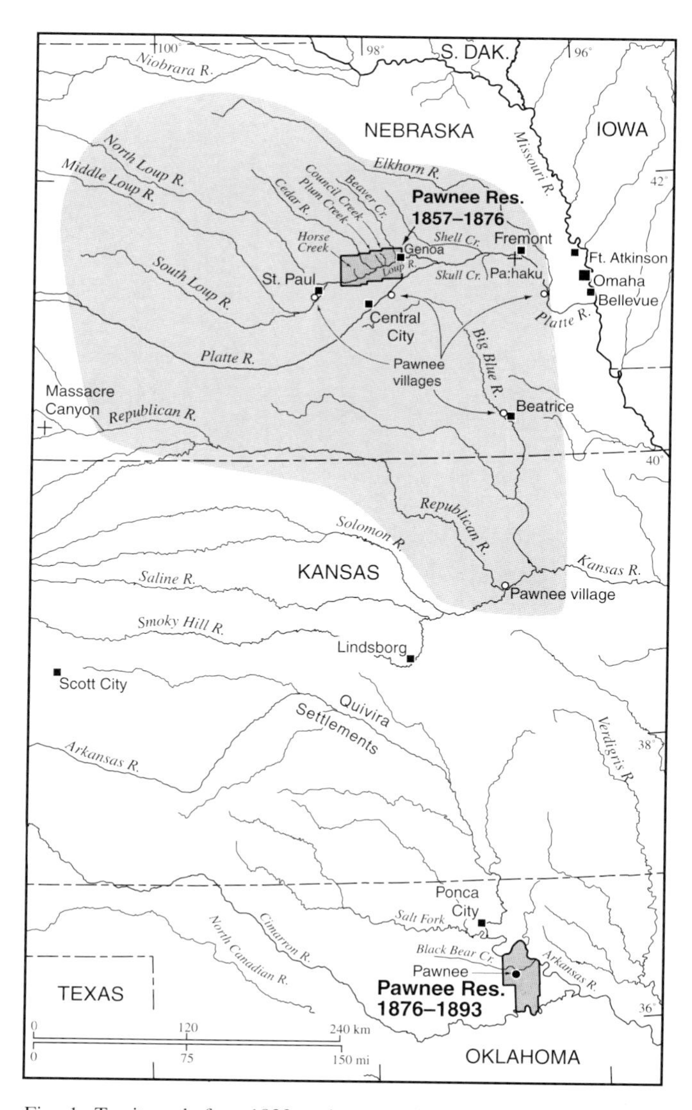

Fig. 1. Territory before 1833 and reservations.

Table 1. Skiri Village Names

Murie 1914, 1981	*G.A. Dorsey 1904*	*G.A. Dorsey 1907a*	*Gilmore 1924*
turi·kaku 'Center Village'	Turíkaku 'Center Village'	Center Village	Tuhrikakuh 'Center Village'
kitkahahpakuhtu? 'Old Village'		Four Band Village	Kitkahapahuhtu 'Old Village'
1. Yellow Star, or Yellow Dwelling, bundle	Akarakáta [*akarahkata*] 'Yellow Dwelling'		Karah-kata 'Yellow Dwelling Village'
2. Red Star, or Red Lodge Pole, bundle	Skauwahákitáwiu [*ckawahahkitawi?u?*] 'Leading Fortune Woman'[a]		
3. White Star, or White Dwelling, bundle; also Mother Born Again	Atirátatariwata [*atira tatariwa·ta?*] 'Mother Born Again'		
4. Big Black Meteoric Star, or Black Dwelling, bundle; also Sphere on Top	Liwidutchok [*riwiru·caku*] 'Round on Top'		
tuhicpi·?at 'Village Stretching out in Bottomlands'	Tuhitspiat 'Village in Bottom'	Village in the Bottom	Tuhitpiat 'Stretching in Bottomlands Village'[b]
1. *tuhicpi·?at* bundle			
2. *cahikspa·ruksti?*, or 'Wonderful Being', bundle[c]	Tcaihíxpáruxti 'Wonderful Man'		Tšahiks Paruksti 'Wonderful-Men Village'
tuhkickita 'Village on a River Branch'	Tuhkitskita 'Village on Creek'		Tuhkitskita 'Branch Village'
tuhwa·hukasa 'Village Stretching across a Hill'	Tuwhahúkasa 'Village Standing Over Hill'	Village on the Hill	Tuhwahukasa 'Village Straight across a Hill'
1. *tuhwa·hukasa* bundle			
2. Morning Star bundle[d]			
tuhu·caku 'Village in a Ravine'	Tohóchuck 'Village in Ravine'	Village in the Ravine	Tuhučaku 'Ravine Village'
tuhwara·kaku 'Village in Thick Timber'		Village on the Wooded Hill	Tuhwarakaku 'Thick Timber Village'
arikarahkucu? 'Big Elk'	Aríkararíkuts [*arikara·rikucu?*] 'Big Elks'	Big Elk Village	Arikarakuču 'Big Antlered Elk Standing Village'
arikara·riki 'Small Standing Elk'	Arikaraíkis 'Standing Elks'	Little Elk Village	Arikarkih 'Small Antlered Elk Standing Village'
akaahpaksawa 'Skulls Painted on Tepee'	Akapaxsáwa 'Skulls Painted on Tepee'	Buffalo Skull Painted Village	Akapahšawa 'Skull Painted on Tepee Village'
cti·kska·tit 'Black Ear of Corn'	Stiskáatit 'Black Corn Woman'	Fools the Wolves Village; also Black Ear of Corn[e]	Stin-katit 'Black Ear of Corn Village'
cti·sarikusu? 'Fish Hawk'		(Fish Hawk)[f]	Skisarikus 'Fish Hawk Village'
tu·rawi?u? 'Part of a Village'	Turáwiu 'Half on Hill Village'	One Half Village	Turawi 'Part of a Village'
ckirira·ra 'Wolves in Water'[g]	Skirirara 'Wolves Standing in Water'	Wolves Standing in Water Village	Skididala 'Coyotes Standing in Water Village'
pahuksta·tu? 'Squash Vine'		Pumpkin Vine	Pahukstatu 'Pumpkin Vine Village'
	Háricahahákata [*haripahahahkata*] 'Red Calf'		
			Kirrit-tara kata 'Sunflower Village'

[a]This name is enigmatic. It seems to be the name of the 2 ears of corn in the bundle; however, Murie (1981) gives the 2 corn names as Female White Fortune and Female Leader of Cornstalks.

[b]Gilmore says that the *tuhicpi·?at* bundle is also known as the *haripahahahkata* (Yellow Calf Skin) bundle. He speaks of this as one of the 4 leading bundles in Old Village; this is contradictory with Murie's list.

[c]This bundle and the North Star bundle were tribal bundles, rather than village bundles, and belonged to no particular village (Murie 1914:551).

[d]The Morning Star bundle was also a tribal bundle; its owner happened to live in Village Stretching Across a Hill.

[e]Dorsey and Murie (1940:78) give Black Ear of Corn as an alternate name for a bundle called Fools the Wolves, belonging to a village of the same name.

[f]Dorsey and Murie (1940:78) give Fish Hawk as the name of a bundle belonging to Village in the Woods (actually Village in Thick Timber), not listed by Dorsey.

[g]Dorsey and Murie (1940:76) translate this as Coyote-in-Water Village.

Source: Parks 1979:232–234.

south of the Republican River (Parks 1979a; Champe and Fenenga 1974:93).

Language

Pawnee is one of four documented languages of the Northern branch of the Caddoan language family. It is spoken in two distinct but mutually intelligible dialects, Skiri and South Band.* Although there was a tendency among Skiri and South Band speakers to develop a mixed dialect earlier in the twentieth century, the two dialects by and large maintained their integrity through the close of the century. Older speakers in the early twentieth century claimed that when the South Bands lived apart, there were differences in their speech, suggesting earlier dialectal differentiation among them that disappeared after the three groups began living together. However, no systematic differences among South Band speakers have been documented (Lesser and Weltfish 1932:3–4). Earlier in the century there was also a tradition that the *kawara·kis*, a group or village reputedly within the Pitahawirata band, spoke a dialect similar to Arikara, but there is no recorded evidence to substantiate the claim (Parks 1979:200).

The two Pawnee dialects were most closely related to Arikara, a language often treated as a divergent dialect of Pawnee and frequently said to be an offshoot of Skiri. However, Arikara and Pawnee were mutually unintelligible, and Arikara shares as many linguistic features with the South Band dialect as it does with Skiri (Lesser and Weltfish 1932:4; Parks 1979:201).

History, 1541–1803

The earliest historical reference to the Pawnee comes from the sixteenth-century narrative of Capt. Juan Jaramillo, a member of the exploring expedition headed by Spanish general Francisco Vásquez de Coronado, whose party in 1541 traveled into the central Plains as far north as present Lindsborg, Kansas. There they reached Quivira, comprised of several ancestral Wichita villages, and they were told that beyond it was Harahey, a place like Quivira with similar settlements; later a chief of Harahey visited them (Winship 1896:590). Since Harahey is a rendition of the Wichita name for the Pawnee, it is generally accepted as a reference to the Pawnee villages to the north (Hodge 1907–1910, 1:532; Fletcher in Hodge 1907–1910, 2:213).

No Spanish or French expedition is known to have reached the Pawnee villages until the early eighteenth century, but a number of explorers ascended the Missouri during the seventeenth century and acquired indirect knowledge of the Pawnee that is reflected on maps of the period. The party of Louis Jolliet and Father Jacques Marquette, for example, reached the mouth of the Missouri River in 1673, and the name Pana appears on the Marquette map of 1673–1674, shown east of the Pahoutet (the Iowa) and northeast of the Maha (Omaha). In 1682, the expedition of Réné-Robert Cavelier, sieur de La Salle reached the mouth of the Missouri River and learned of the Pana nation 200 leagues to the west and the Panimaha (Weddle 1987:119). Drawing on information from the La Salle expedition, Jean-Baptiste Louis Franquelin placed the Panimaha on his 1688 map in a number of locations along the western course of the Platte and on a northern fork that is clearly the Loup River (Tucker 1942: pl. XIA). Based on their placement on the Marquette and Franquelin maps, the Pawnee were clearly well known to the French.

There are other references to the Pawnee in late seventeenth century French accounts that indicate knowledge of them but again suggest little or no direct contact. In the 1680s, Nicolas Perrot noted that the Pawnee and Iowa generally used dried buffalo dung for fires because wood was extremely scarce among them (Blair 1911–1912, 1:124). In 1700, Gabriel Marest wrote that the Kansa and Pani lived in the Missouri River valley, although neither he nor any other Frenchmen had visited them (Nasatir 1952, 1:6).

Despite Marest's statement, in the 1690s Spanish reports of relations between the Navajo and Pawnee attest to the presence of French traders among the Pawnee. One document mentions that a Navajo war party returned with captive Pawnee children and beheaded them after the Spaniards refused to ransom them. In 1697, when a Navajo party made an excursion onto the Plains, its members were killed by Pawnees accompanied by Frenchmen. The next year a Navajo party returned to exact vengeance and destroyed three Pawnee villages and a "fortified place." The victorious party returned home laden with spoils that included French trade goods (A.B. Thomas 1935:13–14).

In the central Plains the early decades of the eighteenth century witnessed a period of French and Spanish exploration and rivalry, during which the Pawnee became only slightly better known to Europeans. The source of French activity and interest in the Missouri region shifted from New France to the lower Mississippi River. In a 1702 memoir, Pierre Le Moyne, sieur d'Iberville, provided a list of the tribes of the Missouri Valley that includes the Panis and Panimahas, and he, as well as his younger brother Jean Baptiste Le Moyne, sieur de Bienville, documented new exploration on the Missouri (Nasatir 1952, 1:8). Hubert reported that where the Rivière des Panis (the Loup) forms three branches, a number of Pawnee villages were located (Nasatir 1952, 1:12). In 1714, Étienne Venyard, sieur de Bourgmont ascended the Missouri River to the mouth of the Platte and later continued north to the Arikara villages (Giraud 1958:7). In 1723, Philippe de La Renaudière, who joined Bourgmont as an engineer, mentioned a Pawnee village of 150 lodges located 15 leagues up the River of the

*The phonemes of South Band Pawnee are: (voiceless unaspirated stops and affricate) *p*, *t*, *č*, *k*, *ʔ*; (voiceless spirants) *s*, *h*; (resonants) *w*, *r*; (short vowels) *i*, *e*, *a*, *u*; (long vowels) *i·*, *e·*, *a·*, *u·*. The stop *č* phonetically is [ts] before consonants and in word-final position. The Skiri dialect has three short vowels *i*, *a*, *u* and three long vowels *i·*, *a·*, *u·*, as well as stress v́. This orthography follows the analysis of Parks (1976).

Panis; farther upriver were 8 additional villages, about a half-league from one another (Margry 1876–1886, 6:394). Information accumulating during this period allowed Guillaume Delisle to compile his 1718 map, showing what is evidently the Loup River, on which is the legend "Les Panis, 10 Villages," and farther north "Les Panimaha, 12 Villages" (Tucker 1942: pl. XV). Since those are the traditional and historical locations of the South Band and Skiri, respectively, this period is the first one when accurate historical and cartographic data for the Pawnee become available.

The reports of Spanish exploration during the opening decades of the eighteenth century yield less information. In 1706, Juan de Ulibarrí led an expedition to El Cuartelejo, a Plains Apachean village near present Scott City, Kansas. The Apaches there told of a Pawnee war party, accompanied by Frenchmen, that had come to attack their village but had been driven away. They told him of five larger rivers, on one of which, Sitascahe—apparently either the Republican or Platte—were two large Pawnee villages. He also learned that the Apaches captured Pawnee slaves whom they sold to the Spaniards and that the Pawnee in turn took Apache slaves whom they sold to the French (A.B. Thomas 1935:69–70, 265) (fig. 2). In 1719, when Gov. Antonio Valverde retraced much of Ulibarri's route during a pursuit of Comanches and Utes, he met a camp of Apaches on the Arkansas River that had been ambushed by a party of Frenchmen united with Pawnees and Wichitas. The following year, in response to the French approach from the northeast, Valverde dispatched an expedition of soldiers and Indians under the command of Pedro Villasur to negotiate with the French. In August, when they were on their summer hunt, the Pawnee, accompanied by a party of French soldiers and Indian allies, destroyed the Spanish force either at the forks of the Platte or near the Platte-Loup junction. That military disaster caused the Spaniards to retreat beyond the Sangre de Cristo Mountains in 1720 and not return to the central Plains for more than 80 years (A.B. Thomas 1935:38–39).

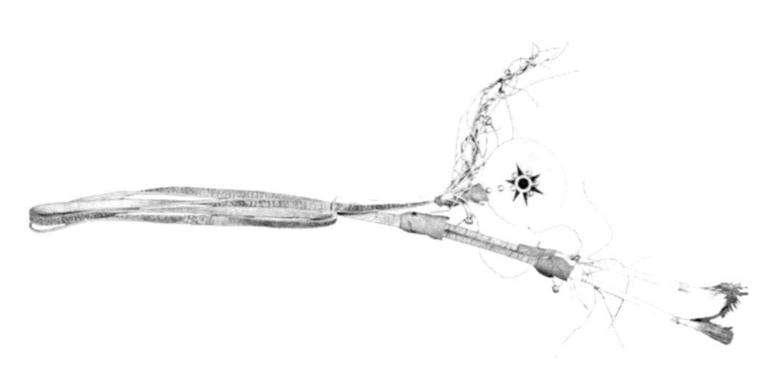

The British Mus., Mus. of Mankind, London: 5199.

Fig. 2. Identification medallion given to captives to ensure their safe return to their tribes (Gibbs 1982:58). Captives could only be released by consent of Pawnee elders, and then were sent home with gifts of clothing and robes. The disk is red-painted buffalo hide with a Morning Star symbol cut out of the center. The hide strap is ornamented with yellow, red, and orange porcupine quillwork, brass hawk bells, and red-dyed horsehair. Collected by Friedrich Paul Wilhelm of Württemberg, 1823; diameter of disk 11.4 cm.

Over the next four decades the French continued to have sporadic contact with the Pawnee. The Mallet brothers, Pierre and Paul, when seeking a new route to Santa Fe in 1739, reached the Platte River, where they visited the Panimaha at the mouth of the Loup River (Margry 1876–1886, 6:455–456). In 1752, French traders led by Jean Chapuis and Louis Feuilli left Fort de Chartres and visited the Pawnee in the course of their expedition to open a trade route to Santa Fe (Nasatir 1952, 1:42). In 1758, Louis Billouart de Kerlérec, governor of Louisiana, reported that the Panimaha, living on the Platte River 25 leagues from its mouth, numbered 600 men bearing arms. They traded with French voyageurs who came from Canada via Michilimackinac to the upper Mississippi and Missouri rivers (Nasatir 1952, 1:50–55).

In 1767, three years after the founding of Saint Louis, the Pawnee were drawn into the developing Missouri River fur trade. In that year Capt. Don Francisco Ríu was sent to Saint Louis to take charge of relations with the Indians beyond the Missouri—to keep them loyal to Spain and to keep the British traders out of the territory west of the Mississippi River. A year later Ríu listed the tribes for which traders had been licensed, and among them were the Pitahawirata (Pani-Topage), who make their first appearance in the historical record here, as well as the Panimaha and Panis (Nasatir 1952, 1:66). On November 15, 1777, more than a decade after Louisiana passed to the Spanish, Lt. Gov. Francisco Cruzat prepared a report for Bernardo de Gálvez, governor-general of Louisiana, that provided more accurate information on two Pawnee tribes: the Kitkahahki, mentioned for the first time in the historical record, living in a village on the Republican River, and the Chawi, residing on the west bank of Skull Creek (the Barcal archeological site) below the Platte River. In his report Gálvez stated that these two tribes had always engaged in hunting, which provided skins of beaver, buffalo, and otters, as well as deer, for the fur trade (Houck 1909, 1:143–144). In a subsequent report Cruzat named the traders who had been granted licenses to trade with the tribes on the Missouri, as well as the value of their merchandise; one license was given for the trade with the Kitkahahki, and two were given for the trade with the "Panis," one presumably with the Chawi and the other with either the Pitahawirata or Skiri (Houck 1909, 1:138–139).

In 1777 Athanase De Mézières, and later Cruzat and other Spanish officials, also reported that a band of approximately 300 Panimahas separated from the other Skiris on the Loup River and moved to the Red River, where they joined the Taovaya. They chose a site between the Taovaya and the Cadodacho that was 180 leagues from Natchitoches, attracted there by the trade with Louisiana and the desire to join the Nations of the North—the Kitsai,

Tawakoni, Iscanis, Taovaya, and Tonkawa—against their enemies, the Osage. They lived there until the nineteenth century (Houck 1909, 1:140; Bolton 1914, 1:23–24, 2:122).

The Pawnee were mentioned in Gov.-Gen. Esteban Rodríguez Miró's 1785 report on the Missouri River valley, which locates the "Pani" (the Chawi and Pitahawirata) on the right bank of the Platte River, the Panimaha farther upstream on the Loup River, and the Kitkahahki on the Republican River (Nasatir 1952, 1:119–127). Until the end of the Spanish regime in Louisiana, the Pawnee figured prominently in the records of the fur trade (Nasatir 1952, 1:208–211).

At the time of the Louisiana Purchase in 1803, the Pawnee had been trading with both the French and Spaniards for at least a century. Based on Spanish records, French voyageurs from Canada were reaching the Pawnee perhaps as early as the end of the seventeenth century and certainly by the first two decades of the eighteenth century. The beginning of Pawnee trade with the Spanish of Santa Fe was as early as 1714, although references to it are few (Giraud 1958:16; Margry 1876–1886, 6:436–437), but Spanish traders were visiting the central Plains soon after the French had begun trading there. However, French traders were more liberal in their trading policy and were able to move more goods more easily over long distances. Consequently, the French had a greater impact on and more influence among the Pawnee and other tribes of the region.

History, 1803–1875

Although the expedition led by Meriwether Lewis and William Clark passed up the Missouri River east of the Pawnee villages without actually visiting them, the explorers did obtain information on the locations, size, economy and trade, and life of the Pawnee bands, as well as a report that in 1803 the Pawnee had suffered from a smallpox epidemic that greatly reduced their population (Moulton 1983–, 3:395–398). The Skiri were on the Loup River at the Palmer archeological site, and the Chawi and part of the Kitkahahki—the latter a group that had migrated north from the Republican River—were on the south bank of the Platte, midway between the points where the Loup and Shell Creek enter the Platte from the north, at the Bellwood site.

The first of the American expeditions to visit the Pawnee was that of Lt. Zebulon M. Pike, who, at the beginning of his exploration of the southwestern parts of Louisiana Territory in 1806, reached the Kitkahahki village on the Republican River, known as the Hill site. A Spanish expedition under Lt. Facundo Malgares had just left the village, and Pike raised the American flag there. His map locates the Chawi below the mouth of Shell Creek, at the Linwood site, and the Skiri at the Palmer site (Wedel 1986:156–157). Maj. George C. Sibley, whose goal was to make peace among the Pawnee, Osage, and Kansa and to foster their allegiance to the American government, in 1811 visited two Pawnee villages, the Skiri and the South Band at the Horse Creek site. He reported that the Kitkahahki had left their Republican River village to settle on the Platte while the three South Bands had abandoned all their villages south of the Platte River and moved to an area south of the Skiri village on the Loup River (Brooks 1965).

Other major travelers and expeditions that left reports of varying detail include those of Maj. Stephen H. Long in 1819 (James in Thwaites 1904–1907, 14:199–250); Paul Wilhelm, Duke of Württemberg in 1823 (Wilhelm 1973:388–397); William H. Ashley and Jedediah S. Smith in 1824 (Dale 1941); John Treat Irving, Jr. (1835), who visited the Pawnee in 1833 with Treaty Commissioner H.E. Ellsworth; Charles Augustus Murray in 1835 (1839); Col. Henry Dodge in 1835 (Dodge 1861); Capt. John C. Frémont in 1842 (Jackson and Spence 1970, 1); Maj. Clifton Wharton in 1844 (Wharton 1925); Lt. James Henry Carleton in 1845 (Pelzer 1943); William Clayton in 1847 (Clayton 1921); and Lt. John W. Abert (1848).

In 1818, the United States government, represented by William Clark and Auguste Chouteau, signed separate, but identical, treaties with each of the four Pawnee bands (Kappler 1904–1941, 2:156–159). The treaties established friendship between the signatories and acknowledged that the Pawnee were under the protection of the United States. They were followed in 1825 by another treaty, signed at Fort Atkinson, in which the Pawnee were treated as a single tribe comprised of four federated bands (Kappler 1904–1941, 2:258–260). Its purpose was to regulate trade with Whites and to limit that trade to citizens of the United States, to insure that the Pawnee refrained from selling or trading arms to hostile tribes, and to provide penalties for violations.

Until the early 1830s the only sustained contact between the Pawnee and Whites had been through the fur trade, which continued to support and expand their way of life. Traders provided them with guns and other manufactured goods in exchange for robes, which came from an increased output during the two communal hunts that formed an integral part of their annual economic cycle. In the late 1820s, for example, in addition to their own needs, the Skiri produced 200 packs of 10 robes a year, while each of the three other divisions produced 600–700 packs. Yet during the early nineteenth century the Pawnee continued to be on the periphery of the Saint Louis fur trade, never given a permanent trading post, but served only by resident traders after the summer and winter hunts.

Beginning in the 1830s and continuing for almost a half-century, the Pawnee were subjected to an incessant, ever-increasing interplay of outside forces, mostly destructive, that radically changed their lives. One was White emigration and transcontinental travel on the Oregon Trail, which followed the Platte River directly through Pawnee territory. As the century progressed, emigration swelled, putting increased demands on the limited natural resources of the region—on the buffalo herds and other game upon which the Pawnee depended for food, on the forage that they needed for their horses, on the wood they needed for their houses and for fuel, and, ultimately, upon the very land that they considered their own. Simultaneous with that early emigration was another encroachment, the forced removal of tribes from east of the Mississippi River to land west of it, increasing the native population of the eastern Plains by approximately 30 percent and creating even more subsistence demands on an already economically uncertain environment.

In 1833, at the Clarks village site, the four bands of Pawnee signed a far-reaching treaty, the first to expropriate Pawnee territory (Kappler 1904–1941, 2:416–418). Under the terms of this treaty the Pawnee ceded all their lands south of the Platte River in exchange for which they were to receive 12 annual payments of $4,600, and were promised agricultural implements, blacksmiths, demonstration farmers, a mill, and a school, as well as military protection. Those benefits were given on condition that they settle in permanent farming villages and give up their semiannual hunts.

Missionary efforts began in 1834 with the arrival of the Presbyterians John Dunbar and Samuel Allis, sent by the American Board of Commissioners for Foreign Missions. For five years, they maintained a mission at Bellevue, on the Missouri River, a location that required their traveling to the Pawnee villages (Wedel 1985). In 1839 they selected a site for the mission and its farms on Council and Plum creeks on the north side of the Loup Fork, some 8 to 15 miles from the Pawnee villages, and moved there in 1841. That year Allis was appointed the first government teacher to the Pawnee and opened a school for Pawnee children, while George Gaston became the first government farmer. Two years later a teacher, three farmers, two blacksmiths, and two helpers joined the new settlement; but over the ensuing three years relentless Sioux attacks on the Pawnee made life so hazardous for the missionaries and government employees that they abandoned the settlement.

The treaty of 1833 marked a turning point in Pawnee history. For the first time their villages and garden lands were confined to the area north of the Platte River, forcing the Chawi, Kitkahahki, and Pitahawirata to relocate. By 1841 they had removed and built a large, combined village, the Mission site, between Plum and Council creeks on the north bank of the Loup. At the same time the Skiri abandoned their Palmer site village and established a new one on Cedar Creek, where it joins the Loup, about four miles above the Mission site.

White emigration and Indian removal from the east brought two other devastating effects to the Pawnee: disease and increased warfare. Throughout the century a relentless series of epidemics took a deep, steady toll on their population. There were smallpox epidemics in 1825, 1831, 1838, and 1852; a cholera epidemic was spread by the '49ers, followed by measles and diphtheria in 1864.

Even more demoralizing than disease was the loss of life from the unremitting attacks of their enemies, particularly the Sioux. The Pawnee had always been at war with most Plains tribes. Their only friends had been the Arikara, Mandan, and Wichita. They had also enjoyed intermittent peace with the Omaha, Ponca, and Otoe but only because they had inspired fear in those tribes. With all others there was a perpetual state of conflict. After the treaty of 1833, the Pawnee gave up their weapons and renounced warfare, agreeing to take up new lives as agrarians, ostensibly to be protected by the U.S. The effect of this new life of dependency, combined with severe population loss from disease, left the Pawnee vulnerable to their enemies. The Sioux, in particular, vowed a war of extermination, and for a period of 40 years after the treaty, the Pawnee, lacking weapons and unprotected, endured constant attacks by Sioux war parties that cumulatively inflicted major losses of life. The Sioux also contributed to Pawnee starvation and a hazardous life by ruining their tribal hunts, ransacking the stored food in their villages when the people were away on communal hunts, and burning the earthlodges in their villages at every opportunity.

Incessant Sioux attacks forced the Pawnee to abandon their Loup River villages in 1846 and establish new ones farther east at various sites on the south side of the Platte River. In 1855 their agent reported their locations—the Kitkahahki were living at the Linwood site, the Skiri at the McClaine site, and the Chawi at the Leshara site—as well as the tribe's desire for a new treaty that would establish a reservation south of the river, which would serve as a buffer to protect them from the Sioux (Champe and Fenenga 1974:78). Pawnee life there, however, continued to be plagued by adversity: their harvests were inconsistent, and their communal hunts were thwarted by the Sioux and Cheyenne. Moreover, in 1854, Nebraska Territory was opened to settlers, who began to encroach on Pawnee territory on the north bank of the Platte. That encroachment, combined with periodic starvation, triggered occasional thefts and other minor incidents between Pawnees and Whites that set in motion a drive among the new settlers for the removal of the Pawnee from Nebraska.

On September 24, 1857, under the Office of Indian Affairs' new reservation policy, which was a response to the public's demand for land and the government's need to protect the native populations in new territories, the Pawnee concluded a treaty at Table Creek that established a 15-by-30-mile reservation for them on the Loup River (Kappler 1904–1941, 2:764–767). It required them to return to the north side of the Platte within a year of its ratification in April 1858. After the summer hunt in 1859, they moved to the new reservation, on which Genoa, Nebraska, a Mormon settlement, had been established in 1857 as a way station for immigrants traveling the Mormon

Trail to Salt Lake City. When the Pawnee arrived to take possession of the reservation, the Mormons abandoned Genoa, which then became the site of the Pawnee agency, and the Pawnee established three contiguous villages where Beaver Creek joins the Loup River. The Skiri occupied the two western villages, and the South Bands lived together in the largest village.

In the decade after the Pawnee settled on their reservation, government efforts at acculturation remained largely ineffectual. Although some Pawnees were conscious of the gradual disappearance of the buffalo and became amenable to an agricultural way of life based on individual families and the acceptance of formal education, most continued their communal buffalo hunts, despite the strong opposition of their agents, while Pawnee women largely maintained traditional horticulture, and young men continued to raid tribes to the south for horses. In 1862 the Genoa Manual Labor School opened (fig. 3), but in the late 1860s only one Pawnee child in 10 attended it; moreover, after boys came of age they dropped out of school and took up hunting and raiding, while girls left to get married (Lesser 1978:20–21).

The effort to assimilate the Pawnee intensified under President Ulysses S. Grant's Peace Policy, under which administration of the Nebraska reservations in the Northern Superintendency was given in 1869 to the Hicksite branch of the Society of Friends. The Quakers' assimilationist policy had as its ultimate goals the allotment of Indian lands, the establishment of farms, and the education of Indian children—goals that were not achieved while the Pawnee lived in Nebraska. In 1871, for example, the agent had 6,000 acres on the north side of the Loup surveyed and divided into 10-acre plots to be allotted to each family and planned a sale of 50,000 acres of reservation land south of the Loup River, the proceeds to underwrite the initial costs of those farms. However, the project did not materialize because of Sioux raids (Milner 1982:27–116).

From 1864 to 1877 the Pawnee furnished scouts who served with the U.S. Army during the Plains Indian wars (fig. 4). The first enlistment of 95 scouts, organized under Frank North, a clerk and interpreter in the trader's store at the Pawnee Agency, served in the 1865–1866 Powder River Expedition against the Sioux, Cheyenne, and Arapaho, who were committing depredations along the Platte River road. In 1867, when the transcontinental line of the Union Pacific Railroad was under construction from central Nebraska to southeastern Wyoming, a battalion of four companies of Pawnee scouts was enlisted to patrol the rail line and protect its crews from Sioux and Cheyenne harassment. In 1869 the army again went on the offensive with the goal of driving the Sioux and Cheyenne out of the Republican River buffalo range, and enlisted Pawnee scouts to serve in the campaign. The Pawnee dealt a decisive blow to the Cheyenne Dog Soldiers. In the following year the scouts again guarded the railroad, and in January 1871 they were mustered out (Dunlay 1982:147–164).

Nebr. State Histl. Soc., Lincoln: top: RG 270.PH-12; bottom: RG 4422.PH-37.

Fig. 3. Genoa Manual Labor School on Pawnee Res., Genoa, Nebr. top, Children at the school in 1872. bottom, Tailoring class. Photographer and date not recorded.

After 1870, despite Pawnee service for the U.S. Army, the tribe continued to be deprived of weapons and left unprotected from Sioux attacks on their reservation. At the same time the Union Pacific Railroad and the Homestead Act brought to the country surrounding the Pawnee Reservation an influx of settlers who by 1873 had taken all land with timber, water, and easily tilled soils and had cut down most of the riparian woodlands. Settlers trespassed on the reservation and cut down so much timber that they threatened the Pawnee subsistence base.

In August 1873, while the Pawnee were on their summer hunt in southwestern Nebraska, a combined force of nearly 1,000 Oglala and Brule Sioux attacked them, killing almost 100 Pawnees and ruining the hunt. The incident, which occurred in what is now known as Massacre Canyon, gave rise to a faction that sought to migrate to Indian Territory, a part of which, in fact, moved south in late 1873 to join their friends the Wichita. The Oglala thwarted the Pawnees' winter hunt in 1873, and the Brule raided their villages in January 1874. That year the Indian agent forbade a summer hunt, and drought and insects destroyed their crops, creating a growing sentiment for moving. Although the Quakers administering the Pawnee

RULING-
HIS-SON

reservation opposed relocation of the tribe, fearing that it would retard acculturation, their efforts were undermined by state and federal representatives, who were committed to consolidating the Nebraska tribes in Indian Territory.

In October 1874 tribal leaders agreed to give up their reservation in Nebraska and migrate. In February 1875 some 1,760 Pawnees had gathered among the Wichita. Meanwhile, the Pawnee agent had selected for them a reservation on Cherokee land between the forks of the Arkansas and Cimarron rivers, south of the Osage reservation, and in March 1875 tribal leaders formally accepted the land. A site for the new agency was selected on Black Bear Creek near present Pawnee, Oklahoma. That year the Pawnee at the Wichita Agency and the remaining 400 Pawnees in Nebraska moved to their new reservation (Lesser 1978:27–33; Wishart 1979:400–401).

Culture, Late Eighteenth to Mid-Nineteenth Centuries

Set on a terrace above a river, a Pawnee village was a collection of earthlodges (fig. 5) varying in number from 40 to as many as several hundred. Occasionally, villages were surrounded by a defensive sod embankment, but generally they lacked fortification. Although the density of lodge arrangement within the village was approximately four to an acre, there was no order in the placement of lodges, and the spaces between them were generally narrow, filled by paths for walking and pens made of stakes in which horses were kept during the night. A few paces east of each lodge was an open platform or arbor that during the summer served as a shelter and as a structure upon which corn and squash could be dried. Large bell-shaped cache pits, often 6–10 feet deep, for dried horticultural produce were also located outside the lodge.

Structures

A circular, dome-shaped structure, the earthlodge varied in diameter from 30 to 60 feet, with some small ones no more than 23 feet in diameter. The topsoil of its interior floor was removed to a depth of several inches to a foot. In the center of the floor was the fireplace, an unlined basin some eight inches deep and three to four feet in diameter. Set up midway between the fireplace and the exterior wall were 6, 8, or 10 weight-bearing posts that were 12 to 18 feet high, connected at the top by stringers. Standing three or four feet inside the perimeter of the lodge was a second series of smaller, shorter posts that numbered from eight to 20 and that were also connected with stringers. Set against those stringers were closely spaced poles, the lower ends of which were set into the ground at the base of the lodge wall; they comprised the foundation for the sloping wall that enclosed the dwelling area. Making up the foundation of the roof were pole rafters that ran from the top of the wall to the frame of the smokehole that formed the apex of the lodge directly over the fireplace. Both wall and roof rafters were covered by layers of willows and grass and, finally, a layer of sod or earth some 12 inches deep. An entry vestibule, approximately 12 feet in height, seven feet in width, and 13 feet in length, was similarly framed by foundation posts and wall poles and covered with earth. The lodge generally faced east, opening away from storms and winter winds (J. B. Dunbar 1880:273–275; G.A. Dorsey 1904b:xiv–xv; J. Dunbar 1918:599–600; Wedel 1986:160).

Along the north and south sides of the interior of the lodge were sleeping platforms, about two feet above the floor, that were wide enough to accommodate two to four individuals. In an ordinary lodge there were 8–10 beds on each side, separated by willow mats (G.A. Dorsey 1904b:xv). At the west end of the lodge, opposite the doorway, was a sacred space, generally marked by a small raised platform of earth or wood that served as an altar, on which were placed a buffalo skull and other sacred objects (fig. 5). A sacred bundle and other religious paraphernalia were suspended from one of the rafter poles above the altar. The places of honor, as well as the beds of honor, were those on either side of the altar.

Beside the fireplace was at least one post, hooked at the top, from which cooking pots were suspended. On the floor were spread mats woven of rushes. Near the door on the north and south sides of the lodge interior, between the sleeping platforms and the central roof supports, was a mortar made from a hollowed-out log that the women who lived on that side used for grinding corn. In the same areas cache pits were dug into the ground to store food and personal possessions when the occupants were on communal hunts. In winter a sweatlodge was frequently constructed inside the lodge (G.A. Dorsey 1904b:xvi).

Lodge construction was a cooperative endeavor undertaken by women, who were the owners of the house. Depending on quality of materials and construction, the life expectancy of the structure varied but generally did not exceed 10 to 15 years. Usually two, but sometimes as many as 10, families lived in them, each one having its

top, U. of Wyo., Laramie, Amer. Heritage Center:B-H 537 ea; Smithsonian NAA: bottom left, 1299-B; bottom right, 98-10377; bottom center, Southwest Mus., Los Angeles: N35627.

Fig. 4. Scouts and warriors. top, Scouts of 1864–1877. back row, left to right, Walking Sun (Chawi), Leading Fox (Skiri), Rush Roberts, Sr. (Skiri), and Simond Adams (Skiri); seated, Wichita Blaine (Pitahawirata), High Eagle (Pitahawirata), Robert Taylor (Kitkahahki), and Billie Osborne (Skiri). Photograph by Aubrey Ewert Merryman, 1929. bottom left, White Horse (Pitahawirata), wearing a Civil War pattern military jacket and holding a tomahawk and revolver. His hairstyle and the multiple earrings that he wears were favored by Pawnee men. Photograph possibly by William H. Jackson, 1860s–1870s. bottom center, Crooked Hand (Skiri, b. ca. 1830, d. 1873), a warrior in Nebr. and father of Simond Adams. Ambrotype probably by S.R. Nichels, about 1854–1870. bottom right, Ruling-His-Son (also Chiefly Fox, Pitahawirata, b. ca. 1830, d. 1928), a survivor of Massacre Canyon. He wears a feather headdress and bear claw necklace and holds an eagle feather fan. Photograph by Aubrey Ewert Merryman, © 1927.

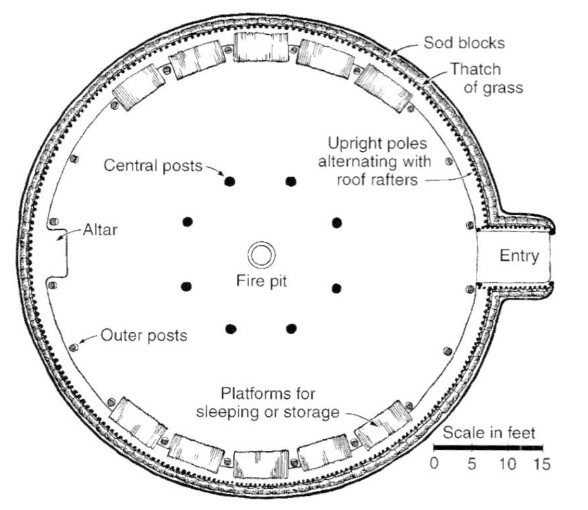
Sod blocks
Thatch of grass
Upright poles alternating with roof rafters
Central posts
Altar
Entry
Fire pit
Outer posts
Platforms for sleeping or storage
Scale in feet
0 5 10 15

top, Nebr. State Histl. Soc., Lincoln: RG2065.PH-1-4; center left, Southern Methodist U., DeGolyer Lib., Dallas, Tex.: AG82.152.5; center right, Field Mus., Chicago: 71673 (A113529); bottom left, Kans. State Histl. Soc., Topeka; bottom right, Weltfish 1965:89.

Fig. 5. Earthlodges. top, Portion of a village of earthlodges at the forks of Beaver Creek and the Loup River near Genoa, Nebr. Photograph by William Henry Jackson, 1871. center left, Interior of Sitting Bull's earthlodge. Photograph by Thomas Croft, about 1896. center right, Detail of rush mat. Collected by George A. Dorsey, Pawnee Res., Okla., 1902; overall length 218 cm. bottom left, Sacred bundle formerly belonging to an individual killed at Massacre Canyon in 1873. It has a bison hide wrapping that is held together by 3 leather straps; all are covered with red ocher pigment. Under the straps are 3 arrowshafts, a raccoon penis bone used as a meat fork, and a catlinite pipe. Radiography of the bundle in 1988 revealed its contents to include beads, 8 hawk skins, and a single eagle talon. The bundle, donated by the family of Dolly Moore in 1987, is on exhibition in a plexiglass case over the altar area on the west side of a reconstructed earthlodge at the Pawnee Indian Village Mus., Republic, Kans. Length 64 cm. Photograph by Barry Worley, 1998. bottom right, Architect's plan of an earthlodge.

separate part of the lodge with its own furniture. The number of occupants also varied, smaller lodges housing 12–18 individuals and larger ones accommodating up to 50 people. The lodges of chiefs, priests, and doctors were exceptionally large since they were used for ceremonial gatherings as well as domiciles (J. B. Dunbar 1880:275; Murie 1981:7; Wedel 1986:161).

On level ground outside every village there were one or two game grounds, well worn tracks where males played the hoop and pole and similar games. On bluffs or other high ground overlooking villages were cemeteries in which the dead were interred.

The Pawnee built two types of dwellings for use on their communal hunts. On the summer hunt they constructed a "side dwelling" (*aka·ririwis*) (fig. 6) that was a half-bowl-shaped framework of bent saplings, open in the front but otherwise covered with hides (Weltfish 1965:167–169). During the winter hunt they lived in conical hide tepees built on a three-pole framework that supported 12 to 20 poles each about 16 feet long. Like the earthlodge entrances, tepee doors usually faced east (J. B. Dunbar 1880:272–273; J. Dunbar 1918:603).

Okla. Histl. Soc., Oklahoma City: 5057.

Fig. 6. Skiri women in camp. They are working in front of a summer "side dwelling" covered with canvas. A canvas-covered tepee is behind them. Woman in center is working on a skin with a hide scraper. A wooden mortar and pestle are to the right. Photograph by William S. Prettyman, north of present Pawnee, Okla., 1889.

Subsistence

The Pawnee economy was based on an annual round that regularly alternated between cultivation and hunting, supplemented by gathering. In the eighteenth century and earlier, horticulture seems to have had a much greater relative importance in the Pawnee economy. After the acquisition of the horse, the introduction of metal and other trade goods from Euro-Americans, and the concentration of their population in larger villages, the Pawnee encountered environmental problems that militated against year-round residence in their permanent villages. Those problems included an insufficient quantity of fuel and game as well as decreasing pasturage for their herds of horses. In response to those pressures of local resource depletion, the Pawnee made two annual communal hunts to the high prairie buffalo range lying to the west, northwest, and southwest of their villages that consumed up to seven months of the year. Thus, in the nineteenth century, buffalo hunting, supplemented by that of other large game, had assumed an importance equal to that of horticulture.

• HORTICULTURE The Pawnee horticultural tradition relied on the cultivation of small family plots assigned to women by the village chief. The plots, ranging in size from one-half to one and one-half acres, were located in the rich soils along creeks and in the river bottoms, extending as far as 10 miles from the village. Where not bordered by a stream bank, plots were fenced off by bushes and tree branches woven together. To work the soil Pawnee women had three tools: a hoe made of a trimmed and sharpened buffalo scapula with a wooden handle, a simple digging stick, and an antler rake. The bone hoe was still in common use when the Pawnee left Nebraska in the 1870s.

For the Pawnee, corn was their most important crop, since it had religious as well as dietary significance. They grew four subspecies—flint, flour, sweet corn, and popcorn—in 10 varieties in the late nineteenth century and in as many as 15 varieties earlier. Of the 10 varieties two were flints—one yellow, the other varied in color—and five or six were flour corns in five different colors—blue, speckled, white, yellow, and red. In addition to those, they also raised one yellow sugar (or sweet) corn as well as an archaic white flour breed known as 'holy corn' that was grown solely to provide ears to be placed in sacred bundles. Crops with no religious connotations included seven varieties of squash and pumpkin, eight varieties of beans, melons, and sunflowers (Will and Hyde 1917:306–308; Weltfish 1965:119–123).

Horticultural activity began in late April or early May, when the women cleared their fields of vegetation, broke up the sod with hoes and digging sticks, and formed the soil into small hills a foot or more in diameter and one to two feet apart. They planted corn seed in the hills, and planted beans in the spaces between them, where the bean plants could use the cornstalks for support. Squash were planted in separate plots. After they had planted the fields, the women generally hoed and weeded them twice before leaving on the summer hunt.

The harvest began in late August or early September, when the village returned from its summer hunt. In the mid-nineteenth century the corn yield in a good year was estimated at 25 to 30 bushels per acre. The first stage of the harvest was a week-long gathering of green corn, which was first roasted in a pit; then the kernels were cut off the cob and dried on hides. Following the initial corn harvest the women picked beans and, after drying them, they brought in the pumpkin harvest. Smaller pumpkins were cut into pieces to dry, while larger ones were cut into rings that, once dried, were braided into pumpkin mats. In mid-October came the second stage of the corn harvest, the gathering of the mature corn, in which men as well as women participated. The ears were taken to the village and spread out to dry, after which the kernels were cut from the cobs for storage. For some prime ears the kernels were left on the cob and their husks drawn back and braided together with other ears. After the loose corn and beans were dry, they were put into sacks, and they, together with braided corn and squash mats, were stored in cache pits. In years when there were abundant harvests and when there were successful buffalo hunts, the stored garden produce was sufficient to carry the Pawnee into the following year (Weltfish 1965:238–253; Wedel 1986:163–64). The Pawnee raised corn only for their own needs (J. B. Dunbar 1880:276).

• HUNTING The summer hunt generally began in June or early July, after the second hoeing of the corn, and lasted until late August, when the blazing star began to flower, indicating that it was time to return to the villages to harvest the crops. The winter hunt commenced in late October or November, after the harvest had been completed, the ceremonial season had concluded, and house repairs had been made. It extended through March or April, until provisions ran out and it was time to return home to begin the horticultural cycle again.

Except for a few aged and ill individuals who were unable to travel, the entire village set out on the communal hunts, traveling six to eight miles a day in columns that stretched for several miles and covering a total area of several hundred miles in any given hunting season. For the Skiri the hunting route extended west along the Loup and Platte river valleys, focusing particularly on the area around the Platte Forks, but extending south and west. The hunting territory of the other three divisions, who often traveled together, was the country on the south side of the Platte and then south and west to the Republican River country that extended as far south as the Smoky Hill and Arkansas rivers and into eastern Colorado (Weltfish 1965:171–177; Wedel 1986:167).

The favored method of hunting was the surround, in which men on well-trained horses encircled a herd and forced the animals into a milling mass. If the animals broke out or if the terrain were too rough, they ran the animals down, shooting them from horseback. When attacking the herd, Pawnee men preferred to use a bow with metal-tipped arrows rather than a gun, and they often used lances. Although buffalo was the primary game animal hunted, the Pawnee also took elk, pronghorn, deer, and bear on the hunts (Wedel 1986:167).

On a successful hunt thousands of pounds of meat and fat were produced, and what was not consumed after a kill was preserved for later consumption. Meat was sliced into thin sheets 18 to 30 inches in size, dried, then packed in parfleches for storage. The hunts produced other necessities for Pawnee life, particularly large quantities of hides, including those for trade, as well as sinew for sewing and bones for various tools. Winter hides were tanned and used for robes, while summer hides were processed for tepee covers, clothing, bags, and ropes. Pawnee women excelled in the dressing of hides (fig. 6), producing robes that were superior to those of neighboring tribes (J.B. Dunbar 1880: 279; Wedel 1986:166–169).

• GATHERING Although their gardens and hunts provided the Pawnee with the bulk of their diet, the wild vegetables, berries, fruits, seeds, nuts, and tubers that grew in the vicinity of their villages and along the routes of their hunting trips provided essential supplements. They made extensive use of prairie turnip (*Psoralea esculenta*) and groundnut (*Apios americana*) tubers, as well as Jerusalem artichoke (*Helianthus tuberosus*) and bigroot morning glory (*Ipomoea pandurata*) roots. Other favored items that grew within reach of their villages were hog-peanuts (*Amphicarpaea bracteata*), wild plums, chokecherries, ground plums, currants, and riverbank grapes (Wedel 1986:164).

Technology

Although much of their material culture was similar or identical to that of surrounding Plains tribes, the Pawnee made many characteristic articles. The manufacture of some articles was known to nearly every adult male or female, but the techniques of manufacture of other articles were specialized knowledge confined to a small number of individuals. Nearly all women, for example, knew the techniques of processing animal hides as well as making buffalo-horn spoons, while all men made bows (Weltfish 1965:366).

Women manufactured pottery vessels in globular jar and bowl forms, using a paddle and anvil technique, with a stamped exterior surface that was often smoothed and polished. Collared jars were distinguished by multiple loop handles linking the collar to the shoulder. Pottery decoration consisted of incised or trailed lines arranged into designs of parallel diagonal lines or opposed parallel diagonal lines, as well as herringbone and chevron patterns. Those pots, used for boiling food over a fire, were made until the mid-nineteenth century, by which time they were completely replaced by metal cooking vessels (Weltfish 1965:145; Grange 1968).

Another common craft among women was the manufacture of large bulrush mats, which were finely woven and used as floor coverings in both earthlodges and tepees. Several items whose manufacture was limited to a small number of female specialists included: wooden mortars, which were made from hackberry or cottonwood logs hollowed out with live coals and set upright in the lodge floor to be used for grinding corn; "black ropes," woven from buffalo hair, which men used as belts to fasten their robes; wooden bowls, which were carved from cottonwood or oak burls, polished, and used as eating utensils; and coiled willow gambling baskets, six to eight inches in diameter and two to three inches deep, that were used in dice games (fig. 7) (Weltfish 1930, 1965:365–366, 382–385). After obtaining yarn from traders, certain Pawnee women became specialists in weaving multicolored belts worn by boys and girls of good families, as well as by young women; sometimes men also twisted them around their heads to serve as a turban, with the fringes hanging down on both sides of the face and eagle feathers inserted at the back of the head (Weltfish 1937:152–153, 1965:377).

Among men the most commonly manufactured items were arms. For bows, the favorite wood was Osage orange (*Maclura pomifera*), followed in descending order of preference by black hickory *(Carya texana),* Kentucky coffeetree (*Gymnocladus dioica*), and red or green ash (*Fraxinus pennsylvanica*). Choice bows were made of red cedar, while formerly some bows were also made of rib bone or elkhorn. Although every man also made his own bowstrings out of sinew, only specialists manufactured arrowshafts, which were made of red-osier dogwood (*Cornus stolonifera*) sprouts of a year's growth. Most quivers were made from elkskin prepared to be impervious to moisture, although some were made of otter or panther skins with their fur retained. Those quivers symbolized rank: only chiefs could use otter skin, and only the bravest warriors could use panther skin (J.B. Dunbar 1880:277–279; Weltfish 1965:376, 389–391).

After weaponry, pipes were the most significant possession of men, who smoked them for both relaxation and ritual. They, too, were manufactured by specialists, who used ash for pipestems and catlinite, obtained through trade from quarries in southwestern Minnesota, for bowls (fig. 7) (Weltfish 1965:392–396).

Clothing and Adornment

The dress of both sexes, young and old, was simple. Until they reached six years old, boys and girls generally went naked. At the age of six girls began wearing a loose-fitting buckskin skirt fastened with a drawstring. Men considered moccasins and a breechcloth essential wear, and generally wore leggings that covered the legs from waist to ankle. In winter they wrapped a buffalo robe (fig. 8), and later in the nineteenth century a blanket, over their bodies, while in the summer they might wear a thinly dressed skin or a light blanket. Standard women's dress comprised moccasins, leggings that extended from the knees to the ankles, a skirt that covered the area from the waist to the knees, and a loose, sleeveless blouse that was suspended from the shoulder by straps. In the nineteenth century, except for moccasins, women's garments were made of trade cloth if the individual could afford it; otherwise they, too, were made of soft, thinly tanned hide. Both men and women sometimes wore a handkerchief or piece of cloth tied around the head like a turban. They also pierced their ears for earrings, which both sexes often wore in large numbers.

On formal occasions men wore attire that denoted rank and achievement. A symbol of high status was the man's skin war shirt that was decorated on the sleeves with

left, Field Mus., Chicago: 71597; center, Detroit Inst. of Arts: 81.618; right, Smithsonian, Natl. Mus. of the Amer. Ind.: 14/1569.

Fig. 7. Containers. left, Wooden bowl carved in the form of a duck. Brass tacks serve as the eyes. Collected by George A. Dorsey, 1902; diameter 26 cm. center, Dark brown wooden bowl. Collected by M.G. Chandler, about 1920; length 30.2 cm. right, Coiled willow gambling basket with 6 painted plum pit dice. Collected by William Wildschut before 1926; diameter 22.9 cm.

Field Mus., Chicago: left, 16235; right, 16237.

Fig. 8. Roaming Scout (b. ca. 1845, d. 1916), a government scout and prominent Skiri religious leader, wearing a painted buffalo robe and the insignia of a war leader. Each village sacred bundle contained the insignia, which a war leader borrowed from the bundle's priest before setting out on an expedition. Over his shoulders he wears an otterskin collar. left, Front view. Over each side of his chest is a flint arrowhead encircled by a braid of sweetgrass; he carries a pipe, stem upright. right, Rear view. Hanging down the middle of the back is the otter's head, over the left shoulder is the skin of a swift hawk representing a warrior, and over the right shoulder is an ear of corn representing Mother Corn. Tied around his waist is a braided buffalo hair rope (Murie 1981, 1:136–137). Photographs by Charles H. Carpenter, St. Louis, 1904.

enemy scalp hair and embroidered with porcupine quills. So also was a jacket made of beaver or otter skins and ornamented with beads. Other special shirts were made of fine cloth fringed with swan's down and heavily beaded. Before setting out on a war party, a distinguished leader's regalia (fig. 8) comprised an entire otterskin, split down the middle and worn over the shoulders, otter head hanging down the man's back; the skin of a swift hawk hanging over his left shoulder and a dried ear of corn representing Mother Corn hanging over his right shoulder; and on either side of his chest was a flint arrowhead encircled by braided sweetgrass (Murie 1981:136–137; Weltfish 1965:375–376).

Turbans, commonly worn in the winter for warmth, indicated status (fig. 9) as did other items of clothing (fig. 10). Wildcat skin represented the highest warrior rank, while fox skin denoted second rank for the Skiri (big squirrel for the South Band), and a white or red handkerchief or any calico represented third rank. The eagle feather war bonnet, also a status symbol, was worn by those who could afford one. Bonnets sometimes had one or two trailers that reached to the ground (J.B. Dunbar 1880–1882:280–281; Weltfish 1965:376).

Women made clothing from deer and elk skins, which are considerably lighter and softer than buffalo hide. In contrast to the practice of dressing buffalo hides, men, as well as women, dressed deer and elk skins, since men also used them for making saddles, bridles, stirrups, and saddle bags. Women also made moccasins, which were constructed of two pieces, a hard sole and softer uppers. For warmth in winter they sometimes made soft-soled moccasins of buffalo hide with the hair turned inside, or they wrapped the feet in dried grass or calico when wearing standard hard-soled footwear. Skiri moccasins reached just below the ankle, while those of the South Band extended above the ankle (Weltfish 1965:372–373).

Smithsonian, NAA: top left, 1296; bottom left, T-17398; bottom right, 1227; top right, Histl. Mus. Bern, Switzerland: NA 18.

Fig. 9. Men and women's clothing. top left, Kitkahahki men: Terarawest or Stopped with Horses wearing finger-woven turban; Lasharachieks or Humane Chief wearing leggings beaded with bear pawprints, wrapped in a painted buffalo robe and holding a pipe tomahawk; Assonoocottuk or As a Dog But Yet a High Chief wearing a painted buffalo robe, bear claw necklace, and a headdress; Lasharaturaha or Good Chief, wrapped in a blanket and wearing a peace medal; Lasharootoorowootowy or Difficult Chief wearing fringed skin leggings with beaded leg bands, peace medal, and necklaces of beads and shell, holding a pipe tomahawk. Photograph by William Henry Jackson, 1868–1871. top right, Headdress of ermine skin covered at the front in red stroud. The central design and the rosette are quilled hide. Quillwork has a yellow background and orange and blue design elements. The stroud is bound with green silk ribbon and edged with white seed beads. Small brass bells are tied to the ermine skin. Edges of the quilled design at front-center are bound with red ribbon, and the corners opposite the rosette have streamers of green and blue ribbon. The rosette, surrounded by pink- and blue-dyed down, has green ribbons at its center (J. Thompson 1977:159). Collected by L.A. Schoch, 1837; length 37 cm. bottom left, Mary Esau Murie, wife of James R. Murie, wearing a buckskin dress decorated with elk teeth and beaded moccasins. Photograph by Charles Carpenter, Louisiana Purchase Exposition, St. Louis, Mo., 1904. bottom right, Women from the Loup Fork village, Nebr. They are wearing stroud cloth dresses; the 2 girls on the right are wearing overshirts of cloth and multiple bead necklaces, while the 4 on the left are wrapped in commercial blankets. Photograph by William Henry Jackson, 1868–1871.

Men's hairstyles were varied, although the most common one was what the Pawnee called an "Osage cut," where the head was shaved on both sides, leaving a ridge of hair extending across the middle of the head from front to back, and the hair hanging down from the back of the head was braided (fig. 4). Men also wore their hair in two braids that hung down over the shoulders, while some wore a single braid from hair gathered at the crown of the head (Parks 1965–1998). Sometimes colored string or buckskin was plaited in the braids. Others wore their hair loose, brushed back off the forehead. Men carefully plucked all facial hair, including eyebrows, formerly using their fingers but later in the nineteenth century using spiral coils of wire.

Women's hairstyle was more uniform. They preferred to part the hair in the middle and braid it on each side, tying the ends with buckskin. Among girls and young women the part in the hair was often painted with vermillion (J. B. Dunbar 1880:268–269; Weltfish 1965:407).

Social Organization

• SOCIAL AND POLITICAL STRUCTURES The village was the fundamental unit of Pawnee social organization. Membership in it was inherited through the mother. Skiri and South Bands shared social organization, but the discussion features the better-documented Skiri (Parks 1979a).

Among the eighteenth-century Skiri there were at least 13 villages, and perhaps as many as 19 or more, most of which were joined into a confederacy that shared a common political organization and ceremonial complex. Although each village had a name, it was not always a distinct physical entity, since its earthlodges were dispersed and it might adjoin another village. In the nineteenth century, after the formerly numerous villages had coalesced into a single one, village identity remained strong because it was defined by two interrelated parameters, one religious, the other social.

Each village had its own creation myth that told how its founder had been created by a star or constellation and how that star had given the founder a sacred bundle representing its power (*wa·ruksti·*). When the founder died, his bundle and his chieftaincy were passed on to his son. That paternal inheritance continued, so that a village chief (Skiri, *ri·sa·ru?*, South Band *re·sa·ru?*) was considered to be a direct descendant of the founder and was the owner of the village sacred bundle. The bundle thus represented the sacred charter of the village, sanctioning its political organization and serving as the focus of its ceremonial life. Because all the people of a village were regarded as descendants of the founder and his wife, the village was conceived to be a large extended family, all of whose members had a common origin, a common creator, and in their sacred bundle a common source of supernatural power to which they could turn.

The social function of the village was to regulate marriage and thereby guard its bundle, insuring that it would always be kept within the village. Consequently, the village was endogamous, at least in principle prohibiting marriage outside it. Women rarely left the village into which they were born, but men sometimes married outside it and then went to the wife's village to live (Murie 1914:549).

Smithsonian, NAA: left, 1280A; center, 57258; right, 1305B.

Fig. 10. Prominent Pawnee men. left, Petalasharo the Younger, Chawi band (b. 1832, d. 1874). He wears heavily beaded buckskin leggings and shirt decorated with locks of hair. His bearclaw necklace, beaver headpiece with eagle feathers, and the pipe are signs of his status. His face is painted with lines. Photograph by Julian Vannerson and Samuel A. Cohner, Washington, D.C., 1857–1858. center, Echo Hawk, Kitkahahki band (b. 1855, d. 1924), wearing beaded leggings and moccasins, a cloth shirt, and multiple necklaces. His fringed tobacco pouch is beaded with a bird design. Photographed about 1900. right, Eagle Chief, Pitahawirata band, wearing beaded moccasins and a vest with 1st lieutenant shoulder boards on it, multiple necklaces, and Abraham Lincoln peace medal issued in 1862. He wears multiple ball and cone earrings and metal arm bands. Photograph by DeLancey Gill, 1900.

Each Skiri village had a sacred bundle that was a source of identity and power for its members. It enshrined the village history and contained the paraphernalia for performing its distinctive ceremony. At least two bundles belonged to the Skiri federation as a whole and had the primary purpose of maintaining political unity, although both had additional functions. The Skull bundle was part of the Four Pole ceremony, which commemorated the federation itself; the North Star bundle was primarily associated with the Chiefs' ceremony. The Evening Star bundle and the four leading bundles (Yellow Star, Red Star, White Star, and Big Black Meteoric Star) (fig. 11) were de facto tribal bundles, which also retained their original village functions. The Evening Star bundle and its priest were superior to all others, and it was the foremost bundle in horticultural activities. Subordinate to it and paramount over the others were the four leading bundles. The Morning Star bundle had an intermediate status between village and band functions. It had the unique distinction of demanding a human sacrifice, but in more general terms it provided for fertility and success in war.

For matters of tribal concern there was a joint council composed of the hereditary chiefs of the villages and a number of elected chiefs whose offices, gained through meritorious deeds, were not inherited. Each village had one hereditary chief. The exception was Old Village, which had four chiefs representing its four bundles. Although in principle all the hereditary chiefs were equal in rank, the four of Old Village alternated the position of leader, who presided over the council, every six months over a two-year cycle. Their bundles represented the semicardinal directions, and the two chiefs of the north bundles served during the winter while the two chiefs of the south bundles served during the summer.

At council meetings the four chiefs of Old Village sat at the altar at the west end of the lodge. Each of the other village chiefs took the "seat" assigned to his village in a pattern that radiated from the altar. These chiefs' seats were along the north and south walls, with the majority on the north, creating a dual, or north-south organization that permeated Skiri political and religious organization. According to tradition, they reflected the locations of the villages relative to that of the village in which the federation was established.

Although the chiefs had certain rituals of their own, including the admittance of a new chief into their ranks, the primary function of the council was the planning and regulation of the semiannual tribal buffalo hunt. In this role, as in other political affairs, a chief was a regulator, not an authoritarian ruler. Even though chiefs had considerable authority, their decisions were generally based on consensus. Like his celestial forebear, the chief was supposed to be a guardian of the people who was concerned with their wishes and needs. Even though the office was hereditary, the man chosen to fill it had to demonstrate humility, generosity, and sagacity, because a jealous or aggressive temperament was considered unbefitting a chief.

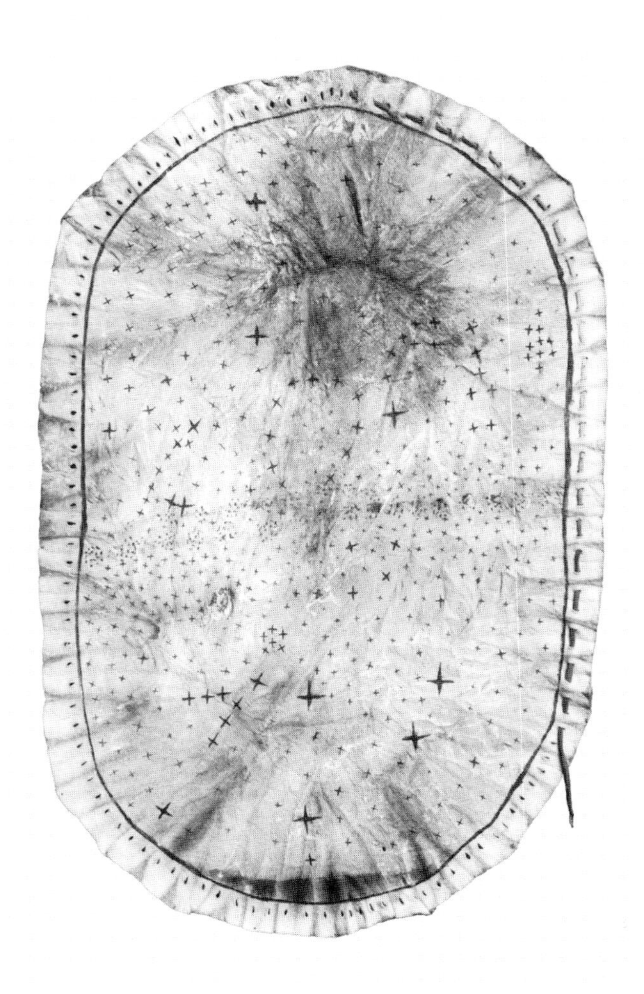

Field Mus., Chicago: 71872.10.

Fig. 11. Star chart, a map of the heavens kept in a buffalo scalp bag that hung from the Big Black Meteoric Star bundle, one of the 4 leading Skiri village bundles. The map, on a piece of soft buckskin, depicts stars that the Heavens instructed a visionary to draw on it, including the Milky Way that crosses the chart in the middle. A band of yellow pigment, representing the yellow western sunset, transects the upper oval end inside the black border; a double band of red and yellow pigments, representing the eastern sunrise, transects the lower oval end inside the border. Twice yearly, the map in its bag was carried in a race from the ceremonial lodge to a stream, where it was ritually cleansed (Murie 1981, 1:95–98; Chamberlain 1982:185–205). It was formerly owned by Roaming Scout, who entrusted it to the museum in 1906; length 66.5 cm.

The priest (*kurahus* 'old man'), an intermediary between humans and the supernatural forces of life, was the symbol of ceremonial leadership. He conducted the ceremonies to promote group welfare—to insure abundant crops and successful hunts, as well as to assure tribal unity and success in war. As a consequence, he had to know the extensive rituals for the sacred bundles. The organization of the priests was parallel to, but separate from that of the chiefs, and they used the same seating arrangement in ceremonies. The principal priest of the Skiri was the Evening Star bundle priest, who was followed in rank by the four leading bundle priests. These five were responsible for conducting the bundle ceremonies. With the partial exception of the Morning Star bundle ceremony, the Evening Star priest was required to know the entire ritual for each major bundle and, when the need arose, to conduct it. The four leading priests were expected to be similarly knowledgeable, since after the Evening Star priest officially opened a ceremony, one of them would generally assume the role of officiator. Which one of the four men then took that role in the ceremony was determined by the same schedule for the alternation of leadership among the leading chiefs.

The priests of the other bundles stood in the same relationship to the Evening Star and four leading priests as did the chiefs of their villages to the four leading chiefs. In reality, these priests were subordinate priests, who knew the ritual of their bundles but had no important role in most major ceremonies. This hierarchy was similarly reflected in the seating arrangement of priests in the lodge: the five high priests sat behind the altar at the west end of the lodge, and the other bundle priests took their assigned positions along the north and south walls.

Entirely distinct from the political and religious organization of chiefs and priests was the shamanistic organization. Comprising it were secret medicine societies, the members of which were doctors (*kura·ʔuʔ*). In contrast to the priest, who was concerned with group welfare, the doctor was a curer of the sick and thus ministered to the welfare of the individual. Similarly, the priest was associated with celestial powers, whereas the doctor obtained his powers from terrestrial beings, primarily animals.

The medicine society was a loose association of members who shared certain curative powers. Usually a society included several noted doctors, a few novices, and a large number of attached members who took part in the dancing but who did not know the society's secrets. There were a number of these societies, each of which held ceremonies early in the spring and again in the autumn. The underlying conception of those ritualistic ceremonies was the purification and renewing of the powers resident in the sacred objects of the society.

Distinct from the medicine societies was an organization functioning on the band or tribal level and known as the Doctors' (or Medicine) Lodge. It was a permanent organization comprising the most prominent doctors, who had applied for seats in the lodge and had performed successfully. Its leaders were doctors who had mastered the secrets of all the medicine societies. Together they held two day-long ceremonies, one in the spring and another in the summer, and then a spectacular month-long ceremony in the early fall. The fall ceremony was an occasion for the members to demonstrate publicly their powers through displays of hypnotism and sleight-of-hand, both of which were thought to be important in the control of disease.

The doctor's position was not inherited. Frequently the son or nephew of a doctor succeeded him, but he did so only after having apprenticed to him for years. The protégé might be any young man who showed a strong interest in learning the doctor's art and who willingly went through the long, arduous, and expensive learning process to succeed his teacher at his death. Thus, Skiri doctors were primarily trained, and did not always achieve their status through visions as in many Plains tribes.

• SOCIETIES Cross-cutting band and village organization were the secular societies, similar to those of other Plains tribes, that were both military and social organizations and had either public or private functions (table 2). The insignia of each society was its one or two staffs, or lances, from which the designation *ra·risuʔ* 'lance (society)' derives. Members of each society had their distinctive dress and often a special hair style or manner of painting themselves. Each society also had its individual musical instruments as well as its own dances and songs that were performed publicly. On war parties men grouped themselves into their societies.

One group, the more powerful and prominent, comprised established societies that were in some way sanctioned by the leading bundles. These Murie (1914:558–560) called "bundle societies." They had varying public functions: some served for war, either leading in the line of battle or supporting the camp police when called upon by the chief, while others served as soldiers on the communal hunt, taking charge when the hunt chief delegated that authority to the society (Murie 1981, 1:98).

Table 2. Men's Societies

Pawnee name	*English name*	*Band*
	Bundle Societies	
ra·risaru·saʔ	Horse Lance Society (also Two Lance Society)	S, C
ra·rispahat	Red Lance Society	S, C, K, P
ra·ristarahaksuʔ	Brave Raven Lance Society	S, C
ra·risickirihki	Wolf Lance Society	S
ra·risku·hat	Loon Lance Society	S
pakska·tit	Black Head	K
tirupahe	Fighting Lance	C, K, P
kicita	Knife Lance	S
hatuhka	Last on Trail (Coming Behind)	S, C, K, P
	Private (Non-Bundle)-Societies	
asi·cakahu·ruʔ (Skidi), *ase·cakahu·ruʔ* (South Band)	Wild Horse	S, C, K, P
hiruskaʔipi·raʔuʔ	Children of the Iruska	S
ka·ka·wa·ruksti?	Holy Crow	S, C, K, P
ra·risaruskucuʔ	Big Horse Lance Society	C
ra·riska·kaʔ	Crow Lance Society	S, K
pakspa·hukasa	Roached Head	S
asa·kipiri·ruʔ	Young Dog	S, K
not recorded	Circumcised (Mischievous)	C

C=Chawi, K=Kitkahahki, P=Pitahawirata, S=Skiri

Membership in the bundle societies was generally, although not exclusively, gained through kinship ties, with a member being succeeded at death by a relative. Among the Skiri, members came from the entire tribe, and whenever a society held a meeting the seating arrangement in the lodge was fixed: members were assigned to either the north or south side according to their bundle and village affiliation. There was, moreover, a seasonal alternation in leadership between the north (winter) and south (summer) sides, similar, but not identical, to that of the chiefs.

A second group was private organizations that rivaled or imitated the recognized societies. They were formed by ambitious young men who had visions in which they were called upon to form a new society. These organizations did not have any public functions or official recognition, although in time of need their members frequently volunteered their services and the society thereby gained social prestige. Most were short-lived, since they were held together only by the personality and enthusiasm of their leaders (Murie 1914).

• SOCIAL STRATIFICATION Pawnee society was socially stratified into two groups, the upper classes and the commoners. The dichotomy was largely determined by hereditary rights, since members of leading families inherited their positions, which were sustained by religious sanctions and reinforced by economic position. Other individuals did not have that advantage and were socially insignificant unless they raised their position through their own efforts—by achieving success in war, by joining men's societies, or even by becoming a doctor. But that achieved status accrued to only the individual during his lifetime and could not be passed on to offspring (Holder 1970:144–156).

Holding highest rank was the hereditary chief. Succession was always patrilineal, generally passing to the eldest son. Sometimes the direct heir might decline the responsibility or might be unfit for the office, and then another more suitable male relative would fill it. Enjoying only slightly less prestige were subchiefs, who did not inherit their positions but were elected to them. Some came from prominent families, while others were commoners. All had distinguished themselves in war and on the hunt and had exhibited the chiefly traits of generosity and self-restraint. Once elected to the position, a chief was given a permanent seat in their chiefs' council and occupied it until his death.

Each hereditary chief selected a warrior assistant (*ra·hikucuʔ*) whose responsibilities were to insure that the chief's decisions were executed, to preserve order in the village, and to assist in the preparation of ceremonies. He in turn appointed three village police (*ra·ripakusuʔ*) to assist him. Unlike the chief, who was a peacemaker and guardian of the village, these men were strong and aggressive, respected because of their physical abilities as well as position. The office of warrior assistant tended to run in upper-class families, but could be achieved by anyone. Another secular position accorded high status was that of warrior (*ra·wira·kis*, *rara·wira·ris*), an achieved rank that afforded social prominence to a commoner who was successful in war and hunting and who made sacrifices to the leading sacred bundles.

The position of priest was outranked only by that of the hereditary chief. Because the priest alone knew all the ritual and complex lore of the sacred bundles, and consequently had mastered a prodigious amount of knowledge and thus power, he commanded respect from the people. That knowledge was acquired only after a long, arduous, and expensive process, and priests, like doctors, guarded their knowledge. Knowledge was power and a life-sustaining essence, and to divulge everything one knew shortened one's life.

Ranking just below the status of priest was that of the doctor, whose position was based on the ability to control and manipulate supernatural power. That power enabled him to cure, as well as to witch other individuals, causing misfortune or even death.

Two other positions that carried modest but respected status in Pawnee society were those of the crier (*pattikus*, South Band *paktikus*) and the errand man (*taru·cuhus*, South Band *taru·ciʔus*), which were associated with ritual activities. An older, respected man, the crier announced ceremonies and political decisions to the village, and sometimes publicly recited rituals of instruction. For every ceremony, secular or religious, there were two errand men, who always sat near the entrance inside the lodge, one on the north side and the other on the south side. Their duties were to tend the fires, cook and serve food for offerings and feasts, and in other ways assist the leaders of a ceremony. Because they were always present, the errand men learned most ceremonies, including the songs and even many secrets; and although they could never use that knowledge officially, they were accorded respect and a comfortable social position.

Commoners in Pawnee society were people without position, wealth, or influence. Constituting approximately half the population, they were people who had no social ambitions or were unsuccessful. Their lodges were small and poorly furnished, and they had few or no horses. They were, consequently, objects of upper-class charity. Below them in status were people who had violated tribal custom or in some other way had become social outcasts and lived on the outskirts of the village. In the late nineteenth century many of these individuals gravitated to the fringes of White settlements (Parks in Murie 1981, 1:10–11).

• KINSHIP Although the village was conceived to be a large kin group, the basic kinship unit was the extended family living in an earthlodge. At its head was an older woman who had built the lodge and owned it, together with her husband. The woman's younger sisters might live there as well, since sororal polygyny was common. Their unmarried sons and their daughters and daughters' spouses comprised a second generation, while the daughters' children made up the third generation. In addition, one or more other families, generally related, might live in the earthlodge, especially in one of a chief, priest, or doctor, which was of exceptional size and could accommodate large ceremonial gatherings.

Postmarital residence was ordinarily matrilocal, following a pattern in which a young man joined his wife's parents' household and performed various services for his in-laws, including hunting. Later, after a man had established himself as a good provider and protector of his family, he and his wife might establish a lodge of their own. During communal hunts, the lodge household often broke up into smaller units, each formed around a capable hunter, that lived in a tepee or summer arbor; and sometimes members of different households might re-form into new units that pooled resources, and later they might continue those household realignments when returning to the earthlodge village.

The women of the lodge insured its stability and continuity. The oldest woman, a grandmother, coordinated the work of the younger women and cared for the children. Middle-aged women performed most of the household labor, including cooking and gardening, while the youngest women, either unmarried daughters or junior wives, looked after the needs of the men living in the lodge. Men, in contrast, were relatively loosely tied to the household, in part because they married out of it and in part because their lifestyle meant that they spent less time there. In addition to hunting, young men devoted much of their time to the activities of their societies and to war expeditions, while middle-aged and older men were involved in village political and social activities that kept them away from the lodge. Boys, young men, and older men, in particular, were transient, frequently spending nights or longer periods in other households. Although the mature man spent more time in his wife's lodge, he never considered it to be his true home, which was the lodge of his mother and sisters.

The kinship system was bilateral and generational. Conceptually a father's brother was a father, a mother's sister was a mother, a man's brother's child was his child, a woman's sister's child was also her child, and children of siblings of like sex were siblings to each other. All these features were extended throughout the system to all collateral lines. Although a father's sister was called mother, a mother's brother was called uncle. In addition, the Pawnee had features of a lineal Crow-type classification. Thus, cross-cousins were not siblings: the mother's brother's children were termed children, while the father's sister's children were called mother and father. Moreover, the children of one's grandchildren were termed children, and the parents of one's grandparents were called mothers and mother's brothers.

Patterned social behavior among relatives was either respectful or jocular. Respect obtained between children and their parents, or between any individuals to whom the parent and child terms were extended. Relations between siblings of the opposite sex were formal, while among brothers there was a lifelong respect for seniority. A relationship analogous to that between younger and older brother was that between nephew and maternal uncle, in that at puberty a boy would go to live in the lodge of either his uncle or his older brother and there receive instruction and training, which included sharing either the uncle's or brother's wife, and in fact calling his uncle's wife "wife" and his uncle's children "my child." Moreover, at the death of an uncle or an older brother, a man would frequently marry the older man's widow.

The most pronounced joking relationship existed between grandparents and their grandchildren and extended to all relatives among whom there was this relationship. The joking, which represented a relaxed relationship, was typically humorous, critical, and vulgar, often referring to marriage. Between a child and his close grandparent the joking was only in fun; but with other, more distant relatives who called each other by grandparent-grandchild terms, marriage was frequent. Similarly, a joking relationship obtained between a young man and the wives of his older brother and uncle because it also included a frequent spousal relationship (Lesser 1930, 1979; Weltfish 1965:20–37).

Life Cycle

After the first sign of pregnancy an expectant mother and her husband had to observe certain prohibitions. A woman, for example, was forbidden to use any form of knife to prepare or cut food, since it was believed that to do so would sever the umbilical cord and cause the child to bleed to death; and she refrained from drinking with a horn spoon or from an earthenware vessel used as a dipper, since the sound residing in it would carry through her to the child and cause it to be born deaf.

At the first sign of labor the husband unbraided his hair to wear it loose and left the lodge for a period of four days, since his presence was believed to increase the difficulty of birth. When labor began, a midwife gave the woman medicine to induce an easy birth, and when the child was born the midwife cut the umbilical cord and later wrapped it in buckskin for the mother to keep in a work box throughout her life. After the midwife washed the infant and placed it on a cradleboard (fig. 12), she bestowed a name upon the baby and gave it to the mother's relatives. Then she placed the afterbirth on a wad of grass, which she wrapped in a piece of buckskin and carried into the woods, where she placed it on a tree.

Children were usually nursed until three years old. Their grandmothers took charge of their early training, and later both grandparents were more actively involved in training children than were parents. Grandmothers taught girls to prepare food, dress hides, and do other women's tasks, while grandfathers instructed boys to make bows and arrows and to play games. Early training included instruction in tribal and family ethics, topics largely inculcated through myths and etiological stories. In addition to grand-

U. of Okla. Lib., Western Hist. Coll., Norman: Cunningham Coll.:144.

Fig. 12. Couple with child in cradleboard. Cradleboards were made by the father's relatives and were decorated with carved and painted symbolic designs, such as the morning star represented here (Von Del Chamberlain 1982:24, 58–60). The child is secured to the cradleboard with finger-woven yarn sashes. Photograph by William S. Prettyman, about 1885.

parents and parents, the mother's brother generally took an active interest in the education of his sisters' sons and daughters, generally giving them as much attention as a father would. On the paternal side, children also had the same rights in their father's sister's lodge that they had in their parents' lodge. The father's sister's husband, in fact, became teacher and to some extent guardian of his wife's brothers' daughters; and if his wife should die, he might marry his wife's niece or even her daughters, if she already had a husband (G.A. Dorsey and Murie 1940:93–95).

When a girl reached her first menses, if she were the daughter of a bundle keeper, she moved into a small lodge outside the earthlodge and remained there with her grandmother for the duration of her menstrual period, since the odor of menstrual blood was believed to destroy the power of sacred objects, and even to render doctors themselves powerless. At the end of her period, the girl's grandmother bathed, reclothed, and purified her with cedar smoke. Subsequently, the two retired to this lodge at every menstrual period, until the girl married (Roaming Scout 1907; G.A. Dorsey and Murie 1940:95–96).

When a boy reached puberty, his mother's brother's wife took charge of him and initiated him to sex. Previously he had gone naked; from now he wore leggings and dressed as a man. From then until he married, he continued sexual relations with his aunt, particularly when his uncle was off hunting or traveling with a war party. Thus, for a period of four or five years the young man, and perhaps his brothers as well, would be a junior husband for this woman, creating a temporary state of polyandry.

Marriages, at least among the upper-class Pawnee, were usually arranged between families. A young man was considered ready only after he had reached maturity, had killed buffalo, and had gone on at least one successful war party, preferably capturing horses, thereby demonstrating that he would be a good provider for a family. After he had demonstrated his readiness, his mother's brother would inform the young man that he was ready for marriage and perhaps announce that he had selected a wife for him; or the young man himself would tell his uncle that he wished to marry and might mention the name of a young woman he desired. Once the young man's family had agreed on a potential wife, an older man, usually a priest, together with the young man, went to the young woman's lodge and the old man explained the reason for their visit. Later, the girl's uncle, and perhaps her brothers as well, would discuss the potential marriage and reach a decision. If the marriage were approved by both families, there was a formal exchange of gifts between them, and then the young man moved into the lodge of his wife's family (G.A. Dorsey and Murie 1940:97–101; Grinnell 1891).

Among other families, marriages were less formal. One night, after the family had gone to bed, a young man might enter the lodge of a young woman he wished to marry and get into her bed. In the morning, the girl's family would discuss the suitability of the young man, and if they approved of him he would move into their lodge.

At death, the preparation of the body and the burial itself varied according to the status of an individual in Pawnee society. When a man or woman of high status was about to die, the family dressed the body in the person's best clothing; and immediately after death the body was painted with red ointment, which gave the skin a smooth, healthy appearance and signaled to the deceased in the spirit land that the person had been well cared for on earth. If a male had been a member of a men's society, his ceremonial paraphernalia was placed with him and his face was painted in the style of the society. Finally, the body was wrapped—usually in a buffalo robe, but also in a rush mat or trade blanket—and securely tied in preparation for burial (Roaming Scout 1907; G.A. Dorsey and Murie 1940:101–107; Wedel 1986:171).

Individuals of high status and others with a family or relatives were buried on a hill outside the village. Men's graves were located on the higher slopes, while women's and children's were on the lower slopes (Wedel 1986:171). For a chief, a wooden lodge might be constructed in the grave and the corpse placed inside it. A man's most valued possessions would be hung from poles at his grave or be placed in the grave, while a woman's possessions—the things she had on her bed, including the cross sticks on the bed frame—would be buried with her. If a person had no relatives or was an inadequate provider for his wife or family, he would be wrapped in his robe, dragged outside the village, placed in a natural hole, and covered with rocks. A poor person with no relatives might be thrown over a bank into a river or, if the village were traveling, his body might be rolled up in whatever he wore and then abandoned (Roaming Scout 1907; Wedel 1986:171).

After a variable period of mourning there was a ritual "wiping of tears" ceremony and death feast for the family of the deceased that formally concluded the mourning. For a chief the period might last several months, but for most men of high status the period was five days. For a poor person the family mourned and fasted three days. At the end of the period, the deceased's family and friends assembled in the family's lodge, where his personal effects had been gathered together and were then distributed to the people present. Afterward a smoke offering to the earth was made, and then the officiant, generally an old man or a chief, washed the faces of the mourners and gave them a ritual drink of water; then the other people in the lodge washed their own faces, all thereby symbolically washing their tears and ending their mourning. Sometimes an old man or priest would deliver an oration, and then the mourners ate a meal cooked by the chief's wife that marked the end of the fasting that had begun after the person's death (Roaming Scout 1907).

When a woman lost her husband, she was supposed to mourn for a year; and if he were a man of prominence she might mourn for as long as two years. During that period she would live with either her own family or her deceased husband's parents. When she resided with her husband's parents, it was understood that at the end of the mourning period she would become the wife of either her husband's younger brother or his sister's son. If the widow were childless, she invariably returned to her parents' lodge, and once the mourning period was over she married again. Should she marry outside her husband's family, she was considered not as desirable as at her first marriage, and the gifts to her family were considerably less.

Men mourned for their wives for at least two, and sometimes three, years. Most men would not consider remarrying until they had gone on a successful war party, taken scalps, and captured horses—acts that formally terminated their period of mourning and symbolized their eligibility for remarriage (G.A. Dorsey and Murie 1940:104–105).

Religion and Healing

The ceremonial life of the Pawnee was dominated by the priests with their sacred bundles and the doctors with their medicines. Although both shared a general concern with the supernatural and attempted to control natural phenomena, they differed markedly in their objectives, the deities invoked, and the means by which they sought to achieve their ends. Those differences closely approximate the distinction between religion and magic, and, similarly, the roles of the two ritual specialists represent the distinction between priest and shaman.

There were certain similarities in the rituals of both priests and doctors. In every ceremony the participants painted themselves. They also made offerings of tobacco and food (always corn and meat), and incensed both ritual objects and themselves. But beyond those similarities, which broadly define a ritual event, there were striking, fundamental differences.

• PRIESTS AND BUNDLE CEREMONIES Since the position of priest was divinely ordained at the time of creation, his functions, like those of the chief, were prescribed. His role was that of a mediator between the deities of the heavens and the people, an intermediary who sought to achieve good fortune and an orderly world through ritual and sacrificial offerings. The priest himself had no supernatural power; he only knew the complex ritual and sacred knowledge that were necessary to the performance of his office.

The deities of the priests were heavenly beings that were arranged hierarchically. At the top was Tirawahat (*tiráwa·hat,* South Band *tira·wa·hat* 'this expanse [of the heavens]'), an amorphous being who created the universe and was identified with the totality of the heavens. Subordinate to him were Evening Star and Morning Star, followed by Sun and Moon and other stellar deities who were involved with various aspects of the creation of the world. All these powers constituted a pantheon that controlled the universe at large. They were responsible for the weather, plant growth, fertility, and other generalized human concerns.

The priests' rituals were distributed over a long ceremonial season that began in the spring and continued through the fall. With few exceptions, each ceremony in the sequence was a measured liturgy that lacked drama. In the liturgies there were several solemn ritual acts (sacrifices and offerings) interspersed with long cycles of songs that recounted events in mythological times. The songs were fixed in form and were long and repetitive, with an emphasis on detail. In intent, the entire sequence sought to gain the attention of the deities and to seek favor by supplication and sacrifice as well as by acknowledgment of their deeds.

Bundles symbolized the history of a group of people and its covenant with the deities. There were several types of them, but they all had in common an origin in an earlier supernatural experience or encounter. During that experience the deity instructed the visionary to make up a bundle of various objects, some to recall what had happened in the vision and some to be used by him in subsequent rituals. Bundles were aggregates of the two kinds of physical objects, the symbolic and the ritual, wrapped up in buffalo hides, which served as casings.

There were two general types of bundles. The ones designated *cuharipi·ru?* (South Band *cu?uhre·re·pi·ru?*) were village or band bundles and were more important. The other type, *karu·su?* ('sack'), was any lesser bundle belonging to an individual.

Most ceremonies occurred at fixed times during the year when certain natural phenomena signaled the appropriate time. The Thunder (or Creation) Ritual of the Evening Star bundle, for example, which initiated the ritual season, was held after the first thunder in the spring, about the time of the spring equinox.

Three ceremonies occurred at variable times. The New Fire ceremony took place whenever a war party brought back to the village the appropriate trophies, generally scalps. The human sacrifice to the Morning Star and the North Star Offering were held only after a man had dreamed that he should sponsor one of these ceremonies, and consequently they were not necessarily annual events. Two other ceremonies also depended on a visionary for their occurrence. The Young Corn Plant ritual commenced when the priests noted that the newly planted corn had grown to a certain height. However, during the preceding year a man dreamed that he was the one to insure that the ceremony would be held, and during the winter hunt he obtained the meat necessary for it. The Corn Planting ceremony of the Skull bundle depended on a woman who dreamed during the preceding winter buffalo hunt that she must sponsor the ritual, and then she had to get a brother to obtain the necessary meat. It was the only ceremony in which women played a major role and the visionary was traditionally a female.

• DOCTORS AND THEIR CEREMONIES The doctor's position was not prescribed. Although he could achieve it directly from a vision experience, he generally attained the position after a long apprenticeship. At birth every Pawnee child came under the influence of a certain animal who was later to be his guardian. The identity of this animal became known either directly through a vision or, more frequently, by enabling a doctor who had power from that same animal to cure the person when he was ill. Once the person knew the identity of his guardian, he could apply to that animal lodge to learn its secrets and become a doctor himself. By means of further signs he could go on to learn the secrets of other medicine societies and progress upward in status and power.

The doctors' deities were earthly powers, particularly animals. Among them there was no fixed pantheon, only an amorphous group of different animals, each possessing similar powers that could be used by humans. Some, like the bear, were thought to be especially powerful; but all animals, even insects, figured in the mythology of the doctors. Each could potentially bless a man and endow him with power, which was always basically the same: the power to cure disease or illness, to hypnotize and witch, and to perform magical feats. Unique among the Pawnee was the belief in underground or underwater animal lodges, in which different varieties of animals met, organized in the same manner as the doctors in the Doctors' Lodge. During visions, Pawnees were frequently taken into these lodges and given the powers of the animals there. Such sites included Pahaku (fig. 13), Guide Rock, Nebraska, and Waconda Spring, Kansas (Parks and Wedel 1985).

The medicine societies and the Doctors' Lodge were two separate organizations with different ceremonies. Medicine societies were composed of doctors whose power came from the same animal as well as any novices whom those doctors had admitted. Several societies—like the Bear, Buffalo, and Deer—were common to all the Pawnee, while others, like the Blood Doctors of the Skiri, were specific to one band. The Doctors' Lodge was a corporation of sorts that met several times a year. Each of the Pawnee bands had its own Doctors' Lodge. Its members were leading doctors from the medicine societies who had applied for a seat (or booth) in the Doctors' Lodge, had performed successfully, and consequently had been given permanent status in the organization, where they represented their medicine society. Among the societies represented in the Skiri Doctors' Lodge in the mid-nineteenth

Nebr. State Histl. Soc., Lincoln: RG2963.PH:24.

Fig. 13. Pahaku (*pa·háku* 'mound on the water'), a Pawnee animal lodge site below the bluff, on the south bank of the Platte River, 6 miles west of Fremont, Nebr. The bluff rises 180–200 feet above the normal river level. It was said to be the first animal lodge known to the Pawnee as well as the source of the Skiri Doctors' Lodge (Parks and Wedel 1985:153–155). Photograph by Arthur Anderson, 1925.

century were the Bear, Deer, Black-tailed Deer, Buffalo, Eagle, Fish Hawk, and Coyote.

The individual medicine societies generally met at least twice a year, in the spring and in late summer or early autumn. The spring meetings included a renewal ritual in which the members, like keepers of sacred bundles, opened their bundles and thurified them in the smoke of sweetgrass. The fall ceremonies of the medicine societies were similar to the spring meetings and lasted no more than several days; they were held in a circular shelter of green boughs, similar to the Sun Dance enclosure of other Plains tribes. All other doctors' ceremonies were held in an earthlodge, generally that of the leading doctor of the particular organization.

The doctors, apart from several short rituals, concentrated their activity into one massive performance, the Thirty-Day ceremony or Doctors' Lodge, near the end of the ritual season. For the Skiri it was the Thirty-Day ceremony (*tawaru·kucu?* 'big performance'), during which the doctors lived in their lodge for a month. The purpose of these rituals was to demonstrate the doctors' powers, to convince the people of their mysterious abilities, and to inspire awe. Unlike bundle ceremonies, the doctors' ceremonies were staged events in which drama predominated. The doctors impersonated their animal guardians and practiced legerdemain. Early Euro-American accounts tell of men being shot dead and brought back to life, body parts amputated and then restored, corn plants grown from seed before the eyes of spectators, and many similar feats. Those acts were impressive, gaining for their doctors a reputation as skilled magicians (Grinnell 1889:375–388). Besides the sleight-of-hand performances, each doctor had his own songs that commemorated the original vision experience upon which his power was based. The songs were fixed in their general form, but each had its individual peculiarities. Each doctor and his apprentices, dressed like and imitating their animal mentor, accompanied the doctor's song with dancing. The dances were a reenactment of the personal encounter between the doctor and his supernatural source of power, the animal; and to validate that encounter, the doctor sought by legerdemain to perform miracles in a staged setting.

• CALUMET CEREMONY The widespread Calumet ceremony, which Fletcher and Murie (1904) called the Hako (*raktara·?iwari·hus*, South Band *raktara·?iwari·?us* 'waving the pipestems'), was a religious ritual in which one individual adopted someone in another social group, either a different band or tribe. The ceremony was initiated by a "father" and a group of his kindred, numbering from 20 to 100 individuals. The father was a wealthy individual, usually a chief, who, together with his relatives, could afford the lavish gifts that were given to the "son" and his relatives, who were also of high social standing and able to afford reciprocal gifts. A man could initiate the ceremony at any time, since it was not a part of the annual ritual calendar, and would take his party to the "children's" village, where there were four days of elaborate rituals that ended with the consecration of a child in the "children's" family, followed by songs, prayers, and dancing that sought blessings for the child and his family—to bring to them the promise of children, long life, and plenty, as well as to establish bonds between two social groups that were as strong as kinship (Fletcher and Murie 1904).

History, 1875–1998

At the time they left Nebraska, most Pawnees still clung to their traditional village life. After moving onto their new reservation, each of the four bands settled on large, separate tracts of land and, initially, farmed the band tract cooperatively after government farmers broke the land for cultivation. There the Pawnee settled into a pattern of life much like the one they had known in Nebraska and for a short time maintained an attenuated form of their old village life in which the chiefs, priests, and doctors continued to organize Pawnee social, economic, and religious activities.

During the early period on the reservation, the produce of the band farms, as well as that from the agency farm, constituted the Pawnees' basic food supply. The principal crop was corn, supplemented by beans and squash, and increasingly by wheat, oats, potatoes, and other vegetables. For years, however, that supply proved inadequate because of natural misfortunes such as drought, insects, and hail storms. Crop failures made the tribe dependent on government rations or on food purchased with their annuity funds, which also were inadequate. In 1875–1876 the tribe attempted a buffalo hunt, but that proved to be futile, and so their meat supply also had to come from government rations.

No more than one-third of the Pawnee reservation was suited for cultivation, and since grazing land was plentiful, the government in 1878 issued cattle to the tribe. Because the livestock received good care and the tribe asked for more, there was an attempt to develop a stock-raising program, and in summer 1880 the Pawnee were issued 400 heifers and bulls. However, by 1882 the program ended in failure after disease took many animals during the first winter; later the Pawnee killed most of the remaining stock whenever they wanted meat or wished to sell hides to traders (Lesser 1933:36).

One of the provisions of the congressional act of 1876 that established the Pawnee Reservation was allotments in severalty. Each family head or single person over 21 years of age who so desired was to be allotted 160 acres of land, and a certificate of individual ownership was to be issued by the commissioner of Indian affairs. If an allotee occupied and cultivated his land for five successive years, he was entitled to receive a patent in fee simple for the allotment, inalienable for 15 years thereafter. Many young and progressive Pawnees took individual farm lands as soon as they could be surveyed, and the agency carpenter assisted them in constructing frame houses. In 1882, despite a concerted drive by agency officials to get families to relocate, there were only 55 families living on individual farms, and they often had to camp in tepees for long periods while waiting for the necessary surveying and assistance in house building.

Meanwhile, most members of the tribe continued to reside in their band villages, where the priests, chiefs, and doctors opposed the move to individualized farming and the changes in Pawnee village life that it entailed. Their resistance was reinforced by the lax and inefficient methods of government officials, who also were often dishonest. After 1882 when the independent Pawnee Agency was merged into a combined one for the Ponca, Pawnee, and Otoe that was located in Ponca City, the agent spent only one or two days a week with the Pawnee. Nevertheless, by 1890 most Skiris and a large proportion of Chawis lived in houses on their own farms, dressed like contemporary Whites, and spoke English in daily life. Most Kitkahahkis and Pitahawiratas were on allotted tracts as well, but many still lived in earthlodges, and only those who attended school spoke English and dressed like Whites.

During the first two decades of their residence in Indian Territory, poor health and a rapid decrease in population brought discouragement to Pawnees and hampered programs intended to improve their lives. Immediately after relocation malarial fevers began to afflict them, taking a heavy toll, and later many died of tuberculosis and pneumonia. Moreover, the housing built for them did not make any provision for sanitation; most did not have outhouses and none of the houses had wells, so that water for drinking and cooking had to come from creeks or springs. In 1883 the tribe had for the first time the services of a physician, who taught them how to sink wells and maintain their water supply, but for more than a decade there was constant strife between him and the Pawnee doctors (ARCIA 1883:77). Not until about 1900 did Pawnees begin to go to agency physicians after realizing that their own doctors were unable to cure their illnesses (Lesser 1933:40–42).

For many years the agency educational program was no more successful than the one for developing farms and houses. Once the new Pawnee Industrial Boarding School began operation, it could accommodate no more than one-quarter of the school-age Pawnee population and could not provide facilities for even those who were registered (ARCIA 1882:79). Instruction in industrial arts—in manual arts and farming for boys, in housekeeping and sewing for girls, and reading for both—was at best minimally successful, leading the agent to comment in 1881 that the school was only nominally "industrial" (ARCIA 1889; Lesser 1933:42–45).

In 1879 the Office of Indian Affairs broadened its educational program by establishing off-reservation boarding schools. The first of these institutions was Carlisle Indian Industrial School in Carlisle, Pennsylvania, which provided academic training through 10 grades and initiated an "outing system" designed to give Indian children experience in White society. Thirteen Pawnees enrolled in Carlisle when it opened, and several years later Pawnee enrollment increased to 19. Meanwhile, Pawnees also attended Hampton Normal and Agricultural Institute in Virginia, a school for Blacks that developed a program for Indians. When Chilocco and Haskell schools opened, Pawnee children were sent to them as well, and by 1889 most Pawnee children of school age were enrolled either in the agency or off-reservation schools (Lesser 1933:42–44; Tousey 1939:273–353).

Until 1887, whenever legal disputes arose among Pawnees, the parties preferred to take their issues to the agent; but in 1889, when the tribe requested it, the Pawnee Court of Indian Offenses was established, assisted by an eight-member Indian police force formed in 1882. The court comprised three Pawnee judges, who adjudicated settlement of estates, adjustment of debts, destruction of property, divorce, and drunkenness. Both court and police continued until 1893 when the Pawnee became citizens of the United States and were then subject to territorial law.

In 1884 the Pawnee agreed to lease 150,000 acres of reservation grazing land to White cattlemen. That agreement, which marked the beginning of the alienation of the Pawnee Reservation, worked against government programs to make the Pawnee self-sufficient, since the money realized from the leases supported most of the tribe and encouraged many individuals to accept a life of idleness. Three years later Congress passed the Dawes Severalty Act, and in 1889 President Benjamin Harrison opened the Territory of Oklahoma to White settlement on lands not assigned to tribes and on excess Indian land sold as a result of the Dawes Act.

In 1892 the Office of Indian Affairs moved to complete the allotment of tracts in severalty among the Pawnee and, for those already living on plots they had chosen and were cultivating, to confirm their possession of them. That summer a special allotting agent came to the Pawnee Agency and drew up 797 allotments in severalty. The Skiri band took allotments north of the town of Pawnee; Chawis, west of town; Pitahawiratas and Kitkahahkis south and east. The agent reserved 840 acres for the school, agency, cemetery, and religious purposes. The residue land, 169,320 acres, was to be purchased from the tribe. In compensation for the surplus lands the Pawnee received an advance of $80,000, with the balance of the sale price to be deposited in the U.S. Treasury as a trust fund, as well as an agreement to continue their perpetual annuity of $30,000. The agreement was ratified March 3, 1893, and that same year the ceded lands were opened for settlement.

In selecting their own tracts Pawnees had chosen the best land on their reservation, and as a result their allotments were scattered. Consequently, when the ceded land was opened to settlement there was an immediate influx of White settlers who lived among and on all sides of them, and the modern town of Pawnee sprang up within a year, drastically changing Pawnee life. At the same time the Pawnees' legal status changed. They were free citizens of the United States, and the agent no longer had executive power to control their acts and behavior. The Whites who settled among the Pawnee were anxious to do business with them, since combined tribal income from the down payment on their lands, from their annuity payment, and from interest on the land sale amounted to $177,000 in 1893. That income, together with money generated from the system of leasing Indian farm lands, worked even more strongly against government efforts to make farmers or tradesmen of the Pawnee (Lesser 1933:67–68).

After 1906, as a result of the Curtis Act, the Pawnee no longer had a tribal government. Although not organized politically during the first three decades of the twentieth century, the Pawnee tradition of hereditary chiefs was still a respected one, and the chiefs acted for the tribe in dealing with U.S. officials. Then in the early 1930s, when President Franklin D. Roosevelt inaugurated the Indian Reorganization Act and the Oklahoma Indian Welfare Act, a non-assimilationist program, the Pawnee supported it. The program, which recognized the existence of Indian communities, sought to give them the legal status and economic resources to continue their tribal existence as long as they chose.

In 1936 the Pawnee drafted a tribal constitution that was adopted by a substantial majority in January 1938. It established two governing bodies for the tribe: a Chiefs', or Nasharo, Council comprised of eight individuals having hereditary rights to chieftainship and elected every four years; and a Business Council made up of eight individuals elected every two years. Hereditary chiefs could not be members of the Business Council. The active governing body was to be the Business Council, which spoke and acted for the tribe as well as transacted its business. The Nasharo Council, in contrast, was essentially a symbolic body that had the right to review Business Council actions involving tribal membership, tribal claims, and treaty rights.

In 1932 Pawnee education was aided by construction of a new school building to replace the one destroyed in a fire in 1904. The native-stone structure had eight classrooms, a large auditorium, and a central heating and air conditioning unit, making it one of the most modern and best equipped facilities in the Indian Service. However, in 1942, when the commissioner of Indian affairs ordered that all Indian agencies in the state be abolished, except for the offices in Anadarko and Muskogee, the school was closed and only two employees were left to staff the Pawnee facility. Eventually the agency offices were moved from the agency grounds to offices in downtown Pawnee (Franks and Lambert 1994:219).

During the decades after establishing a tribal constitution Pawnee leaders had to learn the complexities of administering a tribal organization that had in the past been handled by government agencies, but, because tribal officials lacked the requisite training, the local agent's office continued for many years to administer the tribe as it had been doing. From after World War II until the late 1950s, Congress reversed the policies of the Roosevelt administration and again promoted assimilation of American Indians. In the 1960s, when the forces of assimilation and termination waned, Indian communities were included among the minority groups to be helped by federal social programs.

Immediately after reorganization in 1937, Pawnee leaders sought to regain the Pawnee Reserve, comprising the lands surrounding the agency that had not been alloted. In 1957 the Department of Interior granted the Pawnee the right to use the reserve lands, but it did not give the tribe title to them. In 1968 Congress returned ownership to the tribe, recognizing that the land had been given to the Pawnee in exchange for their lands in Nebraska. In 1975 two additional 20-acre tracts that had been separated from the reserve lands were returned to the tribe (Tyson 1976:94–98). In 1964, 1,898 Pawnees shared in the per capita distribution of a land claims settlement that, through the Indian Claims Commission, compensated the tribe for loss of lands in Kansas and Nebraska (Lesser 1978:x).

In 1962 the tribe acquired the former Pawnee Indian School, which had been vacant for 20 years, and in 1979 leased the school building to the Bureau of Indian Affairs to serve as the offices of the combined agency for the Pawnee, Otoe, Tonkawa, Kansa, and Ponca tribes. At the same time the Pawnee tribal office moved to a smaller structure in the old school complex; and in 1980 a new tribal "roundhouse"—a social center designed after the former band roundhouses that were used for dances and other events—was dedicated nearby. In the late 1980s and early 1990s the Pawnee, like most tribes throughout Oklahoma, managed a bingo operation and a tobacco sales operation (Franks and Lambert 1994:219–221).

Culture, 1875–1998

During the first 15 years after their move to Indian Territory, the Pawnee experienced a rapid loss of traditional culture that was driven by government efforts to transform their economic and material life and simultaneously to suppress tribal customs. The changes in Pawnee life undermined the power of traditional leaders more fundamentally than the opposition from government officials. The hereditary chief, for example, had traditionally been the "father" of his people—a religiously sanctioned leader who accumulated greater material wealth than others through his prowess on the warpath and hunt and through contributions from his people, and who, in turn, dispensed that wealth to his people as an act of paternal generosity whenever the need arose. Gradually, the chief's traditional role became less relevant as ownership of homes and farms enabled individual Pawnees to be materially independent of both chief and tribe. Similarly, the role and importance of priests and doctors waned as the former religious and healing ceremonies lost their significance in a world that had changed economically, socially, and medically. The ritual demonstrations of sacred bundles had practically ceased by 1892, as the last priests who knew the rituals died and associated ceremonial paraphernalia were buried with them. The last great Doctors' Dance was performed in 1878, although the short spring and summer dances continued irregularly.

Other social institutions came under attack. Beginning in 1881 agency officials began to interfere with marriage customs: with polygyny, especially the sororate; with first marriages of young girls, often 14 years old, to older men; and with divorces that were effected simply by mutual consent. By 1890 the agent claimed that those customs had been suppressed and that many Pawnees would seek a missionary to perform marriage ceremonies (ARCIA 1890:197; Lesser 1933:45–47). Agency personnel attempted to prevent dancing, gambling, and feasting, which were important social activities that kept families away from their farms for long periods and resulted in neglected crops.

Although by 1890 the Pawnee were relatively prosperous materially and had adopted most of the material culture of their White neighbors, they had not regained the independence they had formerly known. Consequently, like many other Plains tribes, they were receptive to a nativistic movement when the Ghost Dance spread to the Plains in 1890. In 1891, when Frank White, a Kitkahahki, was visiting the Comanche and Wichita after they had adopted it, he participated in their dances, learned the doctrine, and observed its early forms of organization and leadership as taught by Sitting Bull, the Northern Arapahoe who had introduced the Ghost Dance to the tribes in southern Indian Territory. After returning home, White taught the doctrine and songs to South Band friends, urging them to reject the farm and other work encouraged by White society.

The Pawnee, excited over doctrine that foretold a return to their former way of life, embraced the Ghost Dance at once. Within the first year of its introduction, approximately two-thirds of the tribe were under White's influence. Adherents, who danced all day and late into the night, would fall to the ground, go into a trance, and awake to tell of visions in which they saw deceased relatives living happily in a Pawnee world as it existed before the presence of Whites. To regain that world, followers of the movement believed they had to put the forms of Euro-American culture aside. They stopped working, and consequently throughout the Ghost Dance period Pawnee agents tried to suppress the dancing, but it continued, generally in secret, until about 1900.

In late 1892 five Pawnees visited Sitting Bull for two months, and while they were among the Arapaho, one of them, Joe Carrion, had a vision in which he was given a different perspective on the Ghost Dance. In it he was told that individual Pawnees could obtain sanctions themselves to innovate forms of the Ghost Dance, whereas previously only White, who portrayed himself as a prophet, could sanction them to do anything. That doctrine, which was readily accepted, initiated a reorganization of the Pawnee Ghost Dance that enabled various individuals who had visions to develop their own forms of the dance. Moreover, Carrion was given the gift of the hand game, which later became a special development of the Ghost Dance, and, with the sanctions that his vision allowed, various prophets appeared among the Pawnee. By 1895 the reorganized Ghost Dance was a four-day ceremony. After the fourth day of dancing, the participants rested and then generally held a hand game. Later, however, hand games were interspersed in the dancing during the four-day period.

The Ghost Dance was a stimulus for the revival of old cultural forms—doctors' ceremonies, men's society songs and dances, and games—all of which contributed to a partial renaissance of Pawnee culture. Primary among them was the hand game, formerly a gambling game for men, that developed into the Ghost Dance hand game ceremony. It required an altar at the west side of the lodge, where the hand game bundle containing the items used in the game were displayed and behind which sat the leaders. The ceremonial game began with a smoke offering, followed by the hand games themselves, the intervals between games filled with Ghost Dance songs and dancing. At the end there was a ceremonial food offering and a feast (Lesser 1933:124–321).

Beginning in 1892 and continuing through the first decade of the twentieth century, there were other cultural revivals, prominent among which were partial reconstructions of former men's societies. Among the many that were reconstituted were the Horse Lance, Crow Lance, Wolf Lance, Fighting Lance, Last on Trail, Crazy Dog, Roached Head, and Young Dog societies (table 2). For each organization, members chose leaders and revived songs, dances, and costumes, as well as renewed old ritual paraphernalia when they existed or attempted to make replicas of old sacred objects when they no longer existed. In contrast to the former societies, which limited participation in performances to its male members, the revivals were performed on behalf of all the people and everyone, including women, could participate in the dancing. Women were even employed as singers in a Skiri Wolf Lance society performance in 1900. The important role of women, as well as dreams, in Ghost Dance period revivals is illustrated in the revival of the One Horn Lance society, which in 1893 took its modernized form from the dreams of a woman who was told how to reconstitute the entire ceremony (Murie 1914:638; Lesser 1933:112–115).

During this period there was also a limited revival of the ceremonies of doctors' societies. Some activities, like the Doctors' Dance and the Buffalo Dance, had not actually ceased during the last decade of the nineteenth century, but the impetus of Ghost Dance period revivals gave them a new lease on life. Others, like the Bear society ceremonies, were thought to be lost, but again the vision became a mandate that their performance be revived, and early in the twentieth century a woman was responsible for its performance among the Pitahawirata after she dreamed that she must sponsor it and convinced the few older men who knew parts of the ceremony to pool their knowledge in order to conduct it (Murie 1981, 2:319–394; Lesser 1933:106–112).

Other revivals included dances. The modern form of the Skiri Iruska, or war dance, related to the Omaha grass dance, was borrowed from the Oglala Sioux in 1887, when three Skiri men visited Young Man Afraid of His Horses. In 1911 it was reformed by Eagle Chief (fig. 10) (vol. 4:631). A variant was organized in 1894 when Sitting Bear, a Kitkahahki, had a series of dreams in which he learned the songs and forms of the dance. Although this form died out in 1903, it was revived in 1912. Roaming Chief, a Chawi, also dreamed songs and another form of the modern Iruska ritual during the early Ghost Dance period, and it later spread to the Pitahawirata (Murie 1914:624–630). Many old games, including the men's hoop and pole and moccasin games and the women's stick dice and plum seed dice games as well as shinny and double ball were revived (Lesser 1933:116–117).

Peyotism reached the Pawnee at the same time that the Ghost Dance was introduced. There are several accounts of its origin. One ascribes it to the Quapaw, whom two Pawnee youths visited in 1890 and who brought home several peyote buttons but little knowledge of the ritual. Later, an Arapaho visiting the Pawnee taught the few converts the ritual and then the movement began to grow. Frank White immediately took over leadership of the Peyote religion and elaborated the ritual, adding many Christian elements to it (Murie 1914:636–638). Another account attributes the introduction of the Peyote religion to White, who learned it at the same time he learned the Ghost Dance, while visiting the Comanche and Wichita (Lesser 1933:60). Yet another source says that Eagle Flying Above obtained the ritual from the Arapaho in 1890 (LaBarre 1938:113). By 1916 the ritual had 45 adult adherents, chiefly among the Pitahawirata.

By 1930 most of the revivals of traditional Pawnee life had ceased. The doctors' dances and most of the society dances had come to an end, although some, like the Iruska and Young Dog Dance, continued. The hand games also continued but had lost their religious meaning, becoming important occasions for fun and recreation rather than serving as religious events, a development that continued throughout the twentieth century.

In October 1943 two veterans of World War I sponsored a feast for the leading men and women of the tribe and planned a homecoming celebration to honor World War II veterans. In July 1946 the war dance that comprised the main form of the celebration was given to the veterans at the event. The Pawnee Indian Homecoming Celebration became an annual four-day event sponsored by the Pawnee Indian Veterans' Association (fig. 14).

In the late twentieth century some traditional dances—the Young Dog Dance and the Iruska—continued in attenuated form but they were social dances that lacked their former ritualism. Most dances featured pan-Plains powwow dancing. The Pawnee regularly celebrated Veterans' Day and Memorial Day with dances at which families often honored some member and individuals had Pawnee names formally bestowed on them as symbols of tribal identity.

Hand games also continued at least once or twice monthly. Families sponsored them to celebrate birthdays and the furloughs of young people serving in the armed forces, while organizations sponsored them as fund-raising events. They, too, lacked their former ritualism and religious significance. Since moving to Oklahoma the Pawnee and Wichita made annual reciprocal visits every summer

Fig. 14. Veterans' Homecoming, Pawnee, Okla. left, Cover of program for the Homecoming Celebration, 1947. Photograph is of Rush Roberts, Sr., the oldest Pawnee veteran, an army scout, 1876–1877. center, Sam Young placing an eagle feather in the roach of a new Pawnee straight dancer, Norman Ross Rice. Watching are 4 chiefs, representing each band. Photograph by William H. Howell, 1982. right, Cover of the program of the 45th annual Homecoming Celebration, 1991. Painting shows a Pawnee Scout with Pawnee servicemen in uniforms of World War I, World War II, Korea, Vietnam, and Desert Storm. Painted by Charles W. Chapman, 1991.

during which the two tribes engaged in dancing, hand games, and other social activities (Blaine 1982).

The only twentieth-century religious survival was an attenuated form of the mourning feast given on the fourth day after death. In the 1990s, with the deaths of the last speakers of Pawnee, the feast took the form of a dinner, but lacking speeches and prayers in Pawnee, its religious significance ended.

The Native American Church continued with a small but active membership. Most Pawnees belonged to the Indian Methodist and Indian Baptist churches, and some joined the Full Gospel Church.

Population

The earliest Pawnee population estimate is 2,000 "Panas" families, cited for the opening of the eighteenth century (Iberville in Nasatir 1952, 1:8). It is unclear whether this number represents all the Pawnee divisions, but it suggests a population in excess of 10,000, assuming a minimum of five individuals in a family. A 1758 estimate for the Skiri specifically is 600 warriors (Kerlérec in Nasatir 1952, 1:8, 52). A 1796 estimate by Jean-Baptiste Truteau (Nasatir 1952, 2:384) numbers the Panimaha (Skiri) at 600 lodges and the "Panis" (South Bands) at 800 lodges. In his 1785 report Miró (Nasatir 1952, 1:126) gives the following figures for "men capable of bearing arms" in each of the Pawnee divisions: 350 for the Skiri; 400 for the "Panis," apparently the Chawi and Pitahawirata combined; and 220 for the Kitkahahki. A similar set of figures for men was given in 1804 by Pierre Chouteau: 400 Skiri, 500 "Panis," and 300 Kitkahahki (Nasatir 1952, 2:760). In 1805, however, Lewis and Clark gave slightly higher figures for "warriors": 280 Skiri, 400 Chawi, and 300 Kitkahahki (Lewis and Clark 1832:708–709). In 1791 Pedro de Nava, writing from Santa Fé, gave figures for the "armed men" of two Pawnee groups, 700 for the "Panana" and 600 for the "Huitauyrata" (Pitatahawirata), which, combined, approximate the preceding figures (Nasatir 1952, 1:148). In 1798 Zenon Trudeau attributed 800 men to the "Panis" on the Platte River (Nasatir 1952, 2:539), apparently an estimate for the South Bands only.

Population figures based on actual counts and more accurate estimates begin with the 1806 figure of Zebulon Pike (table 3). It and later figures show an approximate 35 percent drop in the Pawnee population of 10,000 from the preceding century, a loss undoubtedly attributable to the smallpox epidemics late in the eighteenth century and in 1803.

Although there are few nineteenth-century population figures for each of the four Pawnee divisions, the existing ones indicate that the Skiri were the largest and the Pitahawirata the smallest band. In 1840, the population distribution by band was 1,906 Skiri, 1,823 Kitkahahki, 1,683 Chawi, and 832 Pitahawirata (ARCIA 1840:319). In 1882 there was the same general distribution: 416 Skiri, 307 Kitkahahki, 271 Chawi, and 251 Pitahawirata (ARCIA 1882:77). In the twentieth century band intermarriage made separate population figures relatively meaningless, although Pawnees continued to claim membership in one of the four bands as a prerequisite for voting in tribal elections.

Table 3. Pawnee Population, 1806–1996

Year	*Population*	*Source*
1806	6,223	Pike 1810:239
1819	6,500	James in Thwaites 1904–1907, 17:153
1840	7,500	J.B. Dunbar 1880:254
1847	8,400	J.B. Dunbar 1880:254
1856	4,686	J.B. Dunbar 1880:254
1867	2,935	ARCIA 1867 [1868]: 396
1872	2,447	ARCIA 1872:224
1879	1,440	J.B. Dunbar 1880:254
1892	798	ARCIA 1892:396
1901	629	ARCIA 1902:698
1906	649	ARCIA 1906:319
1930	770	U.S. Congress. House. Committee on Interior and Insular Affairs 1953:517
1950	1,149	U.S. Congress. House. Committee on Interior and Insular Affairs 1950:430
1966	2,011	Mizen 1966:242
1996	2,500	Tiller 1996:526

Synonymy

The contemporary name Pawnee comes from a Dhegiha Siouan term that originally designated alien or unrelated peoples, specifically those living west of the Dhegiha tribes. The Osage term *ppáðį* retains this meaning, while *ppáðįmąhą* is said to designate the Pawnee proper (Dorsey 1883; La Flesche 1932:126, phonemicized), although it is the common name for the Skiri (see below). A related set of Osage terms is *ppáį* 'Pawnee' and *ppáįmąhą* 'Skiri Pawnee' (La Flesche 1932:126, phonemicized). The same name designating the Pawnee appears as Omaha and Ponca *ppáðį* (Fletcher and La Flesche 1911:102; Parks 1988), Kansa *ppáyį* (Rankin 1987:120), Iowa and Otoe *pánʸi* (Parks 1988), and Winnebago *pa·ní* (Kenneth Miner, personal communication 1987). The form Paní has also been recorded as the Osage name for the Pawnee (Maximilian in Thwaites 1904–1907, 24:299).

The Dhegiha name was borrowed into Pawnee as *pa·ri*, a self designation that as late as the mid twentieth century was recognized by Pawnee speakers as a non-native form (Parks 1965–1998). The name was also borrowed into Algonquian languages as Fox *apa·ni·ha* (Ives Goddard, personal communication 1999), Kickapoo *pa·ni·ha* (Paul Voorhis, personal communication 1987), Ottawa pahneug (Tanner 1830:316), and Peoria-Miami pānia (Gatschet 1895b).

A related form occurs in Sioux as Teton *pʰaláni* (Buechel 1970:733), Santee and Yankton *pʰadáni* (S.R. Riggs 1890:403; J.P. Williamson 1902:133), and in Assiniboine as *pʰanáni* and *pʰanána* (Parks and DeMallie 1996:239).

Yankton distinguishes Pawnee from Arikara by modification of the form as *itókax pʰadani* 'south Pawnee' (J.P. Williamson 1902:133) and *hútab pʰadani* 'downstream Pawnee' (J.W. Cook 1880–1882); cf. *wazíyata pʰadani* 'Arikara (lit. northern Pawnee)'. An anomalous Yankton form is Padani Mašteta 'Pawnee in the warm (land)' (Anonymous 1884:33).

Early French renderings of the name are based on the preceding Siouan or Algonquian forms. The earliest recorded example appears on Marquette's 1673–1674 map as Pana or Pana Maha (Tucker 1942:pl. V). Other French renderings include Pani, 1674 Jolliet map (Tucker 1942:pl. IV); Panys, 1680s (Perrot in Blair 1911–1912, 1:124), Pana, 1702 (Iberville in Nasatir 1952, 1:8), Panis, 1703 (Delisle's map in Tucker 1942:pl. XIII), Panis, 1714 (Bourgmont in Giraud 1958:16), Panane (Villiers du Terrage 1921:255; Wedel 1936:3), Pananis, 1740 (Beauharnois in Nasatir 1952, 1:33), and Panissas, 1700 (Tonti in Delanglez 1939:232). The most common Spanish renderings are Panana or Pananas, 1719 (Twitchell 1914, 2:189); other variants are Panni and Pannis, 1716 (Hidalgo in Hatcher 1927:59, 60).

English and American forms include Paunee, 1786 (Anonymous 1794:24), Panis, 1795 (Mackay in Nasatir 1952, 1:357), Panees, 1797 (McDonnell in Nasatir 1952, 2:502); Pānias proper, Pânee, 1805 (Lewis and Clark 1832:708–709), Pawnies and Panise, 1815–1817 (Carter 1934–1962, 15:963, 305). Other spellings include Paneas, Panzas, Paonis, and Poenese (Hodge 1907–1910, 2:216).

In the seventeenth and eighteenth centuries, Pawnee in its variant spellings was often a generic or shortened name used interchangeably for the Arikara, Pawnee, and Wichita. Designations for the Arikara and Wichita generally had a modifier after Pawnee to specify the identity of those groups (see "Arikara" and "Wichita," this vol.). One such name, White Pawnee, was ambiguously applied to both the Pawnee, cited as White Pani (Le Page du Pratz 1774:map), and to the Wichita, cited as White Pania, 1804–1805 (Lewis and Clark in Moulton 1983–, 3:445). The name derives from their residence on the White River in Kansas (modern Neosho and Grand rivers). In the nineteenth century the name Pawnee came to be applied exclusively to the South Band Pawnee, until later in the century the name was extended to the Skiri as well.

Most Caddoan tribes shared a common name for the Pawnee, the origin of which is unclear: Caddo *awáhih* (Chafe 1979), Kitsai *awa·hi* (Mooney 1893, phonemicized), and Wichita *awá·hí·h* (David S. Rood, personal communication 1987; Parks 1987). Undoubtedly related to that designation is Arikara *awá·hu*, the name of an Arikara band or village and sacred bundle, often erroneously translated as 'left behind', that is not known to have been applied to the Pawnee (Lesser and Weltfish 1932:9; Parks 1979a:214–229). The Caddoan name was borrowed as Tonkawa *ˀawa·hey* 'Pawnee' (Hoijer 1949:5).

The Caddoan name appears in various forms from the Coronado expedition and later sixteenth century Spanish accounts: for example, Arache, Arahei, and Harahey, 1541 (Jaramillo in Winship 1896:588, 590); Arche and Haxa, 1565 (Casteñeda in Winship 1896:503, 505); and Axa, 1553 (Gomara in Winship 1896:492). For other variants, see Hodge (1907–1910, 1:532). In French and Spanish sources the name appears as Ahuachés, 1719 (La Harpe in Margry 1876–1886, 6:310); Ouacee, 1774 (Gaignard in Bolton 1914, 1:202, 301); Aguages and Aovages, 1777 (Ripperda in Bolton 1914, 2:132, 136); Aovajes and Aavage, 1778 (Croix in Bolton 1914, 2:216, 228); Ouass and Ovaes, 1778 (De Mézières in Bolton 1914, 2:174, 181); Ollaés and Aiiaes, 1779 (De Mézières in Bolton 1914, 2:241, 318); Guahes, 1785 (Vial and Chaves in John 1994:50, where erroneously identified as Iowa); and Aguajes, 1830 (Berlandier 1969:117).

Among many Plains tribes a common designation for the Pawnee is 'wolf people', generalized from the name of the Skiri band. Names with that meaning are Arapaho *hó·xeihi·néni·te·n* (Zdeněk Salzmann, personal communication 1975) or *hô·xéihî·nénnoˀ* (Ives Goddard, personal communication 1990), cited also as aħ-i'-hi-nin (Hayden 1862:326); Cheyenne *hoˀnéhetaneoˀo* (Glenmore and Leman 1985:201; Curtis 1907–1930, 6:158), cited also as Ho'ni-hĭtä'n-eo (sg. Ho'ni-hĭtä'n)-(Mooney 1907:424), Honehetan (Petter 1913–1915:582), and Hóh-ni-tánn (Maximilian in Thwaites 1904–1907, 24:222); Crow *čê·tmače·* 'wolf man' (Medicine Horse 1987:15), cited also as Ts´ĕt-matsĕ (Curtis 1907–1930, 4:180); Hidatsa *cé·šaruxpa·ka* (Jones 1979; Parks 1987), cited also as Sãjeruchpaga (Maximilian in Thwaites 1904–1907, 24:275); Mandan *xrat ruwą́k* (Hollow 1970:323) or *xrate ruwąka·ki* (Mauricio J. Mixco, personal communication 1998), cited also as Cháratä-numangkä (Maximilian in Thwaites 1904–1907, 24:250) and Xaratenumanke (Will and Spinden 1906:215); and Kiowa *kûyk'yàgɔ̀* (Laurel Watkins, personal communication 1979). A Comanche name with the same meaning is Kuitar'-i (Gatschet in Hodge 1907–1910, 2:216), which has been recorded and translated as Kwitara'-a 'skinned buttocks' (ten Kate 1884:9) and Kwitaraa 'les fesse excoriées' (ten Kate 1885:136), also recorded as Quitara 'big feces' (Scott 1890), apparently folk etymologies. An early Cheyenne name that is reputably a metonymical reference to wolves is Paoneneheo 'ones with projecting front teeth', also recorded as Paoninihiéu 'having the front teeth projecting', the former given by Petter (1913–1915:582) as a name for the Pawnee and the latter given by Gatschet as a Cheyenne division (Hodge 1907–1910, 2:216).

Based on the preceding designation used by other tribes, Pawnees sometimes refer to themselves as *ckírihki kuru·riki* 'ones who look like wolves' (Parks 1965–1998). Two related tribal names for the Pawnee are borrowings of the name Skiri, generalized to the other bands as well: Arikara *sčí·ri* (Parks 1986:46); and an alternative Sioux designation, Teton *sčíli* (Buechel 1970:733), Yanktonai *sčídi* (Curtis 1907–1930, 3:141, phonemicized).

An anomalous designation is Comanche *witsapa·i?* (pl. *witsapa·ini·*), which is said to refer to either a tuft of hair on the head or Pawnee sorcery (Robinson and Armagost 1990:149). The Lipan Apache name *?ídà bá·šàš* is composed of 'enemy' and an unexplained modifier (William E. Bittle, personal communication 1976).

The common sign language designation for the Pawnee is 'wolf'. It is made by extending the index and second fingers of the right hand upward from the right side of the head, palm facing out, to represent the narrow, sharp ear of the animal (Mallery 1881:472–473; W.P. Clark 1885:279–280). Sometimes both hands are used to make the same sign on each side of the head (Hadley 1893:128). An alternative sign, reported only for the Sioux, is to pass the right hand "from the back part of the right side of the head, forward seven or eight inches," representing 'shaved heads,' in which only the scalp lock is left (Mallery 1881:472). The latter sign is reflected in the name Shaved Heads (Sage 1846:155).

Bands

The Pawnee had no name for the four bands as a whole. The bands were known to themelves and to each other by their band names. Contrary to some sources (Hayden 1868:401; Gatschet in Hodge 1907–1910, 2:216), the Pawnee term *cahriksicahriks* (South Band), *cahiksícahiks* (Skiri) is a generic term that means 'Indian', in contrast to White person, and is not a self-designation (Lesser and Weltfish 1932:4–5; Parks 1965–1998).

The Pawnee name for the Skiri is *ckí·ri*, which derives from the stem *ckirir-* 'wolf, coyote'. The Pawnee form has been borrowed as Osage Ckíci and Kansa Ckíyi (Dorsey in Hodge 1907–1910, 2:590), Wichita *ackí·ri·h* (Parks 1988; David Rood, personal communication 1998), as well as the Arikara and Sioux forms above. In American sources the name is cited as Skee′de (Morgan 1871:196); Skee-e-ree, 1805 (Lewis and Clark 1832:709); Skeeree and Skere (E. James 1823, 1:478; 2:365); and Ski′di (J.B. Dunbar 1880:244). The most common spelling of the name in twentieth-century sources is Skidi.

The meaning of the name is reflected in the French designation *Loups* 'wolves', frequently in combination with the modifier Pawnee or another term. Citations include Loups, 1794 (Trudeau in Nasatir 1952, 1:209); Pania Loup, Loups, 1804–1805 (Lewis and Clark in Moulton 1983–, 3:396, 26); Loos (Gass 1807:23); Indiens-Loups (Gass 1810:22); Paunee Loups (Atkinson 1826:7); and Pawnee Loup (Irving 1835, 2:13). Spanish sources have Lobos, 1795 (Mackay in Nasatir 1952, 1:357; 1805, Twitchell 1914, 2:483). English sources have Wolves, 1804–1805 (Lewis and Clark in Moulton 1983–, 3:396), and Wolf Indians (Gass 1807:23).

In early historical sources the most common designation for the Skiri is Panimaha, a borrowing from the Dhegiha Siouan name, which is Omaha *ppáðįmąhą* 'upstream Pawnee' (Dorsey 1890:79; phonemicized), Osage *ppáðįmąhą* (La Flesche 1932:126, phonemicized), Kansa *ppáyįmáhą* (Rankin 1987:120), and Quapaw *ppanimáha* 'Pawnee' (Rankin 1991:109). The name was borrowed as Creek Pa-nĭ-mahû (Grayson in Hodge 1907–1910, 2:590), Illinois Panimaha (Gravier 1700), and Shawnee *pa·nimoho* 'Pawnee' (Ives Goddard, personal communication 1999).

Variants of the name Panimaha in European and American sources include Panimaha, 1683 (La Salle in Margry 1876–1886, 2:323), Panis mahas, 1758 (Kerlérec in Nasatir 1952, 1:52), and Pawnee Mahas, 1816 (Chouteau 1816). Occasionally the name was shortened to Maha, as Mahah (Sage 1846:153) and Mahas, 1845 (Gregg in Thwaites 1904–1907, 20:301). For other spellings, see (Hodge 1907–1910, 2:590–591).

The Pawnee name for Chawi is *cawí·?i* (Lesser and Weltfish 1932:8; Parks 1965–1998), which has no known origin. It was borrowed as Arikara *sawí·?At* (Lesser and Weltfish 1932:9; Parks 1970–1990), Wichita *cawí·?a* (Parks 1988), and Kansa *ccamí* and *ccawí* (Dorsey in Rankin 1987:31). Spelling variants of the Pawnee form in American sources are Tsca-we (E. James 1823, 2:lxxxv), Chä′-we (Morgan 1871:286), Chau-i (Grinnell 1889:215), and Chowees (ARCIA 1861:213).

In American sources the Chawi are most commonly designated the Grand Pawnee. Variant citations are Parnee, Pania Proper, and Grand par, 1804–1805 (Lewis and Clark in Moulton 1983–, 3:395); and Panias propres (Gass 1810:417); Grand Pawnee (Z.M. Pike 1810:143); Grand Pana, 1845 (Gregg in Thwaites 1904–1907, 20:301, said to be a Canadian usage); and Grands (ARCIA 1861:213). The meaning of those names is reflected in Kansa *ppayįxci* 'real Pawnee' (Dorsey in Rankin 1987:120, phonemicized) and Osage Páyiⁿqtai (Dorsey in Hodge 1907–1910, 1:238).

The Pawnee name of the Kitkahahki band is *kitkahahki* 'little earthlodge village' (Lesser and Weltfish 1932:7; Parks 1965–1998). That form is reflected in Arikara *tItkAháhtš* (Lesser and Weltfish 1932:9; Parks 1970–1990) and Wichita *kítkahat* (Parks 1988). Spelling variants of the Pawnee form are Ket-ka-kesh (James 1823, 2:lxxxv), Kattahawkees (ARCIA 1861:213), Kit′-kä (Morgan 1871:286), and Kit′-ke-hak-ĭ (J.B. Dunbar 1880:246).

The Kitkahahki were most commonly known as the Republican Pawnee, variants of which name are: republicks, 1804–1806 (Lewis and Clark in Moulton 1983–, 3:397, 398), Pānias Republican, 1805 (Lewis and Clark 1832:709), Pawnees republic (Z.M. Pike 1810:143), Pawnee Republican (Irving 1835, 2:13), and Republicans (ARCIA 1840:95).

In Dhegiha Siouan related designations occur, based on the term for 'turkey': Omaha Zizíka-ákiðisį or Zizíka ákisí (Dorsey 1890:397, normalized) and Kansa *síkka hákisį* (Dorsey in Rankin 1987:126). The rendition Ze-ka-ka (E. James 1823, 2:lxxxv) reflects the Omaha form.

The Pawnee form of the Pitahawirata band name is *pi·taha·wíra·ta* 'man going downstream' (Lesser and

Weltfish 1932:7; Parks 1965–1998), which has been spelled as Guitaboiratas, 1785 (Vial and Chavez in John 1994:50, where erroneously identified as the Cheyenne name for the Kiowa), Huitauyrata, 1791 (Concha in Nasatir 1952, 1:148), Pe-tou-we-ra (E. James 1823, 2:lxxxv), Pe-tä-hä′-ne-rat (Morgan 1871:196), Pethä′nerat and Pethowerats (Keane in Stanford 1878–1885, 1:530), and Tapahowerat (ARCIA 1861:213, a misspelling). It has been borrowed as Arikara *wi·tAhawíra·tA* (Lesser and Weltfish 1932:9; Parks 1970–1990), Wichita *wí·tá·wíra·ʔa* (Parks 1988), and Omaha witaháwiðatá (La Flesche in Dorsey 1890:413, normalized). The Kansa name *míttaháwiye*, identified as Kitkahahki Pawnee (Dorsey in Rankin 1987:92), is properly the name Pitahawirata.

Historically, the Pitahawirata are most commonly known as the Tappage (from French *tapage* 'racket') (E. James 1823, 1:351) or Noisy Pawnee. Variants of those forms are Noisy Pawnee and Pitavirate Noisy Pawnee (Treaty of 1818, in Kappler 1904–1941, 2:157), Tappage Pawnee (Irving 1835, 2:13), Pawnee Tappage (Treaty of 1848, in Kappler 1904–1941, 2:571), Tapage (Parker 1840:51), and Tappa (ARCIA 1861:213).

Sources

There are several chronological accounts of Pawnee history from the early historic period through the nineteenth century: Hyde (1951) provides a comprehensive history but is often unreliable; Champe and Fenenga (1974) present a succinct, useful chronological summary; and Wedel (1986) focuses on the Kitkahahki occupation of the Republican River valley. Two summaries of nineteenth-century Pawnee history are Lesser (1933:1–53) and Wishart (1979a). Accounts of the Pawnee agency prior to the tribe's removal to Indian Territory include J.S. Clark (1942, 1943) and Milner (1982), the latter of which discusses the responses of the Pawnee to the Society of Friends's attempts to implement the government program of assimilation.

Substantive descriptions of Pawnee life begin in the nineteenth century with accounts by explorers, travelers, and military officers. The earliest is George Sibley's 1811 journal (G.P. Brooks 1965), followed by the accounts of Edwin James on Stephen H. Long's expedition in 1818–1820 (Thwaites 1904–1907, 14:199–250) and of Paul Wilhelm, Duke of Württemberg (1973). John Treat Irving, Jr. (1955), who visited the tribe in 1833 with Treaty Commissioner H. E. Ellsworth, presents a rich description, while Charles Augustus Murray (1839) provides a vivid account of a summer hunt in 1835. Other military accounts include those of John C. Frémont (Jackson and Spence 1970, 1), James Henry Carleton (1943), and John W. Abert (1848).

Reports of early missionary activity among the Pawnee that include descriptions of tribal life are those of the Presbyterians John Dunbar (1918) and Samuel Allis (1887, 1918), whose letters are printed in Wedel (1985); the Moravians Gottlieb F. Oehler and David Z. Smith (1914); and the Friend Benjamin Hallowell (1973). Platt (1892, 1918) presents the reminiscenses of a contemporary school teacher among the Pawnee.

The role of the Pawnee in nineteenth-century intertribal warfare, particularly with the Cheyenne and Sioux, is depicted in Grinnell (1915) and R. White (1978), respectively. The service of Pawnee men as scouts for the U.S. Army is recounted in Ware (1911), Grinnell (1928), Bruce (1932), Danker (1958, 1961, 1961a), and Dunlay (1982). Accounts of the Sioux attack on the Pawnee at Massacre Canyon are Riley (1973) and J.W. Williamson (1922).

Modern ethnographic accounts begin in the late nineteenth century with valuable overviews of Pawnee culture by John B. Dunbar, son of the missionary John Dunbar (J. B. Dunbar 1880, 1880a, 1880b, 1882) and by Grinnell (1889:215–408). They are followed in the early twentieth century by the works of professional anthropologists, foremost among which is the account of Skiri social organization and religion by George A. Dorsey and James R. Murie (1907), the latter a member of the tribe. Part of that monograph was edited by Spoehr (1940). The introduction to G.A. Dorsey (1904b) offers a summary of Skiri culture. Murie (1914) is a description of men's societies, doctors' societies, and early twentieth-century dances; it also includes an overview of Skiri social organization. Weltfish (1965), a synthetic ethnography of the Skiri based on fieldwork between 1929 and 1935, is the most comprehensive published account of nineteenth-century Pawnee culture. Holder (1970) contrasts Plains horticultural tribes, including the Pawnee, with nomadic groups, offering an insightful portrayal of northern Caddoan culture. Richard White (1983:147–211) discusses the nineteenth-century Pawnee in a changing environment and the development of tribal dependency.

Pawnee, and more specifically Skiri, religion is richly documented in numerous publications. Fletcher describes a thanksgiving ceremony (1900) and the Calumet dance (Fletcher and Murie 1904); G.A. Dorsey (1907a) discusses social organization; Wissler (1920) provides information on sacred bundles; Linton (1922, 1922a, 1923, 1923a, 1926) describes several religious ceremonies, including the sacrifice to the Morning Star, as well as the Doctors' Lodge. Based on collaborative work with Clark Wissler at the turn of the century, Murie (1981) (vol. 17:251) is the most comprehensive description of Skiri ceremonialism as well as South Band doctors' rituals that survived into the twentieth century. Other accounts of the sacrifice to the Morning Star include Wissler and Spinden (1916) and Thurman (1979). Lesser (1933) describes in detail the Ghost Dance among the Pawnee and its evolution into the Ghost Dance hand game.

There are extensive collections of Pawnee mythology and oral traditions, foremost among which are Grinnell (1889:25–213, 1892b, 1893a, and 1894), G.A. Dorsey (1904b, 1906, 1906a), Weltfish (1937), and Parks (1994:377–402). Pawnee music is described in Densmore (1929), while Evarts (1965) is a sound recording of Skiri music made by Weltfish in 1936. Kinship is described in Morgan (1871), G.A. Dorsey and Murie (1907), Lesser (1930, 1933, and 1978), and Lounsbury (1956). Aspects of Pawnee star lore are described in Buckstaff (1927) and Fletcher (1902, 1903), while Von Del Chamberlain (1982) is a detailed summary of the topic. Marriage customs are described by Grinnell (1891), and Pawnee names for and uses of plants are presented in Gilmore (1912). Will and Hyde (1917) describe Pawnee horticulture.

The locations of prehistoric and historic village sites are described in Wedel (1936). Parks and Wedel (1985) inventory the locations of the animal lodges that were the sources of power for Pawnee doctors and that constitute a sacred geography of Pawnee territory

Descriptions of the Pawnee language include grammatical sketches by J. B. Dunbar (in Grinnell 1889:409–437) and Weltfish (1936) and a grammar of the South Band dialect by Parks (1976). J.B. Dunbar (1900) compiled a dictionary. Pawnee language texts are presented in Weltfish (1937) and Parks (1977:65–90). Roaming Scout (1907) is an important collection of Skiri texts recorded by G.A. Dorsey and Murie on wax cylinders from a religious leader; these texts have been translated and edited for publication by Douglas R. Parks. The relationship of Pawnee to other northern Caddoan languages is portrayed in Lesser and Weltfish (1932) and Parks (1979).

Blaine (1980) provides a bibliography of sources on Pawnee history and culture. Blaine (1990) is a detailed account of Pawnee removal during the period 1870 to 1875, a subject also summarized by Wishart (1994). Blaine (1997) presents reminiscenses of early twentieth-century Pawnee life.

Wichita

WILLIAM W. NEWCOMB, JR.

Since 1835, when they first signed a treaty with the United States, a number of once autonomous but culturally similar tribes and subtribes have been known collectively as the Wichita (ˈwĭchĭtô). Before their consolidation the principal groups were the Taovaya, Tawakoni, Iscani, Wichita proper, Waco, and Kitsai. The Iscani disappeared in the last decades of the eighteenth century, and apparently other groups in earlier years also became extinct or were absorbed by others. The Waco emerged as a separate village group in the second decade of the nineteenth century. The name Wichita is drawn from one of the smaller and historically less prominent tribes.

Most of the progenitors of the modern tribe spoke Wichita, a Northern Caddoan language, which had several dialects.* The Kitsai, who became amalgamated with the Wichita during the reservation period, spoke a distinct Northern Caddoan language, more closely related to Pawnee than to Wichita (Parks 1979:203; "Kitsai," this vol.).

History Until 1845

Contact, 1541–1601

The first contact ancestral Wichita groups had with Europeans was in summer 1541 when Francisco Vásquez de Coronado and his army discovered the scattered settlements that they called Quivira along the Little Arkansas River, the farthest near the Smoky Hill River in Kansas (Winship 1896:590; Hammond and Rey 1940:304; Bolton 1949:427–428; Wedel 1942:12, 1959:585–587; M.M. Wedel 1982:121). These people were variously portrayed as comprising six or seven settlements, or as inhabiting 25 villages, some reported to be as large as 200 houses. The people were extensively tattooed, lived in grass houses, hunted bison, and cultivated maize, beans, and squash. The archeological remains of the people of Coronado's Quivira are known as the Little River focus of the Great Bend phase (Wedel 1968:371).

In 1601 Juan de Oñate, governor of New Mexico, led another expedition to Quivira where he met an encampment of 5,000–6,000 tattooed and nearly naked Indians, probably about 25 miles northeast of present Ponca City, Oklahoma (Hammond and Rey 1953; Bolton 1916:199–267; Newcomb and Campbell 1982). The Spaniards termed these Indians Escanjaque, after the word they uttered in greeting, but their name for themselves was Aguacane. They were composed of eight "pueblos" whose home territory likely lay along the North Canadian River in western Oklahoma (fig. 1). They may have spoken a Wichita dialect (Newcomb and Campbell 1982:37) and were primarily bison hunters. Of the 600 movable dwellings in their camp, one kind was circular, dome-shaped, and covered with bison skins or grass; the other was similar to the hide-covered conical tepees the Spaniards had seen used by Apaches.

The Aguacane volunteered to join Oñate in a campaign against a nearby people of a "Great Settlement," whom they blamed for the murder of two Spaniards. Not only were the two peoples old enemies, but they "killed and ate each other" (Hammond and Rey 1953:843). Oñate rejected the offer.

The Great Settlement was about 21 miles beyond the Aguacane encampment, probably on the Walnut River, just above its junction with the Arkansas near present Arkansas City in southern Kansas (Wedel 1942:18–20, 1959:223; Newcomb and Campbell 1982:30). The archeological remains have been designated as the Lower Walnut focus of the Great Bend phase. The natives' name for themselves was not recorded, but they were later called Jumanes (or Jumanos), a name employed indiscriminately by New Mexican Spaniards for any Indians who painted or tattooed their bodies (Scholes and Mera 1940:274; Newcomb 1961:225–226).

The Great Settlement extended along both sides of the river for three or four days' travel, perhaps a distance of 30 miles. Estimates of the number of houses ranged from more than 1,200 to close to 2,000, and more houses could be seen in the distance. One member of the expedition guessed that the population of the settlement was 20,000. The Spaniards also were told that this settlement was small compared to others located to the north, and the Aguacane indicated that there were other dispersed settlements farther down the Arkansas. The houses were the distinctive

*The phonemes of Wichita are: (voiceless stops) *kʷ*, *t*, *k*, *ʔ*; (voiceless affricate) *c*; (voiceless spirants) *s*, *h*; (resonants) *w*, /r/ (*r*, *n*), *y*; (short vowels) *i*, *e* ([ɛ], [æ]), *a*; (long vowels) *i·*, *e·*, *a·*; (overlong vowels) *i:*, *e:*, *a:*; (high pitch) v́; (low pitch) unmarked; (unpredictable secondary stress accompanying low pitch) v̀. The phoneme /r/ is pronounced as an alveolar flap or tap or as the nasal [n], depending on the environment; in this orthography these major allophones are written distinctly as *r* and *n*. This phonemic analysis and the transcription of Wichita words follow David S. Rood (vol. 17:580-586).

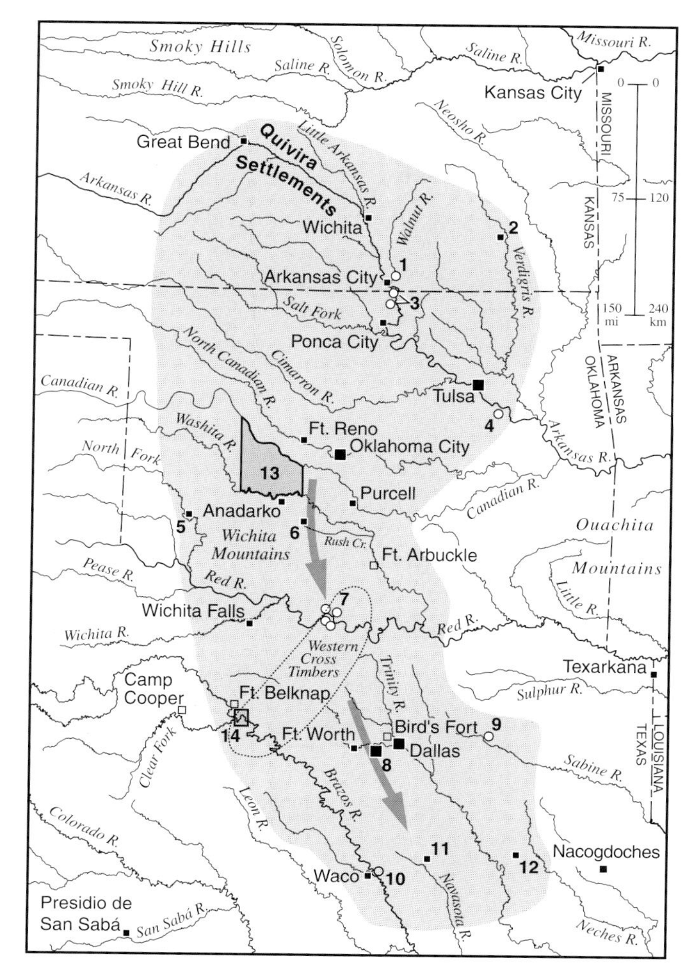

Fig. 1. Wichita territory in the late 16th to early 18th centuries, showing villages and southward migration in the 18th century. 1, Great Settlement, which stretched along both banks of the Walnut River for 30 miles; 2, Taovaya villages and town of Neodesha; 3, Taovaya villages; 4. Tawahoni village; 5, Wichita village and town of Lugert; 6, Wichita village and town of Rush Springs; 7, "Spanish Fort" villages; 8, Waco and Kitsai villages and town of Arlington; 9, Tawakoni and Iscani twin villages; 10, Tawakoni and Waco villages; 11, Tawakoni village and town of Tehuacana; 12, Kitsai village and town of Palestine; 13, Wichita Reservation, 1872–1901; 14, Brazos Reservation, 1854–1859.

grass-covered lodges that the Wichita continued to construct until the late nineteenth century. They were built 30–40 paces apart, clustered in groups of 30–40. These clusters were separated from one another by 200–300 paces, and gardens of corn, beans, and squash occupied these intervals and extended beyond them but not out of sight of the houses (Hammond and Rey 1953:754, 844–845, 847).

When the natives of the settlement discovered the Spaniards approaching, accompanied by Aguacanes, a number of their warriors challenged them to battle by throwing dirt in the air, said to be a "universal sign of war" in that land (Hammond and Rey 1953:753). But Oñate was able to meet them peacefully, apparently by employing the sign for peace—arms stretched toward the sun, then touched to the chest (Hammond and Rey 1953:855). Presents were exchanged; the Indians gave the Spaniards the small beads they wore around their necks, ears of corn, and "some round loaves of corn bread as big as shields and two or three inches thick" (Hammond and Rey 1953:753, 857).

The Aguacane had informed Oñate that these enemy people held a Spaniard captive. Ostensibly to gain his freedom, six or eight natives were seized and placed in chains, including the principal chief, whom Oñate referred to as catarax (Hammond and Rey 1953:754). Miguel, an Aguacane, later related that this settlement had two chiefs, a "main one and a lesser one" (Hammond and Rey 1953:874). Various members of the expedition described the people of the settlement, presumably men, as dark, well-built, and mostly naked, although "some wore buckskin hanging to the knee" (Hammond and Rey 1953:857). They painted their bodies and painted "stripes extended from eye to ear" (Hammond and Rey 1953:842), apparently referring to tattooing.

Migration and Change, 1719–1803

French explorers probing westward from the Mississippi valley were aware of groups ancestral to the Wichita by 1673. Their maps indicate Paniassa villages scattered along the Arkansas River valley in Oklahoma and Kansas (Tucker 1942; Delanglez 1943). In 1719 a French trader, Jean-Baptiste Bénard de La Harpe, established a post near modern Texarkana just above the great bend of the Red River. In August, accompanied by two Kitsai guides and about eight other men, La Harpe traveled by horseback to the Tawakoni settlement on the south bank of the Arkansas River below Tulsa, Oklahoma, near the town of Leonard (M.M. Wedel 1981a:28, 1982:124).

La Harpe and his party were ceremoniously met some distance from the settlement by the principal Tawakoni chief and six chiefs of other "nations," all mounted on beautiful horses. Following mutual assurances of friendship, the French were presented with cornmeal bread mixed with squash and smoked meat. La Harpe was provided with a fine horse, and the group proceeded to the settlement. There the Indians had La Harpe dismount, and two eminent men, with heads bowed, carried him to the chief's dwelling where he was seated on a buffalo robe spread over a platform. The leading men encircled him, and one after another put a hand in his as a token of goodwill. La Harpe presented the young Tawakoni chief with muskets, powder, balls, and cloth, and the chief gave La Harpe an eagle-feather headdress adorned with many colored feathers, and two "calumet feathers" (probably pipestems), one for peace and one for war (Margry 1876–1886, 6:288–290).

About 7,000 persons had come to see the strangers, and during the next several days the elaborate calumet ceremony was conducted for the French by the Taovaya and Iscani chiefs, both of whom were old men. The calumet was danced, speeches made, and presents exchanged. On the second day of the ceremony La Harpe was carried to an arbor, his face was painted, and was presented with 30 buffalo robes, rock salt, tobacco pressed into loaves, some mineral pigments, and an eight-year-old Apache captive. The chief said that 17 other captives had been eaten a week before, apparently in a ritual feast. La Harpe learned that the settlement would be abandoned in November for the winter hunt, from which the Tawakoni would not return until March (Margry 1876–1886, 6:291–292).

At almost the same time that La Harpe reached the Tawakoni settlement on the Arkansas, Claude-Charles Dutisné, heading westward from the mouth of the Missouri River, reached a Taovaya village, probably located on the Verdigris River near modern Neodesha in southeastern Kansas (M.M. Wedel 1982:124). This village had 130 grass houses and 200–250 warriors; another village of the same size was located several miles upstream. The population of each village was about 1,000–1,250; between them they had only about 300 horses, but they reluctantly traded to Dutisné two horses and a mule with a Spanish brand. The Frenchman learned that the Taovaya were at war with the Apache, ate Apache captives, and used leather armor to protect their horses. In warfare they skillfully employed the bow and arrow as well as a long lance tipped with the blade of a European sword. He was told there were other Wichita villages to the west and northwest.

In 1748–1749, deserters from French Louisiana making their way from the Arkansas Post on the Lower Arkansas River to New Mexico passed through two Wichita villages about one and one-half miles apart on the west side of the Arkansas. These are identified as the Deer Creek (34KA3) and Bryson-Paddock (34KA5) archeological sites, in northern Oklahoma (M.M. Wedel 1981a:4, 1982:127; Thomas 1940:82–89; Wedel 1959:533–534). Their population was variously estimated at 1,500–2,500, and one of the villages was fortified with a stockade and ditch. Identified as Panipiqués and Jumanos, one or perhaps both villages were probably mostly Taovayas (M.M. Wedel 1982:127). For a time this was an ideal location since in the late 1740s the Comanche and some or all of the Wichita-speaking groups agreed to a mutually advantageous peace, which made the Taovaya prosperous middlemen in the lucrative trade between the Comanche and the French. French traders could ascend the Arkansas as far as these villages by boat, and the villages were easily accessible to the nomadic Comanche (Febre et al. 1749).

By 1757 these villages had moved far to the south out of the Arkansas drainage to the Red River just west of the Western Cross Timbers, about 50 miles east of Wichita Falls, Texas. A fortified Taovaya village was built on the north side of the river (the Longest site 34JF1), and an Iscani village was located a short distance downstream. By 1765 a village of the Wichita proper was north of the Taovaya village, and the Iscani village was south of the river (apparently the Upper Tucker site 41MU17) (Bell, Jelks, and Newcomb 1974:269–271).

According to a captured Spanish soldier, Antonio Treviño (who lived in the village in 1764), and from what is known about the site archeologically, the fortification consisted of an oval-shaped palisade about 88 by 130 yards, situated in the middle of a dispersed village on the north bank of the river. It was constructed of split logs set vertically in the ground; outside the palisade was an earthen rampart about four feet high, and beyond it a ditch about four feet deep and more than 12 feet wide. Inside were four underground chambers large enough to shelter all noncombatants (Bell, Jelks, and Newcomb 1974:84–85, fig. 26).

About the same time the Taovaya were establishing their fortress on the Red River, to the east the Tawakoni and a band of the Iscani were also migrating south. Before 1742 they were on the Canadian River, but soon afterward migrated to the Red River, and in the 1740s moved farther south into Texas (M.M. Wedel 1981a:32). They apparently first settled in a twin village located on the upper Sabine River, probably at what is known as the Pearson site (41RA5), about 50 miles east of Dallas (Johnson and Jelks 1958; Duffield and Jelks 1961). The migration put many miles between them and their Osage enemies, and it gave them easier access to the French at Natchitoches (John 1975:305–306).

The southward migration of the Wichita tribes in the mid-eighteenth century brought them into closer contact with the Spaniards of Texas, and into a relationship that was uneasy, sometimes hostile, and never wholly resolved. When the longstanding anti-Apache policy of the Spaniards was reversed in 1757, a mission and presidio were built for the Lipan Apache on the San Sabá River in west-central Texas. This was a clear signal to the Wichita that the Spaniards had allied themselves with the Apache, ancient enemies of the Wichita. Consequently, in spring 1758 a combined Indian force sacked and burned the mission, killing two of the missionaries and eight others. Composition of the attacking force is only partly known, but it did include Comanches, Hasinais, Bidais, Tonkawas, Kitsais, almost certainly Yojuanes, probably Taovayas, and others. In the following year Col. Diego Ortiz Parrilla, commander of the San Sabá presidio, with an army of over 600 men, rode northward from the presidio to surprise and decimate a Yojuane camp, then continued northward to attack the fortified Taovaya village on the Red River. Armed with French firearms, supported by other Wichita allies, and apparently assisted by the Comanche, the Indians inflicted a stinging defeat to Parrilla, even capturing his two cannons (Parrilla 1759; Bell, Jelks, and Newcomb 1974:260–265).

Soon afterward, in response to Tawakoni overtures of peace relayed through Caddo intermediaries, Fray Joseph de Calahorra, a veteran Spanish missionary at Nacogdoches, with a small retinue of soldiers and settlers joined along the way by about 100 Caddoes, visited the twin Tawakoni and Iscani villages. They were met, as was customary, about 10 miles out and were escorted in. Only a "street" separated the Tawakoni and Iscani villages, which totaled 47 large dwellings. The villages had 250 warriors. Located in a meadow with the houses, streets, and gardens, there was abundant pasturage for the "fine breeding horses" they raised. Several miles from the villages was fertile farm land where they communally raised and shared equally in the abundant harvest of maize, beans, and squash. The villagers were also constructing a fort with an underground shelter to defend themselves (Johnson and Jelks 1958:412).

The Tawakoni-Iscani settlement on the Sabine probably was abandoned before 1770, perhaps because of dissension over their relationship with the Spaniards or attacks by the Osage. They and apparently other migrant Wichita groups reestablished themselves in small and relatively impermanent scattered settlements and villages on the middle reaches of the Trinity and Brazos rivers and the headwaters of the Navasota.

After the transfer of Louisiana from France to Spain in 1769, Athanase De Mézières became the Spanish commandant at Natchitoches. In autumn 1771 he concluded a treaty of peace with the Taovaya, Tawakoni, Iscani, and Kitsai, and during the following decade he made three tours to their villages. In his 1779 tour he visited for the first time the Spanish Fort villages on the Red River. There were 37 grass lodges on the north bank, apparently of the Wichita proper, and 123 in the Taovaya village on the south bank. Each lodge had 10–12 beds, and De Mézières estimated there were more than 800 men and youths in the two villages. Although it was April, each lodge had 27–34 bushels of dried corn as well as beans and squash. They also raised large quantities of watermelons and tobacco. They dressed in skin shirts, leggings, and moccasins, and their shields, tepee covers, and horse equipment were also of skins. De Mézières was particularly impressed by the women's industry. He noted that women as well as men participated in their system of government. Men could become "petty chiefs" not through inheritance but through their own abilities (Bolton 1914, 2:201–204).

Consolidation and Subjugation, Nineteenth Century

By the opening of the nineteenth century the peoples who were to compose the Wichita tribe were scattered in small villages from southwestern Oklahoma to east Texas. They faced a declining population, poor trading relationships in Spanish Texas and with Americans who were filtering westward, and continued enmity of other tribes.

The Spanish Fort villages suffered from a smallpox epidemic in 1801, leaving about 400 men, half the number of a quarter-century earlier (Sibley 1832:723). There was at that time a Tawakoni village on the north bank of the Red River and on its south side villages of the Taovaya and Wichita proper. The principal chief of the three villages was Awakahea (or Awahakei) of the Tawakoni village, who died in 1811. No agreement could be reached on his successor, and each group went its own way (Garrett 1946:403; Bell, Jelks, and Newcomb 1974:289–301). When the villages dispersed, part or all of the Tawakoni, subsequently known as the Huico (Waco), the name of one of their bands (John 1982–1983:416, 434), moved south to the Brazos in the vicinity of other Tawakoni settlements, establishing their village at the location of Waco, Texas (the Barron Branch site, 41ML95).

The Waco and their Tawakoni allies came into conflict with Anglo-Americans soon after Stephen F. Austin and other empresarios began to attract colonists to their Spanish land grants in southeast Texas in the 1820s. In 1824, when a Waco war party in pursuit of Tonkawas was blamed for killing a White man, the settlers retaliated by surprising the war party and slaying 12 of them (Wilbarger 1889:204–205). In June 1824, commissioners were dispatched to the Brazos River villages to seek peace. Most of the Waco were away on a buffalo hunt and an expedition against the Osage. The Waco village contained 60 houses, and the inhabitants had about 400 acres of corn, beans, squash, and melons under cultivation. It was estimated that they could raise no more than 100 warriors. There was also a Tawakoni village, three miles below the Waco village on the east side of the Brazos, which had only seven houses; this was probably the Gas Plant site (41ML1) (Bell, Jelks, and Newcomb 1974:45–49). At both villages defensive dugouts had been created by digging shallow pits and throwing the excavated dirt up around them (De Shields 1912:67; Berlandier 1969:44).

When the Mexican government ordered Austin to destroy the Waco village, he invited the East Texas Cherokee to participate in a joint campaign against them. Although the Mexican government rescinded its order, in 1829 the Cherokee assaulted the Waco village, exacting a heavy toll. The following year the Cherokee attacked a Tawakoni village at Tehuacana on the headwaters of the Navasota, but this village apparently was not abandoned until after an unsuccessful Texas Ranger assault on it in 1835; the Waco village was vacated about the same time.

About the same time that the Waco, Tawakoni, and Kitsai were being driven from central Texas, the United States government made contact with Wichita peoples north of the Red River. The dragoon expedition led by Col. Henry Dodge in 1834 visited a Wichita village in Devil's Canyon near modern Lugert, Oklahoma (Wheelock 1834; Catlin 1841, 2:70–75). It paved the way for the Camp Holmes treaty of 1835 in which the Indians agreed to peace and perpetual friendship with one another and with the United States. It was the first treaty of the Wichita with the United States, it eased the Osage threat, and it established the usage of the term Wichita as their collective name (Harper 1953; Kappler 1904–1941, 2:435–439).

The Waco, Tawakoni, and Kitsai retreated well beyond the rapidly expanding Texas frontier to establish villages in the upper valleys of the Trinity and Brazos and the lower Wichita rivers. But it was not far enough to escape the increasingly aggressive Texans, who in 1841 assaulted

Kitsai and Waco villages on the West Fork of the Trinity near present Arlington and caused their abandonment.

In September 1843 the Republic of Texas signed a peace treaty at Bird's Fort on the Trinity River with a number of Indian groups including the Waco and Tawakoni, which established a boundary between the settlements and Indian country (Winfrey and Day 1959–1966, 1:242–245). However, raids against settlers' horses continued, primarily by Waco and Tawakoni (Winfrey and Day 1959–1966, 2:50–53).

Culture, 1850–1875

Subsistence

Until the reservation era the Wichita pursued a varied subsistence pattern, sharply divided by sex: men hunted, women gardened. When game was scarce, greater reliance could be placed on the women's gardens, and when floods, droughts, or other conditions harmed or destroyed the gardens, game could be more intensively sought by the hunters.

Throughout much of their history the Wichita followed a semisedentary seasonal cycle. They remained in their settlements throughout the spring and summer while the women worked the gardens. Following the harvest they abandoned their settlements to become tepee-dwelling hunters.

The gardens were typically located along the terraces of rivers and smaller streams, where the women cultivated maize, beans, squash, gourds, and tobacco. Muskmelons and watermelons probably were acquired from French traders during the first half of the eighteenth century. By the mid-eighteenth century the gardens were enclosed with brush or rail fences to keep out horses and other livestock. Men hunted bison primarily, but also deer, elk, bear, antelope, and other game. A variety of wild fruits (some of which, like plum trees, were apparently cared for), berries, nuts, and other plant products were utilized. Fish were not eaten (Bolton 1914, 2:202; G.A. Dorsey 1904a:4; Curtis 1907–1930, 19:37).

The women dried surplus garden produce and stored it in hide bags, both in their lodges and in underground cache pits. Their method of preserving squash was first mentioned in the eighteenth century by De Mézières (Bolton 1914, 2:202), who observed that squash were cut into long narrow strips, flattened by pounding, woven into mats (braided according to G.A. Dorsey 1904a), and then dried (fig. 2). They were easily stored and were an important item in the trade with the Comanche and other nonhorticultural Indians. Surplus meat was smoked or sun-dried. Green corn was roasted or boiled in pottery vessels with other vegetables and meat; dried corn was ground into meal as needed in wooden mortars (fig. 3) and also on stone slabs. Cornmeal was often made into large round loaves and baked in the ashes (Curtis 1907–1930, 19:37).

Settlement Pattern

Wichita communities in the sixteeenth and seventeenth centuries are well characterized as scattered or dispersed settlements. Matrilineally related relatives lived close to one another in a cluster of grass lodges in the midst of cultivated fields, next to other similar clusters, which were near others, often extending for considerable distances in favored locales.

Smithsonian, NAA: left, 89-16387; right, 89-16392.

Fig. 2. Braided squash. left, Woman peeling squash strips. right, With finished braided squash mat. Photographs by Edward S. Curtis, © 1927.

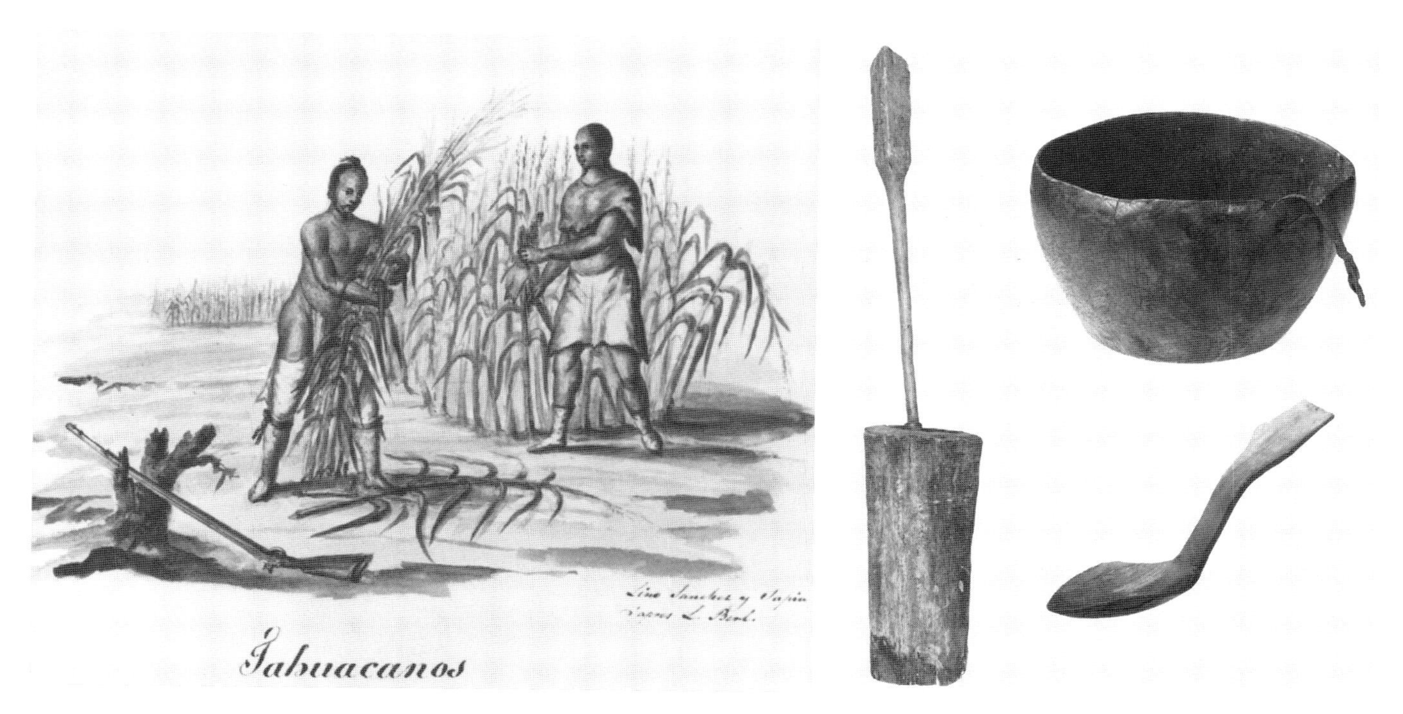

left, The Thomas Gilcrease Inst. of Amer. Hist. and Art, Tulsa, Okla.; center, Field Mus., Chicago: 59354; Smithsonian, Dept. of Anthr: top right, 6878; bottom right, 6887.

Fig. 3. Subsistence and implements. left, Tawakoni of the Brazos Valley harvesting corn. The man wears a breechcloth, moccasins, and leggings. The woman wears a short skirt, short poncho, and moccasins with attached leggings. Watercolor by Lino Sánchez y Tapia, 1834–1838, after a sketch by Jean Louis Berlandier. center, Mortar and pestle, used by women to grind corn. Collected by George A. Dorsey, Wichita Res., Okla., 1901. Height of mortar, 67 cm. Length of pestle, 113 cm. right, Wooden bowl, carved from a tree burl, and a buffalo horn spoon. Collected by Edward Palmer, 1868. Diameter of bowl 24 cm, length of spoon 22 cm.

Hostilities during the early historic period must have been sporadic; they did not force the Wichita into more compact and secure settlement patterns. The spread of the horse complex, the introduction of firearms, depopulation, and the other factors related to European invasion forced them to abandon their dispersed settlements during the eighteenth century for compact villages, often built near similar villages. Some villages soon came to be fortified.

Structures

The beehive-shaped grass lodges of the Wichita (fig. 4) were substantial dwellings that varied from 15 to 30–40 feet in diameter and were constructed of cedar posts and cross-beams surrounded by upright poles sunk into the earth and lashed together at the top (Douglas 1932b). Willow rods were lashed to the upright poles and covered with grass thatching (Curtis 1907–1930, 19:38). The lodges and arbors described by members of Oñate's expedition (Hammond and Rey 1953) did not differ materially from those described 300 years later. Originally each lodge had two small willow and grass doors, low and narrow, one on the east, the other on the west, and vestigal doors on the north and south sides, which had earlier been used ceremonially (G.A. Dorsey 1904a:4–5). Six to as many as 12 beds, constructed of light poles and raised well above the floor, were arranged around the interior walls. Beds were covered with bison hides, and painted hide curtains were hung around the beds to afford privacy. A slight excavation was made in the center of the lodge for a fire. The fireplace was considered sacred as many offerings and medicinal preparations were made there. A small smoke vent was provided near the top of the roof. A three to four-foot peak, formed from bundles of tightly wrapped grass, capped the apex of the lodge, and from its base four poles extended for about three feet, one pointing in each of the cardinal directions. They symbolized the deities of the directions, and the peak symbolized the Wichita creator god. As late as 1900, 90 percent of the Wichita lived in grass lodges (Kiowa Agency 1931).

Adjacent to the lodges were several kinds of arbors, the largest being oval in floorplan and like the lodges in construction except that they were open-sided and had a raised floor, providing a shady retreat for work and relaxation. Raised platforms, 10 to 20 feet square, reached by notched tree-trunk ladders, were employed for drying corn, meat, and squash. At one time, small sleeping platforms were constructed for the confinement of young women. When hunting, the Wichita used hide tepees, which apparently were like those of the Plains Apache; they also constructed some form of sweatlodge (Bolton 1916:260; G.A. Dorsey 1904a:4–5).

Clothing and Adornment

During the first centuries of European contact Wichita peoples dressed for the climate. In warm weather men wore little more than a breechcloth and moccasins, and

top, Smithsonian, NAA: 43,676-A; inset, based on Nabokov and Easton 1989:146.

Fig. 4. Wichita grass lodge. top, "Ska-wa-cer's home." Traditional grass lodge, open sunshades, storage platforms (some covered with canvas), cultivated gardens in the foreground, and a log cabin with chimney are evident. Two other home sites are visible in the distance. Photograph by W.J. Lenny and William Sawyers, Purcell, Indian Terr., 1888–1891. inset, Sketch of framework of grass lodge. bottom left and bottom right, Mr. and Mrs. Miller and unidentified young man building a grass lodge, at the Southern Plains Mus., Anadarko, Okla. Photographs by John Schweitzer, 1952.

women a short skirt (fig. 3). In cold weather a robe was added. Hide moccasins appear to have been aboriginal, and after the adoption of horses, leggings were added. By 1834, Wichita attire had been considerably altered. Catlin (1841, 2:74) remarked that the women wore dresses reaching from chin to ankles, fringed and ornamented with rows of elk teeth.

The most striking feature of Wichita personal appearance was extensive tattooing, said to have been revealed in a vision by the buffalo. Men were tattooed on both eyelids, with a short horizontal line extending from the outside corner of each eye. Short tattooed lines also extended downward from the corners of the mouth. On the back of their hands were clawlike designs, placed there after a boy had killed his first bird. Small crosses, symbolizing war honors, were tattooed on the arms and chest and represented the stars of Flintstone Lying Down Above, the mythic guardian of warriors. They also pierced their ears, usually in four places, and suspended numerous ornaments from them.

Women's tattoos were less individualistic but even more intricate than those of men. A tattooed line ran down the bridge of the nose to the upper lip, encircled the mouth, but just before the lines met below the lower lip the ends turned downward to the chin. Between these two lines were two other parallel lines, and all four terminated at the chin and intersected with a line along the chin line. This chin-line tattoo ran from ear to ear, above which were tattooed a row of solid trangles. Other triangles were tattooed on the neck and upper breast and a series of parallel zigzag lines coursed up and down the arms. The breasts, including the nipples, were tattooed with several short lines, and around them were tattooed three concentric circles, said to prevent pendulous breasts in old age. The tattooing of women was a form of social identification that distinguished them from female captives and from the women of other tribes (G.A. Dorsey 1904a:2–3).

Social Organization

A woman, her husband, unmarried children, and married daughters with their husbands with children composed the basic social and economic unit. A family might occupy one lodge, or perhaps several close together if the family was large, and the oldest woman of such households was its head and supervisor. Other related families built their dwellings nearby. The women of the household cooperatively tilled the gardens, gathered firewood, tanned hides, sewed clothing, prepared food, and built houses. During menses, husband and wife did not sleep in the same lodge, and normal female duties were suspended.

The men helped in the physically more demanding tasks of house-building. During the hunting season, the household groups were broken up, but they maintained cohesiveness by pitching their tepees close to one another. Before European pressures forced alterations in Wichita life, it is probable that the matrilineal emphasis was greater than it was in later years (Schmitt and Schmitt 1952:59).

Kinship

The Wichita used the terms 'brother' and 'sister', and behavior appropriate for siblings, to include all cousins. A child lived in the same household with the children of his maternal aunt (his mother's sister), and, in fact, because men sometimes married sisters, she also might be married to the child's father.

A person termed his mother's sisters 'mother', qualifying the term with 'little' or 'big' depending upon whether they were younger or older than one's biological mother. Similarly, a father's brothers were 'little' or 'big' fathers. Inasmuch as the Wichita practiced the levirate, a custom in which a man marries his brother's widow, the brothers of a child's father were potential fathers. A father's sister was also termed and treated as a 'big' or 'little' mother, but a mother's brother, who lived elsewhere if married, was termed uncle. In the grandparental generation all relatives were referred to as grandfather or grandmother, with the qualifying 'big' or 'little' depending upon the relative age of the connecting grandparent. Reciprocally, all grandchildren of a person's siblings were termed grandchildren (Schmitt and Schmitt 1952:11).

Life Cycle

At the birth of a child a mother moved to a tepee pitched near her lodge. Husbands were barred from entering the tepee until four days after the birth lest they cause mother and child to become ill. Expectant women were attended by experienced, elderly midwives. Shortly after birth an older woman took the infant to a river, where she held it aloft and offered prayers to the moon and the creator god. The child was then immersed in the river and prayers were addressed to the powers of the water. A woman chosen for her good health would construct a cradle using materials ritually prepared by the father (fig. 5). If the child grew to be healthy, the cradle might be purchased and used by other families (G.A. Dorsey 1904a:11–12; Curtis 1907–1930, 19:41).

Children were often named prior to birth as a consequence of dreams of the mother or other relatives. Later, they might be given another name based on some personal mannerism or significant act. People who were experiencing poor fortune or continued illness often changed their names in later life by means of a name-giving ceremony or through purchase (G.A. Dorsey 1904a:8; Curtis 1907–1930, 19:40).

Fathers played an important role in the instruction of their sons in hunting, the use of weapons, and the other male skills. Mothers and the other women of the household trained girls in female activities. Girls approaching marriageable age (said to be 16 years) were kept away from men and boys. Families of marriageable boys usually arranged, through go-betweens, marriage with the family of the chosen girl, ideally a girl of the same village. But if a girl's parents favored a particular boy for a son-in-law the procedure might be reversed; this may have been more common prior to reservation days. Marriages were formalized by giving presents to and a feast for the bride's relatives (G.A. Dorsey 1904a:9–11).

A newly married couple lived in the household of the bride's parents, and the new son-in-law was expected to perform a number of duties for the family, the most important being to supply them with meat. His standing with the family depended upon how well he fulfilled this and other obligations. If the bride's parents were not satisfied with his behavior, he was sent home, thus constituting divorce. The relationships between in-laws, particularly those of the opposite sex, were always reserved and formal. Thus, a man's mother-in-law might talk to him through his wife rather than directly to him, and a man would never tease or

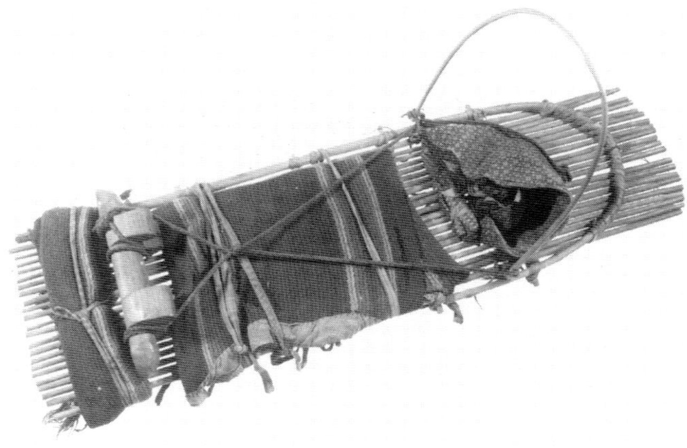

top, Smithsonian, NAA: 1338-A; bottom, Smithsonian, Dept. of Anthr.: 152944.

Fig. 5. Cradles. Shortly after the birth of a child, the father sought out a woman who was of good health to make a cradle. The father cut and peeled 24 willow rods, which he gave to the woman. She then painted the rods and plaited them in the form of a flat mat bound with sinew. top, Women with child in cradleboard. The woman on left is wearing multiple ball-and-cone earrings. Photograph by James Mooney, 1891. bottom, Cradle having knitted wrappings, a sunshade of calico, and a zoomorphic footrest. Collected by James Mooney, 1891. Length 84 cm.

joke with a mother-in-law no matter how successful or prestigious he might become.

When a person was on the verge of death, relatives began to gather around, and all relatives were expected to be present when the body was buried. Nonrelatives took charge of the last rites, because the souls of the dead were believed to attempt to persuade relatives to join them. Relatives cut their hair in mourning, close relatives cutting off more than distant ones. Burial generally occurred two to four days after death, in a shallow grave over which was erected a shedlike structure. Prayers were addressed to the earth. The corpse's head was oriented to the east, and graves were normally located on hills near the villages. A man's war gear was buried with him except for his shield, which was given to a friend who knew its medicine. The family of the deceased often impoverished itself through giveaways. Relatives mourned for four days and surviving spouses for several months (G.A. Dorsey 1904a:12–16; Curtis 1907–1930, 19:42; Schmitt and Schmitt 1952:11–14; Schmitt 1952).

Political Organization

The dispersed settlements of the early historic period were clearly autonomous but also in contact with other related settlements. Chiefs wielded considerable authority within their communities and were accorded respect and obedience by their followers. Chiefs acquired their position through their bravery, generosity, kindness, and the reciprocal love and respect of their people. They were elected by the head warriors who controlled village affairs through their ability to demote a chief if his performance was unsatisfactory. However, retiring chiefs frequently nominated an outstanding young man to fill their position (G.A. Dorsey 1904a:6; Curtis 1907–1930, 19:43). The primary responsibility of chiefs may have been conducting the calumet ceremony, which established and maintained relationships with other groups.

A "lesser" or second chief was called 'the one who locates', referring to his duty of being constantly on the lookout for better village sites. He was also responsible for the removal of the village and for laying out new village sites. How long aboriginal settlements were maintained in one location is unknown, but by the eighteenth century and the onset of frequent removals, selection of new village sites had become a vitally important task. Next in the hierarchy were the medicine men, who conducted important ceremonies. One of their number filled the important office of crier. Helpers or assistants might become highly ranked medicine men after years of apprenticeship. Social status for the remaining population was determined by wealth and prowess in war (G.A. Dorsey 1904a:6–7).

During the eighteenth century, with continuing population decline, migration, warfare, and the other changed conditions imposed by the European onslaught, the traditional political stucture was not able to hold the various tribal components together, much less to lead them to consolidate their depleted and scattered villages into effective entities. The Iscani, for example, split into at least two bands, and the Tawakoni in Texas splintered over relations with the Spaniards. During the nineteenth century, the authority of some particularly able village chiefs, as in the case of Awakahea, expanded in that they were recognized as the leaders of several villages (John 1982–1983). But there were few such leaders, and their successors were unable to hold various factions together.

Warfare

Wichita captives among the Pueblos in 1541 and the animosity of the Aguacane for the Wichita of the Great Settlement in 1601 indicate that conflict was present before European intervention. Whatever its nature, after the advent of Europeans and the development of bitter competition between tribes for firearms, horses, and European goods, intertribal strife apparently increased dramatically. The traditional enemies of the Wichita were the Plains Apache, Osage, and Tonkawa. Captives of both sexes and all ages were tortured and eaten, apparently in response to religious beliefs (Margry 1876–1886, 6:291–292). By the mid-eighteenth century captives had become an important article of commerce, and cannibalism disappeared prior to the nineteenth century.

Militarily, the Wichita reached their peak in the mid-eighteenth century. Nonetheless, they were not aggressive in that their migrations were prompted in large part by a desire to distance themselves from enemies, and the fortifications they built were for defensive purposes. Warfare consisted of small raiding parties, composed of a handful of volunteers, whose aim was to steal horses, take scalps, and capture women. Men painted depictions of their war deeds on tepees and robes. Victorious war parties were received in their villages with rejoicing, sparking scalp and victory dances. The death of any warrior required ritual expiation on the part of the leader, after which the entire village mourned for four days. War tales could be narrated only during the winter, when men gathered at night to relate their war deeds (G.A. Dorsey 1904a:7, 15).

Mythology

In 1719 La Harpe reported that the Wichita venerated "a great spirit" under diverse forms and offered to him the first fruits from their gardens (Margry 1876–1886, 6:296). This was 'Man Never Known on Earth', the creator who was closely associated with the sun, Man Reflecting Light (G.A. Dorsey 1904a:26; Newcomb 1961:270–272).

According to one origin myth (G.A. Dorsey 1904a:25–29), before any celestial beings were created, Man Never Known on Earth was alone and in darkness. After the land was created floating on water, he made the first humans and placed them on the earth. They were the moon, Bright Shining Woman, and the morning star, Having Power to Carry Light, who was regarded as the founder of Wichita culture. Bright Shining Woman was the protector of women and source of procreative power for humans, animals, and plants.

Everything they needed to live was given to them through dreams. Moon received the four Corn Mothers (different types of corn) to nourish the people. Morning Star journeyed to the east where he found a grass lodge inhabited by Star That is Always Moving who taught him how to makes bows and arrows and to hunt. When Star That is Always Moving wounded a black and white deer, he initiated the cycle of day and night. Sun told Morning Star to return to Moon, after which the people multiplied. Morning Star taught the men to make offerings after successful hunts, then he and Moon ascended to the sky where the people offered prayers to them.

A separate origin myth tells of a great flood during which most people and animals were drowned. As Wind journeyed forth and dried the land he discovered a woman lying on the ground who, after giving birth to a female child, sunk into the earth. The child was raised by Wind in the underwater home of the beaver. There she married and gave birth to a boy, Morning Star, who led the people out of the beaver lodges, gave them corn, and taught them to hunt (Curtis 1907–1930, 19:53–56).

Woman Forever in the Water was the primary water power and granted health and well-being as well as protecting the virtue of women whose husbands were absent. The earth was the great keeper of medicines and the mother of everything. Prayers were also offered to many other stars, meteors, and the various winds. Four distinct epochs were recognized as constituting the world cycle, the last of which was believed to lead to the destruction of the present world and the beginning of a new world cycle (G.A. Dorsey 1904a:18–21; Curtis 1907–1930, 19:44–48).

Religion and Ceremonies

Every sort of object might contain or could be imbued with more than natural qualities. Animals often assumed special power and appeared to men in dreams or visions to become their spirit helpers, but there was no structured vision quest. All spiritual knowledge was believed to come from dreams and visions. To disregard instructions given by spirits brought ill fortune to the offender, as spirits knew at all times the thoughts of the individual (Curtis 1907–1930, 19:47). Deities and spirit-helpers were spoken of as "dreams" and divided into 'above dreams' and 'dreams down here', the later classified as 'dreams living in water' and 'dreams closest to man' (G.A. Dorsey 1904a:20).

The Wichita believed in a continuing existence after death in a spirit world, where they held the same social standing as in life; those who had taken their own lives were unable to enter (G.A. Dorsey 1904a:14). According to La Harpe, the dead departed in a great canoe under the guidance of a black man with horns who took warriors and other reputable people to a prairie where there were buffalo in abundance, and others to a dry, barren place where life was difficult (Margry 1876–1886, 6:296).

Semisecret religious societies were responsible for maintaining and strengthening relationships with the important deities who controlled tribal welfare. Membership in these societies was apparently open to anybody who wished to join, and in the early years of the twentieth century 14 dance societies, three of which were composed of women and some of which were probably secular, were remembered (Curtis 1907–1930, 19:43–44).

The most important of these was the Deer Dance, a ceremony of the medicine men, which was held three or four times a year during the warm months. Last performed in 1871 (G.A. Dorsey 1904a:16), it was thought to remove evil influences, promote abundant crops, good health, long life, and general prosperity. The rite, which originated in a vision of the 'red bean man', took place in a ritually constructed lodge. Attended by both male and female shamans, the dance involved smoke offerings; the opening of medicine bundles; trance states possibly induced by the ingestion of mescal beans (*Sophora secundiflora*), during which the participants received power from animal visions; and conjuring acts. The ceremony was led by a chief shaman dressed as a deer. Offerings to various gods also were made, and following a feast the ceremony was concluded with a foot race open to all tribal members (including women), which presumably gave participants great endurance on the warpath (Curtis 1907–1930, 19:64–71).

Another important ceremony was that of the calumet in which feathered pipestems were presented to a prominent person or chief of a neighboring tribe. First described by La Harpe in 1719, its performance was thought to confer lasting benefit to the tribe (Margry 1876–1886, 6:290–292).

Other ceremonies, originating in visionary experience, involved the use of sacred bundles, the bear medicine bundle being one of the most important. Rain bundle ceremonies were held annually for both the maturation of corn and the calling of the buffalo. These ceremonies were held in ritually purified lodges and involved singing and the opening of the bundles. The Surround the Fire ceremony was directed to the spirit of the dogwood tree for the increase and health of children (Curtis 1907–1930, 19:72–85). The Many Dogs and Horn societies performed ceremonials for success in war. Victorious war parties participated in numerous scalp dances, four of which were led exclusively by women (G.A. Dorsey 1904a:17).

A Wichita secret society of sorcerers was reported, whose members could cause "silent death" to their enemies. Membership in the society required sacrificing the life of a relative or a close friend. This was accomplished by procuring a lock of hair or some possession of the victim and placing it either in the knurl hole of a tree for "slow death" or in the mouth of a toad, which was then killed, for "fast death." Poisoning was also practiced. Those found guilty of witchcraft would be killed and their bodies left on the open plain without ceremony (Curtis 1907–1930, 19:57–59).

History Since 1846

Reservation Period, 1846–1901

When Texas achieved statehood late in 1845 it retained claim to public lands; Indians living in the state became the responsibility of the federal government, in effect denying them any claims to land within the state. In 1846 and again in 1850 the federal government negotiated treaties with all the local Indians it could assemble, by which the Indians acknowledged that they were under the protection of the United States (Winfrey and Day 1959–1966, 3:43–61, 130–136). In 1853 the Texas legislature authorized the federal government to establish Indian reserves on vacant Texas land. The Waco, Tawakoni, and remnants of other tribes—Caddo, Delaware, Shawnee, and Tonkawa—were soon gathered on a reserve on the upper Brazos River. But nearby Texas settlers became so hostile and menacing that by June 1859 it was evident that the reserves would have to be abandoned. In August 1,050 Indians of the Brazos Reservation, including approximately 375 Wacos and Tawakonis, escorted by federal troops, made the trek to the Leased District in Indian Territory, purchased by the government from the Choctaw and Chickasaw (Winfrey and Day 1959–1966, 3:193–209; Bell, Jelks, and Newcomb 1974:295–298; Elam 1971:314–317).

The Wichita north of the Red River had in October 1858 abandoned their village on Rush Creek, following its destruction by Maj. Earl Van Dorn with four companies of cavalry, coincident to a battle with the Comanche. They fled to Fort Arbuckle, where Indian agent Elias Rector, anticipating abandonment of the Brazos Reservation, designated a reservation for them all. But the Wichita, now considered a single tribal entity, were hardly well settled before they were uprooted by the Civil War. The bulk of the tribe fled to Kansas in the winter of 1862–1863 and remained there until 1867. The site of one of their refugee camps is now the city of Wichita, Kansas (Bell, Jelks, and Newcomb 1974:299–302).

Although the Wichita were returned to their old homes along the Washita River after the Civil War, they were unable to secure government recognition of their right to its possession. In autumn 1872, a reservation embracing 743,610 acres between the Canadian and Washita rivers and west of 98° longitude, was agreed to by the Wichita, but Congress never ratified the agreement. The Waco and Tawakoni (late of Texas), the Wichita from north of the Red River, and the Kitsai established themselves in what the agents termed separate "neighborhoods" (Randlett 1901; Schmitt 1950:155). Each group had a chief and one of them was acknowledged as head chief of the tribe. By the end of the reservation period the position of local chief had disappeared. These tribal (or subtribal) fragments were too weak to rebuff or reject overtly whatever policies or actions the government might wish to impose.

In 1878 the Kiowa-Comanche and Wichita agencies had been combined, and after the reservations were broken up official reports seldom dealt specifically with its various tribes. Agents often were able to exact compliance with governmental policy by withholding annuities and trust funds. This enabled them to discourage attendance at the summer and fall dances, which frequently lasted as long as 10 days. In 1882 the Wichita were settled at Rush Springs south of the Washita River (Elam 1971:372).

Although the Wichita were reported to have about 100 acres under cultivation as early as 1869, it was a consequence of women's labors (ARCIA 1869:382). Typically the women enclosed garden patches of three to four acres with split rail fences, in which they grew corn, squash, watermelons, and a variety of garden vegetables. Efforts to induce the Wichita to become American-style farmers were furthered by plowing fields for them and planting in rows for easy cultivation of corn (and later cotton).

As late as 1875 it was reported that many of their farms were still worked with hoes by the women. Occasional floods, frequent droughts, and grasshoppers often destroyed or severely reduced crop yields, discouraging farming by whatever means by either sex. Wichita men felt it was degrading to labor in the fields, and most of them did not become willing farmers until the twentieth century. They were interested in raising horses, not cattle or crops. They regarded themselves as hunters, and with their agent's approval, continued to pursue bison in off-reservation hunts until the animal's virtual extinction.

A boarding school was opened near the Wichita Agency in 1871, which emphasized agricultural arts for boys and domestic training for girls.

Attempts to convert the Wichita to Christianity were less overt than those associated with farming. A Baptist mission was established in 1878, and its success was credited to Tula-Mico (Tulsey-Micco), a Seminole Baptist missionary. By 1880 a meeting house had been constructed with donated funds for its 70 members. Services attracted 100–300 persons (ARCIA 1880:75).

When the Ghost Dance swept the plains, the Wichita embraced the movement enthusiastically (fig. 7). Throughout the summer of 1891 they danced (Mooney 1896:902–903), but when the millennium failed to arrive, the Ghost Dance attracted fewer and fewer followers. Despite opposition by the authorities, reservation Indians, apparently including the Wichita, continued to dance until at least 1917.

The religious use of peyote was also adopted by the Wichita as early as 1889, as it was highly compatible with the Surround the Fire ceremony (*hacthiyas* 'fire tied around'). La Barre (1938:120) noted that many medicine bundles contained peyote before a Kiowa named Old Man Horse introduced the Peyote religion to the Wichita, about 1902. In 1924, the Wichita sent representatives to the annual meeting of the Native American Church indicating their continued interest in the sacramental use of peyote (Stewart 1987:226).

The Wichita resisted the determined efforts of the Cherokee Commission, under the provisions of the Dawes

Heard Mus. Lib., Phoenix, Ariz.: 120.

Fig. 6. Wichita commissary building in Indian Terr., 1872. Former U.S. Army Capt. Trustrim Connell stands in the door with Wichitas. Photograph by William S. Soule.

Smithsonian, NAA: top, 1353-b; bottom left, 1317; bottom right, 1353-c.

Fig. 7. Ghost Dance. top, Men on horseback following a woman with arms extended, one of the early manifestations of a trance state. A sweatlodge frame is in the foreground. bottom left, Tawakoni Jim, the principal chief of the confederated Wichita, Waco, and Tawakoni tribes, a judge on the Court of Indian Offenses in 1888 (Mooney 1896:438), and a voice against the allotment of the reservation. bottom right, Dance leaders with ritual paraphernalia. The woman holds corn, pipe, a staff with crossbar, and a full birdskin, probably an eagle. The man holds a painted shield, corn, and a pipe and wears a painted shirt. Photographs by James Mooney, 1893.

Severalty Act of 1887, to break up their reservation. They were discouraged from seeking and for a time denied legal counsel, and then they were offered about 50 cents an acre for their "surplus" land. But on June 4, 1891, 152 Wichitas out of an adult male population of 227 were persuaded to sign an agreement with the commissioners. Litigation over what the Wichita had agreed to, and the Choctaw and Chickasaw claims to reservation lands, postponed dismemberment of the reservation until December 1900. A Supreme Court decision then led to allotment in severalty, compensation of $1.25 an acre for surplus land, and the opening of the reservation in 1901 (B.B. Chapman 1933, 1944; Wright 1951:260; Newcomb 1976).

The Twentieth Century

Allotment of the reservation meant not only a drastic reduction in land holdings but also destruction of the last vestiges of the old neighborhoods since families had to scatter out to establish homes on their allotments, often at considerable distance from their old residences (Randlett 1901). Even when families moved to potentially more productive lands, most could not plant a crop in 1901, and those who were able to do so suffered from a serious drought that summer. With no annuity or other funds due, and near starvation, the beginnings of postreservation life were bleak for the Wichita.

By the second decade of the century the number of Christian denominations active among the agency's Indians, in addition to the Baptists, included the Methodist Church, Reformed Church of America, Reformed Presbyterian Church, and Mennonites. By this time the Peyote religion had spread to the Kiowa, Comanche, and Wichita agency, and it was reported that peyote was used by approximately 50 percent of the Indians there (Stinchecum 1917).

The Wichita adopted a constitutional tribal organization following the congressional enactment of the Oklahoma Indian Welfare Act in 1936. Its governing body was composed of a chairman, vice-chairman, treasurer, secretary, and three other members, elected for four-year terms of office. Among economic ventures, the tribe in 1974 built a 30,000-square-foot office building in Anadarko (fig. 9), which it leased to the Bureau of Indian Affairs. The Wichita joined with the Caddo and Delaware tribes as WCD Enterprises, Inc., to undertake light industrial and other ventures, and a number of buildings were completed in an industrial park. When the federal Riverside Indian Boarding School in Anadarko was closed in the 1950s, its 2,500 acres reverted to the three tribes, and 10 acres of this land were set aside for the Wichita. Through revenue sharing and donations a community building, dance pavilion, and picnic and camping areas were built. The tribe also benefited from various government programs, apart from those of the Bureau of Indian Affairs, particularly during the Great Society years of the 1960s, obtaining funds to improve the nutrition of low-income families and for an improved water system. The tribe began a number of programs aimed at preserving the tribal heritage and identity, including projects to record tribal songs; however, by 1998 there was no one fluent in Wichita.

In the early 1970s, the Wichita Indian tribe pursued compensation from the United States for the taking of Wichita aboriginal lands within the present states of Kansas, Oklahoma, and Texas. The Wichita were authorized to file their claim before the Indian Claims Commission even though the deadline for submitting such claims had already expired. The case was transferred to the Court of Claims, which in 1981 determined that the Wichita were not entitled to compensation and dismissed the petition "on the basis that the tribe had abandoned the lands . . . being claimed by the time the United States acquired sovereignty over Kansas and Oklahoma in 1803 and Texas in 1845" (Bureau of Indian Affairs 1985b:1). In 1983, the United States Court of Appeals reversed the dismissal and asked for the United States Claims Court to determine the boundaries of Wichita aboriginal lands. Such a finding was never issued by the court because in

left, Smithsonian, NAA: 56,392; right, Field Mus., Chicago: 59,363.

Fig. 8. Dance bustles. left, Harvest Dance with man in center wearing a bustle. Photograph probably by William E. Irwin and Jack Mankins, 1893–1901. right, Bustle made of eagle, crow, and other feathers on a buffalo hide base. Collected by George A. Dorsey, 1901. Length 95 cm.

Fig. 9. Life in the 1990s. top left, Wichita tribal administrative building, north of Anadarko, Okla. Built in 1978, this building houses the tribal museum, finance office, higher education office, and enrollment office. Photograph by Gary McAdams, 1998. top right, Dava Beartrack, a princess of the Kitikiti'sh Little Sisters. Organized in 1993 by Gary McAdams, Eva Cozad, and Cleta Ataddelty, this group teaches girls traditional dancing and culture from the diverse Okla. tribes. Photograph by Ardina McAdams, 1998. bottom left, Virgil Swift, Wichita commander of the Okla. Southwest Chapter of the Vietnam Veterans and treasurer of the Wichita tribe, holding the American flag with the 1997 Veterans' princess Eva B. Wolfe (Kiowa). They prepare for the grand entry at the Wichita Annual Powwow Dance. Photograph by Ardina McAdams, 1997. center right, Wichita Annual Powwow, Wichita Night. left to right, Stuart Owings, Thomas Arnold, and Jimmie Reeder, drumming and singing Drum Dance songs as they circle the arena. Photograph by Ardina McAdams, 1997. bottom right, Rock Springs Church, Baptist, north of Anadarko, which serves not only the Wichita, but also the Caddo, Pawnee, Seminole, Creek, Choctaw, Delaware, Comanche, and Kiowa tribes. Its founder was John McIntosh, a Creek Indian born in Indian Terr. who arrived among the Wichita in the 1870s. The first church was constructed in 1880; the present church was built in 1910. The open-sided building is used for outdoor services and overflows at funerals and revivals. Photograph by Ardina McAdams, 1998.

1985 the Wichita Tribe settled all claims by accepting $14,000,000, with both the United States and the tribe agreeing not to seek further review or appeal of the case.

Population

The documents of the 1540 Coronado expedition at first glance appear to be internally contradictory concerning the settlement patterns in Quivira and at odds with the population figures of the Oñate expedition 60 years later. Coronado reported that he visited or heard of 25 villages in Quivira (Winship 1896:582), but Jaramillo, who accompanied him, wrote that there were "six or seven settlements, at quite a distance from one another, among which we traveled for four or five days" (Winship 1896:590). Coronado may have noted some sort of geographical or political divisions of the settlements; and following this line of reasoning it is possible the expedition passed through six or seven "settlements" each composed of three to five "villages." The villages had "as many as 200 houses" (Winship 1896:577). Using 8 to 10 occupants per lodge, the figure employed by Oñate 60 years later, the villages had 1,600–2,000 inhabitants, and Coronado's Quivira a total population of 40,000–50,000. It should be noted that the settlements were unequal in size.

Population data, gained from members of the 1601 Oñate expedition who were interrogated the following year in Mexico City, reported that the Great Settlement contained variously 1,200, 1,700, and "close" to 2,000 lodges (Hammond and Rey 1953:846). But in their three-day scout alongside the settlement they failed to reach its far end. One soldier estimated the settlement's population at 20,000, and at 8–10 persons per lodge this estimate is reasonable. There was general agreement that there were other settlements up and down the river, and two soldiers learned that other settlements were larger than the one they visited.

By 1719, when Europeans next visited the Wichita, there had been a dramatic decline in the native population. The dispersed village La Harpe visited on the Arkansas apparently had a population of 6,000 (Margry 1876–1886, 6:289). The village Dutisné reached, presumably of Taovaya, and the other village nearby had between them 2,080–2,600 persons. Even if the contact-period population has been overestimated and the 1719 population underestimated, it is apparent that there had been a major and catastrophic population loss.

During the remainder of the eighteenth century Wichita population continued to decline, and disease is mentioned frequently in the documents of the period. In the 1770–1780 decade, for example, primarily following the estimates of De Mézières, all the Wichita peoples, including the Kitsai, had a population of 3,000–4,000. Early in the nineteenth century, after being "again ravaged by smallpox" (Mooney 1910:948), the consolidated tribe had a population of about 2,600. Their nadir population was reached in 1896 when they numbered 365 (G.A. Dorsey 1904a:2).

Population figures for the first decades of the twentieth century are confusing, as the Wichita were often counted with other groups. For example, in 1900 the "Wichita and affiliated tribes," excluding the Caddo, numbered 428 (ARCIA 1900, 1:648), while according to Mooney (1910:949) during the same period "the whole Wichita body [was estimated at] . . . only about 310, besides about 30 of the confederated Kichai remnant." Fourteen years later, the combined Wichita and Caddo population amounted to 1,094 (ARCIA 1914:81), probably almost equally divided between the two tribes (cf. Fletcher 1907a:181). Adding to the confusion is the enumeration of 597 Wichita in 1930 (ARCIA 1930:44) as compared to "300 Wichita and Kichai" reported the same year by the census; however, this source noted that "since there were 645 Indians in Caddo County not reported by tribe, it is quite likely the the numbers of both the Wichita and the Caddo are considerably understated by the census enumeration" (U.S. Bureau of the Census 1937:41, 59).

The undercount must have continued into the following decades, with perhaps 460 Wichita residing on the reservation in 1945 (U.S. Congress. House. Committee on Interior and Insular Affairs 1953:715). By 1960, over 700 Wichitas were living in the northern portion of Caddo County (U.S. Department of Health, Education, and Welfare 1960:15). The number dropped to 470 in 1972 (U.S. Department of Commerce 1974:478–479). In 1984 the total enrollment for the Wichita tribe was 1,170, with about half that number residing on the reservation (The Confederation of American Indians 1986:243). In 1989, the number of reservation residents was reported at 869 (Bureau of Indian Affairs 1989:5). Tribal enrollment grew to 1,912 members in 1998 (Jonelle Fields, communication to editors 1998).

Synonymy†

The name Wichita, now the designation of formerly separate tribes or bands, was originally the name of one village group. The earliest citation is on the 1718 Delisle map, where it appears as Ouachitas (Tucker 1942: pl. XV). Other French versions are Ousita, 1719 (La Harpe in Margry 1876–1886, 6:293); Ouedsitas, 1772 (de Mézières in Bolton 1914, 1:289); and Ouitcitas, 1807 (Robin in Hodge 1907–1910, 2:949). Spanish variants include Ovagitas, 1723 (Barcia 1723:288); Ovedsitas, 1771–1772 (Bolton 1905:91); Guachitas, 1786 (Cabello in Bell, Jelks, and Newcomb 1974:379); Guichitas (Treviño et al. 1765; Cabello 1784, both in Bell, Jelks, and Newcomb 1974:388, 379); Huichita, 1809 (Salcedo in Bell, Jelks, and Newcomb 1974:387); and Huichites, 1828 (Mier y Terán in Ewers 1969:149, n. 231). Later American variants reflect the modern spelling; for example, Whitchetaws and Witcheta,

†This synonymy was written by Douglas R. Parks based in part on a draft by Newcomb and Ives Goddard.

1807 (Sibley 1922:94); Wichetas, 1847 (Neighbors 1847:4); Wichetaws (Schoolcraft 1851–1857, 6:689); and Witchita (Marcy 1853:69).

Borrowings of the name by other tribes, probably dating to the postreservation period, include Caddo *wiċitah* (Chafe 1979), Kansa *mítsitta* (Dorsey 1883c, retranscribed), Osage Witsită (Dorsey 1883), Quapaw *wísitta* (Dorsey 1883b, retranscribed), Shawnee *wi·čita* (Voegelin 1938–1940, 5:414), and Creek *wicíta* (Haas 1942).

In the twentieth century the Wichita name for themselves was *kirikirˀi·s* 'raccoon eye(s)' (Lesser and Weltfish 1932:10; David S. Rood, personal communication 1987), said to be a reference to tattoos around the eyes (Scott 1912–1934). Formerly, this self-designation was also the name of one band, later generalized to the other groups (Lesser and Weltfish 1932:11; Lesser 1979:260). Historical citations of the name are Quicasquiris, 1719 (La Harpe in Margry 1876–1886, 6:289), more correctly Quirasquiris, 1720 (Beaurain in Margry 1876–1886, 6:289); in the nineteenth century it was recorded as Kiddĕkĕdissĕ (ten Kate 1884:10) and Kĭ'tikĭti'sh (Mooney 1896:1095). The designation is reflected in Pawnee *kiriku·ruks* and its Arikara cognate *čirikú·nUx*, literally 'bear eye(s)' (Parks 1965–1990, 1970–1990). The Pawnee name was borrowed into Omaha as kí·¢i-kú-¢uc (Dorsey 1880a).

A similar, related name occurs in Dhegiha and Chiwere Siouan as Omaha-Ponca *ppáðį wasábe* (Dorsey 1878 in Hodge 1907–1910, 2:949, retranscribed; misidentified as Caddo in Fletcher and La Flesche 1911:102) and Iowa-Otoe-Missouria *pʰánʸi waθéwe*, literally 'black bear Pawnee' (Dorsey 1879 in Hodge 1907–1910, 2:950, retranscribed). This name appears in Illinois as Pani8assa and Paniassa (Gravier 1700), which appear in late seventeenth- and early eighteenth-century French sources as Paniassa, 1673–1674 (Marquette in Tucker 1942: pl. V), Pancassa, 1680 (La Salle in Margry 1876–1886, 2:168), Paneassa, 1688 (Franquelin in Tucker 1942: pl. VIA), Paniouassa and Panioussa, 1720 (Beaurain in Margry 1876–1886, 6:289, 290). Later variants and mistranscriptions are in Hodge (1907–1910, 2:949).

A related eighteenth-century French designation was *Panis noirs,* 1742 (Fabry de la Bruyère in Margry 1876–1886, 6:4746) and 1751 (La Jonquière in M.M. Wedel 1981a:46), translated as Black Pani (Charlevoix 1761, 2:246). Lewis and Clark (Moulton 1983–, 3:445) reported that the Wichita were "formerly known by the name of the *White* Panias," an anomalous designation.

In the seventeenth and eighteenth centuries the Wichita groups were often designated by the generic name Pani, used interchangeably for the Pawnee, Arikara, and Wichita, usually cited as Panis (Gaignard in Bolton 1914, 2:82, 85; Sibley 1832:723; M.M. Wedel 1981a:18–25), Panies, 1807 (Sibley 1922:69), and Pana (Garraghan 1927:312; M.M. Wedel 1973), which in the nineteenth century came to be applied exclusively to the South Band Pawnee. However, designations for Wichita groups generally used a modifier to specify them. The phrase "Little Pawnees," for example, was reportedly used to differentiate the Wichita from the Pawnee of Nebraska (Carter 1934–1962, 19:59).

In the eighteenth and nineteenth centuries another common name used by the French for the Wichita was *Panis Piqués* 'tattooed Pawnees'. It is cited as Panipiques, Panipiquets, and Panipiquetes, 1749 (Febre et al. in Bell, Jelks, and Newcomb 1974:333), Paunee Piqûe, 1805 (Lewis and Clark 1832:721), Pānias picqué (Jefferson 1804), Pawnee Piquas (James 1823, 2:104), and Pânies-Piqués, 1839–1840 (Tixier 1940:151). Similarly, Spaniards sometimes designated the Wichita, and perhaps specifically the Waco, as Flechazos, 1785, 'pricked ones' (Vial and Chavez in John 1994:51). The name is cited in American sources as Pawnee Picts (Hildreth 1836:160), Pania Pickey, 1804 (Lewis and Clark in Moulton 1983–, 3:445) or simply Picks, 1837 (Dougherty 1838:16), as well as Skin Pricks, 1804 (Lewis and Clark in Thwaites 1904–1907, 1:190), and Prickled Panis or Freckled Panis (Buchanan 1824:155), and Speckled Pani (Imlay 1793:231).

The preceding designation referring to tattooing is reflected in several tribal names for the Wichita generally. The Cheyenne name is Evxsohetan 'tattooed people' (Petter 1913–1915:583), cited also as Hew'sóitäneo (sg. Hew'sóitän)-(Mooney 1907:426). Two names reflect tattooing of the breast: Comanche Pitchinavo 'tattooed chests' (ten Kate 1885:136) and Otoe *bá·ðe grexé* 'spotted breast' (Parks 1988). Others refer to facial tattooing: Kiowa *ṫó·-kút* 'face mark' (Laurel Watkins, personal communication 1979), cited also as Do'gu'at (Mooney 1896:1095); and Kiowa-Apache *goní̜čéˀí̜šį́na* 'they have painted face' (Bittle 1952–1953).

Other tribal designations that are descriptive of Wichita culture are Comanche Sonikanik 'grass houses' (ten Kate 1885:136) and Kiowa *é·-ṗǫ́·-dɔ̀* 'pumpkin braid' (Laurel Watkins, personal communication 1979; La Barre 1935). The Arapaho name Hinásau, also recorded as Hinásso (Gatschet in Hodge 1907–1910, 2:949), is of unknown origin.

In the eighteenth century, the Spanish of New Mexico often designated the Wichita as Jumanos and Jumanes. However, the name, which is generally interpreted to mean 'striped', has been applied to various entirely distinct groups that practiced tattooing or facial painting (see Hodge 1907–1910, 1:636; Bolton 1911, 2:66–84; J.D. Forbes 1959; M.M. Wedel 1981a:33–35).

The sign language gesture for Wichita symbolized tattooing. One sign used the extended forefinger of the right hand to make a circle or ring several times around the eyes or over the right cheek, or even over the breast, all representing the parts of the body that were formerly tattooed (Mallery 1881:476; W.P. Clark 1885:403; Scott 1912–1934; G.A. Dorsey 1904a:2–3). An alternate gesture was to extend the fingers and thumb of the right hand, semiclosed, and repeatedly bring the hand toward the face, nearly touching it, imitating the motion of tattooing (Mallery 1881:476).

• TAOVAYA The origin of this band name is unknown but is possibly from their name in an extinct dialect of Wichita. The spelling is Bolton's (1914; Hodge 1907–1910, 2:705) normalization of the Spanish variants. The only French recordings are Toayas and Toajas, 1719 (La Harpe in Margry 1876–1886, 6:289, 290). The earliest Spanish recording is Tabas, 1542 (Jaramillo in B. Smith 1857, 1:160), if this is the same. Eighteenth and early nineteenth century Spanish recordings include Tauaïasés and Tavaïases, 1770 (De Mézières in Bolton 1914, 1:211, 215); Taoüiaches, 1779 (De Mézières in Bolton 1914, 2:241); Taouaiazés, 1771 (De Mézières in Bolton 1914, 1:256); Tavayas, 1772 (de Ripperda in Bolton 1914, 1:270); Tavoyache, 1774 (Gaignard in Bolton 1914, 2:85:); Tahuayas, 1795 (Troike 1964:387); Taobayaces, 1778 (Croix in Bolton 1914, 2:228); Tabuayases, 1804 (Salcedo in Nasatir 1952, 2:749); Taouayaches, 1807 (Robin in Hodge 1907–1910, 2:707); Tahuaiasses, 1830 (Berlandier 1969:143–145); and Tamayacas, 1828 (Mier y Terán in Ewers 1969:149, n. 231). For other variants in early Spanish documents, see Bolton (1914) and references in Hodge (1907–1910, 2:706–707).

Examples of American spellings include Towaahack, 1805 (Sibley 1832:723); Towiache and Towe-ash, 1807 (Sibley 1922:40, 94); Toweaches (Schermerhorn 1814:26); Towaches (Morgan 1871:55); Towiash (Latham 1856:104); Toyash (Hildreth 1836:160); and Towoashe (Domenech 1860, 1:444). For other variant forms see Hodge (1907–1910, 2:705). The form Tawehash, which is Mooney's (1896:1095) transcription of the name he obtained as the Caddo and Kitsai form, is often cited as a standardized spelling of this band's name (Hodge 1907–1910, 2:705; Swanton 1952:303).

• TAWAKONI The Wichita form of this name is *tawa·kháriw* (David S. Rood, personal communication 1987), recorded also as *tawa·kháriwa* (Parks 1988; Gatschet in Hodge 1907–1910, 2:704), the origin of which is obscure. It was borrowed as Caddo *tawákunih* (Chafe 1979), Kitsai tawăkăru (Mooney 1893), Tonkawa Tawákal (Gatschet in Hodge 1907–1910, 2:704), and Quapaw *ttahúkkaní* (Dorsey 1883b, retranscribed).

In European and American sources the name occurs in numerous recognizable variants, including Teucarea, 1542 (Jaramillo in B. Smith 1857, 1:160); Touacara, 1719 (La Harpe in Margry 1876–1886, 6:289); Tavakavas, 1742 (Fabry de la Bruyère in Margry 1876–1886, 6:492); Tuacanas, 1772, 1777 (De Mézières in Bolton 1914, 1:289, 2:145); Taovacanas, 1779 (Galvez in Bolton 1914, 2:243); Taguacanes, 1778 (Bonilla in Bolton 1914, 2:165); Tahuacanas and Tahuacanes, 1804 (Salcedo in Nasatir 1952, 2:749); Tawakenoes, 1805 (Sibley 1832:723); Toweca (Gallatin 1836:117); Towiachs, Towakenos, Tawacani and Towacarro (Latham 1856:102–104); and Yo-woc-o-nee (Marcy in Schoolcraft 1851–1857, 5:712). For other examples, including misprints, see Hodge (1907–1910, 2:704). A French corruption was Trois Cannes, 1712 (Pénigaut in McWilliams 1953:156), as if literally 'three canes', which occurs as Three Canes, 1805 (Sibley 1832:723), and misprinted as Three Cones (Schermerhorn 1814:25) and Three Cranes (Alcedo in G.A. Thompson 1812–1815, 4:515).

Quiscat, an eighteenth-century village named after a chief, occurs in several forms, including Quiscat, 1779 (De Mézières in Bolton 1914, 2:277); and Quiscate and Quisquate, 1787 (Vial in Hodge 1907–1910, 2:346). Another eighteenth-century village named after a chief occurs as Flechazo (Bolton 1914, 2:277; Chabot 1932:8) and Flechasos (Cabello 1786).

• ISCANI This name occurs in the eighteenth century and has been thought to be an earlier designation for the Waco (Bolton in Hodge 1907–1910, 2:1002). Variants include Isconies and Ysconies, 1684 (Mendoza in Hodge 1907–1910, 2:1002); Ascani, 1719 (La Harpe in Margry 1876–1886, 6:289–290); Hiscanes, 1749 (Parrilla in Bolton 1914, 1: 211); Yscanis, 1770 (De Mézières in Bolton 1914, 1:211); Iscanis, 1772 (De Mézières in Bolton 1914, 1:284); Yscan, 1770 (Chirinos in Bolton 1914, 1:222); Niscaniche, 1774 (Gaignard in Bolton 1914, 2:85); Yascale, 1759 (Parrilla in Bell, Jelks, and Newcomb 1974:333); and Yxcanis (Chabot 1932:8).

• WACO The Wichita form of this name is *wi·ko·*, which is of unknown etymology (David S. Rood, personal communication 1998). Examples of borrowings are Caddo we′ku and wi′ko (Gatschet in Hodge 1907–1910, 2:888), Kitsai weko (Mooney 1893), Tonkawa *weyko?* (Hoijer 1949:36), and Quapaw Wi′-ku (Dorsey 1883b). Spellings in European and American sources reflect the Wichita form. Early French variants include Quaineo, 1718 (Delisle in Tucker 1942: pl. XV); and Huanchané, Huané, and Honechas, 1719 (La Harpe in Margry 1876–1886, 6:277, 289). Spanish forms are Huecos, 1830 (Berlandier 1969:125–126; Austin 1829) and Wacos (Sánchez 1926:265). American forms include Wachos (Gallatin 1836:117); Wacoah and Wico (Hildreth 1836:166, 177); Whacoe, 1807 (Sibley 1922:94; Burnet in Schoolcraft 1851–1857, 1:239); and Wecos (Domenech 1860, 2:25).

• TOKANE The Wichita form of this name, *tó·kanne?e* (David S. Rood, personal communication 1987; Lesser 1979:260; Parks 1988), survived into the late twentieth century as a band name. The earliest citation of it is Thacanhé, 1700 (Iberville in Margry 1876–1886, 4:374). In the late nineteenth century it was recorded from Dhegiha Siouan speakers as Osage Tu′-ka-nyi (Dorsey 1883), Kansa *ttókkale* (Dorsey 1883c, retranscribed), and Omaha Tu-ká-¢a (Dorsey 1880a), all of which were mistakenly glossed as Tawakoni (Hodge 1907–1910, 2:704). It also appears in the late nineteenth-century form Tooc-a-nie Kiowas, the name of a group said to be part Wichita and part Kiowa (Richards in ARCIA 1875:289).

This band name is also the source of one Comanche designation for the Wichita, *tuhka?naai?* (Robinson and Armagost 1990:123) or *tu·hkanai* (Jean Charney, personal communication 1987), cited also as Tokǘnai (Curtis 1907–1930, 19:229), a borrowing that was generalized to all the Wichita bands. It has subsequently been folk etymologized. Thus one citation, Do′kănă, is translated as 'tattooed people' (Mooney 1896:1095), while other sources cite and translate the form as To-can-a 'dark lodges' (Scott 1890) and Toûghkanne 'dark, gloomy houses' (ten Kate 1885:136) or Tōĕchkanne 'dusky lodges' (ten Kate 1884:373), the last three meanings said to be a reference to the grass lodge.

• AKWITS The name of this Wichita group has been recorded several times but does not appear in the historical literature. The first citation is Akwech (Hodge 1907–1910, 1:34, based on information provided by James O. Dorsey), where it is given as a Wichita subtribe. The Wichita form, recorded in the early twentieth century, is *akʷi·c* (Lesser 1979:260).

• QUIVIRA The name Quivira, Quibira, or Aguivira that Coronado's expedition, 1541 (in Hodge 1907–1910, 2:147) gave to Wichita settlements in the sixteenth century cannot be identified with any modern Wichita name. Although it was said to derive from the Wichita self-designation *kirikirʔi·s* (Hodge 1907–1910, 2:346), that association is unlikely. Historical variants of the name include Quiuira, 1554 (Gomara 1587:470), Quivirenses, 1788 (Alcedo 1812–1815, 4:305), and Quivera (Schoolcraft 1851–1857, 4:28). See Hodge (1907–1910, 2:347) for other forms.

• MENTO For a 50-year period in the late seventeenth and early eighteenth centuries, the name Mento appears in French sources as a designation for the most southerly of three Wichita groups, although sometimes the term may have been used for the Wichita in general. The origin of the name is obscure; the Illinois word assumed in the explanation of M.M. Wedel (1981a:21–25, 1973a:161–162) does not exist (Ives Goddard, personal communication 1998). The earliest recording of it appears to be Matora, 1673–1674 (Marquette map in Tucker 1942: pl. V). Other variants are Meintens, 1697 (Louvigny in Tucker 1942: pl. XIV); Mentous, 1700 (Tonti in M.M. Wedel 1981a:21; Delisle in Tucker 1942: pl. XIII); Mentos (La Harpe in M.M. Wedel 1973a:161; Fabry de La Bruyère in Margry1876–1886, 6:474); and Mantou, 1702 (Iberville in M.M. Wedel 1981a:33), cited as Manton in Margry (1876–1886, 4:599). For later citations see Hodge (1907–1910, 1:844).

The only recorded tribal citation is a late nineteenth century Kansa form *mą́ttowe* (Dorsey in Hodge 1907–1910, 1:844, retranscribed).

Sources

A number of studies have focused on various aspects of Wichita history. Harper (1953, 1953a, 1953b) emphasizes trade and diplomacy between 1719–1835. Her broader and more ambitious study of Spanish and French interaction with Southwest Indians between 1540 and 1795 places the Wichita within this larger context (John 1975). Elam (1971, 1979) presents historical accounts of the Wichita to 1868 and 1895, respectively. The brief articles by Bolton (1910:701–706, 1910a:1002) and Mooney (1910:947–950) on various Wichita subgroups are now rather outdated. The probing studies of Wichita ethnohistory by M.M. Wedel (1971, 1981a, 1982), particularly of the Coronado expedition and the journeys of La Harpe and Dutisné, are essential to comprehending the location, cultural nature, and the forces that affected the Wichita from the sixteenth through the eighteenth centuries. La Harpe (in Margry 1876–1886, 6:239–306) and De Mézières (in Bolton 1914) provide first-hand accounts from the eighteenth century. For later centuries and an extensive bibliography see Bell, Jelks, and Newcomb (1974). Winfrey and Day (1959–1966) reproduce documents relating to the Wichita in Texas. Blaine (1982) discusses the historical relationship between the Wichita and the Pawnee. M.L. Tate (1986) covers the Wichita in his annotated bibliography of the Indians of Texas. Tiller (1996:536–537) gives a social and economic profile of the Wichita Tribe in the mid-1990s.

G.A. Dorsey (1904a) presents a succinct description of Wichita culture and a large body of mythology. Curtis (1907–1930, 19:35–104) also describes Wichita culture, emphasizing religion and mythology. Newcomb (1961:247–277, 1967) provides summaries. Wichita kinship is described in Schmitt and Schmitt (1952) and Lesser (1979). Extensive field notes recorded by Karl and Iva Schmitt in the 1940s are deposited in the Western History Collections of the University of Oklahoma; they were not utilized in the preparation of this chapter. Linguistic investigations have been made by Lesser and Weltfish (1932), Taylor (1963, 1963a), Rood (1976), Chafe (1979), and Parks (1979).

Kitsai

DOUGLAS R. PARKS

The Kitsai (ˈkētsī), extinct as a tribal entity, were a small Northern Caddoan tribe. Throughout most of the historical period there appear to have been two Kitsai groups, a southern one allied with Caddo groups, primarily the Cadohadacho, and a smaller northern group allied with the Wichita proper. During most of the eighteenth and the first half of the nineteenth centuries, the southern division lived in villages in north- and east-central Texas, primarily in the area between the Trinity and Brazos rivers (fig. 1). In the mid-nineteenth century, after the remaining Kitsai in Texas settled on a reservation with the northern group and the Wichita in Oklahoma, they lost their identity as a tribe and were subsequently treated as a Wichita band.

Linguistically, Kitsai is a distinct Northern Caddoan language that is intermediate between Pawnee-Arikara and Wichita.* Despite the tribe's location on the southern Plains and its close historical affiliations with Caddo groups and the Wichita, the language is more closely related to Pawnee than it is to Wichita (Mooney 1896:1095; Lesser and Weltfish 1932:1; Parks 1979:203).

Throughout their history, the Kitsai were allied with the ancestral Wichita tribes (the Wichita proper, Tawakoni, Waco, and others) and with various Caddo groups, such as the Cadohadacho, Nabedache, and Nacogdoche. They also allied themselves with Tonkawa and Comanche. Their enemies included the Hasinai, Plains Apache, and Osage.

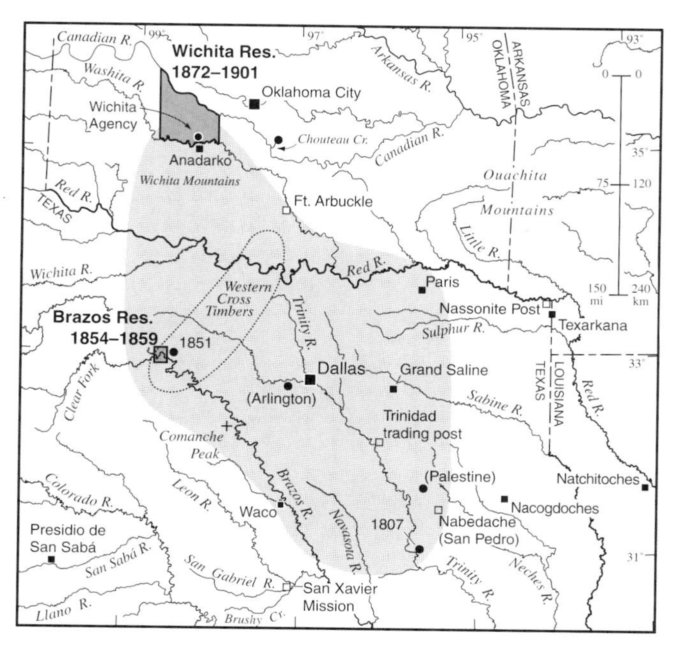

Fig. 1. Kitsai territory, early 18th to mid-19th century, and subsequent reservations, all jointly used by the Wichita.

History, 1700–1859

The earliest references to the Kitsai occur at the end of the seventeenth century, when the French began exploring the country west of the Mississippi and the Spaniards were exploring eastward through Texas. The first references occur in lists of tribes comprising, and allied to or at war with, the Hasinai in eastern Texas and adjoining areas of Louisiana (Joutel in Margry 1876–1886, 3:409; Casañas de Jesus Maria in Hatcher 1927:287). Those lists mention the Kitsai only by name and do not provide any information about them. The first direct reference to them appears in André-Joseph Pénigaut's narrative account of Louis Juchereau de Saint-Denis's exploratory journey to the Red River. In 1712, when Saint-Denis's party visited a Hasinai village, Pénigaut witnessed the return of a war party that had raided a Kitsai village. The Hasinai had taken six Kitsai captives but had killed and eaten four of them on the way back to their village. Subsequently, the Hasinai ritually sacrificed the two surviving prisoners and then ate them, too (Pénigaut in McWilliams 1953:153–156).

The first references to Kitsai locations occur at the end of the second decade of the eighteenth century. In a 1718 memoir Jean-Baptiste LeMoyne, sieur de Bienville, governor of Louisiana, lists Kitsai among the Caddo groups living along the Red River. At that time, one Kitsai group, at least, lived with several Caddo groups in a single village located 150 leagues up the Red River from its mouth (Swanton 1942:55). In 1719, while Jean-Baptiste Bénard de La Harpe was building his Nassonite Post on the Red River, near present Texarkana, he sent du Rivage up that river with merchandise to give to nomadic tribes with whom La Harpe wished to make an alliance. Du Rivage traveled 70 leagues westward and, near present Paris, Texas (R.K. Harris et al. 1965:359–360), met a party comprised of members of several tribes—among them Kitsais, Nabedache Caddos, and two groups of Tonkawas—and

*The phonemes of Kitsai are: (voiceless stops) *t*, *k*, *ʔ*; (voiceless spirants) *s*, *h*; (nasal) *n*; (resonants) *w*, *r*, *y*; (short vowels) *i*, *e* ([ɛ]), *a*, *u*; (long vowels) *i·*, *e·* ([ɛ·]), *a·*, *u·*; (stress) v́ (Bucca and Lesser 1969).

also obtained two Kitsai guides who returned with him to the Nassonite Post. Although the meeting site apparently was not a village, du Rivage's report places the Kitsai in the area of the upper Trinity River in north-central Texas at the opening of the eighteenth century. In 1742, when André Fabry de la Bruyère was sent by Governor Bienville to explore the Arkansas and make alliances with the tribes there, he encountered Kitsai and Tawakoni three days' journey above the Red River (Margry 1876–1886, 6:492).

In a 1745 memorial to the Spanish king, requesting missions to serve the tribes of central Texas, Father Francisco Xavier Ortiz included the Kitsai, who at that time continued to live in the area of the upper Trinity, Brazos, and Red rivers (Bolton 1915:153–154). Several times in subsequent years Kitsais were reported to be at San Xavier Mission, located near the junction of the San Gabriel River and Brushy Creek. In 1758, after the Spanish built a mission at San Sabá for the Lipan Apache, their enemies, the Kitsai joined a combined force that included Taovaya, Caddo, Tonkawa, and Comanche, to burn the mission ("Wichita," this vol.).

In 1769, after Spain acquired Louisiana from France, Athanase De Mézières, the newly appointed Spanish lieutenant-governor at Natchitoches, had the task of winning to Spain the allegiance of the "Nations of the North," among whom were the Kitsai, ancestral Wichita groups, and Tonkawa. In 1770 De Mézières went to the Cadohadacho village on the Red River and extracted from chiefs of the formerly hostile Kitsai and several Wichita groups a commitment to peace. In October 1771 those chiefs went to Natchitoches, where the treaties were solemnized (Bolton 1914, 1:92–95). In the following year De Mézières was sent on an expedition to the Upper Brazos River to cement the new friendship with the Nations of the North and to secure information on their locations, customs, and numbers. His initial stop on that tour was the Kitsai village on the east side of the Trinity River, near present Palestine, Texas. It comprised 30 lodges and 80 warriors. Although on the west side of the river, opposite their village, were villages of the Iscani and Tawakoni, De Mézières stated that the Kitsai maintained a close union with the neighboring Cadohadacho and Texas (Tejas) Indians. During his stay with the Kitsai, De Mézières supplied them with a bonded trader from Natchitoches, the settlement where they traded buffalo and deer skins for arms, ammunition, and other goods (Bolton 1914, 1:101). On a trip in 1778, De Mézierès, after traveling 18 leagues north of Bucareli, found a small village of Kitsai who had separated from the larger one. This village, which had 20 warriors, was in the vicinity of present Grand Saline, Texas, where local salines allowed the villagers to obtain salt for their own use as well as a commodity to trade (Bolton 1914, 2:191).

For the subsequent 50 years after De Mézières' visits, the Kitsai remained living in the same area east of the Trinity River, just north of the Nabedache (San Pedro) and Texas settlements and east of the Waco and Tawakoni, whose villages were on the east side of the Brazos River, near present Waco, Texas. In 1805, John Sibley (1832:721) reinforced De Mézières' observation that the Kitsai maintained a close relationship with the Caddo, when he wrote that the Kitsai "speak the Caddo language, look up to them as their fathers, visit and intermarry among them, and join them in all their wars." In 1820 and again in 1828 they continued to trade primarily at Nacogdoches and also at Trinidad (Padilla 1920:52; Sanchez 1926:282–283; Stephen F. Austin in Bell, Jelks, and Newcomb 1974:306–307), but by the end of the decade an expanding Texas frontier began to overwhelm them and other tribes in central Texas.

During the next decade the Kitsai, Waco, and Tawakoni moved north to the upper valleys of the Trinity, Brazos, and lower Wichita rivers in order to distance themselves from the aggressive Texans. In 1835 the Kitsai and several Wichita groups, together with the Comanche, signed the first treaty with the United States government, establishing peace and friendship between the tribes and the United States as well as treating the Kitsai for the first time as a "band" of the Wichita (Kappler 1904–1941, 2:435–439). Peace, however, was not forthcoming since Texas settlers continued to grow more hostile toward the Indian population. In 1841, for example, a group of Texans attacked the Kitsai and Waco villages on the West Fork of the Trinity River, near present Arlington, and forced their abandonment. In 1846 the Kitsai were reported to be living on the Brazos, 100 miles north of Comanche Peak, and to have suffered a loss in population because of smallpox and war with Texans (P.M. Butler in Bell, Jelks, and Newcomb 1974:294). In 1851, their village was in a valley on the left bank of the Brazos River, about 15 miles below the Clear Fork of the Brazos. Six miles upstream were the villages of the Waco and Tawakoni, and the three groups were said to be organized as separate bands under a head chief named Acaquash (Samuel Cooper in Bell, Jelks, and Newcomb 1974:294).

During this period, and perhaps earlier, a group of Kitsai had taken up residence near the Wichita in southwestern Oklahoma. They were noted to be with the Wichita there as early as 1837, and in 1843 they were reported to be living in a village in the Wichita Mountains. In 1851 Jesse Stem stated that there were only 38 Kitsais on the Brazos Reservation and that within the last two years two-thirds of the tribe had joined the Wichita and were living in the Wichita Mountains (ARCIA 1851:261). They remained in that area until 1858, when they accompanied their Wichita neighbors, who then also included Wacos, to Fort Arbuckle. In 1852 some Kitsais were reported living on Chouteau Creek, an affluent of the Canadian River (Marcy 1853:93).

In 1854 the Texas legislature authorized the United States government to select land for Indian reservations in Texas. For the Kitsai, Caddo, Tonkawa, and two Wichita groups, Gen. Randolph B. Marcy selected 18,576 acres on the Brazos River, near the mouth of Clear Fork, to be known as the Brazos Reservation. The people who settled on it immediately began to cultivate land and build American-style houses, and some of the men enlisted as scouts. Nevertheless, the surrounding White population became increasingly hostile, and in 1858, after relations between the tribes and the White population had continued to deteriorate, Gov. H. R. Runnels and Gen. Sam Houston petitioned the federal government to remove the Indians. The following year the remaining Kitsais on the Brazos Reservation, together with the remnants of the other tribes there, were moved to the Wichita Agency in Oklahoma, which was located on the site of an old Kitsai village (Bell, Jelks, and Newcomb 1974:295–303).

Culture

Subsistence

The Kitsai subsistence pattern, like that of other Caddoan tribes, was a semisedentary one, based on horticulture, hunting, and gathering. The Kitsai lived in their villages from spring until fall, during which time women planted and cultivated gardens. Crops included corn, beans, cucurbits, cantelopes, and watermelons. Kitsai women were noted for their industriousness and for raising a surplus of corn, and perhaps other crops as well, that was regularly traded in European settlements in the eighteenth century.

In addition to the produce of their gardens, Kitsai women relied on the roots and fruit of various wild plants. They collected nuts, acorns, and the fruit of medlars. Out of the medlars they made a bread that De Mézières considered very palatable.

After their crops were harvested in the fall and cold weather had set in, the Kitsai went on extended hunts that lasted until spring, when the horticultural cycle began again. Their hunts yielded an abundance of both buffalo and deer, the meat of which they dried and retained for their own use throughout subsequent seasons. The surplus of buffalo and deer hides was used for trade, enabling Kitsai to procure guns, powder, balls, and other merchandise for their defense and support (De Mézières in Bolton 1914, 1:285–286).

Warfare

There are numerous references in historical sources to the Kitsai participating in Plains warfare, and particularly horse stealing. Nevertheless, they were noted as being less aggressive than most other tribes toward Europeans and, given their size, probably less aggressive toward larger, more warlike tribes like their enemies the Osage, Hasinai, and Apache (De Mézières in Bolton 1914, 1:286). Like other tribes of the region, the Kitsai practiced ritual cannibalism.

Kinship and Marriage

The Kitsai kinship system was generational in type, and among Caddoan tribes it most closely resembled that of the Wichita (Lesser 1979). Terms were used for grandfather and grandmother, father (including father's brother), mother (including mother's sister), mother's brother, father's sister, brother and sister (differentiated by sex of speaker and extended to all parallel and cross cousins), child, and grandchild. A feature unique to the Kitsai, not shared by the Wichita, was use of the mother's brother term reciprocally for nephew/niece; thus a man called his sister's children by the same term that they called him.

Residence after marriage was matrilocal. In addition to terms for parent-in-law, husband, and wife, three other affinal terms were used, none of which was generationally specific: males married into the family, spouses of males married out of the family, and individuals of the same sex married into the same family (for example, two men married to sisters).

The Kitsai practiced both the levirate and sororate, which were not generationally restricted; thus, marriages might occur between individuals classed in the grandparental and grandchild generation. They practiced the levirate and sororate not only after the death of a spouse, but during life as well. Individuals extended husband and wife terms to the same-sex siblings of husband and wife. Consequently, a man considered the sisters of his wife as also being his wives, while a woman considered the brothers of her husband as also being her husbands. Obligatory joking characterized these relationships. Moreover, a younger brother customarily went to live with an older married brother, resulting in the practice of fraternal polyandry (Lesser 1979:265). Polygyny was also practiced.

The relationship between a child and his parents was formal. Questions of sex and arrangement of marriage were left to the grandparents, whose relationship to grandchildren was an open, joking one. This freedom between alternate generations was a distinctive characteristic of the Kitsai system, reflected in the fact that parents of grandparents were classified with parents, and the children of grandchildren were classified with child terms.

Religion

Little is known of Kitsai religion and even whether the basic distinction between priests and shamans existed as it did among other Northern Caddoan tribes. Historical statements hint at the existence of doctors' societies and practices similar to those found among the Pawnee and Arikara. The Comanche, for example, were said to detest the Kitsai in particular because of their powers of sorcery (David G. Burnet in Schoolcraft 1851–1857, 1:237).

At the end of the nineteenth century, the Kitsai and Wichita learned the Ghost Dance doctrine from the Caddo. At first, they manifested only slight interest in it, but, in

Kans. State Histl. Soc., Topeka.

Fig. 2. Clothing. The woman wears a German silver concho belt and wrist bands. The seated man wears a breastplate of hairpipes and a fur-wrapped braid. The woman wears soft-soled moccasins and fringed leggings. Photograph possibly by William Soule, 1869–1875.

1891, when Sitting Bull, the Arapaho Ghost Dance leader, visited them and "gave the feather" to their leaders, they embraced the dance "heart and soul" (Mooney 1896:903).

History After 1860

After the remaining Kitsais moved from the Brazos Reservation, they merged with the Wichita and over the ensuing half-century lost their distinct identity. By the early twentieth century they had been completely assimilated by the Wichita (Curtis 1907–1930, 19:36), although the last fluent speaker of the language survived into the 1940s (Bucca and Lesser 1969:7). For an account of their later history, see "Wichita," this volume.

Population

The earliest population figures, for the 1770s, cite 80 (De Mezieres in Bolton 1914, 1:285) or 90 warriors (Merino y Moreno in Bolton 1914, 2:165). In 1805 and 1809, the number of warriors was estimated at 60 (Sibley 1832:722) and 50–60 (Salcedo in Bell, Jelks, and Newcomb 1974:290).

A total population of 300 was estimated for the years 1849 (Schoolcraft 1851–1857, 1:518) and 1857 (ARCIA 1857:260); 500 was also estimated for 1855 (Whipple, Ewbank, and Turner 1855:9). By 1893 the population had dropped to 52 individuals (Mooney 1896:1095).

Synonymy

The Kitsai self-designation is kítsias (Lesser and Weltfish 1932:10), recorded also as Ki′tsäsh (Mooney 1896:1095), an ethnonym that has no other known meaning. Its exact phonemic form in Kitsai is still uncertain. The same name was used by other Caddoan tribes; thus, Caddo *kí·ca(h)iš* (Chafe 1979), recorded also as Ki′-tchēsh (Gatschet in Hodge 1907–1910, 1:683); Pawnee *kí·cas* (Lesser and Weltfish 1932:10; Douglas R. Parks 1994); and Wichita *kí·che·s* (David S. Rood, personal communication 1987; Douglas R. Parks 1980). Another Wichita designation is kíkiskitsu (Lesser and Weltfish 1932:10). Forms of the same name occur in neighboring Dhegiha Siouan languages; for example, Kansa *gíčaži*, Omaha *kkiðíčaš*, and Osage *kíčaži* (James O. Dorsey in Hodge 1907–1910, 1:683, retranscribed). Recordings of the same designation used by other tribes include Tonkawa Ki′tchas (Gatschet in Hodge 1907–1910, 1:683) and Creek Kitsasĭ (Grayson in Hodge 1907–1910, 1:683).

French renderings of the name are probably based on the Caddo form. Examples with initial k are Keychies, 1701 (Pénigaut in French 1869:73); Kitsaiches, 1712 (Bruyère in Margry 1876–1886, 6:492); and Kitaeches and Kitaesechis, 1714 (Pénigaut in Margry 1876–1886, 5:502; Pénigaut in French 1869:120). A nineteenth-century form is Kichaes, 1830 (Berlandier 1969:141). Examples of renditions with initial qu are: Quidahos, Quidehaio, 1719 (Mustel and du Rivage in French 1846–1853, 3:72); Quidehais, 1719 (La Harpe in Margry 1876–1886, 6:277); and Quiches, 1731 (Anville in Hodge 1907–1910, 1:683). The form Cassia, 1687 (Joutel in Margry 1876–1886, 3:409–410), which occurs in a list of non-Caddo tribes allied to the Hasinai, has been identified as Kitsai, but that identification is doubtful (Swanton 1942:9).

Spanish renderings are: Quitxix (pronounced [kičiš]) and Quizi, 1691 (Casañas de Jesus María in Hatcher 1927:287); Quituchiis, 1748 (Villa-Señor in Hodge 1907–1910, 1:683); Quitseis, 1771–1772 (Bolton 1905:91); Quichais, 1778 (Ybarbo in Hodge 1907–1910, 1:683); and Quichaais, 1790 (Census in Hodge 1907–1910, 1:683); Quitseys, 1770, Quitseis, 1772, Quitreis, 1778, the latter a misprint (De Mézières in Bolton 1914, 1:148, 285, 231); Quisseis, 1772 (de Ripperda in Bolton 1914, 1:320); Quisenzes, 1772 (de la Peña in Bolton 1914, 2:21); and Quitseis or Quicheis, 1799 (Cortés 1989:87). Several

Okla. Histl. Soc., Arch. and Manuscripts Div., Oklahoma City: 5457.

Fig. 3. Kai Kai, the last speaker of the Kitsai language and the primary linguistic consultant of Alexander Lesser, in her mid-80s (Bucca and Lesser 1969:7). Photograph by Alexander Lesser, near Anadarko, Okla., 1929–1930.

forms have an additional final syllable of nasal consonant plus vowel: Quicheigno, 1774, Quitseings, 1777 (Ripperdá in Hodge 1907–1910, 1:683), and Quitzaené, 1865 (Pimentel in Hodge 1907–1910, 1:683). Misreading g for q are: Guichais, 1792 (Texas State Archives in Hodge 1907–1910, 1:683) and Guitzeis (Morfi in Hodge 1907–1910, 1:683).

Nineteenth-century English-language renditions of the name are also variant forms of Kitsai, usually with medial [č]: Keychies, 1805 (Sibley 1832:722); Keechy, 1846 (Senate Document in Hodge 1907–1910, 1:683); and Keechies (ARCIA 1846:894); Kiche, 1840 (Wallace in Hodge 1907–1910, 1:683); Kitchies and Koechies (Schoolcraft 1851–1857, 1:237, 518); Kichis, 1853 (Senate Document in Hodge 1907–1910, 1:683); and Kichais (Whipple, Ewbank, and Turner 1855:76). With medial [ts] are: Keetsas, 1845 and Kitsoss, 1838 (Arbuckle in Hodge 1907–1910, 1:683). Misprints include Hitchies, 1847 (David G. Burnet in Schoolcraft 1851–1857, 1:239) and Hitchi, 1856 (Latham in Hodge 1907–1910, 1:683).

Several references are shortened forms comprising only the initial syllable of the name Kitsai. Examples are: Keyes, 1805 (Sibley 1832:722); and Kyis, cited in addition to the form Keyeshees, 1815 (Brackenridge 1962:81, 87). The use of the initial syllable of a tribe's name as a shortened designation was current among French fur traders in the late eighteenth and early nineteenth centuries.

There is no recorded Plains sign language designation for the Kitsai, but the Kitsai are said to have introduced sign language to the Caddo (W.P. Clark 1885:94).

Sources

There are no general accounts of Kitsai culture. The only extant account is a two-page summary of the tribe that De Mézières wrote when visiting the Tribes of the North in 1772 (Bolton 1914, 1:285–86). There is a detailed description of Kitsai kinship (Lesser 1979). In most historical sources Kitsai culture is characterized as similar or identical to that of the Wichita and Caddo groups with whom they were closely associated. Alexander Lesser conducted linguistic fieldwork with the last fluent speaker of Kitsai in 1929 and 1930 (fig. 3), and a description of Kitsai phonology was published (Bucca and Lesser 1969).

Assiniboine

RAYMOND J. DeMALLIE AND DAVID REED MILLER

Language

The Assiniboine (aˈsĭnĭˌboin) are a Siouan-speaking people linguistically most closely related to the Sioux and Stoney.* Despite long-repeated assertions that they originated as an independent tribe in the seventeenth century when they broke off from the Yanktonai Sioux (Keating 1824, 1:405; Mooney and Thomas in Hodge 1907–1910, 1:102), neither linguistic nor historical evidence supports this folk tradition. Linguistically, Assiniboine is coordinate with the other Sioux dialects, no closer to one than the other, suggesting that Assiniboine separated from the Sioux at the same time the other Sioux dialects were differentiating from one another. The Stoney developed from the Assiniboine and became an independent tribe, probably during the eighteenth century (see "Stoney," this vol.).

Assiniboine is spoken in two distinctive but mutually intelligible dialects. One characterizes the population on Fort Belknap Reservation in Montana and on Mosquito-Grizzly Bear's Head and Carry The Kettle reserves in Saskatchewan; the other characterizes the population on Fort Peck Reservation in Montana and on the Ocean Man, Pheasant Rump, and White Bear reserves in Saskatchewan (Parks and DeMallie 1992:247–250).

Territory

In the seventeenth century Assiniboine territory extended westward from Lake Winnipeg into central Saskatchewan. Archeological materials from this region, known as the Mortlach Aggregate, have been proposed as representing the prehistoric and protohistoric Assiniboine (Walde 1994). Historical sources suggest a westward expansion of Assiniboine territory during the eighteenth century through the parklands of central Saskatchewan and into eastern Alberta, but rather than an actual migration, this may simply reflect increasing knowledge of the western prairies by Hudson's Bay and other European traders (Ray 1974; Russell 1991). Of eight Assiniboine bands listed in 1808 by Alexander Henry the Younger, only one occupied territory within the boundaries of the United States, along the Souris River in North Dakota (Ray 1974:95). Migrations during the early nineteenth century shifted Assiniboine territory southward, and by 1840 three-quarters of the tribe lived on the Missouri in the area of Montana. In the mid-nineteenth century Assiniboine territory stretched east to west from Wood Mountain to the Cypress Hills and north to south from the North Saskatchewan River to the Milk and Missouri rivers (fig. 1) (Denig 1930:396–397). By the twentieth century Assiniboine reservations and reserves were located in Montana and Saskatchewan, within the area they occupied during the previous century.

Relation to the Sioux

The earliest historical reference to the Assiniboine dates to the *Jesuit Relations* of 1640, from which it is clear that the Naduesiu (Sioux) and Assinipour (Assiniboine) had distinct tribal identities. The 1697 map by Jean-Baptiste Louis Franquelin depicts the Assiniboine north and west of the Lake of the Assiniboines (Lake of the Woods), with the Sioux to the south in the area of Minnesota (M.M. Wedel 1974a). One of the Sioux groups is given as Hoheton (*hóhet*^{h}*ų*) 'Assiniboine village', suggesting that the separation of the Assiniboine and Sioux was a more gradual process than written and oral historical accounts imply.

The earliest account of the development of hostilities between the Assiniboine and Sioux was recorded in 1700 by the trader-explorer Pierre-Charles Le Sueur (in C. Delisle 1702). When the Cree began to obtain guns from British traders at Hudson Bay they increased their attacks on the Assiniboine and Sioux; because of their more northerly location, the brunt of these attacks fell on the Assiniboine. Recognizing their vulnerable position, the Assiniboine made peace with the Cree and intermarried with them. This gave the Assiniboine access to trade goods, but by allying with the Cree they became enemies to the Sioux. If this tradition is historically correct these events must have occurred after 1670 when the British established the first permanent trading post, York Factory, on Hudson Bay.

*The phonemes of Assiniboine are: (voiceless unaspirated stops and affricate) *p, t, č, k, ʔ*; (voiceless aspirated stops and affricate) p^{h}, t^{h}, $č^{h}$, k^{h}; (glottalized stops and affricate) *ṗ, ṫ, č̇, k̇*; (voiceless spirants) *s, š, x, h*; (voiced spirants) *z, ž, γ*; (glottalized spirants) *ṡ, ṧ, ẋ*; (nasals) *m, n*; (voiced semivowels) *w, y*; (oral vowels) *i, e, a, o, u*; (nasal vowels) *į, ą, ų*; (primary stress) v́. For many speakers, particularly younger ones, the voiceless unaspirated stops and affricate are lax and often voiced intervocalically and initially before a vowel. This phonemic analysis and the transcription of Assiniboine words follows the analysis of Douglas R. Parks and Raymond J. DeMallie (1996).

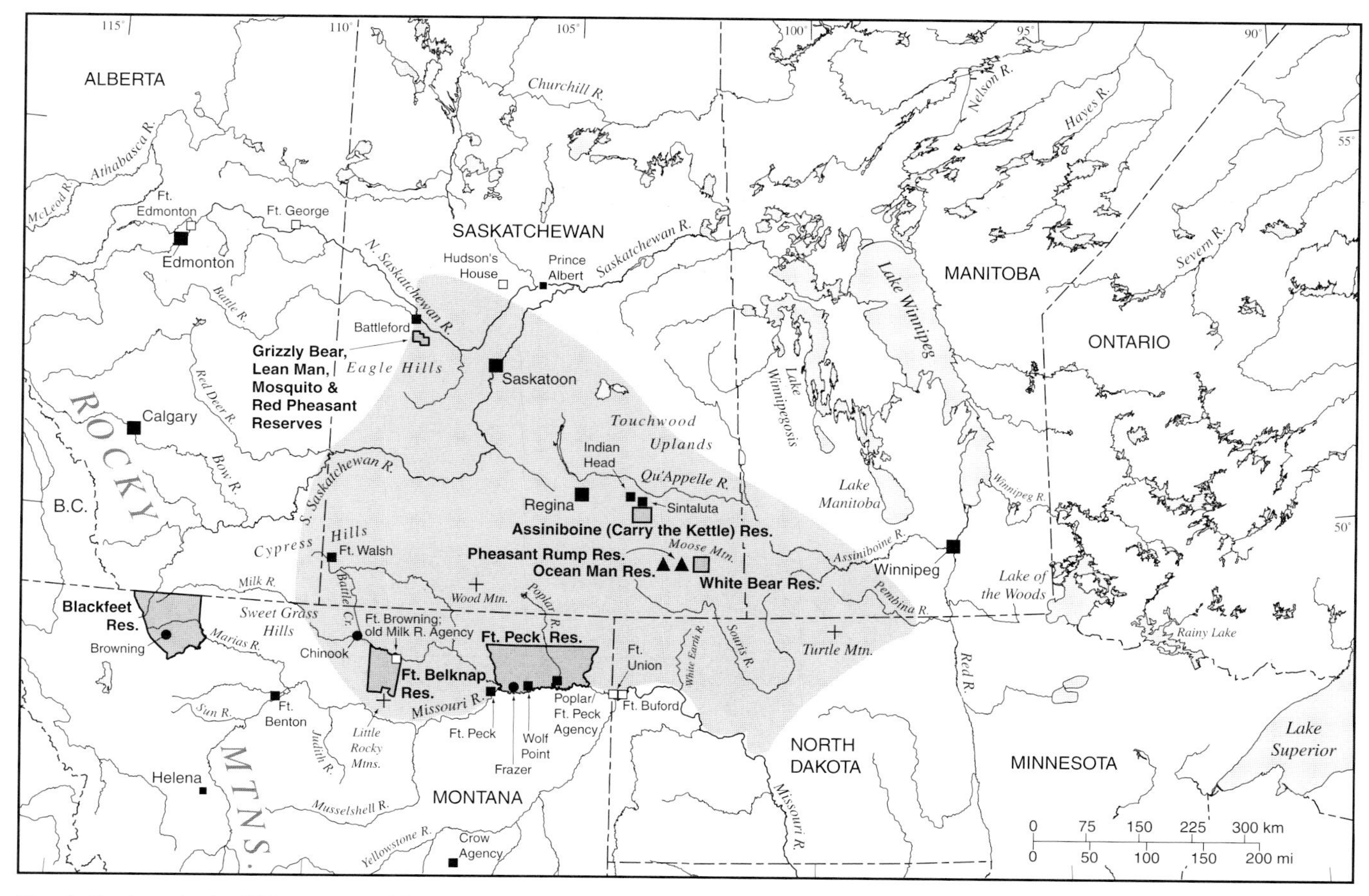

Fig. 1. Territory in the 19th century, with modern reservations and reserves.

Most later accounts of the separation of the Sioux and Assiniboine are obviously mythologized, and they involve the widespread Plains motif of conflict between two leaders, usually over a woman, that results in each taking his people in a different direction (Keating 1824, 1:405–406; Nicollet 1838–1839 in DeMallie 1976:262).

History, 1650s–1869

The first mention of the location of the Assiniboine is given in the *Relations* for 1657–1658, when they were described as living about 100 miles from Lake Nipigon (JR 44:249; Ray 1974:6). The earliest reported direct contact between Europeans and the Assiniboine took place in 1678; Daniel Greysolon Dulhut, visited them in an unsuccessful attempt to establish peace between the Assiniboine and Sioux. In 1684 Dulhut established a post on Lake Nipigon to trade with the Assiniboine and their Cree allies (Ray 1974:11). At this time Assiniboine territory stretched from Rainy Lake on the southeast, west and north to the Touchwood Uplands, where Hudson's Bay Company trader Henry Kelsey (1929:6) met them in 1690–1691. Groups of Assiniboine and Cree continued to visit French traders at Lake Nipigon and Lake Superior, and traveled by canoe down the Churchill, Nelson, and Hayes rivers to trade with the Hudson's Bay Company at York Factory (under French control 1694–1714). There they obtained the firearms that gave them military advantage over their enemies. More than 400 Assiniboines went to York Factory in 1684 (Radisson 1961:227; Ray 1974:12, 14). Trade "gangs" under the leadership of "trading captains" developed into specialized intertribal networks that entailed close relationships between Woodland Assiniboine and the Cree (D.R. Miller 1987:58–63; Sharrock 1974; Morantz 1982).

By controlling access to York Factory the Assiniboine and Cree positioned themselves as middlemen between the European traders and the tribes to the west. Ray (1974:19) argued that during the early eighteenth century, in search of sources of beaver, these northern or Woodland Assiniboine expanded their territory westward into the woodlands between the Churchill and Saskatchewan rivers. This movement engaged the Woodland Assiniboine in hostilities with the Chipewyan as well as the Blackfoot, Gros Ventre, and other groups to the west.

In the southern portion of Assiniboine territory the westward expansion of the Plains Assiniboine through the parkland area of Saskatchewan paralleled that of the Woodland Assiniboine in the north. In 1755 Hudson's Bay Company trader Anthony Henday traveled westward from

York Factory and met Assiniboine groups as far west as Alberta. He reported Assiniboines camping peacefully with Gros Ventres and Blackfoot (Ray 1974:21–22).

The distinction between the two groups of Assiniboine was an ecological one. From late spring to early fall the Woodland Assiniboine subsisted largely on fishing and the hunting of waterfowl at the abundant lakes in the forested area, while the Plains Assiniboine hunted buffalo on the prairies. During winter both groups of Assiniboine followed the buffalo and other big game into the parklands (Ray 1974:31–32).

The westward movement of the Assiniboine during the eighteenth century also reflected pressure from the Sioux, who, gaining access to firearms from French traders, began an aggressive push northward, fighting with the Assiniboine, Cree, and Ojibwa (D.R. Miller 1987:64).

Competition between British and French traders led the French to establish trading posts in Cree and Assiniboine territory in southern Manitoba and Saskatchewan to discourage the Indians from making the long trek to Hudson Bay. From the 1730s through the 1750s the French posts obtained some of the best furs in exchange for alcohol and other luxury goods, but because of the difficulty of transporting goods by canoe the French lacked the quantity of arms and ammunition, kettles, and other metal goods that could be obtained at York Factory. After the French withdrew in the late 1750s British traders began to build posts for the Assiniboine trade. To protect their interests against the rival North West Company, the Hudson's Bay Company relented on its century-long policy of centralizing trade at the bay and opened posts in Assiniboine country beginning in 1774 (Ray 1974:53, 91, 126).

The introduction of horses during the second half of the eighteenth century brought about major changes in Assiniboine life. In 1754–1755 Henday found Assiniboines in eastern Alberta using horses for transport, but they were not yet riding them. By 1766, William Pink reported a small group of Assiniboines in the Prince Albert area with many horses; he mentioned that they had abandoned the use of canoes. A report by Alexander Henry the Elder in 1776 confirms that by that date the western Assiniboine bands were known for their large horse herds. Their primary source of horses was trade with the Blackfoot and Gros Ventre (Ray 1974:156–158). In 1777 the Assiniboines' profitable middleman position in the trade between Europeans to the east and the Blackfoot and Gros Ventre to the west was undercut by the building of a Hudson's Bay Company post, Hudson's House, near Gros Ventre country. Hostilities between the Gros Ventre and Blackfoot on the one side, and the Assiniboine and Plains Cree on the other, soon escalated (Fowler 1987:42). Cut off from the horse trade, the Assiniboine developed a reputation for being the poorest tribe on the plains in horses, dependent on dog travois for transporting goods when traveling (Denig 1961:96). In 1830 the Assiniboine were reported to own only two horses per lodge (J.H. Bradley 1896–1923, 4:288).

In the eastern and southern areas of Assiniboine territory horses were introduced in the 1760s, though in somewhat lesser numbers; here the primary source was trade with the Mandan villages. By the 1790s the Assiniboine were fully integrated into the Plains horse-raiding complex (Ray 1974:156, 159–161). The principal motivation for Assiniboine warfare was the need to obtain horses for both economic reasons and prestige (Denig 1930:470).

Throughout the eighteenth century the direction of Assiniboine movements was toward the northwest. In the 1790s North West Company trader Alexander Mackenzie reported that the western Assiniboine bands were located in eastern Alberta, near Fort George, on the North Saskatchewan River, while some lived in the woodlands north of the river. The journal of Duncan M'Gillivray, written at Fort George in 1794–1795, mentions three Assiniboine bands in the vicinity: during the winter, the Strong Wood and Grand River bands constructed buffalo pounds nearby, and members of the Canoe band came to the fort to trade (McGillivray 1929:34–35, 51; Ray 1974:170). An enumeration of Assiniboine bands by Alexander Henry the Younger in 1808 mentions only a single Woodland band, the Swampy Ground Assiniboine (Gough 1988–1992, 2:376). Hudson's Bay Company reports document that in 1823–1824 a group of Assiniboines, Plains Crees, and Métis were living near Ft. Edmonton, while the Strong Wood Assiniboine lived farther to the northwest on the McLeod River (Ray 1974:94–95, 98). These northwesternmost Assiniboines were the remnants of the Woodland Assiniboine, some of whom moved farther west to the Rocky Mountains where they developed an autonomous tribal identity as the Stoney.

During the late eighteenth century the majority of the Assiniboine migrated to the south and they abandoned the lower Assiniboine River and the Red River in the eastern portion of their territory (Ray 1974:104). Henry's 1808 discussion of Assiniboine bands suggests that two-thirds of the Assiniboine lived between the Qu'Appelle and Souris rivers; the remaining third was spread to the northwest, largely between the South Saskatchewan and Battle rivers (Gough 1988–1992, 1:375–376).

The causes for the Assiniboine migration are multiple. A major factor undoubtedly was the smallpox epidemic of 1781–1782. Between one-third and one-half of the Assiniboine population was estimated to have succumbed, after which the survivors began to move south (Denig 1930:396; Ray 1974:105–107; D.R. Miller 1987:89–90). Another factor was the attraction of the Mandan villages, important trade centers where horses and horticultural products could be obtained. Traders from Spanish Louisiana ascending the Missouri River in pirogues loaded with guns and other goods also presented new trade opportunities. The plentitude of buffalo on the Missouri was another factor. Finally, Fort Union, constructed by the American Fur Company in 1829 on the Missouri above the confluence of the Yellowstone—a location chosen by an

Assiniboine chief, the leader of the Rock band—provided a permanent trading post for the Assiniboine (Larpenteur in Coues 1898, 1:109). Edwin Denig, long-time fur trader at Fort Union, reported that the first movement to the Missouri began as early as 1777, reflecting the escalation of warfare with the Blackfoot and Gros Ventre. Assiniboine bands continued to move gradually from the Saskatchewan area south to the Missouri River until 1825. An additional 60 lodges (the band that became known as the Northern People) migrated there in 1839 (Denig 1930:395, 403, 1961:68–70).

Severe population loss resulted in the restructuring of Assiniboine society. The number of bands proliferated, most of them small and positioned strategically between the Missouri River and the Blackfoot. Just as the population was rebounding, smallpox struck again in 1837–1838; two-thirds of the Assiniboine died. Of the 250 lodges at Fort Union, only 30 survived (D.R. Miller 1987:95–96; Denig 1930:397, 399), a loss that left the Assiniboine vulnerable to attacks from the enemies who surrounded them: Crow, Blackfoot, Gros Ventre, Hidatsa, and Sioux. The Plains Cree remained their only allies (Denig 1961:89).

In 1851 the Assiniboine sent representatives to the multitribal council convened by the United States government at Horse Creek, near Fort Laramie. There they signed their first treaty with the United States, which promised peace among the tribes as well as with the United States and designated boundaries for the tribes, thereby laying the foundation for the establishment of reservations. Although they were not signatories to it, the Assiniboine were mentioned in the Blackfoot treaty of 1855, by which they were given the right to hunt, with the Blackfoot, in lands west of the mouth of Milk River (Kappler 1904–1941, 2:594–596, 737).

Despite treaties, intertribal warfare continued on the northern plains. The increased demand for buffalo hides, dried buffalo meat, and pemmican for trade with the Whites put greater pressure on the herds. The expanding Métis population was a new factor. They were well armed, and after about 1870 increasing numbers of Métis hunted between the South Saskatchewan and the Missouri rivers. The buffalo herds, equally vital for the Assiniboine and the Métis, began to diminish.

Historically disposed to forming intertribal camps, many Assiniboines joined in alliances, individually or as family groups, for short-term tasks such as war expeditions or long-term relationships fused by intermarriages and men's society memberships (Milloy 1988; S.R. Sharrock 1974). The multitribal encampment reported in 1868 (Cowie 1913:297–321) in the Cypress Hills illustrates this social pattern.

The movement of many other Indian and Métis groups into the region along the Missouri between the White Earth and Milk rivers prompted the establishment in 1866 of a U.S. military post, Fort Buford, three miles east of Fort Union. The next year, reflecting the decline of the fur trade, Fort Union was abandoned. Under the Montana Superintendency, in September 1869 Milk River Agency at Fort Browning was established for the Assiniboine, Gros Ventre, River Crow, and some Sioux groups (DeMallie 1986:28–29; D.R. Miller 1987:103–104).

Culture, Mid-Nineteenth Century

Social Organization

Assiniboine society was organized in autonomous bands, each of which had its customary territory (Denig 1930:430–431). Bands were bilateral, although women after marriage normally joined the husband's band. Kinship terminology was of the Dakota type, in which father and father's brother were classed together as father, and mother and mother's sister were classed together as mother; parents' opposite-sex siblings were uncle and aunt. The children of all fathers and mothers were brothers and sisters to one another, and children of aunts and uncles were called cousins (Rodnick 1938:37). Kinship terms were used for address, and the customary patterns of kinship behavior gave structure to daily life. For example, a man was forbidden to speak directly to his parents-in-law; however, a man could lessen the tension of this avoidance relationship and allow for some communication by presenting his parents-in-law with a scalp taken in battle (Denig 1930:503–504; Kennedy 1961:17; Rodnick 1938:38–39).

The core of a band was a group of related families, usually comprising a number of brothers and cousins. Each nuclear family had its own lodge, a buffalo-hide tepee constructed on a three-pole foundation (Rodnick 1938:29; Lowie 1909:14–15). An average size tepee was 31 feet in circumference, requiring 12 hides for the cover, and could house a family of eight, as well as two or three visitors. To the right of the doorway as one entered was storage space, followed in sequence by a place for a widowed grandmother; the man of the household, with his first wife; then their children; and finally, space for male visitors (fig. 2). At the back of the lodge was the honor place, where a visiting brother-in-law or other relative might stay. To the left of the doorway was storage space, beyond which were, in sequence, a place for an unmarried grandfather or uncle; for cowives; and, toward the back, for female relatives or visitors (Denig 1930:507–508, 578, pl. 75).

The Assiniboine observed a clear division of labor between men and women. Young men went to war, but after marriage their primary concern was with hunting, which occupied about one-third of a man's time (Denig 1930:505). Men made all their tools and weapons, provided and cared for the family's horses, and trapped furbearing animals. Women would sometimes accompany men on the hunt to help with the butchering. In camp, women dressed the skins and cut up and dried the meat (fig. 3). The labor necessary to process buffalo hides was so great that a successful hunter took more than one wife. They made the

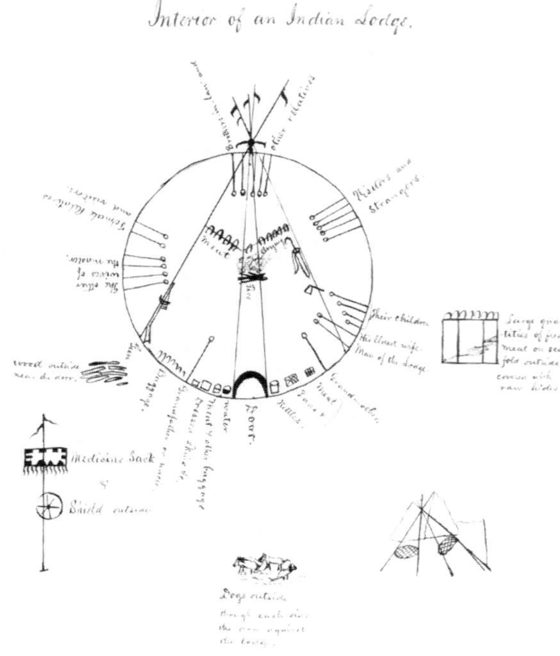

left, U. of Okla. Lib., Western Hist. Coll., Norman: 152; right, Smithsonian, NAA: Denig ms. 2600-b (42514-B).

Fig. 2. Camp and utilization of tepee space. left, Camp with several skin tepees, storage racks, Red River cart, and men smoking a pipe. Photograph by George Anderton, near Ft. Walsh, Sask., 1878. right, Sketch of tepee layout. Individuals slept with their feet toward the center of the lodge, where the fire was located, directly under the smoke hole. At night, the lodge door was locked using a wooden paddle attached to the skin door frame and adjacent tepee poles; this device prevented dogs and strangers from entering (Denig 1930:507–508). Drawing by Edwin T. Denig, about 1854.

family's clothing as well as the tepee cover, cooked, cared for young children, gathered wood and hauled water, and were responsible for packing, unpacking, and setting up the tepee when the camp moved (Denig 1930:505). Sometimes a man, as the result of a vision, rejected male roles, dressed in women's clothes, and engaged in the work of women (Lowie 1909:42).

Political Organization

The band represented a large extended family, headed by a chief *(hųká)*. The chief addressed band members collectively as "my children," underscoring the significance of kinship as the basis for political organization. The position of chief was not hereditary but was based on merit. The chief's family was ordinarily the largest and most prestigious in the band; therefore, when a chief died he was usually replaced by a relative. Because generosity was an important qualification for leaders, wealth was a prerequisite for chieftainship. In addition to the leader of the band, other chiefs might also be recognized. From time to time one of these other chiefs might move off and start a new band (Denig 1930:403, 432–435, 449; Rodnick 1937, 1938:35).

The band was the largest political unit; there was no overarching political structure for the Assiniboine as a tribe. When a number of bands came together for ceremonies, buffalo hunts, or to plan war expeditions, they camped in a circle, in which each band occupied its own section and maintained its autonomy (Rodnick 1938:33).

A chief had no authority to compel action but was the leading member of the band council. All men who achieved success in war or hunting were recognized as members of the council. Decisions of the chiefs and council were carried out by the Soldiers' society, whose members were appointed by the council. Some 20–30 percent of the council members served as soldiers *(akíčʰita)*. The function of the soldiers was to serve as police, maintaining order within the camp and supervising hunts and camp moves. They had the authority to punish transgressors by destroying their property (Denig 1930:436).

The arrangement of a camp reflected the political structure of the band. In the center of the camp circle was the Soldiers' Lodge, where the band council met. Some of the soldiers were always present in the lodge, which also served as a men's social center. Leisure time was devoted to gambling; men preferred plum pit dice and the hand game. Women did not attend councils or even go into the Soldiers' Lodge (Denig 1930:436, 444–445, 569; Rodnick 1938:35). Chiefs and soldiers had the right to wear eagle-feather headdresses and bear claw necklaces (Denig 1930:449, 593).

Crimes, even murder, were considered private matters, to be resolved by the parties involved. They were not dealt with in any formal way by the chief or the council (Denig 1930:448, 452–455).

right, Milwaukee Public Mus., Wis.:112055.

Fig. 3. Meat preparation. Throughout the 20th century hunting was an important subsistence activity. left, Edward "Buster" Moore hanging a recently killed deer. Photograph by Jessie Hawley, Ft. Belknap Res., 1995. right, Woman drying meat on a pole extending from the tepee. If not placed high off the ground the camp dogs, visible in the background, would devour the meat. The painted tepee of Nosey is in the background. Photograph by Sumner Matteson, Ft. Belknap, Mont., 1905–1906.

Subsistence

Buffalo provided the basis for Assiniboine subsistence. When the buffalo congregated in the summer, so did the Assiniboine. During the fall when the herds dispersed the large camps also broke up, individual bands eventually settling in sheltered river bottoms for the winter.

Three methods of buffalo hunting were used. Larger camps utilized the surround method. In preparation, the soldiers prohibited individual hunting. The camp crier announced the time decided on by the council for the surround. Mounted hunters, under the oversight of the soldiers, surrounded the herd. Between 80 and 100 hunters could kill 100–500 buffalo in an hour. Hunting was done with bows and arrows since guns were too cumbersome to load on horseback. The buffalo tongues, as well as other meat, were taken to the Soldiers' Lodge. The man who killed an animal claimed the hide and choicest pieces of meat. Distinctive marks on each man's arrows helped minimize conflict over kills. All men and women who aided in butchering were entitled to take meat for their families. Women sliced the meat into thin sheets and dried it in the sun, after which it would keep for about a year (Denig 1930:455–456, 530–531, 542, 582).

The second method was the park or buffalo pound, which was the main means of hunting buffalo before the introduction of horses and guns. By the mid-nineteenth century it was still practiced only by the Assiniboine and Plains Cree. A circle of posts was constructed at the base of a bluff, enclosing about an acre. On the top of the bluff, extending outward in funnel shape, were piles of earth and stone, each large enough to conceal a person. When scouts reported a herd in the vicinity, a religious specialist expert in calling buffalo approached the herd on horseback, covering himself with a buffalo hide. Imitating a buffalo calf, he slowly led the herd to the pound. When the herd was well into the funnel, the people hiding there stood up and shouted, driving the animals toward the precipice and over the edge. The animals were then slaughtered using guns and bows and arrows. A small camp could "throw" 300–600 buffalo at a time, requiring two to three days for butchering. In the early 1850s there were three pounds in the vicinity of Fort Union, all in active use by the Assiniboine (Denig 1930:532–534; Kennedy 1961:100–103).

A third method of hunting was the approach, in which single hunters, armed with guns, stalked buffalo. During the winter, snowshoes were essential for this form of hunting; sometimes buffalo might be driven into deep snow where they could be easily killed by the hunters (Denig 1930:534–535).

In butchering, a buffalo carcass was cut down the backbone and lengthwise along the belly so that the hide was removed in two pieces. After tanning, the two pieces were sewn together with sinew. Each hide required at least three days of work to process into a robe. The average number of hides a woman could tan during the course of a winter was 18–20, although some women were able to produce 25–35 (Denig 1930:540–541).

Both horse and dog travois were used to transport goods, but because they owned relatively few horses, the Assiniboine made greater use of the dog travois throughout the nineteenth century than other tribes. They also constructed bull boats to ferry goods and people across streams (Denig 1930:579; Rodnick 1938:30).

In addition to buffalo, Assiniboine hunted other game, including elk, deer, bighorn sheep, and antelope. Grizzly bears were occasionally hunted, sometimes in their dens during the winter; killing a grizzly ranked second to killing an enemy and was counted among a man's brave deeds. Furbearing animals, including wolves and foxes, were hunted and a large variety of animals and birds were eaten. Wild plants, including prairie turnips, wild rhubarb, artichokes, a wide variety of fruits and berries, and rose hips, suplemented the diet (Denig 1930:408, 499, 536–538, 544, 583; Rodnick 1938:27).

Religion and Ceremonies

Assiniboine religious life centered around the concept of wakan (*wakʰą* 'holiness'), designating anything that was incomprehensible to humankind. The elements of the physical world, including all animals and plants, were considered spirits, each a manifestation of wakan. The creator was designated Wakan Tanka (*wakʰą tʰąka* 'great holiness'), but was not personified. The spirits were omnipresent and omnipotent, and humans could call on their power for good or for evil (Denig 1930:486).

Through prayer, including the requisite burning of sweetgrass (fig. 4), pipe offerings, sacrifices, weeping, and self-mortification men could gain the pity of the spirits. Assiniboine believed that the world was created for human beings, who fulfilled it and provided the reason for its existence. Spirits provided security to individuals against the insecurities of the world. On the vision quest a young man fasted and prayed for a spirit to visit him and bestow power for war, hunting, or curing. If successful, he constructed a medicine bundle according to his vision. This brought him success and was ultimately buried with his body (Denig 1930:483–484, 486–489, 498; Rodnick 1938:46–47).

Some men, through repeated visions, became specialists in wakan. *wįčʰášta wakʰą* 'holy men' were ceremonial leaders who also had power to find lost objects, cause illness by shooting evil medicine into others even at a great distance, cure by removing evil from a victim's body, and interpret dreams. Holy men whose reputations spread beyond their local band were very few; Denig estimated that there were only six to eight such famous holy men (he calls them diviners) during the mid-nineteenth century. *pʰežúta wįčʰášta* 'medicine men' used herbs and other medicines revealed in visions to heal the sick and wounded. Sweatbaths were also used in curing. Both men and women were curers; women did not actively seek visions, but powers for healing other women and serving as midwives were sometimes given to them in dreams (Denig 1930:422–428, 492–494; Rodnick 1938:53–54).

The most important religious ceremony was the Sun Dance (*tʰičáx wačʰípi* 'lodge-building dance'), which was held each June and brought together the scattered Assiniboine bands. For practicality, two or more Sun Dances might be held in different parts of Assiniboine country (Rodnick 1937:408). Individuals frequently performed the Sun Dance, a four-day ritual, in fulfillment of a vow made in time of danger, for example, on a war expedition.

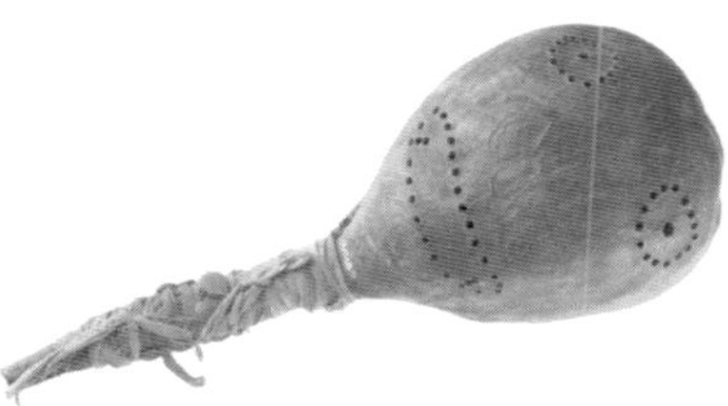

Smithsonian, NAA: left, 34055-A, center, 34054-T, top right, 3175 (neg. 98-41036); bottom right, Field Mus., Chicago: 60189 (neg. 111411.9).

Fig. 4. Medicine men and sacred objects. left, Painted tepee of Nosey. center, Nosey, also known as Yellow Lodge, inside his tepee holding a pipe and sweetgrass. Photographs by Sumner Matteson, Ft. Belknap, Mont., 1905–1906. top right, Medicine bag and other ritual paraphernalia. Photograph by William T. Thompson, The Man Who Took the Coat Res., now known as Carry the Kettle Res., Sask., 1892. bottom right, Medicine rattle made of rawhide sewn with sinew. Perforations represent eyes and a mouth (VanStone 1996:13). Collected by George A. Dorsey, Ft. Peck Res., Mont., 1900; length 28 cm.

Men practiced self-mortification, including piercing their chests with skewers attached by ropes to the center pole. Women also danced and made offerings of small bits of flesh cut from their arms or legs. Cloth and other objects to be sacrificed were hung from the center pole (fig. 5); it was said that anyone who attempted to appropriate them after the conclusion of the ceremony would be struck by lightning. The Sun Dance provided the setting for subsidiary rituals as well, including the performances of animal dreamers and mysterious performances of tricks and sleight of hand by holy men (Denig 1930:488–489; Lowie 1909:58–62; Rodnick 1938:48–50).

Next to the Sun Dance, Horse Society rituals were the most sacred. Both men and women belonged to the society, whose members had medicines for doctoring horses as well as people. Their ceremonies, which were held every two or three years, lasted two days and had as their focus the initiation of new members. They prayed that the tribe would obtain many horses and that children would grow up free from sickness (Rodnick 1938:50–52; Lowie 1909:57–58; Ewers 1956).

The Fool Society (*witkókax wač^hípi* 'fool-maker dance'), a men's society, performed two-day ceremonies the primary purpose of which was to give members powers for war and hunting. They also had power for doctoring eyes. Held once a year in the summer, at the time of the Sun Dance, society members performed, wearing masks (fig. 6); those of younger members had slits for eye holes while those of older members had no eye holes at all; they depended on their sacred power to see. During ceremonies they spoke "backward," saying the opposite of what they meant. They were said to be imitating Inktomi (*įktómi*), the trickster–culture hero. Their ritual centered around the killing and butchering of a buffalo or cow. Walking through the camp, each member carried a blood-filled bladder bag with which they squirted people, particularly their sisters-in-law, with whom men had a joking relationship. After the clowning of these public performances, the members retired to their society lodge, where they doctored anyone with eye problems (Rodnick 1938:40, 52–53; Lowie 1909:62–66).

top, Milwaukee Public Mus., Wis.: SWM-1-F-562; bottom, Smithsonian, NAA: 34054-L.

Fig. 5. Sun Dance, Ft. Belknap, Mont. top, Shinny game. The Sun Dance Lodge is in the background center, and tepees of the camp are on the left. bottom, Building the medicine lodge. Nosey is in the background at left giving directions. Photographs by Sumner Matteson, 1905–1906.

A series of men's societies was closely associated with warfare but also had sacred significance (table 1). Their primary activities were public performances of dances that perpetuated the memory of members' brave deeds and inspired young men to emulate them. Each society had distinctive rules, regalia, songs, and dances. The Brave, or No Flight, Society, for example, had two decorated lances that officers carried into battle. They were obliged to thrust them into the ground and not retreat until the enemy was vanquished or until released by one of their own. Society members were primarily younger men, although the Buffalo Bull Society consisted of middle-aged men and leaders (Denig 1930:556–564; Lowie 1909:66–74).

In 1872, when the Assiniboine made peace with the Sioux—apparently the Yanktonai—they received the Grass Dance, the diagnostic feature of which was crow belts, feather bustles worn by four (or seven) officers in the society. The society dances were elaborate rituals involving the reenactment of war deeds and a feast in which the bustle wearers charged a pot of cooked dog meat and speared pieces that were then presented to honored men (Lowie 1909:66–69; Kennedy 1961:125–150). The Grass Dance developed into the modern powwow dance during reservation times.

Women also had societies, though very little is known of them. The Dance without Robes (*t^hąč^hó wač^hí* 'unclothed dance') was a society whose officers were old women. They performed circle dances as well as the Warbonnet Dance, the latter involving the giving away of property. Men joined in both dances. The Female Elk Society was a sacred organization whose members once each year performed a dance imitating elk; presumably it was a ritual promoting fertility (Kennedy 1961:121–124; Rodnick 1938:8).

Warfare

Warfare was integral to Assiniboine culture. Without participating in war parties it was impossible for a male to achieve adult status, to gain respect, and to marry (Kennedy 1961:46–56). There were two types of warfare, horse stealing raids and war expeditions. The horse raids were essential for increasing tribal herds, but if a raiding party was discovered by the enemy, some might be killed

Smithsonian, NAA: top right, 34054-K; Smithsonian, Handbook of North Amer. Indians Photo. Coll.

Fig. 6. Fool Society activities at Fort Belknap Res., Mont. top left, Al First Sound, ceremonial leader, in his lodge. The blue zigzags on his arms represent the Thunder Bird (lightning), carrier of messages to the Creator. Gray or white clay on his face and body represents the White Gray Owl Old Man or Creator. The ritual staff is decorated with the hoofs or dewclaws of deer or elk. Staff in hand, mask and clothing on, he is ready to go out and make his selection of the Fool Dance warriors or clowns from fellow tribal members. top right, Fool Dancers jubilant over having killed the "sleeping buffalo." Photograph by Sumner Matteson, 1905–1906. bottom left, Rifleman clown during the mock hunt. bottom center, Al First Sound cutting the liver into pieces to give to each clown, and 2 additional pieces to be thrown to the morning and evening stars. bottom right, Clown throwing his piece of meat through the lodge smokehole. top left and all bottom, Photographs by J.W. Wellington, 1952.

Table 1. Men's Societies

Denig 1854	*Lowie 1908–1909*	*Phonemic Retranscriptions and Translations*
Brave (No Flight)	No Flight, nampe′c owa′tc	*nąp^{h}éš owáč^{h}i* 'no-flight dance'
Bull	Buffalo, tatañga watci′bi	*t^{h}at^{h}ą́ka wač^{h}ípi* 'buffalo bull dance'
Circumsized		
Crow	Crow, kaxō′ kona′gitcī′a	*k^{h}ąγí ok^{h}ónakič^{h}iye* 'crow society'
Duck	Duck, paru^{n}′taje watcī′bi	*p^{h}aγų́ta wač^{h}ípi* 'duck dance'
Fox	Fox, toka′n owa′tc	*t^{h}ok^{h}ána owáč^{h}i* 'kit fox dance'
Mice Comrades (Provision Stealers)		
Soldiers		
Wolf Pups	Whelp (Wolf Pup), cuñ gcindja	*šųkč^{h}į́č*a 'pup'
	Brown Crane, peha^{n}′ri^{n}	*p^{h}ehą́ γi* 'brown crane'
	Crazy, ajū′-owatc	
	Dirty, icka^{n}′ watcī′bi	*įšką́ wač^{h}ípi* 'lustful dance'
	Grass, pejū′ owatc, or pejī′ mi^{n}knañgeō′watc	*p^{h}eží owáč^{h}i* 'grass dance', or *p^{h}eží mįkną́ke owáč^{h}i* 'grass worn around the waist dance'

Sources: Denig 1930:434–435, 558–564; Lowie 1909:66, 70–74. Lowie also recorded additional societies or ceremonies by name only. Phonemic transcriptions by Raymond J. DeMallie and Douglas R. Parks.

on either side. This set off a cycle of revenge war parties (Denig 1930:470).

The organization of a raiding or war party was first discussed in the Soldiers' Lodge. When a plan was approved, the leader of the expedition fasted and sought a vision. If the vision was favorable, the leader invited the men he wished to accompany him to come to his lodge for a dog feast, and explained the intention of the expedition (Denig 1930:544; Lowie 1909:28; Rodnick 1938:41, 1939).

The night before a horse-stealing expedition was to set out the members of the party met in the Soldiers' Lodge, where they performed the night-long Crow Dance. In the morning they left the camp, singing the Wolf song. The leader wore a wolf skin on his back and all the members of the party painted their faces red. Horse-stealing parties went on foot, each man taking extra moccasins. If during the expedition the leader had a dream of failure, the party would turn back (Denig 1930:494, 544–545).

When the party reached enemy country they spread out, communicating by signals such as wolf howls or owl hoots. Horse raids took place under cover of darkness. After taking horses from a camp or village, the raiders reassembled at a prearranged spot where the horses were distributed among them, often with much dissension. As they approached their village they signaled their return by setting fire to the prairie. Frequently they gave away all the horses taken, and their names were sung in praise throughout the camp. If a member had been killed on the raid, the party returned loudly grieving the loss (Denig 1930:546–547).

War expeditions were organized to seek revenge against the enemy by taking scalps. Such expeditions might number 100–300 men, but very large parties usually failed in their objective for lack of overall leadership. Before the war party set out a holy man was consulted to divine the outcome of the expedition. Some men went on foot, others on horseback. Scouts were sent out to report the location of the enemy camp. The warriors painted their faces red and dressed for battle in their finery, which included fringed shirts and leggings, headdresses, and sacred war charms. Some men, particularly those who were mounted, carried a buffalo rawhide shield on the left arm, painted and decorated according to their visions. The attack took place at dawn, each warrior operating individually. Their weapons included bows and arrows and guns for fighting at a distance, and lances, war clubs, and battle axes for hand-to-hand fighting. Sometimes pairs of men challenged one another and fought between the two sides, publicly displaying their bravery (Denig 1930:548–554; Lowie 1909:28–33).

If the expedition succeeded in killing enemies without loss to themselves, the whole party blackened their faces as a symbol of joy. They sang the victory song as they reentered their camp and presented the scalps to those who had lost relatives in war, thereby releasing them from their period of mourning. If a member of the party was killed, his relatives smeared their faces and clothes with white clay as a symbol of mourning. They wailed, cut their hair, gashed their arms and legs, and put on ragged clothes. No victory celebration was held if the number of losses exceeded the number of scalps taken (Denig 1930:555–556).

A successful expedition celebrated with two types of dances. The Victory, or Scalp, Dance (*wakté wač^hípi* 'killing dance') was a circle dance in which both men and women participated, the women carrying the scalps on five-foot long staffs. The scalps were stretched on small hoops, the inside painted red. Women also carried weapons or wore regalia that their male relatives had used in war. Between rounds of dancing, men recited their brave deeds, each of which entitled a man to wear an eagle tail feather. Killing enemies in battle counted for nothing if members of the party failed to touch the fallen body and bring home the scalp, which was proof of the enemy's death. The second dance, the Circle Dance (*ówį̨x wač^hípi* 'circling dance'), was performed only by women and gave them an opportunity to sing the praises of their victorious male relatives (Denig 1930:557–558; Lowie 1909:30; Rodnick 1938:43).

The killing of enemies was believed to please the spirits. If enemies were taken alive they were tortured and put to death. In warfare, the bodies of slain enemies were mutilated in order to insult the enemy (Denig 1930:480, 485, 491–492).

Life Cycle

Before a birth, men and children left the lodge while the mother was assisted by older women, one of whom cut the umbilical cord. The mother knelt, grasping two poles set upright in the ground and pressing her abdomen against a crosspiece. If the birth were difficult, a medicine man might be summoned to administer medicines (Denig 1930:429, 516; Lowie 1909:38).

Assiniboine women sometimes practiced abortion by forceful blows to the abdomen. Infanticide was also practiced, especially if the father had deserted the woman, leaving her without a provider (Denig 1930:429, 521).

Newborns were placed in buckskin cradles, which were sometimes attached to cradleboards obtained from the Plains Cree and Plains Ojibwa. The navel cord was enclosed in a small decorated pouch that hung from the cradle and was later attached to the child's clothing (Denig 1930:519; Kennedy 1961:34; Lowie 1909:25).

Babies received a name three to four weeks after birth. A successful warrior or a holy man bestowed the name for which he received a horse that he led around the camp while calling out the new name. Girls' names were generally kept throughout life, but young men frequently received new names in recognition of their first brave deed. After counting many coups a man might receive the name of a deceased grandfather or other male relative (Denig 1930:517, 519; Kennedy 1961:33–35; Lowie 1909:38–39; Rodnick 1938:55–56).

Children were weaned at two to three years of age. About the same age a child's ears were pierced, without ceremony, often by a grandmother. Children were trained by their same-sex parent. Parents did not strike or punish their children but scolded them and instructed them in proper behavior (Denig 1930:513, 520; Rodnick 1938:56–57).

Men taught their sons to hunt and use weapons. Youths sacrificed their first kill by butchering the animal and leaving it for the crows, magpies, and wolves to devour, offering a prayer for future success in hunting and war. By the age of 18 they were proficient as hunters and had joined their first war expedition, although some went to war as young as the age of 12 (Denig 1930:535, 542; Rodnick 1938:41).

At the time of a girl's first menstruation she was isolated in a small lodge or shelter erected near the family tepee. In earlier times this custom was repeated at each menstruation, but it was apparently abandoned by the mid-nineteenth century. Some girls bore children at age 15, but the usual range for childbearing was 18 to 35. The average number of children a woman bore was two to five, although some had as many as eight (Denig 1930:513, 524; Lowie 1909:39; Kennedy 1961:33).

Men married between the ages of 20–25, while women married after the age of 12. A suitor might play a courting flute outside a girl's lodge or resort to love medicines in order to persuade her to run off with him. Since virginity at the time of marriage was highly valued, as a precaution female relatives would wrap a cord around a girl's body and legs before she went to bed. The proper form of marriage required a man to send a horse and some cooked meat to the girl's lodge. If her family refused the offer he might send another horse and other presents. Once the offer was accepted the girl went to the man's lodge to live there as his wife. The new couple could not live with the wife's family because of the practice of in-law avoidance; a man did not enter his parents-in-law's lodge. Until children were born the man was "owned" by his parents-in-law and was obligated to hunt for them. A man had the right to marry his wife's younger sisters as co-wives. At the death of a spouse a man waited a year before remarrying, while a widow might wait as long as three years (Denig 1930:510–512, 590; Rodnick 1938:59–63; Kennedy 1961:27–32).

A man had the right to divorce his wife, though this seldom happened after the couple had children. In such cases the older children stayed with the father and the younger ones went with the mother. Adultery and barrenness were reasons for divorce (Denig 1930:512).

When a person died, the relatives and friends wailed, calling out their kin relationship to the deceased and cutting their hair and gashing their bodies. They begged the spirit of the deceased to leave them and travel to the land of spirits. The mourners wailed until the body was buried. When a warrior died his body, dressed and painted as for war, was first wrapped in a blanket. His weapons were placed with the body, which was then wrapped in a buffalo robe on which the deceased had painted depictions of his brave deeds. The whole was again wrapped in a rawhide and securely tied. Scaffold burial on the limbs of a large tree was the usual means of disposing of the body, which was oriented with feet to the south and head slightly elevated. In the summer a body might be buried in the ground, on the top of a hill. A man's war horse was killed at his grave, to take him to the spirit world. A very respected warrior or chief was sometimes buried in a tepee, in a sitting position as though still alive, the lodge tightly closed and left to disintegrate in the elements.

The bodies of less prominent individuals were treated less elaborately. Weapons and tools were placed with the body for use in the afterlife. A woman's favorite dogs might be killed at her grave. A funeral flag of red cloth was erected over the grave, particularly that of a child. Fluttering in the wind, its purpose was to ward off carrion-eating birds and animals. When the scaffold rotted and fell to earth the bones were gathered up and buried (Denig 1930:491, 493, 570–574).

The person who prepared the body for burial, usually an old man, cut off a lock of hair and preserved it for a year or two; then it was purchased by a near relative, who paid a high price in horses, blankets, and other goods. During the first year after death it was customary to visit the grave two or three times, wailing, offering smoke with a pipe, praying to the spirit. A feast was prepared and eaten at the grave, and some of the food was left for the deceased (Denig 1930:570, 575; Kennedy 1961:164–168).

Clothing and Adornment

The Assiniboine, less eager than many other tribes to adopt European goods, continued to make and use native manufactured implements in the mid-nineteenth century. They had few guns, which put them at a disadvantage in war expeditions against enemies. They preferred clothing of their own manufacture (figs. 7–8) to the coats, shirts, and pants offered by traders. Most clothing was made of tanned hide, although cloth garments were worn during the summer. Cloth was valued because it was light and retained its warmth when wet, but it was not as durable as hide. Both men and women wore light blankets during the summer and buffalo robes for warmth in the winter (Denig 1930:464–465, 584, 588, 1961:95).

Men's shirts and leggings were made of antelope or deer hide, but cloth or blanket material was preferred for breechcloths. During the winter men wore capotes, hooded coats made from trade blankets. Women's dresses were of buffalo cow hide, with short leggings of elk skin, which reached to the calf. Both men and women wore rawhide-soled buckskin moccasins, which during the winter were insulated with buffalo hair.

For ceremonial occasions, including going to war, clothing was decorated with porcupine quillwork or beadwork. A quilled war shirt and leggings, trimmed with locks of

left, Mont. Histl. Soc., Helena: 955-380; center, Smithsonian, Dept. of Anthr: 392952 (79-3840); Smithsonian, NAA: 76-13370.

Fig. 7. Women's clothing. left, Mrs. Standing Bear wearing a cloth dress and a blanket; child wearing Euro-American clothing; Mrs. White Boy wearing a dress with ribbon appliqué skirt and cowrie shell (or elk teeth) decorated bodice. She also wears a wide brass-studded belt with pendant hanging to the ground and is wrapped in a commercial blanket. Photographed about 1890–1900. center, Female doll made of decorated rawhide and buckskin, crafted by Juanita Tucker, Ft. Belknap, Mont., 1955; height 29 cm. right, Woman wearing buckskin-fringed dress decorated with beadwork. The child's cradle is in a swing made of hide and rope. Photograph by Edward S. Curtis, 1905–1908.

human hair, was valued at a horse (the equivalent of 10 buffalo robes); if trimmed with ermine skins, the value doubled. Dentalium shells from the Northwest Coast, obtained through Indian trade networks, were highly valued, especially for decorating women's dresses. Glass beads, obtained from White traders, were used extensively to decorate clothing and moccasins, and beaded strips were sewn to men's blankets. Assiniboine beadwork tended to use large, relatively simple designs on white backgrounds that, stylistically, were similar to the beadwork done by the Plains Cree. Most designs were geometric, with some floral motifs. The technique ordinarily used was the overlay stitch, which gave a smooth surface, in contrast to the lazy stitch used by many other Plains tribes, including the Sioux, which produced a characteristic ridged surface. Small brass hawk bells were used to decorate clothing, and brass and silver wire and other ornaments were valued as arm bands and earrings. In earlier times native dyes were used to color porcupine quills, but by the mid-nineteenth century scraps of colored cloth were boiled with quills to dye them. Paints obtained from traders, particularly Chinese vermillion, chrome yellow, and verdigris, were used, most importantly for face painting (Denig 1930:584–591; Lowie 1909:19–26; Kennedy 1961:90; VanStone 1983, 1996).

Girls were tattooed at the age of 12 to 14. Designs included a round spot on the forehead, lines from both ends and the middle of the mouth down the chin, transverse lines on the cheeks, and rings around the wrists and upper arms. The purpose for this was decorative. Men might be tattooed only after having struck an enemy. Their tattoos often were much more extensive, covering the chest and both arms (Denig 1930:522, 592; Lowie 1909:17).

History, 1869–1960s

United States

In 1869, when the Montana Assiniboine were assigned to the Milk River Agency, they comprised two divisions. The Upper Assiniboine bands, led by Long Hair and Whirlwind, were intermarried with the Gros Ventre; the Lower Assiniboine, comprising the Canoe Paddler band, led by Red Stone, were associated with the Yankton, Yanktonai, and Santee Sioux who had recently moved to the area (Special Agent A.S. Reed quoted in D.R. Miller 1987:107). As game became scarcer, all these groups became dependent on government rations.

In May 1873 the agency was moved to Fort Peck, a trading post built in 1867 by the Durfee and Peck trading company above the confluence of the Milk with the Missouri to serve the Lower Assiniboine Canoe Paddler bands of Red Stone (648 people), Broken Arm (416 people), Bobtail Bear (480 people), and Red Snow (400 people), as well as a band of Sioux under a chief named Long Sioux (1,236 people, described by Agent A.J. Simmons as "confederated with Assiniboines"), and the Yankton-Yanktonai

a
b
c
d
e

led by Struck by the Ree (4,960 people). Also in 1873 a new subagency called Fort Belknap was built one mile southwest of present Chinook, Montana, to serve the Upper Assiniboine bands, which were listed as the North band (1,100 people), Stone or Rocky band (1,070 people), and Dogtail band (425 people), as well as the associated Gros Ventre (1,321 people) and River Crow (1,162 people) (D.R. Miller 1987:116–117). By the late 1870s the River Crow had left Fort Belknap and joined the Mountain Crow at their agency on the Yellowstone (Hoxie 1995:104).

Jurisdictional boundaries for the new agencies were ambiguous, and White settlers occupied land without regard for Indians. Contracts for supplying Indian annuities to the agencies made valuable contributions to the development of commerce in Fort Benton and Helena. During the final years of the buffalo robe trade the lawlessness of the transborder region was epitomized by the "whiskey forts," which existed solely to dispense illegal alcohol (Sharp 1955). By the late 1860s the Cypress Hills had become the last refuge for the buffalo. Competition among the Assiniboine, Plains Cree, Métis, Blackfoot, and others hunting there escalated into warfare (Milloy 1988:115).

In April 1873 a group of White trappers collecting wolf skins attacked without provocation an Assiniboine camp in the Sweet Grass Hills. On May 1, 1873, more "wolfers," having lost several horses in a Plains Cree raid, set out to punish the perpetrators. On Battle Creek in the Cypress Hills the wolfers came upon 40 lodges of starving Assiniboines led by Little Soldier. Fortifying themselves with whiskey, the wolfers attacked the camp, killing 16 people and mutilating their bodies. Protests from Agent A.J. Simmons failed to bring the wolfers to justice, and this event became known as the Cypress Hills Massacre (Allan 1983; Goldring 1973; D.R. Miller 1987:118–120).

In 1876 Fort Peck Agency was moved 75 miles east to the mouth of Poplar River, although the Assiniboine camps at Wolf Point were not relocated. Indian agents encouraged periodic buffalo hunts to supplement inadequate agency supplies, but by the late 1870s the herds were rapidly diminishing and hunting implied the risk of armed conflict both with the Métis and with other Indian tribes. The Assiniboines at Fort Peck were reported to be starving during the winter of 1880 because of delayed shipments of supplies; many were forced to eat their horses, then live on wild turnips, flagroot, and small game (DeMallie 1986:47). By the winter of 1882–1883 the buffalo herds were gone. Over the next several winters many deaths from starvation and malnutrition occurred at Fort Peck and Fort Belknap (D.R. Miller 1987:132–142).

The Northwest Peace Commission arrived at Fort Peck in December 1886 to negotiate new reservation boundaries and extinguish title to lands in exchange for 10 years of annuities. In January 1887 the commission visited Fort Belknap, and the agreements were ratified in May 1888. In 1895 railroad rights of way and gold mining in the Little Rocky Mountains necessitated a further land cession and a reduction of the southern boundary for Fort Belknap Reservation (Kappler 1904–1941, 1:261–265, 601–604; D.R. Miller 1987:142–147).

Canada

The process of settling the Assiniboine on reserves began with their signing Treaty No. 4 with Plains Cree and Plains Ojibwa bands on September 15, 1874, by which they ceded much of southern Saskatchewan and south-central Manitoba (Canada. *Indian Treaties and Surrenders* 1891, 1:313–321). On September 9, 1875, "Stonies" (Canadian Assiniboines) led by Piapot, Pheasant Rump, and Striped Blanket (Ocean Man) signed an adhesion to Treaty No. 4 at Qu'Appelle Lakes. On September 25, 1877, the Assiniboine bands led by Long Lodge, Man Who Took the Coat, Poorman, and Lean Man signed Treaty No. 4 at Fort Walsh (ARDIA 1877:xxxi).

Fort Walsh, a North-West Mounted Police post, was built in 1875 near Battle Creek in the Cypress Hills; it also became the Indian agency. By 1878 all Treaty No. 4 Assiniboine bands in the vicinity were receiving rations there. In spring 1879 Man Who Took the Coat requested that his people be allowed to select their reserve and settle permanently, and a farm was established for them 27 miles

top left, Ind. U., William Hammond Mathers Mus., Bloomington: W1755; Smithsonian, Dept. of Anthr.: a, 129832 (78-12370), d, 165003 (74-5662); center, Field Mus., Chicago: b, 16261, c, 60169; e, Royal Sask. Mus., Regina: 193; bottom left, Smithsonian, NAA: 76-13356; bottom center, Prov. Arch. of Man., Edmund Morris Coll.: 6; bottom right, Sask. Arch. Board, Regina: R-A 7664A.

Fig. 8. Men's clothing. top left, George Rustler wearing a horned headdress with ermine strip and feathers. He wears a buckskin shirt and leggings with painted circles and lines and geometric beadwork and is holding a feather wand. Photograph by Joseph K. Dixon, Crow Res., Mont., 1909 or 1912. a, Swan skin war bonnet captured from an Assiniboine by the Crow Chief Bear in Water. Collected by J. Isham Allen before 1888; length 57.2 cm. b, Mirror case with 2 attached bags. The front has a pink background and a modified hourglass design with beadwork in light and dark blue, green, and red. The left bag is for paint; the right bag contains circular brass earrings. A broad beaded carrying strap of red wool stroud with buckskin is attached with thongs. Collected by E. F. Wilson, Ft. Peck Res., Mont., about 1892; length of mirror case 52 cm. c, Golden eagle wing fan. It is made of a partial wing, the base wrapped with a strip of patterned cloth to form a handle. Collected by George Dorsey, Ft. Belknap Res., Mont., 1900; length 59 cm. d, Soapstone war club truncated at one end and grooved for lashing to handle. It is bound the entire length with skin, which still has its fur; a horsetail pendant is attached and a single turkey feather; the base is bound with red stroud. Collected by George F. Cooks before 1892; length 63.5 cm. e, Beaded belt with geometric designs in red, white, and green on red background. Purchased from Albert Eayeshappie, 1921; length 86 cm. bottom left, Black Eagle wrapped in buffalo robe and holding an eagle feather fan. Photograph by Edward S. Curtis, 1905–1908. bottom center, Big Darkness, Carry the Kettle band, wearing a horned headdress, beaded buckskin shirt, leggings and moccasins. He is holding a pipe and beaded bag. Photograph by Edmund Morris, Sask., 1910. bottom right, Chief Masketo (Mosquito) (b. 1834) from Mosquito Res., Eagle Hills, Battleford district, Sask., wearing a fringed buckskin shirt and leggings with geometric designs and an eagle feather bonnet. He is holding a pipe and beaded bag with floral designs. Postcard photograph before 1937.

northeast of Fort Walsh (E. Dewdney 1880, 1880a). The band led by Mosquito signed Treaty No. 6 on August 29, 1878, at Battleford (Canada. *Indian Treaties and Surrenders* 1891, 2:35–49). They accepted a reserve in the Eagle Hills where, by 1879, they were receiving annuities. In summer 1882 Mosquito's band was joined by those of Grizzly Bear's Head and Lean Man. Together they became known as the Battleford Stoney band.

Economic desperation by the winter of 1881–1882 resulted in the decision to relocate the Indian groups away from the international boundary and the Cypress Hills. Under protest, the bands of Long Lodge and Man Who Took the Coat were removed northeast to the vicinity of Indian Head, where new fields were already plowed and planted for them. Piapot's band joined them, but when he learned that he would not be recognized as leader of the three bands, he chose to move to a reserve of his own in the Qu'Appelle Valley. After Long Lodge's death in 1885 his band was joined with that of Man Who Took the Coat, and the Assiniboine reserve was resurveyed to accommodate the population using the treaty formula of 128 acres per person. After the death of Man Who Took the Coat in 1892, his brother Carry The Kettle became chief.

The bands of Pheasant Rump and Striped Blanket were settled on adjacent reserves surveyed in 1881 at the west end of Moose Mountain. In 1898 Department of Indian Affairs officials recommended that they be removed to White Bear, a Plains Cree reserve nearby. They surrendered their reserves in 1901 and the lands were sold and opened for settlement (Tyler and Wright 1978).

Reservation and Reserve Life

The close relationship between the Assiniboine and Plains Cree in Saskatchewan continued the tradition of intertribal bands. Piapot's band, for example, was called "Cree Talkers," and one mixed Cree-Assiniboine band was identified as Plains Cree (Rodnick 1938:34; Mandelbaum 1940:166). At Fort Peck and Fort Belknap reservations, and at White Bear Reserve after 1901, Assiniboines shared their lands with other groups: at Fort Peck, with Sioux and landless Plains Cree; at Fort Belknap, with Gros Ventre and Cree-Métis; and at White Bear, with Cree and Saulteaux (D.R. Miller 1994).

The first reservation communities comprised subagency buildings with houses constructed nearby; gardens and fields were established contiguously to make use of communally organized labor. Assiniboines quickly learned about agriculture and stock raising, and in both the United States and Canada, government officials praised their industriousness. The scale of agriculture was limited by factors of size of field in relation to capacity to harvest and thresh crops or to store seed and root crops. After 1896 the Canadian Indian Department, reversing its previous policy, allowed Indian farmers to use their own resources to buy mechanized agricultural implements to increase production, but that policy also resulted in increased indebtedness and coincided with a policy encouraging land surrenders and sales to establish trust funds that would minimize the administrative costs of more productive bands (C. Beal 1994; S. Carter 1990).

Assiniboines on the Montana reservations were limited to gardens and small fields until lands were individually allotted. Beginning in 1902, the bulk of both reservations was leased to White cattle companies. In 1909 the first allotments at Fort Peck were made, but they were not fully surveyed and conveyed until 1913. Unallotted lands were declared surplus and opened to homesteading in 1917. Fort Belknap Reservation was first allotted in 1921; all land was allotted to the Indians, leaving no surplus for non-Indian homesteading (D.R. Miller 1987:155–158, 168).

With the passage of the Indian Reorganization Act in 1934, tribes in the United States were given the opportunity to write constitutions and to incorporate for economic purposes. Fort Belknap incorporated in 1935, but Fort Peck rejected the act, preferring to maintain the general council established under the constitution that they adopted in 1927. Not until 1960 did Fort Peck adopt a constitution that established a tribal executive board to govern the reservation (Lopach, Brown, and Clow 1990:104–106; Fowler 1987:95–96; Bureau of Indian Affairs 1978:56, 64).

In the 1930s Assiniboine tribal enterprises were liquidated by the Bureau of Indian Affairs, which continued to control reservation economies. During World War II, in addition to those Assiniboines who joined the armed forces, many others moved off reservation for employment in war-related industries. After the war, many did not return; for example, in 1951, one-third of Fort Belknap Assiniboines lived off reservation. Some participated in the BIA relocation program, which took them to Chicago and other cities. Most ultimately returned to the reservations (Fowler 1987:98–101).

In the 1950s the discovery of oil on Fort Belknap and Fort Peck offered the potential of economic support for the tribes. When leases were finally approved, the government insisted that royalties be paid to individual landowners rather than to the tribes (Fowler 1987:107).

Cultural Innovations, 1880s to 1950s

Innovations during the reservation period revealed the viability of Assiniboine culture. The Tea Dance (*ktų́s wač^{h}ípi* 'drunken dance'), which the Assiniboine borrowed from the Blackfoot in prereservation times, involved the drinking of large quantities of tea and the mimicking of drunken behavior. The dance was revived in 1891 at Fort Belknap, with both men and women participating. The dance included giving away property by the sponsor. Eventually it apparently merged with the Dance without Robes and the Warbonnet Dance (Rodnick 1938:8; Fowler 1987:65–66).

In 1890 the Arapaho introduced the Ghost Dance to the Gros Ventre at Fort Belknap; it spread to the Assiniboine

left, Prov. Arch. of Man., Winnipeg, Edmund Morris Coll.: 292; right, Natl. Cowboy Hall of Fame, Okla. City: 79.26.2503.

Fig. 9. Drummers. left, Men around a large drum. Women behind them wear feather headdresses and long breastplates of hairpipes and beads. Photograph by Edmund Morris, Carry the Kettle Res., Sintaluta, Sask., 1908. right, Men singing and beating drums at the Wild Horse Stampede. The event, begun in 1921, has continued through 1998, growing into a professional rodeo with contenders from Canada, the United States, and Australia. Photograph by Ralph Russell Doubleday, Ft. Peck Res., Wolf Point, Mont., about 1935.

as the *wač^{h}ékiye wač^{h}ípi* 'prayer dance'. Though they held dances for about two years, they did not accept Ghost Dance doctrines (Rodnick 1938:8). The ceremony was revived in 1902, when Kicking Bear and Short Bull, Sioux Ghost Dance leaders from Pine Ridge Reservation, visited Fort Peck and Fort Belknap and instructed the Assiniboine in the Ghost Dance. Incorporated in these dances were sacred red and white paint, feathers, and medicines for healing, which Assiniboines received through the mail from Jack Wilson (Wovoka), the Northern Paiute Ghost Dance prophet, in exchange for money and goods. Fred Robinson, a Fort Peck Assiniboine, subsequently introduced the Ghost Dance to various Assiniboine and Sioux reserves in Saskatchewan (Dangberg 1957; J.H. Howard 1984:175–178). The Assiniboine did not perform Ghost Dances very long, but they continued for some years to use the medicines provided by the prophet.

Although the Ghost Dance was of minor significance to the Assiniboine, they enthusiastically embraced the ritual hand game that passed from tribe to tribe in association with the Ghost Dance (Mooney 1896:817; Lesser 1933:124–130, 309–337). The Assiniboine learned the hand game from the Gros Ventre about 1900 (Rodnick 1938:11). In earlier times the hand game was played to gamble, but the new hand game was a religious ceremony in which no gambling occurred (Denig 1930:569; Lowie 1909:17–18; Rodnick 1938:124).

In 1920 the Fort Belknap Assiniboine received the Rabbit Dance from the Pine Ridge Sioux. Called the Owl Dance by the Assiniboine, this is a dance for couples in which the man, on the outside of the circle, places his right hand on his partner's shoulder and takes her right hand in his left. The lyrics of the songs celebrated the victory of Indian soldiers over the Germans in World War I (Rodnick 1938:123).

In the reservation context the Grass Dance, which also originated with the Sioux, became the predominant dance form at the Fourth of July celebration and other public dances. During the early years of the twentieth century the dance was reorganized as a secular event. By the 1940s crow belts were no longer so important to the Grass Dance and greater attention was paid to American flags and their keepers, both male and female. They symbolized Assiniboine pride in their participation in the World Wars (Fowler 1987:161–162, 210).

The Sun Dance was held at Fort Belknap in association with the Fourth of July celebration until 1952, after which it was discontinued. Attendance at the celebration dwindled in subsequent years, since the Sun Dance had been the main attraction (Rodnick 1938:124; Fowler 1987:162).

History and Culture, 1960s to 1990s

When the federal War on Poverty began in 1964, jobs proliferated on the reservations and many Assiniboines returned from urban communities. The U.S. Department of Housing and Urban Development provided the first modern housing (Fowler 1987:115–116).

Cultural and Religious Renewal

Cultural events included annual powwows—Red Bottom at Frazer and Wadopana at Wolf Point, both on Fort Peck Reservation, and Milk River at Fort Belknap Reservation. In Canada, at least from the late 1970s, powwows were held at Carry The Kettle, White Bear, and Mosquito reserves and at Ocean Man after 1994. Masquerade dances at Halloween, as well as other special event dances, continued early reservation practices.

In Canada, the Mosquito, Lean Man, and Grizzly Bear's Head reserves held Sun Dances ("Lodges") annually beginning in the 1960s. The 1980s brought an active revival of traditional religious activities in Montana as well. Ceremonies that had been dormant for two decades were revitalized. Contemporary annual Sun Dance ceremonies were begun at Fort Peck in 1980, and by the end of the decade additional lodges were held each summer at Fort Belknap. Canadian Sun Dance leaders contributed significantly to the revival at Fort Belknap. The Fort Peck ceremony continued annually with the exception of 1986, when the Assiniboines were invited to hold their Sun Dance at Browning, Montana, on the Blackfeet Reservation.

Sweatlodge ceremonies were held throughout the year, in advance of major ceremonies or independently for special purposes. Other rituals historically practiced in conjunction with the Sun Dance, such as the Fool Dance and Horse Dance, were not a regular part of the modern revival. At the Fort Belknap Sun Dance in 1986 a Horse Dance was performed by Assiniboine visitors from Battleford. In 1993 a group of Fool Dancers from Fort Peck visited the last evening of the Milk River Celebration at Fort Belknap, interrupting the dancing and bringing healing blessings at a time when tensions threatened the community.

The keepers of Assiniboine hand game bundles at Fort Belknap and Fort Peck were still called upon occasionally to hold games for divination and prayer (Fowler 1987:211–212). Other regularly held ceremonies included feasts sponsored by families or individuals, as well as marriage and naming ceremonies. They were usually associated with giveaways and served as expressions of generosity and respect. The ceremonial use of pipes was central to all religious practice.

For practitioners of traditional religion, Ghost or Four-Day Feasts, occurring within four days after a death, were often held in conjunction with church funerals. Wakes, or night-long vigils with the body, were standard practice before funerals. A memorial giveaway took place on the one-year anniversary of a death.

Most of the Assiniboine joined Christian churches but felt little conflict between church membership and participation in traditional rituals (Fowler 1987:228). At Fort Belknap a Roman Catholic mission was established in 1886 and a Presbyterian mission in 1904 (Rodnick 1938:13). Catholicism predominated at Fort Belknap, and Catholic missions were also established at Fort Peck and on the Canadian reserves. Presbyterians were also active at Fort Peck. For a time, the Mormon Church ran a school on the Fort Peck Reservation, and Mormons also missionized at Carry The Kettle Reserve. Presbyterian and United Church missions were established on Canadian reserves as well. Fundamentalist churches also gained converts among the Assiniboine.

Fig. 10. Eulogy by Gilbert Horn at the burial of Phyllis Hawley Anderson, also known as Stands Above the Water. A traditional burial covering of boughs and sage was erected over the cedar coffin made for her ashes, a smudging ceremony was held, and a riderless horse was led to the burial ground. Honor songs were sung and a feast and giveaway followed the burial. Although the body had been cremated, because she had been living in B.C., it was considered a traditional burial. Photograph by Jessie Hawley, Ft. Belknap Res., Mont., 1998.

Higher Education

Assiniboine educators, parents, and politicians were active in the movement for Indian-controlled schools at all levels. Fort Peck Community College was chartered by the Fort Peck Tribes in 1978 and achieved accreditation in 1989. The college included in the curriculum courses in Fort Peck Reservation history as well as separate courses in Assiniboine and Sioux culture, language, and history. The Native American Educational Services College–Fort Peck site offered B.A. degrees in community development starting in the early 1980s. Fort Belknap College was established in 1982 and received accreditation in 1988. Each of these institutions taught the native languages, all of which, by the 1990s, had become endangered. Only a handful of fluent speakers, most elderly, preserved linguistic knowledge on the Montana reservations.

In Canada Assiniboines enrolled in universities in Saskatchewan or in one of the campuses of Saskatchewan Indian Federated College, where, beginning in the mid-1980s, Assiniboine history, culture, and language courses were offered.

Political Organization and Economy

At Fort Belknap, the constitution was modified in 1974 to provide for an elected tribal council of 12 individuals serving staggered two-year terms. According to the constitution six councilmen must be Assiniboines, six Gros Ventres. The council elected its own officers. At Fort Peck, the tribal executive board, established in 1960, was the governing body. It also consisted of 12 members, elected at large every two years (Bureau of Indian Affairs 1978:56, 64).

On the Montana reservations, Assiniboines created opportunities for economic development. On Fort Peck Reservation, an industrial park serviced by a railroad spur was built at Poplar with financial assistance from the Economic Development Administration, in the Department of Commerce, from 1968–1973 (Bureau of Indian Affairs 1978:71–72). From 1975 to 1992, A & S Industries, owned by the Fort Peck Tribe, manufactured camouflage nets for the Defense Department under a joint contract with a tribally owned factory on the Devils Lake Sioux Reservation in North Dakota (renamed Spirit Lake Reservation in 1996). In 1986 A & S Industries developed a sheet metal stamping division. By the late 1990s, the plant pursued private sector manufacturing.

A second industry at Fort Peck, begun in 1968, involved electronic subassemblies for West Electronics. Labor-intensive technology was the key to creating employment opportunities. The need for workers to come from both ends of the reservation gave rise to the Fort Peck Transportation Authority in 1984.

Assiniboines in key administrative positions in the Fort Peck government implemented a uniform commercial tax code in 1985. They successfully defended taxing authority over the Burlington Northern Railroad right of way across the reservation in a test case that resulted in a Supreme Court decision.

Oil and gas development began in the early 1950s, providing income for the tribe as well as for those individuals on whose land the resources were located. The Fort Peck Tribes' Mineral Office, established in 1981, employed its own geologist. The Wolf Point Community Organization, at Fort Peck, pursued a variety of Indian-owned businesses, from a casino to joint-venture manufacturing, each of which created employment and investment opportunities.

Fort Belknap was less successful in pursuing economic development. Ranching, farming, and leasing land remained primary economic activities.

In Canada, White Bear Reserve, contiguous to Moose Mountain Provincial Park, developed a resort and golf course in 1986. In 1993 the band opened a casino on the reserve, but it was closed by the provincial government. Following a compact between the province and the Federation of Saskatchewan Indian Nations, five casinos were authorized, including the Bear Claw Casino at White Bear, which opened in 1995. White Bear was also involved in oil and gas development and a series of small business ventures on the reserve. Carry the Kettle Reserve developed a potato farm, buffalo pasture, and a plastics factory. The Pheasant Rump and Ocean Man reserves were engaged in purchasing and improving land and in creating the infrastructure necessary for the reestablished reserves, including housing, schools, sanitation, and roads.

Land Claims

The Montana Assiniboine sought compensation for the loss of lands designated in the 1851 treaty. Their first claim was filed in the U.S. Court of Claims in 1927 and an award was made in 1933. However, following the federal government's practice of applying offset provisions, whereby the cost of supporting tribes on reservations was deducted from awards, the Assiniboine were found to be still in debt to the United States and the award was declared null and void. The Assiniboine brought the claim to the Indian Claims Commission in 1950 and 1954, only to have it dismissed. In 1979 the Assiniboine Claims Council was reorganized and representatives from Fort Peck and Fort Belknap appeared before U.S. Senate hearings. Congressional legislation was secured in October 1980 that allowed the claim to be returned to the U.S. Court of Claims in 1981. The Court decided in the Assiniboines' favor and awarded over $16 million (Wetsit 1982). The Fort Peck and Fort Belknap Assiniboines shared proportionally in the award.

In 1974 the Assiniboines at White Bear presented a claim to the government of Canada on behalf of the descendants of the former Pheasant Rump and Ocean Man bands, whose members had been amalgamated into the White Bear Reserve when their own reserves were surrendered in 1901. Contending that the surrenders were made under duress and were tainted by the self-interest of public officials, who benefited personally from subsequent sales of reserve lands, the claim was validated and negotiations were begun in 1982. In 1984 the government awarded $19 million. In 1990 Pheasant Rump and Ocean Man reserves were reestablished. Most of the claim settlement was used to purchase the necessary land base.

Mosquito-Grizzly Bear's Head and Lean Man reserves received a treaty land entitlement claim settlement in 1992 as one of 27 bands whose reserves were originally surveyed at a smaller size than they were legally due under treaty. More than 20,000 acres were involved, and the settlement amounted to more than $8.5 million, which was primarily intended for use in purchasing land to be converted to trust status (Saskatchewan Treaty Land Entitlement 1992). In 1998 the descendants of Grizzly Bear's Head and Lean Man awaited federal negotiation of their claim for the surrender of their reserves in 1905. Carry The Kettle Reserve was awarded $24 million in 1996 for treaty land claims (fig. 11).

Fig. 11. Carry The Kettle Res. members signing the Treaty Land Entitlement Specific claim settlement with representatives of Canada, the province of Sask., and the Federation of Saskatchewan Indian Nations. left to right, Cora Thomson, Trustee, signing document; Councilor Howard Thomson; Elsie Koochicum, the land claims coordinator for the Band; and Chief Joe O'Watch wearing a buckskin jacket. Drummers are at left. Photograph by Bernice Saulteaux, Carry The Kettle First Nation Band Hall, south of Sintaluta, Sask., June 6, 1996.

Population

Historical population figures for the Assiniboine are of uncertain accuracy (table 2). Mooney (1928:13) estimated the pre-1780 population at 10,000. Subsequently, the most significant factor affecting the Assiniboine population was a series of devastating epidemics. The smallpox epidemic of 1780–1781 was estimated to have reduced the population by one-third to one-half. The 1819–1820 epidemic of measles and whooping cough may have again reduced the population by half (Ray 1974:105–108). By 1838 the Assiniboine had regained about 30 percent of their population, but in that year smallpox, brought by steamboat to the upper Missouri region, resulted in the loss of as much as as 60 percent of the population. Assiniboine losses would have been even higher, but some 200 lodges had been vacinated by Hudson's Bay Company traders. The population was slow to recover, and other smallpox epidemics struck the Assiniboine in 1856–1857 and 1869 (Denig 1930:399, 1961:71–72; D.R. Miller 1987:100; Ray 1974:191).

Besides resulting in overall population loss, the epidemics decreased the number of individuals per lodge. Eighteenth-century estimates range from 8–14 individuals per lodge, while post-1838 estimates vary from 4.5 to 6. Discussing the 1819–1820 epidemic, Ray (1974:108) calculated that the number of men per lodge dropped from four to two.

Assiniboine population figures in the reservation period are not much more reliable (tables 3–4). Most available figures represent only resident populations and fail to differentiate the Assiniboines from other groups living on the same reservations and reserves. Because of extensive intermarriage, particularly with the Plains Cree and Ojibwa in Canada; the Gros Ventre, landless Cree, and Rocky Boy Cree at Fort Belknap; and the Sioux, Turtle Mountain Chippewa-Cree, and landless Cree at Fort Peck, many individuals have mixed heritage. The payment of claims money and enrollment restrictions forced individuals to declare a single tribal affiliation.

Synonymy†

The name Assiniboine comes from Ojibwa *assini·-pwa·n* 'stone enemy', where historically the designation 'enemy' came to be applied specifically to the Sioux, hence 'stone Sioux' (David H. Pentland, John D. Nichols, personal communications 1998); in Ojibwa orthography this is asinii-bwaan (J.D. Nichols and Nyholm 1995:14). This Ojibwa form of the name has been cited, often with the plural suffix *-ak*, as Assinniboan, 1804 (Lewis and Clark in Moulton 1983–, 3:432), Ussinibwoinug (Tanner 1830:316), Ausinabwaun (N.H. Parker 1857:13), Assiniebwannuk (P. Jones 1861:178), Asinibwanak (Cuoq 1886:77), and Assinipwanak (Gatschet in Hodge 1907–1910, 1:105). Other citations of

†This synonymy was written by Douglas R. Parks.

Table 2. Prereservation Population

Date	*Number of Lodges*	*Individuals per Lodge*	*Number of Men*	*Total Population*	*Source*
1789	200			1,600–2,000	Mackenzie in Lamb 1970:116–117
1794	230	14		4,508	M'Gillivray in Milloy 1988:72–73
1809	850	11[a]	2,000	9,350	Henry the Younger in Gough 1988–1992, 2:375–376
1822–1823	450	7	1,350	3,150	McDonald in Ray 1974:108
1823	3,000		7,000	28,000	Renville in Keating 1824, 1:396
1838	1,000–1,200[b]	6		6,000–7,200	Denig 1930:396, 1961:68, 72
1838	750–820[c]	4.5		3,375–3,690	Denig 1930:396, 431, 1961:79
1850	1,500			4,800	Culbertson 1952:137
1863				5,000	Palliser in Ray 1974:191

[a]Estimate from Peter Fidler, 1815 (Ray 1974:108).
[b]Mont. only.
[c]500–520 lodges in Mont.; 250–300 in Canada; postepidemic figures.

Table 3. Reservation Population, United States

Date	*Fort Belknap Reservation*	*Fort Peck Reservation*	*Total*
1875	3,500	1,998	5,498
1885	700	1,672	2,372
1895	763	716	1,479
1905	689	573	1,262
1916	639	640	1,279
1921	657	777	1,434
1926	581	840	1,421
1935	674		
1978	3,954[a] enrolled 1,797 resident, enrolled	7,504[a] enrolled 4,300 resident, enrolled	
1990	2,180[a]	5,782[a]	
1998		4,129 enrolled	

[a]Includes other tribes.

SOURCES: Rodnick (1938:70–71); Bureau of Indian Affairs (1978:56, 64); 1990 and 1998 figures provided by Fort Belknap and Fort Peck tribes.

Table 4. Reserve Population, Canada

Reserve	*1970*	*1979 on/off reserve*	*1994*	*1997*
Carry The Kettle (I.R. 76)	734	608/349	535	696
Grizzly Bear's Head (I.R. 110), and Lean Man (I.R. 111);			70	
Mosquito (I.R. 109)	387	374/142	280	512[b]
White Bear (I.R. 70)[a]	916	621/597	635	686

[a]Includes Assiniboine, Saulteaux, and Cree.

[b]The three bands combined.

SOURCES: Department of Indian Affairs and Northern Development (1970); Indian and Northern Affairs Canada (1981); Statistics Canada (1994); Indian and Northern Affairs Canada (1998).

the name reflect the Plains Cree form *asini·pwa·t* (Mandelbaum 1979:8; H. Christoph Wolfart, personal communication 1987), which also occurs variously with the plural ending *-ak* as Assine poetwak, 1786 (David Thompson in Glover 1962: 40), Asseeneepoytuck (Franklin 1824:168), Assinibuaduk, 1846–1852 (Kurz 1937:142), Assini-poytuk (J. Richardson 1851:51), and A-si-ni-poi′-tuk (Hayden 1862:381). In Sweet Grass Plains Cree the Assiniboine are *opwa·si·mo·w* (Bloomfield 1934:138; Mandelbaum 1979:8; vol. 17:439), also the name for the Stoney (Bloomfield 1930:296).

Beginning with the earliest French recordings in the seventeenth century and continuing through the nineteenth century, the most common designation for the Assiniboine is a rendering of the Ojibwa name, which appears with a final r, l, or n from Proto-Algonquian *θ, depending on dialect and date (Pentland 1978). Two seventeenth-century citations with r above reflect the form in Old Algonquin: Assinipour, 1640 (JR 18:231), Assinipoüars, 1670–1671 (JR 54:192). Most seventeenth- and eighteenth-century French renditions have l, the pronunciation in early Ottawa and after about 1700 in other dialects; examples are Assinipoüalac, 1667 (JR 51:55, 57), Assiniponiels, 1669 (Marquette in Gallatin 1836:123), Assenidoualaks, 1678, and Assinipoualacs, 1684 (Dulhut in Margry 1876–1886, 6:21, 51), Assiniboels, 1695 (Frontenac in Margry 1876–1886, 5:63), Assinipoils, 1700 (Le Sueur in Margry 1876–1886, 6:82), Assilibouels, 1702 (Iberville in Margry 1876–1886, 4:600), Assinipoual, 1703 (Lahontan 1905, 1:304), Assiniboiles and Assinipoiles, 1716 (Vaudreuil and Bégon in Margry 1876–1886, 6:496, 500), Assiniboils, 1730, assiliboilles, 1738–1739, and Assiniboels, 1744 (La Vérendrye in Burpee 1927:50, 318, 445), Assiliboels, 1750 (La Jonquière in Burpee 1927:485), Osinipoilles, 1776 (A. Henry 1901:277), and Assenipovals (Alcedo 1786–1789, 4:557). Contemporary citations that have a final *t*, but which may be mistranscriptions for *l*, are Assinibouets, 1681 (Du Chesneau in NYCD 9:153) and Arsenipoitis (Barcia 1723:238).

With the subsequent gradual shift of Ojibwa *l* to *n*, which spread from west to east, Ojibwa forms of Assiniboine with final *-n* began to appear early in the eighteenth century, and by the end of the century they had become common, especially among Saint Louis traders and Spanish Louisiana officials (Lewis and Clark in Moulton 1983–, 3:432). Examples are: Assinibouanes, 1722 (Pachot in Margry 1876–1886, 6:517), Assiniboins, 1776 (A. Henry 1901:277), Nasseniboines, 1795 (Fotman in Nasatir 1952, 1:332), Osniboine, 1796 (Carondelet in Nasatir 1952, 2:391), Assiniboine, 1796 (Council of State in Nasatir 1952, 2:435), and Assiniboines, 1795–1796 (McKay in Nasatir 1952, 2:492).

In the late seventeeth and through the eighteenth century, the Cree form of the name with final *t* was also used. Examples are: Asenepoets, 1684 (Radisson 1961:227); Assinae Poets, 1690 (Geyer in H. Kelsey 1929:xxxiii); mountain poets, 1691 (H. Kelsey 1929:7); Sinnae Poets, 1717 (Hudson's Bay Company 1717); Senipoetts, 1729 (York Factory Post Journal quoted in Ray 1974:14); Esinnepoet and sinepoats, or stone Indians, 1743 (Isham 1949:44, 115); Asinepoet, 1754–1755 (Henday in Burpee 1907:331); and Assineapoet, 1795, Assinnepoiet, 1798, Assinipoiet and Assinepoiet, 1799 (William Tomison in Alice M. Johnson 1967:16, 118, 146, 160).

Most nineteenth-century spellings of Assiniboine have final *-n*, as in the modern form. Examples are: Asseniboanes, 1803–1804 (Tabeau 1939:102), Assiniboins and Ossiniboins, 1804 (Lewis and Clark in Moulton 1983–, 3:230, 237), Assineboines, 1809 (Henry in Gough 1988–1992, 2:375), Essinaboin (Secretary of War 1832:64), Assinaboine (ARCIA 1839:498), Assinnaboin (Drake 1848:6), Assinepoins, 1849 (ARCIA 1850:70), and Assinniboine (Hind 1863, 2:148).

Other European and American recordings refer to the Assiniboine as 'rock' or 'stone' Indians; for example, Guerriers de pierre, 1658 (JR 44:249), Guerriers de la Roche, ca. 1700 (Perrot 1864:232), Stone Indians (David Thompson, 1786, in Glover 1962:40; Lewis and Clark, 1804–1805, in Moulton 1983–, 3:432), Sioux of the Rocks (ARCIA 1850:77), Stone Sioux, 1804–1805 (Lewis and Clark in Moulton 1983–, 3:432), and Stoney (Keane 1878:536) or Stonies, 1886 (C.N. Bell in Hodge 1907–1910, 1:105). Although Stoney has come to refer specifically to the Stoney of Alberta (see "Stoney," this vol.), the designations Stonie, Stony, or Plain Stoney are also used for the Assiniboine on the Mosquito-Grizzly Bear's Head Reserve, Battleford Agency, Saskatchewan (Canada. *Indian Treaties and Surrenders* 1891, 2:317–319, 2:44–47). That usage has continued through the twentieth century. The interpretation of the name Assiniboine as 'one who cooks by the use of stones' (William Jones in Hodge 1907–1910, 1:102)—exemplified by Stone Roasters (Tanner 1830:51)—is incorrect, since the second element *pwa·n* of the compound *assini·-pwa·n* is not related to the stem *apwe·-* 'to roast' (Hewitt in Denig 1930:381; David Pentland, personal communication 1998).

The Assiniboine name for themselves is *nakʰóta*, the same self designation used by all other Sioux groups (Denig 1930:381; Parks and DeMallie 1996:185). Reflecting that common identity are several tribal names that refer to the Assiniboine as Sioux. Thus, the Kootenai designation for Assiniboine, Khluhlamá'ka 'cut heads off' (Curtis 1907–1930, 8:168), is a common name for Sioux. Other names among surrounding tribes that designate the Assiniboine as Sioux with a modifying element include Arapaho *ni·ho·nihté·no·tinei* 'yellow foot Sioux' (Loretta Fowler personal communication 1988, retranscribed) and tu-natni 'begging Sioux' (Mooney 1896:1018); Nez Perce *wihneńí·pelu· ʔisequ̇́·lkt* 'walking cutthroat (i.e., walking Sioux)', often shortened to *wihneńí·pelu·* 'walker' (Aoki 1994:886). A nineteenth-century Hidatsa designation is *ita·hacki pahcitakua* 'Sioux in the west' (Thomas Say in James in Thwaites 1904–1907, 17:304, phonemicized), based on the ethnonym *ita·hacki* 'long arrow', the Hidatsa name for the Sioux (Matthews 1877:159, phonemicized).

Some tribal designations associate the Assiniboine with Cree; thus, Sarcee *iči to nišiná* 'wood-in Cree' (Eung-Do Cook, personal communication 1990) and Blackfoot *ni·tsísina·wa* 'original Cree' (Frantz and Russell 1989:325), cited also for Piegan and Blood as Ni'tsíssinaia 'real Cree' (Curtis 1907–1930, 18:186) and for Piegan as nitsí-sĭnna 'real Assiniboine' [i.e., Cree] (Curtis 1907–1930, 6:155).

Several related tribal designations refer to the Assiniboine as 'yellow bone,' the source of which is now obscure: Crow *huliší·le* (Curtis 1907–1930, 4:180; Medicine Horse 1987:15), Hidatsa *hiruší·ri* (Jones 1979:29; Matthews 1877:148; Maximilian in Thwaites 1904–1907, 24:275), Mandan *hú·si·ka* (Parks 1987). The Arapaho name 'yellow foot Sioux' (above) is apparently a related form.

The name for Assiniboine in all Sioux dialects is *hóhe* (Curtis 1907–1930, 3:141; Buechel 1970:733), the origin of which is obscure but which has been variously interpreted as 'revolted' (Keating 1824, 1:380), 'rebels' (Gallatin 1836:123), 'seine (put) in place', 1838–1839 (Nicollet in DeMallie 1976:262), 'fish eaters', 1854 (Denig 1930:396), and 'hoarse voice' (H.L. Scott 1912–1934). Variants include Hoha (Keating 1824, 1:396), and Hohays, 1830 (Snelling 1936:38). It was borrowed into Cheyenne as *hóheeoʔo*, pl. (Petter 1913–1915:582; Curtis 1907–1930, 6:158), which has been reanalyzed as 'cradled ones' (Glenmore and Leman 1985:201). Another Teton Sioux designation is *wazíyata wičʰáša* 'northern men' (Buechel 1970:733).

Several tribal names fit no apparent pattern. The Arikara designation *psíʔaʔ* has no literal meaning (Parks 1986:3), although it has been erroneously associated with the stem *psi* 'to be wintry' (Curtis 1907–1930, 5:151). Another recorded Arikara form, Páhoak-sá (Maximilian in Thwaites 1904–1907, 24:214), is *wa·hukAxá* 'sides of head shaved' (Pawnee *pa·hú·kasa*), the name of an Arikara band (Parks 1979a:232) but not otherwise documented as a term for Assiniboine. The Gros Ventre name *nɔ́ɔkinéíh*, pl. *nɔɔkinéíhinɔh* (Taylor 1994:36), recorded as Naut te nay in (Fidler 1800:fo. 17bʳ) and Natyinéhĭn (Curtis 1907–1930, 5:154), is the cognate of Ottawa *na·towe·ssi* 'Sioux'. A Blackfoot name *ká·yispa·wa* refers to an Assiniboine hair style (Allan R. Taylor, personal communication 1987).

A translation of the name of one Assiniboine band, the Canoe Paddlers, is sometimes generalized to the tribe; thus, Blackfoot *aya·hkio·hsi·tapiwa* 'boatman, canoeist' (Frantz and Russell 1989:325), Gros Ventre *ʔíítóóúhɛkííénnɔh* 'rowing men' (Taylor 1994:37). The Arikara borrowed the Assiniboine name for this band as *watópA* to designate the Fort Peck Assiniboine (Parks 1991, 3:404).

The common Plains sign for Assiniboine is a gesture that signifies cutting off a head, the same sign used for Sioux. Usually an additional sign denoting a specific Assiniboine band follows it (W.P. Clark 1885:50). The sign for the Canoe band, for example, simulates the motions of paddling in a canoe, first on one side of the craft and then on the other. The latter sign is also often used alone to designate the Assiniboine as a tribe (H.L. Scott 1912–1934). The sign for a large abdomen or corpulent body, which designated the Gros Ventre, was used for the Assiniboine as well (Mallery 1881:461–462).

Bands

The earliest mention of Assiniboine bands is by John McDonnell who, writing between 1793–1797, reported Les gens des canots, or Canoe "tribe"; Les gens des filles, or Girls tribe, Les gens du bois fort, or Wood tribe; and the Watombagh-e-ma-ton, or Gens du Grand Diable (Masson 1889–1890, 1:278, 288). Meriwether Lewis and William Clark, 1804–1805 (Moulton 1983–, 3:429–432) provide the next list of bands. The first band is Ma-ne-to-par, Band lar Gru (French *Bande de la Grue*), Crane or Canoe, which is their rendition of Assiniboine *watóp^{h}a*, with M written for *w* and the addition of an unexplained syllable ne. The second name, Na-co-ta O-ee-gah, Gens des fees or Girls (French *Gens des Filles*), is *nak^{h}óta wič^{h}įčana.* O-ee-gah is a miscopying of a spelling something like Ou-ce-jah, with *-na* 'diminutive' omitted. The third name is Na-co-ta Mah-ta-pa-nar-to, Big Devils (Gens des grand Diable), which is again preceded by *nak^{h}óta.* The transcription of *watóp^{h}axnat^{h}ų* again writes M for *w*. Big Devil is not a translation of the band name, but rather is the traders' designation for the contemporary chief of that band, also known as The Gauche (Left Hand) and He Who Holds the Knife (Denig 1930:400).

There are five extensive lists of Assiniboine bands recorded in the nineteenth and early twentieth centuries (table 5). A list presented in Rodnick 1938:34 is not

Table 5. Assiniboine Band Names

Henry 1808 (Gough 1988–1992, 2:375)	*Maxmilian 1832–1834 (1839–1941, 1:440–441)*	*Nicollet 1838 (DeMallie 1976:262–263)*	*Denig 1854 (1930)*	*Lowie (1909)*	*Retranscription and Translation*
1. Canoe and Paddling	1. Oatópabine, les gens des canots	1. Watopenans, canoeists	1. Wa tó pap pe nah, Gens des Canots	1. Watō′pabin, Paddlers	1. *watóp^{h}ana, watóp^{h}apina* (pl.) 'paddler(s)'
2. Little Girl	2. Itschíabine, les gens des filles		2. We ché ap pe nah, Gens des Filles	2. Witcī′abin	2. *wič^{h}įčapina* 'girls'
3. Paddling and Foot	3. Watópachnato, les gens de l'âge	3. Watopar̄'ndate, boats covered with skins	3. Watō′paxna-o^{n}\`wa^{n}, or Watō′paxnatu^{n}	3. Wato′paxnatu^{n}, Those who propel boats	3. *watóp^{h}axnat^{h}ųwą*
4. Red River					
5. Rabbit					
6. Stone or Rocky	6. Jatónabine, les gens des roches	6. Inhantonwanyans, village on the rocks	6. É an tó an, Gens des Roches	6. I^{n}′ya^{n}to^{n}\`wa^{n}bin, Rock-People	6. *įyąt^{h}ųwąpina* 'rock villagers'
7. Those Who Have Water for Themselves Only		7. Minishnan-atowan, village of lone water	7. Minne she nák a to, Gens du lac		7. *miní išná at^{h}ų́wą* 'village at lone water'
8. Eagle Hills					
9. Saskatchewoine					
10. Foot					
11. Strong Wood					
	12. Tschántoga, les gens des [sic] bois				
	13. Otópachgnato, les gens du large				
	14. Taníntaüi, les gens des osayes			14. Tani^{n}′tā\`bin, Buffalo Hip	
	15. Chābin, les gens des montagnes			15. Xe′bina, Mountain People	15. *xépina* 'mountain (people)'
		16. Tchan r̄tata, flexible wood		16. Tca^{n}xta′d^{a}	16. *č^{h}ąxtáta*
		17. Rheatonwan, village on the mountain		17. Xe′nato^{n}wan, Mountain People	17. *xe ʔát^{h}ųwą* 'village at the mountain'
		18. Wichiyenans or Hohes			18. *wįc^{h}íyeną* or *hóhe*
		19. Iya openaka, those who speak in a sharp manner			19. *įyóp^{h}enaka* 'sharp voice'

(continued on next page)

Table 5. Assiniboine Band Names (continued)

Henry 1808 (Gough 1988–1992, 2:375)	*Maxmilian 1832–1834 (1839–1941, 1:440–441)*	*Nicollet 1838 (DeMallie 1976:262–263)*	*Denig 1854 (1930)*	*Lowie (1909)*	*Retranscription and Translation*
		20. Wakpatowan, those who make a village on the river			20. *wakpát^{h}ųwą* 'river village'
				21. Tca^n′xe wintca′cta, People of the Woods	21. *č^{h}ąxé wį̀č^{h}ášta* 'wood mountain people'
			22. Wah zé ab or To kúm pe, Gens du Nord	22. Wazī′a wintca′ct^a, Northern People	22. *wazíyam wį́č^{h}ašta* 'northern people'
				23. U^{n}ska′ha, Roamers	
				24. Hu′decā`bin^E, Red-butt	24. *hútešana, hútešapina* (pl.), 'red bottom (people)'
				25. Wacī′azi hyā bin, Fat-Smokers	25. *waší azínyapi(na), waší azíhyapina*
				26. Cuñktcē′bi, Canum Mentulae	26. *šųkč^{h}épi(na)*, 'dog penis (people)'
				27. Cahī′a iye′skābin, Speakers of Cree	27. *šahíya iyéskapina* 'Cree speakers'
				28. Icna′umbis^a, Those-who-stay-alone	28. *įšná ų́piša* 'always lives alone'
				29. Ini′na u′mpi	29. *inína ų́pi* 'lives quietly'

NOTE: Phonemic transcriptions and translations by Raymond J. DeMallie and Douglas R. Parks.

included in table 5 since it repeats the names in Lowie (1909), sometimes with slightly different translations of band names. Also omitted is a 1939 list by J.L. Long (Kennedy 1961:190–191), which repeats Lowie's list and adds 20 names, apparently of local groups not otherwise identified.

Sources

Primary historical accounts by fur traders and explorers that present information on the Assiniboine include Kelsey, 1691–1697 (Kelsey 1929); La Vérendrye, 1730–1751 (Burpee 1927); Henday, 1754–1755 (Burpee 1907); Henry the Elder, 1776 (A. Henry 1901); Cocking, 1792–1793 (Burpee 1908); Thompson, 1784–1812 (Glover 1962); M'Gillivray, 1794–1795 (Morton 1929); and Henry the Younger, 1799–1814 (Gough 1988–1992).

The fullest history of the Canadian Assiniboine is Ray (1974), which focuses on the Assiniboine in the fur trade. Russell (1991) reviews eighteenth-century Assiniboine history in relation to the Plains Cree. Histories of the Montana Assiniboine include Rodnick (1938:1–22), DeMallie (1986), Fowler (1987), and D.R. Miller (1987).

The ethnographic accounts by Denig (1930, 1961), written in the 1850s, present an extensive and detailed picture of Assiniboine culture by a fur trader who spent two decades at Fort Union and was married to an Assiniboine woman. Ethnographic field studies include Curtis (1907–1930, 3), Lowie (1909), Rodnick (1938), and Ewers (1955a, 1956). J.L. Long (in Kennedy 1961), a tribal member, recorded cultural data and personal narratives in the 1930s under the auspices of the Montana Writers' Program (originally published in Writers' Program 1942).

Oral traditions are published in Lowie (1909, 1960b), Kennedy (1961), and D. Phillips (1979). D. Kennedy (1972) presents the memoirs of a Canadian Assiniboine chief.

For the linguistic classification of Assiniboine see Parks and DeMallie (1992). The earliest linguistic publication on Assiniboine is Denig (1854). Hollow (1970) presents Assiniboine phonology. Levin's (1964) grammar is unreliable. An unpublished dictionary and collection of texts have been compiled by Parks and DeMallie (1996, 1983–1988). Farnell (1995) includes Assiniboine narratives, simultaneously spoken and signed, and presents them with movement transcriptions in Labanotation.

Assiniboine art and artifacts are described in Lowie (1909), Dusenberry (1960), Ewers (1982), and VanStone (1996).

Significant collections of Assiniboine artifacts are found in the American Museum of Natural History, New York, and the Field Museum of Natural History, Chicago.

Stoney

IAN A.L. GETTY AND ERIK D. GOODING

Language and Territory

The Stoney (ˈstōnē) are the northwesternmost Siouan-speaking peoples of the Great Plains. Often confused with the closely related Assiniboine, the Stoney are identified in the fur trade period as comprising two groups, the Mountain Stoney and the Wood Stoney (Parks and DeMallie 1992:248–250; E.D. Cook and Owens 1991:145; Andersen 1968, 1970). The Stoney are part of the Sioux-Assiniboine-Stoney language continuum* and are the only Siouan group who live entirely in Canada (Parks and DeMallie 1992).

The contemporary Stoney live on five reserves in Alberta (fig. 1) (Dempsey 1986a; Laurie 1957–1959, 1:1). The Mountain Stoney consist of the Bearspaw, Chiniki, and Wesley (Goodstoney) bands, who share the largest of the Stoney reserves, located at Morley, Alberta (Indian Reserve 142, 143, 144), as well as two satellite reserves, Big Horn (I.R. 144A) and Eden Valley (I.R. 216). The Stoney Reserve at Morley, established in 1879, contains 109 square miles along the Bow River, about 30 miles from Calgary. The bands were named after the three Stoney chiefs who attended Treaty No. 7 in 1877. The 5,000-acre Big Horn Reserve, about 100 miles north of Morley, just below the Kootenay Plains, is composed of members of the Wesley Band. The Eden Valley Reserve, also comprising 5,000 acres, is about 80 miles south of Morley.

The Wood Stoney comprise the two northernmost bands, living on reserves located about 50 miles west of Edmonton. The Alexis Reserve (I.R. 133) is at Lac Sainte Anne near the town of Glenevis, and Paul's Reserve (I.R. 133A) is on Lake Wabamun near the town of Duffield.

It is likely that all the Stoney groups interacted with one another during the precontact period and were joined by other Assiniboine or Sioux families over the centuries. The Bearspaw elders tell of groups migrating west to the mountains to escape the diseases decimating tribes farther east (MacEwan 1969:22). Historically their territory ranged from the plains, where they hunted buffalo, to the Rocky Mountain foothills and watersheds, where they trapped fur animals and hunted big game. By the fur trade era (marked by the arrival of the Hudson's Bay Company in 1670) Stoney were allied with the Plains Cree and inveterate enemies of the Blackfoot tribes and their Sarcee allies. Around the beginning of the eighteenth century the Mountain Stoney made peace with the Kootenai and Shuswap of interior British Columbia and formed close alliances with them.

History, 1690s–1870s

Little is known about the Stoney in the early contact period. The "Mountain Poets" encountered by Henry Kelsey in 1690–1691 when he journeyed along the Saskatchewan River may have been Stoney groups (Laurie 1957–1959, 1:5). When Hudson's Bay Company trader Anthony Henday (Hendry) wintered in central Alberta in 1754–1755, he acknowledged the assistance of "Assiniboine" families who were doubtless Stoneys (MacGregor 1954).

The Stoney came into regular contact with European traders after the 1770s when the rival trading companies, the Hudson's Bay Company and the North West Company, rapidly built posts at Fort Edmonton and near Rocky Mountain House. They traded furs and meat for goods imported from Europe and central Canada. The Wood Stoney inhabited the lake and forest region west of Edmonton, extending to the headwaters of the North Saskatchewan and Athabasca rivers (Andersen 1968:50). This period brought profound change for all Plains tribes as the buffalo herds began to diminish during the mid-nineteenth century.

Along with economic change came the first Christian missionaries. From 1840–1848 Robert T. Rundle, an English Methodist, was sent to Rupert's Land to serve the community of Fort Edmonton (Rundle 1977). Each summer he traveled along the foothills from Rocky Mountain House to the Bow River to proselytize among the Stoney

*The phonemes of the northern dialect of Stoney (spoken by the Wood Stoney on the Alexis and Paul reserves) are: (lax unaspirated stops and affricate) *p*, *t*, *č*, *k*, ʔ; (voiceless aspirated stops and affricate) *pʰ*, *tʰ*, *čʰ*, *kʰ*; (glottalized stops and affricate) *ṗ*, *ṫ*, *ċ*, *k̇*; (voiceless spirants) *s* ([θ], [s]), *š* ([ṣ], [s], [š]), *x* ([x̣], [x]), *h*; (voiced spirants) *z* ([ð], [z]), *ž* ([ẓ], [z], [ž]), *γ* ([ʁ], [γ]); (nasals) *m*, *n*; (semivowels) *w*, *y*; (short oral vowels) *i*, *e*, *a*, *o*, *u*; (long oral vowels) *i·*, *e·*, *a·*, *o·*, *u·*; (nasal vowels [phonetically long]) *į*, *ę*, *ą*, *ǫ*, *ų*; (stress) v́. The lax series is voiced intervocalically; the velar fricatives may be pharyngealized, especially by older speakers. A phonetic glottal stop is present before phonemic initial vowels. The southern dialect (spoken by the Mountain Stoney on the Morley Reserve) has a voiceless aspirated series corresponding to both the aspirated and glottalized series of the northern dialect, contrasting with a voiced series. This phonemic analysis follows the transcription in E.-D. Cook (1995); information on dialect differences and transcriptions of Stoney words in this chapter are from Eung-Do Cook (communications to editors 1998).

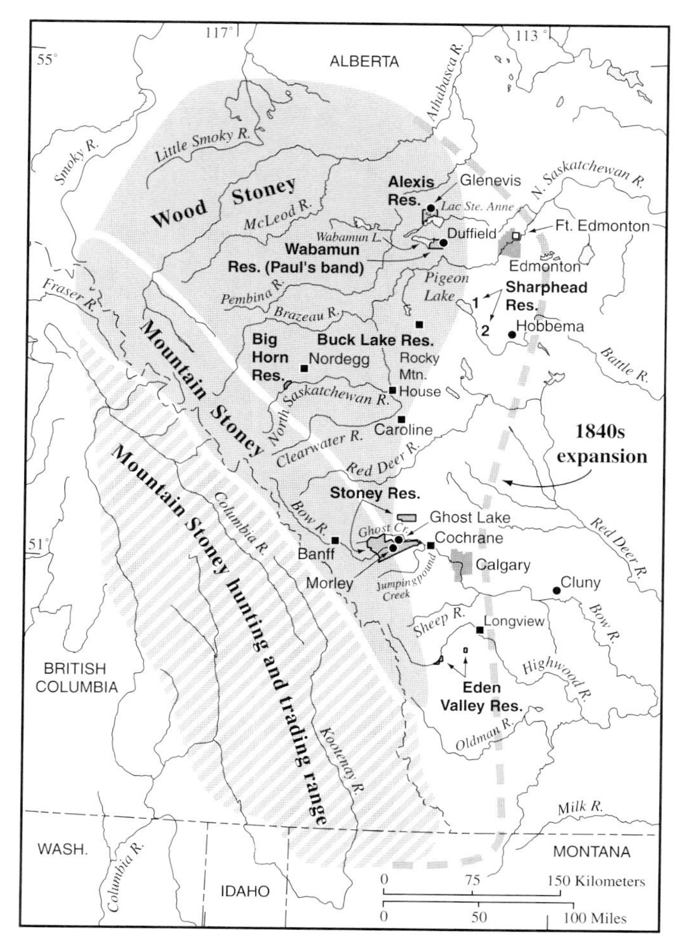

Fig. 1. Territory in the early 19th century, with modern reservations, towns, and cities.

and their Plains Cree allies, whose territory extended from northwest of Edmonton as far south as Chief Mountain (in northern Montana) and into interior British Columbia (Laurie 1957–1959, 1:22; Snow 1977:18–26). Rundle preached to the encamped families at every opportunity and left a lasting legacy of spirituality. His replacement, Thomas Woolsey, arrived from England in 1855. In 1860 George McDougall arrived in Edmonton with his family and began to build the infrastructure for the Methodist Church in western Canada. Mission posts were started at Pakan (Victoria) and Pigeon Lake (Hutchinson in Rundle 1977). In 1873 the most southerly Methodist mission was established by McDougall and his son, John C. McDougall, at Morleyville, on the Bow River, where the Stoney Reserve was surveyed in 1879.

Culture

Stoney subsistence patterns reflected their adaptation to various environments extending from the prairies to the forest lands of the eastern slopes of the Rocky Mountains. The Alexis and Paul's bands resided in a forest and lake region where they relied on a mixture of hunting, trapping, and fishing (Andersen 1968). To the south of Rocky Mountain House, the Bearspaw, Chiniki, and Wesley groups occupied the foothills and headwaters along the front range of the Rocky Mountains. They relied mainly on big game such as moose, elk, deer, bighorn sheep, and wood buffalo, supplemented by beaver and muskrats as well as the traditional gathering of wild plants and fruits and the occasional purchase of processed foods from the trading posts. Because of their close proximity to the plains, the various Stoney groups relied on a mixture of resources from the forests and plains; their lifeway closely resembled the horse and buffalo culture of neighboring Plains groups (Laurie 1957–1959, 1:2; Andersen 1968). When hunting buffalo the Stoney preferred the pound technique perfected by their Assiniboine relations.

In addition to buffalo, the Stoney also hunted moose, deer, elk, and other animals. They borrowed from the Shuswap the technique of snaring moose using rawhide ropes suspended over the moose trails. Unlike most Plains tribes, fish were important to the Stoney diet. They were caught using three-tined spears, arrows, hooks and lines of bone and twisted inner bark of willow, and fish traps (Curtis 1907–1930, 18:164, 166).

Bows were made from birch, willow, or serviceberry and backed with sinew for strength. Arrows were made from serviceberry shoots (Curtis 1907–1930, 18:166).

The Stoney lived in local bands, characteristically made up of patrilineal extended family groups that camped together for large-scale hunts and religious ceremonies. Each band was led by a chief recognized for his abilities and inherited influence. Primarily nomadic, the more northerly groups would gather near lakes to engage in intensive fishing and during the winter months the family units would spread out into protected areas in the river valleys (Snow 1977:xii; Curtis 1907–1930, 18:167).

Stoney kin terminology was largely identical to the Assiniboine, but with the addition of distinctive terms for father's brother and mother's sister. Stoney men classified their brother's children as "stepchild," reflecting the prevalence of the levirate, which maintained an ongoing relationship between families even after a man's death (Curtis 1907–1930, 18:169–170).

Marriage was negotiated between two families. Customarily, horses were presented to the girl's family, if the marriage was approved, the girl was escorted by her relatives to the husband's tepee. Cross-cousin marriage was regularly practiced, as was polygyny (Curtis 1907–1930, 18:171).

The Stoney had a single men's society, the Soldiers (*akíčʰita*), composed of young, unmarried men known for their bravery. Their society lodge was pitched in the center of camp, where the Soldiers lived, always ready to mediate disturbances and defend the camp against enemies. The Soldiers were believed to have spiritual power; however, they lost their power when they married and were no longer members of the society (Curtis 1907–1930, 18:167–168).

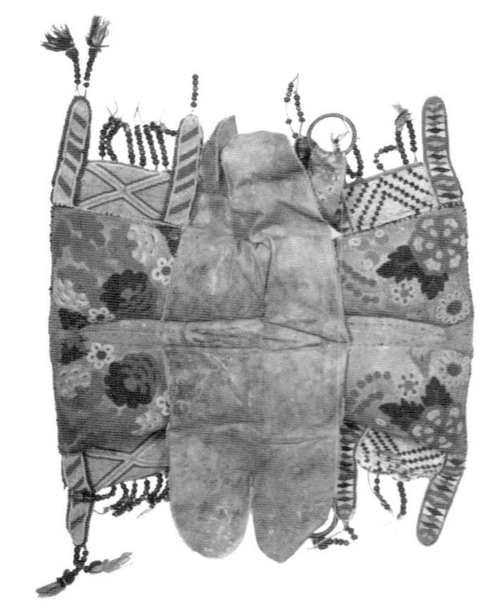

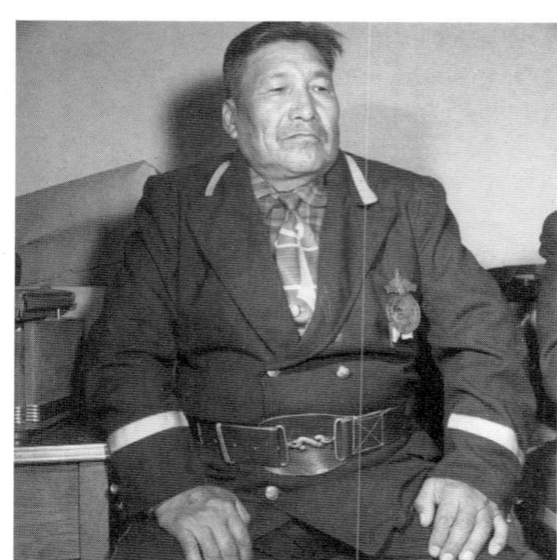

Glenbow-Alberta Inst., Calgary: top left, NA-7-54, top center, ND-14-25, center right, AF-3598, bottom left, NA-1241-210, bottom right, NA-2557-22; Prov. Arch. of Alta., Edmonton: H. Pollard Coll.: top right, P-170, center left, P-56; bottom center, Prov. Arch. of Man., Winnipeg: Edmund Morris Coll.: 165.

Fig. 2. 20th-century life. top left, William Snow, a medicine man of the Wesley Band, seated at entrance to spruce-bark-covered tepee. A canvas tepee is in the background. Photograph by Dan McCowan, probably Banff, Alta., 1948. top center, Children from Banff or Stoney Res., Alta., beside their play tepee made of flour sacks. The girl on the left has a beaded belt and wears a large shell necklace. The boy on the right wears leather cuffs in imitation of adult male attire and holds 2 painted drums. Photograph probably by Norman Luxton, 1915–1920. top right, Chief White Head or Hector Crawler (b. 1850, d. 1933) and wife Nancy during Banff Indian Days wearing heavily beaded clothing including gauntlets, belt, vest, and yoke on dress. He holds a decorated gun case and she holds a feather fan. Both wear eagle-feather headdresses and stand in front of a painted skin tepee. Photograph by Harry Pollard, near Cochrane, Alta., 1916. center left, John Hunter on a horse decorated with painted hands on flank and shoulder. He pulls a travois with two small children on it. To the left is Peter Ear wearing beaded breechcloth and moccasins, fringed cloth leggings and a fur collar. Both men hold lances. To the right is Dan Wildman, Sr., mounted, pulling travois and holding a bow and arrows. Photograph by Harry Pollard, Stoney Res., Morley, Alta., 1907–1910. center right, Man's pad saddle. The saddle is elaborately beaded with geometric designs and large pink and mauve flowers with green leaves at each corner. Blue flowers with yellow centers and green leaves decorate the interior sections. Collected by John Alfred Kidd, Morley, Alta., before 1907; length 53 cm. bottom left, Lazarus Dixon, Bearspaw Band, in hunting clothing at Banff Indian Days. He has a medicine bag tied to his fur belt; feathers and the head and foot of a tundra swan are around his neck. Photograph by Fern Gully, 1938–1948. bottom center, Chief Peter Wesley (d. 1935) and the painter Edmund Morris. Wesley's fur jacket has decorations of ermine strips on the sleeves and beaded shoulder epaulets. His leggings are also decorated with beaded strips and ermine. Photographed at Morley, Alta., 1908. bottom right, Isaac Twoyoungmen (b. 1900, d. 1965), chief of Wesley Band and a member of a delegation that boycotted the federal election in June 1962, the first they were eligible to vote in, fearing that voting would lead to infringements of their treaty rights. He is wearing a medal depicting a sun over a mountain range with the inscription "Friendship, Loyalty, Progress." His suit with gold stripes and the "snake belt," a Canadian militia uniform of about 1900, were presented to him when he was elected chief in 1960. Photographed in Calgary, Alta., 1962.

The primary dwelling for the Stoney was the tepee, which appeared in two forms. During the time of dog transport, prior to the introduction of horses in the early 1700s, the main habitation was the three-pole Plains-style hide tepee, which was constructed of buffalo or moose hides. The second form was a spruce bark–covered tepee used in semi-permanent encampments (fig. 2 top left). Other shelters were used, such as permanent pole and moss dwellings in the shape of a tepee, and temporary structures constructed from pine, spruce, and fir branches (Snow 1977:4–5).

Stoney spirituality was incorporated into every aspect of life. One of their forms of ritual expression was the Sun Dance, and they practiced many other ceremonies, including the naming of children, spiritual quests, rites of passage, and communal celebrations (Lowie 1909; Snow 1977:5–7). Individuals sought spiritual power and guidance on the vision quest, which was typically held at sacred areas in the mountains. After the arrival of missionaries, traditional religious beliefs and ceremonies began to incorporate Christian elements, including Sunday services, the singing of Cree hymns, and Bible teachings. The Christian presence became firmly rooted when reserves were established near mission stations, including those of the Roman Catholics at Alexis in 1842, the Methodists at Morley in 1873, and the Presbyterians at Paul's about 1899 (Snow 1977:16–26; Laurie 1957–1959, 1:30–37; Andersen 1968:74, 120).

History, 1870s–1970

The Stoney participated in two modern treaties with Canada. Treaty No. 6 was concluded with the Cree Nations at Fort Pitt and Fort Carlton in Saskatchewan in August 1876, and a year later Chief Alexis signed an adhesion to the treaty at Edmonton on August 21, 1877 (A. Morris 1880:360–361). The Sharphead people were initially listed as Pigeon Lake Indians in the 1877 treaty paylists and then described as Sharphead's Band in 1878. They followed a traditional lifeway of hunting and fishing in the Pigeon Lake area just west of the four bands of Plains Cree at Hobbema, Alberta, under Chiefs Ermineskin, Samson, Muddy Bull (now Louis Bull Band), and Bobtail (now Montana Band) (Titley 1991). By 1882 they had moved to Wolf Creek and Battle River where in 1885 a 42.4-square-mile (22,912 acres) reserve was set aside for the Wolf Creek Stoney or Sharphead people. Within five years illness reduced the population by 60 percent, and the Sharphead families dispersed to escape the devastating epidemics. In 1894 the Indian Department deemed the Sharphead Reserve (I.R. 141) to be abandoned (Titley 1991). In the early 1890s Sharphead survivors moved onto other Stoney reserves, a few to Alexis and Morley; but the majority, 61 members, settled on the Paul Reserve in 1890–1892. Chief John Sharphead retired to the Morley Reserve along with three or four other families, and a similar number joined the Samson and Ermineskin Cree reserves at Hobbema. The official surrender of the reserve was taken in 1897 under questionable circumstances, nor was the decision acceded to by the majority of male members as required by the Indian Act. In the 1990s the Sharphead descendants organized to attempt to reconstitute the band and receive compensation for the loss of their original reserve.

Under the terms of Treaty No. 7 made in September 1877 at Blackfoot Crossing (located on the Bow River south of Cluny on the Siksika Reserve of the Blackfoot), the Bearspaw, Chiniki, and Wesley groups were specifically limited to settling on reserve lands in the vicinity of Morleyville (later Morley) where the Methodist mission was located. The mission included a church, orphanage school, agricultural crops, a sawmill, and a trading post. At the time of the treaty Stoney territory extended from the Athabasca headwaters down along the headwaters of the Brazeau, North Saskatchewan, Clearwater, Red Deer, Ghost, Bow, Jumping Pound, Sheep, Highwood, Pekisko, and Old Man river watersheds, and extended into northern Montana, Idaho, and the interior of British Columbia. John C.

McDougall served as an advisor and translator to the Stoney leaders at Treaty No. 7, where he signed as a witness to the consenting signatories who marked an X by their names recorded in the Cree language. At this time, the Wesley people camped in the northern part of their territory on the Kootenay Plains and the Red Deer River area; the Chiniki group camped in the Bow valley from Morleyville to Banff; and the Bearspaw were divided into two groups that camped south of the Bow River along the foothills. The southern camp was known as the Dixon Band after their headman, James Dixon, and they later formed the core population of the Eden Valley Reserve.

The completion of the Canadian Pacific Railway in 1885 and the concurrent establishment of nearby Banff National Park had an immediate impact upon Stoney hunting practices and their relative isolation from Canadian civilization. They remained largely independent of government assistance during the 1880s, but eventually even the big game came under pressure from resource development adjacent to the Morley Reserve. Around 1895, several families under the leadership of Peter Wesley (Moosekiller) (fig. 2 bottom center) moved back to the Kootenay Plains area and began a quest for their own permanent reserve. Since 1900 several additions to the land base at Morley have been made, beginning in 1914 with Rabbit Lake Reserve (I.R. 142B), containing 12,742.60 acres, now part of Stoney Reserve. In 1929 compensation monies from the Ghost Lake dam were used to buy two ranch properties of 1,547.99 and 427.9 acres. In 1945 a loan of $500,000 was made to the Morley bands from the federal government, which they used to purchase two more properties, the Coppock Ranch comprised of 7,012.57 acres and the Crawford Ranch containing 1,865 acres. In the 1950s the Stoney tribal council used a portion of the loan funds to make purchases of 985.9 acres, 1,914.3 acres, and 1,120 acres along the Highwood River west of Longview. These were consolidated into Eden Valley Reserve.

To the north in the Kootenay Plains area west of Nordegg, Alberta, the Big Horn Reserve was set aside by the provincial and federal governments in 1947–1948. Although the elders understood that additional lands would be added to it, the reserve remains at its original location and size. The Big Horn group continues to petition the federal government to fulfill their treaty land entitlement in accordance with the spirit and intent of Treaty No. 7. They remain caught between a jurisdictional dispute under the 1930 Natural Resources Transfer Act (subsequently called the Constitution Act of 1930) by which Canada could force the Alberta government to make lands available for Indian reserve purposes to satisfy a treaty land entitlement. Additions to the Stoney land base include the purchases of the 2,490.24-acre Two Rivers Ranch near Morley in 1976; the 468.69-acre Nelson property near Longview in 1979; the 318.94 acres of farm land near Caroline in 1982; the 320-acre Cartwright land adjacent to Eden Valley Reserve in 1984; the 2,489.69-acre Richard Copithorne Ranch east of Morley in 1986; and parcels of 8.56 acres at Scott Lake Hill in 1981 and 160 acres from Oland Construction at Morley in 1980 (Stoney Tribal Administration 1986).

The rapid social and economic changes following World War II shaped Stoney culture and social attitudes. At the same time individuals continued their traditional lifeways, acting as hunting and fishing guides in the mountain valleys, and continuing to hunt, fish, and trap despite the creation of designated conservation parks that restricted their access to Crown lands, with no regard to treaty rights.

Renewal of Self-Government, 1970s–1990s

The Stoney at Morley assumed more control over their administration affairs in 1968 under the new self-government policies of the Canadian government. One of the first decisions made by the tribal council in 1969 was to start research into treaty land claims. The catalyst was the hydroelectric dam, jointly planned by Calgary Power (subsequently TransAlta) and the Alberta provincial government, on the North Saskatchewan River three miles upstream from the Big Horn Reserve (W.E.A. Getty 1975). The resulting reservoir flooded lands used by the Big Horn Stoney, including burial grounds, Sun Dance lodges, fur trap lines, hunting grounds, camping sites, and grazing lands (Snow 1977:101–103). Nine years following this loss, the Alberta provincial government transferred 1,277.91 acres to the federal government for the use of the Big Horn people, but it has not acknowledged their aboriginal and treaty land claim.

In the 1960s vast deposits of natural gas were discovered under Stoney reserve lands at Morley. People were partly self-sufficient from big game hunting, trapping, and gathering, but during the 1970s the people benefited from gas royalties, which encouraged ranching, a sawmill operation, tourism, and business enterprises. Income from the mineral royalties was shared through per capita distributions (which peaked in the early 1980s but were eliminated in the late 1990s), and band funds were used for housing construction, community infrastructure, employment, education scholarships, and many other community services such as health, recreation, business development, and treatment centers. After peaking at over $50 million dollars in the early 1980s, gas revenues declined steadily to one-quarter of the peak years (Stoney Tribal Administration 1986).

Education and job training were funded by federal employment training programs. The Oral History Program, begun in 1970, recorded hundreds of interviews with elders, with a focus on land claims, aboriginal and treaty rights, teachings, and recording traditional place-names. In 1972 the research and language programs were united into the innovative Stoney Cultural Education Program, which recorded oral history, worked to preserve the Stoney language, and developed educational curriculum materials (Snow 1977:135–136).

The Stoney Economic Development department began to implement the socioeconomic plan prepared for the council in 1970 (Underwood, McLellan, and Associate Ltd. 1970). The Stoney Indian Park was developed as a tourist camping facility on the banks of the Bow River and Bowfort Creek (where the 1832 Hudson's Bay Company trading post was located). A gas service station and food store were constructed in 1975, and the Stoney Wilderness Centre operated during the 1970s at Chief Hector Lake (the former site of a YMCA summer camp for non-Indians) (Snow 1977:137, 158).

The Stoney benefited dramatically from the rise in natural gas revenues. The Stoney Health Centre was opened in 1973, a modern administration building was opened in 1978, and cattle ranching was expanded at the S.T.A.R. ranch (Stoney Tribal Agricultural and Ranching). Gas revenues were used to purchase agricultural and ranching lands totaling 6,273 acres at a cost of $8,790,000 (Stoney Tribal Administration 1986). Tribal funds were used to enhance community services including fire trucks, social and health services, the Stoney Medicine Lodge for drug abuse treatment, an elders' center, and a day care center. Dozens of new homes were built or renovated, fences built, roads upgraded, and septic systems installed at a cost of over $31 million dollars from 1976–1986, after which gas revenues rapidly declined.

In 1989–1990 the first specific claim for the Stoney was validated by the Canadian federal government for negotiation involving lost gas royalties. As a result of the unauthorized loss of mineral rights when the Ghost Lake hydroelectric dam was constructed in 1930, the Stoney people received a $19.6 million settlement in 1990. Twelve million dollars was put in a trust fund, $4 million was marked for economic development, and $3 million was distributed to the 3,000 band members.

The Nakoda Lodge opened in May 1981 as a conference center and base camp for the Wilderness School. The Chief Chiniki Restaurant and handicraft shop was built on the Trans Canada Highway at the exit to the Morley townsite in 1979, which was expanded in 1988 to serve the Calgary Winter Olympics. The adjacent Nakoda Learning Centre contains a museum and art gallery, library, archives, films and photographs of the Stoney people (Nakoda Lodge Brochure 1998). The indoor Chief Goodstoney Rodeo Centre was built in 1982–1983.

The Morley Community School, opened in 1985, provides bicultural education to over 500 students from kindergarten to high school. In 1986 "control over all educational Programs in Morley was transferred from the Department of Indian and Northern Affairs to the Stoney Education Authority. We view this accomplishment with pride and dignity and see it as one of the best means of investing in our most precious legacy—our children" (Stoney Tribal Administration 1986).

Since the mid-twentieth century, the Stoney have experienced a renewal in traditional spirituality. In particular, the Sun Dance (outlawed under the Indian Act until 1951) was more openly and frequently sponsored (fig. 3 top). There was an attempt to bridge the cultural gap between ceremonialists and Christian believers through the North American Indian Ecumenical Gathering held annually at the Stoney Indian Park beginning in 1972 (Snow 1977:142–149). Elders, medicine men and women, clergymen, ceremonial leaders, political militants, and young people were drawn to this spiritual gathering and celebration of culture. They shared their spiritual teachings and powers, centered around the

Nakoda Inst., Morley, Alta.

Fig. 3. The continuation of traditional culture in the 1970s. top, Jake Rabbit's Sun Dance lodge frame with Mt. Laurie in the background, Stoney Res., Morley, Alta., June 1978. center, George Ear (b. 1910, d. 1994), well-known story teller, relating a tale to the younger generation, Stoney Indian Park, Morley, Alta., 1974. bottom, Frances Snow (b. 1928) demonstrating the preparation of moose hide, Stoney Wilderness Centre camp, Nakoda Lodge, Stoney Res., Morley, Alta., June 1978. Photographs by Warren Harbeck and Tommy Snow.

sacred fire that burned day and night throughout the conference. According to Chief John Snow, "Often people would gather around the Sacred Fire for prayers, meditations, telling stories, sharing experiences, and encouraging one another in the journey of life" (Stoney Tribal Administration 1986). The last gathering was held in 1992.

In the 1990s the Stoney conducted tribal business and conversation in the Stoney language. During the summer Stoney groups hosted powwows and traveled throughout Canada and the United States dancing, singing, and assisting in the powwows of other peoples. The Stoney held Round Dances and feasts to mark Thanksgiving, Christmas, and New Year's celebrations. They were famous for their singing abilities, and several singing groups, including the Stoney Park, Eya-hey Nakoda, Chiniki Lake, Ta-Otha Spirit, Little Boy, and Logan Alexis singers were award winners.

The Alexis and Paul reserves enjoyed a degree of prosperity from oil and gas revenues beginning in the 1970s. Although small (Alexis has 15,259 acres; Paul has three reserves totaling 18,112 acres), both communities are close to non-Indian services in nearby towns and the city of Edmonton. The Alexis people opened a school in 1990 that was expanded to accommodate a high school in 1994. As members of the Yellowhead Tribal Council based in Enoch (a neighboring Cree reserve), they have emphasized educational and employment opportunities off their reserves. The band operates a convenience store and gas station and provides community services.

The Paul Reserve facilities include a band administration office, arena, day care, health clinic, treatment center, and seniors' home. Their main economic enterprise is an 18-hole golf course. The community school serves kindergarten to grade 9.

Population

Like their Assiniboine relatives, the Stoney suffered significant population loses from epidemic diseases after contact, but there are no reliable population statistics from before the reserve period. Population counts were 556 in 1877 (Treaty Paylist 1877), 647 in 1885 (Dominion of Canada. Department of Indian Affairs 1886), and 570 in 1895 (Dominion of Canada. Department of Indian Affairs 1897). In 1997 the population of Alexis Reserve was 1,219; Paul Reserve, 1,428. Morley Reserve registered 3,393 among the Bearspaw, Chiniki, and Wesley Bands, but 479 of these lived on Eden Valley Reserve and 133 lived on Big Horn Reserve (Department of Indian Affairs, personal communication 1998).

Synonymy†

The Stoney refer to themselves as *nak*^{h}*óta* (northern dialect), pronounced [nak^{h}óda] in the southern dialect and written Nakoda in the practical orthography used for both dialects (Eung-Do Cook, communication to editors 1998; Scott 1912–1934). The same term of self-designation is used by the Assiniboine and, in its cognate forms, by the Teton, Yankton-Yanktonai, and Santee Sioux. The Stoney use the same term to refer to the Assiniboine and Sioux (Laurie 1957–1959, 4:93). To differentiate themselves from the Assiniboine, the Stoney modify the name with the term *iyéska* (Paul *í·ska*; Morley *iyéθka*): (Morley) nakóda iyéθka (Laurie 1957–1959, 4:93). They also use *iyéska* (pl. *iyéskapi)* alone as their self-designation (Parks and DeMallie 1985; Allan R. Taylor, personal communication 1998), cited as Eeaiska, 1809 (Henry the Younger in Gough 1988–1992, 2:393), Escab (Franklin 1823:104), Yes-kaȟ-be (Barker 1890:177), and Eeyaythka (Laurie 1957–1959, 4:93). The Assiniboine refer to the Stoney as *t*^{h}*éhą nak*^{h}*óta* 'far off Nakota' (Lowie 1909:34; Parks and DeMallie 1996:272). A similar designation is Gros Ventre Niniwi-nátyinéhĭn 'northern Assiniboine' (Curtis 1907–1930, 5:154).

Surrounding tribes commonly designate the Stoney as 'Assiniboine', a name that literally means 'stone' or 'stone Sioux.' The Plains Cree call both Stoney and Assiniboine *asini·pwa·t* 'stone Sioux' (H. Christoph Wolfart, personal communication 1987); the Ojibwa use the same name, *assini·-pwa·n* (Baraga 1878–1880:246, phonemicized). In Sweet Grass Plains Cree the Stoney are *opwa·si·mo·w* (Bloomfield 1930:296), literally 'Sioux speaker' (Wolfart in vol. 17:439), also the name for the Assiniboine (Bloomfield 1934:138). The Crow designation is *mi·mi·naxpâ·ge* 'stone people' (Medicine Horse 1987:15), in contrast to the name for the Assiniboine, which means 'yellow bone'.

The contemporary designation Stoney derives from the preceding name. In the nineteenth century, variants in English translation became commonplace. By the late nineteenth century the plural form Stonies had become the most common name among the English in Canada (C.N. Bell in Hodge 1907–1910, 1:105). Other forms include Stone and Stoney, 1878 (Keane in Stanford in Hodge 1907–1910, 1:105) and Sioux of the Rocks (ARCIA 1850:77).

Another common designation for the Stoney refers to their location along the Rocky Mountains. The earliest recorded name is Mountain Poets, 1690–1691 (Kelsey in Russell 1991:180) or Mountain Sioux, which reflects the Cree name. Other forms include Rocky Mountain Sioux (MacEwan 1969:22), Mountain Stoneys (Maclean 1896:21), and Rocky Mountain Stoney Indians (Christie 1874:34).

The Blackfoot and Blood name for the Stoney is *sa·hsáísso?kitakiwa* (Frantz and Russell 1989:221), rendered also as saxsísokitaki (Uhlenbeck and van Gulick 1930:213) and *sa·xsáso·kitaki* (Allan R. Taylor, personal communication 1987), which has been translated literally as 'mountain dwellers' (Curtis 1907–1930, 18:186). The Piegan name was recorded as Saȟsís-sókitaki (Curtis 1907–1930, 6:155).

Two anomolous Gros Ventre designations for the Stoney are *níįkin?ihíhk?i* (sg.) 'far jumper' and *niih?ɔ́tɔɔhéíhích niih?ɔ́tɔɔhéíhích* (pl.) 'having tight pants', the latter a relatively recent name (Taylor 1994:297).

†This synonymy was written by Douglas R. Parks.

In the Plains sign language, the sign of cutting the throat, which designates the Sioux and Assiniboine, is also used for the Stoney (Mallery 1881:462; W.P. Clark 1885:50; H.L. Scott 1912–1934). That sign is reflected in another Stoney self-designation wàpeṁaksa 'cut throats' (Barbeau 1960:164), also cited as wapamathe (Snow 1977:8).

Divisions

Beginning at the very end of the eighteenth century, in the fur trade literature two groups are recognized, the Mountain Stoney and the Wood Stoney. Previous to that time it is impossible to distinguish the Stoney from the Assiniboine.

• MOUNTAIN STONEY This group was designated the Strong Wood Assiniboines, 1794 (M'Gillivray in Morton 1929:34) and 1809 (Henry the Younger in Gough 1988–1992, 2:376; Maclean 1896:21), Thickwood, 1878 (Keane in Stanford in Hodge 1907–1910, 1:105), and Plains Assiniboine (H.L. Scott 1912–1934).

• WOOD STONEY This group, which lived in the forest, was known as the Swampy Ground Stone Indians, 1799 (James Bird in A.M. Johnson 1967:202), Swampy Ground Assiniboines, 1809 (Henry the Younger in Gough 1988–1992, 2:376; Maclean 1896:21) and Swampy Ground (H.L. Scott 1912–1934). They were also known as the Tshanha'ndabing 'woods people' or Wood Stonies (Barbeau 1960:164).

Sources

The primary ethnographic sources on the Stoney are Barbeau (1960), Laurie (1957–1959), Lowie (1909), Curtis (1907–1930, 18:163–176), Niddrie (1992), and Snow (1977) for the Mountain Stoney and Andersen (1968) for the Wood Stoney.

The most informative nineteenth-century primary sources include Rundle's journals, 1840–1848 (Rundle 1977); the writings of Thomas Woolsey, 1855–1869 (Dempsey 1989), the Earl of Southesk's narrative, 1859–1860 (1875); the Palliser expedition, 1857–1860 (Spry 1968); and the writings of John McDougall (1911, 1970).

Twentieth-century sources include Breton (1920), Pocaterra (1963), MacEwan (1969), Munroe (1969), Medicine (1970), Andersen (1970), Getty and Larner (1972), W.E.A. Getty (1974, 1975), Larner (1972, 1976), Dempsey (1986a), Harbeck, Kaquitts, and Snow (1980), Chumak (1983), Jonker (1983, 1988), Notzke (1985, 1987, 1987a), P. Parker (1990), Titley (1991), and Treaty No. 7 Elders et al. (1996).

Stoney language information is found in Laurie (1957–1959), Bellam (1976), Harbeck, Kaquitts, and Snow (1980), A.R. Taylor (1981), Shaw (1985), E.-D. Cook and Owens (1991), Parks and DeMallie (1992), and E.-D. Cook (1995). Chiniki Research Team (1987) presents material on place-names.

Material on education is found in Botari (1996), Gibson (1983), and Harbeck (1973).

Major museum collections of Stoney materials are in the Glenbow Museum, Calgary, Alberta; the Luton Museum, Banff, Alberta; the White Museum of the Canadian Rockies, Banff; the Canadian Museum of Civilization, Hull, Quebec; and the Nakoda Learning Centre at Nakoda Lodge, Morley, Alberta.

Blackfoot

HUGH A. DEMPSEY

Language

The Blackfoot (ˈblăkˌfoŏt) are of Algonquian linguistic stock* and since historic times have been divided into three tribes: Blackfoot, Blood, and Piegan (ˈpāˌgăn), spelled Peigan in Canada. The Piegan developed northern and southern divisions, separated in the postreservation period by the United States–Canadian boundary. Allied to the confederated Blackfoot tribes were the Athapaskan-speaking Sarcee and the Algonquian-speaking Gros Ventre. The Gros Ventre separated from them after 1861 (Fowler 1987:49).

Prehistory

There are different opinions as to how long the Blackfoot have been plains dwellers. The belief that they were woodland dwellers who drifted onto the plains from the region of the Eagle Hills in Saskatchewan in the immediate precontact period has been rejected by Indians and some anthropologists (Thompson in Glover 1962:254; Hlady 1964:45–48; Walde 1894:126). Rather, there is a tradition that the Blackfoot resided between the North Saskatchewan and Bow rivers for an extended period prior to contact (Wissler 1910:17). The Blackfoot lifeway at the time of first European contact was predominantly Plains, with little or no discernible influence from woodland cultures of the Subarctic.

Territory and Environment

Blackfoot territory in the early historic period has been reconstructed as extending southward from the North Saskatchewan River to the Milk River, a tributary of the Missouri (fig. 1) (Heron in Chesterfield House 1823). This territory, bounded by the Rocky Mountains to the west and by the mouth of the Vermilion River on the east, consisted primarily of short-grass plains interspersed by deep coulees and streams running from west to east (Wissler 1910:8–13). During the summers, some streams dried up completely, as did many of the sloughs and lakes. Aspen, poplar, and birch were the main trees that managed to survive in the coulees. In the north, clumps of trees and bushes provided some shelter, while to the west, the tree-covered foothills of the Rocky Mountains were a primary source of lodgepole pine.

The weather was marked by hot dry summers and long cold winters, which often were interrupted by mild spells caused by warm chinook winds blowing across the mountains. Spring was often cool and wet, while autumns were warm and dry. The spring and summer were marked by violent thunderstorms, which were of religious significance to the tribes, while winter blizzards made traveling impossible for days at a time.

Culture Before Contact

The Blackfoot referred to the precontact period as the time when dogs were used either as pack animals or for drawing travois (fig. 2) (Ewers 1960:44–48).

The dwelling of the Blackfoot was the tepee, fashioned by women from six to eight buffalo cowhides. The poles were of lodgepole pine, which women attached to pack dogs to drag from camp to camp. Tepee covers were held in place by a combination of pegs and stones. On the open prairie, thousands of stone tepee rings still mark encampments throughout the Blackfoot hunting grounds (Forbis 1970:26–27; L.B. Davis 1983).

Technology

The main weapons of the Blackfoot were bows and arrows, lances with stone points, shields, and war clubs. A shield was almost three feet in diameter, large enough for a man to hide behind. They were made from the thick neck hide of the buffalo bull and could repel an arrow or lance thrust (Glover 1962:242). Such shields are illustrated at several pictograph sites in Blackfoot country, including some fine examples at Writing-on-Stone, Alberta (Conner and Conner 1971:15).

*The phonemes of Blackfoot are: (voiceless unaspirated stops) *p*, *t*, *k*, *ʔ*; (voiceless spirants) *s*, *h*; (nasals) *m*, *n*; (semivowels) *w*, *y*; (short vowels) *i*, *a*, *o*; (long vowels) *i·*, *a·*, *o·*; (diphthongs) *ai* ([ay], [ey], [ɛ], [æ]), *ao* ([aw], [ɔ]), *oi* ([ɔy], [ü]); (high pitch) v́, v́·, v́v́, (falling pitch) v̂·, v̂v. There are also vowel sequences. Word-final vowels are voiceless; some speakers do not pronounce word-final *-wa*, retaining the preceding vowel as voiced.

This phonemic analysis follows Frantz (1991:1–6). In his orthography the phonemes are written as follows: p, t, k, ’; s, h; m, n; w, y; i, a, o; ii, aa, oo; ai, ao, oi; (high pitch v́, v́v́, (falling pitch) v́v. Uncredited Blackfoot forms in italics in this chapter are from Frantz and Russell (1995) and Donald G. Frantz (communication to editors 1998); where so credited, forms in synonymies have been phonemicized by Allan R. Taylor.

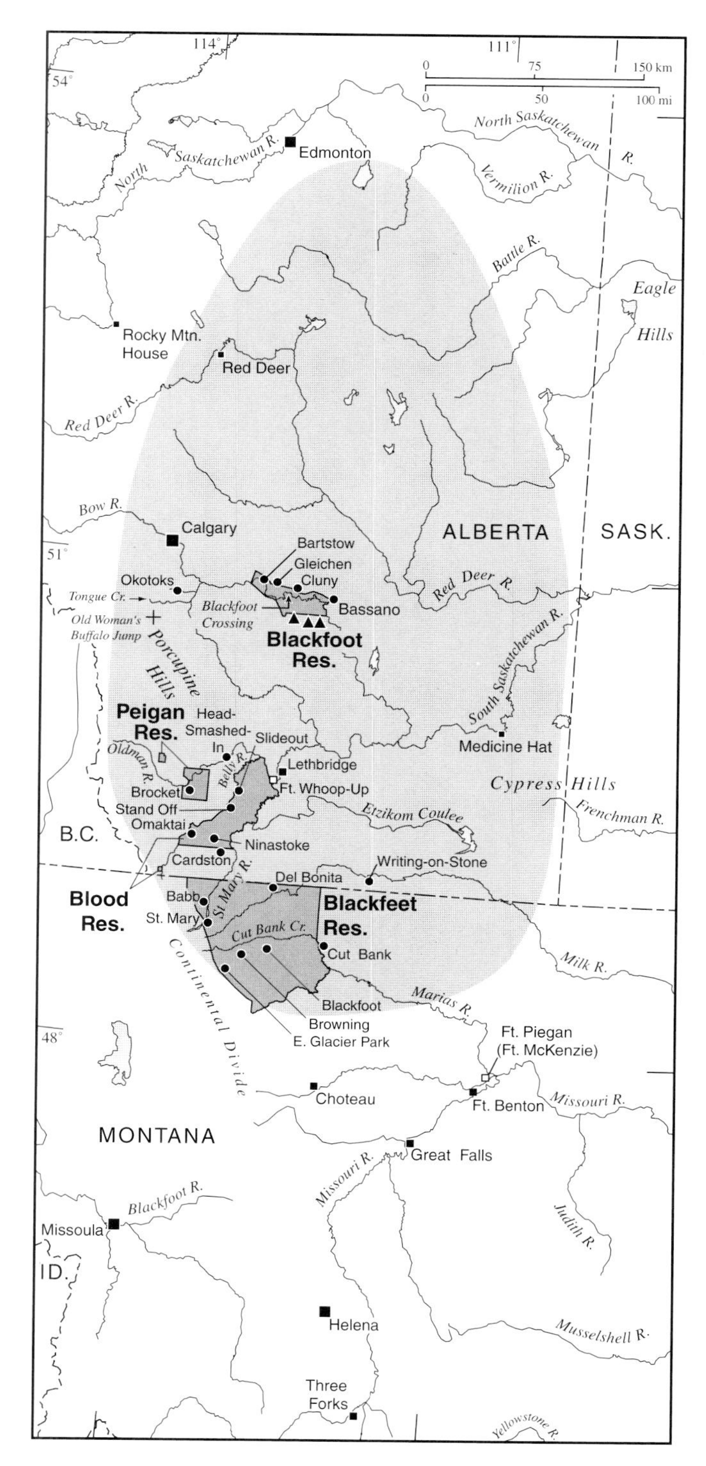

Fig. 1. Territory about 1800 with modern reservations and reserves.

Tools and weapons were made primarily of bone, wood, and stone. Tanning tools, such as scrapers, fleshers, and beamers, were fashioned from bone, with the scrapers having flaked stone blades. Vessels were made of clay, wood burls, and animal paunches, while ladles were of animal horn or wood.

Warfare

Skirmishes with enemy tribes undoubtedly occurred, particularly when hunting parties made incursions into enemy territory. If an attack was made upon an unsuspecting camp, the mortality rate could be high, but if two parties met on the open prairie, few fatalities occurred. The attacking parties lined up in rows facing each other just within the range of arrows and lances. Warriors placed their shields protectively in front of themselves and fired arrows at the opposing side until the honor of both forces had been satisfied (Glover 1962:242).

Subsistence

• BUFFALO SURROUND Of all the animals within their hunting grounds, the buffalo was the most important to the Blackfoot. Its flesh was called *ni·tá?piowahsini* 'real food', in contradistinction to all other flesh, believed to be inferior. In addition to its use for food, the buffalo provided many articles of utilitarian and religious value, including clothing, lodges, tools, drinking vessels, and storage containers.

The prehorse Blackfoot had several methods of hunting buffalo. One of the most popular was the surround, where hunters approached a small herd and drove it into a semicircle on the open prairie or sometimes into an enclosure made of dog travois placed upright in the earth and tied together to form a fence (Ewers 1960:45). The buffalo were then systematically killed with lances and arrows. Another method saw a hunter cover himself with the skin of a calf or wolf and approach the herd close enough to make a kill. After a snowstorm, hunters might drive buffalo into coulees where they floundered in the deep snow and were easily killed.

Perhaps the most successful hunting method was known as the *pisská·ni* 'buffalo jump' (Grinnell 1892:230) ("Environment and Subsistence," fig. 7, this vol.). In the autumn or early winter, hunters enticed a herd to the edge of a cliff and then stampeded the buffalo over the precipice. Those not killed by the fall were trapped below and dispatched with arrows and spears. In this way, a Blackfoot band might secure enough food to last for several weeks.

Buffalo jumps may have predated Blackfoot occupancy of the region. Archeological sites, notably Head-Smashed-In Buffalo Jump in southwest Alberta, have been dated at 3000 B.C. (Vickers 1986:61). Such sites were used because of the particular conditions along the foothills of the Rocky Mountains for this type of hunting. Not only was the area a favorite wintering ground for buffalo, but also steep cliffs provided ideal jump sites. These usually had a northern exposure because the prevailing winds prevented the animals from picking up the scent of the hunters and their camps (Verbicky-Todd 1984:111).

When a jump site was chosen, rocks, buffalo dung, or other materials were formed into piles, creating a V-shaped, irregular pair of drive lines, which extended for a

top, Glenbow-Alberta Inst., Calgary: NC-2-219; bottom left, Southern Methodist U., DeGolyer Lib., Dallas, Tex.: Ag82.102.1; bottom right, William Farr, Missoula, Mont.

Fig. 2. Travois. top, Blood woman with travois laden with tepee furnishings including backrests. The horse in the background has an eagle-feather headdress, hairpipe breastplate, and bag hanging from its saddle. Photograph by Arthur Rafton-Canning, Lethbridge, Alta., © 1910. bottom left, Dog travois. Photographed about 1890s. bottom right, Winter travel with travois. Blood woman from Canada leaning over the travois to shield her baby from being photographed. Photograph by Joseph Herbert Sherburne, Browning, Mont., 1898.

mile or more back from the cliff edge. The piles were high enough for people to hide behind during the actual hunt (Wissler 1910:35–36).

Before the drive began, holy men and women performed rituals involving songs, prayers, and the use of the *i·nísskimmi* 'buffalo stones' (fig. 3), frequently ammonites. The first of these, according to the Piegan, was believed to have been given directly by the buffalo spirit to Weasel Woman, who used it to attract the herds (Wissler and Duvall 1908:85).

Once a herd had been sighted, *áwaʔki·ksi* 'callers-in' were sent to lure the animals to the jump. Sometimes the buffalo callers allowed the animals to catch their scent and move off in the direction desired. At other times the men briefly showed themselves so that the buffalo would move but would not stampede. During this period of the hunt, which might take several days, the young men were constantly on the move, running along the outer perimeter of the herd to control their direction of travel (Dempsey 1957).

Peabody Mus. of Salem, Mass.: E26372.

Fig. 3. Buffalo stone made of flint. A rawhide cord covered with red ocher is attached so it can be worn around the neck. Collected by Frank G. Speck, before 1947; length with cord 40 cm.

Once the buffalo were within sight of the drive lines, the other hunters took their places behind the rock piles. Then, one man who had been chosen to act as a decoy came forward to entice the buffalo along the final leg of their journey. Wearing a buffalo robe complete with head and horns, he traveled ahead of the grazing herd, moving in and out of their view. These actions aroused the curiosity of the animals and, as they entered the wings of the drive lines, the other hunters suddenly jumped up, waving robes and shouting. As the buffalo stampeded forward, they were discouraged from leaving the narrowing lane by the people hidden behind the stone piles. If a buffalo went over the cliff and escaped unharmed, the jump had to be abandoned for several years, as it was believed that the animal would warn the other buffalo about the site (Verbicky-Todd 1984:120).

When the buffalo jump was successful, larger numbers of animals than needed were often killed as the herd stampeded over the cliff. However, the drive was not always successful. Sometimes the herd would not move according to plan but would stampede away. On other occasions, the buffalo would swerve from the drive lines, trampling to death anyone who stood in their way.

The Blackfoot located their hunt camp close to the base of the cliff, and from there the women came to butcher the animals. Because the hunt was a communal activity, the meat was shared equally among all the families who participated. On return to camp, prayers of thanksgiving were offered, followed by several days of feasting. If the weather was cold, the meat was kept on racks away from the dogs, but in warmer weather it was cut into strips and sun-dried.

The last buffalo jump was used by the Blood Indians during the winter of 1868–1869 and among the Piegans about 1874; however, this method of hunting buffalo had fallen out of common use by the 1850s when the availability of guns and horses rendered the system obsolete (Verbicky-Todd 1984:132–133).

• HUNTING AND GATHERING Other large mammals in Blackfoot territory included the grizzly bear, black bear, deer, elk, antelope, mountain sheep, and mountain goat. Lesser mammals sometimes used for food included the porcupine, rabbit, and squirrel. Domestic dogs were seldom eaten, and fish was used as food only in times of starvation (Wissler 1910:40). Birds were not primary sources of food although ducks, geese, swans, and prairie chickens were eaten when buffalo was not available.

Among the plants commonly used for food were a variety of berries, including serviceberries, blueberries, chokecherries, bullberries, and raspberries. Of these, serviceberries and chokecherries were the most widely used, particularly in making pemmican. This dish consisted of a mixture of pulverized dried meat, pounded dried berries, and hot marrow fat. It would keep for many months, stored in rawhide sacks, and was eaten cold or hot. Wild turnips, camas, rosebuds, and prickly pears also were eaten. Most vegetable foods were roasted or baked, while meat was boiled or baked over hot coals. One method of boiling was to place hot stones in a fresh paunch filled with water, and adding meat and berries to make soup (Wissler 1910:25–27).

History, 1730 to 1855

After 1730, the Blackfoot began to acquire their first horses. Fur trader David Thompson was told about the Piegans' reaction to the first sight of horses, ridden by their enemies, the Eastern Shoshone; they named the new animal "big dogs" (Thompson in Glover 1962:241–242), but subsequently called them "elk dogs" (Umfreville 1790:202).

During this period, the Blackfoot gained an advantage when they received their first European guns through Plains Cree middlemen. Thus, mounted on horses from the south and carrying firearms from the east, the Blackfoot rode into a new era. They had not yet seen a European but they were affected dramatically by his technology. By 1754, when they were visited by Anthony Henday, a Hudson's Bay Company trader, the Blackfoot were familiar with axes, knives (vol. 4:362), kettles, and other metal objects and had adapted a completely equestrian lifestyle (J.G. MacGregor 1972:29).

With horses, the Blackfoot expanded their methods of hunting, changed their concept of wealth, and increased their personal possessions. The horse enabled them to hunt buffalo by the chase, to carry more objects in their travels, and to move greater distances in a day. Their tepees increased in size, winter pasturage became a consideration in their lives, and more leisure time became available to develop artistic and religious pursuits (Ewers 1955:300–305).

Tribal wealth was measured in horses, with the sizes of herds varying at different periods of history. Around 1830, the Blackfoot and Blood were estimated to have owned about five horses per lodge while the Piegan had about 10 (Bradley 1923:288). Other surrounding tribes such as the Crow, Nez Perce, and Eastern Shoshone were considered to be richer in horses. Some Blackfoot had only one horse, while one Blood band in 1854 still used dogs as their beasts of burden. However, generosity was a prequisite of leadership so surplus horses were loaned to poorer tribal members when required for hunting and moving camp (Hanks and Hanks 1950:124).

Next to hunting, the most important change in daily life caused by the acquisition of the horse was in the rapid escalation of warfare. Blackfoot men who owned few or no horses were encouraged to take them from enemy tribes. At the same time, incursions by mounted hunting parties, particularly from tribes west of the Rocky Mountains, became more frequent and the Blackfoot horses themselves became the objects of plunder. Small raiding parties coursed the plains in the summer, seeking out enemy camps and attempting to run off their horse herds (Dempsey 1990:4). In addition, increased mobility made it easier for the Blackfoot to travel in large bands.

The Blackfoot began trading with Europeans on a regular basis in the 1780s. The early traders did not build forts within their lands. Instead, Blackfoot trading parties traveled north in spring and autumn to carry their goods to forts on the North Saskatchewan River. The primary goods offered in trade were dried meat, buffalo robes, horses, and a few furs (Coues 1897, 2:529–530). As a result, the tribes were able to acquire European trade goods but were not obliged to alter their hunting and subsistence patterns as did some of their northern neighbors.

By the early nineteenth century, the Blackfoot were feeling the pressure of the better-armed Plains Cree and Assiniboine raiders from the north and east. During this time, the Piegan withdrew to the Missouri River and foothills regions, while the Blood centered on the Bow and Belly rivers, and the Blackfoot remained near the Red Deer River. The area immediately south of the North Saskatchewan River became a no-man's-land which at certain times of the year was dominated by the Blackfoot but at other times was overrun by Plains Cree and Assiniboine (J.G. MacGregor 1967:20–22).

The Blackfoot usually maintained friendly relations with the British traders, taking their goods to Fort Edmonton or Rocky Mountain House. The British sought to develop trade relations with the transmontane tribes who had beaver, who were enemies to the Blackfoot. Attempts were made by the Blackfoot to prevent the sale of firearms to these tribes, but the fur traders' discovery of mountain passes north of the Blackfoot hunting grounds thwarted their efforts.

American traders and trappers coming up the Missouri River from the south initially were treated as enemies. This hostility has been attributed to several sources, including the killing of two Piegans by the Meriwether Lewis and William Clark expedition in 1806, and the differences in fur-gathering methods of the British and Americans. British trading companies built forts and encouraged the Indians to bring in their furs and robes; American mountain men trapped their own furs and avoided any dealings with the Indians (O. Lewis 1942:27).

This hostility between the Blackfoot and Americans was exacerbated with the construction of a fort in 1810 at Three Forks, on the Missouri, at the edge of Blackfoot hunting territory (Wishart 1979:45). In 1823, the Blackfoot drove out another group of trappers from the Missouri Fur Company, which resulted in the withdrawal of American trappers from the upper Missouri (Wishart 1979:45–48).

In 1831, the American Fur Company made peace with the Blackfoot tribes and built Fort Piegan (later Fort McKenzie) at the forks of the Marias on the upper waters of the Missouri. From that time on, the Blackfoot became keen traders who pitted American against British to get the best prices for their goods. However, American relations with the Blackfoot remained precarious, and any attempt to trap in Blackfoot country was violently opposed (Wishart 1979:62).

Culture in the Nineteenth Century

As a nomadic people, the Blackfoot tribes were divided into numerous bands, which were basically small bilateral family groups with membership determined primarily through the father (Wissler 1911:20). Most marriages were outside the band, and those that did occur between members of the same band involved couples with no blood relationship (Dempsey 1982:93). During periods of good hunting, several bands, or an entire tribe, might remain together, but more often they dispersed into smaller units. Bands had little or no formal structure, other than the recognition of a leader, and membership often varied according to hunting success, internal disputes, or other factors. When a band became too large, it would divide into two or more smaller bands, which might travel or hunt together at certain times of the year. Poorer band members made the most frequent changes in band affiliation, following leaders who could best provide for their needs. Care of the poor was a primary responsibility of all band leaders (Dempsey 1982:97).

In 1870 there were reported to be nine bands each among the Blood and Northern Blackfoot and 15 bands among the Piegan (Ewers 1958:97). Bands had distinctive names, often given because of an incident or characteristic of the group. Some examples among the Blood during the mid-nineteenth century were the Followers of the Buffalo, Fish Eaters, All Short People, Many Fat Horses, and Black Elks. In the South Piegan there were the Don't Laugh, Fat Roasters, Skunks, Short Necks, and Small Robes. The Blackfoot bands included the Bad Guns, Liars, Strong Ropes, All Medicine Men, and Big Provision Bags. The North Peigan had the Big Buffalo Chips, Gopher Eaters, Lonesome Mourning, Hairy Noses, and Lone Fighters (Wissler 1911:21; cf. Curtis 1907–1930, 6:23; Grinnell 1892:208–209). Whenever several bands or an entire tribe camped together in spring or summer, each family and each band had a specific place within the circle (Wissler 1918:268, 1911:22; Grinnell 1892:225).

Political Organization

The government of each Blackfoot tribe centered upon the band, each of which had a recognized leader. His appointment was not hereditary and a man retained his position only as long as he could offer effective leadership (Dempsey 1982:96–97). If he failed to do so, his people shifted their allegiance to another man. Frequently, upon the death of a chief, leadership did pass to a son or nephew, either because of family influence or because the individual had learned the ways of political leadership by observing the actions in his household.

Generally, a band leader had an outstanding record of success in warfare and was regarded as generous to the poor in his distribution of war booty or inherited wealth (Dempsey 1982:97). Larger bands might have subchiefs who were honored men and who formed a council where the band leader presided (Wissler 1911:25). The primary function of the band leaders was to help keep social order and peace within the band. Establishing equitable settlements for murders or other crimes, maintaining friendly relations with other bands, and acting as magistrate and mediator—all were part of the band leader's duties (Wissler 1911:24–25). The chiefs met frequently, and the leader of the most influential band was usually recognized as the head civil chief for the entire tribe. Often he was a good orator who had a large personal following and had a reputation for wisdom and diplomacy (Maclean 1895:252–253). The role of civil chief was most significant during the summer encampment when all the bands were together.

In time of war or danger, the leadership of a band or of the entire tribe was assumed by a war chief. He was a leading warrior who on other occasions may have taken little or no interest in band government. During the crisis, he assumed complete control; but when peace was restored, the recognized civil chief returned to his normal leadership role (Maclean 1895:252–253).

Annual Cycle

The annual movements of a band reflect the climate and buffalo. In late October or November, the bands established separate camps along wooded river bottoms with easy access to grass for horses and timber for fuel. Some of the favorite wintering grounds were near the Porcupine Hills, the confluence of the Belly and Saint Mary rivers, along the Battle River, the upper waters of the Missouri, and the valleys of the Milk and Marias rivers (Doty 1966:17–26; Crooked Meat Strings, in Hanks papers).

By late November, with increasing snowfall, the band would choose small areas in heavily timbered areas for protection from the wind, where they set up their permanent winter camp. If wood and grass were exhausted, a day's journey would suffice for establishing a new camp. Otherwise, one location might last for the entire winter. Beaver bundle owners kept a calendar count with a bundle of sticks and announced the time when the geese would fly north. Buffalo were hunted when possible throughout the winter, and the length of hair on the buffalo embryo foretold the coming of spring.

In spring, the people ventured out onto the prairies, and the bands would separate into smaller camps because the buffalo herds were scattered. Activities included hunting, gathering new tepee poles from the foothills, visiting trading posts, and replacing worn out lodges and equipment. The Medicine Pipe ceremony was held immediately after the first spring thunder was heard. Women and children dug prairie turnips (*Psoralea esculenta*), and horses fattened on the spring grass (Uhlenbeck 1912:1–8).

In early summer the buffalo migrated to the open plains. At this time they often occupied the eastern range of their hunting grounds, particularly the area near the Cypress Hills. Camps were moved frequently to provide grass for the horse herds. The bands comprising each of the three Blackfoot tribes congregated in tribal camps where the leading chief organized the summer buffalo hunts that provided food, hides for new tepees, and as many as 300 buffalo bull tongues for the Medicine Lodge. Following a successful hunting season, each Blackfoot tribe held its own Medicine Lodge ceremony when the serviceberries ripened, usually during August (Uhlenbeck 1912:2–4; Grinnell 1892:264). From there the bands separated again to hunt on the open prairies, sometimes staying in large camps if there were enough buffalo to support them.

By autumn, the Blackfoot were ready to visit the trading posts again before choosing their winter camps. These fall camps sometimes were in proximity to buffalo jumps, or pounds, for even after they obtained horses, they did not abandon this ancient form of hunting. The fall buffalo hunt was the most important of the year. Berries were collected and pemmican was made for winter consumption, along with a large store of dried meat. Robes were prepared for trade, and hunting continued into the winter (Uhlenbeck 1912:12).

The only crop known to the Blackfoot was native tobacco (*Nicotiana quadrivalvis*), which was planted in the spring and was left untended until harvest. After the introduction of trade tobacco, the native variety was used primarily for religious purposes, and the activities associated with planting and harvesting became complex sacred rituals (A. Johnston 1987:52).

Structures

By the mid-nineteenth century, the availability of horses as a means of transportation enabled the Blackfoot to enlarge their tepees. Ordinary family lodges were made from 12–14 buffalo skins and between 20–30 poles. The women used a four-pole foundation in erecting tepees and always faced the doorway to the east. The ears of the tepee, which regulated the draft, were controlled by two poles that fitted through eyelets cut in the upper corners of the ears (Wissler 1910:99, 104).

The Blackfoot possessed very few painted lodges, which were owned only by chiefs (Maximilian in Thwaites 1904–1907, 23:104). The basic designs painted on the exterior of Blackfoot tepees included symbols for mountains, foothills, prairies, the night sky, Pleiades, Ursa Major, sun, moon, morning star, rainbow, and puffballs. In addition there were stylized representations of animals or birds, such as the otter, mountain sheep (fig. 4), beaver, eagle, and buffalo, each representing a spirit helper or protector of the lodge. Songs, special altars, flags, and medicine bundles accompanied many of the designs, most of which derived from visions and could be transferred from one owner to another (Grinnell 1901:650–667).

A few leading warriors had lodges made of 30 buffalo skins. These ostentatious symbols could be owned only by someone who had performed an outstanding war deed of dual significance. For example, one Blackfoot gained this honor by defeating two armed enemies who were riding the same horse; one of these men he deliberately knocked off the right side of the horse and the other off the left. Because of this audacious war deed, he was entitled to own a tepee that had two fireplaces and two entrances. The structure was so large that the covering was made in two sections, each forming a load for a horse-drawn travois (Dempsey 1972:63; Grinnell 1901:650).

Clothing

Blackfoot clothing was similar to that of other northern plains tribes (figs. 5–6). In 1810, fur trader Alexander Henry the Younger, when describing Blackfoot men, said:

> Their dress consists of a leather shirt, trimmed with human hair and quillwork, and leggings of the same; shoes are of buffalo skin dressed in the hair; and caps, a strip of buffalo or wolf skin about nine inches broad, tied around the head. Their necklace is a string of grizzly bear claws. A buffalo robe is thrown over all occasionally. Their ornaments are few — feathers, quillwork, and human hair, with red, white, and blue earth, constitute the whole apparatus (Coues 1897, 2:525).

Blackfoot women's costumes were described in 1833:

> It is a long leather shirt, coming down to their feet, bound round the waist with a girdle, and is often ornamented with many rows of elk's teeth, bright buttons, and glass beads. The dress wraps over the breast, and has short, wide sleeves, ornamented with a good deal of fringe... The lower arm is bare. The hem of the dress is likewise trimmed with fringes and scalloped. The women ornament their best dresses, both on the hem and sleeves, with dyed porcupine quills and thin leather strips, with broad diversified stripes of skyblue and white glass beads (Maximilian in Thwaites 1904–1907, 23:103).

Division of Labor

Women were the owners of the tepees and furnishings. Their duties included the pitching and striking of the lodge, packing, cooking, manufacturing and decorating most clothing, caring for infants, training girls, making and decorating parfleche bags and tepee liners, and the general maintenance of the lodge (Wissler 1911:27–28). They also helped the men in butchering during hunts, collecting lodge poles, and saddling the horses. The men provided food, protected the camp, manufactured certain religious and war objects, looked after the horses, trained boys for manhood, and carried out raids upon enemy tribes. They also painted religious symbols on rattles, shields, robes, and tepees (Wissler 1911:27).

Variant sexual behavior, although uncommon, was culturally accepted. Women who chose to take aggressive roles were referred to as manly hearted women; usually they signified their intentions as teenagers when they joined horse raiding parties (O. Lewis 1941). Later, they affected male dress, took wives, and maintained positions of leadership, either as warriors or shamans (Goldfrank 1945:11, 48–49). In 1844, fur trader John Rowand reported meeting a woman who was leading a Blackfoot war party that he claimed consisted of 1,000 men and more than 200 women (MacEwan 1971:47). In the late nineteenth century, there were well-known manly hearted women among the Piegan (G.R. Pratt 1981:3–5).

Berdaches also existed among the Blackfoot. They wore women's dresses and were in demand as wives because of their physical strength in carrying out womanly duties and for their artistic abilities. Their deviant behavior was attributed to being inhabited by spiritual forces. In Blackfoot (Blackfeet dialect), a berdache was *áya·ki·hkaʔsiwa* 'acts like a woman' (Schaeffer 1965:221–223).

top, McGill U., McCord Mus., Notman Photographic Arch., Montreal: 2160; bottom left, Smithsonian, NAA: 55,991; bottom right, Prov. Arch. of Alta., Edmonton: P 52.

Fig. 4. Camps. top, Canvas tepee with horse herd nearby. The man wears a breastplate made of strips of fur and dragon sideplates from muskets and holds a Winchester Centerfire rifle, model 1873 (Pohrt 1969; Harry Hunter, communication to editors, 1998). He also wears a wide belt and a knife case decorated with brass tacks. Photograph by William Notman, Blackfoot Res., near Gleichen, Alta., 1889. bottom left, Canvas-covered tepee painted with mountain sheep. In 1940 the tepee was owned by Frank Red Crow, Blood. Medicine bundles are hanging on a tripod. Photograph by Thomas B. Magee, Browning Mont., about 1900. bottom right, Inside a sacred lodge, where men and women sit around the medicine pipe bundle. A painted tepee liner is behind them. Photographed about 1910.

top left, Amer. Mus. of Nat. Hist., New York: 316639; Glenbow-Alberta Inst., Calgary, Alta.: top center: NA-3981-9; top right: NA-3281-3; bottom left, Bureau of Ind. Affairs, Washington: 1279; bottom center, Dept. of Ind. and Northern Affairs, Que.

Fig. 5. Clothing and headdresses. top left, Mountain Chief, southern Piegan (b. 1848, d. 1942), wearing traditional upright feather headdress decorated with white skins of ermine trapped in winter. Such a headdress was considered sacred, often protecting the wearer in battle. His right hand holds a lance; his left, a horse effigy, which may reflect his ties to the Black Horse Society, which he started and which had its own dances and giveaways (Ewers 1969:279). Photograph by Joseph K. Dixon, Crow Agency, Mont., 1909. top center, Man and woman in studio. The woman is wearing a cloth wing dress decorated with beads and buckskin fringe. She carries a knife belt decorated with brass studs and wears multiple metal bracelets. The man's jacket of military cut has strips of beadwork over the shoulder and an ammunition belt decorated with brass studs. He holds a Winchester Rimfire rifle, model 1866, and quirt and wears beaded moccasins. Photograph by Alexander J. Ross, Calgary, Alta., 1886. top right, Acustie, northern Peigan, wearing horned headdress with ermine strips. Photograph by Frederick Steele and Co., Winnipeg, Man., 1890s. bottom left, Julia Wades-In-Water, Chief Wades-In-Water, and Mae A. Coburn, who, as chairman of the Investigating Committee of the Welfare Society spoke on behalf of her tribe in 1933. Julia, the only Indian policewoman at that time, is wearing a fringed buckskin dress with painted designs on skirt and a heavily beaded yoke as well as dentalium earrings. The chief is wearing beaded clothing, including moccasins, floral leggings, gauntlets, vest, and a Sioux-style eagle feather warbonnet; his breechcloth is made up of strips of fabric. Photographed 1940s. bottom center, James Gladstone or Many Guns, Blood (b. 1887, d. 1971), member of the Crazy Dog Society, who served in the Canadian Senate from 1958 to 1971. Photographed in Ottawa, probably 1958. bottom right, Billy Young Pine, Blood, from Stand Off, Alta., wearing a horned fur bonnet, beaded necklace, and sequence-decorated arm band. He is holding a dance quirt. Photograph by John Running, 1984.

Life Cycle

When a woman was ready to give birth, she separated from the men in the camp and was cared for by medicine women. Close contact with her at this time could result in a man losing his sacred powers. After the umbilical cord was cut with an arrowhead, the child was washed, prayers were given, and the child was painted red (Grinnell 1896:286). The Blackfoot believed in reincarnation, and boys born with birthmarks were said to be carrying scars or battle wounds from a previous life (Wissler 1911:28).

At the time of birth, a baby was given a personal name by the mother. Sometimes this was based upon the first thing she saw after the birth. A short time later, the father arranged

a, Pitt Rivers Mus., U. of Oxford, U.K.: 1893.67.1; b, Mus. für Völkerkunde, Berlin: IV B 303b; c, Canadian Mus. of Civilization, Hull, Que.: 71429; d, State Histl. Soc. of Wis., Madison: 44595; e, Field Mus., Chicago: 51563; f, Histl. Mus. Bern, Switzerland: 74.410.26 a-b; g, Smithsonian, Dept. of Anthr.: 674.

Fig. 6. Men and women's clothing. a, Man's shirt, made of 2 skins, quilled shoulder and striped sleeves, with rosettes and hair tassels along the arms. The chest and back have colorful quilled squares while the shoulders have rectangular bands over them. Painted onto the shirt are images of bows, guns and a horse. Collected by E.M. Hopkins, 1842; length 118 cm. b, Legging made of light brown antelope leather, with fringed border and dark brown strips painted in 5 rows. Attached are short leather fringes sewn with sinew, scalp-hair and horse-hair tufts, and 2 bells. The sinew wrappings are overlain with white, yellow, and blue porcupine quills. Collected by Herzog von Württemberg, 1867; length at center 98 cm. c, Rosa Running Rabbit wearing a painted skin robe over a beaded dress. Photograph, cropped, by Harlan I. Smith, near Gleichen, Alta., 1928. d, Legging of native tanned hide with white, blue, and faceted purple glass bead decoration. Collected by Joseph Laframboise, about 1830; length 55 cm. e, Woman's dress made of 2 matched skins. The yoke is decorated with black and white pony beads and a deer tail. Inset pieces of red and blue trade cloth are outlined with seed beads; alternating blue and green beads decorate the hem. Collected by George A. Dorsey, 1897; length 120 cm. f, Knife blade set into a red wooden handle and sheath made of rawhide. The sheath is decorated with turquoise and white pony beads, and bird quills of orange, natural white, and black, secured with a single line of sinew stitching. Collected by A. A. Von Pourtalès, 1832; length of knife 29 cm, length of case 26 cm. g, Pair of soft-soled moccasins. Collected by George Gibbs, before 1862; length 26 cm.

to have the child officially named by an older relative or an important person in the camp. If the name was chosen by a man, it might relate to his own war experiences. Both men and women gave names honoring sacred animals and holy powers, and often a family name no longer in use would be passed down. A girl's name would remain unchanged throughout her life. A boy was given his first name in a sweatlodge ceremony when he was a few weeks old; but he could earn a succession of new names as a result of war exploits, hunting prowess, or religious experiences (McClintock 1910:395–401).

Boys and girls played together until about five years of age, when a male relative began training the boy and older sisters or the mother began to teach the girl. At an early age all children were taught to be obedient, to respect the numerous religious restrictions, and to be quiet in the presence of elders. Boys were taught to use the bow and arrow, to guard and round up horses, to follow game trails. They were also exhorted to be warriors and to die fighting in battle. Girls began by collecting firewood and water, and learned to cook, tan, sew, and pack. They were encouraged to be sober and serious minded and to emulate the women who sponsored the Medicine Lodge (Grinnell 1892:189–190; Wissler 1911:29).

There were no special puberty rites. However, the first game killed by a boy and the first quillwork or beadwork accomplished by a girl usually resulted in the family giving a feast. When a boy reached adolescence, he might be given a derisive name and thus encouraged to go to war to earn a new one (Middleton 1953:116). Boys often joined war parties at the age of 13 or 14, acting as servants in making fires, cooking, and looking after the camp while the warriors scouted and raided enemy camps. This was considered to be part of a boy's training and he did not expect to share in the booty. After two or three trips as a servant, he could expect to be invited to join a raiding party as a full member (Grinnell 1892:251).

Between the ages of 15 and 20, and before marriage, a young man might seek a vision to gain power. A sweatlodge was constructed by the youth for a chosen medicine man who would sweat and pray for the young man's success. After this the boy offered a pipe to the medicine man who then prepared the youth for a fast in the mountains or at some dangerous place, such as a steep cliff or near a burial ground. The boy fasted for four days and if a vision occurred, it usually consisted of a spirit helper appearing in human form. It gave him advice on his future life, stipulated taboos, and indicated the type of religious object, song, or ritual to use in maintaining communication with his spirit helper. Details of the vision would be revealed only to the medicine man who sometimes assisted in interpreting their meaning (Curtis 1907–1930, 6:79–81).

Field Mus., Chicago: 2864.

Fig. 7. Menstrual shelter used by the Blood tribe. Photograph by Edward P. Allen, Alta., 1897.

After reaching marriageable age, successfully participating in war raids, and acquiring wealth in horses, a young man began courting. Often he met a girl on her way to gather wood or water, or near her tepee at night. Girls might encourage a suitor by making him a pair of moccasins. Direct communication was generally discouraged by the girl's parents, since virginity was held in great esteem (Wissler 1911:8–9).

Marriage was arranged in a number of ways, depending upon the wealth and status of the participants. Negotiations were held between the father and his prospective son-in-law or between the two male parents. Once agreement was reached on a marriage, there was an exchange of gifts, usually two or three horses or their equivalent, with the groom and his family making a payment about double the amount received (Bradley 1923:272). In some instances, the payment was made by the groom's family only. Marriage among wealthier families involved gift exchanges of 15 or more horses (Grinnell 1892:211–217). The bride generally moved to her husband's camp, but exceptions were frequent, particularly when the bride was from an affluent family (McClintock 1910:184–188). Band exogamy was preferred but was not strictly enforced (Dempsey 1982:95).

Polygyny was common, with the number of wives being limited only by a man's wealth. It was said that only very poor men had fewer than three wives (Grinnell 1892:218), while one Blood reportedly had 23 wives lodged in two separate tepees (Dempsey 1982:102). Normally the first wife was the senior member of the female household and was referred to as the "sits beside him" wife. Often she was consulted about additional marriages and sometimes encouraged her husband to take additional wives to share the work load. It was common for a man to marry one or more sisters and to marry the widows of his brothers. Joking was prescribed between a man and his wives' sisters. While sororal polygyny was practiced, it was not institutionalized. Mother-in-law avoidance was strictly practiced (Wissler 1911:8–12).

If a woman was lazy or unfaithful, a man might divorce her by sending her back to her parents and demanding the repayment of the bride price. Similarly, a woman might divorce her husband on the grounds of cruelty or neglect; if reconciliation was not possible, arrangements were made to return the gifts to the husband's family or to arrange for another marriage for the woman and to make a settlement between the old and the new husband (Wissler 1911:13).

When a man was near death, he was dressed in his best clothes and his personal possessions were placed around him. After he died, the camp site was abandoned as the Blackfoot believed his spirit would remain in the area before leaving for the sand hills. The tepee in which the man died was sometimes sewn up and used as a death lodge; four lines of stones, one in each direction, were laid on the ground, as the mark of a chief or prominent warrior (Dempsey 1956:177). Otherwise the body was placed on a scaffold, in a tree, or on a high hill. Underground burial was not practiced. Before death, an individual might request certain personal belongings to be placed with the body. The remaining wealth, including horses, was distributed by the family according to the wishes of the deceased (Wissler 1911:31). After the death of a man who was not well liked or stingy, band members might raid his property. A man's horse might be killed to provide him with transportation to the sand hills, the land of the dead; among poorer families, the tail and mane were cut off and placed with the body (Wissler 1911:30–32).

Women were treated in a similar fashion, but horses were not killed, nor were burial lodges constructed for them. A woman's personal possessions were wrapped up with the body.

The name of the deceased was not uttered again after the person's death. Women mourners cut off their hair, gashed their legs, and wailed. Male mourners cut their hair and left the camp, either on a raid or to visit another band. During the period of mourning, men wore old or worn out clothing and lived simply, while women carried out the wailing ritual at frequent intervals. A mourner might cut off a finger joint. In their sorrow, owners of medicine bundles might destroy or desecrate them because they had failed to avert the death. To prevent this, a bundle was often taken by a previous owner and, after the mourning period, a ceremony was held and the bundle was returned (Wissler 1911:31).

Warrior Societies

The warrior societies, known as All Comrades, were age graded, each society having its own regalia, dance, and rituals. In 1833 seven of these societies were noted, each graded and ranked according to rank and accomplishments (Maximilian in Thwaites 1904–1907, 23:116–117). Subsequently, the Blood, Piegan, and Blackfoot were found to each have varying numbers of these societies. For example, those among the Piegan, beginning with the youngest, were the Pigeons, Mosquitoes, Braves, All Brave Dogs, Front Tails, Raven Bearers, Dogs, Kit Foxes, Catchers, and Bulls (Wissler 1913:369).

These societies usually originated in a vision experience during which a sacred power gave the specific rites, paints, dress, and songs that characterized the society. For example, the Catchers society was established through a vision of two spirit beings, each bearing a pipe, and leading a procession from the Sun to the visionary (Wissler and Duvall 1908:121; Curtis 1907–1930, 6:22; McClintock 1910:455). The younger societies, such as the Doves or Mosquitoes, consisted of young men who played pranks on adult members, who were expected not to complain about their behavior (McClintock 1910:448–450). Mature warriors joined societies whose functions were to act generously to elders and to the poor, to carry out disciplinary measures, to protect the camp from surprise by enemies, to know the location and movements of the buffalo, and to hold feasts and competitions with the other societies. The most dangerous assignments were given to the Braves, consisting of the oldest unmarried men (Curtis 1907–1930, 6:6–17).

When bands united in the spring, these societies camped in a circle within the larger camp circle, their tepees being used as meeting places for the camp leaders (Grinnell 1962:224). At this time the members of younger societies might offer pipes to the leaders and members of older societies in order to purchase from them the rites and privileges of membership. Once a man sold his rights, he lost his membership, and had to purchase rights to the next society in the hierarchy (Grinnell 1892:222; Dempsey 1956:48). Each society had an elder member who was a camp crier, announcing society news and the results of war expeditions. The same individual advanced through the grades with one group until his death (Curtis 1907–1930, 6:18). Those societies comprised of successful warriors had the highest status. Among the Piegan, the Bulls were considered to be the oldest society, having controlled the use of buffalo jumps in the prehorse period.

When a camp circle was established, several societies were given the responsibility for patrolling the area, controlling the hunts and protecting the band. Minor internal disputes were brought before the tribal chief, who acted as magistrate. Serious crimes, such as murder, required all band members to pay the required penalties to the surviving relatives in order to avoid further bloodshed (Maclean 1895:254–255). Tribal leadership depended heavily upon the All Comrades, and successful cooperation with them was essential. One of the societies was selected to direct the camp when it moved (Curtis 1907–1930, 6:16–17). Anyone hunting buffalo prior to an announced tribal hunt might have his clothing and weapons destroyed and his horses and meat seized. Men caught leaving on a raid during times of peace might also be punished (Bradley 1923:279–280).

Warfare

Raids, primarily for horses, were carried out by small parties of young men under the leadership of a more experienced warrior. A leader was chosen because of his past successes, which indicated that his war medicine was strong enough to protect the expedition and to ensure success. Raids were frequently carried out in spring and summer when the bands were together. Occasionally, winter raids were made during storms when tracks would be obscured. Very often, the leader chose relatives for his war party because he knew of their reliability and the spoils would be kept within the family. A young unmarried man went to war about three times a year, once in winter and twice in summer, but after marriage he went about twice a year. Before setting out, the leader called the party to his tepee where they sang and offered prayers (Crooked Meat Strings in Hanks papers).

Leaving on foot at dawn, each warrior took a light pack containing a bow and arrows or gun, bullets and powder, knife, extra moccasins, awl, and sinew. After arriving in enemy territory the men constructed a war lodge out of branches and leaves. Scouts returning to this camp uttered the cry of a crane and kicked over a pile of sticks when the enemy was found. Then, after the others had sung an honoring song, he told them of his discoveries. Where possible, the raid was made at dawn, the party attempting to take as many horses as possible without being detected. The best race horses and buffalo runners were inside the enemy camp, often tethered to the owner's tepee. Pack horses and poorer animals grazed near the camp, with young boys acting as herders.

If a raid was successful, warriors would paint their faces black and ride into the camp circle, firing guns and singing victory songs. If any of the party was killed, a scout went ahead to a hill near the home camp. As people watched, he picked up a stone and placed it on the ground; each stone indicated one man dead or missing.

If the enemy attacked the Blackfoot, or if a person was killed while on a raid, particularly an outstanding leader, a revenge raid might take place. An older relative of the deceased would take a pipe to the chief and ask him to smoke. If he accepted, he would form a war party of 100 or more mounted men. The goal of such a revenge party was to kill as many of the enemy as possible and to gain war honors through being the first to count coup on a particular enemy warrior (Schaeffer 1948–1969). Counting coup consisted of touching the enemy with a club or whip without necessarily causing him any harm (Grinnell 1892:245–250). In 1865, a revenge party of 80 Blackfoot, Blood, Piegan, and Sarcee attacked a camp of Assiniboines and Plains Crees and killed 29 men and women who were going for water (Dempsey 1980:60–61). Other traditional enemies included the Eastern Shoshone, Crow, Flathead, Pend d'Oreille, and Kootenai.

Religion

Blackfoot religion was based upon the belief that the Sun was the major deity, his wife was the Moon, and Morning Star was their son. Thunder also was a major spirit. The Sun gave success in war and hunting, health, long life, and happiness (Grinnell 1892:258). Star legends abounded within Blackfoot mythology while many creatures of the air—eagles, bluebirds, ravens—had sacred powers. Generally speaking, any animate or inanimate object could possess power. Forces under the earth, underwater, or associated with night, such as the owl, often were considered to be evil.

The world was created by a trickster-creator named Napi (*ná·piwa*) (Grinnell 1892:137), often explained as 'Old Man' by a folk-etymology. He was responsible for the creation of the natural environment but also embodied within himself good and evil, wisdom and foolishness, bravery and cowardice. A number of features within Blackfoot country, such as the Oldman River, Tongue Creek, and Okotoks, are named for Napi or his exploits. One of the most important archeological sites in southern Alberta, the Old Woman's Buffalo Jump, was identified in Blackfoot mythology as the place where the first marriage of men and women took place. Because Napi was denied a bride, he was said to have turned himself into a pine tree, which became a landmark of the area for many years (John Yellowhorn, personal communication 1961).

Medicine bundles were the basis for most Blackfoot rituals (fig. 8). Although the composition of bundles varied, most of them contained the basic objects necessary to perform a ceremony, including sweetgrass, tobacco, and paint. The individual objects around which a bundle was organized included pipes, scalp shirts, weasel tail decorated suits, tepee flags, otter skins, knives, lances, shields, and bridles. The sacred objects were wrapped in skins or cloth and were kept in rawhide (Wissler 1912:67–288).

Among the most sacred possessions were the sacred pipe bundles and the Beaver bundle (Wissler 1912:168–203). Although each pipe had a distinctive name and perhaps had some unique powers, all had similar rituals associated with them, and the owners were distinguishable by their hairstyles and face paint. A loose society of sacred pipe owners existed; they usually met after the first spring thunderstorm to open and renew their bundles. Bundles also were opened to transfer ownership, renew the tobacco, or to fulfill a vow.

When the Medicine Lodge, a form of the Plains Sun Dance, was adopted by the Blackfoot, probably early in the nineteenth century, the bundle practice was extended to that ritual. The woman who made the initial vow to sponsor the ceremony acquired a *na·towáʔsa* 'holy turnip' bundle from a previous sponsor and used the objects within it for her rituals. The basic elements of the Medicine Lodge included the woman's vows, a period of fasting, cutting of sacramental buffalo tongues, construction of a 100-willow sweatlodge, raising of a center pole and erection of the holy lodge, ceremonies by the weather dancers, and counting of coups.

Once it was in place, the Medicine Lodge was used by warrior societies and other religious groups to perform their own rituals. A self-torture ritual also occurred within the lodge. As an entire tribe might be gathered for the ceremony, the opportunity was taken for transferring ownership of sacred pipes, tepee designs, and other religious objects (Wissler 1918:225–270).

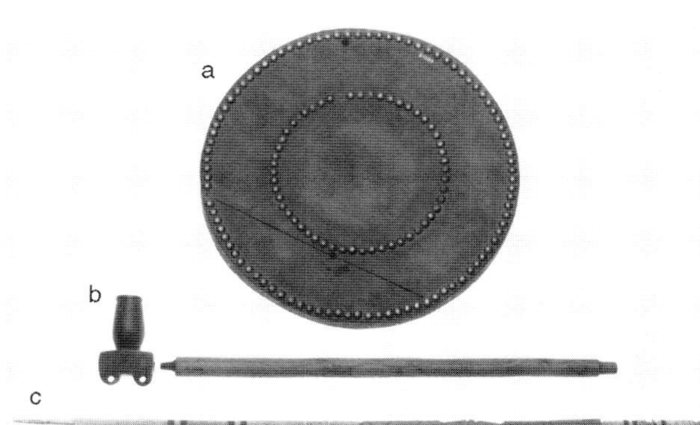

Glenbow-Alberta Inst., Calgary: top left: NA-991-16; top right, NA-991-62; bottom left, Field Mus., Chicago: a, 51580; b, 51568; c, 51679; bottom right, Mont. Histl. Soc., Helena: 955-557.

Fig. 8. Sacred Smoke ceremonies. top, All Smoke ceremony, held any time of the year. top left, Ben Calf Robe at dawn, carrying the offering that had been the center of the All Smoke ceremony during the night. The offering represents an enemy warrior, crowned with 7 eagle feathers, representing the 7 Blackfoot brothers who went to live in the sky and became the Big Dipper. The offering was taken to a hill, where the songs and prayers of the evening would be carried into the sky. top right, left to right: Ben Calf Robe, Amos Leather, and One Gun performing the final rites of the All Smoke ceremony. At the end of the singing, the clay altar is destroyed and the offering laid across it. Everyone gives a war whoop, indicating that they have been victorious over their enemy, represented by the offering. top left and right, Photographs by William D. Marsden, Blackfoot Res., Cluny, Alta., 1959. bottom left, Smoking paraphernalia. a, Tobacco cutting board, made of wood with 2 circles of brass tacks as decoration. b, Pipe and stem made of stone and wood with 2 small holes carved under the pipe. c, Pipe tamper, a carved wooden stick that is painted and decorated with pink, black, yellow, and blue seed beads. Collected by George A. Dorsey, Blood Res., 1897; length of tamper 60.5 cm (others to same scale). bottom right, Medicine Smoke ceremony held only in association with the medicine bundle, here the Beaver bundle, being opened. back row, 2 unidentified men, James Stingy, Philip Arrow Top, Louis Bear Child with drum, John Bear Medicine with drum, and Three Calves with rattle. front row, Mrs. Night Gun, George Bull Child. During the ceremony Three Calves blessed and painted a number of buffalo stones for the photographer, who had been adopted into the tribe (Willcomb 1970:45). Photograph by Roland H. Willcomb, Cut Bank Creek, Mont., early 1940s.

History, 1855 to 1990

The first of many major events which were to change the lives of the Blackfoot occurred in 1855 when they made a treaty with the United States government. At that time, consideration was being given to building a railroad across the plains for which a vast region of Montana and adjacent territories was required. In exchange for an exclusive hunting ground, annuity payments, and other benefits, the Blackfoot and other tribes were expected to surrender their rights to the region and agree to live in peace.

The negotiations, held at the mouth of the Judith River, were carried out by the newly appointed governor of Washington Territory, Isaac I. Stevens. Representing the

Indians were chiefs from the Blackfoot, Blood, Piegan, Gros Ventre, Nez Perce, Flathead, and Plains Cree tribes. The Blackfoot and other tribes agreed to maintain perpetual peace with the government and with other tribes adhering to a treaty that permitted settlers to live or travel through their territories; and to allow for the construction of roads, telegraph lines, military posts, and Indian agencies. In return, the Blackfoot were given a huge reservation "bounded on the south by a line drawn eastward from the Hell Gate or Medicine Rock passes to the nearest source of the Musselshell River, down that river to its mouth, and down the Missouri to the mouth of Milk River to the forty-ninth parallel (the Canadian border); on the north by this parallel; and on the west by the Rocky Mountains" (Ewers 1958:217). They also were promised goods and annuities of $20,000 annually for 10 years, plus $15,000 annually during the same period for agricultural training to promote the goals of assimilation (Farr 1984:5). At this time the first agency was established at the fur trading post of Fort Benton. In 1869, the agency was moved to a more accessible location five miles north of Choteau, Montana (Ewers 1974:112).

A decade later the government considered the Blackfoot hunting territory to be too large, and after the creation of the territory of Montana in 1864, pressure by White settlers resulted in new treaties in 1865 and 1869. Although never ratified, they succeeded in reducing the reservation to a fraction of its original size. Further cuts were made through executive orders in 1873 and 1874 and by agreements in 1888 and 1895 (Ewers 1974:132–164).

Increased Wealth

The demand for buffalo hides for use in the industrial East suddenly gave the tribes a commodity that they could easily supply. This in turn increased the buying power of the Blackfoot and gave them a level of affluence previously unknown to them. The most dramatic changes occurred in the sizes of their horse herds. A Piegan named Many Horses, considered the wealthiest member of the tribe in the 1860s, was said to have owned about 500 head (Ewers 1955:29). Ownership of 100 or more animals became common.

Similarly, women possessed more copper kettles, knives, and axes, while tepees made of canvas became a further mark of status. However, the demand for more goods brought independent traders directly into Blackfoot hunting grounds and, for the first time, a significant number of intermarriages with White men began to take place. These were primarily among the South Piegan and Blood, whose hunting grounds were in close proximity to the Missouri River trading posts.

Farther north, the Blackfoot and northern bands of Blood gradually withdrew from the Battle River area and abandoned their trade with the Hudson's Bay Company. Like their southern neighbors, they began taking their trade to the Missouri River where there was a constant demand for buffalo robes. The British, with difficult water routes to the East, were in no position to compete with the traffic of the Missouri in moving large shipments of robes to market (Sharp 1955:34–35).

Loss of Hunting Grounds

Within a few years of the signing of the 1855 treaty, White people began trickling into Montana. First there were free traders, missionaries, and government officials. Then the discovery of gold along the mountains brought a flood of prospectors, merchants, and ranchers. The influx resulted in a number of clashes between Indians and Whites, reaching such proportions by 1866 that Montanans were referring to the troubles as a "Blackfoot war" (Dempsey 1980:56–65). Dissatisfaction over the failure of the government to abide by the treaties led to a series of raids against settlers, miners, and traders encroaching on Blackfoot territory. In turn, these raids inhibited the Indian agents from recommending the ratification of the treaties (Ewers 1974:109–111). These events culminated in the first and only United States military action against the Blackfoot. In January 1870, cavalry and infantry under command of Maj. Eugene Baker attacked Heavy Runner's peaceful camp of Piegan, killing 173 persons, mostly women and children (Sharp 1955:149). Due to popular sentiment aroused by this incident, a congressional decision was made no longer to employ army officers as Indian agents. The Blackfoot response was to ask for peace, recognizing that the brutal war tactics of the army made them a formidable enemy.

The incident drove a number of camps across the border to Canada, but there they were subjected to the unlimited sale of whiskey by American traders at Forts Whoop-Up, Standoff, and Slideout. The ownership of the British possessions had been transferred to Canada in 1869, but authorities had no means of enforcing law and order after the withdrawal of the Hudson's Bay Company. Accordingly, enterprising American merchants discovered that they could operate within the legal vacuum of the Canadian prairies, selling whiskey and repeating rifles to the Blackfoot (Sharp 1955:33–54). In 1873 it was estimated that 600 barrels of liquor were traded to the Blackfoot, and that between 1868 and 1873, 25 percent of the tribe died as a result of alcohol consumption and drunken brawls (ARCIA 1873:252; Ewers 1958:259). In 1874 the North West Mounted Police were sent to the region to put down the illicit traffic. The effect upon the Blackfoot tribes was dramatic. The sale of alcohol was halted, and the Indians made rapid strides in replacing their depleted horse herds and restoring order over their lives (Morris 1880:248).

This respect for the Mounted Police made it possible for the Canadian government to arrange for the signing of Treaty No. 7 at Blackfoot Crossing on the Bow River, southern Alberta, in September 1877 that involved little or no negotiation. As one of the commissioners, James F. Macleod, was an officer in the Mounted Police, the Blackfoot willingly signed the treaty even though they did not fully understand the terms. Most of the Blood, Blackfoot, and North Peigan tribes at this time accepted Canadian authority and abandoned all claims south of the United States border (Dempsey 1977, 1977a; Getty and Smith 1978).

Through this treaty, they surrendered their hunting grounds of approximately 50,000 square miles in Canada in return for reserves based on a population of five persons per square mile. They also were promised perpetual annuity payments of $25.00 annually for chiefs, $15.00 for councillors, and $5.00 for all other men, women, and children, as well as implements for farming or cattle for ranching, and an assortment of tools, flags, medals, and ammunition. Because European settlement had not yet begun in western Canada, the Blackfoot had free choice of reserve lands. Most of them selected reserves near favorite wintering places: the Blackfoot at the Blackfoot Crossing of the Bow River, the Blood on the Belly River, the North Peigan near the Porcupine Hills, and the Sarcee—part of the confederacy—west of Fort Calgary (Maclean 1896:49–50).

Initially, none of the Indians chose to live on their reserves but preferred to hunt the diminishing herds of buffalo. In Canada, the Mounted Police made no attempt to keep them confined but permitted them to roam and to subsist for themselves. In the United States, some attempt was made to force the Indians onto their reservation, but with little success while buffalo herds still existed. In 1878, the South Piegan, under the leadership of White Calf, had a successful summer hunt, but in the following winter few buffalo could be found. By 1884, unsuccessful buffalo hunts led to over 300 South Piegan deaths from starvation (Samek 1987:44–45).

Early Reservation Period, 1880–1945

By 1880, the Blackfoot were effectively split into four geographical locations. In Montana, the South Piegan finally moved onto their reservation where they became known as the Blackfeet, while in Canada the North Peigan, Blood, and Blackfoot went to their allotted lands. In 1884, an attempt was made to determine the exact boundaries of the South Piegan reservation, but not until 1888 did Congress ratify the agreement that provided them with a greatly reduced reservation, and by another agreement in 1895 the western portion of the reduced reservation was ceded and opened for settlement. Each agreement provided annuity payments of $150,000 for tools, livestock, and other subsistence goods over a 10-year period (Farr 1984:10). The funds were intended to assist the Blackfeet in adapting to reservation life and becoming self supporting, but the programs were relatively unsuccessful (Samek 1987:62).

Although the American Blackfeet and Canadian Blackfoot developed independently in different countries, there were many similarities (see Samek 1987). All turned to farming and ranching as a means of livelihood; log houses replaced tepees; Roman Catholic ("History of the Canadian Plains Since 1870," fig. 2, this vol.), Methodist, and Anglican missionaries built boarding schools that took children away from their homes; and the ration house became the center of reservation life. By the late 1880s most reserves had introduced cattle ranching and by the turn of the century a few families were self-supporting through this enterprise, or through coal mining, haying, or lumbering. Farming also was moderately successful on some reserves, but the introduction of mechanized farming about 1920 was not successfully adopted by the Blackfoot. As long as they could work with horses they were able to compete, but most were unable to obtain the funds for machinery or to meet the demands of the newer technology. Extremely cold winters, a period of drought from 1917 to 1920, and a fluctuating economy resulting from World War I combined to further worsen farming conditions. Returning veterans also increased competition for cash income jobs (McFee 1972:54).

Beginning about 1907, the Blackfoot were pressured to surrender lands for White settlement. The Peigan in Canada were persuaded to give up part of their land in 1909 and the Blackfoot in 1911 and 1918 (Dempsey 1986:8, 33). The Blackfeet in Montana were allotted individual lands from 1907 to 1912, and the remainder of the reservation area was opened for settlement (Farr 1984:99). In 1918, permission was granted for Indians to dispose of their allotments. As a result, many Montana Blackfeet sold their lands to Whites and were left indigent. In 1921, the Board of Indian Commissioners reported severe poverty. Each elderly Blackfeet received 12 pounds of meat; and small amounts of coffee, flour, and beans were given as monthly rations (BIC 1921:54–57).

Through the Indian Reorganization Act of 1934, the piecemeal sale of Blackfeet land in Montana was halted. The tribe adopted a constitution, and a council of 13 was elected semiannually to manage tribal funds and property, regulate criminal behavior, and encourage cultural traditions (Ewers 1958:323–324; Rosier 1999).

Of the four Blackfoot tribes in Canada and the United States, only the Blood were able to resist all attempts to reduce the size of their reserve, which continued to be the largest in Canada. Because of the differences in land surrender policies, no individual allotments were issued in Canada; as a result, even though two of the Canadian reserves were reduced in size, their remaining land was entirely Indian occupied, thus permitting a degree of cultural integrity. The Montana Blackfeet, on the other hand, found their reservation interspersed with non-Indian settlers.

These differences had the effect of isolating the Canadian Blackfoot from their neighbors while their American relatives were constantly thrust into the larger society. As a result, there have been differences in the development of the two groups. For example, a noticeable loss of language occurred at a much earlier date on the Blackfeet Reservation. An appreciation of education, particularly higher education, was more noticeable in Montana earlier than on the Canadian reserves. However, the persistence of religious rituals and secret societies was more evident among the Canadian groups than among the Montana Blackfeet.

In the 1920s and 1930s education was firmly in the hands of government or church institutions. Farming and ranching were only marginally successful, and the introduction of irrigation to the Blackfeet Reservation did not bring the prosperity that many expected.

With the outbreak of World War II many young men served in the armed forces, where they learned skills that after the war were more valuable off reservation. In addition, government policies made it easier for Indians to obtain a good education. As a result, many Montana Blackfeet participated in the relocation program and moved to urban areas throughout the United States.

Postwar Development, 1945–1980

After 1945 the Canadian government began to provide more adequate funds to assure better schools, improved health services, economic and industrial development, and the encouragement of self reliance. Unlike their American counterparts, the Canadian Blackfoot tended to remain on their reserves. Because their reserve lands were more fertile than in Montana, Canadian Blackfoot developed a stronger agricultural base.

During the postwar period the American Blackfeet increased their involvement with stock raising and initiated programs for educational training, but financial problems and land leasing made it difficult to keep government loan cattle from being repossessed (McFee 1972:58–59). After the U.S. House of Representatives passed Concurrent Resolution 108 in 1953, demanding early termination of federal responsibility for Indian lands in trust, the Blackfeet continued to lose increasing amounts of land.

By the 1960s, the graduates of integrated schools began to assume more important roles in the communities. Most employees on the reserves were Indians, including band managers, welfare officers, public works staff, stenographers, nurses' aides and, in some areas, teachers and nurses. Other Indians preferred to leave their reserves to work in cities. Attempts were made to introduce small industries to the reserves and, while not all were successful, some proved to be economically viable. Among these were a mobile home factory, pencil-making factory, tourist resort, retail stores, post peeling plant, commercial potato industry, upholstering factory, and garment factories. Communications networks also were established, including the *Kainai News*, Blackfoot Radio, and *Blackfoot Community News*. A media center for the production of videos was developed by Blood entrepreneurs.

With the introduction of electricity to Canadian reserves in the 1970s, television became a major factor in language loss. Whereas before television most preschool children spoke Blackfoot, within a few years English became the language of the young. From that time on, an increasing number of Canadian households began to consider English to be their primary language, while in Montana the Blackfoot language was fast becoming a rarity. In both countries, courses in the native language were initiated.

Living conditions improved considerably for all Blackfoot in the immediate postwar period. Beginning with small welfare houses in the 1950s, the services improved so that by the 1970s many Canadian families were living in modern houses with running water, septic tanks, and natural gas or propane heating. The Montana Blackfeet suffered a severe flood in 1964 that led to an emergency federal appropriation of 5.5 million dollars for new construction, roads, dams, and canals on the reservation. New houses were built, but by 1969 only 32 percent of families had modern housing. Construction programs contributed another 110 houses and the Mutual Help housing program of the Federal Housing Administration also provided homes for those who helped build the houses (McFee 1972:61–63).

Although opportunities for education and employment improved, many serious problems remained. The removal of restrictions on obtaining liquor by the American Blackfeet in the 1950s and the Canadian Blackfoot during the 1960s caused an immediate social upheaval. Whereas it was always possible for the Blackfoot to obtain liquor from bootleggers, there was enough social stigma attached to the practice that it was not a major problem. However, the legalizing of bars and taverns turned surreptitious individual drinking into a family affair, which wreaked havoc in the communities.

A high unemployment rate also remained a problem. Work on the reserves focused primarily on tribal administration, ranching, and farming. However, many Blackfoot farmers were obliged to lease their lands because of machinery costs and lack of access to bank loans.

As educational services improved, the facilities for the Blackfoot included schools and colleges on the reserves as well as integrated services in nearby White communities. One noteworthy project in 1976 was the establishment of the Blackfeet Community College on the Blackfeet Reservation and Red Crow College on the Blood Reserve. During the same period, Mount Royal College in Calgary opened Old Sun Campus on the Blackfoot Reserve and Red Crow College on Blood Reserve. In addition, the University of Lethbridge developed an Indian Studies program designed chiefly for Blackfoot students.

The social life of most reserves centered around rodeo, hockey, basketball, and other Indian-organized sports. Rodeo, in particular, reached a high degree of organization under the Indian Rodeo Cowboy Association, a semiprofessional body organized in 1962 by the Blackfoot tribes (Mikkelsen 1987:16). Most reserves constructed modern indoor arenas for both rodeo and hockey.

The 1980s and 1990s

By the 1980s and 1990s, the Blackfoot tribes retained many of their ceremonies and religious societies. In Canada, their reserves were among the nation's largest, providing an internal unity that encouraged the retention of traditional customs. A relatively small migration to cities left much of the population intact, giving the young an opportunity to learn from their elders. Similarly, some religious activities were never curtailed.

The Medicine Lodge ceremony was held during the summer on the Blood Reserve and was reintroduced to the Peigan Reserve. The Horn Society and Women's Society persisted among the Blood and were reintroduced to the Blackfoot. Several medicine pipes were still in the care of their keepers; museums repatriated others. Each reserve had persons who gave prayers and painted and performed religious ceremonies for those who requested them.

At the same time, many elements of pan-Indianism were evident in all Blackfoot communities. Powwows and Indian Days were common (fig. 9), with costumes reflecting the current styles of the northern plains. A form of self-torture ritual was reintroduced, borrowed from the Northern Cheyenne and Sioux and practiced separate from the Medicine Lodge. Some Blackfoot also participated in communal sweatbaths, although historically such rituals were not used by the people at large. For purposes of cultural preservation, the Blackfoot tribes developed programs to teach language, dance, craft work, and history, using elders as their primary sources.

Social and economic problems persisted. Alcoholism, drug use, child neglect, and family violence were major concerns. Modern rehabilitation centers were opened on most reserves, their programs using an appreciation and understanding of native culture as part of their treatment.

Fig. 9. 20th-century celebrations of the Southern Piegan, Blackfeet Res., Browning, Mont. top, Camps at the North American Indian Days. Photograph by Thomas F. Kehoe, 1956. bottom, Giveaway by the Bird Rattler family in honor of Richard Lee Bird Rattler, who was killed in an automobile accident. left to right: Joe Bird Rattler, Jr., George Old Person holding portrait of Richard, and drummers Philip Many Hides and Jim White Calf. Photograph by Thomas F. Kehoe, Blackfoot Res., July 1972.

Fig. 10. Activities of the 1990s. left, Southern Piegan William Old Chief being congratulated on being elected chairman by Ed Little Plume. The Southern Piegan tribal flag is behind them. Photograph by Joe Fisher, Browning, Mont., 1998. right, Northern Peigan students from the Napi's Playground Elementary School, Peigan Res., Brocket, Alta., in Ottawa to see the capital and to lobby the government for a new fine arts center for the reserve. The Northern Peigan flag is being displayed. Photograph by Shari Narine, 1998.

However, death rates due to alcohol-related traffic accidents and diseases as well as murders were inordinately high (Knox 1980).

Unemployment reached 75 percent of the adult population. Increasing numbers of families found it necessary to migrate to the cities in search of work. There, social problems increased for families who were unable to break out of the welfare cycle (Brody 1971).

However, the problems were offset by many achievements. A program of Indian irrigation farming was underway on the Blood Reserve; oil and gas production was important on the Blackfoot Reserve; computer technology showed some success in programs designed and run by Blackfoot Indians; and a number of artists such as Henry Standing Alone, Al Many Bears, and Gary Schildt received recognition for their work.

Population

The population of the Blackfoot tribes varied over the years, being affected primarily by smallpox epidemics of 1780, 1837, 1849, and 1869 (table 1). Other diseases such as measles, scarlet fever, tuberculosis, and scrofula also accounted for many deaths.

The number of intermarriages between the Montana Blackfeet and non-Indians doubled by 1930, comprising three-quarters of the population under 30. By 1950 over 85 percent were of mixed-blood descent (Ewers 1958:327). Because of differences between Canada and the United States in legally defining Indians, no record of intermarriage has been kept in Canada. By comparison with the Blackfeet, however, the extent of intermarriage in Canada has been estimated to be less than 25 percent.

Fig. 11. Morning prayers on the occasion of the trip to Wyoming where highly valued Indian mustangs were to be purchased for the tribe. Photograph by Joe Fisher, near Browning, Mont., 1995.

Synonymy†

For the Blackfoot tribes as a group there are two native self-designations recorded in the nineteenth century. One is *saokí·tapi·ksi* 'prairie people', rendered Chokitapix, 1875 (Jean L'Heureux in Dempsey 1972:84), Sokitapi (sg.) (E.F. Wilson 1887:12), Sowké-ta-pe (Lanning 1882), and Sawketakix, 1885 (Hale in Hodge 1907–1910, 2:571). Another, probably less common, expression is

†This synonymy was written by Douglas R. Parks, based in part on a draft by Ives Goddard.

Table 1. Blackfoot Population, 1780–1997

Year	*Blackfoot*	*Blood*	*Peigan/Piegan*	*Total*	*Sources*
1780	—	—	—	15,000	Mooney 1928:13
1810	500 men	200 men	700 men	1,400 men	A. Henry in Coues 1897, 2:530
1814				8,000	Schermerhorn 1814:42
1823	4,200	2,800	4,200	11,000	T. Heron in Chesterfield House [Journals] 1823
1830				30,000	L. Cass in Schoolcraft 1851–1857, 3:609
1855	1,750	2,450	2,450	6,550	I. Stevens in Schoolcraft 1851–1857, 6:698
1859	2,400	2,000	2,600	7,000	J. Rowand in Hind 1859:116
1872	3,568	2,508	4,184	10,260	J. L'Heureaux in Dempsey 1961:12
1885	2,400	2,800	3,100	8,300	H. Hale 1885:698
1909	795	1,174	2,666[a]	4,635	Mooney in-Hodge 1907–1910, 2:571
1970	2,355	4,262	11,334[b]	17,951	Neville 1970:26; U.S. Bureau of the Census 1973:188
1987	3,658	6,882	9,425[c]	19,865	Indian and Northern Affairs Canada 1987:00053; Bureau of Indian Affairs 1987:7
1997	4,849	8,522	17,815[d]	31,186	Indian and Northern Affairs Canada 1998:38, 40; Wanda Glaze, communication to editors 1998

[a] 471 Registered Peigan Indians in Canada and 2,195 Blackfeet Indian Reservation residents in the U.S.
[b] 1,413 Registered Peigan Indians in Canada and 9,921 Blackfeet Indian Reservation residents in the U.S.
[c] 2,232 Registered Peigan Indians in Canada and 7,193 Blackfeet Indian Reservation residents in the U.S.
[d] 2,938 Registered Peigan Indians in Canada and 14,877 enrolled tribal members, Blackfeet Tribe, Mont.

ni·tsí?poyiwa 'people who speak one language', reflected in the recordings Netsepoyè (Maclean in Hale 1885:107) and Nitsipoie (E.F. Wilson 1887:13).

The generic Plains Cree name for the Blackfoot is *ayahciyiniwak* 'alien people; enemy' (Lacombe 1874:325; Bloomfield 1934:34; H. Christoph Wolfart, personal communication 1987). Early European recordings reflect the Woods Cree form of the name with *θ* (phonetically [ð] between vowels) for the *y* in the penultimate syllable of the stem, and some renderings appear to lack the first syllable or to have *iy* for *ay*; for example, Hiattchiritiny, 1737 (Beauharnois map in Burpee 1927: opp. 116; segment *-rit-* perhaps miscopied); Atchue-thinnies, 1738 (Norton in Davies 1965:249; cf. 292, 318); Archithinue, 1754 (Henday in Burpee 1907:337); Earchethinues, 1743 (Isham in Rich 1949:113; used for both Blackfoot and Crow); Ye-arch-a-thin-a-wock (Pink 1767, entry for 4/30/1767; cf. 9/26/1767, 5/2/1768, 5/4/1768); Yachithinnee, Yeachithinnee, 1776 (Cocking in Rich 1951:67, 168).

The Cree name was borrowed into Ojibwa as *aya·ččinini* (Baraga 1878–1880, 1:29, phonemicized), which seems to be reflected in the forms Iactchejlini and Ihateheouilini, 1750–1753 (Legardeur de St. Pierre in Margry 1876–1886, 6:640, 643).

Apparently the Cree also called the Blackfoot 'Slaves', 1809 (Henry in Gough 1988–1992:2, 376), in Cree *awahka·n* (Grinnell 1892:158, retranscribed), a term generally used to designate Athapaskan groups to the north. An early French designation was Gens du large, 1794 (M'Gillivray in Morton 1929:31).

Over time the name of the Blackfoot tribe specifically was extended to designate more inclusively the Blood and Piegan as well. Because of the consequent difficulty of sorting out the referents of the terms meaning literally 'black foot', those names are discussed below under the names of the Blackfoot tribe.

Blackfoot tribe

The native self-designation for the Blackfoot tribe is *siksikáwa* '(person having) black feet' (Frantz and Russell 1989:241), from which translation the English name derives. Although the traditional explanation for this name is that it refers to the coloring of their moccasins, the origin of the ethnonym is obscure. In the historical literature this name appears as Siksekai or Seksekai, 1832–1834 (Maximilian in Thwaites 1904–1907, 23:95; L.H. Morgan 1871:289); Satsikaa (Hale 1846:219); and Sixikowex (Lacombe 1886:81). Misprints or erroneous forms include Sitkeas and Sasitka (Schoolcraft 1851–1857, 3:252, 4:688); and Sikcitano (Canada. Department of Indian Affairs 1902:125). The form *siksikáíkoana* 'Blackfoot man' is reflected in several citations: Sixhiekiekoon, 1808 (Henry 1799–1814:819); Sichekiekoon, 1809 (Henry in Gough 1988–1992, 2:393); and Saxoe-koe-koon (Franklin 1822:109).

The English name Blackfoot, probably translated from Cree, appears variously as Blackfooted Indians, 1722 (Cocking in Burpee 1908:111) and later as Blackfoot Indians, 1798 (Sutherland in Alice M. Johnson 1967:132) or simply Black foot, 1782 (Walker in Rich 1952:282), with the plural forms Blackfeet, 1786 (Anonymous 1794:24), Blackfoots (Manchester House Journals, III/25/1788), and Blackfeets, 1800 (Bird in Alice M. Johnson 1967:235). In the late twentieth century there was a generally standardized distinction in local usage between Blackfoot (pl. Blackfoots) for those people living in Canada and Blackfeet (pl. Blackfeets) for those in the United States.

French designations are Indiens aux Pieds noirs (Mackenzie 1802a:176) or simply Pieds-noirs, 1827 (Amérique Septentrionale, map in Maelen 1827:leaf no. 47); 1841 (Point 1967:40). Other forms in European languages have the same literal meaning; for example, German Schwarzfüssige (Güssefeld, map 1797, in Hodge 1907–1910, 2:571; Mackenzie 1802b:79).

In Algonquian languages the designation is a translation of *siksikáwa*: Woods Cree *kaskite·waθasit*, literally 'person with black soles', which first appears as Koskitow-Wathesitock, 1772 (Cocking in Burpee 1908:110–111; cf. Franklin 1822:109). The Plains Cree form is *kaskite·wayasit* (Faries 1938:24; H. Christoph Wolfart, personal communication 1987), from which comes Kuscahtaiwiahsittuck, 1811 (Henry in Coues 1897, 2:537). The Ojibwa form is *makkate·wanasit* (pl. *-ak*, phonemicized, Gatschet 1882, in Hodge 1907–1910, 2:571), cited also as Macateoualasites or Pieds Noirs, 1757 (Bougainville 1908:189) and Muccataihoositeninnewog, 1809 (Henry in Gough 1988–1992, 2:393); the Fox name is *me·mahkate·wanasite·ha* (pl. *-ki*, phonemicized, Gatschet 1882, in Hodge 1907–1910, 2:571). The Cheyenne name is *mo?OhtávEhahtátaneo?O* (sg. *mo?OhtávEhahtátane*) (Glenmore and Leman 1985:201), also recorded as Moqtávhatätä'n (Mooney 1907:422) and Moxtavàtatan (Petter 1913–1915:582). Similar is Gros Ventre *wɔɔ?ɛtɛ́ɛ́níhtɛɛk?i* (Taylor 1994, 1:83), recorded also as Wáotänihtäts (Curtis 1907–1930, 5:154). Languages farther east have names with the same meaning: Shawnee Mkatewetitéta (Swanton 1952:396) and Ottawa Mukkudda Ozitunnug (Tanner 1830:316).

Designations in Siouan languages have the same meaning. The Crow name is *itšipíte* (Medicine Horse 1987:15), which occurs as Aitche jibbla minnach Baga (*itšipíte wiraxpâ·ke*, 'black feet people'), 1805 (McKenzie in W.R. Wood and T.D. Thiessen 1985:249). The cognate Hidatsa form is *icíšipíša* (Jones 1979:32; Parks 1987), which occurs as Aitché shilbisha wrach baga (*icíšipíša ruxpá·ka* 'black-foot people'), 1805 (McKenzie in W.R. Wood and T.D. Thiessen 1985:249) and as both Black foot Indians itze-su-pe-sha and Les Noire Indians at-te-shu-pe-sha-loh-pan-ga, 1819–1820 (E. James in Thwaites 1904–1907, 17:304). The Mandan name is *šipsí* (Hollow 1970:227;

Parks 1987). Sioux forms are Teton, Yankton, and Yanktonai *sihásapa* 'black foot' (Curtis 1907–1930, 3:141; Buechel 1970:733; J.P. Williamson 1902:18); the Assiniboine form is identical, *sihásapa* (Parks and DeMallie 1988:346), cited also as Seehasap, 1809 (Henry in Gough 1988–1992, 2:393). It is also the same in the Dhegiha languages: Osage *sísape* and Kansa *sísábe* (Robert L. Rankin, personal communications 1987, 1990); Omaha *sísabe* (phonemicization of Fletcher and LaFlesche 1911:102), Ponca *sísabe* (J.H. Howard 1965:133). Winnebago *sí·sé·p* has the same meaning (Kenneth Miner, personal communication 1987).

Tribes west and south of the Blackfoot that employ names with the same meaning are Flathead *sčq̓ʷáyšin* 'black foot', truncated in the late twentieth century to *sčq̓ʷe* (Giorda 1877–1879, 2:35, retranscribed; Sarah G. Thomason, personal communication 1994); Colville-Okanagan *stq̓ʷˁayxnx* 'black foot person' (Mattina 1987:168); Spokane Schḳwaíshĭni 'black foot people' (Curtis 1907–1930, 7:165); and Kootenai Katskakílsaka 'blackened legs' (Curtis 1907–1930, 7:168). Perhaps related to the preceding or a borrowing of one is the Nez Perce name *ˀisq̓óyxnix*, the derivation of which is not known (Aoki 1994:1081) but is said to mean 'deceptive' (Curtis 1907–1930, 8:163).

On the southern Plains the Kiowa name is *tʰǫ̀·-kʰǫ́·-gɔ́* 'black legs' (Laurel Watkins, personal communication 1979) and the Plains Apache name is bìgá·sìtʽè·cí· 'their legs black' (Bittle 1952–1953). A Comanche recording Tuhuvti-ómokat (Gatschet 1884, in Hodge 1907–1910, 2:571) also means 'black legs'.

Pawnee *asúhka·tit* and Arikara *xUhkátit* both mean 'black moccasin' (Parks 1965–1990); the Arikara form does not mean 'black foot' (contra Curtis 1907–1930, 5:151).

Another, reputedly old, Cheyenne designation is pó-o-mas 'blankets whitened with earth' (Hayden 1862:290), recorded also as Póomŭ'ts 'gray (i.e., unpainted) robe' (Mooney 1907:422).

An anomalous form is Sarcee *goží* 'goose' (Eung-Do Cook, personal communication 1990). The Arapaho and Shoshone names for the Blackfoot are borrowings (see Piegan and Blood below).

The Plains sign language gesture for the Blackfoot has several variants. One is to make the signs for 'moccasin' and 'black' (W.P. Clark 1885:68), a reflection of the northern Caddoan names. Another sign is made "by extending the right thumb and forefinger at right angles to each other and placing them about the front of one of the legs below the knee—forefinger on the left side—the hand is then carried down toward the foot and outward in a sweeping curve above the instep"; no satisfactory explanation of this sign was ever recorded (H.L. Scott 1912–1934). Other reported sign language variants are equally obscure in their reference but do designate a moccasin or legwear (see Mallery 1881:462–463).

One list of Blackfoot bands was recorded in the late nineteenth century (Grinnell 1892:208–209). The names of those bands are presented in tables 2–4.

Blood tribe

The Blackfoot name for the Blood tribe is *ká·ína·wa* 'many chiefs' (Allan R. Taylor, personal communication 1994; Frantz and Russell 1989:130). It appears as Kaĭnna and Kahna 1832–1834 (Maximilian in Thwaites 1904–1907, 23:95), Ke'na (Hale 1846:219), Kai'-e-na (Hayden 1862:256), Ki'-na, 1861 (L.H. Morgan 1959:200), Ka-na-ans, 1872 (Jean L'Heureux in Dempsey 1961:12), Kenna (Butler 1874:266), Kena (Hale 1885:1), and Kai'-nah (Grinnell 1892:209). The derived form *káínaikoana* 'a Blood Indian man' was recorded as Kine-ne-ai-koon, 1808 (Henry in Gough 1988–1992, 2:393) and Kainoè-koon (Franklin 1822:109).

The Blackfoot name was borrowed into Arapaho as *koúnehe·noˀ* (*kóunéhe·*, sg.) (Ives Goddard, personal communication 1990), recorded also as ka-wi'-na-han and erroneously translated as 'black people' (Hayden 1862:326). It was borrowed in Gros Ventre as *kɔ́ɔ́wunɛ́hɛɛɔh* (*kɔ́ɔ́wunɛ́hɛɛˀ*, sg.) (A.R. Taylor 1994, 1:89).

The name Blood is a translation of the Woods Cree name *miθko-iθiniwak* 'blood people', which was recorded as Mithco, 1767–1791 (G. Williams 1969:207); Mithco-Athinuwuck, 1772 (Cocking in Burpee 1908:110); Mecoethinnuuck, 1809 (Henry in Gough 1988–1992, 2:393) and Meethnothinyoowuc (Franklin 1822:109). The Plains Cree form is *mihko·wiyiniw* (Bloomfield 1984:138). The source of the Cree name is unknown, although several writers have recorded stories explaining its origin (Maximilian in Thwaites 1904–1907, 23:95; Hayden 1863:256). In Ojibwa the name was recorded as Misquoeninnewog, 1809 (Henry in Gough 1988–1992, 2:393).

The English designation Blood appears variously as Bloody Indians, 1772 (Cocking in Burpee 1908:110);

Table 2. Blackfoot Bands

Grinnell 1892:208–209	*A.R. Taylor 1994a*
Puh-ksi-nah'-mah-yiks, Flat Bows	Flat Bows, Smashed Flat Bows
Mo-tah'-tos-iks, Many Medicines	Medicine Men All Over
Siks-in'-o-kaks, Black Elks	Black Elks
E'-mi-tah-sai-yiks, Dogs Naked	
Sai'-yiks, Liars	Liars; Crees
Ai-sik'-stŭk-iks, Biters	Biters
Tsin-ik-tsis'-tso-yiks, Early Finished Eating	Early Finished Eating
Ap'-i-kai-yiks, Skunks	Skunks

Table 3. Blood Bands

Grinnell 1829:209	*Hayden 1862:264*	*Frantz and Russell (1989)*
Siks-in′-o-kaks, Black Elks	sik-si-no′-kai-īks, Black Elks	
Ah-kwo′-nis-tsists, Many Lodge Poles		
Ap-ut′-o-si-kai-nah, North Bloods		
Is-tsi′-kai-nah, Woods Bloods		
In-uhk′-so-yi-stam-iks, Long Tail Lodge Poles		
Nit′-ik-skiks, Lone Fighters	ni-tet′-ska-īks, They that fight by themselves	
Siks-ah′-pun-iks, Blackblood		
Ah-kaik′-sum-iks		
I-sis′-o-kas-im-iks, Hair Shirts		
Ah-kai′-po-kaks, Many Children		
Sak-si-nah′-mah-yiks, Short Bows		
Ap′-i-kai-yiks, Skunks		
Ahk-o′-tash-iks, Many Horses		
	i-ni′-po-i, Buffalo rising up	
	mum-i′-o-yīks, Fish-eaters	
		akáístaʔaowa, Many Ghosts
		akáóki·na·wa, Many Graves

Table 4. Piegan Bands

Grinnell 1829:209-210	*Hayden 1862:264*	*Taylor 1994a, based on Uhlenbeck 1934*	*Frantz and Russell (1995)*
Ah′-pai-tup-iks, Blood People	a′-pe-tup-i, Blood People	aápaitapiks, Blood People	
Ah-kai-yi-ko-ka′-kin-iks, White Breasts	kai′-it-ko-ki′-ki-naks, White-breasted Band	kaìékaukèkiniks, White Breast People	*kayikkaoʔki·ki·ksi*, White Chest Clan
Ki′yis, Dried Meat		káiis, Dried Meat	
Sik-ut′-si-pum-aiks, Black Patched Moccasins	si-ka′-tsi-po-maks, The Band with black patched moccasins	sikátsìpamaiks, Black Patched Moccasins	
Sik-o-pok′-si-maiks, Blackfat Roasters		sikoxpóxsimaiks, Black Fat Melters	
Tsin-ik-sis′-tso-yiks, Early Finished Eating		siniksístsauyìks, Eat Before Others	
Kut′-ai-īm-iks, They Don′t Laugh	ko-te′-yi-mīks, The Band that do not laugh	kαtáiimiks, Not Laughers	*káta'yayimmi·ksi*, Never Laughs Clan
I′-pok-si-maiks, Fat Roasters	e-pōħ′-si-mīks, The Band that fries fat	ixpóxsimaiks, Fat Melters	
Sik′-o-kīt-sim-iks, Black Doors	si-kōħ′-i-tsim, The Band with black doors	síkoxkitsimaiks, Black Door People[a]	
Ni-taw′-yiks, Lone Eaters		nitáuyiks, Lone Eaters	
Ap′-i-kai-yiks, Skunks	a-pi-kai′-yiks, The Polecat Band	ápekaììks, Skunks	
Mi-ah-wah′-pīt-sīks, Seldom Lonesome			*miá·wa·hpitsi·ksi*, Never Lonesome Clan
Nīt′-ak-os-kit-si-pup-iks, Obstinate	ne-ta′-ka-ski-tsi-pup′-īks, People that have their own way, that listen to no one		

(continued on next page)

Table 4. Piegan Bands (continued)

Grinnell 1829:209-210	*Hayden 1862:264*	*Taylor 1994a, based on Uhlenbeck 1934*	*Frantz and Russell (1995)*
Nit'-ik-skiks Lone Fighters		nitáitskaiks, Lone Fighters[b]	*ni?táítsskaiksi*, Lone Fighter Clan
I-nuks'-iks, Small Robes	a-mīks'-eks, Little Robes	ináksiks, Small Robes	
Mi-aw'-kin-ai-yiks, Big Topknots		myɔxkínaiaiks, Hard Topknots	
Esk'-sin-ai-tŭp-īks, Worm People	is-ksi'-na-tup-i, The Worm people	isksínaitskaiks, Bug People	
I-nuk-si'-kah-ko-pwa-īks, Small Brittle Fat		inaksikakoxpùyiks, Small Soft Grease People	
Kah'-mi-taiks, Buffalo Dung		kàmíxtáiks, Buffalo Chips	
Kut-ai-sot'-sĭ-man, No Parfleche			
Ni-tot'-si-ksis-stan-iks, Kill Close By			
Mo-twai'-naiks, All Chiefs		motúiinaiks, Chiefs All Over	
Mo-kŭm'-iks, Red Round Robes			
Mo-tah'-tos-iks, Many Medicines	mo-ta'-tōts, The Band that are all medicine men	motátosiks, Medicine Men All Over[c]	
	sus-kso'-yīks, The Band with hairy mouths	itstsóyiks, iststsóyike, Rough Mouth People[d]	
	e-ka-to'-pi-staks, The Band that have finished packing, as bales of anything		
		moxkɑ́miks, Pelicans	
		nitáisiksikimisimàiks, Lone Coffee Makers	
		saxkókiniks, Short Necks	
		sikokóóyiks, Black Lodges	
			immoyíssksisi·ksi, Hairy Nose Clan, or *ko·tsa·ki·yi?ta·ksi*, Padded Saddle Clan
			ksikksisóka?simi·ksi, White Robe Clan
			ómahkokatáóoyi·ksi, Gopher Eater Clan

[a]Said by Uhlenbeck to be a branch of the Black Patch People.
[b]Said by Uhlenbeck to be a branch of the Fat Melters.
[c]Said by Uhlenbeck to be "the ancient name of the motúiinaiks."
[d]Said by Uhlenbeck to be a branch of the Blood People (aápaitapìks).

Bloods, 1795 (Tomison in Alice M. Johnson 1967:21); Bloodies (Hind 1859:116); and Blood People and Blood Blackfoot (L.H. Morgan 1871:289). It is cited in German as Blut Indianer (Mackenzie 1802b:79 and Walch map 1805, in Hodge 1907–1910, 1:643) and in French as Indiens du Sang (Mackenzie 1802a:176) and Gens du Sang (Duflot de Mofras 1844, 2:342).

The same meaning occurs in the designations used by various Indian tribes: Assiniboine *wéwįčʰašta* 'blood man' (Parks and DeMallie 1988:427), recorded as Waiwitchusha, 1811 (Henry in Gough 1988–1992, 2:393); Santee *wéwičʰašta* (J.P. Williamson 1902:19) and *wéwičʰaša*; Yanktonai and Teton *wéwičʰaša* (Buechel 1970:576; Curtis 1907–1930, 3:141); Crow *i·rwače·* 'blood man' (Medicine Horse 1987:15), recorded earlier as Í- matsě (Curtis 1907–1930, 4:180); Flathead Snguls'chi 'blood people' (Giorda 1877–1879, 2:38), recorded also as Sĭnhuhlschi (Curtis 1907–1930, 7:165); Spokane Sníhulischí (Curtis

1907–1930, 7:165); Kootenai wanmukantĕk 'blood people' (Curtis 1907–1930, 7:168).

In the sign language the gesture for the Blood is made by drawing the forefinger across the lips (Curtis 1907–1930, 18:186).

Two lists of Blood bands were recorded in the nineteenth century (Hayden 1862:264; Grinnell 1892:208–209). The names in them are presented in table 3.

Piegan tribe

The Blackfoot name for the Piegan tribe was *pi·kániwa*, also *pi·ʔkániwa* (sg. *pi·kani*, *pi·ʔkáni*), from which the English designation Piegan derives. It has no known linguistic derivation, although because of erroneous associations with other words it is frequently said to mean 'scabby robes', 'badly dressed robes', or 'chapped skin' (Hayden 1862:256; Curtis 1907–1930, 18:187).

Throughout the historical literature this tribe has been known by a rendition of its own name. Examples that reflect the Blackfoot form include Pikani, 1840 (Wilkes 1845, 4:471); Pikun′-i (Hayden 1862:256); Pe-kan′-ne (L.H. Morgan 1871:289); Pi-kŭn'-i (Grinnell 1892:209); and Pikuni (Shultz 1926:3). The derived form *pi·káni·koana* 'a Piegan Indian man' is reflected in several recordings: Pe kan ne koon, 1808 (Henry in Coues 1897, 2:537); Peganoe′-koon (Franklin 1822:109); Piega-ne-ko-en (L'Heureux 1878:12); and Pieganekowex (Lacombe 1886:81).

The Blackfoot form was borrowed into Plains Cree as *pi·kano-iyiniw* and *piye·kano-iyiniw* (Lacombe 1874:553). The compounding form *pi·kano* is reflected in several historical renditions: Pikaraminoüaches, 1736 (La Vérendrye in Burpee 1927:248); Pegonow, 1772 (Cocking in Burpee 1908:111); Pekenow (Manchester House Journals entry for 10/8/1787; cf. 3/13/1787, 10/23/1787); Pekanow, 1792 (Fidler in Alice M. Johnson 1967:15n); Pikenow, 1800 (Thompson in Dempsey 1966:8); Picaneaux (Mackenzie 1802a:176); Pecaneaux (Schoolcraft 1851–1857, 5:179); and Peaginow (Butler 1874:266). These early forms were superseded in English and French by those without the final vowel: Paegan (Umfreville 1790:103); Piegans, 1794 (M'Gillivray in Morton 1929:34, cf. 31); Peagans, 1808 (Thompson in M.C. White 1950:28, cf. 178); Pegans (Franklin 1822:108); Pagans, 1835 (Russell 1955:32); Piekán (Hale 1846:219); and Piagan, 1872 (L'Heureux in Dempsey 1961:12). Other variants are given in Hodge (1907–1910, 2:246–247).

The Woods Cree form of the name, *pi·kano-iθiniwak* (pl.), is reflected in two historical recordings: Pekunnoethinnuucks, 1809 (Henry in Gough 1988–1992, 2:393) and Peganoo-eythinyoowuc (Franklin 1822:108). The Ojibwa form was recorded as Pekumnoeninnewog, 1809 (Henry in Gough 1988–1992, 2:393).

The spelling and pronunciation of English Piegan (ˈpāˌgăn, formerly pēˈāˌgăn or pēˈāgŭn) and French Piégane (Lacombe 1874:325) reflect the Cree form with *piye·kan-*. In Canada the English spelling Peigan is preferred, while in the United States the accepted spelling is Piegan.

Borrowed forms of the name Piegan appear in several neighboring Indian languages: Assiniboine *pikána* (Parks and DeMallie 1988:327), cited as Pegan, 1809 (Henry in Gough 1988–1992, 2:393); Yanktonai Píḳkan (Curtis 1907–1930, 3:141); Crow *pi·akále·* (Medicine Horse 1987:16); Cheyenne *péékánE* (Glenmore and Leman 1985:201; Curtis 1907–1930, 6:158); and Shoshone Pak′ ke nah (Ballou 1880–1881), recorded also as Pi ke (Gebow 1859), Pah kee (Hill 1877), Par′ keeh (Stuart 1865), and Paw-kees, 1819–1820 (Say in E. James in Thwaites 1904–1907, 17:299).

Two similar English designations, Muddy Water Indians, 1772 (Cocking in Burpee 1908:111) and Muddy River Indians (Manchester House Journals, entry for 7/9/1787), assume derivation of the name Piegan from Cree *pi·kan* 'it is muddy water'. Such a Cree form, however, is not a likely ethnonym, even though a Blackfoot etymology of the name cannot be found.

Other tribal names for the Piegan are Gros Ventre *cɔɔsʔi* 'enemy' (A.R. Taylor 1994, 2:109); Kutenai Sánhla 'bad ones' (Curtis 1907–1930, 7:168); Flathead Schĭkoí (literal meaning unknown; Curtis 1907–1930, 7:165); and Sarcee *cidó osgona* (literal meaning unknown; Eung-Do Cook, personal communication 1990).

Three lists of Piegan bands were recorded in the late nineteenth and early twentieth centuries (Hayden 1862:264; Grinnell 1892:208–209; Uhlenbeck 1934). Those names, together with modern transcriptions and translations, are presented in table 4.

Sources

Two major bibliographies list sources on the Blackfoot tribes, B.R. Johnson (1988), an annotated alphabetical listing, and Dempsey and Moir (1989), arranged by subject. Ewers (1958) provides the best historical overview, a claims case chronology of the Montana Blackfeet (1974), a comprehensive ethnography focusing on the integration of horses in Blackfoot culture (1955), a general introduction to the Blackfoot (1944), and a study of crafts (1945). McClintock (1910) presents a very readable account of Blackfoot culture.

For the specialist, the most comprehensive works are the studies by Wissler on material culture (1910), social life (1911), sacred bundles (1912), societies (1913), the Sun Dance (1918), and mythology (Wissler and Duvall 1908).

Grinnell (1892) contains adventure stories, legends, and accounts of daily life. Uhlenbeck (1911, 1912) presents collections of texts in the Blackfoot language, while Frantz and Russell (1989) is a Blackfoot-English dictionary. Hellson (1974) and A. Johnston (1987) present data on Blackfoot ethnobotany.

Goldfrank (1945) is a study of historical changes in Blackfoot social life; Hanks and Hanks (1950) examines the historical relationship between the Blackfoot and the Canadian government. Harrod (1972) is a study of the missionization of the Blackfoot. Carriker et al. (1976:28–30) is a guide to early Blackfoot language works by Jesuit missionaries. Two works deal with the Blackfeet Reservation in Montana: Farr (1984) is a historical study from 1882–1945, and McFee (1972) presents a brief historical summary and an analysis of the modern period. Samek (1987) is a comparative study of the effects of U.S. and Canadian policy on the Blackfoot from 1880 to 1920.

Dempsey (1972, 1978, 1980) present biographies of Crowfoot, Charcoal, and Red Crow, nineteenth-century leaders; biographical sketches of these and other prominent Canadian Blackfoot are also in MacEwan (1971). Two accounts by Blackfoot themselves are Mountain Horse (1979), a Blood Indian, and Bullchild (1985), a Piegan.

In addition, there are a number of accounts by fur traders that contain significant data. Two of the best are the early nineteenth-century writings of David Thompson (Glover 1962) and of Alexander Henry the Younger and David Thompson (Coues 1897). Important travelers' accounts include Maximilian (1843; in Thwaites 1904–1907, 22–24), Paul Kane (1859; Harper 1971), and Catlin (1841; see also Truettner 1979).

A number of museums in North America and Europe hold good collections of Blackfoot material. Among the best are the Glenbow Museum, Calgary, Alberta; Provincial Museum of Alberta, Edmonton, which houses the impressive Scriver Collection (Scriver 1990); National Museum of the American Indian, New York; Smithsonian Institution, Washington; American Museum of Natural History, New York; British Museum, London; Field Museum of Natural History, Chicago (VanStone 1992); Canadian Museum of Civilization, Ottawa; Southwest Museum, Los Angeles; Denver Art Museum; and Royal Ontario Museum (Brownstone 1993).

Sarcee

HUGH A. DEMPSEY

The Sarcee (ˌsärˈsē) a small Athapaskan-speaking* group, originated as part of the woodland-dwelling Beaver Indians of the Subarctic. In the period immediately before European contact, they became a transitional people who hunted on the plains but wintered in the woodlands with their parent group. Early in the eighteenth century, when Crees armed with weapons from European traders penetrated westward, a wedge was driven between the Beaver and the Sarcee. Already adapted to a plains lifestyle, the Sarcee abandoned the last vestiges of woodland life and remained on the plains. In 1772–1773, Matthew Cocking recognized them as a distinct tribe of "Equestrian Indians" (Burpee 1908:110), and in 1790 they were described as "a small tribe which has separated from the main body, and now harbor in some country about the Stony [Rocky] Mountains, where they keep to themselves, for not many have as yet appeared at any of the trading-houses" (Umfreville 1954:103).

Origins

Sarcee legends explain their separation from the Beaver. In the most common story, the entire tribe was crossing a large lake in midwinter when a woman noticed an animal's horn protruding from the ice. As she struck it with an ax to free it, the ice cracked, separating the tribe into two divisions (W.A. Tims 1929:7). Another tale relates the separation to a dispute over the killing of a dog (Leslie 1977:7). A third account mentions a quarrel between two chiefs that led to the formation of two distinct bands that subsequently separated (Jenness 1932:3). After their separation from the Beaver, the Sarcee allied with the Blackfoot for purposes of survival (Wilson 1888:243; Curtis 1907–1930, 18:91, 141).

*The phonemes of Sarcee are: (plain voiceless stops and affricates) *d*, *λ*, *ʒ*, *ǯ*, *g*, g^{w}, *ʔ*; (voiceless aspirated stops and affricates) *t*, *ƛ*, *c*, *č*, *k*, k^{w}; (glottalized stops and affricates) *ṫ*, *ƛ̇*, *ċ*, *č̇*, *k̇*; $\dot{k}^{w}$; (voiced fricatives) *l*, *z*, *ž*, *γ*; (voiceless fricatives) *ł*, *s*, *š*, *x*, *h*; (nasals) *m*, *n*; (semivowels) *y*, *w*; (vowels) *i*, *a* (low front), *o* (partly rounded low back), *u* ([o], [u]); (high tone) v́, (low tone) v̀, (mid tone) v̄. In the analysis of Cook (1984) there are also geminate vowels, which may have the same or different tones; younger speakers may also have contrastive long vowels: *i·*, *a·*, *o·*, *u·*. In an alternative analysis in which only two tones are taken as phonemic, high tone is v́ and low tone unmarked.

This inventory of phonemes is given by Cook (1984), who represents them with the following symbols: d, dl, dz, dj, g, gw, '; t, tl, ts, tc, k, kw; t', tł', ts', tc', k', kw'; l, z, j, γ; ł, s, c, x, h; m, n; y, w; i, a, o, u; i·, a·, o·, u·; and the same marking of tones.

Territory and Environment

By 1815, the Sarcee hunting grounds were described as the territory between the Red Deer and Battle rivers, bounded on the east by Beaverhill Lake and on the west by the Rocky Mountains (Hudson's Bay Company 1967:15). By the mid-nineteenth century they had moved farther south, along the Bow and Red Deer rivers, on the northwest fringe of the Great Plains (fig. 1). Alternately at war and peace with the Plains Cree, and Stoney, the Sarcee consistently fought the Crow, Kootenai, Flathead, Northern Shoshone, and Assiniboine (Curtis 1907–1930, 18:91).

The major portion of the Sarcee hunting ground was short-grass plains dotted with aspen and willow. Heavier growths of poplar and birch were found along the streams, while the area closer to the mountains abounded in spruce and pine. Winters were long and cold, with deep snow, particularly in the foothills, limiting winter travel. Springs were often cool and wet, while summers were hot and autumns warm and dry.

Culture in the Early Nineteenth Century

As part of the Blackfoot confederacy, the Sarcee often ranged far south into their allies' hunting grounds and camped with them, particularly with the Blood and Blackfoot. Despite their alliance with the Blackfoot tribes, the Sarcee often had violent disagreements with them, striving to assert their independence. In some instances open conflict with one Blackfoot tribe caused them to seek refuge with another. Perhaps because of this independence, a trader in 1811 wrote that they had the reputation of being "the bravest tribe in all the plains, who dare face ten times their own number" (Henry in Coues 1897, 2:737).

During the mid-nineteenth century, the Sarcee successfully maintained a balance between independence and reliance upon the Blackfoot. They became bilingual, using their own language within their camps but speaking Blackfoot to their allies and to the fur traders. They adopted most aspects of Plains Indian life but wherever possible they added their own distinctive features.

Subsistence

The Sarcee depended on buffalo hunting, which formed the basis of their economy. In late autumn, they used jumps or

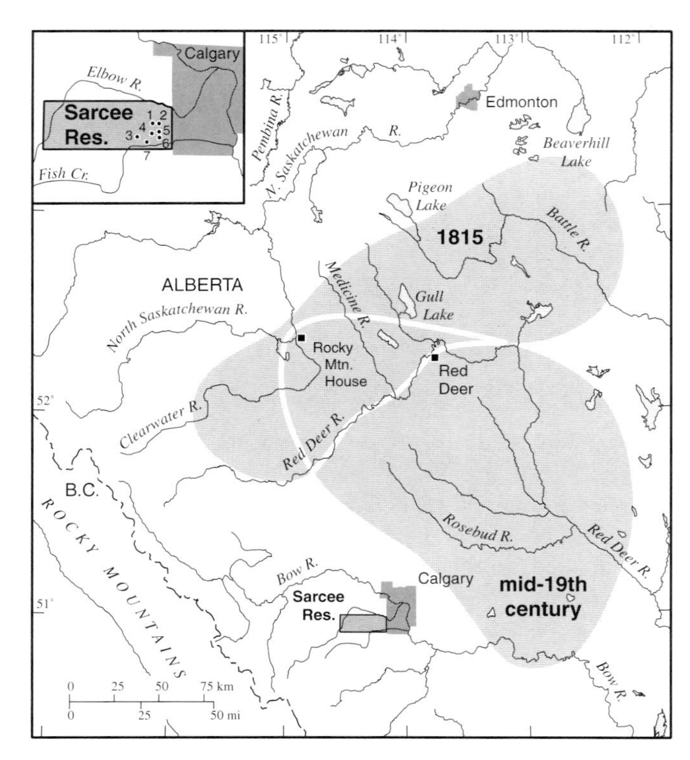

Fig. 1. Sarcee range in the early 19th century showing southward shift from 1815 to mid-19th century, area of continuous use 1815–1850s, and 20th-century reserve. Inset, Sarcee Res. and villages: 1, White Elk; 2, Starlight; 3, Crowchild; 4, Night; 5, Wolf; 6, Two Guns; 7, Otter.

pounds to kill large numbers of buffalo. The meat was dried and stored, and some of it was pounded and mixed with dried berries and fat to make pemmican (fig. 2). At this time of year, coyotes, wolves, and foxes were caught in deadfalls, an individual hunter having 7–10 such traps (Curtis 1907–1930, 18:93, 95). Buffalo also provided skins for clothing and shelters, and bones for tools.

Other food animals included antelope, deer, elk, mountain sheep, mountain goat, porcupine, rabbit, and squirrel. Fish and domestic dogs generally were not eaten. Eggs and ducks, geese, and swans were consumed in lesser quantity. Prairie turnips, serviceberries, blueberries, and chokecherries (fig. 2) were the primary vegetables and fruits gathered and eaten (Curtis 1907–1930, 18:99).

Social and Political Organization

The Sarcee were divided into bands, each composed of a number of closely related families (table 1). Bands hunted and camped together and each recognized a leader, often the senior male member, whose authority was exerted through popular support and through the weight of his own prestige. The kinship system, which formed the basis of social organization, was bilateral, recognizing relationships through both the father and mother. No positive rule for determining band membership was recorded, and a family could change band affiliation at any time. Marriages

Glenbow-Alberta Inst., Calgary:-NA-667-338.

Fig. 2. Maggie Big Belly pulverizing dried meat, which is then mixed with serviceberry mash to make pemmican. Photograph by Arnold Lupson, Sarcee Res., Alta., 1920s.

Table 1. Sarcee Band Names

1. *gooǯí-tii cúut̓ína*	'Blood Sarcee'
2. *λí gu γana*	'killed by smoke'
3. *míċida niciλ̓aná*	'his small robe'
4. *náciis t̓íiná*	'turning the head away'
5. *mo γá-kuk̓aacílná*	'his lodge cut off (at bottom)'
6. *čáǯi γá mitċidáá-yina*	'his three-year-old buffalo robe'
7. *mo γá gúčowná*	'his large lodge'
8. *cúut̓ína-tii-yina*	'genuine Sarcee'

SOURCE: Curtis (1907–1930, 18:102); phonemicized by Eung-Do Cook, personal communication 1991.

usually took place between members of different bands, and the couple generally lived with the wife's family, which the new husband was expected to help support. Band constituency was fluid; a leader attracted a following that would stay with him only as long as he was successful. There was no tribal chief, but on formal occasions, such as a visit to a trading post, the most influential band chiefs would speak on behalf of the whole tribe (Jenness 1932:10–11; Curtis 1907–1930, 18:102, 161).

Because of the severity of the winters, the Sacree often camped for weeks at a time in the protective valleys within their hunting grounds, venturing out only in pursuit of buffalo. In the spring they divided into smaller family units consisting of one to a dozen families to hunt, make war, renew their tepee poles, and to replace worn lodge covers. In early summer the bands came together, sometimes joining one of the Blackfoot tribes, to hold individual society dances and the tribal Sun Dance. The summer camp was organized by band, each having its place in the camp circle, with the tepees of the band chiefs erected in the center of the circle (Jenness 1932:13; cf. Curtis 1907–1930, 18:103).

In the fall and again in the spring, visits were made to Rocky Mountain House or Fort Edmonton to trade buffalo robes, skins, dried meat and horses to the Hudson's Bay Company. In winter, the entire tribe often camped within the same river valley, with bands situated one or two days' riding distance of each other to facilitate winter visiting (Jenness 1932:12).

Technology

The tools and weapons of the Sarcee were traditional objects made of wood, bone, and stone, as well as metal tools and utensils obtained from traders. Scrapers, fleshers, and beaming tools used in tanning were made of bone, with the scrapers being fitted with flaked stone or metal blades. Axes were made of sharpened moose or elk antlers. Weapons consisted of the sinew-backed serviceberry or chokecherry bow and arrow, lance, war club, flintlock, knife, and shield. Containers were made of rawhide, animal paunches, and the whole skins of smaller mammals. Copper trade kettles were also used.

The only dwelling used by the Sarcee was the tepee, usually made of 12–14 buffalo skins, with six more forming an interior lining. Like the Blackfoot, they used a four-pole foundation. The wind flaps, which regulated the draft, were controlled by two poles that fitted through eyelets. This style made the tepee distinctive from that of Stoney and Plains Cree Indians, who fitted their poles into pockets sewn into the flaps.

The tepees were owned by women, who were responsible for their erection and dismantling. However, if a tepee bore a painted religious design, this was owned and painted by male members of the household. Although not common, such designs were created either as a result of visions or through transfer from a previous owner (fig. 3) (Leslie 1977:8).

The horse was the primary means of transportation, although the dog was used by poorer families as a beast of burden. The travois, dragged by horses or dogs, was the only vehicle; it was a frame made of poles with a rack for carrying a family's possessions. Horse gear was often embellished with bead decoration as was the clothing of men, women, and children (fig. 4).

Life Cycle

During pregnancy, Sarcee women observed food restrictions so the child would be born strong and healthy. Although girls were sometimes named at birth, a boy remained nameless for a week or two until arrangements could be made for a medicine man or elder warrior to choose an appropriate name. A girl's name remained with her throughout life; but as a boy entered adolescence, he was given a derogatory name and encouraged to perform a brave deed that would entitle him to receive a man's name. Then he would usually be given one that had been owned by a deceased relative (Curtis 1907–1930, 18:104–105; Jenness 1932).

Children remained with their mothers until the age of 9–10, when boys became the responsibility of their father or uncle, who taught them to ride, hunt, and undergo the religious rituals expected of a young man. Women taught their daughters tanning, sewing, beading, and other household arts (Jenness 1932:18–19).

At the age of 14 or 15, a boy joined his first war party, often serving in a menial capacity, gathering firewood and cooking rather than participating in the raid itself. After proving his courage, a boy was recognized as a full member of a war party and was entitled to a share of captured horses. Having distinguished himself in warfare, the youth was again given a new name, and was usually sponsored by his father for membership in the Mosquito society. After this his place in the tepee was no longer at the side with the women, old men, and children, but in the back, at the place of honor opposite the entrance (cf. Jenness 1932:20). Some young men became dandies, and spent many hours attending to their hair and face paint, disdainfully rejecting menial tasks. Often such youths posed on nearby hills or paraded where girls went to fetch water, returning to camp only for their meals.

There were no puberty ceremonies. A girl's virginity was closely guarded, both for family prestige and to permit her to participate in certain ceremonies at the Sun Dance. Courtship usually began with furtive glances while the girl went about her chores, and, if encouraged, the young man tried to be alone with her. This frequently happened while moving camp, when a young man could more easily talk to a prospective wife (Wilson 1888:246). If they decided to marry, arrangements were made by the parents and an exchange of gifts took place between the families. The girl might offer newly made moccasins to the prospective groom. If these were accepted and a return gift given, betrothal was expected (Jenness 1932:23). It was the responsibilty of the bride's family to provide a new tepee and furnishings to the couple and a gift, including horses, to the groom's family, which they returned two-fold to the bride's family (Curtis 1907–1930, 18:107; Honigmann 1956:25–28).

Because of the high mortality rate among men due to hunting and war, there were more women than men, and polygyny was common. A man often married sisters, as well as a deceased brother's widows. The first wife was addressed as "elder sister" by all other wives. Sexual joking was practiced between a man and his sisters-in-law and a woman and her brothers-in-law, whether married or not. Uncles and aunts were classified as older brothers and sisters, except for mother's sisters, who were also called mother. Father's brothers had the greater responsibility in training male children, though a boy might receive gifts from his maternal uncles. Fathers' and mothers' sisters were treated with great respect. A man's relationship to his father-in-law was minimal and mother-in-law avoidance

Glenbow-Alberta Inst., Calgary: top, NA1020-53, bottom left, NA-667-570; bottom right, United Press International, New York.

Fig. 3. Decorated tepees. top, Painting of 2 male figures smoking pipes on a tepee belonging to Crow Collar. Log house with sod roof and a horse travois leaning on poles are nearby. Photograph possibly by John W. Tims, about 1890s. bottom left, Men painting a conventional design of circles at the bottom border, which represent fallen stars, and a top design, representing the sky and constellations. Photograph by Arnold Lupson, 1920s–1930s. bottom right, Tepee painted with the Bee design, which was originally owned by Many Wounds who sold it to Crow Child of the Sarcee Res. Chief Harold Cardinal, president of the Indian Assoc. of Canada, left, and Chief Jim Shot Both Sides, right, with Queen Elizabeth II after a meeting that reaffirmed the provisions of 19th-century treaties regarding land, health services, education, and economic development. Photographed near the Calgary airport, July 1973.

was practiced. A woman interacted more freely with both her parents-in-law (Honigmann 1956; Jenness 1932:24).

A man could punish an adulterous wife by cutting off her nose or ear, or less severely, some of her hair. He might threaten to attack the guilty man and demand payment in horses. He might also divorce his wife. In rare cases, a woman might attack an unfaithful husband, or the guilty woman. She might leave her husband and return to her family, keeping the tepee and her other possessions (Honigmann 1956:29–31).

When a man was dying he was dressed in his finest clothes, painted with red ocher according to his society membership. After death, the body was placed on a platform in a tree, raised on a scaffold, or left inside a tepee that was then sewn shut. A man's horse may have been killed so that his spirit could use it to travel to the land of the dead. Wives, as a sign of mourning, gashed their legs, cut their hair short, and dressed in old and ragged clothes. On occasion, women also severed a finger at the joint (Jenness 1932:38). The spirit of a dead person immediately traveled

Fig. 4. Beaded clothing. left, Big Knife or Old Knife dressed for participation in the Calgary Stampede. He wears beaded moccasins and a horned headdress decorated with ermine and carries a beaded blanket strip. The horse is decorated with a beaded face mask bearing the initials "KWC." Photograph by Arnold Lupson, 1919. right, Big Knife's wife and daughter. The woman wears a velveteen dress with ribbon appliqué on the skirt and a heavily beaded yoke; she wears an upright feather headdress and a cowrie shell choker. The young girl's dress is of hide with a beaded yoke; she also wears a beaded belt and moccasins. Photograph by William J. Oliver, Alta., 1911.

eastward to Great Sand Hills, where it lived with other ancestors in small tepees, cohabitating freely regardless of kin relationships. Some spirits roamed about on earth and made themselves known by whistling (Curtis 1907–1930, 18:110–111).

Men's Societies

The men's societies normally originated in a vision experience of the founder who gave the requisite songs and dress to other members (P.E. Goddard 1914). There were five such societies: Mosquito, Dog, Painted Red, All Associate, and Bird. Membership cut across band affiliations. Younger men first joined the Mosquitos and then progressed to more senior societies. Generally, membership was through purchase, with leadership positions requiring the most goods. After a few years, membership would be sold, and a man would join a new society. The Dog and Painted Red were made up of middle-aged men, while the younger men predominated in the other societies (Jenness 1932:41).

The societies gathered during the summer preceding the Sun Dance, when they inducted new members. Each society in turn held a four day ceremonial, erecting its own special tepee in the center of the camp circle next to those of the chiefs. During this period the society leaders assumed control of the camp. Those who disobeyed the society leaders risked having their tepee pulled down and cut to pieces (P.E. Goddard 1914:465). The Dog and Painted Red society members acted as police for the communal buffalo hunt and distribution of meat, and the Painted Red also policed the Sun Dance. Each society member had his own medicine bundle, which he used for secret rituals as well as for public ceremonies (Jenness 1932:42).

Religion

Morning and evening prayers were directed to the Maker of the Earth, as protection from evil spirits and to insure good dreams. The Maker was the creator, whose dwelling was above in the eastern sky. After sweatlodge ceremonies (fig. 5), offerings to the Maker were hung on trees (Jenness 1932:68). Personal power was gained through dreams that came either spontaneously or during a vision quest (Curtis 1907–1930, 18:112). Young men went to hilltops where they fasted for visions; others received spirit helpers, sacred songs or tepee designs through dreams. Men going to war often sought the advice of a medicine man who, through a vision, might be able to predict their future success or failure. Power gave prosperity, long life, the ability to heal, or protection from death or capture in war. Visions were kept secret and sacred objects were created to invoke the power (Jenness 1932:69). Medicine objects (fig. 6), songs, and rites could be transferred through purchase, and older objects were the most powerful and costly.

Glenbow-Alberta Inst., Calgary: NA-667-637.

Fig. 5. Sweatlodge participants. Heated rocks and a prayer cloth attached to a pole are nearby. Photograph by Arnold Lupson, 1920s–1930s.

Glenbow-Alberta Inst., Calgary: top, NA 667-782; Canadian Mus. of Civilization, Hull, Que.: bottom left, V-D-137 (neg. 73-3701); bottom right, V-D-37 (neg. 92-859).

Fig. 6. Medicine bundle ceremony and sacred paraphernalia. top, Tom Many Horses's wife dancing with medicine pipe. Photograph by Arnold Lupson, 1920s. bottom left, Tobacco cutting board made of wood and decorated with brass tacks. Traces of red paint are in the 4 corners. Collected by Edward Sapir, Sarcee Res., Alta., before 1922; length 29.2 cm. bottom right, Bandolier made of 4 strands of yellow painted seeds strung as beads with owl feathers at one end and a brush of horse tail at the other. An elderly woman, Bird's Hat, made this and other bandoliers for her male relatives to protect them from gunfire after having seen one in a vision. Collected by Diamond Jenness, Sarcee Res., Alta., 1921; length with feathers 85 cm.

The most revered religious objects were the medicine bundles, two of which were highly prized, the Beaver Bundle and the Medicine Pipe Bundle. Each bundle had its own origin myth, songs, and rites. The Beaver Bundle was associated with the cultivation of tobacco and the Sun Dance, and its rites were held before the society dances in the spring during a tobacco planting ceremony. It was also used to call buffalo and contained several buffalo stones, small stones resembling buffalo that were believed to bring good luck in hunting (Jenness 1932:79; Curtis 1907–1930, 18:118). The Medicine Pipe bundle was opened at the first sound of thunder in the spring, at which time a special dance was held (fig. 6). The Bear Knife Bundle was a war medicine that could be transferred by means of a ceremony in which the knife was hurled at the new owner (Curtis 1907–1930, 18:113–114).

Painted tepees were regarded as sacred possessions. In 1921, the Sarcee owned the rites to make 11 such tepees (Jenness 1932:91; Curtis 1907–1930, 18:116–118).

Eagle trapping was a highly developed ritual process involving numerous religious prohibitions and prayers. When eagles were trapped, the hunters carried them carefully, walking slowly and thanking the powers for success. The eagles were laid in the eagle-trapping tepee at the place of honor opposite the doorway, with buffalo stones set up between them and the central fireplace. A dance was held and sacred songs were sung. If any buffalo stones fell over during the night, it meant that the eagle trappers would continue to have success. When the trapping was completed, a feast was given, after which the eagles were ritually skinned (Curtis 1907–1930, 18:95–99).

The most important religious ceremony was the Sun Dance, celebrated in July or August when the saskatoon berries were ripe. One hundred buffalo tongues were required for offerings and a feast. Lasting nine days, the ceremony was held in fulfillment of a vow made by a woman who was a virgin or who was unquestionably faithful to her husband. The vow was usually given for the healing of the sick or the safe return of a family member from a war expedition. The first four days involved a 100-willow sweatlodge ritual and movement to the site of the dance. On the fifth day the Sun Dance lodge was constructed and the following four days were dedicated to dancing for power and renewal. Vows made by young men were fulfilled at this time, as each was pierced on the chest and attached by thongs to the center pole. Other men vowed to fast in a specially made hut within the Sun Dance lodge. Women who had remained faithful in marriage could vow to consume a sacramental portion of dried buffalo tongue, thereby receiving special blessings for their entire families (P.E. Goddard 1919:271–282; Jenness 1932:47–57).

History

Throughout the period of recorded history, the Sarcee have been closely identified with the Blackfoot, camping and hunting with them but maintaining their separate identity. They suffered a major loss during the smallpox epidemic of 1837–1838 and by the middle of the nineteenth century they normally hunted along the Red Deer and Bow rivers. In 1855, James Doty described them as "British Indians, who neither hunt or trade on American soil" (Doty 1966:25), yet within a decade they were commonly traveling into Montana Territory with the Blackfoot.

In 1869–1870 another smallpox epidemic reduced the number of Sarcee lodges from 50 to 12. In addition, Montana traders discovered they could sell whiskey and repeating rifles from forts in southern Alberta without fear of arrest. Although Canada had assumed jurisdiction of the area from Great Britain, no means existed for enforcing law and order.

During the next five years, intertribal killings, starvation and poverty plagued all the tribes of the region. In 1874, the situation became so bad that the Canadian government sent the North West Mounted Police to put down the illegal traffic in alcohol and guns. In 1877, the government negotiated Treaty No. 7 with the Sarcee as well as the Blackfoot tribes and the Stoney. Signing on behalf of the Sarcee was Bull Head, who was chosen head chief, while Many Horses, The Drum, and Eagle Robe were named as minor chiefs. A total of 255 Sarcee were entered on the Canadian government rolls (table 2).

The Sarcee first accepted a common reserve with the Blood and Blackfoot along the Bow River (Sarcee 145). However, in 1883, after the disappearance of the buffalo, the Sarcee received a reserve of their own just west of Calgary, comprising 108 square miles. The size of the reserve was based on the treaty provision of five persons per square mile (Morris 1880:369).

During the first 15 years on their reserve, the men spent much of their time hunting in the nearby foothills or working for farmers and ranchers in the district. The proximity of the reserve to Calgary also provided a market for hay, firewood, berries, and other products. At the same time, the town was a continuing source of social problems, while the reserve itself became a haven for indigent Indians from other tribes, particularly the Plains and Woodland Crees, who had gravitated to Calgary.

Separated from the Blackfoot, the relatively small Sarcee population found it difficult to maintain the Sun Dance and the exchange of medicine bundles. Yet, in 1895 the Indian agent complained that they were "more tenacious of their customs and superstitions than other Indians" (Dempsey 1986a:40).

Shortly after settling on the reserve, Anglican missionaries opened a school and were diligent in their efforts to convert the tribe to Christianity. However, by 1896 the missionary complained that not a single adult on the reserve had been converted.

The introduction of cattle ranching in 1896 heralded a new era, and within a decade some families became self-supporting. Whereas Sarcee had difficulty in adjusting to farming, the cattle industry was a vocation that they could accept.

From 1896 until 1945, the economic development of the Sarcee was minimal. During these years, sickness, mostly tuberculosis, was responsible for a high death rate, with 12 births and 30 deaths in 1896 being typical. By 1924 the population had slipped to 160 individuals, and the problem became so acute that a doctor was appointed Indian agent in order to combat tuberculosis. His efforts met with success, and a gradual improvement in health conditions became evident.

The early years of the twentieth century also marked the period when speculators coveted the valuable reserve lands. Attempts were repeatedly made to force the sale of parts of the reserve, but in each instance the Sarcee refused. The only land loss occurred in 1931 when some 600 acres were sold to hold the backwaters of a reservoir, and in 1952 when 940 acres were sold for a military camp. Those 940 acres were returned to the Sarcee in 1996.

The proximity of the reserve to Calgary was both an asset and a liability. In 1962, the Sarcee became one of the first reserves in Alberta to lose all school facilities when the decision was made to bus students to the city. Although this provided access to excellent educational facilities, and several Sarcees went on to pursue academic studies, the closing of reserve schools exacerbated the problem of cultural loss as few opportunities existed for language or cultural training. In 1992, an elementary school was built on the reserve, and a high school in 1994.

The Sun Dance and medicine pipe ceremonies became moribund, and few visible forms of native religion remained. However, the interest in traditional dress, music and dance persisted, encouraged in part by the Sarcee Indian Days, which began in 1961, and by their active involvement in the Indian encampment featured annually since 1923 at the Calgary Stampede (Starlight 1983:24). Groups such as the Broken Knife Singers became well known throughout the region. Very few families remained conversant in the Sarcee language in the 1990s.

The Sarcee in the 1970s established a cultural center on the reserve and later added the Sarcee People's Museum. With a resident population of about 850 in 1987 (Canada.

Table 2. Population, 1780s–1997

Year	*Tents*	*Men*	*Total*	*Source*
1780s	90		650	Thompson in Glover 1962:240
1801	35	120		Mackenzie 1802:lxvii
1801	70			Fidler in Josephy 1961:324
1810	90	150		Henry in Coues 1897, 2:532
1824	100			Franklin 1824, 1:170
1841	50	100	350	Simpson 1841
1843	45		350	Rowand in Maclean 1896:10
1859	45		360	Hind 1859:chap. 13
1870	40		420	Sully 1870
1870	12			Butler 1874:370
1877			255	Dempsey 1971:5
1924			160	Dempsey 1971:8
1971			475	Dempsey 1971:8
1987			889	Canada. Indian and Northern Affiars 1987:52
1997			1,264	Canada. Indian and Northern Affairs 1988:41

Indian and Northern Affairs 1987:52), the Sarcee occupy a reserve roughly 6 by 18 miles on the outskirts of Calgary. Within the reserve, the standard of living was rural; farming and ranching were the primary occupations, along with employment related to tribal administration. Although there were employment opportunities available on the reserve, these competed with the city for the attention of tribal members (Sarcee Executive Staff 1983:18–19).

Within the reserve, the degree of integration has varied widely, from those who speak only English in their homes and are employed in the city, to others who prefer more traditional ways. Modern houses and good roads are common throughout the reserve. Facilities include a sports arena, museum, cultural center, administration offices, rodeo grounds, and churches. An annual Indian Days has been one of the largest in southern Alberta, and the permanent powwow pavillion demonstrates how serious the Sarcee are about preserving their traditions.

Some small industries were established on the reserve, including a service station, gravel pit, cattle company, and theatrical group. Another project on the reserve was the creation of Redwood Meadows, a housing project and golf course. This land, leased to non-Indians for a period of 99 years, provided the construction of modern houses as well as a source of employment and income for the reserve (Sarcee Executive Staff 1983:18).

Synonymy†

The name Sarcee, also spelled Sarsi, has no known source. It is the name by which the tribe has almost invariably been known in the historical and contemporary literature. Variant eighteenth- and nineteenth-century spellings include: Sussee and Sussou, 1775 (Graham in Williams 1969:211); Susee, 1790 (Umfreville 1954:103); Sessews (Fidler 1792–1793); Circees, 1794 (M'Gillivray in Morton 1929:37); Sesseu, 1800 (Bird in Johnson 1967:232); Sarcees (Mackenzie 1802:lxvii); Surcees, 1816 (Harmon 1957:199); Sassee (Franklin 1824, 1:170); Circus, 1835 (Douglas in Jenness 1938:4); Sarcis and Sassis (Maximillian 1843:242) Ciriés (Gairdner 1841:257); Searces, 1856 (Fort Sarpy Journal in McDonnell 1940:164); and Sarxi (Wilson 1888:243). For additional variants see Hodge (1907–1910, 2:468).

Two designations refer to the Sarcee as Beavers: Plain Beaver, 1872 (L'Heureaux in Dempsey 1961:12) and Castors de Prairies (Petitot 1891:362). The second represents the historical derivation of the Sarcee from the Beaver Indians of the Subarctic.

There are few recorded Plains tribal names for the Sarcee, in large part because most tribes did not know them or associated them with the Blackfoot. Two of the most widely known are variants of the name Sarcee itself. The Blackfoot designation is *sa·hsí·wa* (Allan R. Taylor, personal communication 1987), recorded as Siksika Sussekoon, 1808 (Hodge 1907–1910, 2:468), Sa se (Lanning 1882), Pegan saȟsí, Blood sáȟsi (Curtis 1907–1930, 6:155), and saxsí(ua) (Uhlenbeck and Van Gulik 1930:186). Numerous sources relate this name to a putative word Sa-arcez (Petitot 1883:652), sa arsi (Henry in Gough 1992, 2:382), or something similar, meaning 'not good', but that derivation is incorrect.

The Plains Cree name *sa·si·w* (sg.) (vol. 17:438), *sasi·w* (Bloomfield 1984:234), is also a variant of the form Sarcee and has no underlying meaning in the Cree language. It appears in historical sources as Sussew (Manchester House Journal, July 9, 1787), Sussewuck (pl.) or Woody Country Indians, 1772 (Cocking 1908:111), Sarséwi (Petitot 1883:652), and Sŭsíu (sg.), Sŭsiwŭk (pl.) (Curtis 1907–1930, 18:158).

The Cheyenne name was Sásapán (Curtis 1907–1930, 6:158), recorded also as Sasap, Sasapan (Petter 1913–

†This synonymy was written by Douglas R. Parks.

1915:583). It was said to be a borrowed term (Curtis 1907–1930, 6:158), probably from Blackfoot or Cree.

The Sarcee designated themselves *cúùt̓ínà* (in the practical orthography Tsúùt'ínà). Although the name has been translated by tribal members as 'many people' (Eung-Do Cook, personal communication 1987) and elsewhere as 'nation tribe' (Curtis 1907–1930, 18:162), both derivations are improbable. In the 1990s this name was sometimes used in English, often spelled Tsuu T'ina or Tsu T'ina. The form Tsô-Ottinè (Petitot 1891:362; cited in Hodge 1907–1910, 2:468) was said to mean 'people among the beavers', but that is an erroneous translation of the name.

Anomalous names are Stoney Cha^{n}-togábi^{d}n, phonemicized *č^{h}ąt^{h}ókapina* 'small woods enemy' (Curtis 1907–1930, 18:176); Crow Isashbaȟáts 'bad robes' (Curtis 1907–1930, 4:180); Kiowa *pɔ̀-kí-gɔ̀* 'thigh flesh' (Laurel J. Watkins, personal communication 1979; Mooney 1898:160); Ottawa Ussinnewudj Eninnewug 'stone mountain men' (Tanner 1830:316); and Kootenai Tcō'kō or Tsū'qōs, underlying meaning unknown (A.F. Chamberlain 1892:8).

The gesture obtained from Sarcee for their self-designation in the Plains sign language represents a stutterer. It is made by extending the first two fingers of the right hand forward, back up, from the right corner of the mouth, with the thumb extended below the fingers. The two fingers are then raised up from the thumb several times, in imitation of a person stuttering (Scott 1912–1934). The Blackfoot are reputed to call the Sarcee "heavy talkers" (James W. Schultz in Scott 1912–1934), apparently a reference to this sign.

Another sign for Sarcee obtained among the Blackfoot imitates the flattening of the nose to signify a duck's bill. It reputedly derived from a Sarcee preference for eating duck meat, but that interpretation is probably a folk etymology (Scott 1912–1934). In the late nineteenth century, Kiowa in Oklahoma remembered a sign for the Sarcee—a sweeping motion of the right hand across the thigh—that reflected their name for the tribe and was also the sign for the Brule Sioux (Mooney 1898:160).

Sources

The best source on Sarcee history and culture is Jenness (1932). Other brief, general works include E.F. Wilson (1888), Maclean (1896), Curtis (1907–1930, 18), and Dempsey (1986a). Topical studies include linguistics: Cook (1972, 1984), P.E. Goddard (1915), and Sapir (1925); kinship: Honigmann (1956); societies, religion, and traditions: P.E. Goddard (1914, 1919), Honigmann (1944, 1945, 1949), and Simms (1904a).

A number of fur traders made passing reference to the Sarcee, but more frequently they were included with the Blackfoot when any ethnographic descriptions were provided. The best of these accounts are from 1790 (Umfreville 1954) and Alexander Henry, 1809–1811 (in Coues 1897, 2).

From 1879 to 1916, the annual reports of the Canadian Department of Indian Affairs contain regular reports, some quite detailed, from the Sarcee Indian agent.

Among the best collections of Sarcee artifacts are those in the Canadian Museum of Civilization, Ottawa; National Museum of the American Indian, New York and Washington, D.C.; and the Glenbow Museum, Calgary, Alberta.

Plains Cree

REGNA DARNELL

The term Plains Cree (ˈkrē), is ambiguous in the ethnographic literature, sometimes referring to a linguistic variety of Cree and sometimes to a cultural adaptation to buffalo hunting on the Plains that flourished briefly from the early nineteenth century until the disappearance of the buffalo around 1880. Moreover, the Plains Cree, along with their Assiniboine allies, were the last tribe to move onto the Plains in historic times (cf. Russell 1991). As a result, they have frequently been dismissed as a hybrid culture resulting from the European fur trade, assimilating traits of the Europeans and of their neighbors, particularly the Assiniboine (whom they dominated politically) and the Woodland Ojibwa (Jenness 1932:317).

The main body of the Cree were Subarctic boreal forest hunters (vol. 6:196–207, 217–230, 256–270). The West Main Cree (speakers of Eastern Swampy and Western Swampy Cree) and the East Main Cree (speakers of East Cree) are far better known ethnographically. The boundary between the Western Woods Cree and the Plains Cree is virtually impossible to draw clearly, due to poor historical records, particularly during the fur trade period, and to the disappearance of the Plains buffalo adaptation, which defined the Plains Cree culturally in historic times. The term Plains Cree is most often applied to speakers of the variety of Cree having *y* from Proto-Algonquian **l*, without regard to historical ecological adaptation, but the northern Plains Cree speakers have been treated in the *Handbook* as part of the Western Woods Cree (vol. 6:256–270).

Language

Because language is crucial to the maintenance of Plains Cree cultural identity, understanding of the Plains Cree throughout their history is best approached by way of the emergence of a distinct dialect.* Cree is a Central Algonquian language closely related to Ojibwa, Fox, and Menominee. Its dialects are defined by the reflexes of Proto-Algonquian **l*. Ancestral **l* merged with *y* in Plains Cree and with *n* in Western Swampy Cree and most varieties of Eastern Swampy Cree; it appears as *δ* in Woods Cree, *r* in a few small areas, and remains as *l* in the Moose dialect of Eastern Swampy Cree (Michelson 1939; Pentland 1978; vol. 6:52–66). Plains Cree was also spoken at Rocky Boy's Reservation near Havre, Montana, and, at least in the early twentieth century, at Turtle Mountain and Spirit Lake Reservation, North Dakota (Wolfart 1973:9). These communities in the United States, south of historical Cree territory (fig. 1), were formed after the Northwest Rebellion of 1885.

Although Cree formed a dialect continuum, there was a major break in intelligibility between Eastern Swampy and Western Swampy (vol. 6:55). The boundaries between Woods and Western Swampy Cree and between Woods and Plains Cree were considerably more permeable. That is, movement and contact from north to south were more flexible than those from east to west; once in their historic locations, the Plains and Woods Cree retained little contact with their Eastern Woodlands heritage; however, this impression may be an inadequate description of the situation at the boundaries. D. Meyer (1985) describes the historical interaction of Plains Cree in east-central Saskatchewan with the Shoal Lake (Swampy) Cree of west-central Manitoba. Intermarriage was not uncommon (Neil McLeod, personal communication 1998).

Although the sound system of Cree is well known, there was considerable phonetic variation within Plains Cree, reflected in the development of practical orthographies with variant marking of vowel length (and number of vowels), preaspiration of stops, and voiced variants of stops. Orthographic problems were further compounded by widespread but unstandardized use of the syllabic writing system introduced by Anglican missionary James Evans in the mid-nineteenth century (vol. 17:174–176). A standardized Roman orthography proposed by C. Douglas Ellis (1973, 1983) on the basis of his work with Eastern Swampy Cree was restated by Pentland (1977) and adopted, for example, in the Cree language program at the Saskatchewan Indian Federated College, Regina. It was similar to the system used in at least some parts of Manitoba, Alberta, and other parts of Saskatchewan.

*The phonemes of Plains Cree are: (voiceless stops and affricate) *p, t, c, k*; (voiceless fricatives) *s, h*; (voiced nasals) *m, n*; and (voiced semivowels) *w, y*; (short vowels) *i, a, o*; (long vowels) *i·, e·, a·, o·*. Northern Plains Cree lacks *e·*.

This phonemic analysis follows Wolfart (1973; vol. 17:430). Phonemicizations of Plains Cree words in this chapter not in Bloomfield (1984) have been provided by David H. Pentland (communication to editors).

The increasingly standardized roman practical orthography uses this phonemic transcription, with long vowels indicated by a macron (ā) (Pentland 1977; Ellis 1983) or a circumflex accent (â) (Ahenakew 1987). For the officially standardized but locally variable syllabic orthography see vol. 17:175 (where the consonant below *s* shall read *š*).

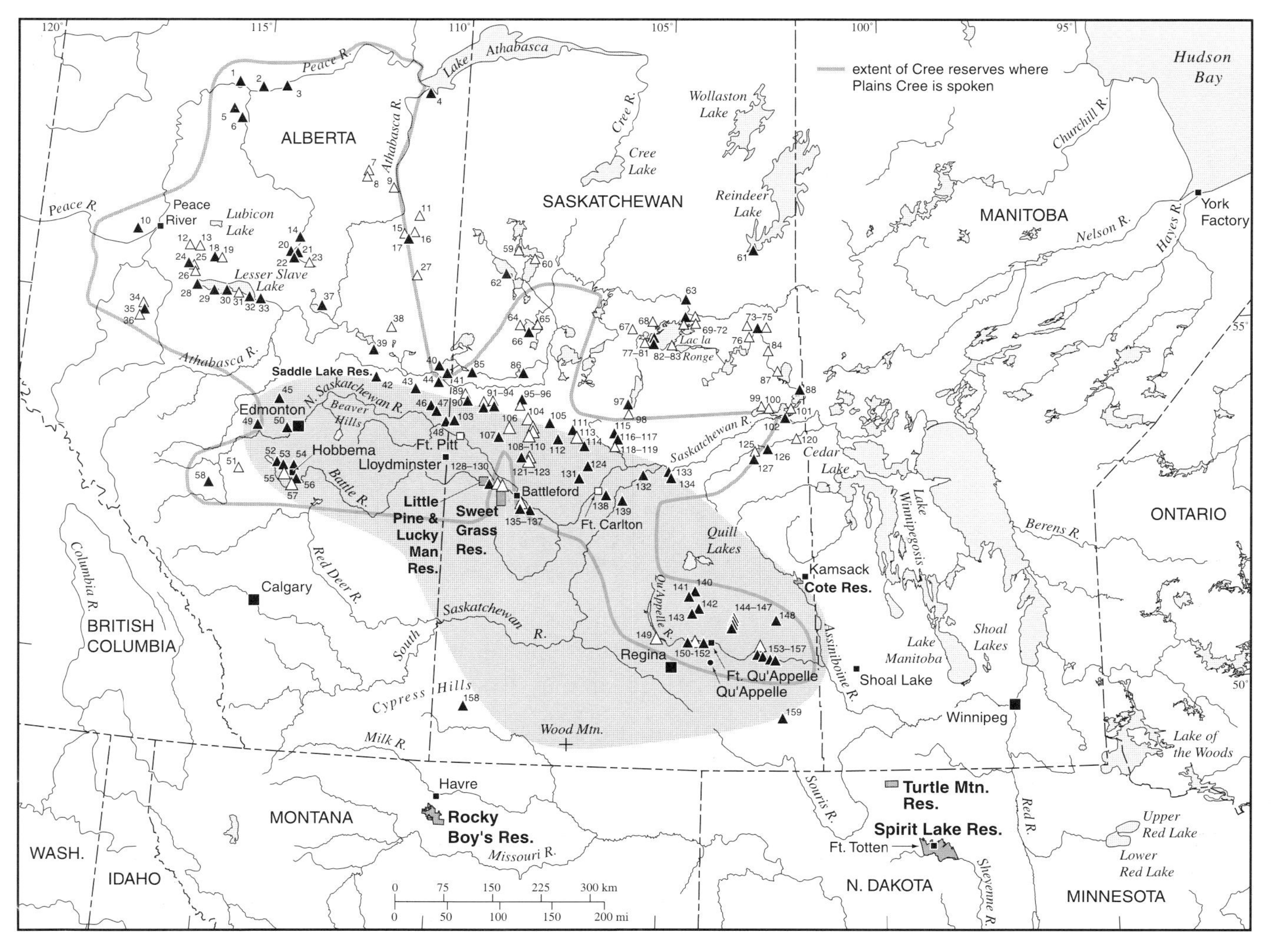

Fig. 1. Plains Cree territory 1860–1870 (Mandelbaum 1979:13). For northern Plains Cree speakers see vol. 6:256–270. Reserves and reservations mentioned in the text are named on the map, while all other affiliated reserves are numbered on the map and named below. Reserves that are shared with other tribes are indicated with an asterisk. Alberta: 1, Beaver Ranch 163; 2, John d'Or Prairie 215; 3, Fox Lake 162; 4, Chipewyan 201*, 5, Tall Cree 173A; 6, Tall Cree 173; 7, Namur River 174A*; 8, Namur Lake 174B*; 9, Fort McKay 174*; 10, Peace River Crossing 151A; 11, Clearwater 175*; 12, William McKenzie 151K; 13, Utikoomak Lake 155B; 14, Wabasca 166C; 15, Gregoire Lake 176A*; 16, Gregoire Lake 176B*; 17, Gregoire Lake 176*; 18, Utikoomak Lake 155; 19, Utikoomak Lake 155A; 20, Wabasca 166B; 21, Wabasca 166D; 22, Wabasca 166A; 23, Wabasca 166; 24, Pakashan 150D; 25, Halcro 150C; 26, Freeman 150B; 27, Janvier 194*; 28, Sucker Creek 150A; 29, Drift Pile River 150; 30, Swan River 150E; 31, Assineau River 150F; 32, Saw Ridge 150H; 34, Sturgeon Lake 154A; 35, Sturgeon Lake 154; 36, Sturgeon Lake 154B; 37, Jean Baptiste Gambler 183; 38, Heart Lake 167*; 39, Bear Lake 131; 40, Cold Lake 149B*; 41, Cold Lake 149A*; 42, White Fish Lake 128; 43, Kehiwin 123; 44, Cold Lake 149*; 45, Alexander 134; 46, Puskiakiwenin 122; 47, Unipouheos 121; 48, Makaoo 120; 49, Wabamun 133A & 133B*; 50, Stony Plain 135; 51, Buck Lake 133C*; 52, Pigeon Lake 138A; 53, Louis Bell 138B; 54, Ermineskin 138; 55, Samson 137A; 56, Samson 137; 57, Montana 139; 58, Sunchild 202. Saskatchewan: 59, Turnor Lake 193B; 60, Churchill Lake 193A; 61, Southend 200; 62, Turnor Lake 194; 63, Grandmother's Bay 219; 64, Canoe Lake 165A; 65, Canoe Lake 165B; 66, Canoe Lake 165; 67, Morin Lake 217; 68, Sucker River 156C; 69, Stanley 157; 70, Stanley 157A; 71, Fort Portages 157C; 72, Old Fort 157B; 73, Wood Lake 184D; 74, Pelican Narrows 184B; 75, Mirond Lake 184E; 76, Sandy Narrows 184C; 77, Little Hills 158A; 78, Little Hills 158B; 79, Little Hills 158; 80, Kitsakie 156B; 81, Lac La Ronge 156; 82, Fox Point 157D; 83, Fox Point 157E; 84, Birch Portage 184A; 85, Bighead 124; 86, Waterhen 130; 87, Amisk Lake 184; 88, Sturgeon Weir 184F; 89, Ministkwan 161A; 90, Ministkwan 161; 91, Makwa Lake 129; 92, Makwa Lake 129B; 93, Makwa Lake 129C; 94, Makwa Lake 129A; 95, Meadow Lake 105; 96, Meadow Lake 105A; 97, Montreal Lake 106; 98, Bittern Lake 218; 99, Pine Bluff 20A and 20B; 100, Muskeg River 20C; 101, Budd's Point 20D; 102, Cumberland 20; 103, Seekaskootch 119; 104, Thunderchild 115D; 105, Chitek Lake 191; 106, New Thunderchild 115C; 107, New Thunderchild 115B; 108, Moosomin 112F; 109, Moosomin 112E; 110, Saulteau 159A*; 111, Big River 118; 112, Witchekan Lake 117; 113, Big River 118A; 114, Atakakup 104; 115, Little Red River 106D; 116, Montreal Lake 106B; 117, Little Red River 106C; 118, Sturgeon Lake 101A; 119, Sturgeon Lake 101; 120, Carrot River 27A; 121, Saulteau 159*; 122, Moosomin 112B; 123, Moosomin 112; 124, Mistawasis 103; 125, Carrot River 29A; 126, Shoal Lake 28A; 127, Red Earth 29; 128, Poundmaker 114; 129, Sweet Grass 113B; 130, Sweet Grass 113A; 131, Muskeg Lake 102; 132, Muskoday 99; 133, James Smith 100; 134, Cumberland 100A; 135, Grizzly Bear's Head and Lean Man 110 and 111; 136, Mosquito 109; 137, Red Pheasant 108; 138, Okemasis 96 & Beardy 97; 139, One Arrow 95; 140, Day Star 87; 141, Poor Man 88; 142, Muskowekwan 85; 143, Gordon 86*; 144, Little Black Bear 84; 145, Star Blanket 83; 146, Okanese 82; 147, Peepeekisis 81; 148, Minoahchak 230*; 149, Last Mountain Lake 80A*; 150, Piapot 75*; 151, Muscowpetung 80*; 152, Pasqua 79*; 153, Shesheep 74A*; 154, Sakimay 74*; 155, Cowessess 73*; 156, Kahkewistahaw 72; 157, Ochapowace 71; 158, Nekaneet 160A; 159, White Bear 70*.

Territory

Cree speakers moved west as a result of game depletion in the area east of Lake Winnipeg resulting from the fur trade in the late eighteenth and early nineteenth centuries. The Plains Cree adapted fully to their new environment, which imposed many changes on their prior Eastern Woodlands culture (Mandelbaum 1979:326ff.). Although some Crees certainly moved west, others were as far west as the Peace River well before European contact (Smith 1987:435). Cree locations were known for this period only through French sources, and the French were always behind the Cree in westward expansion. J. Smith (1987:439–440) believed that the ancestral Cree had spread throughout the prairies by 1400, citing the extreme lack of intelligibility between the Plains Cree dialect of Alberta and its Woodlands counterparts. In J. Smith's (1987:440–443) view, the Cree were motivated by depletion of game rather than by warfare in their western movement; guns were not adapted to boreal forest warfare and provided a largely psychological advantage.

D. Meyer (1983a:45) suggested that by the 1700s the Cree had spread through northern Alberta, south onto the Plains and north into the Northwest Territories. If the Cree were pre-European in their western phase, they should be equated with the Clearwater Lake complex of northern Manitoba and Saskatchewan, leaving a clear boundary between Cree and Athapaskan. Clearwater Lake remains are dated by radiocarbon between the late 1400s and the early 1700s; European trade goods are not present. If the ancestral Blackfoot were indeed driven south by the Cree, D. Meyer (1983a:46) suggested this occurred in the 1400s rather than the 1600s as proposed by McCullough (1982) on the basis of materials from Lac La Biche, Alberta.

Although archeologists have suggested different origins for the Cree (Wright 1971; D. Meyer and D. Russell 1987), it seems clear that the ancestors of the historical Plains Cree emerged in the parkland zone between the boreal forest and the prairies (Ray 1974). There were ancestral Cree in northwestern Manitoba by A.D. 900 and in southern Manitoba and northern Saskatchewan by 1500 (Wright 1971:3; VanStone 1983:1).

J. Smith (1976) argued that only the name Cree was extended to Indians already living farther west and that the westward movement theory (Petitot 1883) reflected limited French knowledge of the western Indians. French forts reached the foothills of the Rockies only a decade prior to the Treaty of Paris in 1763; after the French cessions, the Hudson's Bay Company moved into the interior, its competition with the North West Company ending only with their merger in 1821. In the intervening period, Cree had to spend less time traveling to trading posts, but game was depleted around the posts. Smallpox and influenza epidemics beginning in 1781 and lasting until 1838 cost over half their population (vol. 6:258). Some of these Cree became more dependent on the trading posts; others moved south onto the Plains and became buffalo hunters. When Father Pierre Jean de Smet visited the Plains Cree in 1845, they were fully adapted to life on the Plains, engaged in warfare for territory and goods (Mandelbaum 1940:178).

History to 1876

Emergence of the Plains Cree

The Plains Cree emerged historically through a combination of migration and territorial expansion between about 1670 and 1810. The fur trade of the late eighteenth century, centered in the Saskatchewan and Red river systems, provided a base for Cree expansion to the Rocky Mountains in the west and the Plains to the south (Milloy 1988; Ray 1974; Thistle 1986).

Initial expansion of the Cree was motivated by trade rather than warfare and preceded trade in firearms (Milloy 1988:5). The Cree allied themselves with the Assiniboine at York Factory by 1690. As they moved southwest into the Plains, the two tribes formed a trade and military alliance against the Blackfoot. The Cree and Assiniboine provided the Blackfoot with guns, which proved useful in their efforts to displace the Shoshone from southern Alberta (Milloy 1988:6). The Shoshone, who obtained horses by warfare, were so successful that the Missouri River tribes allied themselves in protest. As the Shoshone were cut off from the Mandan, their source of guns and other trade goods, the Blackfoot were able to move southwest, leaving the Cree to clear out Gros Ventre opposition to expansion in the north (Milloy 1988:9). The Cree, controlling local tribal relations because they controlled access to guns, developed a seasonal rhythm of spring trading to the south and winter hunting of beaver, meeting annually with the Blackfoot in March (Milloy 1988:11). By 1813, the Cree were at peace with the Blackfoot and supplying guns to them as well as to the allied Mandan-Hidatsa (Milloy 1988:16).

By 1776, Canadian traders had reached the South Saskatchewan River. The Cree remained middlemen between them and the western tribes because their visits were irregular and their supplies uncertain. The Cree continued to provide beaver for furs and provisions, giving them money for European goods. Until the traders reached the prairie edge, the horse was of little use and buffalo were not a significant part of the Cree adaptation (Milloy 1988:18, 20).

In the 1790s, the Plains Cree emerged as a unique group, exploiting the buffalo in the border between the parklands and prairies. Because of the double ecological zone, they had more options than other tribes, hunting in the Woodlands in the plentiful summer season and moving into the Plains to hunt buffalo in times of winter scarcity (Milloy 1988:21–22).

The Cree in the Saskatchewan River valley remained primarily Woodlands in their adaptation, depending on the beaver, the canoe, and the fur trade, although they had some contact with the Plains. They trapped in the winter and traded with the Blackfoot and the Hudson's Bay Company in the spring and summer. Horses were used as pack animals to enable buffalo hunting seasonally (Milloy 1988:23–24).

By 1770, the South Saskatchewan River Cree had obtained enough horses to divide themselves between horse and canoe adaptations. Horses became increasingly important as the trading posts moved west. They came to depend more on provisioning and less on furs per se. As beaver were depleted, provisioning became a matter of dried buffalo meat and fat. The transition was complete by the 1790s (Milloy 1988:25–27). The Blackfoot turned to the buffalo even earlier than the Cree. The new adaptation, moreover, made the Cree-Blackfoot alliance nonfunctional, although the Cree were virtually unique during this period in retaining a range of alternative strategies (Milloy 1988:29–30).

Between 1790 and 1810, Cree control over trade broke down, largely because they could not obtain the horses necessary to hunt buffalo, and the whole region was characterized by political instability. The Cree need for horses caused them to break their alliance with the Blackfoot in favor of the Flathead and the Mandan and Hidatsa (Milloy 1988:31–36). The Cree and their Assiniboine allies provided guns for use against the Sioux and left their women and children with the Mandan and Hidatsa while they waged war. For economic motives, including the availability of corn to supplement their own provisions for warfare, they increased the military capacity of the Mandan and Hidatsa (Milloy 1988:43–46).

Between 1806 and 1836, the Cree maintained their middleman position between the Mandan and Hidatsa and the European trade, obtaining European goods by exploiting the competition between the Hudson's Bay Company and the Canadian traders (Milloy 1988:47–49). The southwestern Cree obtained horses through an annual spring fair at the Mandan and Hidatsa villages. Trade included prestige items such as eagle feathers as well as European trade goods, firearms, horses, agricultural products, and buffalo (Milloy 1988:49–51). However, the Mandan-Hidatsa held sufficient control of the trade to escalate horse prices and seek direct contact with the European traders. The Cree were squeezed out because the prices of beaver remained steady; they responded by not paying their debts. Attempts to blockade the Mandan and Hidatsa from the European traders were unsuccessful; the Cree resorted to stealing horses, causing the alliance to reach a breaking point (Milloy 1988:54–58).

Meanwhile, the Mandan and Hidatsa had consolidated their military position, obtaining guns from the northeast and producing a mounted force that settled their relations with the Sioux, Crow, and Cheyenne. They no longer needed Cree military assistance. The Cree responded by breaking away from their Assiniboine allies (who opted for strategies of war and blockade) and seeking peace with the Mandan and Hidatsa. By the early 1820s, however, the Cree and Assiniboine rejoined forces in war and horse stealing.

The Horse Wars

In the period between 1810 and 1850, the Cree had become a full Plains tribe, although they were still plagued by their inability to acquire horses. The fortunes of the Plains Cree were enhanced by their relative population increase; they escaped smallpox infection and received more medical aid from Europeans than their fellow Plains tribesmen (Milloy 1988:69, 72). This was the period of florescence of Plains Cree culture.

The fortunes of war also went well. The Blackfoot sued for peace in 1819, defeated by a Kootenai-Crow-Cree alliance. They retreated to the Hudson's Bay post at Edmonton, away from the center of action, without their horses (Milloy 1988:85–89). The issue became whether the allied Cree and Assiniboine or the Blackfoot would control the Upper Missouri; buffalo robes had become the most important item of trade (Milloy 1988:92–104).

The Buffalo Wars

The buffalo disappeared between 1850 and 1880. Regions were depleted differentially, forcing the tribes into one another's territories and escalating warfare (Milloy 1988:104–105). Throughout this period, the Plains Cree remained on good terms with the traders (vol. 4:370), retaining their political independence but blaming the Métis and the traders for the disappearance of the buffalo. Some Crees tried to combine agriculture on the Mandan-Hidatsa model with winter hunting. Most, however, saw war as the most viable strategy, particularly in light of the instability of the Blackfoot confederacy (Milloy 1988:106–109). The Cree unsuccessfully attempted a "heavily armed migration" west into Blackfoot territory (Milloy 1988:109). By 1871, they were able to hunt buffalo only by sufferance of the Blackfoot (Milloy 1988:118).

Throughout the contact period, most Plains Cree maintained friendly relationships with Whites; they were sufficiently in control of their own cultural choices to adapt various European tools, behavioral patterns, and Christianity (vol. 17:175). The Plains Cree remained dependent on the fur trade for cash income and items of European material culture (vol. 4:348) even after their dependence on the buffalo increased.

In the 1860s, the Cree tried to achieve peace through diplomacy with their Blackfoot neighbors. The Cree chief Poundmaker (whose father was Assiniboine) was adopted by the Blackfoot chief Crowfoot. However, after their defeat at the hands of the Blackfoot in the Battle of Old Man River in 1871, the Plains Cree were forced to ask the Hudson's Bay factor at Edmonton for a treaty (Dempsey 1986a). Treaty No. 4, signed in 1874 at Qu'Appelle, Saskatchewan, covered the territory of southern Saskatchewan. The Plains and Western Woods Cree in central Saskatchewan and Alberta signed Treaty No. 6 at Fort Pitt and Fort Carlton in 1876. As a result, they obtained concessions of short-term payments for tools and equipment and long-term health care provisions not included in earlier treaties. Treaty No. 6 confined the Plains and Woodlands Cree to reserves; by 1880, the buffalo were completely gone.

Culture in the Nineteenth Century

The main source for the following summary is Mandelbaum (1940, 1979), which represents the period 1860–1870, within the memory of the elders during 1934–1935 fieldwork.

At their maximum extent, the Plains Cree extended from central western Manitoba through central and southern Saskatchewan to the foothills of the Rocky Mountains in Alberta (Mandelbaum 1940:165). Along with their Assiniboine allies, they displaced the Sioux, Crow, and Gros Ventre in the south and Blackfoot and Sarcee in the west. They maintained little contact with the Western Woods Cree to the north. The Plains Ojibwa to the east were allies and also late arrivals on the Plains (Mandelbaum 1940:165–166).

The Plains Cree (*paskwa·wiyiniwak* 'plains people') are distinguished from the Western Woods Cree (*saka·wiyiniwak* 'bush people'). Hayden (1862:237) listed 10 bands, most designated by the name of a chief. Skinner (1914a:517) listed 13 bands, three of which he considered of possible mixed ancestry. Mandelbaum (1940:166–167) listed eight major divisions of Plains Cree in the late nineteenth century (table 1) (see also Wolvengrey 1997).

Strictly speaking, the environment of the Plains Cree was parkland rather than plains; however, they are considered a Plains tribe because of their economic dependence on the buffalo. Mandelbaum (1979:274) considered the buffalo pound the major Plains Cree cultural innovation, reflecting a movement from individual to collective hunting techniques. There was little ceremonial elaboration around the buffalo, which may have been the result of the late arrival of the Plains Cree on the plains.

Subsistence

Buffalo were hunted by chute and pound in autumn and early winter when the herds entered the wooded regions. Free chase with horses was used during the spring and summer southward movements of the herds. Less common tactics included natural traps, horsemen surrounding a herd, tracking a single animal, relay hunting by two men, hunters crawling up to a herd, several men approaching a herd under a buffalo robe and calling like a calf to attract the cows, and setting of prairie fires to control movement of herds.

Pemmican was made by pounding dried meat with berries and pouring melted fat over the mixture. Meat was roasted and occasionally baked in a pit overnight. Hot

Table 1. Plains Cree Band Names, Early 20th Century

Skinner 1914a	*Mandelbaum 1940, 1979:9–11*	*Phonemicized Form*
Katepoisipi-wiinuûk (Calling River People; Qu'Appelle band)[a]	Katepwewcɪpɪ·wɪyiniwak (Calling River People)	*ka·te·pwe·wi-si·pi·wiyiniwak*
Wabuswaianûk (Rabbit Skin People)	wapucwayanak (Rabbit Skin People)	*wa·poswaya·nak*
Mämäkitce-wiinuûk (Big Gizzard People)		*mama·hkice·wiyiniwak* (?)
Paskokopa-wiinuûk (Willow People)	paskuhkupawɪyiniwak (Parklands People; Willow Indians)	*paskokopa·wiyiniwak* (?)
Nutimi-iniuûk (Poplar People)	natimɪwɪyiniwak (Upstream People) or amiskwatcɪwɪyiniwak (Beaver Hills People)	*natimiyiniwak, amiskwaci·wiyiniwak*
Cipi-winiuûk (River People)	cɪpɪwɪyiniwak (River People)	*si·pi·wiyiniwak*
Saka-winiuûk (Bush People)		*saka·wiyiniwak*
Masnipi-winiuûk (Painted or Pictured People)		*masinipe·wiyiniwak* (?)
Little Dogs, Piapot's Band		*acimosisak*
Asinskau-winiuûk (Stone People)		*asiniska·wiyiniwak*
Niopwätûk (Cree-Assiniboine)	nehɪopwat (Cree-Assiniboine) or paskwawɪyiniwak (Prairie People)	*ne·hiyawi-pwa·tak, paskwa·wiyiniwak*
	pusakawatcɪwɪyiniwak (Touchwood Hills People)	*posa·kanaci·wiyiniwak*
	waskahɪkanwɪyiniwak (House People)	*wa·skahikaniwiyiniwak*
Tcipoaian-winiuûk (Chipewyan People)		*ci·pwaya·niwiyiniwak* (?)
Sakbwatsûk (Bush Assiniboine)		*saka·wi-pwa·cak* (?)

[a]Also called Kagiciwuinuwûk 'loud voices people', the name of a chief; in 1914 called Kakiwistaihau-wiinuûk 'Fox's people', after his son.

stones were used to boil meat, especially by war parties. The most common meal was thick soup made from berries, meat, fat and turnips. Bones were crushed and boiled for grease, which was stored in buffalo paunches. Women did the food preparation.

Fish was a dietary supplement when hunting was poor; it became more important after the disappearance of the buffalo. Fish weirs (fig. 2) were constructed during spring downriver runs, and winter fish were speared at open places in river ice. Fish were also made into pemmican.

Indian turnip or grassberry was the most important root food. Turnips were dug by the women and dried. Berries were picked by women and girls. Maple sap was collected in early spring and made into syrup and sugar.

Clothing

Men wore a soft buckskin breechcloth tied over a narrow belt at the waist. Men's leggings were made by doubling over a single piece of hide with ornamental fringes. Shirts were worn on ceremonial occasions (fig. 3). Men and women wore buffalo robes at all seasons. Women's dresses were made from two oblong pieces of hide or cloth superimposed on each other. Dresses had detachable sleeves and a back cape (fig. 4). They extended to the middle of the leg. A belt was worn around the waist. Simple leggings covered the lower leg. Clothing of both sexes was decorated with beads or embroidery. Tattoos and facial painting were employed.

Social Organization

Each band exploited its own hunting territory; individuals and families could change bands easily. A band chief (*okima·w*) attracted followers by his war record, wealth, generosity, and hunting ability. He was less a political leader than a highly respected man. A band could have more than one chief and the title was not necessarily hereditary.

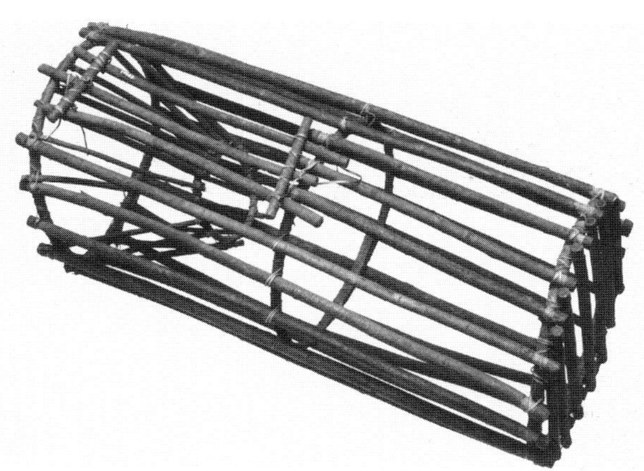

Amer. Mus. of Nat. Hist., New York: top, 16090; bottom left, 16091; bottom right, Field Mus., Chicago: 14983 (neg. A111574).

Fig. 2. Fishing. top, Weir on Battle River, Poundmaker Res., Battleford, Sask. The success of a weir, usually operated at night, depended on its placement in a swift part of the current, which allowed the fish to be carried into the basket. bottom left, Close-up of entrance to fish basket at the same weir. A sweep probably made of willow and netted in the center is lying across the entrance (Mandelbaum 1940:200). Photographs by Pliny E. Goddard, 1911. bottom right, Model fish trap made of willow twigs notched at both ends and lashed to supports with unsmoked hide strips. A door is lifted to remove the fish. Collected by Isaac Cowie, Saskatchewan Valley, Alta., before 1900; length 64 cm.

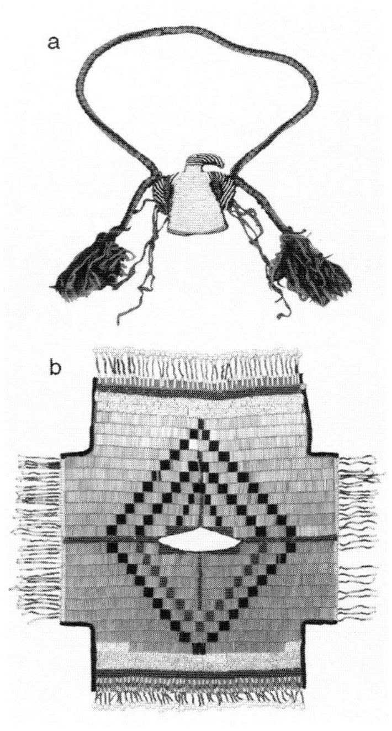

top left, Stark Mus. of Art, Orange, Tex.: 31.78/154; a, Glenbow-Alberta Inst., Calgary, Alta.: AP 721 and b, Lower Ft. Garry Natl. Hist. Park, Selkirk, Man.: HBC 906 (2327); bottom left, Sask. Arch. Board, Regina: R-B693; bottom right, Man. Mus. of Man and Nature, Winnipeg: H4.42.1.

Fig. 3. Clothing and body decorations. top left, Man wearing a fringed buckskin shirt decorated with beaded strips on sleeves and shoulders and quilled rosette on chest. Around his neck is a pouch and what may be a charm on an oval background. He wears bone decorations in his hair, and his braids are fur wrapped. Oil on paper by Paul Kane, 1848. a, Thunderbird charm made by Alex Smith about 1900, for use during the Sun Dance. The thunderbird is cut out of buckskin, one side solidly beaded in blue, the other in white with green stripes on the head and wings. The edges are done in red. The necklace is loosely braided of red and white wool. Collected from Agnes Smith in 1968; height of the thunderbird, 12.5 cm. b, Woman's dance cape, of canvas, decorated with shells and tubular beads in silver, white, red, black, and blue. Collected by Rev. Canon Edward K. Matheson, Battleford, Sask., 1921; length when open 94 cm. top right, Willie Auger, a dancer from Saddle Lake First Nation, Alta., at a powwow. He is wearing matching beaded collar, armbands, and wrist bands and a porcupine hair roach with eagle feather. He holds a staff with the head of a loon carved at the top. Photograph by Bert Crowfoot, 1997. bottom left, Women from the Sweet Grass Res. wearing cloth dresses that reflect intertribal influence as well as Euro-American fashion. The dress on the left appears to be of heavy stroud, possibly blanket material, with sleeves and suspenders cut and sewn, and decorated with appliqué and beadwork. The other two dresses are of a velveteen material decorated with beadwork of floral designs. The netted bodice decoration on the center dress is atypical, while the heavily beaded yoke of the bodice on the right is similar to historical styles. Photograph possibly by Ken W.F. Cooper, near Battleford, Sask., 1936. bottom right, Elkskin dress decorated with quill-wrapped fringe, red cloth appliquéd disks, and beads. Collected by Paul Kane, Ft. Edmonton, about 1846; length 131 cm.

bottom, Field Mus., Chicago: a, 15002, b, 14997, c, 15005 (neg. 111549).

Fig. 4. Buckskin. The preparation of hides was usually women's work. top, Winona Frank rubbing the skin with an oily mixture of animal brains, fat, and liver and then soaking in water. The skin was softened by rubbing it over a rough stone, twisted rawhide, or, as here, on an iron strap fixed to a frame post. center, Wringing the soaked skin. Later the skin was stretched and pulled to make it more pliable for use in making clothing. Photographs by Thomas Kehoe, Little Pine Res., Sask., 1973. bottom, Deerskin dress with detached sleeves and matching leggings, decorated with brown pigment, fringe, and strands of hide. Collected by Issac Cowie, Saskatchewan Valley, 1892; length of c, 103 cm.

Every band had one or two criers who announced daily news throughout the camp circle. They were usually men too old for warfare. They were chosen by the chief and received many gifts from him and other members of the band. Criers were expected to be well dressed and well fed (Mandelbaum 1979:109).

Leading men of the band comprised its council. The chief's crier summoned them by name when an important decision was to be made. The chief outlined the issue, and each man spoke, beginning with the youngest and ending with those of highest rank. The chief then announced his decision, which was transmitted through the camp by the crier (Mandelbaum 1979:108–109). The chief's crier also summoned any man invited by the chief to his tepee. An old respected man was chosen as temporary camp leader during the summer between council meetings. He had to be familiar with the hunting territory and able to make decisions on his own.

Each band had a single warrior society with its own insignia, songs, and dance (Mandelbaum 1979:110–121). A man became a warrior when he was formally invited to sit in the Warriors' Lodge and join the dances. Warriors were chosen by the old men of the band from the ranks of the Worthy Young Men. There was no formal ceremony and most young men were eventually asked to join (Mandelbaum 1979:110–111). Powers were divided between a warrior chief and a peace chief, who led dances but was not necessarily a leader in warfare. The society provided for the needy and policed the buffalo hunt to prevent individuals from ruining the community hunt. Women did not participate in political life.

Warriors and Worthy Young Men attained prestige by dissociating themselves from the sentiments of the common people, especially about material possessions and sexual jealousy. They took on the dreaded task of preparing the dead for burial (Mandelbaum 1979:120).

Lowie (1955:7) noted that the Warriors (*okihcita·wak*) were primarily a club and constituted the only formal society. The elaboration of military societies common to other Plains tribes was not found among the Cree.

Kinship

Cross-cousin marriage was the dominant classificatory principle; although this form of marriage was uncommon in practice, Hallowell (1930) argued that cross-cousin marriage was basic to north-central Algonquian kinship. The equation by male speakers of daughter's husband and sister's son was reflected in other kinship terms as well. The term for cross-cousin was extended to mean "sweetheart"

(Mandelbaum 1979:124). Strict mother-in-law avoidance was practiced. A man could speak to his father-in-law only after presenting him with a scalp he had taken. A woman was expected to be close to her mother-in-law but could not speak to her father-in-law. These avoidance restrictions extended to siblings of the married person. Opposite sex siblings avoided one another. A joking relationship existed between grandparents and grandchildren (Mandelbaum 1979:127). A man could joke with his male cross-cousin, his brother-in-law, and his male parallel cousin. A woman could joke with her male cross-cousin and her grandparents.

Callender (1962) found the Cree cross-cousin terminology more consistent than in Proto–Central Algonquian. Kinship was the persistent idiom of social relationship among Plains Cree; kin terms were readily extended to nonrelatives to structure everyday social interaction.

Life Cycle

No taboos were observed during pregnancy. The baby was not nursed until two days after birth. Moss bags were used, often until the child was old enough to walk. Cradleboards appear to have been introduced by the Hudson's Bay Company. Children were named by shamans soon after birth at a feast prepared by the parents. The name came from a vision of the shaman. A special relationship existed between a person and the man who had named him (Mandelbaum 1979:140–141). Everyday names were used to protect the sacred names.

Children were nursed for a period ranging from one to five years. The mother was not supposed to have intercourse again until the child was weaned. Children were not beaten and were rarely reprimanded. Grandparents spent most time with the children, and elders taught traditional stories. Young men taught boys to hunt and fight. Girls were secluded for four nights at first menstruation; this was the best time for receiving a vision. An old woman stayed with the girl. Otherwise women did not seek visions, although they may have done so in earlier times (Mandelbaum 1979:145–146, 159–162). Many women attained supernatural power; however, female shamans could not lead or vow to perform important ceremonies. A woman's husband or son would have to sing her song during the ritual.

Parents wanted their children to marry within the same band so they would know the family of a potential spouse (Mandelbaum 1979:146). The girl's father took a gift, usually horses, to the man he wanted to marry his daughter. If the boy's parents agreed to the marriage, the bride's family made a new tepee. The groom came and sat down in the tepee beside his bride. His acceptance of a pair of moccasins sealed the marriage. Newly married couples usually lived near the husband's parents. Unmarried women were chaperoned outside the camp. A girl with an illegitimate child was married to an elderly or poor man if the father of

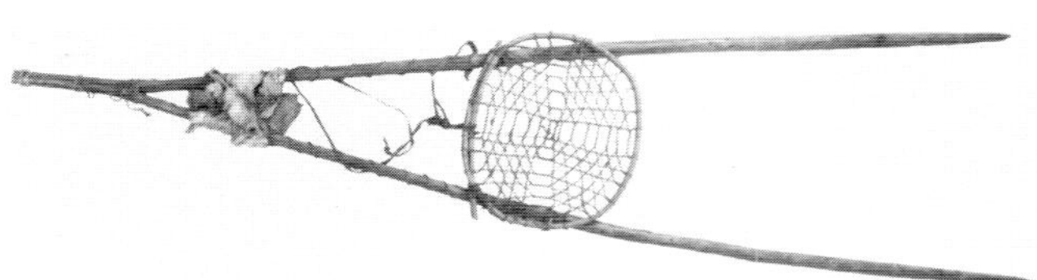

top, Wash. State Histl. Soc., Tacoma:6.03.001; bottom, Field Mus., Chicago: 14993 (neg. A111551).

Fig. 5. Dog transportation. Horses, the preferred method of transportation, were hard to maintain during the severe winters in the far northern plains, so dogs performed much of the work of hauling firewood, meat, and household supplies. They were trained, cared for, and owned by women. top, Dog travois in use. Photographed late 19th century. bottom, Dog travois. Collected by Issac Cowie, southern Alta., 1892; length 233 cm.

the child refused to marry her (Mandelbaum 1979:147). Affinally related families frequently exchanged gifts. If a man's parents were dead, he was expected to live with and support his wife's parents. Wife exchange was practiced if a man wanted another man's wife or if the two men were very close friends. Jealousy was common, but an adulterous wife was often given to her lover. If a marriage was unsuccessful, either partner could return to his parents. Whichever remained kept the children and household property. Both could remarry after a short time (Mandelbaum 1979:150).

Burial was usually by interment (fig. 6), although tree burial was sometimes practiced in the winter. The head always faced north. Tobacco and grease were placed in the grave. Close relatives of the deceased were expected to mourn, usually for four days. Some person of prestige came and combed and braided the mourners' unbound hair and told them when to stop mourning (Mandelbaum 1979:152–153).

Religion

The great spirit and creator of the universe, *kice·-manito·w*, was not personalized. Other spirit powers were intermediaries (J.S.H. Brown and Brightman 1988). There was thought to be a life force in human persons and all other living things (including all things that were classified as grammatically animate in the Cree language). Boys usually sought spirit power through a vision quest at puberty

(Mandelbaum 1979:159). The most important visions were those that made a man a shaman or curer (Mandelbaum 1979:162).

The most important ceremony was the Sun Dance (fig. 7), called *nipa·kwe·simo·win* 'thirst dance' because it involved fasting by participants (Mandelbaum 1979:183–199). The ceremony was directed toward the thunder. The sponsor was a man who had dreamed of thunder. The Sun Dance brought long life for the maker and rain for the people; curing was secondary (Skinner 1919:287). The Sun Dance provided the greatest annual opportunity for social activity, including dancing, gambling, and courtship. (For a detailed description of the Sun Dance at Hobbema, Alberta, see Goddard 1919a.) Between 1884 and 1921 the Canadian government suppressed the Sun Dance performances.

Natl. Arch. of Canada, Ottawa: PA 118766.

Fig. 6. Cemetery of the Calling River People, Crooked Lake Res., Sask. The gable-roofed decorated board houses erected over the graves were unique to this band of Cree. Food and tobacco offerings for the deceased were placed in these structures (Mandelbaum 1940:248). Photograph by Oliver B. Buell, Ft. Quappelle, Sask., 1885.

The smoking tepee (*pi·htwa·wikamik*) was the other important vowed ceremony, fulfilling a pledge to the spirits through an all-night singing session (Mandelbaum 1979:199–204). It was usually held in the spring. The *wi·htiko·hka·nak* or windigo dancers (fig. 8) performed a ceremony that stressed inverted speech and clowning. The windigo (*wi·htiko·w*) is a cannibal monster, but literal cannibalism was apparently not involved in the ceremony. Rather, the cannibal represented chaos, a negation of the existing order (Neil McLeod, personal communication 1998). A buffalo dance was held to ensure abundant herds, not to cure the sick, as is usual on the Plains. Other vowed dances included the prairie chicken, giveaway, horse, elk, bear, bee, calumet bundle, and round; Mandelbaum (1979:343) considered these unique to the Cree and reflective of their Woodlands heritage. Skinner (1919:528–537) mentioned other dances as well, the big dogs, scalp, and open-end tent (an annual memorial to the dead).

Ceremonial elements common to all Cree were smoking a pipe as an offering to the supernatural, material offerings to particular spirit powers, vision songs, prayer, vow to the supernaturals, serving of food (except at curing rituals), purification through a sweetgrass smudge, sweatbath (fig. 7) and medicine bundles (which Mandelbaum 1979 believed were borrowed from the Blackfoot).

History Since 1876

Many of the material gains made by the Cree on their reserves in the late 1870s were lost as a result of the

Sask. Arch. Board, Regina: left, R-B 2759; right, R-A 6094.

Fig. 7. Ceremonial structures. left, Sun Dance lodge where ceremony is taking place. Cloth offerings hang from the center pole. Photographed near Lloydminster, Sask., about 1905. right, Framework of sweatbath. Cloth offerings and dishes of food are visible. Photographed at Cote Res., near Kamsack, Sask., 1939.

left, Sask. Arch. Board, Regina: R-A7671; right, Denver Art Mus., Colo.: 1942.214.

Fig. 8. Windigo Dancers. In Cree folklore the windigos (*wi·htiko·wak*) were a race of cannibalistic giants. The Plains Cree Windigo Dance took place during the Sun Dance and involved 3 days of dancing, clowning, hunting, and feasting by its masked participants who talked "backwards during the dances" (Mandelbaum 1979:204–206). left, Masked dancers from the Sweet Grass Res. The pledger carries a staff with deer hooves attached. He went from tepee to tepee shaking the staff over the heads of those he wished to join him in the dance. Photograph probably by Gerald W.L. Nicholson, 1939. right, Canvas mask, made in 1936 by Fineday, a Plains Cree from the Sweet Grass Res. Collected by David Mandelbaum before 1940; length 52.1 cm.

involvement of Cree and Cree-Métis in the Northwest Rebellion of 1885. Although less than five percent of them had actually been involved in the hostilities, and the Plains Cree had not felt themselves to be at war with the Whites, the rebellion provided the government an excuse to tighten control over the Cree (Stonechild 1986). Several chiefs, including Poundmaker and Big Bear, were imprisoned (vol. 4:91–92). Big Bear attempted unsuccessfully to improve terms of the treaty. The aftermath of the rebellion was traumatic for the Cree, many of whom were newly separated from their kinsmen by an international boundary, groups of Cree having sought asylum in the United States. In 1916, the Rocky Boy's Reservation was established for them in Montana. The Cree had little reason to feel common cause with their Métis kinsmen.

Family trapping territories came into being by the end of the nineteenth century. Many Cree became relatively sedentary, settling near trading posts and mission stations. There were no more communal hunts. The importance of fishing increased with the metal ice chisel and twine gill net (vol. 6:264). Missionary presence—largely Roman Catholic (Oblate) and Anglican—was felt from the 1840s on. Missionaries opposed polygyny, the levirate, cross-cousin marriage, and rituals such as the Sun Dance and shaking tent. The Sun Dance was outlawed by the Canadian government in 1884. Traditional ceremonies continued to be held secretly. Relations between bands declined with sedentary existence around missions.

Traditional culture was maintained fairly intact until after World War II, when Canadian government intervention in isolated communities became more pronounced. Positive benefits from the Canadian government also became available, including health care, welfare and child allowance payments, government housing, and all-weather roads.

Some military veterans built political organizations that lobbied for Indian rights and land. Among these were John Tootosis, Johnny Calihoo, and Edward Ahenakew.

By the 1960s the Plains Cree had developed considerable political self-consciousness (vol. 4:280) and dominated the Indian Association of Alberta (led by Harold Cardinal) and the Federation of Saskatchewan Indians. Cardinal (1969) expressed the concerns of this militant period, in which Cree led the protest against the short-lived Red Paper—the Canadian government's attempt to end the special status of treaty Indians. Joseph Dion (1979), one of the founders of the Métis Association of Alberta ("Plains Métis," fig. 2, this vol.), described persistence of traditional culture in northern Alberta communities. (Many culturally and linguistically Cree persons are legally Métis rather than "status" or "treaty" Indians.) The main political issue of the 1980s involved provincial and federal government failure to settle land claims of nonstatus Indians, those who never signed treaties; the Woods Cree of Lubicon Lake in north-central Alberta rallied national and international support for this battle (J. Smith 1988), obtaining a settlement. Native land claims were entrenched in the Canadian Constitution over the protests of Alberta, particularly, as a producer of mineral and natural resource revenue.

The Cree worked effectively within the band system, each band electing its chief and council every two years. The traditional term for a respected leader, *okimaw*, is reserved for the elders. The elected chief is called *okima·hka·n*, literally 'made chief' (C.D. Ellis 1960).

The Department of Indian Affairs and Northern Development had four districts and five agencies in Alberta and five in Saskatchewan. Loan programs were available to individuals or bands for commercial farms and small businesses. Alberta residential schools were discontinued in 1966, and local school committees increased input into educational priorities for Cree children. Emphasis was placed on traditional language and culture and on obtaining high school and advanced educational credentials for the use and benefit of native communities.

Plains Crees were active in many native organizations, including the Edmonton Native Communications Society, the Treaty Voice of Alberta, the Calgary Treaty Urban Alliance, the Federation of Saskatchewan Indians, and various Native friendship centers.

Language was a paramount issue in the maintenance of traditional culture and Cree identity. Cree language was taught at the Saskatchewan Indian Federated College (which offered a B.A. in Cree Linguistics), the University of Alberta School of Native Studies, Edmonton; and the University of Manitoba, Winnipeg. In addition to linguistic descriptions of Cree (Lacombe 1874, 1874a; Bloomfield 1928, 1930, 1934; Wolfart 1973), Wolfart and Carroll (1981) presented Cree grammar for English speakers in nontechnical contrastive terms. Darnell and Vanek (1973) worked with native speakers to devise teaching materials in syllabic script; and Freda Ahenakew, a Cree woman trained in linguistics, produced a grammar (1987) and a text-based approach to the teachings of traditional Cree speakers (1987a). Many communities in the Prairie Provinces developed their own teaching materials for the language; the theoretical issues of such programs were summarized in Burnaby (1980). The language was also taught on many reserves.

In Alberta and Saskatchewan, language maintenance varied from reserves where virtually no one under 30 spoke the language to those where most children entered school without speaking English fluently. There were more speakers of Cree than any other native language in Canada, approximately half of whom were Plains Cree.

Cultural persistence was evident in religious revival (fig. 9). Powwows and Sun Dances were regularly performed. Even in urban areas, sweatlodges were common. Traditional healers attacked problems of alcohol, drug abuse, and psychosomatic illness (Young, Ingram, and Schwarz 1989). Religious persistence was described in Montana (Dusenbery 1962) and Saskatchewan (Tarasoff 1980). In many Cree communities, there was a renewed emphasis upon learning the traditional skills of bush life and on the way of perceiving reality that accompanies them. Many Crees found no necessary contradiction between Christianity and traditional native religion (for an example from Wabasca, Alberta, see Darnell 1974).

Fig. 9. Native American Church, Rocky Boy's Res., Mont. The Peyote religion, organized under the name Native American Church, has traditions of ritual curing and the seeking of individual visions. It rejects the consumption of alcohol and has shaped the growth of an intertribal Indian identity (S.D. Gill 1982:170–171). top, Log structure where night-long services are held. center, Altar with remains of tobacco placed at the directional points of a half-circle. bottom, Feast after the Peyote ceremony. This occasion was the 50th anniversary of the Native American Church on the reservation. Approximately 60% of the adults on the reserve are active Peyotists, one of the most significant groups of Peyotists on U.S. reservations (Stewart 1987:252–255). left to right, Mary Rose Denny, cutting cake; unidentified girl; Paul Eagleman's granddaughter; Paul Eagleman, William Denny, Sr.; others unidentified. Photographs by Michael Crummett, 1984.

Population

The Plains Cree reached their maximum territory and population about 1860. In 1660, Roman Catholic missionaries recorded 9,000 Cree. In 1809, they were reported to have declined to about 3,000. By 1863, 11,500 were recorded in Canada; in 1860, about 12,500. By 1871, as a result of epidemics and warfare with the Blackfoot, only 7,000 remained (Ray 1974:191). Over half the Plains Cree population was wiped out by smallpox and influenza in recurrent epidemics between 1781 and 1838 (vol. 6:258). These figures, calculated primarily on the basis of number of tents, can be taken only as approximations.

Reserve statistics are more accurate. Population stabilized around 1883, with the Cree in 48 bands, subject to 10 agencies. The lowest population, 6,766, was recorded in 1894. About 1904, a steady rise began. In 1929, 9,016 was the total (Wissler 1936:9–10).

In 1973, there were 17,436 Crees in Alberta and 26,325 in Saskatchewan, for a total of 43,761. More than one-third of Alberta Crees were concentrated at Hobbema and Saddle Lake reserves in the 1970s. The total Plains Cree reserve area in Alberta (27 reserves) is 587,500 acres. In Saskatchewan in 1997 only Lac La Ronge Reserve had more than 6,000 persons (Indian and Northern Affairs Canada 1998:33). By 1990, over 40 percent of the Plains Cree lived off-reserve.

Synonymy†

The name Plains Cree is a geographical designation used to distinguish those groups of Cree who moved from the east and north out of the woodlands and onto the northern Plains. The first recorded designation of the Plains Cree as a distinct entity is an early eighteenth-century reference to the Cree of the Prairies (La Vérendrye in Burpee 1927:25). In the nineteenth century the name Plains Cree was used sporadically as a designation, sometimes as Plain Crees (Hind 1860, 1:318). Usually, however, these people were referred to simply as Cree. For a discussion of the name Cree, see volume 6:227–228.

The Plains Cree name for themselves is *ne·hiyawak* (H. Christoph Wolfart, personal communication 1987), which has been translated as 'those who speak the same language' (Hayden 1862:235). (For a discussion of the etymology of this term and its forms in other dialects, see vol. 6:267–268; for additional variant spellings in historical sources see Hodge 1907–1910, 1:362.) The Plains Cree also called themselves *iyiniwak* 'people', implying 'plain, genuine, natural people' (Lacombe 1874:358; Curtis 1907–1930, 18:158). The Plains Cree are distinguished from other Crees as *paskwa·wiyiniw* 'prairie people' (H. Christoph Wolfart, personal communication 1975; Curtis 1907–1930, 18:158).

A common name for the Plains Cree occurs among tribes immediately south of them, represented by Assiniboine *šahíya* (Parks and DeMallie 1988:351–352; Curtis 1907–1930, 18:176); Crow *sahí·a* (Medicine Horse 1987:16; Curtis 1907–1930, 4:180); Mandan *šahí* (Hollow 1970:223); Hidatsa *šahí·* (A.W. Jones 1979:63), also cited as ša hē (W. Matthews 1877:200); Arikara *šAhíʔA* (Parks 1986:16), also cited as Shahí (Curtis 1907–1930, 5:148); and Cheyenne Sáhéya, noted as a borrowed term (Curtis 1907–1930, 6:158), also recorded as *sáheaʔeoʔO* 'Chippewas' (Glenmore and Leman 1985:201). The Piegan form Sayíw (Curtis 1907–1930, 6:155) and Blackfoot *sá·yi·koana* 'liars' (Allan R. Taylor, personal communication 1974) are apparently the same name. The form has also been attributed to the Sioux, cited as Shi-e-á-la (Hayden 1862:235), but other sources have this as the Sioux name for the Cheyenne (Buechel 1970:733). Although Hayden (1862:235) attributes the origin of this widespread name to the Assiniboine and Sioux, the actual source of it is unknown (cf. W. Matthews 1877:200).

Another common designation for the Plains Cree among northern Plains tribes is 'rabbit' or 'rabbit people'. This name occurs among Sioux groups: Teton *maštíčala wičʰaša* 'rabbit man' (Buechel 1970:733, phonemicized); Santee *maštįča* 'rabbit' (Riggs 1890:309, phonemicized); and Yankton *maštįča oyate* 'rabbit people' (Williamson 1902:41, phonemicized). The Arapaho name is *no·kúhnen* 'rabbit person' (Ives Goddard, personal communication 1990); the Gros Ventre is *nɔɔcih* (sg.), *nɔ́ɔ́chɔh* (pl.) 'rabbits' (Taylor, 1994, 1:186); and Cheyenne *vohkoohétaneoʔO* 'rabbit people' (Glenmore and Leman 1985:201), recorded also as Voxko (sg.), Voxkoeo (pl.) 'rabbits' (Petter 1913–1915:582).

A name with no known underlying meaning is Blackfoot *asinaawa* (Franz and Russell 1989:349; Curtis 1907–1930, 18:186) and *asinááwa* (Allan R. Taylor, personal communication 1974). The Flathead name is Nħutuħtú, which has no known underlying meaning (Curtis 1907–1930, 7:165). In Kootenai the Plains Cree are Kutskiáwi 'liars' (Curtis 1907–1930, 7:168).

Various Subarctic Athapaskan tribes have cognate forms of a general name for the Cree that means 'enemy': Chipewyan *ʔená* (Ronald Scollon and Eung-Do Cook, personal communication 1979), an early recording of which is Annah (A. Mackenzie 1802:291); Hare *ʔeda* (Keren Rice, personal communication 1979); and Kutchin Ana (Petitot 1869).

A different name with no underlying meaning, *dešine*, is the designation of the Cree among several other northern Athapaskan tribes, namely, Beaver, Slavey, Tahltan, and southern Kaskan (Patrick Moore, personal communication 1994).

There was no generally used sign in the Plains sign language that denoted the Plains Cree. Some tribes, like the Assiniboine, Crow, and Arapaho, designated them by the sign for a rabbit, reflecting those tribes' linguistic designation. The Arikara, Hidatsa, and Mandan denoted them

†This synonymy was written by Douglas R. Parks.

by the signs for 'blackened faces', while the Blackfoot also used a compound sign, 'Sioux' and 'to lie', hence 'Sioux liar', to denote them (W. P. Clark 1885:131; Scott 1912–1934).

Bands

Besides the names in table 1, Skinner (1914a:517) gives Omuskego 'Swampy', said to be a major division of the Plains Cree; but he obtained no other divisional names.

The band names that Mandelbaum (1940:11) recorded were grouped into two geographical divisions: (1) the eastern bands, termed *mamihkyiniwak* 'downstream people', composed of the Calling River People, Rabbit Skin People, and Touchwood Hills People; and (2) the western bands, or *natimtwtyiniwak* 'upstream people', composed of the Upstream People, Parkland People, River People, and House People. The Cree-Assiniboine band was sometimes considered to be a member of the western bands and sometimes to constitute a third division called 'Prairie People'.

Sources

The classic source on Plains Cree is Mandelbaum (1940, 1979). Additional viewpoints are found in Lowie (1954, 1955), although he relied on Mandelbaum for data, and Skinner (1914, 1914a, 1919). Cooper (1944), Rossignol (1938a, 1939), Dusenberry (1962), and Tarasoff (1980) provide further information on religious practices. The ethnographic literature suffers from unclear delineation of the Plains Cree from other Cree groups, particularly the Western Woods Cree. Archeological sources helping to disambiguate this situation include McCullough (1982), D. Meyer (1978, 1983), D. Meyer and D. Russell (1987), J. Smith (1976, 1981, 1987), Syms (1977) and J. V. Wright (1971).

Ethnohistorical and historical sources include Milloy (1988), Ray (1974), and Thistle (1986). Important Plains Cree museum collections include those of Cowie (VanStone 1991) and Simms (VanStone 1983) at the Field Museum of Natural History, Chicago, and Mandelbaum's at the American Museum of Natural History, New York.

Plains Ojibwa

PATRICIA C. ALBERS

The Algonquian-speaking Ojibwa (ōˈjĭbwā) were the last of many Eastern Woodlands populations to settle on the plains in historic times. By the mid-nineteenth century, three different populations of Ojibwa ancestry occupied portions of a vast area extending across North Dakota and Montana as well as Manitoba, Saskatchewan, and Alberta. The Plains Ojibwa evolved a unique cultural identity based largely on an equestrian, buffalo-hunting lifeway. The other two are the Plains Métis (this vol.) and the Saulteaux (vol. 6).

The Plains Ojibwa are a newly emergent population, not only because they adopted a way of life different from their ancestors but also because their ethnic origins are composite. Some are descended from the Saulteaux of Ontario, whose language they speak,* but others trace their origins to the Ojibwa, Ottawa, and Huron communities of Minnesota, Wisconsin, and Michigan (Howard 1977:13–14; Peers 1994:3–7). Whether their roots reach back to the northern or southern shores of Lake Superior, many of the Ojibwa who reached the plains lived among, and intermarried with, neighboring Cree and Assiniboine. Indeed, throughout much of their history on the plains, the Ojibwa developed a Plains-oriented identity and way of life in tandem with their Cree and Assiniboine neighbors (S.R. Sharrock 1974; Albers and Kay 1987; Albers 1996).

Movements and Adaptations to the Plains, 1730–1816

Before 1780, the westernmost Ojibwa were reported to be among the groups trading at the Mandan villages, and among those fighting against the Hidatsa and Cheyenne. Notwithstanding their occasional forays to the prairies, early eighteenth-century sources describe a population heavily dependent on the hunting, trapping, fishing, and gathering of woodland resources. As late as 1750, these Ojibwa were still without horses and their principal mode of travel was on foot or by canoe (Hickerson 1956; Coues 1897, 1:225–231; Voegelin and Hickerson 1974:3–7; Howard 1977:14–15; J. Jackson 1982; Peers 1994:14–18).

As the Ojibwa moved west, they became close allies of the Assiniboine and Plains Cree with whom they traded, intermarried, and fought against common enemies, particularly the Sioux and Gros Ventre. By the 1760s, some were traveling through the territories of Assiniboine and Plains Cree between Lake of the Woods and the Assiniboine River (S.R. Sharrock 1974). They did not maintain any firm foothold in the parkland regions bordering the prairies until the 1780s, when a smallpox epidemic wiped out much of the indigenous population in southwestern Ontario and neighboring Minnesota (Ray 1974:96–108; Peers 1994:18–21). Some scholars (Greenberg and Morrison 1981) argue that a new and ethnically mixed population emerged, loosely identified by local traders as Ojibwa. Whatever the case, by the 1790s the Ojibwa were well established in much of the parkland region bordering the prairies along the Red and Assiniboine rivers (Hickerson 1956; Ray 1974:96–100; Sharrock and Sharrock 1974:35–47; Voegelin and Hickerson 1974:8–15; Howard 1977:16–20; Camp 1984; Peers 1994:28–38).

Initially, the Ojibwa moved west as migrant laborers who traveled alone or in small camp groups to take advantage of new opportunities in the fur trade (Peers 1994:8–18). Once they occupied the parklands, some continued to push farther west in search of more productive fur-trapping sites. As early as the 1780s, Ojibwas were observed at trading posts along the Assiniboine River catering to a largely Plains clientele, and by the 1790s, a steadily growing number were utilizing the prairies west of the Red River as far as the Pembina Hills. In the same period, they were reported as far south as the Souris River and in the vicinity of the Qu'Appelle and Saskatchewan rivers, but they did not settle in any of these areas in appreciable numbers until the nineteenth century (Hickerson 1956; Masson 1889–1890, 1:169; Ray 1974:99–102; Howard 1977:17–18; Thistle 1986:70–71; Peers 1994:39–51). When moving onto the prairies west of the Red River and south of the Assiniboine, the Ojibwa hunted and settled peaceably among their neighbors, the Assiniboine and Plains Cree (S.R. Sharrock 1974:109–110; Albers 1996:97–102). But in contrast to their equestrian allies who relied largely on buffalo for subsistence and fur-trade provisions, the

*The phonemes of Saulteaux are: (unaspirated stops and affricate) *p*, *t*, *č*, *k*, ʔ; (spirants) *s*, *š*; (nasals) *m*, *n*; (semivowels) *w*, *y*; (short oral vowels) *i*, *e*, *a*, *o*; (long oral vowels) *i·*, *e·*, *a·*, *o·*; (long nasal vowels) *į·*, *ę·*, *ą·*, *ǫ·*. The oral stops, affricate, and spirants are always voiceless when geminated, usually voiceless word-initially and word-finally, and optionally voiceless in all positions in very careful speech; they are usually voiced word-medially when not geminated or in a cluster with a spirant. Geminate stops are preaspirated in some dialects. Some dialects lack ʔ, or the nasalized vowels, or both.

This phoneme inventory follows the description in Voorhis (1977). Cited Saulteaux words have been phonemicized by John D. Nichols and Roger Roulette (communication to editors 1999).

Ojibwa owned few horses and were principally trappers of small fur-bearing game (Peers 1994:27–38).

In the years after 1797, when much of the region's beaver population perished from epidemic disease, the patterns of production among the westerly migrating Ojibwa became more diversified. Most of them continued to follow a pattern of seasonal hunting and trapping in the parkland oases that jutted onto the prairies along riverbanks and elevated escarpments. Here they joined local Plains Cree and Assiniboine on winter buffalo drives, which provided an ever more important source of supplemental meat during trapping seasons. Some of the Ojibwa even remained in the prairie region year-round, but most returned to more familiar habitat sites in the parklands and forests for fishing in summer, sugar making in spring, and gathering wild rice in autumn. The Ojibwa presence on the prairies was still limited and confined primarily to small family and band groups who lived near or settled among resident Assiniboine and Plains Cree (Harmon 1911:72; Hickerson 1956:274–293; Tanner 1830:57–58, 63–64, 86–87, 96–98, 132, 137, 142; Coues 1897, 1:53, 57, 191, 196, 257, 269; Howard 1977:17–20; Peers 1994:39–61).

During the first two decades of the nineteenth century, the Ojibwa witnessed a further decline in prime fur-bearing animals, an increasing cost in trapping them, and a loss of valued parkland habitats as Europeans and Métis moved into their territorial range. One of the results of these changes was that more Ojibwas chose to move and pursue other economic opportunities, and many of these were to be had on the prairies where horses and buffalo meat had commercial currency (Ray 1974:125–182; Sharrock and Sharrock 1974:30–64; Thistle 1986:51–80; Peers 1994:63–97). Although more Ojibwas were utilizing and living in a prairie environment in the early decades of the nineteenth century, it is difficult to mark precisely the date at which a distinct Plains Ojibwa population emerged. However, it is clear that by 1805 a small core of Ojibwa hunted buffalo, owned horses, and lived on the prairies among Plains Cree and Assiniboine, and that by the next decade, the size of this core population had increased as more of the parkland-based Ojibwa sought more secure economic opportunities on the prairies (Peers 1994:69).

Establishing a New Cultural Identity, 1817–1862

The year 1817 marked a significant turning point in Plains Ojibwa history. Not only was it the date when Ojibwa, along with Plains Cree and Assiniboine, ceded lands along the Assiniboine and Red rivers to the Selkirk Colony, but also it was a time when their trade relations with the Mandan seriously deteriorated and when hostilities with the Sioux escalated over access to buffalo-hunting ranges. It was also a point at which the range and internal diversity of Ojibwa adaptations to the plains were becoming more apparent (Sharrock and Sharrock 1974:53–88; Voegelin and Hickerson 1974:64–121; Milloy 1988:62–68; Peers 1994:92–179).

Environments, Locations, and Named Groups

During this period, the majority of Plains Ojibwa remained in a transitional environmental position, where buffalo hunting was combined with procuring other big game species and where trapping, fishing, and the gathering of parkland and woodland resources remained important to their livelihood (Ray 1974:96–100; Howard 1977:31–34; Peers 1994:80–83, 144). Although dependent on the prairies in varying ways and degrees, most Ojibwas remained in parkland locations along the Assiniboine, Qu'Apelle, and Saskatchewan rivers (fig. 1). They included within their ranks the *onikami·wininiwak* 'Portage People', mistowaiau-wininiûk (?) 'Winnipeg People', and kipaukaning-wininiwûk (?) 'Qu'Appelle River People' (Skinner 1914c:481). Their principal commercial alliances were forged with the British, and in their westernmost locations, they maintained close ties with Plains Cree and Assiniboine. In the years after 1820, Ojibwa established even closer associations with the newly emergent Métis communities. Especially in locations east of the Turtle Mountains, the Ojibwa commonly hunted buffalo with Métis as far south as Devils Lake, and after 1850, a few joined the Métis in their migrations to the plains of Alberta and Montana. Some of these Ojibwa were probably included among those identified as the *ša·kana·šši·wininiwak* 'English People' (Skinner 1914b, 1914c; A. Ross 1957:98–99; Spry 1968:137; Hind 1971:46, 53; Ray 1974:96–100; S.R. Sharrock 1974:113; Voegelin and Hickerson 1974:119–137; Peers 1994:66–69, 104, 160).

It was not until the 1820s and 1830s that an established and truly distinctive population of mounted and buffalo-dependent Ojibwa emerged on the plains (Howard 1977:21–23). As their presence on the prairies took hold, more Ojibwas broke away from the parklands and forests to join their plains-adapted relatives. In the mid-nineteenth century, steady waves of Ojibwa newcomers were drawn to the western plains not only because resources continued to dwindle in the eastern parklands and prairies but also because economic opportunities were awaiting them in the hide trade (Ray 1974:147–154; Sharrock and Sharrock 1974:68–69; Peers 1994:99–139). The Ojibwa who became the most plains-oriented in their lifeway occupied and traveled an area that extended west across the prairies from the Turtle Mountains to the eastern edge of the Cypress Hills. They were a fully equestrian people dependent primarily on bison for subsistence and exchange. The largest body of this population was located between the Assiniboine and Souris rivers (Ross 1957:255–257; Ray 1974:205–207; Sharrock and Sharrock 1974:68–69; Voegelin and Hickerson 1974:127–128; Howard 1977:21–23; Albers 1996:104–107) and most certainly included the *mikkinakk wači·winiwak* 'Turtle Mountain People' and *mo·swači·wininiwak* 'Moose Mountain People' (Skinner 1914c:481; Howard 1977:73). A portion of these Ojibwa

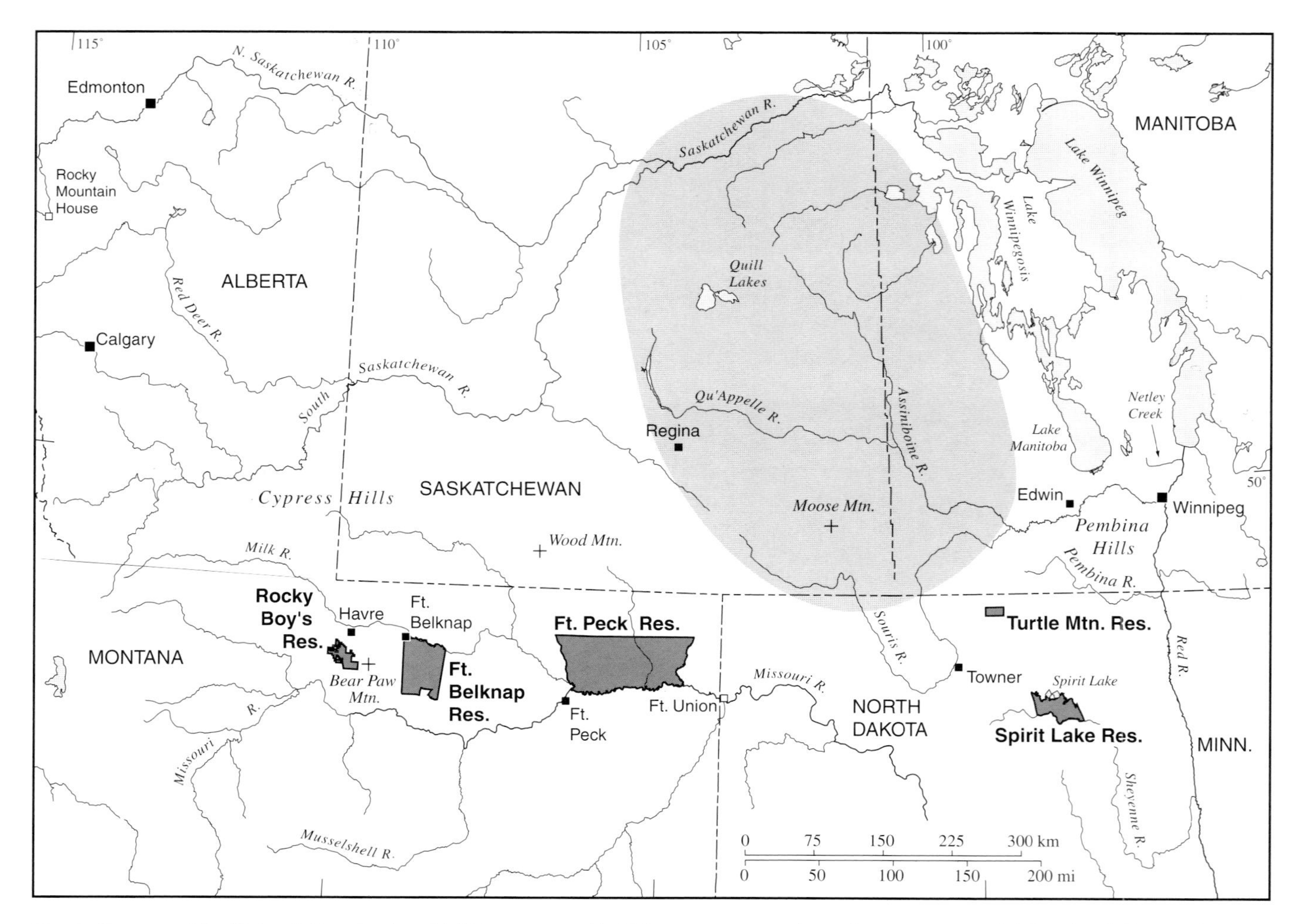

Fig. 1. Range used by Plains Ojibwa in the mid-19th century, with 20th-century reservations. For reserves, see "Plains Cree," fig. 1, this vol.

formed a large fortified village called *pišikki ka·-tta·t* 'Buffalo Lodge' located near Towner, North Dakota, which was destroyed by Yanktonai in 1824–1825 (Howard 1976, 1977:21–22). In the next decade, some of them were reported among the Plains Cree and Assiniboine trading with Americans at Fort Union on the Missouri (Anonymous [Fort Sarpy] 1940a:130; Ewers 1957a:24–33; Sharrock and Sharrock 1974:65–66; Ray 1974:147–154).

After the epidemics of the 1830s, which wiped out large segments of the local Plains Cree and Assiniboine populations, the Plains Ojibwa became a more dominant population on the plains straddling the Souris River (Kurz 1937:84, 234–235; Ross 1957:269–272; Denig 1961:71–73; Ray 1974:187–192; Sharrock and Sharrock 1974; Voegelin and Hickerson 1974: 103–104, 120–137; J.F. Taylor 1977; Trimble 1986). Other Plains Ojibwa moved farther west and lived in the region of the Wood Mountains and Cypress Hills among predominately Plains Cree and Assiniboine groups. These were the *mittikwači·wininiwak* 'Wood Mountain People' and the *inina·ntaka·wininiwak* 'Cypress Hill People' (Cowrie 1913:302–303, 308–310; Skinner 1914c:481; Larpenteur 1933:92; Denig 1961:102–111; W. Fraser 1963:25; Boller 1972:292; Albers 1996:108–115; Peers 1994:187–189). Save for the difference of their language and ethnic identification, these Plains Ojibwa were very much a part of a regional body politic that included the allied Plains Cree and Assiniboine (S.R. Sharrock 1974; Ewers 1975; Mandlebaum 1979: 105; Albers and Kay 1987:67–74; Albers 1993:112–114; Peers 1994:96, 187).

Subsistence

The vast and ecologically varied region covered by the Plains Ojibwa created a cultural canvas on which diverse connections were drawn to the plains as well as Eastern Woodlands (Skinner 1914b; Howard 1961, 1977:1–5). In the earliest mentions of their life on the plains, the Ojibwa were reported to hunt buffalo largely during the fall and winter in small groups under the direction of a buffalo dreamer or poundmaker, using surround and impounding techniques (Skinner 1914c:498; Tanner 1830:63; Howard 1977:26–28; Peers 1994:142–144). In later years, buffalo were procured more often in two large annual hunts, one in the summer for meat and another in the fall for meat and robes. In the manner of the neighboring Assiniboine and Plains Cree, these hunts involved a variety of equestrian chase techniques under the supervision of a hunt leader chosen by the band chief and council. This leader, in turn, selected warriors, or *okiččita·k*, who were empowered with absolute authority to scout and police a hunt (Skinner 1914c:494–499; Howard 1977:24–26).

Since Plains Ojibwa lived much of the year either in the parklands proper or at parkland oases in the midst of the prairies, they also hunted and trapped a variety of other game, including moose, elk, white-tailed and black-tailed deer, rabbit, muskrat, and quail. Indeed, for those living closest to the parklands, some of these species probably remained important in local food supplies (Law 1953:22; Howard 1977:28–30; Peers 1994:144). The Plains Ojibwa also fished, and once again, those closest to the parklands spent more of their summer season engaged in this activity (Howard 1977:31; Peers 1994:22–24, 128–130). Also, those closest to the parklands continued their reliance on wild rice, maple sugar, and other woodlands plant resources, while the ones living on the plains became more dependent on vegetable foods such as wild turnips (Howard 1977:32–33; Peers 1994:22–24, 28–29, 81–82). In both prairie and parkland environments, Plains Ojibwa were reported to grow native and imported crops, from corn to potatoes (Howard 1977:33; Moodie and Kaye 1982; Peers 1994:69–72,81–82).

U.S. Military Academy, West Point Mus. Coll.: 553.

Fig. 2. Interior of hide-covered tepee. The man on right wears a fringed hide coat and leggings with quilled or beaded geometric designs. He has a powder horn and knife scabbard and is smoking a pipe. The women wear cloth dresses and puckered moccasins. Hanging on the tepee wall are snowshoes, pouch and powder horn, decorated mittens, gun, hatchet, bow, and skins of birds and animals. Watercolor by Peter Rindisbacher, near Red River Colony, Man., 1822–1825.

Technology

Various aspects of material culture also expressed their dual affiliations. The Plains Ojibwa used the hide tepees of the Plains as well as the bark or reed lodges of the Eastern Woodlands (Skinner 1914b:316). They fashioned rawhide parfleches and buckskin backrest banners much like their Plains neighbors, but they also made containers from birchbark and wove baskets from willow (Howard 1977:40–44, 1980; Brasser 1984; Peers 1994:147–149). Their beadwork entailed geometric and floral motifs, while their dress and moccasin styles were adapted from Plains and Eastern Woodlands sources (fig. 2) (Howard 1977:60–72; Brasser 1987; Peers 1994:149–152, 190–192). They also adopted the Plains-style travois, although many of them used canoes and Red River carts for transporting their supplies and belongings (Skinner 1914b:317; Howard 1977:45–49; Peers 1994: 154).

Social Organization

The Ojibwa were identified with territorial names, derived largely from the locations in which particular groups lived. As among the neighboring Plains Cree and Assiniboine, these territorial groupings were composed of nomadic, loosely organized bands with shifting memberships (Howard 1977:73). Closer to their ancestral Eastern Woodlands life, some of the Plains Ojibwa were associated with village settlements as well. Some of these were located at permanent sites near places such as Netley Creek and the Turtle Mountains, and they were occupied fairly continuously from the winter through spring seasons (Howard 1977:22; Peers 1987:153). Village and band groups were under the direction of a head chief, often hereditary, with limited powers and a series of secondary chiefs who achieved their positions through generosity, diplomatic skills, and successes in warfare. These chiefs formed a loosely structured council that appointed distinguished warriors to assist in maintaining community order. Some of the *okiččita·k* were also members of various men's societies, including the Big Dogs who were connected with the same organization among neighboring Plains Cree (Skinner 1914c:482–493; Howard 1977:75–80).

The Plains Ojibwa employed a Dakota-type kinship system in which parent-in-law and sibling avoidance were practiced. They possessed a number of named, exogamous patrilineal clans, including the Thunderbird, Moose, Bear, and Sturgeon. These groups were nonlocalized, and it was customary to extend hospitality to visitors with the same clan affiliation. First marriages were generally arranged by parents or other guardians; divorce was easily obtained. Residence tended to be virilocal (Skinner 1914c: 481–482; Howard 1977:73–74, 84–87, 225–226).

Religion

In relation to their religion and ceremonial life, the Plains Ojibwa were also in a transitional cultural position. Their dualistic cosmology, evident in the struggles of the thunderbirds (fig. 3) and water panthers, was very much a part of an Eastern Woodlands heritage, as were the Midewiwin or Medicine Lodge, and the Wabano or Shaking Tent ceremony (Skinner 1920; Howard 1977:111–119, 133–152; Peers 1994:155, 168). Other rituals were adopted after the Ojibwa moved to the plains. The Grass Dance (*maškossi·wiššimowin* or *pwa·niššimowin*), Sun Dance (*ni·pa·kwe·ššimowin* 'Thirsting Dance'), and the Clown society (*wi·ntiko·kka·nak*), also performed among the Assiniboine and the Plains Cree, were three of these. The Smoking Tepee ceremony and Trade Dance (*manta·ˀitiwin*) were shared with Plains Cree as well (Skinner 1914c:500–511, 1919a; Howard 1952, 1977:153–180; Vennum 1982:44–63; Brown and Brightman 1988:195–196; Peers 1994:144; Pettipas 1994:56–61).

The Plains Ojibwa encouraged both independence and responsibility in their people. Children were praised for their skills, talents, and self-reliance but were also taught to respect their family, community, and the spiritual world (Hilger 1959; Schneider 1990:139; Albers 1994). Most life-cycle events were marked by special rituals, which included elaborate death feasts held in honor of the deceased (Howard 1977:220–228).

A Changing Landscape, 1863–1917

The year 1863 marked the date of the second Pembina Treaty (the first one in 1851 was never ratified) and the second major land cession in Plains Ojibwa history. Under the provisions of this treaty, portions of their easternmost territory were ceded to the United States and a 640-acre reservation was created north of the Pembina River. Lands in the Turtle Mountains and other areas the Plains Ojibwa frequented were not covered by this or any other treaty. Indeed, until the early 1870s, the vast majority of Plains Ojibwa remained outside the jurisdiction of any treaty and were not formally connected to either the United States or Canada (Dusenberry 1954; Albers 1996:114–116).

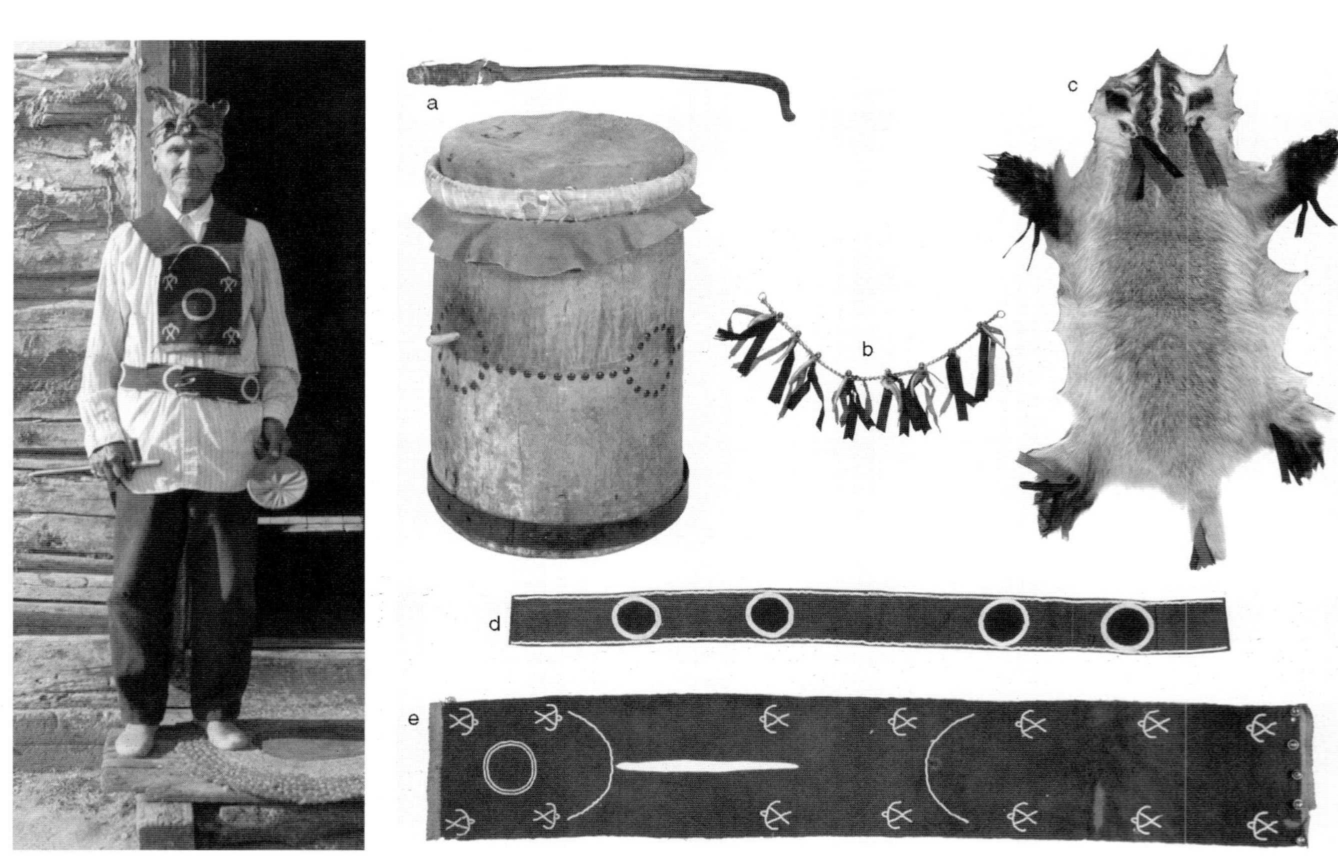

Milwaukee Public Mus., Wis.: a, 65165/27301 a–d; b, 65185/27301; c, 65186/27301; d, 65184/27301; e, 65183/27301.

Fig. 3. Articles used in religious ceremony. left, John Daniels, a medicine man wearing the neckpiece and belt of a Thunderbird war bundle. Made about 1850–1880 and passed down to Daniels, the items had lost their sacred significance by the time of purchase in 1958 (Howard 1977:107–108). Daniels is holding his shaman's pipe and in his left hand his "sucking doctor" rattle, neither item associated with the war bundle. He wears a head handkerchief, because a warrior always wore a head covering (Howard 1963–1965: pl. 14). Photograph by James H. Howard, Long Plain Res., Edwin, Man., 1958. a, Midewiwin drum made of wood and metal. The middle of the drum is decorated with metal tacks and the bottom is painted green. The drumhead is of hide, held by a ring made of wood, textile, and metal. The drumstick is of wood with fabric wrapped around the top. b–e, War bundle collected from John Daniels, original owner unknown. b, Necklace made of metal chain with 8 large badger claws, brass beads, and red and black silk ribbons; length 40 cm. c, Badger skin with red and black silk ribbon dangles, to be worn on the back; length 69 cm. d, Belt of red and dark blue wool trade cloth, white glass seed beads, and dark blue silk grosgrain edging; length 107 cm. e, Thunderbird tunic and belt, the neckpiece made of red wool cloth, white and blue-black glass seed beads and brass bells; bells may have been added by James Howard; length 132 cm. Collected by James Howard, Long Plain Res., Man., 1958.

In 1871, under Treaties No. 1 and 2, Plains Ojibwa living in Manitoba ceded land to the Canadian government and were assigned several small reserves within their home territory, while most of those living in Saskatchewan were not placed on reserves until well after the signing of Treaty No. 4 (Canada 1891, 1912; Cumming and Mickenberg 1972:119–130; Morris 1880). Many of these Plains Ojibwa included populations whose economic orientations were divided between parkland and prairie habitats, and consequently, these groups were among those seeking refuge in the Cypress Hills in the late 1870s during the final collapse of the northern bison herds, and they faced the abrupt adjustment of turning their backs on one way of life to take a new one on reserves (Spry 1976a). Even though a large segment of them took treaties with Canada and remained in that country, there were many, whose territorial range included the United States, who did not and who continued to base their livelihood on bison hunting. However, most of the Plains Ojibwa were not recognized by the United States in various treaties that covered the western plains of North Dakota and adjoining regions in Montana (Dusenberry 1954; Sharrock and Sharrock 1974:127–139; Albers and Kay 1987:80–82; Albers 1996:116).

Throughout the 1880s and early 1890s, there were many Plains Ojibwa among the larger number of Indians and their Métis relatives that began to be referred to as "landless." These were groups of varying sizes who migrated throughout areas west and northwest of the Turtle Mountains seeking their survival wherever they could find it. They included not only Little Shell and his followers who spent some of their time in the Wood Mountains and at Fort Peck living with kin intermarried among the Montana Assiniboine, but also those once denied enrollment at Turtle Mountain who traveled and lived in central Montana and adjoining areas of Saskatchewan. Some of these Ojibwa joined forces with Plains Cree who were married either to Crows or Assiniboines in the area of Fort Belknap, the Bear Paw Mountains, and the Mussellshell River, while others stayed with Cree and Assiniboine in the vicinity of the Cypress Hills (Bottineau 1900:114; Hesketh 1923:112; Dusenberry 1954, 1965:97–98; Bennett 1969:148–155; H. Peterson 1978; Dempsey 1984:59, 92; Peers 1994:186–188, 201, 205; Albers 1996:114–116).

It took many years for most of these Plains Ojibwas to gain trust lands and a legally recognized affiliation with either the United States or Canada, although some under the name of the Little Shell Band of Montana remained unrecognized in 1998 (W. Byran 1985:98–103). Under an executive order, the Turtle Mountain Reservation, composed of 22 townships, was created for Plains Ojibwa and a portion of their Métis relatives in 1882, but two years later, it was reduced by another executive order to only two townships. This reservation grew smaller as squatters and prospective settlers intervened politically to legitimate the removal of prime agricultural lands on the reservation from the hands of the Plains Ojibwa and Métis (Bottineau 1900; Hesketh 1923; Delorme 1955a; Howard 1959; Camp 1984; S.N. Murray 1984; Schneider 1990:125; Miller 1994:231–236). Unable to survive within the reduced reservation, many Ojibwas left to move farther west during the late 1880s and to join forces with various Plains Cree–Ojibwa populations who were labeled as "landless." After the Northwest Rebellion of 1885, some of the "landless" Plains Ojibwas settled on largely Plains Cree reserves in Saskatchewan, but others remained in Montana where they intermarried and settled successfully on the Blackfeet, Flathead, Crow, Northern Cheyenne, Fort Peck, and Fort Belknap reservations (Bennett 1969:142–155; Dempsey 1984:96–105; Miller 1994:237–238; Albers 1996:116). In 1917, another executive-order reservation, named after the Plains Ojibwa leader, Rocky Boy, was established for a segment of the remaining Plains Ojibwas, Plains Crees, and Métis in Montana while others continued landless through the 1990s (Dusenberry 1954, 1958, 1962, 1965; W. Bryan 1985:72–83; Miller 1994:238).

Reservation and Reserve Life, 1918–2000

Plains Ojibwa have adapted to reserve and reservation life in varied ways. Although most of the political and economic aspects of their former way of life have been abandoned, many features of their language, kinship system, and ceremonial life have persisted until the 1990s.

Missionary and government efforts in Canada and the United States brought change, but they also generated resistance (Dusenberry 1962; Miller 1994; Pettipas 1994). As with neighboring native groups in the northern prairies and parklands, the Plains Ojibwa were encouraged to farm early on but only a few had sufficient lands, technical means, and capital to make agriculture successful (S. Carter 1990). At Turtle Mountain, this situation was complicated by allotment and a large population of allotees, many of whom were assigned public domain lands off-reservation in the Dakotas and Montana. Allotment contributed both to a further scattering of a portion of the Ojibwas and to the leasing of lands to outsiders by those who did not migrate (Miller 1994:234–236).

Some Ojibwas turned to petty commodity production in trapping and craftswork, as well as seasonal wage-labor jobs in construction and farmwork, supplemented by subsistence hunting, fishing (fig. 4), and gathering, to make their livelihood. Some received advanced educations and secured full-time employment in occupations from nursing and mechanics to law and teaching (Law 1953:77–80; Howard 1977:235–237; Cuthand 1978:31–42; S.N. Murray 1984; W. Byran 1985:73–74; Schneider 1990:125–126).

By World War II, few Ojibwas could depend on a mixed economy of subsistence work and seasonal labor any more. Larger numbers attempted to enter the labor market on a full-time basis, but jobs were scarce near their home communities. Eventually, some left their reservations to

Natl. Arch.: top, 75-ED-6-1212-64Z; bottom, 75-CP-111-60-15.

Fig. 4. Economic activities at Turtle Mountain Res., N. Dak. top, Employees of Chippewayan Authentics, a joint tribal and Bureau of Indian Affairs enterprise, active 1964–1966, created to provide employment for members of the reservation. The men are carving wooden animal figures that were sold by museums and other organizations. Photograph by Don Morrow, 1964. bottom, Fisherman at Fish Lake after a heavy rain. Photograph by Wayne L. Skow, 1960.

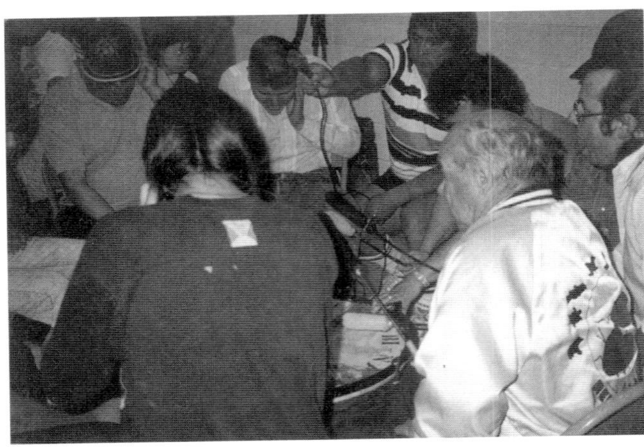

Turtle Mountain Community College, Belcourt, N. Dak.

Fig. 5. Life in the 1990s. top, Turtle Mountain Res. drummers at powwow; man with microphone wearing striped shirt is Verlin Dubois; to his left David J. Ripley, Terry Baker, and Boy Joe Fayant with light-colored jacket. Photographed June 1993. bottom left, Waylon Whitford, 4-year old from Rocky Mountain House, Alta., receiving his annual $5 stipend from the Canadian Dept. of Indian and Northern Affairs as stipulated in Treaty No. 6. Photograph by Rob McKinley, 1998. bottom right, Leslie Peltier at June 1993 powwow. top and bottom right, Photographer not recorded.

find work in the cities, while many of those who remained behind faced a life of chronic unemployment (Delorme 1955a; Howard 1977:237; Schneider 1986:135–151, 1990:130–131). Beginning in the late 1960s this trend was reversed, at least partially, when the United States and Canadian governments developed programs to mitigate the effects of poverty and to foster economic development. Many different kinds of jobs emerged in Plains Ojibwa communities, funded largely through federal programs for housing, education, and health, although some of this employment was cut back in the 1980s. After the 1970s, many jobs were also created in privately owned and tribally run enterprises (fig. 4), from supermarkets to gambling casinos, and many of these contributed to local economic growth (Howard 1977:237; Schneider 1990:135–136).

In the twentieth century, the political destinies of Plains Ojibwa continued to be affected by their trust relationships with the Canadian (fig. 5) and United States governments. In Canada, band governments were run by elected chiefs and councils, and they followed policies shared with other treaty populations in the prairie provinces (Sanderson 1984). In the United States, the Turtle Mountain and Rocky Boy's reservations were governed by an elected chair and council. Here the "traditional" or "full-blood" Plains Ojibwa made up only a small segment of the populace, although at Turtle Mountain this group held important leadership roles in ceremonial affairs and occupied titular, hereditary positions with advisory functions (Dusenberry 1954; A. Thompson 1973; Howard 1977:237–238; Schneider 1990:132–33).

Despite the small size of the traditional Plains Ojibwa population in the United States, which probably never amounted to more than a few thousand people, they have been active in promoting both the retention and reintroduction of traditional culture in their communities, including the Sun Dance and the Grass Dance in the form of the modern powwow (Howard 1952, 1977:197–214; Tarasoff 1980; Schneider 1990:138; Vennum 1982; W. Bryan 1985:78–79; Pettipas 1994:135–139, 179, 183–189). The traditional community has also been called upon for assistance in developing bilingual and bicultural educational programs (Schneider 1990:136). In Canada, more so than in the United States, the Plains Ojibwa and Plains Cree languages continue to be learned at home and spoken by many adults. Similar efforts have been made in Canadian communities to preserve aspects of traditional culture in areas of ritual and craftswork (Howard 1977:238). Not all expressions of Plains Ojibwa culture found their outlets in formats drawn from the past; indeed, some of the most creative and vibrant late twentieth-century cultural pathways followed new avenues including the Native American Church (Howard 1977:215–217; Couch and Marino 1979; Pettipas 1994:191–192) and the artistry of Plains Ojibwa painters (Dewdney 1978; Warner 1990). Throughout the twentieth century, the Plains Ojibwa displayed a continued inventiveness in preserving and redefining their culture (Schneider 1990:140).

Synonymy†

The name Plains Ojibwa is a geographical designation introduced by Skinner (1914:477) to differentiate Ojibwa groups on the plains from woodland Ojibwa groups. Throughout the twentieth century these people were known variously as Ojibwa, Chippewa, Bungi, Saulteaux, Plains Ojibwa, and, later, western Ojibwa (Peers 1994:xvii).

The names Ojibwa and Chippewa are variant renderings of *očipwe·*, originally the self-designation of a band living north of Sault Sainte Marie and in the twentieth century the self-designation of groups in the eastern part of Plains Ojibwa country and some western communities (Peers 1994:xv–xvii), including those in North Dakota and Montana. Chippewa is the preferred usage in the United States and southern Ontario, while Ojibwa, and particularly Ojibway, is preferred throughout the rest of Canada. For variant spellings see volume 15:768–769.

Plains Ojibwa speakers in the eastern part of their territory also use the self-designation *aniššina·pe·* 'human being; Indian', that is commonly used by woodland Ojibwa groups but not used by western Plains Ojibwa groups (Peers 1994:xv). For discussion and variant spellings of the term, see volume 6:241.

In western Manitoba and Saskatchewan the Plains Ojibwa are most commonly designated Saulteaux ('sōtō), locally as well as officially, a usage of French Canadian traders that became established in the early nineteenth century (Howard 1977:7; Peers 1994:xv–xvii). This name is also applied to groups to the east; for discussions and spelling variants see volumes 6:254–255 and 15:769–770.

†This synonymy was written by Douglas R. Parks.

Hudson's Bay traders in the eighteenth and nineteenth centuries referred to the Plains Ojibwa, as well as the Northern Ojibwa, as Bungees (1800, Alexander Henry the Younger in Coues 1897, 2:533), also spelled pung'ke, 1743 (Isham in Rich 1949:191), Bungays (Hind 1860, 1:333), and Bungi (Howard 1977:7). The term is a borrowing from Ojibwa *panki·* 'a little', said to be a native plea when interacting with traders (Bishop 1975:203). Throughout the twentieth century the Plains Ojibwa also used the name Bungi as a self-designation, but more commonly in the United States than Canada (Skinner 1914:477; Howard 1977:7). For discussion of the term, see volume 6:241.

There are few terms designating the Plains Ojibwa specifically. In North Dakota, and perhaps in Montana, Plains Ojibwa sometimes refer to themselves as *nakkawininiwak*, glossed 'those who speak differently [from Ojibwa]' (Howard 1977:6–7, phonemicized), or *nakkawe·wininiwak* (John D. Nichols, communication to editors 1999), borrowings from Plains Cree *nahkawiyiniwak* and *nahkawe·wiyiniwak* (vol. 6:241, vol. 17:438). The Ojibwa of Minnesota are said to refer to Plains Ojibwa as *maškote-aniššina·pe·* 'prairie people' (Howard 1977:7, phonemicized). However, most neighboring tribes do not differentiate them from Cree. The upper Missouri tribes, for example, use the same term for both Cree and Ojibwa: Assiniboine *šahíya* (Parks and DeMallie 1996:250), Mandan *šahí* (Robert C. Hollow, personal communication 1975), Hidatsa *šahí·* (Jones 1979:63), and Arikara *šAhiʔA* (Parks 1970–1990).

Sources

There has been a tendency in both the anthropological and historical literature to submerge the Plains Ojibwa with other tribes. Reflecting their long history of intermarriage and collaboration with neighboring peoples, information on this group is found not only under Saulteaux, Ojibwa, and Chippewa but also under Plains Cree, Assiniboine, and Métis.

The best primary sources on early Ojibwa adaptations to the Plains are the published journals of Charles Jean Baptiste Chaboillez (Hickerson 1959), Duncan M'Gillivray (Morton 1929), Daniel Harmon (1820), Alexander Henry the Younger (Coues 1897; Gough 1988–1992) and David Thompson (Coues 1897; Tyrrell 1968), and the recollections of the captive John Tanner (1830). The Hudson's Bay Company Archives in Winnipeg contains a wealth of unpublished records. Several excellent summary works have used these and other sources (Hickerson 1956; Ray 1974; Russell 1991; S.R. Sharrock 1974; Sharrock and Sharrock 1974; Camp 1984; Thistle 1986), but by far the most complete and exhaustive coverage of Plains Ojibwa early history is found in the work of Peers (1987).

For the period between 1817 and 1863, Peers's (1994) work provides the best historical overview of Plains Ojibwa in Canada, while other works cover their situation in the United States (Ewers 1957a, 1968, 1974a; Howard 1961, 1976, 1977; Sharrock and Sharrock 1974; Voegelin and Hickerson 1974). Important primary source materials for this period are found in published sources (Maximilian 1843; in Thwaites 1904–1907, 22–24; Larpenteur 1933; Kurz 1937; Ross 1856; Denig 1961; Kane 1859; Harper 1971; Hind 1860) and in unpublished records at the Hudson's Bay Company Archives; the Saskatchewan Archives Board, Regina; and Manitoba Archives Board, Winnipeg.

Published materials on Plains Ojibwa history from 1863 to the modern era focus largely on the populations who settled on reservations in the United States, either at Turtle Mountain (Bottineau 1900; Hesketh 1923; Law 1953; Delorme 1955, 1955a; Howard 1959; C. Gourneau 1989; P. Gourneau 1973; Murray 1984; Camp 1984, 1987, 1990; Saint Ann's Centennial 1985; Schneider 1986, 1990) or Rocky Boy's (Dusenberry 1954, 1965; Rego 1977; H. Peterson 1978; Couch and Marino 1979; W. Bryan 1985; Burt 1987). There are primary source materials on Plains Ojibwa in the United States at the Montana Historical Society, Helena; North Dakota Heritage Center, Bismarck; and in the military and the Department of the Interior records at the National Archives in Washington, D.C., Kansas City, and Denver. Very little has been written about the modern histories of Plains Ojibwa in Manitoba and Saskatchewan, and much of what exists describes their experiences in very general terms or in the context of other ethnic groups, especially the Plains Cree and Métis (Cowie 1913; Giraud 1945; Sharp 1954; Dusenberry 1962; Fraser 1963; Spry 1968, 1976a; Cumming and Mickenberg 1972; Bennett 1969; Sprenger 1972; A.E. Thompson 1973; Woodcock 1976; Cuthand 1978; S. Dewdney 1978; J.S.H. Brown and Brightman 1988; Pettipas 1994; Tarasoff 1980; Dempsey 1984; Sanderson 1984; Carter 1990; Warner 1990).

Primary ethnographic source material is contained in the works of Skinner (1914b, 1914c, 1919a, 1920) and Howard (1952, 1977, 1980). A few studies have looked at aspects of Plains Ojibwa art (Brasser 1984, 1987) and ceremonialism (Couch and Marino 1979; Tarasoff 1980; Vennum 1982; Pettipas 1994). A small amount of ethnographic information can also be found in the context of their relations with neighboring populations, including the Mandan (Bowers 1950), Hidatsa (Bowers 1965), Assiniboine (Rodnick 1938; Kennedy 1961; Miller 1987), Sioux (Albers 1974; Howard 1976), and Plains Cree (Skinner 1914; Dusenberry 1962; Mandelbaum 1979; Fromhold 1981). Museum collections include materials located at the Turtle Mountain Chippewa Heritage Center in Belcourt, North Dakota; the North Dakota Heritage Center; Milwaukee Public Museum; Manitoba Museum of Man, Winnipeg; the American Museum of Natural History, New York; and the Canadian Museum of Civilization in Hull, Quebec.

Plains Métis

DIANE PAULETTE PAYMENT

In North American, people of mixed American Indian–European descent number in the millions and reside in all parts of the continent. Unknown numbers have passed into Euro-Canadian and Euro-American communities; others identify as Indians, on or off reservations. Only in certain historical circumstances, which arose most notably around the Great Lakes and in western Canada, have people of mixed ancestry maintained distinct communities or personal identities neither Indian nor White. Of these, most but by no means all would identify themselves by the term Métis (ˈmā,tē, ˌmāˈtēs; vol. 6:370).

Language

An important feature of Métis culture was the emergence of a distinct composite language. Michif (or Mitchif) was based primarily on Plains Cree and Canadian French with a distinctive Saulteaux or Ojibwa element (Bakker 1991:11–20, 1997:248–276).* In addition to Michif, Métis communities speak or have spoken three other languages—Michif French, such as is spoken in Saint Laurent, Manitoba; Michif Cree, as at Ile à la Crosse, Saskatchewan; and Michif Saulteaux, as at Turtle Mountain Reservation, North Dakota (Lavallée 1990). There were dialectic distinctions in Michif according to various regions but uniformity in how the French and Cree components combine: the noun phrase was French; the verb structure was Cree; and the syntax was Cree with French and probably some English influence (J.C. Crawford 1985:233). Michif was widely spoken in the nineteenth century and in the late twentieth century was still spoken fluently by the elders in many Métis communities and understood by others, although English was the first language of the generations under the age of 40. One of the reasons for this was the negative attitude of non-Métis toward Michif, which was derisively called a jargon or incorrect French in Saint Laurent and in Batoche, Saskatchewan. In Montana, Michif speakers were mockingly referred to as *bonjours* in reference to their "foreign" language and status. During the late twentieth century Michif gained academic recognition (Bakker 1990, 1991, 1997; J.C. Crawford 1985; Douaud 1985; Lavallée 1990; Laverdure and Allard 1983; Papen 1984), and a Michif Languages conference was sponsored by the Manitoba Métis Federation in 1985. It was taught only at the college level in North Dakota, but in the western Canadian provinces there was a movement toward the recognition and promotion of the language and its inclusion in the school curriculum.

*The phonemes of the Cree component of Michif are: (voiceless unaspirated stops and affricates) *p*, *t*, *č*, *k*; (voiceless spirants) *š*, *h*; (nasals) *m*, *n*; (semivowels) *w*, *y*; (short oral vowels) *i*, *a*, *u*; (long oral vowels) *i·*, *e·*, *a·*, *u·*; (nasal vowels) *į*, *ę̄*, *ų*.

The phonemes of the French component of Michif are: (voiceless unaspirated stops and affricate) *p*, *t*, *č*, *k*; (voiced stops and affricate) *b*, *d*, *ǯ*, *g*; (voiceless spirants) *f*, *s*, *š*, *h*; (voiced spirants) *v*, *z*, *ž*; (nasals) *m*, *n*, *nʸ*, *ŋ*; (resonants) *r*, *l*; (semivowels) *w*, *y*; (oral vowels) *i*, *ɪ*, *ɛ*, *æ*, *a*, *ɑ*, *ɔ*, *u*, *ü*, *œ*; (nasal vowels) *æ̨*, *ą*, *ų*, *œ̨*.

These phoneme inventories follow Bakker (1997:80).

Italicized terms referring to Métis culture in this chapter are in standard French orthography.

Origins: Territories

The Métis never occupied a clearly bounded "tribal" territory; it is more appropriate to place emphasis on local communities and resource areas and directions of historical movement and migration than to suggest a long-term or exclusive possession of any region (fig. 1) (J.C. Peterson and J.S.H. Brown 1985:xxii; Ens 1989:map 8). Métis communities and individuals were to a great extent people in motion (J.C. Peterson 1985:37). Born, in good part, of the fur trade, they followed its vicissitudes and were caught up, first in the supplanting of the trade by American settlers in the lower Great Lakes in the early 1800s, and then in its displacement to the north and west when Canada, the nation to the east, established its hold on the old Hudson's Bay Company chartered territory of Rupert's Land in 1869–1870.

Métis as an expanded twentieth-century ethnic designation encompassed several groups with rather diverse roots. During the French regime, the Montreal-based fur trade became firmly established in the Great Lakes and its traders and explorers, of whom the most famous were the La Vérendrye family, extended French knowledge of the plains to the foothills of the Rockies. Grand Portage, Minnesota, on the northwestern shore of Lake Superior, became a base for expansion of both French and Ojibwa along the waterways of the Canadian Shield, down the Winnipeg River to Lake Winnipeg and the plains and parklands beyond (Gilman 1992). No White women were among the coureurs de bois, and Ojibwa traders, like other native groups, regarded both adoption and marriage as good means of establishing solid trading alliances. By

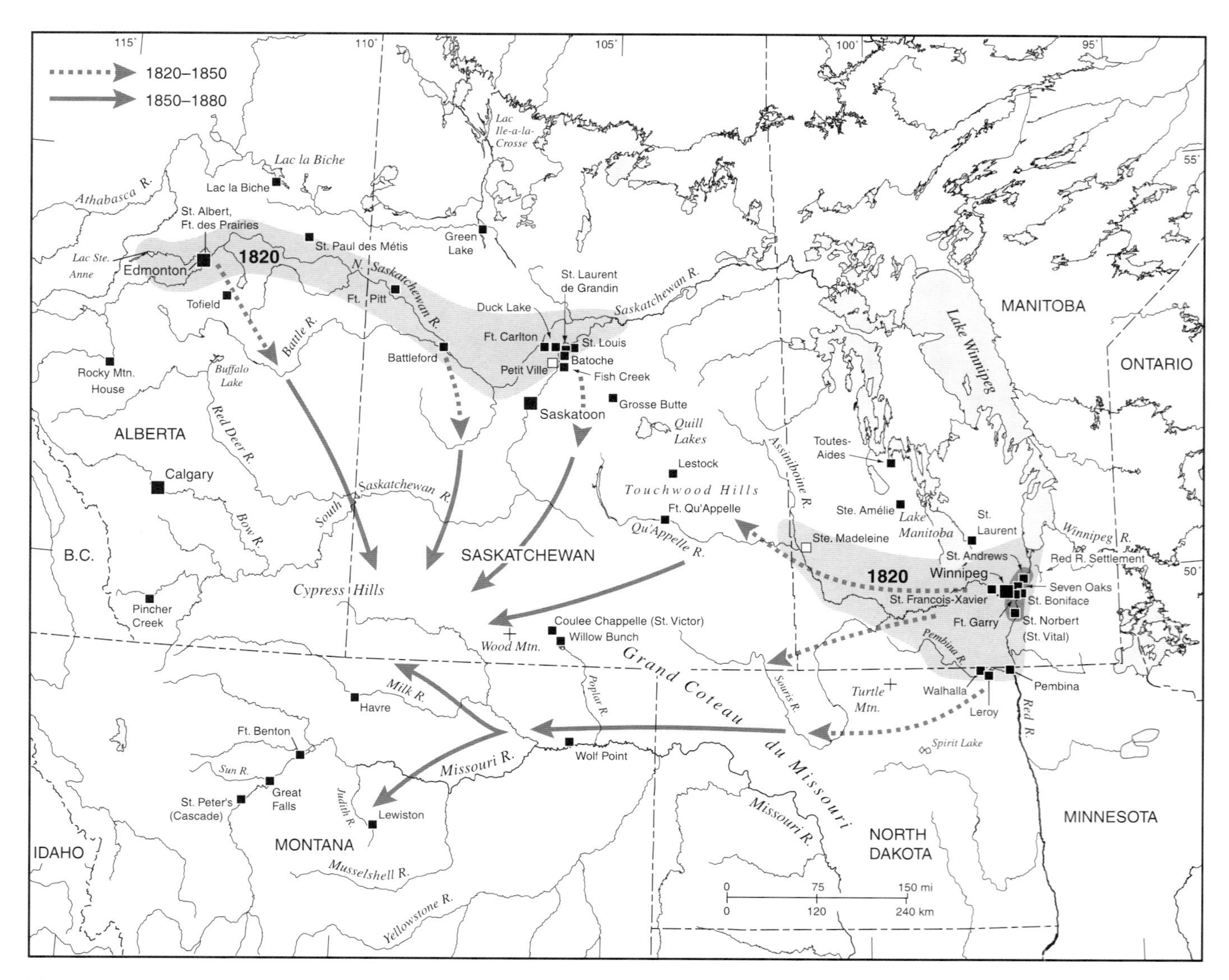

Fig. 1. Areas of settlement around 1820-1880, with Red River Settlement in darker shading, and later seasonal shifts for hunting.

1763 with the French cession of Canada to Britain, Ojibwa-French unions were an established pattern.

In the following years, under the increasingly Scottish-dominated entrepreneurship that led to the founding of the North West Company (1779–1784), the Montreal trade expanded into Plains regions that had been formerly occupied by Cree and Assiniboine but were abruptly depopulated by the smallpox epidemic of 1781–1782. Among the voyageurs of the time, especially of the laboring echelons, were increasing numbers of Métis, often members of families whose fathers had gone free from fur trade contractual employment to subsist as trappers and trade provisioners. These men, known as *gens libres* 'freemen', and their families, may be seen as founders of a distinctive Métis identity on the plains, especially as they moved into buffalo hunting and pemmican manufacturing in the Red River area of southern Manitoba and beyond.

By the early 1800s, Métis homelands on the plains included settlements and seasonal camps in present-day Wisconsin, North and South Dakota, Minnesota, Montana, as well as Manitoba, Saskatchewan, and Alberta. Gathering places included Prairie du Chien, Wisconsin; Devils Lake and Pembina, North Dakota; Saint Boniface, Manitoba; and Fort des Prairies, Alberta. Around 1840 the Métis of the northern plains began establishing *hivernements* or wintering camps at Wood Mountain, in the Qu'Appelle valley, and in the Saskatchewan River district. They also gathered around the fur trade posts of the American Fur Company at Pembina and Saint Paul. In 1843 some winterers and traders of the Fort Edmonton area relocated to the mission of Lac Sainte Anne, Alberta; and in the early 1860s a farming settlement was established nearby at Saint Albert (B.J. Dawson 1979; Tardif 1961).

External Relations

Throughout the nineteenth century, Métis interacted with both parent groups. They pursued trade and political alliances with the Plains Ojibwa, Plains Cree, Assiniboine, and Blackfoot and often acted as intermediaries between them and Euro-Americans and Euro-Canadians. They also resisted the attempts of both the North West Company (1784–1821) and of the Hudson's Bay Company (post-1821) to control them. They defeated the Sioux at Grand Coteau in 1851, resisted the colonization endeavors of the Hudson's Bay Company at the Battle of La Grenouillère (Seven Oaks) in 1816, and defended their territorial and political rights in the Red River Rebellion in 1869–1870. The failure to secure these rights after Manitoba's entry into the Canadian confederation in 1870 resulted in a military confrontation with the Canadian government known as the Northwest Rebellion in the Saskatchewan district in 1885. Subsequently, the Métis sought redress mainly through constitutional means, forming political associations in all three prairie provinces to actively pursue land claims and national rights.

Culture

Society and Way of Life

The Métis society that emerged on the Plains in the early nineteenth century reflected the cultural traits of both its native and European ancestors. Plains Ojibwa, Plains Cree, *Canadien* (French-Canadian), and Scottish customs and beliefs blended in various degrees and new social groups emerged. Scholars have generally emphasized the distinctions between the two historical groups, Métis and "Halfbreeds," and distinguished them according to their fur trade tradition (the French-Canadian North West Company versus the English Hudson's Bay Company). Métis society at Red River was both complex and varied. There were important ethnic and cultural differences between the two populations of native and European parentage but there was also interaction along political and occupational lines, especially after the union of the two fur trade companies under the name of the Hudson's Bay Company in 1821 and the resettlement of families in the parishes of the Red River Settlement, in close proximity to each other (Gallagher 1988).

There was intermarriage between members of prominent trading families such as the children of Narcisse Marion and Andrew McDermott, while the offspring of hunting and freighting families tended to marry within their own group (Spry 1985). The extended family, which included parents, children, grandparents, and a network of *la parenté* (blood relatives, relatives through marriage, and cousins to the third degree) from both sides, was an important feature of Métis society. Cross-cousin marriages were common in Saint Boniface and at Batoche (Payment 1990:40–42) until the 1920s. A few intermarried extended families often formed a community, for example, the Dumonts of Petite Ville, the Trottiers of Prairie Ronde, and the McGillises of Coulée Chapelle. The elder "grandfathers" and "grandmothers" were respected for their knowledge and wisdom; when widowed they usually resided with or in close proximity to one of their married children (Payment 1990:38–39).

Métis society was essentially patriarchal much like its Plains Cree, Plains Ojibwa, Scottish, and *Canadien* parent societies although there is evidence that native women had a more egalitarian role in the preagricultural economy of the Plains (Albers and Medicine 1983). Women played a complementary role to men in the fur trade, and they have been referred to as "center and symbol in the emergence of Métis communities" (Crown 1983). Children of marriages according to the "custom of the country" commonly resided with their mothers if their European fathers departed. The arrival of missionaries was accompanied by an emphasis on Christian marriages (La Société historique de Saint-Boniface 1991:54–70; parish register of Saint Boniface 1818–1860), but customary marriages persisted well into the twentieth century, especially in isolated settlements. According to a Métis account, the custom of *emprunter* or the "borrowing" of a spouse was quite common in the case of a separation (Payment 1990:42–43). By the late nineteenth century, Métis women were the principal educators and transmitters of cultural values and beliefs. The adoption of children, whether in the case of a childless couple (for example, Gabriel Dumont and Madeleine Wilkie) or from a spouse's previous marriage was general practice.

According to Duke Redbird (1980:6), "the Metis had developed a way of life that was co-operative, rather than competitive." This meant the sharing of resources, nonaccumulation of material goods, and a social status based on ability rather than wealth. Europeans and Americans often considered Métis traders and farmers superior to hunters although the Métis themselves held capable hunters in high regard. Their values were not readily understood or accepted by nonnative peoples in the nineteenth century and resulted in disparaging and misleading accounts (A. Ross 1856; Milton and Cheadle 1865). Métis joie de vivre and concern for the known present rather than the unforeseeable future were interpreted as idleness and improvidence, and their independent character was often mistaken for arrogance.

Métis settlement on the plains in the first half of the nineteenth century reflected a migratory lifeway. They occupied river lots in the Red River parishes of Saint Boniface, Saint Andrew's, Saint Norbert, and Saint François-Xavier but traveled regularly to hunting and trading camps to the south and northwest. A large number of seasonal camps such as Wolf Point, Montana; Grosse-Butte, Saskatchewan; and Buffalo Lake, Alberta; were erected in the 1860s and 1870s. Some such as Petite-Ville were the precursors of settlements such as Saint Laurent de Grandin (founded in 1871), but most were abandoned for more suitable locations. After the 1870s or the period of agricultural settlement by Euro-Americans and Canadians, many Métis relocated to maintain the custom of separate community settlement. They gathered in Havre and Lewistown, Montana; Saint Joseph, later Walhalla, North Dakota; Sainte Amélie and Toutes-Aides (Lake Manitoba); Willow Bunch and Green Lake, Saskatchewan; and Pincher Creek and Lac la Biche, Alberta.

Some Métis whose lifeway was closer to their Indian brethren "took Treaty" or settled on reserves in western Canada. Métis were included in Treaties No. 3, 4, and 6 (of the seven numbered treaties of northwestern Ontario, Manitoba, Saskatchewan, and southern Alberta) in the 1870s, but an 1880 amendment to the Indian Act excluded "half-breeds" from both the provisions of the act and the treaties (Dickason 1992:279–280). However, many Métis continued to reside "illegally" on reserves or on their fringes.

Political Tradition and Armed Resistance

The concept of Métis nationhood on the Plains can be traced to the settlements at Pembina and the Forks of the Red and Assiniboine rivers in the early 1800s. It was expressed more explicitly during the power struggles between the North West and Hudson's Bay companies that resulted in armed conflict at La Grenouillère in 1816. Some writers have described the Métis as pawns of the Nor'Westers in this struggle, but Métis oral traditions (Falcon's song) and testimonies (petition of 1815 cited in Corrigan and Barkwell 1991:9–10; Shore 1991) suggest they were defending their own interests and rights as a nation indigenous to the Northwest. By the late 1840s, the Métis were in the avant garde of their compatriots in their political aspirations. Contrary to the half-breeds who aspired to assimilate into the British-Protestant world of their usually higher-ranked fur trader fathers (J.S.H. Brown 1980), the Métis developed a tradition of resistance to the political and economic control exercised by the Hudson's Bay Company.

Métis social control was inspired by elements of native Plains tradition such as elected chiefs, communal rights (*droits des gens*), and restitutive justice. Leaders were chosen for a specific time and activity. For example, Jean-Baptiste Wilkie led the Pembina buffalo hunt in 1840; Pierre-Guillame Sayer and Louis Riel, Sr., challenged the trade monopoly of the Hudson's Bay Company in 1849; and Cuthbert Grant (at La Grenouillère, 1816) and Louis Riel, Jr. (1869–1870 and 1885) (fig. 2) led armed resistances. According to Redbird (1980:6), Métis also gained status among their peers by their ability to compromise and diffuse conflict. Laws or regulations were usually passed on orally and ratified or changed at public assemblies but increasingly codified by 1870 (List of Rights of 1869–1870 in Manitoba and "Laws and Regulations of the Colony of St. Laurent, Saskatchewan" in 1873). The local governing body of the Hudson's Bay Company in the Red River Settlement, the Council of Assiniboia (1822–1869), recruited its members from the pro-Company religious and social elite after 1835; as a result only a few prominent

left, Glenbow-Alberta Inst., Calgary: NA-1899-8; right, Manitoba Culture, Heritage, and Citizenship, Historic Resources Branch, Winnipeg.

Fig. 2. Leaders of the Métis movement. left, Métis Association of Alberta at Edmonton, 1932. front row, left to right: Jim Brady, secretary; Rev. Father Constant Falher (parish priest from Grouard); Joseph F. Dion, president; Rev. Bishop Guy; Malcoln F. Norris; and Peter Tomkins, Sr.; back row, Joseph Miville Déchêne, member of the provincial legislative assembly; Félix Calihoo; Léonidas Alcidas Giroux, member of the provincial assembly; and Peter Tomkins, Jr. Photographer not recorded. right, Statue of Louis Riel, Jr., leader of the Northwest Rebellion, who was convicted of treason and executed in 1885. Not until 1992 was he formally recognized as a founding father of Manitoba. Photographed on the legislative building grounds, Winnipeg, May 1996.

Métis were appointed to the council (Dorge 1974:58). Pro-free trade and nationalist Métis *Canadiens* such as Narcisse Marion, Louis Riel, Sr., and Louis Letendre *dit* Batoche were not nominated to the council although they had prestige and influence among the Métis. Furthermore, no hunters or freighters were appointed. Nonetheless, both Métis groups were represented in local courts, acted as constables, and presented numerous petitions dealing with trade and agriculture. The paramilitary organization of chiefs or *gouverneurs* and 10 captains or *soldats* was used on the buffalo hunt (Giraud 1986, 2:143) and during battle, for example the Northwest Rebellion of 1885.

The Métis also attempted to negotiate agreements or treaties with the American and Canadian governments. In 1863 a treaty was signed with the Red Lake and Pembina bands of Chippewa, most of whom were of Chippewa-Cree and French-Canadian origins. According to article 8, each "male adult half-breed or mixed blood" could obtain a 160-acre homestead (Kappler 1904–1941, 2:855). A reservation was established at Turtle Mountain in 1882, but the issue of Métis right of admission remained unresolved. After protracted negotiations, land cessions, and the implementation of eligibility lists, citizenship and residence rules between 1892 and 1906, over one-third of the claimants were disqualified (G.S. Camp 1987:161–179). Meanwhile, while "waiting for the day that never comes" (Dusenberry 1965:101), many original Turtle Mountain Métis had relocated farther west to Montana or returned to Canada. The Métis in Manitoba and the Northwest Territories (present-day Saskatchewan and Alberta) also experienced loss of political power in their struggle to safeguard their land rights and cultural traditions.

In 1869, the Hudson's Bay company began negotiations with the British and Canadian governments for the transfer of Rupert's Land, without consultation with its inhabitants. Unauthorized Canadian surveys and the arrival of land speculators in their homeland set into motion an organized Métis resistance under Louis Riel. The Métis National Committee stopped a survey party in the parish of Saint Vital, Manitoba, and ordered patrols on the Pembina trail to stop the new governor-designate, William McDougall, from traveling north of Pembina. The Métis based their actions on the laws of the prairie and established a regulatory council or *sénat métis*. In November 1869, the Métis occupied the Hudson's Bay Company's Fort Garry (Winnipeg), and conventions of French and English-speaking Métis met to discuss the issue of transfer. Riel and his council drafted a List of Rights. In December, a provisional government was established and its flag, a fleur de lys with a four-leaf clover and bison on a white background, flew at Red River (Schmidt 1912:76). Métis from both groups participated in the negotiations with the Canadian government and elected members to the 1870 convention, which chose Riel as president. The provisional government negotiated the terms of the Manitoba Act of 1870, which provided for provincial status, a land reserve of 1.4 million acres (566,580 ha), and official status for the French language and Roman Catholic confessional schools. Riel declared: "no matter what happens now, the rights of the métis are assured by the Manitoba bill: it is what I wanted—*My mission is finished*" (quoted in L.H. Thomas 1982:742).

Representation and active participation in the government and judiciary were means by which the Métis hoped to direct their integration into the Canadian system. But their rights in the new province were not respected. By 1879 they were a minority in the Manitoba legislature (Friesen 1979:33–47), and the land reserve was being appropriated by newcomers (Sprague 1988). The Métis resisted the encroachment on their lands in the Red River valley, but most were compelled to relocate farther north in the Lake Winnipeg and Lake Manitoba region and in Saskatchewan, Alberta, North Dakota (Turtle Mountain region), and Montana (along the Sun and Musselshell rivers). They maintained their political tradition of elected leaders and council in Saint Laurent de Grandin (Payment 1990:145–146) and in Willow Bunch (Rondeau and Chabot 1970) but were not represented in the government of the Northwest Territories in the late 1870s and early 1880s.

The refusal of the Canadian government to confirm Métis riverlot claims along the Qu'Appelle and South Saskatchewan rivers and in Saint Albert led them to submit several petitions in this period. The unrest led to constitutional and then armed resistance in the South Saskatchewan district at Duck Lake, Coulée des Tourond (Fish Creek), and Batoche in 1885. Louis Riel, who was teaching school at Saint Peter's mission in Montana (near Cascade), went to Saskatchewan to lead his compatriots in *la guerre nationale*. On March 18, 1885, the provisional government of Saskatchewan was established with an elder, Pierre Parenteau, Sr., as president and Gabriel Dumont as military adjutant. Riel also selected a people's council or *exovidate*. The Métis under Dumont fought the North West Mounted Police and local militia at Duck Lake on March 26 and met the Canadian River North West Field Force under the command of Gen. Frederick D. Middleton at Fish Creek in April. The engagements ended in a qualified victory for the Métis who then retreated to Batoche where they dug trenches and laid ambushes, waiting for the Canadian offensive to resume. On May 9, Middleton and his army of over 800 attacked Batoche with cannon and a Gatling gun. The Métis, numbering around 250, held the Canadian army in check for three days (R.F. Beal and R.C. Macleod 1984; Hildebrandt 1985).

The military defeat at Batoche forced some Métis to seek at least temporary refuge in the United States, in Minnesota, North Dakota, and Montana. The armed resistance, and especially Riel's execution in November 1885 (vol.4:91), had important political repercussions for the Métis in western Canada and in the northwestern United States. They were increasingly isolated from the political mainstream and discriminated against as a "rebel people."

But the Métis struggle for recognition and justice persisted. In 1887 the Métis of Manitoba formed the Union Nationale Métisse de Saint-Joseph to promote their culture and defend Riel's cause. During the 1890s, politicians such as Roger Marion of Saint Boniface and Charles-Eugène Boucher of Batoche defended Métis interests.

The early 1900s were years of displacement and isolation in the wake of increased immigration. Many Métis fought for Canada during the two world wars, but the recognition that they received on the battlefield was not maintained upon their return (J.D. Harrison 1985:79–82). The Depression of the 1930s fostered the formation of organizations to combat both the lack of political power and poverty. The Métis Association of Alberta was founded in 1932 under the leadership of Jim Brady, Peter Tomkins, Malcolm F. Norris, and Joseph F. Dion (fig. 2). The Métis became a strong political force, reiterating the demands of Riel and Dumont for a land base, economic assistance, and political rights. In response, the government of Alberta appointed a commission chaired by Judge Albert F. Ewing to inquire into the condition of the Métis. One of the positive results of the inquiry was the establishment of eight Métis settlements, which eventually attained a certain level of local self-government (Pocklington 1991; C.E. Bell 1994). The Saskatchewan Métis Association was established in 1938, and some Métis associated themselves with socialist parties such as the Canadian Commonwealth Federation in the 1940s and 1950s (Barron 1990).

The 1960s witnessed the revitalization of political associations and nationalist thought. Métis leaders such as Howard Adams were influenced by the American Black Power movement (H. Adams 1975). New associations were established in Manitoba, Ontario, and British Columbia. Confronting the Canadian government's White Paper of 1969 and the Constitution Act of 1982, western Métis representatives became dissatisfied with sharing representation with non-status Indians. From 1970 to 1983, the Native Council of Canada alone had represented Métis interests on the national level, but in 1983 the Métis National Council was formed to secure distinct Métis representation (J.S.H. Brown 1988:1345). In the United States Métis do not have official status as such.

Economy

Métis economic tradition placed more emphasis on sharing resources rather than on accumulating personal property (Manuel and Posluns 1974:19, 53). However, Métis merchants, whether employed by the Hudson's Bay Company or working independently, adopted the principles of capitalist enterprise and free trade (in the context of opposition to the commercial monopoly of the Hudson's Bay Company). There was evidence of a class system based on occupation and wealth in the fur trade, with the Métis generally part of the laboring class (St. Onge 1989; Bourgeault 1984; Dobbin 1981). The Métis worked at a variety of occupations in the nineteenth century, namely as voyageurs, freighters of merchandise, and servants in the fur trade posts. Some Métis achieved the position of clerks and post managers, but few became commissioned officers. As they usually spoke several languages, their role as interpreters was invaluable and their knowledge of the land brought them employment as scouts and guides to visiting explorers and travelers.

The Métis buffalo hunt (fig.3) was often depicted as a primitive way of life associated with a nomadic lifeway and the "the love of the chase" (A. Ross 1856:108–118; G. Stanley 1963:8, 18). However, the hunt was a rational and adaptive response to life in a restricted economy and helped the Métis exploit the most abundant resource in the plains, at least before 1860 (Coutts 1988:148). The buffalo hunt was a viable business and the main source of food and other products. The Métis were the provisioners of pemmican for the fur trade posts and the Red River Settlement. Both men and women were involved in the hunt and the production of pemmican.

top, Royal Ont. Mus., Toronto: 912.1.26; bottom, Man. Mus. of Man and Nature, Winnipeg: H4-4-13.

Fig. 3. Hunting with horses. top, *Half Breeds Running Buffalo*. Probably sketched during the artist's travels with Métis hunters near Ft. Garry, June 1846. The chase lasted about one hour and extended over 5–6 square miles with a total of about 500 buffalo killed. The hunters threw articles of apparel next to their kills to denote their own prey (Harper 1971:71–72). Oil on canvas by Paul Kane. bottom, Pad saddle of the type used by hunters. It is hand sewn and made of smoke-tanned hide, stuffed with grass or hair. The stirrups are carved of wood. Porcupine quills were used for the decoration, with brown, red, white, blue, yellow, and purple colors. Collected by Paul Kane, 1845–1846; length 52 cm.

The Métis hunt was only one activity in a seasonal network of complementary activities that included small-scale farming, fishing, freighting, and independent trading. Spring was the time of the major buffalo hunt, followed by other activities such as maple sugaring. In the summer, grain crops such as wheat and oats were raised and wild rice and roots were harvested. In the fall, the second hunt took place, accompanied by fishing and trapping (fig. 4), while winter was the time to hunt, trap, and cut firewood. A harsh environment, rudimentary technology, shortages of capital, and poor access to markets seriously limited agricultural productivity. Agriculture in Red River was hampered by recurring droughts, floods, and locusts. As a result, the Métis practiced a mixed economy, drawing upon a wide variety of resources to achieve a successful response to environmental and social conditions.

By the 1840s, independent Métis merchants such as Antoine Gingras, Joseph Rolette, Jr., and Norman Kittson conducted a brisk trade across the Canadian–United States border, between Saint Boniface (Red River Settlement) and Saint Paul, Minnesota (R.R. Gilman, Gilman, and Stultz 1979). In 1849, the Hudson's Bay Company challenged the activities of the free traders. Pierre-Guillaume Sayer (Serre) was tried and convicted "for illicit trade with the Natives" in Red River but was freed as a large crowd outside the courtroom cried "le commerce est libre." The confrontation illustrated the determination of the Métis to oppose the commercial monopoly of the Hudson's Bay Company. During the 1850s and 1860s, the transport trade to Saint Paul and northwestern trading posts increased. The trains of Red River carts hauled furs, pemmican, and skin goods on the return trip north. The trade in buffalo robes and hides prospered in these decades (Ens 1989:122–125). In the 1870s, the Métis of Saint Albert moved south to Buffalo Lake to be closer to the last herds (R.F. Beal, Foster, and Zuk 1987). The robes were exported to Fort Benton, Montana, a central point for the American trade. The commerce attested to the enterprise and adaptability of the Métis; but along with the spread of the railroads and White hunters, it precipitated the destruction of the northern herds. Overhunting resulted in the disappearance of the buffalo from the Plains by the late 1870s. In the following decades, the Métis were gathering buffalo bones to be ground for fertilizer, in the last phase of a once profitable industry.

The 1880s onward also saw the decline of fur-bearing animals and the northward retreat of the fur trade that fostered other economic strategies. The emergence of a market-oriented agrarian economy by 1900 altered traditional patterns of resource use, forcing the Métis to revise their seasonally regulated economy. The settlers of East Prairie Settlement, Alberta, devised a new adaptive strategy, systematically combining at least three resource bases (trapping, farming, and ranching, supplemented with wage labor

Glenbow-Alberta Inst., Calgary: PA 2218-26.

Fig. 4. Abraham Plante, Métis trapper with his dog and rifle; snowshoes rest against the log cabin. Skins, including weasel or ermine, mink, marten, fox, lynx, and northern coyote are hanging from a pole behind him. Photograph probably by James Brady, in the foothills of the Rockies, Alta., 1930s.

and welfare) and regulating exploitation to meet subsistence requirements and ensure resource conservation (Driben 1985:111, 128).

In the 1930s, the main issues were poverty and unemployment. Communities such as Saint Louis, Saskatchewan, and Saint Laurent were economically diversified and self-sufficient, but many Métis were living on the fringes of Indian reserves or White settlements in shanty towns, where they struggled to make a living as hired labor. Other subsistence activities included wild produce harvesting, berry picking, and senega root digging. Some Métis were involved in commercial fishing and dairy farming, but the majority were neither full staple producers nor wage laborers. They remained largely an impoverished underclass (St. Onge 1989:127).

The struggle and conflict over land claims greatly affected the economic well-being of the Métis. The confirmation of customary land grants was the foremost issue in Manitoba and the Northwest Territories while in North Dakota and Montana, the "landless people" attempted to secure a land base. The Manitoba Act of 1870 recognized the Métis system of riverlots, hay privilege, and common grazing. Section 32 guaranteed possession of lands already occupied without title whereas section 31 stated that 1.4 million acres would be "reserved for the benefit of the half-breed residents." But these rights were undermined by a series of contrary and possibly unconstitutional amendments that in effect abrogated the original provisions of the Manitoba Act (Mailhot and Sprague 1985:1–30). Scrip (certificates negotiable for land or money) was subsequently established to deal with claims under section 31 (fig. 5). Money scrip, in particular, being personal rather than real property and payable to the bearer, was largely exempt from regulations and led to speculation, fraudulent sales, and transfers. The system facilitated the selling of scrip certificates for ready cash rather than their use to claim lands and prevented the establishment of a land base for the Métis in Manitoba and the Northwest Territories. Many Métis settlers had difficulty meeting stringent residency and cultivation requirements in order to obtain title to their lands while others could not afford the registration (entry) fee. Riverlot claimants in the Northwest Territories were required to purchase land in excess of the 160-acre homestead grant, and by the 1920s mortgages and tax arrears forced many off their farms (Payment 1990:273–281).

The transfer of Crown lands to the provinces in 1930 put pressure on the "road allowance people," as poor Métis who resided on lands reserved for roads came to be known (M. Campbell 1973:1992). The Métis of communities such as Sainte Madeleine, Manitoba, were actually evicted and their lands appropriated for pasture by Euro-Canadian farmers under the Prairie Farm Rehabilitation Act (Zeilig and Zeilig 1987). Across the border, the impoverished Chippewa-Cree of Turtle Mountain were losing their lands (G.S. Camp 1987:180–195) while the landless Canadian Cree

No 7410
Dominion of Canada
No 7410
Department of the Interior
This is issued as called for by Certificate form G No. 981
Issued by the North West Half Breed Commission.
The Bearer hereof is entitled to an allowance of
One hundred and sixty Dollars in any purchase
OF DOMINION LANDS.
$160.00
$160.00
Issued at the Department of the Interior at Ottawa,
this Fifteenth day of December 1885
Entered

Natl. Arch. of Canada, Ottawa: RG 15, Vol. 1391 (C-132171).

Fig. 5. Scrip. Canceled scrip certificate issued in 1885 for $160 by the North West Half Breed Commission of Canada's Department of the Interior. In 1879, the Dominion Lands Act acknowledged Métis title and provided for land grants in the territory outside of Manitoba. In 1885, every Métis head of family in the North-West Territories and outside Manitoba became eligible to receive scrip in "extinguishment" of aboriginal title. A scrip certificate could be exchanged for money or land or equivalent value.

of Hill 57 near Great Falls, Montana, were subsisting in squalid conditions (Dusenberry 1965:103).

In Canada in the 1930s, several settlement schemes were brought forth by provincial governments to "rehabilitate" the Métis. The Alberta government established eight farm colonies in northern Alberta in the 1930s, providing the only collective land base for the Métis in North America.

Although the Métis lacked control of affairs in the settlements, they had access to social services, individual farm incomes, and a trust fund (Pocklington 1991). In the 1940s, a similar colonization scheme was implemented in Green Lake, Saskatchewan, and cooperative farmers were established in Lestock and Willow Bunch (Barron 1990). However, these cooperative agricultural schemes were imposed and controlled by governments who doubted Métis competence, discouraged initiative, and did not provide required resources. Contrary to their intent, they often became repositories of poverty and dependency.

The 1950s were years of increased migration to urban areas in search of employment. In an effort to again address persisting Métis poverty, the Manitoba government commissioned an inquiry into the "facilitation of the social integration and economic advancement of people of Indian ancestry" in the province (Lagassé 1959). By the mid-1950s, welfare formed about one-half the income of some Métis in urban centers such as Winnipeg. In the north, a decline in fur resources accompanied by falling demand for furs resulted in increased unemployment and marginalization in the 1960s. Some Métis found employment as tourist guides, in highway construction, and on fur and fish farms. But when asked to sum up the economic situation of the Métis, an elder at Duck Lake, Saskatchewan, replied: "we are a class of poor people" (Aimé Dumont, personal communication 1983). The Métis demonstrated resiliency and initiative throughout these difficult times, but it was only in the 1970s, as a result of increased self-determination and access to economic programs, that conditions began to improve.

Religion

Métis religion was both dualistic and a syncretism of native and Christian beliefs and practices. According to native tradition, life was based on a harmonious relationship with the land and activities regulated by the cyclical rhythms of nature. Human beings were an integral part of the cosmos (Sioui 1992:8–19). The Métis accepted Jesus and the Bible but "didn't quit their own ways" (D. Young, Ingram, and Swartz 1989:12). According to Redbird (1980:6–7), the Métis were aware of and responded to both views.

Roman Catholicism was formally introduced in the Red River Settlement in 1818 as a result of a petition of the *Canadiens* and their Métis families (La Societé historique de Saint-Boniface 1991:54–56), while the Church of England established its first mission two years later. Many Plains Métis had probably been introduced to Christianity even earlier by their *Canadien* forefathers who settled in the west as freemen. Their "traditional" or "folk" Catholicism was expressed by the persistence of certain rituals and a particular reverence for the priests, even among nonpractitioners (Dion 1979:164–171; Charette 1976:191–197). Church hymns were sung in Cree and images of the saints revered. Both Roman Catholic and Protestant denominations sought to "civilize and Christianize," which implied adopting a sedentary way of life centered on agriculture and abandoning native belief systems. Although the Catholic and Protestant churches were rivals in the Northwest, there is evidence that the Métis themselves did not make distinctions and attended both, depending on their location (Spry 1985:112).

The influence and impact of the missionaries seems to have varied. There is evidence of control and divisiveness (Pannekoek 1991) as well as genuine concern and dedication to an underprivileged community (Huel 1989:29). Some leaders, such as the Roman Catholic bishop Joseph-Norbert Provencher and the Anglican priest William Cockran, were authoritarian and dogmatic, but priests such as the abbés Noel-Joseph Ritchot and Georges Belcourt championed the Métis. Catholic missionaries accompanied the Métis on the hunt, and some, such as Louis Laflèche, were regarded as having shamanistic powers. The Gray Nuns, who arrived in Red River in 1844 and opened many convent schools and hospitals in the Canadian west, recruited sisters among the Métis.

The relationship between the missionaries and the Métis can best be described as ambivalent (Payment 1990:107–144). This is evident in the clergy's response to the Métis resistence movements. In 1869–1870 the Métis believed they had received the support of the missionaries, whereas in 1885 they felt betrayed. The clergy's hostility towards Louis Riel in the Saskatchewan resistance was critical. Riel had indigenized Catholicism and expressed it in terms that were meaningful to the Métis. He was the "prophet of the New World," the Métis were God's chosen people, and the millennium was at hand (Flannagan 1983:96). The Oblates of Mary Immaculate priests of Batoche and neighboring parishes responded to this modification of Catholic beliefs by denouncing Riel as an apostate and Satan's instrument, or at best a lunatic. Deprived of the church's support, the Métis built their own sanctuary to the Virgin Mary and their own place of worship (Payment 1990:123). During the armed conflict some missionaries exchanged information with government agents and the military. As a result Gabriel Dumont, the Métis commander, and others developed mistrust and resentment toward the priests, which increased after 1885.

The Métis remained profoundly religious. They continued to celebrate the feast of their patron, Saint Joseph; and the national feast day on July 24 was both a religious and cultural celebration. Some also practiced native healing, participated in vision quests, and attended "gift giving" ceremonies at neighboring reserves (Payment 1991:30).

The missionaries were usually responsible for schools and promoted the assimilation of the Métis through the imposition of either the French or English language, Christian instruction, and Western values. The Métis often resisted these efforts either passively or actively. When the Oblate Fathers established a boarding school at Saint Paul des Métis, Alberta, in 1895, it was doomed to failure from the start (Sawchuck, Sawchuck, and Ferguson 1981). The Métis resented clerical control and the unfavorable comparison with their French Canadian neighbors. Ultimately, the "prison" school was burned.

The annual summer pilgrimages to Our Lady of Lourdes at Saint Laurent de Grandin, Saskatchewan (fig. 6), and Lac Sainte Anne, Alberta (S. Simon 1995), were attended by both young and old. In a gesture of reconciliation and adaptation, the Christian churches incorporated Indian music and languages into their rituals. In the missionary spirit of defending the underprivileged, some missionaries adopted a militant stance in support of Métis rights and claims (Fumoleau 1977), while Métis priests asserted their heritage and combated prejudice within the church (Lavallée 1986, 1992, 1997). Many Métis youth, however, rebelled and rejected the faith of their forefathers in favor of the beliefs of their Indian foremothers.

Structures

Métis land use, building styles, and decorative artwork reflected dual origins and an implicit Métis culture. The Métis riverlot system of landholding in Red River, Saint Laurent de Grandin, and Lac Sainte Anne was inspired by

Glenbow-Alberta Inst., Calgary: NA-871-1.

Fig. 6. Métis, Cree, and French Canadians summer pilgrimage to the shrine of Our Lady of Lourdes at St. Laurent de Grandin, near Duck Lake, Sask. Photographed July 1928.

the seigneurial system of New France, but with few fences to alter the landscape. It is customary to claim parallel lots 6–12 chains in width (1 chain = 66 feet) and up to two miles deep. The rear of each lot was used for hay and wood.

Métis buildings were distinctive and inspired by both Plains Indian and French Canadian traditions. When they were hunting and trading on the plains, the Métis used tents (fig. 7). Their wintering dwellings were small horizontal log structures with straw roofs and window panes made of skin parchment. The interior was usually plastered with a mud and straw mixture. At one end of the unpartitioned room, there was a mud stove or "chimney" used for cooking and heating (Calihoo 1953:21–22). Homes or buildings in settlements were larger and better finished. The Riel family home in Saint Vital, Manitoba, had

top, Natl. Arch. of Canada, Ottawa: C4164; bottom, Geological Survey of Canada, Ottawa: 613.

Fig. 7. Dwellings and transportation. top, Métis scouts and traders working for the North American Boundary Commission. A Red River covered cart and canvas tent make up their camp, which included a woman wearing Euro-Canadian clothing and 6 children. At least one of the men is wearing an Assomption sash. Photograph by Watson, McCrory, G. Parsons, or J. McCammon (Birrell 1996:115), 1872–1874. bottom, Métis freighters at the settlement of Maple Creek, Sask., relaxing around a cooking stove. The woman (right) wears a traditional shawl and a crucifix. A wagon is behind her. Photograph by T.C. Weston, 1884.

one and one-half stories. Its tenon-and-groove or "Red River" style of construction featured a log frame with an infill of horizontal posts on a fieldstone foundation. The exterior and interior of many houses were finished with a whitewashed plaster or, as in the case of the Riel home, wooden siding (Payment 1988:34). Métis buildings in Saskatchewan and Alberta by 1900 were more typically of horizontal logs notched ("dovetailed") at the corners (Burley, Horsfall, and Brandon 1992:132–133). Métis dwellings often acquired additions to the main building as space was needed. This adaptive usage became widespread during the decades of increased poverty between 1885 and 1940. After the 1950s log homes were replaced with a variety of frame structures, but the penchant for bright decorative colors persisted.

Technology

Métis artwork was expressed in a variety of personal and trade items. Women produced elaborate floral designs as decorations on moccasins, leggings, pipebags, firebags, pad saddles, and other articles (fig. 8). The Métis were called "the flower beadwork people" by the Sioux (S.F. Racette 1991:12–13). After silk embroidery was introduced by the Gray Nuns in Saint Boniface, Métis women added to it the traditional method of using quills and beads on hide (Morier 1979:28–31). The women also wove red willow baskets and mats, braided rugs, and sewed the shawls that the elders wore into the 1950s. The multicolored sash was a clothing item probably inspired by early Northeast Indian and French Canadian tradition (Barbeau 1939:25–26). Originally finger woven, then produced on looms, these versatile items were used as suspenders, as belts over blue capotes, and as ropes, tumplines, or dog harnesses. The sash was an enduring symbol of Métis identity as various groups of Métis adopted a particular pattern to represent them. They also established the Order of the Sash and the Order of the Shawl to honor elders who made outstanding contributions to their people and country.

The Red River cart (fig.7) was perhaps the first distinctive Plains Métis artifact. It was so closely associated with them that the Plains Cree referred to the Métis as "half-wagon, half-man." The cart, made entirely of wood, could be drawn by either horses or oxen. It was used to transport merchandise along the rutted dirt trails between Red River and Saint Paul and to Fort Edmonton and beyond in the Northwest Territories. When the wheels were removed, the cart floated on the river as a raft. In the winter it could be used as a cariole or sleigh (R.R. Gilman, Gilman, and Stultz 1979:15–16). The usually ungreased wooden axles, wrapped with thin strips of buffalo hide called shagganapi, made an excruciating noise as each wheel turned; a train of carts could be heard within a three-mile radius (J.K. Howard 1952:51–57). During the hunts, the carts were drawn up in a circle around the tents as a military enclosure.

The gun was the Métis man's most prized possession, along with his pipe and knife (J.D. Harrison 1985:53). Historically, it was essential for survival in hunt and war. During the days of the buffalo hunt the Métis used big-bore muzzle-loading muskets, which required considerable dexterity and speed while reloading during the chase. The Métis who fought in 1885 had only smoothbore shotguns with the barrels filed off. They later used standard rifles and pistols for hunting.

Identity

Traditional Métis foods included buffalo meat, pemmican, and bannock, accompanied with strong black tea and a pipe of tobacco made of red willow shavings. After the depletion of the buffalo herds, roasted moose and deer meat and small game were eaten. Domestic gardening also added a variety of vegetables to the wild roots and fruit such as pimbinas and saskatoons. In Saint Boniface, Batoche, and Saint Albert, the Métis incorporated French Canadian foods such as meatballs, meat pies, *beignes croches* (irregularly shaped doughnuts), and puddings in their diet (Payment 1990:47–53).

An enduring symbol of Métis identity was its official flag, a white figure eight placed horizontally on a blue background. Its origins go back to the flag carried at the Battle of La Grenouillère in 1816. According to C. Racette (1987:6) the horizontal eight is an infinity sign with two meanings: the joining of cultures and the existence of a people forever while the blue background acknowledged the French heritage of the Métis. The symbol was also expressed in the traditional dances of the Métis, such as the quadrille, in which the dancers move in a figure eight pattern. Other flags were the fleurs-de-lys with shamrock, at times with the buffalo of the provisional government of the Red River in 1869–1870 (C. Racette 1987:14–15) and the religious banners of Saint Joseph, the Immaculate Heart of Jesus, and Mary of the Riel's *exovidate* in 1885 (Payment 1990:154–157).

Music and dance were important features of Métis cultural identity. The fiddle, concertina, harmonica, and spoons accompanied the Red River jig, Scottish reels, and Cree "chicken" dance (fig. 9). Métis music combined features of French Canadian, Scots-Irish, and Saulteaux (Plains Ojibwa) or Cree to form a new style (Lederman 1988:206). Some of the songs, such as "Le fils du roi" and "Courtesan malheureaux" were adaptations of French Canadian folklore, while others were distinctly Métis. Pierre Falcon, the bard of the prairie Métis, composed six satirical songs, the best known being "La Chanson de La Grenouillère." Louis Riel wrote many poems, some of which were put to music. Two well-known compositions are "La Métisse," written during the tumultuous events of 1869-1870, and "Chanson de Louis Riel," composed in Montana in honor of his sister, Henriette. The traditional music was still played by elders in the 1990s, while entertainers Andy Desjarlais, Reg Bouvette, and Ray St. Germain developed a distinctive "country" music style.

a
b
c
d
e
f

9.
Fur collar & trimming

15.
Buffalo skin coat

top left, Natl. Arch. of Canada, Ottawa: C-46498; center left, Metropolitan Toronto Central Lib., Ont.: L-37; bottom left and center, Newberry Lib., E.E. Ayer Coll., Chicago; bottom right, Racette 1991:19; Canadian Mus. of Civilization, Hull, Que.: a, III-D-389 (76-780), b, V-Z-4 (76-895); c, Natl. Gallery of Canada, Ottawa: 9631; d, Man. Mus. of Man and Nature, Winnipeg: H4.12.116; e, New Brunswick Mus., St. John: 41911; f, Lower Ft. Garry Natl. Hist. Park, Selkirk, Man.: HBC 34-30A (2445).

Fig. 8. Métis decoration of clothing and artifacts. top left, *A Halfcast and his two Wives*. The woman on left is carrying an infant in a cradleboard; she is holding a pipe. The man wears a finger-woven Assomption sash, cloth breechcloth, decorated leggings, European hat with fur edging and what appears to be an octopus bag across his chest; he has a powder horn over his shoulder and holds a rifle. All three wear moccasins. Watercolor by Peter Rindisbacher, about 1825–1826. center left, a Métis hunter wearing moccasins, beaded garters, and holding a fringed skin guncase and a beaded item on his lap. Photograph by Humphrey L. Hime, Red River Settlement, 1858. bottom left and center, Front and back of deerskin winter coat embroidered with floral and geometric designs. The man also wears a beaded bag suspended from his Assomption sash and a fringed and decorated knife sheath in the back of his sash. Pen and ink by Frank Blackwell Mayer, St. Paul, Minn., 1851. bottom right, Illustration from *The Flower Beadwork People* (S.F. Racette 1991) showing back and front of Red River coat with bead designs. Original gouache and watercolor by Sherry Farrell Racette, 1991. a, Gauntlets made from tanned, smoked skin, trimmed with black fur. The wrists are lined with burgundy velvet, and multicolor silk embroidery in a floral design decorates the back. This style is typical of late 19th-century Cree-Métis craftwork. Acquired in 1972; length 43 cm. b, Knife and unsmoked hide sheath decorated with woven porcupine quillwork fringes. Quill colors include red, blue, white, green and yellow. The knife is a double-edged iron blade with a black bone handle and circular inlays of brass and white bone. Collected by the Earl of Caledon, 1841–1842; length of knife 30.5 cm, length of sheath 29.5 cm. c, Finger-woven sash with flame design in scarlet, yellow, green, and white woolen yarn. The design and materials are typical of sashes that were popular among the Red River Métis during the early 19th century. Length 40.6 cm. d, Embroidered cap made of deer hide, cotton, and silk, decorated with brightly colored flowers in red, purple, blue, green, and yellow. The Métis floral embroidery was so distinctive that the Sioux and Cree called them the "flower beadwork people" (J.D. Harrison 1985:84). Collected by K.I. Robinson, 1959; length 16 cm, width 13.5 cm. e, Octopus tobacco bag made of red stroud cloth with red, blue, and green tassels. Collected by Henry Youle Hind, Red River region, 1857–1858; length 56.5 cm. f, Man's coat of unsmoked moosehide and painted in the early floral style of the Red River Métis. The coat is styled like a European coat (vol. 4:398), cut full in the back for horseback riding. The quillwork shoulder decorations are reminiscent of military epaulettes. Collected by John Halkett, 1821; length 113 cm.

Métis oral literature included formal narratives, informal storytelling, and political discourse. The stories of the raconteurs had a spiritual and moralistic as well as a practical dimension (see examples recorded by Létourneau 1978). Louis Riel and Louis Schmidt, who were fluent in spoken and written French, wrote accounts. Riel left a collection of letters, diaries, poetry, and political and religious writings comprising over four volumes (G. Stanley 1985). Louis Goulet's memoirs were transcribed by Métis writer and lawyer Guillaume Charette in the 1930s (Charette 1976), and the lifestories of Elizabeth Thérèse Baird née Fisher (1998), Marie Rose Smith née Delorme (Carpenter 1977), and Peter Erasmus (Spry 1976) were also recorded. In the 1920s, the Union Nationale Métisse de St. Joseph du Manitoba formed a historical committee to record the Métis accounts of the Northwest Rebellion of 1885 and subsequently commissioned a celebratory history (de Trémaudan 1982). The publications of Sealey and Lussier (1975), Pelletier (1974), H. Adams (1975), and Redbird (1980) addressed political and social themes. M. Campbell (1973, 1978), LaRocque (1983, 1986), and Culleton (1983) wrote about Métis history from a personal

left, M. Campbell 1995:54; right, Minn. Histl. Soc., St. Paul: 3360.

Fig. 9. Métis dances. left, Fiddle player known as Ole Arcand from a story titled "Le Beau Sha Shoo." The folktale relates how Ole Arcand died, went to heaven, visited with Jesus who gave him this new fiddle song, which was "kinda wile/ full of high stepping and growling/ an we could shore dance to him" (M. Campbell 1995:65). Gouache and watercolor by Sherry Farrell Racette, 1995. right, Dance at Devils Lake, Dak. Terr., about 1870. The fiddlers and men are on the left, while the women and children are on the right. Pencil drawing by Louis Voelkerer.

perspective, addressing contemporary issues such as poverty, alcoholism, and racism. Métis literature and history were also documented on film and video (M. Campbell 1992; H.W. Daniels 1992; C. Welsh 1992), and newspapers such as *New Breed* and *Le Métis* and periodicals such as *Windspeaker* and *The Native Studies Review* provided an important platform for Métis perspectives and issues.

Feasts such as *La fête des Métis* (later called "Back to Batoche Days") in Batoche and the Union Nationale picnic in Saint Vital ensured cultural continuity. Customs such as the New Year's Day paternal blessing and greetings, large family reunions at weddings and wakes, and regular visiting with family and friends persisted.

Social and Political Issues

The 1980s and 1990s were a period of cultural revival, economic development, and political empowerment for the Métis in Canada (fig. 10). The Gabriel Dumont Institute, Saskatchewan; the Louis Riel Institute, Manitoba; and Turtle Mountain Community College, North Dakota initiated educational programs and research promoting Métis values. The homecoming celebrations at The Forks, Winnipeg, to mark Canada's parliamentary recognition of Louis Riel as a founder of Manitoba in July 1992 and "Métis 125" (celebrating the Métis contribution on the 125th anniversary of Canadian confederation), which featured an impressive roster of artists and musicians, exemplify the sense of nation and cultural identity.

Successful political negotiations with the Canadian government gave strength and prestige to the Métis. *Métisisme* (declaration of the Federation of the Métis Settlements of Alberta in 1982) provided key philosophical, legal, and political arguments on the issues of aboriginal land rights and self-government in the Constitution of Canada. The Constitution Act of 1982 identified the Métis as an aboriginal group and the Métis Nation Accord, which was adopted in principle by the federal and provincial governments in 1992, proposed guarantees of negotiated self-government, resource management, and land claims; however, these proposals were not ratified. The Royal Commission on Aboriginal Peoples (1996) addressed issues of Métis identity and assets. The thousands of Métis who resided principally in North Dakota and Montana in the United States continued to lack official status. The residents of Turtle Mountain and Rocky Boy's reservations have Indian status while countless others in communities such as Leroy, North Dakota, and Great Falls, Montana, were absorbed into the American melting pot. In 1996, the Métis Resource Centre located in Winnipeg, Manitoba, opened an Internet site that offered historical, genealogical, cultural, and bibliographical information. The State Historical Society of North Dakota opened a museum in Pembina that featured the role of the Métis in the fur trade.

Métis Nation of Alta., Edmonton.

Fig. 10. Métis in the 1990s. top, Signing ceremony, April 14, 1998, in which St. Margaret's Roman Catholic Church near Tofield, Alta., was turned over to the Métis Nation to be used as the official Métis Church. The flags, one blue for the North West Company, one red for the Hudson's Bay Company, with the infinity symbol, represent the joining of 2 cultures and the existence of the people forever. Photograph by Rafique Islam. bottom, Eric Nystrom, an employee of the Canadian Park Service, demonstrating traditional activities. bottom left, Interpreting fur trade history to visitors at Rocky Mountain House National Historic Site, Alta. On the right are elk hide, a beaver hide, a buffalo powder horn, and a small covered kettle. The interpreter holds a beaver-tail trade knife. bottom right, Drying moose meat for use during winter. Unidentified man at right. bottom, Photographed 1996–1997.

As a result of an amendment to the Canadian Indian Act (Bill C-31) in 1985, some Métis or Nonstatus Indians who had lost their rights through marriage or enfranchisement opted for Indian status. Others, forced off reserves, formed new Métis communities (Hourie 1991:133–139). These developments caused political tensions with native peoples. As Métis become Indians under the Indian Act, their rights as Métis persons were extinguished by abandonment, a process that could only have been halted by the constitutional and legal entrenchment of Métis national rights.

Population

From the period of early gatherings of Métis at Pembina and at The Forks in the Red River valley in the 1790s and early 1800s, the population can only be estimated. The first censuses were incomplete as seasonal occupations required mobility and absence from their main residences. The Métis homeland in the Plains was vast and the custom of seasonal migratory rounds is well illustrated by the fact that many Red River Settlement Métis included in the 1849 census were also enumerated at Pembina in 1850 (Harpole and Nagle 1972). In 1814, Gov. Miles Macdonell reported that there were about 200 Métis, French Canadians, and Scots in the Red River Settlement, which included both Pembina and Saint Boniface (W.L. Morton 1967:49). Rev. Sévère Dumoulin stated that he was ministering to nearly 300 people at the Pembina mission in 1819 and 500 in 1821 (Nute 1942:177, 290). The Red River Census of 1826 reported 3,500 people in the settlement, of which about 80 percent were of mixed origin. According to the Minnesota Territorial Census of 1850, there were about 5,000 Métis in the Minnesota-Dakota territory, about the same as at Red River, which listed "684 half-breed heads of families" in 1849. The Red River censuses between 1849 and 1870 were incomplete. The 1856 census enumerated 816 Métis families, an increase of 132 families since 1849 or over 5,000 people based on an average family size of five (Hind 1860:177); other sources suggested a population closer to 6,000. Hind also stated that the Métis population at Pembina exceeded 500 while that of Saint Joseph numbered 1,200 in 1858 (N.L. Woolworth 1975:20). The first Manitoba census in 1870 reported 5,696 Métis and 4,082 "half-breeds" out of a total population of 12,000 (Canada. Sessional Papers 1871, 20:91). By 1886 the population had decreased to 4,369 Métis and 3,597 "half-breeds."

The Métis population of Pembina–Saint Joseph was about 2,000 in the early 1870s (G.S. Camp 1987:78). In 1880, 101 "heads of families" camped on the Musselshell River, Montana, signed a petition drafted by Louis Riel (Flanagan 1985:183) that suggests a population of about 500 Métis in the Montana Territory. In 1965, Dusenberry (1965:88) reported that there were 4,000 Métis in Montana.

In the post-1870 period in Canada, increasing prejudice and the reluctance to identify themselves as "half-breeds" (the ethnic category used in the censuses) compelled many Métis to report that they were French or Scots. As a result, official numbers were probably greatly underestimated. One report estimated the Métis population of the Northwest Territories (districts of Assiniboia, Saskatchewan, and Alberta) at 5,380 in 1884 (Mailhot and Sprague 1985:12,3). A territorial census in August 1885 reported 2,848 Métis, but this figure does not account for those who sought exile in the United States or were absent from the settlements subsequent to the Northwest Rebellion (Canada. Dominion Bureau of Statistics 1886:11).

Only about 22,000 people in the Prairie provinces identified themselves as "half-breed" in the 1901 census, while the number was 26,660 in 1941. Half-breed as a category was dropped from the Canadian census between 1941 and 1981. In an inquiry commissioned by the Manitoba government, Métis author Jean Lagassé enumerated 23,579 kin in 1958 but reported that voluntary identification was one of his biggest problems (1959, 1:56–57). The 1991 Canadian census identified 98,980 Métis in the Prairie Provinces (Royal Commission on Aboriginal Peoples 1996:table 5.1). But according to Métis association estimates, there were 100,000 Métis in Manitoba, 80,000 in Saskatchewan, and 60,000 in Alberta in 1991 (personal communications 1992).

Synonymy†

The English designation Métis derives from standard French *métis* 'half-breed, half-caste'. It came into use in English during the nineteenth century to designate descendants of Indians, primarily Ojibwa or Cree, and French or French Canadians. In the second half of the twentieth century its usage became more widespread, frequently applied to anyone of mixed Indian and European ancestry. For a discussion of pronunciation variants, see volume 6:370–371.

An old French Canadian variant of the name is *métif*, which occurs as Maitiffs, 1805 (Sibley 1832:730), and Métif, 1818 (McGillivray in J.S.H. Brown 1983:44). The Métis French pronunciation [mɪčɪf] (Papen 1987:247) has been rendered as English Mitchif (vol.6), Michif, and Métchif (J.C. Crawford 1985; Lavallée 1988:ii) especially to designate the language.

Names formerly used in English but considered pejorative in the late twentieth century are half-breed, breed, and mixed-blood. Historically, the most commonly used English designation is Halfbreed, which was first recorded in the Carolinas in the mid-1700s and became a common term in northern colonial English-speaking contexts by the early 1800s. Despite rejection of the designation as derogatory in the late twentieth century, the term continued to be used as a self-designation in some northern communities, primarily near Hudson Bay (J.S.H. Brown 1980a; J.S. Long 1985:157). Although the term mixed-blood has been widely used by English-speaking outsiders in the twentieth century, it has not been used by Métis themselves.

These preceding designations are reflected in the names used in many Indian languages that denote the Métis proper and often any person of mixed Indian-European ancestry. Examples are Cheyenne *ó?xevé?hó?E* 'half White people' (Glenmore and Leman 1985:202); Gros Ventre *kɔh?uníh?ɔɔtɔh* 'half White man' (Allan R. Taylor, personal communcation 1987); Ojibwa *aya·pittawisit* 'one who is half' (Baraga 1878–1880, 1:124, phonemicized); Plains Cree *a·pihtawikosisa·n* 'half son' (Ahenakew and Wolfart 1992:29); Teton and Santee Sioux *wašíčų čʰįča* 'mixed blood, half-breed', literally 'Whiteman child' (Buechel 1970:551; Riggs 1890:536); Yankton Sioux

†This synonymy was written by Douglas R. Parks, incorporating material provided by Jennifer S.H. Brown and Diane Paulette Payment.

dak^{h}óta č^{h}įča, literally 'Dakota child' (J.P. Williamson 1902:79); Assiniboine *sakná* 'half-breed, Métis', cognate with the Sioux term for 'British' (Parks and DeMallie 1988:344); Mandan *šahí* 'Cree; half-breed' (Parks 1987); and Hidatsa *xaxát^{h}ųwą* 'French-Cree, Métis' (Parks 1991a).

Related to the preceding names is the eighteenth- and early nineteenth-century French designation *Bois-Brûlés* or *Broulé* 'burnt wood'. Although rare, some Métis occasionally used it to designate themselves in the twentieth century (Lussier 1981). The name is reflected in Ojibwa *wi·ssa·kkote·winini* 'Métis man', *wi·ssa·kkote·wikkwe·* 'Métis woman', based on *wi·ssa·kkote·* '(partly) burnt forest' (Baraga 1878–1880, 2:421, phonemicized). Another French name is *chicots* (Douaud 1985:83).

A modern Sioux designation is *iyéska* 'interpreter', reflecting the historical social position of mixed peoples (R.E. Daniels 1970:221).

Sources

Krech (1994:126–132) and Friesen and Lusty (1980) are guides to sources on the Métis. Survey studies include J.K. Howard (1952), Giraud (1986), and de Trémaudan (1982). Howard's popular history placed the Métis in a North American context while Giraud's comprehensive ethnological study and de Trémaudan's defensive tract illustrated the cultural biases of the mid-nineteenth century. Some of these themes were reiterated from a Métis perspective by H. Adams (1975). Collections of essays were presented by Lussier and Sealey (1978–1980), J.C. Peterson and J.S.H. Brown (1985, including one of the few articles on the Montana Métis), and Barron and Waldram (1986). J.D. Harrison (1985) is a popular illustrated history that provides a cultural overview of the Métis in Canada up to the 1980s, while J.C. Peterson (1990) reviews the activities of the Métis in the Pembina–Saint Joseph area up to the mid-1880s. Redbird (1980) and Dobbin (1981) present Métis perspectives on both historical and contemporary issues. There was a special issue on the Métis in the *Journal of Canadian Studies* in 1980 and in *Canadian Ethnic Studies* in 1985. Specific community studies include Saint François-Xavier, Manitoba (Ens 1996), Lac La Biche, Alberta (J. Champagne 1990), Buffalo Lake (R.F. Beal, Foster, and Zuk 1987), Batoche (Payment 1990), Sainte Madeleine (Zeilig and Zeilig 1987), Saint Laurent de Grandin (Lavallée 1988), and East Prairie Settlement, Alberta (Driben 1985). Relationships with Christian missionaries have been investigated by Pannekoek (1990) and La Société historique de Saint-Boniface (1991). Architecture and material culture have been documented by Burley, Horsfall, and Brandon (1992), while music has been the subject of Bouchard (1975) and Whidden (1993, 1995). The diary of Marie-Rose Smith, née Delorme (Carpenter 1977), the memoirs of Louis Goulet (Charette 1976), and stories and legends collected by Benoist (1975) and Letourneau (1978) provide firsthand accounts of nineteenth-century customs and lifeways. J.S.H. Brown (1980) and Van Kirk (1980) looked at families and the role of women and children in the fur trade while M. Campbell (1973, 1978) and LaRocque (1983, 1986) shared personal experiences on these themes. A genealogy of the Manitoba Métis was compiled by Sprague and Frye (1983). Louis Riel's life was documented by G. Stanley (1963), Flanagan (1979), Martel (1984), and Siggins (1994), and his writings published in a collection of five volumes (G. Stanley 1985). Gabriel Dumont was the subject of a biography by Woodcock (1976), and the 1885 military engagements have been described by D. Morton (1972), R.F. Beal and R.C. Macleod (1984), and Hildebrandt (1985). The Métis political resistances of 1869–1870 and 1885 and associated land claims have been re-examined by Mailhot and Sprague (1985), Sprague (1988, 1991), Flanagan (1983, 1991), Kermoal (1994), Payment (1996), and Chartrand (1991). The politics of Alberta Métis settlements are the subject of Pocklington (1991), while Corrigan and Barkwell (1991) documented Métis legal traditions in the light of initiatives toward self-determination and control of the justice system.

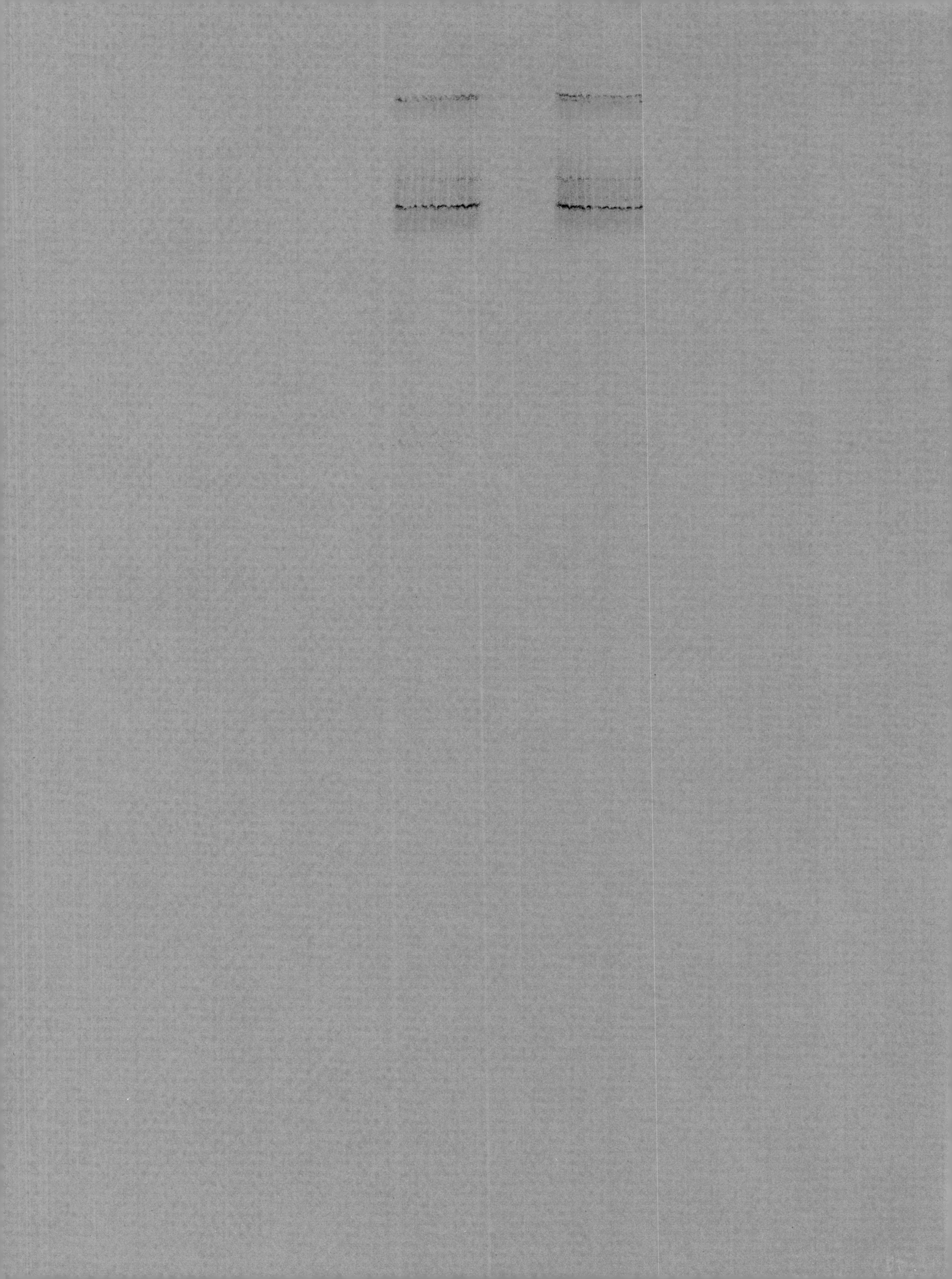